D1568027

The Gallup Poll

Public Opinion 2015

The Gallup Poll

Public Opinion 2015

EDITED BY
FRANK NEWPORT

ROWMAN & LITTLEFIELD
Lanham • Boulder • New York • Toronto • Plymouth, UK

ACKNOWLEDGMENTS

The Gallup Poll represents the efforts of a number of talented and dedicated individuals. I wish to express my gratitude to James Clifton, Chairman and CEO of Gallup, whose continuing vision and commitment to the value of social and economic analysis of the poll data undergirds all that is in this volume. I also acknowledge the central role of the poll staff, including Jeffrey Jones; Lydia Saad; Alyssa Brown, Art Swift, and Tracey Sugar, who compiled the chronology; and all of the authors whose names appear on the bylines within this volume. Kimberly Clarke edited text, selected the graphs and managed the assembly of materials and the publication process. Professor Fred Israel, City University of New York, George Gallup Jr. (1930–2011) and Alec Gallup (1928–2009) deserve special credit for their contributions to the first 37 volumes in this series.

Published in the United States of America by Rowman & Littlefield Publishers, Inc.
A wholly owned subsidiary of The Rowman & Littlefield Publishing Group, Inc.
4501 Forbes Boulevard, Suite 200, Lanham, Maryland 20706, www.rowman.com

Unit A, Whitacre Mews, 26-34 Stannary Street, London SE11 4AB

ISSN 0195-962X

Cloth ISBN-13: 978-1-5381-0023-3 eISBN: 978-1-5381-0024-0

♾™ The paper used in this publication meets the minimum requirements of American National Standard for Information Sciences—Permanence of Paper for Printed Library Materials, ANSI/NISO Z39.48-1992.

Printed in the United States of America

CONTENTS

INTRODUCTION

The Gallup Poll: Public Opinion 2015 contains the findings of the more than 500 Gallup Poll reports released to the American public during the year 2015. The latest volume reveals the attitudes and opinions of individuals and key groups within the American population concerning national and international issues and events of the year, and reports on Americans' views of the economy, their personal financial situation and well-being, and the political arena.

The 2015 volume is the most recent addition to the 42-volume Gallup collection, *Public Opinion, 1935–2015*, the largest compilation of public opinion findings ever published. The Gallup collection documents the attitudes and opinions of Americans on national and international issues and events from Franklin D. Roosevelt's second term to the present.

Shown in detail are results of tens of thousands of questions that the Gallup Poll—the world's oldest and most respected public opinion poll—has asked of the public over the last eight decades. Results of the survey questions appear in the Gallup Poll reports reproduced in the 42 volumes. These reports, the first of which was released on October 20, 1935, have been provided on a continuous basis since that time, most recently as daily updates on Gallup's website, gallup.com.

The 42-volume collection documents public opinion from 1935 to the present in the following six separate and distinct areas:

1. *Measuring the Strength of Support for the President, Political Candidates, and Political Parties*. For over 70 years, Gallup has measured, on a continuous basis, the strength of support for the president, for the congressional opposition, and for various political candidates and parties in national elections.
2. *Monitoring the Economy*. An important Gallup Poll objective has been monitoring the U.S. economy in all of its permutations from the perspective of the American consumer. Gallup now measures unemployment and job creation and assesses Americans' views on economic conditions, the job market, and personal financial concerns on a daily basis—providing a continuous record of this vital component of the U.S. economy.
3. *Gauging and Charting the Public's Mood*. From its earliest days the Gallup Poll has sought to determine, on an ongoing basis, Americans' satisfaction or dissatisfaction with the direction in which the nation appeared to be headed and with the way they thought that their personal lives were progressing. This process also has involved regular assessments of the people's mood regarding the state of the nation's economy as well as the status of their personal finances, their jobs, and other aspects of their lives.
4. *Recording the Public's Response to Major News Events*. Gallup has recorded the public's attitudes and opinions in response to major news events of the last seven decades. Examples include Adolf Hitler's invasion of the Soviet Union, the bombing of Pearl Harbor, the dropping of the atomic bomb on Hiroshima, the assassination of President John F. Kennedy, the moon landing, the taking of U.S. hostages in Iran, the O. J. Simpson trial verdict, the impeachment of President Bill Clinton, the 9/11/2001 terrorist attacks, the Iraq War, Hurricane Katrina and its aftermath, and the election of the nation's first black president in 2008.
5. *Measuring Americans' Views on Key Policy Issues*. A primary ongoing Gallup polling activity has been to document the collective will of the American people in terms of major policy issues and initiatives under consideration by elected representatives. Gallup routinely measures Americans' priorities, including monthly assessments of the most important problem facing the nation, interest in and awareness of issues and pending legislation, and overall sentiments on pressing national issues.
6. *Tracking America's Well-Being and Health*. Since 2008, Gallup has tracked America's subjective well-being and personal health assessments on a daily basis as part of the Gallup-Healthways Well-Being Index.

Two of the most frequently asked questions concerning the Gallup Poll are: Who pays for or provides financial support to the Poll? And who determines which topics are covered by the Poll or, more specifically, who decides which questions are asked on Gallup surveys? Since its founding in 1935, the Gallup Poll has been underwritten by Gallup itself, in the public interest, and by the nation's media. The Gallup Poll also receives financial support from subscriptions to Gallup Analytics, this annual volume, and partners with innovative businesses who are vitally interested in understanding human attitudes and behavior.

Suggestions for poll questions come from a wide variety of sources, including print and broadcast media, from institutions as well as from individuals, and from broad editorial consideration of the key and pressing issues facing the nation. In addition, the public themselves are regularly questioned about the problems and issues facing the nation as they perceive them. Their answers establish priorities and provide an up-to-the-minute list of topic areas to explore through the Poll.

The Gallup Poll, as it is known today, began life on October 20, 1935, as a nationally syndicated newspaper feature titled *America Speaks—the National Weekly Column of Public Opinion*. For brevity's sake, the media quickly came to refer to the column as the Gallup Poll, after its founder and editor-in-chief, Dr. George H. Gallup. Although Dr. Gallup had experimented during the 1934 congressional and 1932 presidential election campaigns to develop more accurate techniques for measuring public opinion, including scientific sampling, the first Gallup survey results to appear in print were those reported in the initial October 20, 1935, column.

Although the new scientific opinion polls enjoyed almost immediate popular success, their initial efforts were met with skepticism from many quarters. Critics questioned, for example, how it was possible to determine the opinions of the entire American populace based on only 1,000 interviews or less, or how one knows whether people were telling the truth. The credibility of the polls as well as their commercial viability was enhanced significantly, however, when Gallup correctly predicted that Roosevelt would win the 1936 presidential election in a landslide, directly contradicting the forecast of the Literary Digest Poll, the poll of record at that time. The Digest Poll, which was not based on scientific sampling procedures, claimed that FDR's Republican challenger, Alfred M. Landon, would easily win the election.

Over the subsequent eight decades, scientifically based opinion polls have gained a level of acceptance to where they are used today to investigate virtually every aspect of human experience in most nations of the world.

In 2008, Gallup began an unprecedented program of daily tracking surveys, interviewing 1,000 national adults virtually each day of the year as part of the Gallup-Healthways Well-Being Index project. Daily interviewing allows Gallup to track important health, well-being, political and economic indicators on a continuous basis and also creates large databases used for detailed analysis of small demographic, political and regional subgroups. The benefits of this major initiative in survey research procedures will be apparent to the reader as he or she reviews the content of this volume.

Frank Newport

THE SAMPLE

Most Gallup Poll findings are based on telephone surveys. The majority of the findings reported in Gallup Poll surveys are based on samples consisting of a minimum of 1,000 interviews.

Design of the Sample for Telephone Surveys

The findings from the telephone surveys are based on Gallup's standard national residential and cell telephone samples, consisting of directory-assisted random-digit telephone samples utilizing a proportionate, stratified sampling design. The random-digit aspect of the residential telephone sample is used to avoid "listing" bias. Numerous studies have shown that households with unlisted telephone numbers are different from listed households. "Unlistedness" is due to household mobility or to customer requests to prevent publication of the telephone number. To avoid this source of bias, a random-digit procedure designed to provide representation of both listed and unlisted (including not-yet-listed) numbers is used.

Beginning in 2008, Gallup began including cellphone telephone numbers in its national samples to account for the growing proportion of Americans who are "cellphone only." Cellphone samples are also based on random-digit-dial procedures using lists of all cellphone exchanges in the United States.

Telephone numbers for the continental United States are stratified into four regions of the country. The sample of telephone numbers produced by the described method is representative of all telephone households within the continental United States.

Only working banks of telephone numbers are selected. Eliminating nonworking banks from the sample increases the likelihood that any sampled telephone number will be associated with a residence.

Within each household contacted on a residential landline, an interview is sought with the adult eighteen years of age or older living in the household who has had the most recent birthday (this is a method commonly employed to make a random selection within households without having to ask the respondent to provide a complete roster of adults living in the household). In the event that the sample becomes disproportionately female (due to higher cooperation rates typically observed for female respondents), the household selection criteria are adjusted to select only the male in the household who has had the most recent birthday (except in households where the adults are exclusively female). Calls made on cellphones do not use the same respondent selection procedure since cellphones are typically associated with a single individual rather than shared among several members of a household.

A minimum of three calls (and up to six calls) is attempted to each selected telephone number to complete an interview. Time of day and the day of the week for callbacks are varied to maximize the chances of reaching a respondent. All interviews are conducted on weekends or weekday evenings in order to contact potential respondents among the working population.

The final sample is weighted so that the distribution of the sample matches current estimates derived from the U.S. Census Bureau's Current Population Survey (CPS) for the adult population living in households with a landline or cellular telephone in the continental United States.

Weighting Procedures

After the survey data have been collected and processed, each respondent is assigned a weight so that the demographic characteristics of the total weighted sample of respondents match the latest estimates of the demographic characteristics of the adult population available from the U.S. Census Bureau. Gallup weights data to census estimates for gender, race, age, Hispanic ethnicity, educational attainment, region, population density, and phone status.

The procedures described above are designed to produce samples approximating the adult civilian population (18 and older) living in private households. Survey percentages may be applied to census estimates of the size of these populations to project percentages into numbers of people. The manner in which the sample is drawn also produces a sample that approximates the distribution of private households in the United States. Therefore, survey results also can be projected to numbers of households.

Sampling Tolerances

In interpreting survey results, it should be borne in mind that all sample surveys are subject to sampling error—that is, the extent to which the results may differ from what would be obtained if the whole population surveyed had been interviewed. The size of such sampling errors depends largely on the number of interviews. The design of the survey methodology, including weighting the sample to population estimates, should also be taken into account when figuring sample error.

The following tables may be used in estimating the maximum sampling error of any percentage. The computed allowances have taken into account the effect of the sample design and weighting upon sampling error for a typical Gallup poll. They may be interpreted as indicating the maximum range (plus or minus the figure shown) within which the results of repeated samplings in the same time period could be expected to vary, 95% of the time, assuming the same sampling procedure, the same interviewers, and the same questionnaire.

Table A shows how much allowance should be made for the sampling error of a percentage near 50% (which produces the largest uncertainty or sampling error; sampling error decreases as the percentages move further away from 50% in either direction).

Let us say a reported percentage is 49% for a group that includes 1,000 respondents. We go to the column for a sample size of 1,000. The number here is 4, which means that the 49% obtained in the sample is subject to a maximum sampling error of plus or minus 4 points. Another way of saying it is that very probably (95 chances out of 100) the average of repeated samplings would be somewhere between 45 and 53, with the most likely figure being the 49 obtained.

In comparing survey results in two samples, such as for men and women, the question arises as to how large must a difference between them be before one can be reasonably sure that it reflects a real difference. In Table B, the number of points that must be allowed for in such comparisons is indicated.

Here is an example of how the table would be used: Let us say that 50% of men respond a certain way and 40% of women also respond that way, for a difference of 10 percentage points between them. Can we say with any assurance that the 10-point difference reflects a real difference between men and women on the question? The sample contains approximately 500 men and 500 women.

TABLE A
Recommended Allowance for Sampling Error of a Percentage

In Percentage Points (at 95 in 100 confidence level)*
Sample Size

	1,000	750	500	250	100
Percentages near 50	4 (3.6)	4	5	7	11

*The chances are 95 in 100 that the sampling error is not larger than the figures shown.

TABLE B
Recommended Allowance for Sampling Error of the Difference

In Percentage Points (at 95 in 100 confidence level)*
Percentages near 50

	750	500	250
Size of sample			
750	6		
500	6	7	
250	8	8	10

*The chances are 95 in 100 that the sampling error is not larger than the figures shown.

Since the percentages are near 50, we consult Table B, and since the two samples are about 500 persons each, we look for the number in the column headed "500" that is also in the row designated "500." We find the number 7 here. This means that the allowance for error should be 7 points, and that in concluding that the percentage among men is somewhere between 3 and 17 points higher than the percentage among women, we should be wrong only about 5% of the time. In other words, we can conclude with considerable confidence that a difference exists in the direction observed and that it amounts to at least 3 percentage points.

DESCRIPTIONS OF GALLUP ECONOMIC MEASURES USED IN THIS VOLUME

Gallup's **Employment/Underemployment Index** provides continuous monitoring of U.S. employment and underemployment and serves as a key adjunct to the U.S. government's monthly tracking. This index—based on the combination of responses to a set of questions about employment status—is designed to measure U.S. employment accurately, in accordance with International Conference of Labour Statisticians standards. Based on an individual's responses to the question series (some of which are asked of only a subset of respondents), Gallup classifies respondents into one of six employment categories: employed full time for an employer; employed full time for self; employed part time, but do not want to work full time; employed part time, but want to work full time; unemployed; and out of the workforce. Using these categorizations, Gallup further divides the workforce into those who are employed and those who are underemployed. Employed respondents are those in the workforce who are either employed full time or working part time but do not want to work full time. Underemployed respondents are those in the workforce who are either unemployed or employed part time but want to work full time. Gallup interviews 1,000 Americans daily—or about 30,000 per month. Because of its daily tracking of other political, business, and well-being measures, Gallup provides insights not available from any other source on the health, well-being, optimism, financial situations, and politics of those who are working or seeking work.

Gallup's **Economic Confidence Index** is based on the combined responses to two questions asking Americans, first, to rate economic conditions in this country today and, second, whether they think economic conditions in the country as a whole are getting better or getting worse. Gallup's Economic Confidence Index is updated daily, based on interviews conducted the previous night, as well as weekly, providing a far more up-to-date assessment than the monthly reports from the other indices, which are often weeks old when issued.

Gallup's **Job Creation Index** is based on employed Americans' estimates of their companies' hiring and firing practices. Gallup asks its sample of employed Americans each day whether their companies are hiring new people and expanding the size of their workforces, not changing the size of their workforces, or letting people go and reducing the size of their workforces. The resulting index—computed on a daily and a weekly basis by subtracting the percentage of employers letting people go from the percentage hiring—is a real-time indicator of the nation's employment picture across all industry and business sectors. Gallup analysis indicates that the Job Creation Index is an excellent predictor of weekly jobless claims that the U.S. Labor Department reports each Thursday. In some ways, Gallup's Job Creation Index is more meaningful than the government's weekly new jobless claims measure, given that not everyone who is laid off files for unemployment. The index may also pick up hiring trends days or weeks before they are manifested in the official unemployment rate or other lagging indicators. Finally, the index measures job creation (hiring) and job loss (letting go) on a continuous basis. This provides additional real-time insight not available from broadly aggregated indicators and unemployment data.

Gallup's **Consumer Spending** measure is calculated from responses to a basic question asking Americans each day to estimate the amount of money they spent "yesterday," excluding the purchase of a home or an automobile or normal household bills. The result is a real-time indicator of discretionary retail spending, fluctuations in which are sensitive to shifts in the economic environment. Changes in Gallup's spending estimates are related to changes in both direction and magnitude of actual consumer spending as reported by the government. Further, Gallup's Consumer Spending measure provides estimates on a continuing basis, giving an early read on what the government eventually reports roughly two weeks after the close of each month. Gallup's continuous surveying allows for analysis of spending patterns on a daily and a weekly basis, which is particularly important to understanding seasonal variations in spending. The spending measure allows business and investment decisions to be based on essentially real-time information.

ABOUT THE GALLUP-HEALTHWAYS
WELL-BEING INDEX®

The **Gallup-Healthways Well-Being Index** includes more than 2.2 million surveys and captures how people feel about and experience their daily lives. Levels of well-being correlate with healthcare (utilization and cost) and productivity measures (absenteeism, presenteeism, and job performance), all critical to organizational and economic competitiveness.

Well-Being Index data provide a comprehensive view of well-being across five elements:

Purpose: Liking what you do each day and being motivated to achieve your goals

Social: Having supportive relationships and love in your life

Financial: Managing your economic life to reduce stress and increase security

Community: Liking where you live, feeling safe and having pride in your community

Physical: Having good health and enough energy to get things done daily

STATE OF THE STATES POLLS

A number of stories included in this volume are based on Gallup's "State of the States" series, analyses that examine state-by-state differences on the political, economic, and well-being measures that Gallup tracks each day.

State of the States stories are based on aggregated data for six-month or full-year time periods, providing large enough samples for meaningful analyses of responses in each of the 50 states and the District of Columbia.

2015 CHRONOLOGY

January 2015

January 7 Twelve killed in terrorist attack at newspaper in Paris

January 21 Israeli prime minister agrees to controversial U.S. Congress appearance

February 2015

February 1 New England wins over Seattle in Super Bowl

February 12 Senate approves Ashton Carter as secretary of defense

February 14 Worst terrorist attack in 30 years in Denmark

February 27 Opposition leader is assassinated in Moscow

March 2015

March 3 Israeli Prime Minister Netanyahu speaks to U.S. Congress

March 4 Justice Department releases report on Ferguson police

March 4 Trial begins in Boston Marathon Bombing

March 17 Netanyahu's Likud Party wins Israeli elections

March 23 Charlottesville police report no evidence in University of Virginia fraternity rape case

March 24 Crash of German jetliner carrying 150 passengers, no survivors

April 2015

April 2 Iran agrees to nuclear deal

April 8 Tsarnaev found guilty in Boston Marathon Bombing trial

April 12 Hillary Clinton officially announces presidential candidacy

April 12 Baltimore riots after the death of Freddie Gray while in police custody

May 2015

May 2 Duchess of Cambridge gives birth to a girl

May 8 Cameron elected to second term as British prime minister

May 12 Eight killed in Amtrak crash north of Philadelphia

May 15 Boston Marathon Bombing jury sentences Tsarnaev to death

May 22 Ireland legalizes same-sex marriage

June 2015

June 17 Man kills nine at Charleston church

June 18 House passes Trade Authority Bill

June 26 Supreme Court declares constitutional right to same-sex marriage

| June 26 | Gunman kills dozens at beach resort in Tunisia |

July 2015

July 1	Cuba and U.S. agree to open embassies
July 10	Confederate flag removed from South Carolina buildings
July 14	Iran agrees to nuclear deal
July 14	Spacecraft reaches Pluto
July 16	Four Marines killed in recruiting center shooting
July 27	Boy Scouts ease ban on gay adults

August 2015

August 6	Republicans hold first 2016 presidential debate
August 14	American flag raised in Cuba
August 20	Greek prime minister resigns as result of economic crisis

September 2015

September 22	Pope Francis visits the U.S.
September 22	Senate blocks abortion ban bill
September 25	John Boehner, Speaker of the House, resigns

October 2015

| October 1 | Gunman kills seven at Oregon Community College |

October 13	Democrats hold first debate
October 15	Obama announces more U.S. troops to Afghanistan
October 22	Hillary Clinton questioned in Benghazi hearing on Capitol Hill
October 29	Paul Ryan is elected Speaker of the House of Representatives
October 30	U.S. sends troops to fight ISIS in Syria

November 2015

November 13	Attacks by ISIS kill dozens in Paris
November 20	Over 25 killed in Mali hotel attack
November 24	Turkey shoots down Russian warplane
November 27	Three killed in Colorado Springs Planned Parenthood shooting
November 30	World leaders gather for U.N. climate talks

December 2015

December 2	San Bernardino social services center shooting results in 14 dead
December 3	Defense Department announces all military combat roles open for women
December 8	GOP candidate Donald Trump calls for ban on Muslims entering the U.S.
December 12	U.N. Climate Summit agrees to global pact

January 02, 2015

CLUSTER OF CONCERNS VIE FOR TOP U.S. PROBLEM IN 2014

by Lydia Saad

Story Highlights

- *Poor government leadership was top problem in 2014*
- *Economy ranked a close second*
- *No issue averaged 20% or more mentions, a first since 2001*

PRINCETON, N.J.—In 2014, four issues generated enough public concern over enough months for at least 10% of Americans, on average, to identify each of them as the nation's most important problem. Complaints about government leadership—including President Barack Obama, the Republicans in Congress and general political conflict—led the list, at 18%. This was closely followed by mentions of the economy in general (17%), unemployment or jobs (15%) and healthcare (10%).

Most Important Problem Facing the U.S. in 2014

Issues averaging 2% or higher

	Yearly average^	Highest monthly result	Lowest monthly result
	%	%	%
Government/Congress/Politicians	18	21	15
Economy in general	17	20	13
Unemployment/Jobs	15	23	8
Healthcare	10	16	5
Immigration	8	17	3
Federal deficit/debt	6	9	3
Ethics/Moral decline	5	7	3
Education	4	6	3
Poverty/Homelessness	4	5	2
Focus overseas/Foreign aid	4	7	1
Gap between rich/poor	3	4	1
Race relations/Racism	3	13	1
Lack of money	3	5	1
Crime/Violence	2	3	1
Judicial system	2	3	1
Lack of respect for each other	2	2	1
Wars/War (non-specific)	2	3	1
Terrorism	2	4	0
Wage issues	2	2	1
National security	2	3	1

^ Based on average of 12 monthly surveys

GALLUP

Beyond the top four issues, 8% of Americans named immigration as the country's most important problem, while 6% mentioned the federal budget deficit or debt and 5% cited ethical or moral decline. All other issues received less than 5% average mentions in 2014.

Some of the issues troubling Americans received uneven attention during the year. In particular, mentions of unemployment were consistently higher in the first half of 2014 than later in the year, reaching 23% in February. Also, race relations, usually mentioned by no more than 2% of Americans as the nation's top problem, surged to 13% in December as recent legal decisions sparked protests nationwide against police treatment of blacks. Similarly, mentions of immigration spiked in July to 17% as thousands of undocumented children from Central and South America created a crisis at the southern U.S. border. But this is the first time since 2001 that no single issue averaged 20% or more for the year.

The year 2014 was also the first since 2007 that the economy was not the top ranking issue, and it was the first year ever in Gallup records that dissatisfaction with government topped the list. Without a dominant issue such as the economy, the Iraq War or terrorism crowding out other issues as they have in years past, this is also only the third time since 2001 when three issues garnered at least 15% in average mentions. Thus, 2014 joins 2013 and 2009 as years when multiple issues emerged as significant top-of-mind concerns for Americans.

Top Four Issues Named Most Important Problem Facing the U.S.

Annual averages of monthly results

	Top ranked issue	Second ranked issue	Third ranked issue	Fourth ranked issue
2014	Government (18%)	Economy (17%)	Unemployment (15%)	Healthcare (10%)
2013	Economy (22%)	Government (20%)	Unemployment (16%)	Healthcare (10%)
2012	Economy (31%)	Unemployment (25%)	Government (13%)	Federal deficit/debt (10%)
2011	Economy (30%)	Unemployment (29%)	Government (12%)	Federal deficit/debt (12%)
2010	Economy (29%)	Unemployment (27%)	Healthcare (13%)	Government (12%)
2009	Economy (40%)	Unemployment (16%)	Healthcare (15%)	Government (7%)
2008	Economy (39%)	Iraq (18%)	Gas prices (10%)	Healthcare (8%)
2007	Iraq (33%)	Healthcare (10%)	Immigration (9%)	Government (8%)
2006	Iraq (26%)	Immigration (10%)	Government (9%)	Economy (9%)
2005	Iraq (22%)	Economy (11%)	Government (8%)	Terrorism (8%)
2004	Iraq (22%)	Economy (19%)	Unemployment (14%)	Terrorism (14%)
2003	Economy (27%)	Iraq (17%)	Unemployment (12%)	Terrorism (10%)
2002	Terrorism (24%)	Economy (22%)	Iraq (9%)	Unemployment (7%)
2001	Economy (14%)	Terrorism (10%)	Ethics/Moral decline (9%)	Education (9%)

GALLUP

Of the top five issues that most concerned Americans in 2014, the economy and unemployment are significantly less dominant than they were even two years ago. At the same time, concerns about government and immigration have been mounting, while concerns about healthcare have consistently simmered at a moderately high level since 2009.

Most Important Problem Facing the U.S. – Annual Averages Since 2001

Average percentage mentioned across monthly measures for each year

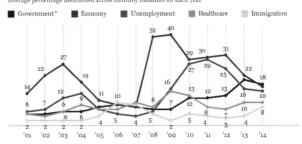

■ Government^ ■ Economy ■ Unemployment ■ Healthcare ░ Immigration

^ Government includes dissatisfaction with President Obama, Congress, other government leaders, ethics of politicians and political conflict

GALLUP

With unemployment and gas prices falling, the U.S. not being involved in any major wars and scaling back operations in Afghanistan, and no acts of domestic terrorism occurring, the factors that have caused Americans to converge on a single pressing concern in the past simply weren't present in 2014. Rather, as mentions of the economy and unemployment have dwindled since 2012, mentions of healthcare and government leadership have grown to join them, forming a set of comparably sized, moderate-level concerns that now define the public's view of what ails the nation.

Not only was this the average picture in 2014, but it remained the state of affairs in the last quarter, suggesting 2015 is starting on a similarly calm note. That is underscored by the significant improvement in the Gallup Economic Confidence Index in late December, reaching positive territory for the first time since before 2008.

The dispersion of public concern seen in 2014 may also have implications for the 2016 presidential election. Should it persist, the lack of a single defining public issue could make candidates' task of honing a message for the election more complex.

Survey Methods

Results for the monthly Gallup Poll Social Series surveys included in this analysis are based on telephone interviews conducted with a random sample of approximately 1,000 adults, aged 18 and older, living in all 50 U.S. states and the District of Columbia. The yearly averages from the combined results are based on the total sample of approximately 12,000 national adults, with a margin of sampling error of ±1 percentage point at the 95% confidence level.

January 06, 2015
ABOUT THREE IN 10 AMERICAN JEWS IDENTIFY AS REPUBLICANS

by Frank Newport

Story Highlights

- *29% of American Jews are Republican, up from 22% in 2008*
- *61% of Jews are Democrats, down from 71% seven years ago*
- *Highly religious and male Jews are most likely to be Republican*

WASHINGTON, D.C.—In 2014, 29% of Jewish Americans identified as Republicans or leaned Republican, little changed in recent years, but higher than in 2008. Meanwhile, 61% of American Jews identified as Democrats or leaned Democratic, down from 71% in the strongly Democratic year of 2008.

The diminished Democratic skew among American Jews in recent years is slightly more pronounced than the same trend among all Americans. The percentage of the general population that identifies with or leans Democratic has fallen by about seven percentage points since 2008, compared with the 10-point drop among Jews. The percentage that identifies with or leans Republican among the general population is up three points, compared with the increase of seven points among Jews.

These results are based on 2014 Gallup Daily tracking interviews with 4,116 Americans who identified their religion as Jewish.

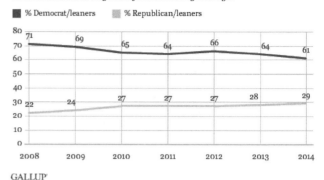

American Jewish Party Identification: Yearly Averages

GALLUP'

Jews in the U.S. are proportionately well represented in Congress, with 28 members of the 535 House and Senate members in the new Congress identifying their religion as Jewish, meaning that about 5% of all House members and Senators are Jewish, compared with the 2% of the adult population. Of these Jewish members of Congress, all are Democrats or independent, with the one exception being newly elected Republican Rep. Lee Zeldin of New York.

Jewish Partisanship Varies by Gender, Religiosity and Education

As is the case with other Americans, Jewish Americans' political leanings vary significantly by religiosity, gender and education. Jewish men are more Republican than Jewish women, highly religious Jews are more Republican than less religious Jews, and Jews with lower levels of education are more likely to be Republicans than those with more formal education.

American Jewish Party Identification: 2014

By religiosity, gender and education

	Republican/leaners	Democrat/leaners
	%	%
Highly religious	42	46
Moderately religious	32	59
Not religious	24	67
Male	36	54
Female	23	68
High school or less	36	49
Some college	32	55
College graduate	30	62
Postgraduate	25	68

GALLUP'

All of these patterns among the Jewish population reflect those evident in the overall U.S. population. The Democratic skew among women is well established, highly religious Americans are more Republican than those who are less religious, and Americans with postgraduate educations are more likely to be Democratic than those with less education.

Two of the Jewish segments with the highest Republican representation constitute a relatively small proportion of the overall Jewish population, which helps explain the two-to-one overall Democratic-to-Republican Jewish ratio. Jews as a group are not very religious, with only 19% classified as highly religious, less than half of the percentage of all Americans who are highly religious (41%).

Jews tend to have higher levels of education on average, leaving only 34% who do not have a college degree, compared with 69% of the general population.

There are few systematic differences in party identification in the Jewish population across age, income or region of country.

Bottom Line

The general Democratic orientation of American Jews is a well-established political fact, although this Democratic slant has decreased marginally in recent years, as it has among the general U.S. population. Given the small sample sizes of the Jewish population in traditional surveys, it is difficult to determine precisely those issues on which Jewish Democrats nationally may differ from Jewish Republicans, although most news accounts suggest that U.S. relations with Israel is certainly one of them. The Jewish Republican minority in the U.S. is politically active, including the efforts of the Republican Jewish Coalition, which will hold its national leadership reception in Washington, D.C., on Jan. 6 with prominent Republican members of Congress expected to be in attendance. The direct influence of Jewish Republicans in Congress may be lessened with the departure of former House Minority Leader Eric Cantor, who was defeated in his Virginia Republican primary election last year.

Survey Methods

Results for this Gallup poll are based on telephone interviews conducted Jan. 2–Dec. 30, 2014, on the Gallup U.S. Daily tracking survey, with a random sample of 4,116 adults who identify their religion as Jewish, aged 18 and older, living in all 50 U.S. states and the District of Columbia. For results based on the total sample of Jewish adults, the margin of sampling error is ±2 percentage points at the 95% confidence level. All reported margins of sampling error include computed design effects for weighting.

January 07, 2015
IN U.S., UNINSURED RATE SINKS TO 12.9%

by Jenna Levy

Story Highlights

- *Uninsured rate down from 13.4% in the third quarter of 2014*
- *Rate has dropped most among blacks and lower-income Americans*
- *Most Americans are covered through employer or self-funded plans*

WASHINGTON, D.C.—The uninsured rate among U.S. adults for the fourth quarter of 2014 averaged 12.9%. This is down slightly from 13.4% in the third quarter of 2014 and down significantly from 17.1% a year ago. The uninsured rate has dropped 4.2 percentage points since the Affordable Care Act's requirement for Americans to have health insurance went into effect one year ago.

The uninsured rate declined sharply in the first and second quarters last year as more Americans signed up for health insurance through federal and state exchanges. After the open enrollment period closed in mid-April, the rate leveled off at around 13%. The

12.9% who lacked health insurance in the fourth quarter is the lowest Gallup and Healthways have recorded since beginning to track the measure daily in 2008. The 2015 open enrollment period began in the fourth quarter on Nov. 15 and will close on Feb. 15.

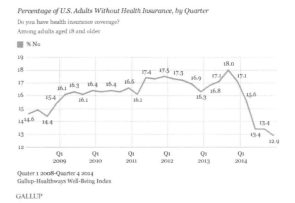

Percentage of U.S. Adults Without Health Insurance, by Quarter
Do you have health insurance coverage?
Among adults aged 18 and older

Quarter 1 2008-Quarter 4 2014
Gallup-Healthways Well-Being Index

GALLUP

The fourth-quarter results are based on more than 43,000 interviews with U.S. adults from Oct. 1 to Dec. 30, 2014, as part of the Gallup-Healthways Well-Being Index. Gallup and Healthways ask 500 U.S. adults each day whether they have health insurance, allowing for precise and ongoing measurement of the percentage of Americans who lack health insurance.

Uninsured Rate Drops Most Among Blacks, Low Income

While the uninsured rate has declined across nearly all key demographic groups since the Affordable Care Act went into effect a year ago, it has plunged most among blacks and lower-income Americans. The uninsured rate among blacks dropped seven points over the past year, while the rate among Americans earning less than $36,000 in annual household income dropped 6.9 points.

The Hispanic population remains a key target of the healthcare law's marketing efforts, as it continues to be the subgroup with the highest uninsured rate, at 32.4%. Still, the percentage of uninsured Hispanics is down 6.3 points since the end of 2013.

Across age groups, the uninsured rate dropped the most among 18- to 25-year-olds, falling 6.1 points from a year ago. The rate fell 5.6 points for 26- to 34-year-olds, and 5.2 points for 35- to 64-year-olds. The percentage of uninsured Americans aged 65 and older has not changed over the past year, likely because most were already covered through Medicare.

Percentage of Uninsured Americans, by Subgroup
Do you have health insurance coverage?

	Quarter 4 2013 %	Quarter 4 2014 %	Net change (pct. pts.)
National adults	17.1	12.9	-4.2
18 to 25	23.5	17.4	-6.1
26 to 34	28.2	22.6	-5.6
35 to 64	18.0	12.8	-5.2
65+	2.0	2.0	0.0
Whites	11.9	8.5	-3.4
Blacks	20.9	13.9	-7.0
Hispanics	38.7	32.4	-6.3
Less than $36,000	30.7	23.8	-6.9
$36,000 to $89,999	11.7	8.7	-3.0
$90,000+	5.8	3.4	-2.4

Gallup-Healthways Well-Being Index

GALLUP

Two in Five Americans Under 65 Have Employer-Based Coverage

The uninsured rate among 18- to 64-year-olds dropped to 15.5% from 20.8% a year ago, with most of the dip reflecting Americans gaining coverage through self-funded plans, Medicaid and Medicare. Those aged 65 and older are excluded from this analysis of health insurance type because most are covered through Medicare.

The 20.6% of U.S. adults under the age of 65 who say they are covered by a self-funded plan is up three points since the fourth quarter of 2013. This is likely because more Americans purchased individual plans through a federal or state health insurance exchange.

The percentage of 18- to 64-year-olds with Medicaid (8.6%) has also increased slightly over the past year, which is not surprising because many states expanded Medicaid eligibility so that more lower-income and lower-middle-income Americans could get affordable insurance. There was also a slight increase over the past year in the percentage of those under 65 with Medicare insurance.

The percentage who get their insurance through a current or former employer declined in the first quarter of 2014, but recovered throughout the year.

Type of Health Insurance Coverage in the U.S. Among 18- to 64-Year-Olds

Is your insurance coverage through a current or former employer, a union, Medicare, Medicaid, military or veterans coverage, or a plan fully paid for by you or a family member?
Note: Primary and secondary insurance combined

	Q3 2013* %	Q4 2013 %	Q1 2014 %	Q2 2014 %	Q3 2014 %	Q4 2014 %
Employer	44.4	44.2	42.5	43.5	43.3	43.4
Self-paid	16.7	17.6	19.3	20.7	20.7	20.6
Medicaid	6.8	6.9	7.9	8.4	8.7	8.6
Medicare	6.4	6.1	6.3	6.9	7.1	7.5
Military/Veterans	4.3	4.6	4.8	4.7	4.9	4.7
Union	2.8	2.5	2.6	2.5	2.4	2.6
(Something else)	3.8	3.5	3.7	3.8	3.6	4.1
No insurance	21.2	20.8	19.0	16.2	16.2	15.5

Gallup-Healthways Well-Being Index
*August-September 2013 only

GALLUP

Implications

The Affordable Care Act has accomplished one of its goals: increasing the percentage of Americans who have health insurance coverage. The uninsured rate as measured by Gallup has dropped 4.2 points since the requirement to have health insurance or pay a fine went into effect. It will likely drop further as plans purchased during the current open enrollment period take effect. The Department of Health and Human Services (HHS) reported that 6.5 million Americans either selected new plans or were automatically re-enrolled into a plan via HealthCare.gov as of Dec. 26, 2014. Prior to this year's open enrollment period, Gallup found that more than half of those who were uninsured planned to sign up, a positive sign. Gallup also found that most newly insured Americans planned to renew their policy or get a different policy elsewhere.

Furthermore, the uninsured rate may drop because the healthcare law's provision requiring businesses with 100 or more employees to provide health insurance to 70% of their workers took effect on Jan. 1. In 2016, companies with 50 or more employees will be required to provide health insurance to 95% of their workers.

Other signs also point to the uninsured rate falling more after this open enrollment period ends. HHS continues to focus on the financial assistance available to enrollees and increasing the fine for not having health insurance: currently $325 per person or 2% of an individual's yearly household income, whichever is greater. Gallup previously found that higher fines would compel more uninsured Americans to sign up.

The uninsured rate could also fall further as more states expand Medicaid. Twenty-seven states and the District of Columbia implemented Medicaid expansion through the Affordable Care Act in 2014, which Gallup found to be a major factor in declining uninsured rates. Pennsylvania expanded Medicaid as of Jan. 1, and Arkansas, Iowa and Michigan approved Section 1115 waivers for expansion, giving the secretary of HHS authority to approve experimental, pilot or demonstration projects that promote the objectives of Medicaid and the Children's Health Insurance Program.

However, closing the health insurance gap may be more challenging this year than last, as those who did not sign up last year may be harder to reach or more reluctant to get health insurance. Additionally, the open enrollment period will be nearly two months shorter in 2015 than in 2014.

Survey Methods

Results are based on telephone interviews conducted Oct. 1–Dec. 30, 2014, as part of the Gallup-Healthways Well-Being Index survey, with a random sample of 43,016 adults, aged 18 and older, living in all 50 U.S. states and the District of Columbia. For results based on the total sample of national adults, the margin of sampling error is ±1 percentage point at the 95% confidence level.

January 07, 2015

IN U.S., NEW RECORD 43% ARE POLITICAL INDEPENDENTS

by Jeffrey M. Jones

Story Highlights

- *Record 43% of Americans are political independents*
- *Democrats maintain edge among those with a party preference*
- *Democratic advantage smaller in 2014 than in 2013*

PRINCETON, N.J.—An average 43% of Americans identified politically as independents in 2014, establishing a new high in Gallup telephone poll trends back to 1988. In terms of national identification with the two major parties, Democrats continued to hold a modest edge over Republicans, 30% to 26%.

Since 2008, the percentage of political independents—those who identify as such before their leanings to the two major parties are taken into account—has steadily climbed from 35% to the current 43%, exceeding 40% each of the last four years. Prior to 2011, the high in independent identification was 39% in 1995 and 1999.

The recent rise in political independence has come at the expense of both parties, but more among Democrats than among Republicans. Over the last six years, Democratic identification has fallen from 36%—the highest in the last 25 years—to 30%. Meanwhile, Republican identification is down from 28% in 2008 to 26% last year.

The latest results are based on aggregated data from 15 separate Gallup telephone polls conducted throughout 2014.

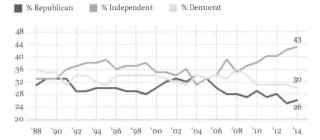

Based on multiple day polls conducted by telephone

GALLUP

These changes have left both parties at or near low points in the percentage who identify themselves as core supporters of the party. Although the party identification data compiled in telephone polls since 1988 are not directly comparable to the in-person polling Gallup collected before then, the percentages identifying as Democrats prior to 1988 were so high that it is safe to say the average 30% identifying as Democrats last year is the lowest since at least the 1950s.

Republican identification, at 26%, is a shade higher than the 25% in 2013. Not since 1983, the year before Ronald Reagan's landslide re-election victory, have fewer Americans identified as Republicans.

The decline in identification with both parties in recent years comes as dissatisfaction with government has emerged as one of the most important problems facing the country, according to Americans. This is likely due to the partisan gridlock that has come from divided party control of the federal government. Trust in the government to handle problems more generally is the lowest Gallup has measured to date, and Americans' favorable ratings of both parties are at or near historical lows. Thus, the rise in U.S. political independence likely flows from the high level of frustration with the government and the political parties that control it.

Democrats' Edge in Party Identification and Leaning Shrinks

Although independents claim no outright allegiance to either major party, it is well known that they are not necessarily neutral when it comes to politics. When pressed, most independents will say they lean to one of the two major parties. For example, last year an average of 17% of Americans who initially identified as independents subsequently said they "leaned" Republican, 15% were independents who leaned Democratic, with the remaining 11% not expressing a leaning to either party.

Since partisan leaners often share similar attitudes to those who identify with a party outright, the relative proportions of identifiers plus leaners gives a sense of the relative electoral strength of the two political parties, since voting decisions almost always come down to a choice of the two major-party candidates. In 2014, an average 45% of Americans identified as Democrats or said they were Democratic-leaning independents, while 42% identified as Republicans or were Republican-leaning independents.

That the three-point Democratic edge was down from six points in 2013, and among Democrats' smaller advantages the past 25 years. Democrats usually hold an advantage in this combined measure of party affiliation. In fact, the only year Republicans held a notable edge since Gallup began tracking independents' political

leanings was in 1991, the year Republican President George H. W. Bush's approval ratings soared after the United States' victory in the Persian Gulf War. Democrats' high point came in 2008, in the final year of George W. Bush's administration and the year Barack Obama was first elected president.

U.S. Party Identification (Including Independent Leanings), Annual Averages, Gallup Polls, 1991-2014

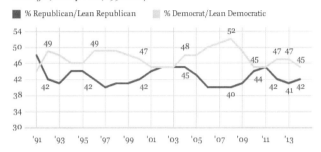

Note: Gallup began regularly measuring independents' party leanings in 1991.

GALLUP

However, the three-point Democratic advantage for all of 2014 obscures the change that occurred during the year. On a quarterly basis, Democrats started out 2014 with a five-point edge, similar to their advantage in 2013. That dipped to two points by the third quarter. In the fourth quarter, likely in response to Republicans' success in the 2014 midterm elections, Republicans held a slight advantage of one point.

Party Identification (Including Independent Leanings), Quarterly Averages, 2014

	% Republican/ Lean Republican	% Democrat/ Lean Democratic	Democratic advantage (pct. pts.)
Quarter 1 (January-March)	41	46	+5
Quarter 2 (April-June)	42	46	+4
Quarter 3 (July-September)	43	45	+2
Quarter 4 (October-December)	44	43	-1

GALLUP

Implications

Since 2008, Americans have been increasingly reluctant to identify with either the Republican or Democratic Party, and now a record 43% claimed political independence in 2014. Given historical trends, 2015 could bring a new record, as the percentage identifying as independents typically increases in the year before a presidential election, averaging a 2.5-point increase in the last six such years.

Although Democrats typically have an advantage in partisanship, that edge shrunk in 2014 and in the last months of the year the parties were essentially on equal footing. With each party controlling part of the federal government—Democrats the presidency and Republicans the Congress—they each will have a say in how the nation addresses its major challenges in the coming year. However, in recent years divided control of government has more often than not resulted in partisan gridlock, and Americans' frustration with the frequent political stalemate is evident. Continued frustration with the government would likely encourage more Americans to identify as independents this year.

Survey Methods

Results for this Gallup poll are based on telephone interviews conducted January–December 2014, with a combined random sample of 16,479 adults, aged 18 and older, living in all 50 U.S. states and the District of Columbia. For results based on the total sample of national adults, the margin of sampling error is ±1 percentage point at the 95% confidence level. All reported margins of sampling error include computed design effects for weighting.

January 08, 2015
U.S. PAYROLL TO POPULATION RATE 44.3% IN DECEMBER

by Ben Ryan

Story Highlights

- *Unemployment continues slide to 5.8%*
- *Hispanics make biggest gains*
- *2014 workforce participation rate remains below previous years'*

WASHINGTON, D.C.—The U.S. Payroll to Population employment rate (P2P), as measured by Gallup, was 44.3% in December, statistically similar to the 44.2% measured in November. The percentage of Americans employed full time for an employer in 2014 did not show a steep end-of-year decline as it did in 2012 and 2013, offering hope that the P2P metric may strengthen more in the new year.

U.S. Payroll to Population Employment Rates

Monthly trend, January 2010-December 2014

% of adult population employed full time for an employer

Gallup Daily tracking

GALLUP

Gallup's P2P metric tracks the percentage of the U.S. adult population aged 18 and older who are employed by an employer for at least 30 hours per week. The latest results are based on Gallup Daily tracking interviews with 26,352 Americans, conducted Dec. 1–30 by landline telephone and cellphone. Gallup does not count adults who are self-employed, work fewer than 30 hours per week, who are unemployed or are out of the workforce as payroll-employed in the P2P metric.

P2P is not seasonally adjusted. However, because of seasonal fluctuations, year-over-year comparisons are helpful in evaluating whether monthly changes are attributable to seasonal hiring patterns or true growth (or deterioration) in the percentage of people working full time for an employer. The P2P rate in December 2014 is up from the rate in December 2013 (42.9%), and similar to the P2P rate recorded in December 2012 (44.4%).

Workforce Participation at 66.3%

Workforce participation among U.S. adults dipped slightly from 66.9% in November to 66.3% in December. Workforce participation measures the percentage of adults aged 18 and older who are working, or who are not working but are actively looking for work and are available for employment.

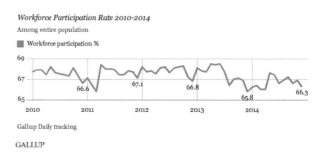

Workforce Participation Rate 2010-2014

Among entire population

Workforce participation %

Gallup Daily tracking

GALLUP

Workforce participation generally falls in the fourth quarter as retirements and layoffs are often pegged to the end of the year. The workforce participation rate has ranged narrowly between lows of 65.8% and highs of 68.5% since January 2010, but the 66.3% in December is among the lowest figures recorded in that time span. Workforce participation since mid-2013 has most often registered below 67%, whereas in prior years it was typically higher than that. This pattern reflects both a growing retiree population and declining participation among those still in their prime working years.

Unemployment Slides to 5.8%, Underemployment Steady

Gallup's U.S. unemployment rate represents the percentage of adults in the workforce who did not have any paid work in the past seven days, for an employer or themselves, and who were actively looking for and available to work. Gallup's unadjusted U.S. unemployment rate fell to 5.8% in December, continuing a relatively steady decline over the past 12 months, and reaching a new low in Gallup's five-year trend.

Gallup U.S. Unemployment Rate Trend, January 2010-December 2014

Percentage of the workforce who are unemployed

Unemployment rate

Gallup Daily tracking

GALLUP

Unlike Gallup's P2P rate, which is a percentage of the total population, traditional employment metrics—such as the unemployment rates Gallup and the U.S. Bureau of Labor Statistics (BLS) report—are based on the percentage of the workforce. While both Gallup and BLS data are based on robust surveys, the two have important methodological differences. Additionally, the primary unemployment rate released by the BLS each month is seasonally adjusted. Although Gallup's employment numbers highly relate to BLS rates, Gallup's numbers tend to have more month-to-month variability, and the unemployment rate that the BLS reports each month does not always track precisely with the Gallup estimate.

Gallup's measure of *underemployment* in December is 15.1%, the same level registered in November, but still lower than what Gallup has measured in prior years. Gallup's U.S. underemployment rate combines the percentage of adults in the workforce who are unemployed (5.8%) and those who are working part time but desire full-time work (9.3%). While Gallup's measure of unemployment fell slightly in December from November, the percentage working part time but who want full-time work rose the same amount, leaving the combined underemployment rate the same.

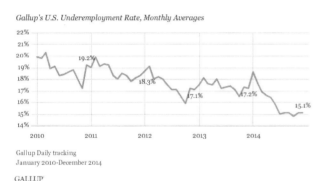

Gallup's U.S. Underemployment Rate, Monthly Averages

Gallup Daily tracking
January 2010-December 2014

GALLUP

Hispanic Unemployment Rate Falls Six Points in 2014

Unemployment fell among Americans in most racial and ethnic groups over the course of 2014 (those of Asian descent were the sole exception), but it fell most among Hispanics. While white unemployment fell from 6.9% in January 2014 to 4.8% in December and black unemployment fell from 12.2% to 9.6%, unemployment among Hispanics fell from 13.1% in January to 7.3% in December 2014.

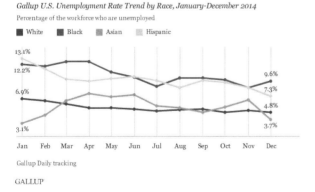

Gallup U.S. Unemployment Rate Trend by Race, January-December 2014
Percentage of the workforce who are unemployed

Gallup Daily tracking

GALLUP

As a result of these changes in the unemployment rates, Hispanics made up 20.4% of all unemployed U.S. adults in December,

down from 24.7% in January. This drop in Hispanic unemployment has been matched by a similar rise in P2P among Hispanics, from 44.3% in January to 49.7% in December—the highest among any ethnic category in the U.S.

Bottom Line

Employment growth has been stronger in the past 12 months than in any year since Gallup began tracking these metrics in January 2010. P2P ended the year a point and a half higher than December 2013, the best performance of any year since 2010. Similarly, unemployment fell by a point and a half, the best performance since 2011. This improvement was shared across all demographics.

However, while workforce participation was stronger in 2014 than 2013, this figure has yet to recover most of the ground lost in the past few years. It remains to be seen whether hoped-for continued strength in 2015 can bring back discouraged workers or if a growing retiree population will drive this figure down even further.

Survey Methods

Results for this Gallup poll are based on telephone interviews conducted Dec. 1–30, 2014, on the Gallup U.S. Daily survey, with a random sample of 26,352 adults, aged 18 and older, living in all 50 U.S. states and the District of Columbia. For results based on the total sample of national adults, the margin of sampling error is ±1 percentage points at the 95% confidence level. All reported margins of sampling error include computed design effects for weighting.

January 08, 2015
U.S. STANDARD OF LIVING INDEX CLIMBS TO HIGHEST IN 7 YEARS

by Justin McCarthy

Story Highlights

- *Index reaches new high of +50*
- *Record 81% of Americans satisfied with standard of living*
- *Sixty-one percent say standard of living is "getting better"*

WASHINGTON, D.C.—Gallup's Standard of Living Index reached a new high of +50 in December, the best score found in seven years of tracking the index. Americans' improved perspective on their personal standard of living comes as they spend more money and begin to view the national economy positively.

The index has labored through a long recovery from its recession-era slump, with lows of +14 in both October and November of 2008, when the global economic crisis erupted. But the latest ratings exceed even pre-crisis levels in 2008, illustrating a remarkable turnaround in how Americans view their standard of living.

The year 2014 started off with better standard of living readings than practically all other monthly readings before, with a +41 in January and February. From March to November, it improved further, but remained in a narrow range of +44 to +47. The +50 rating for December brings the index to an unprecedented level in its seven-year trend.

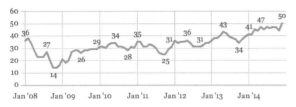

Gallup U.S. Standard of Living Index, Monthly Averages

Right now, do you feel your standard of living is getting better or getting worse?
Are you satisfied or dissatisfied with your standard of living, all the things you can buy and do?

Gallup Daily tracking
The Standard of Living Index is based on a composite of the two questions.

GALLUP

Gallup's Standard of Living Index is a composite of Americans' responses to two questions: one asking whether they are satisfied with their current standard of living, and the other asking whether their standard of living is getting better or worse. The index has a theoretical maximum of 100 (if all respondents say they are satisfied with their standard of living and say it is getting better) and a theoretical minimum of -100 (if all respondents are dissatisfied with their standard of living and say it is getting worse). The current score of +50 indicates Americans are quite positive about their standard of living, but even at its lows in the fall of 2008, Americans evaluated their standard of living positively overall.

Both dimensions of the index have improved by roughly five points over the past year; however, since the nadir of these perceptions in 2008, people's outlook for their standard of living going forward has improved much more than their current satisfaction with it.

Four in Five Americans Satisfied with Their Current Standard of Living

A consistent majority of Americans have expressed satisfaction with their standard of living over the past seven years, ranging from 69% in late 2008 to 81% today. However, after fluctuating in an even narrower seven-point range from 2009 through 2013, it rose from 76% at the end of 2013 to 81% at the end of 2014.

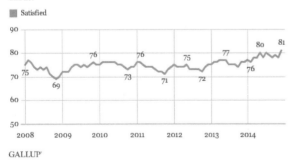

Americans' Satisfaction With Their Current Standard of Living

Are you satisfied or dissatisfied with your standard of living, all the things you can buy and do?

■ Satisfied

GALLUP

Optimism for Improving Standard of Living Reaches New High

While Americans are becoming more satisfied with their current standard of living, they are also becoming more optimistic about its future. Sixty-one percent of Americans now say their standard of

living is "getting better"—a new high, and nearly twice the level it was at its low of 33% in October 2008.

Less than a quarter of Americans (23%) say their standard of living is "getting worse."

Americans' Future Expectations for Their Standard of Living

Right now, do you feel your standard of living is getting better or getting worse?

■ Getting better   ■ Getting worse

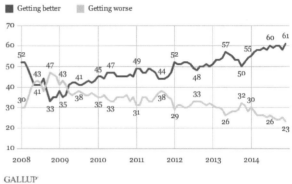

GALLUP

Bottom Line

Though most Americans' personal financial situation probably doesn't change dramatically from one year to the next, an improving economy and soaring stock market likely help them feel better about their own situation. To some degree, this is evident in reports from Gallup's daily tracking data of increased spending. The question defines standard of living as "all the things [they] can buy and do," so perhaps lower gas prices are freeing up dollars for Americans to spend on discretionary items.

While both political parties clamor for the credit of this post-recession glow, where the index will be heading from here is better to focus on. Because how Americans view their standard of living can crumple just as quickly as the economy.

Survey Methods

Results for this Gallup poll are based on telephone interviews conducted Dec. 1–30, 2014, on the Gallup U.S. Daily survey, with a random sample of 13,165 adults, aged 18 and older, living in all 50 U.S. states and the District of Columbia. For results based on the total sample of national adults, the margin of sampling error is ±2 percentage points at the 95% confidence level. All reported margins of sampling error include computed design effects for weighting.

January 09, 2015
U.S. LIBERALS AT RECORD 24%,
BUT STILL TRAIL CONSERVATIVES

by Lydia Saad

Story Highlights

- *Conservatives remain largest ideological group, at 38%*
- *Liberals up one point to 24%, the highest yet*
- *Conservative-liberal gap now smallest in Gallup trends*

PRINCETON, N.J.—Conservatives continued to outnumber moderates and liberals in the U.S. population in 2014, as they have since 2009. However, their 14-percentage-point edge over liberals last year, 38% versus 24%, is the smallest in Gallup's trends since 1992. The percentage of U.S. adults identifying themselves as politically conservative in 2014 was unchanged from 2013, as was the percentage of moderates, at 34%, while the percentage considering themselves liberal rose a percentage point for the third straight year.

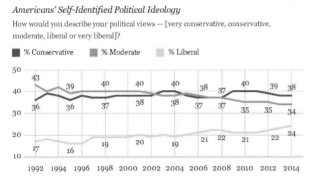

Americans' Self-Identified Political Ideology

How would you describe your political views -- [very conservative, conservative, moderate, liberal or very liberal]?

Based on annual averages of Gallup multiday telephone polls

GALLUP

When Gallup initiated this measure of self-identified political ideology in 1992, the largest group of Americans called themselves moderate, while slightly more than one-third identified as conservative and fewer than one in five as liberal. The conservative-liberal gap at that time was 19 points, and by 1996 it had widened to 22 points, its highest across the trend. Since then, the liberal percentage has swelled and the percentage of moderates has shrunk from 40% to 34%.

These results are based on combined data from Gallup's standalone surveys of U.S. adults, totaling between 16,000 and 45,000 interviews for each year.

Political Polarization Inched Further Ahead in 2014

The one-point uptick in the percentage liberal in 2014 stems from one-point increases in liberal self-identification among both independents and Democrats. The small percentage of Republicans identifying as liberals stayed the same. Longer term, since 2000, all of the rise in liberalism on this measure is owing to Democrats.

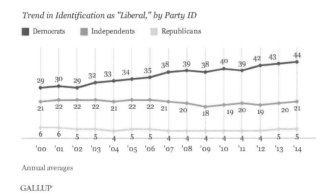

Trend in Identification as "Liberal," by Party ID

Annual averages

GALLUP

At the same time, Republicans' strong tendency to identify with the conservative moniker stayed the same in 2014 at 70%, just under the 73% high point reached in 2012. The percentage of Republicans who consider themselves conservative remains slightly higher today than it was through the mid-2000s, and the pattern is nearly the same with independents. At the same time, fewer Democrats call themselves conservative compared with a decade ago.

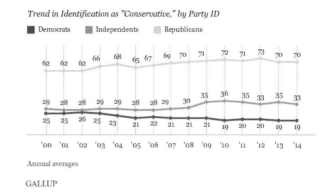

Trend in Identification as "Conservative," by Party ID

Annual averages

GALLUP

Over time, the growth of liberals and conservatives has come at the expense of moderates, a group that has been shrinking as a proportion of every party group, but particularly of Republicans and Democrats. While moderates gained a point back among independents and Republicans in 2014, they remain below their recent highs.

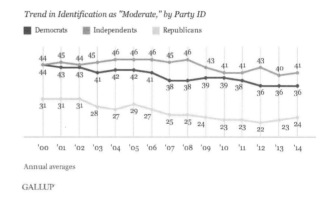

Trend in Identification as "Moderate," by Party ID

Annual averages

GALLUP

As evident in a thorough review of these trends in 2014, moderates still represent the largest segment of independents. Since 2010, Democrats have been more likely to identify as liberals than as moderates. Conservatives continue to dominate Republicans' ranks.

Bottom Line

Over the past 22 years, Americans' ideological bent, or at least their willingness to associate with certain labels, has changed in subtle ways. Although the "liberal" moniker remains the least favorite, it has enjoyed the most growth, while "conservative" is up slightly and "moderate" has waned. But to a large extent, these changes reflect opposing ideological shifts within the parties, not national trends. That helps explain how there could be a record proportion of liberals at a time when Democratic identification was at a long-term low. Likewise, even though 2014 was a strong election year for the Republican Party, Gallup found no increase in conservatism in 2014 compared with 2013. All of this happened at the same time that political independence was peaking, which is to say that ideological polarization and the strength of the two major parties don't necessarily go hand in hand. In fact, one may undermine the other.

Results are based on aggregated telephone interviews from 15 separate Gallup polls conducted in 2014, with a random sample of 16,479 adults, aged 18 and older, living in all 50 U.S. states and the District of Columbia.

For results based on the total sample of national adults, the margin of sampling error is ±1 percentage point at the 95% confidence level.

January 09, 2015
LACK OF TEACHER ENGAGEMENT LINKED TO 2.3 MILLION MISSED WORKDAYS

by Matt Hastings and Sangeeta Agrawal

Story Highlights

- *Just 30% of U.S. teachers are engaged in their work*
- *Actively disengaged teachers average twice as many absences*

This article is the first in a series exploring employee engagement among U.S. teachers as measured by Gallup Daily tracking.

WASHINGTON, D.C.—In the U.S., K-12 schoolteachers who are "not engaged" or are "actively disengaged" at work miss an estimated 2.3 million more workdays than teachers who are "engaged" in their jobs.

Mean Unhealthy Days per School Year and Estimated Additional Missed Workdays

By level of engagement among U.S. full-time teachers

Level of engagement	Share of full-time U.S. teachers	Mean unhealthy days per school year*	Estimated additional missed workdays†
Engaged	30%	10.1	BASELINE
Not engaged	57%	11.3	781,921
Actively disengaged	13%	20.4	1,521,101
TOTAL			2,303,022

Source: Gallup Daily tracking surveys, Jan. 3, 2013–Sept. 30, 2014
*Assumes nine-month school year
†Assumes 3.7 million full-time K-12 teachers (National Center for Education Statistics, 2012); conversion from unhealthy to missed workdays is 0.31

GALLUP

Gallup categorizes survey respondents as "engaged," "not engaged" or "actively disengaged" based on their responses to questions about workplace elements with proven links to performance outcomes. Gallup defines *engaged* teachers as involved with, enthusiastic about and committed to their work. They know the scope of their jobs and constantly look for new and better ways to achieve outcomes. *Not engaged* teachers may be satisfied with their jobs, but they are not emotionally connected to their workplaces and are unlikely to devote much discretionary effort to their work. *Actively disengaged* teachers are not only unhappy, but also act out their unhappiness in ways that undermine what their coworkers accomplish.

Overall, 30% of U.S. teachers are engaged in their work, matching the national average for all workers.

A majority, 57%, of full-time K-12 teachers in the U.S. are "not engaged." They report, on average, 11.3 unhealthy days per school year—days that keep them from doing usual activities—resulting in an estimate of about 3.5 missed workdays per school year. Using engaged teachers as a baseline, all "not engaged" U.S. teachers miss an estimated 781,921 additional days of work each year.

Additionally, about 13% of U.S. teachers are "actively disengaged" in their jobs, somewhat lower than the 18% average for all American workers. These actively disengaged teachers average 20.4 unhealthy days per school year, resulting in slightly more than six missed workdays per school year—more than twice as many missed workdays as engaged teachers reported. Using engaged teachers' absenteeism as the baseline, actively disengaged teachers as a group miss an estimated total of 1,521,101 additional days of work.

Implications

Gallup research has uncovered both individual and business outcomes consistently associated with employee engagement, including well-being, absenteeism, turnover, workers' compensation claims, productivity, customer engagement, workplace safety and profit. Moreover, these findings have been demonstrated across companies and across industries. Here, Gallup adds evidence from the education space to the corpus of engagement findings, indicating that not engaged and actively disengaged teachers miss more work than their engaged colleagues because of poor health. Altogether, the magnitude is substantial, estimated at a total of more than 2.3 million additional missed days each school year in the U.S.

Absenteeism associated with a lack of teacher engagement creates a drain on school productivity. Schools districts must foot the bill for classroom replacements. And when substitute teachers are relied on to execute a regular teacher's lesson plans, often with limited advance notice, it can easily create a suboptimal learning environment for students.

This analysis cannot establish the presence or direction of causality between level of engagement and missed workdays. However, teachers who work in school districts that foster teacher engagement likely are better positioned to face the workplace challenges associated with poor health, including the inability to do usual activities.

Survey Methods

Results are based on telephone interviews conducted Jan. 3, 2013–Sept. 30, 2014, as part of the Gallup Daily tracking survey, for a subgroup of 6,711 self-identified full-time K-12 schoolteachers, from a random sample of adults, aged 18 and older, living in all 50 U.S. states and the District of Columbia. All reported margins of sampling error include computed design effects for weighting.

For results based on the total sample of U.S. teachers, the margin of sampling error is ±1 percentage point at the 95% confidence level.

January 12, 2015
AMERICANS BECOME MORE POSITIVE ABOUT JOBS IN JANUARY

by Frank Newport

Story Highlights

- *45% say it's a good time to find a quality job, highest since 2007*
- *Low point on this measure was 8% in 2009 and 2011*

- *Democrats significantly more positive than Republicans*

PRINCETON, N.J.—Serving as another indication of the public's perceptions of an improving economy, 45% of Americans now say it is a good time to find a quality job, up from 36% in December, and as high as this indicator has been since May 2007.

Percentage in U.S. Saying Now Is a Good Time to Find a Quality Job

Thinking about the job situation in America today, would you say that it is now a good time or a bad time to find a quality job?

■ % Good time to find a quality job

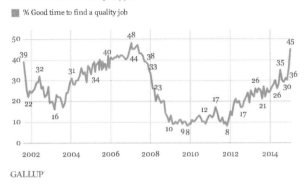

GALLUP

Gallup has asked Americans about their views of the job market on a monthly basis since August 2001, when 39% of Americans agreed that it was a good time to find a quality job. These views became less positive through 2003, but then turned the corner. By January 2007, 48% said it was a good time to find a quality job—the highest Gallup has recorded. Positive views of the job market began to drop that year and dropped further with the onset of the Great Recession, reaching the all-time low of 8% in November 2009 and again in November 2011. Since 2012, these attitudes have been recovering, breaking through the 30% line in 2014 for the first time in six years, and jumping to 45% this month.

These more upbeat perceptions about quality jobs accompany several other Gallup measures that indicate an improved U.S. jobs situation. Gallup's unadjusted unemployment rate for December was down to 5.8%—the lowest in its five-year history—and similar to the 5.6% reported by the government's Bureau of Labor Statistics, which was the lowest since the early months of the recession. Gallup's Job Creation Index—a measure of workers' perceptions of hiring trends where they work—has been at its highest post-recession levels in the latter part of 2014. Mentions of jobs or unemployment as the top problems facing the U.S. have also dropped during much of the past year, and are at only 7% in January, the lowest since October 2008.

Democrats Remain Much More Positive Than Republicans

Americans' views of the job market are influenced by their political orientations, with Democrats (56%) significantly more positive than Republicans (35%). This reflects the general tendency for Americans who identify with the party controlling the presidency to be more positive when asked any number of questions about the state of the nation. Prior to 2009, when Republican George. W. Bush was president, Republicans were significantly more positive on this quality jobs question than were Democrats. Despite the continuing gap between Democrats and Republicans, both groups' attitudes are more positive compared with December's report, when 47% of Democrats and 29% of Republicans agreed that it was a good time to find a quality job.

Differences in views of the job market across population subgroups reflect these underlying political differences. Young people and nonwhites are more likely than those who are older and those who are white, respectively, to say it's a good time to find a quality job. Those currently employed are slightly more positive than those who are not employed.

Is Now a Good Time to Find a Quality Job?

	Yes
	%
National adults	45
Republicans/Leaners	35
Democrats/Leaners	56
Men	49
Women	41
White	39
Nonwhite	58
18 to 34	58
35 to 54	44
55+	35
Employed	48
Not employed	41

Jan. 5-8, 2015

GALLUP

Implications

Americans' views of the availability of quality jobs in the U.S. are improving, and are nearly as good as any time in the past 14 years, providing further evidence that the public is seeing significant economic improvement in the U.S. Still, on an absolute basis, less than half say it is a good time to find a quality job. By comparison, when the researchers at the University of Connecticut and Rutgers University asked this same quality job question of those in the labor force toward the end of the dot-com boom, two-thirds or more responded that it was a good time to find a quality job. The late 1990s may have been a truly exceptional time in recent economic history, and Americans in recent years may have become skeptical because of the recession and wary of becoming too optimistic about the economy. It may also be that the nature of the current jobs recovery—with a continuing absence of higher-paying jobs even as unemployment has come down—is putting a damper on the recovery in positive economic attitudes.

Survey Methods

Results for this Gallup poll are based on telephone interviews conducted Jan. 5–8, 2015, with a random sample of 804 adults, aged 18 and older, living in all 50 U.S. states and the District of Columbia. For results based on the total sample of national adults, the margin of sampling error is ±4 percentage points at the 95% confidence level. All reported margins of sampling error include computed design effects for weighting.

January 13, 2015
U.S. CONGRESS STARTS OFF YEAR
WITH 16% JOB APPROVAL

by Andrew Dugan

Story Highlights

- *New GOP-led Congress has 16% approval, same as in December*
- *History suggests new Congress will receive boost in approval*

WASHINGTON, D.C.—Early into the first session of the new 114th Congress, Americans give the legislative body a 16% job approval rating—matching the December reading of the famously unpopular and divided Congress that preceded it. In contrast to the 113th Congress, Republicans now run both chambers of the national legislature, but so far, there is little evidence that Americans are feeling any warmer about Congress overall. Three-fourths of Americans (76%) disapprove.

Congressional Job Approval Ratings: 2001-2015

Do you approve or disapprove of the way Congress is handling its job?

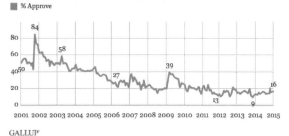

GALLUP

Congressional job approval is rarely high—the historical average stands at 32%—but has hovered at historical lows since late in the George W. Bush presidency, with a brief reprieve during the first year of the Barack Obama presidency. These poorly rated sessions of Congress have varied in partisan composition, but whether controlled by Democrats or Republicans, or split between the two parties, all appear to have left most Americans unimpressed.

Congress's poor track record notwithstanding, there is reason to believe this Congress will at least be rated more popularly going forward than the last two divided Congresses. Typically, elections that hand control of Congress to one party provide an initial uptick in support for the new Congress. For instance, when Democrats took control of both houses in 2007, that Congress began its tenure with a job approval rating 14 percentage points higher than the previous Congress. Likewise, after the historic 1994 midterm elections put Republicans in charge of both houses for the first time in 40 years, Congress began its work with a 10-point bump in its approval rating.

Even in 2011, when Republicans assumed control of the House but not the Senate, Congress temporarily saw its approval spike by seven points.

Only in 2003 did a new partisan makeup of Congress not translate into higher approval; interestingly, then, as now, Republicans won the Senate in the previous election and retained their House majority to earn the right to govern Capitol Hill exclusively. A crucial difference, though, is that the 2003–2005 Congress began its tenure with a 49% approval rating—above the historical norm, and well above where the 114th Congress currently stands.

These results come from Gallup's annual Mood of the Nation poll, conducted Jan. 5–8, 2015. The new Congress was sworn in on Jan. 6, so the poll included a few days before and after the Republicans became the majority party in the Senate as well as the House of Representatives.

Given the timing of this poll—conducted before the body could take action on any substantive items of business—it's premature to judge whether the new Republican-controlled Congress will receive any sort of uptick in support. History suggests it will, though this is not immediately apparent.

Bottom Line

Last Tuesday, 58 freshman House members and 13 new senators were sworn into Congress and, more importantly, the balance of power shifted, giving Republicans control of both houses. At the moment, before Congress has been able to do much legislatively, Americans still give Congress low marks. The 114th Congress begins its tenure with no immediate sign of renewed support, even from Republicans, although it is too early to know what partisans' reactions will be as Congress settles down to action. It is possible that congressional approval will rise, especially if Congress finds itself in a legislative showdown with Obama that rallies Republican support. However, Congress's low ratings in recent years suggest that convincing Americans that Congress is doing a good job will not prove easy for Republican leaders.

Survey Methods

Results for this Gallup poll are based on telephone interviews conducted Jan. 5–8, 2015, with a random sample of 804 adults, aged 18 and older, living in all 50 U.S. states and the District of Columbia. For results based on the total sample of national adults, the margin of sampling error is ±4 percentage points at the 95% confidence level. All reported margins of sampling error include computed design effects for weighting.

January 13, 2015
U.S. ECONOMIC CONFIDENCE INDEX
CONTINUES UPWARD TREK

by Justin McCarthy

Story Highlights

- *Index reaches record score of +4*
- *Third consecutive index reading in positive territory*
- *Half of Americans (50%) say the economy is "getting better"*

WASHINGTON, D.C.—Gallup's U.S. Economic Confidence Index continues to show improvement, averaging +4 for the week ending Jan. 11. The index is up from +1 the week before, and it is at its highest level since Gallup began tracking it daily in 2008. This is the index's third consecutive positive weekly reading.

After nearly seven years in negative territory, the index first moved into positive territory in the final week of 2014. The index was +1 for the week of Dec. 29, 2014–Jan. 4, 2015, and has since improved another three points.

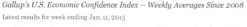

Gallup's U.S. Economic Confidence Index -- Weekly Averages Since 2008
Latest results for week ending Jan. 11, 2015

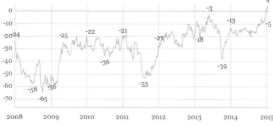

Gallup Daily tracking

GALLUP

The latest figures maintain the long recovery the index has made over the past several years, rising from the low of -65 in October 2008 as the global economic crisis unfolded, as well as a startling drop to -39 amid the U.S. government shutdown in October 2013.

Gallup's Economic Confidence Index is based on Americans' assessments of current U.S. economic conditions and their perceptions of whether the economy is getting better or worse. It has a theoretical minimum of -100, if all Americans thought the economy was poor and getting worse, and a theoretical maximum of +100, if all Americans thought the economy was excellent or good and getting better.

For the week ending Jan. 11, 28% of Americans said the economy was "excellent" or "good," while 25% said it was "poor," resulting in a current conditions index score of +3—the highest score for this component since the first week of 2008. Meanwhile, the economic outlook component measured +5, up four points from the previous week, and is the highest Gallup has recorded since daily tracking began. The outlook score is the result of 50% of Americans saying the economy is "getting better" and 45% saying it is "getting worse."

Economic Confidence Index Components -- Weekly Averages From 2008 to 2015
Latest results for week ending Jan. 11, 2015

■ Current conditions　▨ Economic outlook

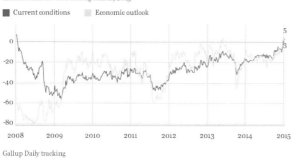

Gallup Daily tracking

GALLUP

Bottom Line

The year is young, but it's off to a good start, in terms of Americans' confidence in the economy. With three positive readings in a row, the index has clearly made progress, although there is much room to improve. Certainly falling gas prices—now at their lowest average since April 2009—are contributing, as well as lower unemployment and improved GDP growth.

The latest index figures are positive, but not overwhelmingly so. However, the overall positive evaluations of the economy have persisted now for three weeks in a row, suggesting some staying power. Continued positive economic news will likely keep Gallup's economic index score in positive territory, although a sudden burst of negative news could easily send it back down. However, with Americans spending more and rating their standard of living at new highs, consumer behavior should help the economy avoid backsliding.

Survey Methods

Results for this Gallup poll are based on telephone interviews conducted Jan. 5–11, 2015, on the Gallup U.S. Daily survey, with a random sample of 3,551 adults, aged 18 and older, living in all 50 U.S. states and the District of Columbia. For results based on the total sample of national adults, the margin of sampling error is ±2 percentage points at the 95% confidence level. All reported margins of sampling error include computed design effects for weighting.

January 13, 2015
HOLIDAYS, WEEKENDS STILL AMERICANS' HAPPIEST DAYS OF YEAR

by Justin McCarthy

Story Highlights

- *Thanksgiving among the three happiest days annually since 2008*
- *Holidays like July 4 (67%), Christmas (63%) top 2014 list*
- *Tuesdays, negative news cycles coincide with least happy days*

WASHINGTON, D.C.—Last year, holidays such as Thanksgiving (68%), Independence Day (67%) and Christmas (63%) were the days when Americans were most likely to say they experienced happiness and enjoyment without a lot of stress and worry. Thanksgiving has been one of the top three happiest days every year since 2008. Certain weekend days, particularly Saturday, July 19 (63%), also ranked among the happiest for Americans in 2014.

Gallup-Healthways Daily Mood: Happiest Days of 2014
Asked of American adults

	% With a lot of happiness/ enjoyment without a lot of stress/worry	Day of the week	Key events
Nov 27	68	Thursday	Thanksgiving
Jul 4	67	Friday	Independence Day
Dec 25	63	Thursday	Christmas
Jul 19	63	Saturday	--
Jan 1	62	Wednesday	New Year's Day
May 26	62	Monday	Memorial Day
May 25	62	Sunday	Weekend day before Memorial Day

Gallup-Healthways Well-Being Index

GALLUP

The results for each year are based on more than 175,000 surveys, conducted daily as part of the Gallup-Healthways Well-Being

Index. As part of the survey, respondents were asked to say whether they experienced each of several emotions "during a lot of the day yesterday." Gallup-Healthways' U.S. Mood Index tracks the percentage of U.S. adults who, reflecting on the day before they were surveyed, say they experienced a lot of happiness and enjoyment without a lot of stress and worry, and vice versa.

Also ranking high among the days Americans felt happiest in 2014 were New Year's Day (62%) and Memorial Day (62%). Though not a holiday, the day prior to Memorial Day, May 25 (62%), also ranked high—likely because it was part of an extended weekend for many Americans.

Weekdays, Negative News Cycles Make Up Americans' Least Happy Days

Weekend days were happier for Americans, on average, than other days of the week, with an average 57% happy on Saturdays and 55% happy on Sundays.

Meanwhile, weekdays were the least happy for Americans. Tuesdays (44%) saw the lowest percentage, on average, who reported feeling happiness or enjoyment, followed by Wednesdays (45%), Thursdays (46%), Mondays (46%) and Fridays (48%).

Of the 84 least happy days, 78 of them were the first four days of the workweek—Monday, Tuesday, Wednesday or Thursday. Additionally, low reported happiness levels often coincided with negative news coverage, as has been the case in the past.

April 8 (37%), a Tuesday, ranked as the least happy day in 2014. That day, pro-Russian uprisings in Ukraine filled the news. It was also the day after the discovery of the Heartbleed Web virus, which made millions of Internet users vulnerable. The next-least-happy day was Sept. 8 (38%), a Monday, and a day after the U.S. launched new airstrikes against the Islamic State militant group.

June 5, Sept. 16, Sept. 23, Oct. 8, Oct. 28 and Dec. 9 also ranked at the bottom of the list, with only 39% of Americans reporting that they experienced happiness on each of these dates. Many of these dates coincide with school shootings and other negative, high-profile events that can be disruptive and disheartening to Americans, although it is not possible to determine with certainty whether these news events were at the root of Americans' less happy mood.

Gallup-Healthways Daily Mood: Least Happy Days of 2014
Asked of American adults

	% With a lot of happiness/ enjoyment without a lot of stress/worry	Day of the week	Key events
Apr 8	37	Tuesday	Pro-Russian protests in Ukraine; Heartbleed bug discovered
Sep 8	38	Monday	Day after U.S. airstrikes against ISIS; Baltimore Ravens terminate contract with Ray Rice
Jun 5	39	Thursday	Shooting at Seattle Pacific University
Sep 16	39	Tuesday	--
Sep 23	39	Tuesday	--
Oct 8	39	Wednesday	First Ebola patient in U.S. dies
Oct 28	39	Tuesday	Antares rocket explodes after taking off in Virginia
Dec 9	39	Tuesday	U.S. Senate committee releases report critical of CIA interrogation tactics

Gallup-Healthways Well-Being Index

GALLUP'

Happiness and Stress Unchanged in 2014

Overall, 48.7% of Americans expressed happiness and enjoyment without a lot of stress in 2014—compared with 48.4% in 2013. The 2014 average is on the higher end of the spectrum of yearly figures since 2008, falling short of the high of 49.1% in 2011.

Meanwhile, stress and worry without happiness and enjoyment dropped slightly to 10.7% in 2014, matching the previous low from 2011.

Overall, both figures have been fairly steady over the past seven years.

Gallup-Healthways Daily Mood: Yearly Averages, 2008-2014
Asked of American adults

■ % With a lot of happiness/enjoyment without a lot of stress/worry
▨ % With a lot of stress/worry without a lot of happiness/enjoyment

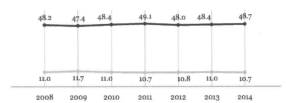

2008	2009	2010	2011	2012	2013	2014
48.2	47.4	48.4	49.1	48.0	48.4	48.7
11.0	11.7	11.0	10.7	10.8	11.0	10.7

Gallup-Healthways Well-Being Index

GALLUP'

Bottom Line

Despite the major economic, political and other changes that have taken place since 2008, Americans' personal levels of happiness have stayed remarkably constant over that period. Within the year 2014, Americans were most happy on holidays and on weekends, and were least happy at the beginning of the workweek.

Workdays don't have to be drudgery, however, if the work people are doing engages them and makes them excited about what they are doing. Gallup has found that engaged employees generally have better moods and lower levels of stress during the workweek than those who are "not engaged" or "actively disengaged."

Survey Methods

Results are based on telephone interviews conducted Jan. 2–Dec. 30, 2014, as part of the Gallup-Healthways Well-Being Index survey, with a random sample of 175,271 adults, aged 18 and older, living in all 50 U.S. states and the District of Columbia. For results based on the total sample of national adults, the margin of sampling error is ±1 percentage point at the 95% confidence level. All reported margins of sampling error include computed design effects for weighting.

January 14, 2015
HEART ATTACKS AND DEPRESSION CLOSELY LINKED

by Dan Witters and Jade Wood

Story Highlights

- *Heart attack doubles the odds of depression diagnosis*
- *Link holds after taking demographics into account*

WASHINGTON, D.C.—U.S. adults who have had a heart attack are twice as likely as those who have not had a heart attack to report being diagnosed with depression at some point in their lives, 30.1% versus 15.0%, respectively.

Heart Attack Occurrence and Lifetime Depression Diagnosis
Has a doctor or nurse ever told you that you have depression?

	All U.S. adults	Have experienced a heart attack	Have not experienced a heart attack
Depression diagnosis at any point over lifetime	17.5%	30.1%	15.0%

Gallup-Healthways Well-Being Index
Jan. 2, 2014-Dec. 16, 2014
Controlling for age, gender, race/ethnicity, education, income, marital status and health insurance status

GALLUP

Importantly, the link between heart attacks and depression holds true after controlling for the effects of age, gender, race/ethnicity, education, income, marital status and health insurance status.

Similarly, those who have had a heart attack are twice as likely as those who have not to say they are *currently being treated* for depression. While 8.1% of those who have never experienced a heart attack currently contend with depression, this figure jumps to 16.5% among those with a history of at least one heart attack.

Heart Attack Occurrence and Current Depression Diagnosis
Do you currently have or are you currently being treated for depression?

	All U.S. adults	Have experienced a heart attack	Have not experienced a heart attack
Currently have or are being treated for depression	10.4%	16.5%	8.1%

Gallup-Healthways Well-Being Index
Jan. 2, 2014-Dec. 16, 2014
Controlling for age, gender, race/ethnicity, education, income, marital status and health insurance status

GALLUP

Overall, in data collected from Jan. 2, 2014, through Dec. 16, 2014, 17.5% of Americans report having been diagnosed with depression at some point in their lifetime, and 10.4% currently have depression or are being treated for it. About one out of every 25 U.S. adults (3.8%) report having experienced a heart attack at some point in their lives.

These results are based on interviews with 164,102 adults in the U.S. conducted as part of the Gallup-Healthways Well-Being Index, of which 6,236 report having experienced a heart attack at some point in their lifetime.

Implications

Heart disease and depression are two of the most costly diseases in the U.S. They affect individuals' quality of life and well-being and create an enormous burden on the U.S. healthcare system and economy. Heart disease is the leading cause of death for men and women in the U.S., and the Centers for Disease Control and Prevention estimates that coronary heart disease costs the U.S. $108.9 billion each year in healthcare services, medications and lost productivity. Depression is the leading cause of disability worldwide among all chronic diseases. Previous Gallup research shows that depression costs U.S. employers $23 billion annually in lost productivity, and those who are unemployed, especially the long-term unemployed, are even more likely to be diagnosed with depression.

These results, however, do not prove that heart attacks increase a person's odds of having depression, but they do show that the two are closely linked. Depression is a known predictor of cardiac problems and is as strong a risk factor for heart disease as diabetes and smoking. Studies suggest the relationship between depression and heart disease develops from underlying behavioral and physiological mechanisms related to depression such as a lack of self-care, self-medicating through food or substances and hormonal and inflammatory problems, which trigger heart disease. Consequently, a depression diagnosis could potentially increase the chance of having heart attack, and being obese—a risk factor for both heart disease and depression—might simultaneously increase the likelihood of having a heart attack and being diagnosed with depression. Depression diagnoses, therefore, can and do pre-date heart attack occurrence.

Dr. Dean Ornish, founder of the Preventive Medicine Research Institute, explains how symptoms of depression can increase the odds of experiencing a heart attack: "Feeling depressed makes it harder to make healthy lifestyle choices. People are more likely to smoke, overeat, drink too much and work too hard when they're feeling lonely and depressed. One patient said to me, 'I've got 20 friends in this pack of cigarettes, they're always there for me and no one else is—you want to take away my 20 friends?' In our research, we've found that people are more likely to make lifestyle choices that are life-enhancing than self-destructive when they're feeling happy and loved."

In addition, substantial research suggests the relationship may also point in the other direction: Those who experience a heart attack will be much more likely to be diagnosed with depression later. After all, a heart attack not only affects the cardiac system, but also it can alter an individual's entire life experience, including his or her autonomy, sense of security and confidence in the future, physical capabilities, and ability to resume living a normal life.

Research also suggests the link between heart attack and depression extends to mortality. Researchers at the Montreal Heart Institute found that those who were depressed were six times more likely to die within six months of their heart attack than those who were not depressed.

The psychological aspects of living with illness must be given proper attention in healthcare. Preventing and recovering from a heart attack and subsequent depression often depends on making positive lifestyle choices and having a strong support network. Symptoms of cardiac issues and depression can overlap—fatigue, disruption of daily routines, sleep disturbance—so it is vital that caregivers assess and treat heart attack and depression simultaneously. And to decrease the prevalence of these connected conditions, healthcare professionals could recommend lifestyle changes to help treat both of them, thus focusing on the connection between heart attack and depression by caring for the whole person.

Survey Methods

Results are based on telephone interviews conducted Jan. 2–Dec. 16, 2014, as part of the Gallup-Healthways Well-Being Index survey, with a random sample of 164,102 adults, aged 18 and older, living in all 50 U.S. states and the District of Columbia. Of these, 6,236 report having experienced a heart attack at some point in their lifetime.

For results based on the respondents reporting having had a heart attack, the margin of sampling error is approximately ±1.1 percentage points at the 95% confidence level. For those who reported never having had a heart attack, the margin of error is ±0.2 percentage points. All reported margins of sampling error include computed design effects to account for the weighting of the data.

January 14, 2015
MENTIONS OF JOBS AS TOP U.S. PROBLEM AT SIX-YEAR LOW

by Rebecca Riffkin .

Story Highlights

- *Seven percent name unemployment/jobs as most important problem*
- *Lowest percentage to mention jobs since October 2008*
- *Economy, government remain most frequently mentioned problems*

WASHINGTON, D.C.—In January, 7% of Americans name unemployment or jobs as the most important problem facing the country. Although this figure is similar to the 8% who cited unemployment or jobs in December 2014, it is the lowest percentage mentioning the issue since October 2008. Mentions of unemployment and jobs are down significantly from a peak of 39% in September 2011.

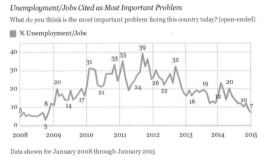

Unemployment/Jobs Cited as Most Important Problem

What do you think is the most important problem facing this country today? (open-ended)

■ % Unemployment/Jobs

Data shown for January 2008 through January 2015

GALLUP

As the job market weakened in late 2008, mentions of jobs and unemployment as the most important problem began to rise. The job market continued to worsen, with unemployment climbing to as high as 10.0% in October 2009, as measured by the Bureau of Labor Statistics. Consequentially, mentions of jobs and unemployment spiked even higher in early 2010, when the issue often ranked as one of the most frequently mentioned. As recently as June 2014, when the U.S. unemployment rate still measured above 6%, unemployment tied with government dissatisfaction and the economy in general as the most important problem, when these issues were mentioned by at least 15% of Americans. Mentions of jobs as the most important problem have generally fallen since then, likely as a result of the improving job market.

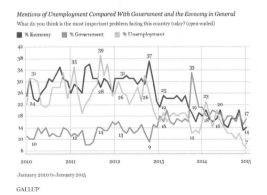

Mentions of Unemployment Compared With Government and the Economy in General

What do you think is the most important problem facing this country today? (open-ended)

■ % Economy   ■ % Government   ■ % Unemployment

January 2010 to January 2015

GALLUP

Unemployment ranks well down the list this month, with government dissatisfaction and the economy in general at the top. In addition to those three issues, at least 6% of Americans mentioned immigration, the federal debt and a decline in moral values as top problems.

Recent Trend for Most Important U.S. Problem

What do you think is the most important problem facing this country today? (open-ended)

	November 2014	December 2014	January 2015
	%	%	%
Dissatisfaction with government	19	15	17
Economy in general	20	13	14
Immigration/Illegal aliens	13	7	8
Unemployment/Jobs	12	8	7
Federal budget deficit/Federal debt	5	5	7
Ethical/Moral/Family decline	3	6	6
Race relations/Racism	1	13	5
Healthcare	7	6	5
Education	4	3	5
Poverty/Hunger/Homelessness	4	4	3
Crime/Violence	1	2	3
Lack of respect for each other	2	2	3

Note: Issues mentioned by 2% or less in January 2015 are not shown

GALLUP

Mentions of racism and race relations fell back to 5% this month, after rising sharply to 13% in December 2014 amid controversy over relations between blacks and white police officers. Despite the downtick, this figure is still higher than the percentage who mentioned race relations before December.

Bottom Line

The 7% of Americans who mention jobs and unemployment as the most important problem facing the country is a noticeable drop from highs seen over the last few years. This is clearly a response to the improved U.S. job market, as demonstrated by the trend in lower unemployment rates as measured by both the U.S. Bureau of Labor Statistics and Gallup Daily tracking. Although Americans are no longer as focused on unemployment as the most important problem, mentions of the economy in general and government remain high and Americans continue to name these issues more than any others as top problems.

Survey Methods

Results for this Gallup poll are based on telephone interviews conducted Jan. 5–8, 2015, on the Gallup U.S. Daily survey, with a random sample of 805 adults, aged 18 and older, living in all 50 U.S. states and the District of Columbia. For results based on the total sample of national adults, the margin of sampling error is ±4 percentage points at the 95% confidence level. All reported margins of sampling error include computed design effects for weighting.

January 15, 2015
U.S. DIVIDED ON WHETHER GOP OR OBAMA SHOULD HAVE MORE INFLUENCE

by Andrew Dugan

Story Highlights

- *U.S. divided on whether Obama or GOP should have more influence*

- *Support for GOP has fallen since last November*

WASHINGTON, D.C.—Americans are divided on which part of their divided government should have more influence over the direction the nation takes—Democratic President Barack Obama (40%) or the Republicans in Congress (43%).

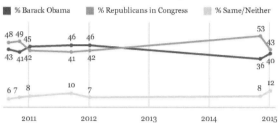

Americans' Preference for Who Should Influence U.S. Direction

Who do you want to have more influence over the direction the nation takes in the next year -- Barack Obama or the Republicans in Congress?

■ % Barack Obama   ■ % Republicans in Congress   % Same/Neither

Note: "Same/Neither" is a volunteered response.

GALLUP

These results come from Gallup's annual Mood of the Nation poll, conducted Jan. 5–8. Republicans have, after their electoral victory last November, assumed control of both chambers of Congress, but appear to have lost their immediate post-election glow. Just after the midterm elections that so decisively favored Republicans, 53% of Americans said they would prefer that Republicans in Congress have more influence over the nation's direction, whereas 36% opted for Obama, for a GOP-tilted spread of 17 percentage points.

The spread is now within the margin of error, though mostly as a result of Republicans losing support—10 points—rather than Obama gaining it. The 40% of Americans now preferring that Obama have the greater influence is only modestly higher than his record low of 36% set in November. Twelve percent of Americans, up from 8% in the last reading, do not choose a side, saying "both" or "neither" should have the greater influence.

Arguably, from the midterm elections until Republicans officially took control of both houses of Congress on Jan. 6, Obama has had greater influence in shaping events. After the midterm elections that delivered a stinging rebuke to Obama and that threaten to make his last two years in office more difficult, the president has unveiled a number of major policy shifts, including a diplomatic outreach to Cuba, an executive action to protect a number of residents living in the U.S. illegally from deportation and concluding a bilateral deal with China on carbon emissions. But while Obama may have seized the agenda at least temporarily, this new gumption has not translated into a noticeably larger amount of Americans preferring Obama on this question.

Still, Obama's standing in the seventh year of his presidency is at least stronger than that of his predecessor, George W. Bush, in 2007. Bush famously called himself the "decider," but by his seventh year in office, few Americans (32%) wanted Bush to decide. More than six in 10 (63%) wanted the Democrats in Congress, and their newly won majorities in both houses, to have greater say over the nation's affairs. At the time, Bush was dogged by a low approval rating (37%). Obama's approval rating, though not spectacular, is better than Bush's was at a similar time in his presidency.

President Bill Clinton, in contrast to his two successors, can claim that he was the more preferred political actor in the seventh year of his presidency, though he seemed to lose significant support over the course of the year. In January 1999—shortly after the House of Representatives voted to impeach the president—55% chose Clinton over congressional Republicans to lead the nation, perhaps as a show of support for a popular president against a hostile Congress. By April, though, the figure had fallen to 44%.

Presidents in Seventh Year of Presidency vs. Congress

Who do you want to have more influence over the direction the nation takes in the next year?

	Prefer sitting president	Prefer opposing party in Congress	President's lead/deficit (pct. pts.)	President's approval rating
Barack Obama		Republicans in Congress		
Jan. 5-8, 2014	40%	43%	-3	46%
George W. Bush		Democrats in Congress		
Jan. 5-7, 2007	32%	63%	-31	37%
Bill Clinton		Republicans in Congress		
Jan. 8-10, 1999	55%	37%	+18	67%
April 13-14, 1999	44%	43%	+1	60%

GALLUP

GOP Support Among Independents Drops

Fewer than four in 10 self-identified independents today say they would prefer that congressional Republicans have the edge in setting the nation's direction, down from a majority (53%) in November. Indeed, about as many independents now say they would like Obama to lead (37%) as say this about the GOP (38%)—a stark turnaround from November, when independents tilted heavily to the GOP. Those affiliated with both major parties, meanwhile, strongly prefer that the leader(s) of their respective parties have the greater influence over the nation.

Americans' Preference for Who Should Influence U.S. Direction by Party ID

	President Barack Obama	Republicans in Congress	Same/Neither
REPUBLICANS			
November 2014	5%	94%	1%
January 2015	5%	88%	5%
INDEPENDENTS			
November 2014	31%	53%	10%
January 2015	37%	38%	18%
DEMOCRATS			
November 2014	76%	13%	8%
January 2015	81%	6%	9%

GALLUP

Bottom Line

Second-term presidents serving their final two years can often seem like reduced figures in the political landscape, as their ability to shape public policy is perceived to diminish. Many factors contribute to this perception. For instance, in the modern era, nearly all second-term presidents have had a Congress controlled by the opposition party in their final two years (only Lyndon Johnson had an allied Congress)—but a main factor is that second-term U.S. presidents are typically less popular than they were in their first terms.

And this erosion in public support in turn reduces the president's ability to influence Congress.

Obama has tried to stay ahead of these historical forces by launching a flurry of policy moves, but the proportion of Americans preferring his guidance on the nation's direction has increased only marginally. Republicans in Congress, for their part, have seen a substantial drop in support from November, just as they begin to try their hand at governing. Ratings of the economy have greatly improved since the November elections, which could be one reason fewer Americans support the GOP. Indeed, the improving economy could eventually give Obama the edge on this measure, perhaps giving him the political momentum. But at the moment, judging by public opinion, it appears the last two years may not be better or worse for Obama, but rather more of the same: a nation divided, with both sides fiercely contesting that they have the mandate to lead it.

Survey Methods

Results for this Gallup poll are based on telephone interviews conducted Jan. 5–8, 2015, on the Gallup U.S. Daily survey, with a random sample of 804 adults, aged 18 and older, living in all 50 U.S. states and the District of Columbia. For results based on the total sample of national adults, the margin of sampling error is ±4 percentage points at the 95% confidence level. All reported margins of sampling error include computed design effects for weighting.

January 15, 2015
WASHINGTON LEADS LARGEST U.S. STATES IN TEACHER ENGAGEMENT

by Matt Hastings and Sangeeta Agrawal

Story Highlights

- *Since 2012, teacher engagement has remained relatively stable*
- *Among top 15 states, Washington has highest percentage of "engaged" teachers*
- *Florida has highest percentage of "actively disengaged" teachers*

WASHINGTON, D.C.—Of the 15 most populous U.S. states, Washington leads in the percentage of teachers engaged in their jobs (35%) followed by Texas, North Carolina, Georgia and Illinois. Florida reports the highest percentage of actively disengaged teachers (17%) followed by New Jersey, New York, Pennsylvania and Michigan.

Gallup categorizes survey participants as "engaged," "not engaged" or "actively disengaged" based on their responses to questions about workplace elements having proven links to performance outcomes. Gallup defines *engaged* teachers as involved with, enthusiastic about and committed to their work. They know the scope of their jobs and constantly look for new and better ways to achieve outcomes. *Not engaged* teachers may be satisfied with their jobs, but they are not emotionally connected to their workplaces and are unlikely to devote much discretionary effort to their work. *Actively disengaged* teachers are not only unhappy, but also act out their unhappiness in ways that undermine what their coworkers accomplish.

Engaged Teachers: 15 Most Populous States	
State	**% Engaged**
WA	35%
TX	34%
NC	33%
GA	33%
IL	32%
VA	31%
CA	31%
PA	29%
NY	29%
AZ	28%
FL	28%
OH	27%
MA	26%
NJ	25%
MI	22%

Source: Gallup Daily tracking surveys, Jan. 2, 2011–Sept. 30, 2014

GALLUP

Actively Disengaged Teachers: 15 Most Populous States	
State	**% Actively Disengaged**
FL	17%
NJ	16%
NY	16%
PA	15%
MI	15%
NC	14%
VA	14%
AZ	13%
OH	13%
TX	13%
GA	12%
CA	11%
MA	10%
IL	10%
WA	10%

Source: Gallup Daily tracking surveys, Jan. 2, 2011–Sept. 30, 2014

GALLUP

These results are based on interviews with 16,529 full-time K-12 schoolteachers conducted Jan. 2, 2011–Sept. 30, 2014, as part of Gallup Daily tracking.

Interestingly, Washington state reported the largest percentage of engaged teachers while also boasting the smallest percentage of actively disengaged teachers. At just 10%, it stands tied with Massachusetts and Illinois for the lowest percentage of actively disengaged teachers.

While no state is completely free of actively disengaged teachers, most states included in the analysis registered percentages of actively disengaged teachers at or less than the national average of 13% for the survey period. Seven states exceeded that figure, meaning they have a larger than average percentage of actively disengaged teachers.

Among them, at 17%, Florida leads large states in the percentage of actively disengaged teachers. New Jersey, New York, Pennsylvania and Michigan round out the top five states with the largest percentage of actively disengaged teachers. Michigan has the lowest percentage of engaged teachers, at 22%.

Although states with the highest percentage of actively disengaged teachers typically have the lowest percentage of engaged teachers, Massachusetts is an exception. Massachusetts has a relatively low percentage of actively disengaged teachers, but also ranks among the lowest for engaged teachers, at 26%. As a result, of the states included in this analysis, it has the highest percentage of teachers in the middle, "not engaged," category.

Teacher Engagement Nationwide Relatively Stable Since 2012

As measured in 2014, 31% of all U.S. teachers were identified as being engaged in their jobs, while 12% reported being actively disengaged. The majority of U.S. teachers, 56%, were not engaged in their work. Employee engagement among U.S. teachers has remained relatively stable since 2012. Moreover, teachers exhibit levels of engagement comparable to estimates for the total U.S. workforce.

Implications

Gallup research has identified a number of outcomes associated with employee engagement, including teacher absenteeism estimated at more than 2.3 million additional missed workdays each school year. School leadership matters as well. Having principals with natural talent for their job enhances the likelihood that teachers will be engaged in their work. Engaged teachers are more likely to yield engaged students who realize greater educational achievement. Given these findings, the impetus to select and develop school principals and teachers based on their natural aptitudes for the role is paramount.

Level of Engagement Among U.S. Teachers

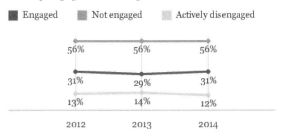

Source: Gallup Daily tracking surveys, Jan. 2, 2011-Sept. 30, 2014

GALLUP

Among the most populous states included in this analysis, the range in estimates of engaged teachers is wide—a 13-percentage-point difference between the top- and bottom-ranking states. This may suggest that some states are more successfully capitalizing on the talent of their teachers than others. However, even for states like Washington, with the highest percentage of engaged teachers coupled with the lowest percentage of actively disengaged teachers, there remains room for improvement. Those looking to improve teacher engagement might be well served by studying the best practices of states with high levels of teacher engagement.

Survey Methods

Results are based on telephone interviews conducted Jan. 2, 2011–Sept. 30, 2014, as part of the Gallup Daily tracking survey, for a subgroup of 16,259 full-time K-12 school teachers, from a random sample of adults, aged 18 and older, living in all 50 U.S. states and the District of Columbia. All reported margins of sampling error include computed design effects for weighting.

For results based on the total sample of U.S. teachers, the margin of sampling error is ±1 percentage point at the 95% confidence level. For state-level estimates, the margin of sampling error for most states is ±4 but is as low as ±2 for larger states and as high as ±7 percentage points for states with smaller populations.

January 15, 2015
AMERICANS' PERSONAL AND U.S. SATISFACTION ON THE UPSWING

by Justin McCarthy

Story Highlights

• *Satisfaction with personal life back to prerecession levels*
• *Satisfaction with U.S. surges nine points since December*

• *32% satisfied with direction of U.S.; among highest in eight years*

WASHINGTON, D.C.—After falling during the economic downturn, Americans' satisfaction with the way things are going in their personal lives has recovered to 85%. Meanwhile, Americans' satisfaction with the direction of the country surged nine percentage points since December to 32%, one of its best readings in the last eight years.

Personal Satisfaction vs. National Satisfaction

In general, are you satisfied or dissatisfied with the way things are going in your personal life at this time?
In general, are you satisfied or dissatisfied with the way things are going in the United States at this time?

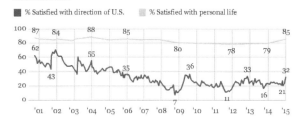

Latest figures from Jan. 5-8, 2015

GALLUP

Large majorities of Americans have expressed satisfaction with their personal lives in each poll since Gallup began asking the question in 1979. The percentage of Americans satisfied with their personal lives reached a low of 73% in July 1979 amid the U.S. energy crisis, while it peaked at 88% in 2003. The latest 85% reading is significantly higher than the previous 78% to 80% figures recorded since President Barack Obama's 2008 election.

Consistent with their tendency to rate their own situations, or local conditions, more positively than national conditions, Americans are much less likely to be satisfied with the way things are going in the U.S. On average, satisfaction with personal life is 43 points higher than satisfaction with the country's direction. The difference between the two was as low as 14 points in the months after 9/11, and as high as 70 points after the 2008 election. Americans' satisfaction with U.S. conditions fell below 30% in March 2006, and has rarely been above that level since the spring of 2007, only surpassing it early in President Obama's first term, around the time of his 2012 re-election and in the current month.

Satisfaction With U.S. Trajectory Continues to Vary by Party Identification

While Americans of different political identifications rate their satisfaction with their personal lives about the same, their satisfaction with the direction of the U.S. varies quite a bit, with those supporting the president's party giving a rosier assessment than others.

As has been the case since Obama's 2008 election, Democrats remain the most satisfied (50%), followed by independents (30%) and Republicans (16%).

For Republicans, the 16% reading in January—up nine points from last month—tops the 3% to 15% range they have stayed within since Obama's election.

Independents' eight-point bump from December's poll nearly matches their previous Obama-era high of 32% in May 2009.

Democrats, meanwhile, climbed 14 points from last month, reaching their highest satisfaction figure since November 2012.

Satisfaction With Direction of U.S., by Party ID

% Satisfied

	Dec. 8-11, 2014	Jan. 5-8, 2015	Change
Democrats	36	50	+14
Independents	22	30	+8
Republicans	7	16	+9

GALLUP

Bottom Line

While the usual political differences persist, Americans' overall increase in satisfaction in January is likely due to economic growth in the U.S. and good news from the stock market. This increased satisfaction is reflected in Americans' growing economic confidence.

All the while, Obama's approval rating has also showed positive momentum in recent months. And while the nation has a host of issues to deal with, 2014 was void of the hyperpartisan drama that sent economic confidence plummeting the year prior. This culmination of positive economic and political factors certainly has helped boost Americans' overall satisfaction with the nation's course.

Survey Methods

Results for this Gallup poll are based on telephone interviews conducted Jan. 5–8, 2014, on the Gallup U.S. Daily survey, with a random sample of 804 adults, aged 18 and older, living in all 50 U.S. states and the District of Columbia. For results based on the total sample of national adults, the margin of sampling error is ±4 percentage points at the 95% confidence level. All reported margins of sampling error include computed design effects for weighting.

January 16, 2015
AMERICANS' LIFE OUTLOOK BEST IN SEVEN YEARS

by Alyssa Brown

Story Highlights

- *54.1% considered "thriving," highest since tracking began in 2008*
- *Future life ratings improved from 2013; current life ratings did not*
- *Blacks', Asians' and young adults' life ratings unchanged from 2013*

WASHINGTON, D.C.—Americans' outlook on life is the best it has been in at least seven years. More Americans were "thriving" and fewer were "struggling" in 2014 than has been the case since Gallup and Healthways began tracking Americans' life evaluations daily in 2008. In 2014, 54.1% of Americans, on average, rated their lives highly enough to be considered thriving and 42.1% were classified as struggling.

Gallup and Healthways measure Americans' life evaluations as part of the Gallup-Healthways Well-Being Index. Gallup classifies Americans as "thriving," "struggling," or "suffering" according to how they rate their current and future lives on a ladder scale with steps numbered from 0 to 10 based on the Cantril Self-Anchoring

Striving Scale. Those who rate their present life a 7 or higher and their lives in five years an 8 or higher are classified as thriving, while those who rate both dimensions a 4 or lower are considered suffering. Respondents whose ratings fall in between are considered struggling.

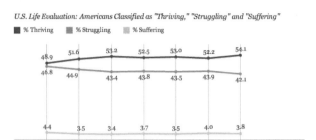

U.S. Life Evaluation: Americans Classified as "Thriving," "Struggling" and "Suffering"

■ % Thriving ■ % Struggling ▨ % Suffering

	2008	2009	2010	2011	2012	2013	2014
Thriving	48.9	51.6	53.2	52.5	53.0	52.2	54.1
Struggling	46.8	44.9	43.4	43.8	43.5	43.9	42.1
Suffering	4.4	3.5	3.4	3.7	3.5	4.0	3.8

2008-2014
Gallup-Healthways Well-Being Index

GALLUP

The rise in Americans' life ratings last year was driven by an improvement in how they evaluate their future lives, rather than their current situation. Americans, on average, rated their future lives a 7.8, up from 7.6 in 2013, which is the highest recorded score on this measure to date. On the other hand, Americans' current life ratings averaged 7.0, unchanged from 2013 and similar to ratings found since 2009. As is typical, Americans' future life ratings were higher than their current life ratings.

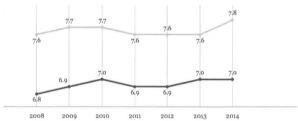

U.S. Life Evaluation: Americans' Current and Future Life Ratings

■ Current life rating ▨ Future life rating

	2008	2009	2010	2011	2012	2013	2014
Future life rating	7.6	7.7	7.7	7.6	7.6	7.6	7.8
Current life rating	6.8	6.9	7.0	6.9	6.9	7.0	7.0

2008-2014
Gallup-Healthways Well-Being Index

GALLUP

Blacks, Asians and Young Americans No More Likely to Be Thriving Than in 2013

A higher percentage of Americans in many key subgroups were thriving in life evaluations in 2014 compared with 2013. Middle-aged Americans, Hispanics, Eastern residents and those earning $120,000 or more annually saw their percentage thriving improve the most. Men's ratings improved more than women's, although women maintain an edge and are still ahead of men in their percent thriving, a pattern seen since 2008.

Importantly, the percentages of blacks, Asians and young Americans who were "thriving" in 2014 are unchanged from 2013, showing that life ratings are not improving across the board. However, because these groups had among the highest life ratings in 2013, they still compare favorably to other groups. The percentages of seniors and those Americans earning $48,000 to $90,000 annually who are thriving improved slightly, but trailed the improvement seen nationally.

Broadly speaking, the life evaluation metric is most strongly linked to income, followed by age. Higher-income Americans and young adults have consistently been more likely to be classified as thriving than their lower-income and older counterparts, the latter group mainly because of their lower projections for their future lives.

Percentage "Thriving," by Subgroup, 2013 vs. 2014

U.S. Life Evaluation

	2013	2014	Difference
	%	%	(pct. pts.)
National average	52.2	54.1	1.9
Male	50.2	52.3	2.1
Female	54.0	55.8	1.8
18-29 years	60.6	60.6	0
30-44 years	56.9	59.8	2.9
45-64 years	48.6	51.2	2.6
65+ years	42.8	44.5	1.7
White	51.9	54.1	2.2
Black	52.9	53.0	0.1
Asian	60.5	60.4	-0.1
Hispanic	52.6	55.3	2.7
Under $24,000	36.6	38.9	2.3
$24,000-$47,999	45.0	47.2	2.2
$48k-$89,999k	58.0	59.6	1.6
$90k-$119,999k	65.2	67.4	2.2
$120k +	70.0	72.5	2.5
East	51.5	54.0	2.5
West	54.1	55.7	1.6
Midwest	51.5	53.1	1.6
South	51.7	53.8	2.1

Gallup-Healthways Well-Being Index

GALLUP

Bottom Line

Americans, on average, rated their lives in 2014 better than in any year since Gallup and Healthways began tracking this metric in 2008, and this likely reflects increasing optimism about their future, finances and the U.S. economy. This uptick in thriving coincides with an increase in Americans' ratings of their standard of living, a rise in their economic confidence at the end of 2014, and more Americans saying now is a good time to find a quality job.

Previous Gallup research shows that Americans' life ratings tend to track closely with their standard of living perceptions and confidence in the national economy. Thus, if Americans' perceptions of the economy and their personal finances continue to climb in 2015, their life ratings likely will rise as well.

Survey Methods

Results are based on telephone interviews conducted Jan. 2–Dec. 30, 2014, as part of the Gallup-Healthways Well-Being Index survey, with a random sample of 176,903 adults, aged 18 and older, living in all 50 U.S. states and the District of Columbia. For results based on the total sample of national adults, the margin of sampling error is ±1 percentage points at the 95% confidence level.

January 16, 2015

AMERICANS' PERSONAL FINANCIAL ASSESSMENTS UP SHARPLY

by Jeffrey M. Jones

Story Highlights

- *In U.S., 47% say they are financially better off than a year ago*
- *Financial assessments much better than in early 2014*
- *Current results approach those of stronger economic times*

PRINCETON, N.J.—Americans are much more likely to report that they are financially better off now (47%) compared with a year ago than to say they are worse off (28%). Last January, more said they were worse off than better off, consistent with most measurements since the Great Recession began. The more positive results this year are closer to what Gallup measured during strong economic times over the past 40 years—such as in the late 1980s and late 1990s—than in sluggish economic times.

Next, we are interested in how people's financial situation may have changed. Would you say that you are financially better off now than you were a year ago, or are you financially worse off now?

Note: percentage "same" not shown

GALLUP

Americans' rosier financial assessments come as falling gas prices have benefited nearly all Americans and rising stock values in the past year have benefited most. The job market by all accounts is better than it was a year ago.

The latest results mark a dramatic turnaround from the recent recession and post-recession years. In May 2009, 54% of Americans said their financial situation was worse and 23% better, the gloomiest assessment in Gallup's 40-year trend. Last year at this time, 35% of Americans said their financial situation was getting better and 42% said it was getting worse.

The most positive personal financial assessments came in the late 1990s and in 2000, when a majority consistently said their financial situation was better than a year prior. Specifically, in 1999, an average of 56% of Americans said they were better off, compared with 21% saying worse off.

Personal Financial Ratings Improve in All Key Subgroups

Americans in all key subgroups see an improved personal financial outlook, with each showing at least marginal improvement in their ratings between the January 2014 and January 2015 polls. Younger Americans and those living in middle-income households saw slightly greater improvements, with increases of 20 and 19 points, respectively, in the percentage of each group saying they are better off financially.

Changes in Assessments of Personal Financial Situation,
January 2014 vs. January 2015

	2014 % Better off	2014 % Worse off	2015 % Better off	2015 % Worse off
All Americans	35	42	47	28
Men	34	41	48	25
Women	36	43	47	32
White	31	44	45	29
Nonwhite	45	39	52	26
18 to 34 years old	41	42	61	24
35 to 54 years old	38	42	45	31
55+ years old	29	42	39	29
College graduate	40	32	56	24
College nongraduate	33	47	44	30
Under $30,000 household income	32	55	36	41
$30,000 to <$75,000	32	44	51	23
$75,000 or more	44	30	56	24
Employed	39	39	53	25
Not employed	30	47	40	31
Republican	31	47	38	34
Independent	31	47	45	29
Democrat	46	31	62	21

GALLUP

Lower-income Americans showed only a slight increase from 32% getting better in 2014 to 36% this year. Lower-income Americans are the only key subgroup who remain more likely to say their situation is getting worse rather than better.

Republicans also saw below-average improvement in their ratings, suggesting that personal financial ratings are not free from political considerations, as Republicans may be reluctant to acknowledge that circumstances of any kind are getting better at a time when the sitting president is a Democrat.

Americans Expect Good Times to Continue

Americans generally believe their financial situations will stay on a positive arc, with 65% saying they expect to be better off a year from now, while 15% expect to be worse off. Americans have generally been optimistic about their financial future. At no point in the last 40 years—even during tough economic times—have more Americans predicted their finances to get worse rather than better.

Looking ahead, do you expect that at this time next year you will be financially better off than now, or worse off than now?

Note: percentage "same" not shown

GALLUP

Even so, the current 65% who expect their finances to improve in the next 12 months is on the high end of what Gallup has measured historically, just six points below the peak of 71% from March 1998.

Implications

Americans' ratings of their personal financial situations have improved greatly over the past year. This is consistent with the improved ratings of Americans' standard of living and growing confidence in the U.S. economy that Gallup recently reported.

The current personal financial situation ratings are now at or near the high levels Gallup measured in the past four decades when the U.S. economy was strong. The improvement is especially notable given that just five years ago, near the end of the Great Recession, Americans gave the bleakest assessment of their personal finances at any time in the last 40 years.

As usual, most Americans expect things to continue to improve over the next year, but the optimism they express about the coming year also exceeds what is typical. Whether Americans' finances actually improve over the coming year will depend in large part on whether the national economy continues to get better, or takes a step back.

Survey Methods

Results for this Gallup poll are based on telephone interviews conducted Jan. 5–8, 2015, with a random sample of 804 adults, aged 18 and older, living in all 50 U.S. states and the District of Columbia. For results based on the total sample of national adults, the margin of sampling error is ±4 percentage points at the 95% confidence level. All reported margins of sampling error include computed design effects for weighting.

January 19, 2015
AMERICANS' SATISFACTION WITH SECURITY FROM TERRORISM DROPS

by Frank Newport

Story Highlights

- *Satisfaction on security from terrorism down 10 points vs. 2014*
- *Still, few Americans mention terrorism as nation's top problem*
- *Democrats are much more positive than Republicans*

PRINCETON, N.J.—Although a majority of Americans remain satisfied with the nation's security from terrorism, this measure has dropped 10 percentage points since last year, from 69% to 59%, and is now back where it was in 2008.

The latest update on Americans' satisfaction with terrorism and other aspects of American life comes from Gallup's Jan. 5–8 Mood of the Nation poll. The interviewing dates for this poll overlapped the Jan. 7 terrorist attack on the headquarters of French newspaper *Charlie Hebdo* in Paris. Although that attack was not against Americans, it received widespread U.S. media attention, likely making the terrorism issue more salient in Americans' minds.

How satisfied are you with the nation's security from terrorism?

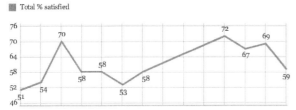

Note: Total satisfied = % very + % somewhat satisfied

GALLUP

Satisfaction with the nation's handling of terrorism over the past 13 years has varied from as low as 51% in January 2002—months after the 9/11 terrorist attacks—to the high point of 72% in January 2012. The measure was at 70% in January 2004, just a few weeks after the Dec. 13, 2003, capture of former Iraqi dictator Saddam Hussein outside his hometown of Tikrit, Iraq.

Despite this year's drop in feeling secure from terrorism, it remains near the top of the list of 27 dimensions of U.S. life tested in this January's poll—below only Americans' ratings of their overall quality of life, U.S. military strength and preparedness, and the opportunity to work hard and get ahead.

Few Mention Terrorism as Most Important Problem

Despite the downturn in satisfaction with how the nation is handling terrorism, Americans' likelihood of mentioning terrorism as the nation's most important problem is little changed over the past four or five years. In the Jan. 5–8 survey, 2% of Americans say terrorism is the most important U.S. problem, dwarfed by mentions of other issues such as dysfunctional government, the economy, immigration, jobs and the national debt. Mentions of terrorism on this measure have been in the low single digits for most of the past eight years.

Views of Terrorism as the Most Important U.S. Problem

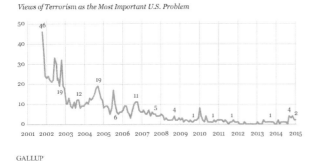

GALLUP

Democrats More Positive About the Nation's Security From Terrorism

As is true with many other measures of the national and economic mood, satisfaction with the nation's security from terrorism is highest among Americans whose party identification aligns with that of the president. This year, with Barack Obama in office, 71% of his fellow Democrats and Democratic leaners are satisfied, compared with 49% of Republicans and Republican leaners. The same pattern has been evident since 2012, the first year Gallup measured this during Obama's presidency.

By contrast, from 2002 through 2008, with George W. Bush in the White House, Republicans were generally much more satisfied than Democrats with the nation's handling of terrorism. The largest partisan gap occurred in 2007, when 69% of Republicans were satisfied, compared with 42% of Democrats.

The decline in satisfaction with terrorism this year is more apparent among Republicans (down 14 points) than among Democrats (down four points).

How satisfied are you with the nation's security from terrorism?
Total % satisfied, by party identification

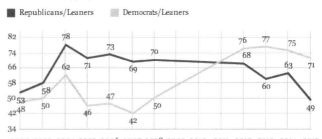

GALLUP

Bottom Line

Although Americans' satisfaction with the nation's security from terrorism has slipped 10 points from last year, it remains in majority territory. It is also one of the four elements of life in the U.S. that Gallup measures about which Americans are most positive. The drop from last year may in part reflect the continuing instances of terrorist activity around the globe, including the ongoing Islamic State conflict in the Middle East and the attack on *Charlie Hebdo*, which occurred while the survey was being conducted. At the same time, few Americans name terrorism as the most important problem facing the nation.

Survey Methods

Results for this Gallup poll are based on telephone interviews conducted Jan. 5–8, 2015, with a random sample of 804 adults, aged 18 and older, living in all 50 U.S. states and the District of Columbia. For results based on the total sample of national adults, the margin of sampling error is ±4 percentage points at the 95% confidence level. All reported margins of sampling error include computed design effects for weighting.

January 19, 2015
U.S. MOOD ON ECONOMY UP, RACE RELATIONS SHARPLY DOWN

by Lydia Saad

Story Highlights

- *Satisfaction with race relations down 25 points to a mere 30%*
- *Satisfaction with the economy up 13 points in past year, to 41%*

• *Security from terrorism dips 10 points, but still high at 59%*

PRINCETON, N.J.—Americans' views about the economy, their overall quality of life and the opportunity to get ahead through hard work are more positive than they were before the 2014 State of the Union address—echoing their improving economic confidence. At the same time, Americans are markedly less satisfied with the state of race relations and, to a lesser extent, with the nation's security from terrorism, with crime and with federal taxes.

Americans' Satisfaction With the State of the Nation -- 2015 vs. 2014

Next, [I'm going to read some aspects of life in America today/we'd like to know how you feel about the state of the nation in each of the following areas]. For each one, please say whether you are very satisfied, somewhat satisfied, somewhat dissatisfied or very dissatisfied.

Total % very/somewhat satisfied

	Jan 5-8, 2014	Jan 5-8, 2015	Change
	%	%	Pct. pts.
State of the nation's economy	28	41	13
Overall quality of life	74	84	10
Opportunity to get ahead by working hard	54	60	6
Availability of affordable healthcare	38	43	5
Nation's laws or policies on guns	40	42	2
Our system of government and how well it works	35	37	2
Government surveillance of U.S. citizens	30	32	2
Quality of public education	39	40	1
Size and influence of major corporations	35	36	1
Size and power of the federal government	33	34	1
Acceptance of gays and lesbians	53	53	0
Quality of medical care	56	56	0
Nation's energy policies	40	39	-1
Nation's efforts to deal with poverty/homelessness	27	26	-1
Influence of organized religion	54	53	-1
Way wealth and income are distributed in U.S.	32	31	-1
The role the U.S. plays in world affairs	40	38	-2
Nation's military strength and preparedness	72	69	-3
Quality of the environment	55	52	-3
Moral and ethical climate	35	32	-3
Nation's policies regarding abortion	38	34	-4
Level of immigration	38	33	-5
Social Security and Medicare systems	42	37	-5
Amount Americans pay in federal taxes	38	32	-6
Nation's policies to reduce or control crime	51	45	-6
Nation's security from terrorism	69	59	-10
State of race relations	55	30	-25

GALLUP

These are the significant changes in how Americans see the country at the start of 2015 compared with the same point in 2014, according to Gallup's annual Mood of the Nation poll. This year's update was conducted Jan. 5–8, spanning the Jan. 7 terrorist attack on the headquarters of French newspaper *Charlie Hebdo* in Paris that took 12 lives and immediately consumed U.S. and world news headlines.

Americans' ratings of the remaining aspects of the country in the poll are largely unchanged, including such widely debated areas as education, the level of immigration, healthcare and the nation's energy policies.

Quality of Life, Military, Economic Opportunity Lead 2015 List

Apart from the changes in the past year, Americans are most satisfied with the overall quality of life in the country. Eighty-four percent are satisfied with this aspect of the nation, including 30% very satisfied and 54% somewhat satisfied. This eclipses the nation's military strength and preparedness, which earns a 69% satisfaction

score. Meanwhile, 59% of Americans remain satisfied with the nation's security from terrorism, keeping this in the top five despite a 10-point decline since 2014.

Other issues about which at least half of Americans are satisfied include the opportunity to get ahead by working hard (60%), the quality of medical care (56%), the influence of organized religion (53%), the acceptance of gays and lesbians (53%) and the quality of the environment (52%).

Americans' Satisfaction With the State of the Nation

Next, [I'm going to read some aspects of life in America today/we'd like to know how you feel about the state of the nation in each of the following areas]. For each one, please say whether you are very satisfied, somewhat satisfied, somewhat dissatisfied or very dissatisfied.

Total % very/somewhat satisfied

	Jan 5-8, 2015
	%
Overall quality of life	84
Nation's military strength and preparedness	69
Opportunity to get ahead by working hard	60
Nation's security from terrorism	59
Quality of medical care	56
Influence of organized religion	53
Acceptance of gays and lesbians	53
Quality of the environment	52
Nation's policies to reduce or control crime	45
Availability of affordable healthcare	43
Nation's laws or policies on guns	42
State of the nation's economy	41
Quality of public education	40
Nation's energy policies	39
The role the U.S. plays in world affairs	38
Our system of government and how well it works	37
Social Security and Medicare systems	37
Size and influence of major corporations	36
Size and power of the federal government	34
Nation's policies regarding abortion	34
Level of immigration	33
Moral and ethical climate	32
Government surveillance of U.S. citizens	32
Amount Americans pay in federal taxes	32
Way wealth and income are distributed in U.S.	31
State of race relations	30
Nation's efforts to deal with poverty/homelessness	26

GALLUP

The rise in Americans' satisfaction with the nation's economy to 41% puts the issue at about the middle of the group of 27 areas rated this year, up from the bottom of the pack last year. At the same time, the downturn to 30% in satisfaction with race relations has moved it from the middle of the list to near the bottom, just slightly ahead of the nation's efforts to deal with poverty (26%). Other issues on which no more than a third of Americans are satisfied are immigration (33%), the moral and ethical climate (32%), government surveillance of U.S. citizens (32%), federal taxes (32%) and the way wealth and income are distributed (31%).

Progress and Setbacks Since 2008

Yet another way to look at the 2015 results is how they compare with January 2008—the last Gallup reading of these measures before Barack Obama took office (the questions weren't asked in early 2009). On that basis, satisfaction is up on six items, led by the availability of affordable healthcare, acceptance of gays and lesbians, the quality of medical care and the level of immigration—all areas where Democrats' satisfaction has surged and independents' has increased, while Republicans' has waned or not changed.

Over the same period, satisfaction is down in seven areas—most sharply on race relations, where it has fallen among all party groups, and the U.S. system of government and how well it works, down mainly among Republicans.

The economy is not on this list of issues that have seen major change since January 2008 because economic confidence did not become deeply negative until later in 2008.

Americans' Satisfaction With the State of the Nation -- 2015 vs. 2008

Items that show significant change since 2008

Total % very/somewhat satisfied

	Jan 4-6, 2008	Jan 5-8, 2015	Change
	%	%	%
Availability of affordable healthcare	25	43	18
Acceptance of gays and lesbians	38	53	15
The quality of medical care in the nation	45	56	11
Level of immigration	23	33	10
Nation's energy policies	31	39	8
Social Security and Medicare systems	31	37	6
Nation's laws or policies on guns	48	42	-6
Size and power of the federal government	41	34	-7
Moral and ethical climate	39	32	-7
Opportunity to get ahead by working hard	68	60	-8
Nation's policies regarding abortion	43	34	-9
Our system of government and how well it works	53	37	-16
State of race relations	51	30	-21

GALLUP

Bottom Line

When Americans settle in to watch Obama deliver his State of the Union address Tuesday night, they will do so feeling better about the economy than a year ago—though still not as content about it as they could be, given that satisfaction stands at 41%. That provides Obama with an opportunity to tout his successes while still asking Congress to support additional economic measures. It also frees him to make proposals that may have seemed extravagant at the height of the recession, such as his plan to subsidize tuition at community colleges for students who meet certain conditions.

Race relations, which elicited high mentions on Gallup's Most Important Problem list in December, has the compound challenge of suffering the sharpest decline in public satisfaction since 2014 and ranking among the lowest issues tested—thus making it a prime topic for the president's attention.

With Obama edging closer to the end of his presidency, he may be speaking as much to the future as to the members of Congress sitting before him. In reviewing his achievements, economic progress is likely to be front and center, but he may also highlight the three issues on which public satisfaction—and particularly Democrats' satisfaction—has increased the most since 2008: healthcare, gay rights, and immigration.

Survey Methods

Results for this Gallup poll are based on telephone interviews conducted Jan. 5–8, 2015, with a random sample of 804 adults, aged 18 and older, living in all 50 U.S. states and the District of Columbia.

For results based on the total sample of national adults, the margin of sampling error is ±4 percentage points at the 95% confidence level. All reported margins of sampling error include computed design effects for weighting.

January 20, 2015
OBAMA AVERAGES 42.6% JOB APPROVAL IN YEAR SIX

by Jeffrey M. Jones

Story Highlights

- *Sixth-year average is Obama's lowest*
- *His recent ratings have been higher; 24th-quarter average is up*

PRINCETON, N.J.—President Barack Obama averaged a 42.6% job approval rating throughout his sixth full year in office, which ended Monday. Although his more recent ratings have been higher, including a 46% average rating last week, his sixth-year average is his lowest yearly rating to date.

Barack Obama's Yearly Job Approval Averages

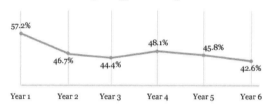

Gallup U.S. Daily tracking

GALLUP

These results are based on Gallup U.S. Daily tracking from Jan. 20, 2014, through Jan. 19, 2015. Obama begins his seventh year in office on Tuesday, also the day of his State of the Union address.

Presidents' sixth year in office has generally been unkind. Across all presidents, the sixth year is the one with the lowest overall average (45.5%), slightly worse than the seventh- and eighth-year averages. The sixth-year average is held down by Richard Nixon's very low sixth-year approval ratings up until he resigned from office in August 1974. Taking Nixon's numbers out of the mix, the sixth-year average would be 48.4%.

Average Approval Ratings for U.S. Presidents by Year in Office, 1945-2015

Year in office	Average approval rating (%)	Number of presidents
First	64.4	12
Second	56.0	12
Third	54.9	12
Fourth	51.5	10
Fifth	51.1	8
Sixth	45.5	8
Seventh	46.5	5
Eighth	46.7	5

GALLUP

Of the six post–World War II presidents before Obama who served a full or partial sixth year in office, three had their worst yearly averages in year six: Dwight Eisenhower, Lyndon Johnson and Nixon.

Not all presidents have had difficult sixth years, though. Bill Clinton averaged 63.8% job approval and Ronald Reagan 59.9% as their sixth year coincided with periods of strong economic growth. Although it was his lowest yearly average of his eight-year presidency, Eisenhower still managed a relatively solid 54.4% approval rating in his sixth year.

But the presidents who were not popular in their sixth year tended to be very unpopular, including Harry Truman, George W. Bush and Nixon, who all averaged below 40% job approval.

Job Approval Averages for Presidents During Their Sixth Year in Office

	Dates of sixth year	Sixth-year average (%)	Number of polls
Truman	January 1950–January 1951	38.6	13
Eisenhower	January 1958–January 1959	54.4	16
Johnson	January 1968–January 1969	41.9	14
Nixon	January 1974–August 1974	25.4	15
Reagan	January 1986–January 1987	59.9	13
Clinton	January 1998–January 1999	63.8	32
G.W. Bush	January 2006–January 2007	37.3	32
Obama	January 2014–January 2015	42.6	349

GALLUP

Obama's Approval Ratings Trending Upward

Even though Obama's sixth year in office was his worst to date, his approval ratings were showing signs of positive momentum in the latter stages of the year. For example, in the last three months of the year—his 24th quarter in office—his approval rating averaged 43.4%, up nearly two full percentage points from the prior quarter.

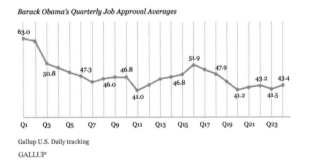

Barack Obama's Quarterly Job Approval Averages

Gallup U.S. Daily tracking
GALLUP

More recently, Obama's ratings have been even higher, averaging 46% job approval last week and the prior two weeks.

Obama's more positive recent approval ratings are likely influenced by two factors. The first is his decision to use executive actions to address the legal status of undocumented immigrants living in the U.S. This move, announced in a nationally televised address in November, was widely supported by Hispanics. In turn,

Hispanics' overall approval rating of Obama climbed, and remains at that higher level today.

Secondly, Americans' assessments of the national economy are improving and are at their highest levels since before the recession. All else being equal, Americans usually rate presidents better when the economy is strong.

Implications

President Obama certainly had a trying sixth year in office as he dealt with challenges abroad—such as the rise of Islamic militants in the Middle East—and faced continued partisan gridlock in trying to address key domestic issues. During the fall months, he registered some of the lowest approval ratings of his presidency. That culminated with Republicans' strong showing in the midterm elections, giving them solid majorities in both houses of Congress.

But since that time, aided by falling unemployment, plummeting gas prices and generally solid economic growth, as well as resurgent support from Hispanics, things have started to look up for Obama.

Historically, most presidents' seventh-year averages are lower than their sixth-year averages. If Obama's positive momentum continues throughout his seventh year in office, he would join Eisenhower as the only post–World War II presidents who saw significant improvement in support during their seventh year in office.

Survey Methods

Results for this Gallup poll are based on telephone interviews conducted Oct. 20, 2014–Jan. 19, 2015, on the Gallup U.S. Daily survey, with a random sample of 42,603 adults, aged 18 and older, living in all 50 U.S. states and the District of Columbia.

For results based on the total sample of national adults, the margin of sampling error is ±1 percentage point at the 95% confidence level.

January 21, 2015
AMERICANS SEE HEALTHCARE, LOW WAGES AS TOP FINANCIAL PROBLEMS

by Art Swift

Story Highlights

- *14% in U.S. cite healthcare, low wages*
- *Top earners name retirement savings, college expenses*
- *Low earners' top concern is "lack of money/cash flow"*

WASHINGTON, D.C.—Healthcare costs and lack of money or low wages rank as the most important financial problems facing American families, each mentioned by 14% of U.S. adults. Fewer Americans than a year ago cite the high cost of living or unemployment, and the percentage naming oil or gas prices is down from 2012.

Gallup has been asking Americans about the most important financial problem facing their family in an open-ended format for the past 10 years. Healthcare this year has returned to the top of the list for the first time since early 2010, when the Affordable Care Act, or "Obamacare," was signed into law. Still, Americans viewed it as an even bigger financial problem in 2007, when a range of 16% to 19% said it was most important.

Most Important Financial Problem in U.S., Recent Trend
What is the most important financial problem facing your family today?

	July 2011	October 2011	2012	2013	2014	2015
	%	%	%	%	%	%
Healthcare costs	12	12	12	10	12	14
Lack of money/Low wages	17	14	18	14	13	14
Too much debt/Not enough money to pay debts	11	13	9	11	10	9
College expenses	7	7	7	9	11	8
Retirement savings	6	5	4	6	6	6
Cost of owning/renting a home	6	7	12	9	8	6
High cost of living/Inflation	9	13	11	11	10	6
Unemployment/Loss of job	9	10	9	7	8	5
Taxes	4	3	5	5	3	4
Lack of savings	2	3	3	2	2	3
Energy costs/Oil and gas prices	7	4	11	5	1	2
Social Security	2	2	1	1	1	2
Stock market/Investments	1	2	1	1	1	1
Transportation/Commuting costs	1	*	1	1	3	1
Interest rates	1	1	*	1	2	1
State of the economy	1	1	*	1	2	1
Controlling spending	*	--	1	1	1	1
Other	2	2	4	2	5	2
None	16	11	11	13	12	17
No opinion	3	3	4	5	3	8

GALLUP

Notably, 6% of Americans see the high cost of living or inflation as their family's biggest financial problem, down from 13% just over three years ago. And in today's era of sub-$50-per-barrel oil, only 2% name energy costs, or oil or gas prices as their most important financial problem, down significantly from 11% in 2012 amid a spike in oil prices.

The percentage who don't mention any financial problem is up five percentage points from last year, to 17%. This sizable uptick suggests that the economic recovery may be reducing the financial problems that families face.

Most Important Financial Problems Vary Across Income Groups

For Americans earning $75,000 or more a year, retirement savings, college expenses and healthcare costs rank as the most important financial problems. Among lower-income Americans, retirement savings and college expenses are less important. Healthcare costs, however, have double-digit-percentage support across the board.

Perhaps not surprisingly, lower-income Americans name "lack of money/cash flow" and "not enough money to pay debts" as their top most important money woes. The stock market or investments, interest rates, retirement savings and controlling spending do not rank among lower-income Americans' top financial problems.

Bottom Line

The American economy continues to recover. With Gallup's Economic Confidence Index in positive territory for the first time since the Great Recession, and with President Barack Obama stating that the U.S. last year had its best year for job growth since 1999, certain financial problems have receded from the nation's memory, while others have persisted in the forefront. Americans have consistently cited healthcare, a topic of fierce debate this decade, as one of the most important financial problems, and it remains so.

Americans' Most Important Financial Problem
By annual household income level

	$75,000+	$30,000 to $74,999	Under $30,000
Healthcare costs	13	18	10
Lack of money/Cash flow	4	14	16
Not enough money to pay debts	6	11	15
College expenses	13	7	7
Retirement savings	14	5	--
Cost of owning/renting a home	6	4	9
High cost of living/Inflation	8	4	5
Unemployment/Loss of job	5	3	8
Taxes	4	4	*
Low wages	2	3	5
Lack of savings	4	4	2
Energy costs	1	2	2
Social Security	*	*	6
Stock market/Investments	2	1	*
Transportation/Commuting costs	*	2	1
Interest rates	1	1	1
State of the economy	1	*	*
Controlling spending	1	*	--
Other	2	2	2
None	18	14	15
No opinion	3	9	8

* Less than 0.5%
Jan. 5-8, 2015

GALLUP

Lack of money and low wages are still an important problem for many Americans, yet unemployment and the high cost of living are mentioned less often than in recent years, as are energy prices. Whether these developments result from a stronger economy or are just not top of mind, Americans' financial worries clearly have shifted over the past few years.

Issues that have remained low-level concerns all decade—including Social Security, the stock market, controlling spending and transportation costs—remain low again this year, suggesting that, good times or bad, Americans are not concerned about these issues affecting their families' financial situation.

Survey Methods

Results for this Gallup poll are based on telephone interviews conducted Jan. 5–8, 2015, on the Gallup Poll Social Series, with a random sample of 804 adults, aged 18 and older, living in all 50 U.S. states and the District of Columbia. For results based on the total sample of national adults, the margin of sampling error is ±4 percentage points at the 95% confidence level. All reported margins of sampling error include computed design effects for weighting.

January 22, 2015
AMERICANS' SATISFACTION WITH FEDERAL TAXES ON LOW SIDE

by Lydia Saad

Story Highlights

- *Barely a third satisfied with taxes, down from 38% in 2014*
- *Satisfaction about taxes ties lowest levels seen since 2003*
- *Nearly half, 46%, dissatisfied and want lower taxes*

PRINCETON, N.J.—Americans' satisfaction with the amount that Americans pay in federal income taxes roughly ties the lowest percentage Gallup has seen in the past 12 years. Thirty-two percent are now satisfied, down from 38% a year ago, but similar to the 33% found in 2003 and 2012.

U.S. Satisfaction With What Americans Pay in Taxes

Please say whether you are very satisfied, somewhat satisfied, somewhat dissatisfied, or very dissatisfied with___the amount Americans pay in federal taxes.

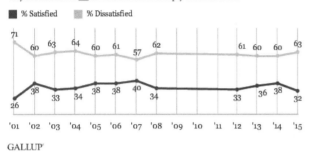

GALLUP

According to the Jan. 5–8 poll, 63% of Americans this year are dissatisfied with the amount Americans pay in taxes. In a follow-up question, most of this group—equivalent to 46% of all Americans—say they would like to see Americans pay less in taxes. Hardly any—4%—would prefer they pay more. An additional 13% are dissatisfied with what Americans pay in taxes, but aren't specific about how it should change.

The 46% who currently want taxes decreased is notably higher than what Gallup has found since 2012. It is only exceeded by the 51% recorded in mid-January 2003, a week after President George W. Bush proposed extending certain 2001 tax cuts and implementing new ones, measures that ultimately became known as the 2003 Bush tax cuts. Gallup did not ask this satisfaction question about taxes from 2009 to 2011.

Americans' Core Positions on Amount Americans Pay in Taxes

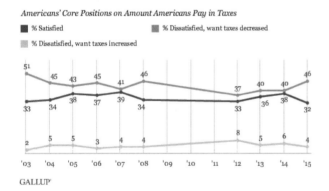

GALLUP

Democrats' Views at Odds With Independents and Republicans

While only 5% of Democrats believe Americans' taxes should be increased, the largest segment, 47%, is satisfied with what Americans pay, while about a third, 31%, think they should pay less. In contrast, the largest segment of independents (46%) and a robust majority of Republicans (61%) are dissatisfied and believe taxes should be decreased.

Majorities of Americans in all income groups, except those in the lowest income bracket, are dissatisfied and believe taxes should be reduced. About as many Americans in households bringing in less than $30,000 per year are satisfied with the amount Americans pay in federal income taxes (39%) as say they should be decreased (31%).

Americans' View of Federal Income Taxes -- by Party ID and Household Income

Jan. 5-8, 2015

	Satisfied	Dissatisfied, taxes should be decreased	Dissatisfied, taxes should be increased
	%	%	%
Democrats	47	31	5
Independents	29	46	3
Republicans	23	61	2
$100,000+	30	53	4
$50,000-$99,999	31	52	4
$30,000-$49,999	26	53	4
Less than $30,000	39	31	4

GALLUP

Just in the past year, Republicans' preference for decreasing taxes has swelled by nearly 20 percentage points—from 44% to 61%—which largely accounts for the increase in this viewpoint nationally. This is also the highest proportion of Republicans holding this view since 2003.

At the same time, independents are only slightly more likely this year than in 2014 to favor decreasing taxes, but they are significantly more likely to feel this way today (46%) than in 2012 (37%). Meanwhile, Democrats' desire for lower taxes has crept up, but remains below where it stood during the recent Bush presidency.

Percentage Favoring a Decrease in Amount Americans Pay in Taxes, by Party ID

Implications

Six years into Barack Obama's presidency, public satisfaction with taxes is at a low ebb, and nearly half of Americans are dissatisfied and would like to see the amount people pay decreased. This decline in satisfaction on taxes is largely driven by Republicans who, prior to hearing Obama's tax reform proposals in his State of the Union address, may have been answering with newfound hope that the enhanced Republican majority in Congress will enact tax cuts. At least, it appears that Bush's initiative on taxes in 2003 may have spurred a similar reaction in Republicans 12 years ago.

It remains to be seen how Republicans, and Americans overall, will react to Obama's call for certain middle-class tax breaks, paired with increases in capital gains and inheritance taxes aimed at the wealthiest Americans. If Americans view this plan as mainly providing significant tax relief for the middle class, it should be received positively. But if Republicans are successful at defining it as an effort to raise revenue to not just pay for middle-class tax credits, but to expand government spending, concern could prevail.

Survey Methods

Results for this Gallup poll are based on telephone interviews conducted Jan. 5–8, 2015, with a random sample of 804 adults, aged 18 and older, living in all 50 U.S. states and the District of Columbia. For results based on the total sample of national adults, the margin of sampling error is ±4 percentage points at the 95% confidence level. All reported margins of sampling error include computed design effects for weighting.

January 23, 2015
AMERICANS' VIEWS ON 10 KEY STATE OF THE UNION PROPOSALS

by Frank Newport, Jeffrey M. Jones, and Lydia Saad

Story Highlights

- *A number of President Obama's SOTU proposals do well in polls*
- *Raising minimum wage, infrastructure spending get high marks*
- *One proposal Americans oppose: Closing Guantanamo Bay prison*

PRINCETON, N.J.—Gallup data reveal how Americans' views line up with 10 key issues raised by President Barack Obama in his 2015 State of the Union address Tuesday night.

1. Raising the minimum wage

We still need to make sure employees get the overtime they've earned. And to everyone in this Congress who still refuses to raise the minimum wage, I say this: If you truly believe you could work full time and support a family on less than $15,000 a year, go try it. If not, vote to give millions of the hardest-working people in America a raise.

Gallup last asked about raising the minimum wage in November 2013, and at that time 76% were in favor of raising it to $9 an hour (from the current $7.25), while 22% were opposed. This included 91% of Democrats in favor, 76% of independents and 58% of Republicans. Separately, Gallup found 69% in favor of increasing the minimum wage to $9 along with establishing automatic inflation-based increases.

Despite this broad support, just 26% of Americans in 2014 said the minimum wage issue is extremely important for Obama and Congress to address. Altogether, 57% called it extremely or very important, but this was overshadowed by the 87% prioritizing veterans' healthcare, 72% prioritizing pay equality for women, and 65% wanting legislation to expand access to preschool. Notably, public demand for action on the minimum wage roughly equals that for passing new immigration reform legislation (58%), and slightly outpaces that for scaling back the Affordable Care Act, also known as Obamacare (53%).

2. Laws to strengthen unions

We still need laws that strengthen rather than weaken unions, and give American workers a voice.

Americans always have been more likely to say they approve than disapprove of labor unions and have historically sympathized with unions over companies in labor disputes. At the same time, the public's appetite for strengthening unions is moderate at best. Thirty-five percent of Americans say they would personally like to see labor unions have more influence than they do today, compared with 27% who prefer less influence and 23% who want their influence kept the same. And Americans widely support right-to-work laws, which prohibit requiring workers to join unions or pay union fees as a condition of employment.

3. Increased spending on infrastructure in order to create jobs

Let's pass a bipartisan infrastructure plan that could create more than 30 times as many jobs per year, and make this country stronger for decades to come.

Gallup research from previous years has shown that the public strongly supports the idea of spending more money on infrastructure projects that would put people to work. One Gallup poll conducted in 2013 asked the question in two ways, one explicitly mentioning spending government money, and the other not, and found 72% versus 77% support across the two wordings.

4. Reform tax code for working/middle class

But for far too long, lobbyists have rigged the tax code with loopholes that let some corporations pay nothing while others pay full freight. They've riddled it with giveaways the super-rich don't need, denying a break to middle-class families who do.

And let's close the loopholes that lead to inequality by allowing the top 1% to avoid paying taxes on their accumulated wealth. We can use that money to help more families pay for childcare and send their kids to college.

Obama made no bones about his desire to increase taxes on corporations and the top 1% of income earners specifically to help ease taxes and household expenses for the middle and working class.

In 2014, 49% of Americans said the middle class pays too much in taxes. Further, 61% said upper-income people pay too little and 66% said the same of corporations. On the surface, this seems consistent with Obama's approach to tax reform.

However, far fewer Americans expressed *the relevant combination* of views to be completely in sync with Obama's redistributive goals. Just 31% say that middle-income people pay too much *and* that upper-income people pay too little. Similarly, 34% say the middle class pays too much *and* that corporations pay too little. The rest, either believe both entities pay the right amount, both pay too much, or some other combination of views.

More broadly, 54% of Americans last April said their tax bill is "fair," but this was the lowest positive reading on this measure since 2001. At the same time, 52% said they consider the amount of federal income tax they pay as too high—indicating that they would welcome some tax relief. The percentage saying their tax bill is too high was the highest figure Gallup has seen on this question since 2008, although still below the 65% found in 2001 before President George W. Bush's first round of tax cuts. Less than one-third of Americans in a January Gallup survey said they were satisfied with the amount Americans pay in federal taxes.

5. Authorizing the use of force against ISIL

Tonight, I call on this Congress to show the world that we are united in this mission by passing a resolution to authorize the use of force against ISIL.

Obama's request for a resolution on ISIL, also known as the Islamic State group or ISIS, is to some degree an "after the fact" element of his speech, given that under his orders as commander in chief, the U.S. military has been launching attacks against ISIL and Islamic militants for months. There is no recent research that directly asks about a congressional resolution on such military action, but Gallup polling from 2014 shows Americans backed the military action after it began.

Gallup data from September show that Americans approve of taking military action "in Iraq and Syria against Islamic militants, commonly known as ISIS," by 60% to 31%. This is slightly below the average support for other military actions Gallup has asked about over recent decades.

6. Lifting the Cuba embargo

In Cuba, we are ending a policy that was long past its expiration date. When what you're doing doesn't work for 50 years, it's time to try something new. Our shift in Cuba policy has the potential to end a legacy of mistrust in our hemisphere; removes a phony excuse for restrictions in Cuba; stands up for democratic values; and extends the hand of friendship to the Cuban people. And this year, Congress should begin the work of ending the embargo.

Gallup last asked about the Cuba embargo in 2009, at which time Americans were more likely to favor (51%) than oppose (36%) ending it. However, the results are consistent with what Gallup found the five times it asked about the embargo between 1999 and 2009. It is unclear if President Obama's recent moves to normalize relations with Cuba may have affected those views. Americans historically have been even more supportive of re-establishing diplomatic relations with Cuba and of ending U.S. restrictions on Americans traveling to Cuba.

7. Reducing carbon emissions

In Beijing, we made an historic announcement—the United States will double the pace at which we cut carbon pollution, and China committed, for the first time, to limiting their emissions. And because the world's two largest economies came together, other nations are now stepping up, and offering hope that, this year, the world will finally reach an agreement to protect the one planet we've got.

Americans favor proposals to set higher emission standards for business and industry (65%) and for automobiles (62%). They show similar support, 63%, for imposing mandatory controls on carbon dioxide emissions. However, their support for all of these proposals, is down considerably from the past. As recently as 2007, 79% or more favored each of these proposals. That decline may be in part related to the economic downturn—Americans tend to be less in favor of environmental protection when the economy is weaker. It may also be due to the shift from having a Republican president less likely to pursue tougher environmental policies to a Democratic president who is more likely to do so.

8. Closing the Guantanamo Bay prison

It makes no sense to spend $3 million per prisoner to keep open a prison that the world condemns and terrorists use to recruit. Since I've been president, we've worked responsibly to cut the population of Guantanamo Bay in half. Now it's time to finish the job. And I will not relent in my determination to shut it down. It's not who we are.

The president appears to be fighting an uphill battle when it comes to Americans' views on closing Guantanamo Bay. Gallup has asked Americans about the Guantanamo Bay prison four times since 2007, prefacing the question by informing respondents that the prison holds "people from other countries who are suspected of being terrorists" and asking if the prison should or should not be closed and move "some of the prisoners to U.S. prisons." A majority has opposed closing the prison each time Gallup has asked the question. Most recently, a June 5–8, 2014, Gallup survey showed that 66% opposed and 29% favored closing the prison.

Attitudes about closing the prison may be related to details about what would happen to the prisoners. A January 2009 Gallup poll that simply asked if the prison should be closed—with no further explanation—found sentiment somewhat more closely divided, with 35% saying it should be closed, and 45% saying it should not.

9. Congressional cooperation

There are a lot of good people here, on both sides of the aisle. And many of you have told me that this isn't what you signed up for—arguing past each other on cable shows, the constant fundraising, always looking over your shoulder at how the base will react to every decision. Imagine if we broke out of these tired old patterns. Imagine if we did something different.

Obama's call for more civility in Washington is music to the ears of at least a segment of Americans, particularly those who cite partisan politics as the nation's top problem. Partisanship, along with a collection of other reasons to be dissatisfied with government, has been one of the most frequently mentioned issues in recent years when Americans were asked to name the most important problem facing the nation. On average, 18% of Americans in Gallup's monthly measures throughout 2014 mentioned dysfunctional government, making it the most frequently mentioned issue, just ahead of the economy at 17%. And dissatisfaction with government remains a top problem so far in 2015, registering 17% in early January.

Although Gallup has not asked directly about Americans' preference for increased political civility, they do show a stronger and increasing preference for political leaders in Washington to compromise in order to get things done rather than stick to their beliefs even if little gets done.

10. Reform the criminal justice system

Surely we can agree it's a good thing that for the first time in 40 years, the crime rate and the incarceration rate have come down together, and use that as a starting point for Democrats and Republicans, community leaders and law enforcement, to reform America's criminal justice system so that it protects and serves us all.

All Americans in general appear to be open to the idea of reforming the criminal justice system, given that the public has a relatively low level of confidence in the system to begin with. In Gallup's annual update on confidence in institutions this past June, 23% of Americans had "a great deal" or "quite a lot" of confidence in the criminal justice system, putting it in the bottom half of all institutions tested. Other evidence shows that the high visibility of the events in Ferguson and New York have eroded confidence in the police and in race relations in general, suggesting that confidence in the criminal justice system could itself be even lower now than it was in June. Aggregated data over the past four years shows that blacks are somewhat more likely to say they have very little or no confidence in the criminal justice system than whites.

A question from a 2013 Gallup poll asking if the American justice system is biased against black people revealed a much more substantial racial divide: 68% of blacks said "yes" compared with 25% of whites.

January 22, 2015
SATISFACTION WITH ACCEPTANCE OF GAY PEOPLE PLATEAUS AT 53%

by Justin McCarthy

Story Highlights

- *Satisfaction still well above previous levels in last 15 years*
- *Sixteen percent dissatisfied with gay acceptance, and want more*
- *Fourteen percent dissatisfied with gay acceptance but want less*

WASHINGTON, D.C.—Against the backdrop of the Supreme Court's recent decision to accept four cases involving whether states can constitutionally prohibit same-sex marriages, a slight majority of Americans (53%) say they are satisfied with the acceptance of gays and lesbians in the U.S. This level is the same as last year but remains higher than those Gallup has measured over the past decade.

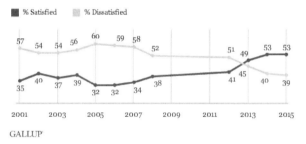

Americans' Satisfaction With Acceptance of Gays and Lesbians in the U.S.
Next, we'd like to know how you feel about the state of the nation in each of the following areas. For each one, please say whether you are -- very satisfied, somewhat satisfied, somewhat dissatisfied, or very dissatisfied. How about the acceptance of gays and lesbians in the nation?

GALLUP

Acceptance of gays and lesbians is one of two issues that saw zero change in Americans' satisfaction levels from the previous year in Gallup's annual Mood of the Nation poll, conducted Jan. 5–8. Only recently have a majority of Americans said they were satisfied with the state of acceptance of gay and lesbian people in the country, surpassing the 50% mark last year for the first time. However, since 2005, satisfaction has grown more on this than any other issue that Gallup has asked Americans about.

In May 2014, Gallup found that 58% of Americans felt gay and lesbian relations were morally acceptable. But Americans' personal opinions about homosexuality do not dictate whether they are satisfied with the current level of acceptance toward it.

Americans Who Want Less Gay Acceptance on the Decline

In a follow-up question that probed Americans who are dissatisfied with the current acceptance of gays for their position, 16% of

Americans indicate they want to see more acceptance while 14% want less. Another 10% are dissatisfied, but don't have a preference for whether there should be more or less acceptance.

As the percentage of Americans satisfied with the acceptance of gays and lesbians has increased markedly since the mid-2000s, there has been a much greater drop in the percentage who are dissatisfied and want less acceptance of gays and lesbians, from 30% to 14%, than of those who want more acceptance, from 20% to 16%.

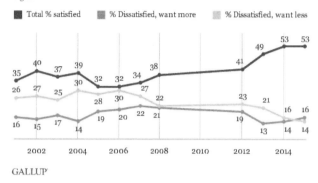

Satisfaction With the Degree of Acceptance
Would you like to see gays and lesbians be more widely accepted in this nation, less widely accepted, or is the acceptance of gays and lesbians in this nation today about right?

GALLUP

The general trend suggests that over time, fewer Americans are dissatisfied because they want less tolerance, and more classify themselves as satisfied. The percentage who are dissatisfied because they want more tolerance has remained fairly stable. This may indicate a broad pattern by which Americans who previously wanted less tolerance of gays and lesbians have become more likely to accept the situation as it is today.

Democrats Remain Most Satisfied With Gay Acceptance, Republicans the Least

Sixty percent of Democrats say they are satisfied with acceptance of gays and lesbians, slightly more than independents (55%) and considerably more than Republicans (43%). Those are the highest measures to date for Democrats and independents. Republicans' satisfaction is down from last year, likely explaining the lack of change in overall satisfaction.

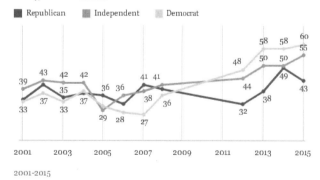

Satisfaction With Acceptance of Gays and Lesbians, by Party Identification
% Very/Somewhat satisfied

2001-2015

GALLUP

Americans who identify with the GOP have been least satisfied with gay acceptance since 2012—an election year that saw the first pro-same-sex-marriage presidential candidate as well as the first openly gay U.S. senator elected to office. Unlike independents and Democrats, Republicans' satisfaction has never reached the 50% mark.

From 2001 to 2008, when few states recognized same-sex marriages, Democrats were generally the least satisfied with gay acceptance. But the issue didn't see large differences between parties until 2007, when Democrats and Republicans were separated by 14 percentage points—the first double-digit difference in opinion between those who affiliate themselves with the two parties.

Bottom Line

To many pro-gay supporters, 2014 was a "banner year" in gay rights as the number of states allowing marriage equality nearly doubled. And while support for same-sex marriage may have inched higher, the events of 2014 didn't sway Americans' collective levels of satisfaction with acceptance of gays and lesbians. While the Supreme Court's decision this spring could put an end to the issue of the constitutionality of same-sex marriage once and for all—or breathe new life into a movement that opposes it—the news might not budge Americans' satisfaction with gay acceptance.

Marriage equality supporters may be satisfied with the string of legal victories at both state and federal levels. Satisfaction with acceptance could also come from an increased exposure of lesbian, gay, bisexual and transgender (LGBT) people in the media. Conversely, some supporters of LGBT equality could be dissatisfied with the 14 remaining states that have not legalized same-sex marriage, or disheartened by state legislation to allow businesses to turn away gay customers on the basis of religious liberty.

Those who oppose marriage equality and other issues important to the gay community could easily feel dissatisfied with gay acceptance related to massive legal battle losses and other high-profile gestures of support for gay people. They could be satisfied, however, if they live in a state where gay marriage is still illegal, or if they feel emboldened by elected officials who continue to fight its legalization.

Survey Methods

Results for this Gallup poll are based on telephone interviews conducted Jan. 5–8, 2015, on the Gallup U.S. Daily survey, with a random sample of 804 adults, aged 18 and older, living in all 50 U.S. states and the District of Columbia. For results based on the total sample of national adults, the margin of sampling error is ±4 percentage points at the 95% confidence level. All reported margins of sampling error include computed design effects for weighting.

January 26, 2015
U.S. OBESITY RATE INCHES UP TO 27.7% IN 2014

by Jenna Levy

Story Highlights

- *Obesity rate up from 27.1% in 2013 and 25.5% in 2008*
- *Obesity rate increased most among Americans aged 65+ since 2008*

- *Americans who are obese have lower well-being*

WASHINGTON, D.C.—The percentage of U.S. adults who are obese continued to trend upward in 2014, reaching 27.7%. This is up more than two percentage points since 2008 and is the highest obesity rate Gallup and Healthways have measured in seven years of tracking it. More Americans who were previously overweight have now moved into the obese category, while the percentage who are at normal weight has remained stable since 2013.

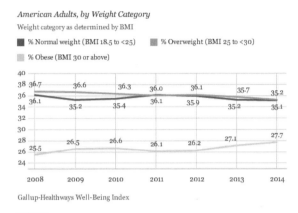

American Adults, by Weight Category
Weight category as determined by BMI

■ % Normal weight (BMI 18.5 to <25)   ■ % Overweight (BMI 25 to <30)
▨ % Obese (BMI 30 or above)

Gallup-Healthways Well-Being Index

GALLUP'

The percentage of Americans who are underweight has remained steady at 2.0%.

These results are based on more than 167,000 interviews conducted in 2014 as part of the Gallup-Healthways Well-Being Index. Unlike government estimates of obesity, the Gallup-Healthways Well-Being Index uses respondents' self-reported height and weight to calculate body mass index (BMI). The Centers for Disease Control and Prevention and government estimates of obesity are slightly different, as they are calculated using clinical measurements of height and weight as part of the National Health and Nutrition Examination Survey (NHANES). The latest NHANES results from 2011 to 2012 reported a 34.9% obesity rate for adults aged 20 or older, not significantly different from data collected since 2003. Another self-reported government survey, the Behavioral Risk Factor Surveillance System, says the obesity rate for U.S. adults aged 18 and older was 29.4% in 2013.

Individual BMI scores of 30 or above are classified as "obese," 25 to 29.9 are "overweight," 18.5 to 24.9 are "normal weight" and 18.4 or less are "underweight." While the Gallup-Healthways data show that just more than 35% of Americans have been classified as "normal weight" from 2008 to 2014, the obesity rate has risen each year except 2011, with at least a quarter of adults having BMIs categorized as obese.

More Americans Now Classified as Morbidly Obese

The World Health Organization further classifies BMI scores of 30.0 or higher into three classes of obesity:

- Obese class I = 30.0 to 34.99
- Obese class II = 35.0 to 39.99
- Obese class III = 40.0 or higher

Those with BMIs of 40.0 or higher—obese class III—are often considered "morbidly obese." According to Americans' self-reports of height and weight, the 4.0% who are classified as morbidly obese in 2014 is the highest Gallup and Healthways have measured in seven years of tracking.

The percentage of Americans in obese class I and obese class II have also increased slightly since 2008. The marginal increases across all three obesity classes have potentially negative consequences as healthcare costs related to obesity continue to rise.

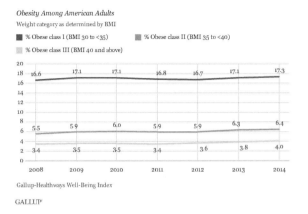

Obesity Among American Adults
Weight category as determined by BMI

■ % Obese class I (BMI 30 to <35)   ■ % Obese class II (BMI 35 to <40)
▨ % Obese class III (BMI 40 and above)

Gallup-Healthways Well-Being Index

GALLUP'

Obesity Rises Most Sharply Among Seniors Since 2008

Obesity rates have increased at least marginally in 2014 compared with 2008 across nearly all major U.S. demographic groups. Since 2008, Americans aged 65 and older have seen the sharpest uptick in obesity, a four-percentage-point increase to 27.4%. This is followed by increases among 45- to 64-year-olds (3.5 points), Americans living in the Midwest (2.9 points) and women (2.8 points). Obesity rates among Hispanics, blacks, and young adults aged 18 to 29 are similar to those found in 2008.

Although the obesity rate among blacks has not changed much since 2008, this group has the highest obesity rate of any major demographic group, at 35.5%. Obesity rates also exceed 30% among Americans aged 45 to 64 and those earning less than $36,000 per year. Young adults aged 18 to 29 are the least likely to be obese (17.7%), followed by those earning at least $90,000 per year (23.1%).

Percentage Obese in U.S. Among Various Demographic Groups
Sorted by change, largest to smallest
Among adults aged 18 and older

	2008	2014	Difference
	%	%	(pct. pts.)
National adults	25.5	27.7	2.2
Aged 65+	23.4	27.4	4.0
Aged 45 to 64	29.5	33.0	3.5
Midwest	26.8	29.7	2.9
Women	23.9	26.7	2.8
Whites	24.3	26.7	2.4
Aged 30 to 44	27.0	29.3	2.3
South	26.9	29.2	2.3
Annual income less than $36,000	30.0	32.3	2.3
Annual income $90,000+	21.1	23.1	2.0
East	24.7	26.6	1.9
Annual income $36,000 to $89,999	25.8	27.7	1.9
West	22.8	24.6	1.8
Men	27.0	28.7	1.7
Blacks	35.0	35.5	0.5
Aged 18 to 29	17.4	17.7	0.3
Hispanics	28.8	28.3	-0.5

Gallup-Healthways Well-Being Index

GALLUP'

Excess Weight Linked to Lower Overall Well-Being

Americans of a normal weight have the highest average well-being (64.5), followed by those who are overweight but not obese (63.0). Underweight Americans (62.2) have lower well-being than those who are overweight. Americans who are obese have the lowest well-being across weight groups.

As Americans become more obese, their well-being declines significantly, as measured by Gallup-Healthways Well-Being Index scores. Adults in obese class III, those considered morbidly obese, had the lowest average well-being of any weight group, at 50.9, in 2014. This compares with 54.7 for those in obese class II and 57.5 for those in obese class I.

The Gallup-Healthways Well-Being Index measures the five essential elements of well-being: purpose, social, financial, community and physical. The Well-Being Index is calculated on a scale of 0 to 100.

Average Well-Being Index Scores, by Weight Category, 2014
Well-Being Index scores on a scale of 0-100

	WBI mean score
Underweight	62.2
Normal weight	64.5
Overweight	63.0
Obese class I	57.5
Obese class II	54.7
Obese class III	50.9

Gallup Healthways Well-Being Index

GALLUP'

Implications

While it is well known that obesity is associated with physical health problems such as diabetes, high blood pressure and other chronic diseases, obesity is also linked to other elements of well-being. Gallup previously found that obese adults experience lower social well-being than their normal-weight or overweight counterparts. Furthermore, higher obesity rates are linked to lower incomes and long-term unemployment, suggesting a relationship exists between obesity and lower financial well-being.

While the relationship between well-being and obesity is reciprocal, previous Gallup research demonstrated that overall well-being influences future obesity outcomes more than obesity influences future well-being. Regardless of the direction of the relationship, this research suggests that helping Americans move from the obese to the overweight and normal weight categories would boost the overall U.S. economy. In addition to reducing healthcare costs, previous Gallup research shows that higher well-being predicts key business outcomes such as lower absenteeism and turnover, as well as fewer workplace safety incidents.

With the obesity rate increasing across nearly all demographic groups since 2008, it is imperative for employers, public health officials and individuals themselves to act to reverse the trend. However, given the link between lower well-being and obesity, these actions should focus on more than just diet and exercise.

"To date, most efforts to curb obesity focus on driving weight loss through diet and exercise, without addressing other aspects of well-being that may contribute to obesity," said Janna Lacatell, Healthways Lifestyle Solutions Director. "The rising obesity rate suggests these efforts have been largely ineffective. While access to evidence-based, proven weight loss programs emphasizing better nutrition and more physical activity is a critical component to reducing obesity, these interventions alone are not enough. To make a truly measurable impact on reducing obesity rates, interventions should also address other factors known to influence weight management, such as financial and social well-being."

Addressing the underlying causes of obesity through a better understanding of all elements of well-being can help more Americans achieve a long-term healthier weight.

Survey Methods

Results are based on telephone interviews conducted Jan. 2–Dec. 30, 2014, as part of the Gallup-Healthways Well-Being Index survey, with a random sample of 167,029 adults, aged 18 and older, living in all 50 U.S. states and the District of Columbia. For results based on the total sample of national adults, the margin of sampling error is ±1 percentage point at the 95% confidence level. All reported margins of sampling error include computed design effects for weighting.

Only three months ago, in mid-October, 39% of Americans approved of Obama's job performance—near his term low of 38%, last reached in September. His approval recovered slightly to 42% by the time of the Nov. 4 midterm elections. Following the elections—after announcing executive actions on immigration and benefiting from an improving economy and falling gas prices—his approval rating has gradually improved, averaging 44% in December and 46% thus far in January.

Survey Methods

Results for this Gallup poll are based on telephone interviews conducted Jan. 23–25, 2015, on the Gallup U.S. Daily survey, with a random sample of 1,527 adults, aged 18 and older, living in all 50 U.S. states and the District of Columbia. For results based on the total sample of national adults, the margin of sampling error is ±3 percentage points at the 95% confidence level.

The Jan. 19–25 weekly average results are based on telephone interviews with a random sample of 3,043 national adults, aged 18 and older. For results based on this weekly sample, the margin of sampling error is ±3 percentage points at the 95% confidence level.

January 26, 2015
OBAMA JOB APPROVAL HITS 50% FOR FIRST TIME SINCE 2013

by Lydia Saad

Story Highlights

- *President's three-day average job rating through Sunday reaches 50%*
- *First time Obama has hit 50% threshold since 2013*
- *In the past month, Obama up most among younger, lower-income adults*

PRINCETON, N.J.—Less than a week after President Barack Obama delivered his State of the Union address to Congress, his job approval rating reached 50% in Gallup Daily tracking conducted Friday through Sunday. This is the first time the president's rating has returned to that level in Gallup's ongoing three-day rolling averages since June 2013.

President Barack Obama's Job Approval Rating

Three-day rolling averages from June 1, 2013, through Jan. 25, 2015

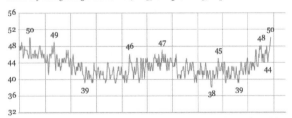

Jun '13 Aug '13 Oct '13 Dec '13 Feb '14 Apr '14 Jun '14 Aug '14 Oct '14 Dec '14 Feb '15

Gallup U.S. Daily tracking

GALLUP

January 26, 2015
ONLY A THIRD OF THE OLDEST BABY BOOMERS IN U.S. STILL WORKING

by Frank Newport

PRINCETON, N.J.—The first members of the huge baby-boom generation in the U.S. have reached retirement age in recent years, and these older boomers are retiring in large numbers, just as Americans in their mid- to late 60s did a few years earlier. While about eight in 10 boomers in their early 50s are in the workforce, the percentage employed drops to about 50% for boomers who are 60, and the proportion accelerates downward with each year of age thereafter. Only about a third of those aged 67 and 68—the oldest boomers—are still working in some capacity.

Baby Boomers' Employment: 2014

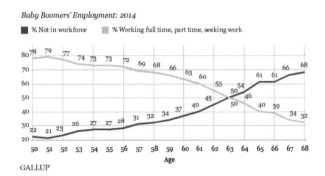

GALLUP

These workforce estimates are based on 134,168 Gallup Daily tracking interviews conducted in 2014 with Americans aged 50 to 68—those born from 1946 through 1964, the post–World War II years commonly used to define the baby-boom generation. Americans are classified as being in the workforce if they report being employed full time for an employer or self-employed, working part time, or not working but able to work and actively seeking employment.

Older Boomers' Retirement the Same as Pre-Boomers Four Years Ago

Much attention has been paid in recent years to pending changes in the work status of aging baby boomers, with some suggestions that boomers may work longer and postpone retirement. While the last boomer will reach age 65 in 2029, the early indications from the available evidence suggest that boomers are retiring "on time." The percentage of 65- to 68-year-olds still in the workforce in 2014 is almost identical to what Gallup measured among the pre-boomers of this age range in 2010. Thus, the vanguard of the boomer generation is retiring at nearly the identical rate as were pre-boomers four years ago.

Employment Among Those 65 to 68: 2010 and 2014

Age	2010: % working full time, part time, seeking work	2014: % working full time, part time, seeking work
65	40	40
66	38	39
67	33	34
68	33	32

GALLUP

This is a short-term comparison, and other Gallup data suggest that from a broader perspective, Americans have been retiring at an older age than they did years or generations ago. And when asked in previous research about their retirement intentions, large numbers of working baby boomers have indicated that they are going to retire after age 65 or not retire at all. Still, the 2010 to 2014 comparison is important because it provides a valuable look at the first group of boomers who have moved past the traditional retirement age of 65 over the past four years, and the results do not support the hypothesis that baby boomers are staying in the labor force longer than those who came immediately before them.

Older Baby Boomers Slightly More Likely to Work Part Time

There are interesting variations by type of work as baby boomers age. The percentage of boomers working part time edges up from around 10% among those in their 50s to 15% among boomers who are 68. This modest increase in part-time work is occurring even as the percentage working full time drops dramatically down to a similar 16% level. Thus, while most of those who abandon full-time working status are leaving the workforce altogether, a small percentage appear to be moving into part-time work. Overall, about half of those still in the workforce at age 68 are working full time, while half are working part time.

Baby Boomers' Employment: 2014

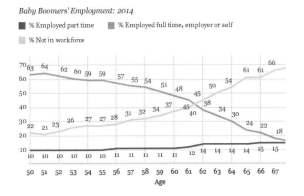

Same Patterns for Men and for Women

At every age increment, male baby boomers are more likely than female boomers to be in the workforce, with remarkably little variation in this pattern across the age spectrum. At age 50, the gender gap in the percentage working full time is 12 percentage points—84% of men working, contrasted with 72% of women. At the other end of the boomer range, the gap is also 12 points, with 38% of men in the labor force, contrasted with 26% of women.

Baby Boomers' Employment by Gender: 2014

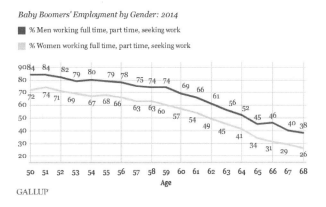

GALLUP

Even though the gap between the workforce participation rate of men and women stays about the same across the baby-boom years, there are subcurrents at work within the broader workforce categories. Both men and women leave the full-time work category as they age, but men drop out of full-time status a little more quickly than women. By age 68, the gap in full-time workforce participation between men and women is eight points, compared with a double-digit gender gap of as much as 20 points in the earlier years. On the other hand, men become somewhat more likely to work part time in their older boomer years, while part-time work stays constant among women. Thus, by age 66, there are more part-time working men than women, a flip from the pattern among younger baby boomers aged 50 to 65.

Part-Time Employment: 2014

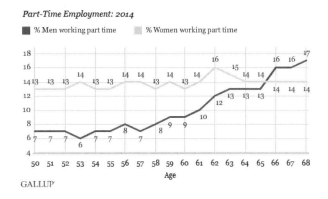

GALLUP

Implications

Despite some expectations that baby boomers will defy the usual working patterns of aging Americans and stay in the workforce longer than those who came before them, the data do not appear to support that expectation. Boomers aged 65 to 68 are retiring at about the same rate as those who were in that age range a few years ago. By age 68, only about a third of boomers are still in the workforce, including just 16% who are working full time. Prior research indicates that from a long-term perspective, the average retirement age has been increasing, but according to these new findings, in the short term, boomers appear to be leaving the workforce in predictable numbers.

The baby-boom generation is large, and the pattern of retirement that appears to be taking place among older boomers thus can potentially have a significant effect on lowering the overall workforce participation rate. This inevitable aging of the U.S. population leaves a smaller percentage of the population working and supporting their elders through Social Security and Medicare. It also means the U.S. could face a shortage of workers without a substantial influx of people from other countries.

The aging baby boomers who do choose to stay in the workforce may have increasing value to employers, and other analyses in Gallup's series on boomers will investigate the employee engagement of these labor segments compared with those who are younger.

The increasing size of the retired labor force of aging boomers will have the potential to affect society in many other ways as well, including changing patterns of housing, travel and leisure, politics and retail commerce, and an increasing need for healthcare services.

Survey Methods

Results for this Gallup poll are based on telephone interviews conducted Jan. 2–Dec. 30, 2014, on the Gallup U.S. Daily survey, with a random sample of 134,168 adults, aged 50 to 68, living in all 50 U.S. states and the District of Columbia. For results based on the total sample of national adults, the margin of sampling error is ±1 percentage point at the 95% confidence level. All reported margins of sampling error include computed design effects for weighting.

January 28, 2015
MAJORITY OF U.S. EMPLOYEES NOT ENGAGED DESPITE GAINS IN 2014

by Amy Adkins

Story Highlights

- *31.5% of U.S. employees engaged in 2014*
- *Engagement at its highest since 2000*
- *Younger workers are least engaged*

WASHINGTON, D.C.—Less than one-third (31.5%) of U.S. workers were engaged in their jobs in 2014. The average is up nearly two percentage points from 29.6% in 2013 and represents the highest reading since 2000, when Gallup first began tracking the engagement levels of the U.S. working population. However, a majority of employees, 51%, were still "not engaged" and 17.5% were "actively disengaged" in 2014.

Gallup defines engaged employees as those who are involved in, enthusiastic about and committed to their work and workplace. The 2014 employee engagement average is based on Gallup Daily tracking interviews conducted from January to December 2014 with 80,837 adults employed for an employer. The 1.9% increase in engagement from 2013 to 2014 represents 2.5 million employees nationwide. Gallup categorizes workers as engaged based on their

responses to key workplace elements it has found to predict important organizational performance outcomes.

U.S. Employee Engagement, 2013 vs. 2014

% Employees	2013	2014
Engaged	29.6	31.5
Not engaged	51.5	51.0
Actively disengaged	18.8	17.5

GALLUP

Engagement Highest Among Managers

Among job categories, managers, executives and officers had the highest levels of engagement in 2014 at 38.4%. This group outpaced every other job category Gallup tracked and saw the greatest gains in engagement from 2013, moving up nearly four points from 34.7%.

At the other end of the spectrum, employees in manufacturing or production jobs recorded the lowest levels of engagement, with an average of 23%. Employees in transportation (25.5%) and service (28.2%) roles also had engagement levels that fell well below the national average.

U.S. Employee Engagement, by Job Category
% Employees engaged

	2013	2014
Manager, executive or officer	34.7	38.4
Farming, fishing or forestry	36	33.6
Professional	30	32.4
Construction or mining	31.5	32.2
Clerical or office	29.3	31.8
Installation or repair	28.5	31.3
Sales	29.2	30.6
Service	27.9	28.2
Transportation	24.1	25.5
Manufacturing or production	22	23

GALLUP

Millennials Least Engaged Generation

Among the generations, traditionalists are the most engaged group, at 42.2%, possibly because the few who work do so by choice and enjoy their jobs. Millennials are the least engaged group, at 28.9%. Although the economy is improving, workers in this generation may not be getting the jobs they had hoped for coming out of college. Gallup's employee engagement data reveal that millennials are particularly less likely than other generations to say they "have the opportunity to do what they do best" at work. This finding suggests that millennials may not be working in jobs that allow them to use their talents and strengths, thus creating disengagement.

U.S. Employee Engagement, by Generation
% Employees engaged

	2013	2014
Millennials	27.5	28.9
Generation X	29.6	32.2
Baby boomers	30.9	32.7
Traditionalists	38.3	42.2

GALLUP

Bottom Line

At 31.5%, employee engagement is at its highest level since Gallup first began measuring the performance indicator in 2000. As Gallup has reported, public perceptions of the economy and job market are increasingly positive following improved GDP growth and lower unemployment. Workers' improved engagement levels could be a reflection of the country's improved economic conditions. Engagement began to drop in 2008 during the financial collapse and continued to fall in 2009, not showing any signs of improvement until 2011, and then reaching its current peak in 2014.

Employee engagement initiatives have also become more commonplace since Gallup first introduced its Q^{12} employee engagement survey in the late 1990s, with nearly 30 million workers being assessed on the instrument along with managerial training. Many organizations increasingly assess their managers on engagement metrics and expect them to maintain employees' engagement levels. Employee engagement levels might be rising to some degree because managers increasingly see engaging employees as a natural part of their duties. Managers are giving engagement more attention than they have in the past, potentially leading to higher engagement percentages.

While 31.5% of U.S. employees are engaged, there are organizations that have doubled this number, perhaps most notably the Gallup Great Workplace Award winners. These organizations excel in their employee engagement strategies and they have realized substantial increases in engagement levels as a result.

Survey Methods

Results for this Gallup poll are based on telephone interviews conducted January to December 2014, on the Gallup U.S. Daily survey, with a random sample of 80,837 adults, aged 18 and older, living in all 50 U.S. states and the District of Columbia. For results based on the total sample of national adults, the margin of sampling error is ±1 percentage points at the 95% confidence level.

January 29, 2015

U.S. BABY BOOMERS MORE LIKELY TO IDENTIFY AS CONSERVATIVE

by Jeffrey M. Jones

Story Highlights

- *Older generations have twice as many conservatives as liberals*
- *Millennials evenly divided between liberals and conservatives*
- *Generational ideology preferences largely consistent over time*

This article is part of an ongoing series analyzing how baby boomers—those born from 1946 to 1964 in the U.S.—behave differently from other generations as consumers and in the workplace. The series also explores how the aging of the baby-boom generation will affect politics and well-being.

PRINCETON, N.J.—Older generations of Americans are much more likely to describe their political views as conservative than as liberal. This includes the large baby-boom generation, of whom 44% identified as conservative and 21% as liberal last year. That 23-percentage-point conservative advantage is less than the 31-point edge for the older traditionalist generation, but greater than those for Generation Xers and millennials. In fact, millennials are about as likely to say they are liberal as to say they are conservative.

Ideological Self-Identification, by Generation, 2014

Generation (Birth years)	Conservative	Moderate	Liberal	Conservative - Liberal gap
	%	%	%	pct. pts.
Millennials (1980-1996)	28	40	30	-2
Generation X (1965-1979)	35	39	23	+12
Baby boomers (1946-1964)	44	33	21	+23
Traditionalists (1900-1945)	48	33	17	+31
All adults	38	36	24	+14

GALLUP

The results are based on aggregated data from 14 separate Gallup polls conducted in 2014, including interviews with more than 16,000 U.S. adults, aged 18 and older.

The ideological differences across the major generations in the U.S. are consistent with generational differences in party preferences, as older generations tend to be more Republican and younger generations more Democratic.

Older generations are also more likely than younger generations to choose an ideological side—liberal or conservative—as opposed to say they are moderate. Whereas 40% of millennials choose the moderate label to describe their political views, 33% of baby boomers and traditionalists do the same.

But those differences in identification as "moderate" do not account for the liberal-conservative differences, as there are increasingly fewer liberals and increasingly more conservatives in each older generation.

Ideological Identification by Generation Fairly Consistent Over Time

Throughout the past two decades, the relative conservatism of each generation has been consistent, even as the members of each generation have aged. Those born before 1946 have been the most conservative generation in every year going back to 1994, based on the percentage of the generation identifying as conservative minus the percentage identifying as liberal. Baby boomers have been less conservative than traditionalists, but more conservative than Gen Xers and millennials each year since 1994, spanning the period when baby boomers moved from being in their 30s or 40s to now, when they are in their 50s or 60s.

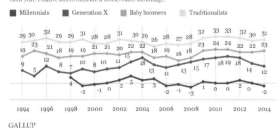

Trend in Conservative Minus Liberal Self-Identification, by Generation, 1994-2014
Figures are the percentage identifying as conservative minus the percentage identifying as liberal in each year. Positive scores indicate a conservative advantage.

GALLUP

The consistency in the relative rank of the generations over time reflects the fairly constant ideological preferences of each generation. Net conservatism among traditionalists typically has been about 30 points, while the conservative edge among baby boomers has about 20 points, and millennials have been close to even.

The ideological preferences of Gen Xers have varied a bit more over time, with the conservative advantage closer to 10 points in the 1990s and mostly in the mid-to-high teens since then. Since 2012, the conservative lead among this generation has shrunk, as there has been a slight drop in conservative identification (from 39% to 35%) and a slight increase in liberal identification (from 21% to 23%). This change has occurred about equally among the younger and older people in Generation X.

These variations in the past two decades could be a product of Gen Xers moving from young adulthood to middle age over the past 20 years, causing them to possibly re-evaluate their priorities and political beliefs.

More broadly, the political mood of the country seems to have affected all generations to some degree, particularly over the past decade. All generations shifted in a slightly more liberal direction in the later years of George W. Bush's presidency, when his approval rating slumped, and to a more conservative direction in the first years of Barack Obama's presidency.

Implications

Given the general consistency in ideological preferences over time, the expectation is that baby boomers' conservative tilt will persist as they continue to age into their 70s and 80s. That has been the pattern for traditionalists, who are that age now and whose ideological profile today looks similar to what it was 20 years ago.

Although the generations' ideology has stayed fairly consistent over time, Americans' ideology as a whole has undergone a gradual shift, with a notable increase in the percentage of Americans identifying as liberal. The data suggest that generational replacement may be a cause of this change, as those now entering adulthood are about as likely to identify as liberal as conservative, while at the same time, the older Americans who pass on are much more likely to be conservative.

Younger Americans' greater likelihood to identify as liberal may be tied to this group's racial and ethnic composition and connected to how this relates to the U.S. political process. The younger generation of U.S. adults is much more racially and ethnically diverse than older generations, and racial and ethnic minorities are much more likely to identify politically as liberal rather than conservative and as Democratic rather than Republican.

The ideological changes evident in the U.S. population more generally also may reflect both younger and older Americans' willingness to use the various political labels to describe themselves. One of the major changes Gallup has documented in recent years is that self-identified Democrats are more likely to describe their political views as liberal than as moderate, while in the past the opposite was true.

Although it is not possible to know from these data if ideological preferences persist throughout people's lifetimes, each major generation's preferences have been largely stable over the past two decades. If these trends largely persist, there should be a continued increase in the percentage of Americans identifying as liberal and decrease in the percentage identifying as conservative in the future,

unless the generation born after 2000 emerges as more conservative than liberal.

Survey Methods

Results for this Gallup poll are based on aggregated telephone interviews conducted January–December 2014, with a random sample of 16,479 adults, aged 18 and older, living in all 50 U.S. states and the District of Columbia. For results based on the total sample of national adults, the margin of sampling error is ±1 percentage points at the 95% confidence level.

For results based on the total sample of 2,977 millennials, the margin of sampling error is ±2 percentage points at the 95% confidence level.

For results based on the total sample of 2,900 Generation X, the margin of sampling error is ±2 percentage points at the 95% confidence level.

For results based on the total sample of 6,513 baby boomers, the margin of sampling error is ±2 percentage points at the 95% confidence level.

For results based on the total sample of 3,778 traditionalists, the margin of sampling error is ±2 percentage points at the 95% confidence level.

Prior years' results are also based on yearly aggregates of Gallup polls, with sample sizes from 15,000 to 44,000.

January 29, 2015
IN U.S., SIX IN 10 DISSATISFIED WITH IMMIGRATION LEVELS

by Andrew Dugan

Story Highlights

- *60% dissatisfied with current level of immigration; 33% satisfied*
- *Republicans more likely this year to be dissatisfied*

WASHINGTON, D.C.—As congressional Republicans weigh whether to file a lawsuit against President Barack Obama for his executive actions on immigration, 60% of Americans say they are dissatisfied with the level of immigration into the country today. This is an increase of six percentage points from 2014, but is comfortably lower than the 2008 high of 72%. By contrast, one-third of Americans are satisfied with current levels of immigration.

Few issues on Gallup's annual Mood of the Nation poll saw such a drop over the past year in the number of Americans expressing satisfaction—or the corresponding climb in those voicing dissatisfaction—as the desired level of immigration. The poll, conducted Jan. 5–8, saw larger drops in such high-profile issues as the nation's security from terrorism (10-point drop from 2014) and a 25-point decline in satisfaction with the state of race relations.

The increasing level of dissatisfaction with current immigration levels comes at a time when immigration is once again a major issue in the political debate. Late in 2014, President Obama issued an executive action protecting some immigrants who are living in the U.S. illegally from deportation. While the move has been politically popular for the president among Hispanic Americans, it is not without controversy. Republicans on Capitol Hill have vowed to undo the measures, and in fact the House has passed a spending bill that includes language to roll back the president's actions. That legislation is unlikely to receive approval in the Senate, but it speaks to the broader partisan conflict unfolding on immigration.

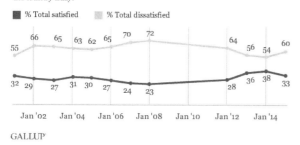

U.S. Satisfaction With Current Levels of Immigration

For each one, please say whether you are -- very satisfied, somewhat satisfied, somewhat dissatisfied, or very dissatisfied. How about -- the level of immigration into the country today?

GALLUP

Importantly, this survey question does not distinguish between legal and illegal immigration. While many Republicans, including Senate Majority Leader Mitch McConnell, are careful to say they support *legal* immigration, the party is nonetheless known for housing many outspoken politicians on this issue, such as influential Rep. Steve King of Iowa, whose anti-immigration rhetoric often does not distinguish between legal or non-legal status.

Nearly Two in Five Want Less Immigration

In a follow-up question that queried Americans who are dissatisfied with the current levels of immigration, the majority—39% of U.S. adults in total—said they would like to see the level of immigration *decrease*. This ranks among the lowest level of Americans who are dissatisfied and express a desire for less immigration since Gallup began asking the question in 2001, even if it is nominally higher than last year's 35%. The share of Americans who are dissatisfied and want more immigration (7%) was unchanged from 2014.

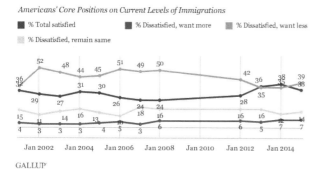

Americans' Core Positions on Current Levels of Immigrations

GALLUP

Fourteen percent of Americans said they were dissatisfied with the current level of immigration in the country, but did not express a specific preference for either increasing or decreasing it.

Republicans Most Dissatisfied With Level of Immigration

More than four out of every five self-identified Republicans say they are dissatisfied with the current level of immigration (84%), a figure that towers above the number of independents (54%) or Democrats (44%) who feel similarly. Moreover, the number of GOP affiliates

saying they are dissatisfied on this issue swelled by 19 percentage points compared with 2014, suggesting that the overall increase in public dissatisfaction with immigration levels is driven primarily by Republicans, perhaps in reaction to the president's actions. However, even among Democrats, dissatisfaction increased by eight points this year.

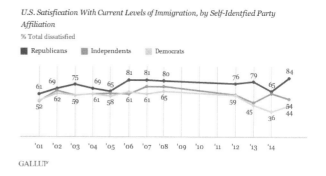

U.S. Satisfaction With Current Levels of Immigration, by Self-Identfied Party Affiliation

GALLUP

Bottom Line

Republican lawmakers who oppose the president's recent executive action on immigration are finding different venues to challenge the decision. This is happening via legislative measures, and will perhaps make it through the court system. The matter will likely weigh heavily on the upcoming Senate confirmation hearings of Attorney General nominee Loretta Lynch.

The president's disputed actions may have had some effect on how Americans perceive immigration levels, providing Republicans additional fodder with which to challenge the president. The number of Americans saying they are dissatisfied with current immigration levels increased by six points and seems mostly driven by self-identified Republicans, although dissatisfaction among Democrats is also up slightly. Still, compared with earlier times this century, a smaller than usual proportion of Americans say they are dissatisfied with immigration levels.

Survey Methods

Results for this Gallup poll are based on telephone interviews conducted Jan. 5–8, 2015, with a random sample of 804 adults, aged 18 and older, living in all 50 U.S. states and the District of Columbia. For results based on the total sample of national adults, the margin of sampling error is ±4 percentage points at the 95% confidence level. All reported margins of sampling error include computed design effects for weighting.

January 30, 2015
IN U.S., 60% SATISFIED WITH ABILITY TO GET AHEAD

by Frank Newport

Story Highlights

- *Satisfaction with upward mobility chances up from 2014*
- *Americans much less satisfied with income/wealth distribution*
- *Democrats least satisfied with mobility chances*

PRINCETON, N.J.—Six in 10 Americans are satisfied with the opportunity for a person in the U.S. to get ahead by working hard. This is up from 54% last year, which was similar to satisfaction levels measured in the prior three years. However, from 2001 through 2008, Americans' satisfaction with the ability to get ahead by working hard was higher, ranging from 77% to 66%.

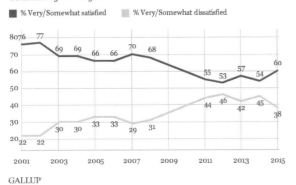

How Satisfied Are You With the Opportunity for a Person in This Nation to Get Ahead by Working Hard?

■ % Very/Somewhat satisfied   ▨ % Very/Somewhat dissatisfied

GALLUP

The latest measurement comes from Gallup's annual Mood of the Nation poll, conducted Jan. 5–8. Clearly, Americans' satisfaction with the chances to get ahead are linked to their views of the economy; when the recession hit and economic confidence dropped, so did Americans' satisfaction with the chance to get ahead. Now that economic confidence is moving back up again, so are views of mobility.

The ability to get ahead by hard work is just one component within the broad spectrum of concerns about economic inequality. Another component is satisfaction with the way income and wealth are distributed. Americans' satisfaction is much lower on this measure, with 31% satisfied and 67% dissatisfied, than on the ability to get ahead.

Are You Satisfied or Dissatisfied With the Way Income and Wealth Are Distributed in the U.S.?

	Satisfied	Dissatisfied
	%	%
Jan 5-8, 2015	31	67
Jan 5-8, 2014	32	67

GALLUP

In recent years, President Barack Obama has addressed both of these issues, calling for a "fair shot" for Americans to be able to get ahead by working hard, while at the same time calling for higher taxes on the rich to help distribute income and wealth more equally. Gallup's measures show that Americans are more dissatisfied with the way financial rewards end up being distributed than they are with the lack of equality of opportunity.

Americans can be placed into four categories based on their responses to these two questions.

- A little less than a third (31%) of Americans are dissatisfied with *both* the opportunity to move up and the current system of income and wealth distribution.
- Another quarter (24%) of Americans are satisfied with both economic mobility and economic equality.

- Most of the rest (35%) are satisfied with the opportunity for mobility in the country, but not the amount of equality.
- A small group (7%) are dissatisfied with mobility, but OK with the distribution of income and wealth.

Satisfaction With Upward Mobility and Income/Wealth Equality

	%
Satisfied with both	24
Satisfied with upward mobility, dissatisfied with income/wealth equality	35
Dissatisfied with upward mobility, satisfied with income/wealth equality	7
Dissatisfied with both	31

Upward mobility: "Are you very satisfied, somewhat satisfied, somewhat dissatisfied, or very dissatisfied with the opportunity for a person in this nation to get ahead by working hard?" Income/Wealth equality: "Are you very satisfied, somewhat satisfied, somewhat dissatisfied, or very dissatisfied with the way income and wealth are distributed in the U.S.?"

Jan. 5-8, 2015

GALLUP

Three-quarters of Americans are dissatisfied with at least one of the two aspects of inequality, but with differing views about which aspect of the system is out of balance. Overall, however, there is clearly more dissatisfaction with the way income and wealth are distributed than dissatisfaction with the chances Americans have to get ahead.

Democrats Most Dissatisfied With Inequality of Results

Roughly the same percentages of Republicans/Republican leaners and Democrats/Democratic leaners are dissatisfied with both aspects of the nation's economic system. However, Democrats are about half as likely as Republicans to be satisfied with both (17% vs. 30%). At the same time, they are significantly more likely to be satisfied with the opportunity to get ahead while feeling dissatisfied with the income and wealth distribution (44% vs. 28%).

Satisfaction With Upward Mobility and Income/Wealth Equality, by Party

	Satisfied with both	Satisfied with mobility, dissatisfied with equality	Dissatisfied with mobility, satisfied with equality	Dissatisfied with both
	%	%	%	%
Republicans/Leaners	30	28	10	29
Democrats/Leaners	17	44	4	32

Jan. 5-8, 2015

GALLUP

Middle-income Americans—the "middle class" toward whom Obama aimed much of his recent State of the Union address—are in fact more likely than those making less than $30,000 or making at least $75,000 to be dissatisfied with both aspects of inequality, and are less likely to be satisfied with both.

Satisfaction With Upward Mobility and Income/Wealth Equality, by Income

	Satisfied with both	Satisfied with mobility, dissatisfied with equality	Dissatisfied with mobility, satisfied with equality	Dissatisfied with both
	%	%	%	%
Less than $30,000	29	34	5	27
$30,000 to <$75,000	15	39	7	38
$75,000 or more	31	32	9	26

Jan. 5-8, 2015

GALLUP

Implications

Despite Obama's and others' concerns that Americans are increasingly unable to have a fair shot at getting ahead, a majority of Americans continue to say they are satisfied with the chance for upward mobility in the nation today. This level of satisfaction fell during the recession, but has inched back up this year as the recovery has taken hold. The years ahead will show whether these views return to pre-recession levels, or whether attitudes have undergone structural change such that public cynicism about mobility becomes stagnant, even when the economy continues to improve.

On the other hand, dissatisfaction is relatively high with the way income and wealth are distributed in the country today, indicating that the public's concern is focused more on the inequality of results as the system plays out, rather than on the chances people have of improving their lot within the system. These attitudes are not new. Gallup polling over the decades has consistently shown that Americans believe money and wealth should be distributed more equally in U.S. society, and have consistently supported higher taxes on the rich to help achieve that aim.

Obama's policy in recent years has increasingly emphasized these broad issues, including his recently promulgated proposals relating to "middle-class economics." His plan to increase taxes on the rich in order to pay for more tax breaks for those who are less rich resonate with underlying American attitudes. His other plans designed to give more Americans a "fair shot" at economic success—such as free community college and expanded pre-K education—may be popular individually, but have less attitudinal support, given that the majority of the public is satisfied with Americans' ability to get ahead if they work hard.

Survey Methods

Results for this Gallup poll are based on telephone interviews conducted Jan. 5–8, 2015, with a random sample of 804 adults, aged 18 and older, living in all 50 U.S. states and the District of Columbia. For results based on the total sample of national adults, the margin of sampling error is ±4 percentage points at the 95% confidence level. All reported margins of sampling error include computed design effects for weighting.

February 01, 2015
**ENGAGED TEACHERS ENJOY
PERSONAL, PROFESSIONAL EDGE**

by Matt Hastings and Sangeeta Agrawal

Story Highlights

- *Engaged teachers report higher levels of purpose well-being*
- *Engaged teachers report higher personal and professional satisfaction*

This article is the third in a series exploring employee engagement among U.S. teachers as measured by Gallup Daily tracking.

WASHINGTON, D.C.—Engaged teachers in the U.S. enjoy a substantially higher level of purpose well-being compared with their less engaged colleagues. Among the nation's "engaged" teachers, 74% are thriving in purpose well-being, compared with just 35% and 12%, respectively, among "not engaged" or "actively disengaged" educators.

Purpose Well-Being by Level of Engagement Among U.S. Teachers

Level of engagement	Thriving	Struggling	Suffering
Engaged	74%	25%	1%
Not engaged	35%	58%	6%
Actively disengaged	12%	48%	39%
All U.S. teachers	45%	47%	9%

Source: Gallup-Healthways Well-Being Index, Jan. 2, 2011-Sept. 30, 2014

GALLUP'

Overall, less than half of U.S. teachers—just 45%—are thriving in purpose well-being, with the majority (56%) struggling or suffering. These findings are consistent with estimates of well-being for the U.S. population more generally, measured as a part of the Gallup-Healthways Well-Being Index. Worldwide, just 18% of adults are thriving in purpose well-being, while in the U.S. this rate increases to 37% thriving.

Gallup categorizes survey participants as "engaged," "not engaged" or "actively disengaged," based on their responses to questions about workplace elements that have proven links to performance outcomes. Gallup defines *engaged* teachers as involved with, enthusiastic about and committed to their work. They know the scope of their jobs and constantly look for new and better ways to achieve outcomes. *Not engaged* teachers may be satisfied with their jobs, but they are not emotionally connected to their workplaces and are unlikely to devote much discretionary effort to their work. *Actively disengaged* teachers are not only unhappy, but also act out their unhappiness in ways that undermine what their coworkers accomplish.

Purpose well-being is one of the five unique elements of well-being, and is understood as people liking what they do each day and being motivated to achieve their goals.

Teacher Engagement Related to Multiple Dimensions of Purpose Well-Being

At 98%—almost universally—engaged teachers agree or strongly agree that they use their strengths to do what they do best every day. In contrast, just 40% of actively disengaged teachers report the same—a more than 50-percentage-point difference—with almost one-quarter disagreeing or strongly disagreeing that they get to use their strengths in this way every day.

U.S. Teachers' Use of Strengths by Level of Engagement
You get to use your strengths to do what you do best every day.

Level of engagement	% Agree/ Strongly agree	% Disagree/ Strongly disagree
Engaged	98%	1%
Not engaged	85%	3%
Actively disengaged	40%	24%
All U.S. teachers	83%	5%

Source: Gallup-Healthways Well-Being Index, Jan. 2, 2011-Sept. 30, 2014

GALLUP'

Again, with near universality, 98% of teachers who are engaged in their jobs agree or strongly agree with the statement, "You like what you do every day." This is eight points higher than the 90% rate of agreement found among not engaged teachers, and 45 points higher than is true for the nation's actively disengaged teachers.

U.S. Teachers' Daily Enjoyment by Level of Engagement
You like what you do every day.

Level of engagement	% Agree/ Strongly agree	% Disagree/ Strongly disagree
Engaged	98%	0%
Not engaged	90%	1%
Actively disengaged	53%	15%
All U.S. teachers	87%	3%

Source: Gallup-Healthways Well-Being Index, Jan. 2, 2011-Sept. 30, 2014

GALLUP'

Seventy-six percent of engaged teachers report having reached most of their goals over the past year, compared with just 35% of actively disengaged teachers and 63% of all U.S. teachers.

U.S. Teachers' Goal Attainment by Level of Engagement
In the last 12 months, you have reached most of your goals.

Level of engagement	% Agree/ Strongly agree	% Disagree/ Strongly disagree
Engaged	76%	3%
Not engaged	61%	8%
Actively disengaged	35%	28%
All U.S. teachers	63%	9%

Source: Gallup-Healthways Well-Being Index, Jan. 2, 2011-Sept. 30, 2014

GALLUP'

In addition to the personal benefits reported above, engaged teachers overwhelmingly identify a positive leader in their lives. In fact, 85% of engaged teachers agree or strongly agree with the statement, "There is a leader in your life who makes you enthusiastic about the future." Comparatively, only 37% of actively disengaged teachers and 67% of all U.S. teachers report the same.

Leadership in Lives of U.S. Teachers by Level of Engagement

There is a leader in your life who makes you enthusiastic about the future.

Level of engagement	% Agree/ Strongly agree	% Disagree/ Strongly disagree
Engaged	85%	6%
Not engaged	63%	14%
Actively disengaged	37%	36%
All U.S. teachers	67%	14%

Source: Gallup-Healthways Well-Being Index, Jan. 2, 2011-Sept. 30, 2014

GALLUP'

Implications

Teachers who are engaged in their jobs enjoy a personal and professional edge compared with their less engaged colleagues across a range of purpose metrics. In a profession plagued with turnover rates approaching 15% to almost 20% for teachers employed at high-poverty schools, the positives associated with teacher engagement cannot be overlooked.

In addition to the individual benefits of an engaged teacher workforce, positive outcomes have been traced to students whom teachers serve, as well as the school systems where they work. Gallup's report on the State of America's Schools highlights a link between teacher engagement and student engagement—and thereby, student achievement. Additionally, a recent Gallup article indicates that the lack of engagement among U.S. teachers results in more than 2.3 million additional missed workdays every year. As such, unengaged educators are likely to affect school budgets in terms of substitute teacher costs, and school success via their classroom absence.

Engagement can serve as a key lever for enhancing well-being, and vice versa. Schools that prioritize both of these as part of teacher professional development efforts might expect a substantial return on their investments, including reduced attrition, daily stress, and use of healthcare services.

Survey Methods

Results are based on telephone interviews conducted Jan. 2, 2011–Sept. 30, 2014, as part of the Gallup Daily tracking survey, for a subgroup of 9,763 self-identified full-time K-12 school teachers, from a random sample of adults, aged 18 and older, living in all 50 U.S. states and the District of Columbia.

For results based on the total sample of U.S. teachers, the margin of sampling error is ±1.5 percentage points at the 95% confidence level. All reported margins of sampling error include computed design effects for weighting.

February 02, 2015
MAJORITIES IN FIVE STATES
APPROVED OF OBAMA IN 2014

by Lydia Saad

Story Highlights

- *Massachusetts and Hawaii most approving of Obama in 2014*
- *Fewer than one in five in Wyoming approved of Obama*

- *Strong regional patterns persist in Obama's ratings*

This story is part of Gallup's annual "State of the States" series, which reveals state-by-state differences on political, economic, religion and well-being measures.

PRINCETON, N.J.—Residents of five states gave President Barack Obama 50% or better job approval ratings in 2014, with Massachusetts and Hawaii leading the list at roughly 53%. Wyoming residents were the least approving, at 19.3%.

Top States, Obama Job Approval	
	%
Massachusetts	53.4
Hawaii	52.5
Maryland	51.9
New York	51.6
California	50.5
New Jersey	49.8
Connecticut	48.1
Rhode Island	47.5
Delaware	47.1
Illinois	46.1

Gallup Daily tracking, January-December 2014

GALLUP'

Bottom States, Obama Job Approval	
	%
Wyoming	19.3
West Virginia	22.3
Idaho	25.1
Utah	28.3
Oklahoma	30.0
Montana	30.2
North Dakota	30.9
Kentucky	30.9
Arkansas	32.0
South Dakota	32.2

Gallup Daily tracking, January-December 2014

GALLUP'

2014 marks the first time in Obama's six years in office that Massachusetts has as much as tied for first in approving of the president's job performance, while Obama's home state of Hawaii has topped the list each year.

Obama's overall rating nationally fell by four points over the same period, from 46.5% in 2013 to 42.4% in 2014. So far in 2015, Obama's approval rating has been better, averaging 46.5% in January. (Note that these averages are based on January to December results and therefore differ slightly from Gallup's other yearly calculation, which uses Obama's inauguration date as the starting point for each yearly average.)

California's fifth-place showing in 2014 is also its highest to date. Meanwhile, Maryland's and New York's appearance in the top four in 2014 is typical for these states.

Wyoming residents have frequently been the least approving of Obama, and repeated that in 2014—for the fourth time. Additionally, the three other states where less than 30% of residents approved last year—West Virginia, Idaho and Utah—have consistently given Obama some of his worst annual approval ratings by state.

These results are based on 177,034 Gallup Daily tracking interviews conducted nationally from January through December 2014. At least 400 respondents were interviewed in each state, and at least 1,000 were interviewed in 40 states. Each state's sample was weighted to match demographic parameters for that state's adult population.

Residents in Handful of Coastal States Give Obama His Highest Scores

The states can be grouped into five categories according to their average 2014 approval scores.

- Well above average = approval ratings exceeding 50%
- Above average = approval ratings between 46.5% and 50%

- Average = approval ratings within four percentage points of (above or below) the 42.4% national average—or 38.4% to 46.4%
- Below average = approval ratings between 34% and 38.3%
- Well below average = approval ratings below 34%

Obama Job Approval by State, 2014

■ Well above average ■ Above average ■ Average ■ Below average ■ Well below average

GALLUP

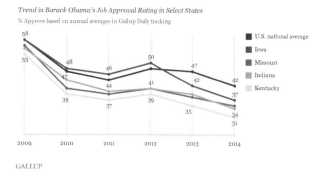

Trend in Barack Obama's Job Approval Rating in Select States
% Approve based on annual averages in Gallup Daily tracking

■ U.S. national average
■ Iowa
■ Missouri
■ Indiana
■ Kentucky

GALLUP

Notably, several of the states where residents give Obama above-average or well-above-average ratings—California, New York and New Jersey—are highly populous. By contrast, Obama's lowest ratings tend to be in states with relatively small populations, such as several in the Rocky Mountain and Midwestern regions. The full results by state are shown below.

Relative State Rankings Mostly Steady Over Time

The basic regional pattern of Obama's 2014 state ratings is similar to what Gallup has found throughout his presidency, with his strongest support coming from the Northeast and Pacific regions, and his lowest in the Rockies, and parts of the South and Midwest. Thus, although his overall yearly approval rating has declined considerably since 2009, it has declined relatively proportionally in most states.

In a handful of states, Obama appears to have lost a bit more ground relative to his peak ratings in 2009 and 2012, including West Virginia, North Dakota, South Dakota, Kentucky, Wyoming, Missouri, Indiana and Iowa. In all but Iowa, Obama's ratings have consistently been below the national average, but there was a significant deficit in Iowa in 2013 and 2014, compared with little difference in the earlier years. Notably, several of these states had important senatorial elections in 2014, and those elections saw Republicans score important victories that ultimately helped the GOP win control of the Senate for the first time since 2006.

The declines in these states more than offset the one- to two-point increases in his approval rating in a handful of small states.

In four states—Virginia, Florida, Oregon and Georgia—Obama's state job approval rating has matched the national average, or come within two percentage points, in every year since 2009, making these potentially valuable bellwether states. However, while Obama carried the first three in both presidential runs, he lost in Georgia, suggesting a greater disconnect between general public sentiment and the electorate in that state.

Bottom Line

Obama ran into political and economic headwinds in 2014 that conspired to make his average job approval rating for the year his lowest yet. Because that was reflected in declines in most state ratings, the basic geographic pattern of his strengths and weaknesses remained about the same. However, the handful of states showing greater-than-average declines bear watching in 2015, because if this continues, and if the Democratic standard-bearer inherits these problems, that could have implications for 2016.

Survey Methods

Results for this Gallup poll are based on telephone interviews conducted Jan. 2–Dec. 30, 2014, on the Gallup Daily tracking survey, with a random sample of 177,034 adults, aged 18 and older, living in all 50 U.S. states and the District of Columbia.

For results based on the total sample of national adults, the margin of sampling error is ±1 percentage point at the 95% confidence level.

Margins of error for individual states are no greater than ±6 percentage points, and are ±3 percentage points in most states. The margin of error for the District of Columbia is ±6 percentage points. All reported margins of sampling error include the computed design effects for weighting.

February 04, 2015
MASSACHUSETTS, MARYLAND MOST DEMOCRATIC STATES

by Jeffrey M. Jones

Story Highlights

- *Massachusetts and Maryland are most Democratic states*
- *Wyoming and Utah are most Republican states*
- *Similar numbers of Republican, Democratic, competitive states*

This story is part of Gallup's annual "State of the States" series, which reveals state-by-state differences on political, economic, religion and well-being measures.

PRINCETON, N.J.—Massachusetts and Maryland rank as the most Democratic states, and Wyoming and Utah are the most Republican, based on the political party identification and leanings of their state residents in 2014. The Democratic advantage in Massachusetts and Maryland exceeds 20 percentage points, while Utah and Wyoming show Republican advantages of more than 30 points.

Most Democratic States
% Democratic/Democratic Lean -
% Republican/Republican Lean

	Democratic advantage
Massachusetts	21.8
Maryland	20.9
Rhode Island	19.4
New York	17.3
Vermont	16.1
California	15.0
Hawaii	14.5
Delaware	13.3
Illinois	12.5
CT and NJ (tie)	11.7

Gallup Daily tracking,
January-December 2014

GALLUP

Most Republican States
% Republican/Republican Lean -
% Democratic/Democratic Lean

	Republican advantage
Wyoming	35.5
Utah	33.1
Idaho	25.2
South Dakota	18.4
Montana	17.7
Alabama	14.1
Kansas	12.3
Tennessee	11.3
North Dakota	11.1
Nebraska	10.9

Gallup Daily tracking,
January-December 2014

GALLUP

The results are based on Gallup Daily tracking interviews throughout 2014 with more than 177,000 U.S. adults. Gallup asks Americans whether they identify with the Democratic or Republican Party. Independents and those who express no party preference are subsequently asked whether they lean more toward the Democratic Party or the Republican Party.

The combined percentage of residents who identify with the Democratic Party or lean toward it, versus the percentage of Republican identifiers and leaners, gives an indication of the relative strength of each party within a state. Nationally, Democrats had a slim three-percentage-point advantage in 2014.

The rank order of the states based on their partisanship has been fairly consistent over time. Since Gallup began reporting on state party identification seven years ago, nine states have ranked in the top 10 most Democratic every year, including Massachusetts, Maryland, Rhode Island, New York, Vermont, California, Hawaii, Delaware and Illinois. New Jersey and Connecticut tied for 10th this year, and one or the other has been in the top 10 every year since 2008. Maine is the only other state to rank among the 10 most Democratic since 2008, tying for 10th in 2008.

There has been more variation in the Republican top 10 over time, with 17 different states appearing at least once since 2008. Wyoming and Utah have been the two most Republican states each year, with Idaho placing third in all but two years. In addition to those states, Kansas and Nebraska have ranked in the top 10 every year. Montana, Alabama, North Dakota and Alaska have been in the top 10 all but one year.

Solid, Leaning and Competitive States

The 10 most Democratic and 10 most Republican states all have party gaps greater than 10 percentage points. Gallup classifies these states as solid Democratic or solid Republican. A smaller set of states show a party advantage of greater than five points but less than 10 points. On this basis, Gallup classifies six states as leaning Democratic (Washington state, New Mexico, Pennsylvania, Michigan,

Maine and Oregon) and five states as leaning Republican (Alaska, Mississippi, Oklahoma, Arkansas and Indiana).

The remaining 18 "competitive" states have a party advantage for either party of no greater than five percentage points. Within this group, Louisiana, Nevada and Ohio are the most competitive states, with less than one percentage point difference between the two parties.

The solidly Republican states are mainly clustered in the northern part of the Mountain West region and in the western Plains states. The solidly Democratic states are largely in New England and the Middle Atlantic region, but also include two of the more populous states, California and Illinois. Many of the Midwestern states are competitive, along with the Southern states bordering the Atlantic Ocean.

Party Identification by State, 2014

■ Solid Democratic ■ Lean Democratic ■ Competitive ■ Lean Republican ■ Solid Republican

GALLUP

There are similar numbers of states in each of the major categories, including 17 solid or leaning Democratic states, 15 that are solid or leaning Republican and 18 that are competitive. Those totals have been fairly consistent since 2011—but continue to mark a major shift away from the Democratic Party since 2008, the apex for Democratic strength nationally in the last 25 years. That year, Gallup classified 29 states as solidly Democratic and an additional six as leaning Democratic, to only five solid or leaning Republican.

Political Composition of the 50 U.S. States
Based on annual state averages of party affiliation from Gallup Daily tracking
District of Columbia not included

	'08	'09	'10	'11	'12	'13	'14
Solid Democratic	29	23	13	11	13	12	11
Lean Democratic	6	10	9	7	6	5	6
Competitive	10	12	18	15	19	19	18
Lean Republican	1	1	5	7	3	2	5
Solid Republican	4	4	5	10	9	12	10
Total Democratic	35	33	22	18	19	17	17
Total Republican	5	5	10	17	12	14	15
Net Democratic	+30	+28	+12	+1	+7	+3	+2

Notes:
-- Solid states are defined as those in which one party has at least a 10-percentage-point advantage over the other in party affiliation (identification + leaning).
-- Leaning states are those in which one party has more than a 5-point but less than a 10-point advantage in party affiliation.
-- Competitive states are those in which the parties are within 5 points of each other in party affiliation.

GALLUP

Nine states saw their classification change between 2013 and 2014. Three states that were competitive in 2013 are now considered leaning, including Pennsylvania (now leaning Democratic), Indiana (now leaning Republican) and Arkansas (also leaning Republican). Minnesota and South Carolina moved to competitive status, from lean Democratic and solid Republican, respectively. Meanwhile, Oklahoma and Alaska shifted from solid Republican to lean Republican, Tennessee from lean Republican to solid Republican and New Mexico from solid Democratic to lean Democratic.

Implications

A state's partisanship is an indicator of how the state will vote in federal and state elections, as well as the types of policies that will become law in those states. Of course, the figures presented here are based on all state residents, and differences in turnout, which usually favor Republicans, can alter the political balance of the state electorate in a given election.

Since 2008, there has been a significant movement away from the Democratic Party both at the national level and in many states. Democrats still maintain a modest advantage in national partisanship, partly because they have an advantage in some of the most highly populated states such as California, New York and Illinois. At the same time, other large states like Florida and Texas are competitive, with Florida showing a slight Democratic edge and Texas a slight Republican one.

In fact, Tennessee and Indiana, which rank 16th and 17th in terms of population, are the most populous states that are either solidly Republican or leaning Republican. The GOP's inability to dominate in many high-population, electoral-vote-rich states underscores the challenges it faces in presidential elections based on the winner-take-all electoral vote system. The GOP can overcome that deficit with better turnout to some degree, but also must carry the vast majority of competitive states in order to win the election.

Survey Methods

Results for this Gallup poll are based on telephone interviews conducted Jan. 2–Dec. 30, 2014, on the Gallup Daily tracking survey, with a random sample of 177,034 adults, aged 18 and older, living in all 50 U.S. states and the District of Columbia.

For results based on the total sample of national adults, the margin of sampling error is ±1 percentage point at the 95% confidence level.

Margins of error for individual states are no greater than ±6 percentage points, and are ±3 percentage points in most states. All reported margins of sampling error include the computed design effects for weighting.

February 05, 2015
U.S. SMALL-BUSINESS OWNERS' OPTIMISM HIGHEST SINCE 2008

by Coleen McMurray and Frank Newport

Story Highlights

- *Small Business Index rose sharply since Quarter 4, 2014*
- *Index almost 100 points higher than at low point in 2010*

- *Small-business owners more positive on revenues, hiring, credit*

PRINCETON, N.J.—U.S. small-business owners are the most optimistic they have been in seven years, according to the latest Wells Fargo/Gallup Small Business Index. The index, at +71, has increased significantly for two consecutive quarters, and reflects optimism in small-business owners' views of both their current situation and their expectations for the future.

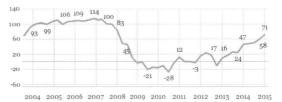

Wells Fargo/Gallup Small Business Index

The Small Business Index consists of owners' ratings of their business' current situation and their expectations for the next 12 months, measured in terms of their overall financial situation, revenue, cash flow, capital spending, number of jobs and ease of obtaining credit.

Index conducted since August 2003 and quarterly from December 2003-January 2015

GALLUP

The latest quarterly Small Business Index survey was conducted Jan. 5–9, 2015. The overall Small Business Index score has increased significantly, from +58 in November and +49 in July 2014. While still below pre-recession levels, the index is the highest it has been since January 2008's +83. The Wells Fargo/Gallup Small Business Index measures small-business owners' views of their present situation and future expectations concerning their financial situation, cash flow, revenues, capital spending, hiring and credit availability.

Small-business owners' evaluations of their present conditions increased to +28, up from +21 last quarter. At the same time, the future expectations component continued to climb to +43, up from +37 in November. Both of these dimensions, like the overall index, are at their highest points since 2008.

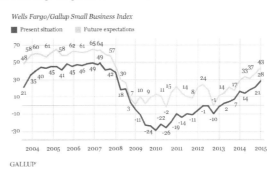

Wells Fargo/Gallup Small Business Index
■ Present situation ▨ Future expectations

GALLUP

The overall rise in the index reflects more positive readings on a number specific dimensions:

- Small-business owners are feeling better about their companies' revenues, with nearly one-half (49%) reporting that their revenues have increased "a little" or "a lot" over the past 12 months. This is a seven-percentage-point uptick from Quarter 4, 2014, and represents the highest reading on this measure since 2007.
- The survey shows a net-positive hiring situation, with more owners reporting hiring over the last 12 months than decreasing their workforce.

- Thirty-four percent of small-business owners report that it has been easy for them to obtain credit, up from 28% a year ago.
- The current survey shows small increases in owners' positive ratings of 11 of the 12 metrics comprising the overall index.

Bottom Line

Small-business owners' improving views of their revenues and other aspects of their businesses have propelled the overall Wells Fargo/Gallup Small Business Index to its highest level since 2008. This continues the general upward movement seen in the index since it reached its low point in 2010, although it remains below the high points registered in the years prior to the Great Recession. Small-business owners' more upbeat views of their operating environments come at a time of generally positive economic trends in economic growth and unemployment, as measured by the government, as well as year-over-year upticks in Gallup's consumer-based reports on employment, company hiring and consumer spending.

Survey Methods

Results are based on telephone interviews with 603 U.S. small-business owners in all 50 states, conducted Jan. 5–9, 2015. The margin of sampling error is ±4 percentage points at the 95% confidence level.

February 06, 2015
OBAMA APPROVAL RATINGS STILL HISTORICALLY POLARIZED

by Jeffrey M. Jones

Story Highlights

- *Avg. 70-point gap in Democratic vs. Republican ratings of Obama*
- *Ties George W. Bush's sixth year as fifth most polarized*
- *Obama, Bush have had most politically polarized job approval*

PRINCETON, N.J.—Throughout President Barack Obama's sixth full year in office, an average of 79% of Democrats, compared with 9% of Republicans, approved of the job he was doing. That 70-percentage-point party gap in approval ratings ties for the fifth-most-polarized year for a president in Gallup records dating back to 1953.

Each of Obama's six years in office rank among the 10 most polarized in the last 60 years, with George W. Bush holding the other four spots. Bush's most polarized years were his fourth through seventh years in office, after the rally in support for him following the 9/11 terror attacks had faded. Clearly, political polarization has reached new heights in recent years, under a Republican and a Democratic president.

Bush's and Obama's approval ratings were most polarized along party lines in their fourth years in office—which has been the case for most presidents because that is the year they seek re-election. Both Bush and Obama saw their polarization scores ease slightly in their fifth year, and go down a bit more in year six. Bush's polarization score dropped even further in his seventh year, as his overall job approval ratings continued to decline.

Presidential Years With Largest Gaps in Approval Ratings by Party, Gallup Polls, 1953-2014

President	Year in office	Dates of year	Avg. approval, Republicans	Avg. approval, Democrats	Avg. party gap
			%	%	Pct. pts.
Obama	4	Jan 12-Jan 13	10	86	76
G.W. Bush	4	Jan 04-Jan 05	91	15	76
G.W. Bush	5	Jan 05-Jan 06	86	14	72
Obama	5	Jan 13-Jan 14	11	82	71
Obama	6	Jan 14-Jan 15	9	79	70
G.W. Bush	6	Jan 06-Jan 07	79	9	70
Obama	2	Jan 10-Jan 11	12	81	69
Obama	3	Jan 11-Jan 12	12	80	68
G.W. Bush	7	Jan 07-Jan 08	73	7	66
Obama	1	Jan 09-Jan 10	23	88	65

GALLUP

No Other Presidents' Sixth-Year Polarization Close to Bush's, Obama's

The structure of job approval in Obama's and Bush's sixth years in office was remarkably similar—with 79% approval among supporters of the president's party, and 9% from supporters of the opposition party. Not surprisingly, Bush and Obama had by far the most polarized sixth years for presidents who served into a sixth year. In Bill Clinton's sixth year, there was an average 53-point gap in his approval ratings, 17 points lower than those of his immediate successors. Clinton's polarization score was a bit lower because his overall approval rating in year six, 64%, was much higher than Bush's (37%) or Obama's (43%). The other presidents serving into a sixth year had polarization scores below 50 points—including Dwight Eisenhower and Ronald Reagan, who were popular at the time, and Richard Nixon, who had historically low approval ratings. Nixon resigned in August 1974, in the middle of his sixth year in office.

Gaps in Approval Ratings by Party for Presidents' Sixth Year in Office, Gallup Polls, 1953-2014

President	Dates of sixth year	Avg. approval, Republicans	Avg. approval, Democrats	Avg. party gap
		%	%	Pct. pts.
Obama	Jan 14-Jan 15	9	79	70
G.W. Bush	Jan 06-Jan 07	79	9	70
Clinton	Jan 98-Jan 99	36	89	53
Reagan	Jan 86-Jan 87	85	39	46
Nixon	Jan-Aug 74	53	13	40
Eisenhower	Jan 58-Jan 59	82	37	45

GALLUP

Obama on Pace to Have Most Polarized Approval Ratings

So far in his presidency, there has been an average party gap of 70 points in Obama's approval ratings, which, if it continues, would be easily the highest for any president to date. Bush is second with a 61-point gap throughout his presidency, followed by Clinton (56) and Reagan (52). The other presidents had party gaps of no more than 41 points.

Obama's more polarized ratings are attributable mainly to lower support from the opposition party than his predecessors received. His average 13% approval rating among Republicans is 10 points lower than Bush's 23% approval rating among Democrats and 13 points below Clinton's 26% approval among Republicans. All other presents had approval ratings of at least 30% from the opposition party.

Average Gaps in Approval Ratings by Party for Presidents, Gallup Polls, 1953-2014

President	Dates of presidency	Avg. approval, Republicans	Avg. approval, Democrats	Avg. party gap
		%	%	Pct. pts.
Obama	Jan 09-present	13	83	70
G.W. Bush	Jan 01-Jan 09	84	23	61
Clinton	Jan 93-Jan 01	26	82	56
G.H.W. Bush	Jan 89-Jan 93	82	44	38
Reagan	Jan 81-Jan 89	83	31	52
Carter	Jan 77-Jan 81	31	57	26
Ford	Aug 74-Jan 77	67	36	31
Nixon	Jan 69-Aug 74	75	34	41
Johnson	Nov 63-Jan 69	40	70	30
Kennedy	Jan 61-Nov 63	49	84	35
Eisenhower	Jan 53-Jan 61	88	49	39

GALLUP'

Obama's approval rating from Democrats, 83%, almost exactly matches the average approval ratings that the prior four presidents received from supporters of their own party.

Implications

Both Bush and Obama were elected with hopes of unifying the country. However, the opposite has happened, at least in the way Americans view the job the president is doing, with presidential evaluations more divided along party lines than ever before. These increasingly partisan views of presidents may have as much to do with the environment in which these presidents have governed as with their policies, given 24-hour news coverage of what they do and increasingly partisan news and opinion sources on television, in print and online.

Operating within this context, Obama is on pace to be the president with the most polarized approval ratings in Gallup's polling history, surpassing Bush. Aside from the initial two months of Obama's presidency, Republicans have consistently rated the job he is doing very negatively—to this point, far worse than supporters of the opposition party have ever rated a president.

Obama's overall job approval ratings have improved modestly to the high 40s in recent weeks, but if he cannot boost his support among Republicans, it is unlikely that his overall approval ratings can go much above 50%. By comparison, during Clinton's last three years in office, when he averaged better than 60% approval overall, his support among Republicans exceeded 30%.

Survey Methods

Results for this Gallup poll are based on telephone interviews conducted Jan. 20, 2014–Jan. 19, 2015, on the Gallup U.S. Daily survey, with a random sample of 177,032 adults, aged 18 and older, living in all 50 U.S. states and the District of Columbia. For results based on the total sample of national adults, the margin of sampling error is ±1 percentage point at the 95% confidence level.

For results based on the total samples of 53,288 Democrats and 50,022 Republicans, the margin of sampling error is ±1 percentage point at the 95% confidence level. All reported margins of sampling error include computed design effects for weighting.

February 06, 2015
MISSISSIPPI, ALABAMA AND LOUISIANA MOST CONSERVATIVE STATES

by Frank Newport

Story Highlights

- *Massachusetts, Vermont and Hawaii are most liberal states*
- *Delaware has highest percentage of moderates*
- *Six of top 10 most conservative states are located in the South*

This story is part of Gallup's annual "State of the States" series, which reveals state-by-state differences on political, economic, religion and well-being measures.

PRINCETON, N.J.—Mississippi, Alabama and Louisiana are the most right-leaning states in the union, with between 46% and 49% of residents in each identifying as politically conservative. Massachusetts, Vermont and Hawaii are the most left-leaning, with 30% of residents in each of those states identifying as liberal.

Top 10 Conservative States

State	% Conservative
Mississippi	48.9
Alabama	46.5
Louisiana	45.7
Utah	44.6
Arkansas	43.8
Tennessee	43.2
Montana	43.1
Idaho	43.0
Oklahoma	42.9
South Carolina	42.3

Gallup Daily tracking, January-December 2014

GALLUP'

Top 10 Liberal States

State	% Liberal
Massachusetts	30.3
Vermont	29.8
Hawaii	29.6
New York	27.6
Oregon	27.5
California	27.5
Washington	27.4
Connecticut	26.9
Maryland	26.7
New Jersey	25.5

Gallup Daily tracking, January-December 2014

GALLUP'

The top 10 most conservative states in 2014 are very similar to the top 10 in 2013, with the exception of Louisiana, which was not in the top 10 list in 2013, but replaced Wyoming in the top 10 this year.

The list of the top 10 most conservative states is also similar to what it was in 2008, the first year Gallup tracked ideology daily. Mississippi was the most conservative state in 2008 and remains the most conservative in 2014, with 49% of residents identifying as conservative in both years. Three states—Louisiana, Oklahoma and Montana—were not in the top 10 list in 2008 but are in 2014, while South Dakota, Wyoming and Texas dropped out of the top 10 list over the past seven years.

Eight of the top 10 most liberal states in 2014 were on the top 10 list in 2013. The other two—Connecticut and Maryland—replaced Delaware and Maine, which appeared in the top 10 in 2013. The only two states in the top 10 most liberal list this year that were not in the top 10 in 2008 are Maryland and New Jersey, and in that year, they came in ranked just below the top 10.

These results are based on Gallup Daily tracking interviews throughout 2014 with 177,034 U.S. adults. Gallup asks Americans if they describe their political views as very conservative, conservative, moderate, liberal or very liberal. The results shown combine the two conservative and the two liberal categories.

Conservative States Mostly in the South; Liberal States on the Coasts

Six of the top 10 most conservative states are located in the South (Mississippi, Alabama, Louisiana, Arkansas, Tennessee and South Carolina). Three others are in the Mountain West (Utah, Wyoming and Idaho), and one is Oklahoma—straddling the Midwest/southern border.

The top 10 liberal states are primarily located in the outer longitudes of the U.S.: touching or close to the Atlantic Ocean (Vermont, Massachusetts, Connecticut, New York, New Jersey and Maryland), and the Far West (Oregon, California, Washington and Hawaii).

The accompanying map displays the "conservative advantage," defined as the percentage conservative minus the percentage liberal in each state. The results for each state are shown in a table at the end of the article and will be available today in Gallup's "State of the States" interactive.

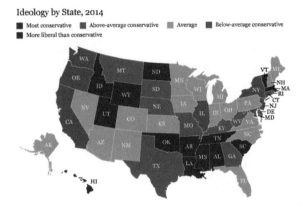

Ideology by State, 2014
■ Most conservative ■ Above-average conservative ■ Average ■ Below-average conservative
■ More liberal than conservative

GALLUP

Some States Ideologically Different From Their Neighbors

Although the general distribution of ideology reflects a clustered regional pattern, history and specific cultural patterns can produce different ideological patterns even among states that share borders. One example of a state that is quite different ideologically from its neighbors is New Hampshire, which is more conservative than the national average, yet borders the two most liberal states in the union: Massachusetts and Vermont. Another example is Illinois, one of the more liberal states in the union, which shares borders with five states that are average or above average in their net conservative rating (Wisconsin, Iowa, Missouri, Kentucky and Indiana).

Delaware Is Most Moderate State

The most moderate states are fairly geographically diverse. Delaware has the highest percentage of moderates of any state in the union, at 44%. The higher percentage of moderates in a given state does not necessarily mean that the state is a swing state politically. Despite the high percentages of residents choosing the moderate label, in many of these states, the remainder of the residents skew significantly conservative or liberal. For example, Rhode Island, Vermont, Massachusetts and New Jersey are all high on both the moderate and the liberal list, meaning that residents in these states eschew the conservative label while being more likely than average

to identify with the other two categories. The same phenomenon occurs with states such as North Dakota and Wyoming, where residents are well above average in choosing either the moderate or conservative label, while avoiding the liberal label.

Top 10 Moderate States

State	% Moderate
Delaware	43.9
Rhode Island	41.2
North Dakota	40.8
Wyoming	40.2
South Dakota	39.9
Alaska	39.3
Vermont	38.8
Massachusetts	38.1
Nebraska	38.0
New Jersey (tie)	37.8
New Mexico (tie)	37.8

Gallup Daily tracking, January-December 2014

GALLUP

Implications

Americans have become slightly less conservative and more liberal in recent years, while at the same time, with a few exceptions, the differences in ideology across the 50 states has generally remained quite stable. The most conservative states both seven years ago and now are mainly located in the South and the Mountain West, while the most liberal states are basically located along the East and West Coasts.

This overview of the ideology of states is based on self-descriptions using a general conservative to liberal scale, and thus measures how each American sums up his or her ideological bent. There can be significant divergences in more specific ideological positioning, such as between those who may be conservative or liberal on economic matters, while holding the opposite position on a social matters. Nevertheless, these results roughly conform with the political orientation of states in elections, and the order is similar to Gallup's state rankings of presidential job approval and political party identification.

Survey Methods

Results for this Gallup poll are based on telephone interviews conducted Jan. 2–Dec. 30, 2014, on the Gallup Daily tracking survey, with a random sample of 177,034 adults, aged 18 and older, living in all 50 U.S. states and the District of Columbia.

For results based on the total sample of national adults, the margin of sampling error is ±1 percentage point at the 95% confidence level.

Margins of error for individual states are no greater than ±6 percentage points and are ±3 percentage points in most states. All reported margins of sampling error include the computed design effects for weighting.

February 09, 2015
FEWEST AMERICANS SATISFIED WITH ABORTION POLICIES SINCE 2001

by Rebecca Riffkin

Story Highlights

- *In 2015, 34% satisfied with abortion policies, lowest since 2001*
- *Satisfaction mostly lower since 2012 than it was from 2001 to 2008*
- *Republicans' satisfaction lower since 2012 than prior to 2008*

WASHINGTON, D.C.—In 2015, 34% of Americans say they are satisfied with current U.S. abortion policies. This is the lowest percentage since Gallup first asked the question in 2001.

Satisfaction With U.S. Abortion Policies

Next, we'd like to know how you feel about the state of the nation in each of the following areas. For each one, please say whether you are -- very satisfied, somewhat satisfied, somewhat dissatisfied, or very dissatisfied. How about the nation's policies regarding the abortion issue?

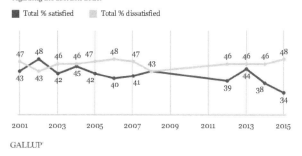

GALLUP

In three of four years since 2012, less than 40% of Americans have been satisfied. Yet between 2001 and 2008, at least 40% were satisfied every year. Gallup asks Americans about their satisfaction with the nation's policies regarding abortion as part of the annual Mood of the Nation poll, conducted in January. The poll was not conducted from 2009 to 2011. Between 2001 and 2008, an average of 43% of Americans were satisfied with U.S. abortion policies; since 2012, the average has been 39%.

Republican Satisfaction With Abortion Policies Lower Since 2012

One factor contributing to the drop in satisfaction with abortion policies is significantly lower satisfaction among Republicans since 2012. From January 2001 to January 2008, after the election of Republican George W. Bush and spanning most of his two terms, at least 39% of Republicans each year said they were satisfied with the nation's abortion policies. Satisfaction among Republicans reached as high as 44% in January 2002, Bush's first year in office. However, since 2012, with Democratic President Barack Obama in office, no more than 29% of Republicans have been satisfied with the nation's abortion policies. And Republicans' satisfaction is particularly low this year, at 21%, an eight-percentage-point decline from a year ago.

Satisfaction among Democrats and independents these past four years has been roughly equivalent to what was observed, on average, from 2001 to 2008. At 46%, Democrats continue to be the most likely of the three party groups to say they are satisfied with the nation's abortion policies. Independents remain more satisfied than Republicans, at 36%.

Between 2001 and 2008, satisfaction among independents and Republicans was remarkably similar, while Democrats were generally only a few points more satisfied than Republicans. However, since 2012, Republicans have been at least eight points less satisfied than independents. In 2015, there is a 15-point gap between Republicans than independents, and 25 points between Republicans and Democrats.

Satisfaction With U.S. Abortion Policies, by Political Affiliation

Next, we'd like to know how you feel about the state of the nation in each of the following areas. For each one, please say whether you are -- very satisfied, somewhat satisfied, somewhat dissatisfied, or very dissatisfied. How about the nation's policies regarding the abortion issue?

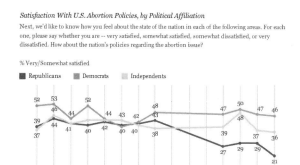

GALLUP

More Who Are Dissatisfied Want Stricter, Rather Than Less Strict, Abortion Laws

Americans who say they are dissatisfied with current abortion policies were asked a follow-up question to learn if they are dissatisfied because they want current abortion laws to be stricter or less strict. This year, of those who are dissatisfied, twice as many prefer stricter rather than less strict laws: 24% want stricter laws, while 12% want current abortion laws to be less strict.

Republicans' overall dissatisfaction with abortion policies has risen from 50% in the Bush years to 62% since 2012, with the 12-point increase distributed mainly among those who want abortion laws to be made stricter and those who want the laws to remain the same (up five points each). The percentage dissatisfied and favoring less strict laws has risen only two points to 7%.

Republicans Have Become More Likely to Want Stricter Laws Since 2008

(Asked of those who are dissatisfied) Would you like to see abortion laws in this country made more strict, less strict, or remain as they are?

	Average under Bush (2002-2008)	Average under Obama (2012-2015)
Republicans		
% Satisfied	42	26
% Dissatisfied, want stricter laws	38	43
% Dissatisfied, want less strict laws	5	7
% Dissatisfied, want laws to remain the same	7	12
Democrats		
% Satisfied	46	47
% Dissatisfied, want stricter laws	16	13
% Dissatisfied, want less strict laws	15	15
% Dissatisfied, want laws to remain the same	12	10
Independents		
% Satisfied	42	40
% Dissatisfied, want stricter laws	23	25
% Dissatisfied, want less strict laws	11	9
% Dissatisfied, want laws to remain the same	10	9

2001 was excluded from averages because President Bill Clinton was in office at the time polling was conducted, in January of that year

GALLUP

At the same time, no meaningful changes have occurred in Democrats' and political independents' views on these questions since Obama became president. Democratic satisfaction with abortion laws averaged 46% from 2002 to 2008, and 47% between 2012 and 2015. Democrats remain the party group most likely to say they are dissatisfied with abortion laws and want them to be less strict, at 15%.

Bottom Line

Americans' satisfaction with U.S. abortion policies has dropped in recent years, mainly because of a decline in satisfaction among Republicans. Compared with the 2002–2008 period, Republicans are now less likely to be satisfied with the nation's current abortion policies. They are now also more likely to say they feel laws should be stricter than was the case before. This shift in attitudes most likely reflects the change from a pro-life Republican president to a pro-choice Democratic one. Notably, Democrats' views have not become more positive after the change in presidential administrations, perhaps because abortion is the law of the land.

This survey was conducted just before a recent proposal from the Republican-controlled Congress to ban all abortions after the mother has been pregnant for more than 20 weeks. While Obama had threatened to veto the bill if it passed, the bill stalled in the House because of pressure from female Republican lawmakers. While this bill failed at the federal level, at least three state legislatures, in Wisconsin, West Virginia and South Carolina, plan to debate a version of the ban. Rank-and-file Republicans are likely to support bills like this, but many independents and Democrats, both of whom are more likely to be satisfied with current abortion laws, may have issues with new legislation, especially if it makes abortion laws more strict.

Survey Methods

Results for this Gallup poll are based on telephone interviews conducted Jan. 5–8, 2015, on the Gallup U.S. Daily survey, with a random sample of 804 adults, aged 18 and older, living in all 50 U.S. states and the District of Columbia. For results based on the total sample of national adults, the margin of sampling error is ±4 percentage points at the 95% confidence level. All reported margins of sampling error include computed design effects for weighting.

February 09, 2015
ECONOMIC CONFIDENCE INDEX HIGHEST IN MINN., LOWEST IN W. VA.

by Justin McCarthy

Story Highlights

- *Minnesota has highest economic confidence score in 7-year trend*
- *Maryland, California, Hawaii, Colorado also sit atop the list*
- *For fifth year in a row, W. Virginia ranks at very bottom*

WASHINGTON, D.C.—Gallup's Economic Confidence Index scores in 2014 were highest in Minnesota—the only state with a non-negative score—followed by Maryland, California and Hawaii. Scores were lowest in West Virginia, Alabama, Kentucky and Mississippi.

Top 10 States, Gallup Economic Confidence Index

	2014
Minnesota	0
Maryland	-4
California	-5
Hawaii	-6
Colorado	-7
Washington	-8
Texas	-8
Massachusetts	-8
Wisconsin	-9
North Dakota	-9

Gallup Daily tracking, January-December 2014

GALLUP'

Bottom 10 States, Gallup Economic Confidence Index

	2014
West Virginia	-42
Alabama	-33
Kentucky	-29
Mississippi	-29
Wyoming	-27
Arkansas	-27
Louisiana	-27
Oklahoma	-26
New Mexico	-26
Tennessee	-25
Missouri	-25

Gallup Daily tracking, January-December 2014

GALLUP'

These results are based on Gallup Daily tracking interviews with 176,702 national adults conducted from January through December 2014, and represent averages for the year. Gallup conducted interviews with at least 450 residents in every state and interviewed 1,000 or more in 41 states.

The Gallup Economic Confidence Index is a composite of Americans' ratings of current U.S. economic conditions and their perceptions of the economy's direction. The index has a theoretical maximum of +100 (if all respondents rate the economy "excellent" or "good" and say it is getting better) and a theoretical minimum of -100 (if all rate the economy "poor" and say it is getting worse).

Nationally, the index averaged -15 for all of 2014. However, scores improved dramatically in the last part of the year, and have consistently been in positive territory so far this year. The ratings reported here, based on averages for all of 2014, do not necessarily reflect current confidence. However, given that there is a decent level of consistency in state rankings from year to year, the relative state rankings may still generally hold even if Americans overall, and in each of the 50 states, are currently more upbeat about the economy.

Gallup has tracked economic confidence ratings at the state level since 2008, and prior to Minnesota's latest rating of zero, no state has had a non-negative annual score. The District of Columbia, which had a score of +18 in 2014, has had positive scores since 2012 and has maintained a significant lead in confidence over residents in the 50 states since 2009.

Though most of the states with the highest index scores are the same as in 2013, Hawaii (-6) and Colorado (-7) moved upward in 2014 after not having made the top of the previous year's list. Washington, Texas and Massachusetts, each with a score of -8, remained in the top 10 from the prior rankings. Wisconsin and North Dakota, both scoring -9, also returned to the top of the list.

Scores in Iowa (-11) and Nebraska (-11)—both of which have regularly been atop the list in recent years—as well as Connecticut (-14) each dipped slightly, and therefore, these states lost their spots among the top 10.

Bottom 10 States Similar to 2013 Rankings

Of the states where residents are least confident about the economy, West Virginia (-42) remains at the bottom—a distinction it holds for the fifth year in a row. Alabama (-33) had also found itself among the bottom states in recent years, but its nine-point drop in 2014 sent it to the second-to-last spot after West Virginia.

Like the upper tier of the list, the bottom tier in 2014 has many repeats from the previous year. Kentucky (-29), Louisiana (-27), Arkansas (-27), Wyoming (-27), Oklahoma (-26) and Tennessee (-25) all remain among the states where residents express the least confidence in the nation's economy. New additions to the list include Mississippi (-29), New Mexico (-26) and Missouri (-25)—each of which slipped several points in confidence in 2014.

Economic Confidence by State, 2014

GALLUP

Gallup has found in the past that there is a political nature to economic confidence, as states where residents have higher confidence tend to be more approving of President Barack Obama, while those with lower confidence are least likely to approve of him. Presidential approval, however, isn't always an accurate barometer of economic confidence. North Dakotans, for example, are among the least approving of Obama but have far greater confidence than residents of most other states as they have enjoyed an oil boom in recent years.

Bottom Line

Confidence in the economy varies significantly from state to state, though it generally tilted negative in 2014, as has been the case in recent years.

Although the yearly average for the Economic Confidence Index was steady in 2014 compared with 2013, improvements seen in late December have carried over into the new year, suggesting the index could gain real ground in 2015. But increases in confidence aren't always felt evenly throughout the country. West Virginia has continually languished at the bottom of the list—as it has on a variety of measures—and many Southern states have too. Pockets of extreme discontent with the economy can hamper national progress, and state rankings such as this one provide an opportunity to see where improvement is most needed.

Survey Methods

Results for this Gallup poll are based on telephone interviews conducted Jan. 2–Dec. 30, 2014, on the Gallup U.S. Daily survey, with a random sample of 176,702 adults, aged 18 and older, living in all 50 U.S. states and the District of Columbia. For results based on the total sample of national adults, the margin of sampling error is ±1 percentage point at the 95% confidence level.

Margins of error for individual states are no greater than ±6 percentage points and are ±3 percentage points in most states. The margin of error for the District of Columbia is ±6 percentage points.

February 11, 2015
N.D. FIRST, CONN. LAST IN STATE JOB CREATION IN 2014

by Lydia Saad

Story Highlights

- *North Dakota ranks No. 1 in worker reports of job creation*
- *Connecticut ranks last, followed closely by Alaska*
- *Job Creation Index inched slightly higher nationally in 2014*

PRINCETON, N.J.—North Dakota maintained its pre-eminent position in Gallup's annual ranking of state job markets in 2014, with employed North Dakota residents providing a strongly upbeat report on hiring conditions where they work—the most positive of any state. Connecticut finds itself at the other end of the spectrum, as workers there reported the worst hiring climate, although still net positive.

Best Hiring Climates	
Gallup Job Creation Index, 2014	
	Index
North Dakota	36
Texas	31
Nebraska	31
Wisconsin	31
Michigan	30
Iowa	30
Utah	30
South Dakota	29
Oklahoma	29
Delaware	29
Washington	29
Oregon	29

Gallup Daily tracking, January-December 2014

GALLUP

Worst Hiring Climates	
Gallup Job Creation Index, 2014	
	Index
Connecticut	16
Alaska	17
New Mexico	18
West Virginia	18
Maine	19
New Jersey	20
Mississippi	20
Kentucky	21
Vermont	21
Rhode Island	21
Alabama	21
New York	21

Gallup Daily tracking, January-December 2014

GALLUP

Gallup's Job Creation Index is derived from full- and part-time workers' reports of whether their employer is hiring and expanding the size of its workforce, not making changes, or letting people go and reducing its workforce.

In North Dakota, 48% of workers in 2014 said their employer is hiring and 12% said their employer is letting workers go, resulting in a +36 Job Creation Index score. By contrast, Connecticut's +16 index score reflects 33% of workers saying their employer is hiring and 17% letting go.

The 2014 state-level findings are drawn from 201,254 interviews with employed adults nationwide, conducted throughout the year as part of Gallup Daily tracking.

Energy Producing and Farm States Dominate the Top Tier

Beyond North Dakota, other states where workers are especially likely to report positive net hiring include Texas, Nebraska, Wisconsin, Iowa and South Dakota—all states that rely on either the energy sector or farming commodities, or both.

Michigan's inclusion among the states with the highest Job Creation Index scores is notable because it represents one of the sharpest turnarounds of any state in the seven years Gallup has measured job creation. Michigan was among the worst-performing states in 2008 and 2009, but with significant improvements in that state's economy, it rose to about average net hiring in 2010, and has ranked among the top-performing states in each of the past two years.

Delaware has followed a similar trajectory, going from one of the lowest-ranking states in 2008 and 2009 to one of the top-ranking in 2013 and 2014. Delaware holds the distinction of being the only state anywhere along the Eastern seaboard to be in the top 10.

Of the 13 states with the best net hiring scores in 2014, most share a border with at least one other state on the list, including North Dakota, South Dakota, Nebraska, Iowa, Wisconsin, Michigan, Texas, Oklahoma, Washington and Oregon. Only Utah and Delaware stand alone, geographically.

Connecticut and Rhode Island Consistently Rank Among the Lowest

Connecticut and Rhode Island tie for compiling the worst collective job creation scores since 2008 and are the only states to have ranked in the bottom 10 each year. New Jersey is not far behind, ranking among the lowest states for net hiring in all but one year.

Connecticut's position at the bottom of the list in 2014 highlights that four of the six New England states had among the lowest Job Creation Index scores last year—the others being Maine, Vermont and Rhode Island. All four also ranked in the bottom 10 in 2013. New Hampshire has occasionally appeared in the bottom tier for job creation, leaving Massachusetts as the sole New England state that has avoided this unwelcome distinction.

Notably, six other low-ranking states last year are geographic pairs: New York and New Jersey, West Virginia and Kentucky, and Mississippi and Alabama—reinforcing that the jobs climate often reflects regional, not just state-specific, factors. The exceptions to this in 2014 were New Mexico and Alaska, both regionally isolated from other hiring-challenged states.

Job Creation Index by State, 2014

■ Above average ■ Average ■ Below average

GALLUP'

Job Creation Continued Its Gradual Recovery

In 2014, the Job Creation Index averaged +26, up from +20 in 2013, and a significant improvement over the slightly negative net hiring average found in 2009.

Gallup Job Creation Index, Annual Averages, Nationwide
Based on U.S. employed adults

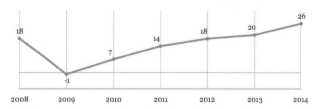

Index represents net new hiring defined as percentage of workers saying their employer is hiring new workers and expanding its workforce minus those saying their employer is letting workers go and reducing the size of its workforce.

GALLUP'

The index was up year over year in most states, but particularly in Oklahoma, Oregon and New Hampshire, where it rose nine points each. At the same time, net hiring failed to improve in a handful of states—North Dakota, Alaska, Hawaii, Delaware, South Dakota, Minnesota, Tennessee and Connecticut—where the index was basically flat in 2014.

Bottom Line

North Dakota maintained its prized position in 2014 as the state where workers sense the most hiring momentum, no doubt reflecting the many economic benefits it is enjoying from its recent emergence as a major oil producer. Workers in North Dakota failed to grow more positive about hiring in 2014, bucking the national trend, which could reflect concern about the potential impact of low international oil prices on North Dakota's oil boom. Nevertheless, the state retained a comfortable lead on Gallup's Job Creation Index in 2014.

Connecticut has consistently ranked in the bottom tier for job creation, and its position at the very bottom in 2014, along with continued low ratings of other New England states and neighboring New York, suggests that is unlikely to change in 2015.

Importantly, however, all 50 states now have positive net hiring scores, and all but three—West Virginia, Alaska and New Mexico—have markedly improved on this measure since these ratings hit their low point in 2009.

Survey Methods

Results for this Gallup poll are based on telephone interviews conducted Jan. 2–Dec. 30, 2014, on the Gallup U.S. Daily survey, with a random sample of 201,254 employed adults, aged 18 and older, living in all 50 U.S. states and the District of Columbia. For results based on the total sample of national adults, the margin of sampling error is ±1 percentage point at the 95% confidence level.

Margins of error for individual states are no greater than ±6 percentage points and are ±3 percentage points in most states. The margin of error for the District of Columbia is ±6 percentage points. All reported margins of sampling error include computed design effects for weighting.

February 12, 2015
U.S. SATISFACTION WITH RELIGION SETTLING AT LOWER LEVELS

by Frank Newport

Story Highlights

- *Overall, 53% satisfied with influence of organized religion*
- *Majority of dissatisfied want religion to have less influence*

PRINCETON, N.J.—A slight majority of Americans, 53%, are satisfied with the influence of organized religion in the U.S. This level of satisfaction has changed little over the past three years, but remains down from what Gallup has measured previously—including higher levels measured in 2001 to 2004—suggesting that Americans' satisfaction with organized religion has settled in at a new baseline.

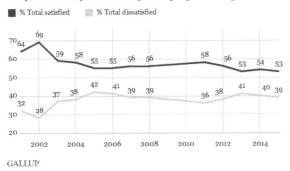

Satisfied or Dissatisfied With the Influence of Organized Religion

■ % Total satisfied   ■ % Total dissatisfied

GALLUP

The latest measurement comes from Gallup's annual Mood of the Nation poll, conducted Jan. 5–8. Satisfaction with the influence of religion comes in sixth on the list of 27 aspects of American life that Gallup measures in the survey.

Nearly two in three Americans (64%) were satisfied with the influence of religion when they were first asked this question in this format in January 2001, exactly eight months before the 9/11 terrorist attacks. Satisfaction rose to its high point of 69% a year later, then dropped below 60% in the years thereafter. Although Americans' satisfaction has fluctuated some from year to year, the basic pattern has been generally stable since 2005, with slightly lower levels of satisfaction recorded over the past three years.

Most of Those Dissatisfied Want Less Influence of Organized Religion

Americans who report being dissatisfied with the influence of religion were asked if they would like to see organized religion have more influence, less influence or keep its influence as it is now. Most of this dissatisfied group, equating to 22% of all Americans, say they would prefer less influence, while 8% would like to see organized religion have more influence.

Over time, the group of Americans who are dissatisfied and want religion to have less influence has consistently been larger than the group who are dissatisfied and want it to have more influence. The gap between these groups grew bigger as overall satisfaction with the influence of organized religion dropped in 2005. There has been little meaningful change in these trend lines in more recent years.

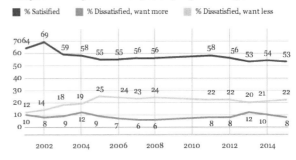

Satisfied or Dissatisfied With the Influence of Organized Religion

■ % Satisfied   ■ % Dissatisfied, want more   ■ % Dissatisfied, want less

GALLUP

The pattern of responses to this expanded question about the influence of religion varies in expected ways across segments of the population defined by their religious service attendance. Satisfaction is at 61% among those who attend religious services weekly—and drops to 47% among those who seldom or never attend.

Most of those who seldom or never attend church and who are dissatisfied want organized religion to have less influence. Those who attend church weekly and are dissatisfied lean toward wanting religion to have more influence. On the whole, however, non-churchgoers are twice as likely to be dissatisfied and to want to see religion have less influence than weekly churchgoers are to be dissatisfied because they want it to have more influence, 33% versus 16%.

Satisfaction With the Influence of Organized Religion, by Religious Service Attendance

	Satisfied	Dissatisfied, want more influence	Dissatisfied, want less influence	Dissatisfied, keep as it is now
	%	%	%	%
Attend church weekly	61	16	4	11
Attend church almost weekly or monthly	60	11	17	8
Seldom or never attend church	47	4	33	10

Jan 5-8, 2015

GALLUP

More generally, these data show that 77% of the most religious Americans are either OK with the current influence of organized religion or are dissatisfied and would like it to have more influence. The percentage of Americans who are in this group drops among the least religious Americans, but still is a majority, at 51%.

Implications

It is clear that Americans' satisfaction with the role of organized religion in society is down from where it was a decade ago. There have been changes in other measures of religiosity over this time period—including most relevantly, a gradual increase in the percentage of Americans who say they have no formal religious identity. This suggests that the drop in satisfaction with the role of organized religion is at least to some degree, a manifestation of more general societal and cultural trends relating to religion.

The drop in satisfaction with organized religion does appear to have leveled off in recent years, although as is the case with many attitudinal trends, it is difficult to predict what might happen in the years ahead. It is also important to remember that this question deals with the influence of *organized* religion. Responses to this question could reflect more of a shift in the way that Americans are conducting the spiritual side of their lives, rather than a definitive shift toward a more secular society. This interpretation is supported by other trends showing that Americans have become more likely to affiliate with non-denominational churches and to eschew identification with formal religions.

Overall, despite changes over time, the majority of Americans today continue to be a member of a church, to attend religious services at least somewhat regularly and to have positive views about the influence of organized religion, while a minority are not at all involved with organized religion and would like to see its influence lessened.

Survey Methods

Results for this Gallup poll are based on telephone interviews conducted Jan. 5–8, 2015, with a random sample of 804 adults, aged 18 and older, living in all 50 U.S. states and the District of Columbia. For results based on the total sample of national adults, the margin of sampling error is ±4 percentage points at the 95% confidence level. All reported margins of sampling error include computed design effects for weighting.

February 12, 2015
AMERICANS FEEL SLIGHTLY BETTER ABOUT FINANCES THAN A YEAR AGO

by Rebecca Riffkin

Story Highlights

- *About half feel "pretty good" about amount of money they have*
- *Half say they feel better about personal financial situation*
- *Both measures up slightly from January 2014*

WASHINGTON, D.C.—Despite the upbeat economic news in recent months and the rise in Americans' overall economic confidence, slightly less than half of Americans say they are feeling "pretty good" about the amount of money they have to spend. This is, however, by a slight margin, the highest level Gallup has measured over the last two years—up from 45% in January 2014 and slightly higher than the 47% recorded in January 2013.

Americans Feeling Slightly Better About the Amount of Money They Have to Spend Since January 2014

Are you feeling pretty good these days about the amount of money you have to spend, or not?

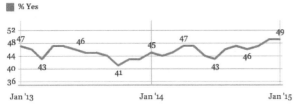

Gallup Daily tracking

GALLUP

Gallup asks Americans each night: "Are you feeling pretty good these days about the amount of money you have to spend, or not?" Americans generally are not overly positive in their responses, with answers staying within the narrow range of 41% and 49% saying they are feeling pretty good over the past two years. The 49% in the last two months, December 2014 and January 2015, are the highest percentage Gallup has found for this question since the beginning of 2013.

More Americans Feeling Better About Their Financial Situation Than a Year Ago

Americans' responses to a separate question asking if they are feeling better about their financial situation are also up modestly to 50% saying they are feeling better from 43% who said the same in January 2014. This is highest percentage saying they are feeling better about their financial situation since 2013.

Americans Feeling Slightly Better About Their Financial Situation

Are you feeling better about your financial situation these days, or not?

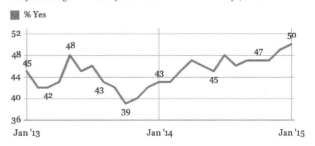

Gallup Daily tracking

GALLUP

These two questions tap into Americans' emotional responses to money and spending, and responses to both have generally increased and decreased in tandem. The lowest percentage over the past two years to answer "yes" for either question Gallup found in October 2013, amid the partial federal government shutdown, when 41% said they felt good about the amount of money they had and 39% said they were feeling better about their financial situation. Positive responses to both questions are at their highest points this year, but even with this increase in positive attitudes, only about half of Americans are willing to say that they are feeling good about either the amount of money they have or their financial situation.

Bottom Line

Americans' responses to these personal spending questions generally parallel their level of confidence in the national economy. Gallup's Economic Confidence Index fell in October 2013, plunging to an average of -35 for the month of October 2013, the same month that Americans' views about their personal finances fell to record lows.

Recently, economic confidence has been rising, and January was the first month since Gallup began tracking when it was positive. Americans' perceptions of their personal finances have also edged up, but much more cautiously, and even now only about half of Americans are willing to say that they feel good about the amount of money they have or their spending. These results suggest that it will take a significant amount of time for the rising economic tide to have a profound effect on Americans' feelings about their personal financial situations.

Survey Methods

Results for this Gallup poll are based on telephone interviews conducted Jan. 2–31, 2015, on the Gallup U.S. Daily survey, with a random sample of 3,590 adults, aged 18 and older, living in all 50 U.S. states and the District of Columbia. For results based on the total sample of national adults, the margin of sampling error is ±2 percentage points at the 95% confidence level. All reported margins of sampling error include computed design effects for weighting.

February 13, 2015

NORTH DAKOTA HAS HIGHEST STATE PAYROLL TO POPULATION RATE

by Ben Ryan

Story Highlights

- *Wyoming had lowest unemployment at 2.6%*
- *West Virginia remains lowest P2P at 35.6%*
- *GDP per capita, economic indexes track with P2P*

WASHINGTON, D.C.—Last year, North Dakota (54.0%) had the highest Payroll to Population employment rate (P2P), as measured by Gallup, among the 50 U.S. states. A cluster of states in the northern Great Plains and Rocky Mountain regions—including Nebraska, Minnesota, Kansas, Wyoming, Utah, Colorado and Iowa—all made the top 10 on this measure. West Virginia (35.6%) had the lowest P2P rate of all the states for the second year in a row.

Top 10 States, Payroll to Population
States with the highest P2P rates

Highest	P2P rate %
North Dakota	54.0
Nebraska	50.5
Minnesota	49.2
Kansas	49.1
Maryland	49.0
Wyoming	48.6
Utah	48.5
Colorado	48.4
Alaska	48.3
Iowa	48.3

Gallup Daily tracking, January-December 2014

GALLUP

Bottom 10 States, Payroll to Population
States with the lowest P2P rates

	P2P rate %
West Virginia	35.6
Florida	38.9
Mississippi	39.0
New Mexico	39.1
Oregon	39.1
Alabama	40.0
Arizona	40.0
South Carolina	40.2
Kentucky	40.3
Nevada	40.7

Gallup Daily tracking, January-December 2014

GALLUP

Gallup's P2P metric tracks the percentage of the adult population aged 18 and older who are employed full time for an employer for at least 30 hours per week. P2P is not seasonally adjusted. These results are based on Gallup Daily tracking interviews throughout 2014 with 353,736 U.S. adults. Gallup does not count adults who are self-employed, work fewer than 30 hours per week, who are unemployed or are out of the workforce as payroll-employed in the P2P metric.

The differences in P2P rates across states may reflect several factors, including the overall employment situation and the population's demographic composition. States with large older and retired populations, for example, would have a lower percentage of adults working full time. The two states with the lowest P2P in 2014, West Virginia and Florida, have two of the largest proportions of residents aged 65 and older, at 17.3% and 16.9%, respectively. Regardless of the underlying reason, however, the P2P rate provides a good reflection of a state's economic vitality.

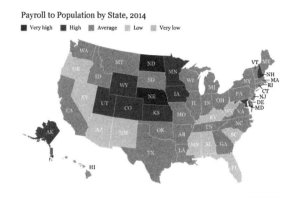

Payroll to Population by State, 2014
■ Very high ■ High ▨ Average ▨ Low ▨ Very low

GALLUP

Aside from the Mountain West and northern Plains states, those states bordering the nation's capital and located in the Northeast also showed higher levels of full-time employment for an employer. Washington, D.C., had the highest P2P rate of any area in the country, at 56.4%, but it is unique in being the only entirely urban region in the survey, heavily dominated by the presence of the federal government, and with one of the lowest percentages of residents aged 65 and older (12.3%).

Wyoming and North Dakota Had Lowest Unemployment Rates

As with P2P rates, states in the northern Great Plains and Rocky Mountain regions—including North and South Dakota, Minnesota, Nebraska and Iowa—were among those with the lowest unemployment rates in 2013. The five states with the lowest unemployment rates were all also in the top 10 for P2P rates in 2014. Similarly, four of the 10 worst-performing states in terms of unemployment were also in the bottom 10 for P2P, and also lowest ranked in 2013.

Gallup's U.S. unemployment rate is the percentage of adults in the *workforce* who are not employed but are looking and available for employment. While P2P reflects the proportion of adults working full time for an employer relative to the entire *population*, the unemployment rate reflects the proportion of adults in the *workforce*—all those working or seeking work—who are not working, but would like to be.

Lowest Unemployment States

	Unemployment rate %
Wyoming	2.6
North Dakota	3.1
Nebraska	3.9
Utah	3.9
Kansas	4.0
Maine	4.1
Iowa	4.3
South Dakota	4.3
Wisconsin	4.5
Colorado	4.6

Gallup Daily tracking, January-December 2014

GALLUP

Highest Unemployment States

	Unemployment rate %
Nevada	9.9
Florida	9.1
California	9.0
New Jersey	8.4
West Virginia	8.3
Rhode Island	8.0
Arizona	7.9
North Carolina	7.6
Connecticut	7.5
New York	7.5

Gallup Daily tracking, January-December 2014

GALLUP

P2P and unemployment are both objective indicators of the employment situation, and as such, there is a great deal of overlap on these two metrics among the best- and worst-performing states. The measures also correspond with the best and worst performers on Gallup's Economic Confidence Index and Job Creation Index, which provide a more attitudinal assessment of the state's economic and employment picture. North Dakota figures in the top 10 and West Virginia in the bottom 10 on both 2014 state lists on these other two measures.

However, across all states, P2P shows a stronger relationship than do unemployment rates with other important economic indicators. For example, P2P tracks positively with state GDP per capita, while unemployment shows little relationship.

P2P and Unemployment by State GDP per Capita

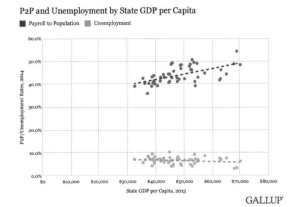

Bottom Line

The top 10 states for P2P tend to have several things going for them, economically. More than half of the states with the highest P2P rates in 2014 ranked in the top 10 for P2P in 2013, thus showing persistent economic strength as the country continues to recover from the Great Recession. Additionally, North Dakota, Wyoming, Nebraska, Utah, Kansas and Iowa in 2014 all ranked in the top 10 states for P2P and bottom 10 for unemployment, indicating these states have particularly robust labor markets. North Dakota, Nebraska, Iowa and Utah ranked in the top 10 on Gallup's Job Creation Index, meaning the positive hiring situation in those states is particularly evident to workers in these states. Alaska, North Dakota and Wyoming also boast the three highest per capita incomes.

By contrast, West Virginia, Florida, Arizona and Nevada in 2014 ranked in the bottom 10 states on P2P rates, and they are among the states with the highest unemployment rates. Many of these same states ranked among the lowest on these measures in 2013 as well. The 2008 recession hit these states harder than it did many others. For instance, Nevada, Florida, and Arizona saw the highest foreclosure rates in the nation, and years later, these states still lag behind others on employment, job creation and economic confidence. As the national economy strengthens in the northern Great Plains and Northeast, these lower-ranking states risk being left behind unless they can find ways to put more of their population into productive full-time employment.

Survey Methods

Results for this Gallup poll are based on telephone interviews conducted Jan. 2–Dec. 30, 2014, on the Gallup U.S. Daily survey, with a random sample of 353,736 adults, aged 18 and older, living in all 50 U.S. states and the District of Columbia. For results based on the total sample of national adults, the margin of sampling error is ±1 percentage point at the 95% confidence level.

Margins of error for individual states are no greater than ±6 percentage points, and are ±3 percentage points in most states. The margin of error for the District of Columbia is ±6 percentage points. All reported margins of sampling error include computed design effects for weighting.

February 13, 2015

ISIS, TERRORISM SEEN AS GRAVER THREATS THAN RUSSIA, UKRAINE

by Art Swift and Andrew Dugan

WASHINGTON, D.C.—Despite the intensifying fighting between Ukraine and Russian-backed separatists before the cease-fire agreement Thursday, Americans place the conflict low on the list of critical threats to U.S. interests in the next decade. Islamic extremists, commonly known as the Islamic State or ISIS, along with international terrorism in general, loom much larger in Americans' minds as a critical threat.

Critical Threats to the United States

I am going to read you a list of possible threats to the vital interests of the United States in the next 10 years. For each one, please tell me if you see this as a critical threat, an important but not critical threat, or not an important threat at all?

	% Critical threat	% Important but not critical threat
Islamic militants, commonly known as ISIS, operating in Iraq and Syria	84	12
International terrorism	84	13
Development of nuclear weapons by Iran	77	16
The military power of North Korea	64	26
The military power of Russia	49	41
The conflict between Israel and the Palestinians	49	41
The conflict between Russia and Ukraine	44	45
The economic power of China	40	44

Feb. 8-11, 2015

GALLUP

The Islamic State has continually been a focal point on the world stage over the past several months as it has brutally executed hostages, including several Americans, leading 84% of their fellow citizens to rank the terrorist group as a critical threat. Americans place the threat from international terrorism in general at the same level.

Only two other issues are considered critical threats by a majority of Americans. Although the U.S. has been conducting talks with Iran to reduce or eliminate Iran's nuclear capabilities, 77% of Americans still view the development of nuclear weapons by Iran as a critical threat. Sixty-four percent view North Korea as a critical threat.

The conflict between Russia and Ukraine, when placed in the context of other global challenges, is not as much of a critical concern to Americans. Yet the situation in Ukraine has severely tested U.S.-Russian relations—to the point that one year ago, half of Americans said they thought the U.S. and Russia were heading back to a Cold War. The U.S. has backed Ukraine's new government, while Russia has advocated for the pro-Russian separatists in eastern Ukraine.

Thousands have already died in nearly a year of fighting between Ukraine and the separatists. But this violence intensified in recent weeks to the point that many policymakers, including possibly President Barack Obama, are considering providing "lethal defensive weapons" to Ukraine. However, Obama said he would wait for the outcome of this week's negotiations in Minsk, Belarus, before deciding.

These results come from the Feb. 8–11 Gallup Poll Social Series World Affairs survey, with interviewing completed before the announcement of the cease-fire agreement.

Before Cease-Fire, Americans Split on Military Aid to Ukraine

Even before Thursday's announcement of the cease-fire that is set to begin Sunday, most Americans (54%) opposed the sending of U.S. military weapons and equipment to Ukraine's government to help combat the separatists. Four in 10 Americans say they favor sending such military assistance, which policymakers and defense analysts often refer to as "lethal aid."

Sending Aid to Ukraine

Do you favor or oppose the U.S. sending military weapons and equipment to the Ukraine government to use in fighting pro-Russian rebels in the eastern part of Ukraine?

	Favor	Oppose	Don't know
Feb 8-11, 2015	40%	54%	6%

GALLUP

Americans Hold Favorable View of Ukraine, With a Third Unfavorable

Gallup has asked Americans about their views of Ukraine on two occasions: this past week, and almost exactly a decade ago, during the country's "Orange Revolution." In 2004–2005, Ukrainians revolted against alleged election fraud, and the protests resulted in a new presidential election. In the midst of this, 67% of Americans said they had a favorable impression of Ukraine, while today that figure stands at 52%. This decline in favorable ratings may be a result of the protracted conflict in Ukraine.

Americans' Opinions of Ukraine

What is your overall opinion of Ukraine? Is it very favorable, mostly favorable, mostly unfavorable, or very unfavorable?

	Very favorable	Mostly favorable	Mostly unfavorable	Very unfavorable	No opinion
	%	%	%	%	%
Feb 8-11, 2015	7	45	29	7	11
Feb 7-10, 2005	9	58	15	3	15

GALLUP

In contrast, 70% of Americans have an unfavorable view of Russia, with 24% viewing it favorably. As recently as 2011, a majority of Americans viewed the former Soviet republic favorably.

Bottom Line

ISIS and international terrorism loom largest in Americans' minds as critical threats to U.S. interests. In a winter that has seen acts of unspeakable terrorism, with Obama seeking authorization for military action against the Islamic State, Americans are clearly concerned about Islamic militants and terrorists. The conflict in Ukraine may not worry Americans as much because they see it as more of a threat to Europe than to the U.S.

Americans prior to the cease-fire opposed the idea of U.S. military aid to Ukraine. Obama has said that sending U.S. troops is unlikely, but that advanced weapons and arming Ukraine's military are on the table should the peace falter. In this combative part of the world, whether the U.S. will wade into the conflict in the near or long term is still an open question. However, with a majority of Americans opposed to U.S. military aid to Ukraine, it appears Obama could have a difficult time of selling a military approach to the American people.

Survey Methods

Results for this Gallup poll are based on telephone interviews conducted Feb. 8–11, 2015, with a random sample of 837 adults, aged 18 and older, living in all 50 U.S. states and the District of Columbia. For results based on the total sample of national adults, the margin of sampling error is ±4 percentage points at the 95% confidence level. All reported margins of sampling error include computed design effects for weighting.

February 16, 2015
NEW CONGRESS HAS SLIGHTLY HIGHER RATINGS, STILL UNPOPULAR

by Andrew Dugan

Story Highlights

- *One in five Americans approve of congressional job performance*
- *Republican support has increased*

WASHINGTON, D.C.—More than a month into the tenure of the Republican-controlled 114th Congress, the partisan makeover of America's legislative body does not appear to have done much for its popularity. One in five Americans say they approve of the way Congress is handling its job, slightly higher than the 16% approval in the final reading for the 113th Congress, from December. Seventy-five percent of Americans disapprove of Congress.

Congressional Job Approval Ratings: 2001-2015

Do you approve or disapprove of the way Congress is handling its job?

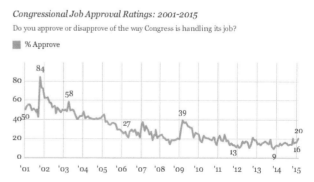

GALLUP

The Jan. 5–8 reading, also 16%, came in a poll that was conducted partially before the new Congress came into office. The current poll, conducted Feb. 8–11, is the first to be fully conducted since the new Congress took office.

In recent weeks, the new GOP-led Congress has considered a number of high-profile bills such as legislation authorizing the Keystone pipeline, and has conducted confirmation hearings for important posts such as secretary of defense and attorney general. However, Americans as a whole apparently have seen little to justify significantly revising their opinions.

No Post-Election Approval Rally Evident So Far

Rarely does anything close to a majority of the public see Congress positively; the legislative body's long-term average approval rating is 32%. But Congresses that result from "wave" elections—contests where one party strongly outperforms the other—usually see an increase in support once their new term begins.

For example, after midterm elections that handed over full control to one party in 1994 and 2006, the new Congress's approval ratings greatly improved, relative to the last reading of the previous Congress. In January 1995, the new Republican Congress was 10 percentage points more popular than the previous Congress, controlled by Democrats, was in December 1994. In January 2007, the new Democratic Congress was 14 points more popular than the prior Congress, controlled by Republicans, was in December 2006.

Congressional Approval and Wave Elections

	Term in office	Party control	% Approval, first poll of new Congress	Dates of first poll	Change in approval (first poll of new Congress minus last poll of previous Congress)
114th Congress	present	Republicans win Senate	20	Feb 8-11, 2015	+4
113th Congress	2013-2015	No party change	15	Jan 7-10, 2013	-4
112th Congress	2011-2013	Republicans win House	20	Jan 7-9, 2011	+7
111th Congress	2009-2011	No party change	19	Jan 9-11, 2009	-1
110th Congress	2007-2009	Democrats win control	35	Jan 15-18, 2007	+14
109th Congress	2005-2007	No party change	45	Feb 7-10, 2005	+4
108th Congress	2003-2005	Republicans win Senate	49	Jan 13-16, 2003	-1
107th Congress	2001-2003	No party change^	50	Jan 10-14, 2001	-6
106th Congress	1999-2001	No party change	50	Jan 15-17, 1999	+8
105th Congress	1997-1999	No party change	41	Jan 10-13, 1997	+7
104th Congress	1995-1997	Republicans win control	33	Jan 16-18, 1995	+10

^2000 election produced a Senate tied 50-50, with then-Vice President Dick Cheney giving Republicans majority control until mid-2001, when a Republican senator switched caucuses to give Democrats control

GALLUP

Many election analysts considered the 2014 midterms a "wave" election, as it not only saw enough GOP Senate candidates win to give that party the majority in that chamber, but it also produced the largest House Republican majority since the Hoover administration in the 1920s.

Nonetheless, in terms of spurring better approval ratings for Congress, the effect of last year's GOP rout has so far been minimal. This could be partly because the 2014 elections saw a less dramatic change in control of Congress—only one chamber changed party control instead of both, as occurred after the 1994 and 2006 elections. It may also be that Americans' widespread dissatisfaction with government is working as a counterweight on the usual

increase in good feeling that occurs when there is a change in party control.

GOP Support for Congress Growing, Still Low

A major reason why approval of Congress increases after a change in party control is that approval ratings among supporters of the new majority party surge. Currently, 27% of self-identified Republicans say they approve of the way Congress is handling its job, up notably from the percentage who said so in January (17%) or December (12%). Democrats' approval rating of Congress is 17% in February and independents' is 18%, basically unchanged compared with January and December.

Change in Approval Ratings of Congress, by Self-Identified Party Affiliation, After Changes in Party Control of Congress

	% First approval rating for new Congress	% Last approval rating for old Congress	Change (pct. pts.)
1994-1995			
Republicans	45	19	+26
Independents	29	25	+4
Democrats	27	27	0
2002-2003			
Republicans	67	61	+6
Independents	43	45	-2
Democrats	38	43	-5
2006-2007			
Republicans	37	32	+5
Independents	28	18	+10
Democrats	39	16	+23
2010-2011			
Republicans	22	7	+15
Independents	16	13	+3
Democrats	24	16	+8
2014-2015			
Republicans	27	12	+15
Independents	18	18	0
Democrats	17	16	+1

GALLUP

But this spike in GOP approval for Congress is much smaller than the swell of support in other Congresses that took office after major "change elections." For instance, support for Congress more than doubled among Democrats once the Democratic majority took over in 2007—from 16% to 39%. And in 1995, when Republicans took the helm of both houses for the first time in 40 years, Republicans' approval of Congress skyrocketed 26 points.

Bottom Line

An organization created to defend the GOP's nascent Senate majority in next year's elections notes on its website that "the U.S. Senate is under new management." And while the promotion of GOP Sen. Mitch McConnell to majority leader has undoubtedly changed the political calculus in Washington, it has done little so far to change most Americans' opinions about Congress.

Given the raft of legislation that may be forthcoming in the following months—involving authorization of use of military force in Iraq/Syria, granting the president greater power in negotiating trade deals, as well as a potentially contentious bill to fund the Department of Homeland Security—there may be significant movement on how the public rates Congress, be it good or bad. But for now, even as Washington adjusts to a new political balance, most Americans seem to be taking their time in assessing the new leadership.

Survey Methods

Results for this Gallup poll are based on telephone interviews conducted Feb. 8–11, 2015, with a random sample of 837 adults, aged 18 and older, living in all 50 U.S. states and the District of Columbia. For results based on the total sample of national adults, the margin of sampling error is ±4 percentage points at the 95% confidence level. All reported margins of sampling error include computed design effects for weighting.

February 16, 2015

AMERICANS INCREASINGLY SEE RUSSIA AS THREAT, TOP U.S. ENEMY

by Jeffrey M. Jones

Story Highlights

- *Russia edges out North Korea as perceived top U.S. enemy*
- *Favorable ratings of Russia sink to 24%*
- *More Americans view Russian military power as critical threat*

PRINCETON, N.J.—Russia now edges out North Korea as the country Americans consider the United States' greatest enemy. Two years ago, only 2% of Americans named Russia, but that increased to 9% in 2014 as tensions between Russia and the U.S. increased, and now sits at 18%.

What one country anywhere in the world do you consider to be the United States' greatest enemy today? [OPEN-ENDED]
Recent trend

	2011	2012	2014	2015
	%	%	%	%
Russia	3	2	9	18
North Korea/Korea (nonspecific)	16	10	16	15
China	16	23	20	12
Iran	25	32	16	9
Iraq	7	5	7	8
Countries in which ISIS operates	--	--	--	4
Middle East (nonspecific)	--	--	2	4
Syria	--	*	3	4
Afghanistan	9	7	5	3
United States itself	2	1	2	2
Japan	*	1	*	1
Saudi Arabia	1	1	1	1
Pakistan	2	2	1	*
Other	9	3	7	7
None/No opinion	10	12	11	13

* Less than 0.5%

GALLUP

The results are based on a Feb. 8–11 Gallup poll, completed just before the international community brokered a cease-fire agreement

between Ukraine and pro-Russian separatists in the country's east region. European leaders had hoped to reach an agreement to head off the possibility that the United States would send weapons and military equipment to Ukrainian military forces.

As Russia has risen in the "enemy" rankings, the two countries that topped the list in the previous three updates—China in 2014 and Iran in 2011 and 2012—have slipped. The percentage mentioning China has dropped eight points over the past year, to 12%, and the percentage mentioning Iran has fallen seven points to 9%.

Nearly Half Now See Russian Military Power as Threat to U.S.

Americans have also become significantly more likely to view Russia's military power as a critical threat to the U.S.—49% now hold this view, compared with 32% a year ago.

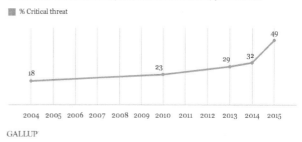

Americans' Perceptions of Russia's Military Power as a Critical Threat to U.S.
Next, I am going to read you a list of possible threats to the vital interests of the United States in the next 10 years. For each one, please tell me if you see this as a critical threat, an important but not critical threat, or not an important threat at all. The military power of Russia

■ % Critical threat

GALLUP

Another 41% currently view Russia's military power as an important, but not critical, threat, down from 49% last year. Seven percent do not consider Russia a threat, down from 17% in 2014.

Despite the increase in perceptions of Russia's military power as a critical threat, the issue still is rated well behind other international challenges such as terrorism generally, the ISIS group specifically, and Iran's development of nuclear weapons.

Favorable Ratings of Russia Tumble

Americans' basic views of Russia are the worst Gallup has measured in its 26-year trend, with 24% having favorable and 70% unfavorable views. Russia's favorable rating has declined 10 points in each of the last two years. Just three years ago, Americans' views of Russia were more positive than negative.

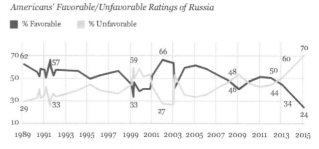

Americans' Favorable/Unfavorable Ratings of Russia
■ % Favorable   ■ % Unfavorable

Note: 1989-1992 wording: Soviet Union

GALLUP

Gallup's trend on ratings of Russia began as the Cold War was ending, and has fluctuated a great deal over its 26 years. For most of that time, Americans have been more positive than negative toward Russia. The major exceptions were during and shortly after the Kosovo situation in 1999, when the U.S. and Russia were at odds over the NATO-led bombing campaign against the Yugoslavians. That included the prior low point in Americans' views of Russia, a 33% favorable rating in April 1999.

Americans' views of Russia also turned more negative just before the start of the 2003 Iraq War, given Russia's opposition to the United States' planned military action, and again after the Russo-Georgian War in 2008. Shortly after coming into office in early 2009, the Obama administration tried to repair relations, with then Secretary of State Hillary Clinton famously giving her Russian counterpart the gift of a "reset button."

Americans' ratings of Russian President Vladimir Putin are even worse than their ratings of the country more generally, as 13% have a favorable and 72% an unfavorable view of Putin. Putin's favorable ratings are similar to what Gallup measured last March, but are down a bit from earlier readings in his second presidential administration, and well below what they were in his first administration from 2000 to 2008.

Implications

Recent U.S.-Russia foreign policy disagreements, including the situation in Ukraine, have taken a toll on U.S.-Russia relations as well as on Americans' opinions of Russia. Americans increasingly see Russia's military power as a threat to the United States, rate Russia the worst they have since the Cold War ended and are more likely to name Russia as the United States' greatest enemy over any other country, including long-standing U.S. foes such as North Korea and Iran.

The feeling appears to be mutual, given that a Gallup World Poll survey of Russians conducted from April to June 2014 found 4% of Russians approving and 82% disapproving of U.S. leadership.

However, because Americans' attitudes about Russia have changed substantially in the past and have been quite positive at times—which has not been the case for countries such as Iran, Iraq and North Korea—if Russian and American policy interests find more common ground, Americans' views of Russia could recover quickly.

Survey Methods

Results for this Gallup poll are based on telephone interviews conducted Feb. 8–11, 2015, with a random sample of 837 adults, aged 18 and older, living in all 50 U.S. states and the District of Columbia. For results based on the total sample of national adults, the margin of sampling error is ±4 percentage points at the 95% confidence level. All reported margins of sampling error include computed design effects for weighting.

February 17, 2015
FREQUENT CHURCH ATTENDANCE HIGHEST IN UTAH, LOWEST IN VERMONT

by Frank Newport

Story Highlights

- *51% of Utah residents attend church weekly, highest in U.S.*
- *Otherwise, highest states on this measure are mostly in South*

- *Lowest weekly attendance found in New England states*

PRINCETON, N.J.—Slightly more than half of Utah residents say they attend religious services every week, more than any other state in the union. Residents in the four Southern states of Mississippi, Alabama, Louisiana and Arkansas are the next most likely to be frequent church attendees, with 45% to 47% reporting weekly attendance. At the other end of the spectrum is Vermont, where 17% of residents say they attend religious services every week.

Top 10 States, Church Attendance		Bottom 10 States, Church Attendance	
States with highest weekly attendance		States with lowest weekly attendance	
	%		%
Utah	51	Vermont	17
Mississippi	47	New Hampshire	20
Alabama	46	Maine	20
Louisiana	46	Massachusetts	22
Arkansas	45	Washington	24
South Carolina	42	Oregon	24
Tennessee	42	Hawaii	25
Kentucky	41	Colorado	25
North Carolina	40	Connecticut	25
Georgia	39	Alaska	26
Texas	39		
Oklahoma	39		

Gallup Daily tracking
January-December 2014

GALLUP'

Gallup Daily tracking
January-December 2014

GALLUP'

These results are based on Gallup Daily tracking interviews throughout 2014 with 177,030 U.S. adults, and reflect those who say "at least once a week" when asked, "How often do you attend church, synagogue or mosque—at least once a week, almost every week, about once a month, seldom or never?" Church attendance self-reports are estimates, and may not reflect precise week in and week out attendance, but provide an important measure of the way in which Americans view their personal, underlying religiosity. In particular, the focus on the top category of "weekly" attendance yields a good indicator of the percentage of each state's population that is highly religious, and for whom religion is likely to be a significant factor in their daily lives.

Ten of the 12 states with the highest self-reported religious service attendance are in the South, along with Utah and Oklahoma. The strong religious culture in the South reflects a variety of factors, including history, cultural norms and the fact that these states have high Protestant and black populations—both of which are above average in their self-reported religious service attendance. Utah's No. 1 position on the list is a direct result of that state's 59% Mormon population, as Mormons have the highest religious service attendance of any major religious group in the U.S.

Five of the six New England states rank among the bottom 10 states for church attendance. Of these, Vermont, New Hampshire, Maine and Massachusetts have the lowest average attendance rates in the nation, with Connecticut not far behind. All other states in the bottom 10 are in the West, including the nation's three states that are as far as one can go in the northwest corner of the country—Alaska, Washington and Oregon. States with average religious service attendance tend to cluster in the middle of the country.

Implications

In his recent National Prayer Breakfast speech in Washington, D.C., President Barack Obama noted, "The United States is one of the most religious countries in the world—far more religious than most Western developed countries." This is certainly true as far as the nation's average religiosity is concerned, but the fact remains that within the U.S. there are stark geographic differences in religiosity. In some states of the union—Utah and Southern states—roughly half of residents report attending religious services weekly, while in others—mostly in the Northeast and the West—a fourth or less of residents attend weekly.

Weekly Religious Service Attendance, 2014

The state-by-state variations in church attendance are significant because attendance is a powerful indicator of underlying religiosity, which in turn is related to Americans' views on life, culture, society in general and politics. For most segments of U.S. society—blacks being the exception—those who are the most religious are also most likely to be Republican, which helps explain the significant relationship between states with the highest church attendance and those that are traditionally red states. Church attendance also provides ties that bind members to their communities, and research shows that at the individual level, those who are most religious have higher well-being than those who are less religious.

There is no definitive answer as to why residents in a state like Mississippi are so likely to be in church on Sundays, while residents in a state like Vermont are so unlikely. Some of the differences reflect the types of people who choose to live in these states, and some reflect the types of religion that are predominant in a given state. A good deal is related to the history, culture and norms that are found in a particular state. Whatever the underlying reasons, it is clear that the cultural practice of attendance at religious services is much more dominant in specific states and regions of the U.S. than it is in others.

Survey Methods

Results for this Gallup poll are based on telephone interviews conducted Jan. 2–Dec. 30, 2014, on the Gallup Daily tracking survey, with a random sample of 177,030 adults, aged 18 and older, living in all 50 U.S. states and the District of Columbia.

For results based on the total sample of national adults, the margin of sampling error is ±1 percentage point at the 95% confidence level.

Margins of error for individual states are no greater than ±6 percentage points and are ±3 percentage points in most states. All reported margins of sampling error include the computed design effects for weighting.

February 18, 2015
OBAMA APPROVAL ON ISSUES, FAVORABLE RATING UP

by Jeffrey M. Jones

PRINCETON, N.J.—Although still relatively low in an absolute sense, Americans' approval ratings of President Barack Obama's handling of the economy and foreign affairs are up significantly from last fall, to 43% and 36%, respectively. His ratings on these issues slumped last year, including a personal low of 31% for his handling of foreign affairs in November.

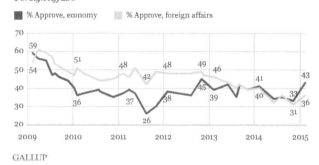

Approval Ratings of President Obama's Handling of the Economy and Foreign Affairs

The recent improvement in Obama's economy and foreign affairs approval ratings mirrors the trajectory of his overall job approval rating, which was 40% in Nov. 3–9 Gallup Daily tracking but was 47% in the latest weekly average, through Feb. 15. The increase has been aided by more positive economic news, including lower gas prices, which have boosted Americans' perceptions of the U.S. economy's health to the best they have been since the 2007–2009 recession.

The more positive economic news may also explain why his economic approval rating has increased more (up 10 percentage points) than his foreign affairs approval rating (up five points) since November. While the economy is getting better, Obama continues to deal with a challenging international environment, including the Ukraine conflict, the Islamic State's presence in Iraq and Syria, as well as the ongoing threats of international terrorism, the Israeli-Palestinian conflict, and North Korea and Iran. As a result, his foreign affairs rating remains on the low side relative to his 2009–2013 ratings.

Obama's economic approval ratings have not been above 50% since the honeymoon phase of his presidency in early 2009. As the economy continued to struggle through much of his presidency, his economic approval bottomed out at 26% in August 2011. It improved rather quickly to 45% by the time of his re-election in November 2012, but subsequently slumped again before the latest rebound.

Obama has been rated higher for his handling of foreign affairs than for his handling of the economy for much of his presidency, but that has changed since mid-2013 in the context of the economic progress and significant international challenges facing the U.S.

Obama's overall approval rating has also generally exceeded his approval for handling both the economy and foreign affairs. This has been the most common pattern for presidents, but there have been many exceptions.

Obama Favorable Rating Back Above 50%

Americans' more basic opinions of Obama—apart from their rating of the job he is doing—have also improved since the fall. Presidents' favorable ratings typically are higher than their job approval ratings. Currently, 51% of Americans say they have a favorable opinion of Obama, up from a personal low of 42% just after last fall's midterm elections. He was last at the 50% level in April 2014.

Personal Favorable Ratings of President Obama

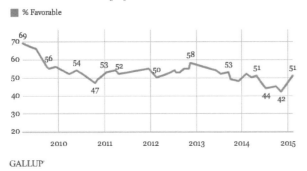

Obama was well liked in 2008, averaging a 61% favorable rating during the year he was first elected. Shortly before his inauguration in early January 2009, his favorable rating surged to 78%, and his first favorable rating as president was a still-healthy 69%. His favorable ratings, like his job approval ratings, began to slide late in his first year as president. However, his favorable ratings have mostly stayed above 50% since 2009, while his approval ratings have typically been lower than 50%.

Obama Favorable, Economic Approval Up Sharply Among Independents

Obama's issue approval and favorable ratings are up at least marginally since November among all party groups. However, independents show much greater increases than the other groups on Obama's economic approval (17 points) and his favorability (12 points). Democrats' ratings on those dimensions were already high to begin with, while Republicans' ratings were and continue to be extremely low.

On foreign affairs, each party group showed only a modest increase from November.

Implications

The 2014 midterms marked one of the lower points in Obama's presidency. This is true in terms of how the public evaluated him but also in the role those lower ratings played in the election outcomes, which gave the Republican Party control of both houses of Congress by healthy margins. Since then, Obama has enjoyed a bit of a comeback, as reflected in his overall approval ratings, his ratings for handling specific issues, and his personal favorable ratings. The improving economy has played a major part in that, as has his plan to use executive actions to address the legal status of millions of immigrants residing in the U.S. illegally. Although the status of those actions are uncertain pending legal challenges, the plan had a positive impact on the way Hispanics view him, and his support among Hispanics remains higher today.

If the economy continues to get better, and if the president can successfully address some of the key international challenges, his ratings may continue to improve. Indeed, his recent job approval ratings in Gallup Daily tracking have been about 50% since the Russia-Ukraine cease-fire agreement late last week.

Change in Ratings of President Obama, November 2014-February 2015, by Political Party

	November 2014 (%)	February 2015 (%)	Change (pct. pts.)
ECONOMIC APPROVAL			
Democrats	70	76	+6
Independents	24	41	+17
Republicans	9	11	+2
FOREIGN AFFAIRS APPROVAL			
Democrats	61	67	+6
Independents	27	29	+2
Republicans	7	12	+5
PERSONAL FAVORABLE RATING			
Democrats	85	86	+1
Independents	35	47	+12
Republicans	12	16	+4

GALLUP

Survey Methods

Results for this Gallup poll are based on telephone interviews conducted Feb. 8–11, 2015, with a random sample of 837 adults, aged 18 and older, living in all 50 U.S. states and the District of Columbia. For results based on the total sample of national adults, the margin of sampling error is ±4 percentage points at the 95% confidence level. All reported margins of sampling error include computed design effects for weighting.

February 18, 2015
MENTIONS OF TERRORISM RISE AS U.S. MOST IMPORTANT PROBLEM

by Rebecca Riffkin

Story Highlights

- *Eight percent of Americans say terrorism most important problem*
- *Highest percentage to name terrorism since January 2010*
- *Government, economy remain most commonly cited problems*

WASHINGTON, D.C.—The 8% of Americans currently naming terrorism as the most important problem facing the U.S. is up six percentage points since January—the highest percentage to mention the issue since January 2010.

The rise in mentions of terrorism this month comes after the *Charlie Hebdo* tragedy and more deaths of Western citizens held hostage by Islamic State militants—including American Kayla Mueller—in Iraq and Syria. It also follows President Barack Obama's request for Congress to authorize military force against the

Islamic State, also commonly known as ISIS, over the next three years.

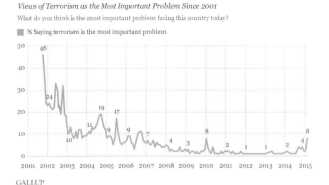

Views of Terrorism as the Most Important Problem Since 2001

What do you think is the most important problem facing this country today?

■ % Saying terrorism is the most important problem

GALLUP

Terrorism was the dominant issue for Americans after the 9/11 terror attacks, with 46% mentioning it in October 2001. This slowly dropped over the following weeks and months, and in February 2009, 3% named terrorism as the top problem. The only other time since then that terrorism showed the type of spike seen this month was in January 2010, a few weeks after a terrorist failed to detonate a bomb on a flight over Detroit.

Government and Economy Still Top Issues

Despite this uptick in mentions of terrorism, it is not the most frequently mentioned problem. Dissatisfaction with government (17%) and the economy (16%) continue to rank as the most commonly named issues. Mentions of healthcare, at 10%, are up five points from January, perhaps related to Americans' worry about the approaching deadline to sign up for health plans under the ACA legislation. More than 5% of Americans also mention unemployment and jobs, education, immigration and a moral/ethical decline.

Most likely related to the same events spurring a rise in mentions of terrorism, there have been modest increases in mentions of national security and the situation in Iraq/ISIS to 4% each.

Bottom Line

Terrorism and the influence of the Islamic State in the Middle East are on more Americans' minds this month, with increases in the percentage of Americans mentioning all of these problems as the most important facing the U.S. In fact, the cluster of issues including terrorism, the situation with ISIS and national security taken together would essentially tie dissatisfaction with government and the economy as the top overall issue.

Whether the heightened concern Americans have about terrorism persists will certainly depend on the amount and nature of terrorist activity affecting the U.S. and its allies in the coming weeks and months. The last American hostage held by the Islamic State was pronounced dead in early February. And recent attacks in Copenhagen are raising fears of home-grown terror attacks in Western Europe and the U.S.

Survey Methods

Results for this Gallup poll are based on telephone interviews conducted Feb. 8–11, 2015, a random sample of 837 adults, aged 18 and older, living in all 50 U.S. states and the District of Columbia. For results based on the total sample of national adults, the margin of sampling error is ±4 percentage points at the 95% confidence level. All reported margins of sampling error include computed design effects for weighting.

Most Commonly Named Problems in February 2015

What do you think is the most important problem facing this country today? [OPEN-ENDED]

	Jan-15	Feb-15
	%	%
Dissatisfaction with government	17	17
Economy in general	14	16
Healthcare	5	10
Unemployment/Jobs	7	9
Terrorism	2	8
Education	5	7
Immigration/Illegal aliens	8	6
Ethical/Moral/Family decline	6	6
Federal budget deficit/Federal debt	7	5
Poverty/Hunger/Homelessness	3	4
Situation in Iraq/ISIS	1	4
National security	2	4

Note: Issues mentioned by 3% or fewer not shown

GALLUP

February 18, 2015
ALASKA LEADS U.S. STATES IN WELL-BEING FOR FIRST TIME

by Dan Witters

Story Highlights

- *Hawaii and South Dakota round out top three well-being states*
- *West Virginia ranks last for the sixth straight year*
- *Hawaii and Colorado only states in top 10 every year since '08*

WASHINGTON, D.C.—Alaska residents had the highest well-being in the nation in 2014, reaching the top spot for the first time since Gallup and Healthways began tracking well-being in 2008. West Virginia and Kentucky rank 50th and 49th, respectively, for the sixth consecutive year. Hawaii and Colorado are on the top 10 list of highest well-being states for the seventh consecutive year.

Alaska rejoins the top five in 2014 after being among this elite group from 2009 to 2011, while Hawaii finished in the top two for the sixth time, improving from the eighth spot in 2013. North Dakota tumbled from the top spot in 2013 to 23rd in 2014. North Dakota's drop was mostly attributable to a drop in its residents' overall life evaluation, coupled with worsened health-related behaviors such as higher smoking rates, reduced exercise and less healthy eating compared with 2013.

All of the 10 lowest well-being states in 2014 have frequented this list in the past.

States With Highest Well-Being in 2014

State	Well-Being Index score
Alaska	64.7
Hawaii	64.5
South Dakota	64.3
Wyoming	63.9
Montana	63.7
Colorado	63.2
Nebraska	63.1
Utah	62.9
New Mexico	62.8
Texas	62.8

Gallup-Healthways Well-Being Index

GALLUP'

States With Lowest Well-Being in 2014

State	Well-Being Index score
West Virginia	59.0
Kentucky	59.8
Indiana	60.0
Ohio	60.1
Mississippi	60.2
Alabama	60.3
Tennessee	60.6
Arkansas	60.7
Michigan	60.7
Missouri	60.8

Gallup-Healthways Well-Being Index

GALLUP'

Well-Being Index by State, 2014

■ Top quintile well-being ■ 2ⁿᵈ quintile well-being ■ 3ʳᵈ quintile well-being
■ 4ᵗʰ quintile well-being ■ Bottom quintile well-being

Gallup · Healthways
Well-Being Index'

These state-level data are based on more than 176,000 interviews with U.S. adults across all 50 states, conducted from January to December 2014. The Well-Being Index is calculated on a scale of 0 to 100, where 0 represents the lowest possible well-being and 100 represents the highest possible well-being. The Gallup-Healthways Well-Being Index score for the nation and for each state consists of metrics affecting overall well-being and each of the five essential elements of well-being:

- **Purpose:** liking what you do each day and being motivated to achieve your goals
- **Social:** having supportive relationships and love in your life
- **Financial:** managing your economic life to reduce stress and increase security
- **Community:** liking where you live, feeling safe, and having pride in your community
- **Physical:** having good health and enough energy to get things done daily

Gallup and Healthways have been tracking well-being since 2008 and updated the Well-Being Index in 2014 to provide a more comprehensive measure of well-being. The Well-Being Index scores for 2014 are not directly comparable to the scores from prior years because they are calculated using the revised instrument and scoring methodology. However, state rankings for 2014 can be compared to rankings from previous years.

As in prior years, well-being in the U.S. exhibits regional patterns. The Northern Plains and Mountain West are higher well-being areas, along with some Western states and pockets of the Northeast and Atlantic. The lowest well-being states start in the South and move north through the industrial Midwest.

Hawaii, Colorado Lead All States With Most Top 10 Rankings

Hawaii and Colorado are the only two states to be in the top 10 for well-being every year since tracking began in 2008. In addition to these two states, 10 others have finished in the top 10 at least three times in the past seven years: Montana, Utah, Minnesota, Nebraska, North Dakota, Iowa, South Dakota, Alaska, Wyoming and Vermont.

Arkansas, Ohio, and Mississippi join West Virginia and Kentucky as the only states that have appeared among the lowest 10 well-being states in all seven years of tracking.

States With the Most Top 10 Finishes in Well-Being (2008-2014)

State	Top 10 finishes
Hawaii	7
Colorado	7
Montana	6
Utah	6
Minnesota	6
Nebraska	5
Alaska	4
North Dakota	4
Iowa	3
South Dakota	3
Vermont	3
Wyoming	3

Gallup-Healthways Well-Being Index

GALLUP'

States With the Most Bottom 10 Finishes in Well-Being (2008-2014)

State	Bottom 10 finishes
West Virginia	7
Mississippi	7
Arkansas	7
Ohio	7
Kentucky	7
Tennessee	6
Alabama	6
Louisiana	5
Indiana	4
Missouri	3
Michigan	3
Nevada	3

Gallup-Healthways Well-Being Index

GALLUP'

Hawaii and South Dakota Each Lead in Two of Five Elements of Well-Being

Alaskans, in addition to having the highest overall well-being, also had the highest ranking in purpose well-being across the nation. Hawaii (financial and physical) and South Dakota (social and community) each lead the nation in two elements of well-being.

West Virginia (purpose and physical) is the only state to rank last for more than one element in 2014.

States With the Highest and Lowest Well-Being in Each Element, 2014

Element	Highest well-being state	Lowest well-being state
Purpose	Alaska	West Virginia
Social	South Dakota	Rhode Island
Financial	Hawaii	Mississippi
Community	South Dakota	Illinois
Physical	Hawaii	West Virginia

Gallup-Healthways Well-Being Index

GALLUP'

Implications

Improving and sustaining high well-being is vital to any population's overall health and economy. Previous Gallup and Healthways research shows that high well-being closely relates to key health outcomes such as lower rates of healthcare utilization, workplace absenteeism and workplace performance, change in obesity status and new onset disease burden. Well-being is also a predictor of business outcomes such as employee engagement, customer engagement, turnover and workplace safety, which can affect a population's ability to reach its economic potential.

High well-being is also strongly related to important societal outcomes such as lower rates of teen pregnancy and crime, as well as higher high school graduation rates and more charitable giving.

Nationally, many aspects of well-being have improved in 2014 to their best levels since measurement began in 2008. For example, life evaluation, which is a key outcome of well-being and a high-level measure of how people think about and evaluate their lives, reached its highest recorded point in the U.S. in 2014. The rate of uninsured Americans fell to a low of 12.9% in the fourth quarter of 2014, indicating that millions of previously uninsured Americans now have insurance. And the Gallup Standard of Living Index reached a seven-year high of +50 by the end of 2014.

Other U.S. metrics point in the opposite direction. Obesity, for example, reached its highest point in 2014, climbing to 27.7%, and is now two full percentage points higher than in 2008. The rise in obesity coupled with improving metrics elsewhere illustrates the need for measuring well-being comprehensively, rather than focusing on one or two aspects.

Regardless of national trends, states' efforts to improve well-being should be customized to meet the needs of city and rural populations alike, always mindful of unique state subcultures. States and local communities can use well-being concepts and the five elements as focal points in designing and implementing initiatives to improve well-being. For example, Blue Zones Project initiatives in California, Minnesota, Iowa, Texas and Hawaii involve multifaceted programs and community actions aimed at improving many aspects of well-being. Specific interventions include working with schools, employers, grocery stores and restaurants to foster healthier choices. Other initiatives include working with governmental and other agencies to enact changes that increase opportunities for healthier lifestyles and community life, such as more walkable and bike-friendly environments, farmer's markets and social activities. But perhaps the most important aspect of a successful program is a strong, uniform and sustained voice from governmental and organizational leadership, which can play a pivotal role in providing the foundation upon which a culture of well-being can be built.

Survey Methods

Results are based on telephone interviews conducted Jan. 2–Dec. 30, 2014, as a part of the Gallup-Healthways Well-Being Index, with a random sample of 176,702 adults, aged 18 and older, living in all 50 U.S. states and the District of Columbia. For results based on the total sample of national adults, the margin of sampling error for the Well-Being Index score is ±0.1 percentage points at the 95% confidence level. The margin of sampling error for most states is about ±0.6 percentage points, although this increases to about ±1.6 points for the smallest-population states such as North Dakota, Wyoming, Hawaii and Delaware. All reported margins of sampling error include computed design effects for weighting.

February 19, 2015
AMERICANS' OPINION OF CUBA HIGHEST IN NEARLY 20 YEARS

by Art Swift

Story Highlights

- *Obama process to normalize relations likely reason for improvement*
- *Equal percentages in U.S. favor ending travel ban, trade embargo*
- *Americans have consistently favored having diplomatic relations*

WASHINGTON, D.C.—As President Barack Obama and his administration work to normalize diplomatic relations with Cuba and loosen travel restrictions between the two countries for the first time in 53 years, Americans now view Cuba more favorably than they have in nearly 20 years. Forty-six percent say they have a favorable opinion of Cuba, up eight percentage points from last year, and a far cry from the 10% favorability rating in 1996.

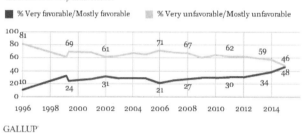

Americans' Opinion of Cuba

What is your overall opinion of Cuba? Is it very favorable, mostly favorable, mostly unfavorable or very unfavorable?

■ % Very favorable/Mostly favorable   ▓ % Very unfavorable/Mostly unfavorable

GALLUP

The percentage of Americans viewing Cuba favorably has been mostly in the 20% to 30% range since 1996. This survey is the first time Gallup has asked Americans for their opinion of Cuba since Obama announced in December that he is working to re-establish diplomatic ties with the communist country. That announcement is presumably the chief reason for the surge in positive feelings toward Cuba, with the president's action probably making it more acceptable to like Cuba.

Policy agreements or disagreements between the U.S. and a country often can affect Americans' favorability ratings of that country. Russia is one example. A longtime Cold War foe, Americans' favorability ratings of Russia soared after the Soviet Union dissolved, but they have soured since the conflict with neighboring Ukraine. France is another. Americans viewed the longtime ally in a highly favorable light for many years until France failed to support the U.S.-led Iraq war in 2003. A decade after the debacle over "freedom fries," though, Americans' favorability toward France has returned to levels seen in the 1990s and before the Iraq war.

Americans' Interest in Re-Establishing Diplomatic Relations With Cuba Strong

While Americans have not always viewed Cuba favorably, they have consistently wanted to re-establish diplomatic ties with the island, severed in 1961 after the U.S. objected to the revolutionary regime led by Fidel Castro.

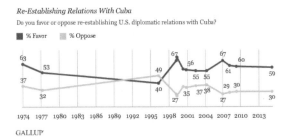

Re-Establishing Relations With Cuba

Do you favor or oppose re-establishing U.S. diplomatic relations with Cuba?

■ % Favor   ▨ % Oppose

GALLUP

The majority of Americans have favored re-establishing diplomatic ties for more than 40 years, with one notable exception. After the U.S. Congress passed the Helms-Burton Act in 1996, tightening the embargo on Cuba, support for reinstating diplomatic relations dropped to 40%. It rebounded, though, by 1999 when it peaked around 70%, and has remained above the majority level ever since.

Americans Want to End Trade Embargo With Cuba

The trade embargo, which was concurrent with the U.S. breaking off ties with Cuba, is another aspect of the relationship that Americans would like to see changed. In Gallup's most recent survey, 59% of Americans said they favor the U.S. government ending its more than 50-year trade embargo with Cuba.

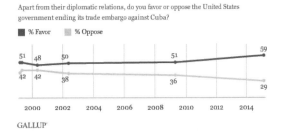

U.S. Trade Embargo With Cuba

Apart from their diplomatic relations, do you favor or oppose the United States government ending its trade embargo against Cuba?

■ % Favor   ▨ % Oppose

GALLUP

This is the highest Gallup has measured since it began asking this specific question in 1999. This support aligns with the other positive views Americans have toward Cuba. Experts say it could be a long time before the U.S. lifts its trade embargo against Cuba, but currently there are bills in Congress with bipartisan support to make the end of the embargo a reality.

Ending Travel Restrictions to Cuba Favored by 59% of Americans

While analysts have said ending the trade embargo may be a long process, there appears to be more momentum in Congress to lift the travel ban to the country. An equal percentage of Americans (59%) support ending of travel ban as do ending the trade embargo.

Bottom Line

Americans are very positive toward Cuba right now and give the island nation the highest favorable rating in 20 years, although still slightly more view Cuba unfavorably than favorably. Americans support re-establishing diplomatic ties with Cuba, ending the trade embargo and ending travel restrictions to the island. Americans' favorable ratings of a country are often motivated by developments regarding that country, and as there appears to be momentum in Congress to change at least some policy initiatives to re-establish diplomatic ties with Cuba, U.S. adults' positive feelings toward the country could continue for some time.

Americans Traveling to Cuba

Apart from their diplomatic relations, do you favor or oppose the United States government ending its restrictions on Americans traveling to Cuba?

	% Favor	% Oppose
Feb 14-15, 2015	59	30
Apr 20-21, 2009	64	27

GALLUP

Survey Methods

Favorable ratings of Cuba are based on telephone interviews conducted in a Feb. 8–11, 2015, Gallup poll with a random sample of 837 adults, aged 18 and older, living in all 50 U.S. states and the District of Columbia. For results based on the total sample of national adults, the margin of sampling error is ±4 percentage points at the 95% confidence level.

Opinions on U.S. policy toward Cuba are based on telephone interviews conducted Feb. 14–15, 2015, on the Gallup U.S. Daily survey, with a random sample of 1,016 adults, aged 18 and older, living in all 50 U.S. states and the District of Columbia. For results based on the total sample of national adults, the margin of sampling error is ±4 percentage points at the 95% confidence level. For results based on the half-samples of 513 national adults in Form 1 and 503 national adults in Form 2, the maximum margin of sampling error is ±5 percentage points.

February 20, 2015
SLIGHTLY MORE AMERICANS SAY U.S. IS NO. 1 MILITARY POWER

by Andrew Dugan

Story Highlights

- *Fifty-nine percent hold this view, up from 53% in 2014*
- *Older less likely than younger adults to say U.S. is top military power*
- *Nearly seven in 10 say it is important for U.S. to be No. 1 militarily*

WASHINGTON, D.C.—As the U.S. military takes on an active role in the fight against the Islamic State group, slightly more Americans, 59%, say the U.S. is the No. 1 military power in the world. This is up six percentage points from February 2014, before the U.S. military became involved in the fight against the Islamic State group, also known as ISIS. Fewer Americans (38%) now say the U.S. is only one of several leading military powers, down from 44% a year ago.

These results come from Gallup's annual World Affairs poll, conducted Feb. 8–11, 2015. The U.S. military has expanded its operations significantly since this time last year, regularly conducting air strikes in Iraq and Syria in an effort to root out Islamic extremists. Additionally, the U.S. now provides military training to anti-government rebels in Syria and the prospect of sending military aid to the besieged Ukrainian government looms large. The U.S. military also played a crucial role in helping countries in West Africa battle the deadly Ebola virus outbreak.

Americans' Views on How U.S. Military Ranks

Do you think the United States is No. 1 in the world militarily, or that it is only one of several leading military powers?

■ % U.S. is No. 1   ▨ % U.S. is one of several leading powers

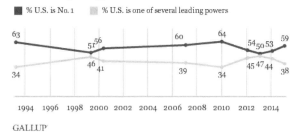

GALLUP

This expanded workload for the U.S. military may be driving the uptick in the percentage of Americans who say the U.S. military is the top in the world, rather than one of several competing powers. While a majority of Americans have said the U.S. has the world's top military power since this question was first asked in 1993, the percentage who say this remains below the high of 64% recorded in 2010. In the following years, as the U.S. continued to withdraw troops from a long-term engagement in Iraq and Afghanistan, smaller percentages of Americans said the U.S. was No. 1 militarily.

Older Americans Less Likely Than Young to Say U.S. Is No. 1 Militarily

Older Americans are less likely than their younger counterparts to say the U.S. is No. 1 militarily. A slim majority of U.S. adults aged 50 and older (54%) say the U.S. is top militarily, well below the 64% of Americans younger than 50 who say the same. Older adults are more likely to have clearer memories of the Cold War and the military prestige the U.S. enjoyed after the fall of the Soviet Union. As such, these older Americans may be more likely to feel that U.S. military power is not as strong now as it was then.

U.S. Views on Stength of U.S. Military, by Age

Do you think the United States is No. 1 in the world militarily, or that it is only one of several leading military powers?

	Aged 18 to 49	Aged 50 and older
U.S. is No. 1	64%	54%
U.S. is one of several leading powers	34%	43%

Feb. 8-11, 2015

GALLUP

Strong Majority Says It Is Important for U.S. Military to Be No. 1

About two-thirds of U.S. adults (68%) say it is important for the U.S. to be No. 1 in the world militarily, up six points from two years ago. Overall, Americans have consistently said it is important for the U.S. military to be No. 1 in the world over the past two decades, emphasizing the importance most Americans place on their country's military preponderance.

Bottom Line

As the U.S. military takes a more active role on the world stage relative to the past few years, more Americans believe their military

is superior. While the U.S. identity has many facets—its inventive economy, democratic tradition and history of being a "melting pot"—America's formidable military has been an important source of national pride. Even after two unpopular military engagements in Iraq and Afghanistan, most Americans continue to see the military power of the U.S. as an important component of the country's global standing.

Importance of the U.S. to Be No. 1 in the World Militarily

Do you feel that it's important for the United States to be No. 1 in the world militarily, or that being No. 1 is not that important, as long as the U.S. is among the leading military powers?

■ % Important   ▨ % Not that important

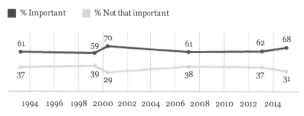

GALLUP

Survey Methods

Results for this Gallup poll are based on telephone interviews conducted Feb. 8–11, 2015, with a random sample of 837 adults, aged 18 and older, living in all 50 U.S. states and the District of Columbia. For results based on the total sample of national adults, the margin of sampling error is ±4 percentage points at the 95% confidence level. All reported margins of sampling error include computed design effects for weighting.

February 20, 2015
AMERICANS SPLIT ON DEFENSE SPENDING

by Justin McCarthy

Story Highlights

- *One in three Americans say U.S. is spending "too little"*
- *Another third of Americans think U.S. is spending "too much"*
- *More Americans now say U.S. military is "not strong enough"*

WASHINGTON, D.C.—For the past decade, Americans have been more likely to say the U.S. government spends too much on defense rather than too little, but today, a slim margin separates these views. While the 32% of Americans saying the country is spending too much is about average for recent years, the 34% saying "too little" is the highest since 2001.

These findings from Gallup's Feb. 8–11 World Affairs poll come as both President Barack Obama and congressional Republicans are seeking to increase defense spending amid threats from the Islamic State, but are not in agreement on how to fund the increases. The U.S. has long held the distinction of having the largest military budget of any nation, and the 2014 budget nearly matched the spending of the 10 next-largest national military budgets. Twenty-nine percent of Americans feel the U.S. budget's size is "about right."

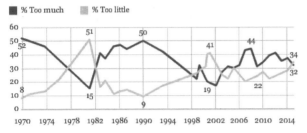

Americans' Views of National Defense and Military Spending

There is much discussion as to the amount of money the government in Washington should spend for national defense and military purposes. How do you feel about this? Do you think we are spending too little, about the right amount, or too much?

■ % Too much ■ % Too little

Note: "About the right amount" not represented on graph

GALLUP

The latest figures show the closest margin between "too much" and "too little" in 10 years, and a shift from last year, when there was a nine-percentage-point margin in the direction of "too much" spending. Americans' views on the size of the defense budget have fluctuated greatly over time, but the public has generally been more likely to say the government spends too much. As many as 50% or more shared this view in the Vietnam War era of the late 1960s and early 1970s, as well as in 1990, after the end of the Cold War and a long military buildup under President Ronald Reagan.

There have been a few times in Gallup's 46-year trend when Americans thought there was too little rather than too much spending on defense. These include 2000–2002, spanning the end of the Clinton administration and the 9/11 terrorist attacks, and January 1981—just months after the nation elected Reagan, who made U.S. military weakness a major theme of his presidential campaign. Over the course of Reagan's administration, he oversaw a 35% increase in military spending.

All Parties Show Increase in Percentage Saying U.S. Spends "Too Little"

Since 2011, the belief that the U.S. is spending too little on defense has grown within each party group, but more so among Republicans (16 points) and independents (12 points) than Democrats (eight points).

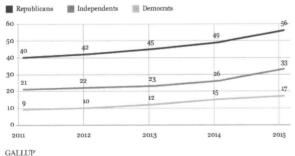

Views of Amount of U.S. Government Defense Spending, by Political Party, 2011-2015
% Who say spending is "too little"

■ Republicans ■ Independents ■ Democrats

GALLUP

More than half of Republicans (56%) today believe the U.S. is spending too little on the military—far more than is true among independents (33%) and Democrats (17%). Gallup has historically found this to be the case when it comes to military spending.

More Americans Now Say Military "Not Strong Enough"

A separate question in the poll asked Americans to assess the U.S. military's strength. Forty-four percent say it is "not strong enough," while 42% say it is "about right" and another 13% believe it is "stronger than it needs to be."

Those views have changed significantly from 2012, when Gallup last asked the question. At that time, a much smaller 32% said U.S. national defense was not strong enough, with 54% believing it was about right.

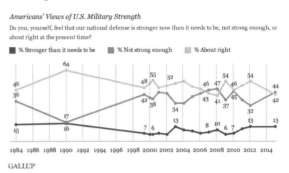

Americans' Views of U.S. Military Strength

Do you, yourself, feel that our national defense is stronger now than it needs to be, not strong enough, or about right at the present time?

■ % Stronger than it needs to be ■ % Not strong enough ■ % About right

GALLUP

Bottom Line

Having witnessed multipronged international turmoil throughout the past year—particularly from the Islamic State—Obama and the GOP-controlled Congress may be able to find some common ground on increases in military spending, which would have the support of a growing number of Americans.

Last month, Gallup found Americans were generally satisfied with U.S. military strength, but their level of satisfaction is down from the past two years and well below where it was after 9/11 and in the early stages of the Iraq War. Combined with the February increase in the percentage saying the U.S. military is not strong enough, public opinion seems to favor increases in defense spending.

Though the White House and congressional Republicans may struggle to agree on how big these increases should be and how they are funded, they can each lean on growing support for an increase within their respective parties.

Survey Methods

Results for this Gallup poll are based on telephone interviews conducted Feb. 8–11, 2015, on the Gallup U.S. Daily survey, with a random sample of 837 adults, aged 18 and older, living in all 50 U.S. states and the District of Columbia. For results based on the total sample of national adults, the margin of sampling error is ±4 percentage points at the 95% confidence level. All reported margins of sampling error include computed design effects for weighting.

February 23, 2015
SEVEN IN 10 AMERICANS CONTINUE TO VIEW ISRAEL FAVORABLY

by Lydia Saad

PRINCETON, N.J.—Even as relations between the leaders of Israel and the United States reportedly deteriorate over disagreement about how to handle Iran's nuclear program, Israel has retained its broadly favorable image in the U.S. over the past year. Seventy percent of Americans now view that country favorably, and 62% say they sympathize more with the Israelis than the Palestinians in the Mideast conflict. By contrast, 17% currently view the Palestinian Authority favorably, and 16% sympathize more with the Palestinians.

Americans' Recent Perceptions of the Israelis and the Palestinians

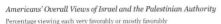

	February 2014	February 2015
	%	%
RATE VERY/MOSTLY FAVORABLY		
Israel	72	70
Palestinian Authority	19	17
SYMPATHIES IN MIDEAST SITUATION		
More with the Israelis	62	62
More with the Palestinians	18	16

GALLUP

These attitudes, from Gallup's Feb. 8–11 World Affairs survey, are unchanged from a year ago, suggesting that neither the evident friction between President Barack Obama and Israeli Prime Minister Benjamin Netanyahu, nor the 50-day conflict between the Israelis and Palestinians in the Hamas-controlled Gaza Strip last year, greatly affected how each is perceived in the U.S.

In fact, Israel's public image in the U.S. has been fairly strong since 2005, with an average 68% of Americans viewing it favorably. But from 2000 to 2004, when hostilities between Israel and the Palestinians were running high, its favorable score averaged 60%. Prior to that, Israel's favorable rating was even more volatile, reflecting other Mideast events, including the 1991 Gulf War, when positive views of Israel soared after that country suffered Iraqi rocket attacks.

Gallup first measured Americans' impression of the Palestinian Authority, the official governing body of the Palestinians, in 2000, and since then, the percentage viewing it favorably has averaged 17%, diverging significantly on only a few occasions. One of these came in 2005, when favorable opinion of the Palestinians increased in polling conducted shortly after Mahmoud Abbas was elected to succeed Yasser Arafat as Palestinian president.

Americans' Overall Views of Israel and the Palestinian Authority
Percentage viewing each very favorably or mostly favorably

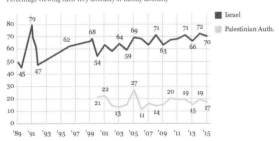

Asked to Choose Sides, Six in 10 Americans Favor Israelis

Americans' tendency to sympathize more with the Israelis than the Palestinians in their regional conflict also peaked in 1991 during the Gulf War, then fell in 1993 as President Bill Clinton led intense Israeli-Palestinian peace talks and more Americans favored

both sides or neither side. Americans remained largely neutral through 2001, spanning several more peace initiatives, when the 9/11 attacks—as well as years of failed peace talks that yielded to heightened Palestinian-Israeli violence—may have fundamentally changed their outlook toward the Middle East. Since 2004, Israel has consistently received the majority share of Americans' sympathies.

Americans' Sympathies in Mideast Conflict
In the Middle East situation, are your sympathies more with the Israelis or more with the Palestinians?

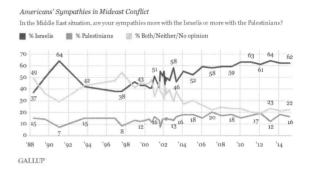

GALLUP

Republicans Nearly Unanimous in Support of Israel

A key reason Americans' sympathy for Israel has solidified at a sizable majority level is that Republicans' support for the Jewish state has increased considerably, rising from 53% in 2000 to more than 80% since 2014—with just 7% choosing the Palestinian Authority. A particularly large jump in GOP sympathy for Israel occurred in the first few years after 9/11 and at the start of the 2003 Iraq War.

Democrats' support for Israel has also risen since 2000, but not quite as sharply as Republicans'. Additionally, the percentage of Democrats sympathizing with Israel fell 10 points this year to 48%, possibly reflecting the tension between Obama and Netanyahu.

Percentage Sympathizing More With the Israelis Than the Palestinians in Mideast Situation
by Party ID

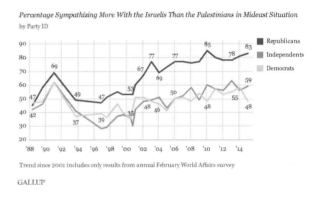

Trend since 2001 includes only results from annual February World Affairs survey

GALLUP

Bottom Line

U.S.-Israel relations have been much in the news over the past year, and tension between Obama and Netanyahu has reportedly worsened since the latter accepted House Speaker John Boehner's invitation to address Congress about Iran this spring—an offer the White House did not sanction. Meanwhile, Israel and the United States share a strong interest in seeing the international terrorist organization known as the Islamic State group, or ISIS, thwarted. Throughout all of this, Israel's positive image in the U.S. remains broadly intact nationally, even as Democrats' sympathy for Israel may have slipped. The percentage of Democrats viewing Israel favorably is also down, currently at 60%, versus 74% a year ago. Positive views of the Palestinian Authority are fairly scarce, but no lower than they have been in recent years.

Survey Methods

Results for this Gallup poll are based on telephone interviews conducted Feb. 8–11, 2015, with a random sample of 837 adults, aged 18 and older, living in all 50 U.S. states and the District of Columbia. For results based on the total sample of national adults, the margin of sampling error is ±4 percentage points at the 95% confidence level.

February 23, 2015

AMERICANS' RATINGS OF NORTH KOREA REMAIN HIGHLY NEGATIVE

by Justin McCarthy

Story Highlights

- *N. Korea the least favorable country for second year in a row*
- *Fifteen percent of Americans say N. Korea the "greatest enemy"*
- *Most Americans perceive the state's military as critical threat*

WASHINGTON, D.C.—Americans' ratings of North Korea remain highly negative, with 9% rating the country favorably and 87% rating it unfavorably. North Korea has consistently ranked among the lowest-rated nations in Gallup's annual rankings for the past decade.

Americans' Favorability Rating of North Korea Since 2000

Next, I'd like your overall opinion of some foreign countries. What is your overall opinion of North Korea? Is it very favorable, mostly favorable, mostly unfavorable or very unfavorable?

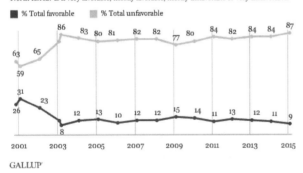

These latest data come from Gallup's Feb. 8–11 World Affairs poll. Like last year's poll, Iran's favorability (11%) was only slightly higher than North Korea's. The two nations have shared the bottom two spots in 10 of the last 11 times Gallup has ranked nations according to Americans' favorability ratings.

Americans' current favorability ratings come as the U.S. National Security Agency definitively identified North Korea as being behind a high-profile cyberattack on Sony Pictures Entertainment in late 2014. The country has also been accused of increasing the number of workers it sends abroad while seizing their wages in an effort to earn money amid economic sanctions from the international community.

This bad publicity has clearly reinforced 12 years of already negative attitudes toward North Korea rather than causing any major shift in opinions. In Gallup surveys conducted in 2000 and 2001, North Korea's favorability ratings were at their height, at 26% and

31%, respectively. A sharp drop in 2002 coincided with then President George W. Bush's naming of the country in his State of the Union address as part of an "axis of evil." Americans' favorability of the country fell to a low of 8% in March 2003 and has not rebounded since.

Not surprisingly given its low favorable ratings, North Korea also ranks high when Americans are asked to name the country they perceive to be the United States' greatest enemy. This year, 15% named North Korea, only slightly behind Russia at 18%.

What one country anywhere in the world do you consider to be the United States' greatest enemy today? [OPEN-ENDED]

Recent trend

	2011	2012	2014	2015
	%	%	%	%
Russia	3	2	9	18
North Korea/Korea (nonspecific)	16	10	16	15
China	16	23	20	12
Iran	25	32	16	9
Iraq	7	5	7	8
Countries in which ISIS operates	–	–	–	4
Middle East (nonspecific)	–	–	2	4
Syria	–	*	3	4
Afghanistan	9	7	5	3
United States itself	2	1	2	2
Japan	*	1	*	1
Saudi Arabia	1	1	1	1
Pakistan	2	2	1	*
Other	9	3	7	7
None/No opinion	10	12	11	13

*Less than 0.5%

GALLUP'

Most Americans Still View North Korean Military as Threat Under Kim Jong Un

Having taken rule in Pyongyang, North Korea, upon the death of his father, Kim Jong Il, in 2011, Kim Jong Un's leadership has not changed Americans' views of North Korea's military power.

While the elder Kim was in power in 2010, 61% of Americans viewed North Korean military power as a critical threat to the vital interests of the U.S. Not much has changed under the younger Kim in the latest poll, which found 64% Americans seeing the state's military as a critical threat. About one in four Americans (26%) view the military in North Korea as an "important, but not critical" threat, similar to the 29% who said so in 2010.

Americans' Views of North Korean Military Power as Critical Threat

Next, I am going to read you a list of possible threats to the vital interests of the U.S. in the next 10 years. For each one, please tell me if you see this as a critical threat, an important but not critical threat or not an important threat at all.

	% Critical	% Important	% Not important
Feb 8-11, 2015	64	26	9
Feb 1-3, 2010	61	29	8

GALLUP'

Bottom Line

Given the consistently low favorability ratings North Korea has received for more than a decade, Americans' negativity is likely to persist unless there is a dramatic change in North Korea's policies. The recent change in the nation's leadership has not brought about a change so far in the human rights violations and antagonistic actions the country has taken toward the U.S. and other nations. In addition, Pyongyang hasn't budged as a result of international sanctions and continues to invest heavily in the state's military and nuclear capabilities.

Survey Methods

Results for this Gallup poll are based on telephone interviews conducted Feb. 8–11, 2015, on the Gallup U.S. Daily survey, with a random sample of 837 adults, aged 18 and older, living in all 50 U.S. states and the District of Columbia. For results based on the total sample of national adults, the margin of sampling error is ±4 percentage points at the 95% confidence level. All reported margins of sampling error include computed design effects for weighting.

February 24, 2015
ARKANSAS, KENTUCKY SEE MOST IMPROVEMENT IN UNINSURED RATES

by Dan Witters

Story Highlights

- *Medicaid expansion, state exchanges linked to greater reductions*
- *No state reported a statistically significant increase in uninsured*
- *Nationwide, full-year uninsured rate drops 3.5 points from 2013 to 2014*

WASHINGTON, D.C.—Arkansas and Kentucky reported the sharpest reductions in their uninsured rates among adult residents since the healthcare law's requirement to have insurance took effect at the beginning of 2014. Oregon, Washington and West Virginia round out the top five. Of the 11 states with the greatest reductions, 10 expanded Medicaid and established a state-based marketplace exchange or state-federal partnership. Montana, which is tied for 10th, is the only exception.

Nationwide, the uninsured rate dropped 3.5 percentage points last year, from 17.3% to 13.8%, the lowest annualized rate across the seven years of Well-Being Index measurement. No state reported a statistically significant increase in the percentage of uninsured in 2014 compared with 2013.

These data, collected as part of the Gallup-Healthways Well-Being Index, are based on respondents' answers to the question, "Do you have health insurance coverage?" These state-level data are based on daily surveys conducted from January through December 2014 and include samples sizes that range from 465 randomly selected adult residents in North Dakota to nearly 17,000 in California.

States With Largest Reductions in Percentage Uninsured, 2013 vs. 2014
"Do you have health insurance coverage?" (% No)

	% Uninsured, 2013	% Uninsured, 2014	Change in uninsured (pct. pts.)	Medicaid expansion AND state exchange/ partnership in 2014
Arkansas	22.5	11.4	-11.1	Yes
Kentucky	20.4	9.8	-10.6	Yes
Oregon	19.4	11.7	-7.7	Yes
Washington	16.8	10.1	-6.7	Yes
West Virginia	17.6	10.9	-6.7	Yes
California	21.6	15.3	-6.3	Yes
Connecticut	12.3	6.0	-6.3	Yes
Colorado	17.0	11.2	-5.8	Yes
Maryland	12.9	7.8	-5.1	Yes
Montana	20.7	15.8	-4.9	No
New Mexico	20.2	15.3	-4.9	Yes

Gallup-Healthways Well-Being Index

GALLUP'

States Embracing Multiple Parts of Health Law Continue to See More Improvement

Collectively, the uninsured rate in states that have chosen to expand Medicaid *and* set up their own state exchanges or partnerships in the health insurance marketplace declined significantly more last year than the rate in states that did not take these steps. The uninsured rate declined 4.8 points in the 21 states that implemented both of these measures, compared with a 2.7-point drop across the 29 states that have implemented only one or neither of these actions.

Change in Uninsured Rate Among States With Medicaid Expansion AND State Exchanges/Partnerships Compared With All Others

	% Uninsured, 2013	% Uninsured, 2014	Change in uninsured (pct. pts.)
States with Medicaid expansion AND state exchanges/partnerships	16.1	11.3	-4.8
States with only one or neither	18.7	16.0	-2.7

Gallup-Healthways Well-Being Index

GALLUP'

Massachusetts Maintains Lowest Uninsured Rate in U.S., Texas the Highest

Overall, Massachusetts has the lowest uninsured rate in the nation for the seventh consecutive year, at 4.6%, followed by 6.0% uninsured in Connecticut and Hawaii. Massachusetts's plan is based on the "Romneycare" model, from which certain aspects of the Affordable Care Act were drawn. The Massachusetts healthcare law, originally passed in 2006, has undergone modifications to accommodate details of the federal law, but maintains its core element mandating that nearly all residents must obtain a minimum level of insurance coverage.

Also for the seventh consecutive year, Texas has the highest uninsured rate at 24.4%, although this percentage is lower than the 27.0% reported in 2013 and is the lowest rate measured to date for Texas.

States with the lowest uninsured rates continue to cluster in the East and upper Midwest. Uninsured rates are highest in the South and the West.

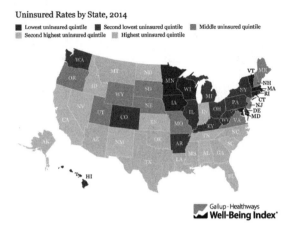

Uninsured Rates by State, 2014

Lowest uninsured quintile ▪ Second lowest uninsured quintile ▪ Middle uninsured quintile
Second highest uninsured quintile ▪ Highest uninsured quintile

Gallup · Healthways
Well-Being Index

Implications

While a majority of Americans continue to disapprove of the Affordable Care Act, it has clearly had an impact in reducing the uninsured rate in the U.S., which declined to its lowest point in seven years by the last quarter of 2014. This trend could be poised to continue, as 55% of Americans who remain uninsured plan to get health insurance rather than pay a fine.

States that have implemented two of the law's core mechanisms—Medicaid expansion and state health exchanges—are seeing a substantially larger drop in the uninsured rate than states that did not take both of these actions. Consequently, the gap in uninsured rates that existed between these two groups in 2013 nearly doubled in 2014.

Many states continue to debate implementing these actions. In addition to New Hampshire last August, Indiana and Pennsylvania both enacted Medicaid expansion in 2015, becoming the 27th and 28th states (plus the District of Columbia) to expand Medicaid. Utah Gov. Gary Herbert continues negotiations with the Centers for Medicare and Medicaid Services to have a plan with revised, more flexible terms than what is detailed in the Affordable Care Act, currently known as the Healthy Utah plan.

Change Analysis Rules

Some states have chosen to implement state-federal "partnership" exchanges, where states manage certain functions and make key decisions based on local market and demographic conditions. For the purposes of this analysis, these partnerships are included with the state exchanges. States with Medicaid expansion that occurred after the midyear point in 2014 were excluded from the "States With Medicaid Expansion and State Exchange/Partnerships" group. For example, New Hampshire, which manages a state-based exchange but did not enact Medicaid expansion until Aug. 15, 2014, is excluded. Michigan, in turn, is included as it manages a state-based exchange and enacted Medicaid expansion effective April 1, 2014. Four states—North Dakota, New Jersey, Ohio and Arizona—decided to expand Medicaid without also administering a state-based exchange or partnership, while several others continue to debate expansion. Pennsylvania enacted Medicaid expansion effective Jan. 1, 2015, and Indiana will do so on Feb. 1. The District

of Columbia, which has expanded Medicaid and has implemented a locally managed exchange, is not included in this analysis.

Survey Methods

Results are based on telephone interviews conducted Jan. 2–Dec. 30, 2013, and Jan. 2–Dec. 30, 2014, as part of the Gallup-Healthways Well-Being Index, with a random sample of 178,072 adults in 2013 and 176,702 adults in 2014, aged 18 and older, living in all 50 U.S. states and the District of Columbia. The margin of sampling error is ±1 to ±2 percentage points for most states, but is close to ±4 percentage points for states with small populations such as North Dakota, Wyoming, Vermont and Alaska. All reported margins of sampling error include computed design effects for weighting.

February 24, 2015
AMERICANS CLOSELY SPLIT OVER PALESTINIAN STATEHOOD

by Lydia Saad

Story Highlights

- *Forty-two percent in U.S. favor a Palestinian state, 38% oppose*
- *Support at lowest point since 2000*
- *Postgrads, liberals and Democrats show the highest support*

PRINCETON, N.J.—Forty-two percent of Americans favor the establishment of an independent Palestinian state comprising the West Bank and Gaza Strip. This is down slightly from 46% a year ago and among the lowest support levels Gallup has recorded since 2000. Nearly as many Americans, 38%, oppose Palestinian statehood, while 20% have no opinion on the issue.

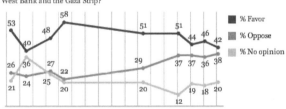

Americans' Support for an Independent Palestinian State

Do you favor or oppose the establishment of an independent Palestinian state on the West Bank and the Gaza Strip?

■ % Favor
■ % Oppose
■ % No opinion

'99 '00 '01 '02 '03 '04 '05 '06 '07 '08 '09 '10 '11 '12 '13 '14 '15

GALLUP

Most demographic subgroups of Americans—men, women, whites, nonwhites and various age groups—are more likely to support than oppose the creation of an independent Palestinian state. However, older Americans buck this pattern, with 43% of those aged 55 and older opposed to it and 41% in favor.

Even greater differences are seen by educational background. Americans with higher levels of education are more likely than those further down the educational ladder to favor Palestinian statehood, and are less likely to say they have no opinion on the matter. Also, Americans with any college background are less likely to oppose statehood than those with no college experience.

Americans' Support for an Independent Palestinian State,
Among Major Demographic Groups

Do you favor or oppose the establishment of an independent Palestinian
state on the West Bank and the Gaza Strip?

	Favor	Oppose	No opinion
	%	%	%
National adults	42	38	20
Men	45	40	15
Women	40	35	25
Whites	43	38	19
Nonwhites	42	36	22
18 to 34	47	32	21
35 to 54	40	36	24
55+	41	43	16
Postgraduate	60	33	7
College graduate only	50	36	14
Some college	42	35	23
No college	34	42	24

Feb. 8-11, 2015

GALLUP

Consistent with Republicans' broadly pro-Israel views, just 33% of Republicans favor creating a Palestinian state, versus 48% opposing it. By contrast, a majority of Democrats favor the proposal. Independents tilt in favor, matching the national average. The pattern is similar by political ideology, with a third of conservatives in favor versus a majority of liberals. Moderates' views fall in between.

Gallup previously reported that Americans are much more likely to say their sympathies in the Middle East conflict lie with the Israelis than with the Palestinians. Nevertheless, more than a third of those who sympathize mainly with Israel favor a Palestinian state. On the flip side, 16% of those who sympathize with the Palestinians oppose it. Among the residual 22% of Americans who express no partiality in the conflict, half take no position on the statehood question, while the remainder are more likely to favor than oppose it.

Americans' Support for an Independent Palestinian State,
Among Major Political Groups

Do you favor or oppose the establishment of an independent Palestinian state on
the West Bank and the Gaza Strip?

	Favor	Oppose	No opinion
	%	%	%
Republicans	33	48	19
Independents	42	38	20
Democrats	52	29	18
Conservatives	32	52	16
Moderates	48	32	21
Liberals	57	25	18
Sympathies in Middle East conflict:			
More with the Israelis	36	52	12
More with the Palestinians	75	16	9
Both/Neither/Unsure	38	13	49

Feb. 8-11, 2015

GALLUP

Notably, the overall decline in support for Palestinian statehood seen since it peaked in 2003 is primarily a function of declining support from Republicans, and to a lesser degree independents, while Democrats' support has generally held up. The drop in Republican support, however, has not been consistent, rising from its all-time low of 29% in 2013 to 41% last year before dropping again to 33% in the most current reading.

Americans' Support for an Independent Palestinian State, by Party ID

Do you favor or oppose the establishment of an independent Palestinian state on the West Bank and the Gaza Strip? (% Favor)

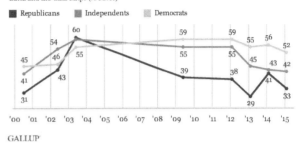

GALLUP

The peak support for Palestinian statehood seen in 2003 came as Republican President George W. Bush was prodding the Israelis and Palestinians to support the so-called road map to peace, focused on a two-state solution. Prior to that, in the last year of Democratic President Bill Clinton's administration, Republican support for statehood was as low as it is today, suggesting that for Republicans, at least, partisanship may play a key role in these attitudes.

Bottom Line

About four in 10 Americans endorse the creation of an independent Palestinian state, on the low end of what Gallup has found since 2000. Americans were much more supportive in 2003, when the players were actively involved in U.S.-led discussions to end the stalemate and Israeli Prime Minister Ariel Sharon—as well as Palestinian leadership—seemed to favor the goal of statehood. Republicans' support has since plummeted, possibly in part because U.S. diplomacy is now led by a Democratic president. But independents' support is also down, and Democrats' has ebbed slightly.

Still, Americans show more support for an independent Palestinian state than might be expected given the relatively low percentages viewing the Palestinian Authority favorably (17%) and sympathizing more with the Palestinians than the Israelis (16%). This suggests Americans at least somewhat separate their views of Palestinian leadership from Palestinians' quest for self-determination. Also, some Americans who side more with Israel but favor statehood may do so believing it will diffuse violence in the region, benefiting everyone.

Survey Methods

Results for this Gallup poll are based on telephone interviews conducted Feb. 8–11, 2015, with a random sample of 837 adults, aged 18 and older, living in all 50 U.S. states and the District of Columbia. For results based on the total sample of national adults, the margin of sampling error is ±4 percentage points at the 95% confidence level.

February 25, 2015

AMERICANS' VIEWS OF U.S. POSITION IN WORLD STEADY

by Jeffrey M. Jones

Story Highlights

- *Satisfaction with U.S. position in world unchanged at 37%*
- *Public divided on whether U.S. rates favorably in world's eyes*
- *Small dip in view that other world leaders respect Obama*

PRINCETON, N.J.—Thirty-seven percent of Americans are satisfied and 61% dissatisfied with the position of the U.S. in the world today. These views are unchanged from last year, even after a series of significant challenges for U.S. foreign policy. Americans' satisfaction is a bit higher than at the end of the Bush administration and at the beginning of the Obama administration, but remains well below where it was in the early 2000s.

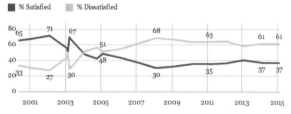

Satisfaction With United States' Position in the World
On the whole, would you say that you are satisfied or dissatisfied with the position of the United States in the world today?

GALLUP

The results are from Gallup's annual World Affairs survey, conducted Feb. 8–11. Americans' satisfaction held steady in the past year, even as the U.S. was forced to deal with the rise of Islamic militants in Iraq and Syria, a dispute with Russia over Ukrainian separatists in the eastern part of Ukraine, heightened tensions between the Israelis and Palestinians, and ongoing policy disagreements involving North Korea and Iran. The lack of change may be attributable to Americans' already high level of dissatisfaction with the nation's world position, with those events and the way the U.S. handled them serving to reinforce the dissatisfaction rather than to worsen or even improve it.

Americans have been more likely to be dissatisfied than satisfied with the position of the U.S. in the world since 2004, about the time it became clear that the U.S. military action in Iraq was running into problems that could—and did—lead to a prolonged U.S. commitment there. Satisfaction fell to a low of 30% in the final year of George W. Bush's administration and remained low in the very early stages of Barack Obama's presidency. Americans' satisfaction is modestly higher now than at that point, but has leveled off.

Gallup has asked the question at least yearly since 2000, but also three times between 1962 and 1966, during the Cold War and early stages of the Vietnam War. In those polls, 43% or 44% of Americans were satisfied with the position of the U.S. in the world.

Consistent with the fact that a Democratic president is deciding U.S. foreign policy, the current poll finds Democrats (57%) much more likely than independents (34%) or Republicans (20%) to be satisfied with the U.S. position in the world.

Americans More Likely to Believe Other Nations View U.S. Positively Than Negatively

Even though Americans are more dissatisfied than satisfied with the U.S. position in the world, they still, by a slight margin, believe the United States rates positively (52%) rather than negatively (47%) in the eyes of the world. These views have changed little since 2010, when they recovered after a downturn during the latter stages of the Bush presidency and the first year of the Obama administration.

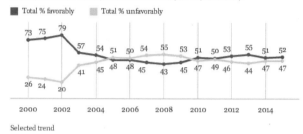

Americans' Perceptions of How U.S. Rates in the Eyes of the World
In general, how do you think the United States rates in the eyes of the world -- very favorably, somewhat favorably, somewhat unfavorably, or very unfavorably?

Selected trend

GALLUP

Americans overwhelmingly believed the international community viewed the U.S. positively from 2000 to 2002, with more than 70% saying this. Those opinions changed dramatically in early 2003 in the lead-up to the Iraq War, when the U.S. had difficulty convincing allies to join the effort and the percentage believing the U.S. rated favorably in the eyes of the world fell to 57%. The United States eventually decided against a certain-to-fail United Nations resolution authorizing the use of force against Iraq, and instead pursued military action with a limited coalition of allies. As the Iraq War continued for a second year into 2005, more Americans thought other nations viewed the U.S. negatively rather than positively, a trend that continued until 2010.

Americans' partisanship colors their opinions of how the international community views the United States. Currently, 69% of Democrats, 49% of independents and 38% of Republicans think the United States rates favorably in the eyes of the world.

Fewer Than Four in 10 Believe World Leaders Respect Obama

After a sharp decline in 2014, Americans' view that leaders of other countries respect Obama has edged lower this year. Thirty-seven percent of Americans now say this, compared with 41% last year, 51% in 2013, and 67% at the beginning of Obama's presidency.

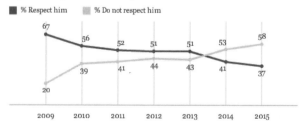

Americans' Perceptions of President Obama's World Standing
Do you think leaders of other countries around the world have respect for Barack Obama, or do you think they don't have much respect for him?

GALLUP

Sixty-one percent of Democrats, 32% of independents and 16% of Republicans think other world leaders respect Obama.

While the 37% of all Americans who say world leaders respect Obama is his worst reading to date, it is not the worst Gallup has measured for any president. In 2007, 21% of Americans thought world leaders respected George W. Bush.

Obama's ratings have been better on this measure than Bush's were, with an average of 51% of Americans believing world leaders respect Obama during his presidency to date, compared with 43% who believed this about Bush when he was president.

Gallup had two measurements of Bill Clinton on the same item—41% in September 1994 and 44% in May 2000.

Implications

Americans continue to be largely pessimistic about the United States' international standing, as most are dissatisfied with the U.S. position in the world and believe world leaders do not respect Obama. Also, they are only slightly more likely to think the U.S. rates favorably rather than unfavorably in the eyes of the world. These views have held steady over the past year in arguably the most challenging year for foreign policy during the Obama administration.

Gallup's trends on these measures dating to 2000 suggest two distinct phases in Americans' perceptions of how the United States ranks on the world stage. The first was a time of high satisfaction and positivity during the economic boom and immediate post-9/11 era, when the terrorist attacks led to a surge in U.S. patriotism and support for government leaders.

The second phase began about the time of the United States' planned military action in Iraq in early 2003, which was largely opposed by the international community, including many traditional U.S. allies. That appeared to cause Americans to re-evaluate the United States' position in the world, seeing it in a much less positive light. Those opinions grew more negative as the U.S. involvement in Iraq continued, and although they have improved modestly in recent years, they have yet to recover to pre–Iraq War levels.

The Obama administration has made a concerted effort to mend international relationships that may have been damaged by the Iraq War, but it, too, has met resistance from the international community over some of its policies, including proposed military action against Syria in late 2013 and a plan to send weapons and military equipment to anti-separatist forces in Ukraine. In both cases, other nations were able to step in and negotiate agreements to avert the use of U.S. force.

Given Gallup's trends on these items, it is not clear if the 2000–2002 or the 2003–present views are more typical of how Americans feel about the United States' world standing. Gallup's 1960s data on Americans' satisfaction with the position of the U.S. in the world potentially indicate that the early 2000s era is more of the exception rather than the rule; thus, Americans may continue to express dissatisfaction with the U.S. position in the world for the foreseeable future.

Survey Methods

Results for this Gallup poll are based on telephone interviews conducted Feb. 8–11, 2015, with a random sample of 837 adults, aged 18 and older, living in all 50 U.S. states and the District of Columbia. For results based on the total sample of national adults, the margin of sampling error is ±4 percentage points at the 95% confidence level. All reported margins of sampling error include computed design effects for weighting.

February 25, 2015
AMERICANS CONTINUE TO SEE UN AS A POOR PROBLEM-SOLVER

by Frank Newport

Story Highlights

- *57% of Americans say United Nations doing "poor" job*
- *Little change over the last three years*
- *Democrats much more positive about the UN than Republicans*

PRINCETON, N.J.—Although there is no shortage of threats to peace and security around the world today, Americans do not see the United Nations doing any better at solving the problems it has had to face than has been the case in recent years. The majority of Americans continue to say the UN is doing a poor job, while slightly more than one-third say it is doing a good job.

Do you think the United Nations is doing a good job or a poor job in trying to solve the problems it has had to face?

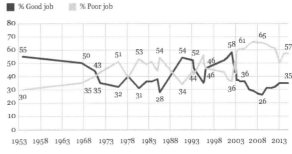

GALLUP

The latest update on these attitudes is from Gallup's Feb. 8–11 World Affairs survey. Gallup first asked about the United Nations in 1953, eight years after the UN officially came into being in October 1945. In the December 1953 survey, 55% of Americans said the UN was doing a good job, while 30% said it was doing a poor job. This positive reaction may have partly reflected the United Nations' role in the Korean War, which ended a few months earlier in July. Ratings of the UN have varied substantially in the decades since, reaching a high of 58% shortly after the 9/11 terrorist attacks, and a low of 26% in February 2009.

Outside of the first reading in 1953, more than half of Americans have given the UN a good rating in only two periods: surveys conducted in 1990 and 1993—before and after the first Persian Gulf War—and in each year from 2000 to 2002. Americans' views of the UN soured in 2003 and have remained relatively low ever since. This drop, at least initially, may reflect the disagreements between U.S. leadership and the United Nations over the U.S. invasion of Iraq.

An average 39% of Americans have rated the job the UN is doing as "good" since Gallup began asking the question 62 years ago, putting the 35% reading over the past three years just below average.

Americans from different partisan persuasions see the United Nations in significantly different ways. Democrats are more than twice as likely as Republicans to say the UN is doing a good job. Democrats are also the only political group to view the UN positively, with 52% saying the UN is doing a good job, compared with 28% of independents and 25% of Republicans.

Do you think the United Nations is doing a good job or a poor job in trying to solve the problems it has had to face, by Party ID

	Good job	Poor job	Don't know/ Refused
	%	%	%
Republicans	25	70	5
Independents	28	61	11
Democrats	52	39	8

Feb 8-11, 2015

GALLUP

This partisan split in attitudes toward the United Nations is not new. Republicans' and Democrats' views of the UN have fluctuated over the past 14 years since Gallup began asking the question on an annual basis, but the gap between the two parties has persisted.

Do you think the United Nations is doing a good job or a poor job in trying to solve the problems it has had to face, by Party ID

% Good job

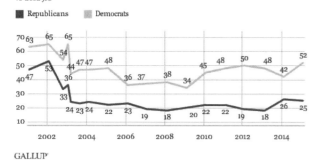

GALLUP

Implications

The charter of the United Nations states that the purpose of the body is to maintain "international peace and security" and "to take effective collective measures for the prevention and removal of threats to the peace, and for the suppression of acts of aggression or other breaches of the peace." There is certainly no shortage of situations where the United Nations could play a role, including fighting in Ukraine, Africa, the Middle East, Syria, Iraq and Afghanistan—but few notable examples of the United Nations taking steps that reduced any of this violence.

Because the wording of Gallup's question asks about the job the UN is doing "in trying to solve the problems it has had to face," the persistence of these world conflicts, wars and often bloody disputes helps explain why Americans tend to say the UN is doing a poor job. In the few instances where Americans have approved of the international body, it has been at times when the United Nations has approved a U.S.-led response to an international crisis, such as the Persian Gulf War.

Many international crises today are not the traditional country-against-country conflicts that typified the wars that preceded the UN's founding, but actions by groups that operate across borders and that have no specific national identity. This may make it more difficult for the UN to actively intervene or remove these "threats to the peace," and may help explain why the UN has been not as actively in the forefront of attempts to address these conflicts. Furthermore, much like Americans' dislike of gridlock in Congress, the UN's inability to come to one mind concerning major problems may further discredit it in Americans' eyes. Whatever the reason, the majority of Americans continue to give the United Nations a poor grade at this juncture in history.

Survey Methods

Results for this Gallup poll are based on telephone interviews conducted Feb. 8–11, 2015, on the Gallup U.S. Daily survey, with a random sample of 837 adults, aged 18 and older, living in all 50 U.S. states and the District of Columbia. For results based on the total sample of national adults, the margin of sampling error is ±4 percentage points at the 95% confidence level. All reported margins of sampling error include computed design effects for weighting.

February 26, 2015
AMERICANS SEE CHINA'S ECONOMIC POWER AS DIMINISHED THREAT

by Jeffrey M. Jones

Story Highlights

- *Forty percent see China's economy as critical threat to U.S.*
- *In 2013–2014, 52% saw China's economy as critical threat*
- *China slides back as perceived top U.S. enemy*

PRINCETON, N.J.—Forty percent of Americans regard "the economic power of China" as a critical threat to the vital interests of the U.S., down from 52% in both 2013 and 2014. Since last year, Americans have shifted more toward viewing China's economic power as an important but not a critical threat, or as not an important threat.

Views of Economic Power of China as Threat to U.S. Vital Interests

Next, I am going to read you a list of possible threats to the vital interests of the United States in the next 10 years. For each one, please tell me if you see this as a critical threat, an important but not critical threat, or not an important threat at all.

The economic power of China

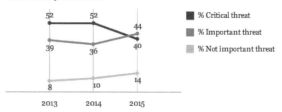

GALLUP

Gallup's annual World Affairs poll finds China's economic power ranking at the bottom of a list of eight different international threats, with ISIS and international terrorism rated as the gravest threats.

The decline in the percentage of Americans viewing China's economy as a critical threat over the past year may be attributable to the rise of other matters on the world stage, such as the Islamic State or ISIS and the situation in Ukraine. Also, by many measures, the U.S. economy has greatly improved while China's has slowed, making the Chinese economy seem like less of a threat than when the U.S. economy was struggling to emerge from recession and the Chinese economy was growing more quickly. Americans' opinions about which country is the world's leading economic power had shifted from the U.S. to China in recent years amid the weak U.S. economy.

China Fades as Top Enemy

Currently, 12% of Americans name China when asked to say which country they consider the United States' greatest enemy. That is down from 20% in 2014 and 23% in 2012. China currently ranks behind Russia and North Korea, after topping the list in 2014 and finishing second, to Iran, in 2012.

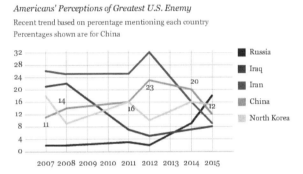

Americans' Perceptions of Greatest U.S. Enemy

Recent trend based on percentage mentioning each country
Percentages shown are for China

GALLUP

China is distinct from the other countries that typically rank among the top U.S. enemies in that it represents primarily an economic threat to the U.S., whereas Russia, Iran, Iraq and North Korea represent more of a security threat.

Favorable Ratings of China Unchanged

Americans' basic opinions of China, notably, are essentially unchanged from a year ago even as Americans see that country's economic power as less threatening and are less likely to name China as the United States' top enemy. Currently, 50% of Americans have an unfavorable opinion of China and 44% a favorable one, compared with 53% unfavorable and 43% favorable in 2014.

For most of Gallup's nearly 40-year trend, Americans have been more negative than positive toward China.

The major exceptions to the general trend were net-positive ratings in 1979, after the U.S. established full diplomatic relations with China, and in early 1989, after President George H. W. Bush's visit.

Americans' views of China became sharply negative after the 1989 Tiananmen Square incident, with a 38-percentage-point drop in its favorable rating, from 72% in February 1989 to 34% in August 1989. These more negative opinions of China persisted over the ensuing decade, with favorable ratings mostly in the 30% range amid ongoing concern about Chinese human rights and tensions over U.S. policy toward Taiwan. Since 2001, Americans have been

a bit more positive toward China as it has made attempts to become more open and involved on the world stage, including joining the World Trade Organization.

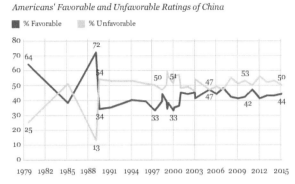

Americans' Favorable and Unfavorable Ratings of China

GALLUP

Implications

Americans view China as a diminished threat, but their basic views of the country are steady, which indicates that the change in perceived threat may have less to do with China itself than with other countries. International events over the past year, particularly the dispute with Russia over the Ukraine situation and the growing influence of ISIS militants in Iraq and Syria, have likely made countries other than China seem more threatening to the U.S.

A U.S. economy that is arguably stronger than at any point since the recession, as well as a slowing Chinese economy, are also possible factors in Americans' seeing China's economic power as less of a threat than in recent years. And as Americans have grown more confident in the health of the U.S. economy, their views of what threatens the U.S. may shift more to security concerns than economic ones.

Survey Methods

Results for this Gallup poll are based on telephone interviews conducted Feb. 8–11, 2015, with a random sample of 837 adults, aged 18 and older, living in all 50 U.S. states and the District of Columbia. For results based on the total sample of national adults, the margin of sampling error is ±4 percentage points at the 95% confidence level. All reported margins of sampling error include computed design effects for weighting.

February 27, 2015
AS NUCLEAR TALKS PROGRESS, 11% IN U.S. SEE IRAN FAVORABLY

by Andrew Dugan

Story Highlights

- *Consistent with past years, 11% see Iran favorably*
- *77% say potential Iranian nukes are a critical threat*
- *Republicans far more likely to say Iran is critical threat*

WASHINGTON, D.C.—As the United States and several other nations continue to negotiate what would be a landmark agreement to limit Iran's production of nuclear weapons, more than eight in 10 Americans view Iran unfavorably (84%). Only 11% have a favorable view of the country. Despite this potential thaw in Iranian-U.S. relations, Americans' views on its longtime foe have remained unchanged for 26 years.

Americans' Favorability Ratings of Iran

Next, I'd like your overall opinion of some foreign countries. What is your overall opinion of Iran? Is it very favorable, mostly favorable, mostly unfavorable, or very unfavorable?

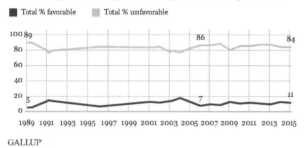

GALLUP

Iran's historical favorable average of 11% is the lowest of 22 countries Gallup asked about in this year's World Affairs poll, conducted Feb. 8–11—a list that includes such prominent U.S. adversaries as Russia, Syria and North Korea.

Since the Islamic Revolution of 1979 toppled the pro-U.S. government in Iran, the two countries have been antagonists, and this has been borne out in U.S. public opinion. When Gallup first asked Americans to rate Iran, in 1989, 5% said they saw the country favorably.

Over the past decade, however, U.S.-Iranian relations have developed an unexpected element of intrigue. In January 2002, then President George W. Bush famously included Iran—along with North Korea and an Iraq then controlled by Saddam Hussein—in what he called "an axis of evil," though Bush's inclusion of Iran in this trio did nothing to damage that nation's already battered standing with Americans. After the American-led invasion of Iraq that altered the political order in the Middle East, Iranian political influence in countries such as Iraq, Lebanon and Syria appeared to grow, often compromising the United States' influence in these places. Furthermore, not long after Iranian President Mahmoud Ahmadinejad—an outspoken U.S. critic—began the first of his two terms as president, a plurality of Americans in 2006 named Iran as America's greatest enemy, a spot it retained for much of Ahmadinejad's presidency.

But more recent events have suggested the two countries may find a way to move beyond this, perhaps to better relations. In 2013, Iranians elected President Hassan Rouhani, a candidate who has publicly stated he is open to working with the U.S. on some matters. With the rise of the Islamic State group in Iraq last year, Iran and the U.S. now have a rare common cause, since neither country is interested in seeing the terrorist group prosper. Meanwhile, the Obama administration has joined other nations in negotiations with Iran aimed at limiting that nation's nuclear program in exchange for relief from economic sanctions.

These efforts may soon bear fruit with some type of multinational agreement, though any deal would not be without its share of congressional critics. And given Iran's low favorability with the American people, it could be a hard sell beyond the halls of Capitol Hill.

Iran's Development of Nuclear Weapons Seen as Critical Threat

Nonetheless, the vast majority of Americans (77%) say the development of nuclear weapons by Iran is a "critical threat," perhaps underscoring the importance of these talks. Another 16% say the threat is important, but not critical. Since 2013, a preponderance of U.S. adults have identified possible Iranian nuclear weapons as a critical threat and the issue has ranked highly compared with other possible threats facing the U.S.

Threats to the Vital Interests of the United States in Next 10 Years:
Development of Nuclear Weapons by Iran

Please tell me if you see this as a critical threat, an important but not critical threat, or not an important threat at all.

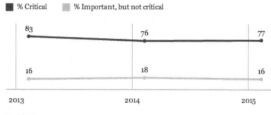

GALLUP

But as the prospect of an agreement—though still far from certain—increases, Democrats are notably less likely to classify the development of an Iranian nuclear bomb as a critical threat compared with Republicans or even with Democratic responses in prior years. Today, 68% of Democrats say Iranian nuclear weapons would be a critical threat, compared with 91% of Republicans. This formidable 23-percentage-point gap, among the highest for the eight threats measured in the Gallup survey, was virtually nonexistent last year, when 86% of Republicans and 80% of Democrats viewed this as a critical threat.

In 2013, the gap between the parties was also a less pronounced one, at 12 points.

Threat Assessment of Development of Nuclear Weapons by Iran
% Saying "critical threat"

	Republicans %	Independents %	Democrats %	Gap: Republican minus Democrats (in pct. pts.)
Feb 8-11, 2015	91	77	68	23
Feb 6-9, 2014	86	69	80	6
Feb 7-10, 2013	91	80	79	12

GALLUP

Fewer See Iran as America's Greatest Enemy

While Americans see Iran no more favorably today than in years past, fewer (9%) in an open-ended question name it as America's greatest enemy, down almost half from last year (16%) and a nearly fourfold drop from the measure's 2012 high (32%). This year, Russia, North Korea and China were all named with more frequency than Iran.

Percentage of Americans Naming Iran as United States' Greatest Enemy

GALLUP

Since Rouhani ascended into office in 2013, fewer Americans have named Iran as their country's biggest enemy. Even if Rouhani's tenure has not seen more Americans view Iran favorably, fewer see it as the nation's main opponent.

Bottom Line

Along with five other nations, U.S. and Iranian negotiators are working to reach an accord satisfactory to all parties. But any agreement will have the herculean task of overcoming a generation's worth of mutual enmity, feelings that are at least partially evident in Americans' low favorable rating of Iran. This is not to say public opinion is immutable—Cuba saw its favorable rating spike by eight points this year in the wake of its announced détente with the U.S.—but attitudes toward Iran may prove a weight on U.S. negotiators and will be reflected in Congress's reaction to any deal. At the same time, stopping Iran from developing a nuclear bomb is a pressing priority for most Americans, meaning policymakers who reject a deal out of hand could feel pressure to promote another solution.

Survey Methods

Results for this Gallup poll are based on telephone interviews conducted Feb. 8–11, 2015, with a random sample of 837 adults, aged 18 and older, living in all 50 U.S. states and the District of Columbia. For results based on the total sample of national adults, the margin of sampling error is ±4 percentage points at the 95% confidence level. All reported margins of sampling error include computed design effects for weighting.

March 02, 2015
GETTING MORE SLEEP LINKED TO HIGHER WELL-BEING

by Justin McCarthy and Alyssa Brown

Story Highlights

- *Positive relationship between more hours of sleep and well-being*
- *For those under age 65, relationship peaks at eight hours of sleep*
- *In U.S., 42% of adults usually get less than seven hours of sleep*

WASHINGTON, D.C.—Americans who report that they usually get more hours of sleep per night have higher overall well-being than those who typically get fewer hours of shut-eye. Getting more hours of sleep is positively associated with having higher well-being, with the relationship peaking at eight hours and leveling off thereafter.

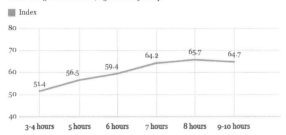

Well-Being Index Scores, by Hours of Sleep

Sept. 5-19, 2014
Gallup-Healthways Well-Being Index

GALLUP

These data are based on interviews with 7,058 U.S. adults conducted Sept. 5–19, 2014, as part of the Gallup-Healthways Well-Being Index. The Well-Being Index measures five elements of well-being: purpose, social, financial, community and physical.

Those who usually sleep seven hours per night have a 4.8-point advantage in their Well-Being Index score over those who typically sleep for six hours. This difference is greater than the well-being advantage for those who sleep six hours versus five hours (2.9 points), and eight hours versus seven hours (1.5 points).

The link between getting more hours of sleep and higher well-being differs slightly by age. For adults aged 65 and older, the relationship peaks at seven hours of sleep. For those under age 65, it peaks at eight hours. For young adults aged 18 to 29, the well-being uptick from seven to eight hours is more pronounced than it is for adults in the middle age groups—4.4 points versus roughly one point, respectively.

Americans aged 30 to 64 who usually get five hours of sleep have significantly lower well-being than those who usually get six hours of sleep, which is not the case for young adults or seniors.

Americans' Well-Being Index Scores, by Age and Hours of Sleep

	Five hours	Six hours	Seven hours	Eight hours
18 to 29	56.5	58.5	62.3	66.7
30 to 44	53.9	57.8	63.2	64.1
45 to 64	55.3	58.8	63.6	64.5
65+	63.3	63.7	68.3	67.7

Sept. 5-19, 2014
Gallup-Healthways Well-Being Index

GALLUP

A strong relationship between sleep and well-being exists, but the direction of the relationship is unclear. Getting more hours of sleep could boost well-being—or those with higher well-being may be more likely than those with lower well-being to get more sleep.

More Than Four in 10 Adults Fall Short of Recommended Amount of Sleep

Forty-two percent of U.S. adults report getting less than seven hours of sleep on a typical night, the minimum number of hours recommended by the National Sleep Foundation for those aged 18 and older. And although young adults who get eight hours of sleep have significantly higher well-being than those who get seven, 67% of 18- to 29-year-olds say they usually get less than eight hours.

Seniors are the most likely age group to get at least seven hours of shut-eye per night, with nearly two-thirds doing so.

Americans' Usual Hours of Sleep, by Age
How many hours sleep do you get at night?

	U.S. adults	18 to 29	30 to 44	45 to 64	65+
	%	%	%	%	%
Less than three hours	1	1	1	1	0
Three to four hours	7	6	8	8	6
Five hours	9	10	9	10	7
Six hours	25	24	27	26	21
Seven hours	27	26	29	27	26
Eight hours	26	26	22	25	30
Nine to 10 hours	6	7	4	4	9
More than 10 hours	0	0	0	1	1

Gallup-Healthways Well-Being Index
Sept. 5-19, 2014

GALLUP

Implications

Previous Gallup research shows that Americans are getting roughly an hour less sleep than they did in the 1940s. Fortunately, the majority of Americans are still getting at least seven hours of sleep per night—the minimum amount recommended by the National Sleep Foundation for those aged 18 and older. But more than four in 10 U.S. adults report that they usually get less than seven hours of sleep per night. This could be a missed opportunity, given that well-being is higher among those who get seven or more hours of sleep than those who get less.

Not getting enough sleep is not only linked to lower well-being for individuals, but it is also costly to the U.S. economy. Employees may not have enough time to sleep because of working long hours, family obligations, insomnia or having poor well-being in other areas. For example, poor physical well-being, social isolation or financial strain could adversely affect quantity of sleep.

Employers can explore interventions to promote the value of sleep and its link to employees' well-being, as it relates to engagement, healthcare costs and productivity. When possible, they may want to allow employees to work flexible hours, which could make it easier for workers to balance work and family demands with getting enough sleep.

Survey Methods

Results are based on telephone interviews conducted Sept. 5–19, 2014, as part of the Gallup-Healthways Well-Being Index survey, with a random sample of 7,058 adults, aged 18 and older, living in all 50 U.S. states and the District of Columbia. For results based on the total sample of national adults, the margin of sampling error is ±1 percentage point at the 95% confidence level.

Each sample of national adults includes a minimum quota of 50% cellphone respondents and 50% landline respondents, with additional minimum quotas by time zone within region. Landline and cellular telephone numbers are selected using random-digit-dial methods.

March 02, 2015

AMERICANS SPLIT ON WORTH OF U.S. BEING NO. 1 ECONOMICALLY

by Justin McCarthy

Story Highlights

- *Half of Americans say it's important for U.S. to be No. 1*
- *Percentage saying this is important is up since 2007*
- *One in six Americans say U.S. is the leading economic power*

WASHINGTON, D.C.—Fifty percent of Americans view it as "important" for the U.S. to be No. 1 in the world economically. This is up from 39% in 2007, when Gallup last asked the question, and is the highest figure since 1993. The other half of Americans (49%) say it is "not that important" for the U.S. to be No. 1, as long as it is among the leading economic powers.

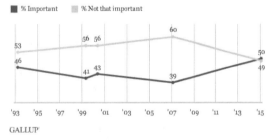

Importance of U.S. Being No. 1 in the World Economically

Do you feel that it's important for the United States to be No. 1 in the world economically, or that being No. 1 is not that important, as long as the U.S. is among the leading economic powers?

GALLUP

These data come from Gallup's Feb. 8–11 World Affairs poll, conducted just months after China overtook the U.S. as the world's largest national economy in terms of purchasing power. Whereas half of Americans now say it's important for the U.S. to be the world's leading economic power, Americans were less likely between 1999 and 2007, when roughly four in 10 said this and about six in 10 viewed being No. 1 as "not that important."

Having been the world's largest economy since the 1870s, Americans—at least in recent decades—may have taken their country's leading economic stature for granted. But as the bloc of BRICS countries—an economic alliance of Brazil, Russia, India, China and South Africa—continues to be an economic force to be reckoned with and has created its own bank, Americans have begun to value being the world's dominant economic power more highly. In recent years, Americans have viewed China in particular as the leading economic power.

Republicans Most Likely to See No. 1 Status as Important

Republicans feel strongest about the importance of U.S. economic dominance; a majority (64%) say it is important for the country to be No. 1 economically. Meanwhile, less than half of independents (48%) and Democrats (41%) agree that it is important.

Since 2000, Republicans have become increasingly likely to say being No. 1 economically is important, while Democrats' views haven't changed. Independents grew less concerned about this between 2000 and 2007, but have since grown significantly more inclined to see it as important.

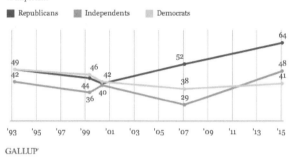

Importance of U.S. Being No. 1 in the World Economically, by Party

% Important

GALLUP

Most Americans Don't View the U.S. as the Sole World Economic Power

While half of Americans say it is important for the U.S. to be No. 1 economically, only 17% believe it actually is. Rather, the vast majority of Americans, 80%, believe the U.S. is but one of several leading economic powers—about the same as in 2010, when 82% held this view.

The 17% who believe the U.S. is the world's No. 1 economy ties for the lowest percentage to say so in the six times Gallup has asked this question. Americans were most confident about the United States' global economic stature in 1999 and 2000, when 40% and 39%, respectively, saw it as No. 1. This view has since waned, dropping to 25% in 2007 before falling again to 17% in 2010, where it remains.

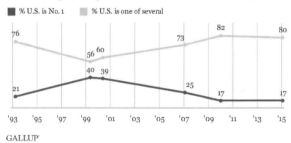

Americans' Views of U.S. as Leading Economic Power

Do you think the United States is No. 1 in the world economically, or that it is only one of several leading economic powers?

GALLUP

Bottom Line

Despite a major recovery in Americans' ratings of the U.S. economy over the past five years, Americans' views about the nation's economic clout in the world haven't changed. A mere 17% say the

U.S. is No. 1 economically, while most say it is one of several leading economic powerhouses. When Gallup in recent years has asked Americans, in a separate question, to say who the leading economic power is, China has overtaken the United States.

At the same time, Americans are now more likely than they have been in the recent past to view being No. 1 as important. As the U.S. cedes its role as the world's dominant economy to China in terms of purchasing power, it could mark a psychological shift for many Americans who, throughout their lives, have seen the United States' world-leading economic role as a given.

Survey Methods

Results for this Gallup poll are based on telephone interviews conducted Feb. 8–11, 2015, on the Gallup U.S. Daily survey, with a random sample of 837 adults, aged 18 and older, living in all 50 U.S. states and the District of Columbia. For results based on the total sample of national adults, the margin of sampling error is ±4 percentage points at the 95% confidence level. All reported margins of sampling error include computed design effects for weighting.

March 04, 2015
SNAPSHOT: U.S. UNINSURED RATE EDGING DOWN IN FIRST QUARTER

by Jenna Levy

Story Highlights

- *Uninsured rate is 12.3% in the first quarter to date*
- *Uninsured rate down 0.6 percentage points from the end of 2014*
- *Gallup will publish first quarter results in early April*

WASHINGTON, D.C.—The uninsured rate among U.S. adults is 12.3% for the first two months of 2015, down marginally from 12.9% in the fourth quarter of 2014.

Percentage Uninsured in the U.S., by Quarter

Do you have health insurance coverage?
Among adults aged 18 and older

	Q4 2014	Q1 2015 To Date	Net difference (pct. pts.)
% Uninsured	12.9	12.3	-0.6

Gallup-Healthways Well-Being Index

GALLUP

The open enrollment period for Americans to purchase a healthcare plan for 2015 through the Health Insurance Marketplace ended Feb. 15, but this deadline was extended to Feb. 22—and even longer for some applicants. Many states extended their enrollment deadlines even longer, and this report does not fully reflect those who obtained health insurance right before the deadline.

The uninsured rate for the first two months of the year is down 0.6 percentage points from the fourth quarter of 2014. Gallup and Healthways will publish the results for the entire first quarter in early April, and if the downward momentum continues, the drop in the uninsured rate may be slightly larger than this preliminary figure.

The results are based on more than 27,800 interviews conducted from Jan. 2 to Feb. 28, 2015, as part of the Gallup-Healthways Well-Being Index. Gallup and Healthways ask 500 U.S. adults each day whether they have health insurance, allowing for precise and ongoing measurement of the percentage of Americans without health insurance.

Implications

The 2015 open enrollment period began on Nov. 15, 2014, and officially ended on Feb. 22 after the Department of Health and Human Services granted an extension past the original closing date of Feb. 15. The deadline was extended only for new participants who had started, but did not finish the enrollment process because of long call center wait times or technical glitches on healthcare.gov. Some states such as New York and Maryland extended this special open enrollment period two weeks to Feb. 28 because of continued website malfunctions. Other states are granting even longer extensions, such as Washington, which is giving residents until April 17 to enroll.

The uninsured rate could decline further in the first quarter if the rate in March—when more interviews will be completed after most enrollment deadlines have passed—remains steady or drops even lower. The Obama administration will also re-open the exchanges from March 15 to April 30 for a special enrollment period aimed at getting those who realize, while paying their taxes, that they must pay a fine for not obtaining healthcare coverage in 2014. This could also drive down the uninsured rate through May. Additionally, Medicaid enrollment is not bound by the open enrollment period, which could allow more uninsured to sign up this month—and throughout the year if more states choose to expand Medicaid. So far, Arkansas and Kentucky have seen the most improvement in uninsured rates as a result of expanding Medicaid and using state-run marketplaces.

Gallup will report complete first quarter results in early April.

Survey Methods

Results are based on telephone interviews conducted Jan. 2–Feb.28, 2014, as part of the Gallup-Healthways Well-Being Index survey, with a random sample of 27,855 adults, aged 18 and older, living in all 50 U.S. states and the District of Columbia. For results based on the total sample of national adults, the margin of sampling error is ±1 percentage points at the 95% confidence level.

March 05, 2015
U.S. FEDERAL EMPLOYMENT RELATED TO HIGHER FINANCIAL WELL-BEING

by Jessica Mangskau and Steve Ander

Story Highlights

- *U.S. federal workers have edge in financial well-being over other workers*
- *Financial differences consistent across income, education*

WASHINGTON, D.C.—U.S. federal government workers are thriving in their financial well-being more than the rest of the workforce. On average, 44% of federal government employees are thriving financially, compared with 34% of all other workers in the U.S.

Financial Well-Being: Federal Workers vs. Non-Federal Workers

	Federal workers	All other workers	Difference
	%	%	pct. pts.
Thriving	44	34	10
Struggling	39	42	-3
Suffering	17	24	-7

Gallup-Healthways Well-Being Index, Feb. 16, 2014-Feb. 15, 2015

GALLUP'

These findings are based on more than 80,000 interviews conducted with U.S. adults, aged 18 and older, who were employed full time from Feb. 16, 2014–Feb. 15, 2015 as part of the Gallup-Healthways Well-Being Index. For each of the five elements of well-being, Gallup classifies respondents as "thriving" (well-being that is strong and consistent), "struggling" (well-being that is moderate or inconsistent), or "suffering" (well-being that is low and inconsistent).

Federal pay has been a topic of debate for years, with differing accounts of whether federal employees are paid more, no more or less than non-federal employees. However, financial well-being is not a direct report of salary, benefits or overall compensation. It is a composite of responses to the perceptions of standards of living, affordability of basic necessities and financial woes based on region of country, family size, cost of living, debt and various other factors that go into subjective assessments of financial situations.

Given this description, it is possible for a person to have a higher salary but experience lower financial well-being. But for those who experience higher levels of financial well-being, they feel as if they can spend time and energy addressing other facets of well-being in their day-to-day lives, including their purpose, social, community and physical well-being. These data show that federal employment is likely associated with higher levels of economic stability and reductions in the stress of providing for a comfortable lifestyle because federal workers report higher financial well-being.

Across Income and Education Levels, Federal Employees Still Thrive More

While some have claimed that federal employees earn more than those working outside the federal government, the differences in financial well-being remain consistent when examining household income levels. A quarter of federal employees whose monthly household income is less than $2,000 are thriving in financial well-being, compared with 15% of workers outside the federal government, a difference of 10 percentage points. While thriving differences between federal and non-federal employees vary somewhat across income levels—such as those households that earn $5,000–$7,499 a month—federal employees consistently have higher financial well-being.

Federal Workers vs. Non-Federal Workers Financial Well-Being, by Monthly Household Income

	Federal workers	All other workers	Difference
	%	%	pct. pts.
Less than $2,000	25	15	10
$2,000 to $2,999	32	21	11
$3,000 to $3,999	33	26	7
$4,000 to $4,999	38	31	7
$5,000 to $7,499	43	38	5
$7,500 to $9,999	56	46	10
$10,000 or more	60	54	6

Gallup-Healthways Well-Being Index, Feb. 16, 2014-Feb. 15, 2015

GALLUP'

The same trends of higher levels of thriving for federal government workers are seen across educational attainment. More than a third (35%) of federal employees with a high school degree or less are thriving, compared with about a quarter (27%) of those working outside of the U.S. government, and these differences continue at each higher level of education, including an eight-point difference in thriving among those with a postgraduate education.

Federal Workers vs. Non-Federal Workers Financial Well-Being, by Education

	Federal workers	All other workers	Difference
	%	%	pct. pts.
High school or less	35	27	8
Some college	41	31	10
College degree	50	41	9
Postgraduate	55	47	8

Gallup-Healthways Well-Being Index, Feb. 16, 2014-Feb. 15, 2015

GALLUP'

In 2012, the Congressional Budget Office found that less educated federal employees made more money than their non-federal counterparts and more educated federal employees made less. Conventional wisdom might suggest then that the differences in financial well-being between less educated federal and non-federal employees would be greater than the differences between those with more education. However, these differences between federal and non-federal employees' financial well-being across education levels are similar, including a matching eight-point difference for those with a high school degree or less and for those with a postgraduate degree. Again, these data suggest that income may not be the basis for high financial well-being.

Implications

Gallup research defines financial well-being as managing one's economic life to reduce stress and increase security. Financial well-being is not necessarily related to absolute income, but rather to approaches to saving and spending and future expectations of job security, among other subjective factors. The survey data indicate that working for the federal government is associated with higher financial well-being when compared with other U.S. workers, holding across income and education levels. Federal workers reporting higher levels of financial well-being could mean good news for the U.S. government because financial well-being is a crucial aspect of overall well-being, which has a significant effect on healthcare costs and engagement on the job.

Many government agencies streamline benefits enrollment for employees that are "opt-out," or able to be set up once and automated to minimize financial stress on a regular basis, such as automated public transportation benefits. Beyond employer benefits, the U.S. Office of Personnel Management (OPM) transparently publishes salary information, which may not be as frequently available in the general workforce, making career paths fairly clear as to one's position in an organization. OPM also guarantees and regulates benefits so federal workers can feel secure that something unexpected will not affect their well-being.

To explain why there may be gaps in financial well-being between federal workers and all other workers, the fact that over 50% of the working population work for small businesses means that if those small business are not thriving, those employees may not be reporting high levels of financial well-being.

Results are based on telephone interviews conducted Feb. 16, 2014–Feb. 15, 2015, as part of the Gallup-Healthways Well-Being Index survey, with a random sample of 80,223 adults, aged 18 and older, employed full time and living in all 50 U.S. states and the District of Columbia. For results based on the total sample of national adults, the margin of sampling error is ±2 percentage points at the 95% confidence level.

March 06, 2015
U.S. INVESTORS APT TO "RIDE OUT" STOCK MARKET VOLATILITY

by Lydia Saad

Story Highlights

- *Most investors likely to take no action amid stock volatility*
- *Fifteen percent are very concerned about recent volatility*
- *Nearly six in 10 say it's a good time to invest in the markets*

PRINCETON, N.J.—Three-quarters of U.S. investors who own stocks say they are very or somewhat likely to simply ride out stock market volatility and take no action, according to the most recent Wells Fargo/Gallup Investor and Retirement Optimism Index survey. This far exceeds the 25% who say they are likely to transfer a portion of their stocks into safer investments and the 11% who would withdraw everything from stocks.

Actions Stock Investors Might Take in Response to Stock Market Volatility

As a result of the recent stock market volatility, how likely are you to do each of the following -- very likely, somewhat likely, not too likely, or not at all likely?

	Very/Somewhat likely
	%
Take no action and just "ride it out"	76
Put additional money into stocks	46
Seek more professional financial advice about how to manage your investments	44
Transfer a portion of the money you have in stocks into cash or other investments, such as CDs and bonds	25
Transfer all of your money out of stocks and into cash or other investments, such as CDs and bonds	11

Based on U.S. investors who have stock investments
Wells Fargo/Gallup Investor and Retirement Optimism Index survey
Jan. 30-Feb. 9, 2015

GALLUP

The Wells Fargo/Gallup Investor and Retirement Optimism Index survey was conducted Jan. 30–Feb. 9 with 1,011 U.S. adults who have $10,000 or more in investments. The survey took place after the stock market gave investors a bumpy ride in December and January, but as the market's strong performance in February was building. Despite some ups and downs at the start of March, the market remains near record highs.

Nearly half of investors with stock investments, 46%, see market volatility as a buying opportunity, saying they are likely to put additional money into stocks. About the same proportion, 44%, are

compelled to seek more professional financial advice to manage their investments amid market turbulence.

The percentage of investors saying they are "very likely" to do any of these things in response to market volatility produces roughly the same rank order of actions, ranging from 44% who would ride it out, down to 3% who would pull all of their money out of stocks.

Three-quarters of investors say they currently own stocks, either as individual stocks or through a stock mutual fund.

In the same survey, the Wells Fargo/Gallup Investor and Retirement Optimism Index was up 21 points to +69. That is the highest for the index since 2007 and reflects investors' improved confidence in their own finances as well as in the economy.

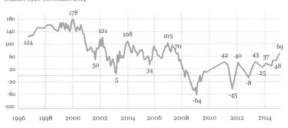

Wells Fargo/Gallup Investor and Retirement Optimism Index
October 1996-November 2014

GALLUP

Investors Remain Bullish on Investing

Although short-term instability in stock markets is par for the course, it could be particularly disconcerting to some investors six years into a bull market that is well past the average length of such markets. Still, reflecting on instability in January, just 15% of stock-owning investors said they are very concerned about the volatility in the market. Another 41% said they are somewhat concerned, while 44% were not too or not at all concerned. Naturally, non-stock-owning investors were less concerned about the volatility given their lack of direct exposure to stocks.

How concerned are you about the recent volatility in the stock market?
Jan. 30-Feb. 9, 2015

	All investors	Investors who own stocks	All other investors
	%	%	%
Very concerned	14	15	12
Somewhat concerned	39	41	33
Not too concerned	33	32	37
Not at all concerned	13	12	17
No opinion	1	0	2

Based on U.S. investors with $10,000 or more in investments
Wells Fargo/Gallup Investor and Retirement Optimism Index survey

GALLUP

Additionally, 58% of all investors in late January/early February said it was a good time to invest in the financial markets. This outpaces the 52% who said this a year ago and is the highest percentage recorded on this measure since 2011.

Bottom Line

The U.S. equity markets looked shaky at the start of winter after a strong fall. The Dow Jones Industrial Average was essentially flat in

December and down nearly 4% in January. But in polling conducted as the markets began to recover in February, investors seemed largely unruffled. More than twice as many saw market volatility as a buying opportunity than as a reason to transfer all stock investments, and most were content to ride it out. A sequence of improved jobs reports in recent months coupled with lower gas prices in early February may have helped lift investors' spirits.

Do you think now is a good time to invest in the financial markets, or not?
Based on U.S. investors with $10,000 or more in investments

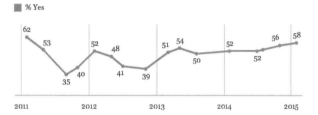

■ % Yes

62 53 35 40 52 48 41 39 51 54 50 52 52 56 58

2011   2012   2013   2014   2015

Wells Fargo/Gallup Investor and Retirement Optimism Index survey

GALLUP®

Survey Methods

Results for this Wells Fargo/Gallup Investor and Retirement Optimism Index survey are based on telephone interviews conducted Jan. 30–Feb. 9, 2015, on the Gallup U.S. Daily survey, with a random sample of 1,011 U.S. investors, aged 18 and older, living in all 50 U.S. states and the District of Columbia. For this survey, investors are defined as adults having investable assets of $10,000 or more.

For results based on the total sample of U.S. investors, the margin of sampling error is ±3 percentage points at the 95% confidence level.

For results based on the sample of 780 U.S. investors who own stocks, the margin of sampling error is ±4 percentage points at the 95% confidence level.

March 06, 2015
IN U.S., PERCENTAGE SAYING VACCINES ARE VITAL DIPS SLIGHTLY

by Frank Newport

Story Highlights

- *More than eight in 10 say vaccinating children is important*
- *More Americans than in 2001 have heard about pros and cons*
- *Six percent say vaccines can cause autism; over half unsure*

PRINCETON, N.J.—A slight majority of Americans, 54%, say it is extremely important that parents get their children vaccinated, down from the 64% who held this belief 14 years ago. Another 30% call it "very important"—unchanged from 2001. The rest, 15%, consider it "somewhat," "not very" or "not at all important," up from 2001.

These results, based on interviews conducted Feb. 28–March 1 on Gallup Daily tracking, follow a relatively large measles outbreak in the U.S. stemming from pockets of unvaccinated children.

This outbreak called attention to the continuing controversy over the possibly serious side effects of vaccines, a hypothesis advanced by some anti-vaccine activists, but vigorously denied by most doctors and scientists. Gallup originally asked questions about vaccines in 2001, the year the mercury-containing preservative thimerosal was removed from most childhood vaccines as a precautionary measure.

How important is it that parents get their children vaccinated -- extremely important, very important, somewhat important, not very important, or not at all important?

	Extremely important	Very important	Somewhat important	Not very important	Not at all important
	%	%	%	%	%
Feb 28-Mar 1, 2015	54	30	11	2	2
Jun 28-Jul 1, 2001	64	30	4	*	1

* Less than 0.5%
Note: % No opinion not shown

GALLUP®

Large majorities within every major demographic group say it is extremely or very important that parents get their kids vaccinated. Views on vaccinating children are related to education and age; those with the highest education levels and Americans aged 30 and older are the most likely to say it is important. Parents of children under 18 and those who are not parents of young children hold similar views on the importance of vaccines.

Percentage Who Have Heard About Disadvantages of Vaccines Nearly Doubles

Overall, Americans are more likely now than in 2001 to say they have heard about both the advantages and the disadvantages of vaccinations for children. Americans remain significantly more likely to have heard about the advantages of vaccines than about the disadvantages, although that gap has closed since 2001—given that the increase in the percentage who have heard about the disadvantages is substantially larger than the increase in those who have heard about the advantages.

How much have you, personally, heard about the advantages/disadvantages of vaccinations for children -- a great deal, fair amount, only a little, or nothing at all?

	A great deal	Fair amount	Only a little	Nothing at all
	%	%	%	%
ADVANTAGES				
Feb 28-Mar 1, 2015	49	34	13	4
Jun 28-Jul 1, 2001	37	36	17	9
DISADVANTAGES				
Feb 28-Mar 1, 2015	30	43	18	9
Jun 28-Jul 1, 2001	15	24	32	28

GALLUP®

Minimal Change in View That Vaccines Are Worse Than Underlying Disease

Although Americans are slightly less likely than they were in 2001 to say vaccines are extremely important, the percentage who say vaccines are more dangerous than the diseases they are designed to prevent has not changed much—9% now versus 6% in 2001.

Six Percent of U.S. Adults Say Vaccines Cause Autism

Six percent of American adults say they believe certain vaccines cause autism in children. Forty-one percent expressly disagree with this claim, while slightly over half of Americans are unsure.

From what you have read or heard, do you personally think certain vaccines do -- or do not -- cause autism in children, or are you unsure?

	Yes, a cause	No, not a cause	Unsure
Feb 28-Mar 1, 2015	6%	41%	52%

GALLUP

The belief that certain vaccines cause autism in children is one of the major controversies surrounding vaccines. This claim is based in part on a now largely discredited article published in a British medical journal in the 1990s, and public pronouncements on the subject by celebrity Jenny McCarthy. Various politicians in the years since have also created controversy with their statements on the issue. The U.S. government's Centers for Disease Control and Prevention denies any connection between the two, saying, "CDC supports the [Institute of Medicine] conclusion that there is no relationship between vaccines and autism rates in children." The American Academy of Pediatrics similarly says, "There is no scientifically proven link between measles vaccination and autism."

There is little variation in views that vaccines cause autism across demographic groups, varying within a few percentage points of the 6% average for the adult population. Younger Americans and those without college educations are most likely to say they are unsure about a causal link, and parents of children under 18—a group that is younger than the overall population—are slightly more likely than others to affirm the link.

From what you have read or heard, do you personally think certain vaccines do -- or do not -- cause autism in children, or are you unsure?

	Yes, a cause	No, not a cause	Unsure
	%	%	%
Total	6	41	52
Male	7	36	56
Female	6	46	48
18 to 29	9	30	60
30 to 49	7	40	53
50 to 64	6	47	47
65+	3	48	47
H.S. or less	6	29	64
Some college	8	36	56
College grad only	7	51	41
Postgraduate	3	75	22
Children under 18	8	39	53
No children under 18	4	46	49

Feb. 28-March 1, 2015

GALLUP

The percentage of Americans who believe that vaccines can cause autism is no higher than average among those who have heard a great deal or a fair amount about the disadvantages of vaccines, suggesting that the belief is not directly tied to the recent news coverage.

Bottom Line

Americans are much more likely now than 14 years ago to report having heard about the disadvantages of vaccines, while at the same time they have grown a bit more likely to have heard about the advantages. Despite increased awareness of the criticisms, the vast majority continue to say that it is important that children be vaccinated. Still, the discussion of vaccine disadvantages may be having some effect, as the percentage who say vaccines are extremely important is down slightly. Additionally, a small segment of the population remains skeptical about the benefits or safety of vaccines—including 9% who say vaccines are more harmful than the diseases they are designed to protect, and 6% who say certain vaccines can cause autism.

Survey Methods

Results for this Gallup poll are based on telephone interviews conducted Feb. 28–March 1, 2015, on the Gallup U.S. Daily survey, with a random sample of 1,015 adults, aged 18 and older, living in all 50 U.S. states and the District of Columbia. For results based on the total sample of national adults, the margin of sampling error is ±4 percentage points at the 95% confidence level. All reported margins of sampling error include computed design effects for weighting.

Each sample of national adults includes a minimum quota of 50% cellphone respondents and 50% landline respondents, with additional minimum quotas by time zone within region. Landline and cellular telephone numbers are selected using random-digit-dial methods.

March 09, 2015
MAJORITY IN U.S. STILL SEE OPPORTUNITY IN FOREIGN TRADE

by Justin McCarthy

WASHINGTON, D.C.—As they have for the past two years, a majority of Americans (58%) continue to view foreign trade as an opportunity for economic growth through increased U.S. exports, while 33% view it as a threat to the economy from foreign imports. The third of Americans who see foreign trade as a threat is on the low side of what Gallup has measured in the past two decades. The greater optimism on trade from 2013 to 2015 comes after a stretch of skepticism between 2005 and 2012.

What Americans Think Foreign Trade Means for the Country
What do you think foreign trade means for America? Do you see foreign trade more as -- an opportunity for economic growth through increased U.S. exports or a threat to the economy from foreign imports?

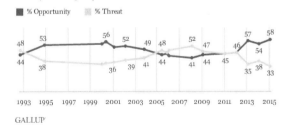

GALLUP

These data come from Gallup's World Affairs poll, conducted Feb. 8–11 with 837 U.S. adults.

The slight decline since last year in the number of Americans who view foreign trade as a threat could reflect lower oil prices and a stronger U.S. dollar. The findings also come as President Barack Obama seeks to reach the multinational Trans-Pacific Partnership

(TPP) trade agreement. If the deal is struck, it will be the largest trade agreement in U.S. history, surpassing the North American Free Trade Agreement (NAFTA) in 1994.

Hope in Foreign Trade Rebounds Among Democrats and Independents

From 2001 to 2011, spanning the entire presidency of George W. Bush and the first two years of Obama's presidency, the percentage of Republicans seeing foreign trade as an opportunity was higher than that of Democrats—in several cases, by double-digit margins. In 2012 and 2013, Democrats grew sharply more positive about trade, even as Republican views languished in the 40% to low 50% range. Opinion among the two party groups converged in 2014, but this year, Republicans' optimism about foreign trade is flat at 51%, while Democrats' has increased slightly, to 61%.

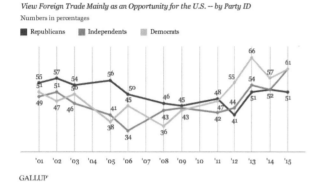

View Foreign Trade Mainly as an Opportunity for the U.S. -- by Party ID
Numbers in percentages

GALLUP'

Despite the increase in Democrats calling foreign trade an opportunity, the TPP deal has arguably encountered the greatest resistance from some Democratic members of Congress, who have concerns about its effect on U.S. jobs and regulations.

Bottom Line

Gallup has found that perceptions of foreign trade may partly relate to Americans' confidence in the economy. And as the economy has improved significantly in the past year, it's likely that public fears about foreign trade have diminished, partly because of Americans' strengthening views of the U.S. economy.

While opinions of the TPP among members of Congress may differ largely along party lines, there is some bipartisan support for the proposed pact, with the Democratic president and GOP congressional members finding at least one area of common ground. Majorities of Americans from both parties—including six in 10 Democrats—appear to agree, seeing opportunity more than they see threats from foreign trade.

Survey Methods

Results for this Gallup poll are based on telephone interviews conducted Feb. 8–11, 2015, with a random sample of 837 adults, aged 18 and older, living in all 50 U.S. states and the District of Columbia. For results based on the total sample of national adults, the margin of sampling error is ±4 percentage points at the 95% confidence level. All reported margins of sampling error include computed design effects for weighting.

March 09, 2015
U.S. EMPLOYEE ENGAGEMENT REACHES THREE-YEAR HIGH

by Amy Adkins

Story Highlights

- *32.9% of U.S. employees "engaged" in workplace in February*
- *This is the highest monthly average recorded in three years*
- *The majority of U.S. workers are still "not engaged"*

WASHINGTON, D.C.—The percentage of U.S. workers engaged in their jobs rose from an average 31.7% in January to an average 32.9% in February. The latest monthly rate of employee engagement is the highest Gallup has recorded in three years and is a full 1.5 percentage points above where it stood in February 2014.

The February 2015 estimate is based on Gallup Daily tracking interviews conducted with 5,993 adults employed for an employer. Gallup categorizes workers as engaged based on their responses to key workplace elements that it has found predict important organizational performance outcomes.

Gallup began its daily survey of U.S. workplace engagement in January 2011. At its peak, the rate of U.S. employee engagement reached 33.8% in March 2011, followed by 33.6% in January 2012. Since then, monthly engagement has consistently averaged less than 33%.

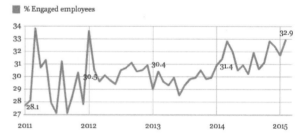

U.S. Employee Engagement, 2011-2015
Monthly averages

■ % Engaged employees

Figures shown are for February of each year

GALLUP'

Recent Engagement and Employment Trends Align

With only a third of U.S. employees engaged at work, half (50.3%) are "not engaged" and 16.8% are "actively disengaged." The slight gain in February engagement may be partially attributable to the nation's economic situation. As unemployment continues to dip and more workers find jobs, companies may be facing renewed issues with retention, leading them to put more emphasis on engagement as a way to keep their workers from seeking new job opportunities.

Recent trends suggest that improvements in engagement coincide with improvements in unemployment and underemployment.

Bottom Line

A decline in the percentage of unemployed and underemployed Americans may have some influence on the percentage of engaged workers. As the job market becomes more competitive, it is possible that companies are putting more effort into engaging their current workers. The slight rise in engagement may also be partly attributable to the workplace "honeymoon effect." Prior Gallup research indicates that newcomers to an organization are more highly engaged than tenured employees. And as more new employees join company workforces, they may be helping to move engagement up.

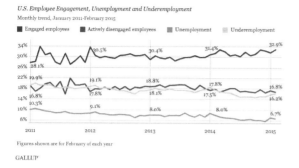

U.S. Employee Engagement, Unemployment and Underemployment
Monthly trend, January 2011-February 2015

■ Engaged employees ■ Actively disengaged employees ■ Unemployment ▢ Underemployment

Figures shown are for February of each year

GALLUP'

Although employee engagement made gains in February, its momentum appears to have slowed considerably. Engagement has stayed consistently below 30% for the first week of March. While the decline in engagement may in some part be the result of declining economic confidence, this dynamic tells only a portion of the story. Engagement is more highly dependent on factors inside the workplace, including manager talent and an organization's overall approach to employee strengths and development.

Employee engagement is a leading indicator of future business success, and Gallup has discovered close ties between engagement and outcomes such as turnover, profitability and productivity. As the percentage of their employees who are engaged at work increases, companies find themselves better positioned to grow. And when they grow, companies consequently help strengthen the economy.

Survey Methods

Results for this Gallup poll are based on telephone interviews conducted Feb. 1–28, 2015, on the Gallup U.S. Daily survey, with a random sample of 5,993 adults employed for an employer, aged 18 and older, living in all 50 U.S. states and the District of Columbia. For results based on the total sample of employed adults, the margin of sampling error is ±3 percentage points at the 95% confidence level. All reported margins of sampling error include computed design effects for weighting.

March 11, 2015
AMERICANS' VIEWS OF NETANYAHU LESS POSITIVE POST-VISIT

by Jeffrey M. Jones

Story Highlights

- *U.S. favorable ratings of Netanyahu down from 45% to 38%*
- *No change in Americans' ratings of Obama or Boehner*
- *Congressional job approval at 18%*

PRINCETON, N.J.—After Israeli Prime Minister Benjamin Netanyahu's much-publicized and controversial address to Congress,

Americans' opinions of him have worsened. His favorable rating is down seven percentage points, to 38%, while his unfavorable rating has increased five points, to 29%. These changes are largely confined to Democrats; Republicans' views are essentially stable.

Opinions of Israeli Prime Minister Benjamin Netanyahu Before and After His March 3 Address to Congress

	Feb. 8-11, 2015	March 5-8, 2015	Change
	%	%	(pct. pts.)
ALL AMERICANS			
Favorable	45	38	-7
Unfavorable	24	29	+5
DEMOCRATS/ DEMOCRATIC LEANERS			
Favorable	32	17	-15
Unfavorable	32	46	+14
REPUBLICANS/ REPUBLICAN LEANERS			
Favorable	60	62	+2
Unfavorable	17	16	-1

GALLUP'

The current rating, based on a March 5–8 poll, came just days after Netanyahu's March 3 address to Congress. Netanyahu's 45% pre-visit rating ranked among the highest Gallup has measured for him.

The address was controversial because House Speaker John Boehner did not inform President Barack Obama about his plans to invite Netanyahu to speak before Congress. Critics of the invitation thought Obama should at least have been notified given the president's predominant role in conducting U.S. foreign policy. Also, Netanyahu planned to use his speech to express his opposition to agreements designed to limit Iran's nuclear capabilities at a time when the U.S., Iran and other nations are actively negotiating such an agreement. Obama did not personally meet with Netanyahu during his U.S. visit.

The March 3 visit appears to have soured Americans'—specifically Democrats'—views of Netanyahu, though he remains more positively (38%) than negatively (29%) rated overall. Thirty-three percent of Americans do not have an opinion of Netanyahu, essentially unchanged from before the visit.

Since February, Democrats have shifted from a 32% favorable/32% unfavorable opinion of Netanyahu to 17% favorable/46% unfavorable. The majority of Republicans, 62%, view the Israeli prime minister favorably.

Obama, Boehner Images Stable

Boehner and Obama, along with Netanyahu, are the chief figures in the controversy. And while Americans' views of Netanyahu have been affected, their opinions of Obama and Boehner have not.

Americans divide evenly in their opinions of Obama—49% favorable and 48% unfavorable—similar to the 51% favorable/48% unfavorable reading from February. The president's February and March favorable ratings are improved from his personal low of 42% last November after the midterm elections. However, they are less positive than his ratings from most of the rest of his presidency.

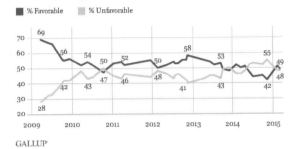

Personal Favorable Ratings of President Obama

Trend since becoming president

■ % Favorable   ■ % Unfavorable

Currently, 27% of Americans have a favorable opinion of Boehner, 49% have an unfavorable one and 24% do not have an opinion of him either way. The last time Gallup measured Americans' opinions of Boehner, in September, he had a 28% favorable rating and 50% unfavorable rating.

Aside from a very brief "honeymoon period" after Boehner took office, Americans have rated him more negatively than positively during his time as Speaker.

Boehner's image among rank-and-file Republicans has not improved since he so prominently aligned himself with Netanyahu. Republicans and Republican leaners continue to have a more negative (43%) than positive (37%) view of Boehner. In September, 47% of Republicans viewed Boehner unfavorably and 36% favorably.

Views of Congress more generally are also largely unchanged—its 18% job approval rating in the current poll is essentially the same as the 20% from last month.

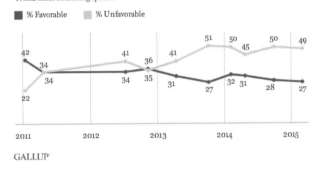

Personal Favorable Ratings of House Speaker John Boehner

Trend since becoming speaker

■ % Favorable   ■ % Unfavorable

Implications

The U.S. and Israel are longtime allies, and this is reflected in Americans' generally positive views of Israel. Those positive feelings have extended to Netanyahu, who typically has been rated more favorably than unfavorably by Americans during his time as prime minister.

However, his recent visit caused him to lose some of that goodwill among the American public, chiefly among Democrats. Democrats are likely taking their cues about the appropriateness of Netanyahu's address and his message on Iran from President Obama, who disagreed both with Netanyahu's addressing Congress and his arguments against a nuclear agreement with Iran.

Israeli voters head to the polls next week to elect a new government and will determine whether Netanyahu and his Likud Party will remain in power. Depending on the results of those elections,

Netanyahu's recent visit may be one more event that contributes to increasing U.S.-Israeli tensions under the Obama and Netanyahu administrations, or may be relegated to a small footnote in the history of U.S.-Israel relations if a new government is elected.

Survey Methods

Results for this Gallup poll are based on telephone interviews conducted March 5–8, 2015, with a random sample of 1,025 adults, aged 18 and older, living in all 50 U.S. states and the District of Columbia. For results based on the total sample of national adults, the margin of sampling error is ±4 percentage points at the 95% confidence level. All reported margins of sampling error include computed design effects for weighting.

March 11, 2015
FEWER AMERICANS SAY WINTER COLDER THAN USUAL

by Rebecca Riffkin

Story Highlights

- *Half of Americans say colder than usual, 18% say warmer*
- *Fewer say 2015 colder than usual than did so in 2014*
- *More ascribe cold temps to normal variation than climate change*

WASHINGTON, D.C.—Despite record-low temperatures in many parts of the country in February, the 51% of Americans who say temperatures in their local area have been colder than usual this winter is down from the 66% who said this about last winter. Eighteen percent of Americans say this winter has been warmer than usual, and 29% say it has been about the same as past winters.

Local Winter Temperatures Compared With Prior Winters

Next, I'd like you to think about the weather in your local area this winter season compared to past winters. Have temperatures in your local area been -- [ROTATED: colder than usual this winter, about the same, (or) warmer than usual this winter]?

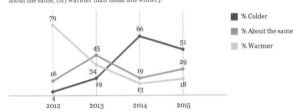

■ % Colder   ■ % About the same   ■ % Warmer

Gallup's March 5–8 Environment poll asked Americans to report on weather conditions in their local areas. Record snowfall covered much of the northeastern U.S. this winter, and at least eight northeastern cities reported record-cold temperatures in February. However, January 2015 was warmer in the Northeast, on average, than January 2014. And cities in the South were as cold in January 2014 as in 2015. The western U.S. also had far less snow than usual in 2015—states such as California and Oregon have experienced snow droughts, and warm weather has quickly melted the snow they did receive.

How Americans in different regions view their local weather mimics these regional variations. More than three in four Easterners (79%) say their winter has been colder than usual. Meanwhile, more than half of Westerners (55%) say their winter has been warmer than usual. A slight majority of Americans living in the South and Midwest say their winters have been colder than usual.

Winter Temperatures Compared With Prior Winters, by Region

Next, I'd like you to think about the weather in your local area this winter season compared to past winters. Have temperatures in your local area been -- [ROTATED: colder than usual this winter, about the same, (or) warmer than usual this winter]?

	East	Midwest	South	West
2015	%	%	%	%
Colder	79	57	55	13
About the same	19	28	34	31
Warmer	2	15	8	55
2014				
Colder	87	87	68	26
About the same	9	10	21	31
Warmer	1	3	9	41

March 5-8, 2015

GALLUP

This year, fewer residents in all four regions say their winters are colder than normal than said so last year. This includes a 30-percentage-point drop in Midwesterners who report colder-than-usual temperatures, from 87% in 2014 to 57% this year, and 13-point drops in the South and West. In 2014, much of the Midwest had extreme cold temperatures, including Chicago with the fourth-most days on record with temperatures at or below zero degrees.

Westerners and those in the Midwest are more likely to say in 2015 that their winter has been warmer than usual than the percentage who said the same in 2014. NASA satellites confirm that the western third of the U.S. have had a warmer-than-normal winter so far in 2015.

Americans Most Likely to Attribute Cold Weather to Normal Variation

Because the topic of climate change tends to come up when extreme weather patterns occur, Gallup asked Americans this year and last year whether they believe that climate change is behind the unusual temperatures they said they are experiencing.

Americans who say this winter's temperatures are colder than usual are less inclined to believe climate change is the cause and are more likely to ascribe them to normal temperature variations. Slightly less than a third of Americans (31%) attribute their reported colder-than-usual winter to normal temperature variations, while 19% say that their local weather is colder than usual because of human-caused climate change.

In contrast, Americans who say this winter's temperatures are warmer than usual are divided on the cause: 9% of Americans who say that their winter has been warmer than usual attribute it to climate change, and 8% say the warmer winter they are experiencing is because of normal variation.

In 2014, more Americans experiencing colder temperatures attributed them to normal variation rather than to climate change.

Implications

Despite record-cold February temperatures in many areas of the country, Americans are less likely to say this winter has been colder

than usual than said so last winter. Americans who say that this winter has been colder than usual are likely to blame normal variations in temperatures, similar to sentiments about last year's winter. But the smaller number of Americans who say this winter has been warmer than usual are divided as to whether it is because of normal variations or because of human-caused climate change.

Americans' Experience of Extremes in Local Weather and the Perceived Cause

Asked of those who say the weather has been colder/warmer than usual: Do you think temperatures are colder/warmer mainly due to—[ROTATED: human-caused climate change (or to) normal year-to-year variation in temperatures]?

	% 2014	% 2015
WINTER TEMPERATURES IN LOCAL AREA		
Colder than usual	66	51
(Due to normal variation in temperatures)	(46)	(31)
(Due to human-caused climate change)	(19)	(19)
(Unsure)	(1)	(1)
About the same	19	29
Warmer than usual	13	18
(Due to normal variation in temperatures)	n/a	(8)
(Due to human-caused climate change)	n/a	(9)
(Unsure)	n/a	(1)

March 5-8, 2015

The perceived cause of warmer temperatures was not asked in 2014

GALLUP

The U.S. Environmental Protection Agency (EPA) warns that climate change is making temperature extremes more common; however, more extreme high temperatures have been observed than extreme low temperatures. Furthermore, the EPA warns that climate change can cause more precipitation, like snow, in big, single-day storms. However, the EPA also makes a distinction between long-term climate change and short-term regional weather changes or events. Discussions about the cause of winter weather changes are likely to continue, as it may be hard for Americans to put year-over-year changes into a longer-term context.

Survey Methods

Results for this Gallup poll are based on telephone interviews conducted March 5–8, 2015, with a random sample of 1,025 adults, aged 18 and older, living in all 50 U.S. states and the District of Columbia. For results based on the total sample of national adults, the margin of sampling error is ±4 percentage points at the 95% confidence level. All reported margins of sampling error include computed design effects for weighting.

March 12, 2015
CLINTON FAVORABILITY, FAMILIARITY BESTS 2016 CONTENDERS
Nearly nine in 10 Americans have an opinion of Clinton

by Jeffrey M. Jones

PRINCETON, N.J.—Hillary Clinton is one of a few potential 2016 presidential candidates to have a significantly higher favorable (50%) than unfavorable (39%) rating among the American public. And the 89% of Americans who are familiar enough with Clinton to have an opinion of her is more than any other potential 2016 presidential candidate. Clinton's relatively high scores on both dimensions give her a better starting position regarding her image than other competitors would have in the 2016 U.S. presidential election.

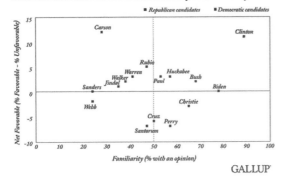

Potential 2016 Presidential Candidates: Familiarity and Favorability

These results are based on a March 2–4 Gallup poll of 1,522 U.S. adults, conducted just as revelations about the private email account Clinton used to conduct business while secretary of state became a major news story, but before her Tuesday press conference addressing questions about the issue.

The graph plots 16 potential candidates—11 Republicans and five Democrats—on a two-dimensional chart displaying their familiarity and favorability ratings. The candidates who appear in the upper-right quadrant are in the most advantageous position at this point as they are both relatively well known and have higher favorable than unfavorable ratings. In addition to Clinton, Republicans Jeb Bush, Mike Huckabee and Rand Paul reside in this space. However, Americans rate each of those Republicans only slightly more positively than negatively, with net favorable scores of +2 or +3, compared with Clinton's +11. And Huckabee and Paul have just slightly above average familiarity. Generally speaking, the further candidates are away from the intersecting lines, the better their image.

Candidates in the lower-right quadrant—including Chris Christie and Rick Perry—are among the better-known candidates, but Americans do not view them positively overall. Joe Biden and Ted Cruz are on the edges of this quadrant. Biden is well known, but opinions of him are equally positive and negative, while Cruz is viewed negatively but has average familiarity. The challenge for these politicians should they run for president is to alter existing perceptions about them so they are more positive than now, or alternatively, to get the smaller group of Americans who are unfamiliar with them to get to know them and view them positively.

Americans view candidates in the upper-left quadrant—including Republicans Marco Rubio, Scott Walker, Bobby Jindal, and Ben Carson and Democrat Elizabeth Warren—more positively than negatively, but these candidates have lower-than-average familiarity. If these candidates can maintain their positive image as they become better known—not an easy task—they would rank among the stronger presidential contenders. Right now, Rubio is closest to crossing that threshold, given that the 47% of Americans familiar with him is only slightly below the 50% average of the 16 candidates, while he has a +5 net favorable score. Carson has a +12 net favorable rating, essentially the same as Clinton's, but is among the least well-known candidates, with 28% of Americans having an opinion of him.

Republican Rick Santorum, Democrat Jim Webb and Bernie Sanders—an independent who may seek the Democratic nomination—have the biggest challenges related to their image because they are largely unknown and not viewed positively by those who do know them.

The full favorability and familiarity ratings among all Americans for each of the 16 candidates tested in the survey appear in the table.

Familiarity and Favorable Ratings of Potential 2016 Presidential Candidates, Based on National Adults

Ranked by % familiar

	% Familiar (have an opinion)	% With favorable opinion	% With unfavorable opinion	Net favorable (pct. pts.)
Hillary Clinton	89	50	39	+11
Joe Biden	78	39	39	0
Jeb Bush	68	35	33	+2
Chris Christie	65	31	34	-3
Mike Huckabee	57	30	27	+3
Rick Perry	57	25	32	-7
Rand Paul	53	28	25	+3
Ted Cruz	50	22	28	-6
Marco Rubio	47	26	21	+5
Rick Santorum	47	20	27	-7
Elizabeth Warren	41	22	19	+3
Scott Walker	38	20	18	+2
Bobby Jindal	35	18	17	+1
Ben Carson	28	20	8	+12
Bernie Sanders	24	12	12	0
Jim Webb	24	11	13	-2

March 2-4, 2015

GALLUP

In forthcoming analyses, Gallup will report the ratings of the potential Democratic presidential candidates among Democrats and the potential Republican presidential candidates among Republicans, giving a sense of how each rates image-wise in the beginning stages of the race for each party's nomination.

Clinton in Slightly Weaker Position Than Last Summer

Gallup conducted a similar analysis of the images of potential 2016 presidential candidates last July. Even as several of these individuals have attracted regular media attention in anticipation of a possible presidential bid, none of these would-be candidates has made significant gains in familiarity. But Perry, Cruz and Christie have moved from net-positive favorable ratings to net negative, while Bush has moved in the other direction.

Then, as now, Clinton was the best-known potential candidate among those rated, but her favorability rating is lower today. Last July, 55% of Americans had a favorable opinion of her and 36% an unfavorable one, for a net favorability score of +19, compared with the current +11 score.

More generally, her favorability ratings have declined in recent years as she has moved from a less overtly partisan role as secretary of state—during which time her favorable routinely topped 60%—to a more clearly partisan role as an expected presidential candidate. Still, even with diminished favorability currently, Americans do not view any of the other well-known candidates as positively as they do Clinton.

Gallup has a long trend line on Clinton's favorable ratings, from her various roles as first lady, U.S. senator, 2008 presidential candidate and secretary of state. At a similar point in early March 2007, before her last presidential campaign, she was better known than now (96% were familiar with her) and had a similar favorability profile (+12, 54% favorable and 42% unfavorable). But her favorable ratings varied over the course of that campaign, including times in which more Americans had a negative than a positive opinion of her. She eventually lost the 2008 Democratic nomination to Barack Obama after starting the campaign as the clear front-runner.

Implications

At this point, slightly less than a year before the first primaries and caucuses, Hillary Clinton is the best-known potential presidential candidate and among the most positively rated. The other possible candidates are all less well known than Clinton at this point, but as Americans get to know them better in the months ahead, these candidates' challenge will be to either maintain or create more positive images.

Right now, Bush and Christie come closest to Clinton in familiarity among the GOP field, and Carson and Rubio come closest to her on favorability. All of these candidates are, however, currently weaker than Clinton on the other of those two dimensions.

The candidates' images will change over the course of the presidential campaign as a result of increased attention from voters, increased media scrutiny, their performance in scheduled debates and how they perform in the early primaries and caucuses.

Because Americans view presidential candidates in largely political terms, many candidates might not end up with favorable ratings much higher than 50%. Regardless of how high a candidate's favorable rating gets, one minimum requirement for being a viable candidate is having a higher favorable than unfavorable rating among the American public.

Survey Methods

Results for this Gallup poll are based on telephone interviews conducted March 2–4, 2015, on the Gallup U.S. Daily survey, with a random sample of 1,522 adults, aged 18 and older, living in all 50 U.S. states and the District of Columbia. For results based on the total sample of national adults, the margin of sampling error is ±3 percentage points at the 95% confidence level. All reported margins of sampling error include computed design effects for weighting.

March 12, 2015
AMERICANS NAME GOVERNMENT AS NO. 1 U.S. PROBLEM

by Justin McCarthy

Story Highlights

- *Gov't listed as top U.S. problem for four months straight*
- *Economy still among top problems*
- *Satisfaction with direction of U.S. at 31%*

WASHINGTON, D.C.—Americans continue to name the government (18%) as the most important U.S. problem, a distinction it has

had for the past four months. Americans' mentions of the economy as the top problem (11%) dropped this month, leaving it tied with jobs (10%) for second place.

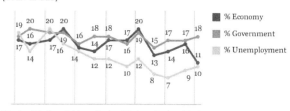

Trends in Top "Most Important" U.S. Problems, March 2014-March 2015

What do you think is the most important problem facing this country today?
[OPEN-ENDED]

GALLUP

Though issues such as terrorism, healthcare, race relations and immigration have emerged among the top problems in recent polls, government, the economy and unemployment have been the dominant problems listed by Americans for more than a year.

The latest results are from a March 5–8 Gallup poll of 1,025 American adults.

While the ranking of the top two problems is similar to what Gallup found in February, mentions of the economy dropped from 16% to the current 11%. In a separate measure, Americans' confidence in the economy had been dipping further into negative territory in late February and early March, but has been improving in recent days.

The state of U.S. healthcare also became less of a problem to Americans in March, as 7% mention it this month, compared with 10% in February.

The latest poll found that terrorism (6%), the situation in Iraq/ISIS (4%) and national security (4%) also ranked among the most cited problems, illustrating that terrorism concerns are still on many Americans' minds.

Most Commonly Named Problems in February 2015 vs. March 2015

What do you think is the most important problem facing this country today?
[OPEN-ENDED]

	February 2015	March 2015
	%	%
Dissatisfaction with government	17	18
Economy in general	16	11
Unemployment/Jobs	9	10
Immigration/Illegal aliens	6	7
Healthcare	10	7
Terrorism	8	6
Education	7	6
Ethical/Moral/Family decline	6	5
Federal budget deficit/Federal debt	5	5
Poverty/Hunger/Homelessness	4	4
Situation in Iraq/ISIS	4	4
National security	4	4
Foreign policy	3	4
Race relations	3	4

Note: Issues mentioned by 3% or fewer not shown

GALLUP

Thirty-one percent of Americans are satisfied with the way things are going in the country. Satisfaction has been stable over the last three months; however, it remains higher than most readings since 2007.

Satisfaction with the nation's direction had declined in 2013 and 2014 after reaching 33% during the 2012 fall presidential campaign. Satisfaction reached an all-time low of 7% in late 2008 as the financial crisis was underway, and an all-time high of 71% in February 1999 amid the dot-com boom.

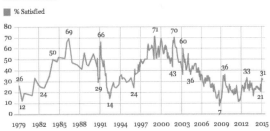

Satisfaction With the Direction of the U.S.

In general, are you satisfied or dissatisfied with the way things are going in the United States at this time?

■ % Satisfied

Latest results from March 5-8, 2015

GALLUP

Bottom Line

While dissatisfaction with government is by no means a new issue to the American people, it has not in recent months been as clearly the leading problem as it is now, given that fewer Americans mention the economy.

Meanwhile, satisfaction with the direction of the U.S. remains relatively upbeat compared with figures from recent years, but two-thirds of Americans continue to be dissatisfied.

Survey Methods

Results for this Gallup poll are based on telephone interviews conducted March 5–8, 2015, with a random sample of 1,025 adults, aged 18 and older, living in all 50 U.S. states and the District of Columbia. For results based on the total sample of national adults, the margin of sampling error is ±4 percentage points at the 95% confidence level. All reported margins of sampling error include computed design effects for weighting.

March 13, 2015

YOUNG BLACK MALES IN U.S. SUFFER WELL-BEING DEFICIT

by Dan Witters and Diana Liu

Story Highlights

- *Among men, blacks have lowest well-being in U.S.*
- *Young black males evaluate own lives far lower than young non-blacks*

WASHINGTON, D.C.—Among U.S. men, blacks have lower well-being than non-blacks, particularly among young men and seniors, according to the Gallup-Healthways Well-Being Index. Black men under the age of 35 have a Well-Being Index score that is at least one point lower than all other groups, a deficit that is statistically significant.

Well-Being Index Composite Score Among Men: Blacks vs. Non-Blacks by Age

	Black Males	Non-Black Males	Difference
All	59.7	61.0	-1.3
18-34	59.1	60.9	-1.8
35-49	59.0	59.2	-0.2
50-64	59.4	59.6	-0.2
65+	63.8	65.7	-1.9

Gallup-Healthways Well-Being Index
Jan. 2-Dec. 30, 2014

GALLUP

These findings are based on nearly 98,000 interviews with American men aged 18 and over, from Jan. 2–Dec. 30, 2014, conducted as part of the Gallup-Healthways Well-Being Index.

Young black males as a group have higher unemployment, lower graduation rates, less access to healthcare and higher incarceration rates than other racial, age and gender groups in the U.S. And in 2014, the particular difficulties this group has in dealings with law enforcement became headline news after events in Ferguson, Missouri, and Staten Island, New York, occurred involving the death of certain young black men at the hands of police. This article explores young black males' well-being, compared with other groups.

The Well-Being Index among black men aged 18 to 34 averages 59.1, 1.8 points lower than the average among all non-black men. The difference is 1.9 points for black men over the age of 65. Among those between the age of 35 and 64, however, there is little difference because blacks and whites in this age range have similar well-being scores.

Well-Being Index Composite Score Among Men by Race/Ethnicity by Age

	White Males	Black Males	Asian Males	Hispanic Males
All	60.7	59.7	63.7	62.3
18-34	60.3	59.1	63.5	62.0
35-49	58.4	59.0	63.6	62.1
50-64	59.2	59.4	64.6	63.0
65+	65.8	63.8	67.1	64.4

Gallup-Healthways Well-Being Index
Jan. 2-Dec. 30, 2014

GALLUP

Asians and Hispanics report the highest levels of well-being among men nationally. Asians in particular hold the highest well-being in every age group, while Hispanics are second-highest in every age group except the over 65 group, where they are surpassed by whites.

Within each racial group, senior citizens have the highest well-being of all age categories. Among blacks, Asians and Hispanics, well-being is also higher among those between the ages of 50 and 64 than among those less than age 50. In contrast, the youngest white males have higher well-being than white men of middle age.

Life Evaluations Much Lower for Black Men Under 35

Similar to well-being generally, young black males' general outlook on their lives is particularly worse than what is reported by young males who are not black. Gallup finds 51.7% of black males ages 18 to 34 rate their life situation well enough to be considered thriving, compared with 59.6% of non-black males in the same age range. There are much smaller differences in life evaluation between blacks and non-blacks at older ages.

Life Evaluation (% "Thriving") Among Men: Blacks vs. Non-Blacks by Age

	Black Males	Non-Black Males	Difference
	%	%	(pct. pts.)
All	50.9	52.5	-1.6
18-34	51.7	59.6	-7.9
35-49	54.5	55.7	-1.2
50-64	47.8	46.8	1.0
65+	46.4	44.2	2.2

Gallup-Healthways Well-Being Index
Jan. 2-Dec. 30, 2014

GALLUP

Also noteworthy is that young black males evaluate their lives worse than black males aged 35–49, a pattern not found across age groups among all U.S. adults or among non-black males, where life evaluation typically is lower among older age groups.

Gallup and Healthways classifies Americans as "thriving," "struggling" or "suffering," according to how they rate their current and future lives on a ladder scale with steps numbered from 0 to 10 based on the Cantril Self-Anchoring Striving Scale. Those who rate their present life a 7 or higher and their lives in five years an 8 or higher are classified as thriving, while those who rate both dimensions a 4 or lower are considered suffering. Respondents whose ratings fall in between are considered struggling.

Implications

Race and ethnicity is associated with well-being for both men and women, as is age. Among all Americans, well-being is higher for young adults than for middle-aged adults, before peaking among seniors. This general pattern is broken among blacks, as the life evaluation of young black men trails that of black men aged 35–49. These findings come at a time when Americans' satisfaction with race relations in the U.S. is sharply lower than what was reported in 2008. In addition, disproportionately high incarceration rates of young black males in the U.S. could potentially result in overestimating their already lower levels of reported well-being, as only non-incarcerated respondents are reached in the ongoing Well-Being Index.

Black men face many challenges in American society. The official unemployment rate for black men is 10.4%, double the rate of 5.2% found for men generally. Amid the jobs deficit, one-quarter of young black men report that they are treated unfairly by police because they are black, higher than what is reported by black women of their age group or older black men.

The well-being shortfall reported by young black men stems from, but also adds to, these challenges. Well-being among populations is related to employment, healthcare utilization, crime, high school graduation rates, poor mental health, and life expectancy, among other outcomes. As leaders of communities continue to discuss ways to help the lives of its citizens, embracing principles of well-being can serve as a critical contribution to this conversation. For young black males in particular, substantially lower well-being also represents a clear opportunity for leaders to make improvements in this arena.

John Hope Bryant, CEO of Operation Hope and a noted thought leader focused on the challenges facing black men in American society today, adds, "There are a myriad of factors that contribute to why young black men's suffering index is so high, but what matters most today—and for our collective American future—is what we do about it in the here and now. And going forward, what every young person in the world wants is a positive expression of what we call 'their life aspirations.' What is needed now are for policy makers, business leaders, thought leaders and community leaders to take this data, and to stand up a Call To Action 3.0. Our lives—and our collective future—literally depends on it."

Survey Methods

Results are based on telephone interviews conducted as part of the Gallup-Healthways Well-Being Index survey Jan. 2–Dec. 30, 2014, yielding a random sample of 97,784 adult men, aged 18 and older, living in all 50 U.S. states and the District of Columbia, selected using random-digit-dial sampling.

For results based on the sample sizes noted below, black respondents for each age category will have a maximum expected error range of about ±2.7 percentage points (life evaluation) and ±0.8 index points (Well-Being Index) at the 95% confidence level. Non-black respondents, in turn, will have a maximum expected error range of about ±0.8 percentage points (life evaluation) and ±0.2 index points (Well-Being Index) at the 95% confidence level.

Sample Sizes

	Black Males	Non-Black Males
All	8,141	89,643
18-34	2,396	18,914
35-49	1,926	18,030
50-64	2,427	26,747
65+	1,392	25,952

Gallup-Healthways Well-Being Index

GALLUP

March 13, 2015
HILLARY CLINTON CLEAR LEADER IN FAVORABILITY AMONG DEMOCRATS

by Andrew Dugan and Justin McCarthy

Story Highlights

- Seventy-nine percent of Dems have favorable view of Clinton
- Her rating is higher than Biden's (64%) and Warren's (37%)
- Clinton most favorable among liberal, moderate/conservative Dems

WASHINGTON, D.C.—Nearly eight in 10 Democrats (79%) have a favorable view of Hillary Clinton. Should she seek her party's 2016 presidential nomination, she would begin the campaign with a commanding lead in favorability ratings over several potential Democratic opponents, including a 15-percentage-point advantage over Vice President Joe Biden and 42-point margin over Massachusetts Sen. Elizabeth Warren.

Favorable Ratings of Potential 2016 Democratic Presidential Candidates

Among Democrats and Democratic-leaners

	Favorable	Unfavorable	Never heard of/no opinion	Net favorable
	%	%	%	pct. pts.
Hillary Clinton	79	13	7	+66
Joe Biden	64	17	19	+47
Elizabeth Warren	37	9	53	+28
Bernie Sanders	21	8	71	+13
Jim Webb	13	12	74	+1

March 2-4, 2015

GALLUP

These results come from interviews with 649 Democrats and Democratic-leaning independents in a March 2–4 Gallup poll. Clinton's candidacy for the presidency, though widely expected, is still officially unannounced. And, at least for the moment, Clinton's presidential ambitions seem almost secondary to the still-unfolding controversy from her decision as secretary of state to conduct official government business through a private email server.

Gallup conducted this poll as the revelations about Clinton's email usage were still coming to light, but the results suggest that Clinton can withstand a few chinks in her armor, at least among the party faithful. Only Biden—a former colleague of hers in the Obama administration and the U.S. Senate—comes anywhere close to Clinton's familiarity and popularity among Democrats. But unlike Clinton, it is far from certain if Biden will even pursue the nomination. Warren—a senator elected in 2012 touting a liberal economic agenda, who has previously denied interest in a White House bid—has a favorable rating of about half of Clinton's (37%). Two other candidates who have publicly expressed interest in the nomination, Sen. Bernie Sanders (I-Vt.) and former Virginia Sen. Jim Webb, both have low favorability.

Of course, it is not that Warren, Sanders and Webb are unpopular with Democrats, at least as measured by the share of Democrats saying they have an unfavorable view of them. Most Democrats do not know these senators or cannot offer an opinion about them. Of some comfort perhaps to Warren and Sanders supporters, among those Democrats who are familiar with the candidates, they are very likely to have a favorable opinion of either politician than not. Webb is roughly even in terms of net favorability.

Gallup asked about two other rumored or speculative candidates in July of last year: Former Maryland Gov. Martin O'Malley and New York Gov. Andrew Cuomo. Both men were also largely unknown to national Democrats, though seen positively among those who were familiar with them.

Clinton Leads With Liberal Democrats and Moderate/Conservative Democrats

Even among Democrats of differing ideologies—liberal versus a moderate/conservative outlook—Clinton's strengths are readily apparent. Liberal Democrats, typically the party stalwarts, give nearly all the candidates higher favorable ratings compared with all moderate/conservative Democrats. Clinton, in particular, receives a resounding favorable rating (86%) from liberal Democrats, and other candidates, notably Elizabeth Warren, see a boost in favorability and name recognition. Even so, except for Biden, all other candidates are much less known when compared with Clinton.

Favorability of Potential 2016 Democratic Presidential Candidates, by Party and Ideology

Ranked by percentage favorable

	Favorable	Unfavorable	Never heard of/No opinion	Net favorable
	%	%	%	pct. pts.
LIBERAL DEMOCRATS				
Hillary Clinton	86	9	5	+77
Joe Biden	72	13	15	+59
Elizabeth Warren	51	7	41	+44
Bernie Sanders	33	5	62	+28
Jim Webb	16	11	73	+5
MODERATE/ CONSERVATIVE DEMOCRATS				
Hillary Clinton	76	16	8	+60
Joe Biden	60	19	21	+41
Elizabeth Warren	29	10	61	+19
Bernie Sanders	14	9	77	+5
Jim Webb	12	12	76	0

Mar. 2-4, 2015

GALLUP

Moderate and conservative Democrats are less positive about all five potential candidates, but mostly because they are more likely not to know the candidates. Again, Clinton leads the pack, with Biden behind her. Warren can boast a respectable net favorable rating with these type of Democrats—a claim neither Sanders or Webb can make—but she is unknown as well.

Clinton's Front-Runner Status, Then and Now

Clinton's position today bears a strong resemblance to her place in the crowded 2008 primary cycle at a similar point in that campaign, with some important distinctions. In early March 2007, 80% of Democrats and Democratic leaners had a favorable view of Clinton, essentially no different from now. But in 2007, then freshman Sen. Barack Obama and former North Carolina Sen. John Edwards enjoyed favorable ratings well above majority levels, and both at that point had higher familiarity levels compared with that of Warren, Sanders or Webb today.

Clinton already had a race on her hands in March 2007, declaring her candidacy, along with Edwards and Obama, months earlier. This time around, however, no popular or well-known Democrat has officially entered the field, and it appears only Biden would begin the race with Clinton's high name identification. Biden, the potential candidate with the least ground to make up with Democrats in terms of his familiarity and generally positive ratings, has given mixed signals on running and is reportedly waiting until the end of the summer to make a decision.

Favorability Ratings of Potential 2008 Presidential Democratic Candidates at the Same Point in the Previous Election Cycle

Among Democrats and Democratic-leaners

	% Favorable	% Unfavorable	Net favorable (pct. pts.)
Hillary Clinton	80	16	+64
Barack Obama	68	9	+59
John Edwards	63	15	+48

March 2-4, 2007

GALLUP

Bottom Line

Clinton's favorable rating among Democrats remains higher than any prospective Democratic presidential rival—none of whom have stated that they are running. At this point in the election cycle, a "more liberal" candidate might not suffice to remove Clinton from the front-runner status she currently enjoys. Favorability ratings are a good indication of a candidate's potential for success given that they embody both name identification and a candidate's image, but it is too early to know how any potential challengers to a Clinton bid for the presidential nomination would end up on that dimension by early 2016 when the primaries and caucuses begin. At this early point in the process, the individual who comes closest to Clinton's favorable ratings is Biden, who has already unsuccessfully sought the Democratic nomination twice.

While Clinton's ascension to the Democratic national ticket is widely seen as inevitable, history shows that such presumptions have been disproven before. But the Democratic field of eight years ago was much more crowded than it is today. The current election cycle is much less contentious, with many of the most influential Democrats rallying their support for her candidacy and little public dissent from the narrative of certitude the party has crafted as 2016 draws nearer.

For Warren, Webb and Sanders, the main problem is not a low favorability or a high unfavorable rating, but rather the large share of Democrats who do not know them at all. Strong majorities have either never heard of or cannot express an opinion about these potential candidates. To challenge a candidate with such widespread name recognition such as Clinton, these candidates must find ways to boost their profile among Democrats.

Survey Methods

Results for this Gallup poll are based on telephone interviews conducted Mar. 2–4, 2015, on the Gallup U.S. Daily survey, with a random sample of 1,522 adults, aged 18 and older, living in all 50 U.S. states and the District of Columbia. For results based on the total sample of national adults, the margin of sampling error is ±3 percentage points at the 95% confidence level.

For results based on the total sample of 649 Democrats and Democratic-leaning independents, the margin of sampling error is ±5 percentage points at the 95% confidence level.

March 13, 2015
CANADA, GREAT BRITAIN ARE AMERICANS' MOST FAVORED NATIONS

by Jay Loschky and Rebecca Riffkin

Story Highlights

- *Americans most favorable toward country's strongest allies*
- *Favorability of France exceeds highest recorded level*
- *Russia less popular than at any time since fall of Soviet Union*

WASHINGTON, D.C.—Americans' current views of foreign nations range from highly positive evaluations of Canada (92% favorable) and Great Britain (90%) to highly negative ratings of Iran (11%) and North Korea (9%).

In Gallup's Feb. 8–11 World Affairs survey, Gallup asked Americans if their overall view of various prominent countries on the world stage is very favorable, mostly favorable, mostly unfavorable or very unfavorable. Based on the ratings, these 22 nations can be divided into four groups: very favorable, favorable, mixed and very unfavorable.

Americans' Views of Foreign Countries

"Next, I'd like your overall opinion of some foreign countries. What is your overall opinion of [COUNTRY]?"

	% Favorable	% Unfavorable
VERY FAVORABLE		
Canada	92	4
Great Britain	90	6
France	82	12
Germany	81	13
Japan	80	15
India	71	21
Israel	70	24
FAVORABLE		
Jordan	57	28
Mexico	55	41
Ukraine	52	36
Egypt	49	41
MIXED		
Cuba	46	48
China	44	50
Saudi Arabia	38	54
VERY UNFAVORABLE		
Russia	24	70
The Palestinian Authority	17	72
Pakistan	15	75
Iraq	15	81
Syria	14	74
Afghanistan	14	80
Iran	11	84
North Korea	9	87

Sorted by total % favorable
Feb. 8-11, 2015

GALLUP

Americans' views of foreign countries generally follow the contours of American foreign policy, with the country's longtime allies ranking highly and countries with which the U.S. has difficult relationships ranking lower. Fellow Western countries and NATO allies are rated higher than all other countries measured, with Canada (92%), Great Britain (90%), France (82%) and Germany (81%) perceived most favorably. Also rated positively are several important strategic and economic partners of the U.S., including Japan (80%), India (71%) and Israel (70%). Notably, Saudi Arabia is viewed unfavorably by a majority of Americans, despite the country's historically strong ties with the U.S. Americans previously rated Saudi Arabia more positively, but those attitudes soured after the 9/11 terrorist attacks, given that many of the attackers were Saudis.

At the opposite end of the spectrum, longtime U.S. adversaries North Korea and Iran have frequently been among the countries with the lowest favorability ratings. Opinions of Iran have been largely stable at low levels since Gallup first began measuring them in 1989 and haven't received a bump despite a recent thaw in relations. North Korea, most recently in the news for issuing its seemingly perennial call to prepare for war with the U.S., is viewed favorably by fewer than one in 10 Americans (9%).

Favorability of France at Record High; Russia Lowest Since Fall of Soviet Union

At 82% in 2015, American favorability toward France has reached its highest level since this question was first asked in 1991. In the aftermath of January's *Charlie Hebdo* terror attack, Secretary of State John Kerry brought musician James Taylor to Paris to sing "You've Got a Friend" to the French people, the surest sign yet that Franco-American relations are in a solid state. Americans' views of their nation's oldest ally have been steadily on the mend since the two countries had a falling out in 2003 over the U.S.-led invasion of Iraq, when only 34% rated France favorably.

With relations heading in the opposite direction in recent years, Vladimir Putin's Russia is now viewed favorably by just 24% of Americans, Russia's lowest rating since Gallup first began measuring American favorability of the Soviet Union in 1989. U.S.-Russia relations remain strained as a result of disagreement on a number of key issues, most notably Moscow's support of ethnic Russian rebels in Ukraine's civil war, a stance that has led the U.S. and its European allies to issue economic sanctions against Russia in the past year.

Americans' Favorable Ratings of France and Russia

■ France (% Favorable)   ▦ Russia (% Favorable)

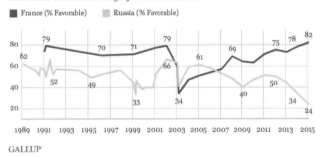

GALLUP'

Americans' Views of India Remain Largely Positive

Americans continue to offer warm views of India, with favorability ratings of the world's biggest democracy largely steady in recent years, standing at 71% in 2015. In Indian Prime Minister Narendra Modi's short time in office, he has established friendly working relations with President Barack Obama, a partnership the U.S. is keen to advance. As India's growing economy is gradually accompanied by increased influence in the region, the U.S.-India relationship is expected to take on added importance, highlighted by January's long-awaited pact allowing American companies to supply India with civilian nuclear technology.

Americans' Favorable/Unfavorable Ratings of India

■ % Favorable   ▦ % Unfavorable

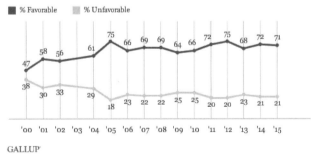

GALLUP'

Recent Shifts in Favorability

While Russia's 10-percentage-point drop in favorability marks the steepest fall over the past year, several countries have experienced a recent boost in goodwill. Following the historic normalization of relations with the U.S., nearly half of Americans (46%) now have a favorable view of Cuba, an eight-point jump since 2014 and Cuba's highest rating since Gallup began measuring its favorability in 1996.

Americans' opinions of traditional Arab allies Egypt and Jordan have seen some improvement as well. Favorability toward Egypt has increased for the second year in a row, up four points to 49% in 2015. Americans have historically held warm feelings toward the Arab nation, although favorability fell from 58% in 2010 to 40% in 2011 in reaction to instability brought on by the Arab Spring. As the political situation in Egypt continues to stabilize behind President Abdel Fattah el-Sisi's authoritarian rule, U.S. opinions of Egypt may climb nearer to previous levels.

Americans are even more positive toward Jordan, expressing favorable views of the country by a 2-to-1 margin (57% favorable vs. 28% unfavorable), a seven-point increase in favorability since 2011. At the time of February's survey, the Jordanian government was heavily bombing ISIS targets in Syria in retaliation for the group's gruesome execution of Jordanian Air Force pilot Moaz Kasasbeh, a campaign likely to draw considerable support from the American public.

Bottom Line

The American public's views of foreign nations largely reflect the countries' relationships with the U.S., with U.S. allies rating highly and countries seen as enemies viewed largely unfavorably. Nonetheless, as evidenced by Americans' relatively dim views of steadfast ally Saudi Arabia, the status of diplomatic relations is not the only factor in determining favorability toward foreign countries. While public opinion of most nations remains relatively steady year after year, favorability ratings are susceptible to changes in response to real-world events, as in the case of rapprochement with Cuba and the deterioration of relations with Russia.

Survey Methods

Results for this Gallup poll are based on telephone interviews conducted Feb. 8–11, 2015, on the Gallup U.S. Daily survey, with a random sample of 837 adults, aged 18 and older, living in all 50 U.S. states and the District of Columbia. For results based on the total sample of national adults, the margin of sampling error is ±4 percentage points at the 95% confidence level. All reported margins of sampling error include computed design effects for weighting.

March 16, 2015
NEITHER MAJOR PARTY CRACKS 40% FAVORABILITY IN LATEST POLL

by Lydia Saad

Story Highlights

- *Americans give GOP 37% favorable rating, Democrats 39%*
- *First time neither party's rating has reached 40%*

• *Republicans' favorability dips after hitting 42% last fall*

PRINCETON, N.J.—Thirty-seven percent of Americans now view the Republican Party favorably and 39% view the Democratic Party favorably. This is the only time since Gallup began tracking the party's images this way in 1992 that neither party has achieved at least 40% favorability from the public.

Americans' Opinions of the Republican and Democratic Parties

■ % Favorable opinion of the Republican Party

░ % Favorable opinion of the Democratic Party

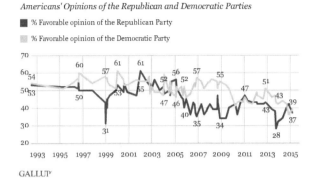

GALLUP

Over the years, Americans' perceptions of the major parties have tended to conform to two patterns. At times—such as in 1992, 1996 and in the post-9/11 years of 2001 through 2005—Americans viewed both parties favorably. At other times, the public viewed one party—typically the Democratic Party—much more favorably than the other. This was evident in late 1998 as the Republican-led U.S. House of Representatives pursued impeachment proceedings against then President Bill Clinton, as well as from 2006 through 2008 as President George W. Bush's popularity waned during the Iraq War; in 2009 at the start of President Barack Obama's presidency; and again in 2013 during the government shutdown, when Republicans' favorable rating plunged to 28%.

Except for a brief spike to 51% for the Democrats after Obama was re-elected in 2012, both parties' ratings have registered below 50% since 2010. The descent to sub-40% ratings for both parties marks a new low in an already inauspicious trend.

Republicans' Favorability Has Dipped Five Points Since Midterms

Republicans' favorable score is down from what Gallup recorded last fall, both before and after the 2014 midterm elections that resulted in the Republicans gaining seats in the U.S. House of Representatives and taking control of the U.S. Senate. Forty percent of Americans viewed the Republican Party favorably last September, and that rose to 42% just after the elections in November before falling in the current survey.

Americans' Views of the Republican Party -- Recent Trend

■ % Favorable   ░ % Unfavorable

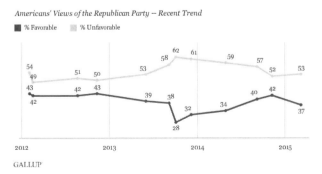

GALLUP

Whether the current dip to 37% represents a return to "normal"—34% viewed the GOP favorably last spring—or reflects specific public concerns about the party's performance since taking power this year, isn't entirely clear. In any case, the current demographic patterns in favorability toward the GOP are roughly similar today to what they were in April 2014, after improving in most categories last fall.

Percentage Viewing the Republican Party Favorably --
Recent Trend by Key Demographics

	Apr 24-30, 2014	Nov 6-9, 2014	Mar 5-8, 2015
	%	%	%
National adults	34	42	37
Men	37	44	38
Women	32	40	37
18 to 34	33	37	37
35 to 54	34	39	32
55 and older	35	47	43
College graduates	28	36	32
Some college	36	48	38
No college	36	42	41
Republicans	73	79	76
Independents	31	37	31
Democrats	9	12	11

GALLUP

Democrats Favorability Remains Near Record Low

Meanwhile, at 39%, Democrats' current favorability is up slightly from the record-low 36% after the 2014 midterms, but is still among the lowest recorded for the party on this measure. By contrast, in the same poll Obama received a 49% favorable rating, up from 42% after the midterms.

Bottom Line

For some time, numerous Gallup trends have been showing Americans largely displeased with government's performance and leadership. Through it all, at least one political party was reviewed well, but now—perhaps because of the constant brinksmanship going on between Obama and the Republican Congress, but maybe for other reasons—both parties are floundering.

Americans' Views of the Democratic Party -- Recent Trend

■ % Favorable   ░ % Unfavorable

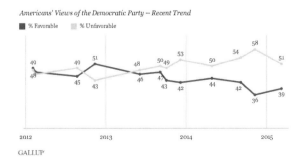

GALLUP

Survey Methods

Results for this Gallup poll are based on telephone interviews conducted March 5–8, 2015, with a random sample of 1,025 adults, aged 18 and older, living in all 50 U.S. states and the District of Columbia. For results based on the total sample of national adults, the margin of sampling error is ±4 percentage points at the 95% confidence level. All reported margins of sampling error include computed design effects for weighting.

March 16, 2015

HUCKABEE, BUSH WELL-KNOWN, WELL-RATED AMONG REPUBLICANS

by Frank Newport

Story Highlights

- *Mike Huckabee and Jeb Bush well known, well liked*
- *Rand Paul and Marco Rubio also well positioned*
- *Chris Christie rates low with conservatives, moderates/liberals*

PRINCETON, N.J.—Of 11 potential candidates for the 2016 Republican presidential nomination, Mike Huckabee and Jeb Bush are the most well known and have the highest net favorable ratings among Republicans and Republican-leaning independents. While Chris Christie is one of the most familiar Republican figures among the party base, he has the lowest net favorable rating.

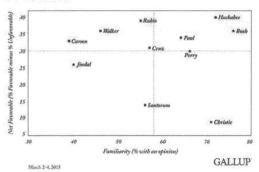

Potential 2016 Republican Presidential Candidates: Familiarity and Favorability
Based on Republicans/Leaners

These findings are based on interviews with 653 Republicans and Republican-leaning independents in a March 2–4 Gallup poll. No major Republican figure has officially announced his or her candidacy at this point, although many have indicated they are seriously exploring the possibility—and a number are making frequent trips to the early caucus and primary states of Iowa and New Hampshire.

Former Florida Gov. Jeb Bush is the best known of the 11 Republicans included in the poll, with 76% of Republicans and Republican leaners knowing enough about him to have an opinion. His top familiarity ranking is not surprising, given that his surname is one of the most famous in contemporary American presidential politics. Former Arkansas Gov. Mike Huckabee—who made a strong bid for the 2008 GOP nomination and who has been a cable

news talk-show host—is almost as well known (72% familiarity rating). Of these two, Huckabee has the slightly higher net favorable rating.

Kentucky Sen. Rand Paul has above-average familiarity, although he is not as well known as Bush or Huckabee, and Paul's net favorable rating—while also above average—is slightly lower than that of the two ex-governors. Former Texas Gov. Rick Perry also has above-average familiarity among Republicans, and his net favorable score is right at average (30%).

Four other Republicans have an above-average net favorable score, but are below average in familiarity. These include, in order of their familiarity scores, Texas Sen. Ted Cruz, Florida Sen. Marco Rubio, Wisconsin Gov. Scott Walker, and physician Ben Carson. Rubio is the most positively evaluated of these four, and has the second-highest net favorable score of any Republican tested—a percentage point below Huckabee's and three points higher than Bush's.

Both New Jersey Gov. Chris Christie and former Pennsylvania Sen. Rick Santorum are handicapped by low net favorable scores. Christie, whose name identification among Republicans is broadly similar to that of Bush and Huckabee, has the lowest net favorable score of any person tested (+9). Santorum, despite placing second to Mitt Romney in convention delegates for the 2012 GOP nomination, has below-average familiarity to go with his low net favorable score. Louisiana Gov. Bobby Jindal is one of the least-known potential candidates measured, and has a slightly below-average net favorable score.

Favorability, Familiarity Are Related

Overall, these data show that eight of the 11 potential Republican candidates measured have net favorable ratings in the 30+ range, although their familiarity scores vary widely. Favorable scores tend to go up as the individuals become better known, but in many instances, so do unfavorable scores. Nonetheless, Rubio, Cruz and Santorum have almost identical familiarity among Republicans, but Rubio's unfavorable rating is only 8%, compared with 21% for Santorum and 13% for Cruz. And Christie and Huckabee have almost identical familiarity, yet Christie has almost twice the unfavorables of Huckabee.

Familiarity and Favorable Ratings of Potential 2016 Republican Presidential Candidates, Based on Republicans/Leaners
Ranked by % familiar

	% Familiar (have an opinion)	% With favorable opinion	% With unfavorable opinion	Net favorable (pct. pts.)
Jeb Bush	76	56	20	+36
Mike Huckabee	72	56	16	+40
Chris Christie	71	40	31	+9
Rick Perry	66	48	18	+30
Rand Paul	64	49	15	+34
Ted Cruz	57	44	13	+31
Rick Santorum	56	35	21	+14
Marco Rubio	55	47	8	+39
Scott Walker	46	41	5	+36
Bobby Jindal	40	33	7	+26
Ben Carson	39	36	3	+33

March 2-4, 2015

GALLUP

Conservative Republicans are more positive than moderate/liberal Republicans about all of the potential candidates except for Christie, although conservatives are barely more positive than moderates/liberals about Bush. Christie's ratings among both groups are low, while Bush enjoys much higher evaluations.

Net Favorable Ratings Among Republicans/Leaners

	Conservative Republicans	Liberal/Moderate Republicans	Difference (conservative minus liberal/moderate)
	Pct. pts.	Pct. pts.	Pct. pts.
Ted Cruz	47	8	39
Mike Huckabee	54	16	38
Rick Perry	45	7	38
Rick Santorum	27	-6	33
Scott Walker	47	19	28
Marco Rubio	50	23	27
Rand Paul	44	19	25
Ben Carson	43	18	25
Bobby Jindal	34	13	21
Jeb Bush	37	34	3
Chris Christie	9	12	-3

March 2-4, 2015

GALLUP

Conservative Republicans are important in the presidential nominating process because they represent more than 60% of all Republicans and Republican-leaning independents and because they tend to be most heavily involved in the primary and caucus voting that determines the nominee. Conservatives are most likely to be positive about Huckabee and Rubio, although a number of other candidates are not far behind, including Cruz and Walker. Christie's net favorable rating among conservative Republicans (+9) stands out as the lowest of all those tested. Santorum, despite his staking out a strong conservative, family values orientation in his 2012 campaign, scores well below average among conservatives, while Jindal and Bush score slightly below average.

Moderate and liberal Republicans are less enthusiastic overall about the candidates, with an average +15 net favorable rating compared with the average +40 among conservative Republicans. Bush gets the highest rating among moderates/liberals, one that is more than twice the average. This gives Bush the advantage of reasonably high ratings among both ideological groups. Rubio also does better than average among moderates/liberals, to go along with his exceptionally high rating among conservatives, and Walker has a similar, although slightly less positive, image. Moderate/Liberal Republicans are by far the most negative about Santorum, giving him a -6 net favorable rating, and they give Texans Perry and Cruz below-average evaluations.

Implications

With the first Republican primary election still about 10 months away, many politicians are still in the "testing the waters" phase of the campaign. Republicans' familiarity with many of these individuals will no doubt increase in the months ahead, and others may jump into the race.

At this early juncture, however, several potential Republican candidates have image profiles among the national GOP rank-and-file that are worth noting. Bush and Huckabee enjoy the best combination of high familiarity and positive evaluations of any of the 11 politicians measured. Bush's image is built on solidly favorable ratings from both conservative and moderate/liberal Republicans, while Huckabee's much more reflects high ratings from conservatives.

At the other end of the spectrum, Christie receives below-average ratings from Republicans in both ideological groups, particularly conservatives, giving him the lowest overall net favorable ratings of any individual measured. Santorum joins Christie as the other candidate with significantly below-average net favorable ratings and, like Christie, suffers from low ratings among conservatives and, in particular, moderate/liberal Republicans.

Rubio and Walker also have net favorable scores that are among the highest measured, but neither is as well known as Bush or Huckabee. Rubio, like Huckabee, does particularly well with conservatives, but unlike Huckabee has a well-above-average rating among moderate/liberal Republicans. Walker too has above-average ratings among both groups of Republicans.

Survey Methods

Results for this Gallup poll are based on telephone interviews conducted March 2–4, 2015, on the Gallup U.S. Daily survey, with a random sample of 653 Republicans and Republican leaning independents, aged 18 and older, living in all 50 U.S. states and the District of Columbia. For results based on the total sample of national adults, the margin of sampling error is ±4 percentage points at the 95% confidence level. All reported margins of sampling error include computed design effects for weighting.

March 17, 2015
IN U.S., WORRIES ABOUT TERRORISM, RACE RELATIONS UP SHARPLY

by Justin McCarthy

Story Highlights

- *Worries about terrorism, race relations increase most since 2014*
- *Concerns about unemployment, affordable energy decrease most*
- *Americans most worried about healthcare, economy and terrorism*

WASHINGTON, D.C.—Out of 15 domestic issues, Americans' concerns about terrorism and race relations have risen most sharply over the past year. The percentage of Americans who worry "a great deal" about the possibility of a terrorist attack (51%) climbed 12 percentage points from 2014 to 2015, while concerns about race relations (28%) surged 11 points. Americans' worries about illegal immigration also climbed over the past year, increasing six points to 39%.

These data are from a March 5–8 Gallup poll, which asked Americans about the degree to which they are worried about each of a list of problems and issues.

Events in the past year such as the terrorist attack on a French newspaper's office, the rise of ISIS and ongoing protests over a white police officer in Ferguson, Missouri, shooting and killing an unarmed black man have likely played a role in the uptick in Americans' worries about a possible terrorist attack and race relations.

Changes in Americans' Levels of Concern About National Problems
% "A great deal" of concern

	2014	2015	Change
	%	%	(pct. pts.)
The possibility of future terrorist attacks in the U.S.	39	51	12
Race relations	17	28	11
Illegal immigration	33	39	6
Crime and violence	39	43	4
Drug use	34	38	4
The quality of the environment	31	34	3
Climate change	24	25	1
The Social Security system	46	46	0
The way income and wealth are distributed in the U.S.	--	46	--
Hunger and homelessness	43	43	0
The size and power of the federal government	48	46	-2
The availability and affordability of healthcare	57	54	-3
The economy	59	53	-6
The availability and affordability of energy	37	28	-9
Unemployment	49	37	-12

"The way income and wealth are distributed in the U.S." was not asked in 2014

GALLUP

On the other hand, Americans' concerns about unemployment have fallen substantially over the last year. While nearly half of Americans (49%) said in 2014 that they had a great deal of worry about the job market, this figure has since dropped to 37%, a level not seen since before the most recent economic recession. Similarly, the percentage saying they worry a great deal about the economy has fallen six points, which is consistent with higher economic confidence over the past year and a slightly higher rate of growth in the national GDP in 2014 than in recent years.

The percentage of Americans who worry about the availability and affordability of energy has also dropped nine points since last year, to 28%.

Healthcare, Economy Are Issues Americans Worry Most About

Overall, Americans worry most about the availability and affordability of healthcare (54%), the economy (53%) and the possibility of a future terrorist attack in the U.S. (51%).

Nearly half of Americans express a great deal of worry about the Social Security system, the size and power of the federal government and the way income and wealth are distributed in the U.S.

On the other hand, Americans express the least amount of concern about climate change—25% have a great deal of worry—confirming that despite widespread news coverage of the implications of changing temperatures, Americans are not highly worried about the issue. Additionally, less than a third of Americans worry a great deal about race relations and the availability and affordability of energy.

Bottom Line

The events of the past year have clearly shifted Americans' relative levels of worry about a number of issues facing the country. Terror attacks in Paris and the rise of ISIS have formed the backdrop to a significant increase in concerns about such attacks taking place on American soil. At home, the racially charged incidents in Ferguson and elsewhere have amped up conversations on racism and police brutality, often creating a wedge within communities.

Americans' Levels of Concern About National Problems -- 2015 Rank Order

Next, I'm going to read a list of problems facing the country. For each one, please tell me if you personally worry about this problem a great deal, a fair amount, only a little, or not at all. First, how much do you personally worry about ... [RANDOM ORDER]?

	A great deal
	%
The availability and affordability of healthcare	54
The economy	53
The possibility of future terrorist attacks in the U.S.	51
The Social Security system	46
The size and power of the federal government	46
The way income and wealth are distributed in the U.S.	46
Hunger and homelessness	43
Crime and violence	43
Illegal immigration	39
Drug use	38
Unemployment	37
The quality of the environment	34
The availability and affordability of energy	28
Race relations	28
Climate change	25

March 5-8, 2015

GALLUP

Meanwhile, gains in unemployment and economic growth and lower gas prices have provided a sense of economic relief to many Americans and have alleviated worries about economic issues.

Survey Methods

Results for this Gallup poll are based on telephone interviews conducted March 5–8, 2015, on the Gallup U.S. Daily survey, with a random sample of 1,025 adults, aged 18 and older, living in all 50 U.S. states and the District of Columbia. For results based on the total sample of national adults, the margin of sampling error is ±4 percentage points at the 95% confidence level. All reported margins of sampling error include computed design effects for weighting.

March 18, 2015
MONTANA RANKS HIGHEST IN EMPLOYEE ENGAGEMENT FOR 2013 AND 2014

by Jim Harter and Bailey Nelson

WASHINGTON, D.C.—Workers in Montana, followed closely by those in Mississippi and Louisiana, had the highest levels of employee engagement in 2013 and 2014. With 22% of workers engaged, the District of Columbia had the lowest employee engagement, followed by New York, Minnesota and Connecticut.

The 2013–2014 employee engagement estimates across states are based on Gallup Daily Tracking interviews conducted Jan. 2013–Dec. 2014, including 166,409 interviews with adults employed full or part time for an employer. Nationally, 31% of workers were engaged during this time period.

Previous Gallup research shows that employee engagement predicts nine performance outcomes for organizations. Business units with engaged workers have 22% higher profitability than those with disengaged workers because they have higher productivity, higher retention rates, fewer accidents on the job and fewer quality defects. As reported in Gallup's 2013 State of the American

Workplace report, strong employee engagement is linked to higher customer engagement. And with benefits such as improved overall well-being and physical health, high engagement is also good news for individuals.

States With Highest Engagement in 2013 & 2014

State	Engaged
	%
Montana	39
Mississippi	37
Louisiana	36
Oklahoma	35
New Mexico	35
Arkansas	35
Texas	34
Florida	34
Alabama	33
Georgia	33

GALLUP

Employee Engagement by State, 2013-2014

■ Highest engagement quintile ■ Second highest engagement quintile ■ Middle engagement quintile
□ Second lowest engagement quintile □ Lowest engagement quintile

GALLUP

Gallup identifies workers as engaged, not engaged or actively disengaged based on their responses to items that assess key workplace elements found to predict important business outcomes.

- **Engaged** employees are involved in and enthusiastic about their work and workplace. Day after day, they are passionate about their jobs and feel a profound connection to their company. They are more productive, drive innovation and promote organizational growth.
- **Not engaged** employees are essentially "checked out." They demonstrate less concern about customers, productivity and profitability. They do not own or feel passionately about their work.
- **Actively disengaged** employees are not just unhappy at work; these employees undermine the accomplishments of their engaged coworkers. They monopolize managers' time, account for more quality defects and quit at a higher rate than engaged employees.

While, for the most part, states with higher percentages of engaged workers have lower percentages of actively disengaged workers, this is not always the case. The District of Columbia, for example, has a relatively low percentage of engaged workers and also a low percentage of actively disengaged workers. Active disengagement tends to be more highly related to labor market trends such as unemployment, underemployment and letting people go.

Connecticut, New York, Michigan and Kentucky Highest in Active Disengagement

There is a four-way tie between Connecticut, New York, Michigan and Kentucky for the highest percentage of actively disengaged workers—21% in each state. Residents of South Dakota, Wyoming, Alaska and Vermont reported the lowest percentages of actively disengaged workers, each with less than 15%. The national average for 2013–2014 was 18% active disengagement. States with higher active disengagement have significantly higher unemployment and underemployment rates than states with lower active disengagement. For example, the eight states with 20% or more actively disengaged workers averaged 8% unemployment and 18% underemployment. In contrast, the seven states with 15% or less actively disengaged workers averaged only 5% unemployment and 14% underemployment. Employees in states with higher active disengagement are also more likely to report that their company is letting people go (16% compared with 13% for those in states with 15% or fewer actively disengaged workers).

States With Highest Active Disengagement in 2013 & 2014

State	Actively Disengaged
	%
Connecticut	21
New York	21
Michigan	21
Kentucky	21
New Jersey	20
Delaware	20
Ohio	20
Pennsylvania	20
Nevada	19
Missouri	19

GALLUP

States With Lowest Active Disengagement in 2013 & 2014

State	Actively Disengaged
	%
Virginia	16
New Mexico	16
North Dakota	16
Texas	15
District of Columbia	15
Montana	15
Vermont	14
Alaska	13
Wyoming	13
South Dakota	12

GALLUP

Implications

There are many factors that correlate with engagement and active disengagement that may help with understanding the engagement differences between states. Previous Gallup research shows that employees in very small companies (fewer than 10 employees) have higher rates of engagement and lower rates of active disengagement—likely related to the psychological ownership and autonomy that is often present in small companies. Gallup finds a similar correlation when comparing state engagement data and U.S. Census Bureau statistics of U.S. businesses: The seven states with the lowest levels of active disengagement are more likely to have a high percentage of firms with fewer than 10 employees than the states with the highest levels of active disengagement. As such, the size of businesses within states may explain some of the state-level engagement differences.

Rates of unemployment and underemployment are also associated with variation in state engagement: There is a general positive correlation between these economic indices and active disengagement. And recent employment statistics and overall U.S. workforce trends suggest that active disengagement has declined in line with decreases in unemployment and underemployment. There are many reasons that may explain the relationship between these economic indices and engagement. A more competitive labor market may boost employers' concern for employees. And Gallup research indicates that newer employees are more engaged than tenured employees—potentially giving states with more new hires a slight engagement advantage.

Knowing why some states have higher employee engagement than others ultimately requires an examination of the management practices of organizations within each state. While there are significant differences in employee engagement across states, Gallup finds even greater differences in engagement across organizations and among manager-led teams within organizations. For example, some organizations have 70% or more of their employees engaged, while others have less than 20% engaged. Within the same organizations, some managers engage nearly every worker they manage, while other managers alienate, or disengage, the employees they manage. Organizations that do the best job of hiring talented managers and do the right things systemically to engage their workforce have a much greater chance to grow. Decisions that affect these practices are made by progressive-thinking organizational leaders and entrepreneurs within each state.

Sangeeta Agrawal provided research assistance for this story.

Survey Methods

Results for this Gallup poll are based on telephone interviews conducted January 2013–December 2014 on Gallup Daily tracking, with a random sample of 166,409 adults, aged 18 and older, living in all 50 U.S. states and the District of Columbia.

For results based on the total sample of national adults, the margin of sampling error is ±1 percentage points at the 95% confidence level.

Sample sizes for states ranged from 488 in Delaware to 15,532 in California in 2013–2014. Margins of sampling error for individual states range from ±1 percentage point to ±6 percentage points at the 95% confidence level. All reported margins of sampling error include computed design effects for weighting.

March 18, 2015
AUSTIN, SALT LAKE CITY LEAD U.S. METROS IN JOB CREATION

by Jeffrey M. Jones

Story Highlights

- *Austin, Salt Lake City Job Creation Indexes are +37*
- *New York, Hartford, San Diego lag in job creation*
- *Most large MSAs have above-average job creation*

PRINCETON, N.J.—Austin, Texas, and Salt Lake City, Utah, have the highest Job Creation Index scores among the 50 largest U.S. metro areas, based on employee reports of hiring activity where they work. San Francisco, Houston and Orlando rank just behind Austin and Salt Lake City in job creation.

Many of the top-ranking metro areas are being boosted by growth in technology jobs, including traditional tech centers in San Francisco and San Jose but also emerging ones in Austin and Salt Lake City. These latter two may be increasingly attractive destinations for tech workers, given salaries that are becoming more competitive for the industry, along with a much lower cost of living than in California. Salt Lake City is also benefiting through growth in

tourism and energy sector jobs. The growth in job creation in both Austin and Salt Lake City also spills over into growth in housing and construction jobs to meet the basic needs of the growing workforce in those areas.

Highest Job Creation Index Scores, 50 Largest U.S. Metro Areas, 2014 Gallup Daily Tracking

	Job Creation Index score
Salt Lake City, Utah	37
Austin-Round Rock, Texas	37
San Francisco-Oakland-Hayward, Calif.	36
Houston-The Woodlands-Sugar Land, Texas	36
Orlando-Kissimmee-Sanford, Fla.	36
San Jose-Sunnyvale-Santa Clara, Calif.	35
Louisville-Jefferson County, Ky.-Ind.	35
Detroit-Warren-Dearborn, Mich.	35
Raleigh, N.C.	35
Portland-Vancouver-Hillsboro, Ore.-Wash.	34

Job Creation Index scores are based on the percentage of workers in each metro area who say their employer is hiring workers and expanding the size of its workforce minus the percentage who say their employer is letting workers go and reducing the size of its workforce.

GALLUP

The results are based on Gallup Daily tracking conducted throughout 2014. Gallup asks working Americans to say whether their employer is hiring workers and expanding the size of its workforce, not changing the size of its workforce, or letting workers go and reducing the size of its workforce. Overall, throughout 2014, an average of 39% of U.S. workers said their employer was hiring workers, compared with 13% who said their employer was letting workers go, resulting in a nationwide Job Creation Index of +26. Reports of job creation are currently quite strong and have improved each year since 2009.

Lowest Job Creation Index Scores, 50 Largest U.S. Metro Areas, 2014 Gallup Daily Tracking

	Job Creation Index score
New York-Newark-Jersey City, N.Y.-N.J.-Pa.	20
San Diego-Carlsbad, Calif.	20
Hartford-West Hartford-East Hartford, Conn.	20
Virginia Beach-Norfolk-Newport News, Va.-N.C.	21
Las Vegas-Henderson-Paradise, Nev.	21
Providence-Warwick, R.I.-Mass.	23
Memphis, Tenn.-Miss.-Ark.	24
Los Angeles-Long Beach-Anaheim, Calif.	24
Pittsburgh, Pa.	24
Riverside-San Bernardino-Ontario, Calif.	24

Job Creation Index scores are based on the percentage of workers in each metro area who say their employer is hiring workers and expanding the size of its workforce minus the percentage who say their employer is letting workers go and reducing the size of its workforce.

GALLUP

Gallup assigns respondents to metro areas using the definitions for metropolitan statistical areas (MSAs) developed by the federal Office of Management and Budget. Each MSA sample is weighted to ensure it is representative of the population of that metro area. Sample sizes range from a low of 745 for Birmingham, Alabama, to a high of 11,362 for the New York City metro area.

Hiring activity appears to be a bit stronger in the larger U.S. metro areas than in the U.S. as a whole, given that all but 15 of the 50 most populous metro areas have Job Creation Index scores higher than the +26 national average. The full data for each of the largest metro areas appear at the end of the article.

The areas with the lowest index scores among the top 50 MSAs are New York, San Diego and Hartford, Connecticut, at +20, and Virginia Beach-Norfolk, Virginia, and Las Vegas at +21. Although these scores are the lowest in a relative sense, they are still strong in an absolute sense.

San Diego and Virginia Beach-Norfolk have large military presences, so reductions in defense spending could be limiting job growth in those areas.

Houston, Salt Lake, Orlando Consistently Among Job Creation Leaders

Gallup previously assessed job creation by metro area for 2012 and 2013 combined. Houston led the other metro areas for that two-year period, but despite an increase in its Job Creation Index score, it was edged out by Salt Lake City and Austin this year. Houston, along with Salt Lake City and Orlando, has ranked among the top five metro areas for both 2012–2013 and 2014.

Meanwhile, New York and San Diego ranked near the bottom in both reports. This is in spite of significant improvement in the Job Creation Index scores for both metro areas this year, including a seven-point increase for New York (from +13 to +20) and an eight-point increase for San Diego (from +12 to +20).

More broadly, each of the 50 largest metro areas had at least a nominal increase in its Job Creation Index score, with the average improvement being eight points. The metro areas with the largest improvements since 2012–2013 are Raleigh, North Carolina, at 14 points, and Sacramento, California; Portland, Oregon; and Detroit, Michigan, at 13 points each. After the improvements, Raleigh, Portland and Detroit now rank among the leading MSAs in job creation. Sacramento had one of the lowest job creation scores in 2012–2013, and now ranks in the middle of the pack.

Implications

The U.S. job market has steadily improved since the depths of the 2008–2009 recession, and the largest metro areas have tended to show an even better job situation than the country as a whole. In particular, metro areas with strong or emerging technology industries rank among those with the greatest hiring activity, based on workers' reports of what is happening at their own workplaces. Metro areas that are successful in attracting workers in a certain growth industry—be it technology, energy or health—will likely reap even greater benefits as the growing job base has snowball effects that lead to job creation in industries, like construction, to support the growing workforce living there.

Survey Methods

Results for this Gallup poll are based on telephone interviews conducted in 2014, on the Gallup U.S. Daily survey, with a random sample of 201,254 employed adults, aged 18 and older, living in all 50 U.S. states and the District of Columbia. For results based on the total sample of workers, the margin of sampling error is ±1 percentage point at the 95% confidence level.

For results based on MSA-level data, the margin of sampling error is no more than ±4 percentage points at the 95% confidence level and is ±3 percentage points for most MSAs. Respondents are assigned to metro area using OMB definitions of metropolitan statistical areas.

March 19, 2015
SAN JOSE AND SAN FRANCISCO LEAD IN ECONOMIC CONFIDENCE

by Andrew Dugan

WASHINGTON, D.C.—The San Jose-Sunnyvale-Santa Clara and the San Francisco-Oakland-Hayward metropolitan areas in California posted some of the highest scores on Gallup's Economic Confidence Index in 2014. San Jose-Sunnyvale-Santa Clara boasted an Economic Confidence Index score of +12, while San Francisco and its surrounding area registered a +9. Both scores are increases from 2012–2013, and the two areas now notably surpass the index score in the Washington, D.C., metro area (+5).

Highest Economic Confidence Index Scores, 50 Largest U.S. Metro Areas, 2014 Gallup Daily

	Index score
San Jose-Sunnyvale-Santa Clara, CA	12
San Francisco-Oakland-Hayward, CA	9
Washington-Arlington-Alexandria, DC-VA-MD-WV	5
Minneapolis-St. Paul-Bloomington, MN-WI	5
Miami-Fort Lauderdale-West Palm Beach, FL	4
Raleigh, NC	1
Seattle-Tacoma-Bellevue, WA	0
Denver-Aurora-Lakewood, CO	0
Austin-Round Rock, TX	0

GALLUP

Additionally, Minneapolis and its surrounding areas, Miami-Fort Lauderdale-West Palm Beach and Raleigh, North Carolina, had positive index scores in 2014. Several of the best performing cities, in terms of economic confidence, are known for their booming technology or research-related sectors, including the famous Silicon Valley, which plays a heavy role in the economies of San Francisco and San Jose and Raleigh's Research Triangle Park.

These results are based on Gallup Daily tracking conducted throughout 2014 in the 50 most populous U.S. metropolitan statistical areas (MSAs). Gallup assigns respondents to metro areas using the definitions for MSAs developed by the federal Office of Management and Budget. Each MSA sample is weighted to ensure it is representative of the population of that metro area. Sample sizes range from a low of 658 for Memphis, Tennessee, to a high of 8,991 for the New York City metro area.

Gallup's Economic Confidence Index is a composite of Americans' ratings of current U.S. economic conditions and their perceptions of the national economy's direction. The index has a theoretical maximum of +100 (if all respondents rate the economy as "excellent" or "good" and say it is "getting better"), and a theoretical minimum of -100 (if all rate the economy as "poor" and say it is "getting worse").

Overall, the average Economic Confidence Index score for the top 50 MSAs was -10, compared with -15 for the entire U.S. Although the index is a measure of how Americans see the *national* economy faring, the different scores from city to city suggest that many Americans judge the state of the country's economy by how well their local economy is performing.

Raleigh saw the largest improvement in its index score from 2012 to 2013, improving 10 points from -9 to +1 in 2014. In 2012–2013, only three metro areas rated the national economy well enough to have a positive Economic Confidence Index score compared with six in 2014, as well as another three metropolitan areas that recorded a score of zero.

The areas with the lowest index scores among the top 50 MSAs are Memphis, at -24, and Birmingham-Hoover, Alabama, at -26. These scores are well below the average index score for the top 50 MSAs, and also trail the national score by a wide margin.

Lowest Economic Confidence Index Scores, 50 Largest U.S. Metro Areas, 2014 Gallup Daily

	Index score
Buffalo-Cheektowaga-Niagara Falls, NY	-18
Indianapolis-Carmel-Anderson, IN	-18
Cincinnati, OH-KY-IN	-20
Kansas City, MO-KS	-20
Pittsburgh, PA	-20
New Orleans-Metairie, LA	-21
Providence-Warwick, RI-MA	-21
Oklahoma City, OK	-21
Memphis, TN-MS-AR	-24
Birmingham-Hoover, AL	-26

GALLUP'

Birmingham also saw the biggest drop in confidence in 2014 relative to its 2012–2013 standing, with its index score falling by seven points.

Implications

In tandem with an improving national economy, the country's largest metropolitan areas are showing signs of strengthening economic confidence. As was seen in Gallup's Job Creation Index, many of the leading cities with the highest index scores have a strong presence in tech or STEM-related fields, an economic specialty that continues to see rapid growth.

March 19, 2015
IN U.S., ABOUT HALF SAY OBAMA DOING GOOD JOB ON ENVIRONMENT

by Justin McCarthy

WASHINGTON, D.C.—As President Barack Obama works to make environmental protection a key issue in the final two years of his administration, about half of Americans (52%) say he is doing a "good job" of protecting the environment. They are less likely to say he is doing a good job of improving the nation's energy policies (39%), a difference seen throughout his administration.

These data, collected March 5–8 as part of Gallup's annual Environment poll, come as Obama places greater focus on environmental issues—from his plan to sign an executive order that all federal agencies cut back their greenhouse gas emissions to a larger effort to reduce such emissions globally.

Shortly after Obama took office in 2009, about four in five Americans said he was doing a good job on the environment (79%), but this figure fell by 2010, consistent with the drop in his overall approval rating. Since 2010, between 51% and 56% have given Obama a positive rating on the environment.

On national energy issues, too, the percentage of Americans who feel Obama is doing a good job has been stagnant in recent years. After a high of 72% in Obama's honeymoon period shortly after taking office, this figure dropped to 43% by 2010 and has remained at about that level in subsequent years, with his current 39% the lowest by two percentage points.

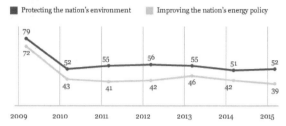

Do you think Barack Obama is doing a good job or a poor job in handling each of the following issues as president?
% "Good job"

■ Protecting the nation's environment ■ Improving the nation's energy policy

NOTE: 2009 question asked: "Do you think Barack Obama will do a good job or a poor job" in each area.

GALLUP'

Obama has recently pushed for an expansion of renewable energy such as solar and wind projects. His administration also seeks tougher standards on oil and coal companies that extract resources from federal lands. Such policies would place restrictions on pollution while creating incentives for investing in renewable energy, which is expected to have some pushback from the GOP-controlled Congress—many of whom argue the incentives favor some businesses over others and misuse taxpayer dollars. Obama's positioning on the relationship of energy policy to environmental protection was exemplified by his veto of congressional legislation that would have authorized the building of the Keystone XL pipeline from Canada through the middle part of the country. His veto was based in large part on safety and environmental considerations, even as pipeline advocates argued that the pipeline would create tens of thousands of construction jobs and decrease U.S. dependence on Middle Eastern oil.

Obama's Ratings on the Environment, Energy Trump Bush's

Americans have consistently held Obama in greater esteem on the environment than they did his predecessor, George W. Bush, whose ratings on environmental protection sank further each year into his administration. Bush received a high "good job" rating of 51% just after he took office in 2001, and this fell to a low of 30% in 2007. His ratings on the environment leveled off in his final year in office, when 31% said he was doing a good job.

Obama vs. Bush -- Protecting the Nation's Environment
Do you think Barack Obama/George W. Bush is doing a good job or a poor job in handling each of the following issues as president?

% "Good job"

■ Obama ■ Bush

| Year 1 | Year 2 | Year 3 | Year 4 | Year 5 | Year 6 | Year 7 | Year 8 |

NOTES:
Question asked in March of each year
2001 question: "Do you think George W. Bush will do a good job or a poor job" in each area.
2009 question: "Do you think Barack Obama will do a good job or a poor job" in each area.

GALLUP'

For the most part, Obama's ratings on energy policy have also exceeded Bush's ratings by year in office. Except for his first year, Bush consistently had higher ratings on the environment than on energy, even though both ratings fell during his administration.

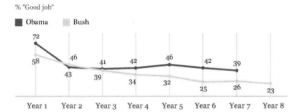

Obama vs. Bush -- Improving the Nation's Energy Policy

Do you think Barack Obama/George W. Bush is doing a good job or a poor job in handling each of the following issues as president?

% "Good job"

■ Obama　　■ Bush

72　58

46　43

41　39

42　34

46　32

42　25

39　26

　　23

Year 1　Year 2　Year 3　Year 4　Year 5　Year 6　Year 7　Year 8

NOTES:

Question asked in March of each year

2001 question: "Do you think George W. Bush will do a good job or a poor job" in each area.

2009 question: "Do you think Barack Obama will do a good job or a poor job" in each area.

GALLUP®

Republicans Give Obama Low Environment and Energy Ratings

Democrats continue to view Obama's performance on protecting the environment most favorably (75%) compared with independents (52%) and Republicans (29%).

All party groups give Obama lower scores for handling energy than for handling the environment. Sixty-eight percent of Democrats, 36% of independents and 13% of Republicans say Obama is doing a good job of improving the nation's energy policy. The gap in environment versus energy ratings is greater for Republicans and independents (16 percentage points each) than for Democrats (seven points).

Views of President Obama's Handling of the Following Issues, by Party

% "Good job," by self-identified party affiliation

	Democrats	Independents	Republicans
	%	%	%
Protecting the nation's environment	75	52	29
Improving the nation's energy policy	68	36	13

March 5-8, 2015

GALLUP®

Bottom Line

Although Obama has just two years left in office, his efforts to make a difference on energy and environmental issues may leave a legacy for his administration. But in the meantime, his domestic and international initiatives over the last five years of his presidency have not made much of a difference in how Americans view his performance on these issues. Obama consistently gets higher ratings for his work on the environment than for his work on energy, something that is also generally true of Bush, his predecessor. Obama's recent decision to veto the Keystone XL pipeline project, citing environmental concerns, most likely highlighted his priorities on these two issues.

Gallup has found that the environment and energy are among the issues Americans worry about least, so while Obama's work in this area may garner attention from politicians, energy companies and environmental groups, these efforts might not mean as much for the nation at large.

Still, Americans continue to favor Obama's performance on environmental and energy policies more than they favored that of the previous president. And when it comes to protecting the environment in particular, Obama has maintained a consistent majority of those who feel he is doing a good job.

Survey Methods

Results for this Gallup poll are based on telephone interviews conducted March 5–8, 2015, with a random sample of 1,025 adults, aged 18 and older, living in all 50 U.S. states and the District of Columbia. For results based on the total sample of national adults, the margin of sampling error is ±4 percentage points at the 95% confidence level. All reported margins of sampling error include computed design effects for weighting.

March 20, 2015

SAN FRANCISCO METRO AREA RANKS HIGHEST IN LGBT PERCENTAGE

by Frank Newport and Gary J. Gates

PRINCETON, N.J.—The San Francisco metropolitan area has the highest percentage of the adult population who identify as lesbian, gay, bisexual or transgender (LGBT) of any of the top 50 U.S. metropolitan areas, followed by Portland, Oregon, and Austin, Texas.

Highest Percentage LGBT Population, 50 Largest U.S. Metro Areas, 2012-2014

LGBT percentages are based on responses to the question "Do you, personally, identify as lesbian, gay, bisexual or transgender?"

	% LBGT
San Francisco-Oakland-Hayward, Calif.	6.2
Portland-Vancouver-Hillsboro, Ore.-Wash.	5.4
Austin-Round Rock, Texas	5.3
New Orleans-Metairie, La.	5.1
Seattle-Tacoma-Bellevue, Wash.	4.8
Boston-Cambridge-Newton, Mass.-N.H.	4.8
Salt Lake City, Utah	4.7
Los Angeles-Long Beach-Anaheim, Calif.	4.6
Denver-Aurora-Lakewood, Colo.	4.6
Hartford-West Hartford-East Hartford, Conn.	4.6

Gallup Daily tracking

GALLUP®

Variation in the percentage who identify as LGBT across the largest metro areas is relatively narrow, with San Francisco's percentage just 2.6 percentage points higher than the national average of 3.6%, and the lowest-ranked metro area—Birmingham, Alabama—one point below the national average.

The top 10 includes metro areas from every region of the country except the Midwest. Given the long history of a visible and politically active LGBT community in San Francisco, the city's ranking at the top of this list is not surprising. Similar to San Francisco, Metropolitan Statistical Areas (MSAs) like Portland, Seattle and Los Angeles in the West, and Boston in the Northeast, are known for their progressive social and political climates and active LGBT communities. Hartford is the capital of Connecticut, which has permitted same-sex couples to legally marry longer than every state except Massachusetts.

MSAs like Austin and New Orleans in the South, and Denver in the Rocky Mountain region, all have reputations as socially progressive cities within states and regions that are much more conservative, perhaps making them regional hubs for the LGBT population.

The ranking of Salt Lake City in the top 10 may seem surprising because Utah is one of the most conservative states in the country. However, the state recently passed a law prohibiting discrimination based on sexual orientation and gender identity in employment and public accommodation, the first state to do so since 2007. The majority of states still do not have such laws on the books.

These results are based on responses to the question, "Do you, personally, identify as lesbian, gay, bisexual or transgender?"— included in more than 374,000 Gallup Daily tracking interviews conducted between June 2012 and December 2014. This is the largest ongoing study of the distribution of the LGBT population in the U.S. on record, and the first time a study has had large enough sample sizes to provide estimates of the LGBT population by MSA.

The number of interviews conducted in each MSA between June 2012 and December 2014 is large enough to allow for estimates of each of the 50 largest metro areas' LGBT population. Each MSA except two had at least 3,000 interviews, with the lowest sample size of 2,674 for New Orleans and the largest of 36,947 for New York. The LGBT percentage, along with the number of completed interviews conducted in each MSA is presented in the accompanying table.

Birmingham Has Lowest Percentage of LGBT

Birmingham, Alabama, with 2.6% LGBT identity, has the lowest percentage of LGBT adults of any of the 50 largest metro areas, followed by Pittsburgh and Memphis, Tennessee. Other MSAs with low percentages of LGBT adults include San Jose, California; Raleigh, North Carolina; Cincinnati; and Houston.

Explanations are likely varied for the particularly low percentages of LGBT adults in some MSAs. Eight of the 10 MSAs with the lowest percentages are in the South or Midwest, the two regions of the country where LGBT identification among adults tends to be lowest and where social stigma toward LGBT people can be relatively high. Alabama, home to Birmingham, has made news lately as its state Supreme Court has resisted implementation of a federal court order to allow same-sex couples to marry. Among the ranked MSAs, Pittsburgh has the highest proportion of seniors in the population. Gallup research has shown that LGBT identity tends to be lower among seniors.

Lowest Percentage LGBT Population, 50 Largest U.S. Metro Areas, 2012-2014

LGBT percentages are based on responses to the question "Do you, personally, identify as lesbian, gay, bisexual, or transgender?"

	% LBGT
Birmingham-Hoover, Ala.	2.6
Pittsburgh, Pa.	3.0
Memphis, Tenn.-Miss.-Ark.	3.1
San Jose-Sunnyvale-Santa Clara, Calif.	3.2
Raleigh, N.C.	3.2
Cincinnati, Ohio-Ky.-Ind.	3.2
Houston-The Woodlands-Sugar Land, Texas	3.3
Oklahoma City, Okla.	3.5
Richmond, Va.	3.5
Nashville-Davidson-Murfreesboro-Franklin, Tenn.	3.5
Milwaukee-Waukesha-West Allis, Wis.	3.5

Gallup Daily tracking

GALLUP

San Jose may be the most surprising metro area to be among the 10 lowest, because it is home to the Silicon Valley and many technology companies that have been among the most vocal supporters of LGBT rights in corporate America. For example, Apple, Google and Facebook all recently signed a friend-of-the-court brief submitted to the U.S. Supreme Court, supporting legalizing marriage for same-sex couples. The low ranking could mean that many LGBT individuals who work in the Silicon Valley choose to live closer to San Francisco and its vibrant LGBT social scene.

Implications

The distribution of LGBT identity across the largest metro areas in the U.S. is relatively narrow, with a range of 3.6 percentage points from the highest to the lowest MSA among the top 50. This mirrors previous analyses of the distribution of the LGBT population across states, which show similarly fairly even distribution, at least in comparison to the many other pronounced geographic differences found on race, ethnic, political and ideological variables.

The lack of sharp distinctions could reflect in part that the geographic MSAs used in this research are large, and for most areas, include significant suburban populations around center cities. The sample sizes involved do not allow for an analysis of center cities per se, but perhaps the LGBT percentage is larger in these areas than in the metropolitan area as a whole.

At the same time, the variation across MSAs does provide interesting information about LGBT identification and its possible relationship to the ideological and legal climate in different metropolitan regions. Certainly, a metropolitan area such as San Francisco has a different history and culture relating to the LGBT population than does Birmingham, and those differences appear in LGBT identification among the areas' residents.

These rankings at least partly may be an indication of where LGBT adults choose to live. But a survey conducted in 2013 showed that only 12% of LGBT adults considered the levels of LGBT social acceptance in a city as a major factor in their decisions about where to live. These rankings could also reflect differences across metro areas in the willingness of residents to identify as LGBT to interviewers. LGBT people who live in MSAs where they experience greater levels of social acceptance and often the legal protections that come with that may be more likely to identify themselves as such compared with LGBT adults living in areas in which there is less acceptance of people of differing sexual orientations. While San Francisco may be one of the most desirable areas in the country for LGBT people to live, it also may be an area where residents feel more comfortable in identifying themselves as LGBT.

Survey Methods

Results for this Gallup poll are based on telephone interviews conducted from June 2012 to December 2014, on the Gallup U.S. Daily survey, with a random sample of 374,325 employed adults, aged 18 and older, living in all 50 U.S. states and the District of Columbia. For results based on the total sample of workers, the margin of sampling error is ±1 percentage point at the 95% confidence level.

For results based on MSA-level data, the margin of sampling error is no more than ±1 percentage point at the 95% confidence level for each MSA. Respondents are assigned to a metro area using the federal Office of Management and Budget (OMB) definitions of metropolitan statistical areas. Gallup assigns respondents to metro areas using the definitions for Metropolitan Statistical Areas developed by OMB. Each MSA sample is weighted to ensure it represents the population of that metro area.

March 20, 2015
HILLARY CLINTON RETAINS STRONG APPEAL TO AMERICAN WOMEN

by Jeffrey M. Jones

Story Highlights

- *Women quite positive toward Clinton, men are divided*
- *Women have long rated Clinton better than men have*
- *Clinton top-rated potential 2016 candidate among women*

PRINCETON, N.J.—Women continue to have a much more positive opinion of Hillary Clinton than men do. Fifty-six percent of women have a favorable opinion of Clinton, while 32% view her unfavorably. Men are evenly divided in their opinions of Clinton.

Americans' Opinions of Hillary Clinton, by Gender
Net favorable is % favorable minus % unfavorable

	Favorable	Unfavorable	Net favorable
	%	%	pct. pts.
National adults	50	39	11
Women	56	32	24
Men	44	45	-1

March 2-4, 2015

GALLUP

The results are based on a March 2–4 Gallup poll, conducted as revelations about her use of a private email account to conduct government business were emerging, but before she publicly addressed the issue. Clinton is expected to officially announce her presidential candidacy for the 2016 election next month. Her combination of high familiarity among the general public and more positive than negative favorable ratings puts her in a more advantageous early position regarding her image than any of her potential 2016 rivals.

Clinton owes much of her strong early position among possible 2016 candidates to her appeal to women. This gender difference in her image ratings is not new; Gallup has previously documented wide gender gaps in views of Clinton while she was first lady, U.S. senator, a presidential candidate in 2008, and most recently, secretary of state.

Not only is there a gender gap in Clinton's overall favorable rating, but all major female demographic groups view Clinton more positively than do their male counterparts, including by age, education, race, marital status and partisanship. In nearly every comparison, Clinton's favorable rating is 10 percentage points higher for women than men in the same subgroup. Her net favorable rating—the percentage who views her positively minus the percentage who views her negatively—is typically 20 points higher for women than for men who share the same characteristic.

Aside from Republican women, each of these groups of women views Clinton more positively than negatively. But her image is more positive among younger women than older women, among

unmarried women than married women, and among nonwhite women than white women, largely reflecting broad partisan differences by subgroup in the U.S. There is only a modest difference in how female college graduates and non-graduates view Clinton.

Americans' Opinions of Hillary Clinton, by Gender and Select Demographics
Net favorable is % favorable minus % unfavorable

	Favorable	Unfavorable	Net favorable
	%	%	pct. pts.
AGE			
Women, 18-49	59	25	34
Men, 18-49	44	41	3
Women, 50+	54	40	14
Men, 50+	44	51	-7
RACE			
Non-Hispanic white women	50	42	8
Non-Hispanic white men	37	56	-19
Nonwhite women	71	10	61
Nonwhite men	59	23	36
EDUCATION			
Women college graduates	62	33	29
Men college graduates	47	49	-2
Women, non-college graduates	55	32	23
Men, non-college graduates	43	44	-1
MARITAL STATUS			
Married women	50	39	11
Married men	40	54	-14
Unmarried women	64	25	39
Unmarried men	49	36	13
PARTISANSHIP			
Democratic/Lean Democratic women	83	11	72
Democratic/Lean Democratic men	74	16	58
Republican/Lean Republican women	26	67	-41
Republican/Lean Republican men	19	77	-58

March 2-4, 2015

GALLUP

Women Most Positive Toward Clinton in Potential 2016 Field

Among all major potential 2016 presidential candidates from either party that Gallup tested in the recent poll, Clinton has the highest favorable rating by far (56%) among U.S. women. Joe Biden ranks a distant second among women in overall favorability (41%), followed by Jeb Bush with 32%. Her +24 net favorable rating also is substantially better than any other possible candidate's rating.

Opinions of Potential 2016 Presidential Candidates, Among Women
Net favorable is % favorable minus % unfavorable
Ranked by % favorable

	Favorable	Unfavorable	Net favorable
	%	%	pct. pts.
Hillary Clinton	56	32	24
Joe Biden	41	34	7
Jeb Bush	32	32	0
Mike Huckabee	29	24	5
Chris Christie	28	31	-3
Rick Perry	22	26	-4
Marco Rubio	22	16	6
Elizabeth Warren	21	14	7
Rand Paul	21	21	0
Ben Carson	18	7	11
Ted Cruz	17	22	-5
Rick Santorum	17	23	-6
Scott Walker	17	14	3
Bobby Jindal	15	13	2
Bernie Sanders	9	8	1
Jim Webb	8	9	-1

March 2-4, 2015

GALLUP

Relative to her competitors, Clinton was not in as same strong a position among women early in the 2008 campaign as she is now. A March 2–4, 2007, Gallup poll shows Clinton's 60% favorable among women at the time was matched by Rudy Giuliani's 61%, with Barack Obama (57%), John McCain (54%) and John Edwards (51%) close behind.

Reflecting her high visibility relative to her other potential rivals in the 2016 campaign, Clinton's 44% favorable rating among men is higher than any other potential candidate, although her -1 net favorable rating trails several Republican candidates' ratings.

Opinions of Potential 2016 Presidential Candidates, Among Men

Net favorable is % favorable minus % unfavorable
Ranked by % favorable

	Favorable	Unfavorable	Net favorable
	%	%	pct. pts.
Hillary Clinton	44	45	-1
Jeb Bush	37	35	2
Joe Biden	37	44	-7
Rand Paul	35	30	5
Chris Christie	34	36	-2
Mike Huckabee	33	31	2
Marco Rubio	30	25	5
Rick Perry	29	38	-9
Ted Cruz	27	33	-6
Rick Santorum	25	31	-6
Scott Walker	24	22	2
Ben Carson	23	9	14
Elizabeth Warren	22	24	-2
Bobby Jindal	20	22	-2
Bernie Sanders	15	17	-2
Jim Webb	14	16	-2

March 2-4, 2015

GALLUP'

Clinton Leads Other Democratic Candidates Among Democrats of Both Genders

Clinton must first win the Democratic nomination before Americans can elect her president. And currently Democratic women and Democratic men view her more positively than any of her potential challengers for the nomination. Eighty-three percent of Democratic women view Clinton favorably, with Biden next at 65%. Clinton's 74% favorable rating among Democratic men exceeds Biden's by 13 points.

Opinions of Potential 2016 Democratic Presidential Candidates, Among Democrats/Democratic Leaners

Net favorable is % favorable minus % unfavorable
Ranked by % favorable

	Favorable	Unfavorable	Net favorable
	%	%	pct. pts.
WOMEN			
Hillary Clinton	83	11	72
Joe Biden	65	16	49
Elizabeth Warren	34	9	25
Bernie Sanders	16	6	10
Jim Webb	11	11	0
MEN			
Hillary Clinton	74	16	58
Joe Biden	61	18	43
Elizabeth Warren	40	9	31
Bernie Sanders	27	10	17
Jim Webb	16	13	3

March 2-4, 2015

GALLUP'

Implications

During her last presidential campaign, Americans' opinions of Clinton varied in response to campaign events. While she is the best known of the potential 2016 presidential candidates, it would not be surprising to see her favorable ratings vary at least slightly between now and the fall of 2016 if she runs for president again. The recent flap over her email use is the kind of event that could cause some changes Americans' opinions of her.

One thing that has been consistent in Clinton's more than two decades in the public eye is that women are much more positive toward her than men are. Should she be able to maintain a positive image throughout a presidential campaign, she will have a decided advantage among more than half of the population that her contenders do not share, making her a formidable contender for president. If the Democratic Party nominates her as their candidate and Americans elect her president, Clinton's bedrock of support among women would likely play a substantial role in that achievement.

To defeat Clinton, her challengers from either party would have to weaken her appeal to women as much as possible and develop an equally strong or stronger advantage among men. That is precisely what occurred in the 2008 nomination contest, when Clinton maintained a slim lead among Democratic women, but with Barack Obama enjoying an even larger advantage among Democratic men.

Survey Methods

Results for this Gallup poll are based on telephone interviews conducted March 2–4, 2015, on the Gallup U.S. Daily survey, with a random sample of 1,522 adults, aged 18 and older, living in all 50 U.S. states and the District of Columbia. For results based on the total sample of national adults, the margin of sampling error is ±3 percentage points at the 95% confidence level.

For results based on the samples of 752 men and 770 women, the margin of sampling error is ±4 percentage points at the 95% confidence level.

March 23, 2015
D.C., SALT LAKE CITY LEAD METROS IN PAYROLL TO POPULATION

by Ben Ryan

Story Highlights

- *Texas boasts three of top 10 metros for P2P*
- *California and Florida dominate bottom 10 metros*
- *Labor force participation tracks most closely with P2P*

WASHINGTON, D.C.—Washington, D.C. (54.1%), and Salt Lake City (52.9%) had the highest Payroll to Population employment rates (P2P) among the 50 largest U.S. metro areas in 2014. The rest of the top 10 metropolitan statistical areas (MSAs) in P2P were distributed widely across the country, but three were in Texas: Houston, Austin and Dallas-Fort Worth. Miami and Tampa, Florida, had the lowest P2P rates, at 38.2% and 39.3%, respectively. Three of the MSAs with the lowest P2P rates were in California: Riverside, Sacramento and Los Angeles.

Highest P2P Rates, 50 Largest U.S.
Metro Areas, 2014

	P2P rate %
Washington-Arlington-Alexandria, D.C.-Va.-Md.-W.Va.	54.1
Salt Lake City, Utah	52.9
Denver-Aurora-Lakewood, Colo.	51.8
Houston-The Woodlands-Sugar Land, Texas	51.5
Minneapolis-St. Paul-Bloomington, Minn.-Wis.	51.3
Austin-Round Rock, Texas	51.1
Dallas-Fort Worth-Arlington, Texas	49.9
Indianapolis-Carmel-Anderson, Ind.	49.4
Seattle-Tacoma-Bellevue, Wash.	49.4
Raleigh, N.C.	49.1

Gallup Daily tracking

GALLUP

Lowest P2P Rates, 50 Largest U.S.
Metro Areas, 2014

	P2P rate %
Tampa-St. Petersburg-Clearwater, Fla.	38.2
Miami-Fort Lauderdale-West Palm Beach, Fla.	39.3
Riverside-San Bernardino-Ontario, Calif.	39.6
Sacramento--Roseville--Arden-Arcade, Calif.	40.2
Las Vegas-Henderson-Paradise, Nev.	41.2
Los Angeles-Long Beach-Anaheim, Calif.	41.6
Detroit-Warren-Dearborn, Mich.	42.2
Providence-Warwick, R.I.-Mass.	42.5
Buffalo-Cheektowaga-Niagara Falls, N.Y.	42.6
Pittsburgh, Pa.	43.2

Gallup Daily tracking

GALLUP

Gallup's P2P metric tracks the percentage of the adult population aged 18 and older who are employed full time for an employer for at least 30 hours per week. P2P is not seasonally adjusted. Gallup does not count adults who are self-employed, work fewer than 30 hours per week, are unemployed or are out of the workforce as payroll-employed in the P2P metric.

These results are based on Gallup Daily tracking conducted throughout 2014 in the 50 most populous U.S. metropolitan statistical areas. Gallup assigns respondents to metro areas using the definitions for MSAs developed by the federal Office of Management and Budget. Each MSA sample is weighted to ensure it is representative of the population of that metro area. Sample sizes ranged from a low of 1,312 for New Orleans to a high of 18,154 for the New York metro area.

Dense urban areas tend to have higher rates of workforce participation, which drives P2P rates up as well. The average P2P rate among the 50 largest MSAs in 2014 was 46.0%, compared with the average of 44.0% for the U.S. as a whole. Nationally, the less densely populated an area is, the more likely adults are to be out of the workforce, while rates of part-time work, self-employment and unemployment remain much more consistent.

Employment Status by Population Density in the United States, 2014
Gallup Daily tracking

	Top quintile, most densely populated	2nd quintile	3rd quintile	4th quintile	Bottom quintile, least densely populated
Employed full time (employer)	46.8%	47.3%	44.6%	42.7%	39.1%
Employed full time (self)	4.9%	4.8%	4.9%	5.1%	6.5%
Employed part time, do not want full time	6.1%	6.7%	6.7%	6.8%	7.2%
Unemployed*	5.5%	4.8%	4.4%	4.1%	4.0%
Employed part time, want full time	7.0%	6.1%	5.9%	5.6%	5.8%
Not in workforce	29.6%	30.3%	33.6%	35.7%	37.3%

*Unemployment figures in this table are as a percentage of the adult population, rather than the labor force as more commonly reported.

GALLUP

Salt Lake City Had Lowest Unemployment

As with P2P rates, MSAs in California and Florida dominate the 10 metros with the highest unemployment in 2014. Tampa registered the highest unemployment rate at 10.8%, followed by Miami at 10.3% and Riverside, California, at 10.2%. Salt Lake City had

the lowest unemployment rate in 2014, at only 3.5%. The Florida MSAs, all of which are in the bottom half in P2P, are also among the highest 10 in unemployment—suggesting their lower P2P rates are not merely a result of having a higher retired population.

While P2P reflects the proportion of adults working full time for an employer relative to the entire *population*, Gallup's U.S. unemployment rate reflects the proportion of adults in the *workforce*—all those working or seeking work—who are not working, but would like to be. Nationally, the U.S. averaged 6.9% unemployment in 2014. Gallup's calculation of unemployment mirrors that used by the government's Bureau of Labor Statistics (BLS) but still differs from it in several ways, including that Gallup's measure is not seasonally adjusted.

Lowest Unemployment Rates, 50 Largest U.S. Metro
Areas, 2014 Gallup Daily

	Unemployment rate %
Salt Lake City, Utah	3.5
Louisville-Jefferson County, Ky.-Ind.	3.9
Austin-Round Rock, Texas	4.7
Columbus, Ohio	4.7
Memphis, Tenn.-Miss.-Ark.	4.8
Denver-Aurora-Lakewood, Colo.	4.9
Raleigh, N.C.	5.2
Buffalo-Cheektowaga-Niagara Falls, N.Y.	5.3
Washington-Arlington-Alexandria, D.C.-Va.-Md.-W.Va.	5.4
Kansas City, Mo.-Kan.	5.5
San Antonio-New Braunfels, Texas	5.5

GALLUP

Highest Unemployment Rates, 50 Largest U.S. Metro
Areas, 2014 Gallup Daily Tracking

	Unemployment rate %
Tampa-St. Petersburg-Clearwater, Fla.	10.8
Miami-Fort Lauderdale-West Palm Beach, Fla.	10.3
Riverside-San Bernardino-Ontario, Calif.	10.2
Virginia Beach-Norfolk-Newport News, Va.-N.C.	9.9
Sacramento--Roseville--Arden-Arcade, Calif.	9.2
Las Vegas-Henderson-Paradise, Nev.	8.9
San Jose-Sunnyvale-Santa Clara, Calif.	8.8
Jacksonville, Fla.	8.8
Los Angeles-Long Beach-Anaheim, Calif.	8.8
Orlando-Kissimmee-Sanford, Fla.	8.6

GALLUP

Five of the top 10 MSAs for P2P also rank in the 10 lowest MSAs for unemployment in 2014: In addition to Salt Lake City, Austin; Denver; Raleigh, North Carolina; and the District of Columbia all make the list. However, Buffalo, New York, also makes it, despite being among the bottom 10 MSAs for P2P. Buffalo ranked last among the 50 largest MSAs on workforce participation, at 61.1%, compared with 66.7% nationally.

Both P2P and unemployment are objective indicators of the employment situation, and as such, there is a great deal of overlap on these two metrics among the best- and worst-performing MSAs. The measures also correspond with the best and worst performers on Gallup's Job Creation Index and Economic Confidence Index, which provide a more attitudinal assessment of an MSA's employment and economic picture. Six of the top 10 MSAs for P2P also rank in the top 10 for economic confidence, and four rank in the top 10 for job creation. Interestingly, Detroit ranks seventh lowest in terms of P2P, but eighth *highest* for job creation, potentially forecasting an improvement in that employment ranking.

Implications

Comparing employment levels among the 50 largest U.S. metropolitan areas in 2014 tells a familiar story. Once again, the biggest factor countering full-time employment is not unemployment, but failure to participate in the labor force at all. According to BLS data, labor force participation declined and unemployment rose sharply in the U.S. in the wake of the 2008–2009 recession. Yet both BLS and Gallup data show that while unemployment has fallen consistently in the intervening years, labor force participation remains at historically low levels.

Higher rates of full-time employment translate not just into higher incomes, but higher well-being, too. American cities that find ways to mobilize working-age adults provide some of the best opportunities to put more Americans back into quality full-time jobs.

Survey Methods

Results for this Gallup poll are based on telephone interviews conducted in 2014, on the Gallup U.S. Daily survey, with a random sample of 353,732 adults, aged 18 and older, living in all 50 U.S. states and the District of Columbia. For results based on the total sample of national adults, the margin of sampling error is ±1 percentage point at the 95% confidence level.

For results based on MSA-level data, the margin of sampling error is no more than ±3 percentage points at the 95% confidence level. Respondents are assigned to metro area using OMB definitions of metropolitan statistical areas.

March 23, 2015
AMERICANS SPLIT ON SUPPORT FOR FRACKING IN OIL, NATURAL GAS

by Art Swift

Story Highlights

- *40% support fracking; 40% oppose it*
- *Older Americans favor fracking more, younger Americans opposed*
- *Republicans solidly support fracking, Democratic support low*

WASHINGTON, D.C.—The practice of hydraulic fracturing, or "fracking," has emerged as a divisive issue across the U.S., reflected in Americans' opinions about it; 40% of Americans say they favor the procedure, while 40% oppose it, and a substantial 19% do not have an opinion. This is amid the Obama administration last week announcing the first nationwide safety rules for fracking.

Fracking is a process of drilling and injecting fluid into the ground at high pressures to fracture shale rocks and release natural gas inside. Developed in the 1940s, fracking became much more widespread in the late 1980s, when oil operators began drilling horizontally, using hydraulic fracturing. In the 1990s, fracking was introduced into shale formations, and it is this practice on a massive commercial scale that is employed throughout the U.S. today. Many credit fracking with contributing to the current "oil boom," which has helped dramatically ramp up the production of oil in the U.S., and even passing Saudi Arabia as the world's largest oil producer. It is also being denounced by environmentalists as causing potential hazards, such as water-table pollution and earthquakes.

This Gallup survey was taken March 5–8, before the U.S. Interior Department unveiled new rules regarding fracking on federal lands and Indian territories, but as the debate rages in states such as New York, Pennsylvania and Oklahoma.

The survey asked Americans whether they favor or oppose "hydraulic fracturing or 'fracking.'" The survey did not further define the process, list pros or cons or measure the degree to which the public has been following the issue. But eight in 10 Americans are willing to give an opinion, with the results split evenly, along with 19% who explicitly said they didn't have an opinion.

Views of fracking are partisan, underscoring the degree to which the fracking debate has become part of today's highly divided political environment. A solid majority of Republicans (66%) support fracking, while 20% oppose it. On the Democratic side, opposition is twice as great as support, 54% to 26%. Independents are more likely to oppose (44%) than to favor (35%) the practice, with 21% having no opinion.

Fracking in the United States

Do you favor or oppose hydraulic fracturing or "fracking" as a means of increasing the production of natural gas and oil in the U.S.?

	Favor	Oppose	No Opinion
OVERALL	40	40	19
POLITICAL PARTY			
Republican	66	20	15
Independent	35	44	21
Democrat	26	54	21
AGE			
18-29	32	44	24
30-49	35	45	20
50-64	46	37	17
65+	52	32	16
ENVIRONMENTAL MOVEMENT			
Active participant	24	53	23
Sympathetic participant	30	49	21
Neutral/Unsympathetic	57	28	16

Mar 5-8, 2015

GALLUP'

Support for fracking is higher among older than younger Americans, which can partly be explained by the relationship between age and partisanship (younger Americans are more likely to identify as Democrats). More than half (52%) of Americans aged 65 and older support fracking, but this support drops to only 32% among 18- to 29-year-olds. Middle-aged Americans are closer to the overall nationwide split on fracking, with those aged 30 to 49 slightly opposing fracking, and Americans aged 50 to 64 slightly favoring the method.

The poll also measures Americans' environmentalism by asking if they are active participants in, or sympathizers to, the "environmental movement." There is a relationship between self-identified environmentalism and opinions about fracking. Twenty-four percent who say they are an "active participant" in the environmental movement favor fracking, 30% who say they are "sympathetic" to this movement (but not active in it) are in favor of fracking, while 57% who would consider themselves "neutral or unsympathetic" to the movement are in favor of the practice.

Bottom Line

Fracking has helped contribute to a substantial increase in natural gas and oil production across the U.S., and now in other parts of the world, and is credited with helping lower its price for the average consumer. At the same time, environmentalists see fracking as harmful to the environment, and the ensuing debate has roiled cities and states that this type of oil production has affected. For instance, Texas is considering "pre-emptive" bills in the state legislature to undo local fracking bans because of the jobs and revenue that hydraulic fracturing is creating. After New York Gov. Andrew Cuomo ordered a ban on fracking in New York last December, some towns in the southern tier of the state, near Pennsylvania where fracking is legal, have threatened to secede from New York because they are missing out on oil revenues from fracking.

These events and countless other local incidents have played into the debate of whether fracking is acceptable in today's America. Opponents of fracking point to a multitude of earthquakes in Oklahoma—585 in 2014, more than the last 35 years combined—as a reason to oppose the procedure. And a report last year stated that Americans who live near oil and gas drilling wells are exposed to fracking-related air pollution in the form of chemicals such as benzene and formaldehyde.

As of now, the public is split evenly in support and opposition of fracking, and as the debate continues, it will be interesting to see if one point of view begins to grab the upper hand in Americans' minds.

Survey Methods

Results for this Gallup poll are based on telephone interviews conducted March 5–8, 2015, with a random sample of 1,025 adults, aged 18 and older, living in all 50 U.S. states and the District of Columbia. For results based on the total sample of national adults, the margin of sampling error is ±4 percentage points at the 95% confidence level.

March 24, 2015
AMERICANS' RATING OF ENVIRONMENT INCHES UP TO RECORD HIGH

by Rebecca Riffkin

Story Highlights

- *In U.S., half rate the quality of the environment positively*
- *Highest percentage to give positive rating since 2001*
- *Reps remain more likely than Dems to give positive rating*

WASHINGTON, D.C.—Half of Americans rate the overall quality of the environment as "excellent" or "good," the most positive views of the environment since Gallup began asking this question in 2001.

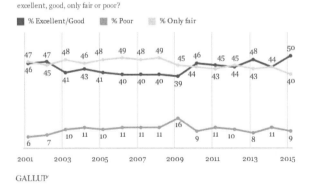

Views of the Quality of the Environment Highest Since 2001

How would you rate the overall quality of the environment in this country today -- as excellent, good, only fair or poor?

These results are based on Gallup's 2015 Environment poll, conducted March 5–8.

The uptick in positive evaluations of the environment is offset by a decline in those rating the environment as "only fair." Forty

percent of Americans rate the environment as only fair, down from 44% in 2014 and the lowest percentage found since 2001. At the same time, the 9% rating the quality of the environment as "poor" is similar to what Gallup has found over the past six years.

Americans' ratings of the quality of the environment dropped in 2003 and didn't rise until 2010. From 2003 to 2009, an average of 41% said the quality of the environment was excellent or good, including an all-time low of 39% in 2009. Since then, coincident with the first full years of the Obama administration, the average has been 47%, similar to the levels recorded in 2001 and 2002.

Republicans and Democrats More Positive About Environment

All partisan groups are a bit more positive about the quality of the environment this year than they were in 2014. Republicans consistently have been the most positive of all party groups about the environment, although the gap narrowed significantly in 2008 leading up to the presidential election. The partisan gap has remained narrow throughout Barack Obama's presidency.

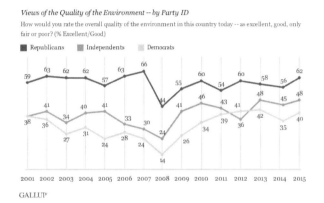

Views of the Quality of the Environment -- by Party ID

How would you rate the overall quality of the environment in this country today -- as excellent, good, only fair or poor? (% Excellent/Good)

Americans Remain More Likely to Think Environment Is Getting Worse Than Better

Unlike the improvement seen in Americans' ratings of the environment today, the percentage who say the quality of the environment is "getting better" has been essentially unchanged since 2009.

But similar to the trend in views about the quality of the current environment, Americans during Obama's presidency have been more likely to say the quality of the environment is getting better than they were to say the same during George H. W. Bush's presidency. When Obama entered office in 2009, Americans' outlook on the environment improved, and it has been fairly stable since.

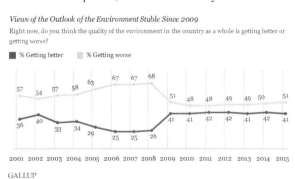

Views of the Outlook of the Environment Stable Since 2009

Right now, do you think the quality of the environment in the country as a whole is getting better or getting worse?

Republicans are slightly more likely than independents or Democrats to say the environment is getting better. The gap between Republicans and Democrats was much larger prior to 2009, but Democrats—and to a lesser degree, independents—became significantly more positive after Obama took office.

Views of the Outlook of the Environment -- by Party ID

Right now, do you think the quality of the environment in the country as a whole is getting better or getting worse? (% Getting better)

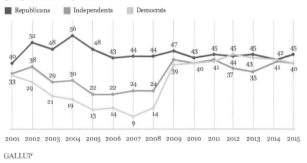

GALLUP

Bottom Line

Americans rate the quality of the environment more positively than they have in the 14 years Gallup has been tracking it. Still, Americans remain more likely to believe the environment is getting worse than getting better.

Democrats especially have become more positive about the environment since President Obama took office in 2009. And the president's recent pro-environment actions—vetoing the Keystone pipeline and announcing fracking regulations—are in line with Americans' generally positive ratings of the job Obama is doing to protect the environment.

Survey Methods

Results for this Gallup poll are based on telephone interviews conducted March 5–8, 2015, on the Gallup U.S. Daily survey, with a random sample of 1,025 adults, aged 18 and older, living in all 50 U.S. states and the District of Columbia. For results based on the total sample of national adults, the margin of sampling error is ±4 percentage points at the 95% confidence level. All reported margins of sampling error include computed design effects for weighting.

March 25, 2015
U.S. VIEWS ON CLIMATE CHANGE STABLE AFTER EXTREME WINTER

by Lydia Saad

Story Highlights

- *Slight majority continue to say effects of warming already evident*
- *No change in percentage worried about the issue, at 55%*
- *Less than half see global warming as a serious threat to them*

PRINCETON, N.J.—Although climate scientists have been in the news describing this winter as a strong signal that global warming

is producing more extreme weather, Americans are no more likely today (55%) than in the past two years to believe the effects of global warming are occurring.

Americans' Belief That Effects of Global Warming Are Already Happening

Which of the following statements reflects your view of when the effects of global warming will begin to happen -- they have already begun to happen; they will start happening within a few years; they will start happening within your lifetime; they will not happen within your lifetime, but they will affect future generations; or they will never happen?

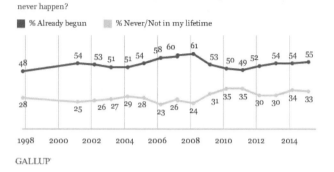

GALLUP

The 2014–2015 winter season brought record warm temperatures to the western U.S. while it delivered record cold to much of the rest of the country and record snowfall in the East. However, this winter has neither created an uptick in new believers that the effects of global warming are manifest nor reduced the ranks of skeptics. A third of Americans believe the effects of global warming will either never happen (16%) or not happen in their lifetime (17%), about the same as in March 2014.

Similarly, as Gallup reported previously, Americans' levels of concern about a number of environmental issues are no higher today than last March, including concerns about global warming. Just over half of Americans, 55%, currently say they worry a "great deal" (32%) or "fair amount" (23%) about the issue, roughly the same as last year and similar to the average over the past six years. Public worry about global warming was higher from 2006 to 2009, and higher still in 1999 and 2000.

Worry About Global Warming/Climate Change

Please tell me if you personally worry about this problem a great deal, a fair amount, only a little or not at all -- global warming or climate change.

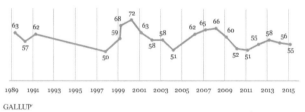

GALLUP

Other Global Warming Trends Also Steady

Three other trends reflecting Americans' concerns and attitudes about global warming tell the same story. Just over a third believe global warming will pose a serious threat to their way of life in their lifetime, a slight majority believe the seriousness of global warming is either underestimated or reported correctly in the news, and a similar majority believe global warming is the result of human activities rather than natural causes.

In the same poll, Gallup found 51% of Americans saying the weather in their area was colder than usual this winter, while 18% said it was warmer and 29% said it was about the same. However, when asked what they attribute it to, most of those in the cold regions believe the extreme cold reflected normal variations in weather. At the same time, just half of those in the warm spots attribute the unusual heat to global warming; the other half think it was normal variation.

Three Measures of Public Belief About Global Warming

Recent trends

	2014 %	2015 %
Do you think that global warming will pose a serious threat to you or your way of life in your lifetime?		
Yes	36	37
No	64	62
Thinking about what is said in the news, in your view is the seriousness of global warming:		
Generally underestimated	33	35
Generally correct	23	21
Generally exaggerated	42	42
Do you believe increases in the Earth's temperature over the last century are due more to:		
Human activities	57	55
Natural causes	40	41

See accompanying question responses and trends for precise question wording.

GALLUP'

Thus, one reason more Americans may not make the connection between unusual weather patterns and global warming is that many more experienced extreme cold than record heat, making the connection less intuitive.

Bottom Line

Americans' global warming views have been in a holding pattern for the past few years. This winter, much of the country experienced either unusually hot, cold or snowy weather, theoretically providing cause for people to reflect on whether they were witnessing normal variation in weather or the effects of global warming. However, most Americans believe the strange weather reflects natural variations, not global warming—and the stability of Gallup's global warming trends underscores this.

Survey Methods

Results for this Gallup poll are based on telephone interviews conducted March 5–8, 2015, with a random sample of 1,025 adults, aged 18 and older, living in all 50 U.S. states and the District of Columbia. For results based on the total sample of national adults, the margin of sampling error is ±4 percentage points at the 95% confidence level. All reported margins of sampling error include computed design effects for weighting.

March 25, 2015
IN U.S., CONCERN ABOUT ENVIRONMENTAL THREATS EASES

by Jeffrey M. Jones

Story Highlights

- *Worry about most problems down after increasing in 2014*
- *Americans are most worried about polluted drinking water*
- *Americans worry least about global warming*

PRINCETON, N.J.—Americans' concern about several major environmental threats has eased after increasing last year. As in the past, Americans express the greatest worry about pollution of drinking water, and the least about global warming or climate change.

Americans' Worry About Environmental Problems

I'm going to read you a list of environmental problems. As I read each one, please tell me if you personally worry about this problem a great deal, a fair amount, only a little, or not at all. First, how much do you personally worry about -- [RANDOM ORDER]?

	% Great deal, 2014	% Great deal, 2015
Pollution of drinking water	60	55
Pollution of rivers, lakes and reservoirs	53	47
Air pollution	46	38
Extinction of plant and animal species	41	36
The loss of tropical rain forests	41	33
Global warming or climate change	34	32

GALLUP'

The results are based on Gallup's annual Environment poll, conducted March 5–8. Gallup trends on many of these items stretch back more than two decades. Last year's increased worry has proved temporary, with the current level of worry on each of the problems back to about where it was in 2013.

Despite ups and downs from year to year in the percentage worried about the various issues, the rank order of the environmental problems has remained fairly consistent over the decades. Americans express greater concern over more proximate threats—including pollution of drinking water, as well as pollution of rivers, lakes and reservoirs, and air pollution—than they do about longer-term threats such as global warming, the loss of rain forests, and plant and animal extinction.

The amount Americans worry about the various threats tends to rise and recede in unison, with concern higher in the late 1980s and early 1990s during the revival of environmentalism, and in the late 1990s and early 2000s amid the economic boom. Since then, Americans' worry has fallen, with concern dipping to record lows on most issues in 2010 or 2011. The current level of worry on each issue remains at or near those record lows.

Consistent with the decline in worry about specific environmental problems, Americans have become more positive about the quality of the environment in recent years. If Americans perceive the environment to be in relatively good shape, it follows they would be less concerned about potential environmental threats to Americans. The more positive views about the environment could be the result of federal, state and local government's as well as individuals' actions to minimize potential environmental threats to U.S. citizens.

The health of the economy may also be a factor in reduced worry about environmental problems. Americans tend to give environmental concerns higher priority when the economy is healthy than when it is ailing, and in recent decades the U.S. economy was arguably its strongest in late 1999 and early 2000.

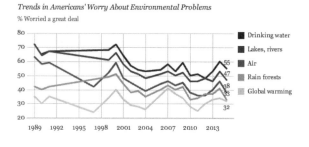

Trends in Americans' Worry About Environmental Problems
% Worried a great deal

GALLUP

Also, the nature of the environmental agenda may indirectly be influencing Americans' concern. The primary focus of the environmental movement has shifted toward long-term threats like global warming—issues about which Americans tend to worry less than about more immediate threats like pollution. Importantly, even as global warming has received greater attention as an environmental problem from politicians and the media in recent years, Americans' worry about it is no higher now than when Gallup first asked about it in 1989.

A final factor is the politicization of environmental issues. This is exemplified by the sharp political polarization in views of global warming. And although concern about environmental issues is lower among both Republicans and Democrats since 2000, it is down more among Republicans. Across the six issues measured in 2000 and 2015, the percentage of Republicans and Republican-leaning independents who worry "a great deal" is down an average of 20 percentage points, compared with an average 10-point decline for Democrats and Democratic leaners.

Worry About Environmental Problems by Political Party, 2000 vs. 2015
% Worried a great deal

	2000	2015	Change
REPUBLICANS/REPUBLICAN LEANERS			
Pollution of drinking water	64	43	-21
Pollution of rivers, lakes, and reservoirs	59	36	-23
Air pollution	50	22	-28
The loss of tropical rain forests	46	24	-22
Extinction of plant and animal species	33	24	-9
Global warming or climate change	29	13	-16
DEMOCRATS/DEMOCRATIC LEANERS			
Pollution of drinking water	76	64	-12
Pollution of rivers, lakes, and reservoirs	71	55	-16
Air pollution	66	53	-13
The loss of tropical rain forests	54	39	-15
Extinction of plant and animal species	53	46	-7
Global warming or climate change	48	52	+4

GALLUP

Democrats worry more than Republicans about all of the issues. Notably, Democrats are more worried about global warming now than they were in 2000, perhaps reflecting the shift in the focus of the environmental agenda toward this issue.

Implications

Americans' concern about a series of potential environmental threats remains on the low end of what Gallup has measured over the past 25 years. Last year's increased worry proved temporary, rather than the start of a trend toward renewed concern about environmental problems.

That diminished concern has both positive and negative aspects for those favoring tougher environmental policies and regulations. The diminished concern may mean the policies and regulations in place are working to protect Americans from environmental threats. However, because of that, and because Americans are less concerned about environmental matters in general, they may be less willing to support policy changes to make those regulations even tougher if they don't perceive pollution and other environmental threats as imminent.

Survey Methods

Results for this Gallup poll are based on telephone interviews conducted March 5–8, 2015, with a random sample of 1,025 adults, aged 18 and older, living in all 50 U.S. states and the District of Columbia. For results based on the total sample of national adults, the margin of sampling error is ±4 percentage points at the 95% confidence level. All reported margins of sampling error include computed design effects for weighting.

March 26, 2015
MAJORITY OF U.S. INVESTORS ANTICIPATE INTEREST RATE HIKE

by Lydia Saad

Story Highlights

- *Half of investors think rates will rise a little, and 5% a lot*
- *Nearly a quarter might pull back on stocks when rates go up*

PRINCETON, N.J.—Before the Federal Reserve recently indicated that it may start raising interest rates this summer, the majority of U.S. investors already thought interest rates would go up. About half said they think interest rates will "go up a little" and another 5% said they will "go up a lot." While few investors expected rates to drop, one-third thought they would stay the same.

U.S. Investors' Outlook for Interest Rates in the Next 12 Months
Based on U.S. investors with $10,000 or more in stocks, bonds or other investments

	Go up a lot	Go up a little	Remain the same	Go down a little	Go down a lot
	%	%	%	%	%
All investors	5	51	34	7	*
Retired	6	51	36	5	*
Not retired	5	51	34	8	*

* = less than 0.5%

Wells Fargo/Gallup Investor and Retirement Optimism Index survey
Jan. 30-Feb. 9, 2015

GALLUP

These findings are from the Wells Fargo/Gallup Investor and Retirement Optimism Index survey for the first quarter of 2015, conducted Jan. 30 to Feb. 9. For this survey, investors are defined as U.S. adults who have at least $10,000 invested in stocks, bonds or mutual funds.

The Fed has not raised interest rates since 2006, after lowering them to practically zero during the recession. That means any increase could be a shock to the market and investors who have become accustomed to extremely low rates. While low rates have been a plus for borrowers, they may have compelled investors to look past CDs and money market accounts now yielding minimal returns, and put more of their investments in the stock market.

In fact, 13% of all U.S. investors, including 17% of retired investors and 11% of nonretired investors, said that low rates have caused them to invest more in the stock market than they are usually comfortable with.

Impact of Low Interest Rates on U.S. Investors' Investment in Stocks

Have the low interest rates in recent years caused you to put more money into the stock market than you are usually comfortable with, or is this not the case?

	Yes, have put more money in stocks than usually comfortable with	No, have not	No opinion
	%	%	%
U.S. investors with stocks	13	86	1
Retired	17	81	2
Not retired	11	88	*

* = less than 0.5%

Wells Fargo/Gallup Investor and Retirement Optimism Index survey
Jan. 30-Feb. 9, 2015

GALLUP

By the same token, rising interest rates could trigger the reverse behavior, driving investors out of stocks and potentially hurting the markets.

In line with this, investors were asked in the Wells Fargo/Gallup survey whether higher interest rates would make them more likely to transfer money out of the stock market and into more conservative investments such as CDs. Most investors said they are "not too likely" (33%) or "not at all likely" (43%) to do this. However, 5% said they are "very likely" and 18% said they are "somewhat likely." That is not a large percentage in absolute terms, but significant in terms of the effect it could have on stock values. Retirees and nonretirees have similar views on this question.

Impact of Rising Interest Rates on U.S. Investors' Sale of Stocks

And if interest rates do go up, how likely would you be to transfer money out of the stock market and into more conservative investments like CDs?

	Very likely	Somewhat likely	Not too likely	Not at all likely
	%	%	%	%
U.S. investors with stocks	5	18	33	43
Retired	5	18	29	46
Not retired	5	18	34	42

Wells Fargo/Gallup Investor and Retirement Optimism Index survey
Jan. 30-Feb. 9, 2015

GALLUP

Bottom Line

The Federal Reserve has reportedly wanted to raise interest rates for some time, but it has continually put caution first and not followed through out of concern for the possible effects on the labor market and inflation. So, even though Federal Reserve Board Chair Janet Yellen notably refrained from describing the board as "patient" in

discussing their intentions on interest rates, that's a long way from a guarantee that rates are going up at their next meeting in April. Still, even before her statement, more than five in 10 investors believed an interest rate hike is likely in the next 12 months, and nearly one in four were poised to pull back on stocks if interest rates go up, making other, safer investments look more attractive.

Survey Methods

Results for the Wells Fargo/Gallup Investor and Retirement Optimism Index survey are based on questions asked Jan. 30–Feb. 9, 2015, on the Gallup Daily tracking survey, of a random sample of 1,011 U.S. adults having investable assets of $10,000 or more.

For results based on the entire sample of investors, the margin of sampling error is ±3 percentage points at the 95% confidence level.

March 26, 2015
COLLEGE-EDUCATED REPUBLICANS MOST SKEPTICAL OF GLOBAL WARMING

by Frank Newport and Andrew Dugan

Story Highlights

- *Educated Reps more likely than less educated Reps to doubt global warming*
- *Democrats with college degrees tend to be less skeptical*
- *Education related to self-reported understanding of issue for both parties*

PRINCETON, N.J.—Republicans with higher levels of education are more likely than those in their parties with less education to say that the seriousness of global warming is "generally exaggerated." By contrast, Democrats with some college or more are less likely than those with less education to believe the seriousness of global warming is exaggerated.

Seventy-four percent of Republicans with a college degree say it is exaggerated, compared with 57% of those with high school education or less saying the same. Democrats are much less likely in general to say that the seriousness of global warming is exaggerated, but those a college degree (15%) are significantly less likely to say this than those with a high school education or less (27%). The relationship between education and views of global warming among independents is generally similar to that shown among Republicans.

These opposing trends by party suggest that higher levels of education reinforce core partisan positions; in this case, Republicans' strong tendency to question or deny global warming and Democrats' inclination to affirm it. The trends also suggest that partisanship rather than education is a main lens through which Americans view global warming and its effects, particularly for those who claim allegiance to one of the two major political parties.

These results come from an aggregation of more than 6,000 interviews conducted as part of Gallup's annual Environment poll conducted each March from 2010 to 2015. Over that time, Americans' views about the seriousness of global warming have been steady: 43% on average have said it was generally exaggerated, 24%

that it was generally correct and 31% have said it was generally underestimated. Longer term, though, Republicans' and Democrats' views about global warming have increasingly diverged.

Views on Seriousness of Global Warming, by Party ID and Education

Thinking about what is said in the news, in your view is the seriousness of global warming -- generally exaggerated, generally correct or is it generally underestimated?

Party affiliation, by education	% Generally exaggerated	% Generally correct	% Generally underestimated
REPUBLICANS			
High school or less	57	18	22
Some college	70	16	11
College graduate	74	14	11
INDEPENDENTS			
High school or less	39	25	34
Some college	50	21	29
College graduate	46	25	28
DEMOCRATS			
High school or less	27	27	42
Some college	19	30	49
College graduate	15	36	48

Aggregated Gallup data 2010-2015

GALLUP

Educated Republicans Less Likely to Worry About, Believe in Global Warming

The tendency for Republicans with college education to be skeptical of global warming is evident in other Gallup trends.

For example, although Republicans tend to be much less likely to worry about global warming than others, Republicans with a college degree are even less likely to worry about global warming "a great deal" than their fellow Republicans. Republicans with more education are also about half as likely as those with a high school education or less to say global warming will pose a serious threat in their lifetime, more likely to say that global warming's effects will never occur, and more likely to say that global warming is caused by natural changes in the environment rather than by human activity.

Republicans' Attitudes and Beliefs Regarding Global Warming, by Education

Among self-identified Republicans, for selected items

Response	High school or less	Some college	College graduate
	%	%	%
Worry about global warming a great deal	23	11	8
Global warming will never happen	24	34	35
Global warming is caused by natural changes in the environment	54	57	66
Global warming will pose serious threat to way of life in your lifetime	29	15	13

Aggregated Gallup data, 2010-2015

GALLUP

The relationship between education and views on global warming among Democrats is in the opposite direction: The most educated Democrats are slightly more likely than less educated Democrats to worry about global warming and to believe it will be a threat in their lifetime. Highly educated Democrats are also much less likely to believe that global warming is the result of natural changes rather than caused by humans. Very few Democrats, regardless of education, say the effects of global warming will never happen.

Democrats' Attitudes and Beliefs Regarding Global Warming, by Education

Among self-identified Democrats, for selected items

Response	High school or less	Some college	College graduate
	%	%	%
Worry about global warming a great deal	45	48	50
Global warming will never happen	5	4	2
Global warming is caused by natural changes in the environment	35	20	13
Global warming will pose serious threat to way of life in your lifetime	49	53	55

Aggregated Gallup data, 2010-2015

GALLUP

Two other questions about global warming follow a different pattern:

- Republicans and Democrats with higher levels of education are both slightly more likely than others in their respective parties to say they understand global warming "very well." The nature of this understanding, however, is obviously quite different between the two groups.
- Republicans' views on whether most scientists believe global warming is occurring vary little by education. Republicans are much less likely than Democrats or independents to say that most scientists believe global warming is happening. Education is strongly related to Democrats' views on this question, with highly educated Democrats more likely than those with less education to agree with the statement.

Bottom Line

Given the scientific nature of global warming, it is not surprising that Americans' understanding and interpretation of its effects could be related to their education levels. Among Republicans and Democrats, education levels have opposite effects, with higher educational attainment linked to more doubt about global warming among Republicans but a greater sense of its reality among Democrats.

In other words, education appears to harden the partisan battle lines, rather than build common bridges. College graduates who are Republicans are actually more likely than college graduates who are Democrats to say they understand a great deal about the issue, but well-educated Republicans find this understanding leads them in a different direction than it does Democrats.

Partisan affiliation more so than education plays the dominating role in the American public's attitudes about global warming today. Education does not mitigate the partisan divide in beliefs about global warming but instead strengthens it.

Survey Methods

Results for this Gallup poll are based on telephone interviews conducted in March of each year between 2010 and 2015, with an aggregated random sample of 6,154 adults, aged 18 and older, living in all 50 U.S. states and the District of Columbia. For results based on the total sample of national adults, the margin of sampling error is ±1 percentage points at the 95% confidence level. All reported margins of sampling error include computed design effects for weighting.

March 27, 2015

CLINTON FAVORABILITY AMONG DEMS BETTER THAN LAST CAMPAIGN

by Jeffrey M. Jones

Story Highlights

- *Clinton +66 net favorability exceeds +58 in 2007*
- *Clinton has larger lead in net favorability over field than she did in 2007*
- *Clinton numbers similar to Gore's in 1999*

PRINCETON, N.J.—Hillary Clinton's net favorability rating among Democrats—defined as the percentage who have a favorable opinion of her minus the percentage with an unfavorable opinion—is higher now than at a similar point leading up to the 2008 presidential election. Her net favorability is also similar to Al Gore's rating early on in the 2000 presidential campaign. The current Democratic field does not appear to present as much competition for Clinton as she faced in 2008.

Favorable Ratings of (Potential) Democratic Presidential Candidates, Among Democrats and Democratic Leaners

Early in year before the 2000, 2008 and 2016 elections

	Favorable	Unfavorable	Net Favorable	Familiarity
	%	%	pct. pts.	%
2016				
H. Clinton	79	13	66	92
J. Biden	64	17	47	81
E. Warren	37	9	28	46
2008				
H. Clinton	77	19	58	96
B. Obama	69	14	55	83
J. Edwards	67	13	54	80
2000				
A. Gore	78	15	63	93
B. Bradley	40	10	30	50

Notes: Net favorable is the % with a favorable opinion of the candidate minus the % with an unfavorable opinion.

Familiarity is the percentage who are familiar enough with the candidate to have an opinion of him or her.

2016 campaign based on March 2-4, 2015 poll; 2008 campaign based on average of March 2-4, 2007 and March 23-25, 2007 polls; 2000 campaign based on Feb. 19-21, 1999 polls.

GALLUP

Besides her lead in favorability ratings over her potential 2016 rivals, Clinton also enjoys an advantage in familiarity over her competition. Ninety-two percent of Democrats know Clinton well enough to have an opinion of her, compared with 81% for Joe Biden and 46% for Elizabeth Warren. Clinton's current level of familiarity is similar to her 96% familiarity before the 2008 campaign and to Gore's 93% in early 1999.

These results on the potential 2016 Democratic candidates are based on a March 2–4 Gallup poll. That poll was conducted as Clinton was being criticized for use of a private email account to conduct official business as secretary of state, but before she publicly addressed the issue.

Gallup has measured Americans' opinions of potential and announced presidential candidates since 1992 to assess whether the public views each favorably, unfavorably or does not have an opinion either way. Ratings from early in the year before the election, compared with the current stage of the 2016 election process, are available for the 2000 and 2008 elections. Those two elections are arguably the most relevant to the coming election because they did not include an incumbent president in the candidate field.

National polls show Clinton the clear leader when Democrats and Democratic-leaning independents are asked to say which of the potential 2016 Democratic candidates they are most likely to support for the nomination. Clinton also had a significant lead over her rivals in 2007 on the same measure. But Clinton may have been more vulnerable in the 2008 campaign than her early lead on the nomination ballot implied because Democrats viewed her major competitors—Barack Obama (+55 net favorable) and John Edwards (+54)—nearly as favorably as they viewed Clinton (+58).

Clinton had near-universal recognition among Democrats in March 2007—96% were familiar enough with her to have an opinion—but Obama and Edwards were familiar to at least eight in 10 Democrats.

At this point, the indications are Clinton will officially announce her 2016 candidacy next month. What is not clear is whether she will have a formidable challenger for the Democratic nomination. Biden and Warren appear to be her most serious potential challengers, but both currently trail Clinton by significant margins on net favorability and familiarity among Democrats.

Given her better net favorable ratings now than in 2007 and her bigger lead on that measure over her closer competitors than before the last campaign, Clinton would start out the 2016 campaign in a more advantageous position than she did in 2008, even though she was the presumed front-runner both times.

Another auspicious sign for Clinton is that her current standing is similar to Al Gore's in the 2000 campaign. Gore was the sitting vice president and the odds-on favorite for the nomination. Former New Jersey senator Bill Bradley challenged Gore for the nomination, but he was far behind Gore early on in net favorability ratings (+30 to +63). He also faced a 43-percentage-point deficit on familiarity, as 93% knew Gore well enough to have an opinion him, compared with 50% for Bradley. Bradley failed to win a single primary or caucus that year.

Should Biden decide to run, Clinton would not be in as strong a position relative to her competition as Gore was in February 1999. Biden's current familiarity and favorability scores are better than Bradley's were at a comparable point in the 2000 campaign.

If Warren decides to run but Biden stays out of the race, the 2016 Democratic nomination campaign may look remarkably like the 2000 campaign at the outset. Warren's net favorable and familiarity scores are essentially the same as Bradley's in early 1999, meaning she would have to overcome a similar deficit to the front-runner that Bradley faced.

To date, Biden has not indicated whether he will seek the nomination. Warren, despite many entreaties to get into the race, has said she will not seek the nomination. Other potential challengers who have given stronger signals they may run—including former Maryland governor Martin O'Malley, Vermont Sen. Bernie Sanders and former Virginia Sen. Jim Webb—are largely unknown to rank-and-file Democrats, and not viewed particularly positively among those who are familiar with them. That certainly could change if any enter the race and become viewed as credible challengers to Clinton, but each would have even more ground to make up on Clinton than would Warren or Biden.

As was the case eight years ago, most political experts have dubbed Hillary Clinton as the clear front-runner for the Democratic presidential nomination. Obviously, similar predictions did not pan out in 2008 as Clinton lost a spirited nomination contest to Obama. But Clinton appears to be in an even stronger position compared with her potential challengers than eight years ago, given clear advantages in both familiarity and favorability. And if Biden decides not to run and no other prominent Democrat unexpectedly gets into the race, Clinton's current positioning would be at least as strong as Al Gore's was before the 2000 campaign, and possibly stronger depending on which Democratic politicians might challenge her.

As in 2000, the Democratic nomination contest may offer little drama if Clinton has a relatively clear path to the nomination. Having a clear path could benefit Clinton, helping her keep a consistent ideological message in the campaign's nomination and general election phases rather than pivoting to the left if a more conservative Democrat challenges her or to the right if a more liberal one challenges her in the primaries. Without serious primary opposition, Clinton could avoid any criticisms of her record, qualifications or positions from her party. She would also have more time to raise money for the general election campaign and make her appeal to the broader electorate than to mainly Democrats.

On the downside, without a serious challenger, she would have less opportunity to hone her messages on the campaign trail and in debates. Further, if the Republican nomination contest is highly competitive, Clinton and the Democrats might struggle to get media attention while the GOP battle plays out. Also, any potential attacks on Clinton's record later in the campaign could harm her standing because the earlier these criticisms occur, the more quickly she can address and move past them.

Survey Methods

Results for this Gallup poll are based on telephone interviews conducted March 2–4, 2015, on the Gallup U.S. Daily survey, with a random sample of 649 Democrats and Democratic-leaning independents, aged 18 and older, living in all 50 U.S. states and the District of Columbia. For results based on the total sample of Democrats, the margin of sampling error is ±5 percentage points at the 95% confidence level. All reported margins of sampling error include computed design effects for weighting.

March 27, 2015

AMERICANS CONTINUE TO VIEW ENERGY SITUATION AS LESS SERIOUS

by Justin McCarthy

Story Highlights

- *Twenty-eight percent call U.S. energy situation "very serious"*
- *Only in 2002 did lower percentage say situation is very serious*
- *Half of Americans say situation is "fairly serious"*

WASHINGTON, D.C.—Fewer than three in 10 Americans (28%) say the energy situation in the U.S. is "very serious," one of the

lowest figures in Gallup's history of asking the question. While this figure has varied widely over the past few decades, the percentage of Americans who feel the energy situation is very serious has declined consistently over the past four years. In Gallup's 38-year trend, only in 2002 did fewer Americans think the U.S. energy situation was very serious.

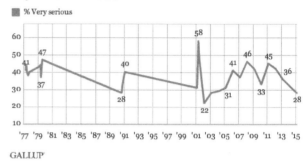

Seriousness of U.S. Energy Situation, According to Americans

How serious would you say the energy situation is in the United States -- very serious, fairly serious or not at all serious?

■ % Very serious

GALLUP

This figure peaked in May 2001 on the heels of California's rolling blackouts, when more than half of Americans described the U.S. energy situation as very serious. But by 2002, that number had fallen to its lowest point, with 22% calling the situation very serious. These two data points straddle the events of 9/11, so the 2002 low may be related to a shift in the attention Americans were paying to the issue. Since then, the percentage has reached as high as 46%, but has been consistently down during the past four years, falling from 45% in 2011 to the current post-2002 low of 28%.

These latest data are from Gallup's annual poll on environmental and energy issues, conducted March 5–8.

In addition to the 28% who say the energy situation is very serious, 50% say it is fairly serious, and 20% not at all serious. As the percentage describing the energy situation as very serious has shrunk since 2011, the percentage saying it is not serious has grown from 7% to 20%.

Perceptions of the energy situation as "very serious" have fallen across all partisan groups over the past four years. The latest drop is largely attributable to Democrats, 29% of whom say it is very serious, down 11 percentage points from 2014. Meanwhile, independents' (28%) and Republicans' (29%) views have held steady.

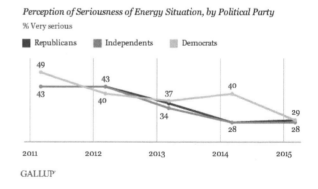

Perception of Seriousness of Energy Situation, by Political Party

% Very serious

■ Republicans ■ Independents ■ Democrats

GALLUP

Bottom Line

As gas prices have been generally lower as of late, so too have Americans' worries about the availability and affordability of energy. Figures from the U.S. Energy Information Administration illustrate how gas prices in the last five years have been more stable than in the previous five. This general stability may be related to Americans' lessened concern about energy. This issue has decreased in prominence in the minds of so many Americans that one in five now say the energy situation is not serious at all. The steep increase in domestic production of crude oil, which strengthens overall U.S. energy independence, may also have something to do with Americans' diminished concerns.

The large majority of Americans continue to view the situation with some degree of seriousness. That may be because energy has a direct impact on Americans' daily lives, so it is hard to dismiss it as unimportant, regardless of the country's current energy situation. For example, changes in gas prices can greatly affect Americans' views on other measures. Still, right now, Americans are less concerned about the U.S. energy situation than they have been at nearly all times over the past four decades.

Survey Methods

Results for this Gallup poll are based on telephone interviews conducted March 5–8, 2015, on the Gallup U.S. Daily survey, with a random sample of 1,025 adults, aged 18 and older, living in all 50 U.S. states and the District of Columbia. For results based on the total sample of national adults, the margin of sampling error is ±4 percentage points at the 95% confidence level. All reported margins of sampling error include computed design effects for weighting.

March 30, 2015
INVESTORS IN U.S. WITH 401(K) VALUE ONE-ON-ONE ADVICE MOST

by Lydia Saad

Story Highlights

- *A third of working investors with a 401(k) say they need advice*
- *One-on-one with financial professional rated most effective*
- *One-quarter rate employer subpar for guiding workers on 401(k)s*

PRINCETON, N.J.—U.S. investors who have access to a 401(k)-type plan at work consider live meetings with human advisers—particularly one-on-one meetings with a financial professional—to be the best way to get information about how to manage their retirement plans. Far fewer say sending information through mobile messaging or posting on social media is "highly effective." Various forms of written communication fall in between.

These findings are from the Wells Fargo/Gallup Investor and Retirement Optimism Index 2015–first quarter survey, conducted Jan. 30–Feb. 9. For this survey, investors are defined as U.S. adults who have at least $10,000 invested in stocks, bonds or mutual funds. About three in four employed investors report they have access to a 401(k)-type retirement savings plan at work. Beyond standard 401(k) plans, that could also mean 403(b) plans commonly used by teachers and other public employees.

U.S. Investors' Views of Possible Sources of Information About 401(k) Plans

Next. I'm going to read some methods an employer might offer to provide its employees information about managing their 401(k)-type plans. For each method, please tell me if you would find that method to be highly effective, somewhat effective, not too effective, or not at all effective.

	Highly effective	Somewhat effective	Not too/Not at all effective
	%	%	%
Offering one-on-one meetings with a financial professional	71	21	8
Sponsoring a seminar or formal presentation	46	36	18
Posting information on your company's internal website	40	40	19
Providing brochures or other written material	33	47	20
Sending you information to your mobile device	21	35	44
Posting information on social media	11	24	63

Based on employed investors with access to a 401(k)-type plan at work

Wells Fargo/Gallup Investor and Retirement Optimism Index survey, Jan. 30-Feb. 9, 2015

GALLUP'

According to these investors, one-on-one meetings with a financial professional are the best way employers can provide employees information about managing their 401(k)-type plans, with 71% calling these highly effective. Employer-sponsored seminars or formal presentations rank second, at 46%, followed by information posted on a company website, at 40%. Confidence drops to 33% for written material such as brochures, 21% for information sent to employees' mobile devices and 11% for information posted on social media.

In terms of the total percentage rating each approach at least somewhat effective, all but social media (at 35%) receive majority confidence, ranging from 92% for one-on-one meetings to 56% for information pushed to mobile devices.

Employed 401(k) investors give their employer generally positive reviews of the job it does in providing employees with information about managing their plan, with about three in four rating it excellent (31%) or good (43%). However, one in four indicate their employer could be doing much better, rating its performance only fair (19%) or poor (6%).

401(k) Investors Need More Help in Picking, Changing Investments

Close to two-thirds of employed investors who currently have a 401(k)-type plan say they can manage their plan by themselves, but 35% say they need advice. Given five areas of investing to choose from, most in the latter group identify knowing which funds to invest in (32%) or knowing when to reallocate funds (29%) as the area they most need help with. While relatively few choose knowing how much to contribute, understanding the tax advantages or tapping retirement money early, 24% say they need help on all or multiple issues.

Bottom Line

Although sponsored by employers, 401(k)-type plans put the onus on workers to save and invest for their retirement using these tax-advantaged accounts. Most investors indicate they are pretty comfortable managing their plan on their own, but a full third say they need advice. A natural place to get that advice is in the workplace, where the employer serves as the intermediary between the investor and the company managing the funds. Most investors are complimentary of the job their employer does of helping workers with the important task of managing their 401(k). But one in four think their employer is not doing a very good job, representing an important information gap that warrants attention.

In December, the Wells Fargo/Gallup Investor and Retirement Optimism Index survey found just 18% of U.S. investors saying they want more financial advice from their employer, per se. Likewise, most employers probably do not want to take responsibility for advising employees about critical financial decisions such as what to invest in and when to reallocate investments in response to market conditions. But given investors' reported needs and views about various sources of information, employers could do more to connect workers who are seeking advice with financial professionals who can personally guide them.

Survey Methods

Results for the Wells Fargo/Gallup Investor and Retirement Optimism Index survey are based on questions asked Jan. 30–Feb. 9, 2015, on the Gallup Daily tracking survey, of a random sample of 1,011 U.S. adults having investable assets of $10,000 or more.

For results based on the entire sample of investors, the margin of sampling error is ±3 percentage points at the 95% confidence level.

For results based on the 416 nonretired investors who have access to a 401(k) plan at work, the margin of sampling error is ±6 percentage points at the 95% confidence level. For results based on the 370 investors who participate in their employer's 401(k) plan the margin of sampling error is ±6 percentage points at the 95% confidence level. For results based on the 182 investors who say they need help in managing their 401(k) plan, the margin of sampling error is ±9 percentage points at the 95% confidence level.

April 01, 2015
MOOD-ALTERING DRUG USE HIGHEST IN WEST VIRGINIA, LOWEST IN ALASKA

by Justin McCarthy

Story Highlights

- *Southern states make up six of the top 10 drug use states*
- *Nationally, 18.9% take drugs to relax "almost every day"*
- *Those who use drugs almost daily have lower well-being*

This story is part of Gallup's annual "State of the States" series, which reveals state-by-state differences on political, economic, religious and well-being measures.

WASHINGTON, D.C.—West Virginians are most likely to report near-daily use of drugs or medications that alter their mood or help them relax, followed by residents of Rhode Island. Southern states make up six of the top 10 highest drug use states, while Alaskans, Wyomingites and Californians are least likely to say they use such drugs almost every day.

States With Highest Drug/Medication Use

How often do you use drugs or medications, including prescription drugs, which affect your mood and help you relax -- almost every day, sometimes, rarely or never?

	% Almost every day
West Virginia	28.1
Rhode Island	25.9
Kentucky	24.5
Alabama	24.2
Louisiana	22.9
South Carolina	22.8
Mississippi	22.3
Missouri	22.2
Indiana	22.1
Oregon	21.9

Gallup-Healthways Well-Being Index
January-December 2014

GALLUP

States With Lowest Drug/Medication Use

How often do you use drugs or medications, including prescription drugs, which affect your mood and help you relax -- almost every day, sometimes, rarely or never?

	% Almost every day
Alaska	13.5
Wyoming	15.5
California	15.8
Illinois	16.0
North Dakota	16.4
New Jersey	16.5
Colorado	16.7
Texas	16.7
Utah	16.8
Maryland/Hawaii	17.3

Gallup-Healthways Well-Being Index
January-December 2014

GALLUP

These data are based on interviews with at least 450 residents of each state from January to December 2014, as part of the Gallup-Healthways Well-Being Index. While the question specifically refers to drugs that "affect your mood or help you relax," the interpretation of that description is left up to respondents and could include prescription drugs, recreational drugs, alcohol or nicotine.

More than one in five residents of Kentucky, Alabama, Louisiana, South Carolina, Mississippi and Missouri report using a drug or medicated substance to alter their mood or relax on a near-daily basis. Indiana and Oregon round out the top 10.

An analysis by the Centers for Disease Control and Prevention found that Southern states are among those with the highest rates for prescribing narcotic painkillers. Southern states also house the most frequent cigarette smokers, according to prior Gallup-Healthways research.

Lower rates of drug and medication use were in a regionally diverse group of states. After the three states that have the lowest drug use rates (Alaska, Wyoming and California), about one in six residents in Illinois, North Dakota, New Jersey, Colorado, Texas and Utah say they use such drugs almost every day.

Americans Who Frequently Use Drugs to Relax Have Lower Well-Being

Nationally, 18.9% of Americans report using a mood-altering substance nearly every day, while the majority, 62.2%, say they never use such drugs. About two in 10 Americans report using drugs or medication rarely or sometimes.

Those who use drugs that affect their mood almost every day have a slightly lower average Well-Being Index score (56.3) than those who use such drugs sometimes (58.9), and a significantly lower score than those who take drugs or medication to relax rarely (61.2) or never (63.6).

Drug/Medication Usage and Overall Well-Being

How often do you use drugs or medications, including prescription drugs, which affect your mood and help you relax -- almost every day, sometimes, rarely or never?

	%	Well-Being Index
Almost every day	18.9	56.3
Sometimes	5.0	58.9
Rarely	13.1	61.2
Never	62.2	63.6

Gallup-Healthways Well-Being Index
January-December 2014

GALLUP

Bottom Line

Americans take drugs and medication, both legal and illegal, for a variety of reasons. Some adults may be taking prescribed medication as a result of an illness, such as depression or anxiety. Meanwhile, others could be using an illegal substance for recreational purposes on a near-daily basis.

While using drugs to relax almost every day is clearly linked to lower well-being, the direction of the relationship is unclear. One possibility is that taking mood-altering drugs or medication nearly every day contributes to lower well-being. But a more probable explanation is that Americans who already have lower well-being are more likely to use drugs or medication to relax or alter their mood, possibly to help cope with challenges related to their low purpose, social, financial, physical or community well-being.

Though the question wording leaves this open to interpretation by the individual respondent, on the whole, those who are the most frequent users of mood-altering drugs have the lowest well-being. States with high percentages of residents who take drugs or medication to relax may be able to reduce these rates by addressing the underlying well-being issues that may compel residents to rely on mood-altering substances.

Survey Methods

Results are based on telephone interviews conducted Jan. 2–Dec. 30, 2014, as part of the Gallup-Healthways Well-Being Index, with a random sample of 176,702 adults in 2014, aged 18 and older, living in all 50 U.S. states and the District of Columbia. The margin of sampling error is ±1 to ±2 percentage points for most states, but is close to ±4 percentage points for states with small populations, such as North Dakota, Wyoming, Vermont and Alaska. All reported margins of sampling error include computed design effects for weighting.

April 01, 2015

MANAGERS WITH HIGH TALENT TWICE AS LIKELY TO BE ENGAGED

by Jim Harter

Story Highlights

- *54% of managers with high talent, 27% with low talent are engaged*
- *Only 35% of U.S. managers are engaged in their workplace*
- *Just 18% of managers have "high degree" of managing talent*

PRINCETON, N.J.—Managers in businesses and organizations who have been identified as having high managerial talent—a natural capacity for excellence—are twice as likely to be engaged (54%) as managers who have limited talent (27%). Those who possess "functioning" or moderate talent are also significantly less likely than the most talented group to be engaged at work.

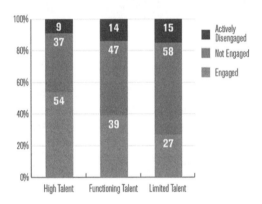

Fifty-four percent of managers who possess high managerial talent are "engaged" at work, while 37% are "not engaged." Conversely, 27% of managers deemed to have "limited talent" are engaged at work, while the majority, 58%, are not engaged in the workplace.

These findings can be found in *The State of the American Manager* report, which contains new insights about managers, and especially the talents that are required for effectively managing teams in organizations. Gallup conceives of talent as the natural capacity for excellence in a given endeavor. Everyone has talent in some areas, but few have the innate talent to become a great manager. Just one in 10 people have the unique blend of innate characteristics that Gallup has found to be predictors of management excellence, including the motivator, assertiveness, accountability, relationships, and decision-making talents. Another two in 10 have "functioning" talent, meaning they possess some of the traits but not all and, with the right coaching, can become successful managers. Just 18% of *current managers* have high talent, which means organizations are missing out on placing the optimal people in managerial jobs 82% of the time.

Managers with high talent lead teams that achieve higher employee engagement, higher productivity and higher employee retention rates, and have more engaged customers and 48% higher profitability. They are also more likely to be brand ambassadors for their organization than those with lesser management talent. Those with high managerial talent are twice as likely as those with low talent to strongly advocate for the products and services of their organizations and twice as likely to say they know what their organization stands for.

Manager Engagement Is Too Low

While 54% of managers with high talent are engaged at work, just 35% of *all* U.S. managers are engaged in their work and workplaces. Fifty-one percent of all U.S. managers are not engaged, and 14% are actively disengaged. Through their impact, Gallup estimates that managers who are not engaged or actively disengaged cost the U.S. economy $319 billion to $398 billion annually.

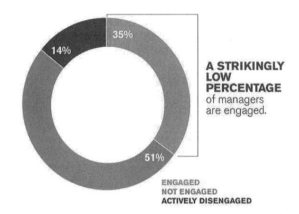

One reason for the high cost is that manager engagement has a direct impact on employees' engagement. Employees who are supervised by highly engaged managers are 59% more likely to be engaged than those who are supervised by disengaged managers—leading to higher productivity, lower turnover, better-quality work, and higher profitability.

Implications

Managers influence everything that gets done in organizations. According to Gallup research, they may occupy the single most important role in workplaces throughout the world. They translate strategy into action and hold employee morale, turnover, productivity, safety and creativity in their hands. A great manager improves lives while improving performance. A poor manager makes workers' lives miserable while destroying performance.

Currently, only slightly more than 30% of employees in U.S. workplaces are engaged in their work and workplaces. This figure has hardly budged in nearly 15 years. But it doesn't have to be that way. Some organizations have 70% engagement or higher, and this hasn't happened by chance. They outpace their competitors in financial performance and make the lives of their employees better in the process. But most organizations are still struggling to improve the morale of their workforces and their performance. There is a root cause: They don't have enough great managers because they have placed people into the position of manager for the wrong reasons. Tenure or success in a prior nonmanager role, while seemingly equitable reasons on the surface, aren't the right reasons. Great managers have different natural talents than average or below-average managers. And they continue to improve if their organization sets the right criteria for building a productive culture.

Managers, through their natural talents, their own engagement and their behaviors explain at least 70% of the variance in engagement across teams. Few organizations have enough great managers. And there is no other job that has as much combined influence on American business success or failure as the manager.

Survey Methods

Estimates of the relationship between managerial talent and engagement and the level of engagement among managers were based on a sample of 2,564 U.S. managers completing Web and paper surveys during September and October 2013. Based on the total Gallup Panel sample of adult managers aged 18 and older, the margin of sampling error is ±2 percentage points, at the 95% confidence level.

Gallup has a four-decade-long history of studying individuals' talents across a broad spectrum of jobs. This has included numerous studies of managerial talents across a wide range of managerial positions. Talent-based assessments, consisting primarily of indepth structured interviews and Web-based assessments, have been designed to predict performance, and large-scale meta-analyses have been conducted examining the predictive validity of the instruments. Thresholds in instrument scores are set with an effort to optimize the probability of selecting high performers. Such thresholds, examined across 341,186 applicants and 70 applicant samples from organizations using managerial assessments, were used to inform the percentage of individuals with high and basic managerial talent. These findings were then cross-validated in a random sample of Gallup panelists (n=5,157). In estimating the percentage of variance in employee engagement that managers account for, multiple regression analysis was conducted across 11,781 work teams examining the relationship between various manager-related independent variables (team members' perceptions of their manager, the managers' engagement and manager talent) and the team's overall engagement as defined by Gallup's Q[12] instrument. The financial value of managerial engagement was estimated using standard utility analysis methods that include the relationship between manager engagement and the engagement of those that report to them, comparing differences between engaged, not engaged and actively disengaged managers. Utility analysis methods also included estimates of the relationship between employee engagement and performance, and literature estimates of the standard deviation of the dollar value of productivity for workers with mean U.S. salary.

April 02, 2015
FOUR IN 10 AMERICANS LOOK FORWARD TO CHECKING MAIL

by Frank Newport and Steve Ander

Story Highlights

- *Older residents most likely to look forward to getting mail*
- *Receiving cards and letters via snail mail has broad appeal*
- *Packages and magazines also evoke positive reactions*

WASHINGTON, D.C.—In a world of email, texts and social media, 41% of Americans nevertheless look forward to checking what is in their mailbox each day. Americans 65 and older are more likely than younger adults to enjoy checking the mail, but 36% of Americans under 30 also feel this way.

Look Forward to Checking the Mail Each Day?
Generally speaking, would you say you look forward to checking what is in the mail each day, or is that something you don't think much about either way?

	Look forward to checking mail each day	Don't think much about checking mail
	%	%
NATIONAL ADULTS	41	58
AGE		
18-29	36	64
30-49	36	63
50-64	41	57
65+	56	44

Mar 27-28, 2015

GALLUP

These data are from Gallup Daily tracking interviewing conducted Mar. 27–28. While more than six in 10 Americans now own a smartphone, and the vast majority of Americans have email addresses and communicate electronically, the results show that checking what the letter carrier brings each day remains a positively anticipated experience for a sizable minority of the public.

Of course, people can receive a wide variety of items in the mail each day, and Americans have a much more positive reaction to receiving some than others. In particular, over 90% of Americans say they have a very positive or positive reaction when receiving personal letters and cards. A sizeable majority of Americans also feel positively about receiving packages (83%) and, to a lesser degree, magazines (60%). Perhaps not surprisingly, sentiments are mostly negative when it comes to receiving letters from businesses, bills and especially advertising fliers.

Reactions to Receiving Types of Mail
Turning to something different, we'd like to know what your reaction is when you receive different types of mail. As I read each type, please say whether your reaction to seeing it in the mail is generally very positive, positive, neither positive nor negative, negative, or very negative?

	Very positive/ Positive	Neither positive nor negative	Very negative/ Negative
	%	%	%
A letter from someone you know	94	3	2
A birthday, holiday or greeting card	93	3	3
A package	83	8	5
A magazine	60	19	18
A catalog	46	24	28
A letter from a business	30	34	34
A bill	29	26	44
An advertising card or flier	22	25	51

Mar 27-28, 2015

GALLUP

The positive response to receiving letters and cards is consistent by age. Ninety-five percent of 18- to 29-year-olds say they feel positively about receiving a personal letter, including 30% who feel very positively, higher than any other age group.

Americans who say they look forward to receiving the mail each day are more positive about getting every type of item than those who don't think much about checking the mail. This difference between the "anticipate mail" group and the more indifferent group is particularly pronounced when it comes to receiving magazines and catalogs. Much of this gap could be due to the consumer and media preferences of those who do not think much about the checking the mail, including the fact that younger and middle-aged Americans may simply be less likely to receive catalogs and magazines.

Reactions to Receiving Types of Mail, by Overall View of Mail

% with Positive Reaction

	Those who look forward to checking mail	Those who don't think much about checking mail
	%	%
A letter from someone you know	97	92
A birthday, holiday or greeting card	96	91
A letter from a business	36	26
A bill	33	24
A package	89	80
A magazine	72	53
A catalog	57	39
An advertising card or flier	27	19

Mar 27-28, 2015

GALLUP

Implications

Despite the electronic revolution in communication and commerce in the last 20 years, millions of Americans continue to be interested in their daily interaction with the U.S. Postal Service (USPS) and associate positive emotions with the mail—in particular, with receiving personal letters and cards. These results, coupled with the previous finding that eight in 10 Americans still visit a post office a few times a year, and that nearly half visit at least once a month, show that the perceived value of old-fashioned mail service is still high among many Americans. While it is likely that people have always had a positive reaction to receiving personal mail, these types of deliveries are probably less and less common in the digital age, explaining why checking the mail on a daily basis may not be as routinely anticipated now as once may have been the case.

These results have mixed implications for the quasi-governmental U.S. Postal Service. While Americans clearly like the thought of receiving personal mail, the actual sending of letters is declining rapidly. The fact that younger Americans are less likely than those older to look forward to receiving their mail each day also suggests the possibility of a dwindling overall interest in mail in the years ahead. As a result of these trends, the USPS has concluded that market-dominant products like first-class mail are becoming less impactful to their business, and has shifted its emphasis to packages. This shift finds support in the attitudes of the American public, who view receiving packages almost as positively as getting personal letters.

Still, the deluge of email, texting and social media updates most Americans receive on a daily basis today may mean that a "fresh" way of communicating—like a personal letter or card—may have increasingly unique value. Cultural practices often move in cycles, and it may be possible that Americans' strong emotional bonds to personal letters and cards means that this "old-fashioned" means of communication could have a renaissance, or at least not become extinct, in the years ahead.

Survey Methods

Results for this Gallup poll are based on telephone interviews conducted March 27–28, 2015, on the Gallup U.S. Daily survey, with a random sample of 1,010 adults, aged 18 and older, living in all 50 U.S. states and the District of Columbia. For results based on the total sample of national adults, the margin of sampling error is ±4 percentage points at the 95% confidence level. All reported margins of sampling error include computed design effects for weighting.

April 03, 2015

INVESTORS MODERATELY CONFIDENT ABOUT RETIREMENT SAVINGS

by Lydia Saad

Story Highlights

- *Nine in 10 retired investors confident they have enough saved*
- *Less than half, however, are very confident*
- *Pattern same with nonretirees' outlook for retirement savings*

PRINCETON, N.J.—Most U.S. investors are generally confident they are financially prepared for retirement, including 88% of retired investors and 76% of nonretired investors. However, less than half (47%) of retired investors are "very" confident they have enough savings to last throughout their retirement, while even fewer nonretired investors, 28%, are very confident they will have saved enough by the time they retire.

U.S. Investors' Confidence in Their Retirement Savings

How confident are you that you will have enough savings [Nonretirees: for retirement at the time you choose to retire; Retirees: to last throughout your retirement]?

	Very confident	Somewhat confident	Not too confident	Not at all confident
	%	%	%	%
Nonretired investors	28	48	13	11
Retired investors	47	41	7	5

Wells Fargo/Gallup Investor and Retirement Optimism Index Survey
Jan. 30-Feb. 9, 2015

GALLUP

These findings are from the Wells Fargo/Gallup Investor and Retirement Optimism Index survey for the first quarter of 2015, conducted Jan. 30–Feb. 9. The Wells Fargo/Gallup survey defines investors as U.S. adults in households with at least $10,000 invested in stocks, bonds or mutual funds. Approximately 40% of U.S. adults meet these criteria.

Among nonretired investors, those with $100,000 or more invested are a bit more optimistic about their future retirement security than those with less than $100,000 invested: 36% in the high-asset group feel very confident they will have saved enough, versus 20% of those with less invested. However, the confidence gap by investor assets widens considerably among retirees. More than half (55%) of retired investors with at least $100,000 in investments are very confident about their savings lasting, compared with a quarter (27%) of those with less than $100,000.

The survey finds little difference in confidence about their future retirement security between nonretired men and nonretired women: 30% versus 25%, respectively, are very confident. At the same time, there is a sizable gender difference among retired investors. Fifty-five percent of male retired investors are very confident they will have enough savings to last throughout retirement, compared with 37% of female retired investors.

U.S. Investors' Confidence in Their Retirement Savings -- by Investment Level

	Very confident	Somewhat confident	Not too confident	Not at all confident
	%	%	%	%
Nonretired investors				
$100,000 or more	36	52	7	4
Less than $100,000	20	42	20	18
Retired investors				
$100,000 or more	55	32	8	3
Less than $100,000	27	58	6	9

Wells Fargo/Gallup Investor and Retirement Optimism Index Survey
Jan. 30-Feb. 9, 2015

GALLUP

U.S. Investors' Confidence in Their Retirement Savings -- by Gender

	Very confident	Somewhat confident	Not too confident	Not at all confident
	%	%	%	%
Nonretired investors				
Men	30	50	11	10
Women	25	46	15	12
Retired investors				
Men	55	36	5	3
Women	37	46	10	7

Wells Fargo/Gallup Investor and Retirement Optimism Index Survey
Jan. 30-Feb. 9, 2015

GALLUP

Younger Nonretired Investors Need Most Help Picking the Right Investments

The survey also asked nonretirees aged 18 to 44—those in the early and middle stages of saving for retirement—to say which of three retirement savings issues they could use the most help with. "Knowing what to invest in" emerged as the clear leader, cited by 32% of respondents. Thirteen percent chose deciding how much to save, and another 13% chose understanding the difference between pretax and after-tax savings tools. The plurality, 41%, said they do not need help with any of these aspects of saving.

In terms of saving and investing towards your future goals, which of the following do you need help with the most?

Based on nonretired investors aged 18 to 44

	%
Knowing what to invest in	32
Deciding how much to save	13
Understanding the difference between pretax and after-tax savings tools	13
None of these	41
No opinion	1

Wells Fargo/Gallup Investor and Retirement Optimism Index Survey
Jan. 30-Feb. 9, 2015

GALLUP

Older Investors Focused on Making Retirement Savings Last, Paying for Healthcare

Gallup presented a different set of retirement issues to investors 45 and older—including nonretirees and retirees. When asked which of four issues they need help with the most, 25% each picked making their savings last throughout retirement and paying for healthcare in retirement. About half as many (12%) said they most need help in understanding tax strategies for withdrawing their savings, and 5% chose understanding their Social Security options. Three in 10 said they don't need help with any of these issues.

(In/As you approach) your retirement, which of the following do you need help with the most?

Based nonretirees and retirees aged 45 and older

	%
Making your retirement savings last throughout your retirement	25
Paying for healthcare in retirement	25
Tax strategies for withdrawing your savings	12
Understanding your Social Security options	5
None of these	31
No opinion	2

Wells Fargo/Gallup Investor and Retirement Optimism Index Survey
Jan. 30-Feb. 9, 2015

GALLUP

Bottom Line

Most U.S. investors are broadly confident they have amassed enough savings to get them through their retirement years, but with the exception of retirees with $100,000 or more in assets and retired men, relatively few truly feel secure. This is especially notable, given that people who are defined as investors for this poll—those who meet the minimum threshold of $10,000 in savings—are almost certainly better prepared for retirement than people with even fewer, or no, investments to speak of.

Investors' less than complete confidence in their retirement security may stem partly from uncertainty about things beyond their control, such as the economy, market stability and major health problems arising. Part, however, may result from a belief that they aren't saving enough or haven't developed a clear retirement plan. While there is no substitute for disciplined savings, younger investors might develop more confidence by seeking expert advice to help ensure they are investing in the right places, while older investors might rest easier with professional guidance in how to make their savings last, taking potential healthcare expenses into account.

Survey Methods

Results for the Wells Fargo/Gallup Investor and Retirement Optimism Index survey are based on questions asked Jan. 30–Feb. 9, 2015, on the Gallup Daily tracking survey, of a random sample of 1,011 U.S. adults having investable assets of $10,000 or more.

For results based on the entire sample of investors, the margin of sampling error is ±3 percentage points at the 95% confidence level.

For results based on the sample of 623 nonretired investors, the margin of sampling error is ±5 percentage points at the 95% confidence level. For results based on the sample of 386 retired investors, the margin of sampling error is ±6 percentage points at the 95% confidence level. For results based on investor class or gender within retired and nonretired investors, the margins of sampling error range from ±6.6% to ±11.5% at the 95% confidence level.

April 06, 2015

NORTH PORT-SARASOTA-BRADENTON, FLORIDA, TOPS LARGE COMMUNITIES IN WELL-BEING

by Dan Witters

Story Highlights

* *North Port-Sarasota-Bradenton, Florida, tops list*
* *California, North Carolina, Texas all have two communities in highest 10*
* *Ohio has five communities in lowest 10*

WASHINGTON, D.C.—North Port-Sarasota-Bradenton, Florida, has the highest Well-Being Index score (64.1) across the 100 most populous communities in the U.S., according to the Gallup-Healthways Well-Being Index. Rounding out the top five are Urban Honolulu, Hawaii; Raleigh, North Carolina; Oxnard-Thousand Oaks-Ventura, California; and El Paso, Texas.

Communities With the Highest Overall Well-Being in 2014

Among 100 most populous metro areas in U.S.

Metropolitan area	Well-Being Index score
North Port-Sarasota-Bradenton, Florida	64.1
Urban Honolulu, Hawaii	63.8
Raleigh, North Carolina	63.6
Oxnard-Thousand Oaks-Ventura, California	63.6
El Paso, Texas	63.6
Austin-Round Rock, Texas	63.4
Provo-Orem, Utah	63.3
San Jose-Sunnyvale-Santa Clara, California	63.2
Washington-Arlington-Alexandria, District of Columbia-Virginia-Maryland-West Virginia	63.1
Winston-Salem, North Carolina	62.9

Gallup Healthways Well-Being Index, 2014

"Metropolitan statistical areas" as defined by the U.S. Office of Management and Budget

GALLUP'

The three communities with a Well-Being Index score of 59.0 or lower are Youngstown-Warren-Boardman, Ohio-Pennsylvania; Toledo, Ohio; and Knoxville, Tennessee. In addition to Youngstown and Toledo, the state of Ohio has three other communities among the 10 ranked lowest for well-being: Dayton, Columbus and Cincinnati. Ohio ranked 46th among the 50 states in well-being in 2014, and is one of five states to have finished among the lowest 10 every year since Gallup and Healthways began measuring well-being in 2008.

Communities With the Lowest Overall Well-Being in 2014

Among 100 most populous metro areas in U.S.

Metropolitan area	Well-Being Index score
Youngstown-Warren-Boardman, Ohio-Pennsylvania	58.1
Toledo, Ohio	58.4
Knoxville, Tennessee	59.0
Dayton, Ohio	59.2
Indianapolis-Carmel-Anderson, Indiana	59.4
Deltona-Daytona Beach-Ormond Beach, Florida	59.5
Scranton--Wilkes-Barre--Hazleton, Pennsylvania	59.5
Columbus, Ohio	59.6
Detroit-Warren-Dearborn, Michigan	59.7
Cincinnati, Ohio-Kentucky-Indiana	60.1

Gallup Healthways Well-Being Index, 2014

"Metropolitan statistical areas" as defined by the U.S. Office of Management and Budget

GALLUP'

As a group, many substantial differences distinguish the lowest well-being communities from the highest. For example, compared with residents of the highest well-being communities, residents of the lowest are 32% less likely to have someone in their lives encouraging them to make healthy choices. They are also 35% more likely to have experienced food insecurity in the last 12 months, 68% more likely to smoke, 26% more likely to be obese, 55% less likely to like what they do each day and 58% more likely to not feel pride in their community.

Some communities that have appeared on these highest and lowest community well-being lists in prior years, such as Boulder, Colorado, and Huntington-Ashland-Ironton, West Virginia-Ohio-Kentucky, are not among the 100 most populous metro areas and therefore are not part of the 2014 reporting.

These community-level data are based on more than 176,000 interviews with U.S. adults across all 50 states and the District of Columbia, conducted from January through December 2014. All reported communities are metropolitan statistical areas as defined by the U.S. Office of Management and Budget. The Well-Being Index is calculated on a scale of 0 to 100, where 0 represents the lowest possible well-being and 100 represents the highest possible well-being. The Gallup-Healthways Well-Being Index score for the nation and for each community comprises metrics affecting overall well-being and each of the five essential elements of well-being:

* **Purpose:** liking what you do each day and being motivated to achieve your goals
* **Social:** having supportive relationships and love in your life
* **Financial:** managing your economic life to reduce stress and increase security
* **Community:** liking where you live, feeling safe and having pride in your community
* **Physical:** having good health and enough energy to get things done daily

Gallup and Healthways have tracked well-being since 2008 and updated the Well-Being Index in 2014 to provide a more comprehensive measure of well-being. The Well-Being Index scores for 2014 are not directly comparable to the scores from prior years because they are calculated using a revised instrument and scoring methodology.

The regional breakdown in well-being scores for communities is largely consistent with Gallup and Healthways state-level results, which show well-being is generally higher in the Northern Plains, Mountain West and West, and lower in the South and Industrial Midwest.

El Paso Leads Large U.S. Communities in Purpose, Physical Well-Being

El Paso is the only community with the highest well-being in more than one element, leading in purpose and physical well-being. Provo-Orem, Utah, leads in community well-being, while Urban Honolulu is No. 1 in financial well-being. Residents of Chattanooga, Tennessee-Georgia, have the highest social well-being.

Youngstown, in turn, is the only community with the lowest well-being in more than one element, trailing in both purpose and social well-being. Toledo has the lowest community well-being, giving Ohio metro areas the lowest spot on three out of five elements. Residents of Columbia, South Carolina, have the lowest financial well-being for large communities, and those of Knoxville have the lowest physical well-being.

North Port-Sarasota-Bradenton, the community with the highest overall Well-Being Index score, does not lead in any element, but is in the top 12 in all five elements. This community is characterized by particularly strong physical, financial and social well-being, ranked second, second and fourth in the nation, respectively, in those elements. Raleigh, Oxnard-Thousand Oaks-Ventura and Chattanooga each have three well-being elements in the top 10.

Implications

The communities with the highest well-being often have many shared characteristics that are much less common among their lower well-being counterparts. The characteristics distinguishing high well-being communities are multifaceted, often spanning multiple well-being elements.

For example, residents of high well-being communities exercise more frequently—an important aspect of physical well-being—but they are also more likely to report that someone close to them encourages them to be healthy, a critical component of social well-being. They are much less likely to be obese, they have fewer significant chronic health conditions, and they feel safe where they live. Those who feel safe where they live are, in turn, more likely to have access to a safe place to exercise and access to fresh produce, which are important community characteristics that are linked to lower levels of obesity.

While those living in high well-being communities are more likely to have basic access to food and healthcare, they are also more likely to manage their money effectively and to live within their means, which are crucial components of financial well-being. People in high well-being communities also report being able to use their strengths on any given day and are more likely to learn new and interesting things, two key aspects of purpose well-being.

Ultimately, residents of the top well-being places in the U.S. are more likely to be thriving across each of the five critical elements of well-being, thus capitalizing on the synergistic benefits of each element acting in concert with one another. This may reflect what is perhaps the most important factor separating the nation's high well-being communities from those with lower well-being: a holistic view of well-being. Leaders in lower well-being communities can study and adapt the distinguishing features of high well-being communities to enhance the overall health of their residents.

"Improving and sustaining high well-being is vital to any population's overall health and economy," says Janet Calhoun, senior vice president at Healthways. "State, local and business leaders should consider specific well-being interventions that make the healthy choice the *easy* choice for their population. A comprehensive long-term environmental strategy creates not only a healthier population, but also a more productive workforce and a more robust economy."

Survey Methods

Results are based on telephone interviews conducted as part of the Gallup-Healthways Well-Being Index survey Jan. 2–Dec. 29, 2014, with a random sample of 176,702 adults, aged 18 and older, living in metropolitan areas in the 50 U.S. states and the District of Columbia, selected using random-digit-dial sampling. Unlike previous years, only the 100 most populous metros—as determined by the U.S. Census Bureau—were reported in 2014. A second requirement is that at least 300 cases are required per metro area for reporting. As such, McAllen-Edinburg-Mission, Texas, and Durham-Chapel Hill, North Carolina, were both excluded from reporting due to an insufficient sample size. These were replaced by the 102nd-largest metropolitan statistical area (MSA) in the U.S.: Lancaster, Pennsylvania.

The "communities" referenced in this article are based on MSAs as defined by the U.S. Office of Management and Budget. In many cases, more than one city is included in the same MSA. The San Jose, California, MSA, for example, also includes the smaller nearby cities of Sunnyvale and Santa Clara in addition to San Jose. Each respondent is attributed to his or her MSA based on self-reports of his or her ZIP code.

Maximum margins of error for the Well-Being Index and the element scores vary according to MSA size, ranging from less than 1 point for the largest cities represented to around ±1.5 points for many of the smallest cities.

April 06, 2015
GOP FIELD FOR 2016 LACKS STAR POWER OF PAST CAMPAIGNS

by Jeffrey M. Jones

Story Highlights

- *Net favorables near +40 for 2016 leaders comparably low*
- *George W. Bush, Elizabeth Dole had +80 scores in 2000*
- *Current field less well known than prior GOP fields*

PRINCETON, N.J.—Mike Huckabee (+40) and Marco Rubio (+39) edge out several other Republicans in their net favorable ratings—the percentage of Republicans who view each favorably minus the percentage who view each unfavorably. But their scores pale in comparison with those for George W. Bush (+85) and Elizabeth Dole (+84) early in the 2000 campaign, and for Rudy Giuliani (+63) at the outset of the 2008 campaign. Bob Dole (+55) also had a higher net favorable rating at the beginning of the 1996 campaign.

Underscoring the relative weakness of the potential 2016 crop of Republican candidates compared with their forerunners in prior campaigns, the candidates with the best scores at this early stage of the 2016 campaign would rank as only third best among the 2008 field, behind Giuliani and eventual nominee John McCain, and as fourth best in the 2000 campaign behind Bush, Dole and Steve Forbes.

Gallup has measured Americans' opinions of presidential candidates since 1992, including favorable and unfavorable ratings for the major Republican contenders in February or March of the year before the 1996, 2000 and 2008 nomination campaigns. The latter two, like the forthcoming 2016 campaign, did not include an incumbent president seeking re-election in either party. Gallup tracked the images of the 2012 Republican candidates but did so in a different question format that does not allow for direct comparisons to the current scores.

The most recent results for potential GOP contenders are based on a March 2–4 Gallup poll. This piece compares just the four most positively rated candidates today relative to the major contenders in past primaries. The data on all 11 potential 2016 candidates included in the early March poll can be found here.

Favorable Ratings of (Potential) Republican Presidential Candidates, Among Republicans and Republican Leaners

Early in year before the 1996, 2000, 2008 and 2016 elections

	Favorable	Unfavorable	Net Favorable
	%	%	
2016			
M. Huckabee	56	16	+40
M. Rubio	47	8	+39
J. Bush	56	20	+36
S. Walker	41	5	+36
2008			
R. Giuliani	76	13	+63
J. McCain	63	21	+42
M. Romney	36	11	+25
2000			
G.W. Bush	88	3	+85
E. Dole	88	4	+84
S. Forbes	60	9	+51
J. McCain	38	6	+32
1996			
B. Dole	70	15	+55
N. Gingrich	54	29	+25
P. Buchanan	35	28	+7

Notes: "Net favorable" is the percentage with a favorable opinion of the candidate minus the percentage with an unfavorable opinion. The 2016 campaign is based on a March 2-4, 2015, poll; the 2008 campaign is based on the average of March 2-4, 2007, and March 23-25, 2007, polls; the 2000 campaign is based on a Feb. 19-21, 1999, poll; the 1996 campaign is based on a March 15-17, 1995, poll. Favorables were not asked in this format early in the 1992 or 2012 campaigns.

GALLUP'

2016 GOP Candidates Held Back by Lower Familiarity

A major factor in potential 2016 candidates' historically weaker net favorable ratings is that none among this group of candidates is as well known as the early front-runners in the past. Jeb Bush is the best known of the potential 2016 GOP candidates, with 76% of Republicans and Republican-leaning independents familiar enough with Bush to have an opinion of him. In past primaries, several candidates have enjoyed a familiarity rating of higher than four of every five Republicans. For example, Elizabeth Dole was familiar to 92% of Republicans and George W. Bush to 91% at a similar stage of the 2000 campaign.

Rubio and Scott Walker currently have very low familiarity scores, comparable to those of McCain in the 2000 campaign and Mitt Romney in the 2008 campaign. Both McCain and Romney emerged as key contenders in those campaigns, but ultimately came up short for the nomination. However, their strong performances set them up for a run in the next presidential election, with McCain winning the 2008 GOP nomination and Romney the 2012 nomination.

From a candidate perspective, being unknown is better than being unpopular. Right now, being unknown is the greater challenge for Walker and Rubio, with roughly half of the party rank-and-file unfamiliar with them. Currently, only 8% of Republicans have an unfavorable opinion of Rubio, and 5% have an unfavorable opinion of Walker. The tendency will be for their favorable ratings among Republicans to increase as they become better known, but their unfavorable ratings should increase at least slightly as well. To the extent each can minimize the increase in negative opinions and maximize the increase in positive opinions as they become better known, it is possible their popularity could rise to approach that of some of the GOP front-runners in past campaigns.

Early Familiarity Scores of Most Positively Rated Republican Presidential Candidates, Among Republicans and Republican Leaners

Early in year before the 1996, 2000, 2008 and 2016 elections

	% Familiar
2016	
J. Bush	76
M. Huckabee	72
M. Rubio	55
S. Walker	46
2008	
R. Giuliani	89
J. McCain	84
M. Romney	47
2000	
E. Dole	92
G.W. Bush	91
S. Forbes	69
J. McCain	44
1996	
B. Dole	85
N. Gingrich	83
P. Buchanan	63

Notes: Familiarity scores are the percentage who are familiar enough with the candidate to have an opinion (positive or negative) of him or her. The 2016 campaign is based on a March 2-4, 2015, poll; the 2008 campaign is based on the average of March 2-4, 2007, and March 23-25, 2007, polls; the 2000 campaign is based on a Feb. 19-21, 1999, poll; the 1996 campaign is based on a March 15-17, 1995, poll. Familiarity was not asked in this format early in the 1992 or 2012 campaigns.

GALLUP'

Although they are by no means unpopular with the GOP base, the better-known Jeb Bush (20%) and Huckabee (16%) do have higher unfavorable ratings among Republicans than most other contenders. Bush and Huckabee still have work to do to become better known among the GOP base, but also would need to work to reduce their unfavorable ratings, or at least keep them from swelling. Both, however, can take heart from McCain's winning the 2008 Republican nomination after beginning the campaign with a 21% unfavorable rating among Republicans.

The 2016 Republican nomination contest is shaping up to be different from the Democratic contest. Republicans will be sorting through a large number of less well-known and currently not highly popular candidates—at least compared with GOP candidates in recent elections—to choose their party's presidential nominee. Meanwhile, the Democratic Party has Hillary Clinton as the clear front-runner, and she is both well known and very popular among Democrats.

The images of the candidates will evolve as the campaign unfolds, and many largely unknown candidates will become better known, particularly if they have noteworthy performances in the debates or do well in early state primaries or caucuses.

But at the outset of the 2016 campaign, the GOP lacks the star power of prior campaigns in having a very well-known and highly popular candidate as the nomination front-runner. That may mean that the Republicans could be in for a protracted nomination battle as a number of similarly rated candidates vie for votes.

However, early popularity is also by no means a guarantee of campaign success. For example, Rudy Giuliani's popularity at the beginning of the 2008 campaign, likely related to his well-regarded handling of the 9/11 terror attacks, faded during a lackluster campaign that saw him struggle to gain a foothold among Republican voters. And Elizabeth Dole could not translate her high name recognition and popularity into a viable 2000 campaign, dropping out before the primaries in part because of George W. Bush's commanding lead in fundraising.

Survey Methods

Results for this Gallup poll are based on telephone interviews conducted March 2–4, 2015, on the Gallup U.S. Daily survey, with a random sample of 653 Republicans and Republican-leaning independents, aged 18 and older, living in all 50 U.S. states and the District of Columbia. For results based on the total sample of Republicans, the margin of sampling error is ±5 percentage points at the 95% confidence level. All reported margins of sampling error include computed design effects for weighting.

April 07, 2015
RAND PAUL BEGINS CAMPAIGN RELATIVELY WELL-KNOWN AMONG GOP

by Andrew Dugan

Story Highlights

- *Paul better known and liked than several presidential competitors*
- *Paul best liked by U.S. Republicans under age 50*
- *Ted Cruz best-liked presidential candidate among conservatives*

WASHINGTON, D.C.—As U.S. Sen. Rand Paul officially began his quest for the Republican presidential nomination Tuesday, nearly seven in 10 Republicans (68%) are familiar with the freshman senator from Kentucky. Paul also enjoys a positive image within the party: A majority of Republicans have a favorable opinion of Paul (51%) while 17% view him unfavorably, for a net favorable score of +34.

Familiarity and Favorability of Rand Paul, Based on Republicans/Leaners

"Next, we'd like to get your overall opinion of some people in the news. As I read each name, please say if you have a favorable or unfavorable opinion of these people -- or if you have never heard of them. How about Rand Paul?"

	% Familiar/ Have an opinion	% With favorable opinion	% With unfavorable opinion	Net favorable (pct. pts.)
Mar 2-4, 2015	64	49	15	+34
Apr 3-4, 2015	68	51	17	+34

GALLUP

These results come from a Gallup poll conducted April 3–4, 2015, just prior to Paul's public announcement that he will seek the 2016 Republican nomination.

Paul's pursuit of the country's highest office begins a new chapter in what has been an unpredictable and rapid rise to national prominence. The son of eccentric Republican congressman and failed three-time presidential candidate Ron Paul, the younger Paul unexpectedly stormed his way into the Senate in the 2010 midterm with significant Tea Party support. Once in office, Paul often found himself at odds with both major parties. In some policy matters, such as foreign relations, Paul has staked positions that have irked influential members of his Republican caucus, while in other matters, such as economics and budgetary policy, he has advocated for outcomes opposed by most Democrats.

But if some of Paul's signature political views stand in contrast to prevailing Republican ideology, it is not evident in his familiarity rating and net favorable score. Among four current and potential GOP candidates Gallup measured, only Jeb Bush, a politician whose candidacy in many ways symbolizes the very "establishment" Paul is seeking to overturn with his presidential bid, is more familiar (81%) to Republican adults. Paul is about as familiar to Republicans as Ted Cruz (65%). Cruz, however, entered the race as the first major GOP candidate on March 23, a move that saw his familiarity rating climb eight percentage points from early March. Florida Sen. Marco Rubio, who is expected to reveal his presidential intentions next week, is slightly less known (60%) than Paul.

Whatever difficulties Paul may have had with senior members of his party in the Senate—his colleague Sen. John McCain once referred to him as a "wacko bird"—appear to have had limited effect on Paul's favorability with Republicans, which stands at 51%. Indeed, while his favorable rating is at statistical parity with that of Bush (53%), the share of Republicans who see Paul in an unfavorable light (17%) is well below that of the better-known Bush (28%).

Familiarity and Favorability of GOP Candidates, Based on Republicans/Leaners

"Next, we'd like to get your overall opinion of some people in the news. As I read each name, please say if you have a favorable or unfavorable opinion of these people -- or if you have never heard of them. How about ...."

	% Familiar/ Have an opinion	% With favorable opinion	% With unfavorable opinion	Net favorable (pct. pts.)
Jeb Bush	81	53	28	+25
Rand Paul	68	51	17	+34
Ted Cruz	65	49	16	+33
Marco Rubio	60	47	14	+33

April 3-4, 2015

GALLUP

Paul Popular Among Young Republicans

Key to Paul's electoral and overall governing strategy is extensive outreach to younger adults, a strategy he may have learned from his father's tech-savvy campaigns. Relatively speaking, Paul is well positioned with younger Republicans—a majority under the age of 50 have a favorable opinion of him (51%). Paul is statistically tied with the better-known Bush (49%) among this group, and he is well ahead of Cruz (37%) and Rubio (32%).

Favorability of GOP Candidates Among Republicans, by Age
% Favorable

	Under 50	50+
Rand Paul	51	51
Jeb Bush	49	57
Ted Cruz	37	59
Marco Rubio	32	59

April 3-4, 2015

GALLUP'

Conservative Republicans Most Favorable to Cruz

Though Paul is closely associated with the conservative Tea Party movement, he is not currently the most well-liked candidate among conservative Republicans. Conservatives—who make up 77% of Republican Tea Party supporters—instead give the highest favorable rating to Cruz, at 63%, while Paul is roughly tied with Bush at just under 60%. Rubio has 53% of conservative Republicans viewing him favorably.

Some of these differences, however, are due to disparities in familiarity. Bush's net favorable score is higher in part because he is the most well known. But he also has the highest unfavorable rating among conservatives, thus giving him the lowest net favorable score of the four, at +30. In terms of net favorability, Paul's +40 puts him well ahead of Bush and tied with Rubio (+41), but still trailing Cruz at +51.

Familiarity and Favorability of GOP Candidates Among Conservative Republicans
Ranked by net favorable

	% Familiar/ Have an opinion	% With favorable opinion	% With unfavorable opinion	Net favorable (pct. pts.)
Ted Cruz	75	63	12	+51
Marco Rubio	65	53	12	+41
Rand Paul	74	57	17	+40
Jeb Bush	86	58	28	+30

April 3-4, 2015

GALLUP'

Bottom Line

Rand Paul's presidential campaign will likely not focus on his libertarian origins or endorse every position his father took in past campaigns. Yet Paul has a legislative record that may not align with mainstream Republican views either, especially in areas of foreign policy or national security issues such as the National Security Agency's surveillance program. Of course, Paul can still point to his battles to reduce federal spending and budget deficits, as well as his advocacy for other conservative causes, as signs of his Republican bona fides.

As Paul tries to gain traction in a brimming Republican field, his opponents will undoubtedly call attention to his supposed political heresies. Time will tell if this strategy is successful in discrediting Paul among the Republican primary electorate—but after spending nearly six years in the Senate staking out controversial political positions, Paul nonetheless enjoys comparably high familiarity and favorability ratings with the GOP.

Survey Methods

Results for this Gallup poll are based on telephone interviews conducted April 3–4, 2015, on the Gallup U.S. Daily survey, with a random sample of 1,023 adults, aged 18 and older, living in all 50 U.S. states and the District of Columbia. For results based on the total sample of national adults, the margin of sampling error is ±4 percentage points at the 95% confidence level. For results based on the total sample of Republicans and Republican leaners, the margin of sampling error is ±6 percentage points at the 95% confidence level.

April 08, 2015
AMERICANS SLIGHTLY MORE POSITIVE TOWARD AFFORDABLE CARE ACT

by Frank Newport

Story Highlights

- *Half of Americans disapprove, while 44% approve*
- *Current attitudes are most positive since October 2013*
- *Blacks and Hispanics the most likely to say ACA has helped them*

PRINCETON, N.J.—Americans' views about the Affordable Care Act (ACA) are more positive now than they were last fall, although overall attitudes remain more negative than positive. Half of Americans now disapprove of the 2010 law, while 44% approve—the narrowest gap since October 2013. By comparison, last November, just after the strong Republican showing in the midterm elections, 56% of Americans disapproved and 37% approved.

Americans' Views of the Affordable Care Act
Do you generally approve or disapprove of the 2010 Affordable Care Act, signed into law by President Obama that restructured the U.S. healthcare system?

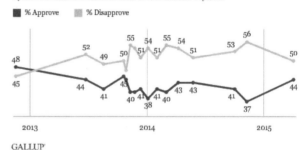

GALLUP'

Americans' support of the Affordable Care Act has fluctuated substantially in recent years, reaching as high as 48% in November 2012, just after President Barack Obama was re-elected, and dropping to as low as 38% in January 2014 and 37% last November. The latest update, based on interviewing conducted April 1–4, shows that Americans have returned to the more positive evaluation of a year and a half ago—albeit one that remains net negative. The shift in attitudes over the past four months may reflect the public's awareness of data showing that the percentage of Americans who are uninsured has dropped substantially since the ACA-mandated open enrollment periods for obtaining insurance began to take effect.

Although opinions of the ACA have become somewhat more positive, Americans' attitudes about the law's impact on their own personal healthcare have not shown much change. The majority of Americans continue to say the law has had no effect on their healthcare so far, while the percentage who say it has hurt their situation continues to be marginally higher than the percentage who say it has helped.

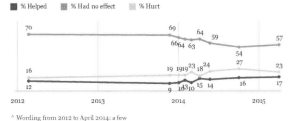

The Affordable Care Act's Perceived Effect on Families

As you may know, a number^ of the provisions of the healthcare law have already gone into effect. So far, has the new law helped you and your family, not had an effect, or has it hurt you and your family?

■ % Helped   ■ % Had no effect   % Hurt

^ Wording from 2012 to April 2014: a few

GALLUP

The Affordable Care Act was partly designed to help those who could not afford insurance to get it, and the data show that several groups that are least likely to be insured—younger, lower-income Americans, minorities—are at least somewhat more likely to be positive about the impact of the healthcare law than others.

- Americans aged 18 to 29 are slightly more likely than those who are older to say the ACA has helped their healthcare situation or that of their family, but almost one in five say it has made their situation worse. The ACA mandated that those under 26 could stay on or be added to their parents' insurance policy, and provided subsidies for younger uninsured Americans to get insurance. On the other hand, the ACA created a requirement that all Americans have insurance, which could be responsible for some of the more negative evaluations among this younger group if they were forced to get insurance they did not want. Most Americans 65 and older are eligible for Medicare, yet three in 10 of this group still say the ACA has either helped or hurt their healthcare situation.
- Americans with lower incomes have been less likely to be insured than those making more, and a slightly higher percentage of those making less than $24,000 a year say the ACA has helped their healthcare situation than is the case among those with higher incomes.
- Blacks and Hispanics are significantly more likely than whites to say the ACA has helped them and their family.

Impact of Affordable Care Act

As you may know, a number of the provisions of the healthcare law have already gone into effect. So far, has the new law helped you and your family, not had an effect, or has it hurt you and your family?

	Helped you and your family	Not had an effect	Hurt you and your family
	%	%	%
AGE			
18 to 29	22	58	18
30 to 49	16	55	24
50 to 64	19	51	28
65+	13	66	17
INCOME			
Less than $24,000	23	53	19
$24,000 to $59,999	19	54	24
$60,000 to $89,999	12	69	19
$90,000+	18	55	27
RACE AND ETHNICITY			
Non-Hispanic whites	13	58	27
Non-Hispanic blacks	26	67	5
Hispanics	27	45	16

April 1-4, 2015

GALLUP

When asked about the impact the ACA will have on their personal healthcare situation in the long term, 32% say it will make it worse—tying the lowest Gallup has measured. This reflects a decline from 38% in October, though these views have fluctuated over the past several years. At the same time, the percentage saying the ACA will make no difference in the long run has gone up. About one in four say it has made their situation better, similar to prior readings.

Americans Say ACA Will Make National Healthcare Situation Worse

Americans' views of the long-term impact of the ACA on the country have remained remarkably stable. In the most recent update, 43% say it will make things worse for the U.S. healthcare situation in the long run, while 37% say it will make things better. This six-percentage-point gap is identical to the gap in overall attitudes about the law.

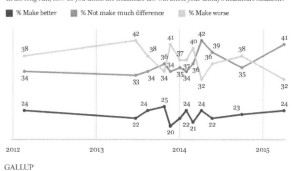

Americans' Views of the ACA's Ability to Improve Families' Healthcare Situations

In the long run, how do you think the healthcare law will affect your family's healthcare situation?

■ % Make better   ■ % Not make much difference   % Make worse

GALLUP

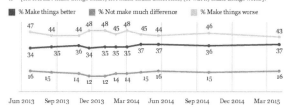

Americans' Views of the Long-Term National Impact of the Healthcare Law

In the long run, how do you think the healthcare law will affect the healthcare situation in the U.S.? Will it -- [ROTATED: make things better, not make much difference, (or will it) make things worse]?

■ % Make things better   ■ % Not make much difference   % Make things worse

June 2013 Asked on Gallup Poll News Service (non-tracking) poll

GALLUP

Implications

The Affordable Care Act remains controversial. Obama and many Democrats point to the demonstrable decrease in the percentage of Americans who are uninsured as an indicator of how successful the law has been. In contrast, Republicans continue to criticize the law, including Republican presidential candidate Ted Cruz, who last month asked his listeners in his announcement speech to "imagine in 2017 a new president signing legislation repealing every word of Obamacare."

Throughout this controversy, Americans as a whole remain more negative than positive about the Affordable Care Act and its impact on their lives and the national healthcare situation. Views of the ACA, however, are modestly more positive than they were last fall.

Americans who are more likely to be affected by the ACA, including young people, lower-income groups and minorities, are at least slightly more likely than others to be positive about the impact of the ACA on their healthcare situations, although significant percentages of most of these groups still say the ACA has hurt them.

Survey Methods

Results for this Gallup poll are based on telephone interviews conducted April 1–4, 2015, on the Gallup U.S. Daily survey, with a random sample of 2,040 adults, aged 18 and older, living in all 50 U.S. states and the District of Columbia. For results based on the total sample of national adults, the margin of sampling error is ±3 percentage points at the 95% confidence level. All reported margins of sampling error include computed design effects for weighting.

April 09, 2015
ABOUT HALF IN U.S. SAY ENVIRONMENTAL PROTECTION FALLS SHORT

by Justin McCarthy

Story Highlights

- *Sixteen percent say gov't doing "too much" to protect environment*
- *Fewer say gov't doing "too little" now than in 1990s and early 2000s*
- *Dems less likely to say gov't does "too little" than before Obama took office*

WASHINGTON, D.C.—Nearly half of Americans (48%) say the U.S. government is doing "too little" to protect the environment, while 16% say it is doing "too much." Roughly a third (34%) say it is doing "about the right amount" in terms of environmental protection. These figures are consistent with the past two years.

Do you think the U.S. government is doing too much, too little or about the right amount in terms of protecting the environment?

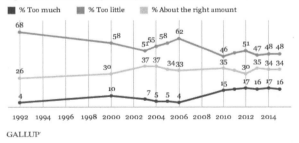

GALLUP

Since President Barack Obama took office, the percentage of Americans saying the government is doing too little to protect the environment has been lower than it was in the 1990s and early 2000s. Meanwhile, the percentage of those who say the government is doing too much has increased since Obama took office.

Gallup first posed the question in 1992, and since then, Americans have always been most likely to say the U.S. government is doing too little to protect the environment. Majorities ranging from 51% to 68% held this belief until 2006. In polls since Obama took office, however, Americans have been less likely to say the government is falling short on environmental protection, though this has remained the dominant view. At the same time, more Americans have said the government is doing too much to protect the environment, reflecting the partisan nature of views of issues such as efforts to reduce industrial pollution and global warming.

These data are from Gallup's annual Environment poll, conducted March 5–8. This comes in a year when the president has ramped up his focus on the environment, with a recent initiative highlighting the link between climate change and its impact on public health through a roundtable discussion with U.S. Surgeon General Dr. Vivek Murthy and Environmental Protection Agency (EPA) Administrator Gina McCarthy. In January, the Obama administration sought to protect over 12 million acres of Alaska's Arctic National Wildlife Refuge. In February, he vetoed congressional legislation that would have authorized the building of the Keystone XL oil pipeline from Canada through the middle part of the U.S. And in March, Obama signed an executive order requiring all federal agencies to cut back their greenhouse gas emissions as part of a larger effort to reduce such emissions globally.

Democrats More Than Twice as Likely as Republicans to Say Government Doing Too Little

Democrats have consistently been more likely than Republicans and independents over the past 15 years to say the federal government could be doing more to protect the environment, but they have been less likely to hold this view since Obama's election. During George W. Bush's administration, significant majorities of Democrats, as high as 79%, said the government was doing too little on the issue, but these majorities diminished during the Obama administration. Independents, too, have waned in their opinion that the U.S. government does too little in environmental protection, from 59% to 67% during the Bush administration and from 46% to 54% during Obama's.

Do you think the U.S. government is doing too much, too little or about the right amount in terms of protecting the environment?
% Too little

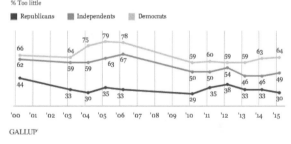

GALLUP

Republicans' views about how the government handles environmental protection, meanwhile, have been fairly stable. Aside from a high of 44% saying it does too little in 2000, the percentage of Republicans holding this view have varied narrowly between 29% and 38%, spanning both the Bush and Obama administrations.

A slight majority of Americans have consistently said Obama has done a "good job" on environmental issues, and he has outperformed his predecessor on the question. But Americans' views about Obama's personal performance and how the government itself has tackled environmental protection break largely along party lines.

Bottom Line

Though Obama's election seemed to have reduced concerns among Democrats and independents that the federal government underperforms on environmental protection, the president's recent environmental protection efforts have not shifted Americans' perceptions. Nearly half continue to say the government does not do enough on this issue.

Americans' views of the EPA, an agency created by Republican President Richard Nixon's administration nearly half a century ago with the mission to protect the environment, have been low relative to most other federal agencies. Though the latest assessment in November 2014 of the EPA's performance is barely higher than in previous polls, Americans regard the agency slightly better than they did when Gallup first asked about the EPA in 2003.

As his second term winds down, Obama's various environmental initiatives, which have taken on a prominent role in his 2015 agenda, may eventually affect Americans' perceptions of the government's efforts to protect the environment. But for the time being, Americans' views have not budged.

Survey Methods

Results for this Gallup poll are based on telephone interviews conducted March 5–8, 2015, with a random sample of 1,025 adults, aged 18 and older, living in all 50 U.S. states and the District of Columbia. For results based on the total sample of national adults, the margin of sampling error is ±4 percentage points at the 95% confidence level. All reported margins of sampling error include computed design effects for weighting.

April 10, 2015
OBAMA'S APPROVAL ADVANTAGE AMONG U.S. JEWS NARROWS

by Frank Newport

Story Highlights

- *Jewish approval of Obama now 54%, eight points above national average*
- *Gap between Jews' and nationwide approval has narrowed recently*
- *Highly religious Jews are least positive about Obama*

PRINCETON, N.J.—For the first quarter of 2015, 54% of American Jews approved of the job Barack Obama is doing as president, compared with an average of 46% among all Americans. That eight-percentage-point gap is lower than the average 13-point gap seen so far throughout Obama's term in office, and is representative of a general narrowing of Obama's Jewish advantage over the last nine months.

A possible weakening of U.S. Jewish support for Obama has been the focus of news media attention in recent months. The administration has embarked on a controversial effort to broker a nuclear agreement with Iran, Israel's longtime avowed enemy, which may have offended some American Jews who see their president as siding more with Iran than with Israel. Adding to the tension, Israeli Prime Minister Benjamin Netanyahu, who strongly opposes a nuclear deal with Iran, got a chilly reaction from the White House when Speaker of the House John Boehner invited him to address Congress last month.

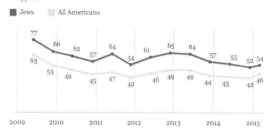

Trend in President Barack Obama Approval Among Jews
% Approve

In a broad sense, Jewish support for Obama has followed the general trajectory of approval among all Americans since the president took office in January 2009—dropping from the initially high "honeymoon" approval ratings in 2009, rising in early 2012 and immediately after his re-election in November 2012, dropping in late 2013 and again last year, and then gaining for the first three months of 2015.

The approval gap between Jews and all U.S. adults has averaged 13 points since Obama took office, but has fluctuated across that period. The gap has been trending downward recently, dropping to 10 points for the second half of 2014, and is now at eight points for the first quarter of 2015.

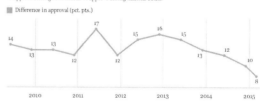

Obama Approval: Difference Between Approval Among Jews and Approval Nationwide
% Approve among Jews minus % approve among national adults

The current findings are based on interviews with 1,022 Americans who identified their religion as Jewish, conducted as part of Gallup Daily tracking from January through March of this year. The larger sample of all Americans is based on 44,101 interviews conducted during the same period.

Jews were particularly positive about Obama in January of this year, with a 61% approval rating, but in the last two months have been much less positive, giving the president a monthly rating of 52% in February and 50% in March—just six and four points, respectively, above the national averages for those two months. If this trend continues, Obama's relative advantage among Jews for the first half of the year would narrow still further. It should be noted that the monthly trends in job approval among Jews are somewhat variable because of the lower monthly sample size of Jewish respondents in Gallup's Daily tracking (usually between 300 and 400 each month).

Highly Religious Jews Least Positive About Obama

An analysis of the aggregate of interviews conducted January 2014–March 2015 highlights several broad differences in approval within the U.S. Jewish population. Jews are the least religious of any major U.S. religious group. The 16% of Jews who report weekly religious service attendance is half the national average of 33% for the same period. The small segment of Jews who attend services weekly are distinctly less positive about Obama than the others, giving Obama a 34% approval rating, compared with much higher approval ratings among Jews who attend services less frequently.

Obama Job Approval Among Jews, by Religious Service Attendance

	Approve	Disapprove	Don't know/ Refused
	%	%	%
Attend weekly	34	60	5
Attend nearly weekly/monthly	53	44	4
Attend seldom/never	58	38	4

Aggregated data: January 2014-March 2015

GALLUP'

Jews With College Degrees, Jewish Women Most Positive About Obama

Almost two-thirds of Jews are college graduates, but among the minority who do not have a college degree—particularly those who have a high school education or less—Obama job approval is considerably lower than the overall Jewish average. The range extends from 39% approval among those who have not advanced beyond high school to 62% among those who have postgraduate education.

Obama Job Approval Among Jews, by Education

	Approve	Disapprove	Don't know/Refused
	%	%	%
High school or less	39	53	8
Some college	48	46	6
College graduate	54	43	3
Postgraduate	62	36	2

Aggregated data: January 2014-March 2015

GALLUP'

Reflecting the gender gap in the general population, Obama approval was 11 points higher among Jewish women than among Jewish men over the past 15 months. Over this same period, approval among the overall national population was 46% among women and 40% among men.

Obama Job Approval Among Jews, by Gender

	Approve	Disapprove	Don't know/ Refused
	%	%	%
Male	48	48	4
Female	59	37	4

Aggregated data: January 2014-March 2015

GALLUP'

Implications

American Jews are more than twice as likely to identify as Democrats than as Republicans, and this partisan skew is reflected in Obama's job approval ratings. Jews continue to approve of the job Obama is doing at a higher level than the national average, although the evidence suggests that this advantage among Jews is narrowing. How much further this gap may shrink in the months ahead remains to be seen, and will depend in part on the future of the relationship between Obama and Israeli leadership. This in turn will reflect the status of the pending agreement with Iran that would restrict that country's nuclear activity in return for a further loosening of economic sanctions. Other administration actions relating to Israel, including support for a possible two-state solution to the Palestinian situation, could also affect Jewish attitudes toward the president going forward.

Survey Methods

Results for this Gallup poll are based on telephone interviews conducted Jan. 2–March 31, 2015, on the Gallup U.S. Daily survey, with a random sample of 44,101 adults, aged 18 and older, living in all 50 U.S. states and the District of Columbia. For results based on the total sample of national adults, the margin of sampling error is ±1 percentage point at the 95% confidence level.

For results based on the total sample of 1,022 Americans who identify their religion as Jewish interviewed between Jan. 2–March 31, 2015, the margin of sampling error is ±4 percentage points at the 95% confidence level.

The margin of sampling error for the entire sample of 221,132 Americans interviewed between Jan. 2, 2014, and March 31, 2015, is ±1 percentage point, and the margin of error for the entire sample of 5,138 American Jews interviewed between Jan. 2, 2014, and March 31, 2015, is ±2 percentage points. All reported margins of sampling error include computed design effects for weighting.

April 13, 2015
IN U.S., UNINSURED RATE DIPS TO 11.9% IN FIRST QUARTER

by Jenna Levy

Story Highlights

- *Uninsured rate down one percentage point from fourth quarter of 2014*
- *Uninsured rate lowest since Gallup and Healthways began tracking in 2008*
- *Down most among lower-income Americans and Hispanics*

WASHINGTON, D.C.—The uninsured rate among U.S. adults declined to 11.9% for the first quarter of 2015—down one percentage point from the previous quarter and 5.2 points since the end of 2013, just before the Affordable Care Act went into effect. The uninsured rate is the lowest since Gallup and Healthways began tracking it in 2008.

The percentage of uninsured Americans climbed from the 14% range in early 2008 to over 17% in 2011, and peaked at 18.0% in the third quarter of 2013. The uninsured rate has dropped sharply since the most significant change to the U.S. healthcare system in the Affordable Care Act—the provision requiring most Americans to carry health insurance—took effect at the beginning of 2014. An improving economy and a falling unemployment rate may also have accelerated the steep drop in the percentage of uninsured over the past year. However, the uninsured rate is significantly lower than it was in early 2008, before the depths of the economic recession, suggesting that the recent decline is due to more than just an improving economy.

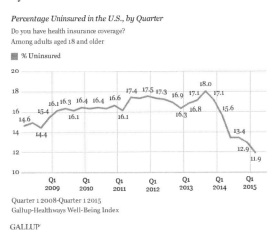

Percentage Uninsured in the U.S., by Quarter

Do you have health insurance coverage?
Among adults aged 18 and older

▨ % Uninsured

Quarter 1 2008-Quarter 1 2015
Gallup-Healthways Well-Being Index

GALLUP

The uninsured rate declined at a slightly slower pace following the second open enrollment period of the federal exchanges compared with the first. The first time around, the uninsured rate fell 1.5 points to 15.6% for the first quarter of 2014 from 17.1% for the fourth quarter of 2013. Comparatively, in that same time frame this year, the uninsured rate fell one point—from 12.9% to 11.9%.

These results are based on more than 43,500 interviews conducted from Jan. 2 to March 31, 2015, as part of the Gallup-Healthways Well-Being Index. Gallup and Healthways ask 500 U.S. adults each day whether they have health insurance, allowing for precise and ongoing measurement of the percentage of Americans without health insurance. The first-quarter results summarize data captured across both pre-deadline and post-deadline dates, so changes in the uninsured rate over the course of the quarter are not reflected.

Uninsured Rate Drops Most Sharply Among Lower-Income Americans and Hispanics

While the uninsured rate has declined across all key demographic groups since the healthcare law fully took effect in January 2014, it has dropped most among lower-income Americans and Hispanics—the groups most likely to lack insurance. The uninsured rate among Americans earning less than $36,000 in annual household income dropped 8.7 points since the end of 2013, while the rate among Hispanics fell 8.3 points. The significant drop in uninsured Hispanics is a key accomplishment for the Obama administration, which led targeted efforts to insure this group as they had the highest uninsured population of all key subgroups. However, despite the gains in insurance coverage among Hispanics and lower-income Americans, these groups still have higher uninsured rates than other key subgroups.

Americans aged 26 to 34 have also seen gains in coverage since the healthcare law went into effect—the uninsured rate among this group is down 7.4 points since the end of 2013, the largest drop

among any age group. Blacks have also seen a substantial drop in their uninsured rate since the fourth quarter of 2013—7.3 points.

Percentage of Uninsured Americans, by Subgroup

Do you have health insurance coverage?

	Q4 2013 %	Q1 2015 %	Net change (pct. pts.)
National adults	17.1	11.9	-5.2
18 to 25	23.5	16.8	-6.7
26 to 34	28.2	20.8	-7.4
35 to 64	18.0	12.0	-6.0
65+	2.0	1.8	-0.2
Whites	11.9	7.7	-4.2
Blacks	20.9	13.6	-7.3
Hispanics	38.7	30.4	-8.3
Less than $36,000	30.7	22.0	-8.7
$36,000 to $89,999	11.7	8.2	-3.5
$90,000+	5.8	3.5	-2.3

Gallup-Healthways Well-Being Index

GALLUP

More Americans Under Age 65 Have Self-Funded Coverage

The uninsured rate among 18- to 64-year-olds dropped to 14.5% in the first quarter of 2015 from 20.8% at the end of 2013, with most of the dip reflecting Americans gaining coverage through self-funded plans, Medicaid and Medicare. Those aged 65 and older are excluded from this analysis of health insurance type because most are covered through Medicare.

The 21.1% of U.S. adults under the age of 65 who say they are covered by a self-funded plan is up 3.5 points since the fourth quarter of 2013. This is likely because more Americans have purchased individual plans through a federal or state health insurance exchange.

The percentage of 18- to 64-year-olds with Medicaid (9.0%) has increased slightly since the requirement for most Americans to carry health coverage took effect. This is not surprising, as many states have expanded Medicaid eligibility so that more lower-income and lower-middle-income Americans can have affordable insurance.

Type of Health Insurance Coverage in the U.S. Among 18- to 64-Year-Olds

Is your insurance coverage through a current or former employer, a union, Medicare, Medicaid, military or veteran's coverage, or a plan fully paid for by you or a family member?

Primary and secondary insurance combined

	Q4 2013 %	Q1 2015 %
Current or former employer	44.2	43.3
A plan paid for by self or family member	17.6	21.1
Medicaid	6.9	9.0
Medicare	6.1	7.3
Military/Veteran's	4.6	4.7
A union	2.5	2.6
(Something else)	3.5	4.2
No insurance	20.8	14.5

Gallup-Healthways Well-Being Index

GALLUP

The percentage of Americans lacking health insurance continued to fall during and after the second open enrollment period that ended on Feb. 15. But the uninsured rate could drop further in the months ahead since the Obama administration established a special enrollment period for March 15 through April 30, aimed at signing up those who realize, while paying their taxes, that they must pay a fine for not obtaining healthcare coverage in 2014.

Some states that run their own exchanges, including Minnesota, Washington and Vermont, also announced special extensions through the end of tax season on April 15. These extended enrollment periods could further drive down the uninsured rate through May, when plans purchased in April go into effect.

Additionally, Medicaid enrollment is not bound by the open enrollment period, which could allow more uninsured to sign up this month—and throughout the year, if more states choose to expand Medicaid. So far, Arkansas and Kentucky have seen the most improvement in uninsured rates as a result of expanding Medicaid and using state-run marketplaces. Finally, the uninsured rate could vary based on underlying dynamics of the workforce and employment rates in the months ahead.

Survey Methods

Results are based on telephone interviews conducted Jan. 2–March 31, 2015, as part of the Gallup-Healthways Well-Being Index survey, with a random sample of 43,575 adults, aged 18 and older, living in all 50 U.S. states and the District of Columbia. For results based on the total sample of national adults, the margin of sampling error is ±1 percentage point at the 95% confidence level.

April 14, 2015

PERCEPTIONS OF TAX FAIRNESS DIVERGING BY INCOME IN U.S.

by Jeffrey M. Jones

Story Highlights

- *Higher- and lower-income Americans less likely to view taxes paid as fair*
- *Middle-income Americans' views steady*

PRINCETON, N.J.—Americans' perceptions of the fairness of their federal income taxes have diverged along income lines in recent years. From 2005 to 2008, roughly six in 10 Americans in each income group said what they paid in income taxes was fair. Since then, higher- and lower-income Americans have grown less likely to consider it fair, while middle-income Americans have remained largely content.

These findings are based on aggregated data from Gallup's annual Economy and Personal Finance poll, conducted each April. The 15-year trend data on perceptions of tax fairness are divided into four groups, which generally correspond to the first and second presidential terms for George W. Bush (2001 to 2004 and 2005 to 2008) and Barack Obama (2009 to 2012 and 2013 to 2015).

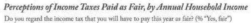

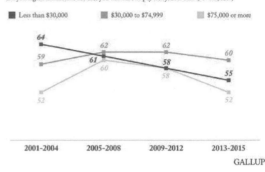

Perceptions of Income Taxes Paid as Fair, by Annual Household Income
Do you regard the income tax that you will have to pay this year as fair? (% "Yes, fair")

■ Less than $30,000   ■ $30,000 to $74,999   ■ $75,000 or more

In the early part of Bush's presidency, lower-income Americans (defined here as those whose annual household income is less than $30,000) were most likely to perceive their tax burden as fair, at 64%. That was far greater than the 52% of higher-income Americans—those whose annual household income is $75,000 or more—who believed their taxes were fair. Appropriately, middle-income Americans fell in between the two groups, at 59%.

By Bush's second term, 2005 through 2008, perceptions of tax fairness converged, with averages of between 60% and 62% of each income group saying their taxes were fair, likely reflecting the impact of the federal income tax cuts enacted in Bush's first term. Higher-income Americans in particular became more likely to say their income taxes were fair.

The basic federal income tax burden for most Americans has not changed since President Obama took office in 2009. The Bush income tax cuts were set to expire in 2010, but Obama and Congress extended them for all taxpayers through 2012 and made them permanent for all but the highest income earners in 2013. As part of the Affordable Care Act, many higher-income Americans have also been subject to higher capital gains taxes and higher taxes to fund Medicare.

Nevertheless, perceptions of tax fairness have shifted modestly by income group over the last eight years, including a six-percentage-point decline in perceived fairness among lower-income Americans and an eight-point decline among higher-income Americans. Even now, however, the majority in each income group believe the taxes they pay are fair, with middle-income Americans most likely to hold that view.

Higher-income Americans' perceptions of tax fairness may to some degree reflect the reality that some are paying more in federal taxes if not federal *income* taxes. But the decline in higher-income Americans' perceived fairness is evident among both those making up to $100,000, whose tax burden has not changed, and those making above it.

There is not an obvious reason why lower-income Americans perceive their taxes as less fair. However, an analysis of the data show that lower-income Americans who identify as Republican have become less likely to view their taxes as fair since Obama took office, while lower-income Democrats' opinions are unchanged. That is a different pattern than that observed among middle-income Americans. Middle-income Republicans are less likely to view their taxes as fair since Obama took office, but middle-income Democrats are more likely to say their taxes are fair. Thus, the trends in views of tax fairness by party offset each other among middle-income Americans, resulting in no change among the group as a whole.

Americans' Perceptions of Tax Fairness Little Changed

Gallup's 2015 update on public opinion toward taxes, conducted April 9–12, shows 56% of all Americans saying the amount of income taxes they pay is fair. That is little changed from the last four years but down significantly from a recent high of 64% in 2003, reflecting the trends by income group discussed previously. The current 56% majority believing their taxes are fair is also higher than what Gallup measured from 1997 through 2001, before the Bush tax cuts took effect.

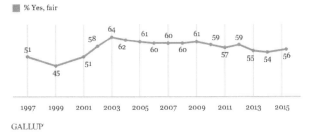

Recent Trend -- Americans' Perceptions That the Income Tax They Pay Is Fair
Do you regard the income tax that you will have to pay this year as fair?

■ % Yes, fair

GALLUP

Gallup's other long-term trend question on taxes asks Americans whether they believe the federal income tax they pay is too high, too low or about right. Typically, a majority regard their taxes as too high, including 51% this year. Most of the rest say their taxes are "about right."

The 51% believing their taxes are too high is little changed from recent years and remains on the lower end of what Gallup has measured historically, likely as a result of the lower income tax rates Americans have been paying since the 2001 and 2003 tax cuts took effect. The record-high 69% saying their taxes were too high was measured in early 1969, after Richard Nixon won the election to replace Lyndon Johnson in the midst of the protracted Vietnam War and the "Great Society" expansion of government programs.

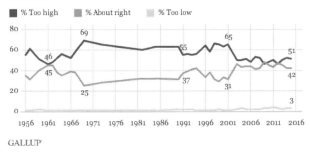

Recent Trend -- Americans' Views of the Amount of Taxes They Pay
Do you consider the amount of federal income tax you have to pay as too high, about right or too low?

■ % Too high   ■ % About right   ■ % Too low

GALLUP

Not surprisingly, higher-income Americans are most likely to say their taxes are too high, with lower-income Americans least likely to agree. In recent years, the differences by income group have not been very large, including 48% for lower-income Americans, 50% for middle-income Americans and 55% for higher-income Americans.

Implications

As Tax Day approaches, more Americans continue to say their taxes are fair than to say they are not. In recent years, though, there has

been a growing disparity in perceptions of fairness by income group. Middle-income Americans are the most likely to believe their taxes are fair, and their views on the matter have changed little. But lower- and higher-income Americans are less likely than roughly a decade ago to view their taxes as fair, even though the tax rates for most people in these groups have not changed.

The disparities in perceptions of tax fairness are not large, and the majority in each income group still see their taxes as fair. It is not essential to the functioning of government for the vast majority of citizens to perceive their taxation levels as fair. However, if more Americans view their taxes as fair, the government's actions and policies may have more legitimacy. Along these lines, between 85% and 90% of Americans said their taxes were fair in Gallup polls conducted during World War II.

Survey Methods

Results for this Gallup poll are based on telephone interviews conducted April 9–12, 2015, with a random sample of 1,015 adults, aged 18 and older, living in all 50 U.S. states and the District of Columbia. For results based on the total sample of national adults, the margin of sampling error is ±4 percentage points at the 95% confidence level.

For results based on three- or four-year aggregates of income groups, the margin of sampling error is ±4 percentage points at the 95% confidence level. All reported margins of sampling error include computed design effects for weighting.

April 15, 2015
U.S. MANAGERS HAVE LOW RATES OF DEPRESSION IN 2014

by Rebecca Riffkin

Story Highlights

- *Less than 4% of managers, transportation workers were depressed*
- *In 2014, 6.3% of service workers said they were currently depressed*
- *Less than 9% of managers have a history of depression*

WASHINGTON, D.C.—In 2014, 3.9% of managers and executives in the U.S. said they were currently suffering from depression—nearly tied with transportation workers, but among the lowest of 14 occupation categories analyzed. By contrast, 6.0% of service workers and 5.9% of professional workers last year reported having or being treated for depression.

As part of the Gallup-Healthways Well-Being Index survey, Americans report whether they currently have or are being treated for depression, as well as whether they have ever been diagnosed as being depressed. Employed Americans also categorize the type of work they do in their primary jobs, which are then broken into 14 broad groups. Because factors such as income and gender have previously been found to have an impact on depression rates, these rates were controlled for age, income, education, marital status, race, gender, full- versus part-time work and health insurance status.

Depression Rates Among Americans of Different Professions

Do you currently have, or are you currently being treated for, depression?

Profession	% Currently have/being treated for depression
Transportation worker	3.8
Manager, executive or official	3.9
Farming, fishing or forestry worker	4.5
Construction or mining worker	4.5
Business owner	4.7
Installation or repair worker	4.9
Sales	5.1
Manufacturing or production worker	5.7
Clerical or office worker	5.7
Physician	5.8
Professional, excluding physicians, nurses and teachers	5.9
Teacher	5.9
Service worker	6.0
Nurse	6.1

Gallup-Healthways Well-Being Index, 2014

Controlled for age, income, education, marital status, race, gender, full- vs. part-time work and health insurance status

GALLUP'

Gallup has recently been focusing on what it means to be a manager in the United States, underscoring the importance of the finding that managers are less likely to report being depressed than are office workers or professional workers, the people with whom managers work closely and often lead. The act of leading may contribute to a lower rate of depression among managers overall, compared with those not in managerial or leadership positions. Or it may be that those who naturally act as leaders, and who are often then promoted to the role of manager, are people less likely to suffer from depression.

Professional workers—the largest occupational category Gallup and Healthways analyzed—join service workers as being significantly more likely to report having depression than the six groups least likely to be depressed, including managers/executives. Depression rates among nurses, physicians and teachers are similar to those found among professional workers and service workers. Transportation workers match managers/executives in their low depression rates, with less than 4% of each group reporting that they are currently being treated for depression. Regardless of occupational category, depression rates are low, with well over nine in 10 workers in every category saying they are not currently depressed or being treated for depression.

Less Than 9% of Managers Report History of Depression

Higher percentages of workers say that a physician or nurse at some point has told them they have depression than say that they are currently depressed. But, as was the case with current depression rates, managers score among the lowest on this history measure, and are the only profession in which less than 9% report a history of depression. This makes managers statistically less likely to have suffered from depression in their lifetime than nine of the 14 professions analyzed.

At least 12% of service workers and manufacturing workers report that they have been diagnosed with depression sometime in their lifetime. This makes them significantly more likely to have a history of depression than managers/executives, business owners, construction workers, transportation workers and farmers.

Overall, in data collected throughout 2014, 17.5% of Americans report having been diagnosed with depression at some point in their lifetime, and 10.4% currently have depression or are being treated for it. Previous Gallup research has found that unemployed Americans are more likely to suffer from depression than employed Americans, which helps explain higher depression rates among the general U.S. population than was found within these professions.

Depression History Among Americans of Different Professions

Have you ever been told by a physician or nurse that you have depression?

Profession	% History of depression
Manager, executive or official	8.9
Transportation worker	9.2
Farming, fishing or forestry worker	9.7
Construction or mining worker	10.1
Business owner	10.3
Physician	10.5
Nurse	10.6
Sales	11.0
Teacher	11.0
Installation or repair worker	11.3
Clerical or office worker	11.7
Professional excluding physicians, nurses and teachers	11.8
Service worker	12.4
Manufacturing or production worker	12.6

Gallup-Healthways Well-Being Index, 2014

Controlled for age, income, education, marital status, race, gender, full- vs. part-time work, and health insurance status

GALLUP'

Bottom Line

Managers and executives are among the occupations least likely to suffer from depression in the U.S. In 2013, Gallup reported that depression was linked to higher rates of absenteeism, costing employers an estimated $23 billion in lost productivity each year, and depression is more prevalent among the long-term unemployed. Depression has also been linked to higher rates of heart attack. And the U.S. Centers for Disease Control and Prevention found that mental illnesses—specifically, depression—were associated with an increased prevalence of chronic diseases, which can cause Americans to leave the workforce.

Gallup and Healthways have previously found that managers have well-being index scores similar to those of professional workers. This indicates that managers don't have higher well-being overall than the professional workers they may be managing, but instead have some unique characteristics that help them avoid depression. Managers may benefit from their work roles, which often allow for more autonomy than other roles, and which could act as a barrier to depression for some. Or possibly the higher responsibility or power managers have could be associated with lower levels of depression. It may also be that the skills often necessary to rise to the level of manager—self-assurance or leadership, for example—make people who possess those traits less likely to be depressed.

Regardless of the cause, depression is a debilitating disease, and managers should work to lower depression rates among their employees in order to lower absenteeism and increase their employees' general well-being.

Survey Methods

Results are based on telephone interviews conducted Jan. 2–Dec. 30, 2014, as part of the Gallup-Healthways Well-Being Index survey, with a random sample of 73,639 adults, aged 18 and older, living in all 50 U.S. states and the District of Columbia. For results based on the total sample of Americans in each profession, the margin of sampling error ranges from ±0.6 to ±1.8 percentage points at the 95% confidence level. All reported margins of sampling error include computed design effects for weighting.

Each sample of national adults includes a minimum quota of 50% cellphone respondents and 50% landline respondents, with additional minimum quotas by time zone within region. Landline and cellular telephone numbers are selected using random-digit-dial methods.

April 15, 2015
MORE AMERICANS SAY LOW-INCOME EARNERS PAY TOO MUCH IN TAXES

by Justin McCarthy

Story Highlights

- *Percentage saying lower-income Americans pay too much is up, at 45%*
- *One in five (21%) say lower-income earners pay "too little"*
- *Forty-six percent say middle class pays "too much"*

WASHINGTON, D.C.—As Americans confront the yearly deadline to pay their federal income taxes, 45% of U.S. adults believe lower-income earners pay "too much." This sentiment is up roughly five percentage points from recent years, but is still lower than a decade ago.

Americans' Views on Tax Burden of Lower-Income Americans
As I read off some different groups, please tell me if you think they are paying their FAIR share in federal taxes, paying too MUCH or paying too LITTLE? First, how about lower-income people?

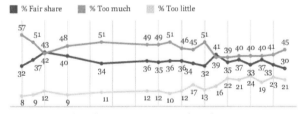

Latest results from April 9-12, 2015

GALLUP

The increase in the belief that lower-income people pay too much is largely attributable to Republicans, a third of whom now hold this view—up from 25% in 2014. The percentage of Democrats saying lower-income people pay too much also increased, from 52% in 2014 to 57% in 2015, while independents' views have been steady, with 44% saying this each year.

When Gallup first polled Americans in 1992 on the fairness of the taxes that various income groups pay, a majority (57%) said lower-income people were paying too much. Gallup also found majorities holding this view in 1993, 1999, 2005 and 2008. Generally, however, between 39% and 49% have said low-income earners pay too much in taxes.

Meanwhile, the percentage of Americans who say lower-income earners are paying "too little" in taxes has increased fairly sharply in the past decade, rising from 10% in 2005 to 22% in 2010. This figure peaked at 24% in 2012—the year in which presidential candidate Mitt Romney made his "47%" comments, characterizing nearly half of the country as individuals who "are dependent upon government, who believe that they are victims, who believe that government has a responsibility to care for them."

These data are from Gallup's annual Economy and Personal Finance poll, conducted April 9–12.

Almost Half of Americans Say Middle Class Overpays in Taxes

Just 6% of Americans say middle-income Americans pay too little in federal taxes. Meanwhile, 46% say the middle class pays too much. While down slightly from a year ago, this remains one of the higher proportions over the past decade to say the middle-income group pays too much, but is sharply lower than Gallup found in the 1990s. Forty-four percent currently say middle-income earners pay "their fair share."

Americans' Views on Tax Burden of Middle-Income Americans
As I read off some different groups, please tell me if you think they are paying their FAIR share in federal taxes, paying too MUCH or paying too LITTLE? First, how about middle-income people?

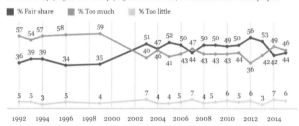

Latest results from April 9-12, 2015

GALLUP

For as long as Gallup has polled on this question, the majority of Americans have said upper-income people pay too little. Currently, 62% hold this view. One in four (25%) say high earners pay their fair share, while just 11% say they pay too much.

Americans' Views on Tax Burden of Upper-Income Americans
As I read off some different groups, please tell me if you think they are paying their FAIR share in federal taxes, paying too MUCH or paying too LITTLE? First, how about upper-income people?

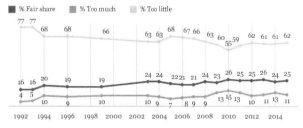

Latest results from April 9-12, 2015

GALLUP

Although the dominant view in the 23 years Gallup has asked the question, the percentage saying upper-income Americans pay too little in taxes has been as low as 55% in 2010, and as high as 77% in 1992 and 1993. The latter possibly reflected Bill Clinton's call for higher taxes on the wealthy, a policy he signed into law in his first term.

Large Majority of Americans Continue to View Corporations as Underpaying

Nearly seven in 10 Americans say corporations pay too little in federal taxes—consistent with views over much of the past decade. Sixteen percent believe corporations are paying their fair share, while fewer than one in 10 (9%) say corporations are overpaying.

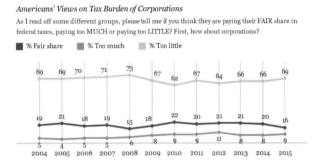

Americans' Views on Tax Burden of Corporations

As I read off some different groups, please tell me if you think they are paying their FAIR share in federal taxes, paying too MUCH or paying too LITTLE? First, how about corporations?

■ % Fair share   ■ % Too much   ▧ % Too little

	2004	2005	2006	2007	2008	2009	2010	2011	2012	2013	2014	2015
Too little	69	69	70	71	73	67	62	67	64	66	66	69
Fair share	19	21	18	19	15	18	22	20	21	21	20	16
Too much	5	4	5	5	6	8	9	9	11	8	8	9

Latest results from April 9-12, 2015

GALLUP'

Bottom Line

Americans have been consistent in their views that high-earners and corporations should pay more in taxes, even as President Barack Obama has sought to shift more of the tax burden onto wealthier citizens and corporations in the U.S. What is a bit more in flux is how Americans view the contributions of lower- and middle-income people.

Political pressure to raise taxes on the rich inevitably sparks discussion of the disproportionate share of federal coffers supplied by the rich—in contrast with the poor, who often pay no income tax. This may explain the increasing view over the past decade that lower-income Americans pay too little in federal income tax, although this seems to have stabilized at just over 20%.

While the majority of Americans believed the middle class paid too much throughout the 1990s, this view waned a bit in the new millennium—likely as a result of the 2001 tax cuts that President George W. Bush put in place. But the most recent two polls have found an uptick to nearly half of Americans saying the middle class is overtaxed, suggesting that the middle class's tax share will continue to be a focal point for political leaders and candidates.

Survey Methods

Results for this Gallup poll are based on telephone interviews conducted April 9–12, 2015, on the Gallup U.S. Daily survey, with a random sample of 1,015 adults, aged 18 and older, living in all 50 U.S. states and the District of Columbia. For results based on the total sample of national adults, the margin of sampling error is ±4 percentage points at the 95% confidence level. All reported margins of sampling error include computed design effects for weighting.

April 16, 2015
MOST AMERICANS SAY HIGHER EDUCATION NOT AFFORDABLE

by Brandon Busteed and Stephanie Kafka

Story Highlights

- *Majority view higher education as available*
- *Less than a quarter (21%) view higher education as affordable*
- *Hispanics most optimistic about availability and affordability*

WASHINGTON, D.C.—A majority of U.S. adults, 61%, believe education beyond high school is available to anyone in America who needs it—down from 67% who felt this way in 2013. However, only a small minority (21%) believe higher education is affordable.

Hispanics More Optimistic About Availability, Affordability of Education Beyond High School

	Yes	No
Do you think education beyond high school is available to anyone in this country who needs it?	%	%
Overall	61	39
Hispanic	73	27
Black	70	30
White	58	42

Do you think education beyond high school is affordable to anyone in this country who needs it?		
Overall	21	79
Hispanic	51	49
Black	19	81
White	17	83

Gallup-Lumina Poll, Nov. 3-Dec. 18, 2014

GALLUP'

These findings are among many releasing Thursday in a report based on the most recent Gallup–Lumina Foundation poll conducted Nov. 3–Dec. 18, 2014.

While the majority of all Americans believe higher education is available to anyone in the U.S. who needs it, some are more likely to feel this way than others do. For instance, Hispanics are more optimistic (73%) than whites (58%) that this type of education is available to all.

Although a majority of all Americans view these educational opportunities as available, few believe it is affordable to those who need it. More than three-quarters (79%) of American adults do not think that education beyond high school is affordable for everyone in the U.S. who needs it, while more than one in five (21%) think it is.

Hispanics are more optimistic in this regard. Fifty-one percent of Hispanics say higher education is affordable, more than twice as high as the 17% of whites and 19% of blacks who say the same. The greater optimism among Hispanics may reflect their increase as a portion of the student body in postsecondary institutions. In fact, the U.S. Department of Education projects that the percentage of Hispanics enrolled in postsecondary programs will increase by 46% between 2009 and 2020.

Implications

If a bachelor's degree is one important way for today's young adults to achieve the American dream, affordability in particular could jeopardize that dream. The average tuition bill for students at a public four-year college has increased by more than 250% over the past three decades—and rising costs are likely a big reason why higher education seems out of reach for many in the U.S. A recent Gallup-Purdue Index study found that 35% of 2000–2014 U.S. college graduates report graduating with more than $25,000 in undergraduate student loan debt, in inflation-adjusted dollars. And while more than half of all adults in the U.S. believe higher education is generally available to those who need it, it is clear that affordability concerns could be placing higher education opportunities at risk for at least some.

The high costs associated with completing a degree beyond high school are also catching U.S. leaders' attention. In January 2015, President Barack Obama announced an initiative that would provide free tuition to students going to community colleges who attend at least part time and maintain a GPA of 2.5 or higher. The proposal is another indication that U.S. leaders share the public's concerns over rising costs in higher education.

Survey Methods

Results for this Gallup–Lumina Foundation poll are based on telephone interviews conducted Nov. 3–Dec. 18, 2014, with a random sample of 1,533 adults, age 18 and older, living in all 50 U.S. states and the District of Columbia. Gallup conducted surveys in English and Spanish.

For results based on the total sample size of 1,533 adults, the margin of sampling error is ±3.3 percentage points at the 95% confidence level. For results based on the total sample size of 123 Hispanic adults and 155 black adults, the margin of sampling error is greater.

April 16, 2015
AMERICANS' OPTIMISM ABOUT FINANCES AT 11-YEAR HIGH

by Art Swift

Story Highlights

- *In U.S., 52% say their financial situation is improving*
- *Highest since 2004 and at majority level for first time since recession*
- *Across income, age and political groups, sentiment higher*

WASHINGTON, D.C.—A majority of Americans, 52%, say their financial situation is "getting better," the highest percentage to say this since 2004. It is also the first time since the recession that this sentiment has reached the majority level.

These data are from a Gallup's annual Economy and Finance survey, poll conducted April 9–12. The percentage of Americans saying their situation is getting better rose nine percentage points from last year.

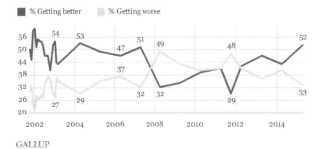

Right now, do you think that your financial situation as a whole is getting better or getting worse?

GALLUP

Gallup has been asking Americans whether their financial situation is getting better or getting worse since 2001. Americans were most positive about the outlook for their personal finances in 2002, when 60% said their financial situation was getting better, while they were least optimistic about their condition in 2011 (29%), as the government showdown over raising the debt ceiling led to instability in the stock market.

There are several possible reasons why Americans are more optimistic this year about their financial situation. Gas prices are about $1.25 per gallon less in the U.S. than they were this time last year, putting more money into American consumers' pockets. Americans are also more positive about the national economy—Gallup's Economic Confidence Index has been generally higher in 2015 than last year—reaching positive territory for the first time in years. The economy has been creating more jobs than in previous years as well, with unemployment at 5.5%, nearly half of what it was five years ago.

Financial Optimism Growing Across Income Groups

Financial optimism has increased across key subgroups this year compared with last year. In every income group, the percentage saying their financial situation is getting better has increased from 2014. The most substantial leap was among those who are making between $20,000 and $30,000 per year. Fifty-one percent of Americans in this income group now say their financial situation is getting better, up from 35% last year. The percentage earning over $75,000 who say their finances are getting better jumped 14 percentage points from last year. However, middle-income earners are only slightly more optimistic than they were last year.

Young adults are the most optimistic about their financial situation, with a commanding 70% saying their situation is improving, up 10 points from last year. In three of the four age groups, the trend is up from last year. Only in one age group, 50–64, was there not much of an increase. This typical pattern in which young Americans are more optimistic about their finances than those who are older is also found in Gallup's economic confidence and standard of living metrics. However, seniors' outlooks are better this year than last year, which might be attributed to improvements in the stock market and retirement accounts recovering.

Not only is there a sizable gap between young and older Americans' views, but there is also a significant divide between Republicans' and Democrats' perceptions of whether their financial situation is getting better. Thirty-eight percent of Republicans say their situation is getting better, while 63% of Democrats say the same. Republicans barely budged from 37% last year, while Democrats jumped 11 points from 2014. Independents' views fall roughly in between the two main parties, with 52% saying that their situation is getting better. This matches the overall percentage of Americans who say this.

Americans Across Income, Age and Political Party Subgroups Saying Financial Situation Getting Better

	2014	2015	Difference
	%	%	pct. pts.
INCOME			
Less than $20,000	29	36	7
$20,000-$29,999	35	51	16
$30,000-$49,999	46	52	6
$50,000-$74,999	46	52	6
$75,000 or more	51	65	14
AGE			
18-29	60	70	10
30-49	54	63	9
50-64	36	38	2
65+	20	33	13
PARTY			
Republican	37	38	1
Independent	42	52	10
Democratic	52	63	11

Apr 6-9, 2015

GALLUP'

This partisan divide could be attributed to allegiances with or against President Barack Obama. It is not uncommon for Americans' views of various national conditions, such as the economy, to vary depending on the party of the president in office. And while the president's actions likely do not directly affect Americans' personal finances, partisanship does affect how Americans evaluate them.

Less Than Half of Americans Say Financial Situation Excellent or Good

Despite the uptick in Americans' financial optimism, when asked to rate their financial situation today, Americans' ratings of their current situation are unchanged. Currently, 46% rate it as "excellent" or "good." This figure has stayed relatively stable during the past decade, with the percentage climbing to 57% in 2003, well before the Great Recession. The low points were in 2010 and 2012, when each year 41% said their financial situation was excellent or good.

How would you rate your financial situation today – as excellent, good, only fair or poor?

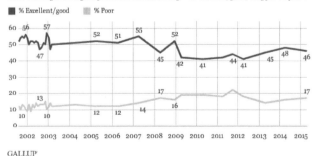

GALLUP'

Bottom Line

For the first time since 2007, more than half of Americans believe that their personal financial situation is getting better, consistent with the rise in Americans' confidence in the national economy more generally. President Obama has stated that the economy has turned a corner and smoother sailing is on the way, and many Americans seem to share that optimism when it comes to their personal finances. While Americans are more optimistic about their future financial situation, their perceptions of the current financial situation have not changed much over the past decade. With economic confidence fluctuating a bit, and Gallup's Economic Confidence Index struggling to stay in positive territory—an important psychological threshold—it is unclear whether 2015 will be a year of sustained warm feelings toward one's finances or a confusing, inconclusive mix.

Survey Methods

Results for this Gallup poll are based on telephone interviews conducted April 9–12, 2015, with a random sample of 1,015 adults, aged 18 and older, living in all 50 U.S. states and the District of Columbia. For results based on the total sample of national adults, the margin of sampling error is ±4 percentage points at the 95% confidence level.

April 17, 2015

MANAGING GOVERNMENT KEY PART OF A PRESIDENT'S IMAGE

by Frank Newport

Story Highlights

- *Americans' ratings of presidents as managers reflect job approval*
- *44% of Americans most recently say Obama can manage effectively*
- *Clinton, Bush and Obama show similar patterns*

PRINCETON, N.J.—Most Americans believe that managing government effectively is an important requirement for a good president, and in recent years, sitting presidents' ratings on this trait have closely matched their overall job approval ratings. Currently, 44% of Americans say that President Barack Obama is an effective manager of government, while 48% approve of the job he is doing overall.

Americans' Ratings of U.S. Presidents: Manage Government Effectively and Job Approval

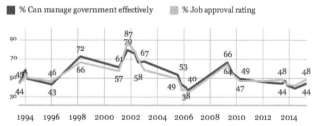

Source: Gallup polls 1993-2015

GALLUP'

The ability to manage government is clearly important to Americans, and previous Gallup research has shown that Americans cite management as one of the top qualities they desire in a president. Gallup has asked Americans from time to time to rate the three most recent presidents—Bill Clinton, George W. Bush and Barack Obama—on their ability to manage government effectively, asking the most recent question about Obama in an April 9–12 survey. The accompanying chart displays the resulting data, along with the job approval rating for the president each time Gallup asked the management question. Clearly, when presidents are doing better on the general job approval measure, as Clinton was in 1998 and as George W. Bush experienced in 2001 and Obama in 2009, they also do better in perceived performance as managers of government. Likewise, when one measure has dipped, so has the other.

Americans' ratings of Obama on the managing government dimension have varied between 66% when he first took office to 39% in the summer of 2014, but in each instance, his contemporaneous job approval rating was within four percentage points of his management score. This gap between views of Clinton and Bush as effective managers and their overall job approval ratings from survey to survey varied more than has been the case for Obama, but reflected the same general pattern. For example, while 79% of Americans said that the label "can manage government effectively" applied to George W. Bush in October 2001, just after 9/11, his job approval rating at that time was also very high, at 87%. When Bush's rating on the management dimension plummeted in 2006, his job approval rating also fell. Clinton's high mark on being an effective manger of government, 66%, came in 1998, a time when his job approval rating was a similarly high 72%.

Overall, the average 52% of Americans who have since 1993 given presidents credit for managing government effectively is only one point different from the 51% average approval rating for the three presidents across the same surveys.

Recent Presidents and Candidates Have Varied Management Experience

That the most recent presidents—including George W. Bush, Bill Clinton, Ronald Reagan and Jimmy Carter—have been state governors, could suggest that Americans appear to want a president with managerial and executive experience. In addition to having been governor of Texas, Bush was also the only president in history to have earned an MBA and was involved in the business world with an oil company in west Texas and as managing general partner of the Texas Rangers major league baseball team.

Still, Americans gave neither Bush nor Clinton more credit for being good managers than they have given Obama, who did not share a state executive background.

Additionally, in the 2012 election, Obama's four years as president ended up trumping candidate Mitt Romney's credentials as a CEO, president of the Salt Lake Organizing Committee for the Winter Olympic Games and Massachusetts governor. Thus, it is difficult to say if prior management experience has a direct bearing on a candidate's probability of being elected president. But it does appear that once in office, Americans use a president's perceived management of government as a criterion for evaluating his overall job performance, rather than viewing management as a separate presidential dimension.

Implications

News story after news story in recent years has focused on apparent governmental managerial wrongdoing in the execution of its responsibilities, including the latest reports of vast cost overruns in the Veterans Affairs' efforts to construct a new facility in Colorado. Americans also cite dysfunctions in the way the government operates as the most important problem facing the country today. There would thus appear to be a strong public appetite for a president who is an effective, efficient manager of government.

The recent record shows that Americans do not tend to differentiate presidents in either an unusually positive or a negative way on their ability to be effective managers, giving presidents ratings on this dimension that basically mirror their overall job approval ratings. This underscores that Americans consider being an effective manager of government as a fundamental requirement for being a good president. Whether Americans are basing their approval of the president at any given time on the state of the economy, the budget, relations with Congress or foreign affairs, they seem to equate good presidential performance with effective management, and vice versa. Americans' perceptions of the president as a good manager are thus a component of how they will evaluate him or her. This suggests that the large group of individuals lining up as 2016 presidential candidates could stress the need for good governmental management as a key part of their efforts to become the next president.

Survey Methods

Results for the most recent Gallup poll cited in this research are based on telephone interviews conducted April 9–12, 2015, with a random sample of 1,015 adults, aged 18 and older, living in all 50 U.S. states and the District of Columbia. For results based on the total sample of national adults, the margin of sampling error is ±4 percentage points at the 95% confidence level. The results for each of the other points in time represented in the research are based on individual surveys, most with samples of approximately 1,000 national adults, and most with a margin of sampling error of ±4 percentage points at the 95% confidence level. All reported margins of sampling error include computed design effects for weighting.

April 20, 2015

U.S. PARENTS' COLLEGE FUNDING WORRIES ARE TOP MONEY CONCERN

by Jeffrey M. Jones

Story Highlights

- *Seven in 10 parents worry about college funding*
- *No other group worries more about any other issue*
- *Lower-income Americans worried about many financial matters*

PRINCETON, N.J.—More U.S. parents worry about having enough money to pay for their children's college education than other Americans worry about any common financial concerns. The 73%

of parents of children younger than 18 who worry about funding college tops the 70% of lower-income Americans who worry about having enough money to pay for medical costs in the event of a serious illness or accident.

Top 10 Financial Worries Among Major U.S. Subgroups, 2001-2015
Figures are percentages who say they are "very worried" or "moderately worried" about the issue.

Subgroup	Financial matter	% Worried
Parents of children younger than 18	Paying for children's college	73
Lower-income households (less than $30,000 per year)	Medical costs in event of serious illness or accident	70
30- to 49-year-olds	Having enough for retirement	69
50- to 64-year-olds	Having enough for retirement	68
Parents of children younger than 18	Having enough for retirement	68
Lower-income households (less than $30,000 per year)	Having enough for retirement	68
Hispanics	Having enough for retirement	67
Hispanics	Medical costs in event of serious illness or accident	65
Lower-income households (less than $30,000 per year)	Maintaining standard of living	64
Married women	Having enough for retirement	64

Based on aggregated data from 2001-2015 Gallup Economy and Personal Finance polls

GALLUP

The results are based on aggregated annual data from Gallup's 2001–2015 Economy and Personal Finance survey. Since 2001, Gallup has asked more than 16,000 Americans how much they worry about each of eight separate financial matters, ranging from having enough money for retirement to making minimum payments on credit cards. The rank order of these fundamental financial concerns has not varied much over time, although the percentage expressing worry in any given year can vary depending on the strength of the economy.

Reflecting that retirement has been the top overall worry each of the 15 years Gallup has conducted the poll, six of the top 10 greatest financial worries by subgroup are about retirement. The six groups with the greatest worry about having enough money for retirement are 30- to 49-year-olds, 50- to 64-year-olds, parents of minor children, those living in lower-income households, Hispanics and married women.

Hispanics' worry about having enough money to pay for a serious medical issue and lower-income Americans' worry about maintaining their standard of living fill the remaining spots in the list of the 10 greatest financial concerns by subgroup.

The table at the end of this article shows the top financial worries for each U.S. subgroup. For most subgroups, having enough money for retirement ranks as the top concern, followed by medical expenses in the event of a serious illness or accident and maintaining one's standard of living.

Given that general pattern, parents' high degree of worry about college funding stands out. And the 73% worried about it is notable because not all parents likely expect their child to attend college, although many more parents may hope or expect their child to go to college than actually will.

Parents thus face twin challenges of paying for ever-escalating college expenses for one or more children and saving for their own retirement. And parents worry a great deal about both, but slightly more about college (73%) than retirement (68%).

As one might expect, parents living in higher-income households worry less about paying for their child's college than those in lower-income households. But a majority, 61%, of parents whose annual household income is $100,000 or more still worry about it.

Parents' Worry About Having Enough Money to Pay for Their Children's College, by Annual Household Income Level

	% Worried
Less than $30,000	85
$30,000-less than $75,000	75
$75,000-less than $100,000	73
$100,000 or more	61

Based on aggregated data from 2001-2015 Gallup Economy and Personal Finance polls

GALLUP

Parents whose income is less than $100,000 are slightly more likely to worry about college funding (77%) than retirement funding (73%), while those whose income is $100,000 or more worry equally about each (61% college and 62% retirement).

Implications

Being a parent can be both rewarding and challenging. Some of parents' greatest challenges are financial, particularly if they hope to send their children to college. This is made clear by parents' worry about paying for college exceeding the level of worry for any other subgroup about any other financial matter. Parents worry more about college funding even more than the most financially vulnerable group—low-income Americans—worry about any financial matter.

High college tuition bills are a financial burden for many American families—particularly those who are low or middle income. Because of high tuition bills, many students accrue large amounts of debt in college that puts them at a bit of a financial disadvantage once they enter into adulthood. Of course, the promise of higher education is that those who earn a degree will be able to secure a well-paying job and thus find financial security of their own, and Gallup polling finds Americans agree with this idea. Though it is well documented that college graduates earn far more over their lifetime than those who do not graduate from college, that finding is not enough to ease parents' worry about how they will pay for their children's education.

Survey Methods

Results for this Gallup poll are based on combined telephone interviews from Gallup's annual Economy and Personal Finance survey, conducted each April from 2001 through 2015. The combined sample is based on interviews with 16,302 randomly selected adults, aged 18 and older, living in all 50 U.S. states and the District of Columbia. For results based on the total sample of national adults, the margin of sampling error is ±1 percentage points at the 95% confidence level.

For results based on the total sample of 4,431 parents of children younger than 18, the margin of sampling error is ±2 percentage points at the 95% confidence level. All reported margins of sampling error include computed design effects for weighting.

April 20, 2015
AMERICANS' MONEY WORRIES
UNCHANGED FROM 2014

by Lydia Saad

Story Highlights

- *Half of Americans have substantial financial anxiety*
- *Worry stable this year, though down from recession*
- *Lacking money for retirement remains top financial worry*

PRINCETON, N.J.—Gallup's Financial Worry metric, which tracks the percentage of Americans worried about multiple common financial challenges, is steady this year at 50%, similar to 49% in 2014. While the metric is down from the 56%-to-61% range seen during the economically challenged period from 2008 through 2012, it remains higher than it was previously.

Americans' Financial Worry

Percentage of U.S. adults "very" or "moderately" worried about three or more financial issues that may affect them, out of seven measured

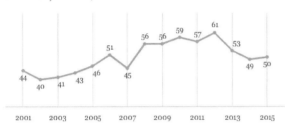

GALLUP

This metric reflects the percentage of Americans who are moderately to highly worried about three or more financial issues out of the seven that Gallup has tracked annually since 2001 as part of its annual Economy and Personal Finance survey. This year's survey was conducted April 9–12.

A variety of financial issues are asked about, ranging from not having enough money for retirement—the most common worry, which 60% of Americans say they are "very" or "moderately" worried about—to not being able to make the minimum payment on credit cards, at 20%. Not being able to afford medical costs associated with a serious illness or accident also ranks high, at 55%, while slightly less than half worry about maintaining their standard of living or paying for normal healthcare. Fewer than four in 10 U.S. adults worry about not having enough to pay their normal monthly bills, or being able to pay their rent or mortgage.

Americans break into four closely sized groups according to their level of financial worry. Roughly one in four are high worriers, worried about six or seven of the seven financial concerns. Another 27% are worried about three to five of these issues, while 25% are worried about one or two and the remaining quarter are worried about none.

Adults in households earning less than $30,000 a year are fraught with financial anxiety, with 44% worried about six or seven of the seven issues, and a combined 72% worried about three or more. The proportion of heavy worriers drops sharply among higher income groups, amounting to just 6% of those households earning $75,000 or more. Accordingly, two major U.S. subgroups associated

with lower income—women and nonwhites—worry significantly more than their counterparts, men and non-Hispanic whites.

Americans' Specific Financial Worries

Please tell me how concerned you are right now about each of the following financial matters, based on your current financial situation -- are you very worried, moderately worried, not too worried or not worried at all?

	Very/ Moderately worried	Not too/ Not at all worried
	%	%
Not having enough money for retirement	60	37
Not being able to pay medical costs of a serious illness/accident	55	43
Not being able to maintain the standard of living you enjoy	46	53
Not being able to pay medical costs for normal healthcare	42	55
Not having enough to pay your normal monthly bills	36	62
Not being able to pay your rent, mortgage or other housing costs	32	63
Not being able to make the minimum payments on your credit cards	20	64

Based on U.S. adults, aged 18+
April 9-12, 2015

GALLUP

In part because of their fairly high income, but also because their stage in life corresponds with lower household expenses and their nearly universal access to government healthcare such as Medicare, seniors are significantly less likely to harbor financial anxiety than younger Americans.

Summary of Americans' Anxiety About Personal Financial Matters

Number of issues Americans are "very" or "moderately" worried about, out of seven issues rated

	No worry (0 issues)	Low worry (1 to 2 issues)	Moderate worry (3 to 5 issues)	High worry (6 to 7 issues)
	%	%	%	%
Total	25	25	27	23
Less than $30,000	13	15	28	44
$30,000 to $74,999	23	27	29	21
$75,000 or more	38	33	23	6
Men	27	26	28	19
Women	22	24	27	27
Married men	29	25	28	19
Unmarried men	27	26	28	19
Married women	25	28	28	19
Unmarried women	20	21	25	33
Non-Hispanic whites	26	26	29	19
Nonwhites	20	24	23	33
18 to 29	23	24	25	28
30 to 49	20	30	26	23
50 to 64	19	23	34	24
65+	41	21	24	15

April 9-12, 2015

GALLUP

An additional item asked as part of the list each year since 2007, but not included in the long-term worry index, is not having enough money to pay college expenses for one's children. This is a relatively low-level concern among all Americans, with 36% saying they are very or moderately worried about it. However, a separate Gallup analysis found that concern about saving for college rises to 73% when focusing on parents of one or more children younger than age 18.

Bottom Line

In January, Gallup found Americans relatively upbeat about their finances at a time when gas prices were tumbling. The 47% then saying they were financially "better off than a year ago" approached the highest levels recorded over the past 40 years, and on par with early 2007. However, Americans' current levels of worry about seven fundamental indicators of financial health suggest they have still not fully recovered from the recession. While they are less worried about everyday financial matters than they were during and immediately after the 2007–2009 recession, Americans remain more worried than they were in the years preceding it.

It's a "good news, bad news" story likely resulting from the gap that still exists between Americans' financial outlook and their reality. A separate finding out of the April poll puts public optimism about their finances at an 11-year high, with 52% saying their financial situation as a whole is getting better. At the same time, Americans' rating of their current finances remains subdued. The 46% describing their finances as "excellent" or "good" falls below the 51%-to-57% range of a decade earlier.

Survey Methods

Results for this Gallup poll are based on telephone interviews conducted April 9–12, 2015, with a random sample of 1,015 adults, aged 18 and older, living in all 50 U.S. states and the District of Columbia. For results based on the total sample of national adults, the margin of sampling error is ±4 percentage points at the 95% confidence level. All reported margins of sampling error include computed design effects for weighting.

April 21, 2015
OBAMA QUARTERLY APPROVAL, AT 46.4%, BEST SINCE MID-2013

by Jeffrey M. Jones

Story Highlights

- *Quarterly approval average improves by three points*
- *Best quarterly average since Obama's 18th quarter*
- *Rating is midrange for presidents in 25th quarter*

PRINCETON, N.J.—President Barack Obama averaged a 46.4% job approval rating during his 25th quarter in office, up three percentage points from the prior quarter. This is his best quarterly average since mid-2013, during his 18th quarter, when he averaged 47.9% approval.

The three-point improvement in the last quarter is the second largest quarter-to-quarter increase in Obama's presidency, behind the four-point increase in his 16th quarter, corresponding with his 2012 re-election. However, since the recent improvement comes after some of his lowest quarterly averages in late 2014, his most recent 46.4% quarterly average still ranks only in the middle of the pack for him.

The gains in Obama's support continued a trend first seen near the end of 2014, when falling gas prices helped Americans' confidence in the economy reach post-recession highs. Although Americans' economic confidence has dipped a little since peaking in early February, it remains better than it has been in the last several years, most likely because gas prices remain low in an absolute sense and the job market has improved considerably.

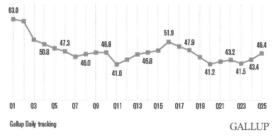

Barack Obama's Quarterly Job Approval Averages

Obama's improved ratings in his 25th quarter may also have been helped by international agreements the U.S. helped broker to address the conflict in Ukraine and Iran's nuclear program. Obama has also re-established formal diplomatic relations with Cuba as one of several steps meant to set a new course in U.S.-Cuba relations.

Obama's 25th Quarter Midrange Compared With Other Presidents

The 25th quarter of a full two-term presidency corresponds with the beginning of the seventh year in office. Obama's average job approval in the 25th quarter ranks third among the five post–World War II presidents elected to two terms—well behind those of Dwight Eisenhower and Bill Clinton, similar to Ronald Reagan's, but much better than that of George W. Bush.

Job Approval Averages for Presidents During Their 25th Quarter in Office

	Dates of 25th quarter	Approval average	Number of polls
Eisenhower	Jan 20-Apr 19, 1959	59.7%	3
Reagan	Jan 20-Apr 19, 1987	46.0%	3
Clinton	Jan 20-Apr 19, 1999	64.6%	11
G.W. Bush	Jan 20-Apr 19, 2007	35.0%	7
Obama	Jan 20-Apr 19, 2015	46.4%	87

Note: Harry Truman, who filled out the remainder of Franklin Roosevelt's fourth elected term starting in April 1945 and was elected in his own right in 1948, averaged 26.0% job approval during his 25th quarter in office, from April 20 to July 19, 1951.

GALLUP

Clinton's 25th quarter was especially noteworthy because it was during that time period that the Senate acquitted him during his impeachment trial. His 25th-quarter average of 64.6% was his second best as president, behind the 66.5% average in his 24th quarter.

Reagan's 25th-quarter average of 46.0% was the lowest of his second term as president, as his administration was ensnared in the Iran-Contra scandal. Bush's 35% average was part of the slump in his approval ratings throughout most of his second term, largely because of the unpopular Iraq War but also due to a series of missteps including the government's response to Hurricane Katrina, his nomination of Harriet Miers to the Supreme Court and plans to sell the rights to U.S. port operations to a United Arab Emirates company.

History offers no guidelines for how Obama's approval rating might change between his 25th and 26th quarters. Eisenhower's and Reagan's approval ratings increased between these quarters, while Bush's and Clinton's ratings declined.

Implications

President Obama's political support has gained positive momentum after suffering last fall around the time of the midterm elections, when his Democratic Party lost control of the U.S. Senate. Obama likely has benefited politically from an improving economy driven by low gas prices and low unemployment, and possibly recent progress in addressing long-standing U.S. challenges on the international stage.

Even so, his 46.4% approval average during his 25th quarter is well below the historical average of 53.3% for all presidents since 1945. Obama's approval ratings have for the most part been below the majority level since he took office, having averaged above 50% in only one quarter since his first year as president. Of course, that quarter was in the fall of 2012, and was enough to ensure his re-election as president.

Survey Methods

Results for this Gallup poll are based on telephone interviews conducted Jan. 20–April 19, 2015, on the Gallup U.S. Daily survey, with a random sample of 44,083 adults, aged 18 and older, living in all 50 U.S. states and the District of Columbia. For results based on the total sample of national adults, the margin of sampling error is ±1 percentage point at the 95% confidence level. All reported margins of sampling error include computed design effects for weighting.

Each sample of national adults includes a minimum quota of 50% cellphone respondents and 50% landline respondents, with additional minimum quotas by time zone within region. Landline and cellular telephone numbers are selected using random-digit-dial methods.

April 22, 2015

CONSERVATIVE REPUBLICANS ALONE ON GLOBAL WARMING'S TIMING

by Andrew Dugan

Story Highlights

- *Majorities of other political identities believe global warming will happen soon*
- *Most conservative Republicans don't think humans cause rising temperatures*

WASHINGTON, D.C.—While notable majorities of all other political party/ideology groups say the effects of global warming will happen within their lifetime, fewer than four in 10 conservative Republicans (37%) agree, a sign of that political identity's strident skepticism on this issue.

Conservative Republicans not only decisively reject the notion that the effects of global warming will happen in this lifetime—a position in sharp contrast to all other political identities—but another 40% say global warming will *never* happen. This is significantly higher than the percentages of moderate/liberal Republicans (16%), non-leaning independents (14%), conservative/moderate Democrats (5%) and liberal Democrats (3%) who say the same.

Americans' Views on Global Warming, by Party and Ideology

Which of the following statements reflects your view of when the effects of global warming will begin to happen -- [ROTATED: they have already begun to happen; they will start happening within a few years; they will start happening within your lifetime; they will not happen within your lifetime, but they will affect future generations; (or) they will never happen]?

	Liberal Democrats	Conservative/ Moderate Democrats	Non-leaning independents	Moderate/ Liberal Republicans	Conservative Republicans
	%	%	%	%	%
Will happen in your lifetime^	89	78	66	64	37
Will affect future generations	9	16	16	18	19
Will never happen	3	5	14	16	40

^ Includes responses "they have already begun to happen," "they will start happening within a few years" and "they will start happening within your lifetime"

Aggregated Gallup data, 2010-2015

GALLUP

These results are based on an aggregate of more than 6,000 interviews conducted as part of Gallup's annual Environment poll each March from 2010 to 2015. Both party affiliation and ideological association are self-reported. The party definitions take into account both respondents' initial party preference—as Democratic, Republican or independent—and independents' leanings toward either party, which are ascertained in a follow-up question. Therefore, the group of "Republicans" reported here includes Republican identifiers and Republican-leaning independents. "Democrats" includes Democratic identifiers and Democratic-leaning independents, and "non-leaning independents" are the residual independents who do not lean toward either major party.

Global warming views are marked by a large partisan gap; Republicans typically treat the concept and consequences of global warming with a heavy dose of skepticism, while Democrats usually express concern about global warming's impact on the environment. To a lesser but still significant extent, Americans describing their political ideology as "conservative"—regardless of party affiliation—tend to cast doubt on global warming and its effects, while ideological moderates and especially liberals are more apt to see the matter as a serious challenge for society.

It is at the intersection of these two key components of one's political identity—party affiliation and ideology—where the sharpest fissures in this debate occur. Gallup has fielded a set of questions designed to measure the public's understanding, skepticism and concern about global warming, and reviewing these data by political identity reveals that for some questions a particular political identity—in this instance, conservative Republicans—is driving the disagreement rather than the entire political party.

Majority of Conservative Republicans Say Global Warming Due to Natural Changes

Policymakers fiercely contest whether global warming is principally due to human-produced pollution or to natural changes in the environment. Of the major political identities, conservative Republicans are the only group in which a clear majority (70%) attribute increasing terrestrial temperatures to natural changes in the environment. By contrast, majorities of Democrats and independents say global warming is due to effects of pollution from human activities. Moderate/liberal Republicans are split on the issue.

Americans' Views on Causes of Global Warming, by Party and Ideology

From what you have heard or read, do you believe increases in the Earth's temperature over the last century are due more to -- [ROTATED: the effects of pollution from human activities (or) natural changes in the environment that are not due to human activities]?

	Liberal Democrats	Conservative/ Moderate Democrats	Non-leaning independents	Moderate/ Liberal Republicans	Conservative Republicans
	%	%	%	%	%
Effects of pollution from human activities	81	67	54	49	27
Natural changes in the environment	16	29	38	47	70

Aggregated Gallup data, 2010-2015

GALLUP'

Earlier this year, the Senate failed to pass a proposal that would have officially recognized human pollution as a cause of global warming; two of the three announced Republican presidential primary candidates—Ted Cruz and Marco Rubio—voted against the measure. Rand Paul was alone among the "official" GOP candidates in supporting the proposal.

Liberal Democrats Alone Say Global Warming Is Serious Threat to Way of Life

Similar dynamics are revealed on another Gallup question, but in an opposite direction. Nearly six in 10 liberal Democrats (58%) assess global warming as a serious threat to their way of life, a judgment not reflected in any of the alternate political identities. Less than half of conservative/moderate Democrats (46%), 35% of independents, 30% of moderate/liberal Republicans and 12% of conservative Republicans agree with this viewpoint. In this instance, then, it is the other "extreme" political identity—liberal Democrats rather than conservative Republicans—whose views diverge with the mainstream opinions of the other political identities.

Bottom Line

President Barack Obama will visit the Florida Everglades on Earth Day to discuss the threats posed to the planet by global warming, which is almost certain to draw both criticism and acclaim. But despite the political volley match, Americans have, for the last several years, reported a consistent viewpoint on this topic: A majority believe the effects of global warming have already begun to happen, and blame human activity for increases in the Earth's temperature.

This stable consensus belies the sharp political divisions that have paralyzed the national government's ability to grapple with this issue, at least in a way that both Congress and the president approve of. While Obama may pursue international accords aimed at combating greenhouse gases, the Republican Congress unabashedly opposes these endeavors. In what amounts to a perfect summation of the distance between the two parties, Obama recently identified global warming as the biggest threat to future generations, while the Republican chair of the Senate Environment and Public Works Committee, James Inhofe, has previously called global warming a "hoax." Inhofe, considered by the *National Journal* as one of the most conservative U.S. senators, undoubtedly represents an extreme viewpoint, just as Obama's heightened language may not accurately capture how many Americans interpret the consequences of global warming.

But even as the viewpoints of Obama and Inhofe—and politicians of a similar ideological profile to either of these two men—might seem irreconcilable, there appears to be evidence that many

Americans agree on issues related to global warming, even if a consensus is not found at the extremes of the American political/ideological spectrum.

Survey Methods

Results for this Gallup poll are based on telephone interviews conducted in March of each year from 2010 to 2015, with an aggregated random sample of 6,154 adults, aged 18 and older, living in all 50 U.S. states and the District of Columbia.

For results based on the total sample of national adults, the margin of sampling error is ±1 percentage point at the 95% confidence level. For results based on the total sample of 1,073 liberal Democrats, the margin of sampling error is ±4 percentage points at the 95% confidence level. For results based on the total sample of 1,536 moderate/conservative Democrats, the margin of sampling error is ±3 percentage points at the 95% confidence level. For results based on the total sample of 916 moderate/liberal Republicans, the margin of sampling error is ±4 percentage points at the 95% confidence level. For results based on the total sample of 1,877 conservative Republicans, the margin of sampling error is ±3 percentage points at the 95% confidence level. All reported margins of sampling error include computed design effects for weighting.

April 23, 2015
U.S. WORKERS' JOB-LOSS FEARS BACK TO PRE-RECESSION LEVELS

by Rebecca Riffkin

Story Highlights

- In U.S., 13% of workers say being laid off very/fairly likely
- Down from 21% in 2010, return to levels seen before recession
- A majority say it is not at all likely they will lose their job

WASHINGTON, D.C.—In the U.S., 13% of employed adults think it is "very" or "fairly" likely that they will be laid off in the next 12 months, down slightly from the 16% who feared job loss a year ago. The percentage who fear being laid off is down from a high of 21% in 2010 and is essentially back to where it was in April 2007, before the Great Recession began.

These results are part of a Gallup trend dating back to 1975. The most recent update is based on Gallup's annual Economy and Personal Finance poll, conducted April 9–12, in which full- and part-time employed adults were asked to predict the likelihood that they will be fired or laid off from their job in the next 12 months.

American workers' job security appears to be influenced by changes in the unemployment rate and the perceived health of the job market. In addition to the heightened concerns about being laid off seen in 2010 through 2013, worry about being laid off also rose to as high as 19% in 1982 during another time of high unemployment.

Overall, the long-term trend shows that, regardless of what is happening in the economy, the majority of workers do not think there is a high likelihood that they will be laid off. Currently, 34% say it is "not too likely" and a majority of 52% say it is "not at all likely" to happen. American workers' perceptions are probably in line with reality, because even in times of high unemployment, nine in 10 Americans who want to work have been employed.

Americans' Fears of Being Laid Off Return to Pre-Recession Levels

Thinking about the next 12 months, how likely do you think it is that you will lose your job or be laid off -- is it very likely, fairly likely, not too likely or not at all likely?

■ % Very/Fairly likely

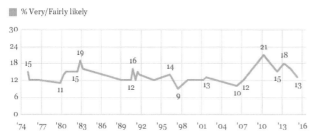

Based on U.S. adults employed full or part time

GALLUP

Majority of U.S. Workers Are Confident They Won't Be Laid Off

Thinking about the next 12 months, how likely do you think it is that you will lose your job or be laid off -- is it very likely, fairly likely, not too likely or not at all likely?

■ % Very/Fairly likely   ▨ % Not too likely   ▨ % Not at all likely

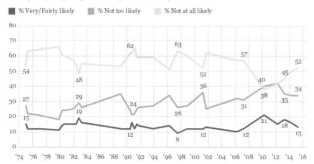

Based on U.S. adults employed full or part time

GALLUP

Across Most Subgroups, Worry About Job Loss Subsides

To gauge changes in job worries by subgroup before, during and after the economic downturn, Gallup aggregated data across multiple years to provide more reliable estimates of worker subgroups. The pre-recession period includes data from 2006 and 2007, when an average of 11% of workers said it was very or fairly likely they would be laid off. The period of heightened job concerns covers 2010 through 2013 (Gallup did not ask this question in the 2008 and 2009 polls), when 18% were worried about being laid off; the current period covers the last two years, when an average of 15% were worried.

The trends show similar patterns in worry among all key subgroups—including by household income, education level, age and gender. All groups saw an increase in worry about losing their job from 2006–2007 to 2010–2013, and most have seen an easing of that worry in the last two years.

Across all three time periods, concerns about being laid off vary most by education and income level. Higher-income workers and those with more education are much less likely to think they will lose their job than lower-income workers and those with less formal education. Younger workers tend to be a bit more worried about losing their job than those who are older, probably because older

workers are more established in their career. Men and women show similar levels of worry.

Perceptions of Being Laid Off in the Next 12 Months, by Demographic Group
% Very/Fairly likely

	2006-2007	2010-2013	2014-2015
ANNUAL HOUSEHOLD INCOME			
Less than $30,000	27	36	27
$30,000 to $74,999	11	17	13
$75,000 or more	4	13	9
EDUCATION			
High school or less	15	26	19
Some college	11	18	14
College graduate	8	12	11
AGE			
18 to 29	12	21	18
30 to 49	12	18	14
50+	9	17	13
GENDER			
Men	11	18	14
Women	11	19	15

Based on U.S. adults employed full or part time

GALLUP

Notably, even among the groups most worried about losing their job, only about one-quarter think that it is likely to happen.

Bottom Line

The changes in workers' concerns about losing their job in recent years are consistent with changes in other recent employment trends. Gallup's Job Creation Index, which measures the percentage of workers who say their employer is hiring minus the percentage who say their employer is letting people go, has steadily increased from the low levels found in 2010 through 2013 and now is among the highest found since October 2008. The unemployment rate has dropped both in Gallup's measures and in measures put out by the Bureau of Labor Statistics. The government's official unemployment statistics found that unemployment dropped below 7% in the last month of 2013, the first time since 2008 it had sunk that low.

U.S. workers seem to be sensitive to changes in the national economy and the job market, which, in turn, affects how secure they feel in their job. It appears the period of heightened concerns about layoffs, seen after the recession, has now ended.

Survey Methods

Results for this Gallup poll are based on telephone interviews conducted April 9–12, 2015, on the Gallup U.S. Daily survey, with a random sample of 472 adults employed full or part time, aged 18 and older, living in all 50 U.S. states and the District of Columbia. For results based on the total sample of employed adults, the margin of sampling error is ±6 percentage points at the 95% confidence level. All reported margins of sampling error include computed design effects for weighting.

April 23, 2015

YOUNG BLACK MALES' WELL-BEING HARMED MORE BY UNEMPLOYMENT

by Dan Witters and Diana Liu

Story Highlights

- *Unemployment negatively affects well-being more for young black males*
- *Attachment to community plummets when out of a job*
- *Reports of safety and security worsen sharply when unemployed*

WASHINGTON, D.C.—Among U.S. men, the gap in well-being experienced by blacks under the age of 35 compared with their non-black counterparts grows still wider when unemployed, according to the Gallup-Healthways Well-Being Index. Compared with the 2.2-point gap in Well-Being Index scores measured among those who are employed, the 2.9-point gap between young black and non-black unemployed men is significantly larger.

Well-Being Index Score, by Employment Status
Among U.S. males aged 18 to 34

	Black males	Non-black males	Difference
Employed	58.4	60.6	-2.2
Unemployed	51.4	54.3	-2.9

Gallup-Healthways Well-Being Index

GALLUP

These findings build on an earlier report showing more broadly that young black males in the U.S. have lower well-being than young non-black males, and this difference is wider than what is found among those between the ages of 35 and 64. Young black males as a group also have higher unemployment, lower graduation rates, less access to healthcare and higher incarceration rates than other racial, age and gender groups in the U.S. And in 2014, the particular difficulties this group has in dealings with law enforcement became headline news resulting from events in Ferguson, Missouri, and Staten Island, New York, involving the deaths of young black men at the hands of police. This article continues to explore the well-being of young black males in comparison with other groups, focusing here on employment status.

These results are based on over 33,000 interviews with American men aged 18 to 34, from Jan. 2 to Dec. 30, 2014, conducted as part of the Gallup-Healthways Well-Being Index. This includes 458 interviews with unemployed black males aged 18 to 34 and another 3,030 interviews with employed black males aged 18 to 34.

Community Well-Being Sinks for Unemployed Young Black Males

Beyond the composite Well-Being Index score, Gallup sees a particularly wide gap in the "community" component of well-being among unemployed young black men.

As one of the five elements of well-being, Gallup and Healthways define community well-being through several individual metrics, including those that measure liking where you live, feeling safe and having pride in your community. Respondents are categorized as thriving, struggling or suffering based on their respective levels of well-being.

While the percentage of people categorized as suffering on the community well-being dimension jumps for all adults when

unemployed, the increase is particularly great among young black males, increasing from an already elevated 25.9% when employed to 43.4% when unemployed. Among non-black males aged 18 to 34, the percentage who are suffering also increases with unemployment, but more modestly than is seen among blacks, from 16.6% to 25.0%.

Community Well-Being, by Employment Status
% "Suffering" in community well-being, among U.S. males aged 18 to 34

	Black males	Non-black males	Difference
	%	%	(pct. pts.)
Employed	25.9	16.6	+9.3
Unemployed	43.4	25.0	+18.4
Difference among unemployed (pct. pts.)	+17.5	+8.4	+9.1

Gallup-Healthways Well-Being Index

GALLUP

The individual metrics that compose community well-being all show similar widening of the well-being gap between black males and non-black males once employment status is a factor. For example, young black males who say they are not proud of the community in which they live climbs from 27.9% among those who are employed to 40.4% when unemployed. Non-blacks also report elevated levels of disagreement, but at a substantially reduced rate.

Pride in Community, by Employment Status
"How strongly do you agree or disagree that you are proud of your community or the area where you live?"
% Disagree, among U.S. males aged 18 to 34

	Black males	Non-black males	Difference
	%	%	(pct. pts.)
Employed	27.9	19.2	+8.7
Unemployed	40.4	25.4	+15.0
Difference among unemployed (pct. pts.)	+12.5	+6.2	+6.3

Gallup-Healthways Well-Being Index

GALLUP

Reports of safety and security among young adult males also suffer when those individuals are unemployed, and even more so among blacks. The percentage of blacks aged 18 to 34 who report not feeling safe or secure goes from 14.7% when employed to 22.5% when unemployed, an increase that more than doubles what is reported by non-blacks.

Feel Safe and Secure in Community, by Employment Status
"How strongly do you agree or disagree that you always feel safe and secure?"
% Disagree, among U.S. males aged 18 to 34

	Black males	Non-black males	Difference
	%	%	(pct. pts.)
Employed	14.7	10.1	+4.6
Unemployed	22.5	13.2	+9.3
Difference among unemployed (pct. pts.)	+7.8	+3.1	+4.7

Gallup-Healthways Well-Being Index

GALLUP

Implications

The relationship between unemployment and well-being—regardless of race, gender or age—is negative and almost certainly reciprocal. When involuntarily outside of the workforce, adults are more likely to be obese; report more daily physical pain, stress and worry; and experience depression. These conditions simultaneously may be a barrier to finding work, while at the same time may be caused or exacerbated by extended unemployment.

But the link between being unemployed and having lower well-being is not always the same across racial divides. The absence of a job affects the well-being of young black males distinctly more so than their non-black counterparts in some key areas of community well-being, underscoring the acute challenges for city leaders. This is exacerbated by official Bureau of Labor Statistics unemployment rates of 12.4% among black men, more than double the 5.1% reported among men in general.

Having a job means having more money to spend, generally affording residents of a community safer living conditions, more opportunities to experience and learn new things, and greater avenues for direct participation in their community. These can have the effect of enhancing pride in the community and satisfaction with it. The absence of a job, in turn, generally leads to less desirable living conditions, more time spent in less safe conditions and a suppressed sense of pride in the area where one lives. In urban areas, where young black males are demographically more likely to reside, the absence of a job exacerbates these differences.

With Americans' satisfaction with the state of race relations sharply down since 2008 and the U.S. Department of Justice report on Ferguson's police department making headlines, the role of good, available jobs may sometimes be understated as a means to enhancing the attachment to community for all residents in any given city, but especially for young black males in particular. John Hope Bryant, CEO of Operation Hope and a noted thought leader focused on the challenges facing black men in American society today, notes, "Young black men are feature actors in a suffering index, because of a lost sense of hope in their lives. The most dangerous person in the world is a person with no hope. We have traditional learning models, and now problem-based learning models. What we need now are aspirational-based learning models. Things that connect education with life aspirations."

Survey Methods

Results are based on telephone interviews conducted as part of the Gallup-Healthways Well-Being Index survey Jan. 2–Dec. 30, 2014, yielding a random sample of 33,549 adult men, aged 18 to 34, living in all 50 U.S. states and the District of Columbia, selected using random-digit-dial sampling. Among these interviews, 3,030 were with employed blacks and 458 were with unemployed blacks seeking to gain employment.

Sample Sizes

	Black males	Non-black males
Total	8,141	89,643
18 to 34	2,396	18,914
35 to 49	1,926	18,030
50 to 64	2,427	26,747
65+	1,392	25,952

Gallup-Healthways Well-Being Index

GALLUP'

For results based on the sample sizes noted above, unemployed black respondents have a maximum expected error range of about ±3.8 percentage points (for suffering, pride in community and safety) and ±1.6 index points (Well-Being Index) at the 95% confidence level. Among employed black respondents, these margins of error reduce to ±1.6 percentage points and ±0.6 index points. Corresponding margins of error for non-black groups are much smaller.

April 23, 2015

AMERICANS AGAIN SAY REAL ESTATE IS BEST LONG-TERM INVESTMENT

by Lydia Saad

Story Highlights

- *Real estate leads four others as best long-term investment*
- *Gold drops to third this year, behind stocks*
- *Preference for bonds at 6%, down from 10% in 2011*

PRINCETON, N.J.—For the second straight year, more Americans name real estate than stocks, gold, savings accounts/CDs or bonds as the best long-term investment. Real estate leads with 31% of Americans choosing it, followed by stocks/mutual funds, at 25%. Meanwhile, gold dropped to third this year, a significant change from 2011 and 2012, when it was the runaway leader.

Americans' Choice of Best Long-Term Investment

Which of the following do you think is the best long-term investment -- [bonds, real estate, savings accounts or CDs, stocks or mutual funds, (or) gold]?

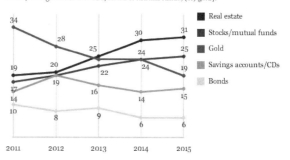

Surveys conducted in April of each year

GALLUP'

The percentages of Americans choosing real estate and stocks are steady this year compared with 2014. This follows three years, from 2011 to 2014, of increasing partiality toward both investments as the housing and stock markets recovered and gold's appeal waned. The public's preference for gold fell five percentage points in the past year, bringing its overall decline since 2011 to 15 points, the largest shift seen among the five investments tracked.

Savings accounts and bonds consistently have been lower on the list, although those identifying savings accounts as the best investment reached 19% in 2012—comparable to stocks and real estate at the time—possibly reflecting Americans' greater desire for stability and security in the first few years after the 2008–2009 financial crisis. This figure has since stabilized near 15%. The percentage choosing bonds has only decreased since Gallup's baseline measure in 2011.

While this trend originates in 2011, an earlier version of the Gallup question that did not include gold shows significant shifts in preference for real estate and stocks between July 2002 and April 2007, with real estate declining from 50% amid the housing boom to 37% when values began to drop, and stocks increasing from 18% to 31% over that same time. Preferences for both then sunk further in 2008 and 2009 as the housing and equity markets suffered severe losses amid a housing mortgage crisis and the resulting global banking crisis and 2007–2009 recession.

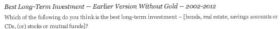

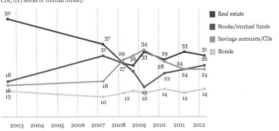

Best Long-Term Investment -- Earlier Version Without Gold -- 2002-2012

Which of the following do you think is the best long-term investment – [bonds, real estate, savings accounts or CDs, (or) stocks or mutual funds]?

■ Real estate
■ Stocks/mutual funds
▨ Savings accounts/CDs
▨ Bonds

GALLUP

Real Estate Favored by All Subgroups

Today real estate is either the top choice or tied for the top choice as the best investment among all major gender, age and income groups. Stocks, on the other hand, faces more competition for second place from gold and savings accounts among some groups.

In particular, and mirroring a pattern seen in the past, nearly as many women, and particularly women aged 18 to 49 years, prefer savings accounts/CDs as prefer stocks. And, savings accounts ranks a clear second among the lowest income group, those earning less than $30,000 annually.

Americans' Choice of Best Long-Term Investment -- Key Subgroup Results

April 9-12, 2015

	Real estate	Stocks/ Mutual funds	Gold	Savings accounts/CDs	Bonds
	%	%	%	%	%
Men	33	26	23	11	4
Women	29	23	15	19	8
Men 18-49	31	29	21	11	3
Women 18-49	28	26	13	23	8
Men 50+	34	23	25	9	5
Women 50+	31	20	18	15	7
18 to 34	25	26	19	21	7
35 to 54	34	27	16	13	6
55+	33	22	22	11	5
$75,000+	33	38	13	9	5
$30,000-$74,999	33	24	23	12	6
Less than $30,000	25	14	21	24	8

GALLUP

Bottom Line

Real estate took a pounding in home values and consumer confidence after the subprime mortgage crisis that started in 2007 spurred the financial crisis of 2008, deepening the 2007–2009 recession. Gold gained appeal during this time, likely due to its tangible quality, but this has proved to be temporary. A return of Americans' confidence in real estate and stocks as solid long-term investments was first evident a year ago, paralleling real-world improvements in these areas. Their continued strength this year indicates that was no fluke. Meanwhile, gold has slipped even further as an attractive way to maintain or grow wealth.

Survey Methods

Results for this Gallup poll are based on telephone interviews conducted April 9–12, 2015, with a random sample of 1,015 adults, aged 18 and older, living in all 50 U.S. states and the District of

Columbia. For results based on the total sample of national adults, the margin of sampling error is ±4 percentage points at the 95% confidence level. All reported margins of sampling error include computed design effects for weighting.

April 24, 2015
CONFIDENCE IN OBAMA'S ECONOMIC DECISIONS RISES IN U.S.

by Andrew Dugan

Story Highlights

* *All major economic leaders saw increase in Americans' confidence*
* *GOP congressional leadership saw biggest one-year gain*
* *One in four do not have opinion of Fed Chair Janet Yellen*

WASHINGTON, D.C.—Half of U.S. adults say they have "a great deal" or "a fair amount" of confidence in President Barack Obama "to do or to recommend the right thing for the economy," a significant rebound from last year's record-low 42%. Moreover, Obama continues to be the most trusted economic actor in Washington among several federal policymakers, including the Democratic leaders in Congress (44%), Federal Reserve Chair Janet Yellen (42%) and the Republican leaders in Congress (38%).

Americans' Confidence in Economic Leaders

As I read some names and groups, please tell me how much confidence you have in each to do or to recommend the right thing for the economy -- a great deal, a fair amount, only a little, or almost none. How about -- [RANDOM ORDER]?

	Great deal/ Fair amount	Only a little/ Almost none	Change in "great deal"/ "fair amount" from 2014
	%	%	pct. pts.
President Barack Obama	50	47	+8
Democratic leaders in Congress	44	53	+9
Federal Reserve Chair Janet Yellen	42	31	+5
Republican leaders in Congress	38	58	+14

April 9-12, 2015

GALLUP

In Gallup's annual Economy and Personal Finance poll, confidence rose for all four leaders, or sets of leaders, compared with last year. This allowed Obama as well as congressional Democratic and Republican leaders to climb out of last year's ratings cellar. Undoubtedly, the general improvement in Americans' economic confidence compared with a year ago played a pivotal part in these more charitable reviews. Gallup's Economic Confidence Index averaged -3 in early April, compared with -16 at the same time in 2014. But even as their scores improved in 2015, none of the four types of leaders has surpassed their historical averages, excepting Yellen, who is in only the second year of her tenure.

While Americans give Obama the highest marks in doing right for the economy—as is typical for the current president—Republican congressional leadership has enjoyed the biggest upswing on this item, a yearly increase of 14 percentage points. Still, a decisive majority (58%) of Americans say they have only a little or almost no confidence in the GOP leadership to make the right decisions for the economy.

Self-identified Republicans were mostly responsible for the higher GOP ratings; their ratings of their party's congressional leadership climbed to 61%, an increase of 18 points. Confidence in GOP leaders also rose among independents and Democrats, but remains low.

Americans' Confidence in Republican Leaders in Congress to Make Right Decisions for Economy, by Party Affiliation

% Great deal/Fair amount of confidence

	2014	2015	Change (pct. pts.)
Republicans	43	61	+18
Independents	20	34	+14
Democrats	16	23	+7

GALLUP

In terms of their public face, Republicans in Congress have largely the same leadership as last year—John Boehner in the House and Mitch McConnell in the Senate. But these leaders have far more leverage over the nation's economic policy after last year's midterm elections, which saw the GOP not only retain control of the House but also take the reins of the Senate. This enhanced role on Capitol Hill may have played a part in Americans', and particularly Republicans', increasing confidence in GOP leadership on the economy, though other evidence suggests the new party in power has had little impact on how the nation views Congress. This month, Congress's job rating stubbornly sits at 15%, essentially unmoved from the historic lows of the last Congress. Previous congressional power shifts, such as in 2007, when Democrats took control, also saw larger gains on this measure (nine points) for that party compared with the year before.

Nonetheless, while Americans' level of confidence in Republican legislative leaders on the economy has improved, it is slightly below Republicans' 15-year average rating (45%) and is even further behind the stronger measures of confidence Republican congressional leaders received for much of the 2003–2006 period, the last time the party had control of both houses of Congress.

Confidence in Congressional Leaders on the Economy, by Party

% Great deal/Fair amount of confidence

■ Democratic leaders in Congress   Republican leaders in Congress

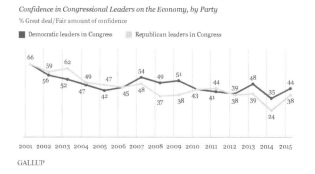

GALLUP

By contrast, Americans' confidence in Democratic congressional leaders is back near its historical mean of 47% after sinking in 2014. But because of the greater year-to-year increase Republicans enjoyed, Democrats' net advantage on this measure has narrowed to six points from last year's 11.

Though Influential, Janet Yellen Remains Unknown to Many

Probably the single biggest policy action that will have an immediate economic impact is in the authority of Federal Reserve Chair Janet Yellen—entirely out of Congress's or Obama's hands. Yellen's likely action to begin raising short-term U.S. interest rates this year may be tantalizing for financial and economic professionals, but for a significant portion of the country (27%), Yellen is too unknown for them to offer an opinion on her performance. Notably, more U.S. adults have at least a fair amount of confidence in her economic recommendations (42%) than those who think otherwise (31%). But she, like her direct predecessor Ben Bernanke, has yet to inspire the same breadth of confidence as the venerated Alan Greenspan, who, in his last year in the position in 2005, generated a 56% confidence score.

Americans' Confidence in Federal Reserve Chairs to Make Right Decisions for the Economy

As I read some names and groups, please tell me how much confidence you have in each to do or to recommend the right thing for the economy -- a great deal, a fair amount, only a little, or almost none. How about Federal Reserve Chairman --

	% Great deal/ Fair amount	% Only a little/ Almost none	% No opinion
JANET YELLEN			
Apr 9-12, 2015	42	31	27
BEN BERNANKE			
Apr 4-7, 2013^	42	38	20
ALAN GREENSPAN			
Apr 4-7, 2005^	56	34	10

^Last poll conducted during their tenure

GALLUP

Despite the apolitical, technocratic nature of the Federal Reserve chair position, Democrats are nearly twice as likely (57%) as Republicans (31%) to express at least a fair amount of confidence in the Obama-appointed Yellen to recommend the right thing for the economy. About a quarter of each party group has no opinion.

Bottom Line

Compared with last year, critical economic metrics such as Gallup's Economic Confidence Index have notably improved, and in tandem, so has the confidence Americans have in the nation's key economic decision-makers, including Obama, congressional leaders of both parties and Yellen. However, Americans' confidence in these leaders can hardly be described as bullish; instead, it is simply more in line with past levels.

Survey Methods

Results for this Gallup poll are based on telephone interviews conducted April 9–12, 2015, on the Gallup U.S. Daily survey, with a random sample of 1,015 adults, aged 18 and older, living in all 50 U.S. states and the District of Columbia. For results based on the total sample of national adults, the margin of sampling error is ±4 percentage points at the 95% confidence level.

April 24, 2015
AN ESTIMATED 780,000 AMERICANS IN SAME-SEX MARRIAGES

by Gary J. Gates and Frank Newport

Story Highlights

- *Approximately 0.3% of adults report marriage to same-sex spouse*
- *0.5% are in same-sex domestic partnerships*

- *About one in six same-sex marriages are in states where it's illegal*

PRINCETON, N.J.—Approximately 0.3% of adults in the U.S. are married to a same-sex spouse, and another 0.5% identify as being in a same-sex domestic partnership. In examining the total population of 243 million U.S. adults, these survey estimates suggest nearly 2 million adults are part of a same-sex couple, of whom 780,000 are married.

Estimates of Same-Sex Marriages and Domestic Partnerships in the U.S.

	% of adults aged 18 and older	Estimated number
Married with a same-sex spouse	0.3	780,000
Unmarried and living with a same-sex domestic partner	0.5	1,200,000
All others	99.2	-

Gallup Daily tracking Jan. 28–Apr. 19, 2015
Based on U.S. Census estimate of 243 million U.S. adults aged 18 and older

GALLUP'

These data are based on 80,568 interviews conducted on Gallup Daily tracking from Jan. 28–April 19, 2015. Overall, approximately 0.3% of all respondents during this time period both identified as lesbian, gay, bisexual or transgender (LGBT) and said they were married, and in a follow-up question, they indicated that they were married to a same-sex spouse. An additional 0.5% of adults identified as LGBT and reported being in a same-sex domestic partnership.

On Tuesday, April 28, the U.S. Supreme Court will hear oral arguments in a set of cases that challenge state bans on marriage for same-sex couples in Kentucky, Michigan, Ohio and Tennessee. This hearing comes two years after the court ruled that the federal Defense of Marriage Act, which prohibited the federal government from recognizing the marriages of same-sex couples, was unconstitutional. At that time, less than half of the states allowed same-sex couples to marry. Today, such marriages are legal in 37 states and the District of Columbia (though disparate rulings by federal and state courts in Alabama have put such marriages on hold there). This rapid legal change brought a surge in marriages among same-sex couples.

The 780,000 American adults who are estimated to be married to a same-sex spouse translates into approximately 390,000 same-sex married couples in the U.S. Similarly, the estimated 1.2 million adults living in a same-sex domestic partnership translates into 600,000 domestic partnership couples. Thus, there is a total of almost a million same-sex couples in the country, of which nearly four in 10 (39%) are married.

At 990,000, Gallup's estimated number of same-sex married or domestic partner couples in the U.S. is significantly higher than past estimates derived from the U.S. Census Bureau's American Community Survey (ACS), which in 2013 put the number of same-sex couples at roughly 727,000. Of this group, more than 250,000 reported they were married. The Census Bureau, however, has cautioned that the ACS estimates of married same-sex couples may not be reliable, as they have determined that a large portion of recorded married same-sex couples may actually be married heterosexual couples who miscoded the sex of one of the spouses.

Separately, analyses of the Centers for Disease Control and Prevention's 2013 National Health Interview Survey put the number of same-sex couples at 690,000, of whom about 130,000 were married by the end of the year. In either case, the number of married

same-sex couples has appeared to increase substantially over the last year.

Bottom Line

The main question before the Supreme Court on Tuesday is whether same-sex couples have a constitutional right to marry. If the court decides the answer is yes when it issues its ruling (likely in June), this means marriage for same-sex couples would become legal in all U.S. states. If the answer is no, it is possible many states that now allow same-sex couples to marry could reinstitute bans. What reinstating bans on same-sex marriage might mean for currently married same-sex couples is not entirely clear.

A second question before the court is whether the 13 states that do not allow same-sex couples to marry must recognize the marriages of same-sex couples who live in those states but were legally married elsewhere. The Gallup data show that approximately 16% of adults who say they are married to a same-sex spouse, or more than 60,000 couples, live in one of the 13 states that do not legally permit same-sex couples to marry.

Survey Methods

Results for this Gallup poll are based on telephone interviews conducted Jan. 28–April 19, 2015, on the Gallup U.S. Daily survey, with a random sample of 80,568 adults, aged 18 and older, living in all 50 U.S. states and the District of Columbia, including 2,610 adults who identified as LGBT. For results based on the total sample of national adults, the margin of sampling error is ±1 percentage points at the 95% confidence level. All reported margins of sampling error include computed design effects for weighting.

April 27, 2015
VIEWS OF HOME BUYING CLIMATE SLIGHTLY LESS POSITIVE IN U.S.

by Jeffrey M. Jones

Story Highlights

- *Slightly fewer Americans say it is a good time to buy a house*
- *Percent expecting local home values to rise highest since 2006*

PRINCETON, N.J.—Americans remain positive about home buying, but are a bit less optimistic than they were in 2013 and 2014. Currently, 69% say it is a good time to buy a house, down from an average 74% during the prior two years, but similar to what Gallup measured from 2009 to 2012. Americans are more positive about buying a house now than they were between 2006 (when home values stopped rising and interest rates increased) and 2008 (after the housing bubble burst). In those years, just over half endorsed home buying.

The latest results are based on Gallup's annual Economy and Personal Finance survey, conducted April 9–12. The slightly less positive views of home buying may have been influenced by lackluster home sales earlier this year, as many parts of the country experienced unusually cold weather. The newest data on home sales, released last week, show there was a surge in sales of existing homes in March.

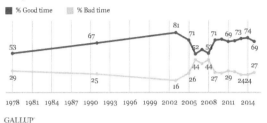

For people in general, do you think that now is a GOOD time or a BAD time to buy a house?

■ % Good time   ▨ % Bad time

GALLUP

Since 1978, Americans have generally been optimistic about the home-buying climate, with majorities saying it is a good time to buy even in times when the economy struggles, including after the housing bubble burst. Thus, the measure likely reflects the value Americans put on homeownership in addition to their views of the prevailing housing market. Although Americans' perceptions of real estate as the best long-term investment sank considerably during the recent recession, prior to that it was the clear leader of four possible choices, and more recently, it has returned to the top spot.

Confidence that it is a good time to buy a home has dropped the most since 2013–2014 among Americans residing in the Western part of the country, with 64% now saying this, down from an average 75%. There were smaller drops among those living in the East and South, while views in the Midwest are steady if not up slightly.

Views of Whether Now Is a Good Time to Buy a House, by Region

	2013-2014	2015	Change
	%	%	pct. pts.
East	72	69	-3
Midwest	75	77	+2
South	72	68	-4
West	75	64	-11

GALLUP

Most Expect Local Home Prices to Rise

Even though Americans are a bit less positive about home buying in general, they expect home prices in their local areas to increase. Currently, 59% expect home prices to rise, 29% believe they will stay the same, and 11% expect prices to decrease. That is the highest percentage expecting an increase since 2006, when 60% expected one.

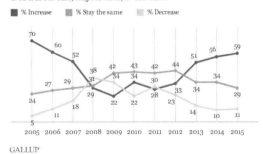

Over the next year, do you think that the average price of houses in your area will increase, stay the same, or decrease?

■ % Increase   ■ % Stay the same   ▨ % Decrease

GALLUP

In recent years, Americans living in the West have been most likely to expect local home values to rise, with 76% predicting an increase this year. Those widespread expectations of higher prices

may explain why fewer Westerners believe now is a good time to buy a home. Southern residents are the next-most optimistic about local home prices, with 61% expecting an increase, followed by those living in the Midwest (51%) and East (46%).

Expectations for Local Home Values Over the Next Year, by Region

	Increase	Stay the same	Decrease
	%	%	%
East	46	36	17
Midwest	51	35	12
South	61	29	9
West	76	17	6

April 9-12, 2015

GALLUP

Implications

Americans remain generally positive about the housing market, although they are slightly less inclined right now to believe buying a home is a good idea than they were during the past two years. It is possible that Americans' current expectations for local home values to rise—the highest in nearly a decade—are causing some to believe conditions favor sellers more than buyers, and that buyers may not be getting as good a value.

It is also unclear to what extent the recent news about surging U.S. home sales may cause Americans to become a bit more positive about home buying conditions. Mortgage interest rates remain low, and higher consumer confidence than in recent years works in favor of continued strong home sales, particularly if the slump in sales earlier this year was mainly because of unusual weather conditions.

But a stronger economy also has persuaded the Federal Reserve Board to consider raising interest rates this year. If higher interest rates make financing a home purchase more expensive, it could dampen the housing market in the coming year.

Survey Methods

Results for this Gallup poll are based on telephone interviews conducted April 9–12, 2015, with a random sample of 1,017 adults, aged 18 and older, living in all 50 U.S. states and the District of Columbia. For results based on the total sample of national adults, the margin of sampling error is ±4 percentage points at the 95% confidence level. All reported margins of sampling error include computed design effects for weighting.

April 27, 2015

IN U.S., FEWER NON-HOMEOWNERS EXPECT TO BUY HOME

by Art Swift

Story Highlights

- *In U.S., 41% of non-homeowners have no plans to buy house*
- *Homeownership down to 61%, lowest in nearly 15 years*
- *Thirty-four percent of Americans rent their primary residence*

WASHINGTON, D.C.—More Americans who do not currently own a home say they do not think they will buy a home in "the foreseeable future," 41%, versus 31% two years ago. Non-homeowners' expectations of buying a house in the next year or five years have stayed essentially the same, suggesting little change in the short-term housing market. As a result, what may have been a longer-term goal for many may now not be a goal at all, and this could have an effect on the longer-term housing market.

U.S. Non-Homeowners' Expectations for Buying a Home

Do you think you will buy a home in the next year, in the next five years, in the next 10 years, or are you unlikely to buy a home in the foreseeable future? (Asked of those who do not currently own a home)

	2013 %	2015 %
Next year	8	7
Next five years	37	36
Next ten years	22	15
Not for the foreseeable future	31	41

GALLUP

One of the long-running facets of the "American dream" has been the ability to buy a house. Yet seven years after the housing market crashed in 2007–2008, it appears that a renewal of zeal for home buying may not yet be evident in the United States. Two years ago, Gallup asked those who did not own a home in the U.S. whether they thought they would buy a house in various time periods in the future. The current Gallup poll shows little movement in Americans' opinions since 2013, except in the sentiment that those who do not own a home say they won't buy one in the foreseeable future. These results come in the same poll that finds a drop in the percentage of all Americans who say it is a good time to buy a house.

Homeownership Rate Lowest in 15 Years

As non-homeowners' expectations for buying a home in the foreseeable future have waned, homeownership rates have also declined from last year. In the April survey, 61% of Americans say they own their primary residence, 34% say they rent, and the remaining 5% have other living arrangements, mostly living with their parents.

That percentage of homeownership is the lowest Gallup has measured in its 15-year trend. The highest percentage of Americans who said they own their home was 74% in a poll in 2005, when the homeownership boom of the 2000s was cresting.

Owning vs. Renting a Home in the United States

Do you own or rent your primary residence?

■ % Own ▨ % Rent

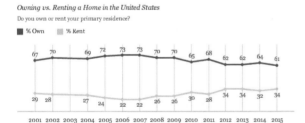

Note: 2005 and 2008 readings reflect annual averages

GALLUP

The percentage of renters is tied for the high since Gallup began asking this question in 2001. The low point for renting occurred in 2006 and 2007 at 22%, just before the U.S. plunged into the Great Recession. Since then, renting has become the norm for about a third of the nation's adults. The U.S. Census Bureau keeps track of homeownership in its surveys. The bureau's most recent estimate of homeownership was 64% in the fourth quarter of 2014, roughly matching Gallup's finding.

Bottom Line

It has been a closely held belief for many in the U.S. that owning a home is a key to eventual personal prosperity. But the Great Recession of 2007–2009 may have changed Americans' ability to act on that belief, given that the housing market has yet to return to pre-recession levels of ownership or home values. It is possible that homeownership will return to previous levels in the years ahead if the economy continues to improve; it is also possible that a "new normal" is occurring in this country, wherein Americans won't be buying a house for the foreseeable future.

For a younger generation that is struggling with student debt, renting a home may be an increasingly safe option. Whatever the reasons, non-homeowners' expectations for buying a home in the near future appear to be waning, and the percentage who say they own their own home is the lowest in nearly 15 years. For an economy that could benefit from a housing recovery for sustained growth this decade, this news may not be the most welcome.

Survey Methods

Results for this Gallup poll are based on telephone interviews conducted April 9–12, 2015, with a random sample of 1,015 adults, aged 18 and older, living in all 50 U.S. states and the District of Columbia. For results based on the total sample of national adults, the margin of sampling error is ±4 percentage points at the 95% confidence level. For results based on the total sample of 324 non-homeowners, the margin of sampling error is ±7 percentage points at the 95% confidence level.

April 28, 2015
FEWER AMERICANS IDENTIFY AS MIDDLE CLASS IN RECENT YEARS

by Frank Newport

Story Highlights

- *51% of Americans say they are in middle or upper-middle class*
- *This is down from the 61% average from 2000 through 2008*
- *48% now say they are in working or lower class*

PRINCETON, N.J.—Americans are considerably less likely now than they were in 2008 and years prior to identify themselves as middle class or upper-middle class, while the percentage putting themselves in the working or lower class has risen. Currently, 51% of Americans say they are middle class or upper-middle class, while 48% say they are lower class or working class. In multiple surveys conducted from 2000 through 2008, an average of more than 60% of Americans identified as middle or upper-middle class.

Gallup began asking this five-part social class question in 2000. In that year, and at several points since, a high of 63% of Americans identified as either upper-middle or middle class. The average percentage placing themselves in the two middle-class categories between 2000 and 2008 was 61%.

Gallup didn't ask the question between 2009 and 2011, but in 2012 and again this year, the combined middle-class percentage dropped significantly, to 50% and 51%, respectively. On the other hand, the percentage of Americans identifying as working and lower class rose to 47% and 48%, up from a low of 33% in 2000.

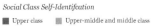

Social Class Self-Identifcation

■ Upper class   ▓ Upper-middle and middle class   ▒ Working and lower class

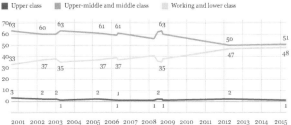

Middle class based on self-identification as upper-middle or middle class. Question wording: If you were asked to use one of these five names for your social class, which would you say you belong in -- upper class, upper-middle class, middle class, working class, or lower class?

GALLUP

There are many ways researchers measure subjective social class. This particular question gives Americans five categories from which to choose. Just 1% of Americans say they are upper class, with the rest spread out in Gallup's April 9–12 survey across upper-middle (13%), middle (38%), working (33%) and lower (15%) class categories. The detailed trends are displayed at the end of this article. Questions which ask respondents to choose only between upper-, middle- and lower-class categories find a larger percentage in the middle-class category than is the case with the five-category measure.

Across all major demographic and political subgroups, identification as middle class or upper-middle class has declined since 2008. In particular, the drop in middle-/upper-middle-class identification by income category has been fairly consistent, between five and nine percentage points in each income group. Overall, even as middle-class identification has dropped across the board, Americans' views of their social class have remained closely tied to their income, as would be expected.

Self-Identification as Upper-Middle/Middle Class, by Demographic Group

	2008*	2012/2015**	Change (pct. pts.)
EDUCATION			
Less than high school	42%	29%	-13
High school graduate	48%	38%	-10
Some college	60%	45%	-15
College graduate	82%	76%	-6
AGE			
18-29	55%	47%	-8
30-49	63%	48%	-15
50-64	65%	49%	-16
65+	65%	62%	-3
INCOME			
Less than $30,000	30%	25%	-5
$30,000-less than $75,000	57%	48%	-9
$75,000 or more	86%	78%	-8
PARTY			
Republicans/leaners	67%	55%	-12
Democrats/leaners	59%	49%	-10

* Aggregate of two September 2008 surveys ** Aggregate of April 2012 and April 2015 surveys

GALLUP

Middle-class identification among those with college degrees has dropped less than it has among those with less education, and older and younger Americans have seen less change in their identification with the middle or upper-middle class than Americans

between the ages of 30 and 64. Republicans are more likely to identify as middle class than Democrats, but both groups have seen roughly even drops in identification with the middle class across time.

Implications

Americans have become less likely to identify as middle class since 2008 and earlier years. One possible explanation focuses on changes in the job market. A big downshift in middle-class identification is found among those with less than a college education, suggesting that increasingly fewer "middle-class" jobs may be available for those without college educations. Further, middle-class identification dropped the most among Americans in their middle-age years, showing that the shifting economy and job market may be most likely to affect the class perceptions of those who are more anchored in their careers, rather than those just starting out or those who are at or near retirement. Similar changes among Republicans and Democrats suggest that politics has not been a major factor in the shift in self-identified class labels.

The percentage identifying as middle or upper-middle class was almost the same in 2012 as it is in 2015, even though the economy, at least as perceived by the public, is in much better shape now than it was in 2012. This could suggest that Americans have shifted into a "new normal" way of looking at their class standing, with the Great Recession having convinced a number of Americans that they are not now, nor are they going to be, middle class, but rather are firmly ensconced in either the working or lower class.

The term *middle class* still resonates with politicians, many of whom are certainly not hesitant to use it to describe those voters their policies are designed to benefit. An exception, however, has been newly announced presidential candidate Hillary Clinton. In her announcement video, she used the term *everyday Americans* to describe her target market, eschewing, at least for the moment, the term *middle class*. As she proclaims on the front page of her campaign webpage: "Everyday Americans need a champion. I want to be that champion." Perhaps Clinton and her strategists are aware that fewer Americans these days see themselves as middle class, prompting the use of more inclusive terminology in their campaign rhetoric.

Social Class Identification 2000-2015

	Upper class	Upper-middle class	Middle class	Working class	Lower class
2015 Apr 9-12	1%	13%	38%	33%	15%
2012 Apr 9-12	2%	11%	39%	33%	14%
2008 Sep 26-27	1%	16%	44%	27%	11%
2008 Sep 5-7	2%	17%	46%	28%	7%
2008 Jun 15-19	2%	19%	43%	28%	8%
2008 Apr 6-9	1%	15%	41%	29%	12%
2006 May 5-7	1%	19%	42%	31%	6%
2006 Apr 10-13	1%	17%	42%	31%	8%
2005 Apr 4-7	2%	14%	47%	28%	9%
2003 Apr 7-9	1%	17%	46%	28%	7%
2003 Jan 10-12	2%	16%	44%	34%	4%
2002 Apr 8-11	2%	18%	42%	31%	6%
2000 Aug 24-27	3%	15%	48%	30%	3%

GALLUP

Survey Methods

Results for the latest Gallup poll are based on telephone interviews conducted April 9–12, 2015, with a random sample of 527 adults, aged 18 and older, living in all 50 U.S. states and the District of Columbia. For results based on the total sample of national adults, the margin of sampling error is ±5 percentage points at the 95% confidence level. Results for the other years represented in this analysis are typically based on samples of approximately 1,000 national adults, for which the margin of sampling error is ±4 percentage points at the 95% confidence level. All reported margins of sampling error include computed design effects for weighting.

April 29, 2015
MORE U.S. NONRETIREES EXPECT TO RELY ON SOCIAL SECURITY

by Jeffrey M. Jones

Story Highlights

- *36% name Social Security as major source of retirement income*
- *Highest percentage in 15 years for nonretirees*
- *401(k) plans still rated as top source for nonretirees*

PRINCETON, N.J.—Although the Social Security program continues to face long-term funding challenges, U.S. nonretirees are more likely to say Social Security will be a major source of income in their retirement than they have been at any point in the last 15 years. The current 36% of nonretirees expecting to heavily rely on Social Security is roughly 10 percentage points higher than a decade ago.

Percentage of U.S. Nonretirees Who Expect Social Security to Be a "Major Source" of Retirement Income

When you retire, how much do you expect to rely on each of the following sources of money -- will it be a major source of income, a minor source of income, or not a source at all?

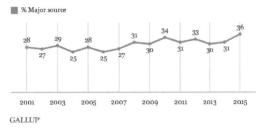

GALLUP

In addition to the 36% of nonretirees expecting Social Security to be a major source of retirement income, another 48% believe it will be a minor source. Fourteen percent do not expect Social Security to be a source of retirement funds for them at all.

These results are based on Gallup's annual Economy and Personal Finance survey, conducted April 9–12.

Generally speaking, the older nonretirees are and the lower their household income is, the more they expect to rely on Social Security as a major source of retirement funds. Close to half of nonretirees aged 55 and older, and of nonretirees whose annual household income is less than $30,000, say Social Security will be a major source of funds.

There are not sufficient sample sizes in any given year's sample of nonretirees to analyze yearly change. However, a comparison of combined data from the 2014–2015 surveys and combined data from the 2005–2006 surveys shows at least modest increases in expected

reliance on Social Security among nonretirees in all age and income groups. There have been proportionately smaller increases among older and lower-income nonretirees, who were more likely to name Social Security as a major source in the past, and greater increases among the groups that were previously less likely to expect to rely on it.

Change in Nonretirees' Expected Reliance on Social Security as a "Major Source" of Retirement Income, by Age and Annual Household Income

	2005-2006	2014-2015	Change
	%	%	(pct. pts.)
AGE			
18 to 34	13	26	+13
35 to 54	30	32	+2
55+	42	48	+6
ANNUAL HOUSEHOLD INCOME			
Less than $30,000	41	45	+4
$30,000 to <$75,000	27	35	+8
$75,000 or more	14	23	+9

GALLUP

Retirement Investment Accounts Continue to Rate as Top Expected Income Source

Even as nonretirees increasingly expect to rely on Social Security in retirement, they are still most likely to name retirement investment accounts, such as 401(k) plans or Individual Retirement Accounts (IRAs), as a major source of retirement funds. Each year Gallup has conducted the poll, 401(k) and other savings plans have topped the list.

Currently, 49% say such plans will be a major source, essentially unchanged from last year but up slightly from an average of 45% from 2009 to 2013. In the past, as many as 58% of nonretired Americans expected to rely on 401(k)s or other retirement savings accounts as a major source of money in retirement. That came in early 2001, shortly after the dot-com economic boom.

Percentage of U.S. Nonretirees Who Expect Retirement Investment Accounts Like 401(k)s or IRAs to Be a "Major Source" of Retirement Income

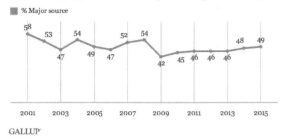

GALLUP

After 401(k) plans and Social Security, the next-most-common expected retirement funding sources are regular savings accounts and CDs (27%), work-sponsored pension plans (25%), part-time work (21%), home equity (21%), and individual stocks or stock mutual fund investments (20%).

In addition to the changes in nonretirees' expectations for Social Security and 401(k) plans over the past 15 years, there have also been modest declines in the percentages of nonretirees expecting pension plans, home equity and individual stock investments to be major sources of retirement income. There have been modest increases in the percentages expecting to rely heavily on regular savings and part-time work.

When you retire, how much do you expect to rely on each of the
following sources of money -- will it be a major source of income, a
minor source of income, or not a source at all?

Based on nonretirees

	Major source	Minor source	Not a source
	%	%	%
A 401(k), IRA, Keogh or other retirement savings account	49	30	19
Social Security	36	48	14
Other savings such as a regular savings account or CDs	27	42	30
A work sponsored pension plan	25	30	40
Part-time work	21	46	31
The equity you have built up in your home	21	38	37
Individual stock or stock mutual fund investments	20	41	36
Money from an inheritance	10	32	57
Annuities or insurance plans	10	33	54
Rent and royalties	9	26	63

April 9-12, 2015

GALLUP

Social Security Is Top Major Source Among Retirees

Gallup has consistently found Social Security to be the clear leader when current retirees are asked about their major sources of income. This year, 59% of retirees say Social Security is a major income source for them. Though the percentage has varied in any given year, a majority have said this each time Gallup has asked the question.

Pension plans have consistently ranked second on the list of retirees' major income sources, with 36% saying so this year. Retirement savings accounts like 401(k) plans and IRAs and retirees' home equity have typically been the third- or fourth-most-common sources. Currently, 25% of retirees name 401(k) plans as a major source and 16% list home equity.

How much do you rely on each of the following sources of income today --
is it a major source of income, a minor source of income, or not a source
at all?

Based on retirees

	Major source	Minor source	Not a source
	%	%	%
Social Security	59	31	9
A work sponsored pension plan	36	21	40
A 401(k), IRA, Keogh or other retirement savings account	25	30	43
The equity you have built up in your home	16	28	53
Individual stock or stock mutual fund investments	14	26	58
Annuities or insurance plans	12	21	65
Other savings such as a regular savings account or CDs	8	43	47
Rent and royalties	8	13	76
Money from an inheritance	6	16	75
Part-time work	3	17	77

April 9-12, 2015

GALLUP

Implications

There has always been a bit of a gap between future retirees' expectations for how much they will rely on Social Security and current retirees' actual reliance on it. To some degree, that may be a product of changes in the laws affecting Social Security. Specifically, many of the Social Security reforms passed in recent decades were designed to affect future generations of retirees but not those who

were receiving benefits or were near the point where they would be. The long-term funding challenges the Social Security system faces may also be a factor in why nonretirees expect Social Security to be less of an income source in their retirement.

Nonretirees are becoming more likely to view Social Security as a major source of their retirement funding than they were a decade ago, although the changes are not dramatic. That may partly compensate for the slight drop in expectations of 401(k) and other investment plans as a major source since then. Fewer Americans are invested in the stock market today than before the recession, even as stocks and mutual funds have been strong investments in the last couple of years.

But even those who are actively saving and investing for retirement are not highly confident their savings will be enough. According to a recent Wells Fargo/Gallup retirement survey, just 28% of nonretired investors are very confident they will have enough savings at the time they elect to retire. Another 48% are somewhat confident. To the degree nonretirees' savings are not sufficient to fund their retirement, nonretirees will have to make up the shortfall somehow. The guaranteed Social Security benefit is an obvious way to do that, if not by also seeking part-time work or scaling back their standard of living considerably.

Survey Methods

Results for this Gallup poll are based on telephone interviews conducted April 9–12, 2015, with a random sample of 1,015 adults, aged 18 and older, living in all 50 U.S. states and the District of Columbia. For results based on the total sample of national adults, the margin of sampling error is ±4 percentage points at the 95% confidence level.

For results based on the sample of 652 nonretirees, the margin of sampling error is ±5 percentage points at the 95% confidence level.

For results based on the sample of 363 retirees, the margin of sampling error is ±7 percentage points at the 95% confidence level.

April 29, 2015
AMERICANS SETTLING ON OLDER RETIREMENT AGE

by Rebecca Riffkin

Story Highlights

- *Thirty-seven percent expect to retire after 65, 32% before 65*
- *Most retired Americans, 67%, report they retired before age 65*
- *Median expected retirement age for nonretirees is 65*

WASHINGTON, D.C.—Nearly four in 10 nonretired Americans, 37%, expect to retire after age 65. This percentage is consistent with recent years, but it is up from 31% in 2009 and nearly three times the 14% who said this in 1995. Thirty-two percent expect to retire before age 65; this is the first time this figure has topped 30% since 2009, but it is still down considerably from the 49% in 1995 who said that they expected to retire before age 65.

The percentage of nonretirees who plan to retire exactly at age 65—the traditional retirement age—has been fairly consistent since the early 2000s, ranging between 24%, where it stands today, and 28%. It was only slightly higher in 1995, at 32%.

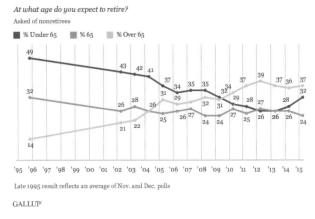

At what age do you expect to retire?
Asked of nonretirees

■ % Under 65   ■ % 65   ■ % Over 65

Late 1995 result reflects an average of Nov. and Dec. polls

GALLUP'

At the same time, a sea change has occurred in preferences for retiring earlier or later than that age point. Prior to 2009, the plurality of nonretired Americans planned to retire before age 65. Since then, the plurality have said they will retire after they reach age 65.

These trends in Americans' expected age of retirement are from Gallup's annual Economy and Personal Finance survey, conducted April 9–12, 2015. As part of that survey, Gallup asked nonretired Americans the age at which they expect to retire, and also asked retired Americans to report the age at which they retired.

In sharp contrast to the finding that about one-third of nonretirees expect to retire before age 65, twice as many of those who have already retired (67%) said they did so before 65. The percentage of retirees who retired before age 65 has been even higher in past years. In the early 1990s, three in four retired Americans reported retiring before age 65.

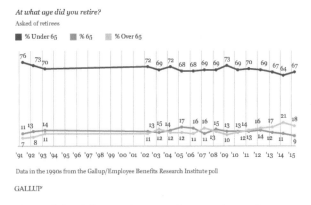

At what age did you retire?
Asked of retirees

■ % Under 65   ■ % 65   ■ % Over 65

Data in the 1990s from the Gallup/Employee Benefits Research Institute poll

GALLUP'

Part of the difference between the age when retirees report retiring and when nonretirees expect to retire may be a generation gap, with current workers expecting to live longer and planning to continue working later in their lives. The long-term trends for both retirees and nonretirees suggest that Americans are continuing to work later in their lives—or planning to do so, if they are not already retired. This does not seem to be the case, however, with baby boomers, as only a third of the oldest in this generation, who are 67 and 68 currently, are still working.

On average, nonretired Americans expect to retire at age 65, similar to averages of between 65 and 67 since 2009. The average age retired Americans report actually retiring has always been lower than nonretirees' expected age of retirement, and is 60 in this year's

survey, matching the average generally found since 2004. Prior to that, the average reported age of retirement was always below age 60.

Implications

Concerns about affording retirement, especially because of the recession, could persuade Americans to wait to retire, or to plan to retire later. A recent Wells Fargo/Gallup Investor and Retirement Optimism Index Survey found that 28% of nonretired investors are "very confident" they will have enough saved when they retire. And the 36% of nonretirees who expect to rely heavily on Social Security to fund their retirement is almost 10 percentage points higher than Gallup found a decade ago. But, many fear the Social Security fund could run out of money before those currently working reach retirement. However, many nonretired Americans who say they plan to retire after the traditional retirement age of 65 could be doing so by choice, rather than out of financial necessity.

Gallup has always found an age gap between when nonretirees say they plan to retire and the age when retired Americans report retiring. Over the past decade, and especially since 2009, an increasing percentage of nonretired Americans report expecting to retire after age 65. Yet a third of nonretired Americans say they expect to retire before age 65, similar to levels in 2009.

Survey Methods

Results for this Gallup poll are based on telephone interviews conducted April 9–12, 2015, with a random sample of 363 retirees and 652 nonretirees, aged 18 and older, living in all 50 U.S. states and the District of Columbia. For results based on the total sample of retirees, the margin of sampling error is ±7 percentage points at the 95% confidence level. For results based on the total sample of nonretirees, the margin of sampling error is ±5 percentage points at the 95% confidence level. All reported margins of sampling error include computed design effects for weighting.

April 30, 2015
NONRETIREES' FISCAL OUTLOOK STILL LAGS PRE-RECESSION LEVELS

by Jeffrey M. Jones

Story Highlights

- *40% positive about finances now and in retirement*
- *30% negative about finances now and in retirement*
- *Outlook has improved since bottoming out in 2012*

PRINCETON, N.J.—Four in 10 U.S. nonretirees report they have enough money to live comfortably now and expect they will have enough to live comfortably when they retire. This percentage is improved from 31% in 2012, but it is still below pre-recession levels. Meanwhile, a still-elevated 30% of nonretirees say they are not living comfortably now and do not expect to be in retirement.

Additionally, there are two smaller groups who predict that their financial situation will change between now and retirement.

The larger of these—representing 22% of all U.S. nonretirees—report having enough to live comfortably now but do not expect to do so after they retire. The percentage in this group peaked at 29% in 2009.

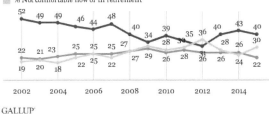

U.S. Nonretirees' Financial Outlook Now and in Retirement

Right now, do you have enough money to live comfortably, or not?

When you retire, do you think you will have enough money to live comfortably, or not?

■ % Comfortable now and in retirement

■ % Comfortable now, not in retirement

░ % Not comfortable now or in retirement

GALLUP

The smaller group, those who say they are not living comfortably now but expect to be in retirement, has ranged between 6% and 10% of nonretirees since 2002 and is currently at 8%.

These results are based on data from Gallup's annual Economy and Personal Finance poll, conducted April 9–12. That poll asks all Americans whether they have enough money to live comfortably right now. Currently, 66% of all Americans, including 63% of nonretirees, say they do. Both figures are up from the post-recession lows but are still not back to where they were before the economic downturn.

Separately, nonretirees are asked if they think they will have enough to live comfortably when they retire. Forty-eight percent of all nonretirees currently think they will, which is again improved from the immediate post-recession years but not as upbeat an assessment as before the recession.

Over time, nonretirees have been consistently more positive about their current financial situation than about their situation after they retire, perhaps because of the uncertainty about the future and what income sources they will draw upon in retirement.

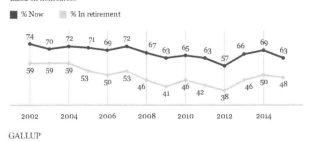

Have/Will Have Enough Money to Live Comfortably Now and in Retirement

Based on nonretirees

■ % Now   ░ % In retirement

GALLUP

Financial Outlook Similar by Age of Nonretirees

Perceptions of current and future finances are similar among those nearing retirement and those who are farther away from it. Between 40% and 45% of nonretirees in all age groups are positive about their ability to live comfortably both now and in retirement, while between 25% and 28% are pessimistic on both questions. Those figures are based on combined data from the 2014 and 2015 surveys.

The major differences in nonretirees' financial outlook are by socioeconomic status, that is, their education and household income level. Roughly six in 10 college graduates and those with higher annual incomes expect their current comfortable financial situation to continue in retirement. Meanwhile, the plurality of those with a high school education or less, and half of those whose annual household income is less than $30,000, say they are not living comfortably now and do not expect that to change when they retire.

U.S. Nonretirees' Financial Outlook Now and in Retirement, by Subgroup

	Comfortable now and will be in retirement	Comfortable now, will not be in retirement	Not comfortable now, will be in retirement	Not comfortable now or in retirement
	%	%	%	%
AGE				
18-34 years	42	22	10	25
35-54 years	40	26	6	28
55+ years	45	23	5	28
EDUCATION				
High school or less	33	21	9	37
Some college	36	26	10	28
College graduate	57	28	3	13
ANNUAL HOUSEHOLD INCOME				
Less than $30K	20	17	12	50
$30K-less than $75K	39	28	7	26
$75K or more	60	29	3	8

Combined 2014-2015 data

GALLUP

College graduates' assessments are nearly back to where they were before the recession. From 2005 to 2007, an average of 59% of nonretired college graduates said they had enough money to live comfortably now and believed they would in retirement. Over the past two years, the average is 57%. But those with some college education, or a high school diploma or less, still trail where they were before the recession, by six percentage points and five percentage points, respectively.

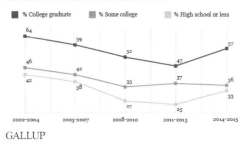

U.S. Nonretirees' Financial Outlook Now and in Retirement, by Education Level

Figures are percentage who say they have enough money to live comfortably now and expect they will have enough to live comfortably in retirement.

■ % College graduate   ░ % Some college   ░ % High school or less

GALLUP

Implications

Americans' financial security was clearly shaken during the 2007–2009 recession and the ensuing years of high unemployment and sluggish economic growth. Now that the economy has picked up steam, Americans are much more upbeat about their current and future financial situation. However, when asked whether they have enough money to live comfortably now, and if they expect to be comfortable financially in their retirement years, U.S. nonretirees are still not as positive as they were before the recession. Further, it appears those of a lower socioeconomic status are further from a full recovery than those of a higher socioeconomic status, whose financial assessments are nearly as positive now as they were before the recession.

Given the prominence of 401(k) and other stock investment plans as an expected major source of retirement income, and that stock values have more than made up the value they lost during the recession, one would think that Americans should be as positive about their current and "golden years" finances as they were a decade ago. However, recent Wells Fargo/Gallup Retirement surveys have found that U.S. investors themselves are a bit skeptical about the stock market as a place to grow one's savings. Also, investors widely favor secure investments that provide lower returns in their retirement accounts over riskier investments with greater growth potential. To these points, the percentage of Americans who own stocks is still well below where it was before the recession.

Nonretirees who are somewhat averse to investing in stocks and who are increasingly likely to see Social Security as a major source of retirement income may not believe their retirement nest egg will be large enough to afford them a comfortable lifestyle after they stop working.

Survey Methods

Results for this Gallup poll are based on telephone interviews conducted April 9–12, 2015, with a random sample of 652 nonretirees, aged 18 and older, living in all 50 U.S. states and the District of Columbia. For results based on the total sample of nonretirees, the margin of sampling error is ±5 percentage points at the 95% confidence level. All reported margins of sampling error include computed design effects for weighting.

April 30, 2015
FRESNO, CALIFORNIA, RESIDENTS LEAST LIKELY TO FEEL SAFE

by Justin McCarthy

Story Highlights

- *Fresno, California, residents least likely to feel safe and secure*
- *Residents of Raleigh, North Carolina, and Boise City, Idaho, most likely to feel safe*

WASHINGTON, D.C.—Less than 64% of adults living in each of three California communities—Fresno, Stockton-Lodi and Bakersfield—agree they always feel safe and secure, making these residents the least likely to feel safe among the 100 most populous U.S. metropolitan areas.

California is not the only state with multiple communities among the lowest 10 in reports of safety and security. Two Ohio metropolitan areas appear on the list: Toledo and the Youngstown-Warren-Boardman community, which straddles the Ohio-Pennsylvania border. In Florida, two communities rank ninth and tenth, respectively: Lakeland-Winter Haven and Deltona-Daytona Beach-Ormond Beach.

U.S. Communities Where Residents Feel Least Safe and Secure

On a 5-point scale, where 5 means strongly agree and 1 means strongly disagree, please rate your level of agreement with the following item: You always feel safe and secure.

	% 4 plus % 5
Fresno, CA	62.7
Stockton-Lodi, CA	62.9
Bakersfield, CA	63.5
Memphis, TN-MS-AR	65.9
Youngstown-Warren-Boardman, OH-PA	66.8
Toledo, OH	67.8
Las Vegas-Henderson-Paradise, NV	68.1
New Orleans-Metairie, LA	68.3
Lakeland-Winter Haven, FL	69.1
Deltona-Daytona Beach-Ormond Beach, FL	69.2

Gallup-Healthways Well-Being Index
January-December 2014

GALLUP'

The 10 communities where residents are least likely to agree they feel safe are rounded out by fourth-ranked Memphis, Tennessee—which also includes areas in Mississippi and Arkansas—seventh-ranked Las Vegas, Nevada, and eighth-ranked New Orleans, Louisiana.

These findings are based on data collected throughout 2014 as part of the Gallup-Healthways Well-Being Index. Nationally, more than three in four Americans (76.5%) responded with a 4 or 5 rating on a 5-point scale. A 5 rating indicates respondents strongly agreed that they always feel safe and secure, and a 1 rating means they strongly disagreed. Among the bottom 10, less than 70% of residents in these areas agreed they felt safe, whereas in the 10 communities where residents felt safest, at least 81.5% of residents agreed they felt this way.

Des Moines, Iowa, Residents Most Likely to Feel Safe and Secure

Residents of Des Moines, Iowa, top the list where residents feel safest, with 85.7% agreeing that they always feel safe and secure, inching out Raleigh, North Carolina, at 84.8%, and Boise City, Idaho, at 84.5%.

The communities topping the list where residents feel safest are diverse—spanning from central Texas to Hawaii—and vary in population. The largest metro area in the top 10 is Austin, Texas, with a population of nearly 2 million, while Des Moines, Iowa, is the smallest, with nearly 600,000 residents.

U.S. Communities Where Residents Feel Most Safe and Secure

On a 5-point scale, where 5 means strongly agree and 1 means strongly disagree, please rate your level of agreement with the following item: You always feel safe and secure.

	% 4 plus % 5
Des Moines-West Des Moines, IA	85.7
Raleigh, NC	84.8
Boise City, ID	84.5
Urban Honolulu, HI	82.6
Provo-Orem, UT	82.5
Winston-Salem, NC	82.2
Ogden-Clearfield, UT	82.1
Colorado Springs, CO	82.1
Omaha-Council Bluffs, NE-IA	81.9
Austin-Round Rock, TX	81.5

Gallup-Healthways Well-Being Index
January-December 2014

GALLUP'

Three states account for more than half of the top 10 communities ranked on residents' sense of security. North Carolina and Utah each have two communities in the top 10 for perceived safety, and Iowa contributes two when including Omaha-Council Bluffs, a metro area Iowa shares with Nebraska.

Also among the metro areas where people reported feeling safest were Urban Honolulu, Hawaii; Colorado Springs, Colorado; and Austin-Round Rock, Texas.

Individuals Who Feel Safe and Secure Have Higher Well-Being

The Gallup-Healthways Well-Being Index score comprises metrics affecting overall well-being and each of the five essential elements of well-being: purpose, social, financial, community and physical. Americans' perceptions of feeling safe and secure strongly relate to their overall well-being. Twenty percentage points separate the Well-Being Index scores of those who agree they feel safe and secure (65.2%) and those who disagree (45.2%). Those who neither agree nor disagree have a Well-Being Index score in the middle, at 53.9%.

While three-quarters of Americans agreed they feel safe and secure in 2014, about one in 10 (9.9%) disagreed.

Feeling Safe and Secure and Overall Well-Being

On a 5-point scale, where 5 means strongly agree and 1 means strongly disagree, please rate your level of agreement with the following item: You always feel safe and secure.

		Well-Being Index score
Disagree (% 1 plus % 2)	9.9%	45.2
3	13.4%	53.9
Agree (% 4 plus % 5)	76.5%	65.2

Gallup-Healthways Well-Being Index
January-December 2014

GALLUP

While there is a strong relationship between overall well-being and perceived safety, shared influencing factors could be shaping both. Someone with high financial well-being, for instance, could afford to live in a community with greater security. And people with high social well-being might have larger social networks, making them feel safer.

The survey item does not specify that respondents should respond in what ways they feel safe and secure. Most likely they are thinking about physical safety, especially related to crime. But if communities focus on improving general safety—perhaps by increasing police forces or establishing neighborhood watch programs—taking such measures could increase overall well-being. Residents who are less concerned about their safety might be more likely to focus on other areas of their well-being. Those who have

a safe place to walk or run, for example, can focus more on their physical well-being. And those who feel safe in their neighborhood are more likely to engage with fellow members of their community.

Bottom Line

The degree to which residents feel safe in a given area has a tremendous effect on a community, including its propensity for economic growth and development. Neighborhoods that residents perceive as being "unsafe," for example, are less likely to attract businesses. At the individual level, though, perception of personal safety could have affect individuals' overall well-being and the way they live their lives. Chronic fear and anxiety that could come from feeling unsafe in a community could negatively influence residents' physical and mental health.

It is no coincidence, then, that most of the communities where residents feel least safe also rank at or near bottom of the Well-Being Index, while many of the communities where citizens feel safest rank at top of the index spectrum.

To view U.S. community well-being rankings, read the full report.

Survey Methods

Results are based on telephone interviews conducted as part of the Gallup-Healthways Well-Being Index survey Jan. 2–Dec. 29, 2014, with a random sample of 176,702 adults, aged 18 and older, living in metropolitan areas in the 50 U.S. states and the District of Columbia, selected using random-digit-dial sampling. Unlike previous years, only the 100 most populous metros—as determined by the U.S. Census Bureau—were reported in 2014. A second requirement is that at least 300 cases are required per metro area for reporting. As such, McAllen-Edinburg-Mission, Texas, and Durham-Chapel Hill, North Carolina, were both excluded from reporting because of insufficient sample size. These were replaced by the 102nd-largest metropolitan statistical area (MSA) in the U.S.: Lancaster, Pennsylvania.

The "communities" referenced in this article are based on MSAs as defined by the U.S. Office of Management and Budget. In many cases, more than one city is included in the same MSA. The San Jose, California, MSA, for example, also includes the smaller nearby cities of Sunnyvale and Santa Clara in addition to San Jose. Each respondent is attributed to his or her MSA based on self-reports of his or her ZIP code.

Maximum margins of error for the Well-Being Index and the element scores vary according to MSA size, ranging from less than 1 point for the largest cities represented to around ±1.5 points for many of the smallest cities.

May 01, 2015

AMERICANS' SPENDING ACTIVITY STABLE BUT UP FROM RECESSION

by Andrew Dugan

Story Highlights

- *Four in 10 Americans say they are spending less money*
- *About a third of U.S. adults reliably say their spending is the same*
- *Americans spending less are more likely to call it a "new normal"*

WASHINGTON, D.C.—As economists and business leaders debate whether the U.S. economy is on the verge of "liftoff," or is stagnating, Americans' changes in their spending patterns are similar to levels they reported in 2012, 2013 and 2014. Importantly, though, the percentage who say they are spending less, 39%, remains well below where it was during the economic downturn.

Americans' Recent Spending Habits

In general, would you say you have been spending -- [ROTATED: more money, the same amount, (or) less money] -- in recent months than you used to?

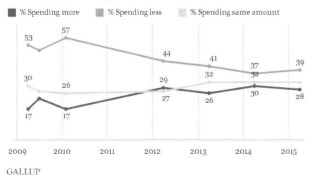

GALLUP

Americans remain most likely to say they are "spending less money," (39%) rather than "spending the same amount" (32%) or "spending more money" (28%). But their perceptions that they are spending less have dropped from as high as 57% when the economy was just emerging from a deep recession in 2010. As the economy continued to recover, the share dropped to a low of 37% last year, similar to where it is this year. Likewise, while the percentage of U.S. adults saying they are spending more (28%) showed no significant change from last year, it is greatly improved from its 2009 and 2010 low of 17%.

To some extent, America's reliable impulse to report "spending less" may partially be the result of social or moralistic pressures that compel some individuals to portray an image of thriftiness, though this may not accurately reflect their behavior. Along those lines, Gallup has repeatedly found that majorities of Americans say they personally prefer saving over spending by a wide margin.

Meanwhile, the share of U.S. adults saying they are spending the same amount of money has shown the least amount of volatility over this period, suggesting a sizable portion of the country has steady financial habits that are at least somewhat removed from larger economic forces.

In line with these findings, Gallup found that monthly spending data for March was essentially equal to that of March 2014.

Americans Who Are Spending Less Continue to Say It's Their "New Normal"

Consistent with previous years, more Americans who say they are spending less estimate that this will become a "new, normal pattern" for them as opposed to a temporary change. In total, nearly three in 10 Americans (29%) say they are spending less money and that this will become a new, normal pattern, while another 10% say they are spending less because of a temporary change in spending patterns. These responses together make up the 39% who say they are spending less. Since 2012, those who say they are cutting back and expect it to be their new normal outnumber those who are cutting back and expect it to be temporary by roughly 3 to 1.

Percentage of Americans Who Are Spending Less and Whether This Is a New Normal or Is Temporary

	Apr 20-21, 2009	Jul 10-12, 2009	Feb 1-3, 2010	Apr 9-12, 2012	Apr 4-14, 2013	Apr 3-6, 2014	Apr 9-12, 2015
	%	%	%	%	%	%	%
SPENDING LESS MONEY	53	50	57	44	41	37	39
-- Will become new, normal pattern	32	32	38	33	31	27	29
-- Temporary change in spending patterns	21	18	19	11	10	10	10

GALLUP

Conversely, a higher proportion of Americans report spending more money for temporary reasons (17%) than say their higher spending will become a new, normal pattern (11%).

Percentage of Americans Who Are Spending More and Whether This Is a New Normal or Is Temporary

	Apr 20-21, 2009	Jul 10-12, 2009	Feb 1-3, 2010	Apr 9-12, 2012	Apr 4-14, 2013	Apr 3-6, 2014	Apr 9-12, 2015
	%	%	%	%	%	%	%
SPENDING MORE MONEY	17	23	17	29	26	30	28
-- Will become new, normal pattern	6	8	7	12	10	11	11
Temporary change in spending patterns	11	15	10	17	16	19	17

GALLUP

Bottom Line

Americans' spending patterns have remained remarkably stable over the past several years, even as the economic recovery has strengthened and the unemployment rate has fallen. Interestingly, the considerable drop in gas prices from one year ago has not translated into an upswing in the percentage of Americans saying they are spending less on what they see as a temporary basis. In March 2014, the average price of gas per gallon in the U.S. was $3.55; last month, that stood at $2.45. But while the year-over-year change in gas prices has been dramatic, on a monthly basis, the price has increased slightly for the past three months in 2015. It may be that the gradual climb in the cost of gas is already eroding Americans' capacity to save, even if the price is well below where it was a year ago.

Survey Methods

Results for this Gallup poll are based on telephone interviews conducted April 9–12, 2015, with a random sample of 1,015 adults, aged 18 and older, living in all 50 U.S. states and the District of Columbia. For results based on the total sample of national adults, the margin of sampling error is ±4 percentage points at the 95%

confidence level. All reported margins of sampling error include computed design effects for weighting.

May 01, 2015

AMERICANS DEEM OBAMA HONEST, LESS SURE OF HIS LEADERSHIP

by Lydia Saad

Story Highlights

- *Slim majority of Americans say Obama is honest and trustworthy*
- *Ratings as honest and good manager are up from last June*
- *His image as a strong leader declined the most since 2009*

PRINCETON, N.J.—A little more than half of U.S. adults consider President Barack Obama to be honest and trustworthy, and the same percentage, 53%, believe he understands the day-to-day problems that Americans face. At the same time, less than half see him as a strong and decisive leader (46%) or as someone who can manage the government effectively (44%). Slightly more than one-third say he has a clear plan for solving the country's problems (36%).

President Barack Obama's Characteristics and Qualities

	Applies	Doesn't apply
	%	%
Is honest and trustworthy	53	45
Understands the problems Americans face in their daily lives	53	45
Is a strong and decisive leader	46	52
Can manage the government effectively	44	55
Has a clear plan for solving the country's problems	36	61

April 9-12, 2015

GALLUP

Perceptions of Obama's personal character—his honesty and his understanding of Americans—have both improved slightly since last June, when 47% of Americans thought he was honest and 48% believed he understood Americans' everyday problems.

The percentage saying he can manage the government effectively is also up five percentage points from his term low of 39% last year. At the same time, the percentages saying he is a strong and decisive leader or has a clear plan for solving the country's problems are essentially unchanged.

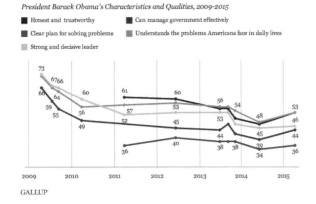

President Barack Obama's Characteristics and Qualities, 2009-2015

■ Honest and trustworthy ■ Can manage government effectively
■ Clear plan for solving problems ▦ Understands the problems Americans face in daily lives
▨ Strong and decisive leader

GALLUP

Presidency Taken Greatest Toll on Obama's "Strong and Decisive" Rating

Over the long term, Obama's image as a strong and decisive leader has declined the most since his earliest days in office, sinking 27 points from 73% in 2009 to 46% today. This outpaces the 16–point decline in his overall job approval rating over the same period, from 64% to 48%. Meanwhile, the percentage saying he can manage the government effectively has fallen 22 points while those saying he understands what Americans face daily has declined 19 points.

These declines in Americans' positive impressions of Obama's presidential qualities happened largely in his first two years in office, but Gallup found his leadership image dropping another five points in 2013, between the months of September and November. This decline likely reflected public displeasure with the partial federal government shutdown and troubled rollout of healthcare.gov occurring at the time, and that rating has not recovered. By contrast, his honest and trustworthy rating, which also fell five points in the fall of 2013 and dropped further to 47% last June, is up to 53% today.

Obama has consistently inspired relative low public confidence that he has a clear plan for solving the nation's problems; the 36% saying he does matches the initial reading from 2011, with little variation in between.

Bottom Line

It is not unusual for Americans' high hopes for a new president—and Americans were optimistic for Obama in 2009—to give way to a certain amount of disappointment and cynicism. The challenges of leading the country eventually reveal the limits of any one person to meet all of them with equal success, and the process of leading inevitably arouses partisan rancor. The declines in Obama's character ratings roughly follow the slide in his overall job approval rating after his initial months in office.

Still, the path of Obama's image on each of the five dimensions has varied slightly, and the trends differ somewhat from the patterns seen for his immediate predecessors. After all of his ratings surged following 9/11, George W. Bush experienced significant declines in how the public viewed his honesty, his ability to manage the government and his possession of a clear plan for solving the country's problems. Bill Clinton, on the other hand, saw his image as someone with a clear plan skyrocket in his second term as the economy picked up steam. Meanwhile, his honesty rating plunged amid the scandals swirling around his impeachment.

Obama's image ratings are well below their peak levels for all five qualities measured in the latest poll, although the majority of Americans again consider him honest and trustworthy and in tune with the problems facing them. Perhaps of greater relevance for his approval rating is that the two key leadership ratings—being a strong and decisive leader and managing the government effectively—continue to register below 50%. An even lower proportion believes he has a clear plan for solving the country's problems, a now-constant feature of his image scores that may have more relevance for his legacy than his job approval rating.

Survey Methods

Results for this Gallup poll are based on telephone interviews conducted April 9–12, 2015, with a random sample of 1,015 adults, aged 18 and older, living in all 50 U.S. states and the District of Columbia. For results based on the total sample of national adults, the margin of sampling error is ±4 percentage points at the 95% confidence level. All reported margins of sampling error include computed design effects for weighting.

May 04, 2015
AMERICANS CONTINUE TO SAY U.S. WEALTH DISTRIBUTION IS UNFAIR

by Frank Newport

Story Highlights

- *63% of Americans say money and wealth distribution is unfair*
- *These attitudes are substantially unchanged over past 30 years*
- *Slight majority of 52% favor heavy taxes on rich as fix*

PRINCETON, N.J.—Despite the growing focus on inequality in recent years, the 63% of Americans who say that money and wealth should be more evenly distributed among a larger percentage of the people is almost the same as the 60% who said this in 1984.

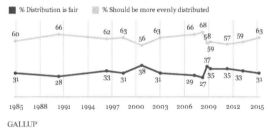

Do you feel that the distribution of money and wealth in this country today is fair, or do you feel that the money and wealth in this country should be more evenly distributed among a larger percentage of the people?

■ % Distribution is fair   ▨ % Should be more evenly distributed

GALLUP

Americans' agreement that money and wealth need to be more evenly distributed reached a high point of 68% in April 2008, in the last year of the George W. Bush administration, and just before the full effects of the Great Recession began to take hold. Americans became slightly less likely to agree with the idea later that year and in surveys conducted in 2009, 2011 and 2013. This year's increase to 63% is close to the average of 62% agreement across the 13 times Gallup has asked the question since 1984. The latest data are from Gallup's April 9–12 Economy and Personal Finance survey.

Americans' views on how money and wealth should be distributed in the country are strongly correlated with their partisanship and ideology. Agreement ranges from 86% among Democrats and 85% among liberals, down to 34% and 42% among Republicans and conservatives, respectively.

Income is also a factor. Those with annual household incomes of at least $75,000 (54%) are considerably less likely than those with incomes below $30,000 (74%) to agree that wealth should be more evenly distributed. Attitudes vary little by age.

The question on the fairness of money and wealth distribution does not include explicit assumptions about the causes of the current unequal distribution of income and wealth, nor does it discuss or imply any particular course of action designed to remedy the situation. Addressing the problem is a moot issue for many Republicans, a majority of whom say the distribution is fair as it is. Most

Democrats, on the other hand, presumably endorse some mechanism by which the distribution of wealth and income could be made less unequal.

Views on Distribution of U.S. Wealth

	Distribution is fair	Should be more evenly distributed	Don't know/ Refused
	%	%	%
National adults	31	63	6
Democrats	12	86	2
Independents	32	61	7
Republicans	56	34	9
Conservatives	48	42	10
Moderates	29	67	4
Liberals	13	85	3
18 to 34	30	66	4
35 to 54	30	64	6
55+	34	59	7
Under $30,000	20	74	5
$30,000 to $74,999	31	62	6
$75,000+	41	54	5

April 9-12, 2015

GALLUP

More than 75 years ago, at the tail end of the Great Depression, the Roper research organization and *Fortune* magazine asked Americans about "heavy taxes on the rich" as one method of redistributing wealth, and found one-third (35%) agreeing that the government should do this. Gallup began asking this question again in 1998, and found Americans' agreement at 45%. Since then, Americans' support for this idea has fluctuated, but has reached a high point of 52% in Gallup's most recent two surveys, conducted in April 2013 and April of this year.

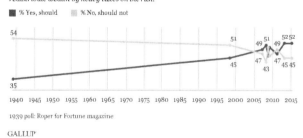

People feel differently about how far a government should go. Here is a phrase which some people believe in and some don't. Do you think our government should or should not redistribute wealth by heavy taxes on the rich?

■ % Yes, should   ▨ % No, should not

1939 poll: Roper for Fortune magazine

GALLUP

As was the case with the basic fairness question, agreement that the government should impose heavy taxes on the rich to redistribute wealth is highly related to partisanship and ideology. Additionally, younger Americans and those with lower incomes are above average in their agreement.

About Half of Americans Are Strong Redistributionists

Analyzing how Americans respond to both questions about inequality shows that nearly half of Americans (46%) are strong redistributionists—in the sense that they believe the distribution of wealth and income is not fair, and endorse heavy taxes on the rich as a way of redistributing wealth. One in four are in essence free-market advocates—sanguine about the distribution of wealth and income and not supporting heavy taxes on the rich. Another 16% say the income and wealth distribution is not fair, but don't endorse heavy taxes as a remedy. A small percentage have the somewhat contradictory views of believing that the distribution is fair but favoring heavy taxes on the rich.

Views on Government Redistribution of U.S. Wealth

	Yes, gov't should redistribute wealth by heavy taxes on rich	No, should not	Don't know/ Refused
	%	%	%
National adults	52	45	2
Democrats	75	23	2
Independents	50	47	3
Republicans	29	70	1
Conservatives	32	66	3
Moderates	56	42	2
Liberals	76	23	1
18 to 34	59	38	3
35 to 54	52	46	1
55+	47	50	2
Under $30,000	61	35	4
$30,000–$74,999	55	44	1
$75,000+	42	57	1

April 9-12, 2015

GALLUP'

Americans' Combined Views of the Fairness of Income Distribution and the Idea of Heavy Taxes on the Rich

	Should tax rich to reduce inequality	Should not tax rich to reduce inequality
Distribution of money and wealth is fair	5%	25%
Money and wealth should be more evenly distributed	46%	16%

April 9-12, 2015
Numbers represent percentage of total national adult population

GALLUP'

Implications

Surveys conducted over the past 30 years have consistently shown that about six in 10 Americans fundamentally believe that the way income and wealth are distributed in the U.S. is unfair. Democrats are much more likely to hold this view than Republicans, helping explain why inequality has been a major focus for President Barack Obama, a core part of the presidential campaign of Hillary Clinton, and a primary talking point when Sen. Bernie Sanders of Vermont recently announced his candidacy.

Although well less than half of Republicans believe that income and wealth distribution in the U.S. is unfair and that wealth needs to be more evenly distributed, GOP presidential candidates have also begun to address the issue, most likely realizing that the issue has currency with independents, Hispanics and other voter groups that could decide the 2016 election. Additionally, the issue has been more of a talking point in discussions of government policy as many news reports have focused on data showing that income and wealth are becoming less equally distributed across the population than was the case in the past.

One way presidential and other political candidates will attempt to differentiate themselves from their competitors concerning inequality will likely be their proposed remedies for it. Democrats

have generally been more likely to endorse government policies designed to reduce the wealth at the top end of the socioeconomic spectrum and help increase it at the bottom. Republicans have been more likely to endorse mechanisms that would make it easier for those at the bottom to move up the economic ladder by their own initiative. Still, given that a not insubstantial 29% of Republicans agree with the idea of heavy taxes on the rich, and that a Republican presidential candidate has to assemble some votes from outside of Republican ranks to win a general election, candidates from both parties will most likely consider a wide spectrum of choices or ways of addressing inequality.

Survey Methods

Results for this Gallup poll are based on telephone interviews conducted April 9–12, 2015, with a random sample of 1,015 adults, aged 18 and older, living in all 50 U.S. states and the District of Columbia. For results based on the total sample of national adults, the margin of sampling error is ±4 percentage points at the 95% confidence level. All reported margins of sampling error include computed design effects for weighting.

May 06, 2015
AMERICANS' VIEWS OF GOV'T HANDLING OF HEALTHCARE UP SHARPLY

by Art Swift and Steve Ander

Story Highlights

- *Satisfaction with handling of healthcare up sharply*
- *Mail delivery satisfaction is nearly universal*
- *Handling of poverty at bottom of list*

WASHINGTON, D.C.—Nearly two years after the debut of the Affordable Care Act, or "Obamacare," Americans are more positive about the work the federal government is doing in healthcare. Forty-three percent say they are satisfied with the government's work in this arena, up 14 percentage points from 2013. Still, 56% say they are dissatisfied.

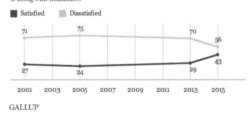

Americans' Satisfaction With the Government's Work in Healthcare
Please say whether you are satisfied or dissatisfied with the work the government is doing with healthcare.

GALLUP'

Gallup has asked Americans to rate their satisfaction with the way the federal government is handling a variety of issues, including healthcare, since 2001. At that time, 27% said they were satisfied with the government's work in healthcare. In two surveys, one conducted in 2005 during the George W. Bush administration and the other in 2013 under Barack Obama, satisfaction with the government's handling of the issue remained below 30%. However, in the most recent Gallup survey, conducted April 29–May 2, satisfaction with these efforts shot up to 43%.

Despite what many considered a botched rollout of the ACA's website, healthcare.gov, as well as much criticism of the program itself, the percentage of Americans enrolling in the government's healthcare program and other insurance programs have exceeded predictions. Likely as a result of Obamacare, the uninsured rate in the U.S. is now the lowest Gallup has tracked since 2008. There have also been modest increases in Americans' views of the Affordable Care Act.

Satisfaction With Government's Work in Healthcare Up Across Party Lines

Americans' higher satisfaction with the government's work in healthcare is reflected across the three major partisan groups. A solid 65% of Democrats this year are content with the government's role in healthcare, contrasted with 39% of independents and 15% of Republicans. While Republican satisfaction is by far the lowest, it is up modestly from 7% two years ago. Satisfaction among Democrats and independents rose 12 and 13 percentage points, respectively.

Satisfaction With Government's Work in Healthcare, by Political Party

	2013	2015	Change
	%	%	(pct. pts.)
Democrats	53	65	12
Independents	26	39	13
Republicans	7	15	8

GALLUP

Mail Delivery Rates Highest, Work on Poverty Lowest

Of 20 different areas included in this year's survey, satisfaction with mail delivery came out on top with 90% of Americans satisfied—which reinforces the U.S. Postal Services' No. 1 ranking among major government agencies in November 2014. That easily outpaces satisfaction with the government's handling of national parks and open space (73%) and its "responding to natural disasters" (71%). At the opposite end of the spectrum, 24% of Americans are satisfied with the government's handling of immigration policy, 23% with "the nation's finances" and 16% with its efforts on poverty.

The U.S. Federal Government's Handling of Major Arenas
Ranked by percent satisfied in 2015

	2013 %	2015 %	Change (pct. pts.)
Mail delivery		90	-
National parks and open space	68	73	5
Responding to natural disasters	75	71	-4
Transportation	57	62	5
The nation's military and national defense	56	57	1
Agriculture and farming	49	55	6
Homeland security	57	53	-4
Public housing and urban development	42	45	3
Energy policy	40	44	4
Healthcare	29	43	14
Environmental issues	42	40	-2
Labor and employment issues	26	40	14
Job creation and economic growth	27	39	12
Criminal justice	42	35	-7
Foreign affairs	39	35	-4
Education	33	34	1
Veterans' issues	38	28	-10
Immigration policy	26	24	-2
The nation's finances	14	23	9
Poverty	19	16	-3

Recent poll conducted Apr 29-May 2, 2015

GALLUP

It's clear that Americans give the government a mixed report card on the list of functions it performs, especially compared with 2013. While some areas of focus for President Barack Obama have seen significant increases in the past two years—healthcare, job creation and labor and employment issues—other areas such as veterans' issues and criminal justice experienced significant drops. These drops likely partly reflect the effect of major scandals involving Veterans Affairs and recent high-profile law enforcement cases in Ferguson, Missouri; Baltimore; and Staten Island, New York.

Bottom Line

While defining a customer for private-sector organizations is largely based on transactions with the business, defining "customers" for the federal government is difficult because of the indirect effects of regulations and the policies. In a broad sense, every resident is a "customer" of the government in numerous ways, even without making a distinct transaction or choice.

Measuring satisfaction with how the government handles various issues—rather than the agencies most responsible or most associated with certain tasks—provides broad metrics that assess governmental effectiveness. Where satisfaction increases significantly over time, there is likely to be a reasonable catalyst for that change. The change might be attributable to government action, from either more effective policies or better coordination among government entities, or it may stem from ineffective policies or management, such as with the recent Veterans Affairs management struggles.

Americans' extremely positive view of the U.S. Postal Service (USPS) and mail delivery may be a result of interacting with the USPS nearly every day. Visiting national parks may also provide a pleasant "customer interaction" for Americans. Overall, Americans may express a high dissatisfaction with government and have low levels of trust in the body in general, but there are several areas of the government's performance that Americans are pleased with.

Survey Methods

Results for this Gallup poll are based on telephone interviews conducted April 29–May 2, 2015, on the Gallup U.S. Daily survey, with a random sample of 2,020 adults, aged 18 and older, living in all 50 U.S. states and the District of Columbia. For results based on the total sample of national adults, the margin of sampling error is ±4 percentage points at the 95% confidence level.

May 07, 2015
U.S. SATISFACTION WITH FEDERAL POVERTY EFFORTS AT NEW LOW

by Jeffrey M. Jones

Story Highlights

- *16% satisfied with federal government efforts on poverty*
- *Satisfaction with poverty usually among lowest for issues*
- *Republican satisfaction has declined since Bush years*

PRINCETON, N.J.—Sixteen percent of Americans are satisfied with the work the federal government is doing to address poverty, a new low in Gallup's 15-year trend. During this time, Americans have never been too satisfied with the government's efforts on poverty; the high point of 26% satisfaction came the first time it was measured in a Sept. 7–10, 2001, poll.

Satisfaction With the Work the Federal Government Is Doing on Poverty

Next, we are going to name some major areas the federal government handles. For each one, please say whether you are satisfied or dissatisfied with the work the government is doing. How about poverty?

■ % Satisfied

GALLUP

The current results are based on an April 29–May 2 Gallup survey that asked respondents to rate their satisfaction with the federal government's work in 20 different areas. The government's handling of poverty ranks last this year, just below its handling of the nation's finances (23%) and immigration policy (24%). Americans are most satisfied with mail delivery, at 90%.

Poverty has also ranked at or near the bottom of this list in prior surveys:

- In 2001, satisfaction with poverty was the lowest-ranked issue, one percentage point behind healthcare at 27%.
- In 2005, satisfaction with the nation's finances, at 23%, edged out poverty and healthcare, both at 24%, for the bottom spot.
- In 2013, Americans were least satisfied with the federal government's handling of the nation's finances at 14%, with poverty next lowest at 19%.

Political Right Leads Drop in Satisfaction With Poverty Efforts

Declining satisfaction among self-identified Republicans and Republican-leaning independents is the primary driver of the decline in satisfaction with federal poverty efforts overall. In 2001 and 2005, when Republican George W. Bush was president, roughly four in 10 Republicans and Republican-leaners were satisfied with government actions to address poverty. Since then, with Democratic President Barack Obama in office, Republican satisfaction has shrunk to 14%. Over this same time, there has been a slight increase in Democratic satisfaction, but nowhere near large enough to offset the decline in Republican satisfaction.

Satisfaction With the Work the Federal Government Is Doing on Poverty, by Political Party

Figures represent percentage satisfied

■ % Republicans/Republican leaners   ■ % Democrats/Democratic leaners

GALLUP

The same general patterns are seen by ideology, with self-described conservatives' satisfaction with poverty efforts down sharply from 36% in 2001 to 16% today, while liberals' satisfaction is up only slightly, from 10% to 17%.

The net result of these changes is that Republicans, Democrats, conservatives and liberals now show roughly equal levels of

satisfaction with U.S. government poverty efforts. There is also little difference in satisfaction among race, education, gender and age subgroups.

Implications

Poverty has been an ever-present problem in the U.S. Although it does not typically rank among the top issues, it consistently registers a modest number of mentions each month when Gallup asks Americans to name the most important problem facing the country.

Over the past 15 years, Americans have never been highly satisfied with government efforts to address poverty, and never has their satisfaction been lower than it is now. The lower level of satisfaction is partly a function of political dynamics whereby Republicans are more likely to be satisfied with government activities when a Republican is president. Republicans typically are also less likely than Democrats to see poverty as an important problem. Because of Democrats' greater concern about the issue and the difficulty the nation has had in greatly reducing poverty, Democrats may still have reason to be dissatisfied with government activity on the issue even when a Democratic president is in office.

Survey Methods

Results for this Gallup poll are based on telephone interviews conducted April 29–May 2, 2015, on the Gallup U.S. Daily survey, with a random sample of 1,011 adults, aged 18 and older, living in all 50 U.S. states and the District of Columbia. For results based on the total sample of national adults, the margin of sampling error is ±4 percentage points at the 95% confidence level. All reported margins of sampling error include computed design effects for weighting.

May 08, 2015
YOUNGER U.S. WORKERS MOST LIKELY TO REPORT WORKPLACE HIRING

by Andrew Dugan

Story Highlights

- *Majority of 18- to 29-year-old workers say employer is hiring*
- *Likelihood to say firm is hiring decreases with age*

WASHINGTON, D.C.—U.S. workers between the ages of 18 and 29 are significantly more likely than older workers to report working for companies that are hiring new people. Gallup's Job Creation Index—a measure of net hiring activity in the U.S.—is +43 among younger workers. This finding is much higher than the +30 among those aged 30 to 49, +21 among those aged 50 to 64 and the much lower +14 for workers aged 65 and older.

These findings come from aggregated Gallup data collected from January to April 2015, involving interviews with more than 65,000 full- or part-time workers. Gallup's Job Creation Index is based on the percentage of workers who say that their place of employment is hiring minus the percentage who say it is letting workers go. The index has been relatively static for the first four months of 2015, averaging +29. In April, it reached +31, its highest score so far this year.

Gallup Job Creation Index, by Age

Based on the percentage of U.S. workers who say their employer is hiring
workers and expanding the size of its workforce minus the percentage who say
their employer is letting workers go and reducing the size of its workforce

	Job Creation Index (Net hiring)
18-29	43
30-49	30
50-64	21
65+	14

Jan. 2-Apr. 30 2015

GALLUP

But whatever the pace of job expansion nationwide, young American workers are the most likely of any age group to report that their companies are expanding. A slim majority, 52%, in this youngest age group say their employer is hiring new people and expanding the size of its workforce, while fewer than one in 10 (9%) say their employer is letting people go and reducing the workforce size. The percentages in other age groups who say that their employer is hiring are nowhere near majority status. Workers aged 30 to 49 are about as likely to say their employer is hiring new people (42%) as say their place of employment is not changing its workforce size (40%). For those aged 50 and older, however, the most common response is that their employer is neither decreasing nor increasing its workforce.

U.S. Workers' Reports of Job Conditions Where They Work, by Age

	Hiring/ expanding workforce	Not changing	Letting go/ reducing workforce
	%	%	%
18-29	52	34	9
30-49	42	40	13
50-64	35	46	13
65+	24	49	10

Jan. 2-Apr. 30 2015

GALLUP

One potential explanation for these findings is tied to young people's likelihood to be recent hires themselves. While the Gallup Daily tracking data do not measure how long a worker has been at his or her current job, one could assume that younger workers are more likely to have been hired more recently than older workers simply because of their age. To that point, the median tenure of 20- to 24-year-old workers was 1.3 years in 2014, according to the Bureau of Labor Statistics, while 45- to 54-year-old workers had been with their current employer for a median of 7.9 years. In other words, because young people are more likely to have recently sought new employment opportunities, they have naturally ended up at organizations and firms that are expanding their workforces.

More generally, younger Americans tend to be more positive than older Americans about the economy—particularly on forward-looking measures. This positivity is evident in younger versus older Americans' confidence in the national economy and reports of their standard of living.

Bottom Line

Young American workers are more likely than any other age group to report that they work for employers who are hiring. In some sense, this may be repetitious: Young employees are more likely to be recent hires, so it is only fitting they should find themselves at firms that are hiring. It is also true that young Americans appear to have a cheerier disposition about the economy, according to Gallup's measures.

Survey Methods

Results for this Gallup poll are based on telephone interviews conducted Jan. 2–Apr. 30 2015, on the Gallup U.S. Daily survey, with a random sample of 65,873 adults, aged 18 and older, living in all 50 U.S. states and the District of Columbia, who are employed . For results based on the total sample of national adults, the margin of sampling error is ±1 percentage points at the 95% confidence level. All reported margins of sampling error include computed design effects for weighting.

May 08, 2015
AMERICANS MORE SATISFIED WITH GOVERNMENT ECONOMIC FUNCTIONS

by Justin McCarthy

Story Highlights

- *U.S. satisfaction up with gov't handling of nation's finances*
- *Satisfaction with work on employment, economic growth also up*
- *Still, majorities dissatisfied on all three measures*

WASHINGTON, D.C.—Majorities of Americans remain dissatisfied with how the federal government handles labor and employment issues, job creation and economic growth, and the nation's finances. But they are significantly more satisfied with the government's handling of these issues than they were in 2013, which marked the low in Americans' views on government efforts to address these issues.

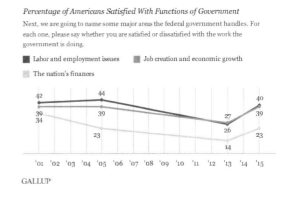

Percentage of Americans Satisfied With Functions of Government

Next, we are going to name some major areas the federal government handles. For each one, please say whether you are satisfied or dissatisfied with the work the government is doing.

■ Labor and employment issues ■ Job creation and economic growth
■ The nation's finances

GALLUP

Americans' increased satisfaction with these functions of government comes at a time when hiring activity is up and confidence in the economy is higher than it has been in the past several years. Further, the unemployment rate as reported by the Bureau of Labor Statistics has dropped from 7.5% at the time of the 2013 poll to 5.5% in March of this year. This uptick in satisfaction also may be related to fewer Americans mentioning unemployment as the most important problem facing the nation in recent months and more saying now is a good time to find a quality job. The latest results in satisfaction with government functions are from Gallup's April 29–May 2 survey.

Of the three measures, Americans' satisfaction with the government's handling of labor and employment issues is up the most since 2013, with 40% now satisfied—a 14-percentage-point jump from 2013. Americans' satisfaction with the government's efforts on job creation and economic growth has increased 12 points to 39%, while satisfaction with the handling of the nation's finances has ticked up nine points to 23%. Still, most Americans continue to be dissatisfied with the government's handling of labor and employment (57%), job creation and economic growth (60%) and the nation's finances (74%).

Democrats and Leaners Most Likely to Be Satisfied With Handling of Employment Issues

Democrats and independents who lean Democratic are about twice as likely as Republicans and independents who lean Republican to be satisfied with the U.S. government's handling of labor and employment issues, 52% vs. 27%. In 2001 and 2005, Republicans were more likely than Democrats to be satisfied on this dimension, reflecting the general pattern of partisans' being more satisfied when the president is from their own party. Still, both party groups have shown more widespread satisfaction since 2013.

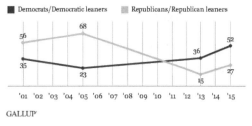

Percentage of Americans Satisfied With the Work the Federal Government Is Doing on Labor and Employment Issues, by Party

Next, we are going to name some major areas the federal government handles. For each one, please say whether you are satisfied or dissatisfied with the work the government is doing. How about labor and employment issues?

■ Democrats/Democratic leaners   ■ Republicans/Republican leaners

GALLUP

The partisan gap in satisfaction with the government's handling of labor and employment was widest in 2005, during George W. Bush's presidency, when Republicans were nearly three times as likely as Democrats to be satisfied. Bush scuffled with predominantly Democratic labor unions during his presidency on a variety of issues ranging from Social Security to workplace safety rules and minimum wage laws.

On job creation and economic growth, as with labor and employment issues, Republicans' and Democrats' satisfaction is closely linked with the party of the incumbent president, and thus Democrats (56%) are much more likely than Republicans (21%) to be satisfied. Under Bush, the majority of GOP leaners were satisfied with his government's handling of the issues, compared with less than a third of Democrats.

Fewer Than One in 10 Republicans and Leaners Satisfied With Handling of U.S. Finances

While Democrats are currently more satisfied than Republicans with the government's handling of the nation's finances, they are not as satisfied as Republicans were in 2001 and 2005 under Bush.

Bottom Line

For all three questions of satisfaction with the federal government's performance on key economic matters, most Americans continue to feel dissatisfied, which makes sense given their net negative assessments of the U.S. economy's current and future standing. Satisfaction with handling of the nation's finances is especially low.

Percentage of Americans Satisfied With the Work the Federal Government Is Doing on the Nation's Finances, by Party

Next, we are going to name some major areas the federal government handles. For each one, please say whether you are satisfied or dissatisfied with the work the government is doing. How about the nation's finances?

■ Democrats/Democratic leaners   ■ Republicans/Republican leaners

GALLUP

Still, the improvements are noteworthy, and reflect the economic progress made, as seen in a variety of government statistics. But while Americans may perceive progress in a variety of areas of government work, they have become increasingly dissatisfied with its handling of poverty, which is related to unemployment and other measures of overall U.S. economic standing.

The survey asks Americans only if they are satisfied or dissatisfied, and does not delve into possible solutions for addressing these economic issues. So Americans could be dissatisfied with the government's handling of them for a variety of reasons. Party breakdowns of Americans' views do shed light on their feelings, however, as those who identify with the current president's party tend to be much more satisfied with the government's handling of these issues under his administration.

Survey Methods

Results for this Gallup poll are based on telephone interviews conducted April 29–May 2, 2015, on the Gallup U.S. Daily survey, with a random sample of 2,020 adults, aged 18 and older, living in all 50 U.S. states and the District of Columbia. For results based on the total sample of national adults, the margin of sampling error is ±4 percentage points at the 95% confidence level. All reported margins of sampling error include computed design effects for weighting.

May 11, 2015
U.S. SMALL-BUSINESS OWNERS' OPTIMISM DIPS SLIGHTLY

by Coleen McMurray and Frank Newport

Story Highlights

- *Small-business owners' optimism fell modestly from first quarter*
- *Optimism remains at highest level in seven years*
- *Owners report downtick in revenues*

PRINCETON, N.J.—In the U.S., small-business owners' optimism is down slightly from earlier this year amid a small decline in owners' ratings of current revenues, according to the latest Wells Fargo/Gallup Small Business Index. Still, small-business owners have been more optimistic this year than at any point in seven years.

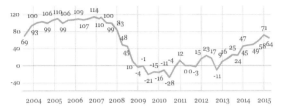

Wells Fargo/Gallup Small Business Index

The Small Business Index consists of owners' ratings of their business' current situation and their expectations for the next 12 months, measured in terms of their overall financial situation, revenue, cash flow, capital spending, number of jobs and ease of obtaining credit.

Index conducted since August 2003 and quarterly from December 2003-April 2015

GALLUP

In the latest quarterly small-business survey, conducted April 6–10, the overall Small Business Index score is +64, down modestly from +71 in the first quarter. While both of these scores are below pre-recession levels, they are the highest since January 2008, when the index was +83.

The slight decline in optimism this quarter reflects modest decreases in how small-business owners feel about both their present situation and the future. The present situation score—how business owners rate current conditions for their businesses—is now at +24, compared with +28 last quarter, while the latest outlook score is +40, compared with +43 last quarter. The latest results are significantly higher than one year ago, when the present score was a +14 and the future score was +33.

Wells Fargo/Gallup Small Business Index

■ % Present situation   ▨ % Future expectations

GALLUP

Several factors may be related to the slight drop in optimism this quarter. The first is a decline in small-business owners' views of their firms' revenues. Forty-two percent of owners say their revenues have increased a lot or a little within the last 12 months, down from 49% in the first quarter. The current score is, however, up from a year ago, when 36% indicated that their revenues had increased. Small-business owners' recent ratings of their revenues are the highest since early 2008, when 45% reported increased revenues.

Business owners also reported modest declines in their perceived ease of obtaining credit in the past 12 months and their projected ease of obtaining credit in the next 12 months. Currently, 25% of owners report that it was very or somewhat difficult to obtain credit in the past 12 months, up from 20% in the first quarter, and 28% expected it would be very or somewhat difficult in the next 12 months, up from 23%. The latest results are similar to the percentages recorded a year ago.

Bottom Line

After reaching its highest level since 2008 in the first quarter of 2015, the Wells Fargo/Gallup Small Business Index fell modestly in the second quarter. But across both of these quarters, the index remains higher than at any point since 2008. Small-business owners' optimism appears to be tempered in the current quarter by owners' perceptions of declining revenues and a slight uptick in their perceived difficulty of obtaining credit. The reports of declining revenues suggest that the downtick in owners' overall attitudes, more than merely reflecting general attitudes about the U.S. economic environment, appears to indicate an actual negative turn in their business performance.

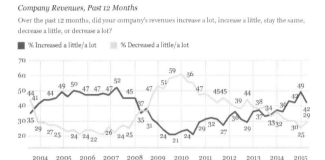

Company Revenues, Past 12 Months

Over the past 12 months, did your company's revenues increase a lot, increase a little, stay the same, decrease a little, or decrease a lot?

■ % Increased a little/a lot   ▨ % Decreased a little/a lot

Wells Fargo/Gallup Small Business Index

GALLUP

Survey Methods

Results are based on telephone interviews with 601 U.S. small-business owners in all 50 states, conducted April 6–10, 2015. The margin of sampling error is ±4 percentage points at the 95% confidence level.

May 11, 2015
MILLENNIALS MOST TRUSTING ON SAFETY OF PERSONAL INFORMATION

by John Fleming

Story Highlights

- *44% of U.S. millennials say their information is kept private*
- *Traditionalists least likely to say companies keep info safe*
- *Various hypotheses for why millennials have this trust level*

PRINCETON, N.J.—In spite of high-visibility data breaches, 44% of millennials in the United States believe that their personal information is kept private "all" or "most of the time" by the businesses or companies they do business with. This is the highest of all major U.S. generational groups.

Just over a quarter of millennials (26%) believe that their personal information is kept private "little" or "none of the time," while the remaining 30% believe it is kept private "some of the time."

On the other end of the age spectrum, the most skeptical generation is traditionalists, Americans aged 70 and older. Twenty-nine percent of traditionalists believe that their personal information is kept private all or most of the time, while just over a third (35%) believe it is kept private a little or none of the time, making this the only generation to have a higher rate of distrust than trust. Thirty-six percent say it is kept private some of the time. Generation X and baby boomers fall in between these two groups, suggesting that expectations of personal privacy are age related.

Belief That Businesses Are Keeping Personal Information Private, by Age Group

In general, how often do you believe that your personal information is actually kept private by the businesses or companies you do business with?

	% All/Most of the time	% Little/None of the time
Millennials	44	26
Generation X	32	28
Baby boomers	32	32
Traditionalists	29	35

Feb. 23-March 3, 2015

GALLUP

Overall, 36% of Americans believe their personal information is kept private all or most of the time, with 31% saying it is kept private little or none of the time. A third (34%) say it is kept private some of the time.

Millennials Defy Expectations for Their Generation

There is a school of thought about millennials and privacy suggesting that because millennials have never known a world without smartphones, apps, the Internet or computers—and the inherent risks to privacy these things pose—they should have lower expectations about the security of their personal information than other generations do. This is because, the thinking goes, everything is available online these days, and even information that is not easily accessible is increasingly vulnerable to hackers. But another perspective argues just the opposite. To its adherents, millennials should actually have higher expectations about the security of their personal information than other generations because they understand how technology works and are fully aware of the inherent risks, but believe technology will keep their personal information safe.

Finally, there is a slightly different version of the latter hypothesis. According to this perspective, millennials should actually have higher expectations than other generations about the security of their personal information simply because they are naïve in the ways of the world—they have no experience to make them think otherwise. In other words, millennials have the least life experience of all generations. A corollary of this view is that members of the oldest generation—traditionalists—should not only have the greatest life experience (and be more jaded or cynical as a result) but the lowest expectations of personal privacy.

Implications

In spite of the oft-heard refrain that millennials are not trusting, these results suggest that in some cases—particularly where the privacy of personal information is concerned—millennials are fairly trusting, at least more trusting than skeptical. Whether this effect is simply the result of life experience and youth, or some other combination of factors, remains to be determined. In recent years, millennials (as well as all other generations) have been exposed to a significant number of high-visibility data breaches. Knowledge of these breaches alone would likely make people question the privacy and security of their online personal information. But millennials seem to rise above this, remaining trusting in the face of an abundance of evidence that their online data may not be very secure.

Survey Methods

Results for this Gallup poll are based on telephone interviews conducted Feb. 23–March 3, 2015, on the Gallup U.S. Daily survey, with a random sample of 1,525 adults, aged 18 and older, living in all 50 U.S. states and the District of Columbia. For results based on the total sample of national adults, the margin of sampling error is ±2.5 percentage points at the 95% confidence level. For comparisons between or within the total sample for each generation, the margin of sampling error is ±5.9 percentage points at the 95% confidence level.

May 12, 2015
DES MOINES, IOWA, LEADS U.S. METRO AREAS IN COMMUNITY PRIDE

by Rebecca Riffkin

Story Highlights

- *Three in four Des Moines residents proud of their community*
- *Scranton residents have the lowest pride, at 50%*
- *New Orleans residents most likely to get community recognition*

WASHINGTON, D.C.—Residents of Des Moines, Iowa, are the most likely to say they are proud of their community, of the 100 most populous U.S. metropolitan areas that Gallup and Healthways surveyed in 2014. More than three-quarters of residents in the Des Moines area agree with the statement that they are proud of the community or area where they live. At the other end of the spectrum, residents of Scranton-Wilkes-Barre, Pennsylvania, are the least likely to express hometown pride, with just half agreeing.

Communities With the Highest and Lowest Reported Pride

On a five-point scale, where 5 means strongly agree and 1 means strongly disagree, please rate your level of agreement with the following items: You are proud of your community or the area where you live.

Communities With the Most Pride	% 4 or 5	Communities With the Least Pride	% 4 or 5
Des Moines-West Des Moines, IA	76.5	Scranton--Wilkes-Barre, PA	50.6
Greenville-Mauldin-Easley, SC	75.1	Youngstown-Warren-Boardman, OH-PA	52.7
Asheville, NC	74.6	Stockton, CA	53.3
Provo-Orem, UT	74.4	Fresno, CA	54.2
Raleigh-Cary, NC	73.8	Toledo, OH	54.2
Bradenton-Sarasota-Venice, FL	71.8	Bakersfield, CA	54.4
Anchorage, AK	71.6	New Haven-Milford, CT	54.7
Oxnard-Thousand Oaks-Ventura, CA	71.5	Albuquerque, NM	55.2
Omaha-Council Bluffs, NE-IA	71.2	Memphis, TN-MS-AR	55.9
Chattanooga, TN-GA	70.2		

Jan. 1-Dec. 31, 2014
Gallup-Healthways Well-Being Index

GALLUP

Greenville, South Carolina; Asheville, North Carolina; Provo, Utah; and Raleigh, North Carolina, round out the top five metro areas with the most community pride. Youngstown, Ohio; Stockton, California; Fresno, California; and Toledo, Ohio, complete the five metro areas with the least pride.

These findings are based on interviews collected throughout 2014 as part of the Gallup-Healthways Well-Being Index. Americans were asked to use a five-point scale—where 5 means strongly agree and 1 means strongly disagree—to rate their level of agreement with the following statement: You are proud of your community or the area where you live. Nationally, 63.5% of Americans responded with a 4 or 5 rating.

In the 10 metro areas leading in community pride, at least seven in 10 residents agree they are proud of where they live. Among the bottom 10, less than 56% agree, but this still means that at least half of residents in each of the 100 largest metropolitan areas feel proud of their community.

Perceptions of Safety and Security Strongly Linked to Community Pride

Americans' pride in their local community is related to a wide variety of factors—one factor is their ratings about how safe and secure they feel. Nationally, 91.3% of Americans who reported feeling safe and secure also reported being proud of their community, while just 2% of those who reported they did *not* feel safe and secure were proud of their community.

Given that relationship, there is some overlap between communities that rank among the best and worst in terms of residents' community pride and their feelings of safety and security. Overall, four of the communities with the highest levels of pride are among the communities in the U.S. with the highest percentage of residents who feel safe and secure: Des Moines, Iowa; Raleigh, North Carolina; Provo, Utah; and Omaha, Nebraska. And six of the communities with the lowest pride are among those with the lowest safety and security rating: Fresno, California; Stockton, California; Bakersfield, California; Memphis, Tennessee; Youngstown, Ohio; and Toledo, Ohio.

New Orleans Residents Most Likely to Receive Recognition for Helping Community

Gallup also asks Americans if they have been recognized for giving back to their community as a way to measure local volunteerism and community service. Residents of New Orleans, Louisiana, are the most likely to agree they received recognition in the last 12 months for helping to improve the city or area where they live, with 28.1% saying they had been recognized. New Orleans is followed by Asheville, North Carolina; Bakersfield, California; Anchorage, Alaska; and Oxnard-Thousand Oaks-Ventura, California.

Communities With Highest and Lowest Community Recognition

On a five-point scale, where 5 means strongly agree and 1 means strongly disagree, please rate your level of agreement with the following items: In the last 12 months, you have received recognition for helping to improve the city or area where you live.

Highest communities	% 4 or 5	Lowest communities	% 4 or 5
New Orleans-Metairie-Kenner, LA	28.1	Fayetteville-Springdale-Rogers, AR-MO	12.5
Asheville, NC	26.4	Deltona-Daytona Beach-Ormond Beach, FL	13.2
Bakersfield, CA	26.0	Harrisburg-Carlisle, PA	13.4
Anchorage, AK	25.1	Ogden-Clearfield, UT	14.0
Oxnard-Thousand Oaks-Ventura, CA	23.6	Provo-Orem, UT	14.1
Little Rock-N Little Rock-Conway, AR	23.3	Dayton, OH	14.3
Greenville-Mauldin-Easley, SC	23.1	Salem, OR	14.8
Allentown-Bethlehem-Easton, PA-NJ	22.6	Madison, WI	15.3
Chattanooga, TN-GA	22.0	St. Louis, MO-IL	15.3
Lakeland-Winter Haven, FL	21.5		

Jan. 1-Dec. 31, 2014
Gallup-Healthways Well-Being Index

GALLUP

Since Hurricane Katrina, volunteers and community service organizations have aided in the effort to rebuild New Orleans. And recently, the city was recognized by CNCS, the federal agency that administers the AmeriCorps program, for being among the top 10 large U.S. cities that produce the highest number of AmeriCorps members per capita. Whether the relatively high rate of civic activity in New Orleans is entirely an outgrowth of the hurricane or if civic duty predates the hurricane isn't clear, but at this point, it is fairly common for New Orleans residents to feel appreciated for giving back to their community, with almost three in 10 agreeing they have been recognized.

Fayetteville-Springdale-Rogers, Arkansas-Missouri, is the city where residents are the least likely to have been recognized for helping their community, at 12.5%. Provo, Utah, one of the cities with the highest reported community pride, also has some of the lowest levels of reported recognition for helping their community, at 14.1%. Another Utah community, Ogden, is also in the bottom five for community recognition, as are Deltona-Daytona Beach-Ormond Beach, Florida, and Harrisburg, Pennsylvania.

Nationally, 19.1% of Americans agreed they have "received recognition for helping to improve the city or area where you live," responding with a 4 or 5 on the 5-point scale.

Bottom Line

Residents who give back to their community can improve other aspects of their well-being. Volunteering can introduce residents to new friends—improving social well-being. It also can give residents a stronger sense of purpose. Indeed, Gallup and Healthways have previously found that Americans who have been recognized for giving back to their communities have higher well-being than those who have not.

While the percentage of residents who are proud of their community varies around the country, at least half of residents in each of the 100 most populous metro areas in the U.S. said they had pride in their community.

There is a strong link between residents' perceptions of feeling safe and secure and their level of community pride. Communities where pride is lacking could work to improve security as a way to improve pride. However, it may be that communities with less pride are also places where crime is more pervasive because people feel less attachment and shared sense of community with their neighbors. Programs focused on increasing local pride could also help residents feel more invested in their community and less inclined to commit crime, thus increasing security.

Survey Methods

Results are based on telephone interviews conducted as part of the Gallup-Healthways Well-Being Index survey Jan. 2–Dec. 29, 2014, with a random sample of 176,702 adults, aged 18 and older, living in metropolitan areas in the 50 U.S. states and the District of Columbia, selected using random-digit-dial sampling. Unlike previous years, only the 100 most populous metros—as determined by the U.S. Census Bureau—were reported in 2014. A second requirement is that at least 300 cases are required per metro area for reporting. As such, McAllen-Edinburg-Mission, Texas, and Durham-Chapel Hill, North Carolina, were both excluded from reporting because of insufficient sample size. These were replaced by the 102nd-largest metropolitan statistical area (MSA) in the U.S.: Lancaster, Pennsylvania.

The "communities" referenced in this article are based on MSAs as defined by the U.S. Office of Management and Budget. In many cases, more than one city is included in the same MSA. The San Jose, California, MSA, for example, also includes the smaller nearby cities of Sunnyvale and Santa Clara in addition to San Jose. Each respondent is attributed to his or her MSA based on self-reports of his or her ZIP code.

Maximum margins of error for the Well-Being Index and the element scores vary according to MSA size, ranging from less than 1 point for the largest cities represented to around ±1.5 points for many of the smallest cities.

May 13, 2015
FIVE MONTHS INTO GOP CONGRESS, APPROVAL REMAINS LOW AT 19%

by Andrew Dugan

Story Highlights

- *Congressional job approval at 19%, essentially unchanged*
- *Approval of GOP Congress similar among Republicans and Democrats*

WASHINGTON, D.C.—Congressional job approval, currently at 19%, remains stuck near historical lows, despite a number of recent high-profile legislative achievements.

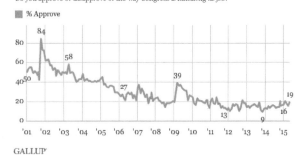

Congressional Job Approval Ratings: 2001-2015

Do you approve or disapprove of the way Congress is handling its job?

■ % Approve

GALLUP'

Over the past month, Congress has confirmed the stalled nomination of Attorney General Loretta Lynch and both chambers passed a bill that was signed into law regarding Medicare. Bills that would authorize limited congressional oversight on any international agreement with Iran and help victims of human trafficking passed the Senate with little or no opposition. The uptick in activity, though hardly historic, is notable compared with the past two Congresses. Those Congresses, marked by divided control of the two chambers, were known for their entrenched partisan gridlock and few legislative accomplishments. And Americans didn't care for their inability to agree—they gave Congress its lowest approval ever over this time period. Gallup found in June 2013, six months into the previous Congress, that gridlock and ineffectiveness were the most frequently cited reason for Americans' disapproval of Congress.

Several months into this new Congress, the accomplishments that have been realized could give one the impression that the

gridlock is softening, particularly over the past month. But these achievements have had virtually no impact on Congress's job approval compared with early April (15%).

And, of course, Congress is far from working perfectly now, even if the pace of work appears to have increased. Most dramatically, the Senate failed to overcome a Democratic filibuster Tuesday afternoon that would give the president enhanced authority in negotiating trade bills, though the May survey was conducted before this occurrence. Legislation authorizing the use of military force in Iraq and Syria to fight ISIS, proposed by the administration and which many members of Congress support, remains stalled.

GOP Congress Has Low Approval Among Republicans

A key reason the current 114th Congress appears to be having more legislative success than the two Congresses before it is that the House and Senate are now under one party's control. Unified GOP control of Capitol Hill should, at least in theory, boost Republicans' overall approval of Congress. But the expected "Republican rally" for Congress has yet to materialize—21% of Republicans and Republican leaners approve of Congress, not much different from the 18% of independents and of Democrats who approve. Nor is Republican support notably higher than the 15% it reached in 2014, despite the decided Republican tilt of this year's legislature.

Congressional Job Approval, by Party Identification

Do you approve or disapprove of the way Congress is handling its job?

	Republicans	Independents	Democrats
	%	%	%
Approve	21	18	18
Disapprove	73	77	80

May 6-10, 2015

GALLUP'

Bottom Line

After years of dysfunction, Congress is moving forward on key pieces of legislation. No longer shackled by split control—though still facing a president of the opposite party—the legislative branch is suddenly finding some areas of agreement. But even if it appears that the gridlock is easing, the overwhelming majority of Americans still disapprove of Congress. If Congress continues passing bipartisan legislation, more Americans might soften their stance. Still, it may be that Americans are largely not aware of or impressed by Congress's recent legislative successes. Or it may be that the hit to Congress's reputation over the last several years—evident in not only dismal job approval ratings but also falling levels of trust and confidence—will take a long time to reverse.

Survey Methods

Results for this Gallup poll are based on telephone interviews conducted May 6–10, 2015, with a random sample of 1,024 adults, aged 18 and older, living in all 50 U.S. states and the District of Columbia. For results based on the total sample of national adults, the margin of sampling error is ±4 percentage points at the 95% confidence level. All reported margins of sampling error include computed design effects for weighting.

May 13, 2015
HILLARY CLINTON'S UNFAVORABLE SCORE TICKS UP

by Lydia Saad

Story Highlights

- *Half in U.S. view her favorably, similar to March and April*
- *Nearly half now view her unfavorably, up from 39% in March*
- *Diminished majority view Bill Clinton favorably, now 59%*

PRINCETON, N.J.—Hillary Clinton's favorable rating from the American people has been steady—near 50%—all spring, but her unfavorable rating has inched higher and is now 46%, up from 39% in March. At the same time, the percentage of Americans with no impression of the former first lady, U.S. senator and secretary of state has gone down.

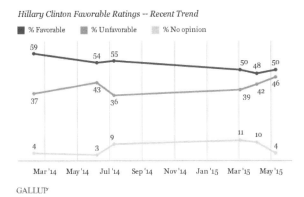

Hillary Clinton Favorable Ratings -- Recent Trend

GALLUP

The last three months have been an important time for Clinton. Since officially launching her presidential campaign in mid-April, she has been deflecting criticism of her exclusive use of a private email address while secretary of state, and more recently, partisan charges of possible conflicts of interest stemming from the Clinton Foundation's reliance on foreign donors. Separately, Clinton is scheduled to testify before the House Select Committee on Benghazi next week.

Against the backdrop of the press swirling around these stories, it may be comforting to the Clinton team as they focus on sewing up the Democratic nomination that most of the increase in her unfavorable rating has occurred among Republicans, not Democrats or political independents. Nearly nine in 10 Republicans now view her unfavorably, up from 75% in March. Over the same period, her unfavorable rating has increased only three percentage points among independents and Democrats, hardly significant except that it has held at this slightly higher level for two months.

Hillary Clinton Unfavorable Ratings, by Party ID

	March 2-4, 2015	April 3-4, 2015	May 6-10, 2015
	%	%	%
U.S. adults	39	42	46
Republicans	75	83	88
Independents	40	43	43
Democrats	10	13	13

GALLUP

Bill Clinton Retains Positive Image

Bill Clinton—whose speaking fees and foundation finances have recently drawn some criticism—is the subject of a renewed debate about whether he is an asset or liability to his wife's campaign. He has lower favorable ratings today than a year ago, but his image remains solidly positive. Currently, 59% of Americans view him favorably and 38% unfavorably. Last June, the figures were 64% favorable and 34% unfavorable—among the most positive for Clinton since he left office in 2001.

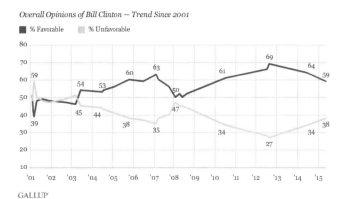

Overall Opinions of Bill Clinton -- Trend Since 2001

GALLUP

Although Hillary Clinton trails Bill Clinton in public favorability by nine points, the gap is narrower among women, nonwhites and seniors, and they are viewed equally positively by Democrats. Hillary Clinton's biggest image deficits relative to her husband are among Republicans, adults under 50 years of age and men.

Americans' Overall Opinions of Hillary and Bill Clinton
Percentage viewing each favorably

	Hillary Clinton	Bill Clinton	Net favorable toward Hillary
	%	%	(pct. pts.)
U.S. adults	50	59	-9
Men	45	56	-11
Women	56	62	-6
Whites	41	51	-10
Nonwhites	72	78	-6
18 to 29	54	63	-9
30 to 49	54	66	-12
50 to 64	48	58	-10
65+	44	49	-5
Men, 18 to 49	50	61	-11
Men, 50+	38	49	-11
Women, 18 to 49	58	68	-10
Women, 50+	55	58	-3
Republicans	11	27	-16
Independents	51	60	-9
Democrats	87	87	0

May 6-10, 2015

GALLUP

Bottom Line

Hillary Clinton has thus far weathered the political storms swirling around her fairly well, with her favorable rating staying close to 50% since March, even as her unfavorable score has edged up, particularly among Republicans. Clinton still has to appear before the House Select Committee on Benghazi and may face further scrutiny over her email practices while secretary of state now that a federal judge has reopened a case probing the matter. For now, her supporters appear to be holding firm. But, should she be looking for ways to burnish her image among independents and Republicans, she might consider more strategic use of her husband on the campaign trail.

Survey Methods

Results for this Gallup poll are based on telephone interviews conducted May 6–10, 2015, with a random sample of 1,024 adults, aged 18 and older, living in all 50 U.S. states and the District of Columbia. For results based on the total sample of national adults, the margin of sampling error is ±4 percentage points at the 95% confidence level. All reported margins of sampling error include computed design effects for weighting.

May 15, 2015

RACE RELATIONS OUTSCORES FOREIGN POLICY AS CLINTON STRENGTH

by Frank Newport

Story Highlights

- *42% say Clinton would do good job on foreign policy as president*
- *Public perceives Clinton's greatest strength would be race relations*
- *Generally mixed reviews of her tenure as secretary of state*

PRINCETON, N.J.—Americans are more likely to say Hillary Clinton would do a good job handling foreign affairs as president than to say she would do a bad job, but this rating is no higher than her rating on the economy and healthcare, and is lower than her rating on handling race relations.

Now, thinking about Hillary Clinton. If she were elected president in 2016, do you think Hillary Clinton would do a good job, a fair job or a bad job handling each of the following issues?

Ranked by percentage "good job"

	Good job	Fair job	Bad job	Good job minus bad job
	%	%	%	pct. pts.
Race relations	44	33	22	22
Healthcare policy	43	25	30	13
The economy	42	29	28	14
Foreign affairs	42	26	29	13
Terrorism	39	29	30	9
Immigration	35	33	30	5
The way income and wealth are distributed in the U.S.	35	31	32	3
The way government operates in Washington	35	30	33	2

May 6-7, 2015

GALLUP

These results are part of Gallup's early look at the American public's view of foreign affairs as an election issue heading into 2016. Americans' views of Hillary Clinton on foreign affairs are particularly interesting at this early stage of the campaign, given that she is by far the most well-known candidate and has a unique background in foreign affairs. This background includes four years as secretary of state, along with eight years as a U.S. senator and eight years as first lady in the White House.

Clinton's prior service could be seen as a major plus for her presidential credentials. Republicans and others, however, have assailed aspects of her tenure at the U.S. Department of State, a time that involved her handling of the terrorist attacks at the Benghazi consulate and her handling of emails while secretary.

Americans give Clinton a net rating on foreign affairs (percentage good job minus percentage bad job) of +13, which is roughly the same as healthcare and the economy, but behind the +22 rating she receives for her potential to deal with race relations. Her ratings on handling terrorism are just behind these others. Americans are least positive about the job Clinton would do in handling two broad issues: the way government in Washington operates and the distribution of income and wealth in the U.S.

Clinton's Perceived Strengths Not in Total Sync With Issue Importance

Clinton's perceived strengths on various issues are not closely synchronized with the importance Americans put on those same issues. The issue Americans think Clinton would handle best—race relations—receives the lowest importance in terms of potential voting considerations. The three issues on which Clinton receives her next highest ratings are spread out across the issue importance spectrum: the economy is at the top of the importance list, healthcare policy in the middle and foreign affairs near the bottom.

A potential negative for Clinton could be the relatively low rating Americans give on her perceived ability to deal with the way government operates. This is one of the top three most important issues for Americans, yet the one on which she receives her lowest ratings.

Importance of Issue and Perceptions of Clinton's Handling of Issues

Ranked by percentage "extremely" or "very important"

	Extremely/ Very important	Clinton: good job minus bad job
	%	pct. pts.
The economy	86	14
The way government operates in Washington	77	2
Healthcare policy	77	13
Terrorism	74	9
The way income and wealth are distributed in the U.S.	71	3
Foreign affairs	61	13
Immigration	59	5
Race relations	55	22

May 6-7, 2015

GALLUP

Clinton's Strength on Foreign Affairs Rated Vastly Different Across Party Lines

As would be expected, there are large differences in how Republicans, independents and Democrats think Clinton would handle various issues as president. Democrats generally expect her to perform well in all of the different areas, Republicans expect her to do poorly in all areas and independents have mixed views. Both Democrats and Republicans rate foreign affairs near the top of their respective rank-ordered lists, but with vastly different absolute ratings. Democrats' net rating of her potential ability to handle foreign policy is +62, independents is +2, and Republicans is −44.

Republicans' and independents' views of Clinton's ability to handle race relations stand at the top of their lists, significantly higher than any other issue. Democrats' ratings of Clinton on this issue are high as well, but no higher than their ratings of her on other issues. Republicans give Clinton the worst ratings on handling government in Washington and the way income and wealth are distributed, and these are near the bottom of the list for Democrats as well.

Clinton will be most likely facing several opponents for the Democratic nomination, even though she is the strong favorite at this point. Democrats say the economy and healthcare policy are the most important issues they will take into account in their vote for president, and they give her high ratings on both.

Americans' Perceptions of Clinton's Handling of Several Issues, by Party ID

% Good job minus bad job

	Democrats	Independents	Republicans
	%	%	%
Healthcare policy	+65	+3	-49
Race relations	+64	+17	-31
Foreign affairs	+62	+2	-44
The economy	+61	+6	-48
Terrorism	+59	-4	-43
The way government operates in Washington	+53	-11	-55
Immigration	+52	-4	-50
The way income and wealth are distributed in the U.S.	+49	-5	-56

May 6-7, 2015

GALLUP

Effect of Clinton's Time as Secretary of State

Americans are somewhat mixed in their evaluations of Clinton's four years as secretary of state, with more Americans rating her tenure as secretary of state as outstanding or above average than rating it below average or poor. The positive group consists of 38% of Americans, while the negative group represents 27%, with the rest saying her job performance was average.

Republicans' criticisms of Clinton's tenure as secretary of state are reflected in the finding that 62% rate her performance in that job as below average or poor, contrasted with Democrats' 63% positive rating of her performance. Independents have mixed opinions, roughly split across the positive, average and negative categories.

Thinking back on her time as U.S. secretary of state from 2009-2013, from what you have heard, read or remember, how would you rate the job Hillary Clinton did as secretary of state?

	Outstanding/Above average	Average	Below average/Poor
	%	%	%
National adults	38	31	27
Democrats	63	33	12
Independents	31	35	26
Republicans	4	29	62

May 6-7, 2015

GALLUP

Bottom Line

Hillary Clinton's experience as secretary of state does not appear to be either an exceptionally strong positive for her or a strong negative

with the U.S. public. Americans rate her potential performance as president on the foreign policy dimension about the same as several other issues and below how she would do on what appears to be a more distinctive strength—her ability to deal with race relations. Looking back, less than half of Americans say she did an outstanding or above average job as secretary of state, a rating that is below her current overall favorable rating.

Republicans generally assume that Clinton would do a bad job on every issue tested were she to become president, although their negative ratings of her potential on foreign affairs are not as low as their ratings of her on other dimensions. This suggests that despite their criticism of aspects of how she did her job as secretary of state, they do not see her ability on foreign affairs to be an exceptional negative compared with their views of other issues she would deal with in the White House. Democrats are quite optimistic about how Clinton would handle all issues as president, and while they rate her highly on foreign policy, this rating is no more positive than other issues' ratings.

Survey Methods

Results for this Gallup poll are based on telephone interviews conducted May 6–7, 2015, with a random sample of 1,016 adults, aged 18 and older, living in all 50 U.S. states and the District of Columbia. For results based on the total sample of national adults, the margin of sampling error is ±4 percentage points at the 95% confidence level. All reported margins of sampling error include computed design effects for weighting.

May 15, 2015
ECONOMY TRUMPS FOREIGN AFFAIRS AS KEY 2016 ELECTION ISSUE

by Jeffrey M. Jones

Story Highlights

- *Economy more important than terrorism, foreign affairs*
- *Importance of foreign affairs no higher than most recent elections*
- *Economy top issue for both Republicans and Democrats*

PRINCETON, N.J.—Eighty-six percent of Americans say the economy will be extremely or very important to their vote next year, a significantly higher percentage than for any other issue. Concerns about terrorism rank high at 74% with foreign affairs further down the list at 61%.

The results are based on a May 6–7 Gallup poll, just as the campaign is getting underway with politicians from both parties officially declaring their candidacies. A forthcoming article on Gallup.com will show how Americans rate the most well-known candidate, Hillary Clinton, on each of these issues.

With a long time span between now and when voters cast their ballots next fall, the issues that prove pivotal during the election could certainly change. However, the economy will likely persist at or near the top of the list as it has done historically in both presidential election years and midterm election years and when the economy was weak, as in 2008, but also when it was strong, as in 2000.

How important will each of the following issues be to your vote for president next year -- will it be -- extremely important, very important, moderately important or not that important? [RANDOM ORDER]

Ranked by percentage extremely/very important

	Extremely important	Extremely/ Very important
	%	%
The economy	43	86
The way government operates in Washington	43	77
Healthcare policy	38	77
Terrorism	42	74
The way income and wealth are distributed in the U.S.	35	71
Foreign affairs	28	61
Immigration	25	59
Race relations	26	55

May 6-7, 2015

International matters have taken on increasing prominence in recent months as the Obama administration has dealt with challenges arising from the growing influence of Islamic terrorists in Iraq and Syria, ongoing conflict in the Middle East and significant policy disagreements with Russia. Terrorism, specifically, ranks fairly high on Americans' list of top election issues, as it typically does. Foreign affairs more broadly, however, ranks behind several issues, including the way government operates in Washington, healthcare policy and the distribution of wealth and income in the U.S. Race relations and immigration have also been major news stories in recent months, but on a relative basis, Americans are less likely to say these issues are important to their presidential vote.

Importance of International Matters to Vote Fairly Typical

Americans' ascribed importance to terrorism and foreign affairs as election issues are no higher than what Gallup has measured in past presidential election cycles. The 74% currently saying terrorism will be extremely or very important to their vote is comparable with the averages of 74% in 2012 and 78% in 2008, but lower than the average of 86% in the 2004 cycle, when the 9/11 terror attacks were still fresh in Americans' memories and the Iraq War was becoming more controversial.

Likewise, Americans were more likely to say foreign affairs was important to their vote in the 2004 election cycle, averaging 68%, than in any other recent election cycle, including 1996 (62%), 2000 (58%), or currently (61%). Gallup did not ask Americans to rate foreign affairs as an election issue in the 2008 or 2012 presidential election cycles.

A historical analysis of Gallup's most important problem question back to 1948 confirms that international matters were more salient for Americans in 2004 than other recent elections. Earlier election years, including those in the 1950s and early 1960s during the early part of the Cold War, and in 1968 with the Vietnam War raging, also had high percentages of Americans viewing international matters as the most important problem facing the country. So far in 2015, 18% of Americans have named an international issue as the most important problem facing the country.

International Issues More Important to Republicans

The economy is the top-ranked issue among Republicans, Democrats and independents, with close to 90% of each party group saying the economy will be important to their presidential vote. Party groups diverge, however, on the importance of international matters. Republicans are more likely than Democrats and independents to mention foreign affairs, with a Republican-Democratic gap of 19 percentage points. There is a smaller but still significant 10-point partisan gap in importance ratings of terrorism.

Percentage of Americans Mentioning International Matters as the Most Important Problem Facing the Country, 1948-2015

Figures are annual averages

Averages in presidential election years and 2015 are displayed

Ratings of Issue Importance to Presidential Vote, by Party

Ranked by Republican-Democratic gap

	Republicans	Independents	Democrats	Republican-Democratic gap
	%	%	%	pct. pts.
Foreign affairs	77	55	58	+19
The way government operates in Washington	85	74	74	+11
Immigration	69	54	58	+11
Terrorism	81	72	71	+10
Economy	89	86	85	+4
Healthcare policy	75	73	83	-8
The way income and wealth are distributed in the U.S.	66	72	76	-10
Race relations	49	46	67	-18

May 6-7, 2015

In addition to the two international issues, Republicans also rate the way government operates and immigration as more important election issues than Democrats or independents. Democrats are more likely than Republicans to say race relations, income and wealth inequality, and healthcare are important to their vote. Independents are more similar to Republicans on healthcare and race relations and more similar to Democrats on inequality.

Implications

A healthy economy is fundamental to helping Americans achieve or maintain financial security, so it is not surprising that it usually ranks as the most important election issue for Americans in good economic times and bad. But the economy is far from the only issue that plays a role in determining election outcomes, and the importance of other issues to voters can make a difference. For example, the heightened importance of terrorism and foreign affairs in the post-9/11 era likely helped George W. Bush win re-election in 2004 in a competitive race with John Kerry because voters thought Bush would better handle both Iraq and terrorism than Kerry would.

Americans are not as concerned with international matters as they were back then, even though foreign policy challenges have been some of the more prominent issues in the news over the past year. At this point, the issue mix for 2016 looks to be fairly typical with the economy the top election issue and terrorism and foreign affairs ranking lower and about where they have been historically.

Survey Methods

Results for this Gallup poll are based on telephone interviews conducted May 6–7, 2015, on the Gallup U.S. Daily survey, with a random sample of 1,016 adults, aged 18 and older, living in all 50 U.S. states and the District of Columbia. For results based on the total sample of national adults, the margin of sampling error is ±4 percentage points at the 95% confidence level. All reported margins of sampling error include computed design effects for weighting.

May 18, 2015
IN U.S., MORE SAY ANIMALS SHOULD HAVE SAME RIGHTS AS PEOPLE

by Rebecca Riffkin

Story Highlights

- *A third of Americans want animals to have same rights as people*
- *Support for this view up from 25% in 2008*
- *Majority, 62%, say animals deserve "some protection"*

WASHINGTON, D.C.—Almost a third of Americans, 32%, believe animals should be given the same rights as people, while 62% say they deserve some protection but can still be used for the benefit of humans. The strong animal rights view is up from 2008 when 25% thought animals' rights should be on par with humans'.

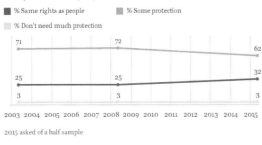

U.S. Support for Animals Having Same Rights as People

Which of these statements comes closest to your view about the treatment of animals: Animals deserve the exact same rights as people to be free from harm and exploitation; animals deserve some protection from harm and exploitation, but it is still appropriate to use them for the benefit of humans; or animals don't need much protection from harm and exploitation since they are just animals?

■ % Same rights as people   ▨ % Some protection
▨ % Don't need much protection

2003 2004 2005 2006 2007 2008 2009 2010 2011 2012 2013 2014 2015

2015 asked of a half sample

GALLUP

Very few Americans, 3%, believe animals require little protection from harm and exploitation "since they are just animals." But, as noted, a modestly increasing minority now believe animals should have the same protection from harm and exploitation as people. Gallup first asked Americans about the rights of animals in 2003 and repeated the question in 2008 and again in the latest May 6–10, 2015, poll.

The percentage of Americans who support the idea that animals' rights should be equal to those of humans increased across all major U.S. demographic groups. Women remain more likely to support this view than men do, but support among both groups has increased by a similar amount since 2008. Similarly, Democrats and Democratic-leaning independents are more supportive of this view

than Republicans and Republican-leaning independents are, but both groups have seen an increase from the last time Gallup asked them. There continues to be little difference between younger and older Americans.

Percentage of Americans Saying Animals Deserve Same Rights as People, by Demographic Group

	2008	2015
	%	%
Men	14	22
Women	35	42
Democrats/Democratic-leaning independents	27	39
Republicans/Republican-leaning independents	19	23
Aged 18 to 49	22	31
Aged 50+	28	33

GALLUP

Most Concern for Treatment of Animals in Circuses, Sports, Research

To further discern Americans' feelings about animal rights, for the first time, Gallup asked Americans about their level of concern for the treatment of animals in various settings. The percentage saying they are "very" concerned ranges from 33% for animals used in research to 21% for animals in the zoo. When combined with those "somewhat" concerned about each, Americans are most concerned about animals in the circus, animals used in competitive animal sports or contests and animals used in research, with just over two-thirds expressing concern about each. They are least concerned about the treatment of household pets, with 46% saying they are very or somewhat concerned.

Americans' Concerns With Animal Treatment in Various Settings

In general, how concerned are you about the way each of the following types of animals is currently treated in the U.S. today -- very concerned, somewhat concerned, not too concerned or not at all concerned?

	Very concerned	Very/Somewhat concerned
	%	%
Animals in the circus	31	69
Animals used in competitive animal sports/contests	32	68
Animals used in research	33	67
Marine animals at amusement parks/aquariums	25	62
Animals in the zoo	21	57
Livestock and other animals raised for food	26	54
Household pets	22	46

May 6-10, 2015
Sorted by "% Very/Somewhat concerned"

GALLUP

Overall, Americans are a bit less concerned about the treatment of marine animals in amusement parks and aquariums (62% are very/somewhat concerned) and animals in the zoo (57%) than about the treatment of circus animals.

The level of concern for marine animals is especially intriguing after documentaries such as *Blackfish* claimed to expose the truth about the treatment and status of animals in captivity. After the release of *Blackfish*, the stock price of SeaWorld dropped substantially, and some lawmakers have discussed banning the use of orcas in shows.

And despite increasing attention focused on the treatment of chickens, cows and other animals mainly used for human food—as exposed in the 2008 documentary *Food, Inc.*—Americans show relatively less concern for how these animals are treated, with 54% at least somewhat concerned, including 26% very concerned.

While the fewest Americans are concerned about the treatment of household pets, still close to half are very or somewhat concerned. This may be prompted by publicity aimed at stopping cruelty toward pets, including a long-running, poignant commercial for the American Society for the Prevention of Cruelty to Animals (ASPCA) showing abused and neglected dogs and cats.

Bottom Line

Animal rights have been top of mind for Americans in recent years because of an increasing number of films and news stories depicting the poor treatment of animals. Congress requested a review of a government-funded animal research lab in late 2014, and cosmetics testing on animals was banned in the European Union in 2013. Ringling Brothers recently announced that it will retire its circus elephants by 2018, a decision that comes after years of allegations of animal abuse and complaints that circus acts are disrespectful to animals. Organized segments of the American public are very vocal about protecting animal rights, with groups such as People for the Ethical Treatment of Animals (PETA) even creating advertisements for prime-time events such as the Super Bowl.

Traditionally, the Bible gives humans domain over animals, and specifies that animals don't have souls—but also warns that righteous men should have regard for the lives of their animals, a view that could still influence religious Americans.

While it is not clear which, if any, of these factors have influenced public opinion, it is clear that Americans have become more likely to believe that animals should have the same rights and protections as people, though this still remains the minority viewpoint.

Survey Methods

Results for this Gallup poll are based on telephone interviews conducted May 6–10, 2015, on the Gallup U.S. Daily survey, with a random sample of 1,024 adults, aged 18 and older, living in all 50 U.S. states and the District of Columbia. For results based on the sample of 497 national adults who were asked about the protection of animals, the margin of sampling error is ±5 percentage points at the 95% confidence level. For results based on the sample of 527 national adults who were asked about their concern for animals in various settings, the margin of sampling error is ±5 percentage points at the 95% confidence level. All reported margins of sampling error include computed design effects for weighting.

May 19, 2015
RECORD-HIGH 60% OF AMERICANS SUPPORT SAME-SEX MARRIAGE

by Justin McCarthy

Story Highlights

- *At 60%, support is up five percentage points from 2014*
- *Gay marriage support reaches new highs in all political parties*
- *One in four say candidates must share their views on the issue*

WASHINGTON, D.C.—Sixty percent of Americans now support same-sex marriage as the Supreme Court prepares to rule on its constitutionality next month. This is up from 55% last year and is the highest Gallup has found on the question since it was first asked in 1996.

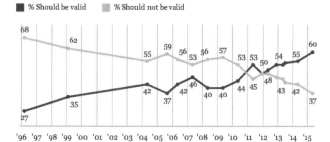

Do you think marriages between same-sex couples should or should not be recognized by the law as valid, with the same rights as traditional marriages?

Note: Trend shown for polls in which same-sex marriage question followed questions on gay/lesbian rights and relations
1996-2005 wording: "Do you think marriages between homosexuals ..."

GALLUP

Public support for the legality of same-sex marriage first reached a majority in 2011, when 53% supported it. Since then, support has ranged from 48% to 55%. The five-percentage-point increase in this year's Values and Beliefs poll, conducted May 6–10, is the largest year-to-year climb since 2011, when support rose by nine points.

Support for the legality of gay marriages in the U.S. has been a fast-changing trend. Just two decades ago, only 27% of Americans backed gay marriage, while 68% opposed. By 2005, the percentage in favor had increased by 10 points to 37%, and by 2010 it had reached 44%.

The record high in support comes roughly one month before the Supreme Court is to issue a ruling on the constitutionality of same-sex marriage. Americans, at this point, are not highly familiar with the case, with 42% following it closely—well below the average 60% for news issues Gallup has measured over the past two decades. Attention to the case is similar among supporters and opponents of gay marriage.

New Highs in Support Across Party Spectrum

Though same-sex marriage continues to be politically divisive, support for its legal status has reached new highs among Americans of all political stripes—with Democrats at 76% support, independents at 64% and Republicans at 37%.

In general, Democrats have been the most likely to say gay marriage should be legal, and Republicans have been the least supportive. Independents typically fall in between but side closer to Democrats than to Republicans.

From a long-range perspective, Democrats' support has increased the most, by 43 points since 1996. That was the year Democratic President Bill Clinton signed into law the now-overturned Defense of Marriage Act (DOMA), which barred federal recognition of state-granted gay marriages. Since then, the Democratic Party has undergone a complete makeover on the issue, and its members have been champions of marriage equality on the state level. Democrats' support for same-sex marriage first reached majority level in 2004, the same year Massachusetts became the first state to legalize it.

Support for Same-Sex Marriage, by Party

Do you think marriages between same-sex couples should or should not be recognized by the law as valid, with the same rights as traditional marriages?

% Should be valid

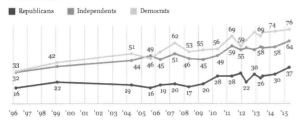

Note: Trend shown for polls in which same-sex marriage question followed questions on gay/lesbian rights and relations

1996-2005 wording: "Do you think marriages between homosexuals ..."

GALLUP

Republicans have consistently been the least likely to say same-sex marriage should be legal, and their support has increased the least since 1996, by 21 points. Between 1996 and 2009, no more than 20% of Republicans believed same-sex marriages should be legally valid. Since then, support has ranged from 22% to 31%, leading up to this year's high of 37%.

The party divide between Democrats and Republicans may hinge largely on the age groups that compose each party. Gallup has found that younger Americans are significantly more likely to lean Democratic, while older Americans skew Republican. And while majorities of each age group under 65 support marriage equality in 2015, those aged 65 and older are still more likely to oppose it. This is a new phenomenon for the 50- to 64-year-old group. Last year, just 48% of these middle-aged Americans supported legally recognizing gay marriage. But in 2015, this figure has climbed to a majority of 54%.

One in Four Americans Say Candidates Must Share Their Views on Gay Marriage

About a quarter of Americans (26%) say they vote for a political candidate solely based on his or her stance on gay marriage. Many others say it is but one of several important factors (43%), and about one in four say it is not a major issue influencing how they vote (26%).

The 26% of American adults who say a candidate must share his or her views on the issue of same-sex marriage is up from just 16% in 2004 and 2008.

Importance of Candidates' Stance on Gay Marriage in How Americans Vote

Thinking about how the gay marriage issue might affect your vote for major offices, would you -- [ROTATED: only vote for a candidate who shares your views on gay marriage, consider a candidate's position on gay marriage as just one of many important factors when voting, or would you not see gay marriage as a major issue]?

	Candidate must share views	One of many important factors	Not a major issue
	%	%	%
May 6-10, 2015	26	43	26
May 8-11, 2008	16	49	33
May 2-4, 2004	16	46	35

GALLUP

Those who are opposed to gay marriage are a good deal more likely to say that a candidate's stance on the issue can make or break whether that candidate receives their vote (37%) than those who are supportive of gay marriage (21%). And both are more likely to say the issue is a defining factor than they have been in the past.

Americans Who Say Candidate Must Share Views on Gay Marriage

% Candidate must share views

	Pro-gay marriage	Anti-gay marriage
May 6-10, 2015	21	37
May 8-11, 2008	2	26
May 2-4, 2004	5	23

GALLUP

On both ends of the political spectrum, this could make same-sex marriage a more salient issue in the 2016 election than it has been previously. While pro–gay marriage voters are more likely to hold a political candidate's feet to the fire than in the past, there is an even larger bloc of anti–gay marriage voters who could reject a candidate for espousing marriage equality.

Implications

National support for marriage equality has been fairly steady in its upward climb, and is more than double what it was in 1996 when Gallup first polled on the issue. A clear majority of Americans now support the issue. The increase among Americans—an increase seen in all major political parties—comes in the midst of a string of legal victories ruling in favor of same-sex couples seeking to be treated equally under the law.

The Supreme Court may issue the final word on the constitutionality of same-sex marriage next month, although it's certainly possible that it may issue a narrow ruling on technical aspects of same-sex marriage law rather than say it should be legal in all states. With the ideological make-up of the court, it could decide that same-sex marriage is not a constitutionally supported right—though this is a less likely outcome, and would go against prevailing public opinion.

While there has been uneven growth in support among Republicans versus Democrats, both groups have become more supportive. The remaining broad partisan divide, however, underscores how contentious the issue will continue to be as the 2016 election process unfolds.

As Hillary Clinton seeks the Democratic nomination in 2016, her support for gay marriage may be even more important as her party embraces the platform more closely than it has in the past. Clinton, like President Barack Obama, changed her stance in 2013 upon her exit from the State Department.

So far, none of the Republicans who have announced their 2016 candidacy support gay marriage, and neither have any potential candidates who are expected to officially throw their hats in the ring. Former Florida Gov. Jeb Bush, who is widely viewed as a top 2016 contender, recently doubled down on his stance against gay marriage—a move consistent with the opinions of rank-and-file Republicans who, despite showing increased support for gay marriage, still oppose it outright. While an anti-same-sex marriage position should not present a challenge for GOP candidates in the primary, it could be more challenging in a general election setting given majority support among all Americans. At the same time, same-sex marriage, like many other moral issues, tends to rank well behind issues such as the economy, terrorism and education when Americans name the issues that are most likely to influence their vote.

Survey Methods

Results for this Gallup poll are based on telephone interviews conducted May 6–10, 2015, on the Gallup U.S. Daily survey, with a random sample of 1,024 adults, aged 18 and older, living in all 50 U.S. states and the District of Columbia. For results based on the total sample of national adults, the margin of sampling error is ±4 percentage points at the 95% confidence level. All reported margins of sampling error include computed design effects for weighting.

Each sample of national adults includes a minimum quota of 50% cellphone respondents and 50% landline respondents, with additional minimum quotas by time zone within region. Landline and cellular telephone numbers are selected using random-digit-dial methods.

May 20, 2015
MAJORITY IN U.S. NOW SAY GAYS AND LESBIANS BORN, NOT MADE

by Jeffrey M. Jones

Story Highlights

- *51% of Americans say people are born gay or lesbian*
- *30% say upbringing, environment determine sexual orientation*
- *New high of 63% say gay relations morally acceptable*

PRINCETON, N.J.—For the first time, a majority of Americans say same-sex orientation is something gays and lesbians are born with rather than something that is determined by their upbringing or environment. Over the past 15 years, Americans had been much more closely divided on the issue. And in the 1970s and 1980s, majorities attributed same-sex orientation to environmental factors rather than innate characteristics.

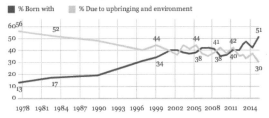

Origins of Same-Sex Orientation: Innate or Environmental?

In your view, is being gay or lesbian -- [ROTATED: something a person is born with, (or) due to factors such as upbringing and environment]?

1977-2008 wording: In your view, is homosexuality -- [ROTATED: something a person is born with, (or is homosexuality) due to factors such as upbringing and environment]?

GALLUP

The current results are based on a May 6–10 Gallup poll that updates several long-standing trend questions on gay and lesbian rights. The poll also finds a new high in support for same-sex marriage.

The question of whether people with same-sex orientation are born that way has been a recent issue in the presidential campaign. Republican candidate Dr. Ben Carson set off a minor controversy when he suggested people "absolutely" choose to be gay or lesbian, citing same-sex activity among prisoners as evidence. He later apologized for those comments. Another Republican candidate, Marco Rubio, addressed the issue directly, saying that while he does not

support same-sex marriage, he does believe people are born gay or lesbian.

Neither viewpoint is out of step with the views of GOP supporters, as Republicans, including Republican-leaning independents, are evenly divided on whether Americans are born gay or lesbian (40%) or whether same-sex orientation is determined by environmental factors (36%). However, even that is a dramatic shift for Republicans, as it represents the first time they have not attributed being gay or lesbian to environmental factors by at least a small margin.

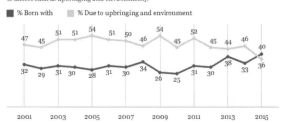

Origins of Same-Sex Orientation, Among Republicans and Republican-Leaning Independents, Recent Trend

In your view, is being gay or lesbian -- [ROTATED: something a person is born with, (or) due to factors such as upbringing and environment]?

2001-2008 wording: In your view, is homosexuality -- [ROTATED: something a person is born with, (or is homosexuality) due to factors such as upbringing and environment]?

GALLUP

Democrats' views have also evolved, although the transformation took place further in the past. In 2001, Democrats and Democratic leaners were divided on the origins of same-sex orientation, but since then have shown a clear tendency to believe that it is an innate characteristic, with 62% holding that view this year.

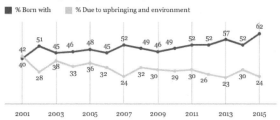

Origins of Same-Sex Orientation, Among Democrats and Democratic-Leaning Independents, Recent Trend

In your view, is being gay or lesbian -- [ROTATED: something a person is born with, (or) due to factors such as upbringing and environment]?

2001-2008 wording: In your view, is homosexuality -- [ROTATED: something a person is born with, (or is homosexuality) due to factors such as upbringing and environment]?

GALLUP

New High Describe Same-Sex Relations as "Morally Acceptable"

In addition to their changing views on the origins of being gay or lesbian, Americans' views on the morality of same-sex relations have also shifted in recent years. Currently, a record-high 63% of Americans describe gay or lesbian relations as "morally acceptable." That became the majority view in 2010. Only a decade ago, a majority thought same-sex relations were morally wrong.

Since 2001, increasing percentages of both Republicans and Democrats say gay or lesbian relations are morally acceptable, though Democrats continue to be much more likely to express that view. Notably, for the first time, a majority of Republicans believe that same-sex relations are morally acceptable. Democrats crossed the majority threshold more than a decade ago.

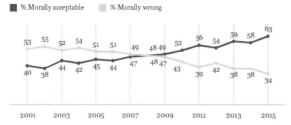

Americans' Views of the Morality of Gay or Lesbian Relations

Regardless of whether or not you think it should be legal, for each one, please tell me
whether you personally believe that in general it is morally acceptable or morally wrong.
How about – Gay or lesbian relations?

■ % Morally acceptable   ▓ % Morally wrong

2006-2008 wording: Homosexual relations; 2001-2004 wording: Homosexual behavior

GALLUP

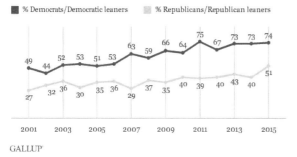

Views of the Morality of Gay or Lesbian Relations, by Political Party

Figures are percentages viewing gay or lesbian relations as "morally acceptable"

■ % Democrats/Democratic leaners   ▓ % Republicans/Republican leaners

GALLUP

Implications

Across a number of different measures, Americans are clearly
becoming more accepting of gays and lesbians, both in terms of
viewing same-sex relations as morally acceptable and supporting
legal same-sex marriage. And this year for the first time, a majority
of Americans say they believe that being gay or lesbian is something
people are born with, rather than a product of their environment.

These trends are evident among Republicans as well as Democrats, although Democrats continue to be much more accepting than
Republicans. Still, this year may mark a key milestone in Republicans' views on same-sex relations. A majority of Republicans now
describe same-sex relations as morally acceptable and they are now
equally likely to view same-sex orientation as an inherent characteristic rather than a choice or a consequence of how people were
raised.

The recent trends toward Americans' increasing acceptance of
gays and lesbians still show no sign of leveling off, and should continue to rise in the future, given that younger Americans are much
more likely than older Americans to express positive views of same-
sex relations.

Survey Methods

Results for this Gallup poll are based on telephone interviews conducted May 6–10, 2015, with a random sample of 1,024 adults,
aged 18 and older, living in all 50 U.S. states and the District of
Columbia. For results based on the total sample of national adults,
the margin of sampling error is ±4 percentage points at the 95%
confidence level.

May 21, 2015
OBAMA FAVORABLE RATING UP, BEST SINCE SEPTEMBER 2013

by Justin McCarthy

Story Highlights

- *At 53%, favorable rating up four points from March*
- *Favorable and job approval ratings usually move in tandem*
- *Favorable ratings continue to vary by party identification*

WASHINGTON, D.C.—Americans' favorable ratings of President
Barack Obama now stand at 53%, up four points from March. This
comes after a year in which these ratings were mostly below 50%
and marks the president's highest score since September 2013.

Personal Favorability Ratings of President Barack Obama

■ % Favorable

GALLUP

A president's favorable ratings are distinct from approval of
his performance; job approval ratings generally tend to be lower.
For the Obama presidency, Gallup trends show the two measures
have changed largely in tandem. As Obama's approval rating has
rebounded nine percentage points from a low of 37% last fall, his
favorable rating has increased 11 points from 42%. The resulting
seven-point gap between Obama's current 46% approval rating and
his 53% favorable rating is slightly larger than the average five-point
gap between these ratings for Obama since he took office.

The gap between job approval and favorable ratings over the
course of Obama's presidency has been as wide as eight points, and
as narrow as two points. The latter took place just after Obama was
re-elected, in November 2012, when his favorable rating was 58%
and his job approval was 56%.

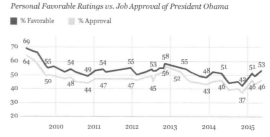

Personal Favorable Ratings vs. Job Approval of President Obama

■ % Favorable   ▓ % Approval

Figures shown only for dates in which favorable and job approval ratings were measured
in the same poll

GALLUP

Independents' Favorable Ratings of Obama Surge Since Last Fall

Obama's favorable rating in the May 6–10 poll reflects increases
compared with November 2014 among Democrats (90%) and

independents (52%). Republicans, on the other hand, continue to be chilly toward the president; their favorable ratings of Obama have been largely flat at low levels since last fall.

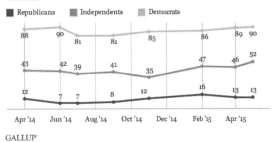

Favorable Ratings of Barack Obama, by Party -- April 2014-May 2015

% Favorable

■ Republicans ■ Independents ▨ Democrats

GALLUP'

Bottom Line

Americans in general are more inclined to give Obama a favorable personal rating than they are to approve of the job he is doing. Obama's favorable and job approval ratings have each improved this year, and his current 53% favorable rating is the highest since late 2013.

The recent increase in how Americans view Obama, and likely also his performance, might have something to do with his attempts to bridge various communities in recent months—such as police and racial minorities, Cuba and the U.S., and members of Congress from both parties who are pro- and anti-trade.

As he serves out his seventh year in office, Obama's favorability is higher than it was in his sixth year, when he received a record-low rating after the 2014 midterm elections. Excluding his first year, when his favorable ratings averaged 62%, his favorables have been fairly steady—as have his job approval ratings.

Depending on how the final 20 months of his presidency go, Obama's relatively buoyant favorability might stand in stark contrast to that of his two predecessors—President Bill Clinton, whose yearly averages peaked in his fifth year and dipped thereafter, and President George W. Bush, whose favorable ratings spiked early on in his presidency and descended rapidly in his second term.

Survey Methods

Results for this Gallup poll are based on telephone interviews conducted May 6–10, 2015, on the Gallup U.S. Daily survey, with a random sample of 1,024 adults, aged 18 and older, living in all 50 U.S. states and the District of Columbia. For results based on the total sample of national adults, the margin of sampling error is ±4 percentage points at the 95% confidence level. All reported margins of sampling error include computed design effects for weighting.

May 21, 2015
AMERICANS STILL SPENDING MORE, STILL NOT ON WHAT THEY WANT

by John Fleming

Story Highlights

- *A majority in U.S. say they are spending more on groceries, 55%*
- *Consumer spending on gasoline is way down from last year*
- *Not as much spending on consumer electronics, leisure activities*

PRINCETON, N.J.—A majority of Americans, 55%, say they are spending more than they did last year on groceries, the area in which Americans continually report spending more.

Spending More Compared to One Year Ago

Are you spending more compared to last year?

	Q2 2014	Q3 2014	Q4 2014	Q1 2015	Pct. Pt. Change (Q2 2014-Q1 2015)
	%	%	%	%	%
TOP 5 CATEGORIES					
Groceries	58	59	57	55	-3
Utilities	42	45	43	45	3
Healthcare	41	42	42	43	2
Cable or Satellite	30	33	33	32	2
Rent or Mortgage	34	32	30	31	-3
BOTTOM 5 CATEGORIES					
Gasoline or Fuel	50	58	31	21	-29
Internet	23	21	22	20	-3
Travel	28	26	24	19	-9
Consumer Electronics	21	20	22	18	-3
Retirement Investments	16	18	19	17	1

Q1 2015 data collected Feb 23-Mar 3, 2015

GALLUP'

Since last June, the top three categories with the highest percentages of consumers saying they are "spending more" (groceries, utilities and healthcare) have stayed in the top five. Of these, only groceries showed a modest decline in the percentage of Americans saying they are spending more (three percentage points), while utilities and healthcare both inched up slightly (three points and two points, respectively). None of these changes, however, are statistically significant.

Consistent with the steep decline in gas prices over the past year, the only category to show a major shift in spending is "gasoline or fuel," in which 21% of Americans in March said they were spending more, compared with 50% in June 2014. Thirteen percent said they were spending less on gas last June compared with 55% this March. The net spending difference has shifted from +37 (spending more minus spending less) to -34.

Over the past nine months, there has been a general but modest decline in net spending across almost all spending categories, driven by a decreasing number of Americans saying they are spending more on each category. The exceptions to this general trend are leisure activities (+3), cable or satellite (+4), utilities (+5) and healthcare (+3), areas where more Americans say they are spending more than a year ago and fewer say they are spending less.

Americans continue to spend more on things they need, but not on things they want. All five categories of discretionary purchases—leisure activities, clothing, consumer electronics, dining out and travel—continue to have negative net spending with substantially more Americans saying they are spending less than last year than those who say they are spending more. As household essentials claim a larger slice of Americans' spending, less remains for discretionary purchases.

Net Consumer Spending Compared to a Year Ago

	Q2 2014	Q3 2014	Q4 2014	Q1 2015	Pct. Pt. Change (Q2 2014-Q1 2015)
TOP 6 CATEGORIES					
Groceries	45	49	46	42	-3
Utilities	30	35	33	35	5
Healthcare	29	34	29	32	3
Rent or Mortgage	23	23	19	19	-4
Cable or Satellite	14	18	18	18	4
Household Goods Such as Cleaning Supplies	23	27	23	16	-7
BOTTOM 6 CATEGORIES					
Leisure Activities	-10	-3	-14	-7	3
Clothing	-9	-5	-5	-9	NC
Consumer Electronics	-10	-11	-12	-13	-3
Dining Out	-18	-12	-16	-18	NC
Travel	-11	-12	-20	-20	-9
Gasoline or Fuel	37	46	-6	-34	-71

NOTE: Net Spending is the percentage of respondents saying they spent more on the category compared to last year minus the percentage saying they spent less.

GALLUP

These data suggest that at least some of the money that is not being spent on gas is going into discretionary spending categories—leisure activities and dining out—which either showed an increase in net spending or showed a modest increase in the percentage of those saying they are spending more today than a year ago. But some of the money that Americans are not spending on gas is going to other non-discretionary categories—cable or satellite, utilities and healthcare. These three categories were among the four to show increases in net spending over the past nine months.

Americans may be letting their gas savings remain in their bank accounts or perhaps moving those funds into savings accounts—rather than actively redirecting them to other areas of spending. Of course, other uses for this gas-driven windfall are possible too.

Implications

After nine months of following Americans' self-reported spending patterns, several conclusions seem warranted. First, net spending—the percentage of Americans reporting that they are spending more within a category minus the percentage saying they are spending less—seems to be fairly stable for all categories except gas or fuel. This could be attributable, in part, to the possibility that self-reports of spending may be less sensitive to actual spending fluctuations than to dramatic shifts in spending, such as the change in spending on gasoline. People may simply be inclined to overlook smaller spending changes when they discuss it. Second, gas prices have actually declined precipitously over the past nine months, and this

decline is clearly reflected in Americans' perceptions of their spending. Third, net spending appears to be on a modest downward trend with the percentage of Americans reporting that they are spending more within a category and the percentage saying they are spending less moving closer together. Finally, the overall order of the spending categories based on net spending hasn't changed much since Gallup began measuring spending in this way. Three of the top four net spending categories back in June 2014—groceries, utilities and healthcare—all remain at the top. Four of the bottom five net spending categories remain at the bottom—travel, dining out, consumer electronics and clothing.

As the summer travel season begins, it will be interesting to see whether American consumers report spending more on gas and whether they say they are spending more on travel and leisure activities.

Survey Methods

Results for this Gallup poll are based on telephone interviews conducted Feb. 23–March 3, 2015, with a random sample of 1,525 adults, aged 18 and older, living in all 50 U.S. states and the District of Columbia. For results based on the total sample of national adults, the margin of sampling error is ±2.5 percentage points at the 95% confidence level. For comparisons between or within the total sample for each generation, the margin of sampling error is ±5.9 percentage points at the 95% confidence level.

May 21, 2015
AMERICANS GREATLY OVERESTIMATE PERCENT GAY, LESBIAN IN U.S.

by Frank Newport

Story Highlights

- *Estimate is similar to what was measured in 2011 and 2002*
- *Latest estimate shows that 3.8% actually identify as LGBT*
- *Estimates are lower among those with the most education*

PRINCETON, N.J.—The American public estimates on average that 23% of Americans are gay or lesbian, little changed from Americans' 25% estimate in 2011, and only slightly higher than separate 2002 estimates of the gay and lesbian population. These estimates are many times higher than the 3.8% of the adult population who identified themselves as lesbian, gay, bisexual or transgender in Gallup Daily tracking in the first four months of this year.

The stability of these estimates over time contrasts with the major shifts in Americans' attitudes about the morality and legality of gay and lesbian relations in the past two decades. Whereas 38% of Americans said gay and lesbian relations were morally acceptable in 2002, that number has risen to 63% today. And while 35% of Americans favored legalized same-sex marriage in 1999, 60% favor it today.

The U.S. Census Bureau documents the number of individuals living in same-sex households but has not historically identified individuals as gay or lesbian per se. Several other surveys, governmental and non-governmental, have over the years measured sexual orientation, but the largest such study by far has been the Gallup Daily tracking measure instituted in June 2012. In this ongoing study, respondents are asked "Do you, personally, identify as lesbian, gay, bisexual or transgender?" with 3.8% being the most recent result, obtained from more than 58,000 interviews conducted in the first four months of this year.

Just your best guess, what percent of Americans today would you say are gay or lesbian?

All numbers are in percentages

	Mean	Less than 5%	5% to <10%	10% to <15%	15% to <20%	20% to 25%	More than 25%	No opin.
2015	23	9	11	14	7	20	33	6
2011	25	4	9	17	9	17	35	8
2002*								
Men	21	8	11	16	9	15	25	16
Women	22	7	14	12	7	17	24	19

*Asked of a half sample with wording, with separate questions:
Just your best guess, what percent of men in the United States today would you say are homosexual or gay?
Just your best guess, what percent of women in the United States today would you say are homosexual or lesbian?

GALLUP

As Gallup pointed out in its initial report of LGBT data in 2012, "Exactly who makes up the LGBT community and how this group should be measured is a subject of some debate," and "There are a number of ways to measure lesbian, gay, and bisexual orientation, and transgender status. Sexual orientation can be assessed by measuring identity as well as sexual behaviors and attractions." Thus, even though these large sample sizes provide great precision regarding the specific measure used, they do not represent the only way to estimate the percentage of the population that is gay or lesbian.

Still, all available estimates of the actual gay and lesbian population in the U.S. are far lower than what the public estimates, and no measurement procedure has produced any figures suggesting that more than one out of five Americans are gay or lesbian. The widely off-the-mark nature of Americans' estimates is underscored by the finding that in the most recent update, from May 6–10, only 9% of Americans estimate that the gay and lesbian population is less than 5%—where Gallup's tracking figure would put it—while at the other end of the spectrum, 33% estimate it as more than 25%.

Part of the explanation for the inaccurate estimates of the gay and lesbian population rests with Americans' general unfamiliarity with numbers and demography. Previous research has shown that Americans estimate that a third of the U.S. population is black, and believe almost three in 10 are Hispanic, more than twice what the actual percentages were as measured by the census at the time of the research. Americans with the highest levels of education make the lowest estimates of the gay and lesbian population, underscoring the assumption that part of the reason for the overestimate is a lack of exposure to demographic data. Still, the average estimate among those with postgraduate education is 15%, four times the actual rate. Younger Americans give higher estimates than those who are older, and women make significantly higher guesses of the gay and lesbian population than men do.

Republicans and conservatives are much less likely than others to consider gay and lesbian relations morally acceptable and to favor legalized same-sex marriage, and Republicans provide estimates of the gay and lesbian population that are somewhat lower than those made by other party groups. Similarly, those who are opposed to

legalized same-sex marriage give modestly lower estimates of the gay population than those who favor it. The causality in these relationships could run both ways; attitudes toward gays and lesbians could be conditioned by views of how prevalent they are in the population, or estimates of their prevalence could reflect underlying attitudes toward the group.

Americans' Estimate of the U.S. Gay/Lesbian Population

By key demographic groups

	Mean estimate %
18 to 29	28
30 to 49	24
50 to 64	21
65+	20
Men	19
Women	27
Postgraduates	15
College graduates	17
Some college	25
High school or less	28

May 6–10, 2015

GALLUP

Americans' Estimate of the U.S. Gay/Lesbian Population

By party, ideology and views on same-sex relations

	Mean estimate %
Democrats	25
Independents	24
Republicans	19
Social liberals	24
Social moderates	24
Social conservatives	21
Same-sex marriage should be valid	25
Same-sex marriage should not be valid	21

May 6–10, 2015

GALLUP

Bottom Line

Americans perceive that more than one in five Americans are gay or lesbian, far greater than the actual rate as measured by self-reports on Gallup Daily tracking. Some of the overestimation may reflect Americans' lack of knowledge about social statistics and demography, which is supported by Americans' historical tendency to overestimate the prevalence of other subgroups in the U.S. population. The overestimation may also reflect prominent media portrayals of gay characters on television and in movies, even as far back as 2002, and perhaps the high visibility of activists who have pushed gay causes, particularly legalizing same-sex marriage. Still, the estimates of gay and lesbian percentages have been relatively stable compared with those measured in 2011 and 2002, even though attitudes about gays and lesbians have changed dramatically over that time.

Results for this Gallup poll are based on telephone interviews conducted May 6–10, 2015, with a random sample of 1,024 adults, aged 18 and older, living in all 50 U.S. states and the District of Columbia. For results based on the total sample of national adults, the margin of sampling error is ±4 percentage points at the 95% confidence level. All reported margins of sampling error include computed design effects for weighting.

May 22, 2015
ON SOCIAL IDEOLOGY, THE LEFT CATCHES UP TO THE RIGHT

by Jeffrey M. Jones

Story Highlights

- *31% say they are socially liberal, 31% socially conservative*
- *This is the first time conservatives have not outnumbered liberals*
- *Conservatives maintain edge on economic issues*

PRINCETON, N.J.—Thirty-one percent of Americans describe their views on social issues as generally liberal, matching the percentage who identify as social conservatives for the first time in Gallup records dating back to 1999.

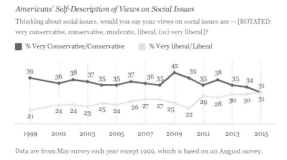

Americans' Self-Description of Views on Social Issues

Thinking about social issues, would you say your views on social issues are -- [ROTATED: very conservative, conservative, moderate, liberal, (or) very liberal]?

Data are from May survey each year except 1999, which is based on an August survey.

GALLUP

Gallup first asked Americans to describe their views on social issues in 1999, and has repeated the question at least annually since 2001. The broad trend has been toward a shrinking conservative advantage, although that was temporarily interrupted during the first two years of Barack Obama's presidency. Since then, the conservative advantage continued to diminish until it was wiped out this year.

The newfound parity on social ideology is a result of changes in the way both Democrats and Republicans describe their social views. The May 6–10 Gallup poll finds a new high of 53% of Democrats, including Democratic-leaning independents, describing their views on social issues as liberal.

Democrats were more likely to describe their views on social issues as moderate rather than liberal from 2001 to 2005. Since then, socially liberal Democrats have outnumbered socially moderate Democrats in all but one year.

Meanwhile, the 53% of Republicans and Republican leaners saying their views on social issues are conservative is the lowest in Gallup's trend. The drop in Republicans' self-identified social

conservatism has been accompanied by an increase in moderate identification, to 34%, while the percentage identifying as socially liberal has been static near 10%.

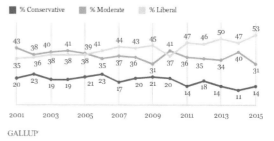

Ideological Identification on Social Issues, Democrats and Democratic Leaners, 2001-2015

GALLUP

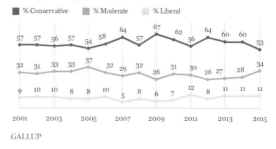

Ideological Identification on Social Issues, Republicans and Republican Leaners, 2001-2015

GALLUP

These trends echo the pattern in Gallup's overall ideology measure, which dates back to 1992 and shows increasing liberal identification in recent years. As with the social ideology measure, the longer-term shifts are mainly a result of increasing numbers of Democrats describing their views as liberal rather than moderate. That may reflect Democrats feeling more comfortable in describing themselves as liberal than they were in the past, as much as a more leftward shift in Democrats' attitudes on political, economic and social issues.

Conservatives Still Lead Liberals on Economic Issues

In contrast to the way Americans describe their views on social issues, they still by a wide margin, 39% to 19%, describe their views on economic issues as conservative rather than liberal. However, as on social ideology, the gap between conservatives and liberals has been shrinking and is lower today than at any point since 1999, with the 39% saying they are economically conservative the lowest to date.

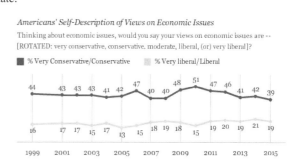

Americans' Self-Description of Views on Economic Issues

Thinking about economic issues, would you say your views on economic issues are -- [ROTATED: very conservative, conservative, moderate, liberal, (or) very liberal]?

Data are from May survey each year except 1999, which is based on an August survey.

GALLUP

Currently, 64% of Republicans identify as conservative economically, which is down from 70% the previous two years and roughly 75% in the early years of the Obama presidency. During George W. Bush's administration, Republicans were less likely to say they were economic conservatives, with as few as 58% doing so in 2004 and 2005. The trends suggest Republicans' willingness to identify as economic conservatives, or economic moderates, is influenced by the party of the president in office, and perhaps the types of financial policies the presidential administration is pursuing at the time.

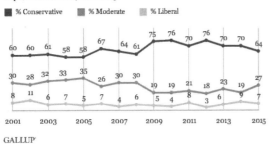

Ideological Identification on Economic Issues, Republicans and Republican Leaners, 2001-2015

Democrats are also contributing to the trend in lower economic conservative identification. While the plurality of Democrats have consistently said they are economically moderate, Democrats have been more likely to identify as economic liberals than as economic conservatives since 2007. The last two years, there has been a 15-percentage-point gap in liberal versus conservative identification among Democrats on economic matters.

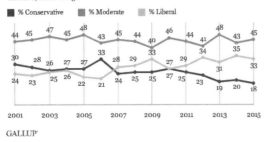

Ideological Identification on Economic Issues, Democrats and Democratic Leaners, 2001-2015

Implications

Americans' growing social liberalism is evident not only in how they describe their views on social issues but also in changes in specific attitudes, such as increased support for same-sex marriage and legalizing marijuana. These longer-term trends may be attributable to changing attitudes among Americans of all ages, but they also may be a result of population changes, with younger, more liberal Americans entering adulthood while older, more conservative adults pass on. Gallup found evidence that population replacement is a factor in explaining changes in overall ideology using an analysis of birth cohorts over time.

The 2016 presidential election will thus be contested in a more socially liberal electorate—and a less economically conservative one—than was true of prior elections. Economically and socially conservative candidates may still appeal to the Republican Party base in the primaries, but it may be more important now than in

the past for the GOP nominee to be a bit less conservative on social issues in order to appeal to the broader general electorate.

And while Americans are less economically conservative than in the past, economic conservatives still outnumber economic liberals by about 2 to 1. As a result, Democrats must be careful not to nominate a candidate who is viewed as too liberal on economic matters if their party hopes to hold the White House beyond 2016.

Survey Methods

Results for this Gallup poll are based on telephone interviews conducted May 6–10, 2015, with a random sample of 1,024 adults, aged 18 and older, living in all 50 U.S. states and the District of Columbia. For results based on the total sample of national adults, the margin of sampling error is ±4 percentage points at the 95% confidence level. All reported margins of sampling error include computed design effects for weighting.

May 26, 2015
OBESITY RATE LOWEST IN HAWAII, HIGHEST IN MISSISSIPPI

by Justin McCarthy and Diana Liu

Story Highlights

- *Nationally, obesity rate rises to 27.7% in 2014*
- *Obesity rates highest in Southern and Midwestern states*
- *Higher obesity rates linked to lower well-being*

WASHINGTON, D.C.—Hawaii residents were the least likely to be obese in 2014, and Hawaii was the only state where fewer than one in five residents are obese. Mississippi had the highest obesity rate in the nation for the second year in a row, at 35.2%.

States With Lowest Obesity Rates	% Obese	States With Highest Obesity Rates	% Obese
Hawaii	19.0	Mississippi	35.2
Colorado	20.3	West Virginia	34.3
Montana	23.5	Louisiana	33.2
California	23.9	Arkansas	33.0
Massachusetts	24.0	Oklahoma	32.6
Idaho	24.2	Alabama	32.1
South Dakota	24.6	Kentucky	31.5
New York	24.7	Indiana	31.4
Minnesota	24.8	Iowa	31.1
Connecticut	24.9	Missouri	30.9

January-December 2014
Gallup-Healthways Well-Being Index

January-December 2014
Gallup-Healthways Well-Being Index

GALLUP

GALLUP

Mississippi and West Virginia have had the two highest obesity rates in the nation since 2012. Five states on the list have had consistently high obesity rates—Mississippi, West Virginia, Louisiana, Arkansas and Kentucky. These states have been among the 10 states with the highest obesity rates every year since Gallup and Healthways began tracking obesity in 2008.

On the other end of the scale, Colorado has consistently had one of the two lowest obesity rates each year since 2008. In addition to Colorado, three states—California, Massachusetts and Connecticut—have been among the 10 states with the lowest obesity rates since 2008.

The national obesity rate continued to rise in 2014 to 27.7%, up from 27.1% in 2013 and significantly higher than the 25.5% recorded in 2008. Since 2013, four states—Nevada, New Mexico, Alabama and Minnesota—have had statistically significant increases in obesity, while only one state, Tennessee, has had a statistically significant decline in obesity.

These data, collected as part of the Gallup-Healthways Well-Being Index, are based on respondents' self-reported height and weight, which are used to calculate body mass index (BMI) scores. Americans who have a body mass index of 30 or higher are classified as obese.

Obesity rates continue to be highest in Southern and Midwestern states and lowest in Western and Northeastern states, a pattern that has persisted since Gallup and Healthways began tracking the obesity rate in 2008.

Obesity Rates, by U.S. State

Higher Obesity Rates Linked to Lower Well-Being

Gallup and Healthways have found a consistent and strong link between obesity and Americans' overall well-being. Therefore, many of the states with the lowest obesity rates are also among those with the highest overall Well-Being Index scores.

Gallup and Healthways define well-being through the five essential elements: purpose, social, financial, community and physical. For each element, respondents are sorted into one of three categories based on their level of well-being: thriving, struggling or suffering. Previous research has demonstrated a link between obesity and lower social well-being, but (excluding physical well-being, of which it is a part) obesity also has a deleterious effect on the other three elements of well-being. Across all elements of well-being, Americans who are obese are more likely to be suffering than those who are not obese.

After controlling for other factors linked to obesity—age, gender, marital status, education, income, race, ethnicity and employment—adults who are obese are:

* 29.3% more likely to be suffering in purpose well-being than those who are not obese
* 14.8% more likely to be suffering in social well-being than those who are not obese
* 33.7% more likely to be suffering in financial well-being than those who are not obese
* 17.5% more likely to be suffering in community well-being than those who are not obese

Percentage Who Are Suffering in Elements of Well-Being, Obese vs. Not Obese

Controls for age, gender, marital status, education, income, race, ethnicity and employment

Element of Well-Being	Obese	Not obese
	%	%
Purpose	17.2	13.3
Social	16.3	14.2
Financial	24.6	18.4
Community	16.1	13.7

Gallup-Healthways Well-Being Index

GALLUP

Bottom Line

The national obesity rate in 2014 was the highest that Gallup and Healthways have measured since starting to track this measure in 2008. In a handful of states, more than a third of the population is obese. Residents in these areas are less likely to eat healthily and exercise, and are more likely to suffer from chronic diseases like high blood pressure, high cholesterol, depression, diabetes, cancer and heart attacks. Obesity-related health problems could drive up healthcare costs and potentially have larger economic implications for states that suffer most.

The strong relationship between obesity and overall well-being suggests that interventions geared toward encouraging exercise and healthy eating, while important, may not be enough to reverse the upward trend in obesity. Gallup has found that Americans' desire to lose weight is not matched by their efforts. The mismatch between desired weight loss and weight loss efforts may stem from deficits in other areas of well-being. For instance, if residents don't have a strong sense of purpose, struggle financially or lack supportive relationships, it will be much more difficult for them to buy healthy food, exercise regularly and achieve their weight loss goals.

"There are proven, effective interventions for helping people lose weight and sustain their weight loss," says Janet Calhoun, senior vice president at Healthways. "For maximum impact, interventions need to go beyond addressing eating habits and physical activity, and include the emotional and social aspects of well-being. Helping people approach change with optimism, resilience and with an awareness of their personal passions are proven techniques for long-lasting behavior change."

Accordingly, members of the medical community, policymakers, employers and others working to combat obesity should seek interventions that address residents' sense of purpose, relationships with their communities, financial health and social networks.

Survey Methods

Results are based on telephone interviews conducted as part of the Gallup-Healthways Well-Being Index survey Jan. 2–Dec. 30, 2014, with a random sample of 176,702 adults, aged 18 and older, living in all 50 U.S. states and the District of Columbia.

The margin of sampling error for most states is ±1 to ±2 percentage points, but is as high as ±4 points for states with smaller populations, such as Wyoming, North Dakota, South Dakota, Delaware and Hawaii.

May 26, 2015
AMERICANS CONTINUE TO SHIFT LEFT ON KEY MORAL ISSUES

by Frank Newport

Story Highlights

- *Americans now more accepting of a number of moral issues*
- *All changes have been in more liberal direction*
- *Biggest shift on gay/lesbian relations*

PRINCETON, N.J.—Americans are more likely now than in the early 2000s to find a variety of behaviors morally acceptable, including gay and lesbian relations, having a baby outside of marriage and sex between an unmarried man and woman. Moral acceptability of many of these issues is now at a record-high level.

Moral Acceptability: Changes Over Time

% Morally acceptable

	2001	2015	Change
	%	%	(pct. pts.)
Gay or lesbian relations	40	63	23
Having a baby outside of marriage*	45	61	16
Sex between an unmarried man and woman	53	68	15
Divorce	59	71	12
Medical research using stem cells obtained from human embryos*	52	64	12
Polygamy (when a married person has more than one spouse at the same time)**	7	16	9
Cloning humans	7	15	8
Doctor-assisted suicide	49	56	7
Suicide	13	19	6
Gambling**	63	67	4
Abortion	42	45	3
Cloning animals	31	34	3
Buying and wearing clothing made of animal fur	60	61	1
Married men and women having an affair	7	8	1
The death penalty	63	60	-3
Medical testing on animals	65	56	-9

Note: Sorted by change in the percentage saying each is "morally acceptable"; unless otherwise marked, issues first measured in 2001

* First measured in 2002

** First measured in 2003

GALLUP'

This latest update on Americans' views of the moral acceptability of various issues and behaviors is from Gallup's May 6–10 Values and Beliefs survey. The complete results for each of the 19 issues tested in this year's survey appear at the end of the article. Gallup has tracked these moral issues in this format since the early 2000s.

The upward progression in the percentage of Americans seeing these issues as morally acceptable has varied from year to year, but the overall trend clearly points toward a higher level of acceptance of a number of behaviors. In fact, the moral acceptability ratings for 10 of the issues measured since the early 2000s are at record highs.

Americans have become less likely to say that two issues are morally acceptable: the death penalty and medical testing on animals. But Americans' decreased acceptance of these practices actually moves them in a more liberal direction.

These results reflect the same type of shift evident in the public's self-reported ideology on "social issues." More Americans now rate themselves as socially liberal than at any point in Gallup's 16-year trend, and for the first time, as many say they are liberal on social issues as say they are conservative.

Key trends in Americans' views of the moral acceptability of certain issues and behaviors include the following:

- The substantial increase in Americans' views that gay and lesbian relations are morally acceptable coincide with a record-high level of support for same-sex marriage and views that being gay or lesbian is something a person is born with, rather than due to one's upbringing or environment.
- The public is now more accepting of sexual relations outside of marriage in general than at any point in the history of tracking these measures, including a 16-percentage-point increase in those saying that having a baby outside of marriage is morally acceptable, and a 15-point increase in the acceptability of sex between an unmarried man and woman. Clear majorities of Americans now say both are acceptable.
- Acceptance of divorce and human embryo medical research are also up 12 points each since 2001 and 2002, respectively.
- Polygamy and cloning humans have also seen significant upshifts in moral acceptability—but even with these increases, the public largely perceives them as morally wrong, with only 16% and 15% of Americans, respectively, considering them morally acceptable.

Gallup will report on a number of these trends in more detail later this week.

Implications

Americans are becoming more liberal on social issues, as evidenced not only by the uptick in the percentage describing themselves as socially liberal, but also by their increasing willingness to say that a number of previously frowned-upon behaviors are morally acceptable. The biggest leftward shift over the past 14 years has been in attitudes toward gay and lesbian relations, from only a minority of Americans finding it morally acceptable to a clear majority finding it acceptable.

The moral acceptability of issues related to sexual relations has also increased, including having a baby outside of wedlock—something that in previous eras was a social taboo. Americans are more likely to find divorce morally acceptable, and have also loosened up on their views of polygamy, although this latter behavior is still seen as acceptable by only a small minority.

This liberalization of attitudes toward moral issues is part of a complex set of factors affecting the social and cultural fabric of the U.S. Regardless of the factors causing the shifts, the trend toward a more liberal view on moral behaviors will certainly have implications for such fundamental social institutions as marriage, the environment in which children are raised and the economy. The shifts could also have a significant effect on politics, with candidates whose positioning is based on holding firm views on certain issues having to grapple with a voting population that, as a whole, is significantly less likely to agree with conservative positions than it might have been in the past.

Survey Methods

Results for this Gallup poll are based on telephone interviews conducted May 6–10, 2015, with a random sample of 1,024 adults, aged 18 and older, living in all 50 U.S. states and the District of Columbia. For results based on the total sample of national adults, the margin of sampling error is ±4 percentage points at the 95% confidence level. All reported margins of sampling error include computed design effects for weighting.

May 27, 2015
IN U.S., SUPPORT UP FOR DOCTOR-ASSISTED SUICIDE

by Andrew Dugan

Story Highlights

- *Sixty-eight percent support euthanasia*
- *Most of the increased support came from 18- to 34-year-olds*
- *Use of word "suicide" does not appear to temper support*

WASHINGTON, D.C.—Nearly seven in 10 Americans (68%) say doctors should be legally allowed to assist terminally ill patients in committing suicide, up 10 percentage points from last year. More broadly, support for euthanasia has risen nearly 20 points in the last two years and stands at the highest level in more than a decade.

When a person has a disease that cannot be cured and is living in severe pain, do you think doctors should or should not be allowed by law to assist the patient to commit suicide if the patient requests it?

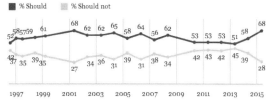

1996-1999 WORDING: When a person has a disease that cannot be cured and is living in severe pain, do you think doctors should be allowed by law to assist the patient to commit suicide if the patient requests it, or not?

GALLUP

These results come from Gallup's Values and Beliefs survey, conducted May 6–10. Typically, firm majorities of Americans have supported physician-assisted suicide for certain types of medical patients, though the magnitude of the support ebbs and flows. In 2001, support for physician-assisted suicide mirrored the current peak—68%—and remained slightly below that level for the ensuing decade. Possibly in response to the accusations of "death panels" that arose during the acrimonious debate surrounding passage of the Affordable Care Act, support dropped to bare-majority levels throughout much of President Barack Obama's first term. Public support for euthanasia fell to a low of 51% in 2013, before rebounding to 58% last year.

This year finds an uptick in support for euthanasia after the high-profile story last year of 29-year-old Brittany Maynard. Dying from terminal brain cancer, Maynard left her home state of California, where physicians are barred from assisting suicide, and ended her life in Oregon, where the practice is legal. Somewhat in response to this well-publicized story, the California state legislature is currently considering a bill that would legalize doctor-assisted suicide.

The larger effect that Maynard's story will have is uncertain, but some notable changes in support are evident compared with last year. The percentage of young adults aged 18–34 who support

doctor-assisted suicide climbed 19 points this year, to 81%. Young adults are now significantly more likely than older U.S. adults to support doctor-assisted suicide.

Support for Doctor-Assisted "Suicide," by Year

When a person has a disease that cannot be cured and is living in severe pain, do you think doctors should or should not be allowed by law to assist the patient to commit suicide if the patient requests it?

% Yes, should be allowed

	May 2014	May 2015	Change
	%	%	pct. pts.
18 to 34 years old	62	81	+19
35 to 54 years old	57	65	+8
55 and older	56	61	+5
Republicans	51	61	+10
Independents	64	80	+16
Democrats	59	72	+13

GALLUP

Meanwhile, support for physician-assisted suicide increased among all three major political affiliations, suggesting no partisan tilt to these changing views.

Use of Word "Suicide" Does Not Diminish Support for Euthanasia

Gallup has also trended a different version of this question that does not mention the word "suicide" but instead asks about doctors being allowed by law to "end the patient's life by some painless means." Americans have historically responded more favorably to the latter wording than the former. This year, both question wordings register nearly identical support, though it is unclear what the longer-term significance of this change may be.

Support for Doctor-Assisted Suicide -- Two Question Wordings

(Form A) When a person has a disease that cannot be cured, do you think doctors should be allowed by law to end the patient's life by some painless means if the patient and his or her family request it?

(Form B) When a person has a disease that cannot be cured and is living in severe pain, do you think doctors should or should not be allowed by law to assist the patient to commit suicide if the patient requests it?

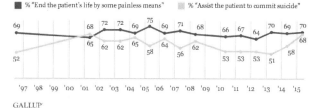

GALLUP

As Gallup has noted before, the fact that one question provides the respondent with a softer description of euthanasia—referring to it as "ending a patient's life by some painless means"—is a likely reason it typically has earned a larger share of support among U.S. adults. The other question, by specifically describing euthanasia as "suicide," introduces an emotionally charged word into an already sensitive subject.

A majority of Americans also say "doctor-assisted suicide" is "morally acceptable," an increase of seven points since 2001. The morality of doctor-assisted suicide has historically been among the most divisive of several moral issues Gallup has tracked since 2001. Once again, question wording is important. This question does not speak to whether doctor-assisted suicide should be permitted, but whether the respondent considers the action morally acceptable. Also of importance is that this item, unlike the two questions examined before, does not provide a larger context as to why or under what conditions doctor-assisted suicide would occur.

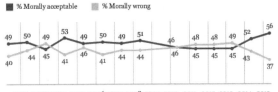

Still, even without the sympathetic background information of the other items, there has been a marked increase in the number of U.S. adults describing doctor-assisted suicide as "morally acceptable." In 2013, less than half of the country said it was morally acceptable (45%), one of the lowest measurements in the question's history. In a swing of 11 points from 2013, now a clear majority say it is morally acceptable.

Bottom Line

Consistent with changing attitudes related to a number of once-controversial social issues, the number of U.S. adults supporting physician-assisted suicide now ties the highest level seen in more than a decade and represents a rebound in support after it receded early this decade. Even the use of the word "suicide" in the description of medical euthanasia appears not to have tempered national support, a break from past years when its inclusion seemed to make some difference in national perceptions.

Survey Methods

Results for this Gallup poll are based on telephone interviews conducted May 6–10, 2015, with a random sample of 1,024 adults, aged 18 and older, living in all 50 U.S. states and the District of Columbia. For results based on the total sample of national adults, the margin of sampling error is ±4 percentage points at the 95% confidence level.

For results based on the sample of 497 national adults in Form A, the margin of sampling error is ±5 percentage points.

For results based on the sample of 527 national adults in Form B, the margins of sampling error is ±5 percentage points.

May 27, 2015
COLORADO SPRINGS RESIDENTS LEAST LIKELY TO BE OBESE

by Rebecca Riffkin

Story Highlights

- *Colorado Springs has the lowest obesity rate, at 19.6%*
- *Baton Rouge has the highest obesity rate, at 35.9%*
- *Obese metro areas lag behind in financial and community well-being*

WASHINGTON, D.C.—Baton Rouge, Louisiana, has the highest obesity rate of the 100 most populous U.S. metropolitan areas that Gallup and Healthways surveyed in 2014. More than a third of Baton Rouge residents, 35.9%, are obese, compared with 19.6% in Colorado Springs, Colorado—the community with the lowest obesity rate. Colorado Springs and San Jose-Sunnyvale-Santa Clara, California, are the only two communities in the 100 most populous metro areas that have an obesity rate of less than 20%.

Highest Obesity Rates, by Community Based on self-reported height and weight	% Obese
Baton Rouge, La.	35.9
Harrisburg-Carlisle, Pa.	35.3
Little Rock-North Little Rock-Conway, Ark.	34.1
Tulsa, Okla.	33.5
Dayton, Ohio	33.5
Memphis, Tenn.-Mo.-Ark.	33.2
Toledo, Ohio	33.1
Bakersfield, Calif.	33.1
Worcester, Mass.	33.0
Indianapolis-Carmel-Anderson, Ind.	32.2

Jan. 1-Dec. 29, 2014
Gallup-Healthways Well-Being Index

GALLUP

Lowest Obesity Rates, by Community Based on self-reported height and weight	% Obese
Colorado Springs, Colo.	19.6
San Jose-Sunnyvale-Santa Clara, Calif.	19.8
Denver-Aurora-Lakewood, Colo.	20.3
Provo-Orem, Utah	20.5
Bridgeport-Stamford-Norwalk, Conn.	21.0
Urban Honolulu, Hawaii	21.2
Boston-Cambridge-Newton, Mass.-N.H.	21.3
North Port-Sarasota-Bradenton, Fla.	21.4
Palm Bay-Melbourne-Titusville, Fla.	21.8
San Francisco-Oakland-Hayward, Calif.	21.9

Jan. 1-Dec. 29, 2014
Gallup-Healthways Well-Being Index

GALLUP

Gallup and Healthways determine obesity rates using self-reported height and weight to calculate each respondent's body mass index (BMI). Americans with a BMI of 30 or higher are considered obese. Nationally, the obesity rate continued to climb in 2014 to 27.7%, up from 27.1% in 2013 and much higher than the 25.5% found in 2008.

Obese Metro Areas Lag Behind in Financial and Community Well-Being

While obesity is clearly tied to lower physical well-being and a higher risk of health problems such as high blood pressure, diabetes, high cholesterol, chronic pain and depression, Gallup and Healthways also discovered that Americans who are obese are more likely to have lower purpose, social, financial and community well-being than those who are not obese, even after taking key demographic variables into account.

Residents of the 10 communities with the highest obesity rates have much lower financial well-being than those living in the 10 communities with the lowest obesity rates. For instance, those living in the most obese communities are much more likely to worry about money and struggle to afford food and healthcare. These findings are consistent with previous Gallup and Healthways research showing that obesity is linked to long-term unemployment and lower incomes.

Additionally, those living in communities with the highest obesity rates have much lower community well-being scores than those residing in communities with the lowest obesity rates. Residents of the former are significantly less likely to be proud of their community and to be satisfied with the city or area where they live.

Bottom Line

As the percentage of obese adults in the U.S. continues to rise, a wide disparity in obesity rates still exists between the communities with the highest rates and those with the lowest. In communities with the highest obesity rates, about one in three residents are obese.

In communities with the lowest rates, about one in five residents are obese.

Percentage Thriving in Five Elements of Well-Being
10 most obese vs. 10 least obese U.S. communities

	Average across 10 most obese communities	Average across 10 least obese communities	Difference
	%	%	(pct. pts.)
% Thriving in purpose well-being	37.6	36.6	+1.0
% Thriving in social well-being	39.8	41.3	-1.5
% Thriving in financial well-being	36.9	43.1	-6.2
% Thriving in community well-being	35.0	40.2	-5.2
% Thriving in physical well-being	29.9	35.7	-5.8

Jan. 1-Dec. 29, 2014
Gallup-Healthways Well-Being Index

GALLUP'

Previous Gallup and Healthways research shows that obesity appears to be more common in smaller communities than large ones. This means that less populated communities, which are not represented in this analysis, could have obesity rates even higher than the 35.9% found in the Baton Rouge metro area.

In addition to obesity being linked to an increased risk of many chronic diseases, carrying extra pounds also appears to be detrimental to other areas of individuals' well-being. For local government and business leaders, the finding that communities with high obesity rates also have lower financial and community well-being scores may be particularly concerning. The most obese communities may have higher percentages of residents burdened with healthcare costs associated with treating obesity-related illnesses, which could have a ripple effect on the broader economy. And if residents in the most obese areas have lower community well-being, crime levels could rise and businesses may move elsewhere.

Government and business leaders at the local level can develop targeted interventions for residents that build upon their community's strengths and help address its weaknesses to make choosing healthy food and exercising regularly easy and accessible.

Survey Methods

Results are based on telephone interviews conducted as part of the Gallup-Healthways Well-Being Index survey Jan. 2–Dec. 29, 2014, with a random sample of 176,702 adults, aged 18 and older, living in metropolitan areas in the 50 U.S. states and the District of Columbia, selected using random-digit-dial methods. Unlike previous years, only the 100 most populous metros—as determined by the U.S. Census Bureau—were reported in 2014. A second requirement is that at least 300 cases are required per metro area for reporting. As such, McAllen-Edinburg-Mission, Texas, and Durham-Chapel Hill, North Carolina, were both excluded from reporting because of insufficient sample size. These were replaced by the 102nd-largest metropolitan statistical area (MSA) in the U.S.: Lancaster, Pennsylvania.

The "communities" referenced in this article are based on MSAs as defined by the U.S. Office of Management and Budget. In many cases, more than one city is included in the same MSA. The San Jose, California, MSA, for example, also includes the smaller nearby cities of Sunnyvale and Santa Clara in addition to San Jose. Each respondent is attributed to his or her MSA based on self-reports of his or her ZIP code.

Maximum margins of error for the Well-Being Index and the element scores vary according to MSA size, ranging from less than 1 point for the largest cities represented to around ±1.5 points for many of the smallest cities.

May 28, 2015
APPROVAL OF OUT-OF-WEDLOCK BIRTHS GROWING IN U.S.

by Jeffrey M. Jones

Story Highlights

- *Six in 10 (61%) say having a baby outside of marriage is OK*
- *Up from 54% in 2012 and 45% in 2002*
- *Most subgroups more accepting than in past*

PRINCETON, N.J.—Sixty-one percent of Americans say having a baby outside of marriage is morally acceptable, a new high by one percentage point and the third straight year that roughly six in 10 Americans have sanctioned this once frowned-upon behavior. In 2002, when Gallup first asked the question, more Americans said having a baby outside of wedlock was morally wrong than said it was morally acceptable.

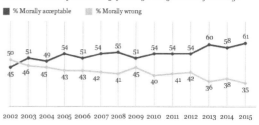

Americans' Views of the Morality of Having a Baby Outside of Marriage

2002 2003 2004 2005 2006 2007 2008 2009 2010 2011 2012 2013 2014 2015

GALLUP'

The 16-point increase in perceived moral acceptability of having a baby outside of marriage is the second-largest increase among the items tracked in Gallup's annual Values and Beliefs poll since its inception, behind only the 23-point jump in moral acceptability of gay and lesbian relations.

Former Vice President Dan Quayle made having a child outside of marriage a political issue in 1992, when he famously criticized the decision of fictional TV news anchor Murphy Brown to have a child. Over the past two decades, the percentage of children born to unmarried parents has increased—and as this trend has continued, Americans have become increasingly comfortable with out-of-wedlock births from a moral perspective.

Gallup's trend on the moral acceptability of out-of-wedlock births shows three distinct periods of support over the last 14 years. The first period, from 2002 to 2004, showed an evenly divided American public, with an average 48% of Americans saying that having a baby outside of marriage was morally acceptable and 47% saying it was morally wrong.

During the second period, from 2005 to 2012, there was a notable shift to the point where a clear majority, averaging 53%, sanctioned out-of-wedlock births.

In the last three years, there has been a further increase—to an average 60% of Americans—saying it is morally acceptable to have a baby outside of marriage.

Growing Social Liberalism a Factor in Greater Acceptance of Out-of-Wedlock Births

Nearly every major demographic or attitudinal subgroup has shown a significant increase since 2004 in their belief that out-of-wedlock births are morally acceptable. Those changes are detailed in a table at the end of this article.

But there is one subgroup—Americans who identify their views on social issues as "conservative"—whose views on out-of-wedlock births have changed little over the past 14 years. Between 2002 and 2004, an average of 35% of social conservatives said having a baby outside of marriage was morally acceptable. Currently, 38% hold this view.

By comparison, over the same period, there has been a 14-point increase among social moderates, to 65%, and a 12-point increase among social liberals, to 77%.

Belief That Having a Baby Outside of Marriage Is Morally Acceptable, by Self-Identified Views on Social Issues

Figures represent average percentages saying "Morally acceptable" during the specified years. Gallup has asked this question annually since 2002.

	2002-2004	2005-2012	2013-2015	Change, 2002-2004 to 2013-2015
	%	%	%	(pct. pts.)
Social liberals	65	72	77	+12
Social moderates	51	57	65	+14
Social conservatives	35	37	38	+3

GALLUP

The growing acceptance of out-of-wedlock births is not just a result of attitudinal change within ideological subgroups, but also of the changes in the size of those groups in the U.S. adult population. From 2002 to 2004, 37% of Americans said they were conservative on social issues. That percentage has dipped to 34% in the last three years, including a record-low 31% this year. Meanwhile, the percentage of social liberals has expanded from 24% in 2002 through 2004 to 30% in the last three years, including 31% this year.

Implications

Americans have grown more liberal in their views on a wide variety of moral issues over the past 15 years. Their greater acceptance of parents having children outside of marriage is one of the bigger changes in moral attitudes during this time, along with Americans' more tolerant views of gay and lesbian relations and of sex between unmarried men and women, which has increased from 53% to 68% since 2001.

The increase in perceived morality of out-of-wedlock births reflects the changing social mores of the U.S., and also perhaps an acknowledgment of the reality that more children are being born to unmarried couples. But the greater number of out-of-wedlock births is not necessarily a positive development for the United States, because babies born to unmarried parents are much more likely to grow up in poverty than those born to married parents. This is largely because out-of-wedlock births are much more common among lower-income Americans than upper-income Americans, and it may speak as much to the greater likelihood that a married household has two incomes as to the benefits of marriage per se. However, a growing body of research indicates that—whatever the underlying causes—children in two-parent households tend to have better academic and emotional outcomes later in life than those born in single-parent households.

It is unclear to what extent Americans are aware of the effects of children being born into single-parent households, and whether greater awareness of those effects might influence how people perceive the morality of unmarried parents having children.

Survey Methods

Results for this Gallup poll are based on telephone interviews conducted May 6–10, 2015, with a random sample of 1,024 adults, aged 18 and older, living in all 50 U.S. states and the District of Columbia. For results based on the total sample of national adults, the margin of sampling error is ±4 percentage points at the 95% confidence level. All reported margins of sampling error include computed design effects for weighting.

May 29, 2015
AMERICANS CHOOSE "PRO-CHOICE" FOR FIRST TIME IN SEVEN YEARS

by Lydia Saad

Story Highlights

- *Americans divide 50% "pro-choice," 44% "pro-life" on abortion*
- *Majority of women, 54%, now pro-choice, vs. 46% of men*
- *Pro-choice ID among Democrats has swelled since 2001*

PRINCETON, N.J.—Half of Americans consider themselves "pro-choice" on abortion, surpassing the 44% who identify as "pro-life." This is the first time since 2008 that the pro-choice position has had a statistically significant lead in Americans' abortion views.

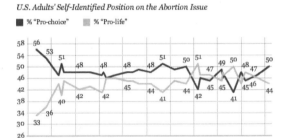

U.S. Adults' Self-Identified Position on the Abortion Issue

Question wording: With respect to the abortion issue, would you consider yourself to be pro-choice or pro-life?

GALLUP

For most of the past five years, Americans have been fairly evenly divided in their association with the two abortion labels. The only exception between 2010 and 2014 was in May 2012, when the pro-life position led by 50% to 41%.

Prior to 2009, the pro-choice side almost always predominated, including in the mid-1990s by a substantial margin. While support for the pro-choice position has yet to return to the 53% to 56% level seen at the time, the trend has been moving in that direction since the 2012 reading.

While Gallup does not define the pro-choice and pro-life terms for Americans, their answers to a separate question about the legality of abortion indicate that those favoring the pro-choice label generally support broad abortion rights, while pro-life adherents mostly favor limited or no abortion rights.

The latest results are based on Gallup's May 6–10 Values and Beliefs poll. Gallup began tracking Americans' identification as "pro-choice" or "pro-life" at least annually in 2001.

Americans' Preference for Extent to Which Abortion Should Be Legal

Results among U.S. adults, and by self-identified abortion position

	U.S. adults	"Pro-choice"	"Pro-life"
	%	%	%
Legal under any circumstances	29	50	4
Legal in most circumstances	13	21	5
Legal in only a few circumstances	36	23	51
Illegal in all circumstances	19	4	37
No opinion	2	2	3

May 6-10, 2015

GALLUP

Modest Gender Gap Seen in Abortion Views Since 2012

The recent increase in the pro-choice side has occurred almost equally among men and women. However, for men, this has not compensated for the larger drop in their identification as pro-choice in 2012. As a result, a slight gender gap has emerged over the last three years, with women more likely than men to be pro-choice. This contrasts with 2001 through 2011, when there was virtually no gender gap.

On a longer-term basis, a higher percentage of women today than in 2001 call themselves pro-choice, while men's identification is about the same.

Trend in Percentage Identifying as "Pro-Choice" on Abortion, by Gender

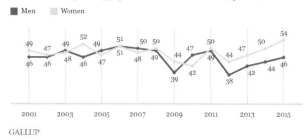

GALLUP

The trends by age and party ID show a similar pattern, with support for the pro-choice label dipping among all age and party groups in 2012, but subsequently returning to 2008 levels or higher.

The biggest change by age since 2001 is that middle-aged and older Americans are more likely to be pro-choice today, while the percentage of young adults who identify with the term is about the same.

Trend in Percentage Identifying as "Pro-Choice" on Abortion, by Age

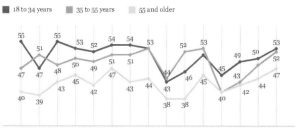

GALLUP

Given the increase in pro-choice support since 2012, Republicans' and independents' identification as pro-choice is about the same today as in 2001, whereas Democrats' pro-choice ID has expanded (to 68%, up from 55%).

Trend in Percentage Identifying as "Pro-Choice" on Abortion, by Party ID

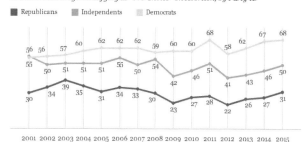

GALLUP

Bottom Line

The pro-choice view is not as prevalent among Americans as it was in the mid-1990s, but the momentum for the pro-life position that began when Barack Obama took office has yielded to a pro-choice rebound. That rebound has essentially restored views to where they were in 2008; today's views are also similar to those found in 2001. Some of the variation in public views on abortion over time coincides with political and cultural events that may have helped shape public opinion on the issue, including instances of anti-abortion violence, legislative efforts to ban "partial-birth abortion" or limit abortion funding, and certain Supreme Court cases. While events like these may continue to cause public views on abortion to fluctuate, the broader liberal shift in Americans' ideology of late could mean the recent pro-choice expansion has some staying power.

Survey Methods

Results for this Gallup poll are based on telephone interviews conducted May 6–10, 2015, with a random sample of 1,024 adults, aged 18 and older, living in all 50 U.S. states and the District of Columbia. For results based on the total sample of national adults, the margin of sampling error is ±4 percentage points at the 95% confidence level. All reported margins of sampling error include computed design effects for weighting.

May 29, 2015
ABORTION EDGES UP AS IMPORTANT VOTING ISSUE FOR AMERICANS

by Rebecca Riffkin

Story Highlights

- *21% will only vote for candidate with same abortion views*
- *Importance of abortion to voting has varied*
- *Abortion more important to pro-life vote than pro-choice*

WASHINGTON, D.C.—The percentage of Americans who say they would only vote for a candidate who shares their views on abortion has been edging up over the past seven years. The 21% who currently say this is, by one percentage point, the highest Gallup has found in its 19-year history of asking the question. The percentage of Americans who do not see abortion as a major issue in their voting decision has declined over the same period, and is now at 27%. Most of the rest (46%) say that abortion is one of many important factors they will take into account.

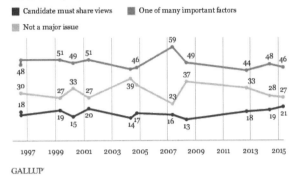

Most Americans Do Not Consider Abortion Top Issue When Voting

Thinking about how the abortion issue might affect your vote for major offices, would you -- only vote for a candidate who shares your views on abortion (or) consider a candidate's position on abortion as just one of many important factors (or) not see abortion as a major issue?

■ Candidate must share views   ■ One of many important factors
■ Not a major issue

GALLUP

Although the percentage of Americans saying they will only vote for a candidate with their same views on abortion has varied since 1996, in all instances, it has clearly remained a minority opinion. The percentage of Americans who say that abortion is one of many important factors they consider when deciding whom to vote for has been relatively stable over the same period, with the exception of a jump to 59% in 2007.

Registered voters, at 19%, are slightly less likely than all Americans to say they will only vote for a candidate who shares their views on abortion. But even among registered voters, the importance of abortion is higher than Gallup has found most years.

Candidates' Abortion Views More Important to Pro-Life Than Pro-Choice

Historically, Americans who self-identify as "pro-life" on the abortion issue have been more likely than self-identified "pro-choice" Americans to say they will only vote for a candidate who shares their views. However, the pro-life advantage is quite narrow in 2015, with 23% of pro-life Americans saying they will only vote for a candidate who shares their views, compared with 19% of pro-choice Americans. The gap was nine points in 2014, and it has been as high as 18 points, in late 2004.

The percentage of pro-choice Americans who say candidates must share their views has increased by four points since 2014, and is up eight points from 2008. The only other year when pro-choice Americans were as likely as they are today to prioritize the issue was in 2001.

Half of Americans (50%) now say they are pro-choice, higher than the 44% of Americans who self-identify as pro-life. This counterbalances the slight advantage that the pro-life side has in how important abortion is to their vote, so that those prepared to only

vote for a pro-life candidate versus those only voting for a pro-choice candidate are even, at about 10%.

Implications

The recent uptick in the importance Americans place on where candidates stand on abortion comes as many states have enacted new or increased abortion restrictions. State lawmakers have passed more than 200 regulations on abortion since 2010, after Republicans gained control of many state legislatures. Republicans in Congress are currently advocating a federal bill banning abortions after 20 weeks of pregnancy, although President Barack Obama is unlikely to sign it.

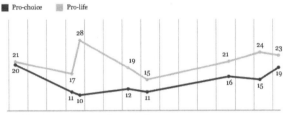

Importance of Abortion to Votes of Pro-Life and Pro-Choice Americans

% Only vote for candidate who shares views

■ Pro-choice   ■ Pro-life

Thinking about how the abortion issue might affect your vote for major offices, would you -- only vote for a candidate who shares your views on abortion (or) consider a candidate's position on abortion as just one of many important factors (or) not see abortion as a major issue?

GALLUP

Abortion is an ever-present issue in presidential campaigns—and a year before the 2016 election, more Americans than in the past say they will only vote for a candidate who shares their views on abortion. So far, the candidates' abortion positions mostly echo their respective party lines, with Hillary Clinton and her leading potential rivals for the Democratic nomination all embracing the pro-choice label, while most of the likely Republican candidates (other than George Pataki) either call themselves pro-life or favor various limits on abortion and abortion funding.

Although abortion is a defining issue to at least one in five Americans, its influence on the 2016 election is likely to be limited as long as each party's candidates continue to espouse their respective party's abortion canon. Only significant deviation from that is likely to compel these abortion-focused voters to either look elsewhere or stay home on Election Day.

Survey Methods

Results for this Gallup poll are based on telephone interviews conducted May 6–10, 2015, with a random sample of 1,024 adults, aged 18 and older, living in all 50 U.S. states and the District of Columbia. For results based on the total sample of national adults, the margin of sampling error is ±4 percentage points at the 95% confidence level. All reported margins of sampling error include computed design effects for weighting.

June 01, 2015
ONCE TABOO, SOME BEHAVIORS NOW
MORE ACCEPTABLE IN U.S.

by Andrew Dugan

Story Highlights

• *Adultery remains least morally acceptable to Americans*
• *Most still frown on polygamy, human cloning and suicide*
• *Over past 15 years, increase in support for all but adultery*

WASHINGTON, D.C.—While a select few actions remain deeply taboo for much of the country, there has been an increasing shift to moral acceptability for some of these over time. Such actions include suicide (which 19% of Americans call "morally acceptable"), polygamy (16%) and cloning humans (15%). On the other hand, "married men and women having an affair" has remained at the bottom of a list of 19 moral behaviors Gallup has measured, with only 8% considering it morally acceptable.

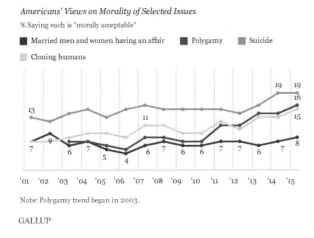

Americans' Views on Morality of Selected Issues
% Saying each is "morally acceptable"

■ Married men and women having an affair   ■ Polygamy   ▨ Suicide
▨ Cloning humans

Note: Polygamy trend began in 2003.

GALLUP

These results come from the May 6–10 Gallup Values and Beliefs poll. Since 2001, this annual poll has gauged the nation's moral sensibilities across numerous behaviors or social issues, including divisive or sensitive topics such as having children out of wedlock, premarital sex, gay or lesbian relations and abortion. Many of the 19 topics rated this year are now judged as morally acceptable by record or near-record percentages of U.S. adults, in tandem with a rising wave of social liberalism.

To some extent, these changing social mores have affected even behaviors that a vast majority of the country routinely judges as "morally wrong." Since 2003, the proportion of U.S. adults saying polygamy is morally acceptable has increased by nine percentage points. Since 2001, cloning humans has seen an increase of eight points; and suicide, a six-point gain. Still, each of these items retains its essence of moral repugnancy in the nation's social consciousness, as resounding majorities describe each of these behaviors as morally wrong.

Even among these taboo topics, married men and women engaging in an affair occupies its own space, in terms of public contempt. Over the past 15 years, no more than one in 10 U.S. adults have ever judged extramarital trysts as moral. This item has always ranked at the bottom of all issues tested in terms of moral acceptability, though at times in previous years it tied cloning humans or

polygamy. In contrast to the continued, nearly universal condemnation of adultery, other topics regarding marriage and who should be having sex with whom have changed remarkably: divorce, sex between an unmarried heterosexual couple, and gay/lesbian relations have all seen double-digit increases in the percentage saying they are morally acceptable.

Older Americans Find More Issues Highly Unacceptable

Gallup has previously defined moral issues as being highly unacceptable when 20% or less of U.S. adults rate them as morally acceptable, which would include suicide, cloning humans, polygamy and adultery in this year's poll.

There is variation in acceptability by age groups. In particular, those aged 65 or older find a wider set of issues as morally beyond the pale: In addition to the four items examined above, U.S. seniors give low moral acceptability scores to pornography (18%) and sex between teenagers (18%). In contrast, young Americans have a more tolerant outlook: There is only one issue—extramarital affairs—that less than 20% of 18- to 29-year-olds rate as morally acceptable.

Moral Issues Americans Find Highly Unacceptable, by Age
% Saying "morally acceptable" at or lower than 20%

	% Morally acceptable
18 to 29	
-- Married men and women having an affair	10
30 to 49	
-- Suicide	17
-- Cloning humans	16
-- Married men and women having an affair	7
50 to 64	
-- Suicide	20
-- Polygamy	12
-- Cloning humans	11
-- Married men and women having an affair	10
65+	
-- Sex between teenagers	18
-- Pornography	18
-- Suicide	16
-- Married men and women having an affair	9
-- Cloning humans	8
-- Polygamy	8

May 6–10, 2015

GALLUP

Bottom Line

Americans today appear to have greater comfort with a host of issues or behaviors that were at one time subject to social stigma. And even among the most taboo behaviors, there is evidence of changing moral judgments, at least in relation to suicide, cloning humans and polygamy.

Why these items are seeing a modest improvement on their perceived morality is hard to determine, though the disproportionately high share of 18- to 29-year-olds labeling them as acceptable may be both telling and predictive. Young adults find just one behavior—affairs between married men and women—highly unacceptable. Provided younger Americans do not shift toward a more culturally conservative stance as they age—and there is reason to believe they won't, given the increasingly liberal views of older Americans—fewer behaviors may eventually be seen as taboo.

But the nation's thoughts on extramarital affairs may be considered an island of stability amid this sea change. Even as much of the country expands the institution of marriage to include gay and lesbian couples, there has been no redefining of the commitment a couple enters into when they get married.

Survey Methods

Results for this Gallup poll are based on telephone interviews conducted May 6–10, 2015, with a random sample of 1,024 adults, aged 18 and older, living in all 50 U.S. states and the District of Columbia. For results based on the total sample of national adults, the margin of sampling error is ±4 percentage points at the 95% confidence level. All reported margins of sampling error include computed design effects for weighting.

June 02, 2015
MAJORITY IN U.S. STILL SAY MORAL VALUES GETTING WORSE

by Justin McCarthy

Story Highlights

- *Seventy-two percent of Americans say U.S. morals in decline*
- *Forty-five percent describe state of moral values as "poor"*
- *Social conservatives most likely to say morals "getting worse"*

WASHINGTON, D.C.—Most Americans (72%) continue to believe the state of moral values in the U.S. is "getting worse," while 22% say it is "getting better." Large majorities have said the state of moral values in the U.S. is declining since Gallup started asking this question annually in 2002.

Americans' Outlook on State of Moral Values in the U.S.

Right now, do you think the state of moral values in the country as a whole is getting better or getting worse?

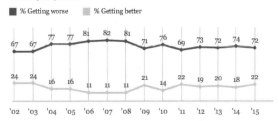

Trend based on Gallup's Values and Beliefs poll, conducted each May

GALLUP

Americans were slightly less pessimistic about the direction of the country's morals in 2002 and 2003, when two-thirds (67%) said it was getting worse. Pessimism peaked between 2006 and 2008, when more than four in five Americans thought the state of moral values was declining.

Social Conservatives Most Likely to Say Morals in Decline

Across most demographic groups, clear majorities of Americans have consistently said the country's morals are deteriorating. But those who identify as social conservatives have consistently been more likely than social liberals to believe the nation's state of moral values is getting worse, with social moderates falling about midway between the two. The liberal-conservative gap was relatively narrow in the first two years Gallup measured this, in 2002 and 2003, but that may have reflected the more positive feelings Americans had about their country in the first few years after 9/11.

Since then, a sizable gap has emerged, with upward of 80% of social conservatives consistently saying the state of morals is getting worse. Meanwhile, social liberals' outlook soured in the last five years of President George W. Bush's presidency, perhaps reflecting their disagreement with the Iraq War. But social liberals then turned sharply less negative upon Democratic President Barack Obama's taking office in 2009, while social conservatives' views have changed little since 2004.

Outlook on State of Moral Values in the U.S., by Social Ideology

Right now, do you think the state of moral values in the country as a whole is getting better or getting worse? (% Getting worse)

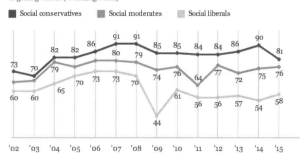

Trend based on Gallup's Values and Beliefs poll, conducted each May

GALLUP

The latest results are from Gallup's annual Values and Beliefs poll, conducted May 6–10. According to the same survey, Americans have become more likely to say they are liberal on social issues and less likely to say they are socially conservative. Additionally, Americans have become increasingly likely to consider certain behaviors morally acceptable than they did in the past.

Americans Most Likely to Rate State of Moral Values as "Poor"

Apart from their perceptions of the direction in which morals are headed, 45% of Americans describe the current state of moral values in the U.S. as "poor," with 34% saying they are "only fair" and 19% rating the state of moral values as either "excellent" or "good."

The percentage who say the state of moral values is currently poor is up slightly from 42% a year ago, and matches the high from 2009 and 2010.

Social conservatives tend to be the most likely to describe the state of U.S. values as poor. This view has increased from as low as 42% in 2003 to a high of 63% in 2013. Currently, 57% of social conservatives say the state of moral values is poor. Social moderates, too, have increased in this view over time, reaching a new high this year of 46%—up from a low of 31% in 2003.

Social liberals, meanwhile, have had less movement in their views of the U.S. being in a state of poor moral values, ranging from a low of 26% in 2011 and 2013 to a high of 36% in 2006 amid the war in Iraq. On average, their views are slightly less negative under the Obama presidency than they were under the Bush presidency.

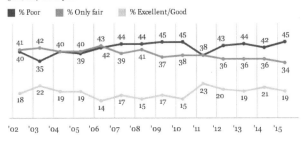

Americans' Views on Current State of Moral Values in the U.S.

How would you rate the overall state of moral values in this country today -- as excellent, good, only fair or poor?

■ % Poor　■ % Only fair　▨ % Excellent/Good

Trend based on Gallup's Values and Beliefs poll, conducted each May

GALLUP'

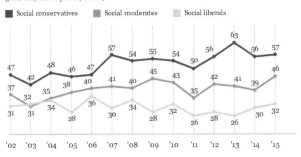

Views on Current State of Moral Values in the U.S., by Social Ideology

How would you rate the overall state of moral values in this country today -- as excellent, good, only fair or poor? (% Poor)

■ Social conservatives　■ Social moderates　▨ Social liberals

Trend based on Gallup's Values and Beliefs poll, conducted each May

GALLUP'

Bottom Line

Americans' views of the state of moral values haven't changed much over the past 13 years. Despite significant shifts in Americans' views on same-sex marriage and other moral issues, as well as the increase in those who identify as social liberals, Americans are about as likely as they were in 2002 to consider moral values in the U.S. to be poor and to say they are heading for further decay.

Perhaps this is because Americans don't answer the questions with such politically charged issues in mind. According to open-ended questions Gallup asked about moral values in 2010 and 2012, Americans' views about the declining state of moral affairs largely reflect a belief that there is a deteriorating collective moral character. That is, their views have less to do with greater acceptance of same-sex marriage or having babies out of wedlock and other hot-button issues, and more to do with matters of basic civility and respect for each other.

Survey Methods

Results for this Gallup poll are based on telephone interviews conducted May 6–10, 2015, with a random sample of 1,024 adults, aged 18 and older, living in all 50 U.S. states and the District of Columbia. For results based on the total sample of national adults, the margin of sampling error is ±4 percentage points at the 95% confidence level. All reported margins of sampling error include computed design effects for weighting.

June 03, 2015
REPUBLICAN CONSERVATIVE BASE SHRINKS

by Frank Newport

Story Highlights

- *Fewer Republicans are socially and economically conservative*
- *Almost one in four in GOP are moderate/liberal on both dimensions*
- *20% are socially moderate/liberal but economically conservative*

PRINCETON, N.J.—The percentage of Republicans and Republican-leaning independents who describe themselves as both social and economic conservatives has dropped to 42%, the lowest level Gallup has measured since 2005. The second-largest group of Republicans (24%) see themselves as moderate or liberal on both social and economic issues, while 20% of all Republicans are moderate or liberal on social issues but conservative on economic ones.

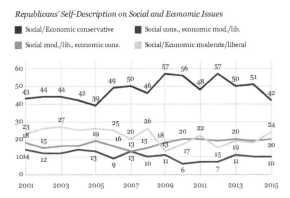

Republicans' Self-Description on Social and Economic Issues

■ Social/Economic conservative　■ Social cons., economic mod./lib.
▨ Social mod./lib., economic cons.　▨ Social/Economic moderate/liberal

Based on Republicans and Republican-leaning independents
Data are from May Values and Beliefs survey each year

GALLUP'

These data are from Gallup's Values and Beliefs poll, which since 2001 has included questions asking Americans to rate themselves as conservative, moderate or liberal on social and economic issues. These trends show not only that Americans as a whole have become less likely to identify as social or economic conservatives, but also that Republicans' views are changing along the same lines.

This change in recent years has been significant. The percentage of Republicans identifying as conservative on both dimensions has dropped 15 percentage points since 2012, largely offset by an increase in the percentage who identify as moderate or liberal on both dimensions. Still, the current ideological positioning of Republicans is not unprecedented; the proportion of social and economic conservatives was as low or lower from 2001 through 2005.

Republicans' Ideology Varies Significantly by Age

The percentage of Republicans and Republican-leaning independents who are conservative on both social and economic issues rises steadily with age. An analysis of aggregated surveys conducted since the 2012 election shows that the size of the social and economic conservative group is twice as large among Republicans aged 65 and older as it is among those aged 18 to 29. This may be good news for GOP candidates who are running on a conservative platform and can assume that older Republicans will constitute a sizable portion of primary and caucus voters. But it is not such good news when it comes to the challenge of energizing a broader base of Republican voters to come out to vote in the typically higher-turnout general election.

Implications

The recent shift in how Republicans view themselves ideologically may have significant implications for the coming GOP presidential nomination fight, particularly in terms of how the candidates will try to position themselves to maximize their appeal. Republican candidates are dealing with a party base that is today significantly more ideologically differentiated than it has been over the past decade. A GOP candidate positioning himself or herself as conservative on both social and economic issues theoretically will appeal to less than half of the broad base of rank-and-file party members. This opens the way for GOP candidates who may want to position themselves as more moderate on some issues, given that more than half of the party identifiers are moderate or liberal on social or economic dimensions.

The caveat in these campaign decisions is that not all Republicans are involved in the crucial early primary and caucus voting that helps winnow the pack of presidential candidates down to a winner. Ideology on both social and economic issues is strongly related to age, and primary voters tend to skew older than the overall party membership. This could benefit a more conservative candidate in the primary process, but that advantage could dissipate in the general election.

Democratic candidates will be dealing with party identifiers who are mostly moderate or liberal on social and economic issues, with a significant divide between these two groups. A forthcoming story will look at the Democratic ideological situation in detail.

Survey Methods

Results for the most recent Gallup poll are based on telephone interviews conducted May 6–10, 2015, with a random sample of 1,024 adults, aged 18 and older, living in all 50 U.S. states and the District of Columbia. For results based on the total sample of national adults, the margin of sampling error is ±4 percentage points at the 95% confidence level.

Results for the aggregated Gallup polls conducted in 2013–2015 are based on telephone interviews with a random sample of 3,587 adults, aged 18 and older. For results based on this sample, the margin of sampling error is ±2 percentage points at the 95% confidence level. All reported margins of sampling error include computed design effects for weighting.

June 04, 2015
MOST AMERICANS CONTINUE TO SAY DEATH PENALTY MORALLY OK

by Art Swift

Story Highlights

- *Sixty percent in U.S. say death penalty morally acceptable*
- *A third of Americans say the procedure is morally wrong*

WASHINGTON, D.C.—As the death penalty continues to lose support in state houses across America, with Nebraska banning the practice last week, 60% of Americans say the death penalty is morally acceptable. While this measure has remained relatively stable over time, the current 60% is on the lower end of acceptance of the death penalty nationwide since Gallup began measuring it in 2001.

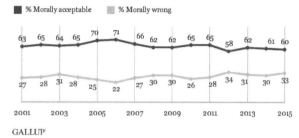

Americans' Views of the Death Penalty as Morally Acceptable
Next, I'm going to read you a list of issues. Regardless of whether or not you think it should be legal, for each one, please tell me whether you personally believe that in general it is morally acceptable or morally wrong. How about -- [RANDOM ORDER]?

GALLUP

Use of the death penalty has been waning for several years. The 35 inmates receiving the ultimate penalty last year in the U.S. was the lowest in 20 years, and the 72 new death sentences delivered in 2014 were the fewest in modern history. Despite these changes, a majority of Americans continue to say they favor the death penalty as punishment for murder, and in the May Gallup Values and Beliefs poll, a clear majority of Americans still say it is morally acceptable to impose the death penalty. Americans' views on the morality of the practice have generally held steady even in light of botched executions, lengthy appeals cases, seven states banning the procedure since 2007 and many states imposing "open-ended moratoriums" on the practice.

When Gallup began asking this question in 2001, 63% said it was morally acceptable, while 27% said it was morally wrong. These percentages recorded in 2001 are not that different from today, though a third of Americans now say the death penalty is morally wrong. The biggest wave of support for its acceptability came in 2006, at 71%, while the low mark was in 2012, at 58%.

Midwest Drops Most in Acceptability of Death Penalty

The Nebraska legislature, officially nonpartisan but dominated by Republicans, voted in April to ban the death penalty. Gov. Pete Ricketts vetoed the bill, but the legislature overrode Ricketts's veto in May. Illinois, another Midwestern state, also banned the death penalty in 2011. And in 2015, the Midwest experienced the sharpest drop among U.S. regions, falling from 69% to 60%.

The South has the highest percentage of Americans who believe the death penalty is morally acceptable of any U.S. region, at 63%.

Moral Acceptability of the Death Penalty in U.S., by Region
% Morally acceptable

	2014	2015
East	54	53
Midwest	69	60
South	60	63
West	60	62

GALLUP

The East has the lowest percentage of those who believe the death penalty is morally acceptable, at 53%, though this is still a majority. Maryland banned the practice in 2013, and New York and New Jersey both ended the death penalty in 2007, leaving only a handful of Eastern states in which capital punishment is still legal.

Republicans Still More Accepting of Death Penalty Than Democrats

Since 2001, the number of Republicans saying the death penalty is morally acceptable has always outweighed Democrats. This year, there is a fairly significant partisan divide on this topic—33 percentage points—as 76% of Republicans express moral acceptance of this practice, while 43% of Democrats say the same.

Moral Acceptability of Death Penalty in U.S., by Party ID
% Morally acceptable

■ Republicans ▨ Democrats

```
                    84
  77  78  77  79       80  76  74  76  77  73  74  73  76

              65
          59      57         55
      53              52         52        52
  50  52                  49      52              47
      47                              42              43

2001  2003  2005  2007  2009  2011  2013  2015
```

GALLUP

Bottom Line

The death penalty has been a topic of considerable public debate for some time. During an era when overall public support for the death penalty was lower than it is today, the practice was ruled unconstitutional by the U.S. Supreme Court in 1972, but reinstated in 1976. Since then, though many inmates have been executed, it can sometimes take decades for condemned inmates to be put to death. In the last 50 years, advancements in the collection and analysis of DNA have helped to exonerate many prisoners. The American public has also witnessed botched executions, with the procedure sometimes taking two hours or more to reach the end result.

A recent cover story in *Time* magazine argues that the death penalty will someday be a thing of the past as a result of the cost of death row incarceration and appeals, Supreme Court challenges and a crime rate that continues to drop. Faced with these expectations and the complicated factors involved in the actual application of the death penalty, Americans still have not materially altered their opinion of whether the death penalty is morally right.

Like so much else in American political life, this is a partisan issue, with the percentage of Democrats who say it is morally acceptable plummeting even further in the past year.

Moral acceptance may remain high even as the death penalty dwindles in actual application. There are times when Americans appear to unite behind a death penalty conviction—as in the case of the Boston Marathon bomber Dzhokhar Tsarnaev, and before him, Oklahoma City bomber Timothy McVeigh—and thus the average American might want the option preserved for such situations.

Survey Methods

Results for this Gallup poll are based on telephone interviews conducted May 6–10, 2015, with a random sample of 1,024 adults, aged 18 and older, living in all 50 U.S. states and the District of

Columbia. For results based on the total sample of national adults, the margin of sampling error is ±4 percentage points at the 95% confidence level.

June 05, 2016
IN U.S., PERCENTAGE STRUGGLING TO AFFORD FOOD AT 7–YEAR LOW

by Shawnette Rochelle

Story Highlights

- *15.8% of U.S. adults struggled to afford food in past 12 months*
- *Lowest percentage recorded since Gallup and Healthways began tracking metric in '08*

WASHINGTON, D.C—In the first quarter of 2015, 15.8% of Americans reported that in the last 12 months they had struggled to afford food for themselves or their families. This is the lowest percentage measured since the Gallup-Healthways Well-Being Index started in 2008.

Percentage of Americans Who Struggled to Afford Food in Past Year, Quarter 1, 2015

Have there been times in the past 12 months when you did not have enough money to buy food that you or your family needed?

■ % Yes

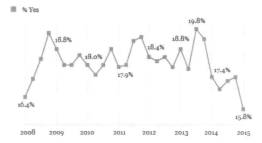

Data reflect Q1 2008-Q1 2015
Gallup-Healthways Well-Being Index

GALLUP

The previous low was in the first quarter of 2008, when 16.4% of Americans reported lacking enough money to buy food for themselves or their families. The percentage peaked in the third quarter of 2013, when nearly one in five Americans said they struggled to afford food.

The decrease in the percentage of Americans agreeing that they have struggled to afford food comes as their financial optimism and perceptions of job creation in their workplaces are at record highs, and as unemployment, as measured by Gallup and the Bureau of Labor Statistics, generally has been declining. Fewer Americans struggling to afford food is a positive sign that the economic recovery could be benefitting some of the poorest Americans.

Across Key Demographic Groups, Fewer Struggle to Afford Food

Across most key demographic groups, the percentage who reported struggling to afford food in the first quarter of 2015 is at least marginally lower than the same period last year, when 17.4% of

Americans reported this. Blacks, Asians, younger Americans and lower-income Americans saw the most improvement in their ability to afford food.

Percentage of Americans Who Struggled to Afford Food in Past Year, by Demographic Group

Have there been times in the past 12 months when you did not have enough money to buy food that you or your family needed?
% Yes

	Q1 2014	Q1 2015	Difference (pct. pts)
AGE			
18 to 29	20.3%	18.0%	-2.3
30 to 49	20.4%	18.9%	-1.5
50 to 64	18.1%	15.9%	-2.2
65+	8.5%	8.4%	-0.1
ANNUAL HOUSEHOLD INCOME			
Less than $24,000	39.9%	37.9%	-2.0
$24,000 to $47,999	19.7%	18.1%	-1.6
$48,000 to $59,999	9.7%	8.9%	-0.8
$60,000 to $89,999	6.8%	5.9%	-0.9
$90,000 or more	4.4%	3.6%	-0.8
RACE/ETHNICITY			
White	13.3%	12.0%	-1.3
Black	30.5%	27.0%	-3.5
Asian	9.5%	6.7%	-2.8
Hispanic	25.2%	23.9%	-1.3

Gallup-Healthways Well-Being Index

GALLUP'

Overall, blacks and Hispanics are about twice as likely as whites to report experiencing difficulty affording food. Those with annual household incomes of $24,000 to $47,999 are half as likely to report this as those living in households earning less than $24,000 a year. Reported struggles to afford food are lower among each successively higher income group, but with smaller differences between income categories.

Women More Likely Than Men to Struggle to Buy Food

Women are more likely to report struggling to afford food than men, a pattern consistent over time. In the first quarter of 2015, 18.3% of women said they struggled to buy food, much higher than the 13.1% of men who reported the same.

Percentage of Americans Who Struggled to Afford Food in Past Year, by Gender

Have there been times in the past 12 months when you did not have enough money to buy food that you or your family needed?

% Yes
■ Male   ■ Female

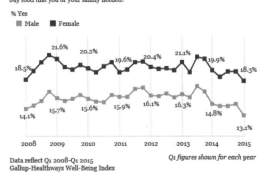

Data reflect Q1 2008-Q1 2015
Gallup-Healthways Well-Being Index

Q1 figures shown for each year

GALLUP'

The higher incidence of single mothers compared with single fathers could explain why more women report struggling to buy food than men. Previous Gallup research shows that single-parent households are much more likely to have difficulty affording food. Single-mother households make up a much larger share of single-parent households in the U.S. than do single-father households. In the first quarter of 2015, Gallup found that 19.3% of single mothers who have never been married with two children reported struggling to afford food versus 13.9% of single fathers who have never been married with two children.

Separated, Divorced Much More Likely to Struggle to Afford Food

Separated Americans are more likely than those of any other marital status group to report struggling to afford food. This is consistent with previous Gallup research showing separated Americans have sharply lower well-being than those of any other marital status group.

Percentage of Americans Who Struggled to Afford Food in Past Year, by Marital Status

Have there been times in the past 12 months when you did not have enough money to buy food that you or your family needed?
% Yes

	Q1 2015
Single/Never been married	20.5%
Married	9.9%
Separated	37.5%
Divorced	24.1%

Gallup-Healthways Well-Being Index

GALLUP'

Both separated and divorced Americans are more likely than married and single Americans to report struggling to afford food in the past 12 months. Having a single income to spend on food as opposed to two incomes, in addition to the loss of personal net worth that often occurs during a divorce or an extended separation, are just two factors that could explain the higher self-reported incidence of struggling to afford food among separated and divorced Americans.

Bottom Line

The percentage of Americans reporting an inability to afford food is the lowest it has been in seven years, an encouraging sign possibly indicating that those who previously struggled to meet this basic need are now feeling the positive effects of the economic recovery. In addition to an improving U.S. job market, world food prices have declined since April 2014, which could be another possible explanation for the dip in the percentage of Americans reporting a struggle to afford food in the past 12 months.

Despite this positive improvement in Americans' ability to afford food, wide disparities in this metric still exist across gender, income, marital status, and race and ethnicity groups.

Survey Methods

Results are based on telephone interviews conducted Jan. 1–March 31, 2015, as part of the Gallup-Healthways Well-Being Index survey, with a random sample of 43,575 adults, aged 18 and older, living in all 50 U.S. states and the District of Columbia. For results based on the total sample of national adults, the margin of sampling error is ±0.6 percentage points at the 95% confidence level.

June 08, 2015

U.S. STANDARD OF LIVING INDEX TIES HIGH OF +52

by Justin McCarthy

Story Highlights

- *May index reading matches previous high in March*
- *Four in five Americans satisfied with standard of living*
- *Sixty-three percent say standard of living getting better*

WASHINGTON, D.C.—Americans' positivity about their standard of living continued to be buoyant in May, with a score of +52 on Gallup's Standard of Living Index. The index has been +50 or higher for the past six months, including the May reading, which tied the high in March.

Gallup U.S. Standard of Living Index, Monthly Averages

Right now, do you feel your standard of living is getting better or getting worse?
Are you satisfied or dissatisfied with your standard of living, all the things you can buy and do?

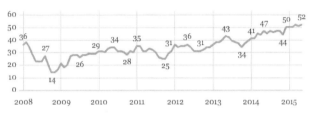

Gallup Daily tracking
The Standard of Living Index is based on a composite of the two questions.

GALLUP

From a long-term view, Americans' opinions of their standard of living have improved since the index reached a low of +14 in October and November 2008 in the midst of the global economic crisis. After gradual increases in the index in the following years, Americans' evaluations of their standard of living returned to early recession levels by 2013. Since then, aside from a gradual decline during the federal government shutdown in 2013, Americans have grown steadily more positive about their standard of living.

Gallup's Standard of Living Index is a composite of Americans' responses to two questions: one asking whether they are satisfied with their standard of living, and the other asking whether their standard of living is getting better or worse. The index has a theoretical maximum of 100 (if all respondents say they are satisfied with their standard of living and say it is getting better) and a theoretical minimum of -100 (if all respondents are dissatisfied with their standard of living and say it is getting worse).

Both Current Standard of Living and Optimism for Its Future Are Steady

In May, 81% of Americans said they were satisfied with their current standard of living, similar to the ratings Gallup has measured

for more than a year. However, the latest reading ties the high point in satisfaction, previously reached in December 2014. Americans have been largely satisfied with their standard of living even at the depths of the recession, with the low point at 69% in 2008.

Americans' perceptions of whether their standard of living is improving or worsening have varied over time. Currently, 63% of Americans say their standard of living is getting better, which is nearly twice as high as the low of 33% in October 2008. The current figure is one percentage point below the seven-year high of 64%, registered in March and April.

Americans' Satisfaction With Their Current Standard of Living

Are you satisfied or dissatisfied with your standard of living, all the things you can buy and do?

% Satisfied

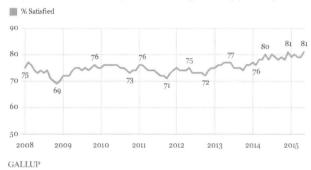

GALLUP

Americans' Future Expectations for Their Standard of Living

Right now, do you feel your standard of living is getting better or getting worse?

% Getting better   % Getting worse

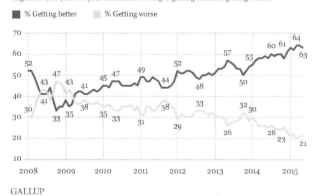

GALLUP

Bottom Line

Though Americans' faith in the U.S. economy has retreated into negative territory as 2015 has progressed, their feelings about their personal standard of living have held steady and even improved. Americans are often much more positive about their personal situation or conditions in their local area than in the broader country. Gallup has found large and consistent differences in how Americans rate personal and local versus national healthcare and health insurance, crime and schools.

Survey Methods

Results for this Gallup poll are based on telephone interviews conducted May 1–31, 2015, on the Gallup U.S. Daily survey, with a random sample of 3,178 adults, aged 18 and older, living in all 50 U.S. states and the District of Columbia. For results based on the total sample of national adults, the margin of sampling error is ±2 percentage points at the 95% confidence level. All reported margins of sampling error include computed design effects for weighting.

June 08, 2015
FEWER YOUNG PEOPLE SAY I DO— TO ANY RELATIONSHIP

by Lydia Saad

PRINCETON, N.J.—Along with the decline in marriages among 18- to 29-year-olds in the U.S. in recent years, Gallup trends on Americans' living arrangements reveal that the percentage of young adults "living together" has hardly budged. This means that not only are fewer young adults married, but also that fewer are in committed relationships. As a result, the percentage of young adults who report being single and not living with someone has risen dramatically in the past decade, from 52% in 2004 to 64% in 2014.

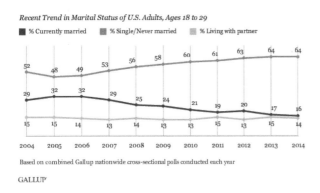

Recent Trend in Marital Status of U.S. Adults, Ages 18 to 29

Based on combined Gallup nationwide cross-sectional polls conducted each year

GALLUP

30-Somethings Gravitating Toward Unmarried Partnerships

Marriage remains the dominant living arrangement for people in their 30s. However, in contrast to the sharp rise in the percentage of 20-somethings leading a single lifestyle, 30-somethings were only slightly more likely to be single in 2014 compared with a decade earlier. This is because, while the percentage of 30-somethings who are married has declined about 10 percentage points, the percentage living together has increased significantly—nearly doubling from 7% to 13%.

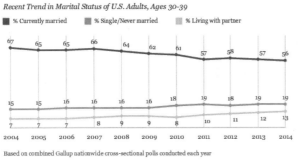

Recent Trend in Marital Status of U.S. Adults, Ages 30-39

Based on combined Gallup nationwide cross-sectional polls conducted each year

GALLUP

Meanwhile, the living arrangements of adults aged 40 and older are largely unchanged. For the past decade, approximately six in 10 reported being married, between 7% and 8% reported being single/never married, and between 3% and 5% reported living together.

These findings are based on yearly aggregates of Gallup's nationwide cross-sectional surveys, encompassing between 15,000 and 32,000 interviews each year.

Broad-Based Increase in Single 20-Somethings

The increase in 18- to 29-year-olds identifying as single and never married is seen across a broad range of subgroups, including by race, education, region and political party.

Still, young Southerners are slightly less likely than their counterparts in other regions to be single, and young whites and Hispanics are less likely to be single than young blacks. Additionally, fewer young women than young men are single, suggesting many women in their 20s are married to men 30 or older. And college graduates are less likely to be single than those with only some or no college education.

Percentage of Adults Ages 18 to 29 Who Are Single/Never Married

	2004	2014	Change
	%	%	pct. pts.
Total aged 18 to 29	52	64	+12
Men	55	68	+13
Women	49	60	+11
Non-Hispanic white	49	61	+12
Non-Hispanic black	66	77	+11
Hispanic	47	61	+14
College graduate	43	55	+12
Some college	52	67	+15
No college	55	66	+11
East	56	66	+10
Midwest	52	68	+16
South	50	59	+9
West	50	64	+14
Republican	43	60	+17
Independent	53	64	+11
Democratic	57	69	+12

Based on combined Gallup nationwide cross-sectional polls conducted each year

GALLUP

Bottom Line

It is widely known that fewer young people today are getting married. But Gallup's data reveal that young adults are not simply swapping marriage for living together, but rather staying single longer. This doesn't necessarily mean young adults are staying out of relationships, just that they are less likely to be making the more serious commitment associated with moving in together—whether in marriage or not. It also doesn't mean they are completely independent. In 2013, Gallup found 14% of adults aged 24 to 34 were living under a parent's roof.

This rise of singledom is particularly evident with 18- to 29-year-olds, increasing by roughly a quarter since 2004, from 52%

to 64%. But it is also evident among adults aged 30 to 39, creeping up from 15% to 19% over the same period.

The important question for society is whether the dramatic shift in living arrangements seen among 20-somethings persists into their 30s, furthering the revolution in U.S. household and family structure. At least attitudinally, Gallup recently found adults in the 18- to 34-year-old age bracket expressing nearly as much desire as older adults to be married, even as they themselves were far less likely to be married currently. But whether that desire among these younger Americans materializes in the coming years remains to be seen.

Survey Methods

Results are based on yearly aggregated data from Gallup Poll Social Series surveys and other multiple-day cross-sectional telephone polls conducted between 2004 and 2014. Each yearly aggregate is based on a minimum of 15,000 interviews with adults, aged 18 and older, and as many as nearly 32,000 interviews. These include interviews with between 1,340 and 3,616 adults aged 18 to 29, and 1,788 to 4,733 adults aged 30 to 49.

For results based on the total sample of national adults in any given year, the maximum margin of sampling error is ±1 percentage point at the 95% confidence level.

For results based on the total sample of Americans ages 18 to 29 or 30 to 39 in any given year, the maximum margin of sampling error is ±3 percentage points at the 95% confidence level.

June 10, 2015
TRUST IN U.S. GOVERNMENT'S TERRORISM PROTECTION AT NEW LOW

by Rebecca Riffkin

Story Highlights

- *67% confident in government terrorism protection*
- *Among highest percentage to worry about being terror victim*
- *Fewer fear a terror attack will happen in next few weeks*

WASHINGTON, D.C.—Two in three Americans say they have a "great deal" or a "fair amount" of confidence in the U.S. government's ability to protect citizens from terror attacks. While this is still a sizable majority, the 67% who are confident is the lowest level that Gallup has measured since it first asked the question after the 9/11 terror attacks.

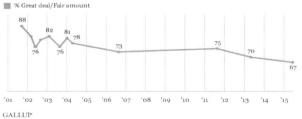

Confidence in U.S. Government to Protect Citizens From Terrorism

How much confidence do you have in the U.S. government to protect its citizens from future acts of terrorism -- a great deal, a fair amount, not very much, or none at all?

■ % Great deal/Fair amount

GALLUP

In 2001, amid the rally in support for government leaders and institutions after the 9/11 terror attacks, 88% of Americans said they had a "great deal" or a "fair amount" of confidence in the U.S. government to protect citizens from future acts of terror. This reading is the highest percentage measured so far.

Confidence in the government remained high between 2001 and 2004, averaging 80% over this period. But on average, 71% have expressed confidence in the four times Gallup has polled on this question since 2004. This decline has come as Americans' trust in government more generally has hit new lows.

More Americans Worried About Becoming Victims of Terror

Slightly less than half of Americans, 49%, are at least somewhat worried that they or someone in their family will become a victim of terrorism. This is up from worry in recent years, and by one percentage point is the highest Gallup has found since February 2003. The last time concern about being a terror victim was significantly higher than this was in the initial weeks after 9/11, when the percentage of Americans who worried about becoming victims of terror reached as high as 59%. Gallup polled often on this topic in the months following the attacks, and by early 2002, 35% were worried about becoming a victim of terror.

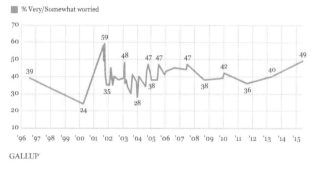

Worries About Becoming a Terrorism Victim Up in 2015

How worried are you that you or someone in your family will become a victim of terrorism -- very worried, somewhat worried, not too worried, or not worried at all?

■ % Very/Somewhat worried

GALLUP

The increase in the percentage of Americans who are concerned about being victims of terrorism is reflected in another recent Gallup question asked each March. This year's update showed a spike in the percentage of Americans who worry a great deal about the possibility of future terrorist attacks in the U.S., rising from 39% in 2014 to 51% this year. This increase is possibly attributable to the growing threat that Americans perceive from the Islamic State group, or ISIS, which now controls substantial parts of Iraq and beheaded three Americans in separate incidents last fall.

Although Americans' worry about terrorism is in the upper range of what Gallup has measured over the last 15 years, their expectations that a terror attack is likely to occur are not. Forty-five percent of Americans think it is very or somewhat likely there will be acts of terrorism in the U.S. in the next few weeks. In 2013, just over a week after the Boston Marathon bombings, 51% of Americans thought it was likely a terror attack would soon hit the country.

Gallup has previously found that the percentage of Americans who fear an attack is imminent has spiked either following attacks or in fear of retaliation, such as in 2003 after the beginning of the Iraq War and in early 2011 after the killing of Osama bin Laden.

Implications

Americans' confidence in the U.S. government to protect its citizens from terrorist events has dropped, which may reflect growing public concern about ISIS in the Middle East and North Africa. The group has killed several Americans, both soldiers and journalists, as well as foreign Christians and Iraqi soldiers. Its continued strength, despite military actions against it in Syria and Iraq, may be disconcerting to Americans.

This elevated public concern could pave the way for an expansion of government anti-terror programs, but lawmakers should be aware that the public still favors limits on such activity. Gallup recently found that 65% of Americans feel the government should take steps to prevent terrorism—but not at the risk of trampling on civil liberties.

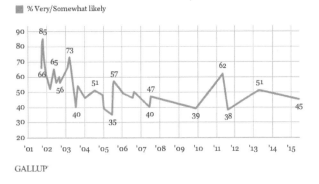

Perceived Likelihood of Acts of Terrorism Occuring in Next Few Weeks

How likely is it that there will be acts of terrorism in the United States over the next several weeks -- very likely, somewhat likely, not too likely, or not at all likely?

■ % Very/Somewhat likely

GALLUP

Survey Methods

Results for this Gallup poll are based on telephone interviews conducted June 2–7, 2015, with a random sample of 1,527 adults, aged 18 and older, living in all 50 U.S. states and the District of Columbia. For results based on the total sample of national adults, the margin of sampling error is ±3 percentage points at the 95% confidence level. All reported margins of sampling error include computed design effects for weighting.

June 10, 2015
AMERICANS STILL SAY LIBERTIES
SHOULD TRUMP ANTI-TERRORISM

by Jeffrey M. Jones

Story Highlights

- *65% say anti-terror efforts should not violate liberties*
- *30% prioritize anti-terrorism over protecting liberties*
- *41% of Americans say government efforts violate their liberties*

PRINCETON, N.J.—The federal government's recent actions to limit the scope of what it can do to prevent terrorism are consistent with Americans' preference to prioritize civil liberties over anti-terrorism efforts when the two come into conflict. Sixty-five percent of Americans say the government should take steps to prevent terrorism but not violate civil liberties, while 30% think any steps to prevent terrorism are justified, even if they violate liberties. In the first few months after 9/11, Americans were more divided on the issue.

The latest results are based on a June 2–7 Gallup poll, conducted after Congress passed and President Barack Obama signed into law the USA Freedom Act, designed to replace the expiring and controversial Patriot Act that was passed after the Sept. 11, 2001, terrorist attacks. These laws help define the scope of government efforts to prevent terrorist attacks against the U.S. Notably, the new law does not authorize the government to collect data on citizens' electronic communications, a secret program that was exposed by former government contractor and now U.S. exile Edward Snowden. However, the government can still obtain those records from the phone companies if it has a warrant.

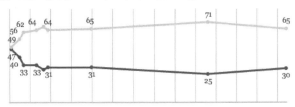

Americans' Views of Tradeoffs Between Anti-Terrorism Efforts and Respecting Civil Liberties

■ % Take all steps necessary to prevent terrorism even if civil liberties violated

▨ % Take steps to prevent terrorism but not violate civil liberties

GALLUP

In January 2002, four months after the 9/11 attacks and with concerns about terrorism still high, 47% of Americans said the government should take all necessary steps to prevent terrorism, even those that violated individual civil liberties, while 49% said anti-terror efforts should stop short of violating civil liberties.

A year after the attacks, in September 2002, Americans showed a greater concern for civil liberties, with 62% saying anti-terror efforts should not violate civil liberties and 33% giving anti-terror efforts the higher priority. Since then, opinion has not fundamentally changed, although the 65% who currently prioritize protecting civil liberties is down slightly from 71% in 2011.

Republicans and Democrats currently hold similar views of whether maintaining security or protecting civil liberties is more important in government anti-terror efforts. Among Republicans and Republican-leaning independents, 66% say civil liberties should be the higher priority and 29% say protecting citizens from terrorism should be. Meanwhile, Democrats and Democratic-leaning independents prioritize civil liberties over security by 64% to 32%.

In January and June 2002, Republicans were more sensitive to security from terrorism than to protecting civil liberties. By September 2002, they shifted toward prioritizing civil liberties and have done so since. They have become even more likely to say civil liberties should be respected with Obama in office than they were when George W. Bush was still president.

Republicans' Views of Tradeoffs Between Anti-Terrorism Efforts and Respecting Civil Liberties

Based on Republicans and Republican-leaning independents

■ % Take all necessary steps to prevent terrorism even if civil liberties violated

▨ % Take steps to prevent terrorism but not violate civil liberties

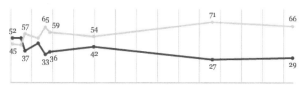

2002 2003 2004 2005 2006 2007 2008 2009 2010 2011 2012 2013 2014 2015

GALLUP

Democrats have always given greater weight to protecting civil liberties, but in the immediate aftermath of 9/11 they showed a closer divide on whether civil liberties or security from terrorism should be the higher priority. Like Republicans, Democrats became more sensitive to protecting civil liberties over time. However, the current results suggest a dip in the percentage favoring the protection of civil liberties, perhaps relating to having a Democratic president—one who called on Congress to pass the USA Freedom Act—overseeing the federal government.

Democrats' Views of Tradeoffs Between Anti-Terrorism Efforts and Respecting Civil Liberties

Based on Democrats and Democratic-leaning independents

■ % Take all necessary steps to prevent terrorism even if civil liberties violated

▨ % Take steps to prevent terrorism but not violate civil liberties

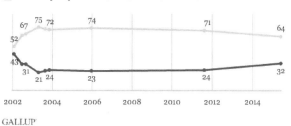

2002   2004   2006   2008   2010   2012   2014

GALLUP

Most Say Terror Efforts Do Not Violate Their Liberties

Some congressional critics of government anti-terrorism methods, most notably Kentucky Sen. Rand Paul, argue that the government has too many powers in this area that violate citizens' rights. The majority of Americans, 55%, disagree, saying they do not believe such government programs violate their civil liberties. But that leaves a sizable minority of 41% who do feel the government is violating their civil liberties. Gallup asked this question for the first time in the June 2–7 poll, so it is not possible to know whether these views differ from those in the past.

Although members of key subgroups vary in the extent to which they believe government efforts to prevent terrorism violate their civil liberties, all groups fall below the majority level. Men are closest at 49%, and are much more likely than women (33%) to believe government anti-terrorism programs violate their civil liberties. There are no differences by political party, although political liberals are more likely than conservatives to say these programs infringe on their liberties. Across age groups, senior citizens are less likely than younger Americans to believe the programs violate their civil liberties.

Implications

The new USA Freedom Act was passed in a public opinion environment very different from that of the 2001 Patriot Act. Once the heightened concern about terrorism evident in the first several months after 9/11 faded, Americans began to place a greater emphasis on protecting civil liberties when thinking about preventing further acts of terrorism. Importantly, those shifts in public opinion occurred long before Snowden exposed the vast government program of collecting data on Americans' electronic communications. And Americans continue to place a greater emphasis on civil liberties even as concern about terrorism has risen amid the growing threat of ISIS.

The change in the public opinion climate, which is reflected in the views of elected representatives, may help explain why the newly passed USA Freedom Act pulls back some of the powers the Patriot Act provided to the government in its efforts to prevent terrorism.

Belief That Government Anti-Terror Efforts Violate Your Civil Liberties, by Subgroup

From what you know or have read about them, do you think the government's programs designed to prevent additional acts of terrorism violate your civil liberties, or not?

	Yes, violate civil liberties	No, do not
	%	%
National adults	41	55
Men	49	47
Women	33	62
18 to 29 years old	44	53
30 to 49 years old	45	51
50 to 64 years old	40	56
65+ years old	30	61
Non-Hispanic white	41	55
Nonwhite	40	54
Democrat/Lean Democratic	40	56
Republican/Lean Republican	42	55
Liberal	48	51
Moderate	41	55
Conservative	38	56
Postgraduate education	41	56
College graduate only	44	54
Some college	46	50
High school or less	35	58

June 2-7, 2015

GALLUP

Survey Methods

Results for this Gallup poll are based on telephone interviews conducted June 2–7, 2015, with a random sample of 1,527 adults, aged 18 and older, living in all 50 U.S. states and the District of Columbia. For results based on the total sample of national adults, the margin of sampling error is ±3 percentage points at the 95% confidence level.

June 11, 2015
VIEWS OF RACE RELATIONS AS TOP PROBLEM STILL DIFFER BY RACE

by Alyssa Brown

Story Highlights

- *13% of U.S. blacks mention race relations as top problem*
- *4% of whites say the same*
- *Blacks more likely than whites to cite unemployment as top issue*

WASHINGTON, D.C.—Black Americans' mentions of race relations as the most important problem facing the U.S. reached 15% in the last quarter of 2014, up from 3% at the beginning of that year. Mentions have remained relatively high since, averaging 13% in the most recent quarter, from April to June 2015. Since early 2014, white Americans' mentions of race relations as a top problem have increased only slightly, from 1% to 4%.

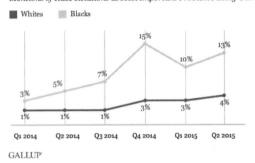

Mentions of Race Relations as Most Important Problem Facing U.S.

GALLUP

The nine-percentage-point gap in the latest quarter between blacks' and whites' mentions of race relations as the top U.S. problem is significantly wider than the narrow gap of no more than four points in any year from 2002 to 2007. A number of high-profile police incidents of unarmed black men in 2014 and 2015 sparked protests across the country and elevated discussion of race relations. Three of the more highly publicized deaths involved Michael Brown in Ferguson, Missouri; Freddie Gray in Baltimore; and Eric Garner in Staten Island, New York.

These findings are based on six quarters of Gallup's monthly measurement of the "most important problem" question from January 2014 through June 2015.

Overall, Americans' mentions of race relations as a top problem increased from 1% in the first quarter of 2014 to 5% in the fourth quarter of 2014, including a reading of 13% in December, and have remained in the 4% to 5% range in 2015. While race relations has risen as a top issue since early 2014, dissatisfaction with government, the economy and unemployment still dominate Americans' list of the most important problems facing the country.

Blacks, Whites Also Differ on Unemployment as Top Problem

The top problems that blacks saw facing the country in the latest quarter were race relations (13%) and unemployment (13%), while whites most often cited dissatisfaction government (18%) and the economy in general (12%).

Blacks have consistently been more likely than whites to perceive unemployment as a top problem, a pattern Gallup has

previously documented. This pattern may reflect real-world differences in unemployment among the groups. The unemployment rate was 10.2% among blacks in May 2015, more than double the 4.7% of whites who were unemployed, according to the U.S. Bureau of Labor Statistics.

Other issues that are more glaring for blacks than for whites are crime and violence as well as poverty, homelessness and hunger. The latter may reflect that blacks have lower average incomes than whites and are more likely to be living in poverty. This is also consistent with a Gallup and Healthways finding that blacks are twice as likely as whites to report having struggled to afford food at least once in the previous 12 months.

Whites are more concerned about the federal budget deficit and debt as well as terrorism, while both groups are equally likely to cite healthcare and education as top problems.

Most Commonly Named Problems Facing the U.S., by Race

What do you think is the most important problem facing this country today? [OPEN-ENDED]
April-June 2015

	Whites	Blacks
Dissatisfaction with government	18%	10%
Economy in general	12%	10%
Unemployment/Jobs	8%	13%
Race relations	4%	13%
Immigration/Illegal aliens	6%	3%
Healthcare	6%	6%
Federal budget deficit/Federal debt	5%	0%
Education	4%	5%
Ethical/Moral/Family decline	5%	3%
Terrorism	5%	1%
Poverty/Hunger/Homelessness	4%	7%
Crime/Violence	1%	5%

Note: Issues mentioned by less than 5% of either group not shown

GALLUP

Implications

After the highly publicized outcry in Ferguson after Brown's death, blacks became just as likely to name race relations as the nation's top problem as they were to name unemployment. And this level of concern has held following riots in Baltimore stemming from Gray's death after Gray was taken into police custody. Whites' mentions of race relations as a top problem did climb slightly over the same time period, but not nearly as much as among blacks.

Just as blacks and whites differ in their views of race relations as a top U.S. problem, they also stand apart in their views on the fairness of the criminal justice system, confidence in police and the need for new civil rights laws. Gallup found last June that 68% of blacks said the American criminal justice system is biased against black people, significantly higher than the 25% of whites who said the same. And while 37% of blacks said they had a "great deal" or "quite a lot" of confidence in the police, 59% of whites said the same. Gallup has also found that blacks are much more likely than whites to say new civil rights laws are needed and that the government should be actively involved in improving minorities' economic and social status.

Blacks' elevated views of race relations as a top problem in the U.S. may persist in the months ahead, after the release of a highly publicized video last week of a white police officer shoving a black teenager in a bikini to the ground in McKinney, Texas.

Results for this Gallup poll are based on telephone interviews conducted April–June 2015, with a random sample of 3,566 adults, aged 18 and older, living in all 50 U.S. states and the District of Columbia. For results based on the total sample of national adults, the margin of sampling error is ±2 percentage points at the 95% confidence level.

For results based on the total sample of 2,698 non-Hispanic whites, the margin of sampling error is ±2 percentage points at the 95% confidence level.

For results based on the total sample of 352 non-Hispanic blacks, the margin of sampling error is ±7 percentage points at the 95% confidence level.

June 12, 2015
MOST IN U.S. SAY LOW GAS PRICES MAKE DIFFERENCE IN FINANCES

by Art Swift

Story Highlights

- *57% say cheaper gas in the last year is making some monetary difference*
- *"Paying down bills" most popular way to spend money saved on gas*
- *The bigger the effect on finances, the more likely to pay down bills*

WASHINGTON, D.C.—U.S. gas prices are nearly a dollar lower than they were a year ago and have been running below their 2014 peak since last spring. But what is the effect of the increase in disposable income on Americans? And where is that money going?

A majority of Americans, 57%, say lower gas prices are making a noticeable difference in their household finances, including 27% who say they are making a "big difference."

The Effect of Gas Prices on Americans' Finances

Gas prices remain nearly $1 per gallon lower than they were a year ago. How much of a difference have these lower gas prices made to your household's financial situation -- a big difference, some difference, only a little difference or no difference at all?

	Big difference	Some difference	A little difference	No difference
Jun 2-7, 2015	27%	30%	25%	17%

GALLUP

The June 2–7 Gallup poll finds only modest differences by income, meaning lower gas prices are not disproportionately helping lower- or middle-income Americans more.

Oil prices began a rapid slide last summer because of oversupply, increased efficiency in production and Saudi Arabia's willingness to allow prices to drop lower than they had been in recent years. After years of prices being higher than $3 per gallon for regular gas, the average price in the U.S. has been lower than $3 since November of last year. In much of the country, gas fell below $2 per gallon as 2015 began, though the average price in the U.S. has been rising recently.

When asked what they are doing with the money they are saving because of lower gas prices, 42% say they are "paying down bills," as opposed to "spending it" (24%) or "saving it" (28%). This suggests that the extra money in Americans' pockets is not bolstering the economy as some predicted in 2014.

While paying down bills could technically be considered a form of spending, it is not spending that generally helps the economy because it covers previous purchases that were already recorded in the nation's gross domestic product. With spending across the U.S. sluggish in the early months of 2015, it is possible that lower gas prices are not contributing to greater spending or GDP growth.

Paying down bills is the most common way consumers are using the money they are saving on gas, regardless of whether they say the savings make "a big difference," "some difference" or "little to no difference" to them financially. Among those who say savings from lower gas prices are making a big difference, a majority (53%) say they are using the extra money to pay down bills, greater than the overall average nationwide. However, using this extra money to pay bills diminishes with lessening financial effect, as those who say lower gas prices have made little to no difference are the least likely to say they are using the extra cash to pay down bills.

What Americans Are Doing With the Money They're Saving on Gas, by Effect on Household Finances

Which of the following are you mainly doing with the money you are saving as a result of lower gas prices -- spending it, saving it or paying down bills?

	Paying down bills	Saving it	Spending it
	%	%	%
National adults	42	28	24
Among those who say lower prices are making "a big difference"	53	22	21
Among those who say lower prices are making "some difference"	45	29	24
Among those who say lower prices are making "little to no difference"	34	31	28

GALLUP

Bottom Line

As gas prices remain below $3 per gallon nationwide, with analysts saying that prices will stay that way for the foreseeable future, many Americans have more money to spend. With GDP growth in negative territory in the first quarter of 2015, the money Americans are not spending on gas isn't necessarily being spent on goods and services, which would bolster the economy. It is possible that people are buying more gas, however, as driving is up from last year, according to researchers at New York brokerage Convergex.

Americans using their newfound savings on gas to pay down bills is not unexpected, as that seems to be their normal inclination when they get extra money. For example, when President George W. Bush spearheaded a rebate for U.S. taxpayers in 2001, more Americans then said they planned to pay bills than opted for saving or spending. Some forecasters have said that the drop in oil has stabilized, so it is also conceivable that Americans may enter a "new normal" of expecting more disposable income and that it may not seem like extra money in time after all.

Survey Methods

Results for this Gallup poll are based on telephone interviews conducted June 2–7, 2015, on the Gallup U.S. Daily survey, with a random sample of 1,527 adults, aged 18 and older, living in all 50 U.S. states and the District of Columbia. For results based on the total sample of national adults, the margin of sampling error is ±3 percentage points at the 95% confidence level.

June 12, 2015

FEWER IN U.S. VIEW IRAQ, AFGHANISTAN WARS AS MISTAKES

by Andrew Dugan

Story Highlights

- *51% say 2003 Iraq War was a mistake, down from 57% in 2014*
- *42% say 2001 Afghanistan conflict was a mistake, down from 49%*
- *Democrats now less likely to see either conflict as mistake*

WASHINGTON, D.C.—Amid a security situation in Iraq and Afghanistan that continues to be contentious, a smaller share of Americans now than last year view the conflict in Afghanistan or the Iraq War as a mistake. A slim majority, 51%, say the 2003 decision to send troops to Iraq was a mistake, down six percentage points from 2014. A little more than four in 10 (42%) say the 2001 military action in Afghanistan was a mistake, also a drop from last year's 49% reading.

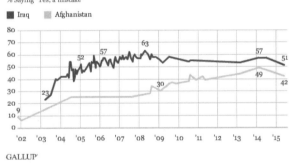

Perceptions That U.S. Made a Mistake in Sending Troops to Iraq and Afghanistan
% Saying "Yes, a mistake"

Official military operations have ended in both Iraq and Afghanistan, but the U.S. is still heavily involved in those countries' security affairs. Over the past year, U.S. military involvement in both countries could be characterized as on the rise, or at least not on the wane. This week, President Barack Obama announced the deployment of an additional 450 troops to Iraq to aid in the fight against the militant group Islamic State, bringing the total number of troops sent since June of last year to 3,550. Obama made good in 2011 on a campaign pledge to withdraw all American troops from Iraq, though he has since had to reverse course as the Islamic State group overran portions of the country.

In Afghanistan, a muscular Taliban insurgency has also complicated Obama's efforts to withdraw troops from that country, a goal most Americans shared when Gallup last asked about it in 2012. In March, Obama announced he would maintain U.S. troop levels, which stand at 9,800, until at least the end of 2015, a break from previous plans for a speedier withdrawal.

Still, these countries' ongoing challenges have not led to a rising level of regret among the American populace for having entered Iraq or Afghanistan. Iraq remains the theater of operations Americans are more likely to see as a mistake, as has been the case since the U.S. began the military campaign in March 2003. Nonetheless, initial support for U.S. involvement was quite positive, but by the summer of 2004 a majority had decided that it was a mistake—a quicker souring on the military action than had occurred in the 1960s after the nation's initial involvement in Vietnam.

The percentage saying involvement in Iraq was a mistake rose to as high as 63% in 2008, and has varied since then, but has stayed above 50%. These most recent findings rank as one of the most "positive" assessments of the Iraq war since September 2006, when the country was evenly divided on this question.

Far fewer Americans have historically considered the Afghanistan military action as a mistake; in fact, at no point has a majority expressed this viewpoint. But the level considering it a mistake has gradually grown as the engagement has worn on, peaking at 49% last year before dipping back down this year.

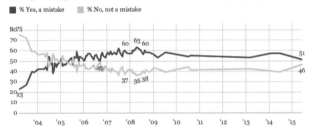

Looking back, do you think the United States made a mistake sending troops to fight in Iraq?

■ % Yes, a mistake   ■ % No, not a mistake

Wording from 2003-2010: "In view of the developments since we first sent our troops to Iraq, do you think the United States made a mistake in sending troops to Iraq, or not?"

GALLUP

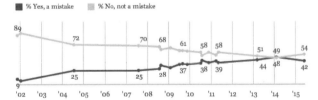

Looking back, do you think the United States made a mistake sending troops to fight in Afghanistan?

■ % Yes, a mistake   ■ % No, not a mistake

Wording from 2001-2011: "Thinking now about U.S. military action in Afghanistan that began in October 2001, do you think the United States made a mistake in sending military forces to Afghanistan, or not?"

GALLUP

Democrats Less Likely Today to See Iraq War as a Mistake

While Republicans remain the political group least likely to express regret for the Iraq or Afghanistan wars, a slight change in Democrats' and independents' views is why a lower proportion of the country now sees either conflict as a mistake. Compared with last year, Democrats are seven points less likely to see Iraq as a mistake and eight points less likely to see Afghanistan as a mistake. Independents saw similar movement on these questions.

Americans' Retrospective Opinions on Wars in Iraq and Afghanistan, by Party
% Saying "Yes, a mistake"

	February 2014	June 2015	Change (pct. pts.)
IRAQ			
Democrats	75	68	-7
Independents	60	52	-8
Republicans	30	31	+1
AFGHANISTAN			
Democrats	61	53	-8
Independents	51	43	-8
Republicans	29	27	-2

GALLUP

Bottom Line

Recent events suggest the chapter has not closed on U.S. military involvement in Afghanistan or Iraq. But even in this context, the percentage of Americans viewing either conflict as a mistake has fallen relative to last year and, for Iraq, the figure is one of the lowest in recent history.

Survey Methods

Results for this Gallup poll are based on telephone interviews conducted June 2–7, 2015, with a random sample of 1,527 adults, aged 18 and older, living in all 50 U.S. states and the District of Columbia. For results based on the total sample of national adults, the margin of sampling error is ±3 percentage points at the 95% confidence level. All reported margins of sampling error include computed design effects for weighting.

June 15, 2015
CONFIDENCE IN U.S. INSTITUTIONS STILL BELOW HISTORICAL NORMS

by Jeffrey M. Jones

Story Highlights

- *Only military, small business top historical averages*
- *Military, small business highest-rated institutions overall*
- *Confidence in organized religion, police at all-time lows*

PRINCETON, N.J.—Americans' confidence in most major U.S. institutions remains below the historical average for each one. Only the military (72%) and small business (67%)—the highest-rated institutions in this year's poll—are currently rated higher than their historical norms, based on the percentage expressing "a great deal" or "quite a lot" of confidence in the institution.

These results are based on a June 2–7 Gallup poll that included Gallup's latest update on confidence in U.S. institutions. Gallup first measured confidence ratings in 1973 and has updated them each year since 1993.

Americans' confidence in most major institutions has been down for many years as the nation has dealt with prolonged wars in Iraq and Afghanistan, a major recession and sluggish economic improvement, and partisan gridlock in Washington. In fact, 2004

was the last year most institutions were at or above their historical average levels of confidence. Perhaps not coincidentally, 2004 was also the last year Americans' satisfaction with the way things are going in the United States averaged better than 40%. Currently, 28% of Americans are satisfied with the state of the nation.

Confidence in U.S. Institutions, 2015 vs. Historical Average for Each Institution
Figures are the percentages with "a great deal" or "quite a lot" of confidence in the institution

	Current year	Historical average	Difference
	%	%	pct. pts.
The military	72	68	+4
Small business	67	63	+4
The criminal justice system	23	24	-1
The medical system	37	38	-1
Organized labor	24	26	-2
Big business	21	24	-3
The police	52	57	-5
Newspapers	24	32	-8
Television news	21	30	-9
The public schools	31	40	-9
The presidency	33	43	-10
The U.S. Supreme Court	32	44	-12
Banks	28	40	-12
The church or organized religion	42	55	-13
Congress	8	24	-16

Current year data are based on June 2-7, 2015, poll. Historical averages are based on all times Gallup has asked about institution, which for most of them dates back to 1973 or 1993.

GALLUP

From a broad perspective, Americans' confidence in all institutions over the last two years has been the lowest since Gallup began systematic updates of a larger set of institutions in 1993. The average confidence rating of the 14 institutions asked about annually since 1993—excluding small business, asked annually since 2007—is 32% this year. This is one percentage point above the all-institution average of 31% last year. Americans were generally more confident in all institutions in the late 1990s and early 2000s as the country enjoyed a strong economy and a rally in support for U.S. institutions after the 9/11 terrorist attacks.

Average Confidence Rating Across All Institutions, by Year
Figures are the average percentage of Americans who have "a great deal" or "quite a lot" of confidence across all institutions

■ % Confident

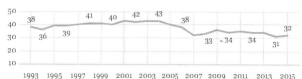

Average is based on the 14 institutions asked annually since 1993, including all institutions asked in 2015 except small business.

GALLUP

Confidence in Political, Financial and Religious Institutions Especially Low

Today's confidence ratings of Congress, organized religion, banks, the Supreme Court and the presidency show the greatest deficits compared with their historical averages, all running at least 10 points below that mark. Americans' frustration with the government's performance has eroded the trust they have in all U.S.

political institutions. Likewise, Americans' confidence in banks fell after the bursting of the housing bubble and the subsequent financial crisis.

The large decline in confidence in organized religion is likely tied to a decline in religiosity overall, but also to scandals that have plagued various religious organizations, most notably the Catholic Church. This year's 42% score for confidence in the church or organized religion is the lowest Gallup has measured for that institution. The prior low was 44% in 2012.

Confidence in the police, at 52% this year, ties the low for that institution recorded in the first year it was measured, 1993. In the past year, the police have been a major focus of news coverage in several incidents in which white police officers' actions resulted in the deaths of black men they were trying to apprehend.

Still, the church and the police rank among the highest-rated institutions, trailing only the military and small business among the 15 institutions tested in this year's poll. Further back in history, the church ranked first or tied for first in all but one survey from 1973 through 1988. Since then, the military has been the top-ranked institution each year except 1997, when small business was first.

Congress is the institution in which Americans express the least confidence this year, with 8% doing so, one point above its 7% rating last year—the lowest Gallup has ever measured for any institution. Congress has ranked last each year since 2010, and a total of 12 times since 1973. Other institutions that have held this unwelcome distinction in the past include big business (nine times), health maintenance organizations (eight), the criminal justice system (six) and organized labor (four). The top- and bottom-rated institutions in each Confidence in Institutions poll are shown at the bottom of this story.

Implications

Americans continue to show lower levels of confidence in most of the major institutions central to U.S. society, with only the military and small business getting ratings in 2015 that are above their historical averages. That speaks to the broader dissatisfaction Americans have with the state of the nation more generally over the past decade as the U.S. has faced serious economic, international and political challenges. Americans have tended to be more confident in U.S. institutions when the economy has been strong, such as in the mid-1980s and the late 1990s and early 2000s. Although Americans are now more upbeat about the economy than they were in 2008–2013, they are not yet convinced that the economy is good, given that their assessments of national economic conditions remain more negative than positive.

Survey Methods

Results for this Gallup poll are based on telephone interviews conducted June 2–7, 2015, with a random sample of 1,527 adults, aged 18 and older, living in all 50 U.S. states and the District of Columbia. For results based on the total sample of national adults, the margin of sampling error is ±3 percentage points at the 95% confidence level. All reported margins of sampling error include computed design effects for weighting.

June 15, 2015
CONFIDENCE IN U.S. BRANCHES OF GOVERNMENT REMAINS LOW

by Justin McCarthy

Story Highlights

- *Americans' confidence in presidency up four points, at 33%*
- *Thirty-two percent have confidence in the Supreme Court*
- *Congress retains the least confidence, at 8%*

WASHINGTON, D.C.—Americans' confidence in each of the three branches of the U.S. government remains low, with confidence in Congress and the Supreme Court near their all-time lows reached last year. Currently, 33% of Americans have "a great deal" or "quite a lot" of confidence in the presidency, 32% are this confident in the Supreme Court, and Congress is still well behind, at 8%.

While Congress has consistently received the lowest confidence rating of the three branches of government, the Supreme Court and the presidency usually track each other closely. This is apart from times when the incumbent president has been extremely popular, as in 1991 and 2002, or exceptionally unpopular, as in 2007 and 2008.

Gallup's June 2–7 poll found confidence in the presidency rising slightly to 33% from 29% last year, which in turn was just four percentage points above the historical low of 25% in 2007. The uptick in confidence in the presidency this year is consistent with Americans' higher job approval ratings of President Barack Obama since last fall.

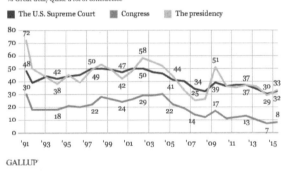

Americans' Level of Confidence in the Three Branches of Government
% Great deal/Quite a lot of confidence

Meanwhile, ratings of the Supreme Court and Congress, which had dropped to record lows in 2014, have barely moved.

Confidence in the Presidency in Obama's Seventh Year Exceeds Bush's

The president in office is not mentioned by name in the confidence in the presidency question, but Americans' evaluations of the sitting president at the time are strongly related to how much confidence Americans place in the presidency as an institution.

Confidence in the presidency as an institution during each year of Obama's presidency has generally been lower than the comparable year in the presidencies of Bill Clinton and George W. Bush. An exception is Obama's first year, when Americans had greater confidence in the institution than in the first years of either Bush or Clinton. Also, in Obama's current year in office, his seventh, confidence in the presidency is higher than the 25% found in Bush's seventh year—the record low—but lower than the 49% in Clinton's seventh year.

Americans' Level of Confidence in the U.S. Presidency, by Term Year
% A great deal/Quite a lot of confidence

	Bill Clinton	George W. Bush	Barack Obama
Year 1	43	48	51
Year 2	38	58	36
Year 3	45	55	35
Year 4	39	52	37
Year 5	49	44	36
Year 6	53	33	29
Year 7	49	25	33
Year 8	42	26	--

GALLUP

The highest confidence rating the presidency has ever received is 72%, in March 1991 during the administration of George H. W. Bush shortly after he had succeeded in pushing Iraq out of Kuwait in the Gulf War. However, by October of that same year, after the Gulf War was over, confidence in the presidency had dropped to 50%.

Average Confidence in the Three Branches Is Low, But Has Been Lower

The average confidence rating for the three branches of government combined is 24%, lower than most previous averages since 1991 and well below the high of 50% that year.

But the average of confidence ratings for the three branches of government has been lower—including in 2008 (23%) and 2014 (22%).

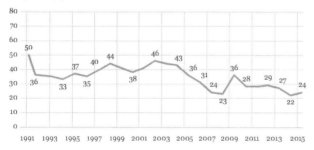

Average of Americans' Confidence Ratings of the Three Branches of Government
% A great deal/Quite a lot of confidence

GALLUP

Bottom Line

Americans' confidence in two of the three institutions that make up the U.S. government—Congress and the Supreme Court—remains near their all-time lows reached in 2014, while confidence in the presidency, although low, is up marginally compared with last year.

For Congress, low confidence in the institution is nothing new to members of the Senate and the House of Representatives, who have also seen low job approval ratings in recent years. Individual members likely aren't as interested in Americans' collective opinions as they are in the views of the voters they must appeal to back home. But the public's extremely low confidence no doubt weighs on Congress at some level.

The Supreme Court, meanwhile, is not directly accountable to the public—and often defies public opinion completely. Although its unelected members serve indefinite terms, confidence in the court is not unsusceptible to a drop in confidence in government as a whole.

Survey Methods

Results for this Gallup poll are based on telephone interviews conducted June 2–7, 2015, with a random sample of 1,527 adults, aged 18 and older, living in all 50 U.S. states and the District of Columbia. For results based on the total sample of national adults, the margin of sampling error is ±3 percentage points at the 95% confidence level. All reported margins of sampling error include computed design effects for weighting.

June 16, 2015
ECONOMIC CONFIDENCE INDEX, GAS PRICES LINKED

by Frank Newport

Story Highlights

* *Current conditions score at -2*
* *Economic outlook score up, at -9*
* *Confidence has tracked with changes in gas prices*

WASHINGTON, D.C.—Gallup's Economic Confidence Index averaged -6 for the week ending June 14. This reading continues the trend in generally lower confidence levels over the last several months, compared with the readings in positive territory in late 2014 and early 2015.

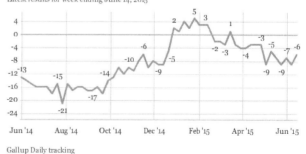

Gallup's U.S. Economic Confidence Index -- Weekly Averages Since June 2014
Latest results for week ending June 14, 2015

Gallup Daily tracking

GALLUP

Gallup's Economic Confidence Index is the average of two components: Americans' views of current economic conditions and their perceptions of whether the U.S. economy is getting better or getting worse. The theoretical maximum for the index is +100, if all Americans say the economy is excellent or good and getting better. The theoretical minimum is -100, if all Americans say the economy is poor and getting worse.

The downturn in Americans' economic confidence so far this year has stemmed more from their negatively tilting expectations for the economy than from their ratings of current conditions. The economic outlook score was -9 for the week ending June 14, based on 43% of Americans saying the economy is getting better and 52% saying it is getting worse. This spring's downtick in expectations is a significant shift; earlier this year, more Americans said the economy was getting better than said it was getting worse. Americans' ratings of current economic conditions, the other index component, are slightly more negative than positive (25% excellent or good and 27% poor), resulting in a score of -2.

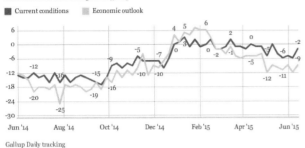

Economic Confidence Index Components -- Weekly Averages Since June 2014

Latest results for week ending June 14, 2015

Gallup Daily tracking

GALLUP

The current drop in confidence marks the largest decline in the index since it plummeted after the government shutdown in the fall of 2013. Unlike 2013, there is no single government action that can be pinpointed as being behind this year's drop, leaving a number of possible causes. But one explanation that fits the data is gas prices, which dropped at the end of last year just as confidence was increasing, and rose again beginning in February just as economic confidence began to decline.

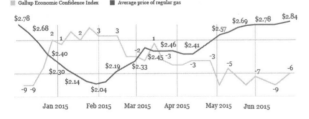

Gallup Economic Confidence Index vs. Price of Regular Gas

Gallup ECI based on weekly averages.
Gas prices based on retail gas prices (in dollars, including taxes, per gallon) as reported each Monday by the U.S. Energy Information Administration.

GALLUP

Although still low on a long-term basis, gas prices have been significantly higher in recent months than the lows of near $2 a gallon to which they dropped at the beginning of the year. Prices nationwide have risen to about $2.80 a gallon over the past several weeks and, concomitantly, the Economic Confidence Index has dropped to well below the break-even point, including the previous week's -9 and last week's -6.

The way gas prices factor into consumers' thinking about the national economy isn't totally clear. But gas prices, along with prices more generally, are one aspect of the economy that consumers come into direct contact with frequently and on an ongoing basis, something that cannot be said about more remote economic factors such as GDP growth and housing sales. The drop to near $2

per gallon may have been so dramatic that it temporarily improved Americans' outlook about the economy, boosting their economic confidence, only to see that lift deflate with the quick return of gas prices to where they had been last November.

Bottom Line

Americans' outlook on the U.S. economy remains more negative than positive, as it has every week since March. Similarly, the price of a gallon of gas, on average, remains much higher than it was at the beginning of the year—albeit still lower than in recent years. Although many varied factors are related to Americans' views of the economy, this relationship suggests that one significant concern weighing on their minds when asked about economic conditions is what they most recently paid for gas at the pump.

Survey Methods

Results for this Gallup poll are based on telephone interviews conducted June 8–14, 2015, on the Gallup U.S. Daily survey, with a random sample of 3,554 adults, aged 18 and older, living in all 50 U.S. states and the District of Columbia. For results based on the total sample of national adults, the margin of sampling error is ±2 percentage points at the 95% confidence level. All reported margins of sampling error include computed design effects for weighting.

June 17, 2015
AS INDUSTRY GROWS, PERCENTAGE OF U.S. SPORTS FANS STEADY

by Jeffrey M. Jones

Story Highlights

- *An average of 60% of Americans sports fans since 2000*
- *Men, upper-income more likely to be sports fans*
- *76% of upper-income men are sports fans*

PRINCETON, N.J.—Although the sports industry is continuing its impressive growth, the percentage of Americans who describe themselves as sports fans has stayed relatively stable over time. Currently, 59% of Americans say they are sports fans, one percentage point less than the average in Gallup's trend dating back to 2000.

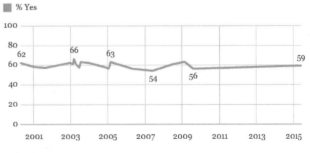

In general, would you describe yourself as a sports fan, or not?

GALLUP

The latest update, from a June 2–7 poll, came as the FIFA Women's World Cup got underway and during the NHL and NBA championship series.

The sports industry has become one of the bigger industries in the United States, mostly because of increasingly expensive rights fees television networks are paying to broadcast the various leagues' games. But the industry also has benefited from increased revenue from merchandise sales, ticket and luxury suite sales and stadium naming rights.

Gallup's sports fan data have shown some minor variation over the last 15 years, but in general, the trend can be characterized as stable at around 60%. Americans were a bit more likely to identify as sports fans from 2000 through 2004 (averaging 61%) than they have been since 2004 (58%). However, it is unclear if this represents a meaningful decline given Gallup's more limited updates of this question in recent years, as well as the possibility that people's willingness to identify as sports fans may vary depending on the time of the year the question is asked. Specifically, Americans appear to be a bit more likely to say they are sports fans in January through March, during the NFL playoffs and NCAA basketball tournament, than in the other months of the year.

Men, Upper-Income Most Likely to Identify as Sports Fans

A majority of U.S. adults in each major demographic subgroup say they are sports fans. Not unexpectedly, men (66%) are much more likely to be sports fans than women (51%). But the poll shows large differences by annual household income, with upper-income Americans (68%) significantly more likely to be sports fans than those residing in lower-income (54%) and middle-income (55%) households.

Upper-income Americans have consistently been much more likely than lower-income Americans to identify themselves as sports fans and have been more likely, or just as likely, as middle-income Americans to say they are sports fans.

Sports Fans by Annual Household Income

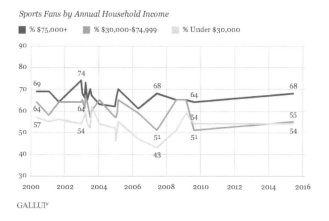

GALLUP

Gender and income each have an independent effect on one's affinity for sports, and the two interact in a way such that upper-income men are especially likely to be sports fans, with 76% saying they are. The effect of income is clear in that upper-income men and women are more likely to be sports fans than their lower- and middle-income counterparts. However, gender appears to have a greater influence than income does, because lower- and middle-income men are more likely than upper-income women to be sports fans.

Sports Fans by Gender and Annual Household Income

	Men	Women
	%	%
$75,000 or more	76	57
$30,000–$74,999	62	48
Less than $30,000	62	50

June 2-7, 2015

GALLUP

There are also significant differences by employment status—65% of employed Americans are sports fans, compared with 51% who are not currently employed. This is not merely related to the fact that men and upper-income people are more likely to be working—employment is related to being a sports fan even after taking into account the effects of gender and income. The data show that 70% of working men and 59% of working women are sports fans, compared with 60% of nonworking men and 45% of nonworking women.

Gallup has not consistently asked about employment status in the same polls in which it measures sports fans, but in the few polls that have included both, the relationships have been apparent.

Additional data on the percentage of sports fans by subgroup appear at the end of the article.

Implications

Sports are a major part of U.S. culture, with roughly six in 10 Americans identifying themselves as sports fans. As a result, sports are a big driver of economic activity, and the market for commerce related to sports is enormous. The attractiveness of sports programming to television networks, Internet websites and advertisers is clear, given that upper-income people, particularly upper-income men, are especially likely to be watching or logging on.

But as the sports industry has continued to grow, the percentage of Americans who identify as sports fans has stayed flat. The link between income and being a sports fan may be one of the factors behind the continued growth. Assuming networks and advertisers are aware of the income-sports fan link, the value of upper-income viewers to networks and advertisers would help explain why league broadcast rights fees are growing. Also, upper-income Americans have more discretionary income to spend on tickets, team merchandise and subscriptions to various sports-related packages to further fuel the sports industry's expansion.

Survey Methods

Results for this Gallup poll are based on telephone interviews conducted June 2–7, 2015, with a random sample of 1,527 adults, aged 18 and older, living in all 50 U.S. states and the District of Columbia. For results based on the total sample of national adults, the margin of sampling error is ±3 percentage points at the 95% confidence level. All reported margins of sampling error include computed design effects for weighting.

June 17, 2015

CONFIDENCE IN RELIGION AT NEW LOW, BUT NOT AMONG CATHOLICS

by Lydia Saad

Story Highlights

- *Less than half of Americans hold the church in high esteem*
- *Confidence dwindled to all-time low among Protestants in 2015*
- *Confidence among Catholics stabilized at improved level*

PRINCETON, N.J.—Americans' confidence in the church and organized religion has fallen dramatically over the past four decades, hitting an all-time low this year of 42%. Confidence in religion began faltering in the 1980s, while the sharpest decline occurred between 2001 and 2002 as the Roman Catholic Church grappled with a major sexual abuse scandal. Since then, periodic improvements have proved temporary, and it has continued to ratchet lower.

Percentage of Americans With a "Great Deal"/"Quite a Lot" of Confidence in the Church/Organized Religion

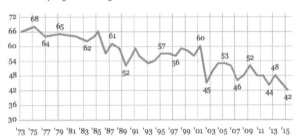

GALLUP'

Confidence Steadies Among U.S. Catholics

U.S. Protestants' confidence in the church and organized religion also hit a new low this year, with 51% now saying they have a great deal or quite a lot of confidence in it. While confidence among U.S. Catholics is also at 51%, this represents a steadying after more than a decade of varying confidence during which their ratings reached as low as 39%.

Although confidence among Protestants has been sliding since 2009, Catholics' has remained above 50% each of the last two years, the first time it has achieved this since 2003–2004. The leadership of the popular Pope Francis, including his recent initiative to hold high-ranking leaders of the Catholic Church accountable for their role in past child sex abuse scandals, may be a factor.

Confidence in the Church/Organized Religion, by Religious Preference — 1973-2015
Percentage with "a great deal"/"quite a lot" of confidence

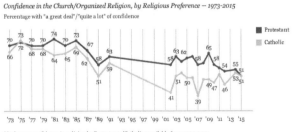

No data on confidence in religion by Protestants/Catholics available from 1992-2001

GALLUP'

Gallup does not have data on confidence in the church broken out by Protestants and Catholics for most of the 1990s, but the earlier trends show that confidence in organized religion fell among both religious categories starting in the mid-1980s, before it recovered somewhat in 1991. Previous Gallup analysis suggests the drop was related to numerous Protestant televangelist scandals. Yet Protestants generally maintained higher confidence in religion than Catholics did during this period.

As low as confidence in the church and organized religion is among Protestants and Catholics relative to the past, it is predictably much lower among nonreligious adults as well as non-Christians. In the latest poll, conducted June 2–7, 10% of the nonreligious and non-Christians combined said they had a great deal or quite a lot of confidence in the church or organized religion.

Confidence in Church/Organized Religion by Religious Preference
June 2-7, 2015

	Protestant/ Other Christian	Catholic	Non-Christian/ No religion
	%	%	%
Great deal/Quite a lot	51	51	10
Some	36	32	27
Very little	10	15	50
None (vol.)	1	1	9
No opinion	2	*	2

* Less than 0.5%
(vol.) = volunteered response

GALLUP'

In addition to serious scandals that have come to light surrounding various religious leaders and church institutions in recent decades, the increase in the share of Americans identifying as nonreligious or as members of a non-Christian faith is another reason that confidence in the church has declined. The total percentage of Americans identifying as Catholic, Protestant or other Christian in Gallup polls has fallen, while the percentage with no religious affiliation has risen considerably.

Implications

The church and organized religion is losing its footing as a pillar of moral leadership in the nation's culture. Once reliably at the top of Gallup's confidence in institutions list, it now ranks fourth behind the military, small business and the police, and just ahead of the medical system. The good news for the church is that it still ranks among the more well-respected institutions at a time when fewer than one in four Americans have confidence in several others, including Congress and the media.

Poor behavior on the part of some religious leaders has caused serious self-inflicted wounds for the church and organized religion—damaging its image among Protestants and Catholics as well as among non-Christians. At the same time, the nation is becoming less Christian and less religious, and those outside of Christianity naturally view the church with less respect. Any progress that organized religion can make in restoring confidence among the faithful may help stabilize its numbers, and perhaps soften others' skepticism.

Survey Methods

Results for this Gallup poll are based on telephone interviews conducted June 2–7, 2015, with a random sample of 1,527 adults, aged

18 and older, living in all 50 U.S. states and the District of Columbia. For results based on the total sample of national adults, the margin of sampling error is ±3 percentage points at the 95% confidence level.

For results based on the total sample of 796 Protestants (including nonspecific Christians), the margin of sampling error is ±4 percentage points at the 95% confidence level. For results based on the total sample of 309 Catholics, the margin of sampling error is ±7 percentage points at the 95% confidence level. All reported margins of sampling error include computed design effects for weighting.

June 18, 2015
DEMOCRATS IN THE U.S. SHIFT TO THE LEFT

by Frank Newport

Story Highlights

- *47% of Democrats are socially liberal and economically moderate/liberal*
- *This is up 17 percentage points since 2001*
- *Democrats remain more liberal on social than on economic issues*

PRINCETON, N.J.—Democratic candidates for the 2016 presidential nomination face a significantly more left-leaning party base than their predecessors did over the last 15 years. Forty-seven percent of Democrats and Democratic-leaning independents now identify as both socially liberal and economically moderate or liberal. This is compared with 39% in these categories in 2008, when there was last an open seat for their party's nomination, and 30% in 2001.

Left-Leaning Democrats

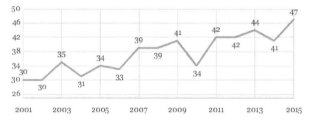

Democrats and Democratic-leaning independents

GALLUP

This combined group of Democrats consists of 25% who are pure liberals—identifying as liberal on both social and economic issues—and 22% who are social liberals but moderate on the economy. At the other end of the ideological spectrum, a scant 7% of Democrats are socially and economically conservative. Most of the rest of Democrats have more mixed ideological leanings, with 18% moderate on both social and economic issues, and 12% socially moderate or liberal but economically conservative.

These data are from Gallup's annual Values and Beliefs poll, which since 2001 has included questions asking Americans to rate themselves as conservative, moderate or liberal on social

and economic issues. The trends for the entire country show a shift toward more liberal self-identification, and that trend is even more pronounced among Democrats on social issues. More than half of Democrats (53%) describe themselves as socially liberal at this point, up from 35% in 2001. On the economic front, Democrats remain most likely to say they are moderate, but among the rest who don't call themselves moderate, economically liberal has become a more frequent self-label than economically conservative.

Democrats Self-Identification on Social and Economic Issues

	%
Socially and economically liberal	25
Socially liberal and economically moderate	22
Socially and economically moderate	18
Socially moderate/liberal and economically conservative	12
Socially and economically conservative	7
Socially moderate/conservative and economically liberal	7
Socially conservative and economically moderate	5

Democrats and Democratic-leaning independents
May 6-10, 2015

GALLUP

Implications

Americans' perceptions of their social and economic views on the ideological spectrum are quite general, and such labels don't always translate directly into specific policy and issues positions. Ideological labels, however, are helpful in understanding voters' positioning in the election year to come. The shift leftward appears to fit with trends on very specific issues such as same-sex marriage.

Primary voters can vary from state to state, but these national trends broadly suggest that Democratic candidates can be somewhat more left-leaning in their policy and issue prescriptions in the 2016 election campaign than in the past.

Democratic front-runner Hillary Clinton faces a more liberal base than she did when she last ran for president in 2008, and no doubt will be calibrating her positions accordingly. The shift in the electorate may help explain the attention being garnered by long-shot candidate Sen. Bernie Sanders of Vermont who has used the label "socialist" to describe himself and who is avowedly liberal across the board. Two other announced Democratic candidates— former Maryland Gov. Martin O'Malley and former Republican senator from Rhode Island Lincoln Chafee—have taken liberal positions in the past. In the 2016 election, they will be seeking to connect with the electorate on that basis, while also attempting to position themselves against Clinton on specific issues.

One consideration for Democratic candidates is the fact that their party's base is somewhat more liberal on social issues than on economic issues, suggesting that candidates may need to temper their liberalism on the economy a little more than they do on their social positions.

A second consideration for Democrat candidates, as always, is the need to be sensitive to the general election demands should they win their party's nomination. While 47% of their party base is socially liberal and either moderate or liberal on the economy, that same percentage among Republicans and Republican independents is only 7%, and some votes from the GOP will be necessary to win in November 2016.

Survey Methods

Results for this Gallup poll are based on telephone interviews conducted May 6–10, 2015, with a random sample of 1,024 adults, aged 18 and older, living in all 50 U.S. states and the District of Columbia. For results based on the total sample of national adults, the margin of sampling error is ±4 percentage points at the 95% confidence level. All reported margins of sampling error include computed design effects for weighting.

June 19, 2015
MEN, WOMEN DIFFER ON MORALS OF SEX, RELATIONSHIPS

by Andrew Dugan

Story Highlights

- *Men and women differ on morality of sex*
- *Biggest gender gap on pornography*
- *Women more likely to accept children born out of wedlock*

WASHINGTON, D.C.—Americans are finding more behaviors or social issues "morally acceptable" than they have in the past, but men and women still differ on several issues, notably those related to sex and relationships. Pornography is the most divisive, with 43% of men finding it morally acceptable versus 25% of women. Notable gender gaps also exist in how men and women view divorce, having a child out of wedlock, polygamy and extramarital affairs.

These findings come from Gallup's May 6–10 Values and Beliefs survey, which is the latest update of a poll that has documented the changing social mores of the country since the early 2000s. This year's survey found a general nationwide shift toward acceptance of once-controversial issues, and even small increases in behaviors widely regarded as morally taboo.

Americans' Views on Moral Acceptability of Selected Issues, by Gender

Next, I'm going to read you a list of issues. Regardless of whether or not you think it should be legal, for each one, please tell me whether you personally believe that in general it is morally acceptable or morally wrong

% saying "morally acceptable"

	Men	Women	Gender gap
	%	%	pct. pts.
Pornography	43	25	18
Married men and women having an affair	12	5	7
Polygamy	20	13	7
Sex between teenagers	40	34	6
Sex between an unmarried man and woman	70	66	4
Gay or lesbian relations	59	66	-7
Having a baby outside marriage	57	65	-8
Divorce	67	75	-8

May 6-10, 2015
Ranked by gender gap

GALLUP

But even against the current of increasing social permissiveness, men and women still have notable disagreements on several issues related to sex, relationships and marriage. Pornography

is the source of the largest discord between men and women. Consistently since 2011, men have been about twice as likely as women to say pornography is "morally acceptable." Nonetheless a clear consensus exists among both genders on this issue, with regular majorities of men and women saying pornography is "morally wrong."

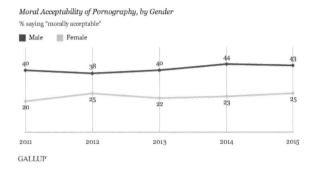

Moral Acceptability of Pornography, by Gender
% saying "morally acceptable"
■ Male ■ Female

GALLUP

Men and women also view two issues that conflict with traditional societal "ideals" of a committed monogamous relationship—adultery and polygamy—differently, although, in both cases, only small percentages of each find them acceptable. Men are seven percentage points more likely to say polygamy or having an affair is morally acceptable. Interestingly, while men regularly have been more likely than women to say polygamy is morally acceptable over the years, attitudes on adultery have fluctuated over time. In 2001, there were no gender differences on this issue. The gap has widened and narrowed in the years since, but the overarching pattern shows men are slightly more likely to find adultery morally acceptable.

Women Now More Likely to View Having a Child Outside of Wedlock as Acceptable

Majorities of both genders now say having a baby outside of marriage is morally acceptable. At 65%, women are slightly more likely than men (57%) to say this. Women's views of the moral acceptability of having children out of wedlock have shifted 19 points since 2002, while the increase has been 14 points among men. Although more women than men this year say having a baby outside of marriage is morally acceptable, this has not always been the case in the past.

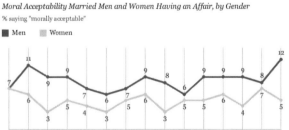

Moral Acceptability Married Men and Women Having an Affair, by Gender
% saying "morally acceptable"
■ Men ■ Women

GALLUP

Also, the percentage of women finding divorce morally acceptable has climbed by nearly 20 points in that time. Today, three-fourths of women find divorce acceptable, which is higher than the percentage of men who do (67%). However, the gap on this issue has not been consistent: Men have been more accepting of divorce than women in some years, while in other years, there have been no significant differences between the genders.

Moral Acceptability of Having a Baby Outside of Marriage, by Gender
% saying "morally acceptable"

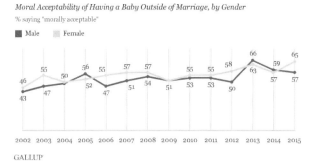

GALLUP

Moral Acceptability of Divorce, by Gender
% saying "morally acceptable"

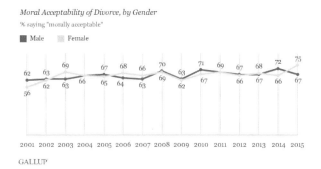

GALLUP

Bottom Line

Perhaps not surprisingly, men and women have different views on the moral acceptability of certain issues related to sex and relationships. Men are more likely to accept behaviors such as pornography or affairs. This year, women are more accepting of divorce or having a child without being married.

Nonetheless, the differences between men and women are mostly a matter of degree rather than of kind. Large majorities of men and women find divorce and having children outside of marriage as morally acceptable. Small majorities of both see engaging in affairs or polygamy in the same way. Though variations exist, for most men and women, the boundaries of what is morally acceptable behaviors in terms of behavior in the sometimes sensitive realm of sex and relationships are mostly the same for men and women.

Survey Methods

Results for this Gallup poll are based on telephone interviews conducted May 6–10, 2015, with a random sample of 1,024 adults, aged 18 and older, living in all 50 U.S. states and the District of Columbia. For results based on the total sample of national adults, the margin of sampling error is ±4 percentage points at the 95% confidence level. All reported margins of sampling error include computed design effects for weighting.

June 19, 2015
IN U.S., CONFIDENCE IN POLICE LOWEST IN 22 YEARS

by Jeffrey M. Jones

Story Highlights

- *52% confidence in police ties 1993 low*
- *Police still rate among most trusted institutions*
- *Democrats show sharp decline in confidence*

PRINCETON, N.J.—While a majority of Americans remain confident in the police, 52% currently express "a great deal" or "quite a lot" of confidence in that institution, tying the low in Gallup's 22-year trend. Confidence has ranged fairly narrowly between 52% and 64% since 1993.

Americans' Confidence in the Police
Figures are percentage with "a great deal"/"quite a lot" of confidence

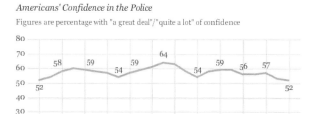

GALLUP

Gallup updated its annual confidence in U.S. institutions question in a June 2–7 Gallup poll. Even at its currently reduced confidence level, the police are still among the highest-ranking institutions, trailing only the military and small business among the 15 institutions tested in the poll.

Overall, 25% of Americans say they have a great deal of confidence in the police, 27% quite a lot, 30% "some," 16% "very little" and 2% "none." The combined 18% who have very little or no confidence in police is the highest Gallup has measured to date. The full results for the trend are shown at the end of this article.

The actions of police in certain U.S. cities—including Ferguson, Missouri; Staten Island, New York; and North Charleston, South Carolina—have recently come under scrutiny after black men were killed while being apprehended by white police officers. These events likely contributed to the decline in confidence in police, although it is important to note that Americans' trust in police has not been fundamentally shaken—it remains high in an absolute sense, despite being at a historical low.

Americans' confidence in the police was last at 52% in 1993, the first time Gallup included police in the list of institutions. That poll was conducted as four white Los Angeles police officers were being tried in federal court for violating Rodney King's civil rights in the 1991 beating of King. The four had earlier been acquitted of criminal charges in state court, which provoked riots in 1992. Two of the four officers were later found guilty of violating King's civil rights.

Democrats Show Largest Loss of Faith in Police

Democrats' confidence in police dropped 13 percentage points over the last two years compared with 2012–2013, a larger change than for any other subgroup. Over the same period, independents' and Republicans' confidence in police has not changed. As a result, Democrats (42%) now have less confidence in police than independents (51%) and remain much less confident than Republicans (69%).

The analysis of a combination of two years' data is necessary to get more stable estimates on smaller subgroups, particularly blacks. Over the last two years, blacks' confidence in police has averaged 30%, well below the national average of 53% and much lower than for any other subgroup. Blacks' confidence is down six points from 2012 to 2013, similar to the four-point drop among all Americans.

Changes in Confidence Ratings of Police, by Subgroup

Figures are percentage with "a great deal" or "quite a lot" of confidence in police

	2012-2013 %	2014-2015 %	Change (pct. pts.)
National adults	57	53	-4
Men	58	51	-7
Women	54	53	-1
White	60	57	-3
Nonwhite	49	42	-7
Black	36	30	-6
Hispanic	60	52	-8
18 to 29 years old	57	50	-7
30 to 49 years old	55	50	-5
50 to 64 years old	55	54	-1
65+ years old	62	58	-4
Postgraduate	63	52	-11
College graduate only	60	56	-4
Some college	56	53	-3
High school or less	53	51	-2
Conservative	60	63	+3
Moderate	57	49	-8
Liberal	51	44	-7
Democrat	55	42	-13
Independent	51	51	0
Republican	68	69	+1
Annual household income $75,000 or more	63	56	-7
Annual household income $30,000 to $74,999	58	57	-1
Annual household income less than $30,000	46	42	-4
Live in big/small city	55	52	-3
Live in suburb	61	57	-4
Live in town/rural area	55	51	-4

Place of residence based on respondent's description as living in "big city," "small city," "suburb of a big or small city," "town" or "rural area."

GALLUP

One reason blacks' confidence has not changed disproportionately over the last two years is that their confidence in the police was already low, and the recent events appear not to have fundamentally changed their already negative views of the police.

Blacks are disproportionately likely to identify as Democrats rather than Republicans or independents, but the data suggest the decline in confidence in police among Democrats has as much to do with politics as race. White Democrats' confidence declined 11 points over the last two years, similar to the 14-point decline among nonwhite Democrats.

The sample sizes are not large enough to break out black Democrats separately, but the limited data suggest their confidence declined no more than that of white Democrats.

The Democratic Party has typically received much higher support from racial and ethnic minorities than the Republican Party, and that is reflected in the greater concern rank-and-file Democrats typically express about matters of race and the greater importance they assign them as a voting issue. As a result, Democrats of all races may be especially concerned about alleged mistreatment of black suspects by white police officers.

Changes in Confidence Ratings of Police, Democrats by Race

Figures are percentage with "a great deal" or "quite a lot" of confidence in police

	2012-2013 %	2014-2015 %	Change (pct. pts.)
White Democrats	60	49	-11
Nonwhite Democrats	48	34	-14

GALLUP

Implications

Although confidence in police is at its low point, the majority of Americans remain confident in this institution and have more faith in it than in most other institutions.

The recent incidents in which black men were killed at the hands of white police officers trying to apprehend them have attracted a lot of media attention, but on a partisan basis they seem to have affected only the way Democrats view the police. The news has had less effect on how blacks specifically view the police, but that is most likely because blacks had far less confidence in the police long before these events happened.

In the future, actions on the part of city governments and police departments to enhance relations with blacks in their communities, along with changes in policing techniques, could result in fewer racially charged incidents with police. That in turn could help restore some of the public's confidence in the police. However, it will likely take much more than that for the police to gain blacks' trust, given the long history of tension between blacks and police.

Survey Methods

Results for this Gallup poll are based on telephone interviews conducted June 2–7, 2015, with a random sample of 1,527 adults, aged 18 and older, living in all 50 U.S. states and the District of Columbia. For results based on the total sample of national adults, the margin of sampling error is ±3 percentage points at the 95% confidence level. All reported margins of sampling error include computed design effects for weighting.

Results for blacks' confidence from the 2012–2013 polls are based on interviews with 219 non-Hispanic blacks and have a margin of error of ±8 percentage points at the 95% confidence level.

Results for blacks' confidence from the 2014–2015 polls are based on interviews with 249 non-Hispanic blacks and have a margin of error of ±8 percentage points at the 95% confidence level.

Each sample of national adults includes a minimum quota of 50% cellphone respondents and 50% landline respondents, with additional minimum quotas by time zone within region. Landline and cellular telephone numbers are selected using random-digit-dial methods.

June 22, 2015

IN U.S., SOCIALIST PRESIDENTIAL CANDIDATES LEAST APPEALING

by Justin McCarthy

Story Highlights

- *More than nine in 10 would vote for a Catholic, black, or woman*
- *Ninety-one percent would vote for a Jewish or Hispanic candidate*
- *Americans show most bias toward socialists (47%), atheists (58%)*

WASHINGTON, D.C.—As the 2016 presidential election field takes shape, more than nine in 10 Americans say they would vote for a qualified presidential candidate who is Catholic, a woman, black, Hispanic or Jewish. Less than half of Americans would vote for a candidate who is a socialist.

Between now and the 2016 political conventions, there will be discussion about the qualifications of presidential candidates -- their education, age, religion, race and so on. If your party nominated a generally well-qualified person for president who happened to be _____, would you vote for that person?

	Yes, would	No, would not
	%	%
Catholic	93	6
A woman	92	8
Black	92	7
Hispanic	91	8
Jewish	91	7
Mormon	81	18
Gay or lesbian	74	24
An evangelical Christian	73	25
Muslim	60	38
An atheist	58	40
A socialist	47	50

June 2-7, 2015

GALLUP

A June 2–7 Gallup poll updated the question—first asked in 1937—about the acceptability of presidential candidates of various background characteristics. The general trend is that Americans have become significantly more accepting over time.

Among religious identities, while the large majority of Americans would vote for a Catholic or Jewish presidential candidate, smaller majorities say they would vote for a candidate who is Mormon (81%), an evangelical Christian (73%), Muslim (60%) or an atheist (58%).

These dynamics can affect 2016 candidates' efforts to attract American voters in the upcoming primaries as well as the general election next year, particularly because the field is shaping up as one that will have some diversity in terms of race, gender and, particularly, religion.

Five declared candidates are Catholics—Republicans Jeb Bush, George Pataki, Marco Rubio and Rick Santorum, and Democrat Martin O'Malley. Two are women—Democratic front-runner Hillary Clinton and Republican Carly Fiorina. Republican Ben Carson is the sole black candidate in the race, while two candidates are Hispanic—Republicans Rubio and Ted Cruz.

Independent Bernie Sanders, who is seeking the Democratic nomination, is the only Jewish candidate in the race. And while a large majority of Americans are willing to vote for a candidate of his faith, Sanders's self-identification as a socialist could hurt him, as half of Americans say they would not vote for someone with that background.

In addition, several candidates have heavily courted the evangelical community—including Republicans Mike Huckabee, Rick Perry, Carson, Santorum and Cruz.

Democrats and Republicans Vary in Support for Candidates From Religious Groups

Democrats and Republicans vary in their support for candidates of particular religious affiliations.

Republicans (84%) are significantly more likely than Democrats (66%) to say they will vote for an evangelical candidate. But Democrats are more likely to say they will vote for a Muslim (73%) or an atheist (64%) than are Republicans, of whom less than half say they are willing to vote for a candidate with either of these belief systems.

Willingness to Vote for President of Various Backgrounds, by Political Party

	Democrats	Independents	Republicans	Difference, Democrats minus Republicans
	%	%	%	(pct. pts.)
An evangelical Christian	66	73	84	-18
Mormon	79	79	84	-5
Jewish	92	86	95	-3
Catholic	95	92	93	2
Hispanic	94	88	91	3
Black	96	89	90	6
A woman	97	89	91	6
An atheist	64	61	45	19
Gay or lesbian	85	73	61	24
Muslim	73	58	45	28
A socialist	59	49	26	33

June 2-7, 2015

GALLUP

Republicans and Democrats differ most in their willingness to vote for a socialist candidate, by 33 percentage points, but socialist ranks last for both parties. The two parties also differ significantly on voting for a gay or lesbian candidate, by 24 points. Majorities of Democrats are willing to vote for a candidate with any of the characteristics mentioned in the poll.

There are no meaningful party differences in willingness to vote for a female, black or Hispanic candidate.

Americans Under 30 the Least Particular on Candidate Characteristics

Gallup also finds wide differences in support for gay or lesbian, atheist, Muslim and socialist presidential candidates by age. Americans between the ages of 18 and 29 are much more likely than those 65 and older to support these four types of candidates. Younger Americans are also slightly more likely to say they will vote for women and Hispanics, by eight points each.

At least two-thirds of adults younger than 30 say they are willing to vote for a candidate with any of the characteristics included in the survey.

Willingness to Vote for President of Various Backgrounds, by Age

	18 to 29	30 to 49	50 to 64	65+	Difference, Youngest minus oldest group
	%	%	%	%	(pct. pts.)
Black	90	91	95	91	-1
Mormon	81	81	79	81	0
Catholic	95	92	94	94	1
An evangelical Christian	75	72	73	74	1
Jewish	91	92	90	89	2
A woman	96	90	96	88	8
Hispanic	95	92	90	87	8
Gay or lesbian	84	79	72	62	22
An atheist	75	63	50	48	27
Muslim	76	67	55	44	32
A socialist	69	50	37	34	35

June 2-7, 2015

GALLUP'

Bottom Line

With more than a dozen candidates running for president, the 2016 field is one of the most diverse Americans have ever seen. On the heels of the historic election and re-election of the nation's first black president, Americans are just as likely to lend their support to black candidates as to women and Hispanics. This suggests that another historic election could be on the horizon with Hillary Clinton, Carly Fiorina, Rubio and Cruz in the race.

Americans' notions about whom they would give their support to are widening, but they are still less than fully supportive of candidates with certain characteristics.

The news is likely worst for Sen. Bernie Sanders. At one point, Americans might have withheld their votes from him because of his Jewish faith—fewer than half said they would support a Jewish candidate in 1937—but today his socialist ideology, given Americans' views on voting for a socialist candidate, could hinder his candidacy more.

To a lesser degree, evangelical Christian candidates may suffer, in that one in four Americans say they will not vote for an evangelical Christian. Candidates of various faiths who court American evangelicals, like Southern Baptists Cruz and Huckabee, or Catholic Santorum, could suffer from their association with the evangelical faithful and the social issues they take firm stances on.

Survey Methods

Results for this Gallup poll are based on telephone interviews conducted June 2–7, 2015, with a random sample of 1,527 adults, aged 18 and older, living in all 50 U.S. states and the District of Columbia. For results based on the total sample of national adults, the margin of sampling error is ±3 percentage points at the 95% confidence level. All reported margins of sampling error include computed design effects for weighting.

June 22, 2015
CONFIDENCE IN U.S. BANKS LOW BUT RISING

by Andrew Dugan

Story Highlights

- *28% have a great deal or quite a lot of confidence in banks*
- *This is 12 points lower than the historical average*
- *Republicans more confident than Democrats in banks*

WASHINGTON, D.C.—Seven years after the worst financial crisis in the U.S. since the Great Depression, the percentage of Americans expressing "a great deal" or "quite a lot" of confidence in banks remains low (28%), but this is higher than their 21% confidence in 2012.

Americans' Confidence in Banks, 1979-2015 Trend

Now I am going to read you a list of institutions in American society. Please tell me how much confidence you, yourself, have in each one -- a great deal, quite a lot, some or very little?

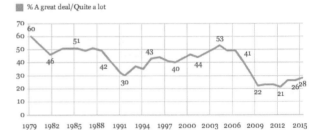

GALLUP'

About half of Americans (45%) have "some" confidence in banks, while 26% have "very little" confidence or none at all.

These results are based on a June 2–7 Gallup poll that included Gallup's latest update on confidence in U.S. institutions. Like confidence in nearly every other major institution Gallup has tested, Americans' current confidence in banks is below the 1979–2015 average of 40%.

But banks' rapid loss of credibility between 2006 and 2009 is the product of more than just a general trend across all institutions. In fact, few institutions have seen such a steep drop in confidence in recent years. In 2004, confidence in banks stood at 53%, near its historical high, amid a lending boom. By June 2009, after that boom went bust, confidence fell to 22%. Three years later, in June 2012, it stood at 21%, as a seemingly endless list of scandals and allegations of misconduct—including a concerted effort by some banks in the U.S. and abroad to manipulate a benchmark interest rate—dogged the financial industry. It has recovered only slightly since then.

Banks have recovered from a precipitous drop in public confidence before. The Savings and Loan crisis combined with the recession of the early 1990s saw confidence in banks tumble from 51% in 1987 to 30% in 1991. As the economy healed, confidence climbed its way back to the 53% reading in 2004.

Americans who express satisfaction with the way things are going in the U.S. are more likely than those who are dissatisfied to say they have confidence in banks, by 39% to 24%. That is part of a broader pattern evident in the data, in which those who are satisfied with national conditions generally tend to express greater confidence in most institutions.

Democrats Have Less Confidence in Banks

In absolute terms, no major political group is especially positive on banks in terms of confidence, though Republicans are slightly more likely to say they have confidence in banks (35%) than are independents (25%) or Democrats (27%).

Americans' Confidence in Banks, by Self-Identified Party Affiliation

Please tell me how much confidence you, yourself, have in banks -- a great deal, quite a lot, some or very little?

	Republicans %	Independents %	Democrats %
A great deal/Quite a lot	35	25	27
Some	47	44	45
Very little/None (vol.)	18	30	28

(vol.) = Volunteered response
June 2-7, 2015

GALLUP

But Democrats are not quite as cool to banks as they were in 2012. That year, fewer than one in five Democrats (19%) had a great deal or quite a lot of confidence in banks, versus today's 27%. Republicans' views have been more static, with 34% expressing this level of confidence in 2012, similar to their 2015 views. Even as some Democratic presidential candidates pledge to break up the largest banks, Democrats have seen a marginal recovery in their views of banks.

Bottom Line

In many ways, the consequences of the 2008 financial crisis continue to haunt the banking industry's image—even as the economy continues to recover from the crash, and nearly all of the government-supplied bailout funds known as TARP have been repaid, according to the Treasury Department. These facts notwithstanding, confidence in banks has seen only slight upward movement from the low levels first encountered in 2009; a more complete recovery of the industry's image with the public has been elusive.

Memories of the crisis, in conjunction with a more recent string of scandals, have likely limited the rehabilitation of banks' image with the American public. But the S & L crisis of the late 1980s provides some hope for industry leaders: The fallout from the crisis led to plunging confidence levels among Americans, but trust was eventually restored, likely related to strong economic growth of the 1990s and the greater accessibility to credit in the 2000s. This example suggests banks could restore some of their lost goodwill with the American public, but currently there is little evidence that this is occurring.

Survey Methods

Results for this Gallup poll are based on telephone interviews conducted June 2–7, 2015, with a random sample of 1,527 adults, aged 18 and older, living in all 50 U.S. states and the District of Columbia. For results based on the total sample of national adults, the margin of sampling error is ±4 percentage points at the 95% confidence level. All reported margins of sampling error include computed design effects for weighting.

June 23, 2015
AMERICANS VIEW QUALITY OF TWO-YEAR, FOUR-YEAR COLLEGES SIMILARLY

by Justin McCarthy

Story Highlights

- *Seven in 10 say quality of four-year college education is excellent or good*
- *Nearly as many rate community college education as excellent or good*
- *About one in three say quality of online college education is excellent or good*

WASHINGTON, D.C.—Americans are about as likely to rate the quality of education that community colleges offer as "excellent" or "good" (66%) as they are to rate four-year colleges this positively (70%). Americans are about half as likely to rate the quality of Internet-based college programs—those offering online-only courses—as excellent or good (36%).

Americans' Views of the Quality of Education at Four-Year Universities, Community Colleges and Online Institutions

From what you know, how would you rate the quality of education offered by each of the following -- as generally excellent, good, only fair or poor? (% Excellent/Good)

	Four-year colleges and universities %	Community colleges %	Internet-based college programs %
Jun 2-7, 2015	70	66	36
Oct 3-6, 2013	68	64	34

GALLUP

These results are based on a June 2–7 Gallup poll. Gallup first asked this question in 2013. Americans' opinions of each form of higher education are essentially the same as in that initial poll, with two- and four-year educational institutions rated similarly on quality and Internet-based programs lagging behind.

Community colleges are front and center in a national debate on the affordability of higher education, with President Barack Obama proposing that the U.S. make community college tuition free. While advocates of higher-education access cheer the greater admission rates at community colleges, these two-year institutions face different challenges, such as lower graduation rates and the task of transitioning students into four-year schools and, ultimately, the workforce. However, Americans view the quality of community colleges similarly to that of four-year schools.

Americans with advanced education rate four-year colleges and universities more highly than community colleges, by nine percentage points, but all other education groups view community colleges and four-year schools similarly.

Adults younger than 30 hold four-year colleges in a bit higher regard than they do community colleges, by 12 points, whereas older Americans' views of the quality of both are similar.

Roughly a quarter of Americans with postgraduate education (27%) believe the quality of online learning is excellent or good, less than the 40% of college-only graduates who say the same. Across age groups, there is relatively little difference in ratings of online education.

	Four-year colleges and universities	Community colleges	Internet-based college programs
	%	%	%
EDUCATION LEVEL:			
Postgraduate	75	66	27
College graduate	77	71	40
Some college	71	74	37
High school or less	63	61	38
AGE:			
18 to 29	70	58	36
30 to 49	72	68	39
50 to 64	69	70	37
65+	65	71	32

June 2-7, 2015

GALLUP'

Bottom Line

Though it may be harder to gain acceptance into and afford four-year colleges and universities, Americans view the quality of education they provide as no better than that of community colleges. However, the public does not rate the quality of online education as positively as that of either two- or four-year colleges.

Gallup has found that although a third of Americans say online programs do a better job of providing broader curriculum choices and good value for their cost, many Americans believe they lack in some key areas including reliable testing and grading, high-quality instruction and their value to potential employers. Online education is not an either/or proposition, as brick-and-mortar colleges routinely incorporate online coursework in their offerings. But in terms of college programs that are solely Internet-based, it seems unlikely that they are going to overtake traditional colleges anytime soon in public perceptions of quality.

Survey Methods

Results for this Gallup poll are based on telephone interviews conducted June 2–7, 2015, with a random sample of 1,527 adults, aged 18 and older, living in all 50 U.S. states and the District of Columbia. For results based on the total sample of national adults, the margin of sampling error is ±3 percentage points at the 95% confidence level. All reported margins of sampling error include computed design effects for weighting.

June 24, 2015
SUPPORT FOR NONTRADITIONAL
CANDIDATES VARIES BY RELIGION

by Lydia Saad

Story Highlights

- *Nonreligious more supportive of nontraditional candidates*
- *Catholics tend to be more supportive than Protestants*
- *Socialist, atheist candidates spark biggest religious support gaps*

PRINCETON, N.J.—Despite tidal shifts over the past 60 years in Americans' willingness to support a well-qualified black, female, Catholic or Jewish candidate for president to the point that these are now widely accepted, significant segments of Americans still don't endorse candidates who are gay or lesbian, evangelical Christian, Muslim, atheist or socialist. No more than three in four Americans say they would vote for candidates from any of these backgrounds. However, that support differs sharply by Americans' religious affiliation.

Americans' Willingness to Vote for Presidential Candidates of Various Backgrounds, by Religious Preference

Between now and the 2016 political conventions, there will be discussion about the qualifications of presidential candidates -- their education, age, religion, race and so on. If your party nominated a generally well-qualified person for president who happened to be _____, would you vote for that person?

Five least widely supported groups

	U.S. adults	Protestant	Catholic	No religion
	%	%	%	%
Gay or lesbian	74	62	82	92
An evangelical Christian	73	82	72	57
Muslim	60	44	69	82
An atheist	58	47	58	91
A socialist	47	28	46	74

June 2-7, 2015

GALLUP'

Currently, 74% of Americans as a whole say they would support a well-qualified candidate for their party's presidential nomination who happened to be gay or lesbian, up from 55% only eight years ago. But this varies from nearly universal acceptance (92%) among adults who profess no religion—including self-identified atheists, agnostics, and those with no specific religious preference—and 82% among Catholics to 62% among Protestants.

Similarly, atheists enjoy broad acceptance from those who don't identify with any religion, 91% of whom say they would support an atheist for president. However, this drops to 47% among Protestants, and is not much higher among Catholics (58%). As a result, the overall percentage who would vote for an atheist stands at 58%.

Americans with no religious preference (57%) are far less likely than Protestants (82%) or Catholics (72%) to say they would vote for an evangelical Christian who is otherwise well qualified. Yet 82% of the nonreligious would back a Muslim, significantly higher than the percentage of Catholics (69%) and Protestants (44%) who would. Evangelicals wind up ahead of Muslims in acceptability to the public, 73% versus 60%, but both groups significantly trail Catholics (93%) and Jews (91%) in this regard.

Socialists provoke the widest religious gap, with 74% of the nonreligious being open to supporting a well-qualified socialist, compared with 46% of Catholics and 28% of Protestants. As a result, less than half of Americans—47%—are willing to entertain the idea of supporting a socialist for president, the only group falling below this threshold.

These deep religious divisions stand in contrast to the unity seen among Protestants, Catholics and the nonreligious when it comes to voting for Catholics, women, blacks, Hispanics, Jews and Mormons—all groups that have achieved broad public acceptance on this measure.

The results by frequency of religious attendance largely mirror those by religious preference. Americans who attend their church or other place of worship weekly or nearly weekly hold views similar to those of Protestants, while those who seldom or never attend look like those with no religious affiliation. However, the nonreligious are still significantly more accepting of most of the nontraditional candidates reviewed here than even infrequent church attendees are.

Americans' Willingness to Vote for Presidential Candidates of Various Backgrounds, by Religious Preference

Between now and the 2016 political conventions, there will be discussion about the qualifications of presidential candidates -- their education, age, religion, race and so on. If your party nominated a generally well-qualified person for president who happened to be _____, would you vote for that person?

Six most widely supported groups

	U.S. adults	Protestant	Catholic	No religion
	%	%	%	%
Catholic	93	94	96	94
A woman	92	91	94	95
Black	92	93	90	94
Hispanic	91	88	93	96
Jewish	91	94	86	95
Mormon	81	80	85	84

June 2-7, 2015

GALLUP

Similarly, in line with the political orientation of the three religious categories reviewed here, Protestants' views about the candidate types tend to be similar to political conservatives', Catholics look most similar to moderates, and the nonreligious are more in line with liberals.

Implications

President John F. Kennedy in 1960 was the first Catholic elected as U.S. president, at a time when 71% of Americans said they would be willing to back a candidate of his faith. That same year, the chances of a black or female candidate winning were nil, with barely half of Americans open to supporting either. Since then, willingness to support a black or female candidate has swelled to more than 90%, and both groups have significantly increased their numbers in elected office, even if not the presidency. Americans have also become more willing to support Hispanics, Jews and, to a lesser degree, Mormons.

While public acceptance of presidential candidates representing these categories is now uniformly high across societal groups, including by religion, the same cannot be said for candidates from what might be termed micro-minority groups. Reluctance among Christians, particularly Protestants, to support gays and lesbians, atheists, Muslims and socialists means presidential candidates with these characteristics could meet with significant resistance. And while President Jimmy Carter described himself as evangelical Christian when he was elected in 1976, that was at a more religious time in U.S. history. Today, nonreligious Americans' coolness toward evangelicals dampens the acceptance of this group's candidates.

Still, there is a broad gulf between attitudes and outcomes. In the decades since Kennedy served, an uninterrupted string of white Protestant males inhabited the White House until the election of Barack Obama in 2008. The chances that an avowed atheist, or a socialist like Bernie Sanders, would be victorious in the general election would depend on not only overcoming broad public disapproval of his or her beliefs, but jumping ahead of more mainstream diverse candidates. These would include Hillary Clinton representing women and Marco Rubio representing Hispanics—candidates who, on paper, are better positioned to break through the oval ceiling.

Survey Methods

Results for this Gallup poll are based on telephone interviews conducted June 2–7, 2015, with a random sample of 1,527 adults, aged 18 and older, living in all 50 U.S. states and the District of Columbia. The candidate characteristics were asked of a random half sample of respondents in Form A. For results based on the total sample of 771 national adults in Form A, the margin of sampling error is ±4 percentage points at the 95% confidence level. All reported margins of sampling error include computed design effects for weighting.

June 25, 2015
JOBS SEEN AS MOST POSITIVE, NEGATIVE PARTS OF U.S. ECONOMY

by Art Swift

Story Highlights

- *More jobs, lower unemployment named best aspect of economy*
- *Lack of jobs, unemployment named worst aspect of economy*
- *"Economy growing" named positive; "big business" named negative*

WASHINGTON, D.C.—The current job climate presents a classic glass half-full/half-empty situation for Americans. When asked what the most positive aspect of the economy is, more Americans cite the availability of jobs and decline in unemployment than any other attribute. But when asked to name the most negative aspect of the economy, they most often mention the continued lack of jobs or unemployment.

Positive Aspects of the U.S. Economy

	%
More jobs/Unemployment is down	23
Economy growing/Improving	14
Businesses are doing better/Entrepreneurship	9
Opportunities/Choices/Freedom	6
Low interest rates/Dollar is retaining value	4
Housing market/Real estate improving	4
American ingenuity/Technology/Innovation	4
Gas/Oil prices going down	3
Stock market improving/Investments	3
Education/Affordable/Improved	3
Increasing minimum wage	2
Government system/Leadership/Capitalism	2
Affordable healthcare/Availability/ACA	1
Increased energy resources/Domestic production	1
Military/Security	1
Trade practices/Not importing as much/Buy American	1
Other	5
Nothing	13
No opinion	16

June 2-7, 2015

GALLUP

In an open-ended question in the June 2–7 survey, Gallup asked Americans to name the most positive and negative aspects about the U.S. economy today. Twenty-three percent say "more jobs/unemployment is down," while about half as many mention "economy growing/improving" at 14%, and 9% cite "businesses are doing better/entrepreneurship."

To explain why Americans may be thinking this way, more Americans in general say it is a good time to find a quality job, though a majority still say it is a bad time to find a quality job. Also, Gallup's Job Creation Index reached a new high in April of +31, another indicator that many Americans believe the job market is improving.

Democrats are more likely than Republicans to say jobs are a highlight of the economy—33% of Democrats cite it as the most positive aspect, while 20% of Republicans and 17% of independents say the same thing.

Lack of Jobs, Big Business Top List of Negatives

Just as jobs top Americans' list of positives, it also tops the list of negatives about the U.S. economy. In this case, 20% of Americans cite "lack of jobs/unemployment" as the most negative aspect of the economy, double the mentions of "big business/corporate greed" at 10%. "Low wages," "income inequality," "government involvement" and "debt" are not far behind.

Although the U.S. unemployment rate is nearly half of what it was five years ago, and Americans are less likely to name it as the most important problem facing the country, many may still be troubled about the types of jobs that are being created or are available. The sentiment that these jobs are low-paying, with weak benefits, is pervasive among many U.S. thought leaders.

Negative Aspects of the U.S. Economy

	%
Lack of jobs/Unemployment	20
Big business/Corporate greed	10
Low wages/Need better paying jobs	8
Income inequality	7
Government involvement/Interference	7
Debt/Deficit	7
High taxes	5
Health insurance	4
Inflation/High cost of living	4
Lack of economic growth/Slow recovery	3
Welfare/Entitlements	3
Government regulation	3
Devaluation of dollar/Low interest rates	3
Affordability/Availability of education	3
Poor workforce/Lazy	2
Too many imports	2
Poverty/Homelessness	2
Gas/Oil prices/Foreign dependence	2
Lack of opportunity/Freedom/Choices	2
Immigration/Immigration policy	1
President Barack Obama	1
Race/Age discrimination	1
Poor stock market/Investments	1
Poor housing market	1
Energy/Lack of energy sources	1
Other	5
None/Nothing	4
No opinion	11

June 2-7, 2015

GALLUP

Politically, 24% of Republicans say jobs are the most negative aspect of the economy, while 19% of independents and 18% of Democrats share that sentiment.

In addition to jobs, other aspects of the economy make both lists. Gas prices are seen as both positive and negative, along with the housing market and health insurance. This suggests that these are far from "settled issues" in Americans' views of the economy.

Bottom Line

Jobs topped both positive and negative lists, which not only illustrates how top-of-mind jobs are when Americans think about the health of the economy, but also that the jury is still out on whether the job market has improved enough to be considered a boon to the economy.

Along with gas prices, the housing market and healthcare made both lists. The fact that these aspects made the list as both a positive and a negative underscores how often there is a difference of opinion on many issues in American life, and that there is far from a consensus on whether the economy is progressing. Broadly speaking, with Gallup's Economic Confidence Index near the 0 neutral point on the scale for several months, Americans are pretty evenly divided as to the state of the economy.

Survey Methods

Results for this Gallup poll are based on telephone interviews conducted June 2–7, 2015, on the Gallup U.S. Daily survey, with a random sample of 1,527 adults, aged 18 and older, living in all 50 U.S. states and the District of Columbia. For results based on the total sample of national adults, the margin of sampling error is ±3 percentage points at the 95% confidence level.

June 25, 2015
LANCASTER, RALEIGH RESIDENTS MOST LIKELY TO SAY HOME IS IDEAL

by Rebecca Riffkin

Story Highlights

- *Nationally, 72.6% say housing is ideal*
- *Dayton, Ohio, residents least likely to say home is ideal*
- *Perceptions of living in ideal home linked to higher well-being*

WASHINGTON, D.C.—Residents of Lancaster, Pennsylvania (78.5%), and Raleigh, North Carolina (78.2%), are the most likely adults in the 100 most populous U.S. metropolitan areas to agree that their house or apartment is ideal for them and their family. El Paso, Texas; Fort Myers, Florida; and Wichita, Kansas, round out the top five communities where residents are most likely to agree their housing situation is ideal.

These findings are based on interviews conducted throughout 2014 as part of the Gallup-Healthways Well-Being Index. Americans were asked to use a five-point scale—where 5 means strongly agree and 1 means strongly disagree—to rate their level of agreement with the following statement: The house or apartment that you live in is ideal for you and your family.

Communities With Highest Percentage of Residents Who Agree Their Housing Is Ideal

On a five-point scale, where 5 means strongly agree and 1 means strongly disagree, please rate your level of agreement with the following items: The house or apartment that you live in is ideal for you and your family.

Highest Communities	% 4 or % 5 (Agree)
Lancaster, PA	78.5
Raleigh, NC	78.2
El Paso, TX	77.7
Cape Coral-Fort Myers, FL	77.4
Wichita, KS	77.1
Tucson, AZ	76.5
North Port-Sarasota-Bradenton, FL	76.4
Allentown-Bethlehem-Easton, PA-NJ	76.1
Charleston-North Charleston, SC	76.0
Omaha-Council Bluffs, NE-IA	76.0

Jan. 1-Dec. 31, 2014
Gallup-Healthways Well-Being Index

GALLUP

Housing needs and what qualifies as an "ideal house" can vary widely across the country and from family to family. Many factors beyond cost affect how individuals view their house or apartment, such as size, location, proximity to public transportation and neighborhood safety. Therefore, residents' ratings of their own homes are important measures for community leaders to use when assessing how local housing matches residents' needs.

Nationally, 72.6% of Americans in 2014 agreed that their housing is ideal, responding with a rating of 4 or 5. Meanwhile, 12.6% disagreed, responding with a rating of 1 or 2. Across the 100 largest metropolitan areas, residents' agreement that their house or apartment is ideal ranges somewhat narrowly between 65.1% and 78.5%.

Dayton, Ohio, Residents Least Likely to Say Their Housing Is Ideal

Residents of Dayton, Ohio (65.1%), are the least likely to say their housing is ideal. Two other Ohio communities, Akron and Toledo, also ranked among the five metro areas where residents are least likely to say their housing is ideal, as does Spokane, Washington. The New York City metro area, infamous for expensive housing, also lags behind in residents' perceptions of their house or apartment being ideal at 67.2%.

Communities With Lowest Percentage of Residents Who Agree Their Housing Is Ideal

On a five-point scale, where 5 means strongly agree and 1 means strongly disagree, please rate your level of agreement with the following items: The house or apartment that you live in is ideal for you and your family.

Lowest Communities	% 4 or % 5 (Agree)
Dayton, OH	65.1
Akron, OH	66.2
Toledo, OH	66.5
New York-Newark-Jersey City, NY-NJ-PA	67.2
Spokane-Spokane Valley, WA	67.6
Colorado Springs, CO	67.8
Columbia, SC	67.8
Portland-Vancouver-Hillsboro, OR-WA	67.9
Seattle-Tacoma-Bellevue, WA	68.2
Virginia Beach-Norfolk-Newport News, VA-NC	68.2

Jan. 1-Dec. 31, 2014
Gallup-Healthways Well-Being Index

GALLUP

Still, even in these lower-ranking communities, around two in three residents say their home is ideal for their family.

Perceptions of Ideal Housing Tied to Higher Well-Being

Americans who agree that their house or apartment is ideal have higher overall well-being than those who disagree that their housing is ideal. The average Well-Being Index score among those who say their housing is ideal is 65.9 out of a possible 100, significantly higher than the 54.6 found among those who are neutral and the 45.3 recorded among those who disagree.

Well-Being Linked With Living in Ideal House
% Thriving shown

	Agree that house or apartment is ideal	Neutral	Disagree that house or apartment is ideal
	Mean score	Mean score	Mean score
Well-Being Index Score	65.9	54.6	45.3
	% Thriving	% Thriving	% Thriving
Purpose	44.7	18.4	11.9
Social	48.3	23.7	15.0
Financial	47.6	21.2	10.7
Community	50.1	9.3	2.2
Physical	38.1	21.8	14.2

Jan. 1-Dec. 31, 2014
Gallup-Healthways Well-Being Index

GALLUP

It is to be expected that the ideal housing measure is closely linked to the broader element of which it is a part—community well-being. However, those who report that their housing is ideal are also significantly more likely to have a stronger sense of purpose, a thriving social life, financial security and physical health than those who are not in ideal housing. This underscores the degree to which there is interplay among the various elements of well-being, and when scores in one element are strong, they likely will be strong in other elements as well.

While the relationship between housing perceptions and the four elements of well-being outside of community well-being is strong, the direction of the relationship is unclear. Americans who are thriving in their financial well-being may be better able to find a house or apartment that satisfies their housing needs and desires. But it is also possible that those living in optimal housing are better able to achieve high purpose, social, financial and physical well-being because they are able to feel comfortable and safe when they are home.

Bottom Line

A number of factors can influence residents' perceptions of whether or not they live in an ideal home for them and their family. The size and price of a home, its location and other factors like a big yard or wheelchair accessibility could all influence whether or not residents perceive their house or apartment as ideal.

It is encouraging that, despite vast differences in Americans' means to purchase or rent a home, a majority of residents in all of the U.S. communities that Gallup and Healthways have studied say that their own home is ideal for them.

The data also reveal that Americans in ideal housing are more likely to have high well-being than those who are not in ideal housing. And while this doesn't prove that ideal housing leads to high well-being in other areas, the link is strong enough that satisfaction with housing may contribute at least a little, making ideal housing a goal worth pursuing.

Results are based on telephone interviews conducted as part of the Gallup-Healthways Well-Being Index survey Jan. 2–Dec. 29, 2014, with a random sample of 176,702 adults, aged 18 and older, living in metropolitan areas in the 50 U.S. states and the District of Columbia, selected using random-digit-dial sampling. Unlike previous years, only the 100 most populous metros—as determined by the U.S. Census Bureau—were reported in 2014. A second requirement is that at least 300 cases are required per metro area for reporting. As such, McAllen-Edinburg-Mission, Texas, and Durham-Chapel Hill, North Carolina, were both excluded from reporting because of insufficient sample size. These were replaced by the 102nd-largest metropolitan statistical area (MSA) in the U.S.: Lancaster, Pennsylvania.

The "communities" referenced in this article are based on MSAs as defined by the U.S. Office of Management and Budget. In many cases, more than one city is included in the same MSA. The San Jose, California, MSA, for example, also includes the smaller nearby cities of Sunnyvale and Santa Clara, in addition to San Jose. Each respondent is attributed to his or her MSA based on self-reports of his or her ZIP code.

Maximum margins of error for the Well-Being Index and the element scores vary according to MSA size, ranging from less than one point for the largest cities represented to around ±1.5 points for many of the smallest cities.

June 26, 2015

INVESTORS MORE ANXIOUS THAN HOPEFUL ABOUT INTEREST RATES

by Lydia Saad

Story Highlights

- *Four in 10 investors say higher rates would hurt their finances*
- *But 43% of retired investors think higher rates will help them*
- *Majority of investors expect interest rate hike in next year*

PRINCETON, N.J.—With the prospect of the first interest rate hike in years still looming, 27% of U.S. investors say higher interest rates would hurt them a little financially, and 16% say it would hurt them a lot. The combined 43% who say higher rates would harm their financial position far outweighs the 24% who say higher rates would help them a little or a lot. One in three say higher rates would not make a difference.

These results are based on the second quarter Wells Fargo/Gallup Investor and Retirement Optimism Index survey, conducted May 22–31, with 1,005 U.S. investors. This survey was conducted before the Federal Reserve opted not to raise rates at its June meeting. For this survey, investors are defined as U.S. adults who have at least $10,000 invested in stocks, bonds or mutual funds, or in a self-directed IRA or 401(k).

While U.S. investors view the prospect of higher interest rates more negatively than positively, this mainly reflects the views of

nonretired investors, half of whom say higher rates will hurt them a lot or a little; just 17% say they will help them. By contrast, 43% of retired investors believe higher rates will improve their financial situation while 23% say they will harm it.

U.S. Investors' Assessment of How Higher Interest Rates Would Affect Their Financial Situation

	Help a lot	Help a little	Make no difference	Hurt a little	Hurt a lot
	%	%	%	%	%
All investors	8	16	33	27	16
Retired	15	28	35	12	11
Not retired	6	11	32	32	18

Wells Fargo/Gallup Investor and Retirement Optimism Index Survey May 22-31, 2015

GALLUP

Past Wells Fargo/Gallup research provides some insights into why retirees are so concerned about interest rates:

- In 2014, one-third of retirees (34%), versus 24% of nonretirees, reported having certificates of deposit (CDs), likely making retirees more sensitive to the low rates recently associated with these savings instruments.
- Earlier this year, Wells Fargo/Gallup found half of retirees saying that CDs and other types of savings accounted for at least a minor part of their retirement income.
- In 2013, 26% of retirees said low interest rates were forcing them to assume more risk with their investments than they would otherwise.
- In the same poll, 14% of retirees said low rates made it necessary for them to work part time.
- Only 13% of retired investors in 2013, compared with 39% of nonretired investors, said they had recently taken advantage of low interest rates to refinance the mortgage on their home.

The nation's central bank has not raised interest rates since 2006, and Federal Reserve Board Chair Janet Yellen has indicated that while she thinks rates should go higher this year, it will be done slowly and only if the labor market and broader economy improves. One member of the Fed board recently said there is a 50% chance he'll back a rate increase in September.

Investors See More Upside Than Downside in Low Rates

While the Fed's policy of low interest rates is controversial in some political and economic circles, the majority of investors (68%) say the benefit of low interest rates to consumer and business borrowers outweighs any costs they create for savers and investors.

An increasing majority of investors are braced for interest rates to rise. Sixty-one percent in May, up from 56% in February, expect interest rates to go up a lot or a little over the next 12 months. Few—just 7%—think rates will go down while about three in 10 expect them to stay the same.

Investor Optimism Holds at Seven-Year High Point

Although Yellen does not believe the economy is showing sufficient strength to raise interest rates right now, investor confidence in 2015 continues to register at the highest level in seven years. The overall Wells Fargo/Gallup Investor and Retirement Optimism Index was

+70 in this quarter. That is similar to the +69 index score in the first quarter, but up from +29 a year ago and is the highest since October 2007. Still, the index remains far from its historical high of +178, recorded in January 2000, and has not exceeded +100 since January 2007.

U.S. Investors' Evaluation of Impact of Low Interest Rates on Consumers

With which of the following statements concerning today's low interest rates would you most agree -- [low interest rates are good for consumer and business borrowers, and these benefits outweigh any costs they create for savers and investors (or) low interest rates hurt savers and investors, and these costs outweigh any benefits they create for consumer and business borrowers]?

	Benefit to borrowers outweighs cost to savers	Cost to savers outweighs benefit to borrowers	No opinion
	%	%	%
All investors	68	26	6
Retired	49	39	12
Not retired	76	20	4

Wells Fargo/Gallup Investor and Retirement Optimism Index Survey
May 22-31, 2015

GALLUP

Wells Fargo/Gallup Investor and Retirement Optimism Index
October 1996-May 2015

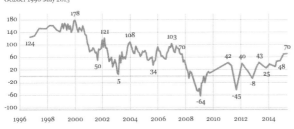

GALLUP

Notably, the stability in investor confidence between the first and second quarters of this year contrasts with the slight decline in Americans' confidence in the economy over the same period as seen in the Gallup Economic Confidence Index. This is likely related to investors' greater exposure to the stock market, which has continued to break records all year.

Bottom Line

For those retirees who financially depend on interest income from savings accounts or CDs, or who want to purchase annuities, today's low rates have been challenging. On the other hand, for working homeowners who have been able to realize huge savings by refinancing their existing home or buying a new home, they have been a financial lifeline.

Those realities are evident in the Wells Fargo/Gallup finding that retirees are more inclined to view low rates in negative terms while nonretirees tend to view them positively. But, in line with the Fed's decision to keep rates near rock bottom for now, both groups believe that, on balance, low rates do more good than harm for consumers as a whole. With investor optimism improving to its highest level in seven years, investors may be getting closer to the point that they can tolerate a rise in interest rates along with the temporary volatility in stocks and bonds it will likely trigger. But with investor confidence still well below the +100 mark, they may not be there quite yet.

Survey Methods

Results for the Wells Fargo/Gallup Investor and Retirement Optimism Index survey are based on questions asked May 22–31, 2015, on the Gallup Daily tracking survey, of a random sample of 1,005 U.S. adults having investable assets of $10,000 or more.

For results based on the entire sample of investors, the margin of sampling error is ±4 percentage points at the 95% confidence level.

June 29, 2015
U.S. INVESTORS PREFER MIX OF HUMAN, DIGITAL FINANCIAL ADVICE

by Jeffrey M. Jones

PRINCETON, N.J.—U.S. investors see online and digital investment tools as complements to the advice they get from a personal financial adviser. Nearly two in three investors say they prefer to get financial advice from *both* sources, including 39% who want advice to come mostly from advisers and 26% who want it to come mostly from digital tools.

Investors' Preferred Experience When Getting Financial Advice

Next we'd like you to think about the type of experience you want when getting financial advice. Do you want the experience to be_____?

	%
Entirely with a financial adviser	23
Mostly with a financial adviser, but with an online or digital component	39
Mostly digital but with access to a financial adviser	26
Entirely online or digital	9
No opinion	3

May 22-31, 2015, Wells Fargo/Gallup Investor and Retirement Optimism Index

GALLUP

While fewer investors want to stick to a single source of financial advice, many more favor using just an adviser (23%) than favor relying solely on digital tools (9%).

The results are based on the May 22–31 Wells Fargo/Gallup Investor and Retirement Optimism Index survey. For this survey, investors are defined as U.S. adults who have at least $10,000 invested in stocks, bonds or mutual funds, or in a self-directed IRA or 401(k).

Although most investors like using both advisers and digital tools, they clearly tilt in favor of human advice. A combined 62% prefer getting financial advice exclusively (23%) or mostly (39%) from a personal financial adviser, whereas a combined 35% prefer mostly (26%) or exclusively (9%) digital advice. Also, when asked to choose between three sources of advice, 50% opt for a strong relationship with a financial adviser, 24% for access to state-of-the-art online or digital investing tools, and 19% for access to on-call financial advisers.

Despite these preferences, investors widely use digital investment sources, with three-quarters saying they use digital tools a lot (19%) or a little (57%). Eighty-five percent of investors report that their primary financial institution offers a variety of online investing tools and services.

Also, investors are just as likely to say digital sources are important as they are to say this about a personal financial adviser when asked to rate each item separately. Specifically, 71% say access to online or digital investing tools is very or somewhat important to them, while 70% say the same about having a strong relationship with a personal financial adviser. Having on-call access to financial advisers or having a trusted friend or family member as an adviser is less important to investors.

Importance of Sources of Financial Advice to Investors
Thinking about different ways to get financial advice, how important are each of the following to you?

	% Very important	% Somewhat important	% Not too important	% Not important at all
Access to online or digital investing tools	33	38	13	16
A strong relationship with a personal financial adviser	37	33	17	12
On-call access to financial advisers, whenever you need them	28	36	20	16
A close friend or family member you trust to provide financial advice	25	30	21	24

May 22-31, 2015, Wells Fargo/Gallup Investor and Retirement Optimism Index

GALLUP'

Digital Advice Has Greater Reach Among Younger Investors

Investors as a whole tend to skew older, but within the investor group, younger investors are more likely than older investors to use digital sources of investment advice, to rate them as important, to say they prefer to use them over other potential sources and to prefer a mixture of digital and human sources of advice.

- Eighty-four percent of investors younger than 50 use digital sources of investment advice a lot or a little, compared with 69% of those aged 50 and older.
- Whereas 61% of older investors say access to digital sources of advice is important to them, a much higher 83% of younger investors rate such access as important.
- Seventy-five percent of younger investors prefer a mix of digital and human sources of investment advice, compared with 57% of older investors. Older investors (30%) are twice as likely as younger investors (15%) to want financial advice entirely from a financial adviser.

Use of, Preference for and Importance of Digital Investing Tools as Source of Financial Advice, by Age
Based on investors

	18 to 49 years old %	50+ years old %
USE OF DIGITAL SOURCES		
A lot	22	16
A little	62	53
NET: A lot/A little	84	69
IMPORTANCE OF SOURCES OF ADVICE		
Strong relationship with personal financial adviser	74	68
Access to online and digital tools	83	61
TYPE OF EXPERIENCE WANTED IN GETTING FINANCIAL ADVICE		
Entirely with adviser	15	30
Mostly with adviser but with a digital component	42	37
Mostly digital with access to adviser	33	20
Entirely digital	9	8
NET: Both financial adviser and digital	75	57
PREFERENCE IF HAD TO CHOOSE		
Strong relationship with financial adviser	43	54
Access to state-of-the-art online/digital tools	30	20
On-call access to advisers	22	18

May 22-31, 2015, Wells Fargo/Gallup Investor and Retirement Optimism Index

GALLUP'

Even though younger investors are more positively disposed toward digital investing tools than older investors are, younger investors are not necessarily ready to abandon financial advisers. The majority of younger investors still prefer an experience that relies mostly (42%) or exclusively (15%) on financial advisers. And if forced to choose, more younger investors, 43%, opt for a strong relationship with a financial adviser than opt for access to state-of-the-art electronic investing tools (30%). Also, nearly three in four younger investors say a strong relationship with a financial adviser is important to them, though that is less than the 83% who say access to digital investing tools is important.

The survey also finds large and consistent differences by age when investors are asked about interest in a variety of specific digital investing tools. These are apparent in tools that help with long-range matters—which may be of less relevance to older investors—including retirement calculators and long-term financial planning tools, but also in tools that address current financial matters like household budgeting and online access to investment accounts.

Interest in Specific Digital Investing Tools, by Age
Based on investors
Figures represent the percentage who are very or somewhat interested in the tool.

	All investors %	18 to 49 years old %	50+ years old %
Tools to help you review and make changes to your existing investment accounts	55	70	43
Long-term financial planning tools	53	70	38
Retirement calculators	50	66	36
Online education courses in financial planning	40	52	30
Household budgeting tools	38	56	24
An automated investment advisory service that uses computer-based portfolio management	33	45	23

May 22-31, 2015, Wells Fargo/Gallup Investor and Retirement Optimism Index

GALLUP'

Implications

Technology has improved Americans' lives in many ways, and that includes getting access to financial advice. Internet websites and smartphone apps now put a wide-ranging set of investment tools at investors' fingertips. Most U.S. investors report that they use these digital tools, and they generally regard them as an important source of financial advice.

But investors still value the advice they get from personal financial advisers, with most preferring a mix of financial advice from a dedicated adviser along with access to digital investing tools. Thus investors tend to see financial advisers and digital investment tools as complementary.

Younger investors' greater likelihood to use digital investing tools and to see them as important suggest reliance on digital tools will only increase in the future. However, because younger investors still very much favor a role for financial advisers, professional advisers will likely continue to play a prominent role in helping Americans make their investing decisions for the foreseeable future.

Survey Methods

Results for the Wells Fargo/Gallup Investor and Retirement Optimism survey are based on questions asked May 22–31, 2015, on the Gallup U.S. Daily survey, of a random sample of 1,009 U.S. adults having investable assets of $10,000 or more. For results based on the total sample of investors, the margin of sampling error is ±4 percentage points at the 95% confidence level. All reported margins of sampling error include computed design effects for weighting.

June 29, 2015
A THIRD OF INVESTORS WORRY ABOUT FINANCIAL ABUSE OF ELDERLY

by Rebecca Riffkin

Story Highlights

- *32% of investors worry about elder financial abuse*
- *One in three investors know a victim of elder financial abuse*
- *Among those who know a victim, 51% worry about such abuse*

WASHINGTON, D.C.—Roughly one in three U.S. investors, 32%, say they worry "a lot" or "a fair amount" about the financial abuse or exploitation of older family members or close friends. Although this represents a sizable number of investors, worry about elder abuse ranks below worry about personal identity theft (57%), cyberattacks on their savings or investments (47%), stock market volatility (42%) and investment scams or frauds (41%).

Most Investors Worry About Identity Theft

How much do you worry about the following types of risks affecting you? Do you worry a lot, a fair amount, only a little or not at all about _____?

	% A lot/A fair amount
Personal identity theft	57
Cyberattacks on your savings or investment accounts	47
Stock market volatility	42
Investment scams or frauds	41
Financial abuse or exploitation of older family members or close friends	32

Asked of U.S. investors
Wells Fargo/Gallup Investor and Retirement Optimism Index, May 22-31, 2015

GALLUP

Gallup asked investors how much they worry about these financial threats as part of the Wells Fargo/Gallup Investor and Retirement Optimism Index, conducted May 22–31. The nearly six in 10 investors who worry about identify theft is similar to what Gallup found in 2009, when two in three Americans worried "frequently" or "occasionally" about identity theft. Lower levels of worry about elder financial abuse no doubt reflect that the other threats are more general forms of fraud and financial insecurity, while elder abuse affects a smaller percentage of the population.

Most Investors Who Know a Victim Worry About Elder Financial Abuse

One in three U.S. investors report personally knowing someone who has been a victim of investment scams or financial abuse targeted at the elderly. These investors who know a victim are more than twice as likely (51%) as those who do not know a victim (23%) to report worrying a lot or a fair amount about elder financial abuse. Investors' age is far less a factor than their personal knowledge of someone who has been victimized in determining how much they worry about elder abuse. Thirty-four percent of investors younger than age 65 are worried, compared with 28% of those 65 and older.

Knowing a Victim of Elder Financial Abuse Makes Investors More Likely to Worry About It

How much do you worry about the following types of risks affecting you? Do you worry a lot, a fair amount, only a little or not at all about: Financial abuse or exploitation of older family members or close friends?

	% A lot/A fair amount	% Only a little/Not at all
Those who know a victim of elder financial abuse	51	49
Those who do not know a victim of elder financial abuse	23	75
18 to 64 years old	34	66
65+ years old	28	71

Asked of U.S. investors
Wells Fargo/Gallup Investor and Retirement Optimism Index, May 22-31, 2015

GALLUP

While elder financial abuse may seem a niche threat at the moment, as the American population ages, the crime could affect more people. The American Institute of Certified Public Accountants, for instance, recently reported that almost half of CPA planners have seen an increase in elder fraud or abuse over the past five years. This abuse can take many forms, including phone and Internet scams, the use of deceit to obtain a person's bank account information or dishonest advice on behalf of trusted individuals, such as brokers or even family members.

The elderly are a prime target because they often live alone, have ample financial resources and because some lack familiarity with newer forms of technology. Declining mental capacity, especially among the elderly suffering from dementia or Alzheimer's disease, can also play a factor in elders' susceptibility to financial abuse. The U.S. government has a website specifically designed to help protect elders and their families from elder fraud and financial exploitation.

Majority of Investors Unlikely to Use Adviser to Prevent Elder Fraud

Almost half of investors (47%) say they are likely to rely on a personal financial adviser to protect themselves or their family members from elder financial abuse in the future.

There are no significant differences across gender, age or investment-level groups in investors' intention to seek advice to help prevent elder abuse for themselves or a loved one.

Investors Divided on Using Adviser to Protect From Elder Financial Abuse

How likely are you to rely on a personal financial adviser to protect you or your family members from elder financial abuse in the future?

	% Very likely/ Somewhat likely	% Not too likely/ Not likely at all
All investors	47	52
Know a victim	53	48
Don't know a victim	44	55
Worry "a lot" about elder financial abuse	47	54
18 to 49 years old	48	52
50+ years old	47	53
Male	45	55
Female	50	49
Less than $100,000 invested	42	57
$100,000 invested or more	51	49

Asked of U.S. investors
Wells Fargo/Gallup Investor and Retirement Optimism Index, May 22-31, 2015

GALLUP

Bottom Line

Elder abuse is not a top concern of investors among several types of potential financial threats they might face, but remains important to about a third of all investors. Similarly, a third of investors personally know an older person who has been financially victimized. Among those who do, about as many are concerned about this form of abuse as are worried about identify theft among investors generally, the top-ranking financial concern. Having a trusted financial professional who can advise investors on major financial decisions or even monitor accounts is one way to avoid being victimized, or to protect loved ones. While close to half of investors are inclined to seek such help in the future, this may depend more on investors' general proclivity to seek advice than on their personal experience with elder fraud.

Survey Methods

Results for the Wells Fargo/Gallup Investor and Retirement Optimism Index survey are based on questions asked May 22–31, 2015, of a random sample of 474 U.S. adults having investable assets of $10,000 or more. For this survey, investors are defined as U.S. adults who have at least $10,000 invested in stocks, bonds or mutual funds, or in a self-directed IRA or 401(k). For results based on the entire sample of investors, the margin of sampling error is ±6 percentage points at the 95% confidence level.

June 30, 2015
TRUST DIFFERS MOST BY IDEOLOGY FOR CHURCH, POLICE, PRESIDENCY

by Andrew Dugan

Story Highlights

- *Conservatives' and liberals' trust differs for most key institutions*
- *Conservatives much more likely to trust the church and the police*
- *Liberals far more likely to have confidence in the presidency*

WASHINGTON, D.C.—In the U.S., liberals and conservatives report markedly different levels of confidence in nearly every key institution Gallup measures, reflecting the general polarization that typifies the country today. The confidence gap—the difference between groups in levels of confidence for a particular institution—is largest for the presidency (by 36 percentage points), followed by the church (27 points) and the police (26 points). Liberals have more confidence in the presidency, while conservatives are more likely to trust the church and the police.

While most institutions elicit sizable gaps in confidence among liberals and conservatives, Congress and TV news, both lowly regarded institutions, generate similar levels of confidence. Conversely, the military and small business are held in high esteem by large segments of liberals and conservatives.

These results are based on a June 2–7 Gallup poll that included Gallup's latest update on Americans' confidence in 15 U.S. institutions.

Confidence in U.S. Institutions, by Ideology

Figures are percentages with "a great deal" or "quite a lot" of confidence in the institution

	Conservatives	Liberals	Difference
	%	%	(pct. pts.)
The church or organized religion	57	30	27
The police	65	39	26
Big business	30	15	15
The military	79	64	15
Banks	32	22	10
Small business	72	63	9
The criminal justice system	28	22	6
Congress	11	9	2
Television news	21	24	-3
The medical system	36	44	-8
The public schools	26	37	-11
The U.S. Supreme Court	27	39	-12
Newspapers	16	35	-19
Organized labor	18	37	-19
The presidency	18	54	-36

June 2-7, 2015

GALLUP

Overall, confidence in most major U.S. institutions continues to linger well below historical norms, suggesting that Americans' dissatisfaction with the central organizations of society is not confined to one political philosophy or viewpoint. But given that ideology represents an individual's values and beliefs, it makes sense that those with different ideological views have more confidence in some institutions than others. These findings shed light on the underlying structure of U.S. society today.

Although the survey question does not name a specific individual, but instead asks about the institution of the presidency, it appears that the incumbent president influences confidence in the institution. Liberals express more confidence in years when a Democrat is president, as is the case now, and conservatives find the presidency more trustworthy when a Republican is in the Oval Office.

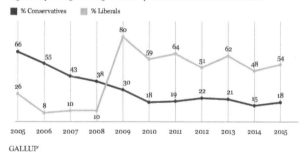

Confidence in the Presidency, by Ideology: Recent Trends

Figures are percentages with "a great deal" or "quite a lot" of confidence in the institution

■ % Conservatives   ■ % Liberals

GALLUP

Conservatives More Confident Than Liberals in Police, Church

Clear majorities of conservatives say they have "a great deal" or "quite a lot" of confidence in the police and in the church, while minorities of liberals say the same. The gap between liberals' and conservatives' confidence in the police grew larger this year, most likely reflecting different reactions to several high-profile situations involving police actions, such as events in Ferguson, Missouri, and Staten Island, New York.

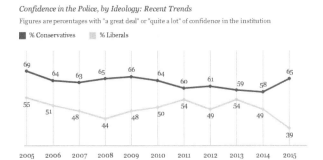

Confidence in the Police, by Ideology: Recent Trends
Figures are percentages with "a great deal" or "quite a lot" of confidence in the institution

■ % Conservatives □ % Liberals

GALLUP

While conservatives remain much more confident in the church than liberals, conservatives' confidence rating has declined recently, from 64% in 2013 to 57% this year.

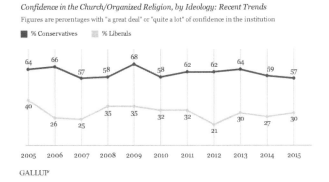

Confidence in the Church/Organized Religion, by Ideology: Recent Trends
Figures are percentages with "a great deal" or "quite a lot" of confidence in the institution

■ % Conservatives □ % Liberals

GALLUP

Liberals Regularly Show More Confidence in Organized Labor, Schools, Newspapers

Despite their overall low levels of confidence in organized labor, public schools and newspapers, liberals habitually express more confidence in these institutions than do conservatives. In particular, liberals' confidence in organized labor is twice that of conservatives.

Bottom Line

Underscoring the different worldviews that liberals and conservatives hold about American society today, these two groups show notable differences in the institutions they find most trustworthy. Majorities of conservatives hold the church and the police in high esteem, two institutions that inspire little confidence among liberals.

Liberals, meanwhile, give heavy support to the presidency, though this is conditional on the incumbent president being a Democrat. Beyond this, liberals have disproportionately high confidence in organized labor, the public school system and newspapers.

Some institutions, such as the military and small business, have the strong confidence of both liberals and conservatives, a reminder that not all institutions are viewed in ideological hues. But those institutions recording the most similar levels of confidence among liberals and conservatives, such as Congress, are those whose confidence levels have sunk to historic or near-historic lows. In other words, several institutions have lost credibility with Americans of varying philosophical stripes, a sign of the broad challenge these institutions have in terms of winning back most Americans' confidence.

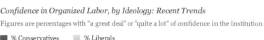

Confidence in Organized Labor, by Ideology: Recent Trends
Figures are percentages with "a great deal" or "quite a lot" of confidence in the institution

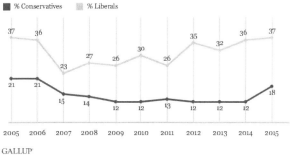

■ % Conservatives □ % Liberals

GALLUP

Survey Methods

Results for this Gallup poll are based on telephone interviews conducted June 2–7, 2015, with a random sample of 1,527 adults, aged 18 and older, living in all 50 U.S. states and the District of Columbia. For results based on the total sample of national adults, the margin of sampling error is ±3 percentage points at the 95% confidence level. All reported margins of sampling error include computed design effects for weighting.

July 01, 2015
U.S. JOB CREATION INDEX HOLDS IN JUNE AT RECORD HIGH OF +32

by Rebecca Riffkin

Story Highlights

- *Index holds at record high of +32 found in May*
- *More companies hiring than keeping workforce the same*
- *Index highest in Midwest at +36, lowest in East at +27*

WASHINGTON, D.C.—Gallup's U.S. Job Creation Index remained high in June at +32. The index score—based on 43% of workers saying their employer is hiring workers and expanding the size of its workforce and 11% saying their employer is letting workers go and reducing the size of its workforce—is the same as what Gallup measured in May, which is the highest Gallup has found for the index.

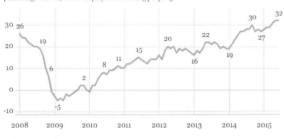

U.S. Job Creation Index, Monthly Averages, January 2008-June 2015

Percentage of U.S. workers who say their employers are hiring new people minus percentage who say their employers are letting people go

Gallup Daily tracking

GALLUP

Gallup began tracking job creation in January 2008 as the Great Recession began taking hold in the U.S. economy. While still at a relatively healthy +26 in January 2008, the index went into a deep dive after the 2008 financial crisis. It bottomed out at -5 in early 2009, and remained negative or close to zero for the rest of that year. The index slowly improved after that, reaching a high of +30 in September 2014. After hovering between +27 and +29 for half a year, the index climbed two points in April and another point in May to reach the current highs.

Gallup's Job Creation Index is based on interviews with 16,572 full- and part-time workers in the U.S., conducted June 1–30 on Gallup Daily tracking. Gallup asks employed workers nationwide each day whether their employer is increasing, reducing or maintaining the size of its workforce.

The percentage of workers who say their company is expanding its workforce is not only well above the percentage who say their company is letting people go, but since April, it has also exceeded the percentage who report their workforce is not changing. So far in the index's history, this has only happened a few times.

Index Highest in the Midwest, Lowest in the East

Over time, the index score in each region has generally followed the national trend, with a steep decline in 2008 through 2009 and improvement since then, including record highs in recent months. No one region has consistently outperformed the other regions over

the last seven years. However, the East continues to slightly lag behind the other regions, as it has since 2013.

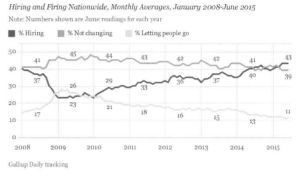

Hiring and Firing Nationwide, Monthly Averages, January 2008-June 2015

Note: Numbers shown are June readings for each year

■ % Hiring   ▓ % Not changing   ░ % Letting people go

Gallup Daily tracking

GALLUP

The index measured +27 in the East, slightly below the high score of +30 found in April, and the lowest of the four regions in June. The index was highest in the Midwest, where it increased to +36, the highest measure for this region yet. The index was unchanged in the West, at +33, but it dropped slightly in the South to +30.

Gallup Job Creation Index, by Region

Based on the percentage of U.S. workers who say their employer is hiring workers and expanding the size of its workforce minus the percentage who say their employer is letting workers go and reducing the size of its workforce

■ East   ■ Midwest   ▓ South   ░ West

Based on monthly averages
Note: Numbers shown are June readings for each year
Gallup Daily tracking

GALLUP

Implications

In addition to the record-high U.S. Job Creation Index score, based on employees' reports of hiring activity at their place of work, Americans' self-reports of their own working situation—as measured in the U.S. Payroll to Population employment rate—is the best since the fall of 2012.

The jobs situation is central to Americans' evaluations of the economy's overall health. And Americans are generally much more upbeat about the state of the U.S. economy now than they have been for the past seven years. However, they still rate economic conditions more negatively than positively overall, and economic confidence is lower now than it was earlier this year.

Survey Methods

Results for this Gallup poll are based on telephone interviews conducted June 1–30, 2015, on the Gallup U.S. Daily survey, with a random sample of 16,572 adults, aged 18 and older, living in all 50 U.S. states and the District of Columbia, who are employed full or part time. For results based on the total sample of employed adults, the margin of sampling error is ±1 percentage point at the 95%

confidence level. All reported margins of sampling error include computed design effects for weighting.

July 01, 2015

MORE SAY ALCOHOL THREATENS AUTO SAFETY THAN POT, PILLS

by Steve Ander and Art Swift

WASHINGTON, D.C.—The vast majority of Americans believe that driving while impaired by alcohol is a "very serious" problem (79%) on the roads today. This swamps public concern about people driving while impaired by prescription painkillers (41%), marijuana (29%) or prescription antidepressants (28%).

Drinking, Drugs and Traffic Safety in U.S.

Do you think people driving impaired by each of the following substances is a very serious problem on the roads today, a somewhat serious problem or not much of a problem?

	Very serious %	Somewhat serious %	Not much of a problem %
Alcohol	79	18	2
Prescription painkillers	41	42	15
Marijuana	29	39	31
Prescription antidepressants	28	36	33

June 24-25, 2015

GALLUP

Still, according to the June 24–25 Gallup survey, most Americans believe people's use of each of the four classes of drugs is at least a somewhat serious problem for traffic safety, but this ranges from a high of 97% for alcohol and 83% for prescription painkillers to 68% for marijuana and 64% for prescription antidepressants.

The question didn't ask Americans to estimate the severity of impairment each substance produces, but to say more broadly how much drivers' use of each substance affects traffic safety. Respondents may be evaluating both the severity of impairment and the prevalence of use by drivers, which may partly explain why more Americans view drinking alcohol as a threat to road safety than they do marijuana or prescription drug use.

Americans' awareness of the dangers of drinking and driving increased in the 1980s, when organizations such as Mothers Against Drunk Driving warned against driving under the influence of alcohol. Yet while marijuana can impair reaction time during driving simulations and in driving tests, some experts, including the Pacific Institute for Research and Evaluation, assert that driving while high is not as serious a problem as driving under the influence of alcohol. But if legalization of marijuana continues across the U.S. and in turn increases usage or emboldens people to take more risks with driving after using marijuana, public attitudes about the threat this poses to driving could change.

Younger Americans Say Drinking Very Serious, Marijuana Not as Serious

Across age groups, Americans aged 18 to 29 (88%) are the most likely to say drinking and driving is a very serious problem, perhaps because of effective communication from anti-drinking-and-driving groups. At the same time, they are the least likely age group

to consider people driving while impaired by marijuana to be a very serious problem (22%). This is consistent with previous Gallup research showing young Americans are the most likely to say they currently smoke marijuana.

While a large majority in each age group say drinking and driving is a very serious problem in regard to road safety, less than half in each group say prescription drugs or marijuana are "very serious."

Drugs, Drinking and Traffic Safety, by Age

Percentage who say problem is "very serious"

	Alcohol %	Prescription painkillers %	Marijuana %	Prescription antidepressants %
18 to 29	88	41	22	29
30 to 49	78	47	27	29
50 to 64	75	37	29	26
65+	74	36	37	28

June 24-25, 2015

GALLUP

Marijuana legalization has occurred largely in states that have voted Democratic in major elections in recent years, including Colorado, Washington and Oregon. Perhaps accordingly, Democrats are significantly less likely than Republicans to consider drivers impaired by marijuana to pose a major safety problem on the roads. Democrats, on the other hand, are a bit more likely than Republicans to believe use of prescription antidepressants poses a very serious threat.

Drugs, Drinking and Traffic Safety, by Political Party

Percentage who say problem is "very serious"

	Alcohol %	Prescription painkillers %	Marijuana %	Prescription antidepressants %
Republicans	78	40	35	25
Independents	78	39	29	28
Democrats	83	43	20	34

June 24-25, 2015

GALLUP

Bottom Line

After more than 30 years of anti-drinking-and-driving campaigns, it seems that Americans—especially younger adults—have gotten the message that drinking and driving is a very serious problem. However, far fewer view marijuana and prescription drugs as a threat to road safety.

With an explosion of prescription drugs in the U.S.—*Time* recently called the abuse of painkillers a "national epidemic"—the lines of how acceptable it is to drive under the influence of these drugs may not be as clearly drawn as they are for alcohol. These drugs may be legal, but abuse and misuse are still possible, and people may not have a clear understanding of when and in what ways they are impaired. In addition, while a growing number of states are legalizing marijuana, Americans are largely not convinced that it impairs drivers enough to cause serious problems on the roads.

It is possible that more Americans say alcohol is a serious problem for road safety because drinking is much more prevalent than using prescription painkillers, antidepressants or marijuana. Nearly two-thirds of Americans say they drink alcohol, whereas 19% report using a mood-altering drug nearly every day and just 7% admit to currently smoking marijuana. Or Americans may believe that these drugs are simply not as harmful as alcohol and can be "managed" more effectively while they drive. For example, it is documented that some who have smoked marijuana may at times be able to over-compensate for their impairment when driving, while drunk drivers may deny that they are impaired at all.

Survey Methods

Results for this Gallup poll are based on telephone interviews conducted June 24–25, 2015, on the Gallup U.S. Daily survey, with a random sample of 1,007 adults, aged 18 and older, living in all 50 U.S. states and the District of Columbia. For results based on the total sample of national adults, the margin of sampling error is ±4 percentage points at the 95% confidence level.

July 02, 2015
SMALLER MAJORITY "EXTREMELY PROUD" TO BE AN AMERICAN

by Art Swift

Story Highlights

- *54% say they are "extremely proud"; 27% are "very proud"*
- *Lower percentage "extremely proud" than immediately after 9/11*
- *Older Americans, Southerners and Republicans most proud*

WASHINGTON, D.C.—As Independence Day approaches, most in the U.S. say they are proud to be an American, including a slight majority, 54%, who are "extremely proud." The percentage saying they are "extremely proud" is slightly lower than in recent years and down from peaks at and around 70% between 2002 and 2004, after 9/11.

Proud to Be an American

How proud are you to be an American -- extremely proud, very proud, moderately proud, only a little proud or not at all proud?

▓ % Extremely proud

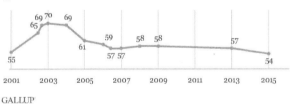

GALLUP

In addition to the 54% who are extremely proud to be an American, 27% say they are "very proud," 14% say they are "moderately proud," 4% are "only a little proud" and 1% state that they are "not at all proud."

These data are from a June 2–7 poll. Gallup has asked this question regularly since 2001. The highest percentage saying they were "extremely proud" to be an American came in 2003, in the months after the Iraq War began and not long after the terrorist attacks of Sept. 11, 2001, when Americans' patriotism surged. It is likely that the aftermath of 9/11 may have produced an anomaly in the levels of "extreme pride" in patriotism.

Older Americans, Southerners and Republicans Lead in "Extreme Pride"

While most Americans are proud to be an American, certain groups are especially likely to say they are extremely proud. "Extreme pride" rises for each succeeding age group, from a low of 43% among those under 30 to a high of 64% among senior citizens.

Extreme pride also varies regionally, from a high of 61% in the South to a low of 46% in the West.

Sixty-eight percent of Republicans say they are extremely proud to be an American, much higher than the 47% of Democrats who say the same. As usual, independents are in the middle, at 53%.

How proud are you to be an American -- extremely proud, very proud, moderately proud, only a little proud or not at all proud?

By age, region and party ID

	% Extremely proud
18 to 29	43
30 to 49	52
50 to 64	58
65+	64
East	50
Midwest	55
South	61
West	46
Republicans	68
Independents	53
Democrats	47

GALLUP

Bottom Line

Americans' likelihood of saying that they are "extremely proud" to be an American has returned to where it was in early 2001, before the 9/11 terrorist attacks. While slightly more than half of Americans are now extremely proud to be an American, more than nine in 10 are at least moderately proud. This suggests that patriotism is still very much alive in the U.S., even if the fervor is slightly less than it was after 9/11.

The reading of 54% in early June is about the same as the 55% recorded when Gallup first asked the question nearly 15 years ago, at the tail end of Bill Clinton's presidency. This indicates that patriotism is not necessarily a fixed characteristic, but can vary depending on circumstances—most notably when the U.S. is under duress, as was the case after the events of 9/11 and the build-up to wars in Afghanistan and Iraq.

Survey Methods

Results for this Gallup poll are based on telephone interviews conducted June 2–7, 2015, with a random sample of 1,527 adults, aged 18 and older, living in all 50 U.S. states and the District of Columbia. For results based on the total sample of national adults, the margin of sampling error is ±3 percentage points at the 95% confidence level.

July 02, 2015

DEMOCRATS REGAIN EDGE IN PARTY AFFILIATION

by Jeffrey M. Jones

Story Highlights

- *Democrats regain edge in party affiliation, 46% to 41%*
- *Parties had been even in the prior three quarters*
- *Democrats typically have an edge*

PRINCETON, N.J.—In the second quarter of 2015, Democrats regained an advantage over Republicans in terms of Americans' party affiliation. A total of 46% of Americans identified as Democrats (30%) or said they are independents who lean toward the Democratic Party (16%), while 41% identified as Republicans (25%) or leaned Republican (16%). The two parties were generally even during the previous three quarters, including the fourth quarter of 2014, when the midterm elections took place.

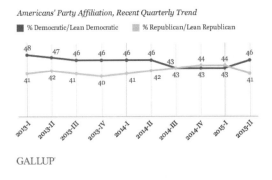

Americans' Party Affiliation, Recent Quarterly Trend

GALLUP

Republicans have seemingly lost the momentum they had going into last fall's elections, which saw them make significant gains in congressional seats, including taking partisan control of the Senate. After those victories, Americans' overall opinions of the Democratic Party worsened while the public grew slightly more positive toward the GOP.

Republicans were able to maintain an even footing with Democrats through the first quarter of this year, but in the second quarter, the percentage of Democratic identifiers and leaners increased by three percentage points while the percentage of Republican identifiers and leaners decreased by three points. As a result, Democrats are now back to where they were in 2013 and early 2014.

The results are based on aggregated data from three Gallup surveys conducted in the second quarter. Gallup's Daily tracking survey also shows a five-point Democratic advantage in party affiliation during the second quarter.

Democrats Usually Lead in Party Affiliation

Gallup has consistently measured Americans' party identification and—for those who initially identify as independents—partisan leanings since 1991. During those 24 years, Democrats have typically held an edge in party affiliation.

There have been a few instances in which Republicans held at least a slight edge for multiple quarters. These include:

- in 1991, after the U.S. victory in the first Persian Gulf War, under Republican President George H. W. Bush

- in late 1994 and early 1995, after the Republican victories in the midterm elections that gave the party control of both houses of Congress for the first time in four decades
- in late 2001 and early 2002, when Americans' support for elected officials including Republican president George W. Bush surged after the Sept. 11 terrorist attacks

At other times, Republicans and Democrats have been relatively even for multiple quarters. Most of these have occurred late in election years in which Republicans fared well, including the 2004 presidential election and the 2002, 2010 and 2014 midterm elections.

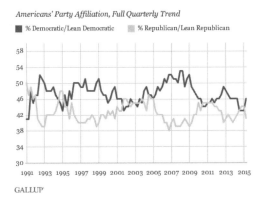

Americans' Party Affiliation, Full Quarterly Trend

GALLUP

As is true now, Republicans have in the past failed to sustain gains in party affiliation for long. And as has occurred multiple times in the past, Democrats have returned to having healthy advantages in party affiliation in the quarters and years that followed prior Republican strong points, such as in 1992–1993, 1996–2000 and 2005–2009.

Implications

Republicans have lost ground versus Democrats over the last three months in terms of the percentage of Americans who align with each party, essentially resetting the political map to what it had been in 2013 and early 2014, and putting the Democrats in a favorable political position as the 2016 campaign is getting underway.

Democratic gains in party affiliation may be partly linked to more positive views of President Barack Obama, whose job approval ratings were near his personal lows last fall but have recovered, perhaps related to low unemployment, lower gas prices than a year ago and an easing of some of the international challenges that faced the U.S., such as the Ukraine-Russia situation.

The recent changes in party affiliation may also reflect Americans' fading memory of the GOP's electoral successes in the 2014 midterm elections that made it the majority party in the Senate while increasing its majority in the House of Representatives. This follows the pattern that occurred after the 1994, 2002 and 2010 elections, when stronger Republican positioning after those elections proved short-lived.

And although Obama and the Republican majority in Congress remain a major focus of the political news coverage, attention is increasingly turning to the 2016 presidential campaign. Here Democrats may be benefiting from having a well-known and relatively popular front-running candidate in Hillary Clinton, which paints a contrast to the large, fractured and generally less well-known field of Republican presidential candidates.

Survey Methods

Results for this Gallup poll are based on telephone interviews conducted April–June 2015, with a random sample of 3,566 adults, aged 18 and older, living in all 50 U.S. states and the District of Columbia. For results based on the total sample of national adults, the margin of sampling error is ±2 percentage points at the 95% confidence level. All reported margins of sampling error include computed design effects for weighting.

July 06, 2015
AMERICANS STILL MORE CONFIDENT IN SMALL VS. BIG BUSINESS

by Andrew Dugan

Story Highlights

- *Small business one of the most trusted U.S. institutions*
- *Big business often one of the least trusted*

WASHINGTON, D.C.—Americans are more than three times as likely to express confidence in small business as they are in big business. Sixty-seven percent of U.S. adults report having "a great deal" or "quite a lot" of confidence in small business, far eclipsing the 21% who are similarly confident in big business. Confidence in small business is up slightly from last year's 62%, while confidence in big business is unchanged.

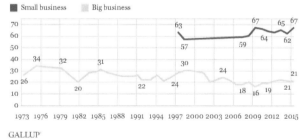

Americans' Confidence in Small Business vs. Confidence in Big Business

Now I am going to read you a list of institutions in American society. Please tell me how much confidence you, yourself, have in each one -- a great deal, quite a lot, some or very little?

% A great deal or quite a lot

■ Small business   ■ Big business

GALLUP

These results are based on a June 2–7 Gallup poll that included Gallup's latest update on confidence in U.S. institutions.

Small business remains one of the most popular institutions in the U.S., and is so far weathering the tide of dissatisfaction that is eroding public confidence in most other institutions. Other than the military, small business is the only major institution in 2015 that is polling above its historical average. Gallup started asking about confidence in small business in 1998, and began updating it annually in 2007, while data trends on other major institutions date back to 1973.

Over this timespan, Americans have reliably reported high confidence in small business—every year, the measure has been well above a majority, including during the 2007–2009 U.S. recession, which dampened public trust for several institutions, particularly those that operate in the economic sphere. For example, in June 2009, confidence in banks and big business fell to lows at the time for each institution, though banks would see confidence fall further. Small business would instead see public confidence climb by seven percentage points to a high of 67%, which is where it stands today.

Confidence in big business, meanwhile, has never been particularly high, peaking at 34% in 1975, then slowly diminishing over the next four decades. Confidence bottomed out at 16% in 2009, and has since improved only slightly to its current 21%. Also of note, big business regularly ranks near the bottom in confidence among major U.S. institutions, and has finished last or tied for last in nine surveys, most recently in 2009.

Bottom Line

Just as Americans are more inclined to trust their local government than the larger federal entity, they are more likely to trust small business, while confidence in big business is in shorter supply. There are many possible reasons for this persistent pattern. Small businesses, as defined by government statistics, are the most likely source of employment for U.S. workers. Because they are more likely to be run or owned by citizens in local communities, they are often seen as more in tune with the needs of local communities than are larger corporations that must pay attention to the decisions of a potentially far-away management structure. And, small businesses are often called the "lifeblood" of the U.S. economy, as President Barack Obama described them in his 2014 Presidential Proclamation of National Small Business Week.

This is not to suggest that big business is not a consequential economic actor. Beyond the success at the marketplace that helped fuel the growth and expansion that made many big businesses "big," some large corporations have had a profound impact on U.S. society. From fast food to culture to technological innovation, there are endless examples of companies whose products have become infused in American lives. But for many Americans, as is true for "big government," the power and political clout that can come with increased size can also be a source of worry and mistrust.

Survey Methods

Results for this Gallup poll are based on telephone interviews conducted June 2–7, 2015, with a random sample of 1,527 adults, aged 18 and older, living in all 50 U.S. states and the District of Columbia. For results based on the total sample of national adults, the margin of sampling error is ±3 percentage points at the 95% confidence level.

July 07, 2015
MOST SMARTPHONE USERS STILL RELY ON COMPUTER FOR WEB PURCHASES

by Lydia Saad

PRINCETON, N.J.—U.S. smartphone users rely on their device for a variety of everyday tasks, including connecting on social media and using email. Nevertheless, when it comes to the marketplace, 74% of U.S. adults with a smartphone say they mainly turn to their computer for making purchases online. Nearly as many also lean more on their computer (62%) than their smartphone (21%) for browsing products or comparing prices online.

AMERICANS' RELIANCE ON THEIR SMARTPHONE VS. COMPUTER FOR VARIOUS TASKS

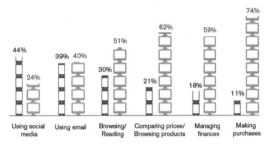

*Percentages using both devices equally, or who don't engage in each activity, not shown

Based on U.S. adult smartphone users
Gallup Panel survey by Web, April 17-May 18, 2015

GALLUP

Far fewer smartphone users rely on their phone than on their computer for window shopping and making purchases online, and relatively few say they spend an equal amount of time doing so on both devices: 11% for browsing products and comparing prices, and 8% for making purchases.

Americans' Use of Their Smartphone vs. Computer for Online Shopping Activities

	More time using phone	More time using computer	Use equally	Use neither/ Don't do this
	%	%	%	%
Comparing prices/ Browsing products	21	62	11	7
Making purchases	11	74	8	7

Gallup Panel
U.S. adults with a smartphone interviewed by Web April 17-May 18, 2015

GALLUP

These results are from a Gallup Panel survey conducted via the Web in April and May with 15,776 U.S. adults who say they have a smartphone.

Smartphones Strongest for Personal Communication

Of the six online activities Gallup measured, using social media such as Facebook, Twitter or LinkedIn is the only activity Americans say they conduct more by smartphone (44%) than computer (24%). Another 13% say they use the two devices equally for this purpose, while 20% say they do not use social media.

Smartphone users have also embraced accessing email by phone. Americans are evenly split in their preferred mode for checking and responding to email: 39% mainly use their smartphone to do so, while 40% prefer using their computer. An additional 20% say they spend the same amount of time on each.

At the same time, the scale tilts toward using a computer for reading online articles (51%), managing finances (59%), comparing prices or browsing products (62%) and making purchases (74%)— four activities that can require a significant amount of time and Internet navigation.

Big Generational Divides in Most Smartphone Activities

While it is well established that far fewer seniors than younger Americans use a smartphone, even seniors who have one are significantly less likely than younger smartphone users to rely on it for several non-telephone-related purposes.

The generational divide falls at the 50-year mark, as similar percentages of 18- to 29-year-olds and those aged 30 to 49 report they mainly use their smartphone—rather than their computer—for most of the activities Gallup measured. However, those percentages drop after age 50. Regardless of age, though, less than half of any age group relies mainly on their smartphone for using email or Internet surfing, and the rate drops to less than a third for browsing products, managing finances and making purchases online.

Those Relying Mainly on Smartphone for Each Activity, by Age

	18 to 29	30 to 49	50 to 64	65+
	%	%	%	%
Using social media	59	55	28	14
Checking or responding to email	48	46	30	19
Browsing the Internet/Reading Web articles	38	37	19	13
Comparing prices/Browsing products	24	27	14	8
Managing finances/Making payments	30	20	10	5
Making purchases online	11	16	6	4

Gallup Panel
U.S. adults with a smartphone interviewed by Web April 17-May 18, 2015

GALLUP

There is a distinction between the two younger age groups for managing finances and making payments online, for which 30% of those aged 18 to 29 versus 20% of those aged 30 to 49 rely mainly on their smartphone. On the other hand, 30- to 49-year-olds (16%) are slightly more likely than younger adults (11%) to use their smartphone for making purchases online. This activity falls into the single digits for those aged 50 and older.

For all activities but email, the percentages relying mainly on their smartphone drop by about half among those aged 50 to 64 versus younger adults, and then sink further among those aged 65 and older. One exception to this is using email, for which the decline by age is not quite as steep.

Bottom Line

With smartphones becoming ubiquitous in the U.S. and most adults owning or having access to a computer, consumers have powerful options for communicating, managing their money and shopping, all of which are made easier by digital technology. But these tasks have varying levels of difficulty, with some being easier to navigate on the larger screens of desktop and laptop computers than on even the biggest smartphones.

Perhaps the online activity most important to the economy is e-commerce, as the convenience of shopping and making purchases "anytime, anywhere" should, in theory, increase consumer spending. As reported this week in the *New York Times*, retailers hoping to maximize these impulse dollars are keen on simplifying the process on smartphones, on which people now spend so much of their time. But smartphone-based commerce has a long way to go, even with the youngest generation, as most smartphone users still prefer to browse and make purchases on a computer. While Amazon offers customers one-click purchasing, thus avoiding the tedium and potential error involved with entering credit card and address information, even this is not a perfect solution for first-time buyers, and is often not available on most other retailer sites. Until that changes, the computer may remain the device of choice for e-commerce, meaning retailers ought to continue optimizing the large-screen online retail experience for consumers.

Survey Methods

Results of smartphone ownership are based on 21,057 national adults interviewed by Web. Results of attitudes and behaviors of smartphone usage are based on 15,766 members of the Gallup Panel who have smartphones. The study was completed April 17–May 18, 2015.

The sample for this study was weighted to be demographically representative of the U.S. adult population, using 2012 Current Population Survey figures.

For results based on this sample, one can say that the maximum margin of sampling error is ±1 percentage point at the 95% confidence level. Margins of error are higher for subsamples. In addition to sampling error, question wording and practical difficulties in conducting surveys can introduce error or bias into the findings of public opinion polls.

July 08, 2015

DEMOCRATS' VIEWS ON CONFEDERATE FLAG INCREASINGLY NEGATIVE

by Jeffrey M. Jones

Story Highlights

- *Most Democrats now view Confederate flag as racist symbol*
- *Republicans' view of flag as symbol of Southern pride unchanged*
- *Americans divided on whether states should stop using flag images*

PRINCETON, N.J.—As South Carolina officials prepare to vote to remove the Confederate flag from the state capitol grounds, a diminished majority of Americans, 54%, down from 59% in 2000 and 69% in 1992, now view the Confederate flag as "a symbol of Southern pride" rather than "a symbol of racism." Democrats' views have shifted from a solid 61% majority viewing the flag as a symbol of Southern pride in 1992 to just 32% holding that view today. Republicans' views are largely unchanged.

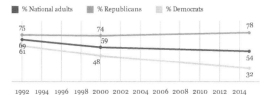

Views of Confederate Flag as Symbol of Southern Pride, by Political Party

Do you, yourself, see the Confederate flag more as a symbol of Southern pride, or more as a symbol of racism?

Note: Independents not shown on graph. Independent percentages were 71% in 1992, 56% in 2000 and 59% in 2015.

GALLUP

Gallup conducted the July 1–5 poll in the days before the Republican-dominated South Carolina Senate voted to remove the Confederate flag from the state capitol's grounds. The South Carolina House, which will take up the measure next, needs a two-thirds majority to pass it before a supportive Republican governor can sign the bill. Gallup's prior poll on the matter, in May 2000, came as an NAACP-led boycott of the state pressured South Carolina to remove the Confederate flag from the top of the state's capitol dome. The government at that time voted for a compromise measure moving the flag to another spot on the capitol grounds.

The issue was reignited last month when a young white male, who had posed for pictures with the Confederate flag, shot and killed nine black members of a South Carolina church.

Whereas 54% of Americans today view the Confederate flag as a symbol of Southern pride, 34%, including 58% of Democrats, believe it to be a racist symbol. The percentage of Democrats viewing the flag as racist is up from 31% in 1992 and 40% in 2000.

Public Divided on Southern States' Displaying Confederate Flag

Americans are divided when asked about Southern states displaying the Confederate flag on official state property. Currently, 47% believe it is all right for them to display the flag on government property or on special license plates available in certain states, while 46% say Southern state governments should stop these practices. In recent weeks, Alabama, Virginia and Georgia as well as South Carolina have made moves to remove the Confederate flag from state property.

Previously, Gallup asked a similar question about the appropriateness of Southern states flying the Confederate flag on top of state capitol buildings. In May 2000, Americans were divided on the matter. In 1992, they were more accepting of the practice, with 55% in favor and 40% opposed.

Republicans generally have endorsed Southern states displaying the Confederate flag, including 67% who support it today. Democrats shared that endorsement in 1992—with 51% saying it was OK to fly the flag on state capitol buildings—but now only 27% believe Southern state governments should display the Confederate flag on government property or license plates.

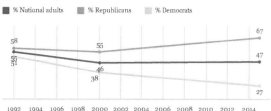

Views of Whether It Is All Right for Southern States to Display Confederate Flag, by Political Party

Note: 2015 question asked about displaying Confederate flag on government property or on special license plates available in the state. 1992 and 2000 question asked about flying Confederate flag on top of state capitol buildings.
Independents not shown on graph. Independent percentages were 56% in 1992, 47% in 2000 and 51% in 2015.

GALLUP

Political Differences Larger Than Racial, Regional Differences

The Confederate flag arguably has greater significance for blacks and Southern residents than for most other Americans. Blacks are, not surprisingly, quite negative in their views of the flag, with 69% believing it is a symbol of racism and 73% saying Southern governments should stop displaying it on government property.

Differences by region, on the other hand, are not as large. Southern residents are slightly more likely than those living in other parts of the country to endorse state governments' display of Confederate symbols, but they are no more likely than Midwesterners to view it as a symbol of Southern pride. Regional differences in the current poll are largely similar to what Gallup measured in 1992, even as many more Americans have migrated to the South from other parts of the country.

The greatest differences in views of the Confederate flag are by political party identification, particularly on the question of whether it is all right for Southern states to display it on government property. Differences by political ideology are nearly as large, with conservatives generally positive and liberals generally negative toward the flag.

Education also has a significant relationship with Americans' views of the Confederate flag: Those with more formal education tend to be more negative toward the flag. Only 29% of postgraduates believe it is OK for Southern states to display the flag on government property, compared with 52% of college graduates only who say the same.

Views of Confederate Flag, by Demographic Group, 2015

	Symbol of Southern pride	Symbol of racism	All right for Southern gov'ts to display	Southern gov'ts should stop practices of displaying
	%	%	%	%
National adults	54	34	47	46
White	64	27	54	41
Black	19	69	20	73
East	49	37	42	49
Midwest	58	33	45	47
South	57	31	52	41
West	51	39	44	50
Republican	78	13	67	27
Independent	59	29	51	41
Democrat	32	58	27	69
Conservative	70	18	63	29
Moderate	53	37	43	51
Liberal	35	55	32	64
Postgraduate	41	48	29	67
College graduate only	46	44	40	54
Some college	59	32	52	45
High school or less	58	28	52	37

July 1-5, 2015

GALLUP'

Implications

As on many other issues, including gun control, abortion and global warming, Republicans' and Democrats' views of the Confederate flag have grown apart. As recently as 1992, a majority of both Democrats and Republicans said the Confederate flag was more a sign of Southern pride than of racism, and both groups were comfortable with Southern states flying the flag on state capitol buildings.

Since the early 1990s, the political parties have become more ideologically homogeneous, mostly because conservative Southern whites who were formerly aligned with the Democratic Party have realigned and are now solidly Republican, as evidenced in their voting for federal and state offices. Today's Democratic Party, with white liberals and racial and ethnic minorities at its core, takes a much more negative view of the Confederate flag.

Fewer Southern states display the Confederate flag in some fashion today than did so in the past, but these changes have not been necessarily driven by widespread public opposition in the

South or the U.S. more generally. Although Americans tend to have a more positive than negative view of what the Confederate flag symbolizes, that level of positivity is less than it was two decades ago. Americans today are also divided on Southern governments' displaying of the flag, which, combined with the sensitivity of the issue, may be enough to motivate even Republican-dominated Southern states to remove the Confederate flag.

Survey Methods

Results for this Gallup poll are based on telephone interviews conducted July 1–3 and 5, 2015, on the Gallup U.S. Daily survey, with a random sample of 2,013 adults, aged 18 and older, living in all 50 U.S. states and the District of Columbia. For results based on the total sample of national adults, the margin of sampling error is ±3 percentage points at the 95% confidence level. All reported margins of sampling error include computed design effects for weighting.

July 09, 2015
MOST U.S. SMARTPHONE OWNERS CHECK PHONE AT LEAST HOURLY

by Frank Newport

Story Highlights

- *52% of smartphone owners check it a few times an hour or more*
- *Young Americans are the most frequent smartphone checkers*
- *Most Americans have smartphone by them all day, many all night*

PRINCETON, N.J.—About half of U.S. smartphone owners check their devices several times an hour or more frequently, including 11% who say they check it every few minutes and 41% who check it a few times an hour. Another 20% of Americans claim to check their phones about once an hour, leaving 28% who check them less frequently.

Next, we'd like you to estimate how often you use your smartphone, including times you look at it, check it or use it for any reason...

	% Smartphone owners
Every few minutes	11
A few times an hour	41
About once an hour	20
A few times a day	24
About once a day	2
Less than once a day	2

Gallup Panel survey via Web and mail, April 17-May 18, 2015

GALLUP'

These data are based on a special Gallup Panel survey conducted among 15,747 U.S. adults who say they have a smartphone. The survey was conducted April 17–May 18 via the Web and included a mail survey component for these questions. The Gallup Panel is a probability-based sample with members in all 50 states.

The frequency with which Americans check their smartphones essentially means that they must be keeping their smartphones by their sides during the day. The data bear that assumption out: 81%

of smartphone users say they keep their phone near them "almost all the time during waking hours."

I keep my smartphone near me almost all the time during my waking hours...

	% Smartphone owners
Yes	81
No	19

Gallup Panel survey via Web and mail, April 17-May 18, 2015

GALLUP

Americans' attachment to their smartphones is so strong that 63% report keeping it near them at night even while sleeping. Some of this may be simple convenience if the phone is checked last thing before going to sleep and first thing upon waking. It may also reflect that many Americans use the alarm clock feature on their smartphone to wake them up each morning.

Most Believe They Check Their Smartphones Less Often Than Others

A Prairie Home Companion host Garrison Keillor is famous for his description of the mythical Minnesota town of Lake Wobegon as a place where all the children are above average. In a similar but reverse fashion, the majority of American smartphone owners perceive that their use of their own device is below average (a mathematical impossibility). Sixty-one percent of owners claim they look at or check their smartphone less often than people they know, including 30% who say they check it a lot less often. Most of the rest say their use is about average, with a scant 11% admitting that they use their phone more often than others.

Compared to people you know, do you look at or check your smartphone...?

	% Smartphone owners
A lot more often than they do	3
A little more often	8
About as often	28
A little less often	31
A lot less often than they do	30

Gallup Panel survey via Web and mail, April 17-May 18, 2015

GALLUP

Why Americans tend to perceive that they monitor their smartphone less often than others is not firmly established. It's possible that Americans either misperceive what others are doing, or that they feel it is a socially undesirable behavior and therefore want to believe that they aren't doing it as much as others. The data show that even among owners who say they check their phone every few minutes, only one-third believe this is above-average behavior, and about half claim that their minute-by-minute monitoring of their smartphone is about the same as others they know. This could reflect the fact that these highly frequent phone checkers are surrounded by family or colleagues who are similar to themselves and engaging in the same type of behavior.

Frequent Smartphone Checking Skews Young

Casual observation in everyday life would lead one to conclude that young people use their smartphone more often than those who are older. The data confirm this, and the differences are remarkable. More than seven in 10 young smartphone owners check their device a few times an hour or more often, including 22% who admit

to checking it every few minutes. That contrasts with the 21% of smartphone owners who are aged 65 and older who check it a few times an hour or more, with a miniscule 3% of that older age group checking it every few minutes.

Next, we'd like you to estimate how often you use your smartphone, including times you look at it, check it or use it for any reason...

	% Every few minutes	% A few times an hour
NATIONAL ADULTS	11	41
GENDER		
Men	12	43
Women	11	38
AGE		
18-29	22	51
30-49	12	47
50-64	6	33
65+	3	18
EDUCATION		
High school or less	7	34
Some college	13	40
College graduate	12	47
Postgraduate	11	43
SMARTPHONE		
iPhone users	12	44
Android users	11	39

Gallup Panel survey via Web and mail, April 17-May 18, 2015

GALLUP

American smartphone owners with a high school education or less are the least likely to check their phones frequently, a finding that reflects the older skew of this group. There is little variation in smartphone checking among owners who have some college, college graduates, and those with postgraduate education. iPhone owners are slightly more likely to check their phone frequently than are Android owners.

Implications

Most American smartphone owners keep their phones near them all day, many even while they sleep, and the majority check their phone at least a few times within every hour. The ubiquitous presence of smartphones in Americans' lives is especially evident among younger Americans, one out of five of whom admits to checking their phone every few minutes.

All of the consequences of this brave new world in which individuals essentially stay in constant touch with the world through their handheld devices are certainly not known at this point, but are being studied with increasing frequency. Certainly the telephone and then radio and then television changed the way people relate to the world, and the smartphone, no doubt, is doing the same. The next report in this Gallup series will delve into the ways in which Americans relate to and think about their phones, including the key question of whether the public feels that the evolution of society into a smartphone-centric culture is a good thing or a bad thing.

Survey Methods

Results are based on 15,747 members of the Gallup Panel who have smartphones, conducted April 17–May 18, 2015. The sample for this study was weighted to be demographically representative of the U.S. adult population, using 2012 Current Population Survey figures. For results based on this sample, one can say that the margin of sampling error is ±1 percentage point at the 95% confidence level.

All reported margins of sampling error include computed design effects for weighting. In addition to sampling error, question wording and practical difficulties in conducting surveys can introduce error or bias into the findings of public opinion polls.

July 10, 2015
U.S. UNINSURED RATE AT 11.4% IN SECOND QUARTER

by Stephanie Marken

Story Highlights

- *Uninsured rate lowest to date in Gallup and Healthways tracking*
- *Sharpest declines found among minorities and lower-income adults*

WASHINGTON, D.C.—The uninsured rate among U.S. adults aged 18 and older was 11.4% in the second quarter of 2015, down from 11.9% in the first quarter. The uninsured rate has dropped nearly six percentage points since the fourth quarter of 2013, just before the requirement for Americans to carry health insurance took effect. The latest quarterly uninsured rate is the lowest Gallup and Healthways have recorded since daily tracking of this metric began in 2008.

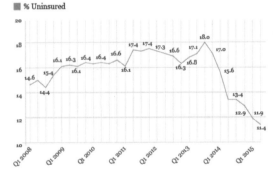

Percentage Uninsured in the U.S., by Quarter
Do you have health insurance coverage?
Among adults aged 18 and older

Quarter 1 2008-Quarter 2 2015
Gallup-Healthways Well-Being Index
GALLUP

The second-quarter results are based on approximately 44,000 interviews with U.S. adults from April 1 to June 30, 2015, conducted as part of the Gallup-Healthways Well-Being Index. Gallup and Healthways ask 500 U.S. adults each day whether they have health insurance, which on an aggregated basis allows for precise and ongoing measurement of the percentage of Americans with and without health insurance.

Gallup's monthly trend indicates that the decline in the uninsured rate took place late in the first quarter—after the Feb. 15 deadline to purchase health insurance—and that the lower rate held steady throughout the second quarter. The uninsured rate fell to 11.3% by March, and the April, May and June averages were similar.

Uninsured Rate Declines Sharply Among Minorities and Lower-Income Americans

From a long-range perspective, the uninsured rate has declined across nearly all key subgroups since 2013. But the sharpest declines have occurred among Hispanics, blacks and lower-income Americans. The uninsured rate among Hispanics declined by 9.6 points from the fourth quarter of 2013—the last full quarter of interviewing before the requirement that Americans carry health insurance took effect. Similarly, the percentage of uninsured blacks dipped 8.9 points over this period. Across major subgroups, those making less than $36,000 in annual household income have seen the sharpest drop—9.9 points since the fourth quarter of 2013.

Percentage of Uninsured U.S. Adults, by Subgroup
Do you have health insurance coverage?

	Q4 2013	Q2 2015	Net change
	%	%	(pct. pts.)
National adults	17.1	11.4	-5.7
18 to 25	23.5	15.9	-7.6
26 to 34	28.2	20.4	-7.8
35 to 64	18.0	11.3	-6.7
65+	2.0	2.0	0.0
Whites	11.9	7.4	-4.5
Blacks	20.9	12.0	-8.9
Hispanics	38.7	29.1	-9.6
Less than $36,000	30.7	20.8	-9.9
$36,000 to $89,999	11.7	8.2	-3.5
$90,000+	5.8	3.6	-2.2

Gallup-Healthways Well-Being Index

GALLUP

More Americans Have Self-Funded Health Plans

To assess changes in insurance type, Gallup and Healthways focus only on those adults aged 18 to 64, given that most Americans aged 65 and older are on Medicare. The percentage of 18- to 64-year-olds who are covered through a plan fully paid for by themselves or a family member was 20.9% in the second quarter, up from 17.6% in the fourth quarter of 2013. Similarly, 9.5% of 18- to 64-year-olds had Medicaid coverage last quarter, up from 6.9% in the final quarter of 2013. The increase in the percentage covered through Medicaid is likely due to the healthcare law provision that expanded the qualifying income levels for Medicaid.

Just under half of 18- to 64-year-olds in the U.S. (43.4%) have health insurance through a current or former employer—a percentage that has stayed relatively stable since the fourth quarter of 2013.

Gallup and Healthways began asking about the source of health insurance using the current question wording in August 2013 in anticipation of shifts in insurance type as a result of the Affordable Care Act. Respondents are asked, "Is your primary health insurance coverage through a current or former employer, a union, Medicare, Medicaid, military or veteran's coverage or a plan fully paid for by you or a family member?" Respondents are also asked if they have secondary health insurance coverage, and if so, what type of coverage. The results reported here are a combined estimate of primary and secondary insurance types.

Type of Health Insurance Coverage in the U.S., Among 18- to 64-Year-Olds

Is your insurance coverage through a current or former employer, a union, Medicare, Medicaid, military or veteran's coverage or a plan fully paid for by you or a family member?

Primary and secondary insurance combined

	Q4 2013	Q2 2015
	%	%
Current or former employer	44.2	43.4
Plan fully paid for by self or family member	17.6	20.9
Medicaid	6.9	9.5
Medicare	6.1	7.6
Military/Veteran's	4.6	4.9
A union	2.5	2.5
(Something else)	3.5	4.1
No insurance	20.8	13.8

Gallup-Healthways Well-Being Index

GALLUP

Implications

The 2015 second-quarter uninsured rate is the lowest rate measured since Gallup and Healthways began tracking the metric at the start of 2008, raising the question of how low the rate can go. Recently, the Supreme Court ruled in the case of *King v. Burwell* to affirm the legality of subsidies provided to those obtaining insurance through the Affordable Care Act via a federal or state exchange. The case represents the second attempt to challenge components of the healthcare law since its implementation, and is a major victory for the law's supporters. Had the Supreme Court ruled differently, the decision would have greatly undermined the Affordable Care Act and likely spurred major changes in the healthcare system—and by extension, the percentages of Americans who are insured and uninsured.

Enrollment for 2016 coverage begins Nov. 1, 2015. The uninsured rate may decline again slightly, although less significantly than it did over this past year, as those who remain uninsured are likely the hardest to engage.

Survey Methods

Results are based on telephone interviews conducted April 1–June 30, 2015, as part of the Gallup-Healthways Well-Being Index survey, with a random sample of 43,575 adults, aged 18 and older, living in all 50 U.S. states and the District of Columbia. For results based on the total sample of national adults, the margin of sampling error is ±1 percentage point at the 95% confidence level. Each quarter dating to Quarter 1, 2014, has approximately 44,000 respondents. Each quarter from 2008 through 2013 has approximately 88,000 respondents.

July 10, 2015
IN U.S., 47% SAY LEGAL MARIJUANA WILL MAKE ROADS LESS SAFE

by Steve Ander and Art Swift

Story Highlights

- *30% of Americans say driving will be "a lot less safe"*
- *Not much difference between states by legal status of marijuana*

- *Older Americans most concerned about marijuana and auto safety*

WASHINGTON, D.C.—As some U.S. states have legalized marijuana for recreational and medicinal use, 30% of Americans say legalization will make driving in those states a lot less safe. Another 17% expect it to make driving a little less safe. Half of Americans, however, say it will not make much of a difference.

Impact of Legalizing Marijuana on Driving

As you may know, certain states have recently made marijuana legal in one form or another. What impact, if any, do you think legalizing marijuana will have on driving in those states? Will it make driving in those states less safe or not make much difference? If less safe, will it make driving a lot less safe or only a little less safe?

	A lot less safe	A little less safe	Not make much difference
June 24-25, 2015	30%	17%	50%

GALLUP

Those in states with some form of legal marijuana are no different in their assessments of its effect on automotive safety than those in states without laws legalizing the drug. Across the 23 states and the District of Columbia that have some form of legalization, 49% say marijuana legalization will not make much difference in driving safety. This is on par with the 52% in the other 27 states who say legalizing pot would not make much of a difference for road safety. Similarly, 29% in states with some form of marijuana legalization say the roads will be a lot less safe, roughly matching the 30% saying the same in states with no legalized marijuana.

State Marijuana Policies and Traffic Safety

As you may know, certain states have recently made marijuana legal in one form or another. What impact, if any, do you think legalizing marijuana will have on driving in those states? Will it make driving in these states less safe or not make much difference? If less safe, will it make driving a lot less safe or only a little less safe?

	Not make much difference	A little less safe	A lot less safe
States with laws legalizing marijuana	49%	19%	29%
States without laws legalizing marijuana	52%	16%	30%

June 24-25, 2015

GALLUP

Marijuana is by far the most-used illicit drug. The Substance Abuse and Mental Health Services Administration (SAMHSA) reported in 2013 that nearly 20 million people had used marijuana in the past month. A 2013 Gallup poll found that 38% of Americans have tried marijuana and 7% admitted they were current marijuana smokers. Legalized pot across the U.S. ranges from recreational to medical purposes, and marijuana use on the whole has increased since 2007. While in many states, medical marijuana has been legal for more than a decade, the legalization of recreational marijuana has started only in the past few years—with four states and Washington, D.C., having laws in place that permit pot use and actually regulating it for tax revenues. Studies have shown that marijuana use affects reaction times, judgment and awareness, but there is no consensus on whether driving while high will adversely affect road safety.

The ultimate impact of marijuana use on traffic safety will be determined both by its effect on one's ability to drive and by how common it becomes for people to drive under its influence. Americans today perceive alcohol as a greater threat to traffic safety than marijuana, which may largely reflect the more widespread use of alcohol than marijuana among Americans and the highly publicized adverse effects of alcohol on driving ability.

Urban Residents' Views Similar to Those of Nonurban Residents

Illicit drug use is higher in metropolitan areas than in rural areas, according to SAMHSA. Yet Gallup finds that Americans living in big cities and urban suburbs are no more likely than those living in all other communities to say marijuana affects driving safety in states where it is legal.

Community Type and Traffic Safety

As you may know, certain states have recently made marijuana legal in one form or another. What impact, if any, do you think legalizing marijuana will have on driving in those states? Will it make driving in these states less safe or not make much difference? If less safe, will it make driving a lot less safe or only a little less safe?

	Not make much difference	A little less safe	A lot less safe
Big cities and urban suburbs	52%	19%	27%
All other communities	49%	16%	31%

June 24-25, 2015

GALLUP

For this analysis, "big city" residents are those living in the 47 U.S. counties that include the nation's largest cities, and "urban suburb" residents are those living in 107 counties that hold the "near-in suburbs" of most major cities and can have characteristics similar to those of big cities. These community segments come from the American Communities Project.

Older Americans See Marijuana as Affecting Auto Safety

While respondents' community type and state policies do not relate to differing opinions on marijuana's impact on driving safety, age does. Specifically, 18- to 29-year-olds (63%) are twice as likely as those aged 65 and older (31%) to see marijuana legalization as not having much effect on traffic safety in states where it is legal. For those aged 50 and older, more than half believe legalization would have some effect on driver safety, while more than half of those younger than 50 say it will make little difference.

Age, Pot and Traffic Safety in U.S.

As you may know, certain states have recently made marijuana legal in one form or another. What impact, if any, do you think legalizing marijuana will have on driving in those states? Will it make driving in these states less safe or not make much difference? If less safe, will it make driving a lot less safe or only a little less safe?

	Not make much difference	A little less safe	A lot less safe
	%	%	%
18 to 29	63	12	24
30 to 49	57	16	26
50 to 64	47	19	32
65+	31	24	39

June 24-25, 2015

GALLUP

Bottom Line

If the trend toward states legalizing marijuana continues, it may affect millions more Americans directly or indirectly in the coming years. Gallup's new study on public views about the effect of legalization on driving will serve as a baseline to measure how these perceptions may change over time.

While the effect of pot use on driving may not be as severe as the effect of alcohol, the National Highway Traffic Safety Administration has stated there are increased risks associated with driving while high. States' efforts to strengthen regulations and enforcement related to driving after smoking marijuana will likely be guided by how frequently accidents can be traced to pot use. And this, in turn, will likely influence public opinion as well.

While the effect marijuana use has on traffic safety is yet to be determined, for now, these data may defuse arguments that increased legalization across the U.S. will influence driver safety. With just 30% of Americans currently saying that an increase in legal marijuana would make driving a lot less safe, and 50% saying it will not make much difference, the pro-legalization forces may have an advantage.

Survey Methods

Results for this Gallup poll are based on telephone interviews conducted June 24–25, 2015, on the Gallup U.S. Daily survey, with a random sample of 1,007 adults, aged 18 and older, living in all 50 U.S. states and the District of Columbia. For results based on the total sample of national adults, the margin of sampling error is ±4 percentage points at the 95% confidence level.

July 10, 2015
AMERICANS' VIEWS OF HEALTHCARE LAW IMPROVE

by Jeffrey M. Jones

Story Highlights

- *Americans' views of ACA best since 2012*
- *Public now evenly divided in views of law*
- *Most continue to say law hasn't helped them personally*

PRINCETON, N.J.—Shortly after the Supreme Court in late June turned back a second legal challenge to the 2010 Affordable Care Act (ACA), Americans' approval of the law rose to 47%, the highest level since 2012. Still, Americans are as likely to disapprove as to approve of the law.

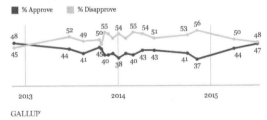

Do you generally approve or disapprove of the 2010 Affordable Care Act, signed into law by President Obama that restructured the U.S. healthcare system?

GALLUP

The results are based on a July 1–5 Gallup poll. On June 25, the Supreme Court issued its decision in the case of *King v. Burwell*. At issue in the case was the Affordable Care Act's provision for tax credits to subsidize individuals' health plans purchased through insurance "exchanges." The law stated that only those who purchased insurance through exchanges established *by states* were eligible for subsidies.

Currently, 16 states have their own exchanges, with individuals in other states having to purchase insurance through federally run exchanges. The Supreme Court ruled that while the language plainly reads that only those in states with state-run exchanges are eligible for the tax credits, the law intended for people to get subsidized coverage through a state-run exchange *or* the federal exchange.

Support for ACA Typically Has Not Been High in the Past

A majority of Americans have typically disapproved of the Affordable Care Act, also known as "Obamacare," since late 2012 when Gallup began asking this version of the question. Opinion of the law before it was passed and immediately after its passage in March 2010 has never been highly positive.

Recent low points in Americans' support for the law came in late 2013 and early 2014, when 38% approved after companies dropped millions of Americans from their insurance plans because the plans did not meet the law's minimum coverage requirements. Those actions clearly contradicted President Barack Obama's pledge that those who liked their insurance plan would be able to keep it under the new law. Approval registered a similarly low 37% last fall after Republicans' strong showing in the midterm elections.

But approval of the law has now increased 10 percentage points in two subsequent polls, rising to 44% in April and now 47% after the court's decision.

Since November, approval of the ACA has increased among all key demographic groups, with the changes for each group generally within a few points of the overall 10-point increase.

Changes in Approval of Affordable Care Act, November 2014 to July 2015, by Subgroup

	November 2014	July 2015	Change
	%	%	pct. pts.
National adults	37	47	10
Men	36	46	10
Women	39	48	9
Whites	29	38	9
Nonwhites	56	68	12
18 to 29	42	54	12
30 to 49	42	49	7
50 to 64	31	45	14
65+	35	41	6
College graduates	48	57	9
College nongraduates	33	43	10
Republicans	8	14	6
Independents	33	41	8
Democrats	74	83	9

GALLUP

As has been the case throughout the law's history, the differences are the greatest among political subgroups, with 83% of Democrats and 14% of Republicans approving. Support for the ACA is higher among nonwhites than whites, younger adults than older adults, and college graduates than college nongraduates.

Majority of Americans Say ACA Has Not Had an Effect on Them Personally

More than five years after the law's passage, many but not all of its provisions have been implemented. Fifty-five percent of Americans currently say the ACA has so far not affected them or their family. This percentage has declined over time as more of the law's provisions have rolled out, including the first two opportunities for Americans to buy health insurance through government exchanges in late 2013/early 2014 and late 2014/early 2015. More Americans say the law has hurt them and their family (25%) than say it has helped them and their family (18%), a pattern that has persisted since Gallup first asked the question in 2012.

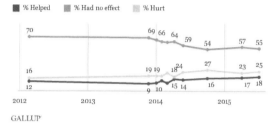

As you may know, a number of the provisions of the healthcare law have already gone into effect. So far, has the new law -- [ROTATED: helped you and your family, not had an effect, (or has it) hurt you and your family]?

GALLUP

As would be expected, Americans who say the law has helped their family overwhelmingly approve of it, and the vast majority of those who say the law has hurt their family disapprove of it. Those who say the law has not affected them are more likely to approve (51%) than disapprove (44%) of it.

Approval of Affordable Care Act, by Reported Effect of Law on Family

	% Helped family	% Had no effect on family	% Hurt family
Approve of ACA	93	51	8
Disapprove of ACA	6	44	90

July 1-5, 2015

GALLUP

To some degree, those relationships reflect the partisan evaluations of the law. Republicans—who widely disapprove of the ACA—are much more likely to say it has hurt their family (40%) than helped it (7%). And Democrats—most of whom approve of the law—are much more likely to say it has helped their family (30%) than hurt it (9%). Whether these reports of the law's effect are accurate assessments or just a broader expression of support for or opposition to the law is unclear.

Implications

Americans' views of the ACA have improved in recent months, but because they were more negative about it previously, now they are merely divided in their assessments of it. The Supreme Court's decision may have helped boost Americans' views of the law, giving it further legitimacy.

Additionally, changes in Americans' party affiliation since last fall could be a factor in the public's more upbeat assessment of the ACA. Americans also view Obama more positively now than they did last fall, and given his close association with the law, more positive opinions of him may translate to more positive opinions about Obamacare.

The Supreme Court's decision makes the future of the law slightly more certain, pending further legislative challenges from Republicans in Congress or legal challenges in court. If Americans elect a Republican president and a Republican-controlled Congress in 2016, this could imperil the ACA. But Republicans would likely need a large enough majority in the Senate to overcome a potential Democratic filibuster if they tried to roll back major provisions of the law or repeal it altogether.

Survey Methods

Results for this Gallup poll are based on telephone interviews conducted July 1–3 and 5, 2015, on the Gallup U.S. Daily survey, with a random sample of 2,013 adults, aged 18 and older, living in all 50 U.S. states and the District of Columbia. For results based on the total sample of national adults, the margin of sampling error is ±3 percentage points at the 95% confidence level. All reported margins of sampling error include computed design effects for weighting.

July 13, 2015
NEARLY HALF OF SMARTPHONE USERS CAN'T IMAGINE LIFE WITHOUT IT

by Lydia Saad

Story Highlights

- *Young women are least able to imagine life with no smartphone*
- *iPhoners more bonded to phone than Androiders, 52% vs. 43%*
- *Four in 10 with smartphone would be anxious if they lost it for a day*

PRINCETON, N.J.—Smartphones emerged as a mass-market product less than a decade ago, yet already 46% of American smartphone users have what might be called smartphone amnesia, agreeing with the statement "I can't imagine my life without my smartphone." A bare majority of U.S. adults, 54%, disagree.

U.S. Smartphone Users' Bond With Their Phones

Do you agree or disagree with this statement: "I can't imagine my life without my smartphone"?

	Agree	Disagree
	%	%
Total	46	54
Men	41	59
Women	51	49
18 to 29 years	51	49
30 to 49 years	48	52
50 to 64 years	42	58
65 and older	40	60
iPhone user	52	48
Android user	43	57
Blackberry/Windows/Other user	27	73

Gallup Panel survey by Web and mail, April 17-May 18, 2015

GALLUP

Smartphone attachment is higher among women (51%) than men (41%), and among younger than older adults. And at each age level, women are more likely than men to say they can't imagine life without their phone. As a result, women under 30 are the most likely of all gender/age groups to feel this way (58%), while men 65 and older are the least likely (35%).

U.S. Smartphone Users' Bond With Their Phones, by Gender and Age

	% "Can't imagine my life without my smartphone"
WOMEN	
18 to 29 years	58
30 to 49 years	54
50 to 64 years	47
65 and older	44
MEN	
18 to 29 years	45
30 to 49 years	43
50 to 64 years	36
65 and older	35

Gallup Panel survey by Web and mail, April 17-May 18, 2015

GALLUP

Additionally, adults with an iPhone are a bit more likely than Android users to feel their life revolves around their device, 52% versus 43%. Although iPhone users report higher household income on average than Android users, and are slightly more likely to be female, these differences don't explain the higher attachment iPhone users feel toward their phones.

Four in 10 Would Experience Anxiety if Their Phone Were Lost for a Day

This kind of attachment may come with a downside, however. Because of their absorption with their device, many smartphone users say that being separated from it can be stressful.

As Gallup previously reported, four in five smartphone users keep their phone close throughout the day, nearly as many check it at least hourly, and three in five sleep near it. And more than one-third of U.S. workers report checking their work email frequently during nonworking hours. Thus, it is not surprising that 42% of all smartphone users say losing their device and not replacing it for a day would make them somewhat (32%) or very (10%) anxious. Another 30% say they would be "not very anxious," leaving just 29% who would not be anxious at all.

Again, young women are the most likely gender/age group to concede they would be anxious if they had to go without their smartphone for a day. Nearly six in 10 women under 30 say this would make them very or somewhat anxious, as do 51% of women 30 to 49 years of age. The rate is closer to 40% for men under 50 and is a third or less among senior men and women.

Seven in 10 Say Smartphone Has Made Their Life Better

Of course, smartphones are not just about compulsion, dependence and anxiety. One likely reason Americans consider their smartphones integral to their lives is that they perceive they are having a positive impact. Overall, 70% of smartphone users say their device has made their life better, including 24% who believe it has made their life a lot better. While a quarter of all smartphone users say their device has made their life neither better nor worse, just 6% say it has made their life worse to any degree.

How Anxious Smartphone Users Say They Would Be if They Lost Their Smartphone for a Day -- by Gender and Age

	% Very/Somewhat anxious	% Not too anxious	% Not anxious at all
WOMEN			
18 to 29 years	58	26	16
30 to 49 years	51	28	21
50 to 64 years	37	33	30
65 and older	33	32	36
MEN			
18 to 29 years	38	34	28
30 to 49 years	40	30	30
50 to 64 years	34	29	38
65 and older	28	30	41

Gallup Panel survey by Web and mail, April 17-May 18, 2015

GALLUP'

As would be expected, crediting their smartphone with a better life is nearly universal (86%) among those who can't imagine their life without it, and 41% of this group says it has made their lives a lot better.

Bottom Line

The smartphone is transformative for those who use it, not only by making their lives better, but by becoming something of a fifth limb. Most take it with them everywhere and sleep with it, and if it goes missing—even for a day—four in 10 would feel a significant level of stress. Although smartphones are quickly replaceable, their owners' potential anxiety about losing them reveals how dependent people have become on them over a relatively short period of time.

Three factors magnify people's bonds with their smartphones: being young, being female and being an iPhone user. And to some extent, these have a compounding effect, such that younger female iPhone users tend to show the highest levels of attachment to their devices, while older male Android users are generally the least attached.

More research needs to be done to understand these dynamics, particularly in terms of the differences by type of phone: Are some operating systems or brands more compelling than others, shaping how users respond to them, or are different types of people simply drawn to different phones? It is also unclear if young women truly have a more intense relationship with their phones or if they are just more willing to admit it.

One thing is certain: People's attachment to their phones is likely to grow in the coming years as smartphone penetration expands toward 100% from the current level near 70%, and as phones add even more features—such as universal Wi-Fi and improved voice control, wallet and online shopping capabilities—that strengthen users' dependence on them.

Survey Methods

Results of smartphone ownership are based on 21,204 national adults interviewed via the Web. Results of attitudes and behaviors of smartphone usage are based on 15,747 members of the Gallup Panel who have smartphones. The study was completed via the Web and mail between April 17, 2015, and May 18, 2015.

July 13, 2015
OLDER RESIDENTS OF DELAWARE HAVE LARGEST WELL-BEING EDGE

by Alyssa Brown and Justin McCarthy

Story Highlights

- *Older adults in Delaware have largest well-being edge relative to state overall*
- *Those aged 55+ also faring well in Oregon, Iowa and New Hampshire*
- *Older residents of Wyoming have smallest well-being edge*

WASHINGTON, D.C.—In all 50 states, residents aged 55 and older have higher well-being than the state's population as a whole. Older Delaware residents have the largest well-being advantage relative to the overall state population, followed closely by Oregon, Iowa and New Hampshire.

States Where Older Americans Have Largest Well-Being Advantage Relative to Statewide Adults

	*Well-Being Score Among Those Aged 55+	^Well-Being Score Among Overall Population	Difference
Delaware	64.2	61.1	+3.1
Oregon	64.5	61.8	+2.7
Iowa	64.9	62.2	+2.7
New Hampshire	64.9	62.2	+2.7
Michigan	63.3	60.7	+2.6
Connecticut	64.5	61.9	+2.6
Pennsylvania	63.7	61.2	+2.5
Idaho	64.4	61.9	+2.5
Kansas	63.6	61.2	+2.4
Florida	64.3	61.9	+2.4
Arkansas	63.1	60.7	+2.4

*Gallup-Healthways Well-Being Index, Jan. 2, 2014-March 31, 2015
^Gallup-Healthways Well-Being Index, Jan. 2-Dec. 30, 2014

GALLUP'

Other states where older adults have a statistically significant well-being edge relative to the overall state population include Michigan, Connecticut, Pennsylvania, Idaho, Kansas, Florida and Arkansas.

Well-being is measured using the Gallup-Healthways Well-Being Index. The Well-Being Index is calculated on a scale of 0 to 100, where 0 represents the lowest possible well-being and 100 represents the highest possible well-being. The Well-Being Index for each state includes five essential elements of well-being—purpose, social, financial, community and physical.

The state where older Americans' well-being advantage is smallest is Wyoming, followed by Alaska, Oklahoma, Nevada, South Dakota, Maine and Vermont. Older adults in California and Texas also have smaller advantages than older residents in other states.

In an absolute sense, Hawaii, Montana, South Dakota, Alaska and Iowa are the top five states for well-being for older Americans—states that also have high well-being rankings for the overall population. States with the lowest well-being for older Americans are also those where well-being as a whole tends to lag behind the rest of the country: West Virginia, Kentucky and Oklahoma. To read more about the well-being of older Americans nationally and by state, read the new Gallup-Healthways report, *State Well-Being Rankings for Older Americans.*

States Where Older Americans Have Smallest Well-Being Advantage Relative to Statewide Adults

	*Well-Being Score Among Those Aged 55+	^Well-Being Score Among Overall Population	Difference
Wyoming	64.0	63.9	+0.1
Alaska	64.9	64.7	+0.2
Oklahoma	61.7	61.0	+0.7
Nevada	62.3	61.5	+0.8
South Dakota	65.1	64.3	+0.8
Maine	63.3	62.4	+0.9
Vermont	63.6	62.7	+0.9
California	63.9	62.8	+1.1
Texas	63.9	62.8	+1.1

*Gallup-Healthways Well-Being Index, Jan. 2, 2014-March 31, 2015
^Gallup-Healthways Well-Being Index, Jan. 2-Dec. 30, 2014

GALLUP

Implications

Previous Gallup and Healthways research shows that older Americans tend to have higher overall well-being than younger Americans do. This analysis reveals that this pattern also holds true in all 50 states. Compared with younger adults, Americans aged 55 and older express more satisfaction with their standard of living, worry less about money, have better access to healthcare, are more likely to have health insurance, eat more fresh produce and are less likely to smoke.

The well-being of older Americans is a critical measure for national, state and local leaders to measure and improve upon. Well-Being Index scores predict important outcomes such as life expectancy, healthcare utilization, new onset disease burden, employment, absenteeism and change in obesity status.

"There are proven and effective interventions that combine social and physical activities to keep people healthy, active and productive as they age," says Joy Powell, Market President at Healthways. "Our research shows that older Americans who are thriving in well-being exercise far more, have less depression and have lower rates of obesity and chronic illness."

As the baby boomer population ages, state leaders should actively monitor and address their older population's well-being deficits. Taking steps to improve on this important metric could significantly benefit older individuals' quality of life and reduce healthcare costs.

Survey Methods

Results are based on telephone interviews conducted Jan. 2–Dec. 30, 2014, as part of the Gallup-Healthways Well-Being Index survey, with a random sample of 173,656 adults, aged 18 and older, living in all 50 U.S. states and the District of Columbia. For results based on the total sample of national adults, the margin of sampling error for the Well-Being Index score is ±0.1 percentage points at the 95% confidence level. The margin of sampling error for most states is about ±0.6 points, although this increases to about ±1.6 points for the smallest-population states such as North Dakota, Wyoming, Hawaii and Delaware.

For the sample of adults aged 55 and older, interviews were conducted Jan. 2, 2014–March 31, 2015. For results based on the

total sample of Americans aged 55 and older (114,388), the margin of sampling error is ±0.1 percentage points at the 95% confidence level. The margin of sampling error for most states is about ±1.5 points, although this increases to about ±2.1 points for the smallest-population states such as North Dakota, Wyoming, Hawaii and Delaware.

All reported margins of sampling error include computed design effects for weighting.

July 14, 2015
AS IN 1999, MOST DO NOT SEE TRUMP AS SERIOUS CANDIDATE

by Andrew Dugan

Story Highlights

- *25% in U.S. consider him a "serious" presidential candidate*
- *Three in 10 view Trump favorably, his lowest in Gallup's trend*
- *Trump's image among Republicans better today than in 1999*

WASHINGTON, D.C.—One in four Americans consider Donald Trump a "serious candidate" for president. Americans view Trump's present bid for the Republican nomination no more seriously now than when the real estate mogul and media personality competed for the Reform Party's nomination in 1999.

Views on Seriousness of Donald Trump's Presidential Campaign

Regardless of whether or not you would vote for him, do you view Donald Trump as a serious candidate for president?

	Yes, serious candidate	No, not serious candidate	Don't know/ Refused
	%	%	%
Jul 8-12, 2015	25	74	1
Oct 8-10, 1999^	23	74	3

^ Question wording: Regardless of whether or not you would vote for the following people, please say whether you would view each as a serious candidate if he or she decided to run for president. How about ... ?

GALLUP

These results come from a Gallup poll conducted July 8–12, roughly a month after Trump joined the 2016 presidential race and instantly made waves in the Republican field. If Trump's fame and colorful personality were not enough to ensure his candidacy attracted media attention, his announcement speech provided the extra incentive. In his nearly hour-long speech, Trump delivered a blistering critique of the current state of affairs in the U.S., asserting, "The American dream is dead." Trump offered his business expertise, his unwavering negotiating style and, less conventionally, his wealth as the ideal antidote to America's ills. But Trump's announcement speech produced considerable controversy; his claim that many immigrants arriving in the U.S. from Mexico are drug peddlers or rapists offended many Americans, and caused several companies to sever business ties with Trump and/or his companies.

Gallup first asked about a Trump presidential bid in 1999. Trump ultimately withdrew from the 2000 presidential race, and the Reform Party nominated Pat Buchanan for president.

Trump has become a fervent critic of President Barack Obama, and has routinely voiced his doubts regarding the authenticity of

Obama's birth certificate, an accusation that carried more weight with Republicans than other political identities. Trump flirted with running for president in 2012 as a Republican, registering a respectable level of support among Republicans in an early poll before eventually declining a bid.

While a consistent percentage of Americans take Trump's presidential candidacy seriously, views by party groups have changed over time. Today, with Trump competing for the GOP nomination rather than a third-party bid, 41% of Republicans say they consider Trump a serious candidate, compared with 20% in 1999. Democrats, meanwhile, take Trump even less seriously as a candidate today (12%) than they did in 1999 (20%), while independents' views haven't changed.

Regardless of whether or not you would vote for him, do you view Donald Trump as a serious candidate for president?

% Yes

	Republicans	Independents	Democrats
	%	%	%
Jul 8-12, 2015	41	25	12
Oct 8-10, 1999	20	27	20

GALLUP

About One in Three Americans View Trump Favorably

While Trump is attracting a lot of attention, the percentage of Americans with a favorable view of him is at a nominal low. Thirty-one percent of Americans see Trump favorably, compared with 43% in March 2011, when he was discussed as a potential candidate for president. Trump's previous low (33%) was in October 1999, when he was actively seeking a presidential nomination.

Favorable Ratings of Donald Trump

Next, we'd like to get your overall opinion of some people in the news. As I read each name, please say if you have a favorable or unfavorable opinion of that person -- or if you have never heard of them. How about Donald Trump?

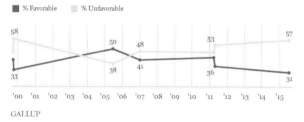

In general, Trump typically has been seen more unfavorably than favorably since Gallup first asked about him in 1999, with the sole exception occurring in 2005, when 50% of the country viewed him favorably and 38% viewed him unfavorably. At the time, Trump starred in the hit show *The Apprentice* and was not actively involved in the political arena.

Trump fares better with Republicans overall, with a 49% favorable rating and 38% unfavorable score. But his high-profile candidacy appears not to have won him any additional admiration among Republicans—his favorable rating among this group is about where it was in 2005. Trump's relatively high unfavorable rating among the GOP gives him a "net favorable" rating among Republicans of +11, well below several other candidates for the nomination. Among Democrats, Trump's favorable rating has cratered, from a high of 49% in 2005 to today's low of 17%.

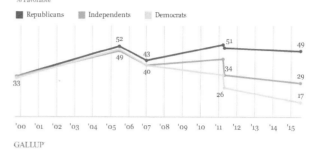

Favorable Ratings of Donald Trump, by Party Identification

Bottom Line

Donald Trump's candidacy has already shaped the presidential race in important ways, such as compelling other Republican candidates to address the issue of illegal immigration more forcefully. Yet even as Trump appears to be a prominent voice in the Republican race, nearly three-quarters of Americans do not take his candidacy for president seriously. The public sees his candidacy as no more credible now than in 1999, despite his decision to run for a major-party nomination this time around and his promise to spend his ample personal wealth in pursuit of his political ambitions.

Survey Methods

Results for this Gallup poll are based on telephone interviews conducted July 8–12, 2015, with a random sample of 1,009 adults, aged 18 and older, living in all 50 U.S. states and the District of Columbia. For results based on the total sample of national adults, the margin of sampling error is ±4 percentage points at the 95% confidence level. All reported margins of sampling error include computed design effects for weighting.

July 15, 2015
TRUMP STRONGER ON ECONOMY THAN FOREIGN AFFAIRS, IMMIGRATION

by Lydia Saad

Story Highlights

- *Nearly four in 10 say Trump would do a good job handling the economy*
- *Confidence in Trump dwindles to 17% on foreign affairs*
- *More doubt him on relations with Mexico than on immigration*

PRINCETON, N.J.—Americans perceive Donald Trump as being able to do a reasonable job of handling the economy as president: 36% say he would do a good job if elected, and 27% say he would do a fair job. However, it is downhill from there for the newly minted Republican presidential candidate. Fewer Americans say Trump would perform well on two other core leadership tasks, with 29% saying he would do a good job on immigration and 17% on foreign affairs.

Americans' Perceptions of Donald Trump's Handling of Issues

Now, thinking about Donald Trump. If he were elected president in 2016, do you think Donald Trump would do a good job, a fair job or a bad job handling each of the following issues?

	Good job	Fair job	Bad job	No opinion
	%	%	%	%
The economy	36	27	34	3
Immigration	29	18	48	4
Relations with China	19	27	47	7
Foreign affairs	17	27	51	6
Relations with Russia	17	25	51	7
Relations with Mexico	17	22	57	4

July 8-12, 2015

GALLUP

An official candidate for only a month, Trump has already waded chin deep into some specific foreign policy areas. He has taken an aggressive stance toward Mexico on immigration, China on trade and President Barack Obama for being too soft on Russia. While Trump's "good job" ratings on relations with each of these nations are about the same, between 17% and 19%, the percentage saying he would do a "bad job" varies from 47% for relations with China—and 51% for relations with Russia—to 57% for relations with Mexico.

Trump's ratings on all six issues tested in the poll are much better among rank-and-file Republicans than among independents or Democrats, as would be expected given that Trump is running as a Republican for the GOP nomination. However, the only issue that a majority of Republicans think Trump would do a good job of handling is the economy.

Perceptions of Donald Trump's Handling of Issues, by Party ID

% Saying he would do a "good job" of handling each

	Republicans	Independents	Democrats
	%	%	%
Economy	56	35	16
Immigration	44	29	11
Relations with China	29	18	6
Relations with Mexico	27	17	5
Relations with Russia	27	16	5
Foreign affairs	23	17	6

July 8-12, 2015

GALLUP

The new Gallup poll, conducted July 8–12, reveals some minor differences in Trump's specific foreign policy ratings when those saying he would do a fair job are factored in. Most notably, while 39% anticipate he would do a good or fair job of handling relations with Mexico, that belief rises to 46% saying the same about China.

Trump Trails Clinton on Core Issue Ratings

The economy, immigration and foreign policy have been challenges for every recent president. It is as much a function of the times as the person occupying the Oval Office. Still, Trump elicits less confidence on each of these issues than the Democratic front-runner, Hillary Clinton—the only other presidential candidate Gallup has evaluated with this question to date. In May, 42% of Americans said Clinton would do a good job on the economy, slightly exceeding Trump's 36%. Clinton had a similar edge over Trump on handling immigration, 35% to 29%, respectively. The former secretary of state generated significantly more confidence on foreign affairs, with 42% saying she would do a good job on that dimension, compared with Trump's 17%.

In addition to Clinton's stronger foreign policy resume helping to explain these gaps, she has a significantly higher favorable rating from Americans: 50% viewed Clinton favorably in May, compared with 31% viewing Trump favorably in the new poll.

Bottom Line

Thirty-one percent of Americans view Trump favorably, including just shy of half of Republicans (49%), and only a quarter perceive him as a serious candidate for president. That's a shaky base from which to campaign, much less defend controversial positions. However, he appears to have some credibility with Americans when talking about the economy, perhaps reflecting his background as a longtime businessman who has built a fortune in real estate and had a successful reality TV show featuring his boardroom skills. Trump's comments on immigration were highly controversial, perhaps contributing to fewer than three in 10 Americans saying he would do a good job on that issue. But it appears he has even less credibility when it comes to handling relations with Mexico and with other countries important to U.S. foreign policy.

Survey Methods

Results for this Gallup poll are based on telephone interviews conducted July 8–12, 2015, with a random sample of 1,009 adults, aged 18 and older, living in all 50 U.S. states and the District of Columbia. For results based on the total sample of national adults, the margin of sampling error is ±4 percentage points at the 95% confidence level.

For results based on the sample of 507 national adults in Form A, the margin of sampling error is ±6 percentage points. All reported margins of sampling error include computed design effects for weighting.

July 16, 2015
RACISM EDGES UP AGAIN AS MOST IMPORTANT U.S. PROBLEM

by Rebecca Riffkin

Story Highlights

- *Nine percent say racism most important U.S. problem*
- *Up from 3% in June, but similar to increases in recent months*
- *Economy, government remain most frequently mentioned problems*

WASHINGTON, D.C.—The percentage of Americans naming race relations or racism as the most important problem facing the country increased to 9% this month, up from 3% in June. Mentions of race relations as a top problem have risen and fallen multiple times over the past seven months as racially charged events have dominated and then faded from the news cycle.

Americans' mentions of racism and race relations as the most important problem facing the country spiked in December 2014 to

13% amid protests over high-profile incidents of police brutality toward blacks in Staten Island, New York, Ferguson, Missouri, and other places across the U.S. This was the highest figure since May 1992, when 15% of Americans said racism was the top problem after the verdict in the Rodney King case sparked riots in many parts of the U.S.

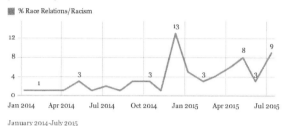

Recent Trend for "Race Relations/Racism" as "Most Important" Problem in U.S.

What do you think is the most important problem facing this country today?
[OPEN-ENDED]

■ % Race Relations/Racism

January 2014-July 2015

GALLUP

For more than a decade prior to December 2014, no more than 5% of Americans had named racism or race relations as the top problem facing the U.S., with the figure often measuring 0%. Still, mentions of racism and race relations in recent months are far below the all-time high of 52% during the civil rights era and race riots in the 1960s.

Following the sharp increase in mentions of race relations in December, the percentage naming this issue fell to 3% in February. Similarly, in May 2015, mentions increased to 8% amid the riots in Baltimore after the death of Freddie Gray, a black man who died in police custody, but dipped back down to 3% in June.

The most recent results are from a Gallup poll conducted July 8–12, a few weeks after nine people were shot at a historic black church in Charleston, South Carolina, which sparked a national debate about the role of the Confederate flag. During the same week as Gallup's recent polling, South Carolina's government voted to remove the flag from its state Capitol grounds.

Economy, Government Remain Most Mentioned Problems

Despite the uptick in mentions of race relations in July, the economy in general and dissatisfaction with the government remain the most frequently mentioned problems, with 13% of Americans naming each.

Mentions of immigration and the federal budget deficit also rank high. Six percent of Americans mentioned unemployment or jobs, the lowest percentage to mention this issue since January 2015. At points over the last few years, mentions of unemployment and jobs as the most important problem have been as high as 39%.

As a whole, however, Americans are divided on the most important problem facing the country. No single issue is named by more than 13% of Americans, with most issues named by less than 5%. This lack of a national focus on a dominant problem may be why many long-term issues, such as the environment and education, rank among the top problems.

Bottom Line

As many Americans debated the role of the Confederate flag in early July, an increased percentage cited racism and race relations as the top problems facing the country. On average, mentions of these

issues have been higher in the past year than in at least a decade. However, the recent trend has been marked by short-lived spikes in response to a major racial event, followed by a decline after the news receded. The major difference, then, appears to be the frequent number of race-related incidents that have made news since last summer. As a whole, though, Americans are divided on what problem is most important in the U.S.

Most Important Problems Facing the U.S.

What do you think is the most important problem facing this country today? (open-ended)

Problem	June 2-7, 2015	July 8-12, 2015
	%	%
Economy in general	13	13
Dissatisfaction with government/Congress	14	13
Race relations/Racism	3	9
Immigration/Illegal aliens	6	7
Unemployment/Jobs	9	6
Ethics/moral/religious/family decline; Dishonesty	5	6
Federal budget deficit/Federal debt	3	5
Poverty/Hunger/Homelessness	5	4
Crime/Violence	3	4
Education	5	4
Healthcare	6	4
Gap between rich and poor	4	3
Judicial system/Courts/Laws	1	3
Terrorism	5	3
Lack of respect for each other	2	3
Environment/Pollution	3	3
Foreign policy/Foreign aid/Focus overseas	3	3

Responses listed by at least 3% of Americans are shown

GALLUP

Survey Methods

Results for this Gallup poll are based on telephone interviews conducted July 8–12, 2015, with a random sample of 1,009 adults, aged 18 and older, living in all 50 U.S. states and the District of Columbia. For results based on the total sample of national adults, the margin of sampling error is ±4 percentage points at the 95% confidence level. All reported margins of sampling error include computed design effects for weighting.

July 16, 2015
REPUBLICANS' APPROVAL OF SUPREME COURT SINKS TO 18%

by Jeffrey M. Jones

Story Highlights

- *Republican approval declines to record-low 18%*
- *Democratic approval climbs to 76%*
- *Largest party gap in views of court to date*

PRINCETON, N.J.—After a historic Supreme Court session that included rulings on same-sex marriage and the Affordable Care Act (ACA), Democrats' approval of the high court has surged to 76% and Republicans' approval has plummeted to a record-low 18%. Americans overall are divided, with 49% approving and 46% disapproving.

The new July 8–12 Gallup poll came after the Supreme Court issued rulings in late June that legalized same-sex marriage nationwide and upheld federal subsidies for health insurance purchased through government exchanges. Those decisions were hailed by President Barack Obama and other Democratic leaders but criticized by Republican leaders. The shift in opinions of the Supreme Court by political party indicates that many Americans are aware of the decisions, as well as the thrust of those decisions politically, and have adjusted their views accordingly.

Supreme Court Job Approval

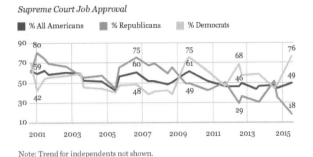

Note: Trend for independents not shown.

GALLUP

Specifically, Republicans' approval of the Supreme Court is down 17 percentage points from September 2014 and down a total of 33 points since last summer. Democrats' approval rose from 47% in September to 76% now—a 29-point gain. Independents' views were largely unchanged, as 46% approved in September 2014 and 49% currently do.

Supreme Court approval among all Americans is up five points since last fall, from 44% to 49%. The current job approval rating is just below the 52% average, which dates back to 2000.

As a result of the partisan changes in opinions of the Supreme Court, Americans' views of it are polarized along party lines more than ever has been the case in Gallup's 15-year trend. The 18% approval among Republicans is the lowest to date, and the 76% approval among Democrats is the highest, albeit by a single percentage point. In 2009, after Obama took office and nominated Justice Sonia Sotomayor to the Supreme Court, 75% of Democrats approved.

The previous high point in political party polarization came in 2012, after the first major Supreme Court ruling on the 2010 healthcare law upheld Congress's ability to fine Americans for not having health insurance. After that decision, 68% of Democrats and 29% of Republicans approved, a 39-point party gap compared with the current 58-point gap.

Partisans' Views of Supreme Court Responsive to Rulings

Supreme Court job approval among all Americans has varied between 42% and 62% in Gallup's 15-year trend. But it has varied even more among Republicans (between 18% and 80%) and Democrats (38% and 76%) during this time. That is because partisans, as is the case in the current poll, have frequently re-evaluated their views of the Supreme Court after it issued rulings that touched on topics that greatly divide Republicans and Democrats.

For example, after the Supreme Court ruled in favor of George W. Bush in the dispute with Al Gore over recounts in Florida presidential voting back in 2000, Republican approval increased 20 points while Democratic approval dropped by 28 points.

As previously noted, the initial Supreme Court ruling on the 2010 healthcare law—issued in 2012—led to a much more positive evaluation of the high court from Democrats along with diminished approval among Republicans.

At this time a year ago, a slim majority of Republicans, 51%, approved of the job the Supreme Court was doing, up from 30% in September 2013. That increase may have reflected support for the court's decision in the "Hobby Lobby" case. The Supreme Court ruled that private companies could, because of religious objections, opt out of the ACA requirement that all health plans must cover contraceptive services.

Over the last 15 years, partisans' views have also responded to presidential appointments to the court. As noted, Democrats' views of the high court became more positive after Obama nominated Sotomayor to the court in 2009. And Republican approval of the Supreme Court improved from 44% in June 2005 to 65% in September 2005 after President Bush nominated John Roberts to the Supreme Court. Republicans' approval rose further to 75% by September 2006 after Justice Samuel Alito, a second Bush appointee, joined the court.

Implications

Americans—specifically Democrats and Republicans—have often changed their opinions of the Supreme Court based on how it has ruled on high-profile decisions. That indicates that many Americans are aware of what the Supreme Court is doing and the public's evaluations have some substance behind them.

Right now, after two major rulings that were consistent with Democrats' policy preferences, Republicans' and Democrats' views of the Supreme Court are more disparate than at any time in the past 15 years. A key question is how long those highly polarized views might persist. Clearly they could shift if the Supreme Court issues another major ruling on a politically divisive issue that pleases Republicans, which in the next term could be invalidating the use of race as a factor in college admissions. More generally, though, the evidence from the trends suggests the major partisan shifts do not persist long, usually diminishing to some degree in the subsequent poll, and possibly showing more substantial change if there is an intervening major Supreme Court event that favors one group of partisans over another.

Survey Methods

Results for this Gallup poll are based on telephone interviews conducted July 8–12, 2015, with a random sample of 1,009 adults, aged 18 and older, living in all 50 U.S. states and the District of Columbia. For results based on the total sample of national adults, the margin of sampling error is ±4 percentage points at the 95% confidence level. All reported margins of sampling error include computed design effects for weighting.

July 17, 2015
U.S. SUPPORT FOR GAY MARRIAGE STABLE AFTER HIGH COURT RULING

by Justin McCarthy

Story Highlights

- *Public support about the same as before Supreme Court ruling*
- *Republicans, seniors remain most opposed to gay marriage*

- *Democrats, adults younger than 30 show greatest support*

WASHINGTON, D.C.—Americans' views on gay marriage are stable following the U.S. Supreme Court's recent ruling that made same-sex marriage a right nationwide. The nearly six in 10 Americans (58%) who say gay marriages should be valid is similar to Gallup's findings in May.

These data are from a July 8–12 Gallup poll, conducted about two weeks after the Supreme Court's 5–4 decision in *Obergefell v. Hodges* legalized gay marriage nationwide. The court's ruling on the practice, which was legal in the majority of states, so far has not affected the way Americans feel about the issue.

Do you think marriages between same-sex couples should or should not be recognized by the law as valid, with the same rights as traditional marriages?

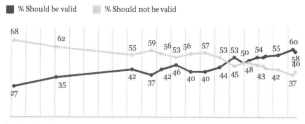

Note: Trend shown for polls in which same-sex marriage question followed questions on gay/lesbian rights and relations
1996-2005 wording: "Do you think marriages between homosexuals ..."

GALLUP'

However, the decision was consistent with American public's opinion on the issue. Americans' support for gay marriage has increased over time, from 27% in 1996, the first time Gallup asked about it, to the current 58%. A consistent majority has favored it since 2011, including a high of 60% in May of this year. The two-percentage-point difference between the May and July estimates is not statistically meaningful.

Politically, Democrats (74%) are most likely to support same-sex marriage, followed by independents (62%). Republicans (30%) remain least likely to support it, with a majority (67%) still opposed.

Support for Same-Sex Marriage, by Group

Do you think marriages between same-sex couples should or should not be recognized by the law as valid, with the same rights as traditional marriages?

	% Should be valid	% Should not be valid
PARTY ID		
Democrats	74	26
Independents	62	35
Republicans	30	67
AGE		
18-29	76	23
30-49	62	37
50-64	52	45
65+	44	52

July 8-12, 2015

GALLUP'

American adults younger than 30 remain the most supportive of gay marriage among age groups. Majorities of those aged 30 to

49 (62%) and 50 to 64 (52%) also say same-sex marriages should be valid.

Bottom Line

Though the Supreme Court's decision has not immediately influenced Americans' overall opinion on the issue of same-sex marriage, this is not to suggest it will not affect opinion in the long run.

Even after a 1967 Supreme Court decision that legalized interracial marriages, Gallup's polling in 1968 found that only one in five Americans (20%) approved of such marriages. It took three more decades to reach a majority of support.

The path to legality of interracial marriage differed from same-sex marriage, though, in that the Supreme Court led public opinion by legalizing something that Americans largely disapproved of at the time. Approval of same-sex marriage, however, has ascended significantly faster, and has enjoyed majority support for a few years before the court's decision. Still, a long view of the trend on gay marriage illustrates that support for it was steady and incremental, and that the movement's big victories in statewide ballot initiatives and legislature-enacted laws had limited effect on public opinion at large.

Survey Methods

Results for this Gallup poll are based on telephone interviews conducted July 8–12, 2015, with a random sample of 1,009 adults, aged 18 and older, living in all 50 U.S. states and the District of Columbia. For results based on the total sample of national adults, the margin of sampling error is ±4 percentage points at the 95% confidence level. All reported margins of sampling error include computed design effects for weighting.

July 17, 2015
DEMOCRATS VIEW U.S. JUSTICES KENNEDY, ROBERTS FAVORABLY

by Jeffrey M. Jones

Story Highlights

- *Republicans have net-negative opinions of Roberts, Kennedy*
- *Republicans have net-positive opinions of Scalia*
- *Ratings of Scalia, Roberts more negative than in past*

PRINCETON, N.J.—More Democrats have a favorable than an unfavorable view of Republican-appointed U.S. Supreme Court Justices Anthony Kennedy and John Roberts, while Republicans' opinions of the justices are much more negative than positive. Democrats' views of another GOP-appointed justice, Antonin Scalia, are more unfavorable than favorable, while Republicans rate him favorably.

Kennedy, Roberts and Scalia are arguably the three most prominent members of the Supreme Court. Chief Justice Roberts and Kennedy often find themselves as the swing votes in cases divided along ideological lines. For example, Roberts sided with the liberal justices to uphold the Affordable Care Act (ACA) in 2012, while Kennedy has been the deciding vote on recent gay rights cases, including the most recent one that legalized same-sex marriage. Scalia is the most vocal member of the court's conservative wing—known for his biting and colorful dissenting opinions.

It appears their high-profile deciding votes on same-sex marriage and the Affordable Care Act have endeared Kennedy and Roberts to Democrats and turned Republicans off to them, even though all were appointed by a Republican president and typically vote more with the court's conservative wing than its liberal wing.

Scalia currently produces a less strong partisan reaction, although Republicans view him a bit more favorably than unfavorably, while the reverse is true for Democrats.

Favorable Ratings of Supreme Court Justices John Roberts, Anthony Kennedy and Antonin Scalia

	All Americans	Democrats	Republicans	Independents
	%	%	%	%
ROBERTS				
Favorable	29	37	23	28
Unfavorable	27	15	43	25
No opinion	44	47	34	46
Net favorable	+2	+22	-20	+3
KENNEDY				
Favorable	29	36	18	30
Unfavorable	21	10	39	18
No opinion	49	53	43	52
Net favorable	+8	+26	-21	+12
SCALIA				
Favorable	29	22	35	28
Unfavorable	27	29	29	25
No opinion	44	49	36	47
Net favorable	+2	-7	+6	+3

July 8-12, 2015

GALLUP

Justices Not Well-Known to Americans

Overall, Americans are not highly familiar with these three justices, as only half or slightly more than half have an opinion of any of them. And none are viewed overly positively by those who do have opinions, with Kennedy's +8 net favorable rating (based on 29% having a favorable and 21% an unfavorable view of him) the best of the three justices included in the July 8–12 Gallup poll.

The poll marks the first time Gallup has measured opinion on Kennedy, but it has asked about Roberts and Scalia previously. Opinions of both justices are less positive now than in the past.

Gallup first asked about Roberts after President George W. Bush nominated him to the Supreme Court in 2005. At that time, he was well liked, with favorable ratings near 50%. Positive ratings of Roberts fell to 39% the next time Gallup asked about him in July 2012—right after he cast the deciding vote in the ACA case. Since then, Americans have largely been divided in their views of him, but are also less likely to have an opinion of him.

Americans are more likely to have an opinion of Scalia now than in Gallup's prior update in 2005. But his image has gone from a mainly positive one to a divided one, mostly because of an increase in negative opinions of him, from 13% in 2005 to 27% today. His favorable rating is similar to what it was a decade ago.

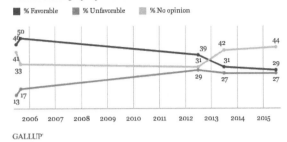

Favorable Ratings of Supreme Court Justice John Roberts

GALLUP

Republicans Fuel Slide in Images of Roberts, Scalia

At the time Roberts was nominated, his net favorable rating among Republicans was +69 (70% favorable, 1% unfavorable). After the 2012 ACA vote, more Republicans viewed him unfavorably (44%) than favorably (27%), while Democrats shifted to a net-positive evaluation of him (54% favorable, 19% unfavorable) from a neutral one.

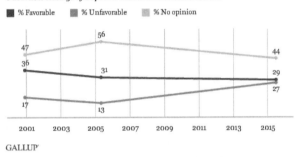

Favorable Ratings of Supreme Court Justice Antonin Scalia

GALLUP

Those views eased in a 2013 update, but after the latest Supreme Court term, which included another Roberts vote to uphold the ACA, Democrats have again grown significantly more positive and Republicans more negative toward him.

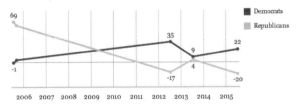

Net Favorable Ratings of Supreme Court Chief Justice John Roberts, by Political Party
Net favorable ratings are the percentage with a favorable opinion minus the percentage with an unfavorable opinion

Note: Trend for independents is not shown to better show Republican and Democratic trends. Independent net favorables were +36 in July 2005, +30 in September 2005, +10 in July 2012, +2 in July 2013 and +3 in July 2015.

GALLUP

Scalia's image has suffered among Republicans, Democrats and independents since 2005, but has suffered the most among Republicans. In 2005, 43% of Republicans had a favorable opinion of him and 7% an unfavorable opinion, for a net favorable rating of +36. Independents (31% favorable, 13% unfavorable) and Democrats (21% favorable, 17% unfavorable) viewed him more positively than negatively then. Democrats' views of Scalia are now more negative than positive, while independents' views are barely more positive than negative.

Even though Scalia has been a consistent conservative vote, Republicans' current widespread dissatisfaction with the high court more generally may be influencing how they feel about him.

Implications

Democrats and Republicans often revise their views of the Supreme Court, depending on how its rulings in major cases fit with their policy preferences. And this year saw dramatic shifts in opinions of the court by political party.

That same phenomenon appears to affect how Americans view individual members of the Supreme Court, even though the justices are generally not well known to Americans. The high court is officially a nonpartisan institution, but the justices' ideological leanings are evident in their voting patterns, and presidents seek to influence the ideological direction of the court through their appointments. Although Kennedy and Roberts are Republican appointees and vote more often with the conservative justices than the liberal ones, their votes in high-profile cases such as those involving same-sex marriage and the Affordable Care Act have seemingly done more to influence how Republicans and Democrats feel about them.

Net Favorable Ratings of Supreme Court Justice Antonin Scalia, by Political Party
Net favorable ratings are the percentage with a favorable opinion minus the percentage with an unfavorable opinion

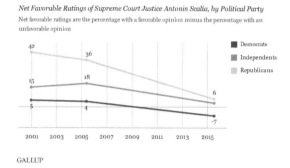

GALLUP

Republicans still hold a marginally positive view of Scalia but are less favorable toward him than in the past. They may give him less credit for voting in a way consistent with Republican policy preferences than they penalize him for being a member of an institution they view so negatively at the moment.

Survey Methods

Results for this Gallup poll are based on telephone interviews conducted July 8–12, 2015, with a random sample of 1,009 adults, aged 18 and older, living in all 50 U.S. states and the District of Columbia. For results based on the total sample of national adults, the margin of sampling error is ±4 percentage points at the 95% confidence level.

All reported margins of sampling error include computed design effects for weighting.

July 20, 2015
OPTIMISM ABOUT U.S. JOB MARKET DIPS IN JULY

by Justin McCarthy

Story Highlights

* *Thirty-eight percent say it's a "good time" to find a quality job*
* *Job market optimism is down from 41% last month*

* *Optimism still higher than at any point between 2008 and 2014*

WASHINGTON, D.C.—Thirty-eight percent of Americans say it is a "good time" to find a quality job, down three percentage points since June and the lowest since December 2014. Still, this is higher than any figure Gallup tracked between 2008 and 2014.

In the nearly 14 years that Gallup has asked this question each month, the percentage of Americans saying it is a "good time" to find a quality job has never reached a majority. The current rating is about where it was when Gallup first polled on the question in August 2001.

The figure peaked at 48% in January 2007, after which it steadily dropped and bottomed out at 8% in November 2009. Optimism about the job market did not change much in the following years, once again hitting the low of 8% in November 2011. Since then, however, it has gradually improved, reaching a recent peak of 45% in January of this year.

Percentage in U.S. Saying Now Is a Good Time to Find a Quality Job
Thinking about the job situation in America today, would you say that it is now a good time or a bad time to find a quality job?

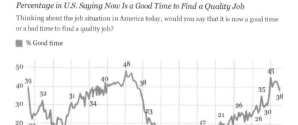

GALLUP

As Gallup has found in the past, Americans' perceptions of the job market are somewhat contingent on their political identification and whether that aligns with the party of the president. Those who identify with or lean toward the Democratic Party (46%) are much more upbeat in their ratings of the current job market than those who identify with or lean toward the Republican Party (29%).

Views of Time to Find a Quality Job, by Subgroup
Thinking about the job situation in America today, would you say that it is now a good time or a bad time to find a quality job?

	% Good time	% Bad time
National adults	38	57
Republicans/Leaners	29	65
Democrats/Leaners	46	49
Men	43	53
Women	34	60
White	37	58
Nonwhite	43	53
18 to 29	51	47
30 to 49	40	56
50 to 64	32	64
65+	29	62
Employed	42	54
Not employed	34	61

July 8-12, 2015

GALLUP

Men are more upbeat than women about the job market, and employed adults more so than those who are not employed. And while adults younger than 30 have a mostly positive view of the job market, this weakens by age group, with those aged 65 and older being the least positive.

Bottom Line

Despite perceptions of a healthier flow of jobs from their own employers and a dropping unemployment rate, these signs might not be enough for Americans to maintain a positive outlook on the U.S. job market. Still, the current outlook is more positive than it has been for most of the past several years. But the majority of Americans have not said it was a good time to find a quality job since Gallup began tracking it in 2001. That may partly reflect a poor job market during much of this time, but it may also reflect Americans' general tendency not to be overly positive about the job market.

Survey Methods

Results for this Gallup poll are based on telephone interviews conducted July 8–12, 2015, on the Gallup U.S. Daily survey, with a random sample of 1,009 adults, aged 18 and older, living in all 50 U.S. states and the District of Columbia. For results based on the total sample of national adults, the margin of sampling error is ±4 percentage points at the 95% confidence level. All reported margins of sampling error include computed design effects for weighting.

July 20, 2015

DEMOCRATIC PARTY RECLAIMS EDGE IN FAVORABLE RATINGS

by Andrew Dugan

Story Highlights

- *Democratic Party seen more favorably than GOP, 42% to 35%*
- *Dems' rating has risen slightly from November 2014 low of 36%*

WASHINGTON, D.C.—As the 2016 presidential race increasingly dominates political news, the favorable ratings for both major parties are still close to their historical lows. Slightly more than four in 10 Americans (42%) view the Democratic Party favorably, while the Republican Party has a favorable rating of 35%. The rating for Democrats is up slightly from March's 39%, while the Republican rating fell two percentage points. The net result is Americans now view the Democratic Party more favorably than the GOP.

These results come from a July 8–12 poll. After their substantial losses in the 2014 midterm elections, Democrats have seen a slight improvement in their political standing. Democrats recently regained the edge in party affiliation they lost last fall, while the approval rating of Democratic President Barack Obama has been slightly higher over the course of this year compared with last.

The Democrats' current favorable rating is more in line with how the American public has seen the party over the course of the Obama presidency. The Democratic Party enjoyed a favorable rating higher than 50% in 2009, but it then fell to the low 40s in 2010. It languished near that level over the next several years, aside from a brief spike in November 2012 to 51% after Obama's re-election.

Meanwhile, Republicans have seen their slight boost in popularity last fall reverse itself. But recent political history shows that Republicans' favorable rating can be fluid. During the government shutdown of October 2013, Republicans saw their favorable rating plunge to 28%. For a brief time, there was chatter among some political pundits that the GOP might fail to pick up seats in Congress in 2014, which would have been a rarity for the opposition party in a midterm election.

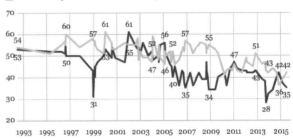

Americans' Opinions of the Republican and Democratic Parties

■ % Favorable opinion of the Republican Party
▨ % Favorable opinion of the Democratic Party

GALLUP

But beginning in late 2013, Republicans saw their favorable rating steadily rise as the Obama presidency was beset with problems. These included the rise of the Islamic State group in Iraq and Syria, and the subsequent execution of American hostages by that terrorist organization, the appearance of Ebola in the U.S., and evidence that the Veterans Administration falsified reports to conceal the waiting times veterans endured to receive medical attention. By November 2014, the American public saw the Republican Party more favorably than the Democratic Party—a rare occurrence in Gallup's trend dating to 1992. The parties' current positioning is a reversal of what it was in November.

Bottom Line

The Democratic Party has regained its edge over the Republican Party in terms of favorability, another sign that it is recovering from its poor 2014 showing. But both parties remain unpopular relative to their historical performance, which suggests neither has the wind at its back going into the 2016 presidential contest.

Survey Methods

Results for this Gallup poll are based on telephone interviews conducted July 8–12, 2015, with a random sample of 1,009 adults, aged 18 and older, living in all 50 U.S. states and the District of Columbia. For results based on the total sample of national adults, the margin of sampling error is ±4 percentage points at the 95% confidence level. All reported margins of sampling error include computed design effects for weighting.

July 21, 2015

OBAMA'S APPROVAL RATING LEVELED OFF AT 46.1% IN 26TH QUARTER

by Jeffrey M. Jones

Story Highlights

- *Obama job approval levels off after showing improvement*
- *Ratings highly stable around 46% during 26th quarter*

- *Nearly matches his term-to-date approval of 47%*

PRINCETON, N.J.—President Barack Obama's job approval rating averaged 46.1% during his 26th quarter in office, which ran from April 20 through July 19. This is essentially unchanged from his 25th quarter average, and shows his approval ratings have leveled off after increasing in each of the prior two quarters.

President Barack Obama's Quarterly Job Approval Averages

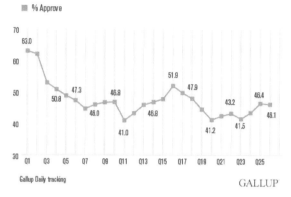

Gallup Daily tracking

GALLUP

Obama's 26th quarter in office was marked by a high degree of stability in views of the president, as nine of Obama's 13 weekly approval averages during the quarter were 46% or 47%. The only exceptions were a single 48% weekly average and three 45% averages.

After enjoying high job approval—typical for all presidents early in their first year in office—Obama's average approval ratings fell below 50% during his fifth quarter. Since then, he has averaged better than 50% in only one quarter, but it was arguably the most important one: the 16th quarter, which coincided with his re-election in the fall of 2012.

His low points as president were the three quarters in which he averaged 41% job approval, including last year just prior to the 2014 midterm elections, which was a factor in the Democratic Party's losses. But after that point, Obama's approval rating climbed for two straight quarters before leveling off in the most recent quarter.

Obama's 26th Quarter Average Is Midrange

Obama is the sixth president since World War II to have served 26 quarters in office. His 46.1% average during this quarter ranks in the middle of the distribution of presidents' 26th quarter averages. Obama's average is similar to Ronald Reagan's 49.7% at the same time in his presidency. Dwight Eisenhower and Bill Clinton had significantly higher job approval ratings during their 26th quarters, while George W. Bush and Harry Truman had significantly lower approval ratings. Since Truman took office shortly after Franklin Roosevelt began his fourth term as president, his 26th quarter did not coincide with the April through July dates of other presidents' 26th quarters.

By the time presidents have been in office 6.5 years, Americans' opinions of them are well established. Historically, presidents' approval ratings have been fairly steady between their 26th and 27th quarters in office. Bush, Clinton and Eisenhower saw slight increases of between one and three percentage points, while Reagan saw a roughly three-point decline.

Truman's average fell a more substantial eight points to 23%, which is the lowest quarterly average for any president in history. That low approval came at a time when Americans listed the Korean War and high cost of living as the most important problems facing the country, and when bribery and corruption in Washington was a major issue.

Job Approval Averages for Presidents During Their 26th Quarter in Office

	Dates of 26th quarter	Approval average	Number of polls
Truman	Jul 20–Oct 19, 1951	30.7%	3
Eisenhower	Apr 20–Jul 19, 1959	62.0%	3
Reagan	Apr 20–Jul 19, 1987	49.7%	3
Clinton	Apr 20–Jul 19, 1999	58.6%	9
G.W. Bush	Apr 20–Jul 19, 2007	31.8%	6
Obama	Apr 20–Jul 19, 2015	46.1%	89

Note: Harry Truman took office during the second quarter of Roosevelt's fourth term.

GALLUP

Obama Has Averaged 47% Job Approval as President

Obama's presidential job approval average to date is 47.4%, which is on pace to be one of the lower averages for post–World War II presidents. Only Truman (45.4%) and Jimmy Carter (45.5%) had lower average approval ratings as president, with Gerald Ford's 47.2% essentially the same as Obama's average. George W. Bush's average was slightly better at 49.4%. Bush's and Obama's ratings are held down to some extent given that they governed in times of record party polarization in ratings of presidents.

Implications

President Obama's approval ratings have stabilized after showing improvement in the fall and winter months. His spring and early summer ratings have been steady around 46%, with weekly averages that rarely stray more than a point or two from that average.

When presidents have been in office for a long time, Americans' opinions of them are largely solidified and resistant to change. Long-serving presidents can still benefit from "rally events," such as when U.S. national security is threatened, but such incidents are rare and presidents likely do their best to avoid such threats emerging in the first place.

In that vein, the president last week announced the U.S. had helped broker a historic agreement to limit Iran's ability to develop nuclear weapons. But the agreement hasn't had any noticeable effect so far on how Americans view the way the president is handling his job, with his approval rating since the announcement holding at about 46%.

Survey Methods

Results for this Gallup poll are based on telephone interviews conducted April 20–July 19, 2015, on the Gallup U.S. Daily survey, with a random sample of 45,080 adults, aged 18 and older, living in all 50 U.S. states and the District of Columbia. For results based on the total sample of national adults, the margin of sampling error is ±1 percentage point at the 95% confidence level. All reported margins of sampling error include computed design effects for weighting.

July 22, 2015
POPE FRANCIS'S FAVORABLE RATING DROPS IN U.S.

by Art Swift

Story Highlights

- *59% have favorable view of pope, down from 76% in February 2014*
- *Christians, conservatives fueling the drop in favorability*
- *Francis seen more favorably than Benedict, less so than John Paul II*

WASHINGTON, D.C.—Pope Francis's favorability rating in the U.S. has returned to where it was when he was elected pope. It is now at 59%, down from 76% in early 2014. The pontiff's rating is similar to the 58% he received from Americans in April 2013, soon after he was elected pope.

The Favorable Ratings of Pope Francis

Please say if you have a favorable or unfavorable opinion of Pope Francis -- or if you have never heard of him.

	Favorable %	Unfavorable %	Never heard of/ No opinion %
Jul 8-12, 2015	59	16	25
Feb 6-9, 2014	76	9	16
Apr 11-14, 2013	58	10	31

GALLUP

After Pope Francis was elected the leader of the 1.2-billion-member Roman Catholic Church in March 2013, he attempted to focus the church on a renewed sense of protecting the poor, on inter-faith relations and on respecting gay and lesbian members of the church. He was lauded in the American news media, with accolades including *Time* magazine naming him the Person of the Year in 2013. The next time Gallup asked about Pope Francis, in February 2014, his favorability had swelled to 76%.

In the current poll, conducted July 8–12, Francis's favorable rating declined, while his unfavorable rating increased to 16% from 9% in 2014. One-quarter of Americans say they have never heard of him or have no opinion, up from 16% in 2014. Now removed from the plaudits of 2013 and the high ratings of 2014, it appears that fewer Americans know enough about the pope to be able to rate him.

Pope's Image Among Catholics and Conservatives Worsens

The drop in the pope's favorable rating is driven by a decline among Catholics and political conservatives, two groups that have been ardent supporters of the modern papacy. Seventy-one percent of Catholics say they have a favorable image of Francis, down from 89% last year.

Pope Francis's drop in favorability is even starker among Americans who identify as conservative—45% of whom view him favorably, down sharply from 72% last year. This decline may be attributable to the pope's denouncing of "the idolatry of money" and linking climate change partially to human activity, along with his passionate focus on income inequality—all issues that are at odds with many conservatives' beliefs.

The pope's image has taken a hit among liberals and moderates as well. Francis's favorable rating among liberals fell 14 percentage

points. Many liberals have criticized the pope for not embracing ordination of women as priests or allowing priests to marry. His papacy is still relatively new, however, and in time he may address these long-standing doctrinal questions more fully.

Favorable Ratings of Pope Francis

	2014 %	2015 %	Change (pct. pts.)
U.S. ADULTS	76	59	-17
Catholics	89	71	-18
Protestants/Other Christians	73	52	-21
Conservatives	72	45	-27
Moderates	79	71	-8
Liberals	82	68	-14

GALLUP

Francis's Ratings Higher Than Benedict's, But Below John Paul's

Pope Francis's 59% favorable rating exceeds the 40% who viewed Pope Benedict XVI favorably in 2010, before he retired in early 2013 after an eight-year papacy. Benedict was plagued by priest abuse scandals in the last years of his papacy. Americans' views of Benedict were higher before 2010, but never as high as the 76% achieved by Francis last year.

Favorable Ratings of Pope Francis, Pope Benedict XVI, Pope John Paul II

	Favorable %	Unfavorable %	Never heard of/ No opinion %
POPE FRANCIS			
Jul 8-12, 2015	59	16	25
Feb 6-9, 2014	76	9	16
Apr 11-14, 2013	58	10	31
POPE BENEDICT XVI			
Mar 26-28, 2010	40	35	25
Apr 18-20, 2008	63	15	22
Jun 1-3, 2007	52	16	32
Dec 16-18, 2005	50	11	39
Apr 29-May 1, 2005	55	12	33
POPE JOHN PAUL II			
Feb 25-27, 2005	78	11	11
Oct 6-8, 2003	73	17	10
Apr 29-May 1, 2002	61	26	13
Dec 28-29, 1998	86	8	6
Aug 8-10, 1993	64	15	21

GALLUP

In contrast, Pope John Paul II, who served as the spiritual leader of the Roman Catholic Church for nearly 27 years, always polled above 60% in the 1990s and 2000s, reaching a high of 86% favora-bility in late 1998. The 64% who have viewed Francis favorably throughout his papacy is below John Paul's average of 72%.

Also, a higher percentage of Americans say they have never heard of Francis than said the same about John Paul II. However, on average, a significantly higher percentage of Americans said they had never heard of Pope Benedict, reaching 39% in 2005.

Bottom Line

Pope Francis is still viewed favorably among Americans, but his image has declined since early 2014. The decline in his favorable rating reflects, in part, the increase in the percentage of Americans who don't have an opinion of the pope, but also a sharp drop in favorable opinions among Catholics and political conservatives.

Pope Francis's image may rebound once he makes his first visit to the U.S. in September. The pope will be traveling to New York, Philadelphia and Washington, D.C., and will be the first pope to address a joint session of Congress. Pope John Paul II's image was boosted by his trips to the U.S. in 1993 and 1999, and Pope Benedict received his greatest favorability rating—63%—when he visited the U.S. in 2008.

Survey Methods

Results for this Gallup poll are based on telephone interviews conducted July 8–12, 2015, with a random sample of 1,009 adults, aged 18 and older, living in all 50 U.S. states and the District of Columbia. For results based on the total sample of national adults, the margin of sampling error is ±4 percentage points at the 95% confidence level.

July 22, 2015

MORE THAN FOUR IN 10 AMERICANS SAY THEY HAVE TRIED MARIJUANA

by Justin McCarthy

Story Highlights

- *Forty-four percent say they have tried marijuana*
- *About one in 10 Americans say they currently smoke pot*
- *Greatest differences in use and experimentation among age groups*

WASHINGTON, D.C.—As Oregon becomes the fourth state to make recreational marijuana use legal, 44% of Americans say they have tried marijuana. This is the highest percentage Gallup has found since it began asking the question in 1969. Back then, a mere 4% admitted to having tried it.

Americans Who Say They Have Tried Marijuana

Keeping in mind that all of your answers in this survey are confidential, have you, yourself, ever happened to try marijuana?

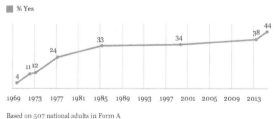

Based on 507 national adults in Form A

Question wording for 1969-1985 trends: Have you, yourself, ever happened to try marijuana?

GALLUP

These data are based on a July 8–12 Gallup poll, which came on the heels of the latest victory for pro-marijuana legalization advocates when, on July 1, Oregon joined Colorado, Alaska, Washington and the District of Columbia in making recreational use legal.

Each time Gallup has polled on the question, Americans have become at least marginally more likely to say they have tried smoking pot, including a six-percentage-point increase in the latest poll. The changes over time may reflect either an increase in the percentage who have tried the drug or an increased willingness to admit to having done so in the past. The latter possibility certainly seems plausible given Americans' growing support for legalizing marijuana in recent decades.

A separate question asks Americans more directly if they smoke marijuana now. Slightly more than one in 10 Americans (11%) say they do, up from 7% in 2013, although the shift is also within the poll's margin of error.

Americans Who Say They Currently Smoke Marijuana

Keeping in mind that all of your answers in this survey are confidential, do you, yourself, smoke marijuana?

	Yes, do	No, do not
	%	%
July 8-12, 2015	11	88
July 10-14, 2013	7	93

Based on 502 national adults in Form B

GALLUP

In comparison, a separate question in the poll finds 19% of Americans say they smoke cigarettes.

Use and Experimentation Differs Most by Age

Gallup used aggregated data from polls in 2013 and 2015 to look at subgroups. The overall averages for use of and experimentation with marijuana in the aggregated data are lower than the estimates for 2015.

An individual's likelihood of using or experimenting with marijuana is higher among certain demographics. Reports of using marijuana, for example, differ significantly by age.

Though Americans younger than age 30 are most likely to say they currently smoke pot (18%), adults between the ages of 30 and 64 are most likely to say they have ever tried it. The latter group includes many baby boomers, who accounted for the sharp increase in admitted use Gallup found between 1969 and 1973. Few adults in the 65 and older age group, which includes the oldest boomers, say they currently smoke marijuana (3%), and they are the least likely to say they have ever tried it (22%).

The more often one attends religious services, the less likely he or she is to admit to using or trying marijuana. Similarly, those who have no religious affiliation are much more likely to say they smoke marijuana (18%) than adults who identify themselves as Catholic (6%) or Protestant (5%).

Men (13%) are more than twice as likely as women (6%) to say they use marijuana. Nearly half of men have at least tried it, compared with 35% of women.

Age, Household Income Make Little Difference in Having Tried Marijuana

Whites and nonwhites are about equally as likely to have experimented with or to currently smoke marijuana. Americans across education and income groups are about equally as likely to say they have tried smoking pot.

Marijuana Usage and Experimentation in the U.S., by Subgroup

	Smoke marijuana	Have tried marijuana
	%	%
Men	13	47
Women	6	35
18-29 years old	18	37
30-49 years old	10	50
50-64 years old	6	49
65+ years old	3	22
White	8	42
Nonwhite	11	39
Democrat	12	48
Independent	11	44
Republican	1	31
Annual income less than $30,000	14	44
Annual income $30,000-$75,000	9	42
Annual income $75,000 or more	7	43
High school education or less	9	42
Some college	12	41
College graduate	10	39
Postgraduate	4	40
No religion/Atheist/Agnostic	18	56
Catholic	6	36
Protestant/Christian	5	39
Attend church seldom/never	14	51
Attend church nearly weekly/monthly	7	38
Attend church weekly	2	27

Based on aggregated data from July 10-14, 2013, and July 8-12, 2015

GALLUP

Current marijuana use, however, does vary among income and education groups. Adults who earn less than $30,000 a year are most likely to say they currently smoke marijuana (14%)—twice as likely as those earning $75,000 or more (7%). And Americans with graduate degrees are less likely to say they are current users (4%) compared with those with college degrees (10%), some college completed (12%) or a high school education or less (9%).

Bottom Line

Pot legalization, once written off as a liberal pipe dream, has found its way to the forefront of political discourse—and onto ballots, where voters in some states have chosen to make recreational use of the substance legal. In even more states, marijuana has been decriminalized or permitted for medical use.

Marijuana is being taken more seriously these days, and pro-legalization advocates are off to a strong start if their successes in Colorado and the Pacific Northwest are any indication of what could soon come to more states. The stigma associated with smoking marijuana appears to be loosening, and Americans may be less shy about revealing their experiences or habits than they have been

in the past. For whatever reason, more Americans than ever before admit that they have smoked marijuana in the past, and there has been an increase in the modest percentage who say they currently smoke it.

Survey Methods

Results for this Gallup poll are based on telephone interviews conducted July 8–12, 2015, with a random sample of 1,009 adults, aged 18 and older, living in all 50 U.S. states and the District of Columbia. For results based on the total sample of national adults, the margin of sampling error is ±6 percentage points at the 95% confidence level. All reported margins of sampling error include computed design effects for weighting.

July 23, 2015
ONE IN FIVE AMERICANS INCLUDE GLUTEN-FREE FOODS IN DIET

by Rebecca Riffkin

Story Highlights

- *One in six, 17%, avoid gluten-free foods*
- *Majority do not think about gluten-free foods*
- *Nonwhites more likely than whites to include gluten-free foods*

WASHINGTON, D.C.—One in five Americans say they actively try to include gluten-free foods in their diet, while 17% say they avoid gluten-free foods. However, the majority of adults, 58%, say they don't think about gluten-free foods either way.

One in Five Americans Include Gluten-Free Foods in Their Diet

Thinking about the food you eat, for each of the following please say if it is something you actively try to include in your diet, something you actively try to avoid or something you don't think about either way. How about gluten-free foods?

	% Include	% Avoid	% Don't think about
All Americans	21	17	58

July 8-12, 2015

GALLUP

In a July poll, Gallup asked 1,009 Americans about the foods they include, or avoid, in their diet as part of its annual Consumption Habits poll. "Gluten-free foods" was included in the list this year for the first time.

There are a number of reasons people may aim for a diet free of gluten, a form of protein found in wheat, rye and barley and their derivatives. For example, gluten can damage the small intestine of people with celiac disease, which is estimated to affect one in 100 people worldwide. However, the Mayo Clinic finds that many people who follow a gluten-free diet have not been diagnosed with the disease. A Mintel Research study found that sales of gluten-free foods increased by 63% between 2012 and 2014, despite a much smaller increase in the percentage of people diagnosed with celiac disease. Based on the new Gallup data, far more U.S. adults say they actively try to include gluten-free foods in their diet than actually suffer from celiac disease.

Nonwhite Americans More Likely Than Whites to Eat Gluten-Free Foods

Demographic differences in those who seek out gluten-free foods are fairly minor. One in three nonwhite Americans say they actively include gluten-free foods, compared with 17% of whites. Age has a modest relationship to use of gluten-free foods, with one in four adults younger than 50 engaging in the practice, compared with 17% of those aged 50 and older. There are not major differences between men and women.

Gluten-Free by Demographics

Thinking about the food you eat, for each of the following please say if it is something you actively try to include in your diet, something you actively try to avoid or something you don't think about either way. How about gluten-free foods?

	% Include	% Avoid	% Don't think about
Male	19	17	59
Female	23	18	58
White	17	17	65
Nonwhite	31	17	45
18 to 49 years	25	15	59
50 years and older	17	19	59

July 8-12, 2015

GALLUP

More educated and wealthier Americans tend to be less likely to include gluten free-foods in their diet than Americans with no college experience and lower-income Americans, respectively, but these differences are also not large.

Gluten-Free by Socioeconomic Status

Thinking about the food you eat, for each of the following please say if it is something you actively try to include in your diet, something you actively try to avoid or something you don't think about either way. How about gluten-free foods?

	% Include	% Avoid	% Don't think about
EDUCATION			
High school diploma or less	26	15	50
Attended college	17	18	64
ANNUAL HOUSEHOLD INCOME			
$75,000 or more	15	19	65
$30,000 to $74,999	21	14	62
Less than $30,000	24	19	50

July 8-12, 2015

GALLUP

Bottom Line

The gluten-free food market has grown substantially in the past five years, as has the introduction of more foods that do not contain gluten. With one in five Americans now seeking to include these products in their diet, the prevalence goes well beyond the roughly 1% of Americans with celiac disease, who have a serious medical reason to avoid gluten. Some Americans may eat gluten-free foods as part of an attempt to lose weight—a variant of a no-carb diet—while others claim it makes them feel better. Although there is some debate over how healthy a gluten-free diet is for those who do not have celiac disease, the percentage of Americans who say they are attempting to include gluten-free food in their diet shows how widespread the practice is.

Survey Methods

Results for this Gallup poll are based on telephone interviews conducted July 8–12, 2015, with a random sample of 1,009 adults, aged 18 and older, living in all 50 U.S. states and the District of Columbia. For results based on the total sample of national adults, the margin of sampling error is ±4 percentage points at the 95% confidence level. All reported margins of sampling error include computed design effects for weighting.

July 24, 2015
SANDERS SURGES, CLINTON SAGS IN U.S. FAVORABILITY

by Lydia Saad

Story Highlights

- *Bernie Sanders's national favorable score doubles to 24%*
- *Hillary Clinton's image slips, now tilts negative, 48% to 43%*
- *Sanders still trails Clinton in favorability among Democrats*

PRINCETON, N.J.—Vermont Sen. Bernie Sanders's favorable rating among Americans has doubled since Gallup's initial reading in March, rising to 24% from 12% as he has become better known. Hillary Clinton's rating has slipped to 43% from 48% in April. At the same time, Clinton's unfavorable rating increased to 46%, tilting her image negative and producing her worst net favorable score since December 2007.

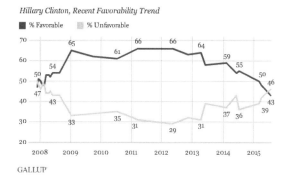

Hillary Clinton, Recent Favorability Trend

GALLUP

Sanders's increased favorability reflects the broader increase in the public's familiarity with him since March. Overall, 44% of Americans are able to rate him today, up from 24% in March. Not only has the percentage viewing him favorably increased, but the percentage viewing him unfavorably has also risen, up eight percentage points to 20%.

Clinton's Inauspicious Rivals

Clinton maintains a higher absolute favorable rating from Americans than any of her official rivals for the 2016 Democratic nomination. In contrast to the relative prominence of numerous candidates on the Republican side, she remains the only Democratic candidate known well enough by a majority of Americans for them to rate her, which helps Clinton maintain a higher overall favorable score.

Sanders is still an unknown to a majority of Americans, with just 44% able to rate him compared with Clinton's 89%. Total familiarity drops still further among the other three announced Democratic candidates: to 23% for former Virginia Sen. Jim Webb, former Maryland Gov. Martin O'Malley at 22% and former Rhode Island Gov. Lincoln Chafee at 17%. With slightly more Americans viewing each of these candidates unfavorably than favorably, their favorable scores reach no more than 11%.

Favorable Ratings of 2016 Democratic Presidential Candidates, Based on U.S. Adults

Next, we'd like to get your overall opinion of some people in the news. As I read each name, please say if you have a favorable or unfavorable opinion of these people -- or if you have never heard of them.
July 8-21, 2015

	Favorable	Unfavorable	No opinion/ Not heard of	Net favorable
	%	%	%	
Hillary Clinton	43	46	11	-3
Bernie Sanders	24	20	56	4
Jim Webb	11	12	77	-1
Martin O'Malley	9	13	78	-4
Lincoln Chafee	6	11	82	-5

Gallup Daily tracking

GALLUP'

The favorable scores of Sanders, Webb, O'Malley and Chafee are not much more encouraging for any of them among their key target audience—Democrats and Democratic-leaning independents. While Sanders's +29 net favorable rating among Democrats is considerably more positive than it is among the general population, still barely half of all Democrats know of him. And the picture is considerably bleaker for the other candidates, none of whom stirs much positive excitement among his or her base or cracks 30% familiarity.

Favorable Ratings of 2016 Democratic Presidential Candidates, Based on Democrats and Democratic Leaners

July 8-21, 2015

	Favorable	Unfavorable	No opinion/ Not heard of	Net favorable
	%	%	%	
Hillary Clinton	74	18	8	56
Bernie Sanders	39	10	52	29
Jim Webb	14	11	75	3
Martin O'Malley	12	10	78	2
Lincoln Chafee	9	8	83	1

Gallup Daily tracking

GALLUP'

Clinton Enjoys Broad Democratic Appeal

Clinton's favorable rating has slipped slightly among Democrats and Democratic-leaning independents since April, falling to 74% from 79%. This partly accounts for her overall decline in favorability among the public. The other factor is a drop among non-leaning independents, from 44% to 36%, while her image among Republicans and Republican leaners is essentially unchanged at 14%.

Among Democrats and Democratic leaners, Clinton is currently viewed more favorably by older than younger adults, by nonwhites than whites and by liberals than moderates or conservatives. However, she retains solid majority favorable scores from all of these groups. And she enjoys equally high ratings from men and women as well as in each of the four major regions of the country.

Sanders's Democratic favorable scores significantly trail Clinton's in all subgroup categories, but he comes the closest to her among whites, men, young adults and liberals. The gap between the two candidates is also closer in the East, where Sanders lives, than in the rest of the country. But he does especially poorly among nonwhites and conservative Democrats, trailing Clinton by more than 50 points in each group.

Favorable Ratings for Top Two Democrats, Based on Democrats and Democratic Leaners
July 8-21, 2015

	Hillary Clinton	Bernie Sanders	Difference
	%	%	
All Democrats/Dem leaners	74	39	-35
Men	71	47	-24
Women	75	32	-43
White	69	50	-19
Nonwhite	80	25	-55
18 to 29 years	62	38	-24
30 to 49 years	76	39	-37
50 to 64 years	76	34	-42
65 years and older	81	45	-36
East	69	49	-20
Midwest	76	37	-39
South	73	36	-37
West	76	35	-41
Liberal	81	53	-28
Moderate	69	32	-37
Conservative	69	15	-54

Gallup Daily tracking

GALLUP'

Bottom Line

Clinton's national image has taken a slight turn for the worse, which is also evident in her image among Democrats. But she remains the only Democratic candidate for president with a national name, and Clinton continues to stand head and shoulders above her next closest competitor—Sanders—in popularity for the presidential nomination.

Survey Methods

Results for this Gallup poll are based on telephone interviews conducted July 8–21, 2015, on the Gallup U.S. Daily survey, with a random sample of 2,374 adults, aged 18 and older, living in all 50 U.S. states and the District of Columbia. For results based on the total sample of national adults, the margin of sampling error is ±2 percentage points at the 95% confidence level.

For results based on the total sample of 966 U.S. adults who identify as or lean Democratic, the margin of sampling error is ±4 percentage points at the 95% confidence level. All reported margins of sampling error include computed design effects for weighting.

July 24, 2015
AMONG REPUBLICANS, GOP CANDIDATES BETTER KNOWN THAN LIKED

by Andrew Dugan

WASHINGTON, D.C.—The GOP presidential field, already 16 candidates strong and brimming with controversy, features a large number of contenders who are familiar to Republicans nationwide. Donald Trump leads the pack as the best-known candidate, at 92%.

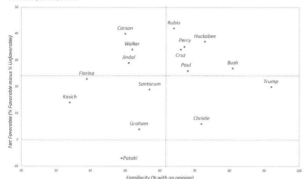

Potential 2016 Republican Presidential Candidates: Familiarity and Favorability
Based on Republicans/Leaners

However, the best-known candidates, Trump and Jeb Bush, are not the best liked. That distinction goes to Marco Rubio and Ben Carson, who enjoy the highest advantage in their net favorable ratings.

These data are based on two weeks of interviewing conducted on Gallup Daily tracking, spanning July 8–21, with a total of 1,028 Republicans and Republican-leaning independents. This was an eventful time on the campaign trail. On July 18, Trump said that longtime GOP senator and 2008 presidential nominee John McCain, a prisoner of war in Vietnam for five years, was not a war hero. Despite nearly universal condemnation of Trump's remarks from other presidential candidates, Trump did not budge from his views.

While Trump is probably the most heavily covered GOP candidate at the moment and is certainly the most well known, he is hardly running against a cast of anonymous or unknown rivals. Besides Trump, three other candidates are familiar to at least 70% of self-identified Republicans, meaning Republicans know enough about the candidate to give him or her a "favorable" or "unfavorable" rating: Bush (81%), Mike Huckabee (73%) and Chris Christie (72%). Another seven candidates enjoy familiarity ratings above bare-majority levels among self-identified Republicans, but below a supermajority of 70%. These candidates include Rand Paul (68%), Rick Perry (67%), Ted Cruz (66%), Rubio (64%), Rick Santorum (57%), Lindsey Graham (55%), Scott Walker (52%) and Bobby Jindal (51%).

Carson, whom half of Republicans are familiar with, nonetheless enjoys a net favorability—the difference between a candidate's favorable and unfavorable ratings—of +40, among the highest of all the candidates, meaning Carson is exceptionally well liked among the smaller subset of Republicans who know him. Other lesser-known candidates, especially Ohio Gov. John Kasich (35% familiarity), are more recent entrants into the field, so their low name recognition may not be a problem for them just yet.

Growing Number of Candidates Well Known and Well Liked

A growing number of candidates are in the "sweet spot" of public opinion, meaning they are comparatively well known among the GOP base as well as comparatively well liked. Rubio has a +42 net favorability, slightly better than Carson's, and 64% of Republicans are familiar with him. Huckabee and Perry also occupy this advantageous space—each is slightly better known than Rubio but is slightly less well liked. Finally, these findings are a reminder of

the importance of campaigning; the best-known, best-liked Republican candidates also happen to be, in many instances, the ones who have been campaigning the longest. Cruz was the first candidate out of the gate, with Paul and Rubio close behind. Bush, meanwhile, officially announced only recently, but his candidacy was far from a secret, and he was engaging in activities that resembled a campaign well before his announcement.

Ratings of 2016 Republican Presidential Candidates: Candidates With Above-Average Familiarity and Above-Average Favorability
Ranked by % Familiar, based on Republicans/leaners

	% Familiar (have an opinion)	% With favorable opinion	% With unfavorable opinion	Net favorable (pct. pts.)
Jeb Bush	81	54	27	+27
Mike Huckabee	73	55	18	+37
Rand Paul	68	47	21	+26
Rick Perry	67	51	16	+35
Ted Cruz	66	50	16	+34
Marco Rubio	64	53	11	+42

July 8-21, 2015

GALLUP

Several Candidates Well Liked But Not Well Known

Three candidates are comparatively well regarded in the GOP field but are not well known. Carson, Walker and Jindal all have essentially the same familiarity rating of about 50%, but each man has a higher-than-average net favorable score. Carson, in particular, has one of the highest net favorable scores of all candidates, at +40.

Ratings of 2016 Republican Presidential Candidates: Candidates With Below-Average Familiarity and Above-Average Favorability
Ranked by % Familiar, based on Republicans/leaners

	% Familiar (have an opinion)	% With favorable opinion	% With unfavorable opinion	Net favorable (pct. pts.)
Scott Walker	52	43	9	+34
Bobby Jindal	51	40	11	+29
Ben Carson	50	45	5	+40

July 8-21, 2015

GALLUP

Pataki Struggling by Wide Margin in Familiarity and Favorability

Five candidates occupy the "no-man's land" of below-average name recognition and below-average favorability. By these metrics, no GOP candidate seems as challenged as former New York Gov. George Pataki. Despite running one of the largest states in the country during a trying time that included the 9/11 attacks, Pataki is familiar to about half of Republicans nationwide (49%). Complicating his chances further, Pataki is more disliked (28%) than liked (21%) among Republicans. He is currently the only candidate in the GOP field to receive a negative "net favorable" score, an unenviable feat. Meanwhile, 2012 runner-up Santorum again finds himself beginning a race in a difficult place in terms of recognition (57%) and likability (+19). Former Hewlett-Packard CEO Carly Fiorina is dogged more by low name recognition (39%) than low likability (+23).

Ratings of 2016 Republican Presidential Candidates: Candidates With Below-Average Familiarity and Below-Average Favorability

Ranked by % Familiar, based on Republicans/leaners

	% Familiar (have an opinion)	% With favorable opinion	% With unfavorable opinion	Net favorable (pct. pts.)
Rick Santorum	57	38	19	+19
Lindsey Graham	55	30	25	+5
George Pataki	49	21	28	-7
Carly Fiorina	39	31	8	+23
John Kasich	35	25	10	+15

July 8-21, 2015

GALLUP

For Trump and Christie, Name ID Outpacing Likability

Two candidates known for their "better to be feared than loved" style of interacting, Trump and Christie, find themselves in the unwelcome position of being well known, but comparatively less well liked. Trump's name recognition is nearly universal, but his net favorability is below average (+20). Given the state of affairs of his contentious campaign, it is hard to foresee his favorable rating rising by a substantial share. For Christie's part, the two-term governor has about as many Republican admirers (39%) as detractors (33%).

Ratings of 2016 Republican Presidential Candidates: Candidates With Above-Average Familiarity and Below-Average Favorability

Ranked by % Familiar, based on Republicans/leaners

	% Familiar (have an opinion)	% With favorable opinion	% With unfavorable opinion	Net favorable (pct. pts.)
Donald Trump	92	56	36	+20
Chris Christie	72	39	33	+6

July 8-21, 2015

GALLUP

Bottom Line

With one of the largest presidential fields in recent history, the Republicans have a number of well-known candidates from whom to choose when the primary campaign gears up. The group of familiar candidates poses clear challenges for candidates who currently have a much lower national profile. In the long run, both types of candidates, the well known and the less so, are aiming to promote their likability as an influential factor in determining GOP voters' decisions.

Survey Methods

Results for this Gallup poll are based on telephone interviews conducted July 8–21, 2015, on the Gallup U.S. Daily survey, with a random sample of 2,374 adults, aged 18 and older, living in all 50 U.S. states and the District of Columbia. For results based on the total sample of national adults, the margin of sampling error is ±2 percentage points at the 95% confidence level.

For results based on the total sample of 1,028 U.S. adults who identify or lean with the Republican Party, the margin of sampling error is ±4 percentage points at the 95% confidence level. All reported margins of sampling error include computed design effects for weighting.

July 27, 2015
DRINKING HIGHEST AMONG EDUCATED, UPPER-INCOME AMERICANS

by Jeffrey M. Jones

Story Highlights

- *Eight in 10 upper-income Americans, college grads drink alcohol*
- *About half of lower-income Americans drink*
- *Beer leads wine as preferred drink in U.S.*

PRINCETON, N.J.—Upper-income and highly educated Americans are more likely than other Americans to say they drink alcohol. Whereas eight in 10 adults in these socioeconomic status groups say they drink, only about half of lower-income Americans and those with a high school diploma or less say they drink.

Self-Reported Alcohol Consumption, by Income and Education

Do you have occasion to use alcoholic beverages such as liquor, wine or beer, or are you a total abstainer?

	% Yes, drink
ANNUAL HOUSEHOLD INCOME	
$75,000 or more	78
$30,000-$74,999	67
Less than $30,000	45
EDUCATION	
College graduate	80
Some college	64
High school or less	52
National adults	64

July 8-12, 2015

GALLUP

The results are based on Gallup's annual Consumption Habits poll, conducted July 8–12.

Overall, 64% of Americans say they drink alcohol, consistent with Gallup's historical trend.

Gallup has consistently found large differences in alcohol consumption among education and income subgroups over time. The income and education differences in drinking are typically larger than those seen by gender, age, race, region and religion.

Americans of higher socioeconomic status certainly have greater economic resources, and can likely afford to buy alcohol when they want to drink. But they also are more likely to participate in activities that may involve drinking such as dining out at restaurants, going on vacation or socializing with coworkers (given the higher drinking rates among working compared with nonworking Americans). The direct connection between drinking and engaging in these activities is not clear from the data, but such a connection could help explain why upper-income Americans are more likely to drink alcohol than other Americans.

While not as powerful a predictor as income and education, religiosity is also strongly related to alcohol consumption. Specifically, 47% of those in the current poll who attend church weekly say they drink alcohol, compared with 69% who attend church less often than that, if at all.

There are also notable differences in drinking by gender, with men (69%) more likely to report drinking alcohol than women (59%). Racial differences are also apparent in that non-Hispanic whites (69%) are significantly more likely to say they drink alcohol than nonwhites (52%). Among age groups, drinking is most common among 30- to 49-year-olds. Detailed percentages by subgroup appear at the bottom of the article.

Drinking Patterns Among Drinkers Also Vary by Income, Education

Not only does the likelihood of whether one drinks alcohol vary by income and education, but so too do drinkers' drinking behaviors and preferences.

For example, nearly half of higher-income and more educated drinkers say they have had a drink within the last 24 hours, compared with one-third or less of non-college graduates and middle- or lower-income drinkers. The differences are especially stark by income, as 47% of upper-income drinkers have imbibed in the last 24 hours, compared with 18% of lower-income drinkers.

When Last Had a Drink of Alcohol, by Income and Education, Among Those Who Drink Alcohol

When did you last take a drink of any kind of alcoholic beverage?

	% Within last 24 hours	% Within last week	% Over one week ago
ANNUAL HOUSEHOLD INCOME			
$75,000 or more	47	29	25
$30,000-$74,999	33	32	34
Less than $30,000	18	45	37
EDUCATION			
College graduate	45	31	25
Some college	31	37	32
High school or less	28	28	43
All U.S. drinkers	35	32	33

July 8-12, 2015

GALLUP

While higher socioeconomic status drinkers are more likely to say they have had an alcoholic drink more recently, they are not more likely than others to report overindulging in alcohol. There are no meaningful differences by income level in the percentage who say they sometimes drink more alcoholic beverages than they should. But, college graduates are significantly less likely than non-college graduates to say they sometimes overdrink.

Sometimes Drink Too Many Alcoholic Beverages, by Income and Education, Among Those Who Drink Alcohol

Do you sometimes drink more alcoholic beverages than you think you should?

	% Yes
ANNUAL HOUSEHOLD INCOME	
$75,000 or more	24
$30,000-$74,999	26
Less than $30,000	27
EDUCATION	
College graduate	18
Some college	30
High school or less	28
All U.S. drinkers	24

July 8-12, 2015

GALLUP

It is unclear if the education differences on overdrinking truly reflect actual behavior, or perhaps reflect that those with more formal education may be less willing to report a socially undesirable behavior in a public opinion survey.

Data from various government and academic studies confirm the relationship between income and alcohol consumption. The studies also indicate upper-income drinkers mostly drink in moderation, but lower-income Americans tend to abstain completely, or to drink heavily.

College Graduates Prefer to Drink Wine

Beer has historically been the alcoholic beverage of choice among U.S. drinkers, and it remains so this year with 42% saying they most often drink beer, compared with 34% for wine and 21% for liquor.

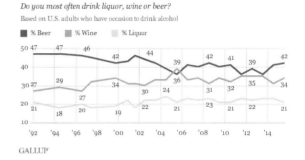

Do you most often drink liquor, wine or beer?
Based on U.S. adults who have occasion to drink alcohol

GALLUP

But beer is not the leading alcoholic beverage among higher socioeconomic status drinkers. Upper-income drinkers are divided in their preference, with 38% preferring wine and 36% beer. Lower- and middle-income drinkers are more likely to prefer beer than wine.

College graduates who drink alcohol show a clearer preference for wine versus beer, 44% to 35%, respectively. Among non-college graduates—particularly those with a high school education or less—beer is the preferred drink.

Alcoholic Beverage Consumed Most Often, by Income and Education, Among Those Who Drink Alcohol

Do you most often drink liquor, wine or beer?

	% Beer	% Wine	% Liquor
ANNUAL HOUSEHOLD INCOME			
$75,000 or more	36	38	21
$30,000-$74,999	44	34	21
Less than $30,000	41	29	26
EDUCATION			
College graduate	35	44	18
Some college	40	35	22
High school or less	52	21	24
All U.S. drinkers	42	34	21

July 8-12, 2015

GALLUP

There are other well-documented demographic differences in a person's favorite alcoholic beverage of choice, with men and younger drinkers clearly preferring beer, while women and older drinkers tilt strongly toward wine.

Implications

Most Americans say they drink alcohol on occasion, but drinking is far more common among upper-income Americans and those with a more formal education. Not only are higher socioeconomic status Americans more likely to drink alcohol, but those who drink do so more often than lower socioeconomic status Americans.

These differences may reflect that upper-income Americans can better afford to purchase alcohol, but upper-income and well-educated Americans are more likely than other Americans to engage in activities in which people commonly drink, such as dining out. Also, because drinking is more common among higher socioeconomic Americans, who presumably are more likely to interact socially with those of similar status, social norms toward drinking may differ among Americans with higher versus lower socioeconomic statuses.

Survey Methods

Results for this Gallup poll are based on telephone interviews conducted July 8–12, 2015, with a random sample of 1,009 adults, aged 18 and older, living in all 50 U.S. states and the District of Columbia. For results based on the total sample of national adults, the margin of sampling error is ±4 percentage points at the 95% confidence level.

For results based on the total sample of 664 drinkers, the margin of sampling error is ±4 percentage points at the 95% confidence level.

July 27, 2015
AMERICANS NOT AVOIDING FAT AND SALT AS MUCH

by Justin McCarthy

Story Highlights

- *Fewer people avoiding fat, more including it in diet*
- *Americans equally as likely to avoid salt as to include it*

WASHINGTON, D.C.—Several recent reports have suggested that fat is not the nutritional hazard it was once presumed to be. This perhaps helps explain why the 47% of Americans who say they "actively try to avoid" consuming it is the lowest level Gallup has measured since it first asked this question in 2002. Conversely, a quarter of Americans say they try to include fat in their diet, while about the same percentage claim they don't think about it.

Americans' Dietary Habits of Eating Fat

Thinking about the food you eat, for each of the following please say if it is something you actively try to include in your diet, something you actively try to avoid, or something you don't think about either way.

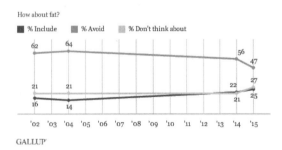

GALLUP

These results are from the Gallup Consumption Habits survey, conducted July 8–12, about a month after news that the federal government's updated *Dietary Guidelines for Americans*, to be issued

later this year, will no longer feature upper limits on total fat intake. The government's Dietary Guidelines Advisory Committee found no health benefit to limiting the amount of total fat in one's diet, whereas past editions of the federal guidelines had suggested limits. The committee did maintain, however, that saturated fat should be limited because doing so could lower the risk of heart disease.

Gallup polling more than a decade ago found more than six in 10 Americans saying they avoid fat in their diet. This dropped to 56% last year, and to less than a majority this year. The one in four Americans who now say they try to include fat in their diet is up from about one in six in the early 2000s.

More Americans Passing the Salt

Americans' attitudes about consuming salt show a similar pattern, with the percentage saying they avoid salt in their diet falling to 39% this year from 46% a year ago. Nearly as many Americans now say they actively try to include salt in their diet (35%) as say they actively try to exclude it.

Americans' Dietary Habits of Consuming Salt

Thinking about the food you eat, for each of the following please say if it is something you actively try to include in your diet, something you actively try to avoid, or something you don't think about either way.

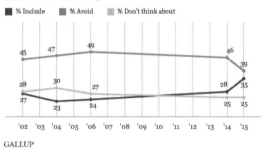

GALLUP

But while government research data may support a retreat from limits on fat intake, that isn't the case for salt—at least for now. There is growing agreement within the nutrition science community that salt is not as harmful to one's health as Americans have been led to believe. Despite this debate, a recent survey by the U.S. Centers for Disease Control and Prevention found that nine in 10 Americans consume too much salt, which increases their risk of hypertension, stroke and heart disease.

Underscoring the difference between Americans' nutritional attitudes and sometimes-conflicting medical evidence, more Americans still say they try to avoid fat than say they avoid salt, and this holds up among all major demographic groups.

Americans' Dietary Habits of Avoiding Fat and Salt

Thinking about the food you eat, for each of the following please say if it is something you actively try to include in your diet, something you actively try to avoid, or something you don't think about either way.

	% Avoid fat	% Avoid salt
Men	42	34
Women	52	43
Whites	44	35
Nonwhites	56	47
18 to 29 years old	44	29
30 to 49 years old	42	41
50 to 64 years old	50	38
65+ years old	53	47

July 8-12, 2015

GALLUP

Bottom Line

Americans' diets, like the health recommendations for them, are constantly evolving, likely influenced over time by scientific research as well as fad diets.

This seems to be the case with fat, which, according to the Dietary Guidelines Advisory Committee, is not something Americans need to limit, as they may have heard they should do in the past—at least in terms of total fat intake.

While scientific input can significantly influence what Americans eat, that doesn't mean Americans always take the advice. In the case of salt, which continues to be a health risk when consumed in excess, Americans appear to have eased their self-restraint, despite contrary advice from government health organizations.

Survey Methods

Results for this Gallup poll are based on telephone interviews conducted July 8–12, 2015, on the Gallup U.S. Daily survey, with a random sample of 1,009 adults, aged 18 and older, living in all 50 U.S. states and the District of Columbia. For results based on the total sample of national adults, the margin of sampling error is ±4 percentage points at the 95% confidence level. All reported margins of sampling error include computed design effects for weighting.

July 28, 2015
ONE IN FIVE AMERICANS SAY MODERATE DRINKING IS HEALTHY

by Rebecca Riffkin
'

Story Highlights

- *Majority say moderate drinking makes no difference to health*
- *28% say one or two drinks a day is bad for health*
- *Americans who drink are more likely to say it is good for health*

WASHINGTON, D.C.—Significantly more Americans believe moderate alcohol consumption is bad for one's health (28%) than believe it is good (17%). The percentage of those viewing alcohol as beneficial is the lowest Gallup has found in this 15-year trend. A slight majority of Americans, 52%, believe drinking in moderation has no effect on one's health.

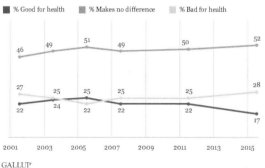

Lower Percentage of Americans Say Moderate Drinking Is Good for Health

Do you, personally, think drinking in moderation -- that is, one or two drinks a day -- [ROTATED: is good for your health, makes no difference or is bad for your health]?

GALLUP

Gallup defines "moderate drinking" as consuming one or two drinks a day, which lines up with the U.S. Centers for Disease Control and Prevention's definition of moderate drinking. These findings are from Gallup's July 8–12 Consumption Habits survey. In the same poll, 64% of Americans said they drink alcohol. This is similar to the national average for the past two decades.

Americans' experiences with alcohol appear to influence their beliefs about the health benefits of moderate drinking. For example, Americans who drink alcohol are more likely to believe it is good for their health (20%) than those who do not drink (12%). Similarly, those who have had a drink in the past day are more likely than those who have had a drink in the past week to believe moderate alcohol intake is good for their health, at 34% and 13%, respectively.

Perceived Health Effects of Drinking by Those Who Drink Alcohol and Those Who Don't

Do you, personally, think drinking in moderation -- that is, one or two drinks a day -- [ROTATED: is good for your health, makes no difference or is bad for your health]?

	% Good	% No difference	% Bad
Don't drink alcohol	12	44	40
Drink alcohol	20	57	21
Had drink in past day	34	55	11
Had drink in past week	13	61	25
Drinking has caused trouble in family	16	46	37
Drinking has not caused trouble in family	18	55	24

July 8-12, 2015

GALLUP

Americans who report that drinking has been a "cause of trouble" in their family are more likely to say that drinking is bad for one's health than those who have not had drinking-related problems in their family (37% vs. 24%, respectively). However, similar percentages of both groups say that drinking is good for one's health.

Groups That Are More Likely to Drink Also More Likely to Say It's Healthy

Population groups that are more likely to report they drink, such as men, those with higher incomes and those with more education, are also less likely to say they believe drinking is unhealthy. For instance, while women are twice as likely to believe drinking in moderation is bad for one's health (30%) as to believe it is good (14%), men are only slightly more likely to say drinking is unhealthy (26%) than to say it is healthy (20%).

The relationship between Americans' drinking habits and their beliefs about the effects of drinking on health is unknown, however. It could be that those who drink are more inclined to believe it is good for their health out of personal experience, or as a way to rationalize their lifestyle choices. Or those who believe drinking is healthy may actively choose to drink as a way to improve their health.

Bottom Line

While the majority of Americans say that moderate drinking does not have an effect on health, those who drink are more likely to believe drinking is good for you than those who do not. The negative effects of heavy drinking, both over the long term and from periodic binge drinking, are well documented and can include liver and brain damage. However, the CDC warns that even moderate alcohol intake can lead to a higher risk of cancer, injuries from falls, violence and motor vehicle crashes. The Mayo Clinic, however, says that one glass of red wine a day can be good for your heart, but warns against beginning to drink just for this health benefit. Other studies have found that a daily glass of alcohol can help with digestion and long life and can lower the chance of diabetes, while still others say these results are overblown. This lack of consensus among the medical community may be one reason U.S. adults remain divided on the health implications of moderate drinking.

Drinking and Health by Subgroup

Do you, personally, think drinking in moderation -- that is, one or two drinks a day -- [ROTATED: is good for your health, makes no difference or is bad for your health]?

	% Good	% No difference	% Bad
GENDER			
Men	20	52	26
Women	14	52	30
RACE			
Whites	18	56	24
Nonwhites	15	44	39
AGE			
18 to 49	17	53	30
50+	25	54	20
EDUCATION			
High school or less	16	45	38
College	18	57	22
ANNUAL HOUSEHOLD INCOME			
Under $30,000	21	46	31
$30,000 to $74,999	16	52	29
$75,000 or more	18	61	19

July 8-12, 2015

GALLUP

Survey Methods

Results for this Gallup poll are based on telephone interviews conducted July 8–12, 2015, with a random sample of 1,009 adults, aged 18 and older, living in all 50 U.S. states and the District of Columbia. For results based on the total sample of national adults, the margin of sampling error is ±4 percentage points at the 95% confidence level. For results based on the total sample of 664 drinkers, the margin of sampling error is ±4 percentage points at the 95% confidence level.

July 28, 2015
U.S. POSTGRADUATES HAVE EDGE IN LIFELONG LEARNING

by Brandon Busteed and Jessica Stutzman

Story Highlights

- *Majority say they learn something interesting every day*
- *Postgrads are only education level that is more likely to agree*

WASHINGTON, D.C.—Nearly three-quarters of U.S. adults with education or training beyond a four-year college degree agree that they learn or do something interesting every day. This is higher than those with a bachelor's degree only (66%), some college or a two-year associate degree (65%), or a high school education or less (63%).

Those With Postgraduate Degrees Most Likely to Be Lifelong Learners

On a 5-point scale, where 5 means "strongly agree" and 1 means "strongly disagree," please rate your level of agreement with the following items:
You learn or do something interesting every day.

	Agree (% 4s + % 5s)
Some postgraduate study/Postgraduate degree	74%
Four-year bachelor's degree	66%
Some college/Technical school/Two-year associate degree from a college	65%
High school or less	63%

Gallup-Healthways Well-Being Index, Jan. 2, 2014–June 1, 2015

GALLUP

Gallup and Healthways ask adults in the U.S. to rate their level of agreement with the statement, "You learn or do something interesting every day," on a five-point scale. Along with other questions, Gallup uses this measure to calculate the extent to which someone is thriving—or strong and consistent—in his or her purpose well-being. Purpose well-being—defined as liking what you do each day and being motivated to achieve your goals—is just one of the five well-being elements that the Gallup-Healthways Well-Being Index measures.

Because factors such as income could affect education levels and, therefore, learning or doing interesting things on a daily basis, the analysis accounted for age, gender, race, income, region and marital status among the percentage who agreed with the statement.

Researchers could measure lifelong learning in a number of quantifiable, activity-based ways, such as asking graduates how many books or articles they have read as well as whether and how often they visit a library or search the Internet for new information. Or researchers could measure it by asking more abstract questions, including whether graduates seek out conversations with people from diverse backgrounds or foreign countries. By asking whether someone agrees that they learn or do something interesting every day, Gallup and Healthways can discern whether graduates are still learning later in life or not.

Bottom Line

Higher education institutions across the U.S. share similar mission and purpose statements. These statements often include a core goal of "fostering lifelong learning" among students and graduates. While this is a commonly shared goal among higher education institutions, it is difficult to identify a way to measure whether students and graduates are indeed becoming lifelong learners.

The Gallup-Healthways Well-Being Index provides a tangible metric with which to evaluate it: The majority of Americans, no matter what their education level, agree that they learn or do something interesting every day. However, when looking at levels of educational attainment, it is not until the postgraduate level that there is a meaningful difference in terms of someone believing that he or she gets to learn or do something interesting every day.

Other factors independent of education level can influence daily learning as well, including the culture of the city or area where one resides. Prior Gallup analyses show that cities with a heavy academic presence tend to score higher in overall well-being, which is supported in part by residents saying that they learn new and interesting things every day. Cities with a strong academic presence likely provide residents with more chances to learn and do interesting things through community events and educational opportunities.

As Americans scrutinize the value of a college degree—from whether it improves their job prospects to whether it helps them become engaged citizens and lifelong learners—it is necessary for colleges and universities to do more to measure and track long-term outcomes, as well as make good on the promises made in their mission statements and touted in admissions brochures.

Survey Methods

Results are based on telephone interviews conducted Jan. 2, 2014–June 1, 2015, as part of the Gallup-Healthways Well-Being Index survey, with a random sample of 251,193 adults, aged 18 and older, living in all 50 U.S. states and the District of Columbia. For results based on the total sample of Americans, the margin of sampling error is ±0.2 percentage point at the 95% confidence level, including computed design effects for weighting.

July 29, 2015
SO FAR IN 2015, MORE AMERICANS EXERCISING FREQUENTLY

by Rebecca Riffkin

Story Highlights

- *55.5% of Americans exercised three or more days in last week*
- *Highest monthly average in seven years of tracking*
- *Hispanics, young adults and men more frequent exercisers*

WASHINGTON, D.C.—More Americans are exercising consistently each week, with 55.5% indicating frequent exercise in June 2015, more than in any month since Gallup and Healthways began tracking this metric in January 2008. In every month this year, more Americans reported exercising for at least 30 minutes three or more days per week than in the same month for the past two years, indicating that Americans' exercise habits may be improving in 2015.

Record Number of Americans Report Exercising in June 2015

Winter low and summer high for each year shown

% Who exercised 30+ minutes for 3 or more days in the last week

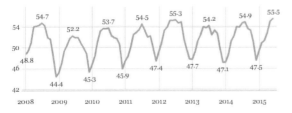

Monthly averages
Gallup-Healthways Well-Being Index

GALLUP

Gallup and Healthways ask at least 500 American adults each day about their exercise frequency. Specifically, these Americans are asked to report how many days in the last seven they exercised for at least 30 minutes.

Exercise follows a seasonal trend in the U.S., with more Americans saying they work out in the summer and less in the winter. The difference in frequent exercise during summer and winter months is typically about seven percentage points.

In the first half of the year, on average, 52.5% of Americans reported exercising for at least half an hour on three or more days of the previous week. This is slightly below the average of 53.0% for the first half of 2012, but up from the same time period in 2013 and 2014, making 2015 the second-highest year-to-date average in this survey. The lowest average occurred in 2009, when 49.3% of Americans reported exercising frequently in the first half of the year, the only time this average has been below 50%.

Average Percentage in U.S. Exercising Frequently in First Half of Year

January through June averages shown

	% Who exercised 30+ minutes 3 or more days in the last week
2015	52.5
2014	51.2
2013	51.4
2012	53.0
2011	50.8
2010	51.1
2009	49.3
2008	51.9

Gallup-Healthways Well-Being Index

GALLUP

Frequent Exercise More Common Among Men, Hispanics and Young Adults

June 2015 reports of frequent exercise vary by demographics. Men are more likely than women to report exercising frequently. Younger adults, aged 18 to 29, are significantly more likely to exercise frequently than those who are older. And Hispanics are slightly more likely to report exercising frequently than whites, and much more likely than blacks.

Among income groups, upper-income Americans are the most likely to exercise frequently, and lower-income Americans are the least likely. Americans who live in the West are more likely to exercise than those in any other region, while those in the South are the least likely. These trends have been consistent over time.

Implications

While frequent exercise seems to dip in the fall and winter, if the current trend continues, 2015 may be one of the best years for exercise rates in the U.S. Research shows that even small improvements in Americans' exercise habits have a positive effect on population health in general, and weight loss and lower obesity rates for individuals more specifically.

Beyond combating weight gain, exercising frequently has many other benefits. Previous Gallup-Healthways research shows that frequent exercise is linked to having a more positive body image and improved emotional health, especially among low-income Americans. Additionally, Americans who set and achieve exercise goals can develop a stronger sense of purpose. And exercising with family and friends can help boost social well-being.

Given these benefits, local leaders may want to encourage frequent exercise as a priority. Some of these interventions could include creating bike paths, improving lighting so residents can exercise safely at night and holding community events that encourage exercise.

Frequent Exercise Rates Among Various Demographic Groups in June 2015

% Who exercised for 30+ minutes 3 or more days in the last week

	% Frequently exercised
GENDER	
Male	58.4
Female	52.7
AGE	
18-29	64.5
30-44	55.4
45-64	52.9
65+	49.7
RACE/ETHNICITY	
Hispanic	58.5
White	55.7
Black	50.3
ANNUAL HOUSEHOLD INCOME	
Less than $36,000	51.4
$36,000-$90,000	56.5
$90,001+	59.4
REGION	
West	61.9
Midwest	54.7
East	53.8
South	52.6

June 1-30, 2015
Gallup-Healthways Well-Being Index

GALLUP'

Survey Methods

Results are based on telephone interviews conducted June 1–30, 2015, as part of the Gallup-Healthways Well-Being Index survey, with a random sample of 14,683 adults, aged 18 and older, living in all 50 U.S. states and the District of Columbia. For results based on the total sample of national adults, the margin of sampling error is ±1 percentage point at the 95% confidence level. All reported margins of sampling error include computed design effects for weighting.

July 29, 2015
AMERICANS' COFFEE CONSUMPTION IS STEADY, FEW WANT TO CUT BACK

by Lydia Saad

Story Highlights

- *Just under two-thirds of U.S. adults drink at least one cup a day*
- *Coffee drinkers average 2.7 cups per day, unchanged from 1999*
- *A quarter say they're addicted, but only 10% want to cut back*

PRINCETON, N.J.—Coffee shops are reportedly the fastest-growing segment of the restaurant industry, yet the percentage of Americans who regularly drink coffee hasn't budged. Sixty-four percent of U.S. adults report drinking at least one cup of coffee on an average day, unchanged from 2012 and remarkably similar to the figure in 1999. Additionally, coffee drinkers currently report consuming just under three cups of coffee per day, also unchanged.

Americans' Coffee Consumption

How many cups of coffee, if any, do you drink on an average day?

	Drink one or more cups per day	Average number of cups per day, among drinkers
	%	
Jul 8-12, 2015	64	2.7
Jul 9-12, 2012	64	2.5
Sep 23-26, 1999	63	2.9

GALLUP'

More specifically, 26% of American adults say they drink one cup of coffee on an average day, 19% drink two, 8% drink three, and 11% drink four or more. The remaining 36% drink none.

In addition to the rapid growth of coffeehouses in recent decades—the number rose by 40% between 1999 and 2005 alone—advances in home brewing machines have enabled consumers to enjoy premium coffee almost anytime, anywhere. And while there are some risks associated with consuming too much caffeine, in moderation the drug is associated with improved concentration and memory as well as potentially lowering the risk of certain cancers, Parkinson's disease and stroke.

Coffee drinkers tend to be older, with 74% of adults aged 55 and older consuming it daily, versus 50% of those aged 18 to 34. Among coffee drinkers, those younger than 35 tend to drink fewer cups per day on average (1.8) than those aged 35 and older, who consume roughly three cups per day. Fewer lower-income than higher-income Americans drink coffee, but lower-income coffee drinkers consume more cups per day than higher-income coffee drinkers (3.8 vs. 2.4 cups, on average).

Coffee Consumption Among Major U.S. Subgroups

	Drink one or more cups per day	Average number of cups per day, among drinkers
	%	
Men	62	2.6
Women	66	2.9
Whites	67	3.1
Nonwhites	59	1.9
18 to 34	50	1.8
35 to 54	66	3.0
55+	74	3.1
$75,000 or more	66	2.4
$30,000 to $74,999	66	2.7
Less than $30,000	58	3.8
East	70	3.1
Midwest	65	3.3
South	63	2.5
West	62	2.2
Employed	63	2.4
Not employed	66	3.2

July 8-12, 2015

GALLUP'

Additionally, whites tend to drink more coffee than nonwhites, and those living in the East and Midwest drink a bit more than those in the West, but there are minimal differences in consumption by gender, education and employment status.

A Pleasant Addiction?

According to WebMD, caffeine can cause "mild physical dependence," and caffeine withdrawal can result in a temporary period of headaches, fatigue, irritability and depressed mood. About one in four coffee drinkers may be familiar with these symptoms, as 26% consider themselves addicted to coffee.

How much coffee does it take to become addicted? Only 10% of those who drink one cup a day consider themselves addicted, but this jumps to 29% among those who enjoy two cups and to 46% among those who have three or more.

Still, just 10% of all coffee drinkers would like to cut back, suggesting that most coffee addicts aren't suffering ill effects from it—at least nothing that a cup of coffee can't fix. And there is no difference in desire to curtail consumption between light versus heavy coffee drinkers, or even between self-described coffee addicts and all others.

In contrast, Gallup typically finds seven in 10 smokers saying they are addicted to cigarettes and about the same proportion saying they would like to quit.

Bottom Line

With research studies showing that moderate coffee consumption has no adverse health effects, and may even have some health benefits, it may be surprising that the proliferation of coffee shops throughout the country hasn't hooked more people or caused current coffee drinkers to consume more. It may be that people are sensitive to their body's tolerance for caffeine and know when enough is enough, creating a natural barrier to consuming ever-increasing amounts. As a result, corner coffeehouses and advanced home brewing machines may make drinking coffee more convenient—and even more pleasant—for people, but they are not stirring Americans to drink more.

Survey Methods

Results for this Gallup poll are based on telephone interviews conducted July 8–12, 2015, with a random sample of 1,009 adults, aged 18 and older, living in all 50 U.S. states and the District of Columbia. For results based on the total sample of national adults, the margin of sampling error is ±4 percentage points at the 95% confidence level. For results based on the sample of 675 coffee drinkers, the margin of sampling error is ±5 percentage points at the 95% confidence level. All reported margins of sampling error include computed design effects for weighting.

July 30, 2015
BAN ON SMOKING IN PUBLIC RETAINS MAJORITY SUPPORT IN U.S.

by Justin McCarthy

Story Highlights

- *Most Americans say smoking in public places should be outlawed*
- *One in four Americans say smoking should be illegal entirely*

- *Women more likely than men to support smoking bans*

WASHINGTON, D.C.—A majority of Americans continue to believe smoking should be made illegal in all public places (58%), as they have since 2011. Forty-one percent are opposed to a total ban in public places.

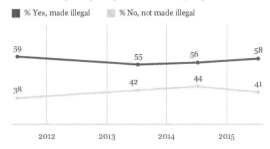

Recent Trend on Americans' Views of Smoking in Public Places
Should smoking in all public places be made totally illegal, or not?

All data based on a half sample

GALLUP

The latest results come from Gallup's July 8–12 Consumption Habits survey, in which 19% of Americans report having smoked cigarettes in the past week, matching the historical low.

Research conducted in 2007 and in prior years showed a lower percentage of Americans in favor of making public smoking illegal, although changes in the survey since 2011 rule out a strict comparison of the two time periods.

In a separate question, Gallup finds much less support for an outright ban on smoking. About one in four Americans (24%) say smoking should be made completely illegal. That is twice the level in 2007 and the highest ever found in Gallup surveys. Still, a large majority of Americans (76%) say smoking should not be made illegal, perhaps reflecting Americans' instincts against making behaviors totally illegal, or reflecting their doubts that such a ban would work in practical terms.

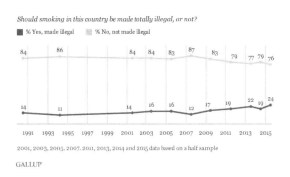

Should smoking in this country be made totally illegal, or not?

2001, 2003, 2005, 2007, 2011, 2013, 2014 and 2015 data based on a half sample

GALLUP

Women are a good deal more likely than men to say that smoking should be banned in public places or made illegal entirely. Among age groups, the older an American is, the more likely he or she is to support a ban on smoking in public places. But Americans of all ages are about equally as likely to support an outright ban.

Bottom Line

Cigarette smoking has been declining gradually in the U.S., from roughly 40% of U.S. adults reporting they smoke in the 1970s to barely 20% today. A solid majority of Americans have favored a total ban on smoking in public places in recent years, although only a minority are in favor of an outright ban on smoking nationwide.

Views on the Legality of Smoking, by Gender and Age

Should smoking in all public places be made totally illegal, or not?
Should smoking in this country be made totally illegal, or not?

	% Yes, made illegal to smoke in public places	% Yes, smoking should be totally illegal
GENDER		
Men	47	19
Women	68	28
AGE		
18-29	46	21
30-49	58	28
50-64	63	21
65+	64	21

July 8-12, 2015

GALLUP

According to the American Nonsmokers' Rights Foundation, as of July 2015, 24 states and the District of Columbia have smoke-free laws for non-hospitality workplaces, restaurants and bars, while 30 have smoke-free laws specifically for restaurants and bars. Municipalities, too, have taken measures to curb public smoking in other areas, such as parks and beaches. Notably, New York City banned smoking in many outdoor spaces, including Times Square.

As public officials have made great efforts to reduce smoking rates, secondhand smoke exposure and smoking-related litter, the public seems to be largely receptive to such measures while still supporting the right of a dwindling minority of Americans to light up, presumably in private.

Survey Methods

Results for this Gallup poll are based on telephone interviews conducted July 8–12, 2015, with a random sample of 1,009 adults, aged 18 and older, living in all 50 U.S. states and the District of Columbia. For results based on the total sample of national adults, the margin of sampling error is ±4 percentage points at the 95% confidence level. All reported margins of sampling error include computed design effects for weighting.

For results based on the sample of 507 national adults in Form A, the margin of sampling error is ±6 percentage points.

For results based on the sample of 502 national adults in Form B, the margin of sampling error is ±6 percentage points.

July 30, 2015
TRUMP GOP FAVORABLE IMAGE DROPS, BUT STILL POSITIVE

by Lydia Saad

Story Highlights

• *Trump viewed favorably in the past week by 51% of Republicans*
• *Image is down from 59% in mid-July, but similar to 53% earlier*

• *Trump's most vocal GOP foes have not made headway*

PRINCETON, N.J.—The controversy Donald Trump created when he questioned the heroism of Vietnam veteran John McCain on July 18 may have reversed the upward momentum the Republican presidential candidate enjoyed in mid-July, although his ratings have mostly reverted to where they were earlier in the month. Last week, 51% of Republicans viewed him favorably, down from 59% the week prior but similar to 53% in the second week of July.

Donald Trump Favorable Ratings -- Recent Seven-Day Averages

Based on Republicans and Republican leaners

	Favorable	Unfavorable	No opinion
	%	%	%
Jul 22-28, 2015	51	40	8
Jul 15-21, 2015	59	34	8
Jul 8-14, 2015	53	38	9

Gallup Daily tracking

GALLUP

Meanwhile, Trump's image among all national adults continues to tilt negative, with 31% viewing him favorably and 57% unfavorably, essentially unchanged this month.

Donald Trump Favorable Ratings -- Recent Seven-Day Averages

Based on U.S. adults

	Favorable	Unfavorable	No opinion
	%	%	%
Jul 22-28, 2015	31	57	12
Jul 15-21, 2015	33	54	13
Jul 8-14, 2015	31	57	12

Gallup Daily tracking

GALLUP

Trump was under fire at the start of July as a number of corporations distanced themselves from the real estate mogul after he accused Mexico of sending immigrants to the U.S. who are not "their best [people]" and who are "bringing drugs," "bringing crime" and "rapists."

Gallup began tracking the favorable ratings of all 16 announced Republican presidential candidates, as well as the five announced Democratic candidates, on July 8, in the midst of the media firestorm over Trump's Mexico comments. In a column published by the *New Yorker* on July 16, McCain was quoted saying Trump had "fired up the crazies," in reference to a large crowd that assembled to hear Trump speak in McCain's home state of Arizona. Trump initially used that to his advantage by sounding populist themes in defense of the Phoenix audience, but the tone changed on July 18 when he suggested McCain's experience as a prisoner of war didn't make him a hero. More recently, Trump has been on the defensive over a statement one of his top aides made diminishing the seriousness of marital rape, and an accusation (now recanted) that Trump has faced on that issue.

Gallup's three-day rolling averages during this period show Trump starting to gain in favorability among Republicans around July 13, peaking at 63% in interviewing conducted July 16–18. His favorability then turned downward following his comments about McCain, reaching 52% in interviewing July 21–23, similar to where he was at the start of tracking. The more recent trajectory of his favorable score is a bit unclear, as it initially rose to 56% in the three-day average through July 26, but has since dipped below 50%.

Donald Trump Favorable Ratings Among Republicans/Republican Leaners
Three-day rolling averages from July 8-10, 2015, through July 26-28, 2015

■ % Favorable

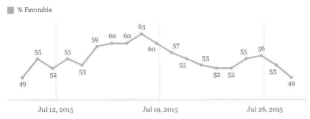

Gallup Daily tracking

GALLUP

Other Republican candidates who either have found or have put themselves in Trump's crosshairs this month include former Texas Gov. Rick Perry, South Carolina Sen. Lindsey Graham and former Florida Gov. Jeb Bush.

Graham and Trump traded verbal insults last week, and at one point Trump upped the ante by urging his supporters to call Graham, giving out the senator's personal cellphone number. Meanwhile, both Perry and Bush have taken strong stands against Trump's statements about Mexico and Mexican immigrants, and have chided Trump for his rhetoric.

Among these three candidates, only Graham's image may have suffered with Republicans, with his favorable rating slipping from slightly positive earlier in July—29% favorable, 24% unfavorable—to slightly negative in the past week, at 25% favorable and 30% unfavorable. By contrast, Bush's and Perry's ratings are largely unchanged.

Ratings of Other Republican Candidates -- Recent Seven-Day Averages
Based on U.S. adults

	Favorable	Unfavorable	No opinion
LINDSEY GRAHAM	%	%	%
Jul 22-28, 2015	25	30	45
Jul 15-21, 2015	30	26	44
Jul 8-14, 2015	29	24	47
JEB BUSH			
Jul 22-28, 2015	52	28	20
Jul 15-21, 2015	55	25	20
Jul 8-14, 2015	54	28	18
RICK PERRY			
Jul 22-28, 2015	48	20	32
Jul 15-21, 2015	52	13	35
Jul 8-14, 2015	49	19	32

Gallup Daily tracking

GALLUP

Bottom Line

Trump enjoyed a bump in Republican favorability earlier this month as he swatted away criticisms from corporate sponsors, took a hard line against illegal immigration and drew crowds of enthusiastic fans. However, since questioning McCain's heroism and getting personal in his attacks on several fellow Republican candidates, he

has lost those gains. Whether those actions are the cause of Trump's slide isn't clear, but they do coincide with it.

The most recent three-day average through July 28 shows Trump with a 49% favorable score, identical to where he started in July. The fact that Trump not only survived the firestorm that erupted in June over his immigration comments, but initially thrived on it, suggests that he has staying power in the GOP race. But it will soon become clear if his image is now suffering either from a delayed reaction to the McCain controversy, or from more recent issues. Either way, these figures will serve as valuable reference points for evaluating the impact of the first Republican candidate debate coming up next week.

Survey Methods

The results reported in this article are based on seven-day averages of telephone interviews conducted on the Gallup U.S. Daily survey in July 2015, including July 8–14, July 15–21 and July 22–28. Each week's average contains a random sample of approximately 1,170 adults, aged 18 and older, living in all 50 U.S. states and the District of Columbia. For results based on the total sample of national adults, the margin of sampling error is ±4 percentage points at the 95% confidence level. Weekly results among Republicans are based on approximately 500 Republicans and Republican-leaning independents and have a margin of sampling error of ±5 percentage points at the 95% confidence level. The three-day rolling averages among Republicans are based on approximately 215 Republicans and Republican-leaning independents for each three-day time period from July 8–11, 2015, through July 26–28, 2015.

July 31, 2015
MORE NONRETIRED U.S. INVESTORS HAVE A WRITTEN FINANCIAL PLAN

by Jeffrey M. Jones

Story Highlights

• *Thirty-eight percent of investors have written financial plan*
• *Many more nonretired investors have plan now than in 2011*
• *About half of investors are following their plans very closely*

PRINCETON, N.J.—Thirty-eight percent of U.S. investors have a written financial plan to help them achieve their investment and retirement goals. Retired investors (43%) are more likely than nonretired investors (36%) to have a written financial plan, as is typically the case. However, the percentage of nonretired investors with a written plan is up significantly since early in 2011 (24%).

A financial plan typically consists of investors' goals—commonly for retirement savings, but also for college savings, insurance needs, taxes and major purchases. Having a written plan with specific goals and formal steps to take should increase the likelihood that people will achieve those goals. Those without a formal written plan may instead have vague notions as to what their financial aims are and how to attain them. Still others may not have even thought about long-range financial matters.

In three separate surveys conducted in 2011, an average 26% of nonretired investors said they had a written financial plan. That increased to an average 31% in 2012 and 35% in 2013 and has been at about that level since.

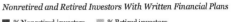

Nonretired and Retired Investors With Written Financial Plans

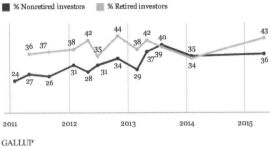

GALLUP

There has been a very slight increase among retired investors since 2011, from an average 37% in 2011 to an average 39% since then.

The rise in the percentage of both nonretired and retired investors with written financial plans coincides with the long-running U.S. stock bull market, the drop in the U.S. unemployment rate, as well as generally improving confidence in the U.S. economy.

The results are based on the Wells Fargo/Gallup Investor and Retirement Optimism Index survey, conducted May 22–31. The survey defines investors as those with $10,000 or more in investable assets.

Overall, 70% of investors say they have a financial plan, but barely more than half of those with a plan, 54%, say it is a written plan. Those figures translate to 38% of all U.S. investors having a written plan. Retired investors are a bit more likely than nonretired investors to say they have a plan and to say it is a written plan.

Financial Plans for Investment and Retirement
Based on investors

	% Have a plan to reach investment goals	% With written plan, among those with a plan	% With written plan, among all investors
All investors	70	54	38
Not retired	69	53	36
Retired	73	59	43

May 22-31, 2015

GALLUP

Investors who do not have a written plan are most likely to cite a lack of time (29%) or not having thought about it (27%) as a reason they do not have a written plan. Another 18% say they do not find written financial plans to be useful.

Most Investors With Plan Follow It Closely, Are Confident in It

Having a financial plan is a key first step in reaching one's investment goals, but those goals will likely be harder to achieve if investors do not follow the plan. The majority of investors with a written financial plan, 53%, say they follow that plan "very closely." Another 39% say they follow it "somewhat closely."

One way investors can keep on track with their financial plan is to review it on a regular basis. The vast majority of investors with a written financial plan, 88%, say they review it at least annually, including 39% who do so more than once a year.

Another way for investors to stay on track with their plan is to enlist the help of a professional adviser. The vast majority of investors with a written plan, 74%, say they developed the plan with the help of an investment adviser, including 80% of substantial investors and 61% of less substantial investors. Substantial investors are those with $100,000 or more of investable assets.

How often do you review your financial plan?
Based on investors with a written financial plan

	%
More than once a year	39
About once a year	49
Every two to three years	5
Every four to five years	2
Less often than that	4

May 22-31, 2015

GALLUP

Investors with a written plan tend to be confident that it is adequately designed to help them reach their goals. Four in 10, 42%, are highly confident of this, with another 48% somewhat confident.

Retirement Is Common Focus of Financial Plans

Nearly all investors with a written plan include retirement as a key component of their saving and investing plan. Ninety-four percent say their financial plan includes retirement income planning, and 88% say it includes a retirement savings plan.

After retirement, other key focus areas are insurance planning, a household budget and an asset allocation plan for investments. Reflecting the generally older age of investors, just 35% say their financial plan includes an education savings plan. Forty-three percent of nonretired investors have education savings as a component of their financial plan, compared with 18% of retired investors.

Retired (76%) and nonretired (57%) investors also differ in the extent to which their financial plan includes estate planning.

Elements Included in Financial Plan
Based on investors with a written financial plan

	All	Nonretired	Retired
	%	%	%
Retirement income planning	94	93	94
A retirement savings plan	88	91	81
Insurance planning	79	81	76
A household budget	76	79	70
An asset allocation plan for your investments	71	70	73
Tax planning	66	62	74
Estate planning	63	57	76
A debt management plan	57	60	52
An education savings plan	35	43	18

May 22-31, 2015

GALLUP

Implications

Although most U.S. investors say they have a financial plan, fewer than four in 10 have gone the extra step to develop a written financial plan. However, that percentage has been growing in recent years. A written plan is a key tool to help investors define their goals and spell out specific steps needed to achieve those goals. The act of developing a clearly defined written plan likely keeps investors more on track for their goals than if they did not have such a plan. Those who do have a written plan appear to be more committed to achieving their goals than those who do not have such a plan—most with a written plan have employed a financial adviser to help develop it, say they follow it at least somewhat closely and say they review it at least annually.

Survey Methods

Results for the Wells Fargo/Gallup Investor and Retirement Optimism Index survey are based on questions asked May 22–31, 2015, on the Gallup Daily tracking survey, of a random sample of 1,005 U.S. adults having investable assets of $10,000 or more.

For results based on the entire sample of investors, the margin of sampling error is ±4 percentage points at the 95% confidence level.

August 03, 2015
DESPITE UNREST, BLACKS DO NOT FEEL MORE MISTREATED BY POLICE

by Frank Newport

Story Highlights

- *18% of U.S. blacks treated unfairly by police within last 30 days*
- *Little changed over the past 18 years*
- *Self-reports of unfair treatment in other settings also stable*

PRINCETON, N.J.—Despite the significant public attention on confrontations between black citizens and police in Missouri, Maryland and New York over the past year, blacks in 2015 express virtually the same opinions about being mistreated by police as they did in 2013. This year, 18% of adult blacks say there has been an occasion the last 30 days when they personally felt they were treated unfairly in dealings with police, which is virtually the same as the 17% recorded in 2013. This is down from as high as 25% in 2004.

Can you think of any occasion in the last 30 days when you felt you were treated unfairly in the following places because you were black? How about in dealings with the police, such as traffic incidents?
Among U.S. blacks

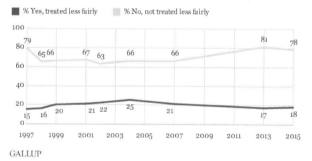

GALLUP

Gallup first asked this question in 1997, when 15% of U.S. blacks reported feeling the police treated them unfairly, and that percentage has fluctuated only minimally in eight surveys since then. These results are from Gallup's Minority Rights and Relations survey conducted with a random sample of 802 U.S. blacks June 15–July 10.

In similar fashion, there has been no increase this year in the percentage of blacks who say that over the previous 30 days they were treated unfairly because of their race while shopping, dining out, at work or getting healthcare. These personal self-reports also have been remarkably stable over the years.

Can you think of any occasion in the last 30 days when you felt you were treated unfairly in the following places because you were black?
Asked of black respondents -- % treated unfairly

	1997	2013	2015*
	%	%	%
In a store where you were shopping	30	24	24
At a restaurant, bar, theater or other entertainment place	21	16	20
At your place of work	21	15	18
In dealings with the police, such as traffic incidents	15	17	18
While getting healthcare for yourself or a family member	--	9	12

*June 15-July 10, 2015

GALLUP

More specifically:

- The highest percentage of blacks reporting unfair treatment because of their race (24%) is in response to a question about shopping in stores. The trend over time on this measure is largely flat, and the lowest percentage saying "yes" is in the two most recent surveys.
- Twenty percent of black Americans say they have been treated unfairly because of their race while dining out or at a bar, theater or other entertainment place. Blacks' perceptions of unfair treatment in these settings are essentially the same now as they were in 1997, and slightly lower than in surveys conducted in 2002 and 2004.
- The trend in blacks' perceived unfair treatment at their workplaces follows a pattern similar to perceptions of unfair treatment while dining out. Eighteen percent report unfair treatment at work now, not meaningfully different from previous years.
- Blacks are least likely to perceive unfair treatment because of their race while getting healthcare for themselves or for a family member. This may reflect that many respondents, particularly younger ones, do not regularly seek healthcare. Gallup has asked this question only three times. The current 12% is not significantly different from the 9% in 2013, and both the 2013 and the 2015 measures are slightly lower than the 20% reading in 2004.

Younger Blacks More Likely to Report Discrimination

There is some variation between broad age and gender groups in reports of discrimination across the five situations. In general, blacks younger than 50 are at least slightly more likely to report discrimination than those who are older, except in the instance of "getting healthcare." Men are more likely than women to report discrimination in dealings with police, but there is little difference by gender across the other four situations.

Can you think of any occasion in the last 30 days when you felt you were treated unfairly in the following places because you were black?
Asked of black respondents -- % treated unfairly

	Aged 18 to 49	Aged 50+	Men	Women
	%	%	%	%
At your place of work	21	13	16	18
At a store, while shopping	29	18	26	23
At a restaurant, bar, theater or other entertainment place	23	15	20	19
In dealings with the police, such as traffic incidents	21	13	23	13
While getting healthcare for yourself or a family member	10	14	13	11

June 15-July 10, 2015

GALLUP

Black Americans' Satisfaction With Their Personal Lives at High Point

The Minority Rights survey contained a question asking Americans how satisfied they are with their lives, and 88% of blacks now say they are very or somewhat satisfied. As was the case in 2013, this is essentially the same as the reported satisfaction among whites, reflecting a significant change from surveys conducted between 2001 and 2008, when whites consistently reported higher satisfaction levels. Blacks' satisfaction with their lives is now higher by one percentage point than at any time over the past 14 years and well above the low point of 80% measured in 2008. On the other hand, whites' personal satisfaction is now essentially tied with its lowest point.

Overall, how satisfied are you with your life — are you very satisfied, somewhat satisfied, somewhat dissatisfied or very dissatisfied?

Total % satisfied (very + somewhat)

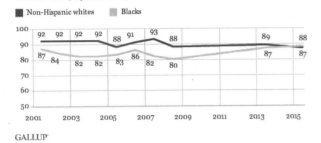

GALLUP

Implications

Perceptions of discrimination for blacks in the U.S. as they go about their daily lives—including interactions with police—have not changed materially over the past 18 years. This is the case even as news reports, social media and other communication sources focus extensively on examples of discrimination, particularly the highly visible deaths of black citizens at the hands of white police. This can be seen as a positive sign that things are not getting worse, or as a negative sign that things are not getting better. Blacks' reports of satisfaction with the way their daily lives are going is at its all-time high point, providing additional evidence that U.S. blacks' views of their general life conditions have not recently deteriorated.

Despite the lack of significant change over time, the fact remains that almost one in five blacks do report having being treated unfairly by police within the 30 days prior to the interview, and—as another example—at least one in four blacks have consistently reported that they felt discriminated against while shopping. The questions ask blacks to report incidents of mistreatment over the past 30 days. It is possible that the percentages reporting such discrimination would be larger if blacks were asked about mistreatment over a longer period. Whatever the case, the data show that instances of perceived discrimination are very real for many blacks in the U.S. today, even if the level of that discrimination has remained fairly constant over the time Gallup has been measuring it.

These self-reports of personal discrimination are different from questions that ask blacks to evaluate their views of the broader situation for U.S. blacks today, including general views of race relations, perceptions of discrimination in local communities more generally and attitudes about the need for new civil rights laws. These measures and others will be discussed in subsequent reports of the results of the 2015 Minority Rights and Relations survey.

Survey Methods

Results for this Gallup poll are based on telephone interviews conducted June 15–July 10, 2015, with a random sample of 2,296 adults, aged 18 and older, living in all 50 U.S. states and the District of Columbia. For results based on the total sample of national adults, the margin of sampling error is ±4 percentage points at the 95% confidence level. For results based on the total sample of 802 non-Hispanic blacks, the margin of sampling error is ±5 percentage points at the 95% confidence level. For results based on the sample of 857 non-Hispanic whites, the margin of sampling error is ±5

percentage points at the 95% confidence level. All reported margins of sampling error include computed design effects for weighting.

August 03, 2015
MAJORITY OF AMERICANS SAY THEY TRY TO AVOID DRINKING SODA

by Rebecca Riffkin

Story Highlights

- *Two in 10 Americans report they include soda in their diet*
- *Little difference between choices of regular soda or diet*
- *Large change in Americans avoiding soda since 2002*

WASHINGTON, D.C.—Americans are more likely to say they actively try to avoid including soda or pop in their diet than 14 other foods, including sugar and fat. At least six in 10 U.S. adults say they are trying to steer clear of these drinks—regardless of whether they are diet or regular.

Most Americans Say They Avoid Soda in Their Diets

Thinking about the food you eat, for each of the following please say if it is something you actively try to include in your diet, something you actively try to avoid or something you don't think about either way.

	% Include	% Avoid	% Don't think about
Diet soda or pop ^	22	62	14
Regular soda or pop ^	22	61	16
Sugar	28	50	22
Fat	25	47	27
Salt	35	39	25
Carbohydrates	44	25	29
Beef and other red meat	63	20	17
Gluten-free foods	21	17	58
Grains such as bread, cereal, pasta and rice	70	14	15
Dairy products	68	13	17
Organic foods	44	11	44
Fish and other seafood	76	10	13
Chicken and other poultry	83	4	12
Vegetables	93	2	5
Fruits	90	1	8

Sorted by % Avoid
^ Indicates asked of half sample
July 8-12, 2015

GALLUP

Americans are most likely to say they actively try to include fruits and vegetables in their diet. Gallup asked 1,009 Americans about the foods they try to include or avoid in their diet as part of its annual Consumption Habits poll in July. Previous Gallup reports have focused on Americans' avoidance or inclusion of gluten-free foods and salt or fat.

Americans appear to be aware of the health benefits of fruits and vegetables, with at least nine in 10 saying they actively try to include each in their diet. At least three in four Americans also say they try to include chicken and fish in their diet, meats that nutrition experts often recommend to help with heart health, in lieu of beef and other red meat—which nevertheless, 63% of Americans still actively try to include in their diet.

In 2015, there are only three types of food that 50% or more of Americans say they actively try to avoid—diet and regular soda and sugar. Historically, Gallup has asked Americans generally about their intake of "soda or pop," but in this year's poll, Gallup asked half of those surveyed about "diet soda or pop" and asked the other half about "regular soda or pop." It appears that Americans don't distinguish between the two, despite the higher sugar and calorie content in regular soda than in diet soda. The results were nearly identical, with 61% reporting they try to avoid regular soda and 62% diet soda.

Regardless of question wording, Americans' attitudes toward including soda in their diet are unchanged since last year. But Americans are far more likely now (61%) than in 2002 (41%) to say they are trying to avoid soda. Likewise, the percentage of Americans who actively include soda in their diet has dropped since 2002, although not as drastically, from 36% to 22%.

Americans' Dietary Habits of Drinking Soda

Thinking about the food you eat, for each of the following please say if it is something you actively try to include in your diet, something you actively try to avoid or something you don't think about either way. How about soda or pop?

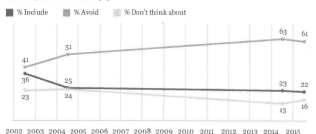

■ % Include   ■ % Avoid   ■ % Don't think about

Specified regular vs. diet soda or pop in 2015, regular soda findings shown

GALLUP'

Americans have also become more likely to report avoiding sugar, from 43% in 2002 to 50% in 2015—although this change is less pronounced than the change in attitudes about soda. Americans' likelihood to either include or avoid fruits, vegetables, chicken, fish or red meat has been largely stable since 2002.

Bottom Line

Americans appear to be aware of the health benefits of eating fruits, vegetables and lean meats such as chicken and fish, with the vast majority of Americans reporting they try to include them in their diet. However, Americans do not always achieve this goal, with 57.7% reporting they had five or more servings of fruits and vegetables at least four days of the last week in 2013.

A majority of Americans report they try to avoid drinking soda, regardless of whether it is regular or diet. This is a drastic change from just over a decade ago. Consumers may say they are trying to avoid soda because of the high-calorie and high-sugar content in regular soda, or the fears of artificial sweeteners used in diet soda. While some doctors agree that a can or two of soda a day isn't harmful to one's health, most advise that lower-calorie and natural beverages, such as skim milk or water, may be healthier choices.

Historical data on these items are available in Gallup Analytics.

Survey Methods

Results for this Gallup poll are based on telephone interviews conducted July 8–12, 2015, with a random sample of 1,009 adults, aged

18 and older, living in all 50 U.S. states and the District of Columbia. For results based on the total sample of national adults, the margin of sampling error is ±4 percentage points at the 95% confidence level. All reported margins of sampling error include computed design effects for weighting.

August 04, 2015

AMERICANS' SATISFACTION WITH WAY BLACKS TREATED TUMBLES

by Jeffrey M. Jones

Story Highlights

- *49% satisfied with way blacks treated, down from 62%*
- *No change in satisfaction with way other groups treated*
- *Increased perception blacks treated unfairly in many situations*

PRINCETON, N.J.—Americans' satisfaction with the way blacks are treated has declined to a new low in Gallup's 15-year trend, now at 49%. This is a sharp drop from two years ago, when 62% were satisfied. Blacks, whites and Hispanics all show significant declines since 2013 in their satisfaction with the treatment of blacks in the U.S.

Satisfied With the Way Blacks Are Treated in U.S. Society

% Very satisfied + somewhat satisfied

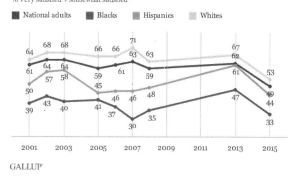

■ National adults   ■ Blacks   ■ Hispanics   ■ Whites

GALLUP'

The results are based on Gallup's 2015 Minority Rights and Relations poll, conducted June 15–July 10 with more than 2,000 national adults, including 800 non-Hispanic whites, 800 non-Hispanic blacks and 500 Hispanics. The drop in satisfaction likely reflects the effects of several high-profile and deadly incidents in the last year involving white police officers and black citizens.

Currently, 33% of blacks are satisfied with the way blacks are treated in society, a decline from 47% in 2013. This decline has occurred even though blacks themselves are no more likely than two years ago to report being treated unfairly in various situations because of their race, including dealing with the police. Blacks' satisfaction levels with the treatment of blacks are now similar to what they were in 2007 and 2008.

A slim majority of whites remain satisfied with the way blacks are treated, but this is down from 67% in 2013. Hispanics' satisfaction with the treatment of blacks has fallen from 61% to 44% over the same time period and is back to where it was in the latter years of George W. Bush's administration.

Politically, Democrats are increasingly less satisfied than Republicans or independents with the treatment of blacks, though all groups' satisfaction levels are down significantly. Democratic satisfaction with the treatment of blacks has fallen from 51% in 2013 to 31% today, while independent levels are down nine percentage points (from 64% to 55%), and Republican levels are down 10 points (from 76% to 66%).

Americans' declining dissatisfaction with the treatment of blacks is specific to blacks and not part of a broader reassessment of how minority groups are treated in the U.S. The poll finds no meaningful change in Americans' satisfaction with the way Hispanics, Asians, Arabs, immigrants and women are treated.

Satisfied With the Way Groups in Society Are Treated, 2013 vs. 2015
Based on national adults

	2013	2015	Change
	%	%	pct. pts.
Hispanics	58	58	0
Asians	78	77	-1
Immigrants	46	44	-2
Arabs	51	49	-2
Women	68	64	-4
Blacks	62	49	-13

GALLUP

The net result of these changes is that Americans now are only slightly more satisfied with the treatment of blacks (49%) than with the treatment of immigrants (44%). Americans are equally satisfied with the treatment of blacks and Arabs. Two years ago, Americans were about equally satisfied with the treatment of blacks and Hispanics, but now a significant gap exists in views of the treatment of the two largest U.S. minority groups.

Americans Perceive Greater Mistreatment of Blacks in Specific Situations

Americans are more likely to believe that blacks are treated unfairly in various situations now than they were in 2007, when Gallup last asked the question. These changes in perceptions include an increase of six points in views that blacks are treated unfairly in dealing with the police to 10-point increases in unfair treatment while shopping. Overall, Americans are most likely to perceive blacks are treated unfairly by police, with 43% saying this occurs.

Changes in Perceptions That Blacks Are Treated Less Fairly in Various Situations, 2007 vs. 2015
Based on national adults

	2007	2015	Change
	%	%	pct. pts.
In dealing with the police, such as traffic incidents	37	43	+6
In stores downtown or in the shopping mall	19	29	+10
On the job or at work	18	26	+8
In neighborhood shops	15	25	+10
In restaurants, bars, theaters or other entertainment places	16	23	+7

GALLUP

Gallup has asked these items periodically since 1997. The 2015 readings for each item are the highest in Gallup's trends.

Much of the increase in perceived unfair treatment of blacks is driven by changes in whites' opinions; in most cases, blacks show modest change on these items since 2007. But blacks were far more likely then, and now, than whites and Hispanics to perceive that blacks are treated unfairly.

Changes in Perceptions That Blacks Are Treated Less Fairly in Various Situations, 2007 vs. 2015
Based on race/ethnic group

	2007	2015	Change
	%	%	pct. pts.
NON-HISPANIC WHITES			
In dealing with the police	31	34	+3
In stores downtown/shopping malls	13	25	+12
On the job or at work	12	20	+8
In neighborhood shops	9	20	+11
In restaurants, bars, theaters, etc.	11	18	+7
NON-HISPANIC BLACKS			
In dealing with the police	73	73	0
In stores downtown/shopping malls	47	52	+5
On the job or at work	53	56	+3
In neighborhood shops	42	46	+4
In restaurants, bars, theaters, etc.	40	42	+2
HISPANICS			
In dealing with the police	51	54	+3
In stores downtown/shopping malls	30	25	-5
On the job or at work	28	29	+1
In neighborhood shops	27	31	+4
In restaurants, bars, theaters, etc.	29	28	-1

GALLUP

Seven in 10 blacks believe that blacks are treated unfairly when dealing with the police, more than double the percentage of whites (34%) who say this. A majority of Hispanics, 54%, agree that blacks are treated unfairly by police.

Implications

Over the last year, several incidents of white police officers killing black suspects they were trying to apprehend have made national news. The effects of those incidents have led to an increase in the U.S. public's perceptions of race relations as the most important problem in the country, a decline in confidence in the police and a significant decrease in Americans' satisfaction with the way blacks are treated in the U.S. Americans are also now more likely to perceive that blacks are treated unfairly in various situations, including dealing with the police, but also at work, when shopping and when visiting restaurants and other establishments.

Blacks themselves would have firsthand knowledge of whether they have been treated unfairly because of their race. And blacks are no more likely now than they were two years ago to say they have been treated unfairly by the police, when at work or when shopping. This suggests much of the rise in concern with the way blacks are treated results from the high-profile media attention focused on the relatively small number of incidents involving black men and white police officers—rather than a broader pattern of mistreatment of all or most blacks.

But the news media are shining a light on troubling incidents of mistreatment of blacks. This media spotlight may lead to efforts to help reduce unfair treatment of blacks by police but also by society more generally. Greater efforts to ensure that blacks are treated fairly could in turn lead to decreases in the percentage of blacks who say they personally have been mistreated, as well as in the percentage of blacks, and all Americans, who perceive blacks get unfair treatment.

Survey Methods

Results for this Gallup poll are based on telephone interviews conducted June 15–July 10, 2015, with a random sample of 2,296 adults, aged 18 and older, living in all 50 U.S. states and the District of Columbia. All respondents had been previously interviewed in the Gallup Daily tracking survey and agreed to be re-contacted by Gallup. For results based on the total sample of national adults, the margin of sampling error is ±4 percentage points at the 95% confidence level.

For results based on the total sample of 857 non-Hispanic whites, the margin of sampling error is ±5 percentage points at the 95% confidence level.

For results based on the total sample of 802 non-Hispanic blacks, the margin of sampling error is ±5 percentage points at the 95% confidence level.

For results based on the total sample of 508 Hispanics, the margin of sampling error is ±7 percentage points at the 95% confidence level.

August 06, 2015
REPUBLICANS VIEW RUBIO, WALKER MOST POSITIVELY ON DEBATE EVE

by Frank Newport

Story Highlights

- *Rubio and Walker at top of list with 38% net favorable ratings*
- *Kasich has lowest familiarity of any candidate; stands to gain*
- *Christie and Trump have less positive images than others in debate*

PRINCETON, N.J.—Just ahead of the first official Republican debate of the 2016 presidential campaign, Republicans give Marco Rubio and Scott Walker the highest net favorable ratings among any of the major 16 candidates running for their party's nomination, followed by Ben Carson, Mike Huckabee and Rick Perry. At the other end of the spectrum, George Pataki, Lindsey Graham and Chris Christie have the lowest net favorable ratings.

Republican Candidates' Familiarity and Image Among Republicans/Leaners
Rank ordered by net favorable

	Favorable	Unfavorable	Net favorable	Familiarity
	%	%	(pct. pts.)	%
Marco Rubio	52	14	+38	66
Scott Walker	45	7	+38	52
Ben Carson	42	7	+35	49
Mike Huckabee	53	20	+33	73
Rick Perry	51	19	+32	70
Ted Cruz	47	18	+29	65
Bobby Jindal	37	9	+28	46
Jeb Bush	52	27	+25	79
Rand Paul	43	20	+23	63
Rick Santorum	40	21	+19	61
Donald Trump	55	37	+18	92
Carly Fiorina	26	10	+16	36
John Kasich	25	10	+15	35
Chris Christie	35	34	+1	69
Lindsey Graham	23	28	-5	51
George Pataki	16	25	-9	41

July 22–Aug. 4, 2015

GALLUP

These data are based on the latest two weeks of interviewing conducted via Gallup Daily tracking, July 22–Aug. 4, with each candidate rated by more than 1,000 Republicans and Republican-leaning independents. Former Virginia Gov. Jim Gilmore entered the race last week and is now included in Gallup's candidate tracking, but his entry was too late for him to be included in these analyses.

These results provide an important update on each candidate's fundamental standing among national Republicans in the election race. As was true two weeks ago, Republicans' familiarity with these candidates varies widely, as do their ratings of each candidate. The table at the end of this article shows the trends in candidate familiarity and net favorable ratings.

The net favorable measure, which simply subtracts the percentage who have an unfavorable opinion from the percentage who have a favorable opinion, is a useful, shorthand way of determining a candidate's relative popularity among their fellow Republicans nationwide. This sentiment is not necessarily related to the candidates' name recognition. Both Walker and Carson, for example, are familiar to only about half of Republicans, yet are viewed quite positively by those who know them. On the other hand, Donald Trump and Christie are much better known, but have well-below-average net favorable scores, with Trump sixth from the bottom on that dimension and Christie third from the bottom.

Other candidates such as Rubio, Huckabee and Perry are both well known and well liked. Graham and Pataki provide a mirror image of that positioning; both are not well known and not well liked among those who know them.

Kasich, Carson and Walker, With Low Familiarity, Stand to Gain From Inclusion in the Debate

The major event in the Republican campaign at this juncture is the inaugural set of debates to be broadcast on Fox News on Thursday. Only 10 candidates will be included in the prime-time debate at 9 p.m. EST; the other seven will debate at an earlier 5 p.m. EST time slot. Fox News determined which candidates would be included in the desirable prime-time event based on an average of national Republican horse race polls. In the end, small differences in average standings among candidates at the low end of the standings determined who ultimately was included in the debate.

Ohio Gov. John Kasich is one candidate who has a great deal to gain by his inclusion in the debate. He was one of the last to announce his candidacy and is familiar to only 35% of Republicans—putting him dead last on this dimension among the 16 candidates Gallup has tracked. His net favorable rating puts him in the bottom half of all candidates. The debate thus provides an important opportunity for him to begin to become better known and more of a player in the campaign.

Physician Carson and former Wisconsin Gov. Walker are also positioned to enhance their relatively weak name identifications, although both are already well liked by those who know them, putting them near the top in terms of their net favorable rating.

Christie and Trump Face Challenge of More Negative Images

New Jersey Gov. Christie does not have a major name identification issue; he is familiar to 69% of Republicans. But Christie has an image problem, with a net favorable rating of +1, meaning that almost as many Republicans who know him have an unfavorable opinion as a favorable opinion. Christie's challenge in the debate, therefore, will be to change his image rather than to become better known.

To a degree, Trump faces the same challenge as Christie. Trump has, by far, the highest familiarity of any of the 16 candidates, but a familiarity that is based more on his history as a businessman and media personality than on anything political. Trump also has the highest unfavorable rating—37%—of any of the candidates. All eyes will be on Trump, who will occupy center stage during the debate, and thus he will have the opportunity to define himself as a candidate to the millions of Americans who, for the first time, will see him in a traditional political setting.

There is some good news for Trump in the latest update of these data. Despite the extraordinary attention he has received in the media in recent weeks, much of it negative, his standing among Republicans has held steady. His current +18 net favorable rating is essentially the same as his +20 net favorable rating two weeks ago.

Perry and Jindal Are Not in Debate, Despite Being Well Liked by Republicans

Former Texas Gov. Perry and, to a lesser degree, Louisiana Gov. Bobby Jindal are two candidates with a significant discrepancy between their images among Republicans and their failure to be included in the prime-time debate. Both are in the top 10 candidates based on net favorability. Perry essentially ties Huckabee with a +32 net favorability rating, based on 51% favorable and 19% unfavorable ratings, and Jindal has a +28 rating, higher than five candidates who will be in the debate (Bush, Paul, Trump, Kasich and Christie). Perry and Huckabee, both former governors from adjacent states, have not only similar net favorable scores but also similar familiarity scores. Huckabee is in the prime-time debate while Perry is not.

Bottom Line

The effect of this much-anticipated debate on the images of the Republican candidates is unpredictable at this point. Trump's presence and the anticipation surrounding the question of who would make it into the prime-time debate will almost certainly mean that the audience will be larger than is typically the case for an event like this six months before the first votes are cast.

Many media observers will focus on highlighting gaffes or high-visibility sound bites that will help them write headlines about who may have won or lost the debate. But the long-term effects of these types of events are not always clear. It's possible that not much will change, particularly given the constrained format in which candidates have only 60 seconds to answer the moderators' questions. In any event, the impact of this particular debate on making lesser-known candidates better known, improving the images of those who are less popular or perhaps hurting the images of other candidates will be measurable in the days that follow Thursday night's event.

Survey Methods

Results for this Gallup poll are based on telephone interviews conducted July 22–Aug. 4, 2015, on the Gallup U.S. Daily survey, with a random sample of 3,147 adults who identify as or lean Republican, aged 18 and older, living in all 50 U.S. states and the District of Columbia. Each candidate was in turn rated by a random subset of Republicans during this time period, with the sample sizes rating each candidate ranging from 1,022 to 1,115. For results based on these samples of Republicans, the margin of sampling error is ±4 percentage points at the 95% confidence level.

August 06, 2015
BLACKS DIVIDED ON WHETHER POLICE TREAT MINORITIES FAIRLY

by Art Swift

Story Highlights

- *52% of blacks say police treat minorities fairly; 48% unfairly*
- *More blacks than whites, Hispanics want greater police presence*
- *Those who see unfair treatment split over need for more cops*

WASHINGTON, D.C.—Black Americans are divided over whether their local police treat racial minorities, including blacks, fairly or unfairly. Fifty-two percent of blacks say local police treat these minorities "very fairly" or "fairly," while 48% say the police act "unfairly" or "very unfairly." In contrast, 73% of national adults, 71% of Hispanics and 78% of whites say the police treat racial minorities fairly.

Fair and Unfair Treatment by the Police

How would you say local police in your area treat racial minorities including blacks -- very fairly, fairly, unfairly (or) very unfairly?

	% Very fairly	% Fairly	% Unfairly	% Very unfairly
NATIONAL TOTAL	23	50	20	5
Non-Hispanic Whites	29	49	16	3
Blacks	8	44	33	15
Hispanics	15	56	23	6

June 15–July 10, 2015

GALLUP

In the wake of high-profile incidents in the past year, including police action involving black Americans in Ferguson, Missouri, Staten Island and Baltimore, Americans have been accustomed to more media portrayals of alleged police brutality. Numerous black Americans have discussed their treatment by police, shining a light on an issue that has been gaining prominence in recent years. This is the first time Gallup has asked this question, so it is not possible to know whether these attitudes have changed from the past. However, prior Gallup research shows that blacks' confidence in police is a bit lower over the past two years, and that, more broadly, nonwhites' views of police officers as honest and ethical declined sharply last year.

More Blacks Than Whites Want Greater Police Presence

The Minority Rights and Relations Gallup survey conducted June 15–July 10, which included an expanded sample size of blacks and Hispanics, reveals that Americans have complex views of how police treat minorities and whether there should be a greater police presence in communities. More blacks (38%) say they want a greater police presence in their local communities than do whites (18%) or Americans more broadly (23%).

In general, though, majorities of these major groups profess wanting "no change" in the police presence in their local community. However, blacks are the least likely to say this at 51%, compared with Hispanics at 59% and whites at 74%. Only small percentages of any group say they want a smaller police presence than currently exists.

Greater Police Presence?
Which would you prefer to see in your local area -- a larger police presence than currently exists, no change (or) a smaller police presence than currently exists?

	% Larger	% No change	% Smaller
NATIONAL TOTAL	23	68	9
Non-Hispanic Whites	18	74	8
Blacks	38	51	10
Hispanics	30	59	10

GALLUP

Those Who Believe Minorities Treated Unfairly Split Over More Cops Needed

Americans who believe minorities have been treated unfairly are somewhat divided over whether there should be a greater police presence in their local communities. Nationally, 73% of adults who believe racial minorities are treated fairly by police say they want the same amount of police officers in their communities, but this drops to 53% among those who think minorities are treated unfairly. Thirty-one percent of the latter group want an increased police presence.

Most blacks who believe racial minorities are treated fairly by police prefer the police presence be kept the same (59%), while 33% want a larger police presence where they live. However, African Americans who say police treat minorities unfairly are divided, with 44% saying they want more police officers and 42% saying they want the same amount of cops in their local area. And U.S. Hispanics feel similarly to blacks—39% who say minorities are treated unfairly want greater police presence, and 40% want the same.

Police Presence and Treatment by Police
Comparing the national total, among blacks, among whites and among Hispanics

	% Treated fairly by police	% Treated unfairly by police
NATIONAL TOTAL		
Want larger police presence than currently	21	31
Want the same amount of police	73	53
Want smaller police presence than currently	7	14
BLACKS		
Want larger police presence than currently	33	44
Want the same amount of police	59	42
Want smaller police presence than currently	8	12
WHITES		
Want larger police presence than currently	18	21
Want the same amount of police	76	65
Want smaller police presence than currently	7	12
HISPANICS		
Want larger police presence than currently	27	39
Want the same amount of police	67	40
Want smaller police presence than currently	6	21

GALLUP

It is telling that among all groups—blacks, whites, Hispanics and overall national adults—who believe minorities have been treated unfairly, relatively small percentages want a smaller police presence in their local communities. This could mean that despite high-profile incidents, Americans recognize that police are needed in their area.

This suggests that while Americans who think minorities are being treated unfairly may want an increased police presence, it is unclear whether they mean more manpower in their communities or perhaps different types of officers, in demeanor or racial makeup.

Bottom Line

Previous Gallup analysis shows that blacks do not feel more mistreated in dealings with police in the last 30 days than they did when asked the same question in 2013. However, when asked a more general question, African Americans are divided on their opinions about whether police treat minorities, including blacks, fairly or unfairly. Whites are more likely to say police treat racial minorities fairly. As calls for police reform in certain segments of the population continue, it is interesting that Americans are not calling for less of a police presence, but rather either the same amount of officers or more officers. This may mean that Americans understand the need and value of police, but may want a different type of police force in the future, or just a change in behavior among current officers.

Survey Methods

Results for this Gallup poll are based on telephone interviews conducted June 15–July 10, 2015, with a random sample of 2,296 adults, aged 18 and older, living in all 50 U.S. states and the District of Columbia. All respondents had been previously interviewed in the Gallup Daily tracking survey and agreed to be re-contacted by Gallup. For results based on the total sample of national adults, the margin of sampling error is ±5 percentage points at the 95% confidence level. For results based on the total sample of 857 non-Hispanic whites, the maximum margin of sampling error is ±5 percentage points. For results based on sample of 802 non-Hispanic blacks, the maximum margin of sampling error is ±5 percentage points.

August 06, 2015
AMERICANS' VIEWS OF BLACK-WHITE RELATIONS DETERIORATE

by Jeffrey M. Jones

Story Highlights

- *47% say black-white relations are good, down from 70%*
- *Blacks' and whites' views also much more negative*
- *58% of Americans still optimistic about future relations*

PRINCETON, N.J.—Americans rate black-white relations much more negatively today than they have at any point in the past 15 years. Currently, 47% say relations between blacks and whites are "very good" or "somewhat good," a steep decline from 70% in 2013. Whites' positive ratings of black-white relations since 2013 have nose-dived by 27 percentage points, from 72% to 45%, while blacks show a smaller but still sizable drop of 15 points, from 66% to 51%.

The results are based on Gallup's Minority Rights and Relations poll, which interviewed more than 2,000 Americans, including more than 800 non-Hispanic whites and more than 800 non-His-panic blacks from June 15 through July 10.

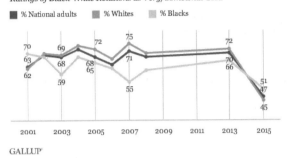

Ratings of Black-White Relations as Very/Somewhat Good

■ % National adults   ■ % Whites   ■ % Blacks

GALLUP

Americans have generally been quite positive about black-white relations in the 15 years Gallup has asked this question. Prior to this year, between 63% and 72% of Americans rated relations between blacks and whites as very good or somewhat good.

Whites and blacks are generally in accord on the state of relations, with 45% of whites and 51% of blacks rating them as good. Whites and blacks have generally had similar and quite positive views over the past 15 years, with a notable gap only in 2007, a year in which blacks' ratings on a variety of measures were more negative.

The most likely explanation for the deterioration in Americans' perceptions of the health of black-white relations since 2013 are the multiple widely reported incidents in which black citizens were killed by the actions of white police officers. Several of those incidents sparked protests or riots.

Notably, as Americans' perceptions of black-white relations have become sharply more negative, their ratings of relations among other racial and ethnic groups are unchanged from 2013, the last time Gallup asked the question.

Ratings of Intergroup Relations as Very/Somewhat Good

Based on national adults

	2013	2015	Change
	%	%	pct. pts.
Whites/Blacks	70	47	-23
Whites/Asians	87	86	-1
Whites/Hispanics	70	69	-1
Blacks/Hispanics	60	60	0

GALLUP

As a result, Americans are now the most negative in their evaluations of black-white relations since Gallup began tracking this measure. In 2013, they were the least positive about black-Hispanic relations. Historically, Americans have believed white-Asian relations to be the most positive.

Americans Remain Optimistic About Black-White Relations in the Future

Even as Americans are much more negative about the state of black-white relations today than they were two years ago, they remain more optimistic than pessimistic about the long-term outlook for the two groups getting along. In fact, the 58% who say a "solution will eventually be worked out" to improve black-white relations is unchanged from 2013. Forty-one percent remain pessimistic about the future, saying relations between blacks and whites "will always be a problem."

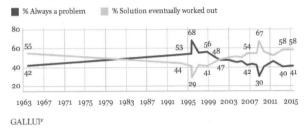

Do you think that relations between blacks and whites will always be a problem for the United States, or that a solution will eventually be worked out?

Based on national adults

■ % Always a problem   ■ % Solution eventually worked out

GALLUP

Americans were more optimistic than pessimistic about the future of race relations the first time the question was asked, by NORC, in 1963. Gallup updated the question several times in the 1990s, a decade marked by the Los Angeles race riots and racially charged court cases, including the Rodney King beating trial and the O. J. Simpson murder trial. Throughout that decade, Americans were more likely to believe that black-white relations would always be a problem than to believe a solution would be worked out. That included an October 1995 Gallup poll conducted shortly after Simpson was acquitted on criminal charges, when a record 68% of Americans said black-white relations would always be a problem.

More recently, Americans have been more optimistic than pessimistic that a solution to black-white tensions would eventually be worked out. This includes a record 67% in November 2008 just after Barack Obama became the first black person to be elected president.

Since 1999, blacks have consistently been more skeptical than whites that a solution to black-white relations will eventually be worked out. Currently, 43% of blacks and 59% of whites predict this will occur. Whites' views have not changed in the past two years, while blacks are slightly less likely now (43%) than in 2013 (48%) to believe a solution to black-white problems will eventually be found.

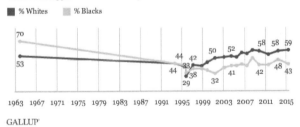

Belief That a Solution to Black-White Relations Will Eventually Be Worked Out, by Race

Trend including polls with sufficient sample sizes of blacks

■ % Whites   ■ % Blacks

GALLUP

Implications

Recent events have likely caused Americans to dramatically re-evaluate their views of the status of black-white relations in the U.S. Americans are much less likely now than two years ago to say relations between blacks and whites are good. At the same time, there has been no change in their generally positive views of relations between blacks and other racial or ethnic groups, and between whites and other racial or ethnic groups. Also, blacks show little change in their overall life satisfaction or reports of being personally treated unfairly because of their race, suggesting that while the public as a whole may be more dissatisfied with the treatment of blacks and see black-white relations are deteriorating, blacks are not experiencing much of a change in their daily life experiences.

Despite their more negative views of the state of black and white relations in the U.S. today, Americans' mostly positive views of the future of black-white relations are unshaken. A majority remains more optimistic than pessimistic that one day black-white relations will no longer be problematic, though whites are more likely to believe this than blacks.

Certainly, what Americans read, hear and see in the media affects their views, and the frequent reports of trouble between black citizens and white law enforcement over the past year have likely caused Americans—black and white—to downgrade their views of relations.

A key question is how long the downturn in perceptions of current black-white relations will persist. Not much will change if there continue to be incidents in which white police officers' actions result in serious harm or death to blacks. But if those incidents stop occurring, they will no longer be top-of-mind for most Americans when asked to assess the state of black-white relations. Should that occur, and absent of any other prominent examples of problematic incidents between blacks and whites, Americans' views of relations between the two groups may once again become positive.

Survey Methods

Results for this Gallup poll are based on telephone interviews conducted June 15–July 10, 2015, with a random sample of 2,296 adults, aged 18 and older, living in all 50 U.S. states and the District of Columbia. All respondents had been previously interviewed in the Gallup Daily tracking survey and agreed to be re-contacted by Gallup. For results based on the total sample of national adults, the margin of sampling error is ±4 percentage points at the 95% confidence level.

For results based on the total sample of 857 non-Hispanic whites, the margin of sampling error is ±5 percentage points at the 95% confidence level.

For results based on the total sample of 802 non-Hispanic blacks, the margin of sampling error is ±5 percentage points at the 95% confidence level.

For results based on the total sample of 508 Hispanics, the margin of sampling error is ±7 percentage points at the 95% confidence level.

August 07, 2015
MANY SMALL BUSINESSES UNAWARE OF PENDING EMV LIABILITY SHIFT

by Coleen McMurray and Frank Newport

Story Highlights

- Many owners unaware of the pending EMV credit card standards
- Quarter 3 index is at 59, down from 71 in Quarter 1
- Small-business owners less positive on revenues

PRINCETON, N.J.—Despite the serious consequences for small-business owners if they don't follow new rules that take effect this fall for credit cards, the latest Wells Fargo/Gallup Small Business Index survey finds that only 32% of owners are aware of the pending changes.

Wells Fargo/Gallup Small Business Index

Have you heard or read about the new EMV liability shift coming in October 2015 regarding point-of-sale credit card purchases and chip-enabled credit card terminals?

	Yes
	%
All owners	32
Accept credit cards	49
Do not accept credit cards	23

GALLUP

The new set of credit card liability rules for businesses will take effect in October. These rules specify that businesses that do not upgrade to credit card equipment that can read new, chip-enabled credit cards will be liable for fraud and security breaches.

One of the reasons for the small-business owners' low awareness of the pending "EMV" rules (which stands for Europay, MasterCard and Visa) is that only 35% of owners in the current Wells Fargo/Gallup Small Business Index, conducted July 6–10, report that they accept point-of-sale credit card payments for purchases. Awareness of the EMV mandate is higher among this group than among those who do not accept such payments, as would be expected, but even among those who accept credit cards, awareness is 49%, compared with 23% among those who do not. Thus, about half of small-business owners who accept credit cards are not aware of the major changes forthcoming this fall.

It appears that a majority of small-business owners who accept credit cards but who do not have chip-enabled technology—about seven in 10—are, at this point, in no rush to comply with the mandate; 29% plan to comply by October, while the majority plan to comply either at a later time (34%) or do not plan to upgrade their systems to comply (21%).

All small-business owners were asked if they believe this liability shift will provide improved protection from fraud—the shift's major objective. Small-business owners are divided in their opinions—42% believe it will greatly or somewhat improve protection, and 42% believe it will improve protection not very much or not at all.

Wells Fargo/Gallup Small Business Index

Just your opinion, how much of an improved protection from fraud will this liability shift provide businesses? Greatly improved, somewhat improved, not very improved or not at all improved?

	Greatly/Somewhat improved	Not very/Not at all improved
	%	%
July 6-10, 2015	42	42

GALLUP

U.S. Small-Business Owners' Optimism Trends Down

U.S. small-business owners continued to be less positive about the economic health of their companies in the third quarter. Optimism declined modestly for the second consecutive quarter this year following a significant jump at the end of 2014 and in early 2015.

The overall index score, which measures small-business owners' views of the economic condition of their companies, is now at 59, down from 71 in the first quarter and 64 in the second. The last time the index saw two consecutive declines was in the third and fourth quarters of 2012. Despite the drop in the current quarter, the index score is still considerably higher than it was in the third quarter of 2014 (49) and in the third quarter of 2013 (25).

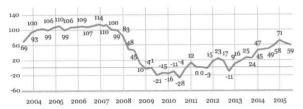

Wells Fargo/Gallup Small Business Index

The Small Business Index consists of owners' ratings of their business' current situation and their expectations for the next 12 months, measured in terms of their overall financial situation, revenue, cash flow, capital spending, number of jobs and ease of obtaining credit.

Index conducted since August 2003 and quarterly from December 2003-July 2015

GALLUP

Several factors may have contributed to the decrease in optimism this quarter:

- Two consecutive drops in small-business owners' positive reports of revenue. In the July survey, 39% of small-business owners reported that their company's revenues increased over the past 12 months, down significantly from 49% in January.
- Slight declines in reports of capital spending. Fewer small-business owners, 25%, plan to increase capital spending in the next 12 months than said the same in April (29%).

Survey Methods

Results are based on telephone interviews with 600 U.S. small-business owners in all 50 states, conducted July 6–10, 2015. The margin of sampling error is ±4 percentage points at the 95% confidence level.

August 07, 2015

AMERICANS LESS POSITIVE ABOUT BLACK CIVIL RIGHTS PROGRESS

by Justin McCarthy

Story Highlights

- *Fewer Americans say black civil rights have improved*
- *Blacks less likely than whites to see improvement*
- *Four in 10 say new civil rights laws needed*

WASHINGTON, D.C.—Americans still widely believe that civil rights for blacks have improved during their lifetime, but the 76% who say this is down from 87% in 2013. Meanwhile, the percentage of Americans who say the situation stayed the same or has worsened (23%) is the highest Gallup has ever found.

These data are from a June 15–July 10 Gallup poll that asked American adults various questions about the state of civil rights for blacks in the U.S. The poll was taken after a year of high-profile deaths of young, black men at the hands of white police officers.

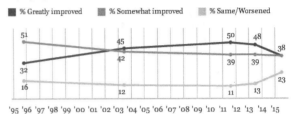

Americans' Views on Progress in Civil Rights for Blacks in the U.S.

Thinking back over your lifetime, how do you feel civil rights for blacks have changed in this country -- would you say the situation has greatly improved, somewhat improved, stayed pretty much the same, somewhat worsened or greatly worsened?

Most recent result based on poll conducted June 15-July 10, 2015

GALLUP

Americans were most positive about civil rights for blacks in 2011, when half said the situation had greatly improved and about four in 10 (39%) said they had somewhat improved. Only 11% said they had stayed the same or worsened.

Only a few years later, more than twice as many Americans (23%) feel civil rights for blacks have stayed the same or have worsened over the course of their lifetimes. Despite this record-high negative view, most Americans feel civil rights have gotten at least marginally better.

Blacks and Whites View the State of Civil Rights for Blacks Differently

There have not been large differences in the percentages of whites and blacks who think black civil rights have improved either greatly or somewhat. But a closer look at the data shows that whites are more likely to fall into the "greatly improved" camp, while blacks tend to believe civil rights have "somewhat improved." Currently, 43% of whites say civil rights for blacks have improved greatly and 36% say somewhat improved, while among blacks, 21% say greatly improved and 49% say somewhat.

Meanwhile, blacks (30%) remain more likely than whites (20%) to say the situation has stayed the same or worsened to some degree.

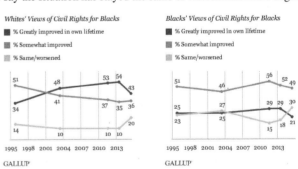

GALLUP   GALLUP

Though majorities of both races feel the situation has improved to some degree, both blacks and whites alike are less likely to feel this way than they have in any previous Gallup poll since 1995.

Hope for Future of Black Civil Rights Improvement Down Among Blacks, Whites

Both whites and blacks are now less likely than in 2008 to be hopeful about the state of civil rights for blacks in the future. Though majorities in the two racial groups believe the situation will have improved in 10 years, this view has fallen about 10 percentage points among both blacks (55%) and whites (67%) since 2008.

Sixty-seven percent of all Americans think black civil rights will improve in the next decade, down from 73% in 2008.

Americans' Views of the Future of Civil Rights Progress for Blacks

Now thinking ahead, 10 years from now, do you think civil rights for blacks will be -- [ROTATED: greatly improved, somewhat improved, the same, somewhat worse (or) much worse]?

% Will be greatly/somewhat improved

	2008	2015	Change
	%	%	(pct. pts.)
All Americans	73	67	-6
Blacks	65	55	-10
Whites	76	67	-9

Polls from June and July in 2008 and 2015

GALLUP

Need for New Civil Rights Laws Receives Greater Support in 2015

More Americans than in any poll over the past 22 years say that new civil rights laws are needed to reduce discrimination against blacks. Four in 10 Americans say new civil rights laws are necessary to protect blacks from discrimination, up from 27% in 2013, and essentially back to where it was in 1993, when Gallup first asked the question.

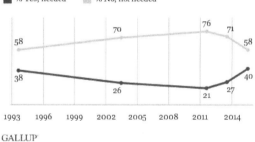

Americans' Views on Necessity of New Civil Rights Laws

Do you think new civil rights laws are needed to reduce discrimination against blacks, or not?

■ % Yes, needed   % No, not needed

GALLUP

A majority of blacks have consistently called for new civil rights laws, though the percentage has varied over time. The current 69% who hold this view is essentially the same as in August 1993, after the federal civil rights trial of the officers who had severely beaten Rodney King.

Whites have consistently been less than half as likely as blacks to feel additional civil rights laws are necessary—currently, 31% say such laws should be passed—again, back to about what white attitudes were in 1993.

Bottom Line

Though the issue of black civil rights is not a new one, the highly publicized events of the past year or so have revived the national conversation on this topic and significantly affected Americans' view of it. And while whites and blacks may see the situation differently, their faith in an improvement of blacks' civil rights has suffered, though it remains much more positive than negative overall.

In some states and municipalities, body cameras for police officers have been proposed or implemented in response to questionable law enforcement activity. But few, if any, discernable pieces of state or federal legislation have emerged in the wake of the Black Lives Matter movement. If a proposed law to improve the state of black civil rights gains any traction, it could stand a better chance now than in the past, as Americans are more amenable to efforts aimed at improvement than they have been, though this remains the minority view.

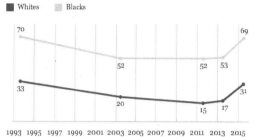

Blacks' and Whites' Views on Necessity of New Civil Rights Laws

Do you think new civil rights laws are needed to reduce discrimination against blacks, or not?

% Yes, needed

■ Whites   Blacks

GALLUP

In the meantime, elected officials and law enforcement alike are working through a sociopolitical landscape that is full of racial tension, and Americans' shifting outlooks on the issue are indicative of this environment.

Survey Methods

Results for this Gallup poll are based on telephone interviews conducted June 15–July 10, 2015, with a random sample of 2,296 adults, aged 18 and older, living in all 50 U.S. states and the District of Columbia. All respondents had been previously interviewed in the Gallup Daily tracking survey and agreed to be re-contacted by Gallup. For results based on the total sample of national adults, the margin of sampling error is ±4 percentage points at the 95% confidence level. For results based on the total sample of whites, the margin of sampling error is ±5 percentage points at the 95% confidence level. For results based on the total sample of Hispanics, the margin of sampling error is ±7 percentage points at the 95% confidence level. For results based on the total sample of blacks, the margin of sampling error is ±5 percentage points at the 95% confidence level. All reported margins of sampling error include computed design effects for weighting.

August 10, 2015
CLINTON'S FAVORABILITY STRONG AMONG BLACK AMERICANS

by Justin McCarthy and Andrew Dugan

Story Highlights

- *Clinton's favorability with blacks towers over other Democrats'*
- *Most Republican candidates have negative image among blacks*

WASHINGTON, D.C.—Hillary Clinton enjoys an 80% favorable rating among U.S. blacks, while two Democratic challengers who have struggled in public exchanges with black activists, Vermont Sen. Bernie Sanders and former Maryland Gov. Martin O'Malley, suffer from low name recognition and favorability among blacks.

Favorable Ratings of Hillary Clinton vs. Other Democratic Candidates, Among Black Adults
Ranked by net favorable

	Favorable	Unfavorable	Familiar	Net favorable
	%	%	%	(pct. pts.)
Hillary Clinton	80	12	92	+68
Bernie Sanders	23	10	33	+13
Martin O'Malley	17	13	30	+4
Jim Webb	11	13	24	-2
Lincoln Chafee	8	11	19	-3

July 8-Aug. 8, 2015

GALLUP

These data come from an aggregated sample of data collected from Gallup's Daily tracking, conducted July 8–Aug. 8, 2015. During this time, two candidates, Sanders and O'Malley, had their campaign events disrupted by black political activists, which caused both candidates political angst.

None of Clinton's Democratic competitors, including former Virginia Sen. Jim Webb and former Rhode Island Gov. Lincoln Chafee, has even a 25% approval rating among blacks, and no more than a third of black adults are familiar with the candidates challenging Clinton for the party's nomination.

As a former Cabinet member to the first black U.S. president and as first lady to another president who received strong backing from blacks, Clinton is poised to inherit some degree of popularity with the black community, which has historically thrown its electoral support behind Democrats. But while Clinton may lead among the current declared candidates, if Vice President Joe Biden enters the race, it could threaten her dominant favorability among blacks, because Biden is nearly as well known as Clinton, and the black community views him quite positively.

GOP Challengers Struggle With Favorability, Name Recognition

Though the Republican Party has historically struggled to attract black voters in modern U.S. politics, there have been some efforts from the party and individual candidates to make their case to black Americans in 2016. But those have done little to alter blacks' positivity toward the GOP, and most GOP candidates for the party's nomination have a negative net favorability among U.S. black adults. Additionally, most GOP candidates are not well known among blacks, similar to their lower familiarity ratings among Americans more generally.

Just one GOP candidate enjoys a positive net favorable rating among black adults: retired neurosurgeon Dr. Ben Carson. Carson is also the sole black candidate of either party at this point in the race. Still, less than half of black Americans (40%) are familiar with Carson.

Because of former Virginia Gov. Jim Gilmore's recent entry into the GOP race, Gallup has not conducted enough interviews with black Americans to include data for him.

Favorable Ratings of GOP Presidential Candidates, Among Black Adults
Ranked by net favorable

	Favorable	Unfavorable	Familiar	Net favorable
	%	%	%	(pct. pts.)
Ben Carson	22	18	40	+4
George Pataki	16	19	35	-3
John Kasich	10	15	25	-5
Carly Fiorina	8	14	22	-6
Lindsey Graham	15	26	41	-11
Rand Paul	15	28	43	-13
Rick Santorum	14	27	41	-13
Chris Christie	23	38	61	-15
Scott Walker	8	25	33	-17
Marco Rubio	12	30	42	-18
Mike Huckabee	16	35	51	-19
Bobby Jindal	7	28	35	-21
Ted Cruz	11	34	45	-23
Rick Perry	13	41	54	-28
Jeb Bush	21	52	73	-31
Donald Trump	20	68	88	-48

July 8-Aug. 8, 2015

GALLUP

Though the black community views New Jersey Gov. Chris Christie and former Arkansas Gov. Mike Huckabee mostly unfavorably, they have the highest net favorability ratings among the candidates with whom a majority of blacks are familiar. This positions Christie and Huckabee better to make inroads with the black community as opposed to candidates such as former Texas Gov. Rick Perry and former Florida Gov. Jeb Bush, whom blacks view highly unfavorably—for example, a majority of blacks (52%) rate Bush unfavorably.

Hands down, Donald Trump is the candidate who will struggle most among blacks. Trump's familiarity among blacks is about on par with Clinton's, but he is deeply disliked. Nearly seven in 10 blacks have an unfavorable view of him—by far the highest negative opinion of any candidate.

Bottom Line

Though the 2016 Democratic primaries are still six months away and the general election more than a year away, Clinton is solidly positioned with blacks, given her high familiarity and positive ratings among the group. Although favorable ratings do not translate directly to electoral support, she fares arguably better among black voters than any other Democratic or Republican candidate at this point in the campaign. Competing Democrats would likely compete better with Clinton for the voting bloc if they boosted their name recognition and, at the same time, boosted their positive image.

Republicans, in contrast, would need to chip away at their poor image among blacks. But they may have a tough time making their case to blacks as to why their policy positions are beneficial to the black community. Several governors or former governors in the race, including Bush, Walker and Perry, have made efforts to limit or eliminate early voting and make the voting process more difficult in general—moves that are widely seen as a rebuff to blacks who don't usually vote for GOP candidates. And many of the candidates have been attacking the Affordable Care Act, even though the White House says it disproportionately benefits black Americans.

At first glance, it may seem impossible to compete with Clinton for the black vote, but a strategy of tapping into her reservoir of black support and eroding a sturdy leg of her base could make all the difference in a tight primary or the general election.

Survey Methods

Results for this Gallup poll are based on telephone interviews conducted July 8–Aug. 8, 2015, on the Gallup U.S. Daily survey, with a random sample of 1,684 black adults, aged 18 and older, living in all 50 U.S. states and the District of Columbia. Each candidate was rated by a random subset of respondents during this time period, with the sample sizes rating each candidate ranging from 414 to 490. For results based on these samples, the margin of sampling error is ±6 percentage points at the 95% confidence level.

August 10, 2015

IN U.S., UNINSURED RATES CONTINUE TO DROP IN MOST STATES

by Dan Witters

Story Highlights

• *Arkansas and Kentucky continue to set pace among states*
• *Medicaid expansion, state exchanges linked to greater reductions*
• *No state reported statistically significant increase in uninsured*

WASHINGTON, D.C.—Arkansas and Kentucky continue to have the sharpest reductions in their uninsured rates since the healthcare law took effect at the beginning of 2014. Oregon, Rhode Island and Washington join them as states that have at least a 10–percentage-point reduction in uninsured rates.

Ten States With Largest Reductions in Percentage of Uninsured, 2013 vs. First Half of 2015

"Do you have health insurance?" (% No)

State	% Uninsured, 2013	% Uninsured, first half of 2015	Change in uninsured (pct. pts.)	Medicaid expansion and/or state/ partnership exchange in 2014
Arkansas	22.5	9.1	-13.4	Both
Kentucky	20.4	9.0	-11.4	Both
Oregon	19.4	8.8	-10.6	Both
Rhode Island	13.3	2.7	-10.6	Both
Washington	16.8	6.4	-10.4	Both
California	21.6	11.8	-9.8	Both
West Virginia	17.6	8.3	-9.3	Both
Alaska	18.9	10.3	-8.6	Neither
Mississippi	22.4	14.2	-8.2	One
North Dakota	15.0	6.9	-8.1	One

Gallup-Healthways Well-Being Index

GALLUP

Seven of the 10 states with the greatest reductions in uninsured rates have expanded Medicaid and established a state-based marketplace exchange or state-federal partnership, while two have implemented one or the other. The marketplace exchanges opened on Oct. 1, 2013, with new insurance plans purchased during the last quarter of that year typically starting on Jan. 1, 2014. Medicaid expansion among initially participating states also began with the onset of

2014. As such, 2013 serves as a benchmark year for uninsured rates as they existed prior to the enactment of the two major mechanisms of the healthcare law.

Through the first half of 2015, there are now seven states with uninsured rates that are at or below 5%: Rhode Island, Massachusetts, Vermont, Minnesota, Iowa, Connecticut and Hawaii. Previously—from 2008 through 2014—Massachusetts had been the only state to be at or below this rate. No state, in turn, has reported a statistically significant increase in the percentage of uninsured thus far in 2015 compared with 2013. Nationwide, the uninsured rate fell from 17.3% in full-year 2013 to 11.7% in the first half of 2015.

These data, collected as part of the Gallup-Healthways Well-Being Index, are based on Americans' answers to the question, "Do you have health insurance coverage?" These state-level data are based on daily surveys conducted from January through June 2015 and include sample sizes that range from 232 randomly selected adult residents in Hawaii to more than 8,600 in California.

States That Have Embraced Multiple Parts of Health Law Continue to See More Improvement

Collectively, the uninsured rate in states that have chosen to expand Medicaid *and* set up their own state exchanges or partnerships in the health insurance marketplace has declined significantly more since 2013 than the rate in states that did not take these steps. The uninsured rate declined 7.1 points in the 22 states that implemented both of these measures by Dec. 31, 2014, compared with a 5.3-point drop across the 28 states that had implemented only one or neither of these actions.

Change in Uninsured Rate Between 2013 and First Half of 2015 Among States With Medicaid Expansion AND State Exchange/Partnership* Compared With All Others

State type	% Uninsured, 2013	% Uninsured, first half of 2015	Change in uninsured (pct. pts.)	% Reduction in uninsured rate
States with Medicaid expansion AND state exchange	16.0%	8.9%	-7.1	44%
States with only one or neither	18.7%	13.4%	-5.3	28%

Gallup-Healthways Well-Being Index
*As of Dec. 31, 2014

GALLUP

Although the 22 states that implemented both mechanisms before Jan. 1, 2015, had a lower uninsured rate to begin with, the 7.1-point drop is larger than what is reported among the other 28 states, and represents a 44% decline since 2013 in the uninsured rate among adults residing there. The 5.3-point drop in the 28 states that have implemented one or neither of the mechanisms represents a 28% decline in uninsured rates. Still, the difference in the *rate of decline* in uninsured rates between the two groups of states has now leveled off, and is unchanged relative to the same 1.8-point gap in the rate of decline measured in midyear 2014.

Implications

Americans' attitudes about the law known as "Obamacare" have become more positive in recent months, and now as many Americans approve of the law as disapprove, a shift from the last several years in which disapproval had consistently outweighed approval. This is happening as uninsured rates for most states have continued to decline. The Supreme Court ruling in the *King v. Burwell* case preserved subsidies for qualifying, low-income adults in states that have defaulted to the federal exchange rather than set up their own locally managed and promoted insurance marketplaces. That decision preserves health insurance for the millions of American adults in those states who have gained health insurance via the federal marketplace in the last two years.

A few states, including Utah, continue to consider Medicaid expansion under modified specifications from what is detailed in the Affordable Care Act. In addition to New Hampshire last August, Indiana and Pennsylvania each enacted Medicaid expansion in early 2015, becoming the 27th and 28th states (plus the District of Columbia) to expand Medicaid. Implementation of this type of expansion in Montana is pending federal waiver approval, and Alaska Gov. Bill Walker has announced that he will proceed with expansion, submitting plans on July 16 to accept federal funds for Medicaid, with a Sept. 1 target date for expansion. While some additional progress can be made, therefore, in the reduction of the uninsured rate via further Medicaid expansion, this mechanism for reduction has likely reached most of its potential unless additional states choose to implement it. As such, the marketplace exchanges that enable people to select and purchase their own plan directly from insurers will likely be the primary means by which the national uninsured rate would be reduced in the immediate future.

Change Analysis Rules

Some states have chosen to implement state-federal "partnership" exchanges, where states manage certain functions and make key decisions based on local market and demographic conditions. For the purposes of this analysis, these partnerships are included with the state exchanges. States with Medicaid expansion that occurred on or after Jan. 1, 2015, were excluded from the "States With Medicaid Expansion and State Exchange/Partnerships" group. For example, Pennsylvania, which manages a state-based exchange but did not enact Medicaid expansion until Jan. 1, 2015, is excluded, while New Hampshire—which expanded in August 2014 and has been excluded in previous analyses—qualified for this one. Four states—North Dakota, New Jersey, Ohio and Arizona—decided to expand Medicaid without also administering a state-based exchange or partnership, while several others continue to debate expansion. Pennsylvania enacted Medicaid expansion effective Jan. 1, 2015, and Indiana did so on Feb. 1. The District of Columbia, which has expanded Medicaid and has implemented a locally managed exchange, is not included in this analysis.

Survey Methods

Results are based on telephone interviews conducted Jan. 2–Dec. 30, 2013, and Jan. 2–June 30, 2015, as part of the Gallup-Healthways Well-Being Index, with a random sample of 178,072 adults in 2013 and 88,667 adults through the first half of 2015, aged 18 and older, living in all 50 U.S. states and the District of Columbia. The margin of sampling error is ±1 to ±2 percentage points for most states, but climbs as high as ±4 percentage points for 2015 results for states with small populations such as North Dakota, Wyoming, Vermont and Alaska. All reported margins of sampling error include computed design effects for weighting.

August 10, 2015
U.S. SUPPORT FOR INCREASED IMMIGRATION UP TO 25%

by Andrew Dugan

Story Highlights

- *Desired immigration level continues to divide public*
- *Share of country saying immigration should be increased is up*
- *Hispanics most likely to say immigration levels should be higher*

WASHINGTON, D.C.—The U.S. public demonstrates no clear preference on what U.S. immigration levels should be. On this contentious issue, 40% say levels should remain where they are, but only slightly fewer (34%) advocate a decrease in the stream of immigrants. One-quarter of the country prefers an increase in immigration levels, the sole response of the three to see a general increase in support over the past 15 years.

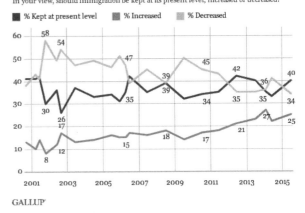

U.S. Adults' Preferences on U.S. Immigration Levels

In your view, should immigration be kept at its present level, increased or decreased?

These results come from Gallup's Minority Rights and Relations survey conducted June 15–July 10, which included an expanded sample of blacks and Hispanics. This practice is often referred to as "oversampling," and allows for a closer look at attitudes and opinions of minority groups whose representation in the sample of a standard poll might otherwise be too small for statistical analysis. In 2013, the last time a comparable methodology was used with respect to this question, U.S. adults reported largely similar attitudes. Gallup has also asked this question in several instances in polls that did not include an oversample of Hispanic and black adults, most recently in June 2014.

The longer-term trends since 2001 are unmistakable: U.S. adults' support for increased immigration is gradually growing. In surveys conducted within a year of the 9/11 attacks, which were perpetrated by 19 individuals who immigrated into the country, near majorities or outright majorities of U.S. adults said immigration levels should be decreased. But as the 2000s came to a close and the current decade has unfolded, support for decreasing immigration has gradually fallen, hitting one of its lowest levels this year. As the country has slowly shifted away from this position, the percentage saying immigration levels should increase has doubled—from 12% in June 2002 to 25% today.

Hispanics More in Favor of Increasing Rather Than Decreasing Immigration

Preferences for changes in immigration levels vary considerably by the respondents' race or ethnicity. Hispanics—half of whom say they are immigrants themselves—are most likely to say immigration levels should be increased (36%), while non-Hispanic whites offer the least amount of support for that proposition (21%). Blacks fall in between the two, at 30%. Despite these differences, the overall trend is similar for all three groups. Support for allowing increased immigration levels hit a low ebb for all races/ethnicities in the years immediately after 9/11, and climbed to new or nearly new highs in 2015.

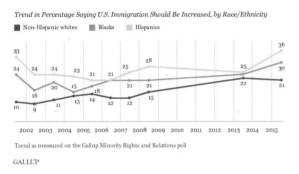

Trend in Percentage Saying U.S. Immigration Should Be Increased, by Race/Ethnicity

Trend as measured on the Gallup Minority Rights and Relations poll

GALLUP

This year's Minority Rights and Relations survey includes a sample of 508 Hispanics, roughly half of whom report being born in the United States and half outside of it. Despite the differences in their country of birth, these two groups of Hispanics do not evince statistically meaningful differences on this question. For both groups, about a third say immigration should be kept at present levels, roughly another third voice a desire to see immigration levels increased and still another approximate third say immigration levels should be decreased.

Preferences for U.S. Immigration Levels Among Hispanic Adults Born in the U.S. vs. Those Not Born in the U.S.

	Born in the U.S.	Not born in the U.S.
Kept at present levels	34%	31%
Increased	39%	33%
Decreased	26%	31%

June 15-July 10, 2015

GALLUP

Nearly Three-Fourths of U.S. Adults Say Immigration Is a Good Thing

Nearly three-fourths of U.S. adults say that, on the whole, immigration is a good thing for the country, a continued affirmation for a practice that has been a core feature of the American experience. While a majority of the country has always agreed with this proposition, the margin has sometimes been more tepid, with a bare 52% agreeing in 2002. Similar to the sentiment that immigration levels should increase, agreement that immigration is a good thing has gradually risen in the years after the 9/11 attacks. In the 2013 and 2015 surveys—both of which included minority oversamples—such agreement reached as high as Gallup has measured since it first asked the question in 2001.

Large majorities of whites (72%), blacks (70%) and Hispanics (81%) say immigration has been a good thing for the country.

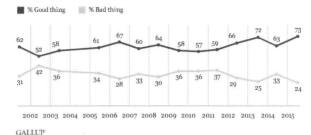

U.S. Adults' Assessments of Immigration's Overall Impact on U.S.

On the whole, do you think immigration is a good thing or a bad thing for this country today?

■ % Good thing   ▨ % Bad thing

GALLUP

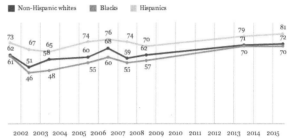

Positive Assessments of Immigration's Overall Impact on U.S., by Race/Ethnicity

% Saying immigration is a "good thing"

■ Non-Hispanic whites   ■ Blacks   ▨ Hispanics

Trends as measured on the Gallup Minority Rights and Relations poll

GALLUP

Bottom Line

Though the U.S. is one of history's great immigrant societies, there is no broad consensus among its citizens today on how or whether immigration levels should change. The current trends suggest that more U.S. adults believe immigration levels should increase than did so a decade ago, but that view still trails the percentage who want levels decreased or kept the same. The growing acceptance of increased immigration levels is evident across racial and ethnic lines, though again this is hardly the predominant position.

But even as the overall specifics may be the subject of continued debate, the notion that immigration is a good thing for the U.S. is something the public widely accepts.

Survey Methods

Results for this Gallup poll are based on telephone interviews conducted June 15–July 10, 2015, with a random sample of 2,296 adults, aged 18 and older, living in all 50 U.S. states and the District of Columbia. All respondents had been previously interviewed in the Gallup Daily tracking survey and agreed to be recontacted by Gallup. For results based on the total sample of national adults, the margin of sampling error is ±4 percentage points at the 95% confidence level.

For results based on the total sample of 857 non-Hispanic whites, the maximum margin of sampling error is ±5 percentage points at the 95% confidence level.

For results based on the total sample of 802 non-Hispanic blacks, the maximum margin of sampling error is ±5 percentage points at the 95% confidence level.

For results based on the total sample of 508 Hispanics, the maximum margin of sampling error is ±7 percentage points at the 95% confidence level.

August 11, 2015
DEMOCRATS SPLIT ON BIDEN PRESIDENTIAL RUN

by Lydia Saad

Story Highlights

- *Democrats split 45% vs. 47% over whether Biden should run for president*
- *Party tilts slightly against Warren running, 36% vs. 49%*
- *Most Democrats would consider voting for Biden, but few certain about it*

PRINCETON, N.J.—As Vice President Joe Biden reportedly deliberates a bid for president while he vacations in South Carolina, a new Gallup poll finds Democrats evenly split over whether he should enter the race. Forty-five percent of Democrats, including independents who lean Democratic, say they want him to run for president in 2016; 47% do not. By comparison, Democrats are less eager to see Massachusetts Sen. Elizabeth Warren, who has maintained she will not run despite grass-roots efforts to encourage her candidacy, jump in.

Democrats' Desire for Additional Democratic 2016 Presidential Candidates

Do you want [name] to run for president in 2016, or not?

	Yes	No	No opinion
	%	%	%
Joe Biden	45	47	8
Elizabeth Warren	36	49	15

Based on Democrats and independents who lean Democratic
Aug. 5-9, 2015

GALLUP

There are currently five major candidates for the Democratic nomination: Hillary Clinton, Bernie Sanders, Martin O'Malley, Jim Webb and Lincoln Chafee. Though Clinton dominates the race, both in national preference polls and in media coverage, some Democrats would like to see a more competitive race to help attract some of the media coverage that the Republican field of 17 is currently monopolizing.

Eight in 10 Democrats Open to Backing Biden

There does not appear to be a large groundswell of support in the Democratic Party for Biden, or for that matter, Warren, to get into the 2016 presidential race to challenge Clinton. But Democrats and Democratic leaners do not widely oppose a Biden candidacy, either.

The Aug. 5–9 Gallup poll finds 19% of Democrats saying they would definitely support Biden if he runs for the 2016 presidential nomination. However, another 61% say they might consider it; 19% say they definitely would not. While Warren has effectively ruled out a run this cycle, if she changes her mind, she would have 15% of Democrats solidly behind her and another 56% willing to consider her.

Gallup asked the same question in reference to Hillary Clinton in January 2007, about a month before she officially joined the race and a year before she made a strong showing in the initial 2008 Democratic primaries. At that time, a third of Democrats said they would definitely support her—about twice the number who are ready to commit to Biden today. But most Clinton supporters still fell into the potential category, with 52% saying they might support her.

Democrats' Potential Support for Joe Biden and Elizabeth Warren

Suppose [name] decides to run for president in the Democratic primary in 2016. Please tell me whether you will definitely support him/her, whether you might consider supporting him/her or whether you will definitely not support him/her.

	Definitely support	Might consider supporting	Definitely not support	No opinion
	%	%	%	%
Joe Biden	19	61	19	1
Elizabeth Warren	15	56	24	6

Based on Democrats and independents who lean Democratic
Aug. 5-9, 2015

GALLUP

Three in Four Democrats View Biden Favorably

Whether or not they would vote for Biden, most Democrats and Democratic leaners—74%—have a favorable view of him, up from 65% a year ago, and similar to Democrats' recent favorable ratings of Hillary Clinton. Just 16% view Biden unfavorably. Biden has been in the news in recent months following the death of his 46-year-old son, former Delaware Attorney General Beau Biden, who succumbed to brain cancer in late May.

Joe Biden Favorability Rating Among Democrats -- Today vs. One Year Ago

	Jul 7-10, 2014	Aug 5-9, 2015
	%	%
Favorable	65	74
Unfavorable	16	16
Never heard of	8	6
No opinion	10	3

Based on Democrats and independents who lean Democratic

GALLUP

Similarly, Biden's image among all Americans has also improved, with nearly half of Americans now holding a favorable impression of him, up from 38% and 39% within the past year. His current 47% to 40% favorable/unfavorable ratio is the most positive Gallup has recorded since immediately after the 2012 election.

Americans' Overall View of Vice President Joe Biden

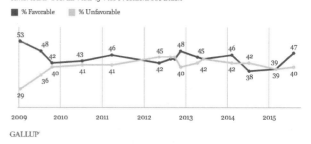

GALLUP

Bottom Line

The vice president has many personal and political factors to consider in deciding whether to pursue a third bid for president. Should Biden emerge as a viable nominee, it would likely be an expensive and bruising battle with Hillary Clinton. But, if Biden is looking for a clear signal from rank-and-file Democrats, this poll doesn't provide one. While nearly half say he should run and most view him favorably, most also view Clinton favorably, and only 19% say they would definitely back him—similar to the percentage saying they would back Warren. Rather than seeking an alternative to Clinton, Democrats may simply believe other candidates, Biden included, deserve a chance—and like to keep their own options open.

Survey Methods

Results for this Gallup poll are based on telephone interviews conducted Aug. 5–9, 2015, with a random sample of 1,011 adults, aged 18 and older, living in all 50 U.S. states and the District of Columbia. For results based on the total sample of national adults, the margin of sampling error is ±4 percentage points at the 95% confidence level. For results based on the sample of 419 Democrats and Democratic-leaning independents, the maximum margin of sampling error is ±6 percentage points. All reported margins of sampling error include computed design effects for weighting.

August 12, 2015
U.S. CONGRESS AND ITS LEADERS SUFFER PUBLIC DISCONTENT

by Andrew Dugan

Story Highlights

- *Congress approval falls to 14% from 17%*
- *Speaker John Boehner records his lowest favorable rating*
- *Republican congressional leaders not popular with GOP base*

WASHINGTON, D.C.—Now on August recess, members of Congress returning to their districts may receive a skeptical reception from constituents, as 14% of U.S. adults approve of the job Congress is doing, down slightly from 17% in July.

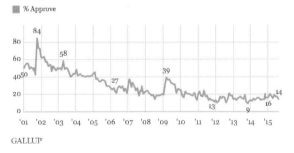

Congressional Job Approval Ratings: 2001-2015

Do you approve or disapprove of the way Congress is handling its job?

GALLUP

These results come from a Gallup poll conducted Aug. 5–9. Congressional leaders can point to a slightly more productive session than was true for the previous two Congresses, such as passing "fast-track authority"—which grants the president enhanced authority to negotiate free-trade agreements—as well as the USA Freedom Act, which significantly revised some provisions of the Patriot Act.

These activities notwithstanding, Congress hasn't gained in popularity among Americans. Moreover, the leaders of the two Republican-controlled chambers, House Speaker John Boehner and Senate Majority Leader Mitch McConnell, are suffering a similar public image problem.

A majority of Americans (54%) have an unfavorable opinion of Boehner, who is in his third term as Speaker. Meanwhile, 23%

view Boehner favorably, down slightly from 27% in March of this year and his lowest favorable rating as House Speaker. Americans have been more likely to view Boehner negatively than positively since 2013.

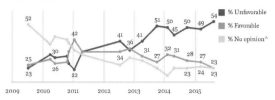

Americans' Overall Opinions of Speaker of the House John Boehner
Based on U.S. adults

Wording prior to 2011: "House Republican leader, John Boehner"
^ No opinion includes those who say they have never heard of Boehner

GALLUP

McConnell is a less well-known figure than Boehner, with nearly four in 10 Americans (37%) saying they have not heard of the senator or registering no opinion of him. McConnell saw his influence on Capitol Hill expand in immeasurable ways after the 2014 midterm elections gave his caucus 54 seats, making him the Senate majority leader. But this promotion has done little to elevate his brand with the American public—nearly twice as many see him unfavorably (41%) as favorably (22%), comparable to ratings of the past several years.

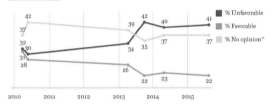

Americans' Overall Opinions of Senate Republican Leader Mitch McConnell
Based on U.S. adults

^ No opinion includes those who say they have never heard of McConnell

GALLUP

Congressional leaders are rarely popular with the public. Boehner's favorable rating today is close to where then House Speaker Nancy Pelosi's stood in October 2010. Back then, 29% viewed her favorably and 56% unfavorably, prior to the widespread Democratic losses in that year's elections. Like Boehner at the beginning of his speakership, Pelosi enjoyed a brief bout of popularity but saw her ratings fall over time.

McConnell's first public rating as majority leader is remarkably similar to that of his chief legislative adversary, Harry Reid, in October 2014, just prior to Reid's losing his job as majority leader. In that poll, 21% had a favorable opinion of Reid, while 45% saw him unfavorably and 34% had no opinion. Both Reid and McConnell have been largely more disliked than liked over their careers as leaders of their respective parties, though a sizable segment of the population does not know them.

Boehner, McConnell Struggle With Republican Support

Although Boehner and McConnell lead the two chambers that often stand in opposition to President Barack Obama, the GOP faithful are hardly enthralled with them. Slightly more Republicans see Boehner unfavorably (42%) than favorably (37%), while 20% have no opinion or don't know him. Independents and Democrats tilt more strongly in the same direction, with majorities holding an unfavorable opinion of the House Speaker.

McConnell breaks even among Republicans, with 34% seeing him favorably and 32% unfavorably. But still another third of Republicans don't know McConnell or haven't heard of him (34%). Anonymity is hardly McConnell's problem among Democrats, as half of self-identified Democrats say they have an unfavorable opinion of McConnell, while 16% see him favorably. McConnell's image with independents also skews negative.

Bottom Line

Even with the August break at hand, Congress is hardly in a position to be satisfied with its accomplishments this year. The legislative branch remains about as unpopular as it was for much of the late Bush presidency and has been throughout Obama's tenure, despite several changes in party control and, correspondingly, in leadership.

Indeed, the main congressional leaders—House Speaker Boehner and Senator Majority Leader McConnell—are not only unpopular figures with the public at large, they are also not particularly well received even among Republicans. For both men, at least on a national scale, the mantle of power has not come with popularity.

Survey Methods

Results for this Gallup poll are based on telephone interviews conducted Aug. 5–9, 2015, with a random sample of 1,011 adults, aged 18 and older, living in all 50 U.S. states and the District of Columbia. For results based on the total sample of national adults, the margin of sampling error is ±4 percentage points at the 95% confidence level. All reported margins of sampling error include computed design effects for weighting.

August 12, 2015

IN U.S., 65% FAVOR PATH TO CITIZENSHIP FOR ILLEGAL IMMIGRANTS

by Jeffrey M. Jones

Story Highlights

- *Support for path to citizenship consistent over time*
- *77% of Hispanics favor a path to citizenship*

- *Half of Republicans back path to citizenship*

PRINCETON, N.J.—Two in three U.S. adults favor a plan to allow immigrants who are living illegally in the U.S. to remain in the country and become citizens if they meet certain requirements over time. Far fewer support allowing those immigrants to remain in the U.S. to work for a limited period of time (14%), or deporting all of these immigrants back to their home countries (19%). U.S. adults' views have been largely stable over the past decade.

U.S. Adults' Preferred Government Policy Toward Illegal Immigrants Living in the U.S.

- % Remain in U.S. and become citizens if meet certain requirements over time
- % Remain in U.S. to work for a limited time
- % Deport all back to home countries

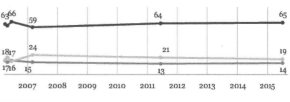

GALLUP

The latest update comes from Gallup's 2015 Minority Rights and Relations poll, conducted June 15–July 10. The poll included larger samples of blacks and Hispanics. Immigration is of special significance to Hispanics, about half of whom are immigrants themselves, according to the poll.

Hispanics (77%) are more likely than non-Hispanic whites (62%) or non-Hispanic blacks (70%) to favor a path to citizenship for immigrants who are in the U.S. illegally. One in five whites, compared with 14% of blacks and 8% of Hispanics, prefer deporting undocumented immigrants back to their home countries.

Hispanics are slightly less likely now than in 2006 (86%) to favor a path to citizenship for immigrants. The 2006 survey was the last time Gallup asked the question in a poll that included an expanded sample of Hispanics. Whites' and blacks' views are largely unchanged since then.

U.S. Adults' Preferred Government Policy Toward Illegal Immigrants Living in the U.S., by Race and Ethnicity

	% Remain in U.S. to become citizens after meeting requirements over time	% Remain in U.S. to work for limited time	% Deport all
Non-Hispanic whites			
Jun 15-Jul 10, 2015	62	15	22
Jun 8-25, 2006	63	19	17
Blacks			
Jun 15-Jul 10, 2015	70	12	14
Jun 8-25, 2006	69	12	17
Hispanics			
Jun 15-Jul 10, 2015	77	14	8
Jun 8-25, 2006	86	8	4

GALLUP

Path to Citizenship Less Appealing to Republicans

U.S. adults' views on the best approach to take with illegal immigrants living in the U.S. differ based on their party identification. At

80%, Democrats overwhelmingly favor allowing illegal immigrants to stay in the U.S. and to have an opportunity to become citizens. Republicans are far less likely to support a path to citizenship, at 50%, but that is still the most common view among this group. Thirty-one percent of Republicans want to see all illegal immigrants deported, while 18% favor allowing them to stay for a limited time to work.

Neither party's views have changed dramatically over the past decade, but Democrats are now a bit more likely to endorse citizenship while Republicans are less likely to do so. The 31% of Republicans who favor deporting all illegal immigrants is up from 20% in 2006, while the percentage of Republicans favoring a path to citizenship is down from 58% to 50%. In 2006, President George W. Bush favored legislation that included a path to citizenship for illegal immigrants.

There has been a 10-point increase since 2006 in the percentage of Democrats who favor a path to citizenship for illegal immigrants.

U.S. Adults' Preferred Government Policy Toward Illegal Immigrants Living in the U.S., by Party Identification

	% Remain in U.S. to become citizens after meeting requirements over time	% Remain in U.S. to work for limited time	% Deport all
Republicans			
2015	50	18	31
2006	58	21	20
Independents			
2015	63	17	19
2006	60	16	22
Democrats			
2015	80	8	11
2006	70	14	14

Note: 2015 data based on June 15-July 10, 2015 poll. 2006 poll based on average of three polls conducted April 7-9, May 5-7 and Jun 8-25, 2006.

GALLUP

Implications

U.S. adults do not express a clear preference on whether immigration levels should be increased, decreased or kept the same, but they mostly agree that immigrants living in the U.S. illegally should be allowed to stay and be given the opportunity to become citizens.

Even so, the federal government has been unable to agree on comprehensive immigration reform over the past 10 years. In 2006, the House and Senate passed differing reform bills but could not agree on a reconciled bill. The Senate passed a bipartisan bill in 2013, but the House took no action on immigration. This is the case even though U.S. adults widely back many of the specific provisions that would go into a reform bill, including increased border security, which has been congressional Republicans' primary concern.

Nearly a decade after a record 19% of U.S. adults named immigration the most important problem facing the country, the issue remains unsettled. President Barack Obama sought to use executive actions to grant legal status to illegal immigrants residing in the U.S., but those moves are on hold pending legal challenges. Senate Majority Leader Mitch McConnell recently said immigration legislation will not be taken up this year or next, ensuring it will remain an issue in the 2016 presidential election.

The issue presents a greater challenge for Republican presidential candidates than Democratic candidates, given widespread Democratic support for a path to citizenship for illegal immigrants. Republicans, on the other hand, are divided, with half supporting a path to citizenship and the other half preferring a measure that stops short of citizenship, including a substantial 31% who want all illegal immigrants deported.

As a result, the party and its presidential candidates face a dilemma in trying to please the many conservative GOP voters who oppose citizenship and represent a core constituency in the primary electorate, along with Republicans who embrace some type of immigration reform. Some party leaders believe advocating immigration reform could shore up Hispanic support for the GOP in the 2016 general election.

Survey Methods

Results for this Gallup poll are based on telephone interviews conducted June 15–July 10, 2015, with a random sample of 2,296 adults, aged 18 and older, living in all 50 U.S. states and the District of Columbia. All respondents had previously been interviewed in the Gallup Daily tracking survey and agreed to be re-contacted by Gallup. For results based on the total sample of national adults, the margin of sampling error is ±4 percentage points at the 95% confidence level.

For results based on the total sample of 857 non-Hispanic whites, the margin of sampling error is ±5 percentage points at the 95% confidence level.

For results based on the total sample of 802 non-Hispanic blacks, the margin of sampling error is ±5 percentage points at the 95% confidence level.

For results based on the total sample of 508 Hispanics, the margin of sampling error is ±7 percentage points at the 95% confidence level.

August 13, 2015
OBAMA GETS LOW MARKS FOR HIS HANDLING OF IRAN

by Justin McCarthy

Story Highlights

- *Only one in three Americans approve of his handling of Iran*
- *Approval of handling of race relations ticks down below 50%*
- *Though improved, approval of handling of immigration still low*

WASHINGTON, D.C.—Only one in three Americans approve of President Barack Obama's handling of the situation in Iran—his lowest rating of eight issues measured in a new Gallup survey. The president's policy toward Iran has been a major focus as he tries to drum up support for the multi-national agreement to limit Iran's nuclear capabilities that Secretary of State John Kerry helped broker. Obama earns his highest marks on race relations, education and climate change, though he does not receive majority approval on any.

Obama's overall approval rating in the poll is 47%. As such, he is rated better for doing his job overall than he is for handling any specific issue, though some of the differences in ratings are within the margin of error. That includes a 41% approval rating for handling the economy and 39% approval on foreign affairs.

Approval Ratings of President Obama's Handling of Issues

Do you approve or disapprove of the way Barack Obama is handling -- [RANDOM ORDER]?

	% Approve	% Disapprove
Race relations	46	50
Education	44	49
Climate change	44	42
The economy	41	56
Terrorism	41	55
Foreign affairs	39	55
Immigration	36	61
The situation in Iran	33	55

August 5-9, 2015

GALLUP

These data are from an Aug. 5–9 Gallup poll, conducted as Congress debates the Iran nuclear deal, which has challenged the usual Democratic allegiances the president has on the hill. As recently as February, Americans gave Iran the lowest favorable rating of 22 countries, and a strong majority felt Iran's development of nuclear weapons posed a "critical" threat to the U.S.

Consistent with partisans' views on other issues, most Democrats, 56%, approve of Obama's handling of the situation in Iran, contrasted with a small minority of Republicans (10%). These ratings among rank-and-file partisans are consistent with the views of the parties' elected representatives—as Republicans are nearly unanimous in their opposition to the deal with Iran, while most Democrats are supportive.

Approval Ratings of President Obama's Handling of Situation in Iran, by Party
% Approve

	Republicans	Independents	Democrats	Gap: Republicans minus Democrats
	%	%	%	(pct. pts.)
Approve	10	31	56	-46
Disapprove	82	58	29	+53

GALLUP

Race Relations Approval Down

While race relations remains the issue Obama receives the greatest approval on (46%), this is down five percentage points from when Gallup last measured it in 2013. It is unclear to what extent his race relations approval rating has been affected by the renewed protests in Ferguson, Missouri. Protests began on the Aug. 9 anniversary of Michael Brown's death, by which time most interviewing on the poll had finished. His approval rating on race relations did not appear to differ in interviews conducted after Aug. 9 compared with those earlier in the field period. The situation escalated after the poll was completed.

Aside from Obama's handling of Iran, his approval is low on immigration (36%)—which, despite this, is up four points from the prior reading from August 2014.

About four in 10 Americans approve of the president's performance on the economy and foreign affairs—similar to their approval on these issues in February. His foreign affairs approval rating is among the lowest of his administration, though it is improved from last fall, when it was 31%. Obama's economic approval rating is essentially the same as the average throughout his presidency.

For most of his presidency, Obama has had higher approval ratings on foreign affairs than on the economy. That may reflect the fact that there were not many notable foreign policy challenges earlier in his presidency. While the economy has improved in recent years, the U.S. has faced a more challenging international environment, including the rise of ISIS and increasing tension with Russia.

Approval Ratings of President Obama's Handling of the Economy and Foreign Affairs

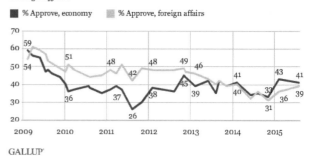

GALLUP

Bottom Line

While Obama's overall approval rating remains improved from where it was in late 2013 and 2014, it has been difficult for him to earn majority public approval on even a single issue. To a large degree, that may be a result of being president at a time of high political polarization, with a very small percentage of Republicans giving him positive ratings on anything he has done.

Amid high-stakes congressional debate over Iran, a mere third of Americans approve of Obama's handling of the situation in the country. Meanwhile, at home, racial unrest has taken hold of the nation's attention and could jeopardize his standing on race relations, one of the issues he has received a majority approval rating on in the past.

If Congress signs off on the nuclear deal with Iran, it is possible that Obama's approval rating on that front could improve. But if Congress votes the deal down, Obama's leadership will have suffered a major blow that could further diminish his rating on Iran, and perhaps his overall job performance rating.

Survey Methods

Results for this Gallup poll are based on telephone interviews conducted August 5–9, 2015, with a random sample of 1,011 adults, aged 18 and older, living in all 50 U.S. states and the District of Columbia. For results based on the total sample of national adults, the margin of sampling error is ±4 percentage points at the 95% confidence level. All reported margins of sampling error include computed design effects for weighting.

August 13, 2015
MANY AMERICANS DOUBT THEY WILL GET SOCIAL SECURITY BENEFITS

by Frank Newport

Story Highlights

- *51% of nonretirees doubt they will receive Social Security*
- *Many retirees are worried their benefits will be cut*

• *Two-thirds say Social Security is in crisis or has major problems*

PRINCETON, N.J.—On the eve of the 80th anniversary of the Social Security system, 51% of nonretired Americans say they doubt the system will be able to pay them a benefit when they retire. These views have fluctuated in recent decades, but the current level of doubt is similar to what Gallup first measured in 1989, when 47% said they would not be able to receive a benefit.

Nonretirees: Will Social Security Pay You a Benefit?
Do you think the Social Security system will be able to pay you a benefit when you retire?

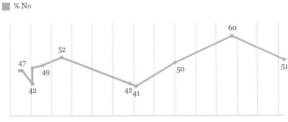

GALLUP

The latest update on Americans' views of Social Security comes from an aggregate of interviews conducted in two recent Gallup surveys, conducted July 8–12, 2015, and Aug. 5–9, 2015.

President Franklin D. Roosevelt signed the Social Security Act into law on Aug. 14, 1935, in the middle of the Great Depression. At the time, Roosevelt was optimistic for the system, saying:

Today, a hope of many years standing is in large part fulfilled. We have tried to frame a law which will give some measure of protection to the average citizen and to his family against the loss of a job and against poverty-ridden old age.

Americans' initial reaction to Social Security appeared to be positive. One of the first questions Gallup asked about the Social Security system was in July 1938, when 78% of Americans said they approved of "the present social security laws which provide old age pensions and unemployment insurance."

Social Security has clearly become a major feature of the U.S. economic landscape in the eight decades since its inception, but changes in the nation's demographic composition have led the Social Security Administration to project that the system's ability to pay full benefits will end in 2034. Americans' doubtfulness about the long-term viability of Social Security thus would appear to have a basis in reality.

Americans younger than 50—most of whom either would be retired or still working in 2034—are the most skeptical that Social Security will be around long enough to pay a benefit, as might be expected. Skepticism is much lower among nonretired workers aged 50 and older, perhaps because they anticipate that they would be grandfathered out of any change in the Social Security system designed to help it remain solvent. Among the small group of Americans aged 65 and older who are still working, only 6% doubt they will get Social Security benefits when they retire.

Retirees Worried About Benefit Cuts

While most Americans aged 65 and older who are still working believe they will get their Social Security benefits, 43% of current retirees predict that eventually there will be cuts in their benefits. This figure is down from 56% in 2010, but up from 32% in 2005. These changes may reflect fluctuations in the economy.

Nonretirees: Will Social Security Pay You a Benefit?
Do you think the Social Security system will be able to pay you a benefit when you retire?

	Yes	No	Doesn't apply (vol.)/ No opinion
	%	%	%
18 to 29	34	64	3
30 to 49	32	63	5
50 to 64	66	30	5
65+	84	6	9

July-August 2015

GALLUP

Retirees: Will Social Security Continue to Pay Full Benefits?
Do you think the Social Security system will be able to continue to pay you full benefits, or do you think there will eventually be cuts in your benefits?

	Continue to get full benefits	Will be cuts in benefits	Doesn't apply (vol.)/No opinion
	%	%	%
July-August 2015	49	43	9
Jul 8-11, 2010	37	56	8
Jan 7-9, 2005	57	32	11

GALLUP

Most Americans Say Social Security System Has Major Problems or Is in Crisis

In the latest survey, 66% of Americans say Social Security is in a state of crisis (21%) or has major problems (45%). The percentages of Americans holding each of these views has varied over the years, reaching a high of 77% in 2010 and lows in 2002 (67%) and this year (66%). But at least two-thirds of Americans have viewed the system as having major problems or as in a state of crisis since 1998. These negative views likely will continue until elected officials in Washington take action to tackle the system's long-term problems or the projections about the system's financial strength improve as a result of shifts in the economy.

Evaluating the Social Security System
Which of these statements do you think best describes the Social Security system -- it is in a state of crisis, it has major problems, it has minor problems or it does not have any problems?

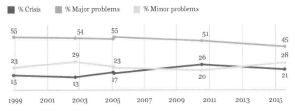

1998-2002 wording: Which of these statements do you think best describes the Social Security system today -- the Social Security system is in a state of crisis, it has major problems, it has minor problems or it does not have any problems?

"It does not have any problems" trend not shown

GALLUP

While Americans aged 18 to 29 and those aged 30 to 49 are equally doubtful they will receive Social Security benefits when they retire, these two groups differ in their perceptions of the state of the system. The younger age group, along with those aged 65 and older, is less likely to say the system is in crisis, while those aged 30 to 49, along with those 50 to 64, are more likely to say it is in crisis. A third of those aged 30 to 49 say the Social Security system is in a state of crisis, twice the percentage among those younger than 30 who say the same.

Overall, a majority in all age groups believes the Social Security system is in a state of crisis or has major problems.

Evaluating the Social Security System, by Age

Which of these statements do you think best describes the Social Security system -- it is in a state of crisis, it has major problems, it has minor problems or it does not have any problems?

	Crisis	Major problems	Minor problems	Does not have any problems	No opinion
	%	%	%	%	%
18 to 29	17	43	35	5	1
30 to 49	33	40	23	3	1
50 to 64	21	51	24	3	1
65+	9	48	32	8	2

July-August 2015

GALLUP

To Ensure Social Security's Future, Americans Prefer Raising Taxes versus Cutting Benefits

There have been many proposals to change the Social Security system to ensure its long-term solvency. Two primary approaches are to raise taxes or to curb the amount of benefits for future Social Security recipients. Given a choice between these two alternatives, Americans tilt 51% to 37% toward saying that taxes should be raised rather than curbing benefits. These attitudes have not changed materially over the past 10 years.

Best Way to Ensure Social Security's Future

If you had to choose one of the following approaches to ensuring Social Security's long-term future, would you rather -- [ROTATED: raise Social Security taxes (or) curb the amount of benefits for future Social Security recipients]?

	Raise taxes	Curb benefits	No opinion
	%	%	%
July-August 2015	51	37	12
Jul 8-11, 2010	49	40	11
Apr 29-May 1, 2005	53	38	9

GALLUP

Younger Americans are more evenly divided in their views on these approaches. Americans aged 50 and older—closer to the point where they will receive benefits—slightly prefer raising taxes.

Implications

Half of nonretirees today, perhaps aware of government projections, say they don't expect to get their Social Security benefits. This is a major economic red flag because Social Security is by far the most relied-upon source of income for retirees. And as more companies do away with defined pension programs, future retirees will need Social Security as a financial base, even as they work to increase their own savings in the years before they retire.

Additionally, Gallup research shows that Americans see tackling Social Security's problems as one of the most effective ways to improve the overall U.S. economy. So far, however, there are few signs that the president or Congress is currently willing or able to address the issue.

The lack of action on tackling Social Security's problems may reflect the fact that the system's inability to pay full benefits is still decades away, according to the latest projections. It is typically easier to face short-term issues than it is to attempt to fix those that are more long term. The lack of action also reflects the difficulties in making changes to a system that is or will be a major source of income for many Americans—changes that will almost certainly negatively affect those paying Social Security taxes or those who are receiving benefits.

One way to encourage legislative or executive action on Social Security is for Americans to pressure their elected officials to makes changes, though this way forward is clouded by the lack of a clear or acceptable way to fix the system. Americans have a slight preference for raising taxes over reducing benefits, but previous research shows than neither of these alternatives receives high levels of support from the U.S. public.

Survey Methods

Results for this Gallup poll are based on telephone interviews conducted July 8–12 and Aug. 5–9, 2015, with two random sample consisting of a total 2,020 adults, aged 18 and older, living in all 50 U.S. states and the District of Columbia. For results based on the total sample of national adults, the margin of sampling error is ±3 percentage points at the 95% confidence level. For results based on the sample of 1,282 nonretirees, the margin of sampling error is ±4 percentage points. For results based on the sample of 738 retirees, the margin of sampling error is ±5 percentage points. All reported margins of sampling error include computed design effects for weighting.

August 14, 2015
SECRETARY OF STATE JOHN KERRY'S IMAGE IMPROVES

by Andrew Dugan

Story Highlights

- *48% have favorable opinion of Kerry, up from 41%*
- *Democrats twice as likely as Republicans to have favorable opinion*

WASHINGTON, D.C.—Secretary of State John Kerry arrives in Cuba on Friday to raise the flag over the once-shuttered U.S. embassy there. Nearly half of Americans (48%) currently view Kerry favorably. This is up seven percentage points from a July poll conducted just prior to the diplomatic breakthrough that led to an agreement regarding Iran's nuclear program.

These data come from an Aug. 5–9 Gallup poll. As secretary of state, Kerry has been instrumental in numerous key Obama administration diplomatic initiatives, including re-establishing ties with Cuba and the international agreement about Iran's nuclear program. The latter in particular may have boosted Kerry's image this year. Slightly more than four in 10 Americans (41%) approved of him in a Gallup poll conducted just days before the agreement was announced.

Americans' Opinions of Secretary of State John Kerry

Next, we'd like to get your overall opinion of some people in the news. As I read each name, please say if you have a favorable or unfavorable opinion of that person -- or if you have never heard of them. How about Secretary of State John Kerry?

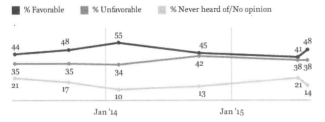

■ % Favorable ■ % Unfavorable ▪ % Never heard of/No opinion

GALLUP

Kerry replaced Hillary Clinton as secretary of state at the start of Barack Obama's second term. His initial favorability reading was 44% in April 2013, while 35% viewed him unfavorably. By the following year, his favorable score had increased to 55%, his highest yet, as Kerry's portfolio of international events expanded to include crises in Ukraine and Syria, and the beginning negotiations of what would become the Iran nuclear deal.

Unlike several of his predecessors, including Clinton, Condoleezza Rice and Colin Powell, Kerry has never enjoyed supermajority appeal. His current reading, though an improvement from earlier this year, is just one point better than his average as secretary of state, and well below the averages of Clinton (63%), Rice (61%), Powell (86%) and Madeleine Albright (62%).

Gallup Historical Ratings of U.S. Secretaries of State

Average of % saying "favorable opinion," while individual is secretary of state

	% Favorable	Tenure	President serving
John Kerry	47	2013-present	Barack Obama
Hillary Clinton	63	2009-2013	Barack Obama
Condoleezza Rice	61	2005-2009	George W. Bush
Colin Powell	86	2001-2005	George W. Bush
Madeleine Albright	62	1997-2001	Bill Clinton
Warren Christopher	40	1993-1997	Bill Clinton

GALLUP

Only Warren Christopher, Bill Clinton's secretary of state during his first term as president, had a lower average rating over his tenure than Kerry's current average. However, as Kerry still has more than a year remaining in office, his average rating is not yet fixed.

Seven in 10 Democrats View Kerry Favorably

Opinions about Kerry vary considerably according to party identification, as perhaps would be expected for a former Democratic senator and nominee for president. More than twice as many Democrats (70%) as Republicans (31%) have a favorable opinion of Kerry. Independents are mixed: 44% view him favorably and 42% view him unfavorably.

Kerry's main improvement in his public image has come among Republicans and independents, rather than the Democratic faithful. Since July, Republicans are 12 points more likely to have a favorable opinion of Kerry and independents are 10 points more likely.

Americans' Opinions of Secretary of State John Kerry, by Party Identification

Next, we'd like to get your overall opinion of some people in the news. As I read each name, please say if you have a favorable or unfavorable opinion of that person -- or if you have never heard of them. How about Secretary of State John Kerry?

	Favorable	Unfavorable	Change in favorable from July 2015
	%	%	pct. pts.
Republican	31	61	+12
Independent	44	42	+10
Democrat	70	14	+1

Aug. 5-9, 2015

GALLUP

Bottom Line

Kerry has been at the forefront of major diplomatic initiatives, including the U.S. rapprochement with Cuba, the international agreement to regulate Iran's nuclear program and his continued efforts to bring resolutions to ongoing conflicts in Syria and Ukraine. And while the public may question the merits of these individual policies, Kerry's labor appears not to have gone unnoticed.

But on a comparative basis, Kerry's favorable ratings are not as high as many of his predecessors in the job. This may reflect the difficult circumstances Kerry is encountering as secretary of state, or the fact that he is serving a president whose approval on foreign policy is low.

Survey Methods

Results for this Gallup poll are based on telephone interviews conducted Aug. 5–9, 2015, with a random sample of 1,011 adults, aged 18 and older, living in all 50 U.S. states and the District of Columbia. For results based on the total sample of national adults, the margin of sampling error is ±4 percentage points at the 95% confidence level. All reported margins of sampling error include computed design effects for weighting.

August 14, 2015
ABOUT ONE IN FOUR AMERICANS SATISFIED WITH U.S. IN AUGUST

by Rebecca Riffkin

Story Highlights

- *Satisfaction slightly lower than earlier in 2015*
- *Economy, government, jobs cited as top problems*
- *Republicans more likely than Democrats to mention immigration*

WASHINGTON, D.C.—Twenty-six percent of Americans are satisfied with the way things are going in the U.S., down slightly from 30% in July. This is also on the lower end of what Gallup has found in its monthly measures of this question throughout 2015, though it is still higher than most 2014 readings.

Generally, less than 30% of Americans have expressed satisfaction with the country's direction since 2007. There were brief spikes in mid-2009 after President Barack Obama took office and again in late 2012 near the time he was re-elected. In fact, today's

26% satisfaction rating is slightly above the average 22% seen over the past eight years. This has been an extraordinarily long spell of subpar satisfaction when compared with Gallup's full trend since 1979. Prior to 2006, ratings lower than 30% were the exception, not the rule.

Satisfaction With U.S., Trend Since 2007

In general, are you satisfied or dissatisfied with the way things are going in the United States at this time?

■ % Satisfied

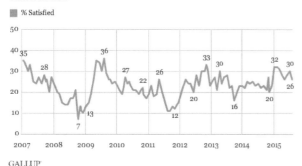

GALLUP

Economy, Government, Jobs Most Important Problems Facing the U.S.

Americans do not have a clear issue in mind when they are asked to name, without prompting, the most important problem facing the country. More than one in 10 mention the economy in general (14%), dissatisfaction with the government (13%) and unemployment or jobs (11%). These three issues have been largely at the top of Americans' minds for several months. Immigration and race relations are also mentioned by more than 5% of Americans this month.

Most Important Problems Facing the U.S.

What do you think is the most important problem facing this country today? (open-ended)

Problem	Jul 8-12, 2015	Aug 5-9, 2015
	%	%
Economy in general	13	14
Dissatisfaction with government/Congress/politicians; poor leadership/corruption/abuse of power	13	13
Unemployment/Jobs	6	11
Immigration/Illegal aliens	7	8
Race relations/Racism	9	6
Poor healthcare/hospitals; high cost of healthcare	4	5
Education/Poor education/Access to education	4	5
Federal budget deficit/Federal debt	5	5
Foreign policy/Foreign aid/Focus overseas	3	4
Terrorism	3	4

Responses mentioned by at least 4% of Americans in August are shown.

GALLUP

The percentage of Americans mentioning each of the specific problems was largely stable between July and August. Mentions of unemployment/jobs increased, despite a relatively strong hiring report from the U.S. government. This increase brings mentions of unemployment back to where they have been for most of 2015, after a lower-than-usual percentage of Americans mentioned unemployment in July.

Slightly fewer Americans say race relations or racism are the top problem this month; however, the percentage who mention it has varied a great deal as racially charged events have entered and faded from the news cycle. This month's polling was completed on the one-year anniversary of Michael Brown's death, which has prompted new protests in Ferguson, Missouri. Those protests escalated the day after polling ended, with the county executive declaring a state of emergency.

Democrats and Republicans Differ on Most Important U.S. Problem

The Aug. 5–9 poll finds Republicans much more likely than Democrats to name the government or immigration as the most important problem. Democrats are more likely than Republicans to cite race relations. This may be related to black Americans being more likely than white Americans to mention race relations as the most important problem, and many black Americans are Democrats.

Most Important Problem by Political Party in July and August 2015

What do you think is the most important problem facing this country today? [OPEN-ENDED]

	Republicans %	Independents %	Democrats %
AUGUST			
Government	14	15	9
Immigration	14	5	7
Race relations	2	6	10
Economy	17	14	12
Unemployment/Jobs	12	8	15
JULY			
Government	21	13	8
Immigration	9	8	5
Race relations	5	7	15
Economy	14	11	17
Unemployment/Jobs	4	8	7

Problems mentioned by more than 5% of American adults in August

GALLUP

Among Republicans, mentions of the government as the most important problem dropped in August. Instead, Republicans were more likely to name unemployment/jobs and immigration in August than in July. This may be fueled by what the Republican 2016 presidential candidates are focusing on in their campaigns, with their first debate prompting many comments about immigration.

Bottom Line

Americans' satisfaction with the way things are going in the U.S. is down slightly from earlier this year. This matches a pattern seen in Gallup's Economic Confidence Index. Americans do not identify a single dominant issue as the most important problem facing the country, but the economy, government and jobs are the ones they are most likely to mention.

Democrats and Republicans differ in their views of the nation's most pressing problem. As the country begins to gear up for the 2016 presidential election, candidates need to find a way to address the many problems Americans identify. If the current mood continues, candidates may find a largely unsatisfied nation that does not identify a single overarching issue as the most important problem facing the country.

Survey Methods

Results for this Gallup poll are based on telephone interviews conducted Aug. 5–9, 2015, with a random sample of 1,011 adults, aged 18 and older, living in all 50 U.S. states and the District of Columbia. For results based on the total sample of national adults, the margin of sampling error is ±4 percentage points at the 95% confidence level. All reported margins of sampling error include computed design effects for weighting.

August 17, 2015
TRUMP FAVORABILITY AMONG WOMEN TYPICAL FOR GOP CANDIDATES

by Stephanie Marken

Story Highlights

- *Trump's favorability among women unchanged after debate*
- *Female Republicans less favorable than male Republicans toward GOP candidates*
- *Trump's gender gap in favorability typical among GOP candidates*

WASHINGTON, D.C.—After Donald Trump's controversial comments about women's issues and about Fox News' Megyn Kelly in particular, many observers are wondering if Trump can muster the female support required to win the GOP primary. Trump has a lower favorability rating among Republican women than among Republican men (50% vs. 59%, respectively). However, this gender gap is fairly typical for many of the current GOP candidates.

Favorability Ratings of Republican Candidates Among Republicans/Republican Leaners

Ranked by gender gap

	Female favorable	Male favorable	Gender gap
	%	%	(pct. pts.)
Ted Cruz	40	56	-16
Rand Paul	38	51	-13
Scott Walker	39	50	-11
Marco Rubio	46	56	-10
Bobby Jindal	32	42	-10
Donald Trump	50	59	-9
Ben Carson	39	48	-9
John Kasich	24	33	-9
Rick Perry	45	53	-8
Chris Christie	36	40	-4
Rick Santorum	36	40	-4
Carly Fiorina	29	33	-4
Mike Huckabee	53	56	-3
Lindsey Graham	24	27	-3
Jeb Bush	53	55	-2
George Pataki	18	19	-1

July 8-Aug. 13, 2015

GALLUP'

These data come from the Gallup U.S. Daily survey, conducted July 8 through Aug. 13 with a random sample of 18,259 adults aged 18 and older, including 7,446 Republicans and Republican-leaning independents. A random subset of respondents rated each candidate during this period, with the sample sizes rating each candidate averaging about 7,490 national adults and 3,021 Republicans and Republican-leaning independents.

Twelve of the 16 Republican candidates asked about receive a significantly higher favorable score from Republican men than from Republican women. The gender gap is 16 percentage points—the widest for any candidate—for Texas Sen. Ted Cruz, closely followed by Kentucky Sen. Rand Paul with a 13-point gap. Carly Fiorina, the sole female GOP candidate, has a slightly higher favorability rating among Republican men (33%) than among Republican women (29%). Former Florida Gov. Jeb Bush, South Carolina Sen. Lindsey Graham, former Arkansas Gov. Mike Huckabee and former New York Gov. George Pataki receive statistically similar ratings from Republican women and men, all within three points of one another.

Gender Gap Also Evident Among National Adults

Among all U.S. adults, men are also more likely than women to view Trump favorably (38% vs. 29%, respectively). As is the case among Republicans, this gender gap is typical for national ratings of GOP candidates. Graham, Bush and Pataki are the only candidates who enjoy similar favorability ratings among men and women nationally; men view all others more positively than women do.

Female Favorability for Trump Appears Unchanged After Debate

Although it may be too soon to measure the full effect of the first GOP primary debate, Gallup data collected Aug. 7–13—the first full week following the debate—show that so far there has been no significant change in Trump's standing among women. Twenty-nine percent of U.S. women viewed him favorably in the weeks before the debate, and 30% viewed him favorably the week after.

Bottom Line

Women in the U.S. are, in general, more likely to identify as Democrats than to identify as Republicans. Further, according to exit polls, 55% of women supported President Barack Obama in the 2012 presidential election. This persistent gender gap in U.S. politics presents a continuing challenge for Republican candidates. Another challenge for Republican presidential candidates is that even among women who identify with or lean toward the Republican Party, women tend to be less likely than men to view GOP candidates favorably.

It is too early to tell whether the first debate—and the comments and media coverage that followed—will negatively affect Trump's campaign among women in the long run. The data so far do not indicate that they have.

The billionaire candidate has since declared that, if elected, he will be "phenomenal to the women," although when pressed about his stance on equal pay for equal work, he refused to comment. Trump has promised a fuller summary of his policies in the coming weeks.

Survey Methods

Results for this Gallup poll are based on telephone interviews conducted July 8–Aug. 13, 2015, on the Gallup U.S. Daily survey, with a random sample of 18,259 adults and 7,446 Republicans and Republican-leaning independents, aged 18 and older, living in all 50 U.S. states and the District of Columbia. Each candidate was rated by a random subset of respondents during this time period, with the sample sizes rating each candidate averaging 7,490 national adults and 3,021 Republicans and Republican-leaning independents. For results based on the total sample of adults aged 18 and older rating each candidate, the margin of sampling error is ±3 percentage points at the 95% confidence level. All reported margins of sampling error include computed design effects for weighting.

August 17, 2015
AMERICANS' SUPPORT FOR LABOR UNIONS CONTINUES TO RECOVER

by Lydia Saad

Story Highlights

- *Nearly six in 10 now approve of unions, up from 48% in 2009*
- *Slightly more want union influence to strengthen than weaken*
- *Majority believe unions are getting weaker*

PRINCETON, N.J.—Americans' approval of labor unions has jumped five percentage points to 58% over the past year, and is now at its highest point since 2008, when 59% approved. In the interim, the image of organized labor had suffered, sinking to an all-time low of 48% in 2009.

Do you approve or disapprove of labor unions?

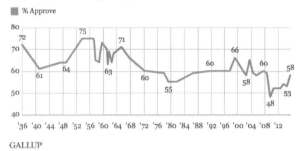

Gallup first asked Americans about organized labor in 1936, a year after Congress legalized private-sector unions and collective bargaining. At that time, 72% of Americans approved of unions. Support remained high into the 1960s, but then dipped through the 1970s until it reached 55% in 1979. It has since varied, reaching as high as 66% in 1999 and as low as the 48% in 2009.

The latest results are from the 2015 installment of Gallup's annual Work and Education survey, conducted Aug. 5–9.

Consistent with the recent increase in approval of unions, the percentage of Americans saying they would like labor unions to have more influence in the country has also been rising, and now stands at 37%, up from 25% in 2009. Meanwhile, the percentage wanting unions to have *less* influence has declined from 42% to 35%, although it remains higher than it was from 1999 through 2008. Instead, fewer today say they want unions' influence to stay the same.

Preferred Change in Power of Labor Unions

Would you, personally, like to see labor unions in the United States have -- [more influence than they have today, the same amount as today, (or) less influence than they have today]?

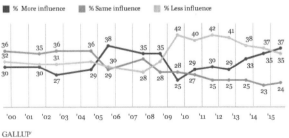

There are a few interesting demographic differences. For example, on both questions, support for unions is higher among women than men. Specifically, 63% of women compared with 52% of men approve of labor unions. Also 41% of women versus 33% of men want unions to have more influence. Favorable views of unions are significantly higher in the East, Midwest and West than in the South. In fact, the South is the only region where less than half of residents approve of unions. Perhaps most positive for the future of unions is the finding that young adults, those aged 18 to 34, are the most supportive of all age groups.

Summary of Americans' Labor Union Views
Aug. 5-9, 2015

	Approve of labor unions	Want unions to have more influence
	%	%
National adults	58	37
Men	52	33
Women	63	41
18 to 34 years	66	44
35 to 54 years	53	32
55 and older	58	37
East	67	40
Midwest	66	40
South	45	32
West	59	38
Republicans	42	18
Independents	52	35
Democrats	79	55

GALLUP

In terms of politics, Democrats are the most supportive of unions, with 79% approving and 55% wanting unions to have more influence. While close to half of Republicans approve of unions, just 18% want them to have more influence—53% want them to have less. The views of independents fall a little closer to Republicans' than Democrats' on both questions.

Americans Perceive Union Power Is Waning

Although Americans have become more pro-union, their perceptions of the outlook for union power haven't changed in the past few years. Fifty-three percent believe unions will be weaker in the future, similar to the result each year since 2011. In most years prior to that, between 41% and 48% thought union power would dwindle, while a higher percentage than today thought it would stay the same.

Outlook for Power of Labor Unions

Thinking about the future, do you think labor unions in this country will become -- [stronger than they are today, the same as today, (or) weaker than they are today]?

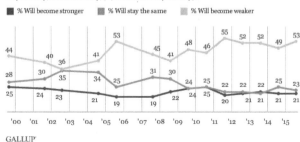

Who Belongs?

Approximately one in eight working adults in the U.S. (12%) belong to a labor union, equivalent to 8% of all Americans. More broadly, 17% of Americans live in a household where at least one person belongs to a union. But, notably, this varies markedly by region, with just 6% of adults in the South living in a union household, compared with 18% in the West and roughly a quarter in the East (24%) and Midwest (23%). Membership is also higher among non-whites (24%) than whites (13%), and among Democrats (24%) than Republicans and independents (13% each). There are smaller differences by gender, and almost none by age.

Bottom Line

With the economy continuing to do better than it did during the recession and the 2008 government bailout of two of the Big Three American auto companies—for which unions' image may have suffered—fading further into history, Americans' views of unions are largely restored to what they were six years ago. The solid majority approve of unions, and most would like to see unions' power strengthened, or at least maintained.

Survey Methods

Results for this Gallup poll are based on telephone interviews conducted Aug. 5–9, 2015, with a random sample of 1,011 adults, aged 18 and older, living in all 50 U.S. states and the District of Columbia. For results based on the total sample of national adults, the margin of sampling error is ±4 percentage points at the 95% confidence level. All reported margins of sampling error include computed design effects for weighting.

August 19, 2015
IN U.S., TELECOMMUTING FOR WORK CLIMBS TO 37%

by Jeffrey M. Jones

Story Highlights

- *Average worker telecommutes two days per month*
- *46% of telecommuters do so during the workday*
- *Most say telecommuters just as productive as other employees*

PRINCETON, N.J.—Thirty-seven percent of U.S. workers say they have telecommuted, up slightly from 30% last decade but four times greater than the 9% found in 1995.

Have you ever telecommuted, that is, worked from your home using a computer to communicate for your job?
Based on employed adults

■ % Yes

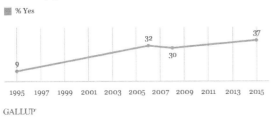

These results are based on Gallup's annual Work and Education poll, conducted Aug. 5–9. Technology has made telecommuting easier for workers, and most companies seem willing to let workers do their work remotely, at least on an occasional basis if the position allows for it. Even though telecommuting has become more common, the growth in the practice appears to have leveled off in recent years. It is unclear how much more prevalent telecommuting can become because it is really only feasible for workers who primarily work in offices using a computer to perform most of their work duties.

Along these lines, telecommuting is much more common among those who have had more formal education, those who are upper income and those who have white-collar professions.

Ever Telecommuted -- by Education, Income and Job Type
Based on employed adults

	% Yes
College graduate	55
Non-college graduate	26
Annual household income $75,000 or more	52
Annual household income less than $75,000	26
White-collar profession	44
Blue-collar profession	16

Aug. 5-9, 2015
Note: White-collar professions are those categorized as being executive/managerial, a professional specialty, technical, sales or administrative.

GALLUP

While a greater percentage of U.S. workers now say they have telecommuted than in the past, telecommuting remains much more the exception than the rule. U.S. workers say they telecommute from home rather than go into the office about two days per month, on average. Nine percent of workers say they telecommute more than 10 workdays—meaning at least half of all workdays—in a typical month.

Number of Workdays Typically Telecommute Rather Than Go to Office
Based on employed adults

	All workers	Workers who have ever telecommuted
	%	%
No days	72	23
One to two days	9	23
Three to five days	8	22
Six to 10 days	2	6
More than 10 days	9	24
Mean number of days	2.3	6.4
Median number of days	0	3

Aug. 5-9, 2015

GALLUP

Among the smaller group of workers who say they have ever telecommuted, the average number of remote workdays is 6.4, and 24% of this group telecommutes more than 10 workdays in a typical month.

The average number of workdays that workers telecommute has not changed much since 2006.

More Telecommuters Foregoing the Office

Telecommuting can take either of two forms. One, perhaps the way people typically think of telecommuting, is an employee working from his or her home office or a coffee shop during normal working hours instead of going into the office. But workers can also telecommute in addition to being in the office by logging on from home during evenings or weekends, when necessary.

In the past, more telecommuters said they most often telecommuted outside of working hours in addition to going into the office during the day. But now they are as likely to say they telecommute during the workday instead of going to the office. This represents a significant shift in the nature of telecommuting, from its use as a supplement to the normal workday to its use as a replacement for being in the office.

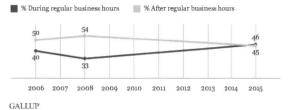

When Telecommuters Are Most Likely to Telecommute

Are you more likely to telecommute -- [ROTATED: during regular business hours instead of going into the office, (or) after regular business hours or on the weekend in addition to going into the office]?
Based on employed adults who have ever telecommuted

■ % During regular business hours ▨ % After regular business hours

GALLUP

Americans Say Telecommuters Just as Productive as Other Workers

Since telecommuting became a reality for many U.S. workers, there has been ongoing debate about whether it is more beneficial or more detrimental to worker productivity. The majority of Americans, including both those employed and not employed, believe workers who work remotely are just as productive as those who work in a business office. The 58% holding this view is up from 47% the first time Gallup asked the question in 1995. This is offset by a drop in the percentage believing telecommuters are more productive than those who work in an office, from 28% to 16%. The net result is a similar proportion believing telecommuters are at least as effective as those who work in offices, given that the 20% who say telecommuters are *less* productive is essentially unchanged since 1995.

Americans' Views of the Productivity of Telecommuters vs. Workers in an Office

Do you think people who work at home using their computers to connect to their business offices are more productive, less productive or just as productive as people who work in a business office?

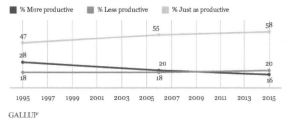

■ % More productive ■ % Less productive ▨ % Just as productive

GALLUP

Telecommuters' opinions are generally similar to those of all Americans. Fifty-six percent believe those who work remotely are just as productive as those who work in offices, while 24% say telecommuters are more productive and 18% say they are less productive.

Implications

Tech giant Yahoo made news in 2013 when CEO Marissa Mayer changed company policy to require all workers to work in a corporate office. Yahoo's policy aside, an increasing number of employers allow workers the flexibility to do their job remotely if it is feasible for their position. More American workers, though still a minority, now say they have telecommuted than said so in three prior Gallup surveys. However, the growth of the practice appears to be slowing.

Moreover, those who telecommute do not do so on a very frequent basis, averaging six days per month with only about one in four telecommuters—the equivalent of one in 11 employed Americans—working remotely from home instead of going to the office on most workdays.

While most assume telecommuting is beneficial to employees, the question remains whether it is beneficial to employers. In one respect, employers might use their telecommuting policy as a way to retain talented workers who may otherwise need to change jobs or stop working altogether. Gallup's workplace research shows that employees who spend at least some time working remotely are a bit more likely to be engaged in their jobs than those who never work remotely.

It is unclear from those relationships whether telecommuting increases engagement or workers who telecommute (and tend to be more highly educated, white-collar employees) are more likely to be engaged in their work in general. Regardless of the causality, Gallup research has consistently demonstrated that companies with a more engaged workforce tend to do better in a variety of business outcomes, including productivity, profitability and customer engagement.

Survey Methods

Results for this Gallup poll are based on telephone interviews conducted Aug. 5–9, 2015, with a random sample of 1,011 adults, aged 18 and older, living in all 50 U.S. states and the District of Columbia. For results based on the total sample of national adults, the margin of sampling error is ±4 percentage points at the 95% confidence level.

For results based on the total sample of 485 adults employed full or part time, the margin of sampling error is ±6 percentage points at the 95% confidence level.

For results based on the total sample of 209 workers who have telecommuted, the margin of sampling error is ±9 percentage points at the 95% confidence level.

All reported margins of sampling error include computed design effects for weighting.

August 19, 2015
MORE AMERICANS SEE THEMSELVES AS "HAVES" THAN "HAVE-NOTS"

by Frank Newport

Story Highlights

- *58% of Americans see themselves as "haves"*
- *More view themselves as "have-nots" than in the past*

- *Majority, however, don't view U.S. as divided along these lines*

PRINCETON, N.J.—The majority of Americans, 58%, consider themselves to be "haves" in U.S. society, while 38% put themselves in the "have-not" group. The percentage of have-nots has more than doubled since 1988, but has been more stable in recent years. Meanwhile, the percentage of haves has held fairly constant, except for a single higher reading during the economic boom in 1998.

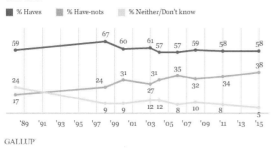

If you had to choose, which of these groups are you in, the haves or the have-nots?

GALLUP

Americans' responses to this question provide a way of looking at inequality in U.S. society—based on Americans' own perceptions of where they are socioeconomically. The latest update is part of Gallup's 2015 Minority Rights and Relations poll, conducted June 15–July 10.

The percentage of Americans perceiving themselves to be have-nots rose in the 10 years between the initial 1988 survey and 1998, while the percentage choosing neither dropped. Since then, the have percentage has settled into a tight range between 57% and 60%. The have-not category has been on more of an upward trajectory, though percentages have fluctuated from year to year.

It is possible that these changes reflect the more difficult economic times ushered in by the Great Recession. It's also possible that the higher visibility of discussions about social inequality has resulted in more people deciding they are on the less fortunate side of the nation's economic divide.

Lower-Income Americans Most Likely to See Themselves as Have-Nots

As would be expected, socioeconomic status is strongly related to a person's tendency to place himself or herself in one of these two groups. There are substantial differences between those in high- versus low-income categories and between those with college degrees and those without.

Self-Placement as Have or Have-Not

	Consider self have	Consider self have-not
	%	%
INCOME		
$90,000+	77	19
$36,000-$89,999	59	35
Less than $36,000	42	53
EDUCATION		
Postgraduate	78	15
College graduate	71	25
Some college	49	47
High school or less	52	44

June 10-July 15, 2015

GALLUP

Still, only a little more than half of those whose annual household income is less than $36,000 say they are have-nots, along with less than half of those with some college or less.

Majority of Americans Don't Think of U.S. as Divided Into Haves, Have-Nots

While all but 5% of Americans are willing to place themselves into a have or have-not category in the survey, more than half say they actually don't view the nation in these terms.

In the current survey, 54% of Americans say they do not think of U.S. society as being divided into groups of haves and have-nots, while 45% do. The percentage of Americans who consider society divided into these two groups has fluctuated over the years, but it was significantly lower in 1988 when Gallup first asked the question, and slightly lower, on average, from 1998 to 2004 than in the years since. The starkest contrast was in 1988, when 26% said that the nation was divided. In 2008, just as the Great Recession was taking a firm hold on the nation's economy, that percentage reached its all-time high of 49%.

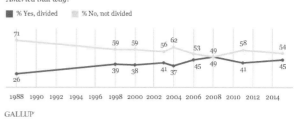

Some people think of American society as divided into two groups – the haves and have-nots -- while others think it's incorrect to think of America that way. Do you, yourself, think of America as divided into haves and have-nots, or don't you think of America that way?

GALLUP

As might be expected, those who believe the U.S. is divided into groups of haves and have-nots are much more likely to identify themselves as have-nots rather than haves (63% to 35%, respectively). Those who do not see the U.S. divided in this way are much more likely to place themselves in the have group (64%) than the have-not group (36%).

Blacks Most Likely to Perceive U.S. as Divided on Economic Lines

There is an interesting pattern in responses to these two questions among whites, blacks and Hispanics. Blacks are much more likely than whites or Hispanics to say they think of the U.S. as being divided between haves and have-nots. But blacks and Hispanics are equally likely to describe themselves as have-nots. These results suggest that blacks are more conscious on a daily basis of inequality in society as a whole than is the case for Hispanics or whites.

Views of Haves and Have-Nots Situation, by Race and Ethnicity

	% Nation is divided into haves and have-nots	% I personally am a have-not
Whites	42	33
Blacks	69	48
Hispanics	37	51

June 15-July 10, 2015

GALLUP

Implications

The stratification of U.S. society into unequal socioeconomic groups has long been a fixture of philosophic, political and cultural debate. It appears to have remained or even expanded as a fairly dominant leitmotif in the ongoing 2016 election, particularly among Democratic presidential candidates. The results of the two questions reviewed in this analysis show that a majority of U.S. adults do not think of American society as being divided along economic lines, and a slightly higher percentage say that if society is divided, they personally are on the haves side of the equation, rather than the have-nots.

These views are somewhat different than they were in 1988, when fewer Americans thought of the U.S. as being divided, and fewer, when asked, put themselves into the have-not category. In recent years, however, there have not been major changes on these indicators.

Historical data for this question is available in Gallup Analytics.

Survey Methods

Results for this Gallup poll are based on telephone interviews conducted June 15–July 10, 2015, with a random sample of 2,296 adults, aged 18 and older, living in all 50 U.S. states and the District of Columbia. All respondents had been previously interviewed in the Gallup Daily tracking survey and agreed to be recontacted by Gallup. For results based on the total sample of national adults, the margin of sampling error is ±4 percentage points at the 95% confidence level.

For results based on the total sample of 857 non-Hispanic whites, the maximum margin of sampling error is ±5 percentage points at the 95% confidence level.

For results based on the total sample of 802 non-Hispanic blacks, the maximum margin of sampling error is ±5 percentage points at the 95% confidence level.

For results based on the total sample of 508 Hispanics, the maximum margin of sampling error is ±7 percentage points at the 95% confidence level.

August 20, 2015
IMMIGRANT STATUS TIED TO DISCRIMINATION AMONG HISPANICS

by Justin McCarthy

Story Highlights

- *One in four Hispanics report mistreatment in past month*
- *Foreign-born Hispanics report more mistreatment than U.S. borns*
- *Hispanics' reports of discrimination lower than blacks' reports*

WASHINGTON, D.C.—About one in 10 U.S. Hispanics say they have experienced discrimination because of their ethnicity over the past month in each of several locations—their place of work, in dealings with police, while getting healthcare and at an entertainment

venue such as a bar or restaurant. Slightly fewer report being discriminated against in a store while shopping (7%). Altogether, 25% of Hispanics have felt discriminated against in at least one of these situations.

Hispanics' Perceptions of Mistreatment in the Past 30 Days

Can you think of any occasion in the last 30 days when you felt you were treated unfairly in the following places because you were Hispanic? How about -- [RANDOM ORDER]?

	% Yes, treated less fairly
At your place of work	11
In dealings with the police, such as traffic incidents	10
In a restaurant, bar, theater or other entertainment place	9
While getting healthcare for yourself or a family member	9
In a store where you were shopping	7
In any of the five situations	25

June 15-July 10, 2015

GALLUP

Half of the Hispanic adults in the sample say they were born in the U.S. (50%), while the other half (49%) were born outside of the country, and the two have significantly different experiences with discrimination.

Hispanics born outside of the country are much more likely than those born in the U.S. to say they have experienced discrimination in each of the situations in the past month. For example, while 18% of foreign-born Hispanics say they were treated less fairly at their place of work because of their ethnicity, only 5% of U.S.-born Hispanics report experiencing workplace discrimination.

Foreign-born Hispanics (15%) are five times more likely than U.S.-born Hispanics (3%) to say they experienced discrimination because they are Hispanic while getting healthcare for themselves or for a family member.

These data are from Gallup's June 15–July 10 Minority Rights and Relations poll, which included a sample of 508 Hispanic adults.

The smallest gap between reports of discrimination between native-born and foreign-born Hispanics is in dealings with the police, such as traffic incidents. On this item, only four percentage points separate U.S.-born Hispanics (8%) and foreign-born Hispanics (12%).

Hispanics' Perceptions of Mistreatment, by Immigrant Status

Can you think of any occasion in the last 30 days when you felt you were treated unfairly in the following places because you were Hispanic? How about -- [RANDOM ORDER]?

% Yes, treated less fairly

	Born in U.S.	Born outside U.S.
	%	%
At your place of work	5	18
In dealings with the police, such as traffic incidents	8	12
In a restaurant, bar, theater or other entertainment place	3	14
While getting healthcare for yourself or a family member	3	15
In a store where you were shopping	2	11

June 15-July 10, 2015

GALLUP

One factor that may explain the gap in discrimination between native-born and foreign-born Hispanics is language. The poll included interviews with Hispanics in both English and Spanish, with those born outside the U.S. much more likely to be interviewed in Spanish than native-born Hispanics. In turn, the analysis shows that reports of discrimination are much higher among foreign-born Hispanics who are interviewed in Spanish than those interviewed in

English. This indicates that language, in addition to ethnicity, may be a key factor in Hispanics' reports of discrimination and in any actual discrimination that occurs.

Hispanics Less Likely Than Blacks to Say They Are Mistreated

The same sequence of questions about discrimination was asked of blacks in the Minority Rights and Relations poll, and for each situation, Hispanics are less likely than blacks to say they experience unfair treatment. While roughly one in 10 Hispanics feel they have been treated unfairly at work and in dealings with police in the past 30 days because of their race, nearly one in five blacks report being treated unfairly in these situations. Blacks are only slightly more likely than Hispanics to feel discriminated against during healthcare transactions.

Blacks' and Hispanics' Perceptions of Mistreatment in the Past 30 Days

Can you think of any occasion in the last 30 days when you felt you were treated unfairly in the following places because you were black? How about -- [RANDOM ORDER]?

% Yes, treated less fairly

	At your place of work	In dealings with the police, such as traffic incidents	While getting healthcare for yourself or a family member
	%	%	%
Blacks	18	18	12
Hispanics	11	10	9

June 15-July 10, 2015

GALLUP

However, the percentage of Hispanic immigrants who say they have been discriminated against is similar to that of blacks. This means that Hispanics as a whole report less discrimination than blacks because native-born Hispanics rarely report discrimination.

Bottom Line

As mistreatment of blacks gains more attention in the media amid Black Lives Matter protests, media coverage about discrimination against Hispanics may fall to the wayside. But the feelings among roughly one in 10 Hispanic adults—and an even higher percentage of foreign-born Hispanics—is that they are not treated fairly by those they work and interact with.

The treatment of Hispanics, particularly of immigrants, takes on special significance as the nation continues to debate immigration reform. The issue has already become a major issue in the 2016 presidential campaign, and Republican front-runner Donald Trump, in particular, has attracted both support and criticism for his unflattering portrayal of Mexican immigrants and a platform that attempts to crack down on illegal immigrants.

Survey Methods

Results for this Gallup poll are based on telephone interviews conducted June 15–July 10, 2015, with a random sample of 508 Hispanics, aged 18 and older, living in all 50 U.S. states and the District of Columbia. Out of 508 interviews with Hispanics, 138 were conducted in Spanish. All respondents had been previously interviewed in the Gallup Daily tracking survey and agreed to be re-contacted by Gallup. For results based on the total sample of Hispanics, the margin of sampling error is ±7 percentage points at the 95% confidence level. All reported margins of sampling error include computed design effects for weighting.

August 21, 2015
POST-DEBATE, IMAGES OF FIORINA, CARSON AND KASICH IMPROVE

by Frank Newport

Story Highlights

- *Net favorable ratings for Fiorina, Carson, Kasich jump up*
- *Images of Paul and Perry suffer in last two weeks*
- *Trump's net favorable rating stable*

PRINCETON, N.J.—The net favorable ratings of three Republican presidential candidates—Carly Fiorina, Ben Carson and John Kasich—improved significantly among Republicans after the Aug. 6 GOP debates. Rick Perry's and Rand Paul's images took a hit. Donald Trump's ratings have remained remarkably stable over the past six weeks.

Republican Presidential Candidates: Net Favorables*

Ranked by Aug. 7-19 net favorables, based on Republicans/Republican leaners

	Jul 8-23	Jul 24-Aug 6	Aug 7-19	Change: Jul 8-23 to Aug 7-19, 2015
Ben Carson	39	36	51	+12
Marco Rubio	42	37	44	+2
Mike Huckabee	38	29	39	+1
Scott Walker	36	36	37	+1
Carly Fiorina	22	14	37	+15
Ted Cruz	35	29	35	0
Jeb Bush	28	24	27	-1
John Kasich	14	18	26	+12
Bobby Jindal	28	27	26	-2
Donald Trump	18	19	17	-1
Rick Perry	36	29	16	-20
Rick Santorum	21	20	9	-12
Chris Christie	6	-2	8	+2
Rand Paul	26	21	6	-20
Lindsey Graham	3	-6	-7	-10
George Pataki	-6	-10	-8	-2
Jim Gilmore	--	--	-11	--

* % Favorable minus % unfavorable, in percentage points

GALLUP

For the purposes of this analysis, Gallup's tracking of the images of the declared GOP candidates is split into three periods—July 8–23, July 24–Aug. 6 and Aug. 7–19—with the last period encompassing the 13 days after the first Republican debates. The net favorable ratings displayed in the accompanying table reflect the percentage of Republicans and Republican leaners who have a favorable opinion of each candidate minus the percentage with an unfavorable opinion.

Key findings:

- Fiorina's net favorable rating is up 15 percentage points since July and 23 points from late July/early August, putting her among the top five candidates on this measure in the latest time period.
- Carson's net favorable rating among Republicans and Republican-leaning independents was already high in the July period, but with a 12-point gain, the physician and former neurosurgeon now has the highest net favorable of any candidate, at +51.
- Kasich is up 12 points since early July, and has moved from having one of the lowest net favorable ratings to an above-average score.

- Former Texas Gov. Perry's image in July was high enough among Republicans to put him up in the ranks of the best-rated candidates. Now, with the 20-point drop in his image after the debate, he is slightly below average.
- Kentucky Sen. Paul was not in as good a position as Perry when Gallup's tracking began in early July, making it worse for him after his rating suffered a large drop of 20 points after the debate. His downturn puts him in the next-to-lowest group of candidates on this image measure, just below Chris Christie and ahead of only Lindsey Graham, George Pataki and Jim Gilmore, whose images are net negative.
- Paul was in the prime-time Aug. 6 debate, while Perry was relegated to the earlier, less highly watched debate. But both men lost considerable ground in the weeks afterward, suggesting it didn't matter which debate they were in. Fiorina, whose image improved significantly, was also in the earlier debate.
- Marco Rubio, Mike Huckabee, Scott Walker and Ted Cruz join Carson and Fiorina as having the most positive images among the 17 candidates—but none of these four saw much change in their images after the debates.
- Graham and Rick Santorum each lost at least 10 points between July and the post-debate period.
- Trump's image among Republicans, despite the media's extensive coverage of his candidacy and his many controversial comments, has remained remarkably constant across this period. His net favorable rating is slightly below the average of the 17 candidates, similar to Perry's score.

Kasich, Fiorina and Carson Have Become More Well-Known

Kasich, Fiorina and Carson, in that order, had the largest gains in familiarity—the percentage of Americans who have formed either a positive or a negative opinion of each—between July and the post-debate period. Walker and Cruz also saw their familiarity scores rise modestly, though their net favorable scores did not improve in the process. Trump, Jeb Bush, Huckabee and Christie are the best-known candidates, and Gilmore, Pataki and Kasich the least known.

Republican Presidential Candidates: Familiarity*

Ranked by Aug. 7-19 familiarity, based on Republicans/Republican leaners

	Jul 8-23	Jul 24-Aug 6	Aug 7-19	Change: Jul 8-23 to Aug 7-19, 2015
	%	%	%	%
Donald Trump	92	91	93	+1
Jeb Bush	82	78	83	+1
Mike Huckabee	74	73	77	+3
Chris Christie	72	70	76	+4
Rand Paul	68	63	72	+4
Ted Cruz	65	65	71	+6
Marco Rubio	64	65	70	+6
Rick Perry	68	69	70	+2
Ben Carson	49	50	59	+10
Scott Walker	52	52	59	+7
Rick Santorum	57	60	59	+2
Lindsey Graham	55	52	53	-2
Carly Fiorina	40	36	51	+11
Bobby Jindal	50	45	50	0
John Kasich	34	36	48	+14
George Pataki	48	42	44	-4
Jim Gilmore	--	--	21	--

* % With a favorable or unfavorable opinion

GALLUP

Despite their jump in familiarity, Kasich, Fiorina and Carson are not in the ranks of those most well-known among Republicans. Notably, only Pataki and Gilmore are less well-known than Kasich. Familiarity scores for Paul and Perry went up slightly, even as their net favorable scores plummeted.

Former Virginia Gov. Gilmore, who left office in 2002, mounted a short-lived campaign for president in 2007 and ran a losing campaign for U.S. senator in 2008, announced his presidential candidacy on July 29. He faces by far the biggest name identification challenge of any of the candidates. Only 21% of Republicans nationwide know enough about him to have an opinion.

Implications

A number of GOP presidential candidates who are well liked face the challenge of becoming better known to significant numbers of Republicans who, at this point, do not know them well enough to rate them. These include Carson—who is still not well known even with his post-debate gains—Walker, Fiorina and, to a lesser degree, Rubio and Cruz.

On the other hand, three candidates who are well known have broad image issues. Trump, despite being hailed as the front-runner based on his standing in GOP horse-race polls, has a net favorable rating of +17 among Republicans, slightly below average, with a 55% favorable rating and a high 38% unfavorable rating. Bush's net favorable rating—at +27—is a little above average, and Christie's +8 is one of the lowest among the candidates.

Trump's situation is perhaps the most fascinating of any GOP candidate. He has over 90% name identification among Republicans and is the major focus of news coverage and social media discussion about the Republican nomination process. His relatively anemic overall net favorable score results from his having a high unfavorable rating. But the 55% of Republicans who like him is similar to the percentages of Republicans who rate Huckabee, Rubio, Carson, Bush and Cruz favorably. Thus, in terms of the pool of Republicans who like a candidate, Trump is on equal footing with these other individuals.

What Trump's high unfavorable ratings will mean down the line remains to be seen. Trump's upside potential may be more limited than, say, that of Rubio—who is less well known but at this point has almost the same favorables as Trump among Republicans, but with a third of the unfavorables. The fact that many Republicans have an unfavorable opinion of Trump is a possible indicator that there are lurking negatives about his candidacy that could spread to other rank-and-file Republicans who now are favorable toward him. Of course, it may also be that those who now have a negative opinion of the business mogul could turn positive as the campaign progresses.

The post-debate jump in familiarity and positive image scores for Carson, Fiorina and Kasich, and the drop for Paul and Perry, show that campaigns and, in particular, debates can make a difference in how partisans rate presidential candidates. At the same time, the stability in Trump's image over time also shows that extraordinary news media coverage and pundit and conventional wisdom don't always translate into changes in the way average Americans view a very well-known candidate.

The next major event on the Republican campaign trail will be the CNN-sponsored debate at the Reagan Presidential Library in California on Sept. 16.

Survey Methods

Results for this Gallup poll are based on telephone interviews conducted July 8–Aug. 19, 2015, on the Gallup U.S. Daily survey, with a random sample of 9,692 Republicans and Republican-leaning independents, aged 18 and older, living in all 50 U.S. states and the District of Columbia. Each candidate was rated by a random subset of respondents during this period, with the sample sizes rating each candidate averaging more than 3,000 Republicans and Republican-leaning independents. Sample sizes of Republicans rating each of the candidates within each of the three time periods ranged between 906 and 1,221. For results based on the total sample of Republicans and Republican-leaning independents, aged 18 and older, rating each candidate at each time period, the margin of sampling error is ±4 percentage points at the 95% confidence level. All reported margins of sampling error include computed design effects for weighting.

August 21, 2015
CAMPAIGN CHALLENGES ASIDE, CLINTON'S IMAGE WITH DEMS STABLE

by Andrew Dugan

Story Highlights

- *Clinton's net favorable score still much higher than other Dems*
- *Bernie Sanders still known by about half of Democrats*
- *Other three candidates still a mystery to most Democrats*

WASHINGTON, D.C.—Democrats' overall opinions of the major Democratic contenders for president have changed little despite six eventful weeks of campaigning. Hillary Clinton remains the best liked among her party faithful. She enjoys a net favorable score of +60, which is essentially where she stood in July. Bernie Sanders is still the next best-liked candidate in the field, with his net favorable stable at +29.

Democratic Presidential Candidates: Net Favorables*

Ranked by Aug. 5-Aug. 18, 2015, net favorables, based on Democrats/Democratic leaners

	Jul 8-21	Jul 22-Aug 4	Aug 5-Aug 18
Hillary Clinton	56	60	60
Bernie Sanders	29	26	29
Martin O'Malley	2	5	0
Lincoln Chafee	1	-2	-1
Jim Webb	3	3	-3

* % Favorable minus % unfavorable, in percentage points

GALLUP

The other three candidates have low net favorable scores among Democrats, partly attributable to their relative anonymity, which showed no signs of change over this period. Aug. 18 marked the sixth week Gallup has been tracking Americans' opinions of 21 candidates who have announced their candidacy for the 2016 presidential nomination of a major party.

Over the course of 2015, Sanders has seen the biggest increase in his favorability rating among Democrats, consequently causing his net favorable score to increase from +13 in March to +29 in July. But for the time period beginning Jul. 8 to Aug. 18, Democrats' views of their party's presidential candidates have been remarkably stable, even as the campaign heats up in unexpected ways. Most notably, Clinton continues to field serious inquiries about her email use as secretary of state. Activists have also confronted several candidates, including Sanders and Clinton, to draw attention to their racial justice agenda. At the same time, Sanders's campaign has had a strong summer, with tens of thousands of supporters flocking to the Vermont senator's events across the country. And Clinton has made major policy addresses on education and the economy.

But if any of this is affecting Democrats' overall impression of the candidates, it is not yet discernable. Clinton remains not only the best-liked candidate, but she is also by far the most well known. Nine in 10 Democrats consistently know enough about her to express an opinion. Sanders remains a distant second in familiarity and has not become any better known to Democrats. In the last two-week period, from Aug. 5–18, about half of Democrats were familiar with Sanders (47%), which is similar to his familiarity in July.

Democratic Presidential Candidates: Familiarity*

Ranked by Aug. 5-Aug. 18, 2015, familiarity, based on Democrats/Democratic leaners

	Jul 8-21	Jul 22-Aug 4	Aug 5-Aug 18
	%	%	%
Hillary Clinton	92	94	94
Bernie Sanders	49	48	47
Jim Webb	25	25	25
Martin O'Malley	22	29	24
Lincoln Chafee	17	18	21

* % With a favorable or unfavorable opinion

GALLUP

The other three candidates are largely unknown to Democrats. In the last two weeks of data, 25% were familiar with Jim Webb, 24% with Martin O'Malley and 21% with Lincoln Chafee.

Bottom Line

The Democratic presidential campaign arguably has not produced quite the same drama that the Republican field has. Periodic bouts of interest or intrigue have emerged, such as Clinton's email scandal and Sanders's growing campaign rallies in the early primary states.

But in recent weeks, Democrats' ratings of the Democratic presidential candidates' images have been highly stable. Clinton is the best-liked candidate running for president among Democrats, as her steady, towering net favorable score demonstrates. Sanders clearly leads the rest of the field in both overall familiarity and favorability, but he still lags well behind Clinton on both metrics. And the images of all five candidates have seen virtually no change since early July, despite ongoing news coverage of their campaigns. But it is early in the process, and the Democrats, unlike the GOP field, have yet to hold a nationally televised debate. It would be premature to say these dynamics are locked in place, but thus far, little has changed.

Survey Methods

Results for this Gallup poll are based on telephone interviews conducted July 8–Aug. 18, 2015, on the Gallup U.S. Daily survey, with a random sample of 8,712 Democrats and Democrat-leaning independents, aged 18 and older, living in all 50 U.S. states and the District of Columbia. Each candidate was rated by a random subset of respondents during this period, with the sample sizes rating each candidate averaging more than 3,000 Democrats and Democrat-leaning independents. Sample sizes of Democrats rating each of the candidates within each of the three time periods ranged between 878 and 1,015. For results based on the total sample of Republicans and Republican-leaning independents, aged 18 and older, rating each candidate at each time period, the margin of sampling error is ±4 percentage points at the 95% confidence level. All reported margins of sampling error include computed design effects for weighting.

August 24, 2015

HISPANICS FROWN ON TRUMP, BUT NOT REST OF GOP FIELD

by Lydia Saad

PRINCETON, N.J.—U.S. Hispanics are still getting to know most of the Republican contenders for president. At this point in the campaign, less than half have formed an opinion of any Republican candidate except Donald Trump and Jeb Bush. Partly because of this, Hispanics' views of most GOP candidates range from mildly positive to mildly negative. The sole exception is Trump, whose favorable rating with Hispanics is deeply negative.

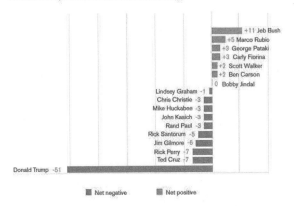

Hispanics' Views of GOP Presidential Contenders

Net favorable (% favorable minus % unfavorable)

+11 Jeb Bush
+5 Marco Rubio
+3 George Pataki
+3 Carly Fiorina
+2 Scott Walker
+2 Ben Carson
0 Bobby Jindal
Lindsey Graham -1
Chris Christie -3
Mike Huckabee -3
John Kasich -3
Rand Paul -3
Rick Santorum -5
Jim Gilmore -6
Rick Perry -7
Ted Cruz -7
Donald Trump -51

■ Net negative   ■ Net positive

Gallup Daily tracking, July 8-Aug. 23, 2015   GALLUP

Gallup began tracking the images of all the major announced candidates for president nightly in early July. Since then, 14% of the roughly 650 Hispanics interviewed have said they view Trump favorably, while 65% have viewed him unfavorably, yielding a net favorable score of -51. This separates Trump from the next-most-unpopular Republicans among Hispanics—Rick Perry (-7), Ted Cruz (-7) and Jim Gilmore (-6), who are viewed far less negatively.

Bush presents the greatest contrast to Trump. Bush's average 34% favorable and 23% unfavorable ratings among Hispanics since July give him a +11 net favorable score—the highest of any GOP candidate. The net favorable scores of Marco Rubio (+5), Carly Fiorina (+3), George Pataki (+3), Scott Walker (+2) and Ben Carson (+2) all tilt slightly positive, although none of these candidates is nearly as well known among Hispanics as Trump and Bush.

In terms of familiarity, only Trump and Bush are recognized by a majority of Hispanics. Eight in 10 have formed an opinion of Trump and about six in 10 of Bush. Familiarity dwindles to roughly 40% for Rubio and Cruz, both Cuban Americans, as well as for Perry and Chris Christie, but drops well below that for all the others.

Trump's Image Among Hispanics as Negative in August as in July

Trump blasted Mexico in his June announcement speech, charging the United States' neighbor to the south with intentionally sending criminals of various kinds over the border, and claiming that, as president, he would compel Mexico to pay for a border wall. Trump has not only stuck to these positions through two months of heavy criticism but also doubled down on them, saying all undocumented residents should be deported and that children born in the U.S. to immigrants in the country illegally should not receive automatic citizenship under the 14th Amendment.

Gallup did not measure Hispanics' views of Trump prior to his presidential announcement, and thus can't quantify how much the candidate's initial remarks about immigrants and immigration have hurt him with U.S. Hispanics. However, since July, his image among Hispanics has remained highly negative, averaging -51 in July and -50 so far in August.

Meanwhile, an interesting shift in Hispanics' ratings of Bush has occurred. His net favorable rating among Hispanics jumped from +1 in July (based on 28% viewing him favorably and 27% unfavorably) to +22 in August (41% favorable, 19% unfavorable), a significant change at a time when no other candidate's image has shown much movement. This could reflect Hispanics' support for Bush's more moderate tone on immigration—at least before he referred to the children of illegal immigrants as "anchor babies." These figures will serve as a valuable baseline to see whether the ongoing criticism of Bush for using the term "anchor babies" hurts him in the Hispanic community.

Clinton the Only Democrat Widely Known Among Hispanics

On the Democratic side, only Hillary Clinton is a familiar figure to a substantial segment of U.S. Hispanics. As a result, she is the only one with a sizable net favorable score. Three-quarters of Hispanics have an opinion of Clinton. With 58% viewing her favorably and 18% unfavorably, she has a net +40 favorable score. This is remarkably similar to Clinton's image among Hispanics in advance of the 2008 presidential primaries, in June 2007, when 63% viewed her favorably and 20% unfavorably.

Bernie Sanders is the next-most-recognized Democrat, known to 25% of Hispanics. Nearly as many view Sanders unfavorably as favorably, giving him a +5 net favorable score. The other Democrats—Jim Webb, Martin O'Malley and Lincoln Chafee—are each known to only 14% of Hispanics and, as a result, have even lower net favorable scores, ranging from +2 to -2.

Bottom Line

Trump has a highly unfavorable image among U.S. Hispanics, but at least for now, this doesn't seem to be tarnishing the rest of the Republican field. As of mid-August, Bush's image among Hispanics had improved as Trump's immigration positions dominated the news. With Hispanics constituting only a small fraction of the Republican

Party, this has not boosted Bush's favorable rating—which has been fairly flat all summer among the Republican base. But, unless his "anchor babies" comment derails him, Bush's recent jockeying with Trump could help warm Hispanic voters to him in the general election should he capture the nomination. For now, Clinton has a modest advantage over Bush in favorability among Hispanics, but she is also much better known than her Democratic competitors.

Hispanics' Views of Democratic Presidential Contenders

Net favorable (% favorable minus % unfavorable)

Gallup Daily tracking, July 8-Aug. 23, 2015

GALLUP

Survey Methods

Results for this Gallup poll are based on telephone interviews conducted July 8–Aug. 23, 2015, on the Gallup U.S. Daily survey, with a random sample of 2,183 Hispanic adults, aged 18 and older, living in all 50 U.S. states and the District of Columbia. Each candidate was rated by a random subset of respondents during this period, with the sample sizes rating each candidate averaging approximately 700 Hispanics. For results based on the total sample of Hispanics, aged 18 and older, the margin of sampling error is ±5 percentage points at the 95% confidence level. All reported margins of sampling error include computed design effects for weighting.

August 24, 2015
AMERICANS' VIEWS OF OIL AND GAS INDUSTRY IMPROVING

by Jeffrey M. Jones

PRINCETON, N.J.—Americans' views of the oil and gas industry continue to improve, with 34% now saying they have a positive view of it. That is up 12 percentage points since 2012, and is one point lower than the 15-year high of 35% from 2003. Ratings have improved as the average price of gas in August has declined more than $1 per gallon since 2012.

Historically, there is a statistically strong, albeit imperfect, relationship between gas prices and Americans' views of the oil and gas industry. From 2001 to 2003—when the August price of a gallon of gasoline in the U.S. averaged around $2, adjusting for inflation—the percentage of Americans rating the industry positively was higher than the historical average of 23%. And views of the oil and gas industry have improved since 2012 as the price of gas has fallen.

Positive perceptions of the oil and gas industry fell to an all-time low of 15% in 2008, when gas prices averaged $4.09 per gallon. Americans' ratings of the industry were also 15% in 2006 when gas was $3.43, a 40-cent increase from the prior year.

Ratings of Oil and Gas Industry Versus Average Price of a Gallon of Gasoline

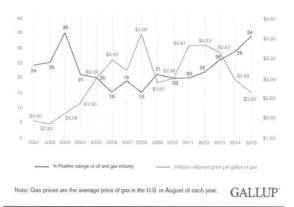

Note: Gas prices are the average price of gas in the U.S. in August of each year. GALLUP

Americans' perceptions of the oil and gas industry were fairly flat from 2009 to 2012, when gas prices were volatile, showing a steep drop in 2009 and then a sharp increase in 2011. During this time, the industry also dealt with negative fallout from the BP oil spill in the Gulf of Mexico, though this did not appear to affect the industry's already low ratings.

The current results are based on Gallup's annual Work and Education poll, conducted Aug. 5–9. Each August, Gallup asks Americans to say whether their views of 25 different business or industry sectors are positive, neutral or negative.

The recent improvement in Americans' views of the oil and gas industry is notable because the industry typically has been one of the poorest rated in Gallup's list. It has had the lowest net-positive ratings, or statistically tied for the lowest, in 12 of the 15 years Gallup has conducted the survey, including every year from 2001 to 2010.

Even with the improved ratings in recent years, the oil and gas industry's net rating in 2015 is -13, based on 34% positive ratings and 47% negative ratings, and oil and gas remains the second-lowest business or industry sector tested. Eighteen percent of Americans are neutral toward it.

Federal Government Now Worst Rated

The federal government is the lowest-rated industry or sector, as it has been now for three of the last five years, including 2011 and 2014. Twenty-five percent of Americans view the federal government positively and 54% negatively. It is the only industry or sector that currently has majority negative ratings.

In addition to the federal government and the oil and gas industry, four other industries have net negative ratings this year, including the pharmaceutical industry, the healthcare industry, the legal field and education. Except for education, Americans typically rate each of these industries more negatively than positively.

The computer industry tops the list, as it has every year except 2006, when it placed second to the restaurant industry. The restaurant industry is also typically rated positively, with a +50 score this year.

Some of the other positively rated industries are the Internet, grocery, farming and agriculture, travel, accounting and retail sectors.

Future Gallup.com stories will outline some of the other notable trends in industry ratings this year.

Ratings of U.S. Industries and Sectors

On another subject, for each of the following business sectors in the United States, please say whether your overall view of it is very positive, somewhat positive, neutral, somewhat negative or very negative. How about -- [RANDOM ORDER]?

	Total % positive	% Neutral	Total % negative	Net (% positive minus % negative)
Computer industry	69	19	10	+59
Restaurant industry	60	27	10	+50
Internet industry	60	22	16	+44
Grocery industry	58	20	19	+39
Farming and agriculture	55	26	17	+38
Travel industry	52	31	15	+37
Accounting	48	37	12	+36
Retail industry	51	30	17	+34
Automobile industry	49	27	22	+27
Publishing industry	40	37	20	+20
Sports industry	43	28	26	+17
Telephone industry	43	29	28	+15
Real estate industry	40	32	25	+15
Television and radio industry	44	22	32	+12
Electric and gas utilities	44	24	32	+12
Movie industry	39	30	29	+10
Advertising and public relations industry	38	29	31	+7
Banking	37	29	33	+4
Airline industry	35	29	32	+3
Education	41	14	43	-2
The legal field	33	27	38	-5
Healthcare industry	39	17	45	-6
Pharmaceutical industry	35	21	43	-8
Oil and gas industry	34	18	47	-13
The federal government	25	18	54	-29

Aug. 5-9, 2015

GALLUP

Implications

Americans' ratings of various industries have been responsive to events affecting the industries historically. One prominent example is the sharp decline in automobile industry ratings, as two of the Detroit Three U.S. automakers needed government bailouts to avoid going bankrupt during the recession, and the subsequent surge in ratings as the industry recovered. The accounting, banking and real estate industries have also seen their images suffer amid scandals or other problems facing each of them.

The oil and gas industry has suffered in the past when gas prices have risen, as well as when the industry was criticized for its record profits. But as gas prices have fallen, which helps consumers but not the industry or governments that rely on oil revenue, Americans' views of the industry have brightened. Still, the oil and gas industry remains one of the more negatively rated industries, though it has relinquished its former status as the lowest-rated industry to the federal government.

Some economists expect to see crude oil prices continue to fall, which would mean gas prices would remain low for the foreseeable future, and may keep Americans' views of the industry trending in a positive direction.

Survey Methods

Results for this Gallup poll are based on telephone interviews conducted Aug. 5–9, 2015, with a random sample of 1,011 adults, aged 18 and older, living in all 50 U.S. states and the District of Columbia.

Each industry was rated by a random subset of approximately 500 respondents. The margin of sampling error is ±6 percentage points at the 95% confidence level. All reported margins of sampling error include computed design effects for weighting.

August 25, 2015

THREE IN 10 U.S. PARENTS WORRY ABOUT CHILD'S SAFETY AT SCHOOL

by Justin McCarthy

Story Highlights

- *One in 10 parents say their child has voiced concerns about safety*
- *Mothers, nonwhite parents most likely to worry about school safety*

WASHINGTON, D.C.—Twenty-nine percent of U.S. parents say they fear for their child's safety at school. This is down from the 33% found immediately after the Sandy Hook school shooting in Newtown, Connecticut, in December 2012, but still above the 25% measured a few months before that incident occurred.

U.S. Parents' Concerns for Their Child's Safety at School

Thinking about your oldest child, when he or she is at school, do you fear for his or her physical safety?

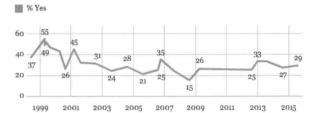

Based on parents of K-12 children
Note: 1977 result of 24% not shown

GALLUP

U.S. parents' fears about school safety reached a high of 55% in April 1999 after the Columbine High School massacre in Colorado. Parents' concern typically peaks immediately following high-profile shootings—as seen in 2001 (45%) after the Santana High School shooting in California, and in 2006 (35%) after a shooting in an Amish schoolhouse in Pennsylvania—and then fades. The low point in parental concern (15%) came in August 2008.

The latest results come from Gallup's Work and Education poll, conducted Aug. 5–9.

Safety and gun control have been at the forefront of news coverage and legislative debate in recent years, as shootings in and out of schools have rocked communities. The tragedy at Sandy Hook initiated an intense legislative debate on gun control, but less than a year after the incident, Americans remained divided on gun control laws.

One in 10 Parents Say Child Has Expressed Concerns About Safety at School

Ten percent of U.S. parents of K-12 students say their child has expressed worries about his or her safety at school. This figure has been fairly consistent since 2003, never straying from the 8% to 12% range.

In the early post-Columbine years, parents were more likely to report hearing such concerns, with one in five saying so in 1999 and in 2001.

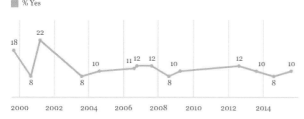

U.S. Parents Who Say Child Has Expressed Concerns About Safety at School

Have any of your school-aged children expressed any worry or concern about feeling unsafe at their school when they go back to school this fall?

■ % Yes

Based on parents of K-12 children

GALLUP

Women, Nonwhites and Lower-Income Parents Most Likely to Worry About Safety

To analyze parents' concerns about school safety by subgroup, Gallup aggregated data from the last five surveys going back to August 2012, when the percentage fearing for their child's safety averaged 25%.

Mothers of K-12 students (34%) are more likely than fathers (24%) to worry about their child's safety at school. And mothers are about twice as likely as fathers to report that their child has expressed concerns about school safety.

Four in 10 nonwhite parents worry about their child's safety at school, far higher than the 23% of white parents who worry. However, the percentage of white (9%) and nonwhite parents (12%) who say their child has voiced concerns about school safety is similar.

Parents earning less than $30,000 per year in annual household income are more likely than parents who earn more to worry about their child's safety and to say their child has expressed concerns about school safety.

Parents' Concerns for Safety at School -- by Gender, Race and Income

	Fear for child's safety at school	Child has expressed worry about safety at school
	%	%
All parents	29	10
Men	24	7
Women	34	13
Whites	23	9
Nonwhites	40	12
Income less than $30,000	41	16
Income $30,000-$74,999	27	7
Income $75,000 or more	24	10

Based on 1,178 parents of K-12 children
Data aggregated from August polls from 2012 through 2015

GALLUP

Bottom Line

Three in 10 parents worry about their child's physical safety at school, and they are not without reason. According to a Quartz analysis, the number of school killings in the U.S. between 2000 and 2010 was one less than the number in dozens of other countries combined.

The most horrifying acts of violence at U.S. schools can leave temporary impressions on parents' psyches. The early 2000s, which were just as much the post-9/11 years as they were the post-Columbine years, ranked high for parental anxiety about school safety, but by 2005, worries for children's safety at school had hit a new low. And despite the unprecedented shock of Sandy Hook, parents' worries are now similar to their historical averages.

Survey Methods

Results for this Gallup poll are based on telephone interviews conducted Aug. 5–9, 2015, on the Gallup U.S. Daily survey, with a random sample of 213 K-12 parents, aged 18 and older, living in all 50 U.S. states and the District of Columbia. For results based on the total sample of parents, the margin of sampling error is ±9 percentage points at the 95% confidence level. All reported margins of sampling error include computed design effects for weighting.

Subgroup analysis represents aggregated data from 2012 to 2015. For results based on the total sample of 645 fathers, the margin of sampling error is ±5 percentage points at the 95% confidence level. For results based on the total sample of 533 mothers, the margin of sampling error is ±5 percentage points at the 95% confidence level. For results based on the total sample of 854 whites, the margin of sampling error is ±4 percentage points at the 95% confidence level. For results based on the total sample of 296 nonwhites, the margin of sampling error is ±7 percentage points at the 95% confidence level. For results based on the total sample of 197 parents whose households earn less than $30,000, the margin of sampling error is ±9 percentage points at the 95% confidence level. For results based on the total sample of 409 parents whose households earn between $30,000 and $74,999, the margin of sampling error is ±6 percentage points at the 95% confidence level. For results based on the total sample of 490 parents whose households earn $75,000 or more, the margin of sampling error is ±5 percentage points at the 95% confidence level.

August 26, 2015
INTERNET INDUSTRY NETS RECORD POSITIVE RATING

by Lydia Saad

Story Highlights

- *Percentage viewing Internet positively jumps to 60%*
- *Industry image improves more among Republicans than Democrats*
- *Older Americans catching up with young adults in positive views*

PRINCETON, N.J.—Six in 10 Americans view the Internet industry either very or somewhat positively, which is up from 49% a year ago and easily the highest positive rating that Gallup has recorded in 15 years.

Positive perceptions of the Internet industry rose from an average 46% between 2001 and 2005 to 52% between 2006 and 2014, before reaching today's 60%. Currently, 16% of Americans view the industry negatively—up from an average 22% from 2001 to 2005—and 22% are neutral toward it.

Americans' Overall View of the Internet Industry

For each of the following business sectors in the United States, please say whether your overall view of it is very positive, somewhat positive, neutral, somewhat negative or very negative. How about the Internet industry?

■ % Very/Somewhat positive

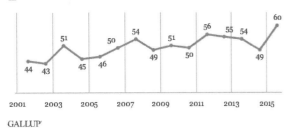

GALLUP

The latest results are from Gallup's Aug. 5–9 Work and Education poll, in which respondents were asked how they view each of 25 business or industry sectors in the U.S. The Internet now ranks third on the basis of net-positive views, behind the restaurant and computer industries. While Americans rate the computer industry slightly better than the Internet industry, views of the computer industry have been fairly flat in recent years; in fact, the current 69% viewing it positively is a few points lower than the 73% peak three years ago.

Americans' Overall View of the Computer Industry

For each of the following business sectors in the United States, please say whether your overall view of it is very positive, somewhat positive, neutral, somewhat negative or very negative. How about the computer industry?

■ % Very/Somewhat positive

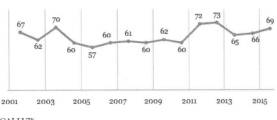

GALLUP

"Internet industry" may mean different things to different people, and Gallup did not define the term in the question, but experts generally define it as companies that provide access to or operate primarily on the Internet. This would include Internet portals and search engines, as well as e-commerce, lifestyle, entertainment and social media sites.

While there is no obvious reason why Americans would have grown more favorable toward the Internet industry in just the past year, Gallup trends indicate that positive perceptions are higher today than the 2006–2014 average among most key demographic groups. It has increased especially among Republicans and independents, while showing little improvement among Democrats.

Longer term, one of the reasons the Internet industry's image has improved since the early 2000s is that older Americans have grown more positive toward it as they have become more familiar with it. From 2001 to 2005, 37% of adults aged 55 and older had a positive impression of the Internet industry and 25% a negative impression, with 39% neutral or unsure. Today, 54% view it positively and 20% negatively, with 26% neutral or unsure.

Positive Views of the Internet Industry, Trend by Time Period
Based on U.S. adults

	2001 to 2005	2006 to 2014	2015	Change since 2006-2014
	%	%	%	pct. pts.
Men	49	57	62	+5
Women	43	48	57	+9
18 to 34	53	58	65	+7
35 to 54	48	53	60	+7
55 and older	37	47	54	+7
Postgraduate	51	62	57	-5
College graduate only	49	53	56	+3
Some college	47	52	65	+13
No college	42	48	59	+11
Republican	46	54	62	+8
Independent	45	50	61	+11
Democrat	47	53	55	+2

GALLUP

Trend in Views of the Internet Industry, by Age
Based on U.S. adults

	Summary of views	2001 to 2005	2006 to 2014	2015	Change since 2001-2005
		%	%	%	pct. pts.
18-34	Total positive	53%	58%	65%	+12
	Neutral/No opinion	27%	24%	22%	-5
	Total negative	19%	18%	13%	-6
35-54	Total positive	48%	53%	60%	+12
	Neutral/No opinion	30%	27%	24%	-6
	Total negative	23%	20%	16%	-7
55+	Total positive	37%	47%	54%	+17
	Neutral/No opinion	39%	31%	26%	-13
	Total negative	25%	22%	20%	-5

GALLUP

Bottom Line

As more Americans have Internet access at home, use smartphones, telecommute and otherwise integrate the Internet in their lives, their perceptions of the industry have improved. The Internet provides services that can enhance people's daily lives, and at least for now, it appears these benefits outweigh any downside Americans may perceive in terms of cost or privacy. One question is whether consumers continue to feel the Internet is on their side, or whether they grow to want more government intervention. However, amid current debate over the merits of various proposed regulations, it is notable that far more Americans have a positive view of the Internet industry than of the federal government, 60% versus 25%, respectively.

Survey Methods

Results for this Gallup poll are based on telephone interviews conducted Aug. 5–9, 2015, with a random sample of 1,011 adults, aged 18 and older, living in all 50 U.S. states and the District of Columbia. For results based on the total sample of national adults, the margin of sampling error is ±4 percentage points at the 95% confidence level. Each industry was rated by a random subset of approximately 500 respondents. The margin of sampling error is ±6 percentage points at the 95% confidence level. All reported margins of sampling error include computed design effects for weighting.

August 26, 2015

HIGHER SUPPORT FOR GENDER AFFIRMATIVE ACTION THAN RACE

by Rebecca Riffkin

Story Highlights

- *67% of Americans support affirmative action for women*
- *Slightly fewer, 58%, support affirmative action for minorities*
- *Women more likely than men to support both programs*

WASHINGTON, D.C.—A majority of Americans say they favor affirmative action programs. However, support is a bit higher for programs aimed at helping women (67%) than for those focused on helping racial minorities (58%).

Majority of Americans Support Affirmative Action Programs
Do you generally favor or oppose affirmative action programs for women?
Do you generally favor or oppose affirmative action programs for racial minorities?

	% Favor affirmative action for women	% Favor affirmative action for racial minorities
U.S. adults	67	58
Men	62	55
Women	72	60
Whites	63	53
Blacks	80	77
Hispanics	74	61

June 15-July 10, 2015

GALLUP

While majorities of men, women, whites, blacks and Hispanics are in favor of affirmative action programs, support varies according to each groups' connection to the program. Women are more likely than men to support affirmative action programs for women, by 72% to 62%, respectively. Blacks (77%) and Hispanics (61%) are more likely than whites (53%) to support affirmative action programs for racial minorities.

These findings are from Gallup's Minority Rights and Relations survey conducted June 15–July 10 with more than 2,000 U.S. adults, including expanded samples of blacks and Hispanics. The last time these questions were asked in 2013, the findings were similar.

White Men Least Likely to Support Either Affirmative Action Program

While still a majority, support among white men trails support among white women for affirmative action programs for women and for minorities. Black women and Hispanic women are more likely than white women to support affirmative action for women, 81% versus 67%, respectively.

While all racial and gender groups' support for affirmative action is higher for programs aimed at women than those aimed at minorities, differences in support for the two programs vary by subgroup. Blacks' level of support for affirmative action targeted at women and minorities are similar. But Hispanics and whites are much more likely to favor programs for women than those for minorities.

Less Than Half of Republicans Support Affirmative Action for Minorities

Support for both types of affirmative action programs differs markedly by political party identification. More than eight in 10

Democrats support affirmative action for women, and 76% support it for racial minorities. Solid majorities of independents also support both types of programs. Republicans are split: Just over half favor affirmative action for women, but fewer than four in 10 favor it for racial minorities.

Support for Affirmative Action Programs, by Men and Women of Different Races
Do you generally favor or oppose affirmative action programs for women?
Do you generally favor or oppose affirmative action programs for racial minorities?

	% Favor affirmative action for women	% Favor affirmative action for racial minorities
Black men	78	74
Black women	81	79
Hispanic men	67	55
Hispanic women	81	67
White men	58	52
White women	67	55

June 15-July 10, 2015

GALLUP

Support for Affirmative Action Programs, by Political Affiliation
Do you generally favor or oppose affirmative action programs for women?
Do you generally favor or oppose affirmative action programs for racial minorities?

	% Favor affirmative action for women	% Favor affirmative action for racial minorities
Republicans	51	38
Independents	63	55
Democrats	83	76

June 15-July 10, 2015

GALLUP

Implications

Affirmative action programs were traditionally created to help avoid discrimination against women and minority applicants at educational institutions, like colleges, and in hiring for jobs. These groups were historically at a disadvantage when applying because of racial or gender prejudice and even legal discrimination. However, some educational institutions are finding alternate ways to increase diversity without affirmative action. And in 2014, the U.S. Supreme Court upheld Michigan's ban on considering race in college applications.

Some claim that affirmative action puts whites or men at an unfair disadvantage, that it can create reverse discrimination or even that it can hurt minorities and women. The U.S. Supreme Court recently announced it would reconsider a case last brought before it in 2013 in which a white woman claims she was denied admission to the University of Texas because of a race-based affirmative action program the university used at that time. Affirmative action may again be an issue in 2016 and could become less used, or even banned, because of this case. However, a majority of Americans of all genders and races continue to support affirmative action programs.

Survey Methods

Results for this Gallup poll are based on telephone interviews conducted June 15–July 10, 2015, with a random sample of 2,296 adults, aged 18 and older, living in all 50 U.S. states and the District of Columbia, including oversamples of black and Hispanic adults. All respondents had previously been interviewed in the Gallup Daily tracking survey. For results based on the total sample of national adults, the margin of sampling error is ±4 percentage points at the 95% confidence level.

For results based on the total sample of 857 non-Hispanic whites, the maximum margin of sampling error is ±5 percentage points.

For results based on the total sample of 802 non-Hispanic blacks, the maximum margin of sampling error is ±5 percentage points.

For results based on the total sample of 508 Hispanics, the maximum margin of sampling error is ±7 percentage points (138 out of the 508 interviews with Hispanics were conducted in Spanish).

For results based on the total sample of 1,148 men, the maximum margin of sampling error is ±5 percentage points.

For results based on the total sample of 1,148 women, the maximum margin of sampling error is ±5 percentage points.

August 28, 2015
RATINGS OF U.S. BANKING INDUSTRY LEVEL OFF

by Jeffrey M. Jones

Story Highlights

- *37% of Americans rate industry positively, 33% negatively*
- *Ratings had improved in each of prior two years*
- *Opinions of banks still trail where they were prerecession*

PRINCETON, N.J.—After two consecutive years of improvement in Americans' ratings of the banking industry, climbing from a low of 25% in 2012 to 40% in 2014, perceptions have leveled off. Now, 37% view the industry positively. The banking industry's image remains better than it was during the economic downturn but is still not back to the more positive levels seen from 2001 to 2007.

Americans' Ratings of the Banking Industry

On another subject, for each of the following business sectors in the United States, please say whether your overall view of it is very positive, somewhat positive, neutral, somewhat negative or very negative. How about banking?

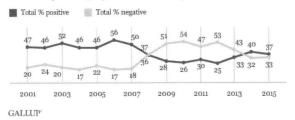

GALLUP

The latest results are based on Gallup's annual Work and Education survey. As part of the poll, Gallup asks Americans for their views on 25 different business or industry sectors, using a 5-point positive-to-negative scale. Banking's +4 net rating (based on 37% rating it very or somewhat positive and 33% very or somewhat negative) is below the average of +16 for all 25 industries, but ranks ahead of several industries with net-negative ratings, such as the federal government, the oil and gas industry, the healthcare industry and the pharmaceutical industry.

Americans were positive toward the banking industry in Gallup's initial annual reading in August 2001, and these upbeat views were consistent through August 2007, a few months before the recession officially began. During this period, an average of 49% of Americans rated the industry positively and 20% negatively, for an average +29 net rating.

In August 2008, as the recession was deepening but a month before the September financial crisis, Americans were evenly divided in their views of the banking industry—36% positive and 37% negative.

From 2009 through 2012, Americans' ratings of banks were substantially more negative than positive, with an average -24 net rating.

After bottoming out at 25% positive (and 53% negative) in 2012, Americans' views of the industry began to recover, with an eight-percentage-point increase in positive ratings in 2013 and a seven-point increase in 2014, enough to push its positive ratings ahead of its negative ratings for the first time since 2007.

Many, but not all, industries have seen increased positive ratings over the last four years. The total 12-point increase in ratings of the banking industry since 2012 exceeds the average three-point increase for the 24 other industries included in the survey.

Changes in Percentage Positive Ratings of Industries, 2012 to 2015

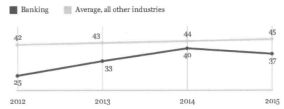

Note: All other industries based on average positive rating of 24 industries (other than banking) tested in the poll

GALLUP

Along with the banking industry, the real estate (up 13 points), oil and gas (up 12 points), travel (up 12 points) and electric and gas utility (up 10 points) industries have shown double-digit increases in their positive ratings since 2012.

Lower-Income Americans Rate Banking Industry Most Positively

Forty-four percent of Americans whose annual household income is less than $30,000 have a positive view of the banking industry, while 26% view it negatively, resulting in a +18 net rating, based on combined 2014–2015 polling. That compares with net ratings of -3 among middle-income Americans (35% positive, 38% negative), and +2 among upper-income Americans (37% positive, 35% negative).

Lower-income Americans did not always view the industry more positively than Americans at higher income levels. Prior to the recession, from 2004 through 2007, net ratings of the banking industry were largely similar by income level, ranging from +29 to +34 among the three income groups.

After the financial crisis and recession, from 2009 to 2012, views of the industry cratered among all income groups, but much more so among upper-income Americans than among middle- or lower-income Americans. The average net rating of the banking industry among upper-income Americans fell a staggering 72 points in the years bracketing the 2008 financial crisis, from +31 to -41, compared with drops of 50 points among middle-income Americans (from +29 to -21) and 39 points among lower-income Americans (from +34 to -5).

Net Ratings of the Banking Industry, by Annual Household Income
Figures are the percentage who rate the banking industry positively minus the percentage who rate the banking industry negatively

	2004-2007	2009-2012	2014-2015
Less than $30,000	+34	-5	+18
$30,000-$74,999	+29	-21	-3
$75,000 +	+31	-41	+2

GALLUP

Upper-income Americans, who are more likely to have money invested in the financial markets, and were probably more likely to be aware of the problems facing U.S. financial institutions as the crisis unfolded, appear to have been more shaken by the industry's problems. Upper-income Americans' ratings of the industry have recovered during the last two years, improving a total of 43 points, from -41 to +2, a greater improvement than for the other income groups. But that improvement left upper-income Americans about as positive toward the industry as middle-income Americans, and still significantly less positive than lower-income Americans.

Among Political Groups, Republicans Most Positive Toward Banks

The Republican Party is sometimes referred to as the party of Wall Street, and ratings of the banking industry by political party are consistent with that description. Forty-six percent of self-identified Republicans view the industry positively and 23% negatively, for a net rating of +23. Meanwhile, independents (35% positive and 36% negative) and Democrats (39% positive and 37% negative) are divided in their views of the industry.

Each political group showed similar declines in ratings of banks after the financial crisis, with the net score for each falling between 50 and 57 points. Republicans' views of banks have improved slightly more over the last two years.

Net Ratings of the Banking Industry, by Political Party Identification
Figures are the percentage who rate the banking industry positively minus the percentage who rate the banking industry negatively

	2004-2007	2009-2012	2014-2015
Republicans	+43	-14	+23
Independents	+25	-30	-1
Democrats	+24	-26	+2

GALLUP

Implications

For now, the positive momentum in Americans' images of the banking industry has halted. Slightly more Americans have a positive than negative view of banks, a much better evaluation of the industry than during the recession and its aftermath, but still lagging behind the more positive images that existed before then.

Gallup has shown a similar pattern in Americans' confidence in the institution of banks, which bottomed out in 2012 and has improved modestly since then, although that increase also appears to be leveling off.

These trends could indicate that those who were most likely to forgive the industry or forget the problems that plagued it have already done so, and the industry may need to convince those with longer memories or greater skepticism that banks have reformed their ways and that the industry has changed for the better. Thus, it appears the banking industry still has work to do to regain the positive image and trust it had before the recession.

Survey Methods

Results for this Gallup poll are based on telephone interviews conducted Aug. 5–9, 2015, with a random sample of 1,011 adults, aged 18 and older, living in all 50 U.S. states and the District of Columbia.

Each industry was rated by a random subset of approximately 500 respondents. The margin of sampling error is ±6 percentage points at the 95% confidence level. All reported margins of sampling error include computed design effects for weighting.

August 28, 2015
AMERICANS' SATISFACTION WITH JOB ASPECTS UP FROM 2005

by Justin McCarthy

Story Highlights

- *More satisfied with health benefits, vacation time*
- *Satisfaction with job security remains near 2014 high*

WASHINGTON, D.C.—Employed Americans' satisfaction with 13 aspects of their current jobs has largely improved in the last decade. The percentages of workers "completely satisfied" with their health benefits and vacation time have increased the most since 2005, each rising at least 10 percentage points.

U.S. Employees' Satisfaction With 13 Job Aspects -- Recent Trend
% Completely satisfied, ranked by 2005-2015 change

	2005	2015	Change over past decade
	%	%	(pct. pts.)
The health insurance benefits your employer offers	27	40	+13
The amount of vacation time you receive	47	57	+10
The retirement plan your employer offers	27	35	+8
The amount of money you earn	25	33	+8
Your chances for promotion	28	35	+7
Your job security	52	57	+5
The recognition you receive at work for your work accomplishments	41	45	+4
Your boss or immediate supervisor	50	54	+4
The amount of work that is required of you	49	53	+4
Your relations with coworkers	69	72	+3
The physical safety conditions of your workplace	68	70	+2
The amount of on-the-job stress in your job	27	28	+1
The flexibility of your hours	62	58	-4

Based on adults employed full or part time

GALLUP

As has been the case since Gallup began polling on aspects of Americans' jobs in 1993, employed Americans are most likely to say they are "completely satisfied" with their relations with their coworkers (72% in 2015) and the physical safety conditions of their workplace (70%). Employed Americans have typically been least likely to say they are completely satisfied with the amount of money they earn (33%) and the amount of stress they have at work (28%).

Smaller majorities of employed adults report being "completely satisfied" with the flexibility of their hours (58%), the amount of vacation time they receive (57%), their job security (57%), their boss or immediate supervisor (54%) and the amount of work that is required of them (53%).

Despite large improvements over the past 10 years in how they view many aspects of their jobs, less than half of employed Americans say they are "completely satisfied" with the recognition they receive at work for their accomplishments (45%) and the health insurance benefits their employer offers (40%). Even fewer are "completely satisfied" with the retirement plan offered (35%) and their chances for a promotion (35%).

These data are from Gallup's Aug. 5–9 Work and Education survey, conducted annually since 2001.

"Complete" Satisfaction With Job Security Remains Near Record High

Fifty-seven percent of Americans are completely satisfied with their job security, near the high of 58% recorded in 2014.

Satisfaction with job security had suffered amid the global economic crisis, falling five points in 2009 to 50%. It didn't recover in the years that immediately followed, and dipped below 50% in 2011 and 2012. By 2014, as Americans' perceptions of job creation at their companies improved, so too did their satisfaction with the security of their own jobs.

U.S. Workers' Satisfaction With Their Job Security
Are you completely satisfied, somewhat satisfied, somewhat dissatisfied or completely dissatisfied with your job security?

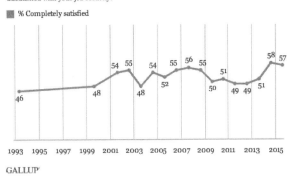

GALLUP

Bottom Line

For the most part, Americans' satisfaction with various aspects of their jobs is higher today than it was in 2005. But despite these improvements, no more than one in three workers are completely satisfied with their salaries, stress levels, chances for promotion and retirement plans.

As the unemployment rate, as measured by the Bureau of Labor Statistics, has improved, so have employed Americans' feelings about their job security. But satisfaction with other aspects of their jobs, such as on-the-job stress, pay and promotion opportunities, still has room for improvement. On a positive note, the large majority of working Americans are satisfied with the safety of their work environment and their relationships with coworkers.

Survey Methods

Results for this Gallup poll are based on telephone interviews conducted Aug. 5–9, 2015, with a random sample of 485 adults employed full or part time, aged 18 and older, living in all 50 U.S. states and the District of Columbia. For results based on the total sample of national adults, the margin of sampling error is ±6 percentage points at the 95% confidence level. All reported margins of sampling error include computed design effects for weighting.

August 31, 2015
ONE IN FIVE EMPLOYED AMERICANS WORRIED ABOUT WAGE REDUCTION

by Rebecca Riffkin

Story Highlights

- *Fewer worried about wage reduction than in 2009 through 2013*
- *Fewer Americans worried about most job aspects than in 2011*
- *Worries about jobs moving overseas constant, but low*

WASHINGTON, D.C.—One in five employed Americans say they are worried their wages will be reduced in the near future. This is noticeably lower than the percentage of Americans who were worried about wage reductions from 2009 through 2013, amid the erratic and uneven economic times after the Great Recession.

One in Five Employed Americans Worry Their Wages Will Be Reduced
Next, please indicate whether you are worried or not worried about each of the following happening to you, personally, in the near future. How about: that your wages will be reduced?

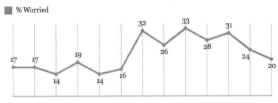

Aug. 5-9, 2015

GALLUP

Between 2003 and 2008, 16% of employed Americans, on average, reported they were worried about their wages being reduced. This percentage doubled in 2009 as unemployment surged to 10% after the financial crisis, and the percentage of workers who were worried remained high through 2013 before falling to 24% in 2014 and 20% today.

This is one of five employment concerns Gallup has tracked annually as part of its August Work and Education survey. Worker concerns peaked on all five measures between 2009 and 2011 and have since receded on each to varying degrees. However, concern about wage loss has decreased the most, falling 13 percentage points since 2011.

Workers' concern about having their hours cut back has declined almost as much, falling 11 points since 2011 to 19% today.

And while concern about reduced benefits remains the top employment worry at 34%, this is down 10 points from a high of 44% in 2011. Fear of being laid off has declined eight points to 22% since 2011, while concern that one's company will move jobs overseas—never a major worry—is down slightly to 9%.

Americans Are Less Worried About Most Aspects of Their Jobs Than They Were in 2011

Next, please indicate whether you are worried or not worried about each of the following happening to you, personally, in the near future. How about ... ?

	% Worried in 2011	% Worried in 2015	Difference (pct. pts.)
That your benefits will be reduced	44	34	-10
That you will be laid off	30	22	-8
That your wages will be reduced	33	20	-13
That your hours at work will be cut back	30	19	-11
That your company will move jobs to countries overseas	13	9	-4

Aug. 5-9, 2015

GALLUP

Since 2003, shifts in workers' fears of employment cutbacks have closely paralleled changes in the U.S. unemployment rate, which peaked at 9% or higher from early 2009 through late 2011, and has subsequently dropped about one point each year.

Bottom Line

As the unemployment rate has declined, fewer Americans are worried about various aspects of their jobs than even a few years ago—including being laid off, but also cuts in pay, benefits or hours. Decreases in worry follow a time line similar to that of other improving economic trends Gallup has found over the past few years, such as its Job Creation Index, the Economic Confidence Index and consumer spending. This could be a positive sign that Americans see their lives returning to the way things were in the early 2000s, although not quite all the way. Or it could be that workers now see conditions as a new reality after the Great Recession and thus not a cause for worry.

Survey Methods

Results for this Gallup poll are based on telephone interviews conducted Aug. 5–9, 2015, with a random sample of 1,011 adults, aged 18 and older, living in all 50 U.S. states and the District of Columbia. For results based on the sample of 485 adults who are employed full or part time, the maximum margin of sampling error is ±6 percentage points. All reported margins of sampling error include computed design effects for weighting.

September 01, 2015

OBAMA JOB APPROVAL DOWN TO 52% AMONG U.S. UNION WORKERS

by Jeffrey M. Jones

Story Highlights

- *Near personal 51% low for Obama*
- *Union members have consistently had higher approval for Obama*
- *Gap between union members and nonmembers is smallest to date*

PRINCETON, N.J.—Leading into this year's Labor Day holiday, 52% of U.S. union members approve of President Barack Obama's job performance, down slightly from 56% in the first quarter of 2015 and one percentage point above his personal low among this group. At the same time, the average rating of the president among those who are not union members has been flat at 46%.

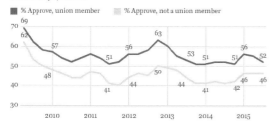

President Obama's Job Approval Rating, by Union Membership
Based on employed adults

■ % Approve, union member   ▨ % Approve, not a union member

Quarterly averages are shown. Latest figure is quarter to date. Gallup did not ask about union membership during Obama's first quarter in office (January-March 2009).

GALLUP

Throughout Obama's presidency, union members have consistently been more likely than nonmembers to approve of the job he is doing, but if these figures hold through the rest of the third quarter, the current six-point gap would be the lowest of his presidency.

The latest figures are based on July 1–Aug. 30 Gallup Daily tracking interviews with 2,684 employed adults who are members of unions and 23,111 employed adults who are not union members. Given the large proportion of Americans who are not union workers, Obama's approval rating among all Americans during this time is also 46%.

Union members are a core Democratic constituency, so it is not surprising that they have been more approving than nonmembers of the job Obama is doing. Obama's job approval rating has averaged 55% among union members since Gallup began tracking approval among this group in the second quarter of 2009. That compares with a 46% average among nonmembers, and 47% among all Americans.

Obama's approval rating among union members has held above the majority level each quarter, with the lows of 51% coming on four separate occasions, most recently in the fourth quarter of 2014.

Other than the 69% recorded during the "honeymoon phase" of his presidency, Obama's approval among union members has been as high as 63%. This occurred during the fourth quarter of 2012, which coincided with his re-election victory.

Currently, his approval rating is an identical 52% among union members who work for the government and union members who work for private-sector employers. Government union workers and nongovernment union workers have typically shown little to no difference in their approval ratings for Obama.

Gap Between Union Members and Nonmembers on Pace to Be Smallest

The trend lines in Obama's approval ratings among union members and nonmembers have risen and fallen together over the six-plus years of his presidency, but with union members' ratings consistently higher, by between seven and 13 points. The smallest gaps prior to the current quarter were seven points during Obama's second quarter, from April to June 2009 (69% union to 62% nonunion), and from April to June 2013 (55% to 48%).

One key reason union members' approval may be lower this quarter could be the president's pursuit of free-trade agreements with Asian nations. Labor unions typically oppose free-trade agreements because of concerns that cheaper imports could result in job losses for American workers.

Also, more of the political attention now is focused on the 2016 election, and Democratic candidates like Bernie Sanders and Hillary Clinton may be talking more about issues union members care about than the president is. In particular, the president's top agenda item at this point is marshaling congressional support for the nuclear agreement with Iran.

One factor that may be preventing Obama's approval among union members from being even lower is that he has taken a number of steps in recent months aimed at expanding workers' rights. Included among these are making an expanded number of workers eligible for overtime pay and attempting to have more workers classified as employees rather than contractors, to make them eligible for greater legal protections.

Union members' approval of Obama was particularly high relative to nonmembers' in 2012, as Obama was campaigning for a second term. In the third and fourth quarters of that year, union members' approval averaged 13 points higher than that of nonmembers.

Implications

Union members have solidly backed Obama throughout his presidency, showing approval nearly 10 points higher than the national average. But their current 52% support for him is on the low end of what Gallup has measured—just one point above his personal low.

Previously, his low points in union-member approval came when his overall approval rating had also been at personal lows, suggesting union members' less positive evaluations at those times were based on the same factors causing other Americans to view him less positively. The current decline in union approval is different because his overall approval rating has been relatively stable at 46%, about five points above his personal low. This suggests the decline in union-member approval in recent months may be a reaction largely confined to this group, possibly in response to the president's actions or policies on trade and his focus on issues of less direct benefit to union workers.

Survey Methods

Results for this Gallup poll are based on telephone interviews conducted July 1–Aug. 30, 2015, on the Gallup U.S. Daily survey, with a random sample of 25,795 working adults, aged 18 and older, living in all 50 U.S. states and the District of Columbia. For results based on the total sample of national adults, the margin of sampling error is ±1 percentage point at the 95% confidence level.

For results based on the sample of 2,684 employed union members, the margin of sampling error is ±2 percentage points at the 95% confidence level.

For results based on the sample of 23,111 employed non-union members, the margin of sampling error is ±1 percentage point at the 95% confidence level.

September 02, 2015
WORKING WOMEN STILL LAG MEN IN OPINION OF WORKPLACE EQUITY

by Lydia Saad

Story Highlights

- *Women twice as likely as men to feel overlooked for promotion*
- *Gender gap in U.S. even greater for pay equity*
- *Perceptions largely unchanged since 2013*

PRINCETON, N.J.—Twelve percent of women say they have been passed over for a promotion or other opportunity because of their gender at some point in their life, similar to the 15% who said this in 2013. By contrast, 5% of employed men, versus 8% two years ago, believe that being male has ever hindered their advancement.

U.S. Workers' Experience With Gender-Based Fairness in Promotions

Have you ever felt you were passed over for a promotion or opportunity at work because of your gender, or not?

	Have felt passed over	Have not felt passed over	No opinion
	%	%	%
AUG 5-9, 2015			
All workers	8	91	1
Men	5	95	*
Women	12	87	*
AUG 7-11, 2013			
All workers	11	88	1
Men	8	91	2
Women	15	85	1

Based on adults employed full or part time

GALLUP

Gallup's Aug. 5–9 Work and Education survey also finds 17% of working women believing they have ever been denied a raise at work because of their gender, within the margin of error of the 13% who said this in 2013. This far exceeds the rate among working men, steady at 4%.

Although the vast majority of men and women believe gender has not been a factor in their ability to advance or to get a raise, 19% of women indicate that at least one of the two types of discrimination has affected them over the course of their working lives, a substantial minority. That compares with 6% of men.

At the same time, equal percentages of men and women say that advancing in their career is extremely or very important to them: 56% of women and 59% of men. However, in a shift from 2013, fewer women today say that career advancement is not important to

them, 19% versus 28%, bringing women into closer alignment with men on this measure.

U.S. Workers' Experience With Gender-Based Fairness in Pay

Have you ever felt you were denied a raise at work because of your gender, or not?

	Have felt denied	Have not felt denied	No opinion
	%	%	%
AUG 5-9, 2015			
All workers	10	90	*
Men	4	96	*
Women	17	83	*
AUG 7-11, 2013			
All workers	8	91	1
Men	4	94	2
Women	13	86	1

Based on adults employed full or part time

GALLUP

Importance of Career Advancement to U.S. Workers

How important is it to you that you advance in your career over time -- extremely important, very important, somewhat important, not too important or not important at all?

	Extremely/Very important	Somewhat important	Not too/Not at all important	No opinion
	%	%	%	%
AUG 5-9, 2015				
All workers	57	23	19	*
Men	59	21	19	1
Women	56	24	19	*
AUG 7-11, 2013				
All workers	54	23	21	1
Men	58	25	15	1
Women	50	21	28	1

Based on adults employed full or part time

GALLUP

Women Less Satisfied Than Men With Current Pay

Beyond their lifetime perceptions of being discriminated against for being a woman, the poll also finds working women lagging working men in current satisfaction with their pay: 20% of women versus 44% of men say they are completely satisfied with the amount they earn. Although working women are slightly less positive than working men about most aspects of their jobs, none of the other differences are statistically significant.

U.S. Workers' Satisfaction With Job Characteristics

Now I'll read a list of job characteristics. For each, please tell me how satisfied or dissatisfied you are with your current job in this regard.

% Completely satisfied

	Men	Women	Difference
	%	%	(pct. pts.)
Your relations with coworkers	72	72	0
The flexibility of your hours	58	57	-1
The health insurance benefits your employer offers	41	39	-2
The retirement plan your employer offers	37	34	-3
Your boss or immediate supervisor	56	53	-3
The amount of on-the-job stress in your job	30	25	-5
The physical safety conditions of your workplace	72	66	-6
The amount of vacation time you receive	61	53	-8
The recognition you receive at work for your work accomplishments	48	42	-6
The amount of work that is required of you	56	48	-8
Your job security	61	52	-9
Your chances for promotion	39	30	-9
The amount of money you earn	44	20	-24

Based on adults employed full or part time
Aug. 5-9, 2015

GALLUP

The current gender gap in satisfaction with pay is markedly higher than what Gallup reported a year ago based on combined 2010–2014 data. Thus, it will be important to monitor future updates to determine if this year's result represents a meaningful shift, whether as a result of real changes in the workplace or heightened sensitivity among women about pay.

Bottom Line

Despite numerous policy and cultural efforts in recent decades to break corporate glass ceilings, integrate women in traditionally male-dominated fields and shine a spotlight on pay equity and advancement, a considerable minority of working women report feeling they were discriminated against at some point in their employment history. The trends are not long enough to establish whether the rates are rising or falling, but working women's beliefs about having suffered gender discrimination have neither improved—nor worsened—since 2013.

To some extent the male-female differences Gallup sees may be explained by certain fundamental differences in the nature of the work that men and women do. For instance, working women are more likely than working men to be employed part time rather than full time. The women surveyed in this poll are also more likely than men to have white-collar professional or administrative jobs, or to work in a service industry, while men are more likely to be in skilled and unskilled blue-collar jobs.

Regardless, divergent gender perspectives about fairness in advancement and pay could have very real significance when it comes to men's and women's life satisfaction, self-esteem, political orientation and broader worldview—implications that employers and policymakers can't ignore.

Survey Methods

Results for this Gallup poll are based on telephone interviews conducted Aug. 5–9, 2015, with a random sample of 1,011 adults, aged 18 and older, living in all 50 U.S. states and the District of Columbia. For results based on the total sample of adults employed full or part time, the margin of sampling error is ±6 percentage points at the 95% confidence level. For results based on the sample of 208 employed women, the margin of sampling error is ±9 percentage points at the 95% confidence level. For results based on the sample of 277 employed men, the margin of sampling error is ±8 percentage points at the 95% confidence level. All reported margins of sampling error include computed design effects for weighting.

September 04, 2015
TRUMP'S IMAGE UP SHARPLY AMONG REPUBLICANS

by Frank Newport

Story Highlights

- *Trump gains 16 points in net favorability in last two weeks*
- *Carson remains leader on favorability, Trump on familiarity*
- *Jeb Bush's favorability edges down*

PRINCETON, N.J.—Donald Trump's net favorable rating among Republicans increased significantly over the past two weeks, putting him among the top six Republicans overall on this measure. Ted Cruz's image also improved, while Carly Fiorina's and Ben Carson's images remain significantly better than they were before the Aug. 6 debate. John Kasich, Jeb Bush and Scott Walker are among those whose images worsened.

Republican Candidate Net Favorable Ratings*: Trends Over Time
Ranked by Aug. 19-Sept. 1 net favorables, based on Republicans/Republican leaners

	Jul 8-21, 2015 %	Jul 22-Aug 4, 2015 %	Aug 5-18, 2015 %	Aug 19-Sep 1, 2015 %	Change, Aug 5-18 to Aug 19-Sep 1 (pct. pts.)
Carson	40	35	48	51	+3
Rubio	42	38	41	42	+1
Cruz	34	29	34	41	+7
Huckabee	37	33	36	38	+2
Fiorina	23	16	32	37	+5
Trump	20	18	16	32	+16
Walker	34	38	37	31	-6
Jindal	29	28	25	23	-2
Bush	27	25	25	19	-6
Perry	35	32	17	18	+1
Kasich	14	15	27	15	-12
Santorum	19	19	14	14	0
Paul	26	23	9	11	+2
Christie	6	1	4	0	-4
Gilmore	n/a	n/a	-9	-6	+3
Pataki	-7	-9	-7	-11	-4
Graham	4	-5	-8	-13	-5

* % Favorable minus % unfavorable, in percentage points

GALLUP

These results are based on a comparison of Gallup Daily tracking across four two-week time periods, from mid-July to Sept. 1, with about 1,000 Republicans and Republican-leaning independents rating each candidate in each period. The complete data are presented at the end of this article.

The chart below displays how well-known (net familiarity, shown on the horizontal axis) and how well-liked (net favorability, shown on the vertical axis) each candidate is in the most recent two-week interviewing period.

Candidates in the upper-right section of the graph have above-average familiarity and above-average net favorable ratings, which is optimal from a candidate campaign perspective. Those in the lower-right section are better known but less well liked, signifying an inability to translate familiarity into positive affect. Those in the upper-left section are not as well known but tend to be better liked, making their major challenge one of becoming better known. And those in the lower left are behind on both dimensions, although some like Kasich and Santorum are just slightly below average on each dimension.

Here are some key insights based on how Republicans view the candidates today and how these views have changed over time:

Donald Trump: Trump's net favorability rating among Republicans climbed 16 points over the last two weeks. This marks a significant shift; Trump's image previous to the last two weeks had been relatively stable despite the extraordinary media attention his candidacy has engendered. He now joins Fiorina and Carson as having chalked up the largest gains on this dimension since mid-July. Trump had near-universal name identification when Gallup tracking began in July, and he retains the distinction of being the best known of the candidates. Still, even with his significant image gains, Trump remains sixth on the net favorability list, trailing Carson, Fiorina, Rubio, Cruz and Huckabee.

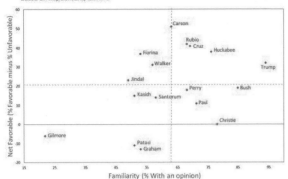

Potential 2016 Republican Presidential Candidates: Familiarity and Favorability
Based on Republicans/Leaners

Ted Cruz: The Texas senator's net favorable rating ticked up seven points in the last two weeks, less than Trump's, but still a significant gain. Cruz now has the third-highest net favorable rating of any candidate, and his familiarity, at 69%, is above average.

Carly Fiorina: Although she was relegated to the earlier "Happy Hour" Fox News debate on Aug. 6, Fiorina received positive reviews for her performance, and the gains she saw after the debate have continued in the last two weeks. Her net favorable score is now 37, up five points from the Aug. 5–18 time period, and up 14 points since mid-July. Her familiarity is also up 14 points over the past eight weeks. CNN, the sponsor of the next Republican debate on Sept. 16, recently made the decision to change its inclusion criteria for the main debate in a way that almost certainly will allow Fiorina to participate. This may help the former Hewlett Packard CEO become even more familiar to Republicans—important to her campaign given her still-below-average familiarity rating of 53%. Her current net favorable score puts her in the top five for all candidates.

Ben Carson: The former neurosurgeon has the distinction of holding the highest net favorable rating, 51, of any of the 17 GOP candidates. Carson, like Fiorina, saw a jump in his net favorability and familiarity after the debate, and he has held on to those gains. Carson's familiarity rating of 63%, however, is still only average.

Jeb Bush: Unlike Trump, Bush has not been able to use his high name identification to his advantage. Bush is the second best known of the candidates, but the former Florida governor has had a bad summer in terms of his image—with a six-point drop in his net favorable score in the last two weeks. Bush's slide puts him just below average on the image dimension, behind eight of his competitors.

Rick Perry, Lindsey Graham and Rand Paul: All of these candidates' net favorable scores have dropped over time. For Graham, this adds insult to injury. He is now the lowest rated candidate at -13, one of three candidates bottoming out in negative territory, along with George Pataki and Jim Gilmore. The path for Perry and Paul has been different. Both had much higher favorability scores in July. Despite Perry's image taking a big hit, it remains essentially tied

with Bush's—just below average. Paul's favorability, on the other hand, is now well below average at 11.

Marco Rubio and Mike Huckabee: Their net favorability and familiarity have not changed much, but both are still well positioned image-wise, with above-average scores on both dimensions. They join Cruz and Trump as the four candidates in the positive, upper-right quadrant of the standings—enjoying both above-average favorability and above-average familiarity.

Chris Christie: The New Jersey governor is notable for his high familiarity, and is third only to Trump and Bush in that regard. But his net favorable score has never been high, and is now at zero—meaning that as many Republicans have an unfavorable opinion of the controversial governor as have a favorable opinion. At this point, Christie ranks among the least-liked candidates.

John Kasich: Although he didn't officially announce he was running for president until July 21, Kasich has made greater gains in familiarity than any other candidate, with his familiarity score shooting up from 34% in mid-July to 51% over the past two weeks. Unfortunately for the Ohio governor, his net favorability score—after rising significantly in the period immediately after the debate—has dropped again over the past two weeks, and he is now essentially back to where he started. Kasich's trajectory is clearly distinct from that of Carson and Fiorina, who also gained familiarity, but who, unlike Kasich, also gained significantly in net favorability.

Bottom Line

The last two months have seen widespread campaigning, media coverage, a highly watched debate and—particularly in the case of Donald Trump—continuing controversy. Tracking changes in each candidate's familiarity and favorability provides a valuable gauge of how all of this is playing out in the minds of the Republican audience.

Despite some political analysts' expectations that Trump's bombastic style and controversial statements could begin to weaken his standing among Republicans, the businessman and TV personality's net favorable score has actually jumped over the past two weeks, and he is now in a much stronger position image-wise than in mid-July. From a broad perspective, these data show no signs yet of an overall backlash among rank-and-file Republicans to his campaign, style or issue positions.

Jeb Bush has begun to criticize Trump directly in videos and speeches, reflecting his campaign's awareness of Trump's standing and Bush's own weakening position. Trump has fought back, and the two best-known candidates are now in a verbal shoving match of sorts. How effective Bush's ads, speeches and appearance in the Sept. 16 debate will be in slowing down Trump's momentum remains to be seen. At this point, the paths of the two best-known candidates have clearly diverged, with Trump going up and Bush going down.

Another group of candidates, including Rubio, Cruz, Huckabee and, to a lesser degree, Walker, started off with positive images but have yet to show signs of significant improvement like Fiorina, Carson or Trump.

The first Republican debate in early August enjoyed extremely high ratings and resulted in significant changes in how Republicans viewed a number of the candidates. The debate on Sept. 16 is the next major milestone in the long, expensive and arduous trek toward the first actual votes to be cast next February.

Survey Methods

Results for this Gallup poll are based on telephone interviews conducted July 8–Sept. 1, 2015, on the Gallup U.S. Daily survey, with a random sample of 13,996 Republicans and Republican-leaning independents, aged 18 and older, living in all 50 U.S. states and the District of Columbia. Each candidate was rated by a random subset of respondents during this period, with the sample sizes rating each candidate averaging about 1,000 Republicans and Republican-leaning independents within each two-week interviewing period.

For results based on the total sample of Republicans and Republican-leaning independents, aged 18 and older, rating each candidate at each time period, the margin of sampling error is ±4 percentage points at the 95% confidence level. All reported margins of sampling error include computed design effects for weighting.

September 09, 2015
ONE IN FIVE VOTERS SAY IMMIGRATION STANCE CRITICAL TO VOTE

by Jeffrey M. Jones

Story Highlights

- *One in five say candidate must share immigration views*
- *Republicans most likely political group to require agreement*
- *Immigrants above national average*

PRINCETON, N.J.—Twenty percent of U.S. registered voters say they will only vote for a candidate who shares their views on immigration, with another 60% saying it will be one of many important considerations they take into account. Registered voters who are Republican, first- or second-generation immigrants or Hispanics are more likely than others to say sharing a candidate's position on immigration is a must in order to win their vote.

Immigration again promises to be an important issue in the 2016 presidential campaign, as the federal government has been unable to pass a comprehensive reform bill. It already has been one of the more discussed issues this year, in large part because Republican front-runner Donald Trump has made the issue the centerpiece of his campaign.

The question was included in Gallup's Minority Rights and Relations poll, conducted June 15–July 10. This is the first time Gallup has asked the question about immigration, so it is not known whether voters' orientation to the issue today is different from the past.

Earlier this year, Gallup found that 19% of registered voters would only vote for a candidate who shares their views on another highly divisive issue—abortion—which is similar to the percentage who say they must agree with a candidate on immigration (20%). But fewer voters said abortion would be one of many important factors to their vote (49%) than say this about immigration (60%), indicating immigration is broadly more important than abortion as a potential make-or-break issue for candidates.

Effect of Immigration on Vote, Based on Registered Voters

Thinking about how the immigration issue might affect your vote for major offices, would you [ROTATED: only vote for a candidate who shares your views on immigration (or) consider a candidate's position on immigration as just one of many important factors (or) not see immigration as a major issue]?

	% Only vote for candidate who shares views	% Consider position as one of many important factors	% Not a major issue
All registered voters	20	60	17
Republicans	27	56	16
Independents	19	65	15
Democrats	18	59	21
Hispanic	25	49	18
Non-Hispanic black	24	46	26
Non-Hispanic white	19	65	15
Self/Parents born in U.S.	19	62	17
Self born in U.S./Parent born in another country	27	54	18
Born in another country	28	47	14

June 15–July 10, 2015

GALLUP

Republicans' greater likelihood of saying they must agree with a candidate on immigration in order to support him or her suggests the issue should be a bigger factor in the Republican primaries than in the Democratic primaries. Republican candidates generally place a high priority on border security and do not favor a path to citizenship for undocumented immigrants residing in the U.S. But some, like Trump, go further, offering a number of additional policies to limit immigration, such as deporting all undocumented immigrants and not granting automatic citizenship to children born in the U.S. whose parents are here illegally.

But in the general election campaign, immigration could work to the detriment of the eventual GOP nominee given immigrants' and Hispanics' above-average desire for agreement with their chosen candidate on the immigration issue, coupled with their generally pro-immigration views.

Although the 24% of blacks who say agreement on immigration is crucial to winning their vote is roughly the same percentage as immigrants, Republicans and Hispanics, nearly as many blacks, 26%, say immigration is not a major issue—higher than for other subgroups.

Hard-Liners on Immigration Not More Likely to Require Candidate Agreement

The basic results by party don't alone indicate whether a more moderate candidate on immigration (such as Jeb Bush or any of the Democrats) or a hard-line candidate on immigration (most notably, Trump) would be more appealing to voters for whom immigration is a make-or-break issue. However, analyzing voting preferences by voters' views on immigration policy indicates it is not necessarily the hard-liners on immigration who are most likely to require agreement on the issue.

Specifically, 21% of registered voters who say all illegal immigrants should be deported say they will only vote for a candidate who shares their views on immigration, essentially matching the national average. Those who favor allowing illegal immigrants to stay and work for a limited time are a bit more likely to say their chosen candidate must agree with them on immigration.

Effect of Immigration on Vote Based on Preferences for Handling Illegal Immigrants Living in the U.S., Based on Registered Voters

	Deport all back to home country	Allow to stay for limited time to work	Allow to stay and work toward becoming citizens
	%	%	%
Only vote for candidate who shares views	21	27	18
Consider position as one of many important factors	63	54	62
Not a major issue	15	16	18

June 15-July 10, 2015

GALLUP'

Although there aren't sufficient cases to analyze these immigration views by voters who identify politically as Republican, the limited data available suggest Republicans in favor of deporting undocumented immigrants back to their country are no more likely than Republicans with more moderate views on the issue to say they would only support a candidate sharing their views on immigration.

Implications

Earlier this year, Gallup found voters ranking immigration as relatively less important as an issue to their vote than the economy, healthcare and the federal government. However, that poll was taken before Trump entered the race. The Minority Rights and Relations poll reported here was conducted mostly after Trump announced his candidacy, finding about one in five registered voters saying they will only vote for a candidate who shares their views on immigration.

Currently, 8% of Americans name immigration as the most important problem facing the country, compared with 6% before Trump entered the race, which suggests his presence has not greatly elevated the issue as a priority for voters, and it may still not be as important of a factor in the election as some of the other issues like the economy and the government.

Nevertheless, immigration has arguably attracted more attention than any other issue in the 2016 campaign thus far, perhaps because of its divisive nature and its complexity, particularly around how to handle the millions of immigrants living in the U.S. who entered illegally but in many cases have established stable and productive lives in this country. And in a close primary or general election contest, even if it is less important than the economy and other issues, immigration could easily tilt the outcome toward one candidate or another.

Survey Methods

Results for this Gallup poll are based on telephone interviews conducted June 15–July 10, 2015, with a random sample of 1,987 registered voters, aged 18 and older, living in all 50 U.S. states and the District of Columbia. All respondents had previously been interviewed in the Gallup Daily tracking survey and agreed to be re-contacted by Gallup. For results based on the total sample of registered voters, the margin of sampling error is ±4 percentage points at the 95% confidence level.

For results based on the total sample of 808 non-Hispanic whites, the margin of sampling error is ±5 percentage points at the 95% confidence level.

For results based on the total sample of 739 non-Hispanic blacks, the margin of sampling error is ±5 percentage points at the 95% confidence level.

For results based on the total sample of 343 Hispanics, the margin of sampling error is ±8 percentage points at the 95% confidence level.

September 09, 2015
GOV'T WORKERS HAPPIER WITH RETIREMENT PLANS, OTHER BENEFITS

by Justin McCarthy

Story Highlights

- *Gov't workers more satisfied with retirement, health insurance*
- *Nine in 10 gov't employees satisfied with vacation time*

WASHINGTON, D.C.—Public and private sector workers are similarly satisfied with most of the 13 job aspects Gallup asks them about, but government employees are more likely to be satisfied with their retirement plans, health insurance and vacation benefits.

Satisfaction With 13 Job Aspects -- Government vs. Nongovernment Employees in the U.S.
% Completely/Somewhat satisfied

	Government employees	Nongovernment employees	Difference
	%	%	(pct. pts.)
The retirement plan your employer offers	82	57	+25
The health insurance benefits your employer offers	80	57	+23
The amount of vacation time you receive	91	74	+17
Your boss or immediate supervisor	88	82	+6
Your job security	87	83	+4
Your chances for promotion	69	66	+3
The amount of work that is required of you	86	83	+3
Your relations with coworkers	96	93	+3
The amount of money you earn	72	70	+2
The physical safety conditions of your workplace	91	91	0
The flexibility of your hours	85	87	-2
The recognition you receive at work for your work accomplishments	76	79	-3
The amount of on-the-job stress in your job	64	67	-3

Based on adults employed full or part time

GALLUP'

These ratings are based on combined data from the last five years of Gallup's annual Work and Education poll, conducted each August since 2001.

The largest gap in satisfaction between government and nongovernment workers is in regard to their retirement plan. While 82% of government employees say they are "completely" or "somewhat satisfied" with their retirement plan, this percentage is much lower among nongovernment employees, with 57% reporting satisfaction.

The gap in satisfaction is nearly as large with health insurance benefits, with 80% of government workers and 57% of nongovernment workers satisfied with the benefits that their employer offers.

Government workers are even more likely to be satisfied with their vacation time than they are with their retirement or health insurance, with 91% saying they are satisfied. While most nongovernment employees, 74%, are also satisfied with their vacation time, there is a 17-percentage-point gap in satisfaction between the two groups.

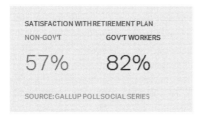

Overall, private sector workers are least satisfied with their retirement plan and health insurance benefits, while government workers are least satisfied with their on-the-job stress.

In addition to vacation time, government workers are most satisfied with their relations with coworkers and the physical safety conditions of their workplace. Coworker relations and workplace physical safety are private sector workers' top-rated workplace aspects.

Bottom Line

Government and private sector employees' views on the various elements of their job make one thing clear: Government employees are much more satisfied than nongovernment employees with the traditional "benefits" of their job—namely, the retirement plan, health insurance benefits and vacation time.

Government benefits vary quite a bit, however, from federal benefits to state government benefits, and this also varies a great deal by state. But many government workers likely have pension plans—something increasingly rare in the private sector—and generous health plans requiring lower out-of-pocket costs than seen in most private sector plans. Government workers may also get guaranteed vacation of two to four weeks (or summers off for public school teachers) and likely all federal holidays.

On the other hand, a federal advisory body found last year that, on average, federal government employees earn more than a third less than their private sector counterparts, but these data show that government employees are just as satisfied, on average, with their pay as are private sector workers. *Historical data are available in Gallup Analytics.*

Survey Methods

Results for this Gallup poll are based on combined telephone interviews from Gallup's 2011–2015 Work and Education surveys, conducted each August with random samples of employed adults, aged 18 and older, living in all 50 U.S. states and the District of Columbia.

For results based on the total sample of 2,949 employed adults, the margin of sampling error is ±2 percentage points at the 95% confidence level. For results based on the total sample of 528 government employees, the margin of sampling error is ±5 percentage points at the 95% confidence level. For results based on the total sample of 2,421 nongovernment employees, the margin of sampling error is ±3 percentage points at the 95% confidence level. All reported margins of sampling error include computed design effects for weighting.

September 10, 2015
SAN ANTONIO-NEW BRAUNFELS LEADS U.S. IN EMPLOYEE ENGAGEMENT

by Amy Adkins and Sangeeta Agrawal

Story Highlights

- *Cities in Texas, Oklahoma and California have most engaged workers*
- *Employee engagement linked to improved business outcomes*
- *U.S. employee engagement at 31.7% in August*

WASHINGTON, D.C.—With 38.1% of its workforce engaged, San Antonio-New Braunfels, Texas, ranked highest in employee engagement among metropolitan statistical areas (MSAs) in 2014. Greater San Antonio was followed by Oklahoma City, Oklahoma, and Riverside-San Bernardino-Ontario, California, at 37.6% and 36.8%, respectively.

Metro Areas With Highest Employee Engagement

Metro Area	% Engaged
San Antonio-New Braunfels, TX	38.1
Oklahoma City, OK	37.6
Riverside-San Bernardino-Ontario, CA	36.8
Tulsa, OK	36.3
Orlando-Kissimmee-Sanford, FL	35.6
Cincinnati, OH-KY-IN	35.0
Miami-Fort Lauderdale-West Palm Beach, FL	34.5
Dallas-Fort Worth-Arlington, TX	34.3
Tampa-St. Petersburg-Clearwater, FL	34.1
San Diego-Carlsbad, CA	34.1

Figures shown are for 2014

GALLUP

Conversely, Buffalo-Cheektowaga-Niagara Falls, New York; San Jose-Sunnyvale-Santa Clara, California; and Minneapolis-St. Paul-Bloomington, Minnesota, ranked lowest in U.S. employee engagement this past year. The employee engagement figures for these metro areas trailed the national leader by 13 to 15 percentage points.

Metro Areas With Lowest Employee Engagement

Metro Area	% Engaged
Buffalo-Cheektowaga-Niagara Falls, NY	23.5
San Jose-Sunnyvale-Santa Clara, CA	24.7
Minneapolis-St. Paul-Bloomington, MN-WI	24.9
Washington-Arlington-Alexandria, DC-VA-MD-WV	25.9
Columbus, OH	26.8
Portland-Vancouver-Hillsboro, OR-WA	27.6
Omaha-Council Bluffs, NE-IA	27.8
Hartford-West Hartford-East Hartford, CT	28.1
Denver-Aurora-Lakewood, CO	28.2
Louisville/Jefferson County, KY-IN	28.3

Figures shown are for 2014

GALLUP

The 2014 employee engagement estimates are based on Gallup Daily tracking interviews conducted January 2014–December 2014, with 52,785 U.S. adults employed full or part time for an employer. MSAs that were represented by at least 300 respondents were included in the results, which includes a total of 53 metro areas.

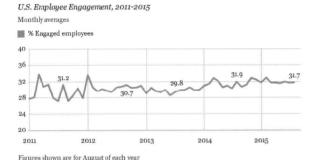

EMPLOYEE ENGAGEMENT: METRO AREAS

BUFFALO	SAN ANTONO
23.5%	38.1%

SOURCE: GALLUP DAILY TRACKING

Nationally, 31.5% of workers were engaged in 2014. Gallup's latest update on employee engagement, from August, finds that 31.7% of U.S. workers are engaged, similar to results from last year but higher than from 2011 through 2013.

U.S. Employee Engagement, 2011-2015

Monthly averages

■ % Engaged employees

[chart showing monthly averages from 2011 to 2015, with data labels: 31.2, 30.7, 29.8, 31.9, 31.7; y-axis from 20 to 40]

Figures shown are for August of each year

GALLUP

Gallup categorizes workers as "engaged," "not engaged" or "actively disengaged" based on their ratings of key workplace elements that predict important organizational performance outcomes. "Engaged" employees are defined as those who are involved in, enthusiastic about and committed to their work. These employees are passionate and creative, and their enthusiasm fuels growth and innovation. Gallup has consistently found links between employees who are engaged in their jobs and the achievement of crucial business outcomes. Companies with highly engaged workforces outperform their peers by 147% in earnings per share and realize:

- 41% fewer quality defects
- 48% fewer safety incidents
- 28% less shrinkage
- 65% less turnover (low-turnover organizations)
- 25% less turnover (high-turnover organizations)
- 37% less absenteeism

Employees who are "not engaged" fail to bring their organizations these types of returns. Not engaged employees are essentially "checked out." They demonstrate less concern about customers, productivity and profitability. They do not own or feel passionate about their work. "Actively disengaged" employees do more than prevent their organizations from growing—they actually try to damage them. These employees are not just unhappy at work; they deliberately undermine the accomplishments of their engaged coworkers. They monopolize managers' time, account for more quality defects and quit at a higher rate than engaged employees.

Buffalo-Cheektowaga-Niagara Falls Highest in Active Disengagement

In 2014, Buffalo-Cheektowaga-Niagara Falls, New York, had the lowest percentage of engaged employees for any MSA. The region also had the highest percentage of actively disengaged employees, followed by Columbus, Ohio, and Louisville-Jefferson County, Kentucky-Indiana. Workers in Richmond, Virginia; Houston-The Woodlands-Sugar Land, Texas; and Oklahoma City, Oklahoma, reported the lowest percentages of actively disengaged employees. Nationally, 17.5% of employees were actively disengaged in 2014.

Gallup has typically found that low levels of employee engagement go hand in hand with high levels of active disengagement, but the two are not necessarily the same because employees who are not engaged may not necessarily be actively disengaged. For example, Minneapolis-St. Paul-Bloomington, Minnesota, ranked near the bottom on employee engagement, but was in the middle of the pack on active disengagement. Also, Richmond, Virginia, had the lowest percentage of actively disengaged workers but was not among the top 10 in engagement, and San Antonio-New Braunfels, Texas, with the highest level of engagement, was not among the 10 lowest on active disengagement.

Metro Areas With Highest Active Disengagement

Metro Area	% Actively Disengaged
Buffalo-Cheektowaga-Niagara Falls, NY	22.6
Columbus, OH	21.8
Louisville-Jefferson County, KY-IN	20.8
Cincinnati, OH-KY-IN	20.8
Detroit-Warren-Dearborn, MI	20.2
Milwaukee-Waukesha-West Allis, WI	20.1
New York-Newark-Jersey City, NY-NJ-PA	20.0
St. Louis, MO-IL	19.7
Hartford-West Hartford-East Hartford, CT	19.6
Omaha-Council Bluffs, NE-IA	19.6

Figures shown are for 2014

GALLUP

Metro Areas With Lowest Active Disengagement

Metro Area	% Actively Disengaged
Richmond, VA	12.4
Houston-The Woodlands-Sugar Land, TX	13.5
Oklahoma City, OK	13.7
Raleigh, NC	14.9
Charlotte-Concord-Gastonia, NC-SC	15.1
Tulsa, OK	15.3
Jacksonville, FL	15.4
San Francisco-Oakland-Hayward, CA	15.5
Austin-Round Rock, TX	15.6
Indianapolis-Carmel-Anderson, IN	15.6

Figures shown are for 2014

GALLUP

Bottom Line

Wide variation exists in employee engagement across the nation's largest metro areas. Gallup has found that employee engagement—or a lack thereof—can be attributed to multiple factors. For example, recent research indicates that engagement is related to economic measures such as unemployment and underemployment. After controlling for household income, metro areas where employee engagement is higher tend to also have lower unemployment and underemployment.

However, the greatest factor in understanding employee engagement is the organization's management practices. Gallup research has found that managers account for at least 70% of the variance in employee engagement scores across business units. Companies must ensure that they are continuously developing managers and providing them with the necessary tools and support to engage employees.

Survey Methods

Results for the city-by-city rankings are based on Gallup Daily tracking interviews conducted January 2014–December 2014, with a random sample of 52,785 adults employed full or part time for an employer, aged 18 and older, living in all 50 U.S. states and the District of Columbia.

For results based on the total sample of employed adults, the margin of sampling error ranges from ±2 percentage points at the 95% confidence level for metro areas with the highest sample size (4,603) to ±8 percentage points at the 95% confidence level for metro areas with the lowest sample size (300). All reported margins of sampling error include computed design effects for weighting.

Results for the August 2015 employee engagement figure are based on Gallup Daily tracking interviews conducted Aug. 1–31, 2015, with a random sample of 6,928 adults employed for an employer, aged 18 and older, living in all 50 U.S. states and the District of Columbia.

For results based on the total sample of employed adults, the margin of sampling error is ±3 percentage points at the 95% confidence level. All reported margins of sampling error include computed design effects for weighting.

September 10, 2015
AMERICANS STILL VIEW AIRLINE INDUSTRY POSITIVELY

by Rebecca Riffkin

Story Highlights

- *35% rate airline industry positively and 32% negatively*
- *Industry has had net-positive ratings since 2013*
- *Industry viewed negatively from 2007 to 2012*

WASHINGTON, D.C.—Americans continue to view the airline industry slightly more positively than negatively, despite the frequent news reports about increased airline fees, cramped seats and customer frustration. The industry's current positive ratings are consistent with what Gallup has found since 2013 and with ratings before the economic downturn. From 2007 through 2012, as was true for many industries, more Americans viewed the airline industry negatively than positively.

Gallup annually asks Americans to rate the airline industry, as well as 24 other business industries and sectors, as part of its August Work and Education poll. Americans rate each industry on a five-point scale ranging from very positive to very negative. The airline industry has a net +3 positive rating this year, based on a combined 35% rating it very positively or positively, and 32% rating it very negatively or negatively. This rating ranks in the bottom third of the industries this year.

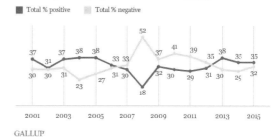

Americans' Ratings of the Airline Industry

On another subject, for each of the following business sectors in the United States, please say whether your overall view of it is very positive, somewhat positive, neutral, somewhat negative or very negative. How about the airline industry?

■ Total % positive   ▓ Total % negative

GALLUP

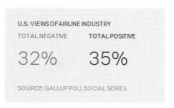

U.S. VIEWS OF AIRLINE INDUSTRY

TOTAL NEGATIVE: 32%   TOTAL POSITIVE: 35%

SOURCE: GALLUP POLL SOCIAL SERIES

The favorability of the airline industry has fluctuated over the years. In 2008, when many industries saw their ratings drop as the economy was in recession, positive ratings of the airline industry fell sharply from 30% to 18%. At that time, record-high gas prices and lower consumer travel expenditures forced airlines to introduce additional fees, increase prices and layoff employees. The resulting negative press, together with Americans' souring attitudes on most industries in 2008, at least partly explains this large net negative rating of -34 at that time. The industry continued to have a net negative rating until 2013, but by a narrower margin.

Younger More Likely Than Older Americans to View Airline Industry Positively

Young adults, those aged 18 to 29, are more likely than older Americans to view the airline industry positively. Based on combined data from 2013 through 2015, 44% of Americans aged 18 to 29 had a positive view of the industry, compared with fewer than four in 10 in all other age groups.

Ratings of the Airline Industry by Age

On another subject, for each of the following business sectors in the United States, please say whether your overall view of it is very positive, somewhat positive, neutral, somewhat negative or very negative. How about the airline industry?

	18-29	30-49	50-64	65+
% Total positive	44	33	35	37
% Neutral	32	35	27	22
% Total negative	21	29	36	34

Combined responses 2013-2015

GALLUP

Younger Americans' more positive views of the airline industry could be attributed to the fact that drastic changes in the industry's history occurred before they were born. No one in this age group was alive before airlines were deregulated in 1978. This move, which was supposed to make air travel less expensive, is what introduced more fees, the bankruptcy of many small airports and several airline mergers. Furthermore, the youngest Americans also became adults and began flying more after airport changes following the Sept. 11 terrorist attacks.

In early 2015, the U.S. Department of Justice announced it was investigating four of the major U.S. airlines for potential and "unlawful coordination" over prices, routes and fees between the airlines. If this did occur among these airlines, it could have hurt consumers by limiting competition and the availability of options between the airlines. Adding to customer complaints in 2015, oil and gas prices are down significantly, but the prices of tickets for flights have remained high.

However, the negative conditions taken as a whole—including mergers, changes in pricing structure, additions of fees and other shifts in the customer flying experience—have apparently not resulted in a significant degradation of the airline industry's image. Americans have been as likely to view the industry positively as negatively over the past several years, and these perceptions are as positive as they have been for a decade.

Survey Methods

Results for this Gallup poll are based on telephone interviews conducted Aug. 5–9, 2015, with a random sample of 1,011 adults, aged 18 and older, living in all 50 U.S. states and the District of Columbia.

Each industry was rated by a random subset of approximately 500 respondents. The margin of sampling error is ±6 percentage points at the 95% confidence level. For results based on the total sample of 270 18- to 29-year-olds, the margin of sampling error is ±8 percentage points at the 95% confidence level. All reported margins of sampling error include computed design effects for weighting.

September 11, 2015

UNION MEMBERS LESS CONTENT WITH SAFETY, RECOGNITION AT WORK

by Andrew Dugan

Story Highlights

- *Union workers less satisfied with workplace safety and flexibility*
- *Union workers more satisfied with employer-provided health insurance*

WASHINGTON, D.C.—In the U.S., employed Americans who report being members of labor unions are significantly less likely than nonunion employees to say they are "completely satisfied" with six of 13 job aspects. These include workplace safety, recognition for accomplishments, flexibility of hours and job security. In only one job aspect, employer-provided health insurance, are union workers significantly more likely than nonunion workers to say they are completely satisfied.

These findings are from an aggregate of interviews conducted from 2011 to 2015 as part of Gallup's annual Work and Education poll. This report compares the 2,586 employed U.S. adults who are not in a labor union with the 393 employed adults who report being in a union.

The largest gap between union members and nonmembers lies in the domain of workplace safety, with 57% of union members

expressing complete satisfaction with their job's safety conditions, compared with 73% of nonmembers.

Satisfaction With 13 Job Aspects -- Union vs. Nonunion U.S. Employees

Now I'll read a list of job characteristics. For each, please tell me how satisfied or dissatisfied you are with your current job in this regard. (% Completely satisfied)

	Union	Nonunion	Difference
	%	%	(pct. pts.)
The physical safety conditions of your workplace	57	73	-16*
The recognition you receive at work for your work accomplishments	35	50	-15*
Your boss or immediate supervisor	45	58	-13*
The flexibility of your hours	52	64	-12*
Your job security	44	54	-10*
The amount of work that is required of you	46	53	-7*
Your chances for promotion	33	37	-4
Your relations with your coworkers	67	70	-3
The amount of on-the-job stress in your job	28	28	0
The amount of money you earn	31	30	1
The amount of vacation time you receive	60	55	5
The retirement plan your employer offers	39	33	6
The health insurance benefits your employer offers	46	35	11*

* Statistically significant

GALLUP

CONTENT WITH WORKPLACE RECOGNITION

NONUNION MEMBERS   UNION MEMBERS

50%   35%

SOURCE: GALLUP POLL SOCIAL SERIES

A slightly smaller gap exists for recognition received at work—35% of union members versus 50% of nonmembers are content. Gallup research shows that frequent recognition of on-the-job accomplishments is an important driver of employee engagement.

Nonunion adults are more likely than union laborers to be completely satisfied with the flexibility of their hours (64% vs. 52%, respectively) and their boss or immediate supervisor (58% vs. 45%). Nonunion workers (53%) are also more likely than union workers (46%) to be satisfied with the amount of work required of them.

There are no statistical differences between the groups on several other dimensions of job satisfaction, including pay, vacation time, employer-sponsored retirement plans and levels of on-the-job stress. Notably, both union and nonunion workers report high levels of satisfaction with their relations with coworkers (67% and 70%, respectively). Coworker relations ranks as the top aspect in terms of satisfaction for both groups.

Employer-provided health insurance is the lone job characteristic for which union workers are statistically more likely to be completely satisfied than their nonunion counterparts, at 46% to 35%. In general, U.S. workers report an increased level of satisfaction with their employer-provided health plan compared with 2005—more so than for any other job characteristic.

Bottom Line

Historically, unions have been instrumental in improving the working conditions of the U.S. labor force, and their efforts have had a lasting effect on contemporary work culture. But labor union membership has declined to about a ninth of the workforce. Americans' approval of labor unions has generally been lower the past few years than in prior decades, including a historic low of 48% in 2009.

Current members of labor unions are significantly less likely than nonmembers to report being completely satisfied with a number of desirable job aspects, including workplace safety and flexibility of hours.

One reason that union members are less likely to be satisfied with several job characteristics is because many so-called "blue-collar" occupations—which generally have high rates of unionization—tend to be in fields that involve low- or no-skilled labor, comparatively more dangerous work environments and other such traits. In these cases, it is likely that fraught workplace conditions helped prompt unionization in the first place and principally explain the job satisfaction differences reviewed here.

Survey Methods

Results for this Gallup poll are based on combined telephone interviews from Gallup's 2011–2015 Work and Education surveys, conducted each August with random samples of employed adults, aged 18 and older, living in all 50 U.S. states and the District of Columbia.

For results based on the total sample of 2,979 employed adults, the margin of sampling error is ±2 percentage points at the 95% confidence level. For results based on the total sample of 393 union employees, the margin of sampling error is ±6 percentage points at the 95% confidence level. For results based on the total sample of 2,586 nonunion employees, the margin of sampling error is ±2 percentage points at the 95% confidence level. All reported margins of sampling error include computed design effects for weighting.

September 14, 2015
AMERICANS' VIEWS OF PHARMACEUTICAL INDUSTRY TAKE A TUMBLE

by Jim Norman

Story Highlights

- *Perennially low-scoring industry loses ground with Americans*
- *Now rated one of the worst industries*
- *Rated higher by Republicans than Democrats*

WASHINGTON, D.C.—Americans' views of the pharmaceutical industry, an often unpopular group that narrowly climbed into the U.S. public's favor last year, slipped back into negative territory in 2015. In Gallup's annual measure of 25 major U.S. business sectors, the percentage of Americans with a positive view of the pharmaceutical industry dropped from 40% in 2014 to 35% this year, while the percentage with a negative view rose from 36% to 43%. This leaves the industry with a negative net-positive rating of -8 in 2015.

Gallup annually asks Americans to rate 25 business and industry sectors as part of its August Work and Education poll. Americans rate each industry on a five-point scale ranging from very positive to very negative. The slide in net-positive ratings for the pharmaceutical industry, from +4 to -8, places it among the lowest-rated industries, which include the legal field (-5), the healthcare industry (-6),

the oil and gas industry (-13) and the federal government, which comes in dead last (-29).

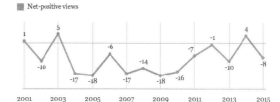

Americans' Overall Views of the Pharmaceutical Industry, 2001-2015

On another subject, for each of the following business sectors in the United States, please say whether your overall view of it is very positive, somewhat positive, neutral, somewhat negative or very negative. How about the pharmaceutical industry?

■ Net-positive views

Net-positive views are the total percentage of positive views minus the total percentage of negative views.

GALLUP

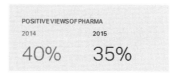

POSITIVE VIEWS OF PHARMA
2014 — 40%
2015 — 35%

Negative Views of Pharmaceutical Industry Nothing New

For many years, the U.S. public has had issues with the pharmaceutical industry. As far back as 1991, 73% of Americans said they considered the high cost of prescription drugs an important reason for rising healthcare costs. Since 2001, when Gallup began testing views of major business and industry sectors every year, the public has had an overall positive view of the pharmaceutical industry only three times: 2001, 2003 and 2014. Since 2003, when Gallup expanded the list to 25 industries, the pharmaceutical industry has consistently ranked in the bottom third of sectors.

Popular business sectors such as the computer, restaurant and accounting industries have regularly registered net-positive ratings more than 30 points higher than the pharmaceutical industry. Only the oil and gas industry, ranked last 10 times, and the federal government, which took the bottom spot the other three years, have consistently scored lower.

Pharmaceutical Industry Has Ranked Low Every Year
Based on net-positive views

Year	Rank
2003	22nd
2004	24th
2005	22nd
2006	20th
2007	22nd
2008	17th
2009	20th
2010	20th
2011	17th
2012	17th
2013	21st
2014	19th
2015	23rd

Net-positive views are the total percentage of positive views minus the total percentage of negative views.

GALLUP

The net-positive rating for all industries combined reached its highest point in more than a decade a year ago (+16), and climbed another point this year (+17). In comparing 2014 and 2015, nine industries lost ground this year in their net-positive ratings, but only education's 13-point slide was bigger than the 12-point drop for pharmaceuticals.

Pharmaceutical Industry's Ratings Often Enmeshed in Politics

The pharmaceutical industry's ratings have fluctuated throughout the years, with the variation often mirroring the changes in the overall ratings for all business sectors. The start of the Iraq War in March 2003 seemed to affect many polling measures positively, and the net-positive ratings for industries overall hit an all-time high of +23 in August of that year, with 22 industries gaining ground. It was also the year that the pharmaceutical industry achieved its highest rating of +5. Five years later, the economic crash plummeted the average score for all industries to a -3, with scores gradually improving since then. The pharmaceutical industry generally followed the same upward path from 2009 (net-positive rating of -18) to 2014 (+4).

However, two of the lowest ratings Americans gave the pharmaceutical industry throughout the years seem to have less to do with the overall mood of the U.S. public. Instead, the net-positive scores of -17 in 2004 and -18 in 2005 likely reflected the major role that attacks on drug companies played in the campaigns of individual Democrats in 2004 and the rocky rollout of the new Medicare plan for prescriptions the following year. Americans' overall negative rating for the pharmaceutical industry shrank to -6 in 2006, but jumped back to -17 in 2007. The industry had double-digit negative scores in 2008, 2009 and 2010 as the battle waged over the Affordable Care Act, but dropped into single digits after the act passed.

Looking at the combined results from the past two years, Republicans give the pharmaceutical industry a +11 net-positive rating, while Democrats rate it at -5. But the differences between the parties shrink considerably when party leaners are included. The rating by Republicans plus leaners drops to +3, and the Democrats-plus-leaners rating rises to -2.

Further muddying the political picture, many of the groups most likely to support Democrats hold the most positive views of the pharmaceutical industry, including ratings of:

- +21 from nonwhites
- +7 from those younger than 35
- +3 from urban residents
- +6 from those with annual household incomes less than $50,000

Implications

Prescription drug prices continue to rise in the U.S., driven partly by the introduction of specialty drugs that can cost as much as $150,000 annually. With few indications that costs will stabilize soon, the issue has moved back onto the national political scene. Vermont Sen. Bernie Sanders, a longtime critic of drug companies who is running for the 2016 Democratic presidential nomination, has announced he will introduce a bill that takes aim at high prescription drug costs through various measures. The combination of constantly rising prices and a presidential campaign in which drug companies are under attack leaves little likelihood that the pharmaceutical industry will gain much ground in public opinion over the next year.

Survey Methods

Results for this Gallup poll are based on telephone interviews conducted Aug. 5–9, 2015, with a random sample of 1,011 adults, aged 18 and older, living in all 50 U.S. states and the District of Columbia.

Each industry was rated by a random subset of approximately 500 respondents. The margin of sampling error is ±6 percentage points at the 95% confidence level. All reported margins of sampling error include computed design effects for weighting.

September 15, 2015
U.S. INVESTORS SAY LOW INTEREST RATES DO MORE GOOD THAN HARM

by Lydia Saad

Story Highlights

- *Investors say the good that low rates do borrowers outweighs harm to savers*
- *Twice as many investors feel helped as feel hurt by recent low interest rates*
- *Six in 10 have taken advantage of low rates with a new or refinanced loan*

PRINCETON, N.J.—As Wall Street and others anxiously await the Federal Reserve Board's decision about raising interest rates at its quarterly meeting on Thursday, more U.S. investors continue to say today's low interest rates do good for consumers by helping borrowers (68%) than say low rates do harm by hurting savers (24%).

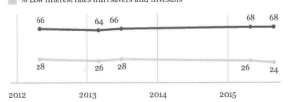

Primary Effect Low Interest Rates Have on Consumers
Based on U.S. investors

■ % Low interest rates good for consumers and business borrowers
□ % Low interest rates hurt savers and investors

Wells Fargo/Gallup Investor and Retirement Optimism Index

GALLUP

Investors' views on this issue have been rock steady since the initial measure in 2012.

Further, twice as many investors say today's low rates are helping their own finances (29%) than say the low rates are hurting them (15%). Low rates especially aid nonretired investors, with 34% saying the rates are helping them financially, whereas 12% say they are hurting them. Retired investors, on the other hand, have the opposite view, with 15% saying the low rates are helping them and 28% say they are hurting them. The majority of both groups, however, say low rates aren't affecting them.

These findings are from the third-quarter Wells Fargo/Gallup Investor and Retirement Optimism Index survey, conducted Aug.

7–16. Investors are defined for this survey as U.S. adults who have at least $10,000 invested in stocks, bonds or mutual funds, a criterion met by 44% of U.S. adults in the current survey.

How Today's Low Interest Rates Affect U.S. Investors

Overall, are today's low interest rates -- [ROTATED: helping you financially, not making much difference or hurting you financially]?

	Total	Retired	Not retired
	%	%	%
Helping you financially	29	15	34
Not making much difference	54	55	53
Hurting you financially	15	28	12
No opinion	1	2	1

Wells Fargo/Gallup Investor and Retirement Optimism Index
Aug. 7-16, 2015

GALLUP

Six in 10 Investors Recently Capitalized on Low Interest Rates

Despite the relatively low 29% of all investors who say that low interest rates are helping their finances, many more investors report having taken advantage of low interest rates to refinance or take out various types of new loans. Overall, 58% of investors say they have taken advantage of low rates in the past two years by doing one or more of the following: purchasing a car (30%), refinancing a mortgage or home loan (17%), purchasing a home (16%), taking out a student loan (9%) or taking out another type of loan (10%).

Not all of these investors may feel the low rate they received on their transaction has "helped" them financially, particularly when it involves taking on a major new expense such as a car payment, mortgage or college debt. But clearly they are better off than they would have been if rates were higher.

Investors Won't Be Shocked by Rate Hike

Despite mounting signs that the Federal Reserve wants to raise rates as soon as is safely possible, investors are no more likely today than in the prior quarter to believe interest rates will rise in the next year. About six in 10 investors predict interest rates will go up a little over the next 12 months, similar to 56% saying this in May. An additional 4% now—versus 5% in May—think rates will go up a lot.

Investors' Predictions for Direction of Interest Rates

Over the next 12 months, do you think interest rates will go up a lot, go up a little, remain the same, go down a little or go down a lot?

	Go up a lot	Go up a little	Remain the same	Go down a little	Go down a lot
	%	%	%	%	%
August 2015	4	58	28	8	1
May 2015	5	56	31	5	2
February 2015	5	51	34	7	*

Wells Fargo/Gallup Investor and Retirement Optimism Index

GALLUP

The trend on this has been remarkably flat all year, possibly indicating that investors' views may be based more on a generalized belief that rates can't stay this low much longer than on whatever they are reading in the news about the Federal Reserve's specific intentions about raising rates this quarter. On the other hand, Federal Reserve Chair Janet Yellen has signaled for much of the year that she wants to raise rates, so perhaps that message has gotten through.

Relatively few investors—17%—say they pay very close attention to U.S. interest rates, but among those who do, more than three-quarters expect rates to rise within the year, either by a little (67%) or a lot (10%).

Bottom Line

Any increase in the Federal Reserve's federal funds interest rate will be a big deal on Wall Street, at least initially. Whether the rate hike puts enough of a damper on consumer spending to slow the economy is an open question that even the Fed can't answer, and is partly why it has been so cautious about making the move. Investors have anticipated a hike in interest rates for some time. This suggests investors wouldn't be shocked if it happens Thursday, possibly limiting the impact it would have on their behavior.

Survey Methods

Results for the Wells Fargo/Gallup Investor and Retirement Optimism Index survey are based on questions asked Aug. 7–16, 2015, on the Gallup Daily tracking survey, of a random sample of 1,006 U.S. adults having investable assets of $10,000 or more.

For results based on the entire sample of investors, the margin of sampling error is ±4 percentage points at the 95% confidence level.

September 16, 2015
"EMAIL" DEFINES CLINTON; "IMMIGRATION" DEFINES TRUMP

by Lydia Saad and Frank Newport

Story Highlights

- *"Email" dominates Americans' recall of news about Hillary Clinton*
- *Donald Trump is most associated with immigration*
- *Americans also mention Trump's style, personality*

PRINCETON, N.J.—Hillary Clinton, the front-runner for the Democratic presidential nomination, has offered specific positions on a variety of issues while campaigning. But when Gallup recently asked Americans to say what they recall reading or hearing about her, one word—"email"—drowned out everything else.

These data were collected as part of a late August Gallup project asking Americans to say what they had read or heard recently about 22 major Republican and Democratic candidates. Each person interviewed was asked about no more than four candidates with whom they were familiar. Clinton's favorable rating among all Americans during the Aug. 24–30 field period tilted slightly negative, with 40% viewing her favorably and 50% unfavorably.

The accompanying word map uses font size to indicate the relative frequency in which specific words (excluding articles, pronouns and neutral or nonspecific words) appeared in the full list of responses for Clinton.

In the verbatim responses from about 750 U.S. adults familiar enough with Clinton to offer an opinion of her, the word "email" came up 329 times, phrased variously as "email," "emails," "email scandal," "email scandals," "that email thing," "email stuff" and "private emails." Relatedly, there were 83 mentions of "server." All of these refer to the controversy involving Clinton's use of private email servers to conduct government business while she was secretary of state.

What Americans Have Heard About Hillary Clinton

Most frequently used substantive words in answer to the question: Please tell me what you may have recently heard or read about Hillary Clinton

Based on 754 U.S. adults familiar with Hillary Clinton
Gallup Daily tracking, Aug. 24-30, 2015

GALLUP

By contrast, there were few mentions of the substantive themes Clinton has talked about on the campaign trail. For example, "economy" appeared on the list only four times, the same number as for "the middle class." "Gun control" appeared seven times, with even fewer mentions of "college" and "capital gains tax." Even the catch-all descriptions "policy" or "policies" were mentioned just nine times.

Republicans' responses were overwhelmingly negative toward Clinton, and Republicans were especially likely to refer to the email issue in negative terms. Republicans also tended to mention "Benghazi," referring to questions about how Clinton handled security for the U.S. diplomatic mission in Libya after the U.S. ambassador and three other Americans were killed in a terrorist attack in 2012.

Even when the responses of the 279 Democrats and Democratic leaners surveyed are isolated in a word map, "email" trumps everything else.

What Democrats Have Heard About Hillary Clinton

Most frequently used substantive words in answer to the question: Please tell me what you may have recently heard or read about Hillary Clinton

Based on 279 Democrats/Democratic leaners familiar with Hillary Clinton
Gallup Daily tracking, Aug. 24-30, 2015

GALLUP

These responses don't necessarily mean Americans are completely unaware of Clinton's policy proposals, where she stands on the issues or her credentials. And the finding that so many Democrats, most of whom (77%) viewed Clinton favorably at the time of the survey, mentioned "emails" is not necessarily a negative, but rather a reflection of news media coverage, for better or for worse. But the frequent mentions of the email controversy certainly suggest that Clinton's attempts to get other messages out to the public, which might either change her image or excite those who already like her, were largely drowned out by the media coverage of the email matter at the time of the survey.

For Donald Trump, Immigration Overshadows Reporter Controversies

While Clinton has been defined by a controversy she first tried to minimize and more recently has tried to quell by apologizing for, Donald Trump is primarily associated with his core campaign issue: immigration.

In verbatim responses from 718 U.S. adults familiar enough with Trump to rate him, the word "immigration" appears 99 times, making it the most frequently used substantive word or term in his word list. This is followed by the phrase "wants to," used 48 times, only four of which are followed by "be president." The rest relate to actions Trump wants to take as president, such as "wants to close the borders," or "wants to make America great again." These came at a time when Trump's national favorable rating was similar to Clinton's: 38% favorable and 51% unfavorable.

What Americans Have Heard About Donald Trump

Most frequently used substantive words in answer to the question: Please tell me what you may have recently heard or read about Donald Trump

Based on 718 U.S. adults familiar with Donald Trump
Gallup Daily tracking, Aug. 24-30, 2015

GALLUP

Twenty-nine people used "policy" or "policies" in response to what they have heard about Trump—a relatively modest number, but more than was the case for Clinton.

Other often-mentioned words are "businessman," "business," "immigrants," "illegal" or "illegals," "border" or "borders" and Trump's "money"—all referring to issues or themes Trump himself is trying to promote.

On the negative side, there are numerous references—often critical ones—to Trump's various "comments" or "statements" in the news, particularly his comments about Mexico and women. While it is unclear if Trump relished or wanted to downplay his quarrel with Fox News anchor Megyn Kelly, a number of people mentioned her by name, with others mentioning Fox News generally or "that female reporter." Similarly, the responses include mentions of TV reporter Jorge Ramos or his Spanish network Univision—referring to Trump's throwing Ramos out of a press conference last month. However, immigration still largely overshadowed these matters.

Then there are the adjectives those interviewed use to describe Trump. Although his supporters consider him "refreshing," "honest," "smart" and "good," others call him "arrogant," "racist," "an idiot," "rude" and a "big mouth." His brash, take-no-prisoners style has clearly filtered through to a portion of the public, and evidently cuts both ways.

Trump's word map based on Republicans, including independents who lean Republican, is highly similar to that based on all Americans, but with less criticism of his personal style and more statements of approval—for example, that he is "good," and "like him." This is consistent with his broadly positive image among Republicans, with 65% viewing him favorably at the time these verbatim responses were collected.

What Republicans Have Heard About Donald Trump

Most frequently used substantive words in answer to the question: Please tell me what you may have recently heard or read about Donald Trump

Based on 295 Republicans/Republican leaners familiar with Donald Trump
Gallup Daily tracking, Aug. 24-30, 2015

GALLUP

Bottom Line

Much of what has been called the narrative of a presidential campaign is interpreted through the filter of the media. Reporters, opinion column writers, editors, bloggers and social media mavens all compete to summarize what they think the stream of information about the candidates is indicating.

What's missing is a solid, empirical sense of what information about the candidates is actually getting through to the average American. These results provide an unfiltered glimpse into what information about the candidates is resonating most with the public.

The data suggest that Clinton has not been able to control the messaging about her and her candidacy, given that the email controversy is the information about her that has been most likely to filter through to the average American.

For Trump, on the other hand, a core component of his campaign—his stance on immigration—is registering with Americans, along with various reactions to his abrasive yet highly reaction-generating style. When Trump is on stage with 10 other GOP candidates in Wednesday night's debate, the way his behavior comes across to viewers will factor into whether he is able to sustain or build on his current momentum.

In some ways, these findings may be counterintuitive. The policy-oriented Clinton was defined most heavily at the time of this survey by controversy stemming from past conduct, while the political novice Trump was better known for his policy positions, namely his focus on immigration.

This analysis has focused on the two candidates with the highest overall name identification at this point in time; future reports will look at the images of other candidates.

Survey Methods

Results for this Gallup poll are based on telephone interviews conducted Aug. 24–30, 2015, on the Gallup U.S. Daily survey, with a random sample of adults, aged 18 and older, living in all 50 U.S. states and the District of Columbia. Hillary Clinton's results are based on 1,095 national adults asked to give their opinion of her as favorable or unfavorable, and 754 with an opinion who were asked to say what they had recently read or heard about her. Donald Trump's results are based on 1,058 national adults asked to give their opinion of him as favorable or unfavorable, and 718 with an opinion who were asked to say what they had recently read or heard about him.

September 17, 2015
MAJORITY OF U.S. INVESTORS CARRY DEBT BUT VALUE DEBT-FREE RETIREMENT

by Justin McCarthy

Story Highlights

- *Nonretirees more likely to say it's "critical" than retirees*
- *Three in four investors have some form of debt*
- *Seven in 10 say certain amount of debt is necessary, acceptable*

WASHINGTON, D.C.—More than half of U.S. investors say it is "critical" to be debt-free in retirement, while another third say it is "important, but not critical." Notably, investors who have not retired yet are much more likely than retirees to say being out of debt is critical.

U.S. Investors' Views on the Importance of Being Debt-Free in Retirement
How important is it to you to be debt-free in retirement?

	Total investors	Retired investors	Nonretired investors
	%	%	%
Critical	56	40	63
Important, but not critical	36	47	31
Not too important	5	6	5
Not important at all	3	7	1

Wells Fargo/Gallup Investor and Retirement Optimism Index
Aug. 7-16, 2015

GALLUP

These findings are from the third-quarter Wells Fargo/Gallup Investor and Retirement Optimism Index survey, conducted Aug. 7–16. Investors are defined for this survey as U.S. adults who have at least $10,000 invested in stocks, bonds or mutual funds, a criterion met by 44% of U.S. adults in the current survey.

Three in four investors have some type of debt, whether that be a mortgage (53%), credit card balance (37%), car loan (35%), student loan (23%) or some other type of debt (12%). The rates are significantly higher for nonretirees than retirees, leading to 83% of all nonretirees having at least one type of loan, compared with 54% of retirees.

Forms of Debt Among U.S. Investors

Do you currently have any of the following types of loans or debt?

% Yes

	Total investors	Retired investors	Nonretired investors
Mortgage or home loan	53	34	61
Credit card balance that carries over from month to month	37	23	43
Car loan	35	26	39
Student loans for yourself or family member	23	5	30
Other outstanding loan or debt	12	4	15
At least one of these forms of debt	74	54	83

Wells Fargo/Gallup Investor and Retirement Optimism Index
Aug. 7-16, 2015

GALLUP

While nonretired investors may be optimistic about achieving debt freedom in retirement, resulting in the large proportion who say achieving that status will be critical, retirees are much more realistic about it. Only 22% of retired investors with debt say being debt-free in retirement is critical, helping to explain the lower "critical" response among retired investors overall. By contrast, 60% of retired investors with no debt say being debt-free in retirement is critical to them.

Half of Investors With Debt Say They Have Made a "Major Effort" to Reduce It

Investors are far from cavalier about their debt. Of those with one or more types of loans or credit card balances, half say they have made a "major effort" to reduce their debt in the coming years, and even more intend to make a "major effort" to reduce it going forward (62%).

Investors take a moderate stand on the prudence of debt, with 70% saying a certain amount is necessary and acceptable. Just 13% embrace the philosophy espoused by some prominent financial experts, such as author and radio host Dave Ramsey, that any amount of debt should be avoided, while an equal proportion (14%) take the opposite view that debt is a powerful tool for growing wealth and should be taken advantage of.

Bottom Line

Investors rely on debt to accomplish a variety of life goals, such as homeownership, paying for college and purchasing a car. While the large majority of nonretired investors put a high value on being debt-free in retirement, retired investors—about half of whom carry debt—are less likely to see that as highly important. Retired investors' views are largely influenced by their own situation in

retirement, while nonretired investors may be answering from a normative perspective about what they would like their financial situation to be (but may not end up actually being the reality) when they retire.

U.S. Investors' Philosophies on Debt

Which of the following comes closer to your beliefs about debt?

	Total investors	Retired investors	Nonretired investors
	%	%	%
Any amount of debt is bad and should be avoided	13	13	12
A certain amount of debt is necessary and acceptable if used sparingly	70	70	71
Debt is a valuable tool for making your money work for you and should be taken advantage of	14	11	15
No opinion	3	6	2

Wells Fargo/Gallup Investor and Retirement Optimism Index
Aug. 7-16, 2015

GALLUP

In any case, American investors take their debt very seriously. The large majority of them are making at least some effort to reduce it now and going forward. This isn't to say that investors see debt as a bad thing—seven in 10 say debt is necessary and acceptable to use sparingly. Just one in eight see all debt as bad, while a similarly sized minority say debt is a valuable tool to leverage.

Survey Methods

Results for the Wells Fargo/Gallup Investor and Retirement Optimism Index survey are based on questions asked Aug. 7–16, 2015, on the Gallup Daily tracking survey, of a random sample of 482 U.S. adults having investable assets of $10,000 or more, including 330 who have any amount of debt.

For results based on the entire sample of investors, the margin of sampling error is ±4 percentage points at the 95% confidence level.

September 17, 2015
GOVERNMENT, ECONOMY, IMMIGRATION SEEN AS TOP U.S. PROBLEMS

by Rebecca Riffkin

Story Highlights

- *No one issue dominates Americans' perceptions*
- *Government, economy, immigration named by more than one in 10*
- *42% say Republicans are better to handle problem, 37% Democrats*

WASHINGTON, D.C.—In September, Americans are most likely to name dissatisfaction with government, the economy and immigration as the "most important problem" facing the country, although no one issue is named by more than one in five Americans. Mentions of the government and immigration are up slightly from August.

Gallup's monthly inventory of Americans' responses to the question "What do you think is the most important problem facing the country today?" shows that government and government dissatisfaction were listed by 17% of Americans in September, while the economy in general was listed by 15% and immigration was listed by 12%. Fewer than one in 10 Americans named all the other responses. A similar lack of consensus was found in August, with no single issue dominating Americans' minds.

Most Important Problems Facing the U.S.

What do you think is the most important problem facing this country today? (open-ended)

Problem	Sep 9-13, 2015	Aug 5-9, 2015	Jul 8-12, 2015
	%	%	%
Dissatisfaction with government	17	13	13
Economy in general	15	14	13
Immigration	12	8	7
Unemployment	8	11	6
Race relations/Racism	7	6	9
Ethics/Morals	7	3	6
Healthcare	6	5	4
Federal budget deficit	5	5	5
Education	4	5	4
Judicial system	4	3	3

Responses listed by at least 4% of Americans in September are shown

GALLUP

The relatively high percentage of Americans who nominate immigration as the top problem may reflect the emphasis it has received in Donald Trump's presidential campaign. However, the current migrant crisis in Europe and the surge of young immigrants from South America in the summer of 2014 may have also influenced this uptick. But economic problems are still a major factor in Americans' minds, with a net of 35% of Americans mentioning an economic issue. Since November 2013, the economy and dissatisfaction with the government have typically been among the top-ranking problems, at times joined by unemployment, immigration and healthcare.

In the past, certain issues have dominated Americans' responses, often corresponding with major events. For example, during the economic downturn, mentions of the economy or unemployment dominated, and during the latter years of George W. Bush's presidency, the situation in Iraq typically topped the list.

Americans More Likely to Say Republican Party Better at Handling Problem

In a follow-up question, Gallup asked Americans which political party they thought could do a better job of handling the problem they named as most important, and the Republican Party emerges with a slight edge. Specifically, 42% of Americans say the Republican Party would do a better job, while 37% say the Democratic Party. Another 23% volunteered that the parties would do the same job, that a third party would do a better job or had no opinion.

Gallup has asked this question on an occasional basis for decades, with a great deal of variation in the responses. Republicans were more likely to be named as the best party to handle the problem in 2014, the parties tied in 2013 and the Democrats were on top by 10 percentage points in September 2012, reflecting Democratic strength in a presidential election year in which Barack Obama was re-elected. But, by way of comparison, Republicans enjoyed a seven-point lead in September 2011, more than a year ahead of the 2012 election, indicating that the current views of party strength are not necessarily predictive of results in the 2016 presidential election.

Among those mentioning the government as the top problem facing Americans, Republicans have the edge as the party deemed better able to handle it, 45% to 34%. Republicans also lead among those who mention the economy as the top problem, 43% to 38%. Those relationships are confounded to some degree by the greater

tendency of Republican Party identifiers than Democratic Party identifiers to mention these issues as the top problem facing the country. On issues Democrats are more likely to name as the most important problem, for example race relations, the Democratic Party is generally viewed as the party better able to handle it.

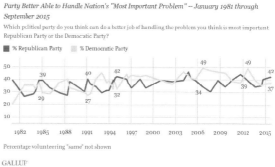

Party Better Able to Handle Nation's "Most Important Problem" -- January 1981 through September 2015

Which political party do you think can do a better job of handling the problem you think is most important, Republican Party or the Democratic Party?

■ % Republican Party   ▨ % Democratic Party

Percentage volunteering "same" not shown

GALLUP

Bottom Line

Unlike 2004, when Iraq was the dominant issue or in 2008 when the economy dominated, the 2016 presidential campaign may be fought over a variety of issues. Donald Trump has made immigration a major campaign issue, and this is an issue that Americans more generally tend to perceive as the most important problem, along with the economy and the government itself. Also, the fact that outsider candidates like Trump and Ben Carson are doing well in the polls at the expense of candidates with government experience could likely be a manifestation of people's dissatisfaction with the government.

Usually, the party that is seen as better at handling the most important problem is the one that wins the election. Just over a year out from the presidential election, Republicans do hold a slight edge on that. However, they had a similar edge in 2011 and lost it before the 2012 election. Much could change between now and the election next year, and it is quite possible that a single issue could rise to prominence in Americans' minds as the most important, and that Americans' perceptions of which party can better handle this problem could shift.

Survey Methods

Results for this Gallup poll are based on telephone interviews conducted Sept. 9–13, 2015, with a random sample of 1,025 adults, aged 18 and older, living in all 50 U.S. states and the District of Columbia. For results based on the total sample of national adults, the margin of sampling error is ±4 percentage points at the 95% confidence level. All reported margins of sampling error include computed design effects for weighting.

September 18, 2015
TRUST IN U.S. JUDICIAL BRANCH SINKS TO NEW LOW OF 53%

by Jeffrey M. Jones

Story Highlights

- *Trust in judicial branch down eight points in last year*
- *Trust in judicial branch still highest of three branches*

PRINCETON, N.J.—Americans' trust in the judicial branch of the federal government has fallen significantly in the past year, and now a record-low 53% say they have "a great deal" or "a fair amount" of trust in it. Trust in the executive and legislative branches also remains near historical lows, but both were up slightly this year.

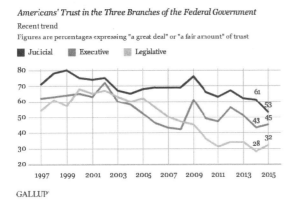

Americans' Trust in the Three Branches of the Federal Government
Recent trend
Figures are percentages expressing "a great deal" or "a fair amount" of trust

Despite this year's drop, the judicial branch retains higher public trust than either of the other branches of government—53%, compared with 45% for the executive branch and 32% for the legislative branch.

PUBLIC TRUST IN JUDICIAL BRANCH
2009   2015
76%   53%
SOURCE: GALLUP POLL

Americans have consistently had more trust in the judiciary than in the other two government branches, but trust in all three has trended downward in an era of widespread dissatisfaction with government. As recently as six years ago, the first year of the Obama administration, 76% said they trusted the judicial branch, 61% said they trusted the executive branch and 45% said they trusted the legislative branch.

The results are based on Gallup's Sept. 9–13 Governance poll, which has measured trust in the three branches of the federal government annually since 2001. Gallup's full trend on trust in government extends back to 1972, with regular updates since 1997.

Trust in Judicial Branch Down Most Among Republicans

The decline in trust in the judicial branch likely stems from the Supreme Court's controversial decisions this year to legalize same-sex marriage and uphold a key provision of the Affordable Care Act allowing Americans to purchase subsidized health insurance through federally run marketplaces.

Democrats cheered those decisions while Republicans criticized them. As a result, the Supreme Court's job approval rating among Republicans plummeted to 18% in July, shortly after the high court's term ended.

In similar fashion, Republicans' trust in the judicial branch has fallen 17 percentage points since September 2014, but trust is essentially unchanged among Democrats, meaning Republicans are mostly responsible for the overall decline in trust. Independents

show a modest six-point drop. Republicans' trust in the judicial branch, now at 42%, is easily the lowest for any party group in Gallup's trend.

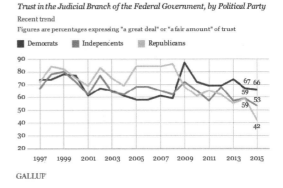

Trust in the Judicial Branch of the Federal Government, by Political Party
Recent trend
Figures are percentages expressing "a great deal" or "a fair amount" of trust

The effect of the Supreme Court's prominent left-leaning decisions is also evident in an increase in the percentage of Americans describing the court's ideology as "too liberal." Now, 37% say this, up from 30% last year and five points above the previous high in Gallup's 22-year trend. The 37% "too liberal" is also five points above the historical high of 32% who said the court was "too conservative" in 2007.

The plurality of Americans have always described the Supreme Court as "about right" ideologically, including 40% this year. Twenty percent currently say it is too conservative.

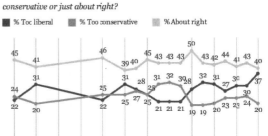

In general, do you think the current Supreme Court is too liberal, too conservative or just about right?

Sixty-three percent of Republicans now say the Supreme Court is too liberal, up from 51% last year. Independents also show an increase in the same direction, from 28% to 35%. Meanwhile, the percentage of Democrats who describe the Supreme Court's ideology as "about right" increased by 15 points to 54%, accompanied by an equal decline in the percentage calling it "too conservative."

Implications

Americans' trust in the judicial branch of the federal government continued to fall this year to a new low of 53%. The decline in trust in the judicial branch over the past several years partly results from broader factors affecting all institutions, namely Americans' widespread dissatisfaction with the way things are going in the country and in the way the federal government operates. But the decline this year is almost certainly a reaction—primarily among Republicans—to the Supreme Court's landmark ruling on same-sex marriage and its turning away the latest legal challenge to the Affordable Care Act.

Views of Supreme Court's Ideology, by Political Party, 2014 vs. 2015

	2014	2015	Change
	%	%	pct. pts.
REPUBLICANS			
Too liberal	51	63	+12
Too conservative	4	11	+7
About right	41	24	-17
INDEPENDENTS			
Too liberal	28	35	+7
Too conservative	22	18	-4
About right	45	43	-2
DEMOCRATS			
Too liberal	13	13	0
Too conservative	46	31	-15
About right	39	54	+15

GALLUP

Americans' opinions of the Supreme Court have been responsive to decisions it has handed down in recent decades, but often those reactions are short-lived. The 2015 rulings, however, appear to be sticking in Republicans' memory, nearly three months after they were handed down. Republicans' trust in the judicial branch is down sharply this year; they are significantly more likely to perceive the court as being too liberal; and still just 26% of Republicans approve of the job the court is doing in the new poll.

Republicans' trust in the judicial branch could be restored with a landmark ruling more in sync with conservative ideology and policy preferences; one possibility would be in a case on Affirmative Action in college admissions, to be heard in the coming term.

But the Supreme Court, even with the erosion in trust, remains more trusted than the executive or legislative branches. To some degree that may reflect the court's less overtly partisan role, although the decisions it makes have clear political implications for many Americans and provoke predictable reactions from those on both sides of the political aisle. Also, the Supreme Court's work is not as constant a presence in the news media as is the work of the president and Congress, which means the judiciary may get less scrutiny than the other branches of the government.

Survey Methods

Results for this Gallup poll are based on telephone interviews conducted Sept. 9–13, 2015, with a random sample of 1,025 adults, aged 18 and older, living in all 50 U.S. states and the District of Columbia. For results based on the total sample of national adults, the margin of sampling error is ±4 percentage points at the 95% confidence level. All reported margins of sampling error include computed design effects for weighting.

September 18, 2015
IN U.S., HALF STILL SAY GOV'T REGULATES BUSINESS TOO MUCH

by Andrew Dugan

Story Highlights

- *About half (49%) say gov't regulates business too much*
- *Near low of 21% say gov't regulates business too little*

WASHINGTON, D.C.—While a sturdy 49% of Americans say the government regulates business too much, a near-low percentage instead say it regulates too little (21%). The latter response has experienced a six-percentage-point drop from 2010, while the former has remained virtually unchanged since 2009. Another 27% of Americans judge the current regulatory approach as about right.

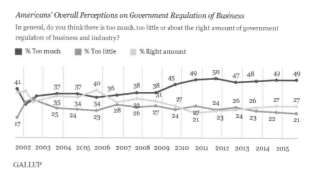

Americans' Overall Perceptions on Government Regulation of Business

In general, do you think there is too much, too little or about the right amount of government regulation of business and industry?

■ % Too much   ■ % Too little   ■ % Right amount

GALLUP

The latest data are from Gallup's annual Governance survey, conducted Sept. 9–13. Moods toward government regulation of business have fluctuated as party control of the White House has changed, though generally more Americans say government regulation of business is too much. But the presidency of Democrat Barack Obama has seen a marked rise in the percentage saying "too much," with the figure typically hovering around 50%. By contrast, the average rate of Americans choosing this response was 36% over the eight years of Republican George W. Bush's administration.

U.S. GOV'T REGULATION OF BUSINESS
TOO LITTLE   TOO MUCH
21%   49%
SOURCE: GALLUP POLL SOCIAL SERIES

In 2009, the first year of Obama's presidency, the percentage saying the government regulates business too much spiked seven points to 45%. This development came in spite of the fact that only about a year prior, the U.S. financial system suffered a major panic attributed to excessive loans by major lending companies, along with a lack of meaningful oversight by governmental entities responsible for regulating major financial companies. It should be noted, however, that this view is not universally accepted. The rise in "too much" has been sustained throughout the Obama presidency, reaching as high as 50% and never falling below the 2009 reading.

As Gallup showed last year, the exponential-like increase in Republicans saying government regulates business too much—climbing from 40% in 2006 to a peak of 84% in 2011—is clearly a major factor in the overall rise in this response rate. This year, about eight in 10 Republicans are in the "too much" camp, far exceeding the percentage of independents (46%) or Democrats (26%) who are similarly aligned.

But a more recent, albeit subtler, shift in overall public opinion also appears evident in this year's survey. The share of Americans saying government regulates business too little is at a near low, and has fallen six points since 2010—with that percentage shifting to the "about right" category, which has, in turn, also risen six points since 2010. While not a dramatic movement, there does appear to be less support for the notion that government regulates business too little.

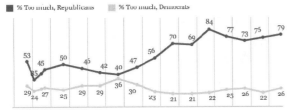

Americans' Views on Government Regulation of Business, by Party

In general, do you think there is too much, too little or about the right amount of government regulation of business and industry?

■ % Too much, Republicans   □ % Too much, Democrats

GALLUP

Perceived Impact Economic Matters Are Having on U.S. Investment Climate

Now I am going to read you some possible situations that could affect the investment climate in the United States. For each one, please tell me whether you think that situation is hurting the investment climate in the United States a lot, hurting it a little, having no effect on it, helping it a little or helping the investment climate a lot.

Sorted by "Hurting it a lot"

	Hurting it a lot	Hurting it a little	No effect	Helping it a little	Helping it a lot
	%	%	%	%	%
Current level of taxes	46	30	14	5	2
Unemployment rate	43	26	12	9	7
Threat of cyberattacks	42	36	19	1	*
Value of the dollar against other currencies	23	36	12	20	5
Current level of interest rates	23	27	15	19	12
Debt crisis in Greece	23	47	22	2	1
Stock market volatility	22	44	15	12	3
Home prices or values	20	20	19	29	8
Slowdown in China	20	42	16	11	4

* Less than 0.5%
Wells Fargo/Gallup Investor and Retirement Optimism Index survey

GALLUP

Bottom Line

Close to a majority of Americans judge government regulation of business to be excessive, as has been the case throughout the Obama presidency. In particular, large amounts of Republicans believe government regulation of business to be too much, suggesting that proposals by GOP presidential candidates to roll back government regulation will be warmly received by their base.

Meanwhile, there is falling support for the notion that the government regulates business too little, even if this idea has played an important role in the platform of competitive presidential candidates such as Democratic Sen. Bernie Sanders.

Survey Methods

Results for this Gallup poll are based on telephone interviews conducted Sept. 9–13, 2015, with a random sample of 1,025 adults, aged 18 and older, living in all 50 U.S. states and the District of Columbia. For results based on the total sample of national adults, the margin of sampling error is ±4 percentage points at the 95% confidence level. All reported margins of sampling error include computed design effects for weighting.

September 21, 2015
INVESTORS SEE TAXES AS BIGGEST DRAG ON INVESTMENT CLIMATE

by Lydia Saad

Story Highlights

- *46% of investors say taxes hurting investment climate a lot*
- *Concern about unemployment nearly as high, but lowest in years*
- *Home values close to being seen as a positive influence*

PRINCETON, N.J.—U.S. investors see the current level of taxes as having the most negative effect on the U.S. investment climate out of nine economic factors they were asked about in the third quarter. Forty-six percent say taxes are hurting the investment climate a lot. Unemployment and the threat of cyberattacks closely follow taxes, while investors see the value of the dollar, interest rates and home prices as far less harmful.

Other matters of less concern to investors include the Greek debt crisis, stock market volatility and a slowdown in China. Roughly one in five investors say each of these hurts the investment climate a lot.

The Wells Fargo/Gallup Investor and Retirement Optimism Index survey was conducted Aug. 7–16, prior to the sharp decline in U.S. stocks starting on Aug. 20 that was triggered by global concern over China's weakening economy. As a result, investors' perceptions of how China's economic slowdown is affecting the U.S. investment climate could be more negative if they were measured today. The same could be said for investors' concerns about stock market volatility. Still, the poll was conducted less than a month after China's already-volatile stock market plunged more than 8% in late July, making major headlines and raising global concerns about weakened consumer demand in that country.

U.S. INVESTORS WHO SAY TAXES HURT INVESTMENT CLIMATE A LOT

46%

SOURCE: WELLS FARGO/GALLUP INDEX

Similarly, less than a quarter of investors in August believed the Greek debt crisis was hurting the U.S. investment climate a lot, even after the matter triggered a major sell-off in the U.S. equities market in late June, likely contributing to a decline in U.S. consumers' economic confidence.

One piece of good news from the poll is that even though unemployment registers among the highest levels of investor concern, the percentage saying unemployment is hurting the investment climate a lot remains well below the levels seen from 2011 to 2013. Concern about housing negatively affecting the markets also fell sharply at the same time.

Also, although none of the nine economic issues measured is seen as more helpful than harmful to the investment climate right now, home values and interest rates come closest. The net-positive perception about home prices is currently -3, based on a combined 37% of investors saying home prices are helping the investment climate a lot or a little and 40% saying home prices are *hurting* the investment climate a lot or a little. The net perception of interest rates is -19, with a combined 31% saying these are helping the investment climate and 50% hurting it.

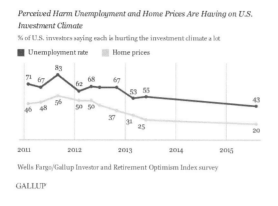

Perceived Harm Unemployment and Home Prices Are Having on U.S. Investment Climate

% of U.S. investors saying each is hurting the investment climate a lot

■ Unemployment rate   Home prices

Wells Fargo/Gallup Investor and Retirement Optimism Index survey

GALLUP

Bottom Line

As of mid-August, U.S. investors were far more concerned about how U.S. taxes and unemployment, rather than economic troubles in Greece and China, were affecting the U.S. markets. While investors' concerns about China have likely increased since that time, their low concerns about Greece less than two months after that country's economic problems spilled over into U.S. markets suggest such global issues have a short lifespan on investors' radar. Meanwhile, nothing has occurred that should have rattled investors' improved perceptions of unemployment and home values. And continued stability in both of these core aspects of the domestic economy should help investors remain calm through any additional globally induced market lurches.

Survey Methods

Results for the Wells Fargo/Gallup Investor and Retirement Optimism Index survey are based on questions asked Aug. 7–16, 2015, on the Gallup Daily tracking survey, of a random sample of 509 U.S. adults having investable assets of $10,000 or more.

For results based on the entire sample of investors, the margin of sampling error is ±5 percentage points at the 95% confidence level.

September 21, 2015
HALF IN U.S. CONTINUE TO SAY GOV'T IS AN IMMEDIATE THREAT

by Frank Newport

Story Highlights

- *49% say government poses immediate threat to rights, freedoms*
- *Republicans much more likely to see government as threat*
- *Americans give very diverse explanations for these views*

PRINCETON, N.J.—Almost half of Americans, 49%, say the federal government poses "an immediate threat to the rights and

freedoms of ordinary citizens," similar to what was found in previous surveys conducted over the last five years. When this question was first asked in 2003, less than a third of Americans held this attitude.

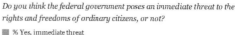
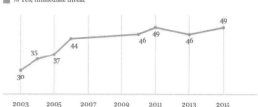

Do you think the federal government poses an immediate threat to the rights and freedoms of ordinary citizens, or not?

■ % Yes, immediate threat

In Sept. 8-10, 2003, and May 20-21, 2013, polls, question was asked of a half sample.

GALLUP

The latest results are from Gallup's Sept. 9–13 Governance poll. The lower percentage of Americans agreeing in 2003 that the federal government posed an immediate threat likely reflected the more positive attitudes about government evident after the 9/11 terrorist attacks. The percentage gradually increased to 44% by 2006, and then reached the 46% to 49% range in four surveys conducted since 2010.

The remarkable finding about these attitudes is how much they reflect apparent antipathy toward the party controlling the White House, rather than being a purely fundamental or fixed philosophical attitude about government.

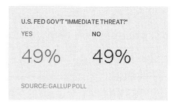

U.S. FED GOV'T "IMMEDIATE THREAT?"

YES — 49%   NO — 49%

SOURCE: GALLUP POLL

Across the four surveys conducted during the Republican administration of George W. Bush, Democrats and Democratic-leaning independents were consistently more likely than Republicans and Republican-leaning independents to say the federal government posed an immediate threat.

By contrast, across the four most recent surveys conducted during the Democratic Obama administration, the partisan gap flipped, with Republicans significantly more likely to agree.

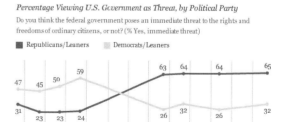

Percentage Viewing U.S. Government as Threat, by Political Party

Do you think the federal government poses an immediate threat to the rights and freedoms of ordinary citizens, or not? (% Yes, immediate threat)

■ Republicans/Leaners   Democrats/Leaners

GALLUP

Republican agreement with the "immediate threat" statement has been higher during the Obama administration than was Democratic agreement during the Bush administration, thus accounting for the overall rise in agreement across all national adults.

What's Behind the Belief That the Government Is an Immediate Threat?

The current survey contains an open-ended question asking those who agree that the government is an immediate threat to explain why they feel this way. This open-ended question was asked once previously, in 2010, but not in any of the surveys conducted during the Bush administration.

Overall, Americans who agree that the government is an immediate threat tend to respond with very general complaints echoing the theme that the federal government is too big and too powerful, and that it has too many laws. They also cite nonspecific allegations that the government violates freedoms and civil liberties, and that there is too much government in people's private lives.

The most frequently mentioned specific threats involve gun control laws and violations of the Second Amendment to the Constitution, mentioned by 12% who perceive the government to be an immediate threat.

In what ways do you see the government posing an immediate threat to the rights and freedoms of its citizens? [Open-ended]

Based on those who believe the federal government is an immediate threat

	% Mentioning
Too many laws/Government too big in general	9
Violations of freedoms/civil liberties	15
Gun control/Violating Second Amendment	12
Too much involvement in people's private lives	10
Socialist government	6
Taking away freedom of speech/Violating First Amendment	6
Taking away freedom of religion	6
Police/Law enforcement violence/arrests	4
Government surveillance of citizens/emails/phone records	4
Marriage issue	4
Overregulation/Too much involvement in business	3
Overtaxing/Taxes too high	3
Healthcare law	3
Failing to secure borders/Illegal immigration	3
Too much spending	3
Government is unfair/picks winners and losers	3
Not focused on needs of country/Puts politics first	3
Too involved in things it shouldn't be	2
Violating separation of powers/No accountability	2
Environmental regulations/EPA	1
Education/School system	1
Other	7
None/Nothing	3
No opinion	4

Sept. 9-13, 2015

GALLUP

Other general complaints enunciated by smaller numbers of those who think the government poses an immediate threat include perceptions that the government is "socialist," that the government spends too much, that it picks winners and losers such as the wealthy or racial and ethnic minorities, that it is too involved in things it shouldn't be and that it violates the separation of powers.

More specific complaints—again voiced by small numbers of those who agree with the threat statement—focus on freedom of speech, freedom of religion, the overuse of police and law enforcement, government surveillance of private citizens including emails and phone records, government involvement in gay marriage issues, overregulation of business, overtaxing, the healthcare law and immigration.

The majority of those who today believe government is an immediate threat, and who answer the open-ended question, are either Republicans or independents who lean Republican. Thus, these open-ended responses tend to reflect the views of Republican-oriented citizens. A look at the smaller number of Democrats who feel the government poses an immediate threat shows that their responses are generally similar to Republicans, with some exceptions. Democrats are somewhat less likely to mention gun control, and also less likely to mention very specific issues such as marriage, taxes, immigration, spending or the healthcare law.

Implications

The fact that almost half of Americans see the federal government as an immediate threat to their lives and freedoms may appear alarming at first, perhaps conjuring an image of Americans worrying that the government will be breaking down their doors and engaging in random arrests of private citizens.

But two findings mitigate against this type of more dramatic interpretation. First, the fact that Democrats and Republicans have flipped in their probability of holding these views when the administration changed in 2009 shows that these attitudes reflect more of a response to the president and disagreement with his policies than a fundamental feeling about the federal government in general.

Second, the explanations offered by those who hold this view reveal more traditional or political types of complaints about things the government is doing, rather than more radical beliefs about the government using power or force against its citizens.

Gallup does not have survey data extending back to the late 1780s when the Constitution was ratified and the federal government began to exercise control over the lives of its citizens. Clearly, there has been tension between the government and the people at many times in history since that point, and it may be that such tensions are a natural part of the system by which the people willingly give up power to government institutions that in turn intrude on their daily lives.

Still, the persistent finding in recent years that half of the population views the government as an immediate threat underscores the degree to which the role and power of government remains a key issue of our time. As a case in point, a question in this same survey asked Americans to name the most important problem facing the nation, and found that issues related to government were the most frequently mentioned. Plus, numerous other measures show that the people give their government some of the lowest approval and trust ratings in the measures' history.

From the people's perspective, then, a focus on the appropriate role for government should be at the forefront of the nation's continuing political discourse and should be a key point of debate in the current presidential election campaigns.

Survey Methods

Results for this Gallup poll are based on telephone interviews conducted Sept. 9–13, 2015, with a random sample of 1,025 adults, aged 18 and older, living in all 50 U.S. states and the District of Columbia. For results based on the total sample of national adults, the margin of sampling error is ±4 percentage points at the 95% confidence level. All reported margins of sampling error include computed design effects for weighting.

September 23, 2015
REPUBLICANS FAVORED ON ISSUES DESPITE WORSE IMAGE

by Jim Norman

Story Highlights

- *Democrats' image still better than Republicans'*
- *Republicans favored over Democrats on key issues*
- *Many Republicans unhappy with GOP, but favor it on issues*

WASHINGTON, D.C.—Less than half of Americans (43%) view the Democratic Party favorably, but the party's image is still better than that of the Republican Party (38%). Neither party has been able to gain favorable opinions from a majority of the public since June 2013, in the early months of President Barack Obama's second term.

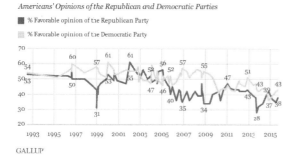

Americans' Opinions of the Republican and Democratic Parties

GALLUP

The Democratic Party's image has been more positive than the Republican Party's since September 2011, except in one survey conducted shortly after the November 2014 midterm elections. The current five-percentage-point advantage for Democrats, measured after intensive months of presidential campaigning for both parties, is about the same as the advantage in July of this year.

Yet while Americans are more likely to view the Democratic Party favorably, they are split on which party is better at keeping the country prosperous. Americans are slightly more likely to say the Republican Party is better at handling whatever issue they personally define as the country's "most important problem," and much more likely to favor the GOP on "protecting the country from international terrorism and military threats."

Americans' Overall Opinions of the Two Parties and Views of the Parties on Issues

	Republican Party	Democratic Party	Democratic Party advantage
	%	%	pct. pts.
Have favorable opinion of party	38	43	+5
Better protect the country from international terrorism and military threats	52	36	-16
Do a better job of keeping U.S. prosperous	46	44	-2
Do a better job of handling the problem you think is most important	42	37	-5

Sept. 9-13, 2015

GALLUP

The Democratic Party has typically held an edge over the GOP on favorability in Gallup's 23-year history of this question. That edge, however, has not extended to Americans' views of which party is better equipped to handle key issues facing the country:

- In five of the last six years, more Americans have said the Republican Party would do a better job of keeping the country prosperous.

- Republicans led Democrats five of the last six years on which party would better protect the country from international terrorism and military threats. In four polls, the GOP led by at least 11 points.
- Democrats trailed Republicans in 2010 and 2011 on which party would do the best job of handling the country's "most important problem," but regained the lead in 2012 and 2013—only to fall behind again after that.

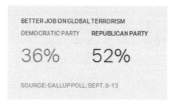

BETTER JOB ON GLOBAL TERRORISM

DEMOCRATIC PARTY   REPUBLICAN PARTY

36%   52%

SOURCE: GALLUP POLL, SEPT. 9-13

From 2006 through 2009—the last three years of George W. Bush's presidency and the first for Obama—Americans had a much more favorable opinion of the Democratic Party than the GOP. They also picked the Democratic Party by large margins to deal with prosperity and "the most important problem."

In 2010, major shifts occurred at the ballot box and in public opinion. Republicans took control of the House in a year when the Democratic image sank to the Republican Party's already-low level, with unfavorable views outweighing favorable ones for the first time in five years. Americans turned from the Democratic Party to the GOP on the issue of prosperity, as an 11-point Democratic lead in 2009 turned into an eight-point Republican advantage. In the years since, Democrats have regained their lead in favorability, but not on the issues.

Republicans Are Major Source of Division

To some degree, the discrepancies in party favorability and issue competency could be based on the popularity of the incumbent president, with Americans tending to favor his party regardless of how they feel about which party can do best on the issues. This appears to have been particularly true when a Democrat is in the White House, as is the case now.

However, the data suggest another factor behind the current *seemingly* contradictory attitudes of some Americans: the willingness of Republicans who are unhappy with the GOP to nevertheless back the party on key issues.

Republicans are currently less likely to have a favorable opinion of their party (78%) than Democrats are to rate the Democratic Party favorably (85%). But, as noted, despite some Republicans' relative lack of enthusiasm for their party, they are more likely to pick the GOP to deal with the issues of national security, prosperity and "the most important problem."

This is a significant change from eight years ago when the nation—just as it is now—was a year away from electing a new president. At that time, Republicans were more likely than they are now to view the GOP favorably, but less likely than now to choose it to deal with any of the three issues. The slight deterioration in Republicans' overall image of their party over the past eight years could reflect the currently fractious state of the party, riven as it is by internal disputes. But with a Democrat in the White House, Republicans apparently come together when asked about their party's ability to handle specific issues.

Americans' Opinions of the Parties, by Partisan Groups for 2007 vs. 2015

	Republicans 2007	Democrats 2007	Republicans 2015	Democrats 2015
	%	%	%	%
Favorable opinion of the Republican Party	83	10	78	10
Favorable opinion of the Democratic Party	23	89	13	85
BETTER PROTECT THE COUNTRY FROM INTERNATIONAL TERRORISM AND MILITARY THREATS				
Republican Party	87	7	96	15
Democratic Party	8	86	3	80
DO A BETTER JOB OF KEEPING U.S. PROSPEROUS				
Republican Party	79	5	92	9
Democratic Party	15	89	6	86
DO A BETTER JOB OF HANDLING THE PROBLEM YOU THINK IS MOST IMPORTANT				
Republican Party	73	4	85	11
Democratic Party	10	86	4	81

GALLUP

Bottom Line

Based on these results, each party has something to feel good about as the 2016 presidential election approaches:

- Republicans can be encouraged because the public favors their party as the best able to protect the nation's prosperity and because the party ahead on this dimension has won the presidential popular vote in 10 of 12 elections.
- Democrats can counter that they have the more positive overall party image, and that in five of the last six presidential elections, the party that has had higher favorable ratings has won the popular vote.

In only one presidential election year—2000—has there been a split, with one party—the Democrats—having higher favorable ratings and one—the Republicans—favored by the public to keep the country prosperous. That year, the popular vote was so close that the Supreme Court wound up deciding the election.

Survey Methods

Results for this Gallup poll are based on telephone interviews conducted Sept. 9–13, 2015, with a random sample of 1,025 national adults, aged 18 and older, living in all 50 U.S. states and the District of Columbia. For results based on the total sample of national adults, the margin of sampling error is ±4 percentage points at the 95% confidence level.

September 23, 2015
5 IMPORTANT THINGS TO KNOW ABOUT U.S. CATHOLICS

by Frank Newport

PRINCETON, N.J.—Pope Francis's first trip to the United States provides a good opportunity to review the state of Catholicism in the U.S. What follows are five important points about Catholics, based on Gallup data that in some cases go back as far as the 1940s.

Catholics Are 23% of U.S. Adult Population

Catholics constituted 23% of the U.S. adult population in 2014, and this percentage has remained fairly steady over the 66 years Gallup has been asking Americans about their religious identification.

Catholics as % of U.S. Adult Population

GALLUP

Since 1948, 25% of Americans, on average, have been Catholic. The percentage was slightly higher than average in the late 1970s and early 1980s, and was slightly lower in the 2000s.

SHARE OF U.S. ADULTS WHO ARE CATHOLIC

23%

SOURCE: GALLUP POLL, 2014

One remarkable aspect of this relatively stable trend is that during the same period, the percentage of Americans who have no formal religious identity has increased from roughly 1% to about 20% today. The rise in those with no religion has been accompanied by a decline in the percentages of Protestants and other non-Catholic Christians, the ranks of which have fallen from as high as 70% of the population, down to about 50% today. Catholics have been able to hold their own—percentage-wise—even as the unaffiliated percentage has risen significantly.

These results are based on Gallup's traditional "stand-alone" polls dating back to 1948. Religious identification is also measured as part of Gallup Daily tracking, and interviews with more than 170,000 individuals in 2014 showed a similar 23.9% of national adults interviewed identified as Catholic.

Almost a Third of U.S. Catholics Are Hispanic

One of the explanations for the stable representation of Catholics in the adult population over time is the increasing percentage of Hispanics in the U.S. population, coupled with the fact that the majority of Hispanics identify as Catholic. In Gallup's 2014 tracking data, 32% of Catholics identified as Hispanic, more than double the representation of Hispanics in the U.S. adult population. Sixty-one percent of Catholics are white, while 3% are black—much lower than the black representation among Protestants.

Catholics No Longer Attend Church Services More Frequently Than Protestants

Catholics' church attendance no longer exceeds Protestants' church attendance. In May 2015, 44% of Catholics said they had attended church within the previous seven days, compared with 45% of Protestants.

Racial and Ethnic Distribution Among Catholics, Protestants and National Adults

	Catholics	Protestants	All national adults
	%	%	%
Non-Hispanic whites	61	70	67
Non-Hispanic blacks	3	17	11
Hispanics	32	8	14

Gallup Daily tracking, January-December 2014

GALLUP

Gallup's historical data show that Catholics' lower recent church attendance is dramatically different from that of the 1950s–1960s. Surveys from the 1950s, for example, showed that more than seven in 10 Catholics reported having attended church in the previous seven days, compared with figures in the 40% range for Protestants. Since then, church attendance among Protestants has remained stable, while it has dropped significantly among Catholics. Catholics lost their church attendance advantage over Protestants in the 1990s.

Catholics' Politics Match U.S. Average

While in Washington, Pope Francis will meet with Democratic President Barack Obama and will make a speech before a joint session of the Republican-controlled Congress. This bipartisanship fits nicely with the party identification of Catholics in the U.S., which is remarkably similar to what is found in the overall population. In 2014, 40% of both Catholics and non-Catholics identified as or leaned Republican, while 43% of both groups identified as or leaned Democratic.

Party Identification Among U.S. Catholics and Non-Catholics

	Catholics	Non-Catholics
	%	%
Republicans/Leaners	40	40
Independents/No lean	14	13
Democrats/Leaners	43	43

Gallup Daily tracking, January-December 2014

GALLUP

This is a different situation from that of other religious groups, whose partisan identification tends to skew in one direction or the other. For example, 47% of Protestants and 71% of Mormons identify as or lean toward the Republican Party, well above the overall 40% of the population who are Republican. On the other hand, 61% of Jews identify with or lean toward the Democratic Party. All of this explains why Catholics have been a key swing group in recent presidential elections, much more so than other religious groups. The tendency for Catholics to mirror the overall population from a partisan perspective is a shift from the past, when Catholics tended to skew significantly more Democratic in their partisan and voting behavior.

Catholics Most Overrepresented in the East, Most Underrepresented in the South

Catholics are overrepresented compared with non-Catholics in the East, are underrepresented in the South and are distributed about equally compared with non-Catholics in the Midwest and West of the country.

The pope will be visiting the District of Columbia, New York and Pennsylvania during his trip to the U.S. New York State has the

highest percentage of Catholics of these three geographic entities, at 36%, followed by Pennsylvania at 28% and then the District of Columbia, below average at 20%.

Geographic Distribution of U.S. Catholics and Non-Catholics

	Catholics	Non-Catholics
	%	%
East	30	19
Midwest	21	21
South	25	37
West	24	23

Gallup Daily tracking, January-December 2014

GALLUP

More broadly, Rhode Island's 45% Catholic is the highest percentage in the nation, while Mississippi's 8% is the lowest.

September 24, 2015
TRUST IN FEDERAL GOV'T ON DOMESTIC MATTERS EDGES TO NEW LOW

by Jeffrey M. Jones

Story Highlights

- *Trust on domestic issues at 38%*
- *Trust on international issues slightly above record low at 45%*
- *Republicans show equally low trust in both areas*

PRINCETON, N.J.—Americans' trust in the federal government's ability to handle domestic problems has fallen further to 38%, a new low. Americans are a bit more likely to trust the government to handle international problems, but at 45%, this is scarcely better than last year's 43% record low.

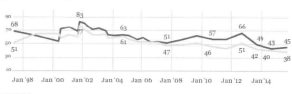

Trust in Federal Government to Handle International and Domestic Problems
Recent trend
Figures represent percent with "great deal" or "fair amount" of trust in the government

GALLUP

From 1972 through 2004, an average 69% of Americans had trust in the government to handle international problems and 62% to handle domestic problems. That period included the record-high 83% trust on international matters and 77% on domestic matters, measured in October 2001, shortly after the 9/11 terrorist attacks.

The results are based on Gallup's annual Governance poll, conducted Sept. 9–13. The poll also finds Americans' trust in each of the three branches of the federal government sits at or near record lows.

Although trust naturally declined after the 2001 peak, it had leveled off a bit near the end of President George W. Bush's first term.

However, in Bush's second term, in which he averaged an anemic 37% job approval, the averages were 56% trust to handle international problems and 52% to handle domestic problems.

TRUST IN U.S. FEDERAL GOVERNMENT
TO HANDLE DOMESTIC PROBLEMS

38%

SOURCE: GALLUP POLL, SEPT. 9-13

President Barack Obama's first term brought renewed trust in the government's ability to tackle international challenges as he wound down the wars in Iraq and Afghanistan. However, the still-struggling economy further eroded Americans' trust in the government to deal with domestic problems. During Obama's first term, which included a spike in both international and domestic trust immediately after the 2012 Democratic convention, Americans' trust on international matters averaged 61%, while it was 48% on domestic problems.

Obama's second term has seen a series of international challenges, including his plans to take military action against Syria in 2013, the recent rise of the Islamic State in Iraq and Syria, and increased tensions with Russia. International trust has averaged 46% during his second term, while domestic trust has averaged 41%.

While the trajectory of these trust measures can be related to the president and his performance, it is important to note that confidence in all three branches of government has been declining in recent years, with 32% trust in the legislative branch the lowest of the three currently.

Democrats More Trusting in Government

Typically, Americans with a party preference express greater trust in the federal government when a president from their favored party is in power. And this year is no exception; Democrats express much greater trust than Republicans in the federal government's ability to handle both domestic and international problems. The fact that the Republican Party controls Congress appears to make little difference in how much Republican identifiers trust the federal government.

Trust in Federal Government to Handle International and Domestic Problems, by Political Party

Figures are the percentage with a "great deal" or "fair amount" of trust

	% Trust International	% Trust Domestic
Democrats	68	56
Independents	43	35
Republicans	25	25

Sept. 9-13, 2015

GALLUP

Notably, Republicans make no distinction in the government's ability to handle domestic or international problems—25% say they trust it in each sphere. This was also the case last year, but in the first five years of the Obama presidency, Republicans were significantly more trusting of the government to deal with international matters than domestic ones.

Currently, independents, and Democrats especially, show more trust in the government on international matters than domestic ones. That has been the case throughout Obama's administration, although the size of the gap has varied during that time.

Implications

Trust in the government is a foundation of representative democracy. Citizens must have faith in their elected leaders to address the issues facing the country. Right now, Americans' trust in the government's ability to handle domestic problems has never been lower in Gallup's trends, which stretch back to the 1970s. Their trust in its ability to handle international problems is only slightly above the historical low.

A sobering reality is that Americans' trust in the government in those two areas was significantly better during the Watergate era. In April 1974, four months before Richard Nixon resigned as president, 51% of Americans trusted the government to handle domestic problems, 13 points higher than today. Trust on international matters at that time was 73%, even after the divisive Vietnam War, although it fell to 56% the next time the question was asked in 1976. The Watergate scandal was the obvious reason trust in government declined in the 1970s.

Now the issues seem to be more related to frustration with the government's inability to solve the problems the nation is facing. To a large degree, that reflects the realities of divided government during the Bush and Obama administrations, but also a more partisan environment in Washington than was the case decades ago. Each president had a time of unified party control but also directed his efforts during that time to issues, namely the Iraq war and healthcare reform, that were arguably not as central to Americans' concerns at the time and served to exacerbate partisan conflict in Washington and among the American public.

The future for trust in government cannot be known. Improvement in the economy over the last several years appears to have done little to reverse the recent decline in trust. From a historical perspective, Americans' trust in the government was eventually restored after Watergate, and a similar comeback in future years and decades cannot be ruled out.

Survey Methods

Results for this Gallup poll are based on telephone interviews conducted Sept. 9–13, 2015, with a random sample of 1,025 adults, aged 18 and older, living in all 50 U.S. states and the District of Columbia. For results based on the total sample of national adults, the margin of sampling error is ±4 percentage points at the 95% confidence level.

All reported margins of sampling error include computed design effects for weighting.

September 25, 2015
THE MORE AMERICANS KNOW CONGRESS, THE WORSE THEY RATE IT

by Frank Newport, Lydia Saad and Michael Traugott

Story Highlights

- *Half of Americans say Congress doing a poor or bad job*
- *Negative views rise to 66% among those highly knowledgeable about Congress*
- *Political awareness is not related to ratings of government*

PRINCETON, N.J.—Americans hold the U.S. Congress in very low esteem, with 49% rating the way Congress is handling its job as poor or bad and 15% rating it as excellent or good. But ratings of Congress are even worse among those who know the most about America's legislative body. Among those who answer four or five questions correctly about how Congress works and who runs it, 66% rate Congress as poor or bad, and 7% rate it as excellent or good.

Rating of U.S. Congress, by Political Knowledge

Columns represent number of political questions answered correctly

	National adults	0	1	2-3	4-5
% Excellent/Good	15	27	19	6	7
% Fair	34	38	32	37	27
% Poor/Bad	49	29	46	56	66
Net positive*	-34	-2	-27	-50	-59

*Net positive is % Excellent/Good minus % Poor/Bad.

June 15-16, 2015

GALLUP

These results are based on a new Gallup study on U.S. adults' attitudes toward Congress. Americans' low evaluations of Congress have been evident across many different measures in recent years, including the current 14% congressional job approval rating and at or near all-time lows in confidence in the legislative branch of government.

Gallup set out to examine what is behind these negative attitudes: Do they arise out of a sense of displeasure rooted in weakly informed assumptions and impressions, or are they serious complaints resulting from paying close attention to Congress and what it is doing? The answer to that question is important because it can help guide efforts by those who care about the legitimacy of this important institution and want to repair its tattered image.

To that aim, Gallup asked Americans a set of five questions measuring their knowledge of specific facts about Congress, its operations and its leadership:

- Do you happen to know how many U.S. senators there are from each state?
- Would you happen to know which chamber of Congress—the House of Representatives or the Senate—is responsible for confirming federal judges?
- For how many years are members of the U.S. House of Representatives elected—that is, how many years are there in one term of office?
- Do you happen to know which political party—the Democratic or Republican—currently has the most members in the U.S. House of Representatives?
- And do you happen to know the name of the majority leader in the U.S. Senate?

The results show that 17% of Americans are highly informed, answering four or five knowledge questions correctly. Another third correctly answered two or three questions, and about a quarter each could answer one or none correctly.

Separately, 20% of Americans report they follow news about national politics very closely, similar to the percentage who correctly answered four or five knowledge questions about Congress. The two measures of political awareness are highly correlated, indicating that the five factual questions serve as an important indicator of both knowledge and political awareness.

Americans' Knowledge About U.S. Congress

Number of factual questions about Congress answered correctly

	%
4-5 correct	17
2-3	33
1	27
None correct	23

June 15-16, 2015

GALLUP

The Knowledgeable Are the Most Negative About Congress

The relationship between Americans' knowledge of Congress's workings and their evaluation of the job it is doing is remarkably strong. Negative ratings of Congress are higher at each level of political knowledge. Only 29% of those who answer none of the five questions correctly think Congress is doing a poor or bad job. This rises to 46% among those answering one question correctly, to 56% among those answering two or three correctly and to 66% among those answering four or five questions correctly. In other words, the more Americans know about Congress, the more likely they are to say it is doing a poor or bad job.

VIEWS OF CONGRESS: "POOR/BAD"

NOT INFORMED	VERY INFORMED
29%	66%

SOURCE: GALLUP POLL, JUNE 15-16

Further, the difference between the excellent/good and poor/bad ratings among those who know little factually about Congress—those who do not answer any of the questions correctly—is -2, a relatively neutral assessment. At the other extreme, the net-positive rating among those who know a great deal—those who answered four or five questions right—is -59.

Thus, Americans who are the most negative about Congress are not making their judgment based on a vague sense of what is happening in Washington, but most likely basing their opinions on a well-informed view of the institution and its operations.

Implications

Evaluations of the job Congress is doing are currently much worse among Americans who know the most about its workings and who are paying the closest attention to who holds power in the institution. There might be many reasons for this, including the underlying relationships between knowledge of Congress and education and age. Highly educated Americans are much more knowledgeable than those with less education and are also much more likely to have negative opinions of Congress. Also, Americans aged 30 and older are somewhat more knowledgeable and more negative toward Congress than those who are younger. There is little significant difference between knowledge and partisanship, showing that this is not a situation driven by traditional politics.

But regardless of how it came to be, the fact that the most knowledgeable about Congress are the most critical has important implications for anyone focused on attempting to narrow the chasm that currently divides Americans and the people elected to represent them. It appears that Congress cannot merely talk its way out of its low ratings, but rather will need to actually perform better to win back public support among those who are paying the closest attention. This puts Congress's image in its members' control. The alternative—if those members of the public who are neither knowledgeable nor paying attention reviewed the institution negatively—would make the prescription for fixing the institution's image far less clear.

The second part of this report will explore the relationship between Americans' views of the U.S. Congress as a whole versus their views of how the Republicans and Democrats in Congress are performing.

Survey Methods

Results for this Gallup poll are based on telephone interviews conducted June 15–16, 2015, on the Gallup U.S. Daily survey, with a random sample of 1,017 adults, aged 18 and older, living in all 50 U.S. states and the District of Columbia. For results based on the total sample of national adults, the margin of sampling error is ±4 percentage points at the 95% confidence level. All reported margins of sampling error include computed design effects for weighting.

September 25, 2015
URBAN COMMUNITIES LEAD U.S. IN ECONOMIC OPTIMISM

by Dante Chinni, Gallup Research Adviser and Guest Contributor

WASHINGTON, D.C.—Americans' views on the U.S. economy heading into the upcoming presidential election have a lot to do with where they live. Small-town and rural America are decidedly dour about the direction of the nation's economy, while large urban and dense suburban places tilt positive or, at worst, just slightly negative.

Americans' Economic Outlook by Community Group
Groups based on American Communities Project

	% Economy getting better	% Economy getting worse	Net getting better (pct. pts.)
Big Cities	53	42	+11
Urban Suburbs	51	44	+7
College Towns	46	49	-3
U.S. AVERAGE	45	50	-5
Hispanic Centers	45	50	-5
Exurbs	43	52	-9
African American South	42	55	-13
LDS Enclaves	41	54	-13
Middle Suburbs	41	54	-13
Military Posts	40	55	-15
Graying America	39	56	-17
Native American Lands	38	58	-20
Rural Middle America	37	58	-21
Aging Farmlands	31	64	-33
Working Class Country	31	64	-33
Evangelical Hubs	30	65	-35

Gallup Daily tracking, January-June 2015

GALLUP

The American Communities Project uses demographic data to break the nation's 3,100-plus counties into 15 types of communities—everything from Big Cities to Rural Middle America. A map

on the American Communities Project website shows how every county is sorted into these community types.

Using Gallup Daily tracking data for the first half of 2015, the American Communities Project analyzed Americans' answers to the question "Right now, do you think the economic conditions in the country as a whole are getting better or getting worse?" on the basis of the 15 community types. Residents of Big Cities and Urban Suburbs were the most positive, with slightly more adult residents in these areas saying the economy is getting better than saying it is getting worse. Residents of College Towns were the next most positive, with roughly the same number saying the economy is getting better as getting worse. And these communities share some important traits. They tend to have large higher-income, college-educated populations. They also tend to be Democratic politically, with all three types voting for President Barack Obama in 2012.

At the same time, adults living in the Evangelical Hubs, Working Class Country and Aging Farmlands are roughly twice as likely to say the economy is getting worse, rather than better. The majority of their populations are rural, with lower college education rates and median household incomes below the national average. And all are heavily Republican; at least 63% of each group voted for Mitt Romney in 2012.

ECONOMY "GETTING BETTER" IN U.S.

EVANGELICAL HUBS	BIG CITIES
30%	53%

SOURCE: GALLUP DAILY TRACKING

The graph that follows displays the percentage of each community that is urban paired with the average percentage in the first half of 2015 saying the economy is getting better. The statistical correlation between the two metrics is strong (0.87 correlation), confirming that urbanicity and economic confidence currently go hand in hand.

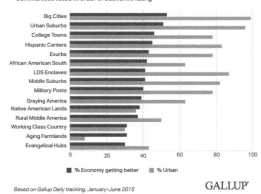

% Urban vs. Positive Economic Outlook Within American Community Groups
Communities listed in order of economic rating

Based on Gallup Daily tracking, January-June 2015

GALLUP

Americans also tend to think the economy is good or bad, improving or stagnating, depending on whether their partisan orientation matches that of the president occupying the White House. And this is largely borne out in the accompanying graph, which displays the percentage of residents in each community who are Democratic or lean Democratic alongside the percentage saying the economy is getting better.

While the relationship between the percentage Democratic and positive economic outlook is strong (0.73 correlation), it is not as strong as the relationship between urbanicity and economic outlook. This is largely because of subdued economic confidence in a few Democratic-leaning areas, namely the African American South and Native American Lands.

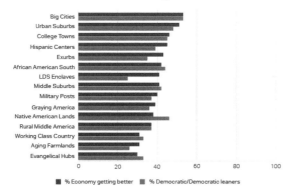

% Democratic vs. Positive Economic Outlook Within American Community Groups

Communities listed in order of economic rating

■ % Economy getting better   ■ % Democratic/Democratic leaners

Based on Gallup Daily tracking, January-June 2015

GALLUP

Further, not only do the 15 groups' views about the direction of the economy differ, but they also vary in how much their outlook has recovered since the recession. In 2009, the more urban and plurality-Democratic communities were already more optimistic about the economy than less urban and Republican-leaning communities, likely reflecting Democrats' greater satisfaction with economic leadership during Obama's inaugural year. However, since then, economic optimism has improved to a greater degree in the more urban, Democratic and/or college-educated communities—such as Urban Suburbs, Big Cities and Hispanic Centers—than in the smaller, rural, less-well-educated and Republican communities, including Evangelical Hubs, Aging Farmlands, Working Class Country and Rural Middle America.

Key Metrics for American Community Groups

Groups based on American Communities Project

	Change since 2009 in % economy getting better	% Urban	% Democratic/ lean Democratic
Urban Suburbs	+17	96	48
Big Cities	+16	99	53
Hispanic Centers	+14	83	39
College Towns	+12	78	45
Exurbs	+12	78	35
Middle Suburbs	+11	82	42
Graying America	+11	63	36
LDS Enclaves	+9	87	25
African American South	+9	63	44
Rural Middle America	+8	50	37
Native American Lands	+8	36	46
Military Posts	+7	78	37
Aging Farmlands	+7	8	26
Working Class Country	+6	30	33
Evangelical Hubs	+4	43	33

Gallup Daily tracking, January-June 2015

GALLUP

Urban Workers Report Best Net Hiring

The pattern is similar in the responses to another Gallup metric—the Job Creation Index—which asks employed adults, "In general, is your employer hiring new people and expanding the size of its workforce, not changing the size of its workforce or letting people go and reducing the size of its workforce?"

Overall, the relationship between community size and perceptions about hiring is similar to that seen between community size and economic optimism. Net hiring (the percentage of employed adults saying their employer is increasing its workforce minus those saying their employer is reducing staff) is +32 or higher in the Big Cities, LDS Enclaves and Urban Suburbs. And the figure is nearly as high in College Towns (+29) and Middle Suburbs (+28). By contrast, net hiring is +20 or below in the less urban Aging Farmlands, Native American Lands, Evangelical Hubs and Working Class Country.

Overall, while the relationship isn't perfect, the more Democratic communities tend to perceive the best hiring conditions, while the Republican communities tend to perceive the worst. However, in this case, the correlation between net hiring and percentage urban (0.88) is much stronger than that between net hiring and percentage Democratic (0.47).

Net Hiring vs. % Democratic and % Urban Within American Community Groups

Groups based on American Communities Project

	Net hiring	% Democratic/ lean Democratic	% Urban
Big Cities	+36	53	99
LDS Enclaves	+33	25	87
Urban Suburbs	+32	48	96
College Towns	+29	45	78
Middle Suburbs	+28	42	82
Exurbs	+27	35	78
Hispanic Centers	+24	39	83
African American South	+24	44	63
Graying America	+24	36	63
Rural Middle America	+24	37	50
Working Class Country	+20	33	30
Military Posts	+19	37	78
Evangelical Hubs	+19	33	43
Native American Lands	+18	46	36
Aging Farmlands	+11	26	8

Gallup Daily tracking, January-June 2015

GALLUP

Implications

These data reveal how the economic divide in the U.S. is strongly linked to proximity to cities as well as to the red/blue political divide. This also means that the different political messages espoused on the political left and right reflect more than just stubborn partisan opinions; they are rooted in real differences in the way their constituencies see and experience the economy after seven years of a Democratic president. People in rural places with lower education rates who also tend to be more Republican really do perceive different economic challenges and realities than those in better-educated urban and more Democratic communities.

Taken together, the numbers show how complicated the electorate is. It's difficult for a candidate to craft an economic message that resonates in all these places. In some areas, the economic pessimism is deep, while in others there is a growing optimism. The difference may help give rise to a 2016 campaign in which the major-party candidates essentially talk past each other, speaking to their urban or rural bases about different economies and different sets of problems.

Dante Chinni is the director of the American Communities Project, a political and socioeconomic research effort partnered with American University and Michigan State University. He is the author of Our Patchwork Nation *and data journalist working with the* Wall Street Journal *and NBC News.*

Survey Methods

This analysis is telephone interviews conducted Jan. 2–June 30, 2015, on the Gallup U.S. Daily survey, with a random sample of 88,667 adults, aged 18 and older, living in all 50 U.S. states and the District of Columbia. The sample size in each community group ranges from 17,932 in the Big Cities and 17,665 in Urban Suburbs down to 244 in Aging Farmlands and 188 in Native American Lands. Aging Farmlands and Native American Lands are the only groups with fewer than 1,100 interviews.

For results based on the total sample of national adults, the margin of sampling error is ±1 percentage point at the 95% confidence level. For most community groups, the margin of sampling error is no more than ±2 percentage points at the 95% confidence level. For Aging Farmlands the margin of sampling error is ±8 percentage points at the 95% confidence level and for Native American Lands it is ±9 percentage points. All reported margins of sampling error include computed design effects for weighting.

September 25, 2015

MAJORITY IN U.S. MAINTAIN NEED FOR THIRD MAJOR PARTY

by Justin McCarthy

Story Highlights

- Six in 10 say third party needed for adequate representation
- Current figure matches high from 2013
- Seventy-eight percent of independents say third party needed

WASHINGTON, D.C.—A majority of Americans, 60%, say a third major political party is needed because the Republican and Democratic parties "do such a poor job" of representing the American people. This matches the high set in 2013. Since 2007, a majority of Americans have generally called for a third party, with the exception of the last two presidential election years.

These latest results come as both the Democratic and Republican parties are experiencing formidable challenges in the 2016 presidential race from unlikely corners of their ranks, including several candidates who have never been elected to a political office. On the Democratic side, independent Vermont Sen. Bernie Sanders has drawn a large following from left-leaning Americans. In the Republican nomination contest, real estate mogul Donald Trump has rocked his GOP competitors with personal attacks and unconventional political statements, and Dr. Ben Carson and former business executive Carly Fiorina are now among the front-runners for their party's nomination. None of these candidates has said they will

seek a third-party bid for the presidency if they don't receive the nomination, but their popularity supports the idea that Americans may be willing to consider candidates outside of the pool of typical politicians.

Americans' Opinions of a Need for a Third U.S. Political Party

In your view, do the Republican and Democratic parties do an adequate job of representing the American people, or do they do such a poor job that a third major party is needed?

■ % Parties do adequate job   ▨ % Third party needed

GALLUP

Americans have been warm to the idea of a third party for at least a decade. When Gallup first asked whether a third party is needed in 2003, four in 10 Americans said it was. The figure climbed in subsequent polls, reaching a majority of 58% in 2007. With the exception of presidential election years in 2008 and 2012, majorities of 52% to 60% of Americans have said a third party is needed to address the inadequacies of the Republican and Democratic parties.

> **NEED FOR A THIRD U.S. PARTY**
>
> PARTIES ADEQUATE   THIRD NEEDED
>
> **38%**   **60%**
>
> SOURCE: GALLUP POLL, SEPT. 9–13

Meanwhile, 38% of Americans in the Sept. 9–13 Governance poll say the two major parties do an adequate job—up from a low of 26% in 2013. However, this is markedly down from 2003, when more than half of Americans (56%) said the two major parties were representing the public adequately. Underscoring this dissatisfaction, less than 40% of Americans said they had a favorable view of either party earlier this year.

Nearly Four in Five Independents Say Third Party Needed

Perhaps unsurprisingly, Americans who identify politically as independents have consistently been most likely to say a third party is necessary. Majorities of independents in every poll since 2003 have had this view, ranging from a low of 56% in 2003 to a high of 78% in the latest poll.

Support for a Third Major U.S. Political Party, by Political Party Affiliation

Numbers in percentages

■ Democrats   ■ Independents   ▨ Republicans

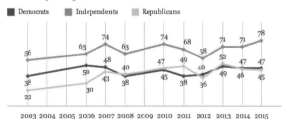

Note: 2007 and 2011 data represent average of two polls

GALLUP

Republicans and Democrats have, for the most part, been about equally likely to voice a preference for a third party, with the percentage in favor of a third party for each group usually less than a majority and well below the percentage of independents.

There have been a few times in the past when one party's supporters were more likely than the other's to believe a third party was necessary. In polls from 2003 to 2007, during Republican George W. Bush's presidency, Democrats were far more likely than Republicans to say a new major party needed to emerge, but the differences between the two groups settled thereafter. In 2011, however, on the heels of the rise of the Tea Party movement, Republicans were 11 percentage points more likely than Democrats to see a third party as necessary.

Bottom Line

Arguably, the U.S. political climate has been ripe for the emergence of a major third party for some time, but that hasn't yet happened.

So far during this election cycle, Americans may be instead expressing their frustration with the parties by supporting candidates such as Sanders, Trump, Carson and Fiorina. The lack of major third party candidates in recent years in part reflects the difficulty such candidates have in obtaining ballot access in the 50 states, securing a place in the debates and raising sufficient funds outside of the traditional two-party system. Businessman Ross Perot, however, had the personal resources to mount an independent campaign in 1992, and ended up with nearly 19% of the popular vote. It is always possible that a similar type of candidate could emerge to tap into the underlying sentiment and become a force with which the two major parties would have to contend.

Survey Methods

Results for this Gallup poll are based on telephone interviews conducted Sept. 9–13, 2015, on the Gallup U.S. Daily survey, with a random sample of 1,025 adults, aged 18 and older, living in all 50 U.S. states and the District of Columbia. For results based on the total sample of national adults, the margin of sampling error is ±4 percentage points at the 95% confidence level. All reported margins of sampling error include computed design effects for weighting.

September 28, 2015
MAJORITY OF AMERICANS SEE CONGRESS AS OUT OF TOUCH, CORRUPT

by Andrew Dugan

Story Highlights

- *Most say lawmakers corrupt, out of touch, favor special interests*
- *Record 48% say their own representative is out of touch*
- *Record 32% say their own member is corrupt*

WASHINGTON, D.C.—However the likely drama over how to fund the government past Sept. 30 unfolds, most Americans appear to have little faith in most lawmakers to do the right thing. Majorities believe that most members of Congress are "out of touch with average Americans" (79%), "focused on the needs of special interests"

rather than the needs of their constituents (69%) and corrupt (52%). Americans are less critical of their own representatives, but substantial percentages say their own member of Congress is out of touch (48%), focused on special interests (47%) and corrupt (32%).

Americans' Views on Their Member and Most Members of Congress

I'd like to ask you about [your member/most members] of Congress. Would you say that [your member/most members] of Congress are …

	Your member %	Most members %
CORRUPT OR NOT CORRUPT?		
Corrupt	32	52
Not corrupt	59	42
FOCUSED ON THE NEEDS OF SPECIAL INTERESTS, OR FOCUSED ON NEEDS OF CONSTITUENTS IN YOUR/THEIR DISTRICT?		
Special interests	47	69
Constituents	43	25
GENERALLY OUT OF TOUCH WITH AVERAGE AMERICANS OR GENERALLY IN TOUCH?		
Out of touch	48	79
In touch	47	20

Sept. 9-13, 2015

GALLUP'

These results come from Gallup's annual Governance poll, conducted Sept. 9–13. By any measure, Congress is not a popular or trusted institution among Americans. The body's current approval rating, 14%, is typical of its ratings over the past several years. Earlier this year, Gallup found that fewer than one in 10 Americans (8%) have a great deal or quite a lot of confidence in Congress.

Traditionally, Americans have been less critical of their own members of Congress, but last year the percentage of U.S. adults saying their own representative deserved re-election dropped to a record low. These uneasy feelings Americans have for Congress may be exacerbated in the coming days, as the prospect of a government shutdown looms. House Speaker John Boehner's unexpected resignation on Friday highlights how acrimonious congressional divisions have become, leading the House Speaker to step down well before his term ends. Speculation is rampant that Boehner's resignation may actually be the action that prevents a government shutdown this week. But if this is true, it could confirm some of Americans' worst impressions of Congress, as it would suggest that simple legislative functions, such as funding the federal government, are enough to thrust the House into leadership turmoil.

Americans Grow More Skeptical of Own Representatives

Gallup has asked these sets of questions in five polls since 1994, providing a glimpse into how Americans have assessed Congress on these dimensions across distinct political periods.

CONGRESS OUT OF TOUCH
YOUR MEMBER   MOST MEMBERS
48%   79%
SOURCE: GALLUP POLL SEPT. 9-13

U.S. adults today are more likely to see Congress as focused on the needs of special interests than they were in 1994. Meanwhile, Americans are slightly more likely today to say their own member of Congress is focused on special interests than on constituents' needs. This year's 47% is nominally the highest figure on record, and up seven percentage points from 2006.

Americans Saying Members of Congress Focus on Special Interests Rather Than on Their Constituents' Needs

■ % Your member focuses on special interests

▒ % Most members focus on special interests

58   65   69 69
42   54   40   46 47

1995 1997 1999 2001 2003 2005 2007 2009 2011 2013 2015

GALLUP'

Americans' views have fluctuated on whether most members of Congress are corrupt. In October 1994—on the eve of a historic Republican wave that swept out many long-serving, powerful congressional Democrats—half of Americans saw most federal lawmakers as corrupt. This fell to 38% in early 2006, but has now climbed back to 52%. Relatedly, Gallup recently found that 75% of Americans perceive corruption to be widespread in the government in general. Nearly a third of Americans (32%) today say their member of Congress is corrupt, 10 points higher than in 2006.

Americans' Views on Whether Members of Congress Are Corrupt

■ % Your member is corrupt   ▒ % Most members are corrupt

50   47   54 52
   38
27   22   32 27

1995 1997 1999 2001 2003 2005 2007 2009 2011 2013 2015

GALLUP'

Over the past five surveys, roughly three in four Americans have judged most members of Congress to be out of touch with average Americans, including 79% this year. The public is more likely to view local members of Congress as in touch, but nearly half (48%) this year say their member of Congress is out of touch, higher than in 2006 (38%) or 1994 (41%).

Americans' Views on Whether Members of Congress Are Generally Out of Touch or in Touch With Average Americans

■ % Your member is out of touch   ▒ % Most members are out of touch

75   77   81 79
   69
41   38   47 48

1995 1997 1999 2001 2003 2005 2007 2009 2011 2013 2015

GALLUP'

Bottom Line

Majorities of Americans view most members of Congress as corrupt, beholden to special interests and out of touch. This is not new and perhaps not even surprising, given the low esteem in which Americans hold the institution. But this cynicism is beginning to influence Americans' views of their own federal representatives, not just the national legislature. Record or near-record numbers of U.S. adults say their local representative is out of touch and focused on serving special interests rather than their constituents.

Congress is under greater-than-usual stress, with the House Speaker's abrupt resignation and a possible government shutdown. Numerous members of Congress have cast this battle as a principled one, even if it results in disruptive outcomes such as a shutdown, or, as is apparently the case, the abrupt resignation of the top lawmaker in the House. But given the large proportion of Americans who believe members of Congress have far less altruistic motives, it is doubtful many Americans will see the showdown as a dispute over how best to serve the nation's interests.

Survey Methods

Results for this Gallup poll are based on telephone interviews conducted Sept. 9–13, 2015, with a random sample of 1,025 adults, aged 18 and older, living in all 50 U.S. states and the District of Columbia. For results based on the total sample of national adults, the margin of sampling error is ±4 percentage points at the 95% confidence level. All reported margins of sampling error include computed design effects for weighting.

September 28, 2015
RECENT GRADS LESS LIKELY TO AGREE COLLEGE WAS WORTH COST

by Steve Crabtree and Sean Seymour

Story Highlights

- *Half of college alumni strongly agree their education was worth the cost*
- *Caring professors raise odds of feeling education was worth it*

Amid recent controversy over rising tuition and mounting student debt totals, half of college graduates in the U.S. (50%) "strongly agree" that their undergraduate education was worth the cost. This figure varies only slightly between alumni of public (52%) and private nonprofit (47%) universities, but drops sharply to 26% among graduates of private for-profit universities.

Half of All U.S. Graduates "Strongly Agree" Their Education Was Worth the Cost

"My education from [University Name] was worth the cost."

	All graduates	Recent graduates (2006-2015)	Public universities	Private nonprofit universities	Private for-profit universities
Strongly disagree	4%	8%	3%	4%	13%
2	6%	9%	5%	7%	15%
3	13%	17%	12%	14%	20%
4	27%	27%	28%	27%	25%
Strongly agree	50%	38%	52%	47%	26%

Based on Web surveys of more than 30,000 U.S. college graduates with Internet access from Dec. 16, 2014–June 29, 2015.

GALLUP'

Recent graduates, those who have obtained their bachelor's degree beginning in 2006, are significantly less likely to strongly agree with this statement. Only 38% of recent alumni strongly agree their education was worth the cost.

The question, which is included in the new 2015 Gallup-Purdue Index study, is particularly relevant given the growing attention on the cost of higher education in the U.S. In November 2014, CNN captured the fervor over the issue with its documentary film *Ivory Tower*. The film cited some alarming statistics: Tuition has been rising at nearly three times the rate of inflation in recent years, and the total amount of outstanding student loan debt in the U.S. has grown to over $1.2 trillion. Presidential candidates from both major parties have already announced proposals for addressing the issue.

GRADUATES WHO "STRONGLY AGREE"
COLLEGE WAS WORTH THE COST

38%

SOURCE: GALLUP-PURDUE INDEX, 2015

Relationships Most Affect Graduates' Perception That Their Education Was Worth the Cost

Some observers have argued that commonly used college rankings such as the ones published by *U.S. News & World Report* each year have actually worsened the situation. They claim that this particular ranking fails to measure many aspects of college life that help students make the most of their college years. Though the 2015 scores assigned to 200 national universities by the *U.S. News & World Report* rankings are clearly related to graduates' likelihood to strongly agree that their college experience was worth the cost, they explain only about one-third of the variation in alumni responses.

The Gallup-Purdue Index was developed to add to education leaders' understanding of the true value colleges provide by identifying and tracking student experiences related to alumni success and well-being after graduation.

Among the most important results from this year's study is the conclusion that having had supportive relationships with faculty members and other mentor figures powerfully influences graduates' estimation of their college experience. Specifically, alumni's strong agreement with any of the following three statements almost doubles the odds that they unreservedly believe their education was worth the cost:

- My professors at [university name] cared about me as a person.
- While attending [university name] I had a mentor who encouraged me to pursue my goals and dreams.
- I had at least one professor at [university name] who made me excited about learning.

The graphic below presents the increase in graduates' likelihood to strongly agree their education was worth the cost if they remembered having each of the listed college experiences. To help isolate the direct relationship between these questions, the analysis controls for graduates' employment status and amount of student loan debt. It also uses results from a five-factor personality scale to help account for personality traits that might cause graduates to rate both their college experiences and their post-college lives positively.

Bottom Line

Amid the heated debate about the costs and benefits of higher education in the U.S., and the finding that recent graduates are less likely to believe their education was worth the cost, the Gallup-Purdue Index brings some positive news: Higher education leaders and other stakeholders have opportunities to increase their university's value to undergraduates. They can do this by focusing on factors that help students make the most of their college years. Key among these factors are relationships with people who can help students stay fully engaged in their education and focused on the future it will help them achieve. In particular, faculty and other mentors can foster these student goals.

The odds of strongly agreeing education was worth the cost are:

1.9x Higher if ... My professors at [University Name] cared about me as a person.

1.9x Higher if ... I had a mentor who encouraged me to pursue my goals and dreams.

1.8x Higher if ... I had at least one professor at [University Name] who made me excited about learning.

1.6x Higher if ... I worked on a project that took a semester or more to complete.

1.6x Higher if ... I was extremely active in extracurricular activities and organizations while attending [University Name].

1.5x Higher if ... I had an internship or job that allowed me to apply what I was learning in the classroom.

1.4x Higher if ... I held a leadership position in a club or organization such as student government, a fraternity or sorority or an athletic team.

1.3x Higher if ... I was a member of a national fraternity or sorority.

1.2x Higher if ... I had a paid job or internship.

Each odds ratio represents the unique variation in the dependent variable (education was worth the cost) associated with each college experience while controlling for the other experiences and for the control variables (employment status, amount of student loan debt and five-factor personality model characteristics).

GALLUP

Survey Methods

Results for the Gallup-Purdue Index are based on Web surveys conducted Dec. 16, 2014–June 29, 2015, with a random sample of 30,151 respondents with a bachelor's degree or higher, aged 18 and older, with Internet access, living in all 50 U.S. states and the District of Columbia.

The Gallup-Purdue Index sample was recruited via the Gallup Daily tracking survey. The Gallup Daily tracking survey sample includes national adults with a minimum quota of 50% cellphone respondents and 50% landline respondents, with additional minimum quotas by time zone within region. Landline and cellular telephone numbers are selected using random-digit-dial methods.

Gallup-Purdue Index interviews are conducted via the Web, in English only. Samples are weighted to correct for unequal selection probability and nonresponse. The data are weighted to match national demographics of gender, age, race, Hispanic ethnicity, education and region provided by the Current Population Survey.

All reported margins of sampling error for the Gallup-Purdue Index of all college graduates include the computed design effects for weighting.

For results based on the total sample of those with a bachelor's degree or higher, the margin of sampling error is ±0.8 percentage points at the 95% confidence level.

For results based on employee engagement of those with a bachelor's degree or higher, the margin of sampling error is ±1.0 percentage point at the 95% confidence level.

In addition to sampling error, question wording and practical difficulties in conducting surveys can introduce error or bias into the findings of public opinion polls.

September 28, 2015
AMERICANS' TRUST IN MEDIA REMAINS AT HISTORICAL LOW

by Rebecca Riffkin

Story Highlights

- *Four in 10 Americans trust the mass media*
- *Ties 2014 and 2012 for the lowest trust level in Gallup's trend*
- *Younger Americans less likely than older to trust the media*

WASHINGTON, D.C.—Four in 10 Americans say they have "a great deal" or "a fair amount" of trust and confidence in the mass media to report the news fully, accurately and fairly. This ties the historical lows on this measure set in 2014 and 2012. Prior to 2004, slight majorities of Americans said they trusted the mass media, such as newspapers, TV and radio.

Americans' Trust in the Mass Media

In general, how much trust and confidence do you have in the mass media – such as newspapers, TV and radio -- when it comes to reporting the news fully, accurately and fairly -- a great deal, a fair amount, not very much or none at all?

■ % Great deal/Fair amount

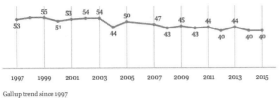

Gallup trend since 1997

GALLUP

Americans' confidence in the media has slowly eroded from a high of 55% in 1998 and 1999. Since 2007, the majority of Americans have had little or no trust in the mass media. Trust has typically dipped in election years, including 2004, 2008, 2012 and last year. However, 2015 is not a major election year.

This decline follows the same trajectory as Americans' confidence in many institutions and their declining trust in the federal government's ability to handle domestic and international problems over the same time period.

AMERICANS' TRUST IN MASS MEDIA

1999	2015
55%	40%

SOURCE: GALLUP POLL, SEPT. 9-13

Trust in the Mass Media Has Fallen More Sharply Among Those Younger Than 50

Trust in the media continues to be significantly lower among Americans aged 18 to 49 than among those 50 and older, continuing a

pattern evident since 2012. Prior to 2012, these groups' trust levels were more similar, with a few exceptions between 2005 and 2008.

Trust Among Democrats Remains Low, But Higher Than Among Republicans

For more than a decade, Republicans and independents have been significantly less likely than Democrats to trust the media. This pattern continues in the latest survey. In 2014, Gallup found that trust among Democrats fell to a 14-year low of 54%, and this figure is essentially unchanged at 55% this year. While more Democrats than Republicans continue to say they trust the media, the percentage of Republicans who report that they trust the mass media increased slightly this year, from 27% to 32%. This increase was offset, however, by a decrease in independents reporting trust, from 38% to 33%.

Trust in Mass Media, by Age
% Great deal/Fair amount of trust
■ 18 to 49 years old   50 or older

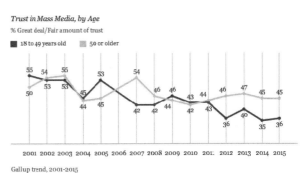

Gallup trend, 2001-2015

GALLUP

Trust in Mass Media, by Party
% Great deal/Fair amount of trust
■ Republicans   Independents   Democrats

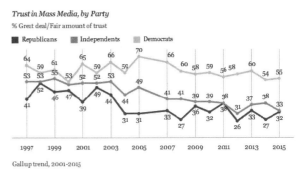

Gallup trend, 2001-2015

GALLUP

Bottom Line

Americans' trust level in the media has drifted downward over the past decade. The same forces behind the drop in trust in government more generally, as well confidence in many U.S. institutions, may also be at work with the media. But some of the loss in trust may have been self-inflicted. Major venerable news organizations have been caught making serious mistakes in the past several years, including the scandal involving former NBC Nightly News anchor Brian Williams in 2015 that some of his firsthand accounts of news events had been exaggerated or "misremembered."

Survey Methods

Results for this Gallup poll are based on telephone interviews conducted Sept. 9–13, 2015, with a random sample of 1,025 adults, aged 18 and older, living in all 50 U.S. states and the District of

Columbia. For results based on the total sample of national adults, the margin of sampling error is ±4 percentage points at the 95% confidence level. All reported margins of sampling error include computed design effects for weighting.

Each sample of national adults includes a minimum quota of 60% cellphone respondents and 40% landline respondents, with additional minimum quotas by time zone within region. Landline and cellular telephone numbers are selected using random-digit-dial methods.

September 30, 2015
FEWER IN U.S. WANT GOVERNMENT TO PROMOTE TRADITIONAL VALUES

by Jeffrey M. Jones

Story Highlights

- *51% say government should not promote any set of values*
- *Americans long have said government should promote traditional values*
- *Americans still favor reduced government role in solving problems*

PRINCETON, N.J.—More Americans say the government should not promote any set of values (51%) than say it should promote traditional values (43%). This is the second time in the past four years Americans have tilted toward saying the government should be neutral on values. For most of the past decade, the public has been divided on what the government's role in this area should be. But even this was a shift from pre-2005, when Americans consistently favored the government's promoting traditional values.

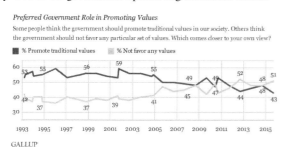

Preferred Government Role in Promoting Values
Some people think the government should promote traditional values in our society. Others think the government should not favor any particular set of values. Which comes closer to your own view?

GALLUP

The movement away from government upholding "traditional" values is in keeping with recent Gallup trends showing Americans becoming more liberal in their views on many specific issues, most notably same-sex marriage and legalized marijuana.

Democrats (62%) are much more likely than Republicans (39%) to say the government should not promote any set of values. Democrats have consistently been more likely to hold this view over time. But one reason Americans as a whole are more likely now than in the past to say government should not promote any set of values is that an increasing number of Republicans hold this view.

The percentages have varied a bit from year to year, but the Republican trend is unmistakable. Whereas an average of 22% of Republicans from 2001 to 2004 thought government should remain value neutral, this has increased to 34% since 2011.

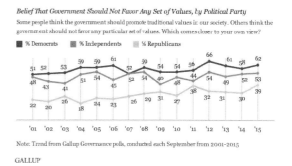

Belief That Government Should Not Favor Any Set of Values, by Political Party
Some people think the government should promote traditional values in our society. Others think the government should not favor any particular set of values. Which comes closer to your own view?

Note: Trend from Gallup Governance polls, conducted each September from 2001-2015

GALLUP

That 12-percentage-point increase compares with an average four-point increase among independents (from 46% to 50%) and a seven-point increase among Democrats (54% to 61%) over the same time periods.

WANT GOV'T TO PROMOTE TRADITIONAL VALUES

43%

SOURCE: GALLUP POLL, SEPTEMBER 2015

Americans Continue to Say Government Should Do Less to Solve Problems

While Americans' views have shifted toward favoring a reduced government role in morality, they have maintained a preference for less government involvement in solving the country's problems. Currently, 55% say the government "is trying to do too many things that should be left to individuals and businesses," while 40% believe the "government should do more to solve our country's problems." Those percentages are similar to the averages of 53% and 39%, respectively, since 1993.

Only once—shortly after the 9/11 terrorist attacks that spurred a rally in public support for government institutions and officeholders—did Americans clearly favor a more active government role over a more limited one. The public was closely divided in its preferences briefly at the beginning of Bill Clinton's presidency in 1993, and favored limited government by a smaller margin from 2006–2008 near the end of George W. Bush's administration, when his approval ratings were very low.

Preferred Government Role in Solving the Nation's Problems
Some people think the government is trying to do too many things that should be left to individuals and businesses. Others think that government should do more to solve our country's problems. Which comes closer to your own view?

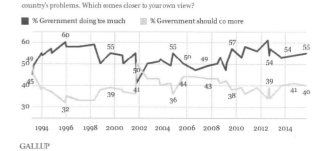

GALLUP

The relative stability in the trend for all Americans masks movement among party groups, reflecting the increasingly homogenous views on this attitude within each party. A majority of Republicans have always believed the government is doing too many things, but that percentage has grown from an average 68% in 2001–2004 to 83% since 2011. Independents have also shown an increase in this sentiment, from 49% to 58%. Meanwhile, Democrats' preference for a less active federal government has declined from an average 37% to 27%, with the change more pronounced since 2012.

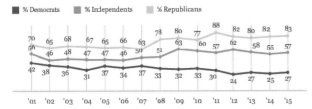

Belief Government Doing Too Much to Solve Nation's Problems, by Political Party

Some people think the government is trying to do too many things that should be left to individuals and businesses. Others think that government should do more to solve our country's problems. Which comes closer to your own view?

■ % Democrats   ■ % Independents   ░ % Republicans

Note: Trend from Gallup Governance polls, conducted each September from 2001-2015

GALLUP

Implications

Americans' growing belief that the government should not favor any set of values represents a shift from the past, and is further evidence of a leftward tilt on matters of morality. That certainly creates a challenge for Republican presidential candidates heading into the next election, particularly those who emphasize moral values issues in their campaigns. And while a values-centered campaign still would appeal to most rank-and-file Republican primary voters, a growing minority of Republicans say the government should not favor any particular values.

At the same time, Americans retain their preference for a more limited government role in solving the nation's problems, inconsistent with the preferences of the Democratic candidates. Although rank-and-file Democrats are more likely to favor government activity to solve the nation's problems than they were in the past, a solid majority of independents and the vast majority of Republicans do not.

These attitudes will help frame the 2016 election but may not decide it, as the state of the nation at that time and the candidates' backgrounds and personal characteristics will also be important. Americans' preferences for the government's role could change, at least around the margins, between now and next November. And the parties' nominees themselves could help shape Americans' views on the proper roles of government if they are able to articulate their messages in ways that resonate with the public.

Survey Methods

Results for this Gallup poll are based on telephone interviews conducted Sept. 9–13, 2015, with a random sample of 1,025 adults, aged 18 and older, living in all 50 U.S. states and the District of Columbia. For results based on the total sample of national adults, the margin of sampling error is ±4 percentage points at the 95% confidence level. All reported margins of sampling error include computed design effects for weighting.

MOST U.S. INVESTORS SAY AREA HOUSING PRICES ARE RISING

by Justin McCarthy

Story Highlights

- *Six in 10 investors say local housing prices on the rise*
- *Large, small investors say homeowning an important investment*

WASHINGTON, D.C.—Roughly six in 10 U.S. investors say housing prices in their area are rising. Just 11% say prices are falling, while a quarter believe prices are stable.

U.S. Investors' Perceptions of the Trend in Housing Prices

Thinking about the housing market in your area, what is your perception of the trend in housing prices?

	Rising a lot	Rising a little	Staying the same	Falling a little	Falling a lot
	%	%	%	%	%
All investors	17	44	26	8	3
Owners	15	46	26	8	3

Wells Fargo/Gallup Investor and Retirement Optimism Index
Aug. 7-15, 2015

GALLUP

These data are from the third-quarter Wells Fargo/Gallup Investor and Retirement Optimism Index survey, conducted Aug. 7–16. Investors are defined for this survey as U.S. adults who have at least $10,000 invested in stocks, bonds or mutual funds, a criterion met by 44% of U.S. adults in the current survey. The large majority of these investors own homes (83%) while a much smaller figure rent (15%). In April, Gallup found that most Americans expected local housing prices to increase.

U.S. INVESTORS ON HOUSING PRICES

RISING A LOT   RISING A LITTLE

17%   44%

SOURCE: WELLS FARGO/GALLUP INDEX

Among all investors who perceive that local housing prices are rising, sentiment is mixed about how increasing prices are affecting their personal financial outlook. About half say rising housing prices make them feel no differently about their discretionary spending or investing in the stock market, while about a third say they are more optimistic about their spending and investments. On the other hand, 56% say rising housing prices make them more optimistic about the economy's outlook, with 24% saying they make no difference.

The vast majority of investors who own their homes see owning property as "important" or "critical" to building wealth. Neither the size of one's investments nor an investor's age appears to influence how a homeowning investor values his or her primary residence as a means of building wealth.

Impact of Investors' Perceptions of Rising Housing Prices on Their Optimism

Does the fact that housing prices in your area are rising make you feel more optimistic, no different or less optimistic about each of the following? How about ... ?

*Among investors who think housing prices are rising

	More optimistic	No different	Less optimistic
	%	%	%
The outlook for the economy	56	24	19
Your day-to-day discretionary spending	32	54	14
Investing in the stock market	32	46	21

Wells Fargo/Gallup Investor and Retirement Optimism Index
Aug. 7-16, 2015

GALLUP

Importance of Homeowners' Primary Residence as a Way to Build Wealth

How important is it to you that your primary residence also serves as a good investment and way to build wealth?

*Among homeowners

	Critical	Important, not critical	Not too important	Not important at all
	%	%	%	%
Homeowners	30	54	12	4

Wells Fargo/Gallup Investor and Retirement Optimism Index
Aug. 7-16, 2015

GALLUP

Bottom Line

A significant majority of investors of varying ages and portfolio sizes see owning property as a way to build wealth. And most investors perceive that housing prices are going up.

However, few say that these price increases are having a real effect on their own day-to-day spending or investments. Instead, the majority of investors who are seeing housing prices increase in their local market say these increases are making them more optimistic about the outlook for the economy.

Survey Methods

Results for the Wells Fargo/Gallup Investor and Retirement Optimism Index survey are based on questions asked Aug. 7–15, 2015, on the Gallup Daily tracking survey, of a random sample of 509 U.S. adults having investable assets of $10,000 or more.

For results based on the entire sample of investors, the margin of sampling error is ±5 percentage points at the 95% confidence level.

For results based on the 438 investors who own their own home, the margin of sampling error is ±6 percentage points at the 95% confidence level.

In addition to sampling error, question wording and practical difficulties in conducting surveys can introduce error or bias into the findings of public opinion polls.

October 02, 2015
HALF IN U.S. ARE FEELING BETTER ABOUT FINANCIAL SITUATION

by Frank Newport

Story Highlights

- *Americans are somewhat more positive now than in 2013*
- *Seven in 10 have enough money to buy what they need*
- *Most Americans say they monitor their spending closely*

PRINCETON, N.J.—Half of Americans, on average, so far this year say they are feeling better about their financial situation. This may not seem like a highly positive state of affairs, but it marks a modest improvement from two years ago, when an average of 43% said they were feeling better about their finances.

Are you feeling better about your financial situation these days, or not?

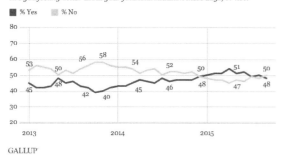

GALLUP

This question is one of a set of personal financial measures Gallup has been asking Americans on a daily basis since 2013. As is the case with most questions that focus on Americans' personal situations and behaviors, these measures have been quite stable over time. Thus, the shift from 2013 when 43% said they were feeling better about their finances and 55% said they were not—a 12-percentage-point gap—to the 50% positive and 48% negative attitudes today—a two-point gap—represents a clear improvement.

AMERICANS' FINANCIAL SITUATIONS

NOT BETTER	BETTER
48%	50%

SOURCE: GALLUP POLL, JAN-SEP 2015

On a more granular level, there has been a slight pullback in these positive attitudes over the past three months; the percentage of Americans who say they are feeling better about their finances has edged down slightly compared with the early months of this year.

This question taps into a sense of how Americans' finances may be changing. Two other measures focus on Americans' attitudes about the current state of their finances, and show major differences in the ways Americans view their money.

Seventy-one percent of Americans so far this year say they have "enough money" to buy the things they need, while less than half as many, 31%, say they have "more than enough money" to do the things they want to do. These two questions indicate roughly equal numbers of Americans who are financially distressed, saying they lack the means to get by on a daily basis, and who are financially flush, saying they have more than they need.

Majority Still Claim They Are Cutting Back on Their Spending

Americans clearly like to believe they are monitoring their spending closely, with 60% so far this year reporting they are cutting back on how much money they spend each week. While this remains the clear majority of Americans, it is down modestly from the average 65% in 2013 who said they were cutting back.

At this time, are you cutting back on how much money you spend each week, or not?

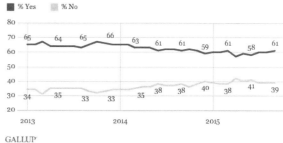

GALLUP

While six in 10 Americans are trying to cut back on their spending, an even higher percentage of Americans, 87% so far this year, agree with the statement, "You are watching your spending very closely." The breadth of this sentiment underscores the value Americans place on appearing responsible about their spending, even among those with high incomes and high net worth.

Implications

These questions reflect not just the reality of how much money people have, but also how they think about their financial situation. Even though Americans are slightly more positive than they were two years ago, they are clearly not greatly optimistic about their financial situation, with just about half saying they are feeling better about it. And while Americans like to feel they are monitoring their spending closely and attempting to control how much they spend, these attitudes have not changed dramatically since 2013.

These attitudes help explain the approach taken by many retailers that continually market their products and services as being discounted and "on sale," even if in some situations the sale price is in reality the normal selling price. For many Americans, buying something appearing to be on sale fits with their views of themselves as careful stewards of their money. Several years ago, leaders at retailer J.C. Penney attempted to adopt a "rational" pricing scheme, which eschewed the constant sale pricing that had been in use previously, and quickly learned their mistake. The approach failed, the CEO who instigated it was fired, and J.C. Penney went back to the consistent sale pricing that it had used previously.

The current results also underscore that most Americans' personal financial situations are quite stable, even as Americans' attitudes about what is happening "out there" in the country at large can undergo more significant shifts in short periods of time.

Survey Methods

Results for this Gallup poll are based on telephone interviews conducted on the Gallup U.S. Daily survey, with a random sample of approximately 3,500 to 4,000 adults, aged 18 and older, living in all 50 U.S. states and the District of Columbia, asked to answer each financial question each month. For results based on the total monthly sample of national adults, the margin of sampling error is ±2 percentage points at the 95% confidence level. All reported margins of sampling error include computed design effects for weighting.

October 02, 2015
DISAPPROVAL OF SUPREME COURT EDGES TO NEW HIGH

by Justin McCarthy

Story Highlights

- At 50%, disapproval of court reaches new high
- Republicans' approval up slightly from record low in July
- Democrats' approval down from record high

WASHINGTON, D.C.—Half of Americans (50%) disapprove of the job the U.S. Supreme Court is doing, while slightly fewer (45%) approve. Although the high court's approval rating is similar to what it has been in recent years, the current disapproval rating is at a new high. Fewer Americans (5%) now have no opinion about the court.

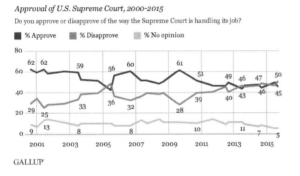

Approval of U.S. Supreme Court, 2000-2015
Do you approve or disapprove of the way the Supreme Court is handling its job?

GALLUP

Although the court's image now tilts negative by five percentage points, that gap is still within the poll's margin of error. This means Americans remain statistically split on the court's image, as they have been in all but one poll since July 2012. Prior to that, majorities had approved of the court's performance in almost all polls from 2000 to 2010, with two exceptions: an approval rating of 48% in June 2008, and a record low of 42% in June 2005 after the court ruled against Susette Kelo in an eminent domain case.

These data are from Gallup's annual Governance poll, conducted Sept. 9–13.

U.S. SUPREME COURT RATINGS
APPROVE   DISAPPROVE
45%   50%
SOURCE: GALLUP POLL, SEPT. 9-13

Party Gap Eases After Record Polarization in July

This July, Democrats' approval of the Supreme Court reached a record high of 76%, while Republicans' approval hit a record-low 18% after the court handed down major decisions legalizing

same-sex marriage and upholding the Affordable Care Act. Two months later, this wide gulf continues to exist in Republicans' (26%) and Democrats' (67%) approval ratings of the court, but the division is not as extreme as it was in July.

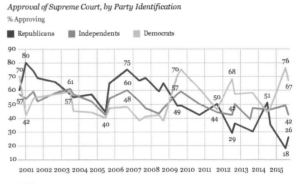

Approval of Supreme Court, by Party Identification
% Approving

■ Republicans   ■ Independents   ▦ Democrats

GALLUP

Bottom Line

Americans remain divided on the job the U.S. Supreme Court is doing, but with disapproval reaching a new high, its image is now the closest it has come in the past 15 years to tilting negative. This may partly reflect the weakening of public confidence in government in recent years. But the court has also been caught in the middle of divisive policy battles that have largely undermined Republicans' approval of the institution, while not helping it with political independents. And as the trend suggests, all of this could change based on the nature of the court's decisions. Already, the court's highest and lowest partisan approval scores in the past 15 years have come from Republicans.

Survey Methods

Results for this Gallup poll are based on telephone interviews conducted Sept. 9–13, 2015, on the Gallup U.S. Daily survey, with a random sample of 1,025 adults, aged 18 and older, living in all 50 U.S. states and the District of Columbia. For results based on the total sample of national adults, the margin of sampling error is ±4 percentage points at the 95% confidence level. All reported margins of sampling error include computed design effects for weighting.

October 05, 2015
INFORMED AMERICANS RATE BOTH PARTIES IN CONGRESS WORSE

by Frank Newport, Lydia Saad and Michael Traugott

Story Highlights

- *Knowledgeable Americans more negative about both parties*
- *Similar to pattern for U.S. Congress in general*
- *Neither party highly positive about own members in Congress*

PRINCETON, N.J.—Americans who are knowledgeable about Congress—based on a five-question quiz—have more negative views of the Republicans and Democrats in Congress compared with those who are less knowledgeable. About half of Americans who answer at least two of the five quiz questions correctly say Republicans and Democrats are doing a "poor" or "bad" job. Fewer than three in 10 Americans who answer none of the questions correctly rate these groups this negatively.

Job Ratings of Republicans in Congress, by Congressional Knowledge Score
Score indicates number of knowledge questions answered correctly, out of five

	Score 0	Score 1	Score 2-3	Score 4-5
	%	%	%	%
Excellent/Good	27	16	9	17
Fair	38	33	36	26
Poor/Bad	29	49	54	56
Net positive*	-2	-33	-45	-39

June 15-16, 2015
*Net positive = % Excellent/Good minus % Poor/Bad

GALLUP

Job Ratings of Democrats in Congress, by Congressional Knowledge Score
Score indicates number of knowledge questions answered correctly, out of five

	Score 0	Score 1	Score 2-3	Score 4-5
	%	%	%	%
Excellent/Good	28	24	11	12
Fair	41	32	41	39
Poor/Bad	27	42	47	49
Net positive*	+1	-18	-36	-37

June 15-16, 2015
*Net positive = % Excellent/Good minus % Poor/Bad

GALLUP

The knowledge scale is based on Americans' awareness of five basic facts about Congress, its operations and its leadership. These results come from a special Gallup study conducted in June, which focused on understanding how Americans' ratings of Congress relate to their political knowledge and attention to news media.

This study found that Americans' views of the U.S. Congress in general are strongly related to their knowledge about Congress, with those who know more about Congress rating the institution overall more negatively. Thus, the finding that ratings of the two parties in Congress are more negative among those who are more knowledgeable fits with this larger pattern.

"POOR/BAD" JOB AMONG MOST INFORMED

DEMS IN CONGRESS	REPS IN CONGRESS
49%	56%

SOURCE: GALLUP POLL, JUNE 15-16

Neither Party Is Rated Highly

Regardless of their knowledge levels, Americans' ratings of the major parties in Congress are not much different from their ratings of Congress as a whole.

Sixteen percent of Americans rate the job Republicans are doing as "excellent" or "good," and 48% rate it as poor or bad. Democrats in Congress—currently in the minority of both chambers, severely curtailing their ability to shape the legislative agenda—are rated slightly better, but still receive a negative review: 19% rate their job performance as excellent or good, versus 41% rating it as poor or bad.

Job Ratings of Congress Overall and Major Parties in Congress
Based on U.S. adults

	U.S. Congress in Washington	Republicans in Congress	Democrats in Congress
	%	%	%
Excellent/Good	15	16	19
Fair	34	34	38
Poor/Bad	49	48	41
Net positive*	-34	-32	-22

June 15-16, 2015
*Net positive = % Excellent/Good minus % Poor/Bad

GALLUP

As would be expected, rank-and-file Republicans and Democrats rate their own party's job performance better than they rate the opposing party's. But Republicans are a bit more critical of Republicans in Congress (23% say they are doing a poor or bad job) than Democrats are of Democrats in Congress (19% say they are doing a poor or bad job).

Still, neither intraparty rating is overly positive, with fewer than three in 10 Republicans (28%) and a third of Democrats (34%) saying their own party is doing an excellent or good job.

Job Ratings of the Two Major Parties in Congress, by Party ID

	U.S. adults	Republicans	Independents	Democrats
	%	%	%	%
REPUBLICANS IN CONGRESS				
Excellent/Good	16	28	16	6
Fair	34	46	32	29
Poor/Bad	48	23	50	64
Net positive*	-32	+5	-34	-58
DEMOCRATS IN CONGRESS				
Excellent/Good	19	8	11	34
Fair	38	26	42	45
Poor/Bad	41	65	45	19
Net positive*	-22	-57	-34	+15

June 15-16, 2015
*Net positive = % Excellent/Good minus % Poor/Bad

GALLUP

Bottom Line

The fundamental finding is that Americans who know the most about how Congress operates are not only the most negative about Congress in general, but also about the Republicans and Democrats in Congress specifically. This reinforces the general conclusion that criticisms of Congress—and the partisan leaders in Congress—are based on a realistic assessment of what these entities are doing rather than a lack of awareness of or interest in what they are doing.

Overall, those with a party preference naturally view their own party's congressional delegation more positively than the other party's, but even those ratings are not overly positive. To some degree, it suggests that Americans' views of the two parties are heavily influenced by their general antipathy toward Congress, not just their feelings toward a particular party.

Survey Methods

Results for this Gallup poll are based on telephone interviews conducted June 15–16, 2015, on the Gallup U.S. Daily survey, with a random sample of 1,017 adults, aged 18 and older, living in all 50 U.S. states and the District of Columbia. For results based on the total sample of national adults, the margin of sampling error is ±4 percentage points at the 95% confidence level. All reported margins of sampling error include computed design effects for weighting.

October 06, 2015
ROLE OF U.S. GOV'T REMAINS KEY SOURCE OF PARTY DIFFERENCES

by Frank Newport

Story Highlights

- *American public essentially divided on role of government*
- *Democrats and Republicans have opposite views*
- *Little change in these attitudes since 2010*

PRINCETON, N.J.—Democrats and Republicans have almost precisely opposite views of the purpose of government in today's society. Fifty-seven percent of Democrats tend to believe the government should take active steps to try to improve the lives of its citizens. The same percentage of Republicans tilt toward the belief that the government should provide only the most basic functions. Independents are evenly divided between the two approaches.

Party Differences in Preferences Regarding Government Activity

Next, I'd like you to think more broadly about the purposes of government. Where would you rate yourself on a scale of 1 to 5, where 1 means you think the government should do only those things necessary to provide the most basic government functions, and 5 means you think the government should take active steps in every area it can to try and improve the lives of its citizens? You may use any number from 1 to 5.

	Democrats	Independents	Republicans
	%	%	%
Prefer a more active government (4 or 5)	57	32	15
Neutral (3)	29	35	27
Prefer a less active government (1 or 2)	14	31	57

Sept. 9-13, 2015

GALLUP

These results, from Gallup's Sept. 9–13 Governance survey, are based on a question that asks Americans to place themselves on a 1-to-5 scale, in which 5 means that "the government should take active steps in every area it can to try and improve the lives of its citizens." At the other extreme, 1 means that "the government should do only those things necessary to provide the most basic government functions."

PREFER A MORE ACTIVE GOVERNMENT

REPUBLICANS	DEMOCRATS
15%	57%

SOURCE: GALLUP POLL SEPT. 9-13

Gallup has asked this question five times since 2010, and taken as a whole, Americans end up being distributed evenly across the positions in their responses. About a third of Americans overall opt for the "1" or "2" position, indicating a desire for a more limited government, and another third opt for the "4" or "5" position, indicating a desire for a more active government. The rest fall in the middle. Americans are also about evenly matched at the most extreme points on the scale, with 20% opting for position 5, the most active possible government, and 17% opting for position 1, the most limited government.

Remarkably, these attitudes have changed little since 2010, underscoring the apparent fundamental nature of the way in which the public looks at the role of government in the U.S.

Implications

Fundamental views of what the government should or should not be doing is at the heart of many of the differences between the two major political parties and their candidates in the U.S. today. These views inform the disparate partisan approaches to solving specific issues of the day, including the economy, jobs, inequality, race relations, healthcare, education, guns and the environment. Democratic candidates tend to assume that government should be used as the means to solve many of these problems, while Republicans generally want to avoid government involvement and to find other ways to address the problems.

The issue of what the government should be doing is not one for which there is a clear majority direction from the citizens of this country taken as a whole. This in turn suggests that political candidates, and the parties they represent, need to recognize that the broad public is conflicted on the issue. While candidates can appeal to their partisan base with rigid positions on the "appropriate role of government" issue, from the broad perspective of the public in general, it is clearly an issue that calls for more flexible debate and discussion.

Survey Methods

Results for this Gallup poll are based on telephone interviews conducted Sept. 9–13, 2015, on the Gallup U.S. Daily survey, with a random sample of 1,025 adults, aged 18 and older, living in all 50 U.S. states and the District of Columbia. For results based on the total sample of national adults, the margin of sampling error is ±4 percentage points at the 95% confidence level. All reported margins of sampling error include computed design effects for weighting.

October 07, 2015
U.S. JOB CREATION INDEX STEADY AT SEVEN-YEAR HIGH

by Justin McCarthy

Story Highlights

- *Index remains at +32 for fifth consecutive month*
- *Government and nongovernment hiring both steady*

WASHINGTON, D.C.—Gallup's U.S. Job Creation Index registered +32 in September for the fifth consecutive month. This is the highest score Gallup has recorded since it began measuring employees' perceptions of job creation at their workplaces in early 2008.

Shortly after Gallup began tracking job creation, the index nosedived as the Great Recession wreaked havoc on the economy. After remaining in negative territory for most of 2009, the index slowly recovered, reaching +30 in September 2014. It then dipped slightly and stayed between +27 and +29 over the next six months. It increased to +31 in April and another point in May to reach the current high, which it has held since.

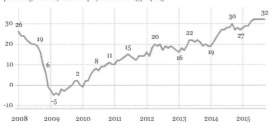

U.S. Job Creation Index, Monthly Averages, January 2008-September 2015
Percentage of U.S. workers who say their employers are hiring new people minus percentage who say their employers are letting people go

Gallup Daily tracking

GALLUP

U.S. JOB CREATION INDEX, SEPTEMBER

+32

SOURCE: GALLUP DAILY TRACKING

The results are based on interviews with 17,284 U.S. full- and part-time workers conducted Sept. 1–30 as part of Gallup Daily tracking. Gallup asks employed workers nationwide each day whether their employer is increasing, reducing or maintaining the size of its workforce. In September, 43% of workers said their employer was hiring workers and expanding the size of its workforce, and 11% said their employer was letting people go and reducing the size of its workforce, resulting in the index score of +32. The "hiring" and "letting people go" percentages have been steady for the last several months.

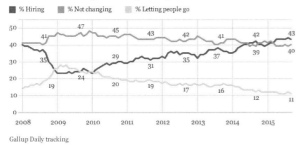

Hiring and Firing Nationwide, Monthly Averages, January 2008-September 2015
Note: Numbers shown are September readings for each year

■ % Hiring   ■ % Not changing   % Letting people go

Gallup Daily tracking

GALLUP

Government, Nongovernment Hiring Both Steady in September

Net hiring in the private sector, where the large majority of U.S. employees work, was +33 for the month of September, the same it has been for five of the past six months.

Government hiring netted +25 in September—similar to scores recorded since April.

Regionally, net hiring was lowest in the East, at +29. The region generally has ranked lowest in workers' perceptions of hiring since

2013. Meanwhile, the Midwest had the highest net hiring score in September, at +34. This is down slightly from +36 in August, which matched the highest score any region has received since Gallup began tracking job creation. Net hiring in the South registered +32, while it was +33 in the West.

Job Creation Index, by Subgroup

	Index Score
Government	+25
Nongovernment	+33
East	+29
Midwest	+34
South	+32
West	+33

September 1-30, 2015

GALLUP

Survey Methods

Results are based on telephone interviews conducted Sept. 1–30, 2015, on Gallup Daily tracking, with a random sample of 17,284 adults, aged 18 and older, who are employed full or part time, living in all 50 U.S. states and the District of Columbia. For results based on the total sample of national adults, the margin of sampling error is ±1 percentage point at the 95% confidence level. All reported margins of sampling error include computed design effects for weighting.

October 07, 2015
CHILDREN A KEY FACTOR IN WOMEN'S DESIRE TO WORK OUTSIDE THE HOME

by Lydia Saad

Story Highlights

- *The majority of women with children prefer homemaking role*
- *Women without children would rather be employed*
- *Men prefer employment regardless of their parenting status*

PRINCETON, N.J.—Having young children at home greatly influences whether women in the U.S. prefer to stay at home or work outside of it. More than half of women, 56%, who have a child younger than 18 would ideally like to stay home and care for their house and family, while 58% of those without young children would rather work outside the home. Having young children makes little difference in men's preferences, with close to three-quarters preferring to work regardless of their parenting status.

These findings are based on combined data from Gallup's 2014 and 2015 Work and Education surveys, encompassing enough interviews to examine Americans' views on the basis of child and employment status for men and women.

U.S. Preferences for Working vs. Staying Home, by Gender and Parenting Status

If you were free to do either, would you prefer to have a job outside the home, or would you prefer to stay at home and take care of the house and family?

	Prefer to work outside the home	Prefer homemaker role
HAVE A CHILD UNDER 18		
Women	39%	56%
Men	72%	26%
DO NOT HAVE A CHILD UNDER 18		
Women	58%	39%
Men	76%	23%

Aggregated Gallup data from 2014-2015

GALLUP

U.S. WOMEN: PREFER TO STAY HOME

NO CHILDREN <18   CHILDREN <18

39%   **56%**

SOURCE: GALLUP POLL

The data show remarkably little difference in the preferences of working versus stay-at-home mothers. Among mothers who are currently employed either full or part time, 40% say they would prefer to work outside the home, and 54% would prefer to stay home. The figures are almost identical among mothers who aren't currently employed: 37% would prefer a job outside the home, while 57% would rather be at home. Meanwhile, there is almost no difference in the lifestyle preference of fathers according to their work status. At least 70% of those employed, as well as those not employed, would rather have a job outside the home.

U.S. Preferences for Working vs. Staying Home, by Gender, Employment and Parenting Status

	Prefer to work outside the home	Prefer homemaker role
HAVE CHILD UNDER 18		
Not employed woman	37%	57%
Employed woman	40%	54%
Not employed man	76%	24%
Employed man	70%	27%
NO CHILD UNDER 18		
Not employed woman	51%	46%
Employed woman	70%	29%
Not employed man	73%	25%
Employed man	80%	20%

Aggregated Gallup data from 2014-2015

GALLUP

Little Change in Recent Attitudes

Gallup trends show little change in men's and women's overall attitudes in recent years, with slightly more than half of women saying that, given the choice, they would prefer to have a job outside the home, and about 45% saying they would rather stay at home caring for the house and family. However, this is a shift from a decade earlier when preferences were flipped, although they varied some during the late 1990s and early 2000s.

Meanwhile, the large majority of men have shown unwavering preference for working outside the home, generally hovering at just under 75%.

U.S. Women's Lifestyle Preference

If you were free to do either, would you prefer to have a job outside the home, or would you prefer to stay at home and take care of the house and family?

■ % Have a job outside the home   ▨ % Stay home, take care of house and family

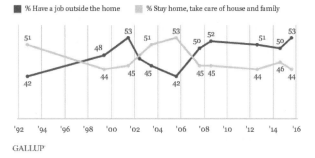

GALLUP

U.S. Men's Lifestyle Preference

If you were free to do either, would you prefer to have a job outside the home, or would you prefer to stay at home and take care of the house and family?

■ % Have a job outside the home   ▨ % Stay home, take care of house and family

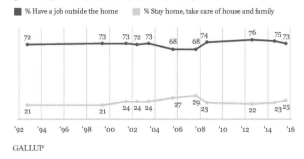

GALLUP

Bottom Line

Having children under the age of 18 is a key factor in whether women would prefer to be employed or stay home, while their current employment status matters relatively little. Among women who don't have young children, employment status makes more of a difference. And for men, neither having a child nor current employment status makes much difference. Men's and women's lifestyle preferences have been fairly stable the past few years, with majorities of both groups overall preferring to work outside the home. While this is consistent with men's views since the early 1990s, women's preference for working outside the home is higher than it was.

Survey Methods

Results for this Gallup analysis are based on combined data from the 2014 and 2015 editions of Gallup's annual Work and Education survey, conducted each August. The total sample for the combined data is 2,403 U.S. adults, aged 18 and older, living in all 50 U.S. states and the District of Columbia. This includes 1,059 men and 984 women.

For results based on the total sample of national adults, the margin of sampling error is ±3 percentage points at the 95% confidence level.

For results based on employment and parenting subgroups within men and women, the margins of error are generally between ±4 and ±8. Three subgroups have higher margins of error of ±10 and ±13, but the reported findings still hold even when accounting for this.

October 08, 2015

U.S. UNINSURED RATE AT 11.6% IN THIRD QUARTER

by Stephanie Marken

Story Highlights

- *Uninsured rate essentially unchanged in third quarter*
- *Rate drops most among Hispanics and lower-income Americans*

WASHINGTON, D.C.—The uninsured rate among U.S. adults aged 18 and older was 11.6% in the third quarter of 2015, essentially unchanged from 11.4% in the second quarter, and down from 11.9% in the first quarter. The uninsured rate has declined 5.5 percentage points since the fourth quarter of 2013, just before the requirement for Americans to carry health insurance took effect in early 2014.

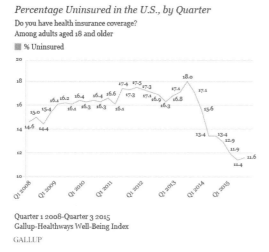

Percentage Uninsured in the U.S., by Quarter
Do you have health insurance coverage?
Among adults aged 18 and older

■ % Uninsured

Quarter 1 2008–Quarter 3 2015
Gallup-Healthways Well-Being Index
GALLUP

Third-quarter results are based on approximately 45,000 interviews with U.S. adults from July 1 to Sept. 30, 2015, conducted as part of the Gallup-Healthways Well-Being Index. Gallup and Healthways ask 500 U.S. adults each day whether they have health insurance, which on an aggregated basis allows for precise and ongoing measurement of the percentage of Americans with and without health insurance.

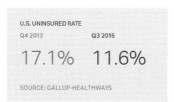

U.S. UNINSURED RATE

Q4 2013   Q3 2015

17.1%   **11.6%**

SOURCE: GALLUP-HEALTHWAYS

Sharp Drop in Uninsured Rate Among Minorities

The uninsured rate has dipped for all key subgroups since late 2013, with the sharpest drops occurring among racial and ethnic minorities and lower-income Americans. The uninsured rate among Hispanics is 29.0% in the third quarter, down 9.7 points from the fourth quarter of 2013. Over the same time period, the uninsured rate among blacks fell 7.5 points.

Across age groups, 26- to 34-year-olds have the largest drop in the percentage uninsured. The rate fell 8.3 points for this age group since the fourth quarter of 2013, followed closely by a 7.6-point dip among 18- to 25-year-olds.

Percentage of Uninsured U.S. Adults, by Subgroup
Do you have health insurance coverage?

	Quarter 4 2013	Quarter 3 2015	Net change
	%	%	(pct. pts.)
National adults	17.1	11.6	-5.5
18 to 25	23.5	15.9	-7.6
26 to 34	28.2	19.9	-8.3
35 to 64	18.0	12.1	-5.9
65+	2.0	1.6	-0.4
Whites	11.9	7.6	-4.3
Blacks	20.9	13.4	-7.5
Hispanics	38.7	29.0	-9.7
Less than $36,000	30.7	22.2	-8.5
$36,000 to $89,999	11.7	9.2	-2.5
$90,000+	5.8	3.0	-2.8

Gallup-Healthways Well-Being Index

GALLUP

More Americans Paying for Own Insurance

To assess changes in insurance type, Gallup and Healthways focus on adults aged 18 to 64 because nearly all Americans aged 65 and older have Medicare. The percentage of 18- to 64-year-olds who are covered through a plan fully paid for by themselves or a family member was 21.2% in the third quarter, up from 17.6% in the fourth quarter of 2013. The percentages of Americans with Medicaid and Medicare insurance also have increased sizably.

Type of Health Insurance Coverage in the U.S., Among 18- to 64-Year-Olds
Is your health insurance coverage through a current or former employer, a union, Medicare, Medicaid, military or veteran's coverage or a plan fully paid for by you or a family member?
Primary and secondary insurance combined

	Quarter 4 2013	Quarter 3 2015	Net change
	%	%	(pct. pts.)
Current or former employer	44.2	43.0	-1.2
Plan fully paid for by self or family member	17.6	21.2	3.6
Medicaid	6.9	9.3	2.4
Medicare	6.1	7.4	1.3
Military/Veteran's	4.6	4.6	0.0
A union	2.5	2.7	0.2
(Something else)	3.5	4.6	1.1
No insurance	20.8	14.2	-6.6

Gallup-Healthways Well-Being Index

GALLUP

Gallup and Healthways began asking Americans about the source of their health insurance using the current question wording in August 2013 in anticipation of shifts in insurance type as a result of the Affordable Care Act. Gallup asks respondents, "Is your primary health insurance coverage through a current or former employer, a union, Medicare, Medicaid, military or veteran's coverage or a plan fully paid for by you or a family member?" In addition, Gallup asks respondents if they have secondary health insurance coverage, and if so, what type of coverage it is. The results reported here are a combined estimate of primary and secondary insurance types.

Implications

The steadiness in the uninsured rate in the third quarter is not surprising given that the open enrollment period for 2015 ended in

February. Similarly, the uninsured rate also held steady between open enrollment periods last year. Open enrollment through the marketplace exchanges will begin Nov. 1, but coverage for many who sign up during that period will not kick in until January 2016. Therefore, the full effect of the 2016 enrollment period on the uninsured rate may not be evident until the open enrollment period ends on Jan. 31.

While proponents of the Affordable Care Act are likely encouraged by the reduction in the uninsured rate since late 2013, it is unclear how much further it will decline. There was a sharp drop in the uninsured rate when Americans were initially able to purchase health plans through government exchanges in late 2013 and early 2014, but there was a much smaller drop during the second enrollment period in late 2014 and early 2015. Future reductions may be even smaller as those who still lack insurance may be particularly resistant to getting it or just harder to reach and guide through the process of getting health insurance.

Survey Methods

Results are based on telephone interviews conducted July 1–Sept. 30, 2015, as part of the Gallup-Healthways Well-Being Index survey, with a random sample of 45,615 adults, aged 18 and older, living in all 50 U.S. states and the District of Columbia. For results based on the total sample of national adults, the margin of sampling error is ±1 percentage point at the 95% confidence level. Each quarter dating to quarter 1, 2014, has approximately 44,000 respondents. Each quarter from 2008 through 2013 has approximately 88,000 respondents.

October 09, 2015

PUBLIC REMAINS WARY OF FEDERAL GOVERNMENT'S POWER

by Jim Norman

Story Highlights

- *Six in 10 Americans think the federal government has too much power*
- *For Obama's second term, number has stayed consistently high*
- *Growing concern this term among Democrats, moderates and liberals*

WASHINGTON, D.C.—Six in 10 Americans think the government has too much power, marking the third year in a row that at least 59% of the public has voiced this view. The 60% recorded in this survey ties the previous high from 2013 for the question, which Gallup has asked annually since 2002.

The solid majorities in 2013, 2014 and this year saying the federal government is too powerful differ significantly from the 51% Gallup measured in 2012. That poll was conducted in the days after the Democratic National Convention that helped propel Barack Obama to a re-election win that year.

During President Obama's first year in office in 2009, the percentage of Americans concerned with the power of the federal government was 51%. By his second year in office, 2010, that percentage climbed to 59%, after the federal government passed the Affordable Care Act. The heightened concern about government power was a key factor in Republicans taking control of the House of Representatives in the 2010 midterm elections. A slight drop to 57% in 2011 was followed by the 2012 drop to 51%.

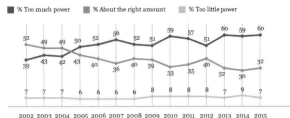

Changing Views on U.S. Federal Government Power

Do you think the federal government has too much power, has about the right amount of power or has too little power?

Overall, the average percentage who thought the government was too powerful during Obama's first term—2009 to 2012—was 54%. This term, the average has risen to 60%.

Democrats, Moderates, Liberals Now More Wary of Government Power

A comparison of the combined results of Gallup's polls in Obama's first term and those in his second term reveal that the rise in concerns over the federal government's power is being driven by Democrats, moderates and liberals. Republicans and conservatives have consistently and overwhelmingly believed the government has been too powerful throughout Obama's presidency. But now a majority of moderates (57%), as well as independents (64%), share that view.

Comparing Americans' Views of Federal Power in Obama's Two Terms

Percentage who think the federal government has too much power

	First term (2009-2012)	Second term (2013-2015)
Democrats	24%	37%
Republicans	81%	80%
Independents	59%	64%
Conservatives	79%	77%
Moderates	44%	57%
Liberals	24%	37%
Blacks	28%	48%
Hispanics	40%	44%
Whites	58%	65%

Combined answers from 2009-2012 and 2013-2015 Gallup Governance surveys

GALLUP

The election of 2014, which saw Republicans gain control of the Senate, had little effect on the views of Democrats, moderates or liberals concerning the power of the federal government. The percentage of moderates believing the government is too powerful has been steady, near 57%, for the past three years, while among liberals, it has maintained a narrow range around 37%.

The largest rise in concern about federal power from Obama's first term to his second has occurred among blacks—a 20-percentage-point increase from 28% to 48%. In the years prior to the election of Obama as the first black president, blacks generally were more concerned than the general public about the federal government having too much power. Obama's victory in the 2008 election led to a huge drop over the next year in the number of blacks having these concerns. Since Obama's re-election, polls the past three years have all shown a resurgence in blacks' concerns about government power.

Conservatives and Republicans show virtually no change, largely because their numbers were already so high during Obama's first term. There is little variation in the general increase from Obama's first term to his second term by age, education, income or gender.

Bottom Line

With four out of five Republicans voicing concerns about a federal government that is too powerful, several major candidates for the Republican presidential nomination have taken notice:

- Ben Carson, who has the highest net favorable rating of any GOP candidate in Gallup tracking, said, "We are in the process right now of learning that our government is far too big—and the bigger it gets, the more taxpayer money it needs to sustain itself."
- Carly Fiorina, whose net favorable numbers have risen significantly, spoke of "the rights of the individual being crushed by a government that's become too big, too powerful and too corrupt."
- Sen. Marco Rubio, whose image is second only to Carson among Republicans, recently referred to the "incredible level of mistrust on anything massive that the government does."

It's not just Republicans who agree that the federal government is too powerful. A majority of independents agree with that view. Less than half of Democrats agree that the government has too much power, and echoing this, Democratic candidates tend to focus on using government as the main instrument to fix perceived problems. The Democratic nominee in next year's general election, however, will need to face the fact that the majority of the country is concerned about the existing level of government power. If the Democrats' campaign in 2016 can pull the percentage of moderates holding that view back below 50%, it could prove to be one of the keys to victory for them.

Survey Methods

Results for this Gallup poll are based on telephone interviews conducted Sept. 9–13, 2015, with a random sample of 1,025 national adults, aged 18 and older, living in all 50 U.S. states and the District of Columbia. For results based on the total sample of national adults, the margin of sampling error is ±4 percentage points at the 95% confidence level.

In addition, two sets of Gallup's annual Governance surveys—four from the years 2009, 2010, 2011 and 2012 and three from the years 2013, 2014 and 2015—were aggregated to create combined results from the first term and the second term of President Obama.

October 09, 2015
AMERICANS' SPENDING ON GASOLINE REFUELS IN THIRD QUARTER

by John Fleming

Story Highlights

- *35% spending more on gasoline, up from 21% in spring*
- *Americans still spending more on groceries*
- *Discretionary spending makes modest comeback*

PRINCETON, N.J.—Americans' reported changes in spending have remained stable in most categories of goods and services over the past year—except for gasoline. The percentage of Americans saying they are spending more or less on gas and fuel has bobbed up and down along with gas prices since June 2014.

Spending on Gasoline Lower Than One Year Ago
Are you spending more compared with a year ago?

	Jun 9-15, 2014	Aug 11-17, 2014	Nov 10-20, 2014	Feb 23-Mar 3, 2015	Aug 6-Sep 10, 2015	Change (August 2014-August 2015)
	%	%	%	%	%	(pct. pts.)
TOP 6 CATEGORIES						
Groceries	58	59	57	55	54	-5
Healthcare	41	42	42	43	43	+1
Utilities	42	45	43	45	42	-3
Gasoline or fuel	50	58	31	21	35	-23
Rent or mortgage	34	32	30	31	35	+3
Home maintenance	31	32	32	30	34	+2
MIDDLE 6 CATEGORIES						
Cable or satellite	30	33	33	32	33	-
Telephone services	31	32	30	30	32	-
Travel	28	26	24	19	30	+4
Leisure activity	24	28	24	24	28	-
Household goods such as toilet paper or cleaning supplies	30	32	29	23	28	-4
Automotive expenses not including gas	27	27	27	24	28	+1
BOTTOM 6 CATEGORIES						
Dining out	22	26	27	23	27	+1
Internet	23	21	22	20	25	+4
Personal care such as toothpaste or cosmetics	25	26	26	21	24	-2
Clothing	22	25	25	22	24	-1
Consumer electronics	21	20	22	18	21	+1
Retirement investments	16	18	19	17	20	+2

GALLUP

At the end of this summer, 35% of Americans said they were spending more on gasoline, which is up from 21% earlier this spring but still nowhere near the levels measured last summer (58%). Americans in the third quarter were nearly as likely to be spending less (31%) as they were to be spending more (35%) on gas and fuel. Just 12% said they were spending less one year ago. The net change in spending (percentage spending more minus percentage spending less) has swung wildly from +46 last year, to -34 this spring, to +4 today.

As Americans head into autumn, a majority, 54%, continue to say they are spending more than they did last year on groceries. This is an area in which Americans have consistently said they are spending more. Across five separate updates since June 2014, the three categories with the highest percentages of consumers saying they are "spending more" (groceries, utilities and healthcare) have remained in the top four in each survey.

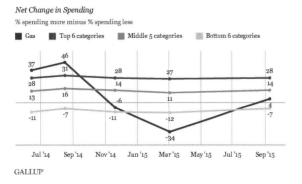

Net Change in Spending
% spending more minus % spending less

These trends continue to illustrate that Americans are still primarily spending more on things they need—but not on things they want. They still say they are spending less, rather than more, than they did in the past year on discretionary purchases such as retirement investments, leisure activities, clothing, consumer electronics, dining out and travel. Nonetheless, there are some signs that discretionary spending is making a modest comeback. Net spending on travel and dining out has become significantly less negative. The 2014 data seem to suggest there is a seasonal effect, so it will be interesting to see whether these changes this year are seasonal (namely, a function of greater spending on travel during the summer travel season) or are more permanent.

Net Change in Spending Compared With One Year Ago
Ranked by net change in spending

	Jun 9-15, 2014	Aug 11-17, 2014	Nov 10-20, 2014	Feb 23-Mar 3, 2015	Aug 6-Sep 10, 2015	Change (August 2014-August 2015)
TOP 6 CATEGORIES						
Groceries	+45	+49	+46	+42	+42	-7
Healthcare	+29	+34	+29	+32	+31	-3
Utilities	+30	+35	+33	+35	+31	-4
Rent or mortgage	+23	+23	+19	+19	+25	+2
Household goods such as toilet paper or cleaning supplies	+23	+27	+23	+16	+21	-6
Telephone services	+21	+17	+16	+20	+20	+3
BOTTOM 6 CATEGORIES						
Retirement investments	-5	+1	-2	-4	-1	-2
Leisure activities	-10	-3	-14	-7	-5	-2
Clothing	-9	-5	-5	-9	-6	-1
Travel	-11	-12	-20	-20	-9	+3
Consumer electronics	-10	-11	-12	-13	-11	-
Dining out	-18	-12	-16	-18	-12	-

GALLUP

Implications

After more than a year of following Americans' self-reported spending patterns, several conclusions seem worth reinforcing. First, net changes in spending—the percentage of Americans reporting that they are spending more within a category minus the percentage saying they are spending less—have been fairly stable for all categories, except gas or fuel. It's possible that people's reports of spending may be less sensitive to modest cost increases or spending

fluctuations than to more dramatic shifts, such as the variations in gas prices over the past year. People may simply be inclined to overlook smaller spending changes in what they report. Conversely, people may interpret stable prices following a big slide as a sort of increase, and adjust their reports to reflect this.

AMERICANS SPENDING MORE ON GAS
AUG 2014   AUG-SEP 2015
58%   35%
SOURCE: GALLUP POLL

Second, the overall order of the categories based on net spending increases hasn't changed much since Gallup began measuring spending this way. Three of the top four net spending categories back in June 2014—groceries, utilities and healthcare—all remain at the top, and four of the bottom five net spending categories remain at the bottom—travel, dining out, consumer electronics and clothing. It is possible that the higher percentages of Americans reporting that they are spending less on these categories reflect an aspirational self-perception—"I'm thrifty and don't waste money"—especially when reporting on discretionary items.

The prior spending report speculated about the effects of the summer travel season, and if Americans would report spending more on gas, travel and leisure activities. The current data—collected at the end of summer—suggest that Americans did in fact report spending more on gas, travel and slightly more on leisure activities.

Survey Methods

Results for this Gallup poll are based on telephone interviews conducted between Aug. 6 and Sept. 10, 2015, on the Gallup U.S. Daily survey, with a random sample of 3,010 adults, aged 18 and older, living in all 50 U.S. states and the District of Columbia. For results based on the total sample of national adults, the margin of sampling error is ±1.8 percentage points at the 95% confidence level. All reported margins of sampling error include computed design effects for weighting.

October 12, 2015
MORE REPUBLICANS NOW PREFER ONE-PARTY GOVERNMENT

by Jeffrey M. Jones

Story Highlights

- *40% of Republicans say one party better, up from 24%*
- *More independents say party control makes no difference*
- *Americans most likely to say party control makes no difference*

PRINCETON, N.J.—In a shift from last year, Republicans now clearly prefer having one party control Congress and the presidency, as opposed to favoring divided party control or saying it makes no difference. Forty percent of Republicans favor one-party control, up from 24% last year. This change makes their views similar to Democrats' views, which are essentially unchanged from last year. Independents are more likely now (45%) than last year (39%) to say party control makes no difference.

Preference for Party Control of the Presidency and Congress, by Political Party

	2014	2015	Change
	%	%	pct. pts.
REPUBLICANS			
Same party	24	40	+16
Different parties	33	26	-7
Makes no difference	38	30	-8
INDEPENDENTS			
Same party	23	23	0
Different parties	32	28	-4
Makes no difference	39	45	+6
DEMOCRATS			
Same party	47	43	-4
Different parties	18	17	-1
Makes no difference	33	35	+2

GALLUP

Since last year's survey, two major political developments have occurred that could be influencing Republicans' views on the best way to distribute party control of government. First, Republicans won a majority of U.S. Senate seats in the November 2014 elections, giving them control of both houses of Congress.

Second, the focus of political attention has increasingly shifted toward the 2016 presidential election campaign and away from President Barack Obama. Republicans may be optimistic about their chances of electing a Republican president, particularly since Democratic front-runner Hillary Clinton has been weakened by the email server controversy.

GOP FAVORING ONE-PARTY GOVERNMENT

2014	2015
24%	40%

SOURCE: GALLUP POLL

Democrats may also be optimistic about winning in 2016, but given that a Democrat currently occupies the White House, their preference for one-party control of government is understandably unchanged.

Although the question seemingly asks Americans for a normative view as to which type of government is best, the practical matter of the president's party has strongly influenced their preferences.

In Gallup's 13-year trend, when a Democratic president (namely Obama) has been in power, Democrats have been more likely to prefer one-party government, and Republicans divided government. When a Republican (namely George W. Bush) has been president, party supporters' preferences have shown the opposite pattern. This suggests partisans may view the party of the president as "fixed" and are answering in terms of how control of Congress should be adjusted to maximize their preferred party's power in Washington.

Unlike partisans, independents' views have been similar regardless of who is in the White House, with the greatest number saying it makes no difference, and more favoring divided government than one-party government.

Preference for Party Control of Congress and the Presidency, by Political Party and Presidential Administration

	Republicans	Independents	Democrats
	%	%	%
OBAMA PRESIDENCY (2009-2015)			
Same party	28	22	42
Different parties	33	32	15
Makes no difference	33	40	38
Same party - different parties (pct. pts.)	-5	-10	+27
BUSH PRESIDENCY (2001-2008)			
Same party	45	21	28
Different parties	18	35	34
Makes no difference	35	39	34
Same party - different parties (pct. pts.)	+27	-14	-6

GALLUP

Americans Overall Most Likely to Say Party Control Makes No Difference

Republicans make up a relatively small percentage of the adult population, 27%, so their sharply increased preference for one-party government this year produces just a slight increase in the percentage of all Americans who favor one-party government, from 30% to 33%.

Meanwhile, the percentage of all Americans preferring divided government has decreased since 2014, from 28% to 24%, and the percentage saying it makes no difference remains essentially unchanged, partly because the independent increase in this view has offset the Republican decline. "No difference" remains the most common response, as it typically has been, among all Americans at 38%.

Do you think it is better for the country to have a president who comes from the same political party that controls Congress, does it make no difference either way, or do you think it is better to have a president from one political party and Congress controlled by another?

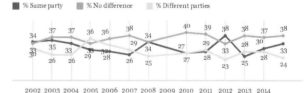

■ % Same party ▨ % No difference ▨ % Different parties

GALLUP

Since 2002, there have been just a few years in which "no difference" was not the most common response. This includes three years when the percentage of Americans who preferred one-party control met or exceeded the percentage not having a preference: 2002, when George W. Bush maintained high job approval ratings a year after the 9/11 terrorist attacks, and the presidential election years of 2008 and 2012. In 2012, a record-high 38% said they preferred one-party control of government in a poll conducted just after that year's Democratic National Convention.

In 2005, when Bush's approval ratings began their descent and Republicans still had control of both houses of Congress, a record-high 36% of Americans favored divided government.

Implications

Given Americans' frustrations with the way the government in Washington is operating—which to a large degree is a function of having divided government—one might expect Americans to be a little more open to having one party control both the president and Congress. But Americans' views on divided government are complex.

To a large degree, their opinions are influenced by partisans' desire to maximize their favored party's power in the current political environment. But in addition to those immediate and practical political desires, many Americans, particularly independents, seem to have normative concerns about giving one party too much power. That attitude would explain why recent eras of one-party government—including 1993–1994, 2002–2006 and 2009–2010—were short-lived. Once the incumbent president in those eras became unpopular, voters gave control of one or both houses of Congress to the opposition party in the next midterm election.

Additionally, a substantial percentage of Americans do not see either one-party or divided control as better than the other. Whether that reflects their own evaluations of how the government has performed under divided versus unified government, or just a more cynical view of government, is unclear.

Thus, Americans may never reach a consensus as to how the government should operate. But even if they did, it would be hard for voters to make it come about. This is especially true in presidential election years, as voters would not know for sure which party would win the White House at the same time they are voting for different members of Congress, all of whom represent narrow geographical areas. It is more feasible for voters to "choose" divided or unified government in midterm elections because the president of the party after the election is known as voters cast their ballots.

Survey Methods

Results for this Gallup poll are based on telephone interviews conducted Sept. 9–13, 2015, with a random sample of 1,025 adults, aged 18 and older, living in all 50 U.S. states and the District of Columbia. For results based on the total sample of national adults, the margin of sampling error is ±4 percentage points at the 95% confidence level. All reported margins of sampling error include computed design effects for weighting.

October 12, 2015
CLINTON MAINTAINS MODEST IMAGE ADVANTAGE OVER SANDERS

by Frank Newport and Andrew Dugan

Story Highlights

- *Hillary Clinton is most popular with Democrats overall*
- *Bernie Sanders beats Clinton among whites, college grads*
- *Sanders still not well known among Democrats*

WASHINGTON, D.C.—Ahead of the first nationally televised Democratic presidential debate Tuesday night, Hillary Clinton maintains a higher net favorable rating among Democrats and Democratic-leaning independents (+52) than her closest rival, Vermont Sen. Bernie Sanders (+40). However, Clinton's 12-percentage-point advantage is less than half of her lead in late July.

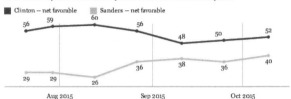

Net Favorable Ratings of Hillary Clinton and Bernie Sanders Among Democrats/Leaners
"Net favorable" equals % with favorable opinion minus % with unfavorable opinion

Note: Data reflect two-week rolling averages beginning July 8-21 and ending Sept. 26-Oct. 10

GALLUP

The smaller gap between Clinton and Sanders reflects changes in both candidates' images in recent months. Sanders's net favorable image has increased from the +26 to +29 range in July and August to +40 in the last two weeks. Clinton's, on the other hand, has gone from +60 to a low of +48 in early September before rising to the current +52.

NET FAVORABILITY RATING

BERNIE SANDERS — +40
HILLARY CLINTON — +52

SOURCE: GALLUP DAILY, SEP 26-OCT 10

Sanders is now familiar to 60% of Democrats, up from 49% when Gallup began tracking this in mid-July. Well over nine in 10 Democrats are familiar with Clinton.

Clinton and Sanders, along with three other announced but not as well-known Democratic candidates—Martin O'Malley, Jim Webb and Lincoln Chafee—will face off on Tuesday in Las Vegas. O'Malley's, Webb's and Chafee's familiarity scores among Democrats were all under 30% when Gallup last tracked them in early September, with net favorable scores near zero among Democrats. Barring a last-minute entrance into the race by Vice President Joe Biden, the debate's attention is likely to focus on the two best-known candidates, Clinton and Sanders.

Sanders Better Liked Among Whites, College Grads

Clinton's and Sanders's images differ among certain segments of the Democratic base—particularly by race, education and age.

Clinton's image is considerably more positive than Sanders's among nonwhites in a large sample of Democrats interviewed Sept. 12–Oct. 10. Clinton also has an advantage among those with a high school education or less, older Democrats, conservatives/moderates and women. Sanders, on the other hand, ties or does better than Clinton among whites, those who have at least some college education, 18- to 29-year-olds, liberals and men.

Perhaps most importantly, Sanders has a seven-point-higher net favorable rating among non-Hispanic white Democrats than does Clinton, underscoring how much Clinton's overall favorability advantage over Sanders is dependent on nonwhites. This particularly includes blacks, among whom Clinton's net favorable rating is 55 points higher than Sanders's.

Net Favorables Among Democrats/Leaners

	Clinton net favorable	Sanders net favorable	Difference, Clinton vs. Sanders
	Pct. pts.	Pct. pts.	
ALL DEMOCRATS	51	38	+13
EDUCATION			
High school or less	54	20	+34
Some college	38	37	+1
College graduate	53	61	-8
Postgraduate	64	62	+2
AGE			
18 to 29	35	43	-8
30 to 49	56	41	+15
50 to 64	59	34	+25
65+	56	34	+22
RACE			
Non-Hispanic white	40	47	-7
Non-Hispanic black	78	23	+55
Hispanic	57	28	+29
IDEOLOGY			
Conservative	41	3	+38
Moderate	49	33	+16
Liberal	58	57	+1
GENDER			
Male	43	44	-1
Female	57	34	+23

Sept. 12-Oct. 10, 2015

GALLUP

Clinton's positive image also depends heavily on Democratic women, among whom Clinton's net favorable rating is 23 points higher than Sanders's. The two candidates are essentially tied among Democratic men.

Sanders has an eight-point higher net favorable rating than Clinton among 18- to 29-year-old Democrats, and among Democrats with undergraduate degrees but no postgraduate study.

Bottom Line

Clinton began the 2016 Democratic campaign in much the same way she entered the 2008 Democratic primary: as the best-known, best-liked candidate and the one most pundits and political analysts viewed as the prohibitive front-runner. Her trajectory since the formal launch of her campaign this year has not been identical to the 2008 campaign. But in both instances, Clinton's own missteps as well as the increasing popularity of a previously underestimated challenger have made the primary contest more competitive than initial assessments might have suggested. Clinton shares the debate stage Tuesday night with a challenger who has greatly narrowed her midsummer advantage in likability among Democrats, at a time when her favorability with national adults has fallen nearly to career lows for the longtime public figure.

The two candidates have already developed distinctly different constituencies within the Democratic base, but it is uncertain how these strengths could play out in voting in the Democratic primaries. Older Democrats have a more positive image of Clinton than of Sanders—something that could play in her favor, given the traditionally higher turnout among older voters. On the other hand, Clinton's less positive image among well-educated and liberal Democrats could hurt her if these groups turn out in significant numbers in the primaries.

But the race is in an early stage, and the performance of Clinton and Sanders in Tuesday's debate—and Biden's possible entry into the contest—may shake things up further. As for the other three candidates, their inability to generate any traction with Democrats over the last several months suggests that this debate may be the point at which they turn their fortunes around, or totally fade into the background.

Survey Methods

Results for this Gallup poll are based on telephone interviews conducted Sept. 12–Oct. 10, 2015, on the Gallup U.S. Daily survey, with a random sample of up to 5,943 U.S. adults identifying as Democrats or independents who lean Democratic, aged 18 and older, living in all 50 U.S. states and the District of Columbia. Each candidate was rated by a random subset of respondents during this period, with the sample sizes rating each candidate ranging from 1,903 to 1,964. For results based on these samples, the margin of sampling error is ±4 percentage points at the 95% confidence level.

October 14, 2015
BIDEN MAINTAINS POSITIVE IMAGE

by Jeffrey M. Jones

Story Highlights

- *49% of Americans view Biden favorably, 37% unfavorably*
- *Opinions of him have been divided most of the last few years*
- *Current views are the most positive since Obama honeymoon*

PRINCETON, N.J.—As Vice President Joe Biden continues to ponder whether to enter the 2016 Democratic nomination campaign, Americans' views of him are more positive (49%) than negative (37%). These views are similar to what Gallup found in its prior update from August and continue to be improved from Americans' divided opinions of Biden through most of his term as vice president.

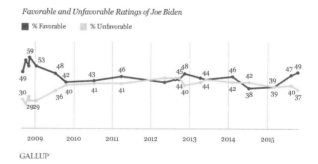

Favorable and Unfavorable Ratings of Joe Biden

GALLUP

As recently as March, equal percentages of Americans had favorable (39%) and unfavorable (39%) opinions of Biden. One reason opinions of Biden have improved in recent months could be Americans' sympathy for him after his son Beau died of cancer earlier this year.

Another reason Biden's favorability may be higher is that many Democrats want to see Biden enter the presidential campaign. They may think the Democratic Party needs an alternative to its weakened front-runner, Hillary Clinton, whom Americans currently view more negatively than positively. In stark contrast to Biden's rising image since March, Clinton's image has worsened since then.

Right now, Bernie Sanders is Clinton's closest challenger, but given his admitted socialist leanings, there are questions about his electability. None of the three other announced Democrats has emerged as a credible challenger to Clinton, though that could change in the days after Tuesday's first Democratic debate.

On only two other occasions since Biden became vice president has Gallup found significantly more positive than negative views of him. These include late 2012 after President Barack Obama and Biden were elected to a second term (48% favorable, 40% unfavorable) and during the "honeymoon phase" of the Obama administration (48% favorable, 36% unfavorable) in 2009. In fact, Biden's current +12 net favorable rating ties that June 2009 reading as the best of his vice presidency.

JOE BIDEN FAVORABLE RATINGS

MARCH 2015	OCTOBER 2015
39%	49%

SOURCE: GALLUP POLL

Prior to his being sworn in as vice president, in late 2008 and early January 2009, Biden's image tilted considerably more positive than negative. This included a personal best 59% favorable rating in a poll conducted in the days after the Obama-Biden ticket won the 2008 presidential election.

Biden Image Better Among Most Key Subgroups

Biden's favorable ratings are higher now than in March among most key subgroups. The sharpest gains in favorability, all near 20 percentage points, are among Democrats, nonwhites and Catholics.

Democrats, as would be expected, have always viewed Biden positively. But their opinions of him have become increasingly positive in recent months, now at 85% favorable, and suggest he likely would be a serious contender for the party's nomination if he entered the race.

Biden's more positive ratings among nonwhites are also noteworthy because support among this group could be decisive in determining the Democratic Party's nominee. While nonwhite Democrats have highly positive views of Clinton, this is not the case for Sanders. Thus, Biden likely would be more competitive with Clinton than Sanders would be among this key Democratic subgroup.

In addition to Democrats and nonwhites, most liberals (74%) and college graduates (62%) view the vice president positively.

Earlier in the year, 35% of Catholics had a favorable opinion of Biden, similar to the national average. Catholics' favorable rating increased to 42% in Gallup's August update, but now sits at 54%. Biden is Catholic, and more Catholics may be aware of that fact after he attended many of Pope Francis's public events during the widely covered U.S. papal visit in September.

Implications

Biden is now viewed as positively among Americans as at any time since he became vice president in January 2009. If he is considering entering the presidential race, he would appear to be well positioned given those relatively positive ratings and his high public profile.

Favorable Ratings of Joe Biden by Subgroup, March 2015 vs. October 2015

	% Favorable, March 2015	% Favorable, October 2015	Change (pct. pts.)
National adults	39	49	+10
Democrats	64	85	+21
Independents	36	42	+6
Republicans	14	19	+5
Liberals	63	74	+11
Moderates	44	55	+11
Conservatives	20	29	+9
Whites	36	43	+7
Nonwhites	47	66	+19
Men	37	49	+12
Women	41	49	+8
18 to 29 years old	34	45	+11
30 to 49 years old	41	46	+5
50 to 64 years old	43	52	+9
65+ years old	38	53	+15
Protestants	37	42	+5
Catholics	35	54	+19
No religion	48	53	+5
College graduates	50	62	+12
Some college	38	39	+1
High school or less	33	45	+12

GALLUP'

Among the announced presidential candidates, only Ben Carson and Carly Fiorina have significantly higher favorable than unfavorable ratings among all Americans, according to Gallup's tracking survey. Marco Rubio, Sanders, and John Kasich have slightly more positive than negative ratings.

To some degree, though, Biden's relatively positive image may reflect his status as a non-candidate. If he officially entered the race, Americans might view him in more strongly political terms. Additionally, the media and his political opponents would give greater scrutiny to his record, and if some of that scrutiny is unflattering, it could negatively affect the way Americans feel about him.

Survey Methods

Results for this Gallup poll are based on telephone interviews conducted Oct. 7–11, 2015, with a random sample of 1,015 adults, aged 18 and older, living in all 50 U.S. states and the District of Columbia. For results based on the total sample of national adults, the margin of sampling error is ±4 percentage points at the 95% confidence level. All reported margins of sampling error include computed design effects for weighting.

October 14, 2015
IN U.S., 59% VIEW PLANNED PARENTHOOD FAVORABLY

by Rebecca Riffkin

Story Highlights

- *Fewer have favorable view of Planned Parenthood than in 1993*
- *23% have "very unfavorable" view in 2015, up from 5% in 1993*

- *Favorability down most among Republicans, from 69% to 35%*

WASHINGTON, D.C.—A majority of Americans, 59%, view Planned Parenthood favorably. Although still positive overall, Americans' current opinions of Planned Parenthood are considerably less favorable than they were in 1993—the last time Gallup asked about the organization—when 81% viewed it favorably.

Planned Parenthood's Favorability Over Time

Next, I'd like your overall opinion of some organizations. Is your overall opinion of Planned Parenthood very favorable, mostly favorable, mostly unfavorable or very unfavorable?

	1989	1993	2015
% Very favorable	29	40	28
% Mostly favorable	50	41	31
% Mostly unfavorable	7	8	14
% Very unfavorable	4	5	23
Total % favorable	79	81	59
Total % unfavorable	11	13	37

GALLUP

Gallup has asked Americans about their views of Planned Parenthood three times: in 1989, in 1993 and in the Oct. 7–11 survey. The most recent poll comes amid significant focus on the organization in the news and throughout social media. The organization's president recently testified on Capitol Hill, largely in response to an anti-abortion group's release of secretly recorded videos that purported to show Planned Parenthood employees discussing potential sales of fetal tissue it recovers from abortions. Planned Parenthood denies these allegations, and has said that the videos were highly edited. The controversy has led to thus far unsuccessful efforts by Republicans in Congress to strip Planned Parenthood of its federal funding.

U.S. VIEWS OF PLANNED PARENTHOOD

FAVORABLE 1993	FAVORABLE 2015
81%	59%

SOURCE: GALLUP POLL

Republicans' Views of Planned Parenthood Changed Most Significantly

The biggest shift in views of Planned Parenthood since 1993 has taken place among Republicans. In 2015, 35% of Republicans say they have a favorable view of the organization, about half of the 69% who had a favorable view in 1993. Independents are also significantly less positive today, with favorable views dropping from 83% to 56%, although independents' views remain more positive than negative. Views of Planned Parenthood among Democrats have changed far less, dropping nine percentage points, from 91% to 82%.

Planned Parenthood's Favorability Has Decreased Most Significantly Among Republicans

Next, I'd like your overall opinion of some organizations. Is your overall opinion of Planned Parenthood very favorable, mostly favorable, mostly unfavorable or very unfavorable?

	% Very/Mostly favorable, 1993	% Very/Mostly favorable, 2015
Democrats	91	82
Independents	83	56
Republicans	69	35
Men	75	55
Women	85	61

GALLUP

Women have historically been more likely than men to view Planned Parenthood favorably. This continues to hold true in 2015, although favorability has dropped among both groups since 1993.

Opinions of Planned Parenthood are closely tied to Americans' views on abortion, because Planned Parenthood provides abortions as well as other reproductive healthcare and sex education for men and women. Currently, 82% of Americans who describe themselves as "pro-choice" on the abortion issue view Planned Parenthood favorably, compared with 33% of those who self-identify as "pro-life." Gallup did not ask the pro-choice/pro-life item in 1993, so it is not possible to know how these opinions may have changed.

Planned Parenthood's Favorability Among Pro-Choice Compared With Pro-Life Americans

Next, I'd like your overall opinion of some organizations. Is your overall opinion of Planned Parenthood very favorable, mostly favorable, mostly unfavorable or very unfavorable?

	Pro-choice	Pro-life
% Very favorable	42	11
% Mostly favorable	40	22
% Mostly unfavorable	10	18
% Very unfavorable	6	41
Total % favorable	82	33
Total % unfavorable	16	59

Oct. 7-11, 2015

GALLUP

Interestingly, 42% of pro-choice Americans have very favorable views of Planned Parenthood, almost identical to the 41% of pro-life Americans who have a very *unfavorable* view—showing how polarized Americans with differing views of abortion are about the organization.

Bottom Line

Planned Parenthood's image among U.S. adults has worsened since 1993. However, absent a more recent reading, the precise effect of the current controversy on Americans' views is unclear. While Republicans have always been less likely than Democrats to have favorable views of Planned Parenthood, the gap has widened significantly since the early 1990s.

This may have been the result of the politicization of Planned Parenthood as well as increased media attention to proposed changes in U.S. and state abortion laws. For example, in May 1993, Congress passed a law that legalized fetal tissue donations after abortions. At the time, many Republicans supported this law. Today, several of those same Republicans were among those pushing to defund Planned Parenthood. The organization only recently announced that it would no longer receive compensation for the medical cost of providing these fetal tissue donations after abortions.

Gallup has observed a similar pattern of party polarization on other issues, including attitudes about global warming and labor unions, to name two examples. While Republican House members and senators' actions and words regarding Planned Parenthood certainly may resonate with their base, they are facing a general public that, as a whole, still views the organization more favorably than unfavorably.

Survey Methods

Results for this Gallup poll are based on telephone interviews conducted Oct. 7–11, 2015, with a random sample of 1,015 adults, aged

18 and older, living in all 50 U.S. states and the District of Columbia. For results based on the total sample of national adults, the margin of sampling error is ±4 percentage points at the 95% confidence level. All reported margins of sampling error include computed design effects for weighting.

October 15, 2015
SOLID MAJORITY CONTINUE TO SUPPORT DEATH PENALTY

by Andrew Dugan

Story Highlights

- *61% of U.S. adults favor use of the death penalty*
- *37% oppose, higher than in the recent past*
- *Blacks more likely to oppose death penalty*

WASHINGTON, D.C.—About six in 10 Americans favor the use of the death penalty for a person convicted of murder, similar to 2014. This continues a gradual decline in support for the procedure since reaching its all-time high point of 80% in 1994.

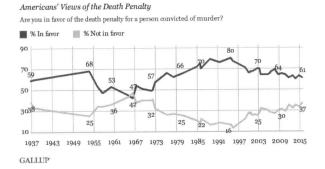

Americans' Views of the Death Penalty
Are you in favor of the death penalty for a person convicted of murder?

■ % In favor ▨ % Not in favor

GALLUP'

Thirty-seven percent oppose the death penalty, slightly higher than in recent years, in part because this year, only 2% of Americans say they have no opinion on the topic.

These results come from Gallup's annual Crime poll, conducted Oct. 7–11, 2015. While the public has, with one exception, favored the death penalty over the 78 years Gallup has asked this question, support for the measure has varied considerably. The low point for support, 42%, came in the 1960s, with support reaching its peak in the mid-1990s and generally declining since that point. Over the past decade, however, there has been minimal fluctuation in the percentage of adults who favor the death penalty, with support always at or above 60%.

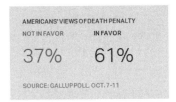

AMERICANS' VIEWS OF DEATH PENALTY

NOT IN FAVOR   IN FAVOR

37%   61%

SOURCE: GALLUP POLL, OCT. 7-11

This reliably high majority of support belies a powerful current of change in recent years that has rendered the death penalty a far

rarer judicial outcome than before. In May, Nebraska became the 19th state (along with D.C.) to ban the death penalty, and the seventh state since 2007. Meanwhile, the number of death sentences issued in 2014 was the lowest since the reinstatement of the punishment in 1976, and the number of executions carried out in 2014 was one of the lowest on record.

Blacks Far Less Likely to Support Death Penalty

A large gulf exists between whites and blacks in their support for the death penalty. In a combined 2014–2015 sample, 68% of whites said they were in favor of the death penalty, while 29% were opposed. Blacks tilt almost as heavily in the opposite direction—55% oppose the death penalty, compared with 39% in favor. This pattern is in alignment with previous Gallup findings, including in 2007. The opposition among blacks may be related to the disparity between blacks making up 42% of the current death row population but just 13% of the overall U.S. population.

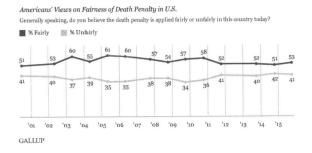

Americans' Views on the Death Penalty, by Race

	% White	% Black	% Hispanic
Yes, in favor	68	39	56
No, not in favor	29	55	43

Combined 2014-2015 data

GALLUP'

The death penalty remains a divisive issue among political partisans, with Democrats (49%) far less likely to be in favor of the punishment than Republicans (82%).

Majority Believe Death Penalty Applied Fairly

Fifty-three percent of Americans say that, generally speaking, the death penalty is applied fairly today in the U.S. While still a majority, this year's rate is below the high of 61% in 2005. Forty-one percent, meanwhile, say they believe the death penalty is applied unfairly.

Americans' Views on Fairness of Death Penalty in U.S.
Generally speaking, do you believe the death penalty is applied fairly or unfairly in this country today?

■ % Fairly ▨ % Unfairly

51 53 60 55 61 60 57 54 57 58 52 52 51 53
41 40 37 39 35 35 38 38 34 36 41 40 42 41

'01 '02 '03 '04 '05 '06 '07 '08 '09 '10 '11 '12 '13 '14 '15

GALLUP'

Plurality of Americans Say Death Penalty Not Imposed Enough

When asked about the frequency with which the death penalty is imposed, 40% of Americans say it is not imposed enough, with the remainder equally divided between saying it is imposed "too often" (27%) or "about the right amount" (27%). The proportion of Americans saying the death penalty is not imposed enough has fallen from a high of 53% in 2005, just as the number of executions has generally gone down over that time period.

Bottom Line

By many metrics—the number of states that have banned the death penalty, the number of executions carried out or the actual population of inmates currently on death row—the death penalty appears to be losing popularity in statehouses and courthouses across the country. But the public at large continues to support the use of the death penalty. A majority continue to assess the punishment as applied fairly, and a plurality wish it were applied more often.

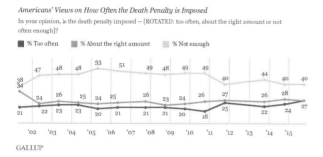

Americans' Views on How Often the Death Penalty is Imposed

In your opinion, is the death penalty imposed -- [ROTATED: too often, about the right amount or not often enough]?

■ % Too often   ▓ % About the right amount   ▒ % Not enough

GALLUP'

But there is no denying that the death penalty is controversial—reflected, at least somewhat, by the deep racial divide it causes. The cascade of exonerations for once-condemned inmates and the plethora of academic literature exploring the alleged disparities in the application of the punishment appear to have made juries less likely to issue a death penalty sentence and legislatures more likely to ban it.

Survey Methods

Results for this Gallup poll are based on telephone interviews conducted Oct. 7–11, 2015, on the Gallup U.S. Daily survey, with a random sample of 1,015 adults, aged 18 and older, living in all 50 U.S. states and the District of Columbia. For results based on the total sample of national adults, the margin of sampling error is ±4 percentage points at the 95% confidence level. All reported margins of sampling error include computed design effects for weighting.

October 15, 2015
BOEHNER IMAGE SLIGHTLY BETTER AFTER RESIGNATION ANNOUNCEMENT

by Jeffrey M. Jones

Story Highlights

- *Favorable ratings up to 31% from 23% before resignation*
- *Independents, Democrats now more favorable toward Boehner*
- *Most do not expect new Speaker to help GOP's legislative cause*

PRINCETON, N.J.—Americans' opinions of House Speaker John Boehner are still negative, but they have improved since he announced last month that he would resign his position. Currently, 31% of Americans have a favorable opinion of Boehner, up from 23% in August. This is his best reading since April 2014.

Last month, Boehner announced he would step down as speaker at the end of October. Boehner may hold his position a bit longer, given that Republicans' search for a replacement is taking longer than expected.

Boehner's tenure has been a rocky one, as he leads an unpopular institution and has had trouble pleasing his own party's supporters,

let alone Americans more generally. Often he has had to choose between pursuing legislation the right flank of his party prefers but that has little chance of becoming law, or working with Democrats to pass compromise legislation that disappoints conservatives, but is necessary to keep the government operating.

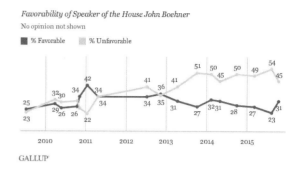

Favorability of Speaker of the House John Boehner

No opinion not shown

■ % Favorable   ▒ % Unfavorable

GALLUP'

Apart from a brief honeymoon period after becoming Speaker in 2011, when 42% of Americans viewed Boehner favorably and 22% viewed him unfavorably, his ratings typically have been more negative than positive. That is not unusual for Speakers, however, as Nancy Pelosi and Newt Gingrich had net-negative favorable ratings for much of their tenures in the position. The more low-key Dennis Hastert fared a little better, with more positive than negative ratings until the end of his speakership. However, Hastert may have benefited from presiding at a time when Americans tended to be a bit more positive toward Congress than is usually the case.

Interestingly, Republicans' views of Boehner are unchanged since Gallup's last measurement in August, while independents and Democrats now view him more favorably. This may be the result of recent attention paid to conservative Republicans' role in forcing Boehner to step down, perhaps leading some independents and Democrats to view him as more of an ally. Nevertheless, Democrats and independents still view him more negatively than Republicans do.

Favorable Ratings of House Speaker John Boehner, by Political Party, August 2015 vs. October 2015

No opinion not shown

	Republicans	Independents	Democrats
	%	%	%
August 2015			
Favorable	37	17	19
Unfavorable	42	57	59
October 2015			
Favorable	36	29	30
Unfavorable	42	43	54

GALLUP'

Tea Party Republicans view Boehner much more negatively than non–Tea Party Republicans do. Thirty-two percent of Republicans (including Republican-leaning independents) who describe themselves as supporters of the Tea Party movement view Boehner favorably, while 59% view him unfavorably. That compares with a more evenly divided evaluation among Republicans who are not Tea Party supporters—34% favorable versus 37% unfavorable.

Most Americans Think New Speaker Will Make No Difference

After resigning, Boehner warned against "false prophets" in the conservative wing of the party who advocate legislative moves that have little to no chance of succeeding, such as the 2013 government shutdown to block funding of Obamacare or more recent discussions to shut down the government over Planned Parenthood's federal funding. Some of those same conservative leaders may see Boehner as the problem and believe a new leader may help the party better achieve its goals.

Most Americans, 66%, do not believe changing leaders will make much difference in helping Republicans pass legislation they favor, though more do predict the GOP will have greater success (23%) with someone new than predict it will be less successful (9%).

The constituency Boehner was trying to warn, namely Tea Party Republicans, is divided about what will happen with a new speaker—49% think the GOP will be more successful while most of the rest say it will make no difference. By contrast, seven in 10 non-Tea Party Republicans—who outnumber Tea Party Republicans by about 2 to 1—believe Boehner's resignation will make no difference. Most Democrats and independents also believe having a new Speaker will not change things.

Views of the Effect a New Speaker of the House Will Have on Republicans' Ability to Pass Legislation They Favor

As you may know, John Boehner announced he would resign as speaker of the House. Just your best guess, do you think having a new Republican leader in Congress will make Republicans more successful in getting legislation they favor passed into law, less successful or will it not make much difference?

	Republicans will be more successful	Republicans will be less successful	Will not make much difference
	%	%	%
National adults	23	9	66
Republicans	38	2	59
Independents	18	7	72
Democrats	15	17	66
Tea Party Republicans*	49	1	49
Non-Tea Party Republicans*	25	4	71

Oct. 7-11, 2015

*The samples of Tea Party Republicans and non-Tea Party Republicans include Republican identifiers and Republican-leaning independents.

GALLUP

Implications

Boehner's decision to step down surprised political observers, but given his unpopularity—including a negative evaluation within his own party—it may have been inevitable. And while the move has led to a softening of Democrats' and independents' negative image of him, it hasn't affected the way Republicans rate him.

As of today, his successor is far from certain after current Majority Leader Kevin McCarthy announced he would not seek the position and none of the other contenders has emerged as a clear front-runner.

Regardless of who succeeds Boehner, the key question is what effect the change will have on Republicans' ability to accomplish their goals. Republicans' internal disagreement may be more about tactics than about substance. Most elected Republicans would probably repeal Obamacare and defund Planned Parenthood if they could, but the question is whether the Republican caucus should spend time on those goals if they cannot realistically achieve them.

As Boehner and like-minded Republicans might argue, the current political environment is not conducive to success on those issues with a Democratic president and enough Democrats in the Senate to successfully filibuster any legislation they oppose.

The Republican Party's image suffered greatly after the 2013 shutdown while not achieving their aim of thwarting Obamacare, although its image soon recovered, and a year later the GOP won control of the Senate and expanded its majority in the House. But that newfound power has not led to Republicans' achieving some of their goals, including regulatory reform, approving the Keystone XL pipeline, reforming taxes and reducing the national debt.

Ultimately, Americans do not think having a new speaker will make much difference, but Tea Party Republicans are more optimistic that it will. Whether their hopes are realized depends on whom the Republicans tap as the new Speaker and whether he or she is inclined to go along with conservatives' wishes, but also how Congress and the president respond to future GOP proposals.

Survey Methods

Results for this Gallup poll are based on telephone interviews conducted Oct. 7–11, 2015, with a random sample of 1,015 adults, aged 18 and older, living in all 50 U.S. states and the District of Columbia. For results based on the total sample of national adults, the margin of sampling error is ±4 percentage points at the 95% confidence level. All reported margins of sampling error include computed design effects for weighting.

October 16, 2015
U.S. EMPLOYEE ENGAGEMENT STEADY IN SEPTEMBER, AT 32%

by Amy Adkins

Story Highlights

- *Engagement stagnant for much of 2015*
- *Monthly averages remain higher than they were from 2011 to 2013*

WASHINGTON, D.C.—In the U.S., 32% of workers were engaged in their jobs in September. While engagement remains higher than it was from 2011–2013, monthly figures have not wavered since the beginning of 2015—consistently trending between 31% and 32%. The lone exception was in February, when the monthly employee engagement average was 32.9%.

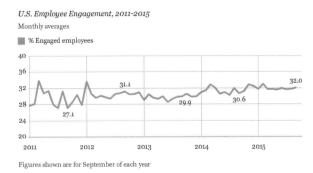

U.S. Employee Engagement, 2011-2015
Monthly averages

Figures shown are for September of each year

GALLUP

The September 2015 estimate is based on Gallup Daily tracking interviews conducted with 6,926 adults working for an employer.

Engaged employees are involved in, enthusiastic about and committed to their work and workplace. Gallup categorizes workers as "engaged" based on their ratings of key workplace elements that predict organizational performance outcomes, such as productivity, profitability and customer engagement. Engaged employees drive the innovation, growth and revenue that their companies need.

U.S. EMPLOYEE ENGAGEMENT, SEPTEMBER

32%

SOURCE: GALLUP DAILY TRACKING

Bottom Line

Thus far in 2015, employee engagement among all U.S. workers has been steady. Employee engagement readings are higher than they were just a few years ago, but the nation's workforce, in aggregate, is seemingly unable to move beyond the 31% to 32% barrier. This static state is aligned with many of the nation's economic indicators—job creation, the Gallup Good Jobs Index and consumer spending have all been flat in recent months.

Survey Results

Results for this Gallup poll are based on telephone interviews conducted Sept. 1–30, 2015, on the Gallup Daily tracking survey, with a random sample of 6,926 U.S. adults employed full or part time for an employer, aged 18 and older, living in all 50 U.S. states and the District of Columbia. For results based on the total sample of employed adults, the margin of sampling error is ±1.8 percentage points at the 95% confidence level. All reported margins of sampling error include computed design effects for weighting.

October 16, 2015
AMERICANS' FAVORABLE RATINGS OF POPE UP AFTER U.S. VISIT

by Justin McCarthy

Story Highlights

- *Favorable rating of 70% up 11 points from July*
- *Ratings up across religious/ideological demographics*
- *Francis's ratings higher than Benedict's, lower than John Paul II's*

WASHINGTON, D.C.—Pope Francis enjoyed a double-digit boost to his favorability after his September visit to the U.S. Seventy percent of Americans now view him favorably—up from 59% in July. The latest rating is closer to the 76% measured in early 2014.

The pope's visit to a trio of East Coast cities last month, which included addresses to Congress and the United Nations General Assembly, was his first to the U.S. While some observers politicized his calls for action on several controversial issues, his visit was widely celebrated by Catholics and non-Catholics alike. The latest

bump in his favorable rating suggests that he successfully connected with Americans during his trip.

Favorable Ratings of Pope Francis, 2013-2015

Please say if you have a favorable or unfavorable opinion of Pope Francis -- or if you have never heard of him.

	Favorable %	Unfavorable %	Never heard of/ No opinion %
Oct 7-11, 2015	70	17	12
Jul 8-12, 2015	59	16	25
Feb 6-9, 2014	76	9	16
Apr 11-14, 2013	58	10	31

GALLUP

U.S. FAVORABILITY: POPE FRANCIS

JULY 2015   OCTOBER 2015

59%   70%

SOURCE: GALLUP POLL

After being elected leader of the 1.2-billion-member Roman Catholic Church in 2013, Francis enjoyed great popularity in American news media, including being named *Time*'s 2013 Person of the Year. By early 2014, his favorability had swelled to 76%.

The pope's favorable rating fell from its previous high when Gallup next measured opinions about him, in July 2015. It's possible that many Americans forgot about him after that initial burst of positive publicity; the percentage not having an opinion of the pontiff rose from 16% to 25%. But his unfavorable rating also climbed during this time, from 9% to 16%, after he weighed in on a variety of issues that are controversial to Americans, including immigration and climate change.

Francis's favorability has rebounded in the latest poll, as more Americans than before are now familiar with him, but there has been no change in his unfavorable rating.

Pope Francis Regains Footing Among Several Demographics

In July, the pope experienced his largest drop in favorability among conservatives, although his favorable ratings among liberals and Catholics themselves also fell substantially. In the latest poll, conducted Oct. 7–11, Francis regained much of his standing with these groups.

Changes in Favorable Ratings of Pope Francis

	February 2014	July 2015	October 2015	Change after papal visit to U.S. (pct. pts.)
U.S. ADULTS	76	59	70	+11
Catholics	89	71	87	+16
Protestants/Other Christians	73	52	67	+15
Conservatives	72	45	63	+18
Moderates	79	71	75	+4
Liberals	82	68	80	+12

GALLUP

Since July, the pope's favorability among conservatives has increased 18 percentage points, higher than the 11-point increase among all Americans. Ratings are also more positive among the other ideological groups, but they have not increased to the same degree. The proportionately larger increase among conservatives partly reflects their lower ratings in the prior poll, meaning conservatives had more room to improve than moderates or liberals. Less than half of conservatives viewed the pope favorably over the summer, while a majority (63%) now have a favorable view of him.

Nearly nine in 10 of the pope's fellow Catholics view him favorably—a 16-point increase from July and nearly back to the 89% from 2014. His favorable rating among Protestants and other Christians is up 15 points to 67%.

Francis's Ratings Still Higher Than Benedict's, Lower Than John Paul's

Generally speaking, Americans rate popes much more positively than negatively. Francis remains markedly more popular than his predecessor, Pope Benedict XVI, whose resignation in 2013 led to Francis's election. Benedict's ratings were middling after his ascension to the papacy in 2005. His favorability climbed to its peak at 63% in 2008 before dropping sharply to 40% in 2010.

Pope John Paul II, however, was the most popular among the three most recent popes, with favorable ratings that ranged from a low of 61% in 2002, after the Catholic priest sex abuse scandal broke, to a high of 86% in 1998.

Favorable Ratings of Pope Francis, Pope Benedict XVI, Pope John Paul II

	Favorable	Unfavorable	Never heard of/ No opinion
	%	%	%
POPE FRANCIS			
Oct 7-11, 2015	70	17	12
Jul 8-12, 2015	59	16	25
Feb 6-9, 2014	76	9	16
Apr 11-14, 2013	58	10	31
POPE BENEDICT XVI			
Mar 26-28, 2010	40	35	25
Apr 18-20, 2008	63	15	22
Jun 1-3, 2007	52	16	32
Dec 16-18, 2005	50	11	39
Apr 29-May 1, 2005	55	12	33
POPE JOHN PAUL II			
Feb 25-27, 2005	78	11	11
Oct 6-8, 2003	73	17	10
Apr 29-May 1, 2002	61	26	13
Dec 28-29, 1998	86	8	6
Aug 8-10, 1993	64	15	21

GALLUP

Bottom Line

By and large, most Americans view Francis favorably, as they have past popes. Among the relatively small percentage of Americans who don't have a positive opinion of Francis, nearly half of them simply don't know who he is or don't have an opinion of him.

Though his recent visit clearly influenced how Americans view him, solid majorities viewed him favorably even before he came to the U.S. And like popes before him, his ratings have fluctuated and likely could continue to fluctuate, depending on his prominence in the news as well as the policies and calls to action he issues as leader of the church.

Francis has made bold statements in his short time in the papacy, and ones that have rankled some U.S. conservatives. And while some people's views of the pope may ebb and flow as a result of the statements he makes, his core favorable rating remains sturdy.

Survey Methods

Results for this Gallup poll are based on telephone interviews conducted Oct. 7–11, 2015, on the Gallup U.S. Daily survey, with a random sample of 1,015 adults, aged 18 and older, living in all 50 U.S. states and the District of Columbia. For results based on the total sample of national adults, the margin of sampling error is ±4 percentage points at the 95% confidence level. All reported margins of sampling error include computed design effects for weighting.

October 19, 2015
QUARTER OF U.S. VOTERS SAY CANDIDATE MUST SHARE VIEW ON GUNS

by Justin McCarthy

Story Highlights

- *The issue is now more salient than in the year after Columbine*
- *Conservatives more likely than others to say issue matters to vote*
- *Americans slightly favor GOP as reflecting their views on gun control*

WASHINGTON, D.C.—More than one in four U.S. registered voters (26%) say they would vote only for a candidate who shares their views on gun control—about double the 11% to 15% who said this in the year after the 1999 Columbine High School massacre. The majority, 54%, say it is one of many important factors in their vote, while 17% do not see guns as a major voting issue for them.

Importance of a Candidate's Position on Gun Control to Americans' Vote

Thinking about how the gun issue might affect your vote for major offices, would you -- only vote for a candidate who shares your views on gun control, would you consider a candidate's position on gun control as just one of many important factors when voting or would you not consider gun control a major issue?

	Only vote for candidate who shares gun views	Consider gun issue one of many factors	Guns not a major issue
	%	%	%
Oct 7-11, 2015	26	54	17
May 5-7, 2000	11	64	23
Jun 25-27, 1999	15	63	21
May 21-23, 1999	14	65	19

Based on registered voters

GALLUP

American voters' views on how gun control relates to their voting behavior have evolved over the past 16 years as discussion on how to combat gun violence has re-emerged with every mass shooting. Last year, a study from the Federal Bureau of Investigation found a sharp rise in mass shootings since 2000. According to the study, the average number of mass shootings per year had more than doubled in 2007 to 2013 compared with 2000 to 2006.

The latest poll, conducted Oct. 7–11, after a mass shooting at an Oregon community college, finds that Americans are roughly twice as likely as they were just after Columbine to say their views on gun control are non-negotiable in how they vote.

Gun Control as Voting Issue Varies by Party, Gun Ownership

Republicans, individuals who identify as conservative, gun owners and those who believe gun control laws should be made less strict are the most likely to say that a candidate must share their views on gun control. At least three in 10 voters in each of these subgroups—including 40% of those favoring less strict gun laws—say they would vote only for a candidate who shares their views on guns. A smaller 21% of those who favor stricter gun laws say they will vote only for a candidate who agrees with them.

GUN CONTROL AS VOTING ISSUE

SINGLE ISSUE **26%**   ONE OF MANY **54%**

GALLUP POLL, OCT 7-11

Importance of a Candidate's Position on Gun Control to Americans' Vote, by Key Subgroups

Thinking about how the gun issue might affect your vote for major offices, would you -- only vote for a candidate who shares your views on gun control, would you consider a candidate's position on gun control as just one of many important factors when voting or would you not consider gun control a major issue?

	Only vote for candidate who shares gun views	Consider gun issue one of many factors	Guns not a major issue
	%	%	%
All registered voters	26	54	17
Conservatives	34	45	17
Moderates	17	57	24
Liberals	22	66	6
Republicans	30	51	16
Independents	22	56	20
Democrats	26	55	13
Own gun	31	51	16
Do not own gun	22	56	17
Want gun laws covering firearms to be more strict	21	59	15
Want gun laws covering firearms to be less strict	40	35	20

Based on registered voters
Oct. 7-11, 2015

GALLUP

Americans Slightly More Likely to Say GOP Better Reflects Their Views on Gun Control

In 1999, Americans were about equally likely to say the Republican Party and the Democratic Party could do a better job of reflecting their own views on gun control, with a slight tilt toward the Democrats. Today, voters are still somewhat divided, but tilt more toward the GOP on the issue, at 46%, compared with 37% for the Democratic Party.

Fourteen percent say neither party does a better job in reflecting their views on gun control. This is about twice as high as the percentage of those who gave this answer in 1999, suggesting greater frustration with both parties on the issue.

Party That Better Reflects Own Views About Gun Control

Which party do you think can do a better job of reflecting your views about gun control -- [the Republican Party (or) the Democratic Party]?

	Republican Party	Democratic Party	Neither (vol.)
	%	%	%
Oct 7-11, 2015	46	37	14
Jun 25-27, 1999	41	45	5
May 21-23, 1999	40	43	9

(vol.) = Volunteered response
Note: Those with no opinion are not shown
Based on registered voters

GALLUP

Perhaps unsurprisingly, nine in 10 Republican voters say their party does a better job. Conservatives (69%) and gun owners (60%) also highly favor the GOP over the Democratic Party when it comes to gun control.

Contrarily, more than three in four Democratic voters (77%) say their party does the better job on gun control. Liberals (74%) and those who do not own a gun (45%) are also most likely to say the Democratic Party does the better job.

Moderates are split between the GOP (38%) and the Democratic Party (39%). Political independents, however, are more likely to prefer the Republican Party (42%) over the Democratic Party (29%) on the issue.

Party That Better Reflects Own Views About Gun Control, by Key Subgroups

Which party do you think can do a better job of reflecting your views about gun control -- [the Republican Party (or) the Democratic Party]?

	Republican Party	Democratic Party	Neither (vol.)
	%	%	%
All registered voters	44	38	14
Conservatives	69	15	14
Moderates	38	39	17
Liberals	17	74	7
Republicans	90	4	4
Independents	42	29	24
Democrats	11	77	10
Owns gun	60	22	17
Does not own gun	39	45	13

(vol.) = Volunteered response
Note: Those with no opinion are not shown
Based on registered voters
Oct. 7-11, 2015

GALLUP

Bottom Line

Much has occurred in the conversation on gun control since a pair of Colorado teenagers killed a dozen fellow students and a teacher in 1999. Today, as was the case when Gallup polled in the wake of the Columbine shootings, Americans are deciding between presidential candidates and their positions on how to address the seeming epidemic of mass shootings.

Most American voters don't identify as single-issue voters when it comes to gun control, however—though a larger percentage do now than did 16 years ago. Still, a majority of them see the issue as an important one that factors into how they choose an elected official.

The Republican Party currently enjoys a slight upper hand on the issue in terms of which party Americans see as better reflecting their own views. But the party is also in less of a position to negotiate, as Republicans and conservatives are more likely to say a candidate must share their views on this issue.

Survey Methods

Results for this Gallup poll are based on telephone interviews conducted Oct. 7–11, 2015, on the Gallup U.S. Daily survey, with a random sample of 855 registered voters, aged 18 and older, living in all 50 U.S. states and the District of Columbia. For results based on the total sample of national adults, the margin of sampling error is ±4 percentage points at the 95% confidence level. All reported margins of sampling error include computed design effects for weighting.

October 19, 2015
AMERICANS' DESIRE FOR STRICTER GUN LAWS UP SHARPLY

by Art Swift

Story Highlights

- *55% say laws on gun sales should be more strict than they are now*
- *Majority do not favor a ban on handguns for average Americans*
- *43% in U.S. have a gun in their house or on their property*

WASHINGTON, D.C.—Fifty-five percent of Americans say they want laws covering the sale of firearms to be stricter than they are now, a distinct rise of eight percentage points from 2014. Fewer Americans than last year want the laws to be less strict, and the proportion who want the laws to stay the same has also declined slightly.

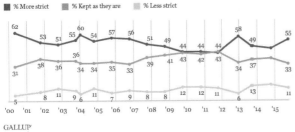

Laws Covering the Sale of Firearms -- Americans' Preferences Since 2000

In general, do you feel that the laws covering the sale of firearms should be made more strict, less strict or kept as they are now?

GALLUP

In 2007, the year of the Virginia Tech massacre, the percentage of Americans who favored stricter laws on gun sales dropped to a bare majority (51%) for the first time in several years. Since then, support for stricter laws had stayed under 50%, except in the wake of the Sandy Hook school shootings in Newtown, Connecticut, in December 2012. At that point, 58% of Americans said they were in favor of stricter laws on gun sales. Although support for stricter laws receded after those shootings, in which a young man fatally shot 20 children and six adults, it has yet to return to the 44% level it was at before that tragedy.

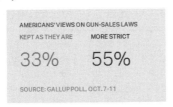

AMERICANS' VIEWS ON GUN-SALES LAWS

KEPT AS THEY ARE: 33% MORE STRICT: 55%

SOURCE: GALLUP POLL, OCT. 7-11

The latest increase, from the Gallup Crime poll conducted Oct. 7–11, came in the days after the most recent high-profile mass shooting, at a community college in Oregon. However, that event seems to have mainly affected Americans' views about laws on gun sales, but not other topics relating to guns.

Independents, Democrats Fueling Trend for Stricter Gun Laws

The rise in the proportion of Americans who want stricter laws on firearm sales can be attributed partly to an increase among certain demographic groups. Support rose among Democrats and especially independents from 2014, and among those who do not personally own a gun. However, support increased even among those who say they own a handgun, from 30% in 2014 to 36% this year.

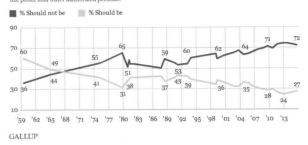

Views on Laws Regarding Gun Sales, by Selected Demographic Group

Those favoring laws that are "more strict than now"

	2014 %	2015 %	Difference (pct. pts.)
Gun owners	30	36	+6
Gun nonowners	57	64	+7
Republicans	29	27	-2
Independents	45	56	+11
Democrats	71	77	+6

GALLUP

Civilian Handgun Possession Should Not Be Banned, Americans Say

The percentage of Americans who favor a law providing that only authorized persons (including the police) would be allowed to possess handguns has remained low since the 1990s. This year, 27%—near the record low—say there should be this type of ban. This trend has been generally declining since Gallup began asking this question in 1959, when 60% said such a law should exist.

Support for Ban on Possession of Handguns, 1959-2015

Do you think there should or should not be a law that would ban the possession of handguns, except by the police and other authorized persons?

GALLUP

In 2015, guns are a part of the fabric of American life and much of its discourse. Overall in the U.S., 43% say they have a gun somewhere in their household, and 28% say they personally own a gun.

Bottom Line

In a maelstrom of debate about guns, Americans have clear-cut views of at least some aspects of the debate. A majority in 2015 say gun sales should be regulated more strictly than they are now, which represents an uptick from last fall; however, it is still slightly lower than in December 2012, immediately after the Newtown school shootings.

But with mass shootings and individual homicides occurring with regularity, the debate will continue over whether there should be restrictions or amendments to firearms purchases or possession. Last week, California's Lt. Gov. Gavin Newsom said he will introduce a state ballot measure for next year that would require ammunition buyers to undergo background checks. President Barack Obama also said he may use executive authority to impose background checks for those purchasing weapons from high-volume firearms dealers.

These are just two examples of initiatives that may or may not gain traction with a public that is disturbed about mass shootings, but evidently divided about how to solve this persistent problem in the 2010s.

Survey Methods

Results for this Gallup poll are based on telephone interviews conducted Oct. 7–11, 2015, with a random sample of 1,015 adults, aged 18 and older, living in all 50 U.S. states and the District of Columbia. For results based on the total sample of national adults, the margin of sampling error is ±4 percentage points at the 95% confidence level. All reported margins of sampling error include computed design effects for weighting.

October 20, 2015

MAJORITY SAY MORE CONCEALED WEAPONS WOULD MAKE U.S. SAFER

by Frank Newport

Story Highlights

- *56% say more concealed weapons would make country safer*
- *Americans overwhelmingly support universal background checks*
- *Americans split on effect of background-check laws on mass shootings*

PRINCETON, N.J.—A majority of Americans, 56%, believe that if more Americans carried concealed weapons after passing a criminal background check and training course, the country would be safer.

Suppose more Americans were allowed to carry concealed weapons if they passed a criminal background check and training course. If more Americans carried concealed weapons, would the United States be safer or less safe?

	Safer	Less safe	No opinion
Oct 7–11, 2015	56%	41%	3%

GALLUP

These results are from Gallup's annual Crime poll conducted Oct. 7–11. In the wake of mass shootings at schools and other public places, some have argued that the shootings could have been stopped if any of the victims had carried weapons. Others argue that having more citizens carrying weapons can lead to more violence and accidental shooting.

STATE OF U.S. IF MORE AMERICANS CARRIED CONCEALED WEAPONS

LESS SAFE	SAFER
41%	56%

GALLUP POLL, OCT. 7-11, 2015

Most states have some sort of permitting process allowing the carrying of concealed weapons, but the requirements and procedures to carry weapons vary significantly by state. The Gallup question did not get into detail on specific requirements other than mentioning that the person with the concealed weapon would have to pass a criminal background check and training course.

Among key subgroups, Democrats and those with postgraduate education are least likely to believe that more concealed weapons would make the U.S. safer. Republicans and gun owners are most likely to say it would make the nation safer. Younger Americans are more likely to choose the "safer" option than those aged 30 and above.

Suppose more Americans were allowed to carry concealed weapons if they passed a criminal background check and training course. If more Americans carried concealed weapons, would the United States be safer or less safe?

By demographic group

	Safer	Less safe
	%	%
NATIONAL ADULTS	56	41
GENDER		
Men	62	37
Women	50	45
AGE		
18 to 29	66	33
30 to 49	56	40
50 to 64	51	46
65+	50	45
EDUCATION		
High school or less	57	40
Some college	65	31
College graduate only	56	43
Postgraduate	35	64
PARTY ID		
Republicans	82	16
Independents	59	39
Democrats	31	67
GUN OWNER		
Yes	74	24
No	48	49
AREA LIVE IN		
Big city	50	47
Suburb	52	47
Town/Rural	63	33

Oct. 7-11, 2015

GALLUP

Strong Support for Universal Background Checks

One of the most commonly advanced proposals relating to gun control is background checks for gun purchasers. President Barack Obama has called repeatedly for legislation mandating such checks, but the most recent effort failed to be passed into law in 2013. For their part, Americans strongly agree with the idea of laws requiring universal background checks using a centralized database for all gun purchases in the U.S. Eighty-six percent favor such a law, while 12% oppose it.

Would you favor or oppose a law which would require universal background checks for all gun purchases in the U.S. using a centralized database across all 50 states?

	Favor	Oppose	No opinion
Oct 7–11, 2015	86%	12%	2%

GALLUP

Americans are more divided, however, on whether a law requiring universal background checks would reduce the number of mass shootings. Slightly less than half think such a law would reduce the number of such shootings either a great deal or a moderate amount, while a little more than half say that it would have little to no effect.

If such a [background-check] law were passed, do you think it would reduce the number of mass shootings in the U.S. a great deal, a moderate amount, a little or not at all?

	A great deal	A moderate amount	A little	Not at all	No opinion
Oct 7-11, 2015	19%	28%	22%	31%	1%

GALLUP

Nearly half of those who favor a law requiring universal background checks doubt it would reduce the number of mass shootings.

Bottom Line

The seemingly continuous incidence of mass shootings in the U.S. in recent years underscores the need for a focus on what can be done to prevent such tragic events in the future. Previous Gallup research has shown that Americans believe a failure of the mental health system to identify individuals who are a danger to others and easy access to guns are more to blame for mass shootings than other causes tested.

Gallup's most recent poll on gun control shows that a majority of Americans favor stricter gun sale laws in this country. At the same time, however, less than half of Americans believe that one such stricter law—universal background checks—would prevent mass shootings. In fact, a majority say that if more Americans carried concealed weapons after passing background checks and training, the nation would be safer.

Previous research shows that three in four Americans are opposed to banning handguns, and Americans in the past have overwhelmingly interpreted the Second Amendment as giving Americans the rights to own guns. All of this research supports the conclusion that Americans believe they should be allowed to own and carry guns, but with more stringent background checks. Americans are inclined to believe that carrying properly permitted guns could make the country safer.

Survey Methods

Results for this Gallup poll are based on telephone interviews conducted Oct. 7–11, 2015, with a random sample of 1,015 adults, aged 18 and older, living in all 50 U.S. states and the District of Columbia. For results based on the total sample of national adults, the margin of sampling error is ±4 percentage points at the 95% confidence level. All reported margins of sampling error include computed design effects for weighting.

October 21, 2015
U.S. CONSUMERS' HOLIDAY SPENDING INTENTIONS BEST SINCE 2007

by Lydia Saad

Story Highlights

- *Consumers estimate spending an average $812 on gifts this season*
- *Highest October estimate since 2007*
- *Fewer than in recent years say they are "spending less" on gifts*

PRINCETON, N.J.—Gallup's initial measure of Americans' 2015 Christmas spending intentions finds consumers planning to spend an average $812 on gifts this season, up from $781 at the same time a year ago, and the highest estimate since 2007.

Americans' Estimated Christmas Spending, 2002-2015

Roughly how much money do you think you personally will spend on Christmas gifts this year?

■ Mean, including zero

'02 $695, '06 $907, '07 $909, '08 $801, '09 $740, '10 $715, '11 $712, '13 $786, '14 $781, '15 $812

Data are for October of each year

GALLUP

The 2015 average spending estimate encompasses a fairly wide range of holiday budgets. According to the Oct. 7–11 telephone survey, about a third of U.S. adults plan to spend $1,000 or more on gifts and another quarter say they will spend between $500 and $999, while about a third will spend between $100 and $499. Another 3% plan to spend less than $100, while 8% say they will not spend anything.

Americans' October Christmas Spending Estimates for 2015

Roughly how much money do you think you personally will spend on Christmas gifts this year?

	Oct 7-11, 2015
	%
$1,000 or more	32
$500 to $999	23
$250 to $499	13
$100 to $249	17
Less than $100	3
None/Don't celebrate	8
Not sure	4
Average (including zero)	$812
Average (excluding zero)	$887

GALLUP

The poll also finds consumers a bit less cautious than last year when asked about how their Christmas spending will compare with the year prior. Although the majority of Americans routinely say they will spend about the same as they did the previous year, the 20% saying they will spend less is down from 24% in October 2014, and is the lowest Gallup has recorded for any October since 2007. It is also markedly lower than the 35% and 33% figures recorded in 2008–2009 during the last recession. Instead, consumers' current mindset about holiday spending appears to be finally restored to the non-recessionary levels seen prior to 2008.

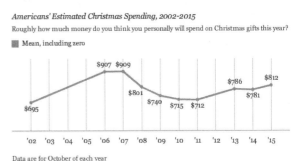

AMERICANS' ESTIMATED CHRISTMAS SPENDING

OCTOBER 2014 — $781
OCTOBER 2015 — $812

GALLUP POLL, OCT 7-11

Perhaps reflecting a desire to appear financially responsible, few Americans ever say they will spend more on gifts in a given year than the year prior, and that remains the case today. The 13% saying this is about average for the past decade.

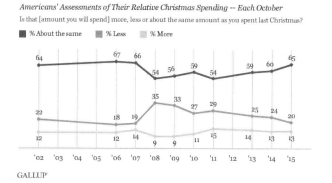

Americans' Assessments of Their Relative Christmas Spending -- Each October

Is that [amount you will spend] more, less or about the same amount as you spent last Christmas?

■ % About the same   ■ % Less   ■ % More

GALLUP

Together, these findings point to improved holiday sales this year compared with 2014. But a cautionary note is in order, as Americans' estimate of the total amount they will spend on gifts can change as the holiday season progresses.

In 2008, consumers' spending estimate plunged nearly $200 between October and November, precipitated by the Wall Street financial crisis, and retail sales wound up falling nearly 5% compared with the year prior. Even in less turbulent times, Gallup has typically found consumers shrinking their spending estimate between October and November.

Americans' Average Christmas Spending Estimates for October and November of Each Year

	October	November	Change
2015	$812	?	
2014	$781	$720	-$61
2013	$786	$704	-$82
2012	--	$770	
2011	$712	$764	+$52
2010	$715	$714	-$1
2009	$740	$638	-$102
2008	$801	$616	-$185
2007	$909	$866	-$43
2006	$907	$826	-$81
2005	--	$763	
2004	--	$730	
2003	--	$734	
2002	$695	$690	-$5
2001	--	$794	
2000	--	$817	
1999	--	$857	

Averages include zero, for those who plan to spend nothing

GALLUP

Bottom Line

After seven years of subdued holiday spending estimates, Gallup's initial 2015 look at Americans' Christmas spending intentions offers more encouragement for retailers than any October estimate since 2007. In addition to the possibility that spending intentions could still crater as the season progresses, the current outlook is a bit out of sync with government data showing weak retail sales this year. But much of that could be explained by the effect lower gas prices have on national spending data. Other data indicate that consumers' discretionary spending is holding up, and the broader health of the economy was fairly strong in the second quarter, growing by 3.9%. Gallup's relatively positive October Christmas spending estimate could signal that consumers are ready to take some of the gas savings they have been holding on to, and invest in some much-needed holiday cheer.

Gallup will issue its final holiday spending report in mid-November.

Survey Methods

Results for this Gallup poll are based on telephone interviews conducted Oct. 7–11, 2015, with a random sample of 1,015 adults, aged 18 and older, living in all 50 U.S. states and the District of Columbia. For results based on the total sample of national adults, the margin of sampling error is ±4 percentage points at the 95% confidence level. The margin of sampling error for the mean Christmas spending estimate is ± $62 at the 95% confidence level.

All reported margins of sampling error include computed design effects for weighting.

October 21, 2015
IN U.S., 58% BACK LEGAL MARIJUANA USE

by Jeffrey M. Jones

Story Highlights

- *Majority favors legal marijuana for third consecutive year*
- *Younger generations more supportive than older generations*
- *Older generations more supportive than they were in the past*

PRINCETON, N.J.—A majority of Americans continue to say marijuana use should be legal in the United States, with 58% holding that view, tying the high point in Gallup's 46-year trend.

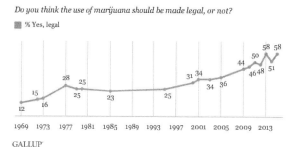

Do you think the use of marijuana should be made legal, or not?

■ % Yes, legal

GALLUP

Americans' support for legal marijuana has steadily grown over time. When Gallup first asked the question, in 1969, 12% of Americans thought marijuana use should be legal, with little change in two early 1970s polls. By the late 1970s, support had increased to about 25%, and held there through the mid-1990s. The percentage of Americans who favored making use of the drug legal exceeded 30% by 2000 and was higher than 40% by 2009.

Over the past six years, support has vacillated a bit, but averaged 48% from 2010 through 2012 and has averaged above the majority level, 56%, since 2013.

The higher level of support comes as many states and localities are changing, or considering changing, their laws on marijuana. So far, four states and the District of Columbia have made recreational use of marijuana legal, and Ohio voters are set to decide a ballot initiative that would do the same this coming Election Day. The topic has been an issue on the 2016 presidential campaign trail, and several candidates have expressed a willingness to let states set their own marijuana laws even though federal law prohibits marijuana use.

AMERICANS FAVORING LEGAL USE OF MARIJUANA

58%

GALLUP POLL, OCT 7-11

Young Adults Consistently More Supportive of Legal Marijuana

Gallup has previously reported that two of the biggest differentiators of Americans' opinions on legal marijuana are age and party identification. Younger Americans, Democrats and independents are the most likely of major demographic and political groups to favor legalizing use of the drug, while Republicans and older Americans are least likely to do so.

Younger Americans have always shown the most support of any age group for making marijuana legal, but this has grown from 20% of 18- to 34-year-olds in 1969 to 71% of those in the same age group today. But even older age groups today are more likely to favor legal marijuana than the comparable age groups in the past. For example, 35% of senior citizens today (aged 65 and older) are in favor of legalization, compared with 4% of senior citizens in 1969. Among all age groups, the increase in support has been proportionately greater over the last 15 years than it was between any of the earlier time periods.

Support for Legalizing the Use of Marijuana, by Age Group, 1969-2015, Selected Polls

	1969	1985	2000/2001	2015
	%	%	%	%
National adults	12	23	33	58
18 to 34 years old	20	32	44	71
35 to 49 years old	11	22	34	64
50 to 64 years old	6	16	30	58
65+ years old	4	13	17	35

Note: Analysis uses combined data from 2000 and 2001 because 2000 survey asked the question of a half-sample of respondents

GALLUP

These patterns by age indicate that one reason Americans are more likely to support legal marijuana today than they were in the past is because newer generations of adults, who are much more inclined to favor use of the drug, are replacing older generations in the population who were much less inclined to want it to be legalized.

But the increase in support nationwide is also a function of attitude change within generations of Americans over the course of their adult lifespans. Gallup's historical data allow for a look at how views on marijuana legalization have changed over time among independent samples of those in the same birth cohorts. For example, Americans who are aged 65 through 79 today—born between 1936 and 1950—are more supportive of making marijuana legal in 2015 than those born in the same years were 15, 30 and 46 years ago. This birth cohort's support has increased from 20% in 1969 to 29% in 2000/2001, and is 40% today.

Support for Legalizing the Use of Marijuana, by Birth Cohort, Over Time

	1969	1985	2000/2001	2015
Year of birth	%	%	%	%
1981-1997	n/a	n/a	n/a	71
1966-1980	n/a	n/a	43	64
1951-1965	n/a	32	35	58
1936-1950	20	22	29	40
1935 and earlier	8	15	18	19

Note: Analysis uses combined data from 2000 and 2001 because 2000 survey asked the question of a half-sample of respondents

GALLUP

Americans born from 1951 through 1965 and from 1966 through 1980 are also more likely to favor legalizing marijuana than they were 15 years ago, with support growing a little more than 20 percentage points within each of these birth cohorts over that time. That exceeds the increases in support for older birth cohorts over the same time.

The oldest Americans, those born in 1935 or earlier, have shown far less change in their attitudes about marijuana over their life spans. The near doubling of support between 1969 and 1985, from 8% to 15%, reflects the dying off of the oldest Americans in that birth cohort during that time period as much as it does attitude change among those from that birth cohort who were still living.

Implications

Americans' support for legalizing marijuana is the highest Gallup has measured to date, at 58%. Given the patterns of support by age, that percentage should continue to grow in the future. Younger generations of Americans have been increasingly likely to favor legal use of marijuana as they entered adulthood compared with older generations of Americans when they were the same age decades ago. Now, more than seven in 10 of today's young adults support legalization.

But Americans today—particularly those between 35 and 64—are more supportive of legal marijuana than members of their same birth cohort were in the past. Now senior citizens are alone among age groups in opposing pot legalization.

These trends suggest that state and local governments may come under increasing pressure to ease restrictions on marijuana use, if not go even further like the states of Colorado, Oregon, Washington and Alaska in making recreational marijuana use completely legal.

Survey Methods

Results for this Gallup poll are based on telephone interviews conducted Oct. 7–11, 2015, with a random sample of 1,015 adults, aged 18 and older, living in all 50 U.S. states and the District of Columbia. For results based on the total sample of national adults, the margin of sampling error is ±4 percentage points at the 95% confidence level. All reported margins of sampling error include computed design effects for weighting.

October 22, 2015
MORE AMERICANS SAY CRIME IS RISING IN U.S.

by Justin McCarthy

Story Highlights

- *Perceptions of rising crime up seven points from 2014*
- *Perceptions of crime not always in sync with federal crime figures*
- *Conservatives, Republicans most likely to say crime is up*

WASHINGTON, D.C.—Seven in 10 Americans say there is more crime in the U.S. now than there was a year ago—up slightly from the 63% who said so in 2014. Meanwhile, 18% say there is less crime, and 8% say the level of crime has stayed the same.

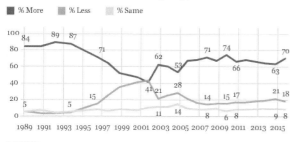

The results are based on Gallup's annual Crime poll, conducted Oct. 7–11.

Since Gallup first began asking Americans in 1989 about their perceptions of crime, majorities generally have said crime had worsened compared with the previous year—with more than 80% holding this view in the late 1980s and early 1990s. Perceptions of greater crime fell over the course of the next decade as actual crime rates dropped, and reached a record low of 41% in 2001 after 9/11. By 2002, though, this figure was back to a majority, and ranged from 53% to 74% in the decade that followed.

Government data on actual crime rates in 2015 will not be released until next year, so it is not possible to know whether Americans' perceptions of rising crime this year reflect what is currently happening in the U.S. In many large cities across the country, violent crime rates have spiked in 2015, suggesting that national crime figures could be on the rise. News reports of this increased violence may account for the uptick in perceived violence in the latest poll.

PERCEIVE MORE CRIME IN U.S. NOW THAN A YEAR AGO

2014	2015
63%	70%

GALLUP POLL

Americans' perceptions of crime, however, are not always on par with reality. Despite government data showing declining violent crime rates in the U.S. over the past two decades, majorities of Americans in Gallup's trend still maintained that crime had increased nationally. Even so, there have been notable declines in the percentage of Americans perceiving more crime when the actual crime rate has fallen, such as in the 1990s.

Government statistics show serious crime decreased nearly every year from 1994 through 2010. According to the U.S. Department of Justice, Bureau of Justice Statistics, the overall violent crime rate for rape, sexual assault, robbery, aggravated assault and simple assault fell from 80 victimizations per 1,000 persons in 1994 to 19 per 1,000 in 2010. In the first decade of that trend, public opinion followed. While 87% of Americans in 1993 said crime was up, this figure dropped to 41% in 2001. But the percentage perceiving more crime shot up again to 62% in 2002—around the time of the Washington, D.C.–area sniper shootings—and has remained fairly high ever since, despite actual crime rates falling in most years.

Though serious crime did increase in 2011 and 2012, Americans' perceptions of crime did not grow in subsequent polls, indicating that actual crime, as measured by federal crime statistics, has not strongly influenced the public's perceptions of crime in recent years.

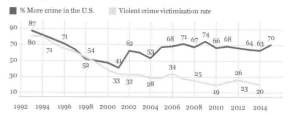

^ Violent crime rate is number of victimizations per 1,000 persons that occurred during the year. Source: Bureau of Justice Statistics, National Crime Victimization Survey, 1993-2014

GALLUP

Crime Victims No More Likely Than Nonvictims to Say Crime Is Up

Americans who say they have been victims of one of a list of eight crimes in the past 12 months are not any more likely to say crime is up than those who were not crime victims, 71% versus 70%, respectively. This is a smaller difference than Gallup has previously found between crime victims' and nonvictims' perceptions, but the differences over the years have never been large.

While majorities of Americans across other demographic and political groups perceive an increase in national crime, the extent of that view varies by subgroup.

Gallup has previously found that women are more likely than men to say crime has increased from the previous year.

Perceptions of greater crime are much lower in the West (64%)—and have been since 2011—than in the East (69%) and the South (71%), while Midwesterners (76%) are most likely to say crime has increased in the U.S. Additionally, those who live in rural areas (75%) are more inclined to say crime is up than those in suburban areas (69%) or cities (68%).

Since President Barack Obama took office in 2009, conservatives (80% this year) and Republicans (79%) have been the most likely to perceive current crime in the U.S. as higher than in the year prior, compared with liberals (57%) and Democrats (65%) who have been much less likely to say crime is up since Obama was elected. This pattern was reversed when George W. Bush was in office, with Democrats being the most likely to perceive an increase in crime.

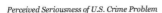

Perceptions of Increased Crime in the U.S., by Subgroup

	2014	2015	Change (pct. pts.)
Men	55	67	+12
Women	71	73	+2
East	60	69	+9
Midwest	65	76	+11
South	70	71	+1
West	53	64	+11
Conservative	68	80	+12
Moderate	66	71	+5
Liberal	47	57	+10
Republican	72	79	+7
Independent	58	69	+11
Democrat	57	65	+8
City	63	68	+5
Suburb	54	69	+15
Town/Rural	68	75	+7
Victim of a crime	65	71	+6
Not a victim of a crime	62	70	+8

October 7-11, 2015

GALLUP

Perceived Seriousness of U.S. Crime Up in 2015

Nearly six in 10 Americans (59%) say U.S. crime is an "extremely" or "very" serious problem—up slightly from 55% in 2014 and just one percentage point below the high for this measure in surveys conducted from 2000 to 2010. About one in three (35%) say the problem is "moderately" serious, while 5% say it's "not too serious" or "not serious at all."

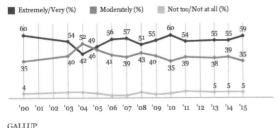

Perceived Seriousness of U.S. Crime Problem

Overall, how would you describe the problem of crime in the United States -- is it extremely serious, very serious, moderately serious, not too serious or not serious at all?

■ Extremely/Very (%) ■ Moderately (%) ▪ Not too/Not at all (%)

GALLUP

Bottom Line

A majority of Americans typically say crime is increasing compared with the previous year, even when government data suggest violent crime is falling. These perceptions have fluctuated significantly over the past 26 years, and although the current 70% who say crime is increasing is up from the last several years, it is still below the levels recorded at a number of times in previous years.

This year, there has been an uptick in Americans' perceptions of crime in the U.S. Although government reports to confirm whether this is the case are not yet available, people may be reacting to news reports of increased violent crime in many major U.S. cities.

Gallup data show that in any given year, about one in four Americans say they or someone in their household was a victim of crime, and 6% or less are the victims of violent crimes. This suggests that news media reports probably have more of an effect on Americans' perceptions of crime in the U.S. than their personal experience with crime.

Survey Methods

Results for this Gallup poll are based on telephone interviews conducted Oct. 7–11, 2015, with a random sample of 1,015 adults, aged 18 and older, living in all 50 U.S. states and the District of Columbia. For results based on the total sample of national adults, the margin of sampling error is ±4 percentage points at the 95% confidence level. All reported margins of sampling error include computed design effects for weighting.

October 22, 2015
DESPITE CRITICISM, NRA STILL ENJOYS MAJORITY SUPPORT IN U.S.

by Art Swift

Story Highlights

- *58% view National Rifle Association favorably*
- *Conservatives, gun owners lead in support for the organization*

WASHINGTON, D.C.—Despite a year of blistering criticism from gun control advocates about the National Rifle Association's hardline stance against gun restrictions amid a spate of mass shootings nationwide, 58% in the U.S. have a favorable opinion of the NRA.

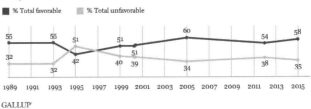

Americans' Views on the National Rifle Association (NRA)

Is your overall opinion of the National Rifle Association very favorable, mostly favorable, mostly unfavorable or very unfavorable?

■ % Total favorable ▪ % Total unfavorable

GALLUP

In a year plagued with mass shootings, including a recent tragedy at a community college in Oregon, there has been a national debate as to whether the NRA, with its ardent support for gun rights, is somehow complicit in these shootings. For example, Democratic presidential candidate Hillary Clinton has blamed the NRA for stifling the movement toward gun control. More broadly, some commentators in the news media and on social media have criticized the NRA for its theory that "a good guy with a gun" may stop "a bad guy with a gun" in mass shootings.

Yet in a Gallup poll from Oct. 7–11, a solid majority of Americans (58%) say they have an overall favorable impression of the NRA. This includes the highest recording of "very favorable" opinions (26%) since Gallup began asking this question in 1989. In December 2012, soon after the shooting at Sandy Hook Elementary

School in Connecticut, 54% of Americans had a favorable impression of the NRA. The highest percentage in Gallup's 26-year trend was in 2005, when 60% of Americans viewed the organization favorably.

AMERICANS' VIEWS ON THE NRA

TOTAL FAVORABLE

58%

GALLUP DAILY TRACKING, OCT 7-11

The lowest favorability rating was in June 1995, when 42% viewed the NRA favorably, at a time when the NRA sent out a fundraising letter calling federal law enforcement agents "jack-booted government thugs" in the wake of the Waco siege in 1993. This low favorability toward the NRA in 1995 was only compounded with the Oklahoma City bombing that spring, one month after the letter was sent to potential donors. This dispute resulted in former President George H. W. Bush publicly resigning from his lifetime membership in the NRA.

Conservative-Liberal Divide Stark in Favorable Impressions of NRA

While Americans overall view the NRA favorably, the favorable-unfavorable divide is pronounced among political ideologies. Among conservatives, 77% have an overall favorable impression of the NRA, contrasted with 30% of liberals. For conservatives this includes 41% who say they have a "very favorable" impression of the group. Ten percent of liberals share the same very favorable impression, with 45% saying that they have a "very unfavorable" opinion of the NRA.

Views of the NRA, by Ideology

	% Conservative	% Moderate	% Liberal
Very favorable	41	21	10
Mostly favorable	36	35	20
Mostly unfavorable	12	23	20
Very unfavorable	4	16	45
Total favorable	77	56	30
Total unfavorable	16	39	65

Oct. 7-11, 2015

GALLUP

Gun Owners Solidly Support the NRA, Non–Gun Owners Mixed

There is also a divide in support for the NRA among those who are gun owners and those who personally do not own a gun. Among gun owners, 78% have an overall favorable opinion of the NRA, while only 20% have an unfavorable opinion. The results are more mixed when examining non–gun owners. Forty-nine percent have a favorable opinion of the group, while 42% view it unfavorably. In the U.S., 28% say they personally own a gun.

Bottom Line

The gun safety organization has been a political advocate for gun rights, lobbying on behalf of particular legislative bills and candidates who support the Second Amendment nationwide, while lobbying against most restrictions on gun ownership. It has also stoked controversy by suggesting that more Americans should be armed in public places, and that guns are not to blame for mass shootings. In short, they believe that gun rights generally should not be restricted. Gallup's survey shows that, even after shootings nationwide, Americans overall still have a favorable opinion of the NRA, as they typically have, suggesting that the public may not be specifically blaming the organization for the crimes of those who commit mass shootings.

Views of the NRA, Among Gun Owners and Non-Gun Owners

	% Gun Owners	% Non-Gun Owners
Very favorable	42	19
Mostly favorable	36	30
Mostly unfavorable	11	20
Very unfavorable	9	22
Total favorable	78	49
Total unfavorable	20	42

Oct. 7-11, 2015

GALLUP

Survey Methods

Results for this Gallup poll are based on telephone interviews conducted Oct. 7–11, 2015, on the Gallup U.S. Daily survey, with a random sample of 1,015 adults, aged 18 and older, living in all 50 U.S. states and the District of Columbia. For results based on the total sample of national adults, the margin of sampling error is ±4 percentage points at the 95% confidence level.

October 23, 2015
OBAMA JOB APPROVAL STEADY IN 27TH QUARTER AT 45.9%

by Jeffrey M. Jones

Story Highlights

- *Average 45.9% approval similar to 46.1% in prior quarter*
- *Obama has been under 50% approval for most of his presidency*
- *Approval midrange compared with other presidents' 27th quarters*

PRINCETON, N.J.—President Barack Obama's job approval rating in his 27th quarter in office, from July 20 to Oct. 19, averaged 45.9%, essentially unchanged from his 46.1% average for the prior quarter.

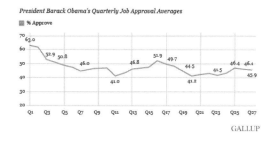

President Barack Obama's Quarterly Job Approval Averages

Obama's daily approval ratings also varied little within his most recent quarter, averaging 46% nearly every week during the quarter.

There were just two modest but notable exceptions. In late August, as U.S. stocks fell in response to concerns about problems in the Chinese economy, his weekly approval rating dipped to 44%. And in late September it rose to 48% during the week of Pope Francis's U.S. trip, which included a widely covered visit with Obama at the White House.

Since he became president nearly seven years ago, Obama has averaged 47% job approval. There have been only five quarters when he had majority approval, with four of those occurring during the first year of his presidency, the so-called honeymoon phase when new presidents tend to be rated positively. The only other time Obama's quarterly approval exceeded 50% was perhaps the most consequential one—the 16th quarter, in which he was re-elected.

Obama's 27th Quarter Midrange Compared With Other Presidents

Obama is the sixth post–World War II president to serve a 27th quarter in office. Two of these—Dwight Eisenhower and Bill Clinton—were rated quite positively at this stage in their presidencies, with average approval ratings of 65.3% and 59.7%, respectively.

In contrast, Harry Truman (23.0%) and George W. Bush (33.2%) were decidedly unpopular at the same point of their presidencies. Truman's 27th quarter average is the worst quarterly average for any president in Gallup's polling history.

Obama's 27th quarter average, along with Ronald Reagan's, is between these two extremes. Reagan averaged 47.0% approval, slightly better than Obama's 45.9%.

Job Approval Averages for Presidents During Their 27th Quarter in Office

	Dates of 27th quarter	Approval average	Number of polls
Truman	Oct 20, 1951–Jan 19, 1952	23.0%	2
Eisenhower	Jul 20–Oct 19, 1959	65.3%	4
Reagan	Jul 20–Oct 19, 1987	47.0%	2
Clinton	Jul 20–Oct 19, 1999	59.7%	7
G.W. Bush	Jul 20–Oct 19, 2007	33.2%	6
Obama	Jul 20–Oct 19, 2015	45.9%	90

Note: Harry Truman took office during the second quarter of Roosevelt's fourth term.

GALLUP

After presidents have served nearly seven years in office, Americans' opinions of them are pretty well established and unlikely to change unless a major international or domestic crisis occurs. Clinton's and Bush's approval ratings did not change between their 27th and 28th quarters. Truman, Eisenhower and Reagan saw modest improvements of a few percentage points.

Implications

Americans' opinions of Obama have been steady this year, holding near 46%. If his approval ratings do not improve dramatically during the remainder of his presidency, his full-term approval rating average, currently 47%, will rank among the lowest for post–World War II presidents, tied with Gerald Ford's and better than only Truman's (45.4%) and Jimmy Carter's (45.5%).

Obama's relatively low approval ratings may be as much a function of the era in which he is governing as it is a reflection on his leadership, management and decision-making. There have been relatively few international crises that helped to boost his public support, as the 9/11 attacks and Iraq War did for Bush, and as similar crises have done for other presidents. Arguably the only "rally event" in Obama's presidency was the capture of Osama bin Laden. Obama also took office during the Great Recession, and the economic recovery since it ended has been slow and uneven.

But Obama is also governing in a time of extreme partisan polarization. In Congress, that has meant political gridlock since Democrats lost control of the U.S. House in the 2010 midterm elections. In the American public, it is evident in his historically low support from the opposition party. Obama's average 13% approval rating among Republicans is on pace to be the lowest job approval rating from the opposition party by a full 10 percentage points, behind Bush's average 23% approval rating among Democrats. By comparison, Clinton averaged 27% approval among Republicans, and presidents before Clinton averaged 40% approval from the opposition.

Survey Methods

Results for this Gallup poll are based on telephone interviews conducted July 20–Oct. 19, 2015, on the Gallup U.S. Daily survey, with a random sample of 45,663 adults, aged 18 and older, living in all 50 U.S. states and the District of Columbia. For results based on the total sample of national adults, the margin of sampling error is ±1 percentage point at the 95% confidence level. All reported margins of sampling error include computed design effects for weighting.

October 23, 2015
FEWER REPORTED CREDIT CARD THEFT VICTIMS IN 2015 THAN 2014

by Rebecca Riffkin

Story Highlights

- *22% had credit card info stolen in past year, down from 27% in 2014*
- *Fewer worry "frequently" about credit card hacks today than in 2014*
- *Victims of credit card theft worry more than nonvictims*

WASHINGTON, D.C.—Twenty-two percent of Americans in 2015 tell Gallup that they or a household member had credit card information stolen by hackers. This is down from 27% who reported the same in 2014.

Fewer Reported Victims of Credit Card Theft in 2015 Than in 2014

Please tell me which, if any, of these incidents have happened to you or your household within the last 12 months. You or another household member had information from a credit card used at a store stolen by computer hackers.

	% Yes	% No
Oct 7–11, 2015	22	78
Oct 12–15, 2014	27	72

GALLUP

In Gallup's 2015 Crime Survey, U.S. adults were asked if they or family members were victims of nine different crimes in the past 12 months. These crimes range from credit card theft to sexual assault. Last year, when Gallup first included credit card hacking on the list, more Americans said they had been a victim of it than of any other crime. Although fewer Americans say they were victims of credit card theft this year, it remains the highest reported crime in 2015.

REPORTED VICTIMS OF CREDIT CARD THEFT IN U.S.

2014	2015
27%	22%

GALLUP POLL, OCT 7-11

2014 was a record year for hacking, in which millions of customers' credit card information was stolen. In response, many banks and credit card companies have sent their customers new cards that contain an embedded EMV chip. These chips help stop hackers from stealing a copy of a customer's credit card, but are not as useful at stopping the theft of online payment credentials. Furthermore, beginning in October 2015, stores that have not upgraded their technology to allow the use of EMV chips for purchases, and instead continue to scan magnetic strips, are liable for the theft of customer information, rather than the credit card company.

Fewer Americans Worry Frequently About Credit Card Theft in 2015

In the same poll, Gallup asks a separate question about how frequently Americans worry about 13 different crimes, such as getting mugged and car theft. This year, 34% report worrying "frequently" and 35% "occasionally" about having their credit card information stolen. While the combined 69% who worry matches the 2014 figure, the percentage who worry frequently is down from 41%, while the percentage who worry occasionally is up.

Frequent Worries About Credit Card Theft Down From 2014

How often do you, yourself, worry about the following things -- frequently, occasionally, rarely or never? How about having the credit card information you have used at stores stolen by computer hackers?

	% Frequently	% Occasionally	% Rarely	% Never
Oct 7-11, 2015	34	35	18	12
Oct 12-15, 2014	41	28	15	14

GALLUP

This indicates that while Americans are concerned about their credit card information being hacked from stores where they shopped, it is less troubling to them now than it was last year.

Victims of Credit Card Theft More Likely to Frequently Worry About It

A majority of Americans (53%) who report that they were victims of credit card theft say they also worry frequently about the crime. This contrasts with 29% of nonvictims who worry frequently about credit card theft. In 2014, Gallup found the same pattern. But victims of credit card theft were more likely to worry about it frequently last year, at 67%, than they are in 2015.

Victims of Credit Card Theft More Likely Than Nonvictims to Frequently Worry About It

% Frequently worry

	2014	2015
Victims of credit card theft	67	53
Nonvictims of credit card theft	32	29

GALLUP

Americans' lessened concern about credit card theft this year results from fewer Americans having fallen victim to this crime, as well as victims worrying less often about it than was the case a year ago.

Bottom Line

The large number of hacks in 2013 and 2014 brought significant changes, including upgrading U.S. credit cards to the chip technology used in the rest of the world. They also helped raise awareness among consumers of the need to monitor credit cards and use safe passwords. And the new chip cards will also lead to the eventual replacement of signatures, which can be forged, with PIN numbers that have to be remembered. But the machines that use these PINs have been slow to roll out, and are costly for retailers and banks to introduce. Furthermore, cards will still be vulnerable to fraudulent purchases online and over the phone, since a card number is still all a thief would need. Therefore, while the decreased number of victims and lower worry found in 2015 are promising, it is unlikely that the threat of credit card theft will disappear in the near future.

Survey Methods

Results for this Gallup poll are based on telephone interviews conducted Oct. 7–11, 2015, with a random sample of 1,015 adults, aged 18 and older, living in all 50 U.S. states and the District of Columbia. For results based on the total sample of national adults, the margin of sampling error is ±4 percentage points at the 95% confidence level. All reported margins of sampling error include computed design effects for weighting.

October 26, 2015
IN U.S., SUPPORT FOR TEA PARTY DROPS TO NEW LOW

by Jim Norman

Story Highlights

- *17% say they consider themselves Tea Party supporters*
- *54%, highest ever, neither support nor oppose the movement*
- *Major drop in support from independents who lean toward GOP*

WASHINGTON, D.C.—Americans' support for the Tea Party has dropped to its lowest level since the movement emerged on the national political scene prior to the 2010 midterm elections. Seventeen percent of Americans now consider themselves Tea Party supporters, and a record 54% say they are neither supporters nor opponents.

The Tea Party emerged in 2009 in opposition to the fledgling Obama administration, and many Americans took sides for or against the movement in the midterm elections the next year. Support peaked at 32% in November 2010, just after those elections, in which Tea Party supporters were widely credited with helping the Republican Party gain control of the U.S. House of Representatives.

As support gradually eroded over the next year, opponents of the Tea Party gained the upper hand and have led supporters in all

10 Gallup polls measuring views of the movement since the start of 2012. Since August 2012, support has failed to reach 25%, and it has fallen below 20% in each of the last two polls.

Do you consider yourself to be [a supporter of the Tea Party movement, an opponent of the Tea Party movement] or neither?

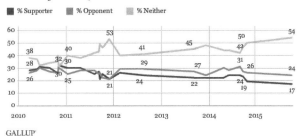

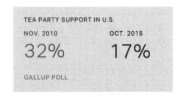

Meanwhile, opposition peaked at 31% just ahead of last year's midterm elections, but has dropped to 24% in the most recent Gallup poll, conducted Oct. 7–11.

Politics and Ideology Drive Support, Opposition

Support for and opposition to the Tea Party movement have been consistently divided along ideological and political lines over the last five years, with Republicans and conservatives the biggest supporters, and Democrats and liberals the strongest opponents.

A comparison of the combined results of the first two Gallup polls measuring Tea Party support, in March and May 2010, and the two most recent polls, from this month and November of last year, reveals where support and opposition are strongest and where the most significant changes have taken place.

Attitudes About Tea Party, 2010 and Now
Support for Tea Party in first two 2010 polls and two most recent polls

	2010 supporter	2014-2015 supporter	Change, 2010 vs. 2014-2015
	%	%	Pct. pts.
Lean Republican	52	23	-29
Republicans	52	38	-14
Republicans + leaners	52	32	-20
Conservative Republicans	63	42	-21
Moderate/Liberal Republicans	32	17	-15

Combined polls from March and May 2010 and from November 2014 and October 2015

GALLUP

Almost two-thirds (63%) of conservative Republicans were supporters in the earliest polls. About four in 10 (42%) still support the Tea Party, but the 21-percentage-point drop since the 2010 polls is second only to the plunge in support from Republican leaners (independents who lean toward the GOP). A majority (52%) of GOP leaners, a key source for Republican votes, were supporters in the 2010 polls, but a 29-point drop has left only 23% still supporting the movement.

On the other side, liberal Democrats were the strongest opponents (61%) in the two 2010 polls, and their opposition was almost as high (59%) in the two most recent polls.

A few groups that were more likely to be supporters than opponents in 2010 have since switched sides, including those 65 and older, and those who are married.

While support for the Tea Party has not increased among any major subgroup since 2010, opposition to it has gone up among one—those with postgraduate education. In the earlier polls, 36% of this group opposed the Tea Party, and that number has grown to 53%. Meanwhile, opposition has dropped in a few groups—18- to 29-year-olds, those with low incomes and unmarried females—because more in these groups no longer have an opinion about the Tea Party.

Bottom Line

Republicans made huge strides in the 2014 midterm elections, including increasing their majority in the House and gaining control of the Senate. However, the Tea Party movement that had played such a huge part in the GOP's 2010 election successes was much less visible this time around. Still, several Republicans elected to the House and Senate with Tea Party support have become major players on the national stage, including presidential candidates Marco Rubio and Ted Cruz. The Tea Party movement has also been tied to the Freedom Caucus, a group of conservative Republican members of the House who have played a key role in the current battle to select a new Speaker.

While the effects of the Tea Party movement on previous elections still resonate, the big drop in support from Republicans and Republican leaners over the past four or five years may indicate that the Tea Party movement's impact on American politics is fading.

As the 2016 campaign approaches, there are some reasons that might change:

- The drop in support for the Tea Party from Republicans and conservatives did not come about because they became opponents of the movement. Rather, the rise occurred in the percentage saying they neither opposed nor supported the movement.
- The previous low in the percentage of Americans who either supported or opposed the Tea Party came in late 2011, a few months before the first primaries of the 2012 presidential campaign. By February 2012, after the first primaries had taken place, the number who supported or opposed had grown by 13 points.

If more Americans begin taking sides on the Tea Party over the next several months as the political campaigns heat up, there's more room for a return to support among Republicans than for an increase in opposition among Democrats.

Survey Methods

Results for this Gallup poll are based on telephone interviews conducted Oct. 7–11, 2015, with a random sample of 1,015 national adults, aged 18 and older, living in all 50 U.S. states and the District of Columbia. For results based on the total sample of national adults, the margin of sampling error is ±4 percentage points at the 95% confidence level.

In addition, two sets of Gallup's polls—two from 2010 and two from last year and this year—were aggregated to create combined results from the first polls and the most recent polls testing attitudes about the Tea Party.

October 26, 2015

**ABOUT HALF OF U.S. ADULTS SAY
LOCAL CRIME IS ON THE RISE**

by Andrew Dugan

Story Highlights

- *U.S. attitudes about local crime trends are stable*
- *Majority of Americans (56%) say local crime problem is not serious*
- *64% not afraid to walk alone at night near home*

WASHINGTON, D.C.—Americans' perceptions of the trend in local crime have been steady in the past year and indeed over the last decade. Almost half of Americans say there is more crime in their local area compared with a year ago (46%), on par with the 41% to 51% range seen since 2005. Another third currently believe there is less crime in their area compared with a year ago, while 18% believe the level of criminal activity is the same.

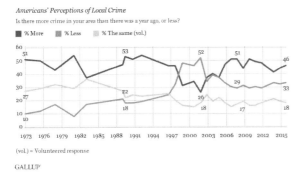

Americans' Perceptions of Local Crime

Is there more crime in your area than there was a year ago, or less?

■ % More   ■ % Less   ▒ % The same (vol.)

(vol.) = Volunteered response

GALLUP

Consistent with historical trends, a Gallup Crime poll conducted Oct. 7–11 shows Americans rate crime in the entire U.S. as much worse than they rate crime in their local area. Seven in 10 Americans believe there is more crime in the U.S. than there was last year, a seven-percentage-point increase from 2014.

Several major cities, including Baltimore, Washington, D.C., and St. Louis, are reporting higher homicide rates compared with last year, though for the most part, homicide rates remain well below the elevated levels recorded in the late 1980s and 1990s. Aggregated data for all of the nation's largest cities so far in 2015 show no signs of a broad trend toward increased violence or criminal activity that might be felt in communities across the country.

Historically, a larger share, though typically not a majority, of Americans say that local crime is on the rise from the previous year, rather than declining. Only between 1998 and 2001 did a higher level of Americans say there was less crime in their area rather than more. In 2005—not an abnormally troubled year in terms of national crime statistics—these attitudes returned to where they have been for most of Gallup's trend. And for the ensuing decade, about half of Americans have consistently assessed crime as on the increase in their local area.

But even if Americans tend to report local crime as increasing rather than decreasing, other Gallup questions indicate that few believe local crime conditions are truly dire. A combined 12% of adults describe the problem of crime in the area they live in as "extremely serious" or "very serious," slightly down from last year's 16%. On the other end of the spectrum, a majority (56%) say the problem of crime is "not too serious" or "not serious at all,"

compared with 50% last year. About a third rate the issue of local crime as "moderately serious."

The 12% who rate the local crime problem as "extremely" or "very serious" is much smaller than the 59% who say the same about the U.S. crime problem.

Meanwhile, in terms of their own personal safety, most Americans (64%) say they would not be afraid to walk alone at night within a mile of their home. This year's reading is similar to those of past polls dating back roughly 20 years. The historical high for this question occurred in 1982, when nearly half of the country said they would be afraid to walk alone at night (48%), but by 1994, that level had fallen below 40%, where it has remained since.

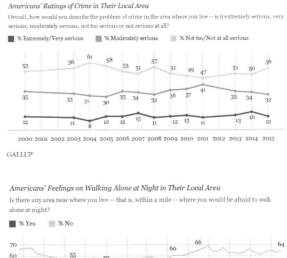

Americans' Ratings of Crime in Their Local Area

Overall, how would you describe the problem of crime in the area where you live -- is it extremely serious, very serious, moderately serious, not too serious or not serious at all?

■ % Extremely/Very serious   ■ % Moderately serious   ▒ % Not too/Not at all serious

GALLUP

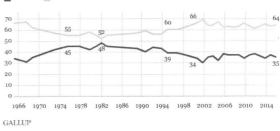

Americans' Feelings on Walking Alone at Night in Their Local Area

Is there any area near where you live -- that is, within a mile -- where you would be afraid to walk alone at night?

■ % Yes   ▒ % No

GALLUP

Bottom Line

While there is no appreciable change in how Americans perceive their local crime conditions relative to last year, a firm plurality say it is on the rise. But to the extent these perceptions are correct, there are few signs that most Americans believe their fundamental safety is in danger in their local communities. A majority rate the problem of crime in their area as not serious, while an even stronger majority say they do not feel unsafe when walking alone at night near their home. Those attitudes remain much more upbeat than Americans' assessments of crime in the broader U.S., as they typically are, most likely because Americans tend to rate local conditions better than national conditions in a variety of areas.

Survey Methods

Results for this Gallup poll are based on telephone interviews conducted Oct. 7–11, 2015, with a random sample of 1,015 adults, aged 18 and older, living in all 50 U.S. states and the District of Columbia. For results based on the total sample of national adults, the margin of sampling error is ±4 percentage points at the 95% confidence level. All reported margins of sampling error include computed design effects for weighting.

October 27, 2015
GRADS OF HISTORICALLY BLACK COLLEGES HAVE WELL-BEING EDGE

by Sean Seymour and Julie Ray

Story Highlights

- *Black HBCU grads are stronger in purpose, financial well-being*
- *College experiences different for HBCU, non-HBCU grads*
- *More black HBCU grads strongly agree they received support*

WASHINGTON, D.C.—Historically black colleges and universities (HBCUs) in the U.S. are battling a number of challenges, including declining enrollment numbers and lower-than-average graduation and retention rates. Despite these challenges, a new Gallup study reveals that black graduates of HBCUs are more likely than black graduates of other institutions to be thriving—strong, consistent and progressing—in a number of areas of their lives, particularly in their financial and purpose well-being.

Black HBCU Graduates More Likely to Be Thriving in Financial, Purpose Well-Being
% Black U.S. college graduates who are thriving in each element of well-being

	HBCU	Non-HBCU	Difference
	%	%	(pct. pts.)
Purpose Well-Being	51	43	-8
Social Well-Being	54	48	-6
Financial Well-Being	40	29	-11
Community Well-Being	42	38	-4
Physical Well-Being	33	28	-5
Thriving in all five elements of well-being	7	7	--

Gallup-Purdue Index, 2014-2015

GALLUP'

These findings are among those featured in the new *Gallup-USA Funds Minority College Graduates Report*. This report is based on the results from Gallup-Purdue Index studies in 2014 and 2015 with 55,812 college graduates aged 18 and older, with Internet access, who received bachelor's degrees between 1940 and 2015. The study included 520 black graduates of HBCUs and 1,758 black graduates of other colleges. These results are based on a Gallup model that accounts for factors such as decade of graduation, student loan debt and parents' education.

The thriving gap between black graduates of HBCUs and black graduates of other schools is largest in financial well-being, which gauges how effectively people are managing their economic lives to reduce stress and increase security. Four in 10 black HBCU graduates (40%) are thriving in this area, compared with fewer than three in 10 (29%) black graduates of other schools.

Of the five elements of well-being that Gallup measures, black graduates of HBCUs are most likely to be thriving in social (54%) and purpose (51%) well-being, which means the majority of them have strong social relationships and they like what they do each day and are motivated to achieve goals. While statistically similar percentages of black HBCU graduates and black non-HBCU graduates are thriving in social well-being, HBCU graduates lead non-HBCU graduates in purpose well-being—less than half of non-HBCU graduates (43%) are thriving in this area.

College Experiences Linked to Thriving After College

Black graduates of HBCUs are more likely than black graduates of other colleges to strongly agree they had the support and experiential learning opportunities in college that Gallup finds are strongly related to graduates' well-being later in life. In turn, these experiences may also contribute to black HBCU graduates being more likely to strongly agree that their colleges prepared them for life after graduation (55%) than black graduates of other institutions (29%).

More than one in three black HBCU graduates (35%) strongly agree that they had a professor who cared about them as a person, a professor who made them excited about learning *and* a mentor who encouraged them to pursue their goals and dreams; only 12% of black non-HBCU graduates strongly agree they had all three experiences.

In fact, black graduates of HBCUs are more likely to strongly agree they had *each* of these experiences, with the gap between HBCU and non-HBCU black graduates widest when recalling having professors who cared about them as people (58% vs. 25%).

Different Experiences for Black HBCU and Non-HBCU Grads
% Black U.S. college graduates who strongly agree

	HBCUs	Non-HBCUs	Difference (pct. pts.)
My professors at My University cared about me as a person.	58%	25%	-33
I had at least one professor at My University who made me excited about learning.	74%	62%	-12
While attending My University, I had a mentor who encouraged me to pursue my goals and dreams.	42%	23%	-19
Felt Support	35%	12%	-23
While attending My University, I had an internship or job that allowed me to apply what I was learning in the classroom.	41%	31%	-10
While attending My University, I worked on a project that took a semester or more to complete.	36%	30%	-6
I was extremely active in extracurricular activities and organizations while attending My University.	32%	23%	-9
Experiential Learning	13%	7%	-6

Gallup-Purdue Index, 2014-2015

GALLUP'

A similar positive relationship exists with experiential learning opportunities—black graduates of HBCUs are more likely to report involvement in applied internships, long-term projects and extracurricular activities.

Implications

Although HBCUs are struggling in a number of areas, their overall success in providing black graduates with a better college experience than they would receive at non-HBCUs needs to be examined more closely and potentially modeled at other institutions. The profoundly different experiences that black graduates of HBCUs and non-HBCUs are having in college may leave HBCU graduates feeling better prepared for life afterward and potentially lead these two groups to live vastly different lives after college.

Survey Methods

Results represent data collected over the course of two years as part of the National Gallup-Purdue Index.

Year one of the study was conducted Feb. 4–March 7, 2014, with a random sample of 29,560 respondents with a bachelor's degree or higher, aged 18 and older, with Internet access, living in all 50 U.S. states and the District of Columbia. The sample was compiled from two sources: the Gallup Panel and the Gallup Daily tracking survey.

The Gallup Panel is a proprietary, probability-based longitudinal panel of U.S. adults that are selected using random-digit-dial (RDD) and address-based sampling methods. The Gallup Panel is not an opt-in panel and includes 60,000 individuals. Gallup Panel members with a college degree and with access to the Internet were invited to take the Gallup-Purdue Index survey online.

The Gallup Daily tracking survey sample includes national adults with a minimum quota of 50 percent cellphone respondents and 50 percent landline respondents, with additional minimum quotas by time zone within region. Landline and cellular telephone numbers are selected using RDD methods. Landline respondents are chosen at random within each household on the basis of which member had the most recent birthday. Gallup Daily tracking respondents with a college degree who agreed to future contact were invited to take the Gallup-Purdue Index survey online.

Year two of the study was conducted Dec. 16, 2014–June 29, 2015, with a random sample of 30,151 respondents with a bachelor's degree or higher, aged 18 and older, with Internet access, living in all 50 U.S. states and the District of Columbia. The sample was recruited using the Gallup Daily tracking survey.

Gallup-Purdue Index interviews are conducted via the Web, in English only. Samples are weighted to correct for unequal selection probability and nonresponse. The data are weighted to match national demographics of gender, age, race, Hispanic ethnicity, education and region. Demographic weighting targets are based on the most recent Current Population Survey figures for the aged 18 and older population with a U.S. bachelor's degree or higher.

All reported margins of sampling error for the Gallup-Purdue Index of all college graduates include the computed design effects for weighting.

For results based on the total sample of black HBCU graduates, the margin of sampling error is ±6.1 percentage points at the 95% confidence level.

For results based on the total sample of black graduates of other schools, the margin of sampling error is ±3.3 percentage points at the 95% confidence level.

For results based on the total sample of those with a bachelor's degree or higher, the margin of sampling error is ±0.6 percentage points at the 95% confidence level.

For results based on employee engagement of those with a bachelor's degree or higher, the margin of sampling error is ±0.8 percentage points at the 95% confidence level.

In addition to sampling error, question wording and practical difficulties in conducting surveys can introduce error or bias into the findings of public opinion polls.

October 27, 2015
GRADUATES EXPOSED TO DIVERSITY BELIEVE DEGREE MORE VALUABLE

by Stephanie Marken

Story Highlights

- *Grads with exposure twice as likely to say degree is worth it*
- *Public college graduates most likely to experience diversity*
- *Grads with exposure more likely to be engaged in jobs*

WASHINGTON, D.C.—Public college or university graduates are more likely than those who graduated from a private university to strongly agree that they were exposed to people of different backgrounds during their collegiate experience. If U.S. college graduates strongly agree that they interacted with people from different backgrounds on a regular basis in college, the odds that they believe their college degree was worth the cost are 2.2 times higher than other graduates who do not strongly agree that they interacted with people from different backgrounds.

The Gallup-Purdue Index explores the perceived value of a college degree by asking respondents the extent to which they believe their degree was worth the cost. The relationship between being exposed to people from different backgrounds and believing their college degree was worth the cost exists even after controlling for personality type, student loan amounts and other collegiate experiences that Gallup has previously demonstrated correlate with the perceived value of a college degree.

Gallup evaluated data from this study as the U.S. Supreme Court prepared to review a potentially landmark case on affirmative action brought against the University of Texas at Austin by applicant Abigail Fisher. Fisher, who first took her case to the U.S. Supreme Court in 2008, contends that the university's affirmative action policy resulted in her rejection by the university. While the Supreme Court sent the case back to a lower court, it has returned to the Supreme Court for another review. The Supreme Court's decision will set a legal precedent that could affect students' exposure to diversity throughout their higher education experience.

Public College Graduates More Likely to Be Exposed to Diversity

Researchers have consistently demonstrated a relationship between exposure to people from different backgrounds in educational settings and positive long-term outcomes, including increases in cultural awareness and a commitment to racial understanding. The Gallup-Purdue Index explores this phenomenon by asking college graduates the extent to which they agree or disagree that they were exposed to people from different backgrounds on a regular basis during their undergraduate experience.

Gallup asked this question of recent college graduates who obtained their degree between 2010 and 2015 because these graduates should be most likely to accurately recall their experiences with diversity. Slightly less than half (46%) of all recent college graduates strongly agree they were exposed to people from different backgrounds on a regular basis during their undergraduate experience. Public college graduates (49%) are most likely to strongly agree they interacted with people of different backgrounds while in college, followed closely by private for-profit graduates (46%) and private not-for-profit graduates (41%).

These results are based on the 2015 Gallup-Purdue Index survey of college graduates. The Gallup-Purdue Index survey is a comprehensive, nationally representative study of U.S. college graduates, aged 18 and older, with Internet access, conducted Dec. 16, 2014–June 29, 2015, with a random sample of 30,151 respondents with a bachelor's degree or higher.

College Graduates' Exposure to People From Different Backgrounds, by College Type

While attending (University Name) I interacted with people from different backgrounds on a regular basis.

	All college graduates	Public	Private not-for-profit	Private for-profit
	%	%	%	%
5 (strongly agree)	46	49	41	46
4	30	31	30	31
3	14	11	16	16
2	7	7	10	5
1 (strongly disagree)	3	2	3	3

Gallup-Purdue Index

GALLUP

Graduates With Greater Exposure More Likely to Be Engaged in Their Job

If recent college graduates strongly agree that they interacted with people from different backgrounds in college, the odds that they are engaged in their current job are 1.4 times higher than other graduates who do not strongly agree with this statement, suggesting a link between exposure to diversity and future work fulfillment for college graduates.

More than half (55%) of recent college graduates who are currently engaged in their job strongly agree that they were exposed to people from different backgrounds during their collegiate experience. In contrast, 35% of recent college graduates who are actively disengaged in their job strongly agree with this statement. Even after controlling for other factors that Gallup has identified, including personality type, student loan amounts and other collegiate experiences, this relationship is linked to employee engagement.

College Graduates' Exposure to People From Different Backgrounds, by Employee Engagement in Current Job

While attending (University Name) I interacted with people from different backgrounds on a regular basis.

	Engaged	Not engaged	Actively disengaged
	%	%	%
5 (strongly agree)	55	43	35
4	23	36	30
3	12	13	16
2	7	7	10
1 (strongly disagree)	3	2	3

Gallup-Purdue Index

GALLUP

Implications

Results from this study indicate that exposure to people of different backgrounds provides graduates with a greater sense of value of the cost of their college degree. While colleges and universities often strive for diversity among their student population, Gallup's research indicates that graduates also view these practices as beneficial in contributing to the overall value of their degree.

For some students, college represents the first opportunity to engage with others from different backgrounds. The Gallup data suggest such students could benefit from more deliberate efforts among colleges and universities to encourage interactions between students from different backgrounds. The upcoming Supreme Court review of the University of Texas's affirmative action policy will have a tremendous bearing on the extent to which colleges and universities can encourage diversity within their student population.

Survey Methods

Results for the Gallup-Purdue Index are based on Web surveys conducted Dec. 16, 2014–June 29, 2015, with a random sample of 30,151 respondents with a bachelor's degree or higher and 4,753 respondents who obtained their degree between 2010 and 2015, aged 18 and older, with Internet access, living in all 50 U.S. states and the District of Columbia.

The Gallup-Purdue Index sample was recruited via the Gallup Daily tracking survey. The Gallup Daily tracking survey sample includes national adults with a minimum quota of 50% cellphone respondents and 50% landline respondents, with additional minimum quotas by time zone within region. Landline and cellular telephone numbers are selected using random-digit-dial methods.

Gallup-Purdue Index interviews are conducted via the Web, in English only. Samples are weighted to correct for unequal selection probability and nonresponse. The data are weighted to match national demographics of gender, age, race, Hispanic ethnicity, education and region provided by the Current Population Survey.

All reported margins of sampling error for the Gallup-Purdue Index of all college graduates include the computed design effects for weighting.

For results based on recent college graduates with a bachelor's degree or higher, the margin of sampling error is ±2.2 percentage points at the 95% confidence level.

October 27, 2015

BEN CARSON WILL BE BEST-LIKED CANDIDATE ON DEBATE STAGE

by Frank Newport

Story Highlights

- *Carson's net favorable score of +60 tops GOP field*
- *Carson's unfavorable rating low compared with Trump, Bush, Christie*
- *Republicans' views of most candidates stable*

PRINCETON, N.J.—Republicans preparing to watch Wednesday night's GOP debate have varying opinions of the candidates vying for their party's nomination. The candidates' net favorable scores range from +60 for Ben Carson to +8 for John Kasich and +10 for Chris Christie. Carson's strength of image is formidable; his net favorable score—the difference between his favorable and unfavorable ratings—is 20 percentage points higher than the next-highest-rated candidate, Marco Rubio. Donald Trump and Jeb Bush both have relatively high unfavorable ratings, pushing their net favorable scores well below those of several other candidates.

Carly Fiorina has the third-highest net favorable rating of the nine Republicans Gallup is now tracking, at +33, followed by Mike Huckabee, Ted Cruz and Trump. Bush, whose familiarity among Republicans is second only to Trump's, has a net favorable score of +19, above only Christie and Kasich.

Carson's big lead on the measure of net favorability is based on his 68% favorable rating, the highest of any candidate, and his 8% unfavorable rating, which is the lowest.

GOP Candidate Images

Among Republicans/Republican-leaning independents

	Favorable	Unfavorable	Net favorable
	%	%	(pct. pts.)
Ben Carson	68	8	+60
Marco Rubio	55	15	+40
Carly Fiorina	46	13	+33
Mike Huckabee	52	20	+32
Ted Cruz	49	18	+31
Donald Trump	58	34	+24
Jeb Bush	50	31	+19
Chris Christie	40	30	+10
John Kasich	26	18	+8

Oct. 13-26, 2015

GALLUP

The upcoming debate at the University of Colorado in Boulder is the third time Republicans will face off this election cycle, following those held on Aug. 6 and Sept. 16. Gallup's candidate image ratings are based on interviews conducted Oct. 13–26 with approximately 800 to 900 Republicans and Republican-leaning independents evaluating each candidate.

Carson and Fiorina Have Benefited Most From Debates

Debates can make at least some difference in the way Republicans view candidates, and the elapsed time since the first debate in early August has been particularly positive for Carson and Fiorina. Just prior to the first debate, Carson's net favorable score was essentially tied with Rubio's, with Fiorina near the bottom of the list. By the eve of the second debate, both Carson's and Fiorina's images had improved significantly, and have stayed the same or edged up further in the time since. Christie's image has also improved, but given his starting point at -2 prior to the first debate, his current +10 net favorable score places him just above Kasich at the bottom of the list.

Notably, Kasich and Bush are the only candidates whose images are worse now than just prior to the first debate, although Bush's current +19 is an improvement over the depths to which he fell just before the second debate. Kasich's image did rise shortly after the first debate, but then fell back again and has remained low since.

Net favorable scores for Rubio, Cruz and Huckabee have not changed much over time.

Trends in Net Favorable Scores: Republican Candidates

Net favorable scores among Republicans/Republican-leaning independents

	Pre-1st debate: Jul 24-Aug 6	Pre-2nd debate: Sep 2-16	Pre-3rd debate: Oct 13-26	Change: Pre-1st debate to present
Ben Carson	+36	+57	+60	+24
Marco Rubio	+37	+34	+40	+3
Carly Fiorina	+14	+32	+33	+19
Mike Huckabee	+29	+31	+32	+3
Ted Cruz	+29	+32	+31	+2
Donald Trump	+19	+27	+24	+5
Jeb Bush	+24	+15	+19	-5
Chris Christie	-2	+3	+10	+12
John Kasich	+18	+16	+8	-10

GALLUP

Republicans' views of Trump have varied over the last three months. Although his current net favorable score is higher than it was prior to the first debate in early August, Gallup's two-week rolling averages show considerable change. His net favorable score rose

going into the second debate in September and fell after the debate, but has now returned to where it was.

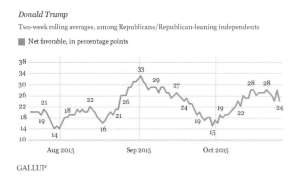

Donald Trump

Two-week rolling averages, among Republicans/Republican-leaning independents

Net favorable, in percentage points

GALLUP

What the Data Mean for the Debate

Carson's "softer" presentation of self in previous debates has worked well for the former neurosurgeon among the GOP faithful, and he goes into the debate Wednesday with high positive ratings and low negative ratings. His main challenge will be to convince future GOP primary voters that he has issue positions and capabilities that would make him a viable choice for their party's nomination.

The debate will be critical for Bush, who to date has not been able to parlay his high name recognition into a strongly positive image among Republicans. A glimmer of good news comes from the trend on his image, which is now a bit more positive than it was just prior to the second debate—but the former Florida governor has a challenging road ahead as he tries to improve his image among Republicans.

Trump will be the most polarizing candidate on stage in the debate, with both the second-highest favorable percentage of any candidate and the highest unfavorable percentage. His variable image thus far suggests that his debate performance Wednesday night could move Republicans in either direction.

Rubio and Fiorina are both in relatively solid positions, with net favorable ratings second only to Carson's. Fiorina's positioning rose significantly after the first debate and has stayed steady since; her goal Wednesday night will be to continue to use the national stage to increase her name identification and positive ratings. Rubio's positive image puts him in a good position to build on his "slow but steady" strategy to have Republicans view him as a viable candidate.

Cruz's and Huckabee's images have been steady over time, and both will want to use the debate to gain more positive ratings and momentum. Christie faces the challenge of attempting to attract positive attention while chipping away at his high negatives, while Kasich's main objective will be to attract attention in general, given that over half of Republicans don't know enough about him to have an opinion.

From a broad perspective, the data show that while the first debate did affect how Republicans viewed a few candidates, there has been general stability since for most candidates. Thus, it may be unlikely that the Wednesday debate—barring a major gaffe or high-visibility moment—will dramatically reshuffle the way Republicans view the candidates vying for their votes.

Survey Methods

Results for this Gallup poll are based on telephone interviews conducted Oct. 13–26, 2015, on the Gallup U.S. Daily survey, with a random sample of 3,133 Republicans and Republican-leaning independents, aged 18 and older, living in all 50 U.S. states and the District of Columbia. Each candidate was rated by a random subset of respondents during this period, with the sample sizes rating each candidate averaging between approximately 800 and 900 Republicans and Republican-leaning independents.

For results based on the total sample of Republicans and Republican-leaning independents, aged 18 and older, rating each candidate, the margin of sampling error is ±3 percentage points at the 95% confidence level. All reported margins of sampling error include computed design effects for weighting.

October 28, 2015
REPUBLICANS' VIEWS OF MCCONNELL NOW TILT NEGATIVE

by Jeffrey M. Jones

PRINCETON, N.J.—Republicans are more likely to have an unfavorable opinion (35%) of Senate Majority Leader Mitch McConnell than a favorable one (30%). Just 18 months ago, Republicans were twice as likely to view him positively (47%) as negatively (23%).

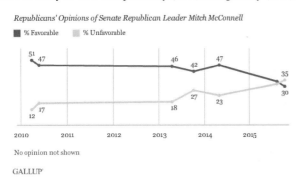

Republicans' Opinions of Senate Republican Leader Mitch McConnell

No opinion not shown

GALLUP

Republicans viewed McConnell favorably from 2010—three years after he became the party's Senate leader—through 2014. During his time as minority leader, his favorable ratings were generally near 50% and his unfavorable ratings near 20%.

That has changed now that Republicans have control of the U.S. Senate, and McConnell is the legislative leader of that chamber. In an August poll, Republicans' opinions of McConnell were evenly divided at 34% favorable and 32% unfavorable. But in the last couple of months, their opinions of him have tilted negative.

Soon-to-be-former Speaker of the House John Boehner is also viewed more negatively than positively by his party base. Like McConnell, Boehner had been rated more positively than negatively by the GOP before this year.

GOP OPINIONS OF MITCH MCCONNELL

FAVORABLE 30%

UNFAVORABLE 35%

GALLUP POLL, OCT 7-11

It is unusual for a legislative leader to be viewed more negatively than positively among rank-and-file supporters of the party.

But Republicans' views of McConnell and Boehner may be suffering this year because the party base is frustrated with the lack of legislative success, even though the GOP has control of both houses of Congress for the first time since 2006. Divided party control of the federal government, with a Democratic president who is unsympathetic to GOP initiatives, is a major impediment to Republicans' achieving their policy goals.

Frustration with the party's congressional leadership helps explain why Republicans are less likely to approve of the job the GOP-controlled Congress is doing (9%) than are Democrats (13%) and independents (16%). Typically, congressional approval ratings are significantly higher among supporters of the majority party.

The Oct. 7–11 poll was conducted before Obama, McConnell and other congressional leaders agreed on a deal this week to raise the debt ceiling limit and fund the government through early 2017. That bipartisan agreement may improve McConnell's image among Democrats and independents, but may not help his cause among the GOP base. Democrats and independents have consistently rated McConnell more negatively than positively, and their ratings of him this year are no worse than they were last year.

McConnell Favorable Among All Americans at New Low

Given the trends in opinions of McConnell by political party, it is no surprise that his 18% favorable rating among all Americans is his worst to date—slightly worse than the 22% he has averaged since October 2013, around the time of the last major federal government shutdown. Currently, 41% of Americans have an unfavorable opinion of McConnell, and 40% are not familiar enough with him to rate him.

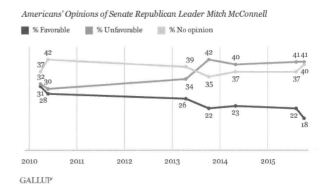

Americans' Opinions of Senate Republican Leader Mitch McConnell

GALLUP

McConnell has never been very popular among all Americans—his best reviews to date came in 2010, when opinions of him were about equally positive and negative. That included 31% favorable and 32% unfavorable ratings in March 2010. By April 2013, opinions of him turned more negative (34%) than positive (26%), and grew significantly worse during the October 2013 shutdown.

Implications

Boehner stunned political observers when he announced he would resign as Speaker of the House, partly because of frustration with his leadership among Republicans in Congress. McConnell, along with presumptive Speaker-to-be Paul Ryan, will now attempt to move the GOP agenda forward.

But McConnell is in little better shape image-wise among Republican supporters nationwide than Boehner was, though the majority leader may be facing less internal pressure from his

Republican Senate colleagues to step aside than Boehner did from his fellow House Republicans.

Whether McConnell can regain past goodwill among his party's supporters is unclear. If the party base is upset with him mainly because the GOP has failed to get legislation it favors passed into law, then prospects of a near-term recovery of his image appear slim. Obama would likely veto Republican-favored legislation, assuming it could pass through a possible Senate filibuster. If the party base is upset with McConnell mainly because it perceives the leadership has not tried hard enough to advance GOP legislation, then a more aggressive approach from him and Ryan may win the majority leader back some of his lost support.

Survey Methods

Results for this Gallup poll are based on telephone interviews conducted Oct. 7–11, 2015, with a random sample of 1,015 adults, aged 18 and older, living in all 50 U.S. states and the District of Columbia. For results based on the total sample of national adults, the margin of sampling error is ±4 percentage points at the 95% confidence level. All reported margins of sampling error include computed design effects for weighting.

October 29, 2015
BLACK DEMOCRATS' LIFE RATINGS SLIP IN OBAMA'S SECOND TERM

by Dan Witters and Frank Newport

Story Highlights

- *Blacks of both parties evaluated lives better after Obama was first elected*
- *White Republicans evaluated lives worse after Obama's first term*
- *Black Democrats' life ratings have partially slipped during second term*

WASHINGTON, D.C.—Within the first two years after President Barack Obama's inauguration in January 2009, blacks' average life evaluation rating increased. Black Democrats' overall rating rose especially sharply, but black Republicans' rating also improved. During Obama's second term, however, black Democrats' average life evaluation rating has worsened, although it remains better than in 2008, before Obama took office.

Life Evaluation by Race and Political Identity*
% Thriving

	2008	2009-2010	Change from 2008 to 2009-2010	2011-2012	2013-2015	Change from 2011-2012 to 2013-2015
	%	%	(pct. pts.)	%	%	(pct. pts.)
Black Democrats	46.6	56.4	+9.8	57.1	52.6	-4.5
White Democrats	45.3	53.7	+8.4	55.1	54.8	-0.3
Black Republicans	50.9	54.7	+3.8	56.2	54.7	-1.5
White Republicans	54.4	51.9	-2.5	51.2	54.9	+3.7

Gallup-Healthways Well-Being Index
* Includes those who lean toward listed party

GALLUP

Gallup and Healthways measure Americans' life evaluations as part of the Gallup-Healthways Well-Being Index. Gallup and Healthways classify Americans as "thriving," "struggling" or "suffering" according to how they rate their current and future lives on a ladder scale, with steps numbered from 0 to 10 based on the Cantril Self-Anchoring Striving Scale. Those who rate their present life a 7 or higher and their life in five years an 8 or higher are classified as thriving.

Black Democrats' life evaluation rating improved by nearly 10 percentage points between the 2008 baseline and 2009–2010, to the point where 56.4% were classified as thriving. The percentage of black Republicans who were thriving also improved, but by less than half that amount.

The percentage of white Democrats who were thriving rose by more than eight points to 53.7%—second only to the improvement seen among black Democrats. Meanwhile, the percentage of white Republicans who were thriving in their life evaluations dropped by more than two points to 51.9%, moving from the highest life evaluation among all groups in 2008 to the lowest during 2009–2010. This realignment was preserved through the end of Obama's first term, with both black Democrats and black Republicans evaluating their lives better than their white counterparts.

The initial shifts in life evaluation after President Obama first took office underscore the power of the presidency in providing a window through which Americans view certain aspects of their lives—even aspects seemingly not directly related to politics. While not the only factors, both the political identification and the race of Americans are related to how Obama's taking office changed their personal life evaluation assessment. White and black Democrats' evaluations improved dramatically, while white Republicans' evaluations fell. But the race factor was seemingly more salient to the small number of black Republicans than was their partisanship, as their life evaluation score rose as well.

However, the apparent effect of Obama's presidency on blacks' and whites' life evaluations seems to have waned during Obama's second term. Life evaluations have dropped somewhat among black Democrats, while among white Republicans they have rebounded to match pre-Obama levels. Black Republicans' life ratings have dropped slightly, by less than two percentage points, while white Democrats' ratings remain essentially unchanged.

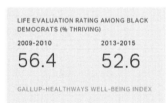

LIFE EVALUATION RATING AMONG BLACK DEMOCRATS (% THRIVING)

2009-2010	2013-2015
56.4	52.6

GALLUP-HEALTHWAYS WELL-BEING INDEX

Under Obama, Blacks' Life Evaluations Improved Most

Despite the recent ups and downs in life evaluations among black Democrats, blacks' average life evaluation rating is more improved relative to 2008 than that of any other racial or party group. Averaging 53.0% since 2013, blacks' overall life evaluation is six points higher than in 2008 and matches the current life evaluation thriving rates of U.S. whites and Hispanics.

All three groups' life evaluation thriving rates have improved by statistically significant amounts since 2008, although the gains among blacks—particularly during the first half of Obama's first term—are much sharper than those seen among whites and Hispanics. The overall improvement in blacks' life evaluations has occurred despite the fact that blacks are the only group to report an overall decline during Obama's second term.

Nationwide, American adults evaluated their lives better in 2014 than in any of the previous six years, improving to 54.1% thriving. This is after four years of mostly stable measurement for life evaluation.

Life Evaluation Among Whites, Blacks and Hispanics
% Thriving

	2008	2009-2010	2011-2012	2013-2015	Change from 2008 to 2013-2015
	%	%	%	%	(pct. pts.)
All U.S. adults	48.9	52.5	53.0	53.7	+4.8
Whites	49.2	51.8	52.1	53.6	+4.4
Blacks	46.9	56.1	56.5	53.0	+6.1
Hispanics	50.6	53.8	53.8	54.5	+3.9

Gallup-Healthways Well-Being Index

GALLUP'

Implications

These data show that something as seemingly distant from Americans' personal lives as the election of a new president and the policies that he advocates can affect the way they view their lives. President Obama's Democratic Party affiliation and his race both had an apparent effect. While both black Democrats and black Republicans' life evaluations improved after he was first elected, the former group saw roughly twice the gain, suggesting that the dual factors of race and party could have driven the change. Among whites, race identity was less of a factor, as white Democrats improved during Obama's first term while white Republicans declined.

The moderate erosion in life evaluations among black Democrats over the course of Obama's second term, coupled with the recovery in life evaluations among white Republicans, has partially dismantled the pattern established during his first. It is possible that the life evaluation ratings of some blacks were adversely affected by the highly publicized civil unrest during Obama's second term, such as the events of Ferguson, Missouri, and Baltimore, Maryland. White Republicans, in turn, may have experienced a boost to their life evaluations during Obama's second term as a result of substantial electoral gains Republicans in Congress made during this period, as well as hopes of retaking the White House in 2016.

Survey Methods

These results are based on telephone interviews conducted Jan. 2–Dec. 30, 2008–2014, and Jan. 2–Sept. 25, 2015, as part of the Gallup-Healthways Well-Being Index, with a random sample of adults identifying as Democrats/Democratic leaners or Republicans/Republican leaners and who also identify as white, black or Hispanic. There were 259,139 such respondents interviewed in 2008, 489,093 adults in 2009–2010, 491,727 adults in 2011–2012 and 91,976 adults in 2013–2015. All were aged 18 and older, living in all 50 U.S. states and the District of Columbia. The margin of sampling error for each reported group is no more than ±1 percentage point in most cases, but climbs closer to ±3 percentage points among black Republicans in the 2013–2015 period. All reported margins of sampling error include computed design effects for weighting.

Sample Sizes of Key Reporting Groups

	Black Democrats	White Democrats	Black Republicans	White Republicans
2008	18,407	119,823	1,329	119,580
2009-2010	32,884	207,084	2,877	246,248
2011-2012	42,039	197,818	4,473	247,397
2013-2015	8,516	35,636	1,053	46,771

Gallup-Healthways Well-Being Index
* Includes those who lean toward listed party

GALLUP'

October 29, 2015
AMERICANS' FEARS ABOUT ROBBERY AND THEFT DOWN IN 2015

by Justin McCarthy

Story Highlights

- *About four in 10 worry about car or home being broken into*
- *One in four worry about muggings, burglaries while they're home*
- *Identity theft, credit card hacking top list of crime worries*

WASHINGTON, D.C.—Americans' concerns about being robbed in a variety of settings fell over the past year, putting these figures at decade-long lows. They are most frequently worried about their cars being stolen or broken into (40%), or their homes being burglarized when they are not home (39%)—both are record lows for the 15-year trend. Additionally, they show slightly less concern about more confrontational robberies such as getting mugged and having their house burglarized while they are home (25% each).

Americans' Worries About Various Theft/Robbery Scenarios
How often do you, yourself, worry about the following things -- frequently, occasionally, rarely or never?

% Frequently/Occasionally worry

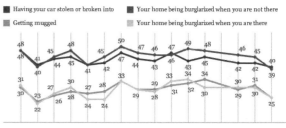

GALLUP'

Worry about each of these crimes reached lows similar to today's readings in 2001, based on the percentage of those who say they "frequently" or "occasionally" worry about them. That was a month after the attacks on 9/11, when Americans' views on a variety of subjects were more positive than usual. Americans' worries about all four of these crimes spiked in 2002–2003 and 2006.

The percentage of Americans worried about the less confrontational crimes—theft involving a car or an unoccupied home—have been up near 50% at several times over the past 15 years. Americans' worry about the more confrontational crimes—muggings and having their home burglarized while they *are* home—has been consistently lower, with peaks of around 33% since 2001.

The latest data are from Gallup's annual Crime poll, conducted Oct. 7–11.

Seven in 10 Worry About Identity Theft, Hacking of Credit Card Info

Though theft and robberies worry a sizable percentage of Americans, identify theft and credit card fraud produce even more anxiety. About seven in 10 say they "frequently" or "occasionally" worry about having computer hackers steal their credit card information from stores they have visited, and the same percentage worry about being a victim of identity theft.

A third of Americans frequently or occasionally worry about having a school-aged child physically harmed while at school, but this rises to 48% among parents of children younger than 18.

Americans' Worries About Various Crimes

How often do you, yourself, worry about the following things -- frequently, occasionally, rarely or never? How about ...

	% Frequently or occasionally worry
Having the credit card information you have used at stores stolen by computer hackers	69
Being a victim of identity theft	69
Having your car stolen or broken into	40
Your home being burglarized when you are not there	39
Having a school-aged child of yours physically harmed while attending school	33
Being a victim of terrorism	27
Getting mugged	25
Your home being burglarized when you are there	25
Being the victim of a hate crime	19
Being attacked while driving your car	17
Getting murdered	17
Being sexually assaulted	16
Being assaulted/killed by a coworker/employee where you work	7

Oct. 7–11, 2015

GALLUP

As the rank-order of crimes indicates, Americans tend to be less worried about more violent crimes. About a quarter say they frequently or occasionally worry about being a victim of terrorism (27%), and about one in five say they worry about being the victim of a hate crime (19%).

Seventeen percent say they worry about being attacked while driving their car or getting murdered, while 16% worry about being sexually assaulted. Being assaulted or killed by a coworker or employee where they work is the crime Americans worry about the least (7%).

Bottom Line

It is a bit peculiar that Americans are less worried about theft and robberies today than at any time in the past decade, given that they perceive crime as being on the rise—although majorities nearly always believe crime is increasing. It will be important to see if the pattern persists in next year's crime update. While fewer Americans are worried about certain crimes, there has been no change in their frequency of worry about others, including being a victim of a hate crime or of terrorism, or having their children physically harmed at school.

The only crimes that the majority of Americans fret over are identify theft and credit card hacking, though these offenses have become common only in the more recent past. Americans tend to concern themselves more with theft than they do murder and sexual assault, suggesting the low prevalence of violent crimes relative to theft offsets their more troubling nature.

Survey Methods

Results for this Gallup poll are based on telephone interviews conducted Oct. 7–11, 2015, on the Gallup U.S. Daily survey, with a random sample of 1,015 adults, aged 18 and older, living in all 50 U.S. states and the District of Columbia. For results based on the total sample of national adults, the margin of sampling error is ±4 percentage points at the 95% confidence level. All reported margins of sampling error include computed design effects for weighting.

November 02, 2015

U.S. CONSUMER SPENDING UP IN OCTOBER, AT $92

by Justin McCarthy

Story Highlights

* *Ranks among highest monthly averages in 2015*
* *Strongest October spending average since 2008*

WASHINGTON, D.C.—Americans' daily self-reports of spending averaged $92 in October, up $4 from September. This is just above the $81 to $91 range seen since January 2015.

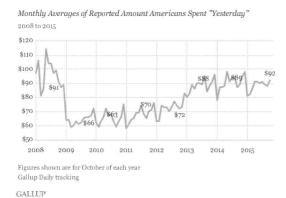

Monthly Averages of Reported Amount Americans Spent "Yesterday"
2008 to 2015

Figures shown are for October of each year
Gallup Daily tracking

GALLUP

Compared with Octobers in prior years, last month's $92 average is similar to readings from 2008 ($91), 2013 ($88) and 2014, but it is significantly higher than the October averages in 2009–2012, which ranged from $63 to $72.

AVERAGE SELF-REPORTED DAILY U.S.
CONSUMER SPENDING, OCTOBER

$92

GALLUP DAILY TRACKING

Depending on November's spending figure, 2015 could follow the autumn spending pattern of the previous two years, as well as those of 2010 and 2011, in which spending increased in both October and November. Monthly averages fell dramatically in the fall months of 2008 as the global economic crisis was unfolding, and stagnated during this period in 2009 and 2012.

September-to-October changes have seen mixed results. In recent years, spending was slightly higher in October. In some years, such as 2009 and 2012, spending dipped slightly or was flat. In 2008, though, average daily spending fell $8 from September to October at the onset of the economic crisis.

Bottom Line

Americans spent more on average each day in October than in September this year, and the October average is among the highest in 2015 so far. Spending during the last three Octobers was higher than during previous Octobers going back to 2008.

November's spending average will be important to monitor. While spending increases are practically a given for the month of December, such increases are not guaranteed for November.

However, Gallup has measured an October–November decline only once, in 2008, as the nation was reeling from the effects of the financial crisis. Other Gallup research shows that Americans are planning to spend more this year on Christmas presents than in recent years, suggesting that the October uptick could be another indicator of robust retail spending as 2015 draws to a close.

Average Reported U.S. Consumer Spending, September–November
Monthly averages

	September	October	November
2015	$88	$92	--
2014	$87	$89	$95
2013	$84	$88	$91
2012	$74	$72	$73
2011	$65	$70	$71
2010	$59	$63	$66
2009	$66	$66	$67
2008	$99	$91	$87

Gallup Daily tracking

GALLUP

Survey Methods

Results for this Gallup poll are based on telephone interviews conducted Oct. 1–31, 2015, on the Gallup U.S. Daily survey, with a random sample of 15,232 adults, aged 18 and older, living in all 50 U.S. states and the District of Columbia. The margin of error for the spending mean is ±$5. All reported margins of sampling error include computed design effects for weighting.

November 03, 2015

U.S. ECONOMIC CONFIDENCE INDEX STEADY AT -13

by Rebecca Riffkin

Story Highlights

* *Monthly Economic Confidence Index steady since July*
* *Index has been below -10 for four months*
* *Weekly index averaged -15 for last week of October*

WASHINGTON, D.C.—Gallup's Economic Confidence Index averaged -13 in October. This is essentially the same as the -14 average for September. The index has declined since peaking at +3 in January 2015, and has remained below -10 for four months.

For the week of Oct. 26–Nov. 1, Gallup's weekly Economic Confidence Index averaged -15, in line with all recent estimates.

MONTHLY U.S. ECONOMIC CONFIDENCE
INDEX, OCTOBER

-13

GALLUP U.S. DAILY TRACKING

Gallup's Economic Confidence Index is the average of two components: how Americans rate current economic conditions and whether they say the economy is improving or getting worse. Since March, Americans have consistently viewed the outlook for the economy more negatively than they have viewed current economic conditions. From a broader perspective, the main cause for the decline in the index since January is the drop in Americans' economic outlook, which has fallen more steeply than their views of the current economy. Both components have been level since August.

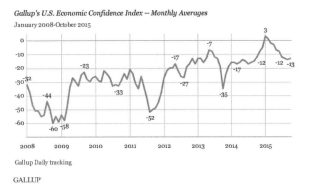

Gallup's U.S. Economic Confidence Index -- Monthly Averages
January 2008-October 2015

Gallup Daily tracking

GALLUP°

In October, 24% of Americans described current economic conditions as "excellent" or "good," while 31% rated them "poor." This resulted in a current conditions average of -7.

The economic outlook average was -19 for this same period. This was the result of 38% of Americans saying the economy is "getting better" and 57% saying it is "getting worse."

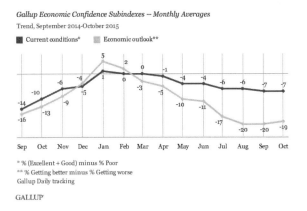

Gallup Economic Confidence Subindexes -- Monthly Averages
Trend, September 2014-October 2015

■ Current conditions*   ■ Economic outlook**

* % (Excellent + Good) minus % Poor
** % Getting better minus % Getting worse
Gallup Daily tracking

GALLUP°

Bottom Line

After peaking at +3 in January, the highest monthly average for the index since 2008, Gallup's Economic Confidence Index has gradually declined, reaching -13 in August and -14 in September. The -13 October average suggests the index has stabilized at its 2015 low. The rise in the index in the fall of 2014 that led up to the January high was the result of improvements in both index components. However, the decline this year has resulted mostly from deteriorating future expectations.

Survey Methods

Results for this Gallup poll are based on telephone interviews conducted Oct. 1–31, 2015, on the Gallup U.S. Daily survey, with a random sample of 15,190 adults, aged 18 and older, living in all 50 U.S. states and the District of Columbia. For results based on the total sample of national adults, the margin of sampling error is ±1 percentage point at the 95% confidence level. All reported margins of sampling error include computed design effects for weighting.

November 03, 2015
U.S. CRIME INDEX STEADY, BUT ID THEFT RISES

by Lydia Saad

Story Highlights

- *Just over one in four households victimized by crime in past year*
- *Rate is similar to recent years, but up slightly from past*
- *Reports of identity theft jump to 16%, highest in Gallup trend*

PRINCETON, N.J.—The percentages of U.S. households and individuals reporting that they have been affected by crime in the past year have not changed much in the past three years. Twenty-seven percent of Americans currently say someone in their household experienced at least one of seven different crimes Gallup has tracked annually since 2000, and 17% of individuals were themselves the victim.

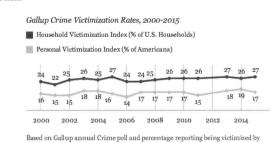

Gallup Crime Victimization Rates, 2000-2015
■ Household Victimization Index (% of U.S. Households)
■ Personal Victimization Index (% of Americans)

Based on Gallup annual Crime poll and percentage reporting being victimized by one or more of seven different crimes.
Poll was not conducted in 2012.

GALLUP°

Today's self-reported crime victimization rates, from Gallup's annual Crime poll conducted by telephone Oct. 7–11 with 1,015 U.S. adults, are similar to what Gallup found in 2013 and 2014. And although there has not been much variation over the years, today's rates are on the higher end of the range seen in Gallup's 15-year trend. The average household victimization rate of 27% over the past three years is a bit higher than the 24% average recorded between 2000 and 2004, and the index has not registered below 26% since 2008.

Both the household and personal victimization indices reflect U.S. adults' responses to questions asking whether they or anyone in their household was the victim of each of seven types of conventional crimes: theft, vandalism, burglary, mugging or physical assault, auto theft, robbery and sexual assault. Those who said yes to the broader question for each crime were subsequently asked whether it happened to them personally or to another family member.

Of the 27% of households affected by crime in the past year, 16% were victimized by one crime and 11% by two or more. Also, 6% of households and 3% of individuals experienced at least one violent crime; the rest were limited to property crimes.

Property Theft and Vandalism Remain Most Common Crimes

Of the seven crimes included in Gallup's crime victimization indices, the most common—both for individuals and for households—is having money or property stolen, as well as having a home, car or other property vandalized. Each of these crimes was experienced by 15% of households in 2015, including by 7% of individuals. Being mugged or having a house or apartment broken into is the next most commonly experienced crime, although with substantially fewer households—4%—affected. The rate drops further for having a car stolen, experienced by 2% of households, as well as having money stolen by force or being sexually assaulted, both 1%.

Household/Self Victim of Crime in Last 12 Months

	U.S. Households Victimized	U.S. Adults Victimized
	%	%
Money or property stolen from you or another member of your household	15	7
A home, car or property owned by you or another household member vandalized	15	7
Your house or apartment broken into	4	4
You or another household member mugged or physically assaulted	4	2
A car owned by you or another household member stolen	2	1
Money or property taken by force, with gun, knife, weapon or physical attack	1	*
You or another household member sexually assaulted	1	1

Oct. 7-11, 2015
* = Less than 0.5%

GALLUP

Mirroring the recent stability in the overall index, the victimization rates for each of the seven component crimes have also been steady.

While Credit Card Theft Is Down, ID Theft Has Doubled Since 2010

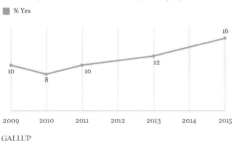

Gallup added two cyber-oriented crimes, credit card fraud and identity theft, to the survey more recently. They are not included in the crime victimization index due to the need to maintain the long-term comparability of the index.

As Gallup reported earlier, the percentage of Americans victimized by credit card theft or fraud fell to 22% this year from 27% in 2014, possibly reflecting fewer hacking incidents occurring at major U.S. retail stores in the past year coupled with increased security features on credit cards.

At the same time, the percentage of Americans reporting that they or another household member was the victim of identity theft rose to 16% this year from 12% in 2013, and is the highest Gallup has recorded of the five times it has been included in the survey since 2009. Ten percent of U.S. adults say the identity theft that occurred in the past year happened to them personally.

Gallup Identity Theft Victimization Trend, 2009-2015

Self or family member was the victim of identity theft in past year

■ % Yes

```
                                                    16
                                           12
10              10
        8
2009   2010   2011   2012   2013   2014   2015
```

GALLUP

Bottom Line

Although the percentage of U.S. adults and households experiencing property and violent crimes has been fairly steady over the past few years, slightly more households are affected now than in the early 2000s. Additionally, the prevalence of identity theft appears to be rising, perhaps reflecting the greater security risks Americans face as they spend more time online.

Gallup will provide additional insights on its crime victimization trend in a forthcoming analysis that focuses on demographic differences in self-reports of crime.

Survey Methods

Results for this Gallup poll are based on telephone interviews conducted Oct. 7–11, 2015, with a random sample of 1,015 adults, aged 18 and older, living in all 50 U.S. states and the District of Columbia. For results based on the total sample of national adults, the margin of sampling error is ±4 percentage points at the 95% confidence level. All reported margins of sampling error include computed design effects for weighting.

November 04, 2015
U.S. JOB CREATION INDEX HOLDS AT SEVEN-YEAR HIGH

by Rebecca Riffkin

Story Highlights

- *Job Creation Index unchanged for sixth month*
- *Job Creation Index holding at seven-year high point*
- *Higher percentage say workplace is hiring than staying the same*

WASHINGTON, D.C.—Gallup's U.S. Job Creation Index averaged +32 in October, the sixth month in a row in which the index has held at this level. This is the highest index score since Gallup began measuring employees' perceptions of job creation at their workplaces in 2008.

U.S. Job Creation Index, Monthly Averages, January 2008-October 2015

Percentage of U.S. workers who say their employers are hiring new people minus percentage who say their employers are letting people go

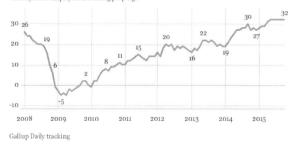

Gallup Daily tracking

GALLUP

When Gallup began measuring job creation in January 2008, the index measured a healthy +26. But it quickly fell, including substantial drops in the fourth quarter of 2008 after the start of the financial crisis. The index hit a nadir of -5 in early 2009, and has slowly rebounded since.

Gallup's Job Creation Index is based on interviews conducted Oct. 1–31 with more than 18,000 American adults who are employed either full or part time as part of Gallup Daily tracking. Gallup asks employed workers nationwide each day whether their employer is increasing, reducing or maintaining the size of its workforce.

In October, 43% of workers said their employer was hiring workers and expanding the size of its workforce, and 11% said their employer was letting people go and reducing the size of its workforce, resulting in the index score of +32.

U.S. EMPLOYEES' PERCEPTIONS OF JOB
CREATION AT WORKPLACE

HIRING	LETTING GO
43%	11%

GALLUP DAILY TRACKING, OCT. 2015

Forty percent of U.S. workers say their employer is "not changing" the size of its workforce. These percentages have been steady for the last several months. Since April, a higher percentage of Americans have said their employer is "hiring" than have said the size of their workforce is "not changing."

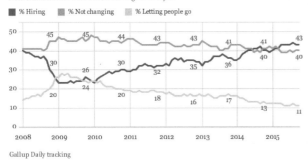

Hiring and Firing Nationwide, Monthly Averages, January 2008-October 2015

Note: Numbers shown are October readings for each year

■ % Hiring   ■ % Not changing   ■ % Letting people go

Gallup Daily tracking

GALLUP

Regional Hiring Steady in October

No regions had significant changes in perceptions of hiring in October compared with September. Net hiring continues to be lowest in the East, at +28, as has generally been the case since 2013. Hiring perceptions were similar in the Midwest (+34), South (+33) and West (+33). Although steady between September and October, hiring in the Midwest has dropped from +36 in August, which tied the highest score recorded for any region since Gallup began tracking this metric.

Job Creation Index, by Subgroup

	Index Score
East	+28
Midwest	+34
South	+33
West	+33
Government	+27
Nongovernment	+34

October 1-31, 2015

GALLUP

Hiring perceptions were steady in both the private sector and among government workers. Net job creation measured +34 among nongovernment workers, where the majority of the country is employed, and +27 among government workers.

Bottom Line

While job creation remains at its current high, the question of how high the index can be expected to go remains unanswered. Gallup's Job Creation Index began in 2008, which means there is not a comparison for robust economic periods such as the dot-com boom in the late 1990s. With less than half of workers reporting that their companies are hiring, it initially would seem plausible that hiring could increase in the future. The size of a small business's workforce is fairly consistent, however, and can't be expected to change frequently, and the majority of workers are employed by small businesses.

The current +32 index comes at a time when unemployment remains low, with the Bureau of Labor Statistics reporting 5.1% unemployment. This is not as good as the rates near 4.0% in 1999 and 2000, but it is one of the better rates in recent times. Even looking at the states with the highest rates of job creation—such as North Dakota—their indexes in 2014 were only slightly higher than the current score for the country as a whole. One future driver of expanded job creation could be more entrepreneurial activity and new business startups, as the number of new businesses being started recently is less than the number that are closing, according to the Brookings Institute. All in all, it is a positive sign that job creation continues at this high point, but it does invite speculation about just how much higher the index can climb.

Survey Methods

Results for this Gallup poll are based on telephone interviews conducted Oct. 1–31, 2015, on the Gallup Daily tracking survey, with a random sample of 18,207 aged 18 and older, who are employed full or part time, living in all 50 U.S. states and the District of Columbia. For results based on the total sample of national adults, the margin of sampling error is ±1 percentage points at the 95% confidence level. All reported margins of sampling error include computed design effects for weighting.

November 05, 2015
SAME-SEX MARRIAGES UP AFTER SUPREME COURT RULING

by Jeffrey M. Jones and Gary J. Gates

Story Highlights

- *Share of married same-sex cohabiting couples up from 38% to 45%*
- *Increases in both states where it had previously been legal or illegal*

PRINCETON, N.J.—More lesbian, gay, bisexual or transgender Americans living with a same-sex partner now report being married

(45%) than did so prior to the U.S. Supreme Court's June 26 decision to make same-sex marriages legal in all 50 states (38%).

Change in Percentage of Married Versus Unmarried Same-Sex Couples After Supreme Court Ruling on Same-Sex Marriage
Based on LGBT Americans

	Jan. 28- June 26, 2015	June 27- Nov. 3, 2015
SAME-SEX COUPLES		
% Married	38	45
% Living together but not married	62	55

Gallup Daily tracking
Note: Since Jan. 28, Gallup has measured sex of spouse/partner for LGBT respondents reporting they are married or living with a partner.

GALLUP

The results are based on Gallup Daily tracking interviews conducted in 2015, including interviews with 4,752 LGBT Americans through June 26, the day the Supreme Court issued its ruling, and 4,172 LGBT Americans since then.

The decision in *Obergefell v. Hodges* and three related cases made same-sex marriage legal nationwide and will dramatically expand and protect the rights of same-sex couples for generations to come. But its immediate and direct impact is mostly limited to same-sex couples in committed relationships.

Gallup's data do not distinguish whether those who identify as LGBT primarily think of themselves as lesbian, gay, bisexual or transgender. This is important because many bisexuals in particular are married or living with opposite-sex partners while most lesbians and gay men marry or live with same-sex partners.

But Gallup does ask those who identify as LGBT, and also report being married or living with a partner, whether their spouse or partner is the same sex as them. Isolating the increase in married versus unmarried LGBT Americans living with a same-sex partner provides the most direct evidence of how same-sex marriages have increased significantly following the *Obergefell* decision.

MARRIED SAME-SEX COUPLES BEFORE
AND AFTER SUPREME COURT DECISION

JAN. 28-JUNE 26   JUNE 27-NOV. 3

38%   45%

GALLUP DAILY TRACKING, 2015

Same-Sex Marriage Rates Up in States Where It Was Already Legal

The practical legal impact of the *Obergefell* decision was to invalidate laws in 13 states that did not recognize same-sex marriages. Since then, the percentage of same-sex married couples increased from 26% to 31% in those states. Prior to *Obergefell*, states that did not recognize or conduct marriages of same-sex couples still had same-sex married couples residing there. But those couples either married elsewhere or considered themselves married even if the state did not. Those spouses' rights were enhanced by the Supreme Court's 2013 ruling in *U.S. v. Windsor* that ensured the federal government would recognize marriages of same-sex couples even in states where such marriages were not recognized by the state.

But states whose laws were not affected by the *Obergefell* ruling have also seen a notable increase in same-sex marriages over the last four months. Currently, 49% of same-sex couples living together in states where same-sex marriages were already legal report being married, compared with 42% prior to the decision. That means same-sex couples living together in these states are now as likely to be married as not married.

Change in Percentage of Married Versus Unmarried Same-Sex Couples Living Together After Supreme Court Ruling on Same-Sex Marriage, by Prior State Law
Based on LGBT Americans

	Jan. 28- June 26, 2015	June 27- Nov. 3, 2015
SAME-SEX MARRIAGE NOT LEGAL IN STATE BEFORE JUNE 26		
% In same-sex marriage	26	31
% Living with same-sex partner but not married	74	69
SAME-SEX MARRIAGE LEGAL IN STATE BEFORE JUNE 26		
% In same-sex marriage	42	49
% Living with same-sex partner but not married	58	51

Gallup Daily tracking
Note: Since Jan. 28, Gallup has measured sex of spouse or partner for those reporting they are married or living with a partner.
Prior to June 26, same-sex marriages were not legally recognized in AR, GA, KY, LA, MI, MO, MS, NE, ND, OH, SD, TN and TX.

GALLUP

Estimated Increase of 96,000 Same-Sex Married Couples

Overall, 3.9% of all Americans identify as LGBT, and 0.4% of all Americans are in a same-sex marriage. The latter figure is up from 0.3% before the ruling.

Those figures can be used to estimate that there are now approximately 972,000 Americans in a same-sex marriage, up from approximately 780,000 before the ruling. Put differently, there are now approximately 486,000 same-sex marriages in the U.S., compared with approximately 390,000 four months ago.

Nearly One in 10 LGBT Now Married to Same-Sex Partner

Among all LGBT Americans, 9.6% currently describe themselves as being married to a same-sex spouse, up from 7.9% before the Supreme Court's decision. There has been a decline in the percentage of LGBT Americans who say they are not married but are living with someone of the same sex, from 12.8% to 11.7%. Nearly half of LGBT Americans, 46.8%, identify as single, likely because LGBT as a group tend to be younger, on average.

Marital Status of LGBT Americans, Before and After Supreme Court Ruling Legalizing Same-Sex Marriage Nationwide
Based on LGBT Americans

	Jan. 28- June 26, 2015	June 27- Nov. 3, 2015	Change
	%	%	pct. pts.
Married to same-sex spouse	7.9	9.6	+1.7
Living with same-sex partner	12.8	11.7	-1.1
Single/Never married	47.4	46.8	-0.6
Married to opposite-sex spouse	14.2	13.4	-0.8
Living with opposite-sex partner	4.8	6.3	+1.5
Divorced	7.1	7.0	-0.1
Separated	2.5	2.1	-0.4
Widowed	2.8	2.8	0.0
N	4,752	4,172	

Gallup Daily tracking

GALLUP

Since June, the percentage of LGBT Americans in opposite-sex marriages has decreased from 14.2% to 13.4%. However, it is still the case that more LGBT individuals report being in opposite-sex marriages than in same-sex marriages. This is likely due to the high proportion of bisexuals within the LGBT population. Other surveys show that bisexuals account for roughly half of the LGBT population, and that the vast majority of bisexuals who report having a spouse or living with a partner are in an opposite-sex relationship.

The decrease in the percentage of LGBT individuals in opposite-sex marriages and the increase in opposite-sex domestic partnerships since June likely reflects changing patterns in the relationship status of bisexual Americans since relatively few gay men or lesbians report having an opposite-sex spouse or partner.

Implications

Just four months after the landmark *Obergefell* decision, there has already been a notable shift toward marriage and away from living together among same-sex couples in the U.S. who live under the same roof. If those trends continue, marriage will soon overtake domestic partnerships as the more common relationship status among committed same-sex couples. In the states where same-sex marriage was legal prior to the Supreme Court decision, same-sex couples are already as likely to be married as they are to be living together.

The Supreme Court's ruling was controversial in many respects but is also reflective of public opinion on the issue. Americans' support for same-sex marriage has grown rapidly in the past decade, particularly in states where same-sex couples could legally marry. And support for same-sex marriage may not have peaked, as more Americans will encounter married same-sex couples routinely in their lives, and younger generations in this country show much greater support for same-sex marriage than do older generations.

Gary J. Gates is Blachford-Cooper Distinguished Scholar and Research Director at the Williams Institute, UCLA School of Law. A national expert in LGBT demographics, he has a Ph.D. in public policy from Heinz College, Carnegie Mellon University.

Survey Methods

Results for this Gallup poll are based on telephone interviews with a random sample of adults, aged 18 and older, living in all 50 U.S. states and the District of Columbia, on the Gallup U.S. Daily survey. Sample sizes and margins of error are shown in the accompanying table:

	Sample size	Margin of error
Pre-Supreme Court decision (Jan. 28-June 26, 2015)		
National adults	148,457	+/-1
LGBT	4,752	+/-2
Non-LGBT	135,643	+/-1
Post-Supreme Court decision (June 27-Nov. 3, 2015)		
National adults	128,771	+/-1
LGBT	4,172	+/-2
Non-LGBT	118,056	+/-1

GALLUP'

November 05, 2015
CARSON BEST-LIKED OF ALL PRESIDENTIAL CANDIDATES

by Andrew Dugan

Story Highlights

- *Carson enjoys highest net favorability with all U.S. adults*
- *Democrats view Carson more favorably than other GOP candidates*
- *About as many blacks who know Carson like as dislike him*

WASHINGTON, D.C.—Political novice Ben Carson retains his formidable edge in popularity over his Republican presidential rivals, with a net favorable score of +59 among Republicans nationwide. But Carson is not only popular with Republicans; he also has a net favorable score of +21 among national adults—the highest of any candidate from either party.

Major-Party Candidate Images for Selected GOP and Democratic Candidates
Among national adults; ranked by "net favorable"

	Party	% Favorable	% Unfavorable	Net favorable (pct. pts.)
Ben Carson	GOP	42	21	+21
Carly Fiorina	GOP	28	22	+6
Marco Rubio	GOP	32	27	+5
Bernie Sanders	Dem.	32	28	+4
John Kasich	GOP	21	17	+4
Mike Huckabee	GOP	32	28	+4
Jeb Bush	GOP	37	39	-2
Ted Cruz	GOP	28	31	-3
Hillary Clinton	Dem.	43	49	-6
Chris Christie	GOP	28	38	-10
Donald Trump	GOP	34	56	-22

Gallup Daily tracking, Oct. 19-Nov. 1, 2015

GALLUP'

The public gives other prominent presidential candidates either a lukewarm or an unfavorable reception, including Marco Rubio (+5), Jeb Bush (-2), Hillary Clinton (-6) and Donald Trump (-22). These results are based on Gallup Daily tracking from Oct. 19–Nov. 1, a period that spanned the third Republican debate.

But as might be expected for a first-time presidential candidate with a limited national profile prior to mounting a campaign, Carson is not as well known as other candidates. Carson's overall "familiarity" score—the total percentage of Americans with a favorable or unfavorable view of him—is 63%, well behind Clinton (92%), Trump (90%) and Bush (76%).

BEN CARSON'S NET FAVORABILITY AMONG U.S. ADULTS

+21

GALLUP DAILY, OCT. 19-NOV. 1

While those candidates were already reasonably well known as the race began, Carson was in no such position. For the period of July 8–21, when Gallup began regularly tracking presidential candidates, Carson's overall familiarity score among national adults was 36%. Few candidates who are still in the field were less well known at that time, including Republicans John Kasich (29%) and Carly Fiorina (30%), and Democrat Martin O'Malley (22%). But Carson, at least partly aided by his debate performances, has seen the most growth on this measure. And he now is about as well known as national political figures such as Rubio, Chris Christie and Ted Cruz.

Carson is well known among Republicans; three in four are familiar with him. And of the three-quarters of Republicans who know him, only a sliver have an unfavorable view of him (8%). Republicans' nearly universal appreciation for Carson is an important reason for his robust popularity nationally. More than four in 10 (42%) U.S. adults identify as or lean Republican, meaning Carson receives high marks from about two-fifths of the country.

GOP Candidate Images Among Republicans

Among Republicans or independents who lean Republican, ranked by "net favorable"

	% Favorable	% Unfavorable	Net favorable (pct. pts.)
Ben Carson	67	8	+59
Marco Rubio	53	15	+38
Mike Huckabee	56	19	+37
Ted Cruz	51	18	+33
Carly Fiorina	44	14	+30
Jeb Bush	52	30	+22
Donald Trump	57	36	+21
Chris Christie	41	31	+10
John Kasich	27	20	+7

Gallup Daily tracking, Oct. 19-Nov. 1, 2015

GALLUP'

Although He Has a Net-Negative Image, Carson Rates Relatively Well Among Democrats

Carson records a -13 net favorable rating among Democrats and independents who lean Democratic, better than most of his Republican rivals and significantly better than the more widely known Rubio, Christie, Cruz, Mike Huckabee and especially Trump. At the same time, Carson is not very well known among Democrats, leaving open the very real possibility that as more Democrats come to know him, they will dislike him, bringing down his net favorable.

GOP Candidate Images Among Democrats

Among Democrats or independents who lean Democratic, ranked by "net favorable"

	% Favorable	% Unfavorable	Net favorable (pct. pts.)
John Kasich	19	19	0
Ben Carson	23	36	-13
Carly Fiorina	18	31	-13
Marco Rubio	20	41	-21
Jeb Bush	26	53	-27
Chris Christie	20	49	-29
Ted Cruz	11	47	-36
Mike Huckabee	13	50	-37
Donald Trump	15	77	-62

Gallup Daily tracking, Oct. 19-Nov. 1, 2015

GALLUP'

Carson Unknown to Most Black Americans

As the sole black candidate running for president in either party, Carson is relatively popular with blacks compared with his GOP rivals. But given the heavy Democratic tilt of black adults, Carson will likely hit a low ceiling on his overall popularity score with this group. At a net favorable of -1, Carson is liked by about as many U.S. black adults as disliked, though the majority (52%) have no opinion of him.

GOP Candidate Images Among Black Adults Nationwide

Ranked by "net favorable"

	% Favorable	% Unfavorable	Net favorable (pct. pts.)
John Kasich	16	12	+4
Ben Carson	23	24	-1
Carly Fiorina	16	19	-3
Marco Rubio	19	29	-10
Jeb Bush	27	48	-21
Ted Cruz	12	35	-23
Chris Christie	17	41	-24
Mike Huckabee	16	40	-24
Donald Trump	17	66	-49

Gallup Daily tracking, Oct. 19-Nov. 1, 2015

GALLUP'

Bottom Line

For the moment, Carson is the most popular major-party candidate—and by a wide margin. While this fact might suggest Carson has a rare bipartisan appeal that the other presidential candidates lack, his popularity is chiefly driven by his extremely positive image among Republicans. Democrats who have an opinion of Carson see him in less negative terms than they see other Republican candidates, but, ultimately, about four in 10 Democrats—a group prone to view any GOP candidate unfavorably because of that candidate's politics—do not currently know Carson.

And that is the situation Carson faces. He enjoys a high familiarity rating among Republicans, but if he is to become a better-known figure nationally, he will have to "introduce" himself to Democrats. If normal political forces prevail, though, it is likely that expanded familiarity will come at the cost of lower popularity. If more Democrats do come to know him—even if they decide they don't like him—it is a sign that his once-improbable campaign is becoming much less so.

Survey Methods

Results for this Gallup poll are based on telephone interviews conducted Oct. 19–Nov. 1, 2015, on the Gallup U.S. Daily survey, with a random sample of 7,121 adults, aged 18 and older, living in all 50 U.S. states and the District of Columbia. Each candidate was rated by a random subset of respondents during this period, with the sample sizes rating each candidate ranging from 1,884 to 2,014. For results based on the total sample of national adults, the margin of sampling error is ±3 percentage points at the 95% confidence level.

For results based on the total sample of 3,180 of Republicans and Republican-leaning independents, aged 18 and older, with about 800 adults, on average, rating each candidate, the margin of sampling error is ±4 percentage points at the 95% confidence level.

For results based on the total sample of 2,900 of Democrats and Democratic-leaning independents, aged 18 and older, with about 800 adults, on average, rating each candidate, the margin of sampling error is ±4 percentage points at the 95% confidence level.

For results based on the total sample of 685 black adults, aged 18 and older, with about 200 adults, on average, rating each candidate, the margin of sampling error is ±5 percentage points at the 95% confidence level. All reported margins of sampling error include computed design effects for weighting.

November 06, 2015
YOUNG, POOR, URBAN DWELLERS MOST LIKELY TO BE CRIME VICTIMS

by Jim Norman

Story Highlights

- *One in four adults younger than 30 are crime victims*
- *City dwellers and the poor also frequent crime targets*

WASHINGTON, D.C.—The young, the poor and those who live in cities are among the most likely targets of crime in the U.S., a study of Gallup polls over the past seven years reveals. All three groups are significantly more likely than the national average (17%) to say they personally were victims in the past year of at least one of seven crimes included in Gallup's index.

Gallup U.S. Crime Victimization Rates, 2009-2015
Percentage of U.S. adults who have personally been the victim of at least one of seven common crimes*

	% Who are victims
U.S. Adults Overall	17%
Age	
18-29	24%
30-49	19%
50-64	15%
65 and older	10%
Annual Household Income	
Less than $30,000	22%
$30,000-$74,999	16%
$75,000 or more	15%
Place of Residence	
City	21%
Rural area or town	16%
Suburb	13%

*Crimes include theft, vandalism, burglary, mugging or physical assault, auto theft, robbery and sexual assault

GALLUP'

Gallup asked U.S. adults in six polls conducted from 2009 to 2015 whether they had personally been the victim within the previous year of one of seven conventional crimes: theft, vandalism, burglary, mugging or physical assault, auto theft, robbery and sexual assault. The rates of personal and household victimization have been steady over this time.

AMERICANS WHO HAVE BEEN VICTIM OF AT LEAST ONE OF SEVEN COMMON CRIMES

17%

GALLUP POLL, OCT. 7-11

Differences in victim rates across various demographic and geographic groups are not large, but age, income and place of residence clearly have an effect:

- The 21% of those describing their place of residence as a "big city" or "small city" who have been crime victims contrasts with 13% of those who say they live in suburbs.

- Those aged 18 to 29 (24%) are more than twice as likely to report being a victim of crime as those aged 65 and older (10%).
- Those at the lowest end of the household income scale are more likely to be victims (22%) than those who earn more.
- Blacks (21%) and Hispanics (21%) are slightly more likely than whites (16%) to report being victims.
- Thirteen percent of those with a postgraduate education have been victims. Those with a postgraduate education tend to have higher incomes and are older, fitting the profile of those with low victimization rates.
- There is virtually no difference by gender: 17% of both men and women report being crime victims.
- Gun owners, at 20%, are slightly more likely than the national average to be crime victims. It is unclear whether owners bought a gun as a result of being a crime victim or whether they were already armed.

Age, Income and Area Interwoven, But Each Matters

Age, income and location of one's residence overlap each other: cities tend to attract adults younger than 30; young adults earn less on average than those aged 30 and older; cities hold a disproportionate number of those with lower incomes.

But with all three groups, the high victimization rates are not just a function of their close relationship to the other groups. Those younger than 30 are most likely to be crime victims no matter where they live or how much they earn. Those with the lowest household incomes are more likely than other income groups to be victims no matter how old they are or where they live. Much of the same is true for city dwellers.

More broadly, a statistical analysis that takes into account the independent effects of age, income and location of residence suggests age is a slightly more important predictor of whether one is a crime victim than where he or she lives or his or her income level.

Bottom Line

Being poor, young or a city dweller is associated with a higher probability of being a target for criminals, with those younger than 30 especially vulnerable to property crimes such as theft, vandalism and break-ins. For younger millennials transitioning to an independent adulthood, the question is how much their vulnerability to such crimes could be lowered.

Survey Methods

Results for this Gallup poll are based on telephone interviews conducted in six Gallup polls on crime conducted in 2009, 2010, 2011, 2013, 2014 and most recently Oct. 7–11, 2015. The aggregate sample for the five polls contains 7,141 adults, aged 18 and older, living in all 50 U.S. states and the District of Columbia. For results based on the subgroups mentioned, the margin of sampling error is ±5 percentage points or less at the 95% confidence level. All reported margins of sampling error include computed design effects for weighting.

November 06, 2015
AMERICANS WITH GOVERNMENT HEALTH PLANS MOST SATISFIED

by Rebecca Riffkin

Story Highlights

- *Uninsured Americans least satisfied with health system*
- *Those with veterans or military insurance most satisfied*
- *Self-insured less satisfied than others who have insurance*

WASHINGTON, D.C.—Americans' satisfaction with the way the healthcare system works for them varies by the type of insurance they have. Satisfaction is highest among those with veterans or military health insurance, Medicare and Medicaid, and is lower among those with employer-paid and self-paid insurance. Americans with no health insurance are least satisfied of all.

Satisfaction With the U.S. Health System Varies by Insurance Type

Primary insurance type	% Satisfied with the way the health system is working
Military or veterans	78
Medicare	77
Medicaid	75
Union	71
Current or former employer	69
Plan fully paid for by you or family member	65
Uninsured	41

Jan. 1– Oct. 31, 2015

GALLUP

In 2015 to date, 67% of Americans are satisfied, compared with 66% in November 2014. Gallup began tracking Americans' satisfaction with the healthcare system in March 2014, at the end of the first Affordable Care Act (ACA) enrollment period. So while it is not possible to compare Americans' satisfaction levels before and after the law took effect, satisfaction has been largely stable since Gallup first measured it.

Americans' satisfaction appears to be influenced by the nature of their health plans, particularly how much they have to contribute to the cost. As a result, those whose plans are subsidized by the government—including military/veteran health plans, Medicare and Medicaid—are the most likely to be satisfied.

Those who receive health insurance through a union are slightly more likely to be satisfied than those who receive it through an employer, while those who pay for their own plan are the least satisfied of those who have some type of insurance. This last group includes Americans who purchased their own health insurance through the exchanges set up as part of the ACA. Their lower satisfaction may result from higher deductibles and co-pays for the most common "Silver" ACA insurance plans than for employer-sponsored insurance plans.

But even with these differences, no less than 65% in any of these groups are satisfied. Only among the uninsured are a majority not satisfied.

The higher satisfaction of military/veterans and Medicare recipients could also be explained by age patterns. Older Americans, who are more likely to have these plans, are more satisfied with the way the healthcare system works for them, regardless of the type of insurance they have. In contrast, the majority of those younger than 65 are on employer plans. Employer plans vary widely, with some

employers paying much of the tab, while others pass the costs on to employees.

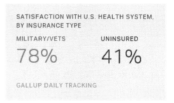

Bottom Line

Americans who get their health insurance through government-sponsored or assisted plans, such as Medicare and Medicaid or veterans insurance, are more likely to be satisfied with the way the healthcare system is working for them than those who have employer-paid insurance or who pay for insurance themselves. There may be a number of reasons for this, such as government plans being more inclusive and having a lower direct cost to the insured person than employer plans or personally paid-for plans. Additionally, the question asks about healthcare generally, and not cost specifically. Therefore, other aspects of the government plans such as access to more specialists, the availability of different services or ease of scheduling appointments may also factor into the higher satisfaction levels.

Survey Methods

Results are based on telephone interviews conducted Jan. 1–Oct. 31, 2015, as part of Gallup Daily tracking, with a random sample of 147,517 adults, aged 18 and older, living in all 50 U.S. states and the District of Columbia. For results based on the total sample of national adults, the margin of sampling error is ±1 percentage point at the 95% confidence level.

Sample sizes and margins of error for adults with different insurance plans are as follows:

Margin of Error and Sample Size for Each Insurance Type

Primary insurance type	Sample size	Margin of error
Military or veterans	5,818	±1
Medicare	39,653	±1
Medicaid	7,477	±1
Union	2,781	±2
Current or former employer	53,071	±1
Plan fully paid for by you or family member	22,816	±1
Uninsured	11,221	±1

Jan. 1–Oct. 31, 2015

GALLUP

November 09, 2015
DEMOCRATS' POSITIVE VIEWS OF CLINTON IMPROVE AFTER DEBATE

by Frank Newport

Story Highlights

- *Clinton's net favorable rating up 14 points since Oct. 13 debate*
- *Sanders remains less well known, and his image has been static*

- *Clinton does much better than Sanders among black Democrats*

PRINCETON, N.J.—Democrats have become increasingly positive about Hillary Clinton since the highly viewed Democratic debate on Oct. 13. Her favorable ratings have increased from 72% for the two-week period just before the debate to 78% now, and her unfavorable rating has dropped from 23% to 15%. Clinton's resulting +63 net favorable rating is now her highest since Gallup began tracking views of the candidates daily on July 8, although still lower than measures taken before she became an active candidate last spring.

Hillary Clinton Net Favorable Rating, Pre- and Post-Oct. 13, 2015, Debate
Among Democrats/leaners

	Sep 28-Oct 12, 2015	Oct 25-Nov 7, 2015	Change
	%	%	(pct. pts.)
Favorable	72	78	+6
Unfavorable	23	15	-8
Net favorable	49	63	+14

GALLUP

Clinton's major opponent for her party's nomination, Vermont Sen. Bernie Sanders, has been increasing his attacks on Clinton in recent weeks, stating in a *Boston Globe* editorial meeting last week that "I disagree with Hillary Clinton on virtually everything," and increasingly focusing on her controversial actions relating to emails while secretary of state.

But the trend in Clinton's image among Democrats provides no evidence that Sanders's attacks are causing her harm so far, particularly in contrast to Sanders's own image, which has been static since just before the Oct. 13 debate. Sanders's current net favorable score of +38 is a point lower than his +39 just before the debate. While the percentage of Democrats who are familiar enough with Sanders to rate him, 64%, is up slightly from the pre-debate period, this remains almost 30 points lower than Clinton's familiarity among Democrats.

Bernie Sanders Net Favorable Rating, Pre- and Post-Oct. 13, 2015, Debate
Among Democrats/leaners

	Sep 28-Oct 12, 2015	Oct 25-Nov 7, 2015	Change
	%	%	(pct. pts.)
Favorable	49	51	+2
Unfavorable	10	13	+3
Net favorable	39	38	-1

GALLUP

Sanders and Clinton, along with former Maryland Gov. Martin O'Malley, will face off in the next Democratic debate Saturday, Nov. 14 at Drake University in Des Moines, Iowa.

Clinton Has Particular Strength Among Black Democrats

As Gallup has seen at previous points in the campaign this year, Sanders's image is far worse among black Democrats than is Clinton's, as evidenced by his +21 net favorable among this group compared with +89 for Clinton. Sanders's weaker image score among black Democrats is partly a reflection of his lower familiarity rating—55% of black Democrats don't know enough about him to rate him. In contrast, 91% are familiar with Clinton, with almost all rating her favorably.

The images of the two candidates are much more similar among white Democrats, with net favorable ratings within five points of each other. Sanders also does much better among liberal Democrats than among conservative and moderate Democrats, although Clinton's image is more positive than his among both of these groups. Sanders has a particular recognition problem among conservative/moderate Democrats, only 53% of whom are familiar with him, compared with 80% of liberal Democrats. Clinton, by contrast, is known to over 90% of both ideological groups.

Net Favorables Among Democrats/Leaners

	Clinton net favorable	Sanders net favorable	Difference, Clinton vs. Sanders
	%	%	(pct. pts.)
ALL DEMOCRATS	63	38	+25
RACE			
Non-Hispanic whites	55	50	+5
Non-Hispanic blacks	89	21	+68
IDEOLOGY			
Conservative/Moderate	55	19	+36
Liberal	73	62	+11

Oct. 25-Nov. 7, 2015

GALLUP

Bottom Line

Sanders continues to be both less well known and less well liked among Democrats than Clinton, his major opponent for the Democratic presidential nomination. Clinton has become even better liked since the Oct. 13 Democratic debate, while Sanders's image has remained essentially static. Sanders appears to be increasing his efforts to "go negative" on Clinton in recent days, and he and O'Malley will have an opportunity to confront her before a national audience on Saturday when the Democrats hold their next debate. This will be a difficult challenge, because over 90% of Democrats are familiar with Clinton, and a growing, and overwhelming, majority of them have a favorable opinion of her. Sanders also faces the challenge of increasing his own name identification, given that a good deal of his net favorable deficit compared with Clinton is a result of his relative lack of familiarity among Democrats. Now, 64% of Democrats know him, up from 49% in mid-July, but Clinton is one of the best-known politicians in America.

If Clinton does win her party's nomination, she will face the challenge of improving her image among all Americans, which at this point is still "underwater," with 44% viewing her favorably and 48% unfavorably. This is slightly improved from recent weeks, but remains significantly less positive than before she became an active presidential candidate.

Survey Methods

Results for this Gallup poll are based on telephone interviews conducted Oct. 25–Nov.7, 2015, on the Gallup U.S. Daily survey, with a random sample of up to 2,971 U.S. adults identifying as Democrats or independents who lean Democratic, aged 18 and older, living in all 50 U.S. states and the District of Columbia. Hillary Clinton was rated by a random subset of 801 Democrats and Bernie Sanders by 764 Democrats during this period. For results based on these samples, the margin of sampling error is ±4 percentage points at the 95% confidence level.

November 10, 2015
RETURNING VETS DON'T FEEL THEIR COLLEGE UNDERSTOOD THEIR NEEDS

by Stephanie Marken

Story Highlights

- *Few vets strongly agree that their college understood their unique needs*
- *Students enrolled while on active duty more positive*

WASHINGTON, D.C.—College graduates who served in the military while enrolled in their undergraduate program are more likely to strongly agree that their college or university understood their unique needs than those who served in the military before enrolling in college. Thirty percent of all military service members and veterans strongly agree that their university understood the unique needs of military service members and veterans. This percentage increases to 40% among those who served while attending college, and decreases to 25% among those who served before enrolling in their undergraduate program.

Percentage of Veterans Who Feel Their University Understood Their Unique Needs, by Enrollment Type

[University name] understood the unique needs of military service members and veterans.

	All military service members and veterans	Enrolled in college while serving	Enrolled in college after serving
	%	%	%
5-Strongly agree	30	40	25
4	18	19	17
3	17	12	20
2	11	8	12
1-Strongly disagree	7	7	8
Don't know/Does not apply	17	15	18

Gallup-Purdue Index, December 2014-June 2015

GALLUP

In 2008, the U.S. Department of Veterans Affairs greatly expanded the education benefits offered to veterans under the Servicemen's Readjustment Act of 1944, often referred to as the GI Bill. This expansion, commonly known as the Post-9/11 GI Bill, provides veterans who served on active duty after Sept. 10, 2001, with unprecedented education benefits, including a living allowance, money for books and the ability to transfer benefits to a dependent.

As a result, veterans and their dependents are enrolling in postsecondary programs at high rates throughout the U.S., forcing colleges and universities to evolve to meet their unique needs, including the need for specialized health services and financial counseling about the education benefits available to this population.

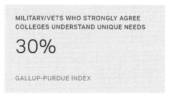

MILITARY/VETS WHO STRONGLY AGREE COLLEGES UNDERSTAND UNIQUE NEEDS

30%

GALLUP-PURDUE INDEX

In its second year, the Gallup-Purdue Index sought to evaluate how institutions are performing in serving this population by asking those who served in the military, before or while they were enrolled in college, the extent to which their university understood the unique needs of military service members and veterans.

College Graduates Who Enrolled in College While on Active Duty More Positive

Less than a third (30%) of all military service members and veterans who served before or during their undergraduate program strongly agree that their university understood the unique needs of military service members and veterans. The percentage strongly agreeing with this statement is higher among those who served while they were enrolled in their undergraduate program (40%) than among those who attended college after serving in the military (25%). These differences suggest colleges and universities have a better grasp of the issues active-duty military service members face in their undergraduate experience than of the issues encountered by returning veterans.

These results are based on the second annual Gallup-Purdue Index study of college graduates. The study is a joint research effort with Purdue University to examine the relationships between the college experience and college graduates' lives afterward. The Gallup-Purdue Index study is a comprehensive, nationally representative survey of U.S. college graduates of all ages with Internet access, conducted Dec. 16, 2014–June 29, 2015, with a random sample of 30,151 college graduates with a bachelor's degree or higher, including 3,722 graduates who have served in the military, which includes the Reserve and National Guard.

Private College and University Grads More Likely to Feel Understood

Military service members and veterans who obtained their undergraduate degree from private colleges and universities are more likely than public college graduates to strongly agree that their college or university understood the unique needs of the military service member and veteran population. About a third of private not-for-profit (36%) and private for-profit (34%) graduates strongly agree with this idea, compared with about a quarter (24%) of public college graduates. The size of institutions may partially explain differences in responses between graduates of public and graduates of private institutions. Military service member and veteran college graduates who obtained their degree from relatively small colleges or universities (with undergraduate enrollments lower than 10,000) are more likely than graduates who obtained their degree from larger colleges or universities (with enrollments of 10,000 or more) to strongly agree with this statement (32% vs. 26%).

Percentage of Veterans Who Feel Their University Understood Their Unique Needs, by College Type and Size

[University name] understood the unique needs of military service members and veterans.

	Private not-for-profit	Private for-profit	Public	Small	Large
	%	%	%	%	%
5-Strongly agree	36	34	24	32	26
4	17	23	18	18	19
3	15	18	19	18	18
2	7	4	14	10	12
1-Strongly disagree	6	7	8	5	8
Don't know/Does not apply	19	15	17	18	18

Gallup-Purdue Index, December 2014-June 2015

GALLUP

Implications

There is tremendous diversity within the military population, and while active-duty and returning service members require some of the same services, other needs differ. Although both groups require knowledgeable financial counselors who understand the complexities of the financial education benefits available to them, active-duty military service members may require more scheduling flexibility, while veterans are more likely to require specialized health services. Data from the Gallup-Purdue Index study indicate that colleges and universities may be more successful at meeting the needs of active-duty military service members than those of veterans. Colleges and universities will continue to benefit from experimentation with programs and support services for this population, as it is important that military service member and veteran programs be tailored to accommodate the diverse needs of these students. Additional results are provided in the Gallup Study of Veteran College Graduates.

Survey Methods

Results for the Gallup-Purdue Index are based on Web surveys conducted Dec. 16, 2014–June 29, 2015, with a random sample of 30,151 respondents with a bachelor's degree or higher, including 3,722 respondents who served in the military including the Guard or Reserve, aged 18 and older, with Internet access, living in all 50 U.S. states and the District of Columbia. For results based on the total sample of military service members and veterans, the margin of sampling error is ±2.3 percentage points at the 95% confidence level.

The Gallup-Purdue Index sample was recruited via the Gallup Daily tracking survey. The Gallup Daily tracking survey sample includes national adults with a minimum quota of 50% cellphone respondents and 50% landline respondents, with additional minimum quotas by time zone within region. Landline and cellular telephone numbers are selected using random-digit-dial methods.

Gallup-Purdue Index interviews are conducted via the Web, in English only. Samples are weighted to correct for unequal selection probability and nonresponse. The data are weighted to match national demographics of gender, age, race, Hispanic ethnicity, education and region provided by the Current Population Survey.

November 10, 2015
IN U.S., WOMEN, POOR, URBANITES MOST FEARFUL OF WALKING ALONE

by Jim Norman

Story Highlights

- *Americans generally are not afraid to walk alone at night near their homes*
- *Those most likely to be afraid not always those most likely to be crime victims*

WASHINGTON, D.C.—While a majority of Americans feel safe enough to walk alone at night in their own neighborhoods, or anywhere within a mile of where they live, the feeling is far from universal. In the U.S., an average 36% over the past seven years have expressed fear about walking alone at night. Fear of walking alone rises to nearly 50% among women, city dwellers and the poor.

These results are based on combined data from the six Gallup Crime polls conducted since 2009, including interviews with 7,141 U.S. adults. During this time, the percentage expressing a fear of

walking alone near their homes at night has been steady, ranging from 34% to 38%. In the longer 50-year history of the trend, the percentage fearful of walking alone has ranged from a low of 30% in 2001, a month after the 9/11 terrorist attacks on New York City and Washington, D.C., to a high of 48% in 1982.

Fear of Walking Alone at Night in Neighborhood, 2009-2015

Is there any area near where you live -- that is, within a mile -- where you would be afraid to walk alone at night?

	Yes, afraid
U.S. adults overall	36%
Annual household income less than $20,000	47%
Annual household income $75,000 or more	26%
Women	46%
Men	26%
Live in big city	49%
Live in rural area	26%

GALLUP

From a broad perspective, fear about walking alone at night is generally higher among groups that are the most likely to be crime victims, including low-income earners and urban dwellers. And among those who have been victims, 49% say they are afraid to walk alone, compared with 33% of nonvictims.

However, those who are the most fearful are not always those who are the most likely to be victims of crime.

- Gun owners are about as likely as Americans overall to be crime victims, but are significantly less likely than others to fear walking alone at night.
- Seniors, those aged 65 and older, are one of the groups least likely to be victimized by crime, but nevertheless are more likely than those aged 30 to 64 to fear walking alone at night near their homes. By contrast, adults younger than 30 are one of the groups most likely to be victims of crime, and a relatively large percentage (43%) fear walking alone at night.
- There is a 20-percentage-point difference between men and women in terms of being afraid to walk alone, with women expressing higher levels of fear, though they are equally as likely to be crime victims.
- Among women, 12% of those aged 50 and older are likely to be crime victims, compared with 22% of those younger than 50. But about 45% in both groups say they fear walking alone at night.

Fear of Walking Alone and Likelihood of Being a Crime Victim, 2009-2015

Percentages who fear walking alone at night and who have been crime victims*

	Fear walking alone	Victims of crime
U.S. adults overall	36%	17%
Personally own a gun	28%	20%
18 to 29 years	43%	24%
30 to 49 years	32%	19%
50 to 64 years	35%	15%
65+	38%	10%
Men	26%	17%
Women	46%	17%
Women, 18 to 49 years	45%	22%
Women, 50+	46%	12%

*Crimes include theft, vandalism, burglary, mugging or physical assault, auto theft, robbery and sexual assault

GALLUP

Fears Not Always Related to Perceptions of Crime Rates

The percentage of Americans who feel safe enough to walk alone at night anywhere in their neighborhoods has been fairly stable since 2003, but that has not been the case concerning attitudes about local crime increasing or decreasing. In Gallup's crime polls going back to 2003, the percentage of Americans saying crime in their area has increased within the past year ranges from 37% in 2004 to 51% in 2006, 2007 and 2009. Over the same period, the percentage of Americans who report feeling safe walking alone at night has remained in a narrower range—from 32% in 2004 to 38% in 2005 and 2011.

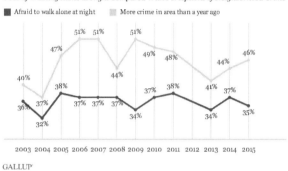

Fear of Walking Alone at Night Compared With Perceptions of Neighborhood Crime

GALLUP

Bottom Line

The sense that a person can walk anywhere near his or her home alone at night without fear, one of the basic measures of how safe and secure Americans feel, has remained fairly stable in recent years. External factors that one might expect to significantly affect this measure—such as a declining national crime rate and a plethora of highly publicized mass shootings—have failed to push fear up or down. Even fluctuations in Americans' sense that crime is increasing or decreasing have not considerably changed their beliefs about whether their neighborhoods are safe at night.

Survey Methods

Results for this Gallup poll are based on telephone interviews conducted in 2009, 2010, 2011, 2013 and 2014 and, most recently, Oct. 7–11, 2015. The aggregated sample for the six polls contains 7,141 adults, aged 18 and older, living in all 50 U.S. states and the District of Columbia. For results based on the subgroups mentioned, the margin of sampling error is ±5 percentage points at the 95% confidence level. All reported margins of sampling error include computed design effects for weighting.

November 11, 2015
CONGRESS'S JOB APPROVAL RATING SLIPS TO 11%

by Jeffrey M. Jones

Story Highlights

- Lowest approval rating this year
- Two percentage points above all-time low

• Republicans are least likely to approve of Congress

PRINCETON, N.J.—Americans' current 11% job approval rating of Congress is its worst rating so far this year. It is also barely better than the all-time low of 9% from November 2013, after the last major government shutdown.

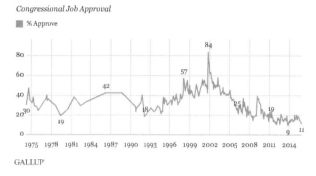

Congressional Job Approval

% Approve

GALLUP

The 86% of Americans who *disapprove* of Congress in the Nov. 4–8 poll ties the high disapproval figure in Gallup's 41-year trend, found in the November 2013 poll and two others.

Congress historically has not received high approval ratings, registering majority approval a small number of times during the economic boom of the late 1990s/early 2000s and after the 9/11 terrorist attacks. That includes a record-high 84% approval in October 2001. But ratings of Congress in recent years have been among the worst Gallup has recorded, rarely reaching 20% since 2011.

Gallup's latest congressional approval rating was obtained shortly after Congress passed bipartisan legislation to avert another government shutdown, and after Republican Rep. Paul Ryan took over as the new Speaker of the House. That change in leadership did not have any immediate positive effect on how Americans view Congress.

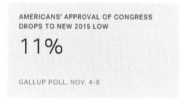

AMERICANS' APPROVAL OF CONGRESS DROPS TO NEW 2015 LOW

11%

GALLUP POLL, NOV. 4-8

The recent compromise fiscal legislation raised the limit the U.S. can legally borrow, and funds the government through 2017. But the deal was not universally hailed, with many Republicans in Congress upset with the party's leadership for not fighting hard enough for conservative fiscal principles. Former House Speaker John Boehner, who in late September announced his intention to resign his post, wanted to complete a deal before stepping down.

Boehner and Republican Senate Majority Leader Mitch McConnell have seen their support from fellow Republicans erode this year, not only among elected Republicans in Washington but also among party supporters nationwide. Gallup's most recent update, from October, found more Republicans having unfavorable than favorable opinions of Boehner and McConnell.

Republicans Least Approving of Congress Among Party Groups

Frustration with the party leadership may explain why Republicans (8%) are slightly less likely to approve of the job Congress is doing than either independents (13%) or Democrats (11%), even though

Republicans have majority control of both houses. Usually, Congress's approval ratings are significantly higher among supporters of the majority party.

Republicans' more negative evaluation of Congress is a recent development. In the first poll Gallup conducted entirely after the GOP assumed control of the Senate earlier this year, Republicans (27%) were significantly more likely than Democrats (17%) and independents (18%) to approve of Congress, consistent with the historical pattern.

But in the spring and early summer months, Republicans' views began to sour, as the party made little progress in achieving its legislative goals. Those views got worse through the summer and early fall—by July, only 11% of Republicans approved of Congress, and their approval since then has slipped further to 8%. Since July, Democrats' and independents' ratings have been consistently higher than Republicans', although Democrats and independents also view Congress quite negatively.

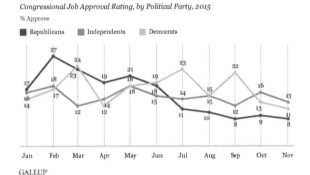

Congressional Job Approval Rating, by Political Party, 2015
% Approve

GALLUP'

Some of the top Republican priorities at the start of this year included approving the Keystone XL pipeline, passing immigration reform, rolling back financial regulations and repealing major parts of President Barack Obama's healthcare law, none of which has been accomplished. More recently, rank-and-file Republicans' disappointment with their congressional leadership may have been reinforced by Congress's failure to block the nuclear deal the Obama administration helped negotiate with Iran and to strip Planned Parenthood of its federal funding.

The Republicans' odds of achieving any of those goals would have been long, given that Democrats can still successfully filibuster legislation in the Senate and Obama can wield his veto pen. But Republicans may be upset with the party leadership, and the GOP congressional majority more broadly, for not being more aggressive in moving their proposals forward and forcing Democrats to filibuster or use the veto.

Implications

A year ago, Republicans were celebrating key victories in the 2014 midterm elections that gave the party control of the Senate and increased their majority in the House. But a year later, rank-and-file Republicans find little to celebrate with Congress, as they give the institution lower approval ratings than Democrats and independents do. As a result, Americans' overall approval ratings of Congress are once again near record lows.

To put Republicans' unhappiness with Congress in perspective, their 8% approval rating of the GOP-led Congress is essentially the same as the 9% approval rating they gave the Democratic-led Congress at the time of the 2010 midterm elections.

Much of Republicans' ire appears directed at the party leadership. Boehner has stepped aside and Republicans have turned over the reins of House leadership to Ryan after a protracted search for a consensus speaker candidate. Gallup will report on Republicans' views of Ryan next week.

Although Ryan, like Boehner and Nancy Pelosi before him, will likely start off his speakership with much political goodwill, that has not had any immediate effect on the way Americans view Congress more generally. Even if Americans support Ryan initially, he will still be forced to navigate a divided federal government and a House Republican caucus that itself is divided. In a poll conducted after Boehner's resignation announcement, most Americans did not believe new leadership would lead to greater GOP success in Congress. But Republicans, particularly those aligned with the Tea Party movement, were more optimistic about the possibilities the change would bring.

Survey Methods

Results for this Gallup poll are based on telephone interviews conducted Nov. 4–8, 2015, with a random sample of 1,021 adults, aged 18 and older, living in all 50 U.S. states and the District of Columbia. For results based on the total sample of national adults, the margin of sampling error is ±4 percentage points at the 95% confidence level. All reported margins of sampling error include computed design effects for weighting.

November 12, 2015

IN U.S., 53% OPPOSE SENDING GROUND TROOPS TO FIGHT MILITANTS

by Justin McCarthy

Story Highlights

- *Fifty-three percent oppose, while 43% are in favor*
- *Majority of GOP, conservatives support use of ground troops*

WASHINGTON, D.C.—As the U.S. intensifies its airstrikes against Islamic State militants in Syria and Iraq, Americans are more likely to oppose (53%) than support (43%) sending U.S. ground troops to these countries to help groups there fight the militants. These figures haven't changed significantly since September 2014 after President Barack Obama launched airstrikes against the Islamic State group and other militant groups.

Americans' Support for Sending Ground Troops to Iraq and Syria
Would you favor or oppose the United States sending ground troops to Iraq and Syria in order to assist groups in those countries that are fighting the Islamic militants?

	Favor %	Oppose %	No opinion %
Nov 4-8, 2015	43	53	4
Sep 20-21, 2014 ^	40	54	6

^ Asked on Gallup Daily tracking after question about approval of military action U.S. was taking against Islamic militants in Iraq and Syria

GALLUP'

The latest data are from a Nov. 4–8 Gallup poll, as airstrikes have intensified in Syria after a lull late last month. The Obama administration announced in October that it would deploy 50 special operations troops on the ground in Syria, after Obama said two years ago that he would "not put American boots on the ground" there.

MORE AMERICANS OPPOSE THAN
SUPPORT GROUND TROOPS IN SYRIA,
IRAQ

FAVOR	OPPOSE
43%	53%

GALLUP POLL, NOV. 4-8

Last year, Gallup found that Americans were more inclined to support the broad concept of U.S. "military action" in Iraq and Syria, with 60% approving. But there was far less support when Americans were asked specifically about sending ground troops, with 40% in favor at that time.

Support for sending ground troops continues to differ by political party and ideology. The issue has been politicized at home, including by Republicans during the presidential debate this week. While several of the candidates—including Florida Sen. Marco Rubio and former Florida Gov. Jeb Bush—have spoken in favor of sending troops, they have questioned the president's strategy, with some candidates suggesting the deployment was late or did not use enough troops to accomplish the task.

A majority of both Republicans (56%) and conservatives (54%) support sending ground troops to Iraq and Syria to combat Islamic State militants.

Meanwhile, less than half of moderates (41%) and political independents (39%) favor the deployment of ground troops. Liberals (31%) and Democrats (37%) are equally or less likely to support that action.

Support for Sending Ground Troops to
Iraq and Syria, by Party and Ideology

	Favor
	%
Conservatives	54
Moderates	41
Liberals	31
Republicans	56
Independents	39
Democrats	37

Nov. 4-8, 2015

GALLUP

Bottom Line

The fairly low level of Americans' support for deploying ground troops could be related to their reluctance to engage in another major military commitment in Iraq, or elsewhere for that matter. A majority of Americans continue to describe the Iraq War as a mistake, and Americans have tended to express much more support for past U.S. actions than for recent military involvements—including in Libya in 2011 after the U.S. conducted airstrikes against the country to enforce a United Nations no-fly zone, and in Syria in 2013 after President Bashar al-Assad used chemical weapons on Syrian citizens. In the latter case, Russia helped broker a deal with the Syrian government, nullifying the need for U.S. military action.

Despite the changing battle landscape and alterations in Obama's approach over the past year, Americans' views on the use of ground troops have not significantly changed.

Survey Methods

Results for this Gallup poll are based on telephone interviews conducted Nov. 4–8, 2015, with a random sample of 1,021 adults, aged 18 and older, living in all 50 U.S. states and the District of Columbia. For results based on the total sample of national adults, the margin of sampling error is ±4 percentage points at the 95% confidence level. All reported margins of sampling error include computed design effects for weighting.

November 12, 2015
BANKS AND PHARMACIES RATE BEST IN CUSTOMER SERVICE IN U.S.

by Art Swift and Steve Ander

Story Highlights

- *Nearly nine in 10 give positive ratings to banks and pharmacies*
- *Customer service ratings improve across older generations*
- *Most consistent ratings seen at clothing/retail stores*

WASHINGTON, D.C.—Out of seven major types of businesses, Americans rate banks and pharmacies best in a survey designed to assess recent, in-person customer service experiences at these institutions. Clothing/retail stores and fast food restaurants garner the lowest percentages of "excellent" service ratings.

Customer Service at a Variety of Businesses

I'm going to list some common businesses that people visit in person. For each one you have visited in the last month, please say, on average, whether the customer service was excellent, good, only fair or poor. If you haven't visited one of these businesses in the last month, please say so. First, how was the service at the _____?

	% Excellent	% Good	% Only fair	% Poor
Bank branch	38	51	9	3
Pharmacy	34	53	10	2
Post office	30	49	15	6
Grocery store	29	58	12	2
Convenience store	20	57	20	3
Clothing or retail store	19	61	18	2
Fast food restaurant	15	54	22	8

GALLUP

Nearly four in 10 Americans said they had an "excellent" experience at a bank branch they visited in the last month, while 34% said the same about the service they received at a pharmacy, and 30% said this about a post office. Fewer than one in five (19%) said they had "excellent" service at a clothing store, and 15% had this service at a fast food restaurant.

To focus on recent customer experiences, Gallup asked Americans about their in-person interactions at these seven businesses that they had visited in the previous month. The percentage visiting the various types of business within this time frame ranged from a low of 54% for post offices to a high of 95% for grocery stores.

These levels show significant differences in perceived customer service in the U.S., but customer service touchpoints are only one major factor in the overall customer experience. These ratings may reflect the overall relationship between a customer and an organization, such as the physical environment and wait times, or other indirect contact with a brand. Also, the ratings may be based on the product and the value the product brings to the person.

"EXCELLENT" RATINGS OF CUSTOMER SERVICE AT A VARIETY OF BUSINESSES

PHARMACY **34%**   BANK BRANCH **38%**

GALLUP DAILY TRACKING

One encouraging sign is that even for the types of stores with lower ratings, a majority say they have had a "good"—if not an "excellent"—experience, suggesting that most customer transactions are viewed positively.

Customer Service Scores Increase by Generation

Different generations of Americans behave differently as customers and have different expectations, and these survey results clearly indicate that ratings of in-person customer service are higher among older than younger generations.

Ratings of Recent Customer Service Experiences in Different Types of Stores, by Generation
% Excellent/Good

	Millennials (1980-)	Generation X (1965-79)	Baby Boomers (1946-64)	Traditionalists (1900-45)
Fast food restaurant	66	66	71	83
Convenience store	74	74	80	83
Post office	76	74	81	86
Clothing or retail store	80	76	83	82
Grocery store	82	85	88	94
Pharmacy	83	85	89	95
Bank branch	84	88	88	95

Based on those who have visited this type of business in the last 30 days

GALLUP

As millennials flock to e-commerce options in the digital age, face-to-face interactions with store employees will become less and less frequent. Traditionalists, those born before 1946, still have significantly more face-to-face interactions than do millennials, especially with banks and pharmacies. In fact, this age group visited pharmacies and bank branches in person more than other age groups by a wide margin.

Generally, face-to-face interactions tend to increase customer loyalty, so if a generation does not frequently interact with store employees, its ratings of the in-person service, when they do experience it, will be lower. To some degree, this observation may explain the paradox that millennials report lower ratings of "excellent" and "good" for the service they receive in post offices (76%) than younger Americans' ratings of "excellent" and "good" for the job the U.S. Postal Service (USPS) is doing overall (81%). Older Americans, who tend to visit the post office more frequently, demonstrate a paradox in high customer service scores, but they showed less support for the job USPS is doing overall—65% rating it as excellent or good.

The lowest variance of customer service ratings across generations is for clothing/retail stores, with "excellent" ratings ranging from 76% to 83%. This relative consistency could stem from these businesses targeting certain audiences—and their sales forces have dedicated, iterative interactions with the customer base, so the customer service is more targeted to the intended audience. For example, clothing stores designed for younger shoppers may not appeal to older Americans, and their sales forces may be less likely to successfully cater to those older customers.

Bottom Line

The nature of customer service in the U.S. is changing rapidly, as more Americans are making purchases online and as businesses implement self-service options at various customer touchpoints. These changes are likely affecting the frequency and type of visits to certain time-honored institutions. For instance, the ability to download and print stamps, and schedule pickups and manage mail delivery online make visiting the post office unnecessary for many customers.

While these changes may improve efficiency in the customer transaction, it means that in-person customer service will have increasingly less influence on how brands are perceived. As the generations shift with millennials becoming an even larger proportion of the customer population, it is incumbent upon these types of businesses to evolve with these key demographic preferences.

At the same time, brick-and-mortar businesses are likely to remain in some form, and research has shown that unsatisfactory customer service is the major issue causing customers to stop buying a product or using a service. So while these businesses transform with the times, strategic investments in customer service cannot be forgotten.

Survey Methods

Results for this Gallup poll are based on telephone interviews conducted Oct. 26–Nov. 3, 2015, on the Gallup U.S. Daily survey, with a random sample of 3,572 adults, aged 18 and older, living in all 50 U.S. states and the District of Columbia. For results based on the total sample of national adults, the margin of sampling error is ±2 percentage points at the 95% confidence level. All reported margins of sampling error include computed design effects for weighting.

November 13, 2015
CANDIDATES' SOLUTIONS TO TOP U.S. PROBLEMS GET MIXED REVIEWS

by Frank Newport

Story Highlights

- *47% of Americans say candidates have good ideas to solve big problems*
- *Republicans are more positive than Democrats*
- *Americans view economy and government as top U.S. problems*

PRINCETON, N.J.—Americans are divided on whether any of the presidential candidates have come up with good ideas for handling the problem they see as the most important facing the country, with 47% saying "yes" and 45% saying "no." Republicans are most positive in their responses, with 60% saying the candidates have come up with good ideas for addressing the specific problem they name, compared with 42% of independents and Democrats who hold that view.

Do Candidates Have Good Ideas?

Based on what you have seen or read, do you think that any of the presidential candidates have come up with good ideas for solving the problem you think is most important, or not?

Do Candidates Have Good Ideas?

Based on what you have seen or read, do you think that any of the presidential candidates have come up with good ideas for solving the problem you think is most important, or not?

	Yes, have come up with good ideas	No, have not	No opinion
	%	%	%
National adults	47	45	8
Republicans	60	32	8
Independents	42	49	9
Democrats	42	53	5

Nov. 4-8, 2015

GALLUP'

Gallup has asked Americans a variant of this question at least once in each of four prior election cycles. In January 1992, for example, only 29% of Americans thought the presidential candidates had come up with good ideas "for solving the country's problems," but by October the proportion had risen to 65%. This shift suggests that perceptions of the candidates' problem-solving ideas may change as the 2016 election year progresses.

Republicans may be more positive than Democrats in their views of the candidates' ideas for several reasons. There are 15 major Republican and three Democratic candidates actively campaigning to succeed Barack Obama as president. The larger GOP field is thus putting forth a much greater volume of proposals than the smaller Democratic field, increasing the probability that Republicans can find a candidate whose ideas for solving problems they agree with.

Secondly, there have been more Republican debates than Democratic debates so far in the campaign. This has given Republican candidates more opportunities to publicly expound on their policies, and rank-and-file Republicans more opportunities to hear their candidates' proposed solutions, than has been the case for Democrats.

Third, the GOP race is arguably getting more media attention, given its highly competitive nature and the novelty of non-politicians Donald Trump and Ben Carson as the current front-runners. That compares with the Democratic race in which Hillary Clinton's status as front-runner seems unlikely to be threatened by her less well-known challengers.

In contrast to the current findings, Gallup found that Democrats were much more positive on this question in January 2008, during another open-seat presidential election year. At that time, there were numerous major contenders running in both parties.

Americans View Economy, Government as Most Important Problems

Regardless of whether they think candidates have come up with good ideas for solving them, Americans' views of the specific problems facing the nation in November show little change from previous months. Mentions of the economy in general are up slightly to 17%, essentially tied with dissatisfaction with government (15%) at the top of the list. Mentions of immigration (9%) remain high, as they have in recent months, followed by unemployment, healthcare, ethics/morals and the federal budget deficit.

Race relations, which as many as 13% of Americans had mentioned last December and 9% in July, dropped back to 3% in this survey, although interviewing was completed prior to the intense focus on race relations over the past week on the University of Missouri's main campus—culminating in the resignation of that university's president on Monday.

Most Important Problems Facing the U.S.

What do you think is the most important problem facing this country today? (open-ended)

Problem	Sep 9-13, 2015	Oct 7-11, 2015	Nov 4-8, 2015
	%	%	%
Economy in general	15	13	17
Dissatisfaction with government	17	16	15
Immigration	12	8	9
Unemployment	8	8	7
Healthcare	6	6	6
Ethics/Morals	7	5	5
Federal budget deficit	5	5	5
Gap between rich and poor	3	3	4
Education/Poor education/Access to education	4	4	3
Guns/Gun control	2	7	3
Race relations/Racism	7	4	3
National security	3	2	3
International issues, problems	3	2	3
Judicial system/Courts/Laws	4	2	3
Environment/Pollution	2	1	3
Terrorism	2	3	3
Poverty/Hunger/Homelessness	3	3	3

Responses listed by at least 3% of Americans in November are shown

GALLUP'

Americans who mention the top two problems—the economy and dissatisfaction with government—are not significantly different in their responses to the "have candidates come up with good ideas for solving this problem?" question than the overall average.

Bottom Line

Record numbers of viewers have watched both the Republican and Democratic presidential debates so far this year. Although some of the high ratings may be attributable to the entertaining candidates running for office, the high viewership levels also suggest that Americans are interested in what the candidates are saying they would do to fix the nation's problems. Less than half of Americans, at this juncture, think that any of the candidates have come up with good ideas for solving the problem they name as the most important facing the nation. That may well change as the campaign progresses, but to date many Americans—particularly independents and Democrats—are apparently still waiting to hear good ideas or haven't fully tuned in to the campaign yet.

Survey Methods

Results for this Gallup poll are based on telephone interviews conducted Nov 4–8, 2015, with a random sample of 1,021 adults, aged 18 and older, living in all 50 U.S. states and the District of Columbia. For results based on the total sample of national adults, the margin of sampling error is ±4 percentage points at the 95% confidence level. All reported margins of sampling error include computed design effects for weighting.

November 13, 2015
UNWILLING PART TIME, UNEMPLOYED ALIKE IN FINANCIAL WELL-BEING

by Dan Witters

Story Highlights

- *Involuntary part-time workers have poor financial well-being*
- *They experience as much food and healthcare insecurity as unemployed*

WASHINGTON, D.C.—The financial well-being of part-time U.S. workers who are seeking full-time work is similar to the financial well-being of the unemployed, according to the Gallup-Healthways Well-Being Index. Thus far in 2015, the financial well-being score for this group, what Gallup calls involuntary part-time workers, is 46.3, compared with 44.6 for the unemployed and 60 for full-time workers who work for an employer. And while 23% of unemployed workers are thriving financially, this is true for just 18% of involuntary part-time workers.

Financial Well-Being, by Employment Status
January-September 2015

	Unemployed	Employed part time, want full-time work	Employed full time by an employer	Self-employed full time	Employed part time, do not want full-time work
Financial well-being score	44.6	46.3	60.0	59.7	65.7
% Thriving in financial well-being	23	18	38	36	45
% Struggling in financial well-being	33	42	41	41	41
% Suffering in financial well-being	44	40	21	23	14

Gallup-Healthways Well-Being Index

GALLUP'

The Organisation for Economic Co-operation and Development (OECD) notes that "involuntary part-time work comprises three groups: 1) individuals who usually work full time but who are working part time because of economic slack, 2) individuals who usually work part time but are working fewer hours in their part-time jobs because of economic slack and 3) those working part time because full-time work could not be found." Someone working as little as a few hours a week would be considered "employed" by the U.S. federal government, which is striking because their financial well-being is similar to a person who does not have a job.

FINANCIAL WELL-BEING SCORE

UNEMPLOYED	INVOLUNTARY P-T
44.6	46.3

GALLUP-HEALTHWAYS WELL-BEING INDEX

These numbers are based on data collected daily from January through September 2015 as part of the Gallup-Healthways Well-Being Index. To assess financial well-being, Gallup and Healthways ask U.S. adults about their ability to afford food and healthcare, whether they have enough money to do everything they want to do, whether they worried about money in the past week and their perceptions of their standard of living compared with those they spend time with. Financial well-being is calculated on a scale of 0 to 100, where 0 represents the worst possible financial well-being and 100 represents the best possible financial well-being.

The financial well-being score for the U.S. as a whole was 59.7 in 2014, the first year Gallup and Healthways measured financial well-being using the current questions. The only group whose well-being score greatly exceeds that is part-time workers who do not want full-time work, registering at 65.7.

Food and Healthcare Insecurity High for Involuntary Part-Time Workers

Consistent with their lower financial well-being, those who work part time but are looking for full-time work are nearly as likely as the unemployed—about three in 10 in each group—to report having lacked enough money for food or healthcare/medicine at least once in the prior 12 months. In contrast, only about 12% of their full-time employed counterparts report similar challenges. Part-time workers who do not want full-time work report the lowest levels of insecurity of all major employment groups, reflecting the typically enhanced socio-economic status of these households.

Food and Healthcare Insecurity, by Employment Status
January-September 2015

	Unemployed	Employed part time, want full-time work	Employed full time by an employer	Self-employed full time	Employed part time, do not want full-time work
% Not enough money for food at least one time in last 12 months	31.7	29.4	11.5	11.1	8.7
% Not enough money for healthcare/ medicine at least one time in last 12 months	29.5	28.3	12.3	15.5	9.2

Gallup-Healthways Well-Being Index

GALLUP'

Involuntary part-time workers and the unemployed also report similar levels of agreement about having "enough money to do everything I want to do." In addition, about half in each group report worrying about money in the last seven days, compared with about one-third of full-time workers.

Key Financial Well-Being Metrics, by Employment Status
% Agree

	Unemployed	Employed part time, want full-time work	Employed full time by an employer	Self-employed full time	Employed part time, do not want full-time work
I have enough money to do everything I want to do.	19.9	24.9	43.3	43.0	51.2
In the last seven days, I have worried about money.	52.9	50.4	34.1	35.2	30.3

Gallup-Healthways Well-Being Index, January-September 2015

GALLUP'

Involuntary Part-Time Workers Slightly Lower in 2015

While involuntary part-time workers experience financial hardships that are very similar to the unemployed, the percentage of part-time workers who want full-time work has shown little decline over the last five years. Since 2010, the percentage of involuntary part-time workers has typically stayed between 8.6% and 9.9% in seasonally unadjusted estimates through 2014. In 2015, however, the reported percentages measured in each of the first three quarters represent five-year lows in relation to the corresponding quarters preceding them, and the 8% estimate for the most recent quarter is the lowest since measurement began.

Implications

As the U.S. economy attempts to recover from the Great Recession, part-time workers who want full-time work endure as a detriment to the progress of financial well-being nationally. These adults are essentially no better off in their overall financial well-being than are the unemployed and, in fact, are less likely to be thriving in their financial well-being.

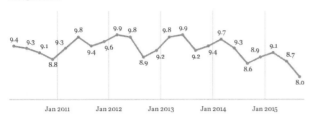

Percentage of Involuntary Part-Time Workers in U.S. Workforce, Trended Quarterly
Among all workers

Since the onset of daily measurement in 2010—the first calendar year after the official end of the Great Recession—the percentage of U.S. workers who were involuntarily working part-time jobs has only recently shown signs of decline.

This decline may signify that Americans are feeling a modest amount of financial relief. Gallup's underemployment rate, which is a combination of the unemployment rate and the involuntary part-time rate, was 14.1% in September, its lowest since daily tracking began in 2010. And given the close relationship between unemployment, involuntary part-time employment and food insecurity, it is likely that the decline in the underemployment rate has played a role in the reduction of food insecurity to its seven-year low, reported earlier this year.

Survey Methods

Results are based on 51,874 telephone interviews conducted with national adults, aged 18 and older, living in all 50 U.S. states and the District of Columbia. Included in this total are 2,622 interviews with adults who are unemployed and 4,171 with adults who are working part time but want full-time work. The margin of sampling error for each reported group is no more than ±2 percentage points, and for large groups, such as employed full time, is less than ±1 percentage point.

November 13, 2015
AMERICANS TILT MORE NEGATIVE TOWARD AFFORDABLE CARE ACT

by Andrew Dugan

Story Highlights

- *44% approve of healthcare law*
- *Since 2012, law has largely been unpopular*
- *Disapproval similar by type of insurance*

WASHINGTON, D.C.—A slight majority of Americans (52%) say they disapprove of 2010 healthcare law known as the Affordable Care Act (ACA) or "Obamacare." Disapproval of the law, which has generated public opposition from its outset, is up four percentage points since July. Approval of the ACA now stands at 44%, down slightly from 47% this summer.

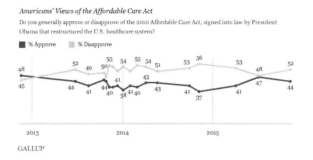

Americans' Views of the Affordable Care Act
Do you generally approve or disapprove of the 2010 Affordable Care Act, signed into law by President Obama that restructured the U.S. healthcare system?
■ % Approve   % Disapprove

The ACA was signed into law a little over five years ago, and it has survived two legal challenges that could have invalidated or fundamentally altered large parts of the law had the Supreme Court ruled differently. But as last week's gubernatorial election in Kentucky demonstrated—where an avowed ACA critic was elected—even if the legal challenges to the ACA are largely settled, the political ones are not.

Since 2013, the year before the law's much-debated mandate for individuals to obtain health insurance took effect, the ACA has been largely unpopular. Disapproval rose to 55% in late 2013 after the technology-troubled rollout of the federal government's health exchanges and the realization that millions of Americans had their insurance policies canceled because they did not meet the law's minimum coverage requirements. Those cancellations directly contradicted President Barack Obama's pledge that those who liked their insurance plan would be able to keep it under the law.

AMERICANS' APPROVAL OF ACA
APPROVE   DISAPPROVE
44%   52%
GALLUP POLL, NOV. 4-8

But over the course of 2014, even as the Obama administration presented solutions for these problems and the uninsured rate among U.S. adults fell dramatically, disapproval remained at or above majority levels. Scorn for the law rose as high as 56% in November 2014, shortly after Republicans won sole control of Congress, with many GOP candidates running promising to support legislation that would undo the law.

While the GOP-dominated Congress has so far been unable to advance a bill that would repeal the ACA wholesale, enthusiasm to repeal the law is hardly diminished among Republicans. Virtually all GOP presidential candidates promise to repeal the law if elected, and nearly nine in 10 rank-and-file Republicans (86%) disapprove of the ACA in the most recent survey. Gallup has previously found that identifying as Republican is the single biggest predictor in determining if a person will disapprove of the law.

ACA Approval Varies Little by Health Insurance Plan

The ACA expands healthcare coverage through various mechanisms, including by expanding eligibility for Medicare and Medicaid, at least for those living in states that have chosen to cooperate in the expansion of these government-run programs. An even greater number of Americans have obtained private health insurance of some variety under the law.

But whether Americans have a private insurance plan or are using Medicaid or Medicare exclusively, they are still more likely to disapprove than approve of the law, according to aggregated data from Gallup's 2014 and 2015 Healthcare polls. A majority of Americans with health coverage disapprove of the ACA, with 56% of Americans with private insurance plans disapproving and 50% of those using Medicaid or Medicare disapproving.

Approval of the Healthcare Law by Type of Insurance Plan

Do you generally approve or disapprove of the 2010 Affordable Care Act, signed into law by President Obama that restructured the U.S. healthcare system?

	Private insurance	Medicaid or Medicare, no private insurance	No insurance
% Approve	41	44	30
% Disapprove	56	50	59

Aggregated Gallup data from Nov. 6-9, 2014, and Nov. 4-8, 2015

GALLUP

Individuals who say they have no insurance, however, tilt heavily toward disapproval of the healthcare law.

Bottom Line

The ACA, or Obamacare, remains the law of the land, overcoming numerous legal challenges—including two that reached the Supreme Court—and unrelenting political opposition. But the law's continued survival and its empirical success in lowering the uninsured rate has not made much difference in how Americans feel about the law. As such, it seems doubtful that the law will be broadly accepted in the U.S. political system in the near future. It will likely remain the target of efforts to repeal or significantly modify it, which could finally prevail if Americans elect a wholly Republican federal government in 2016.

Survey Methods

Results for this Gallup poll are based on telephone interviews conducted Nov. 4–8, 2015, on the Gallup U.S. Daily survey, with a random sample of 1,021 adults, aged 18 and older, living in all 50 U.S. states and the District of Columbia. For results based on the total sample of national adults, the margin of sampling error is ±4 percentage points at the 95% confidence level. All reported margins of sampling error include computed design effects for weighting.

November 16, 2015
APPROVAL OF OBAMA'S HANDLING OF ECONOMY, HEALTHCARE AT 44%

by Justin McCarthy

Story Highlights

- *Both measures at their respective highs since November 2012*
- *Democrats still most approving of Obama's performance on issues*

WASHINGTON, D.C.—Americans' approval of President Barack Obama's handling of the economy and healthcare policy—both at 44%—is at the high for each since November 2012. The president's economic rating was almost as high (43%) in a survey conducted in February 2015.

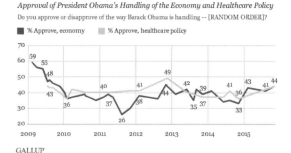

Approval of President Obama's Handling of the Economy and Healthcare Policy

Do you approve or disapprove of the way Barack Obama is handling -- [RANDOM ORDER]?

GALLUP

Americans have not been as approving of Obama's performance on the economy since November 2012, just after the president was re-elected to a second term. The 44% he received then was similar to the 45% right before Election Day. Both scores were major improvements from the sub-40% ratings he'd received during much of his first term—including a record low of 26% in August 2011 after contentious negotiations with Congress to raise the debt limit. Obama's best marks on the economy—between 55% and 59%—came during his first few months in office. Over the past three years, Obama's economic approval rating has fluctuated, reaching a low of 33% in 2014.

The president's approval ratings on healthcare policy have stayed within a tighter range. Americans were least approving of his handling of the issue, at 36%, in February 2010 and in November 2014, when his overall job approval rating was near a record low, and were most approving in November 2012, at 49%. His average approval rating for this issue is 41%.

These data are from a Nov. 4–8 Gallup poll, taken before Friday's Paris terrorist attacks, which appear to have led to a modest rally in support for the president. Obama's overall approval rating rose from 47% in Tuesday to Thursday Gallup Daily tracking to 51% from Friday to Sunday.

The Nov. 4–8 poll also included measures of Obama's handling of foreign affairs (37%) and the situation involving Islamic State militants, commonly known as ISIS, in Iraq and Syria (30%). Both of these ratings would likely be different today, after the Paris attacks. Obama's 37% rating on foreign affairs is consistent with the 36% and 39% ratings he received on the issue in two polls conducted earlier this year, but substantially lower than the majority approval ratings he initially received in his first term in office.

Perhaps unsurprisingly, Democrats remain most approving of the president's performance on the economy (70%) and healthcare (75%), with a smaller majority approving of his handling of foreign affairs (61%). None of these ratings has changed much since a year ago. Conversely, Republicans approve of Obama's performance on these issues the least, with approval ratings just above 10% on each measure. Though still low, these dismal scores are slightly higher than Republicans' single-digit approval of one year ago.

Independents, however, have become significantly more approving of Obama's handling of the economy—up 19 percentage points from last year; healthcare policy, up 10 points; and foreign affairs, up eight points.

At the time the poll was taken, a slight majority of Democrats (53%) approved of Obama's handling of the situation involving the Islamic State, compared with 27% of independents and 10% of

Republicans. While relatively few Republicans approve, they were most likely among political groups to favor the use of ground troops in Syria and Iraq, as Obama has recently committed to doing. The latest developments in Paris could cause Obama to change, or possibly increase the intensity of, his approach.

Changes in Ratings of Obama's Handling of the Issues, by Political Party
November 2014 vs. November 2015

	November 2014 %	November 2015 %	Change (pct. pts.)
ECONOMIC APPROVAL			
Democrats	70	72	+2
Independents	24	43	+19
Republicans	9	15	+6
			.
HEALTHCARE APPROVAL			
Democrats	75	77	+2
Independents	30	40	+10
Republicans	7	12	+5
FOREIGN AFFAIRS APPROVAL			
Democrats	61	61	0
Independents	27	35	+8
Republicans	7	13	+6

GALLUP

Bottom Line

As the unemployment rate hits a seven-year low, approval of the president's handling of the economy has edged up to a recent high. Americans' approval of Obama's handling of healthcare policy is also up to 44%. Both of these are, however, lower than the president's overall approval rating, which was 49% as measured in this same poll and appears to have pushed past 50% in the wake of the Paris attacks. That modest rally in support may have affected how Americans view Obama's handling of specific issues—in particular the situation with the Islamic State and foreign affairs, but possibly also the economy and healthcare.

Obama continues to enjoy majority approval ratings on these issues within his party, and has experienced sizable year-over-year increases in approval among independents. Ratings from the GOP remain low, but have thawed slightly since last year.

Survey Methods

Results for this Gallup poll are based on telephone interviews conducted Nov. 4–8, 2015, with a random sample of 1,021 adults, aged 18 and older, living in all 50 U.S. states and the District of Columbia. For results based on the total sample of national adults, the margin of sampling error is ±4 percentage points at the 95% confidence level. All reported margins of sampling error include computed design effects for weighting.

November 16, 2015
AMERICANS PLAN ON SPENDING A LOT MORE THIS CHRISTMAS

by Lydia Saad

Story Highlights

- *Americans plan to spend an average of $830 on gifts this season*
- *Estimate is up sharply from $720 a year ago at this time*
- *Increase points to solid holiday retail sales*

PRINCETON, N.J.—Gallup's November update of Americans' 2015 holiday spending intentions finds U.S. adults planning to spend $830 on Christmas gifts this year, on average. That is up sharply from the $720 recorded a year ago, and is significantly higher than what consumers have indicated in any November since 2007.

Americans' Christmas Spending Estimate in November of Each Year
Roughly how much money do you think you personally will spend on Christmas gifts this year?

■ Average, including zero

$857 $817 $794 $690 $734 $730 $763 $826 $866 $616 $638 $764 $770 $714 $704 $720 $830

'99 '00 '01 '02 '03 '04 '05 '06 '07 '08 '09 '10 '11 '12 '13 '14 '15

GALLUP

According to the Nov. 4–8 poll, 30% of U.S. adults expect to spend $1,000 or more on gifts, slightly higher than the 25% in the top-spender category a year ago. About one in five will spend between $500 and $999, 14% will spend between $250 and $499, and 19% will spend less than $250. Just 8% say they don't celebrate Christmas or won't be spending anything, while 7% are unsure how much they will spend.

AMOUNT AMERICANS EXPECT TO SPEND THIS CHRISTMAS, ON AVERAGE

$830

GALLUP POLL, NOV. 4-8

Although the average amount all Americans expect to spend is $830, the figure rises to $908 when excluding those who won't spend anything—or, in other words, when limited to U.S. Christmas shoppers.

Americans' Christmas Spending Estimate
Roughly how much money do you think you personally will spend on Christmas gifts this year?

	Nov 19-20, 2014 %	Nov 4-8, 2015 %
$1,000 or more	25	30
$500 to $999	21	21
$250 to $499	15	14
$100 to $249	19	17
Less than $100	5	2
None/Don't celebrate	9	8
Not sure	6	7
Average (including zero)	$720	$830
Average (excluding zero)	$790	$908

GALLUP

Gallup's initial measure of 2015 holiday spending plans, conducted in October, also showed consumers poised to splurge this Christmas, as that month's $812 average spending figure was the highest Gallup had seen in any October since 2007. The consistency between the two months is a bit unusual, as Gallup typically finds

Americans scaling back their spending plans between October and November.

Americans' Christmas Spending Estimates in October and November of Each Year

	October	November	Change
2015	$812	$830	$18
2014	$781	$720	($61)
2013	$786	$704	($82)
2012	--	$770	--
2011	$712	$764	$52
2010	$715	$714	($1)
2009	$740	$638	($102)
2008	$801	$616	($185)
2007	$909	$866	($43)
2006	$907	$826	($81)
2005	--	$763	--
2004	--	$730	--
2003	--	$734	--
2002	$695	$690	($5)
2001	--	$794	--
2000	--	$817	--
1999	--	$857	--

Averages include zero, for those who plan to spend nothing.

GALLUP

According to Gallup's modeling of how prior years' spending forecasts compare with the final November–December retail sales figures for each year, Americans' latest Christmas spending data point to an estimated increase of between 5.1% and 5.8% in U.S. holiday retail sales. This forecast is based on historical comparisons of Gallup November spending estimates to the U.S. Census Bureau's GAFO (General Merchandise, Apparel and Accessories, Furniture and Other Sales) retail sales estimates.

Even at the low end, the predicted range of increased holiday spending would be a considerable improvement over the past decade, when retail sales increases have had a hard time exceeding 3%, and even decreased during the worst of the 2007–2009 economic slump.

*Gallup November Christmas Spending Forecast vs. Holiday Retail Sales^*

■ Year-to-year % change in Gallup's November Christmas spending forecast

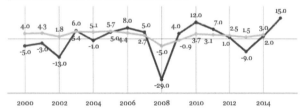
▨ Year-to-year % change in GAFO November/December sales^

^ Holiday retail sales based on average November/December retail sales, according to Commerce Department's GAFO measure of department store and general merchandise store sales

GALLUP

Christmas spending intentions vary greatly by household income. Americans living in households earning $75,000 or more per year plan to spend an average of $1,227 on Christmas gifts this season. This drops to $786 among middle-income earners and to $460 among those earning less than $30,000.

Estimated Christmas spending is also higher among households with children younger than 18 living at home than among those without children at home: $1,092 versus $706.

Regardless of whether Americans follow through with their higher spending intentions, the fact that they are in the mood to do so is a positive sign for the nation's retailers at the end of a slow year. Until now, overall consumer spending has been rather anemic according to U.S. Commerce Department data, typically rising by not much more than 1% in any month this year. However, the latest available GAFO data from September—which are more indicative of the types of purchases Americans make at Christmas—showed an increase of 2.4%. If that holds in the October report, an increase of 5% or more by November and December may not be unreasonable, particularly in light of continued lower gas prices.

Survey Methods

Results for this Gallup poll are based on telephone interviews conducted Nov. 4–8, 2015, with a random sample of 1,021 adults, aged 18 and older, living in all 50 U.S. states and the District of Columbia. For results based on the total sample of national adults, the margin of sampling error is ±4 percentage points at the 95% confidence level. The margin of sampling error for the average Christmas spending estimate is ±$63 at the 95% confidence level.

November 17, 2015
U.S. GIRLS LESS CONFIDENT THEY CAN LEARN COMPUTER SCIENCE

by Elizabeth Keating and Cynthia English

Story Highlights

- *Students, parents, teachers think boys more interested in computer science*
- *Students, parents, teachers think boys more successful in learning it*
- *Fewer female students expect to learn computer science in future*

WASHINGTON, D.C.—American girls in seventh through 12th grades express less confidence than boys do in their ability to learn computer science, according to a recent study by Gallup and Google. Less than half of female students (46%) say they are "very confident" they could learn computer science, compared with 62% of male students.

Confidence in Learning Computer Science Among Seventh- Through 12th-Grade Students

How confident are you that you could learn computer science if you wanted to?

	% Very confident
All	54
Male	62
Female	46

Nov. 19-Dec. 17, 2014

GALLUP

These findings are from a 2014 study by Gallup and Google with random, nationally representative samples of seventh- to

12th-grade students in the U.S., parents of seventh- to 12th-grade students and teachers of students in first through 12th grades.

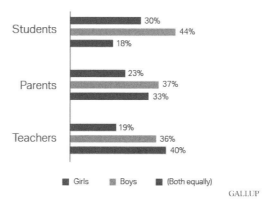

VERY LIKELY TO LEARN COMPUTER SCIENCE, AMONG THOSE IN GRADES 7-12

FEMALE STUDENTS 18%

MALE STUDENTS 35%

GALLUP/GOOGLE STUDY

Female students are also less likely than male students to believe they will learn and do computer science in the future. Male students are nearly twice as likely as girls to say they are "very likely" to learn computer science in the future. Although one in three female students believe they will have a job someday in which they will need to know some computer science, this percentage still trails the 42% of boys who say the same.

Likelihood to Learn Computer Science Among Seventh- Through 12th-Grade Students

	All	Male	Female
How likely are you to learn more computer science in the future? (% Very likely)	27	35	18
How likely are you to have a job someday where you would need to know some computer science? (% Very likely)	38	42	33

Nov. 19-Dec. 17, 2014

GALLUP

Girls Widely Viewed as Less Interested Than Boys in Computer Science

In the U.S., girls are generally viewed as less interested than boys in computer science. Students, parents and teachers are more likely to perceive that boys are more interested than girls in learning computer science, and that boys are more likely than girls to be successful in learning it. Among all students, three in four believe that boys are more interested in computer science, and nearly two-thirds of parents and teachers feel the same.

Perceived Gender Differences in Interest in Computer Science

Who do you think is **more interested** in learning computer science?

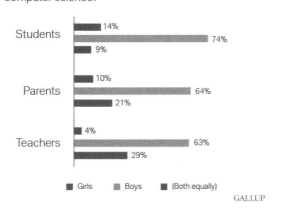

Students
Girls 14%
Boys 74%
(Both equally) 9%

Parents
Girls 10%
Boys 64%
(Both equally) 21%

Teachers
Girls 4%
Boys 63%
(Both equally) 29%

■ Girls　■ Boys　■ (Both equally)

GALLUP

Parents and teachers are more likely than students to say that both genders are equally likely to be interested in and successful in learning computer science. But in all three groups, those who see one gender as having an advantage all lean more heavily toward saying boys are more likely to be interested and to succeed than girls.

Perceived Gender Differences in Success in Computer Science

Who do you think is **more likely to be successful** in learning computer science?

Students
Girls 30%
Boys 44%
(Both equally) 18%

Parents
Girls 23%
Boys 37%
(Both equally) 33%

Teachers
Girls 19%
Boys 36%
(Both equally) 40%

■ Girls　■ Boys　■ (Both equally)

GALLUP

Students and parents were asked how often they see different types of people engaging in computer science on TV and in movies. While about half of students and parents say they see women engaged in computer science in movies and TV shows at least "some of the time," more than a third in each group say they see them in these roles "not very often" or "never."

Perceptions of Computer Science in TV/Film

How often do you see people who do computer science in movies or TV shows who are women?

	Students	Parents
Most of the time	15%	8%
Some of the time	47%	53%
Not very often	31%	30%
Never	5%	5%

November-December, 2014

GALLUP

Bottom Line

Students, parents and teachers in the U.S. are all more likely to view computer science as a male field than a female field. This belief is illustrated in the perceptions among students, parents and teachers that girls are less interested in the field and are less likely than boys to be successful in learning computer science, and girls' own lack of confidence, relative to boys, in their ability to learn computer science. Further, nearly one in three students and parents rarely see female role models in the media to counteract these perceptions.

Parents and teachers may need to more actively encourage their daughters and female students to pursue computer science or work to make computer science learning more appealing to girls. Having more women in TV and movies performing computer science could also help break the stereotype that computer science is more for men. However it is accomplished, getting more girls interested in computer science will be necessary to expand diversity and to increase the pool of qualified job candidates in this rapidly growing field.

Survey Methods

This article includes results from three surveys conducted by Gallup on behalf of Google.

Results for the *Images of Computer Science: Perceptions among Students, Parents and Educators in the U.S.* report are based on surveys conducted with parents, students, teachers, principals and superintendents.

Telephone interviews were conducted for students, parents and teachers currently living in all 50 states and the District of Columbia using a combination of two sample sources: the Gallup Panel and the Gallup Daily tracking survey. The Gallup Panel is a proprietary, probability-based panel of U.S. adults selected using random-digit-dial (RDD) and address-based sampling methods. The Gallup Panel is not an opt-in panel. The Gallup Daily tracking survey sample includes national adults with a minimum quota of 50% cellphone respondents and 50% landline respondents, with additional minimum quotas by time zone within region. Landline and cellular telephone numbers are selected using RDD methods. Landline respondents are chosen at random within each household based on which member had the most recent birthday. Eligible Gallup Daily tracking respondents who previously agreed to future contact were contacted to participate in this study. Parent and student interviews were conducted in English and Spanish. Teacher interviews were conducted in English only.

Student interviews were conducted Nov. 19–Dec. 17, 2014, with a sample of 1,673 students in grades 7 to 12.

Parent interviews were conducted Nov. 19–Dec. 8, 2014, with a sample of 1,685 parents with at least one child in grades 7 to 12.

Teacher interviews were conducted Nov. 25–Dec. 14, 2014, with a sample of 1,013 first- to 12th-grade teachers.

Student and parent samples are weighted to correct for unequal selection probability and nonresponse. Parent data are weighted to match national demographics of age, gender, education, race, ethnicity and region. Student data are weighted to match national demographics of age, gender, race, ethnicity and region. Demographic weighting targets are based on the most recent Current Population Survey.

Teacher samples are weighted to correct for unequal selection probability and nonresponse. The data are weighted to match demographics of age, gender, education, race, ethnicity and region. Demographic weighting targets are based on Gallup Daily tracking information.

All reported margins of sampling error include the computed design effects for weighting.

For results based on the total sample of students, the margin of sampling error is ±3.4 percentage points at the 95% confidence level.

For results based on the total sample of parents, the margin of sampling error is ±3.5 percentage points at the 95% confidence level.

For results based on the total sample of teachers, the margin of sampling error is ±4.0 percentage points at the 95% confidence level.

November 17, 2015
NEW SPEAKER RYAN'S IMAGE POSITIVE AT OUTSET

by Jeffrey M. Jones

Story Highlights

- *42% view Paul Ryan favorably, 29% unfavorably*
- *+13 net favorable rating his highest*
- *Most past Speakers rated favorably when they assumed role*

PRINCETON, N.J.—Speaker of the House Paul Ryan begins his term with generally positive ratings from Americans—42% have a favorable opinion of him and 29% an unfavorable one. His ratings have generally been more positive than negative over the last three years, but Ryan's current +13 net favorable rating is his best to date.

Favorable and Unfavorable Ratings of Paul Ryan

Percentages for "No opinion" are not shown.
Data from one-night poll on Aug. 12, 2012, are not shown (25% favorable/17% unfavorable).

GALLUP

The latest data are from a Nov. 4–8 Gallup poll, conducted shortly after Ryan took over as the new Speaker of the House. Gallup has measured opinions of Ryan at various points since August 2012, when Republican presidential nominee Mitt Romney tabbed him as his vice presidential running mate. Ryan's ratings at that time were only slightly more positive than negative, likely because his presence on the GOP presidential ticket caused Democrats to view him much more negatively than they do now.

Two subsequent readings, taken when Ryan was considered a potential 2016 presidential candidate, showed a slightly wider gap between his favorable and unfavorable ratings, but also a decline in the percentage of Americans familiar enough with Ryan to rate him. In July 2014, 45% of Americans did not have an opinion of Ryan, compared with an average 22% during the 2012 campaign and 29% currently.

His current 42% favorable rating essentially ties with 43% from September 2012 as his high, but in that poll, his unfavorable rating was considerably higher than now—40% compared with 29%.

Most Past Speakers Enjoyed Positive Initial Ratings

Americans have generally rated new Speakers of the House quite positively when they take office. This includes John Boehner (+20 net favorable) in 2011, Nancy Pelosi (+22) in 2007 and Dennis Hastert (+21) in 1999. The exception is Newt Gingrich, whose net favorable was -3 in 1995. However, that is also one of Gingrich's best evaluations in Gallup's trend on him, behind only a +4 net rating (29% favorable, 25% unfavorable) a few weeks after the 1994 midterm elections that led to Gingrich rising to the Speakership.

Ryan should not expect his "honeymoon" to last very long, if history is a guide. Only Hastert maintained more positive than negative ratings two years into his Speakership. But Hastert may have benefited from being less well known than other Speakers, as evidenced by the high percentage not having an opinion of him for much of his tenure. He also governed during a time when Americans were generally satisfied with the way things were going in the United States.

All recent Speakers, including Hastert, left the Speakership rated more negatively than positively, and much worse off than when they started.

Opinions of Speakers of the House -- First and Final Gallup Polls While Speaker

	% Favorable	% Unfavorable	Net favorable
NEWT GINGRICH			
1995 Jan 16-18	34	37	-3
1998 Dec 28-29	38	51	-13
DENNIS HASTERT			
1999 Feb 19-21	31	10	+21
2006 Oct 6-8	27	36	-9
NANCY PELOSI			
2007 Jan 5-7	44	22	+22
2010 Oct 14-17	29	56	-27
JOHN BOEHNER			
2011 Jan 14-16	42	22	+20
2015 Oct 7-11	31	45	-14
PAUL RYAN			
2015 Nov 4-8	42	29	+13

Percentages for "No opinion" are not shown.

GALLUP

Ryan Popular Among Republicans

The poll finds 67% of Republicans have a favorable opinion of Ryan, while 15% have an unfavorable opinion. Both figures are up by about 10 percentage points from Gallup's prior reading, taken in July 2014.

Republicans do not view Ryan quite as positively now as they did when he was running for vice president. In late September 2012, his favorable rating was 85% among the party base.

Favorable and Unfavorable Ratings of Paul Ryan, Among Republicans

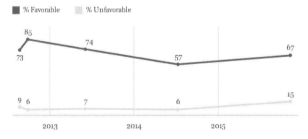

■ % Favorable ░ % Unfavorable

Percentages for "No opinion" are not shown.
Data from one-night poll on Aug. 12, 2012, are not shown (25% favorable/17% unfavorable).

GALLUP

Although Ryan has been rated more positively by Republicans in the past, his current ratings paint a stark contrast with Gallup's most recent reads on Senate Majority Leader Mitch McConnell and former Speaker Boehner from October. Republicans rated both men more negatively than positively.

Implications

As has been the case for recent Speakers, Ryan is entering his new role with more Americans viewing him positively than negatively. Ryan will face a challenge in maintaining those positive ratings, given the trajectory of prior Speakers' favorable ratings. The partisan nature of the role and the association with the unpopular institution of Congress are two likely reasons Speakers become less popular over time.

If Ryan's popularity fades like that of prior speakers, he may follow a downward path among his fellow partisans, as did Boehner—or could remain popular among core party supporters, as did Pelosi. Democrat Pelosi had 62% favorable and 22% unfavorable ratings among Democrats in her final Gallup reading as Speaker in October 2010, not much worse than her initial rating in January 2007. Pelosi's overall ratings turned highly negative because Republicans came to view her so badly. Just 8% gave her a favorable rating while 86% rated her unfavorably in the final Gallup measure of her as Speaker.

Ryan was reluctant to become Speaker, but many Republicans believed he was the only member who could win sufficient support from the conservative and moderate wings of the party. His ability to keep both wings of the party happy will be important in determining how long the honeymoon phase of his Speakership lasts.

Survey Methods

Results for this Gallup poll are based on telephone interviews conducted Nov. 4–8, 2015, with a random sample of 1,021 adults, aged 18 and older, living in all 50 U.S. states and the District of Columbia. For results based on the total sample of national adults, the margin of sampling error is ±4 percentage points at the 95% confidence level. All reported margins of sampling error include computed design effects for weighting.

November 18, 2015
AMERICANS AGAIN CITE COST AND ACCESS AS TOP HEALTH ISSUES

by Rebecca Riffkin

Story Highlights

- *Forty-two percent name either healthcare cost or access*
- *At least 14% of Americans cite cancer, obesity*
- *17% named Ebola last year, versus less than 1% in 2015*

WASHINGTON, D.C.—Americans continue to name the cost of (22%) and access to (20%) healthcare as the most urgent health problems facing the U.S. Obesity and cancer are next on the list, cited by 15% and 14%, respectively. No other issue receives more than 2% of mentions from Americans.

Gallup has asked Americans every November since 2001, and periodically before that, to name the most urgent health problem facing the U.S. Cost of and access to healthcare have generally topped the list since the early 2000s, while Americans most frequently mentioned diseases such as cancer and AIDS in the 1990s and in Gallup's one survey in the 1980s.

Cost and Access Remain Most Commonly Named as Urgent Health Problems

What would you say is the most urgent health problem facing this country at the present time?

	Nov 7-10, 2013	Nov 6-9, 2014	Nov 4-8, 2015
	%	%	%
Affordable healthcare/health insurance; costs	23	19	22
Access to healthcare/universal health coverage	16	18	20
Ebola virus	--	17	*
Obesity	13	10	15
Cancer	10	10	14
Finding cures for diseases	1	3	2
Diabetes	2	2	2
Drug/Alcohol abuse	1	1	2
Government interference	9	2	1
Heart disease	2	2	1
Flu	--	1	1
Mental illness	2	1	1
AIDS	1	1	1
Other	6	3	7
No opinion	13	10	12

* Less than 0.5%

GALLUP'

Other health issues have appeared near the top of the list over the past 15 years, including last year, when Ebola was listed among the top three health concerns. This was most likely in response to multiple Ebola outbreaks in West Africa and a few confirmed cases in the U.S., which prompted widespread media coverage of the disease. This year, less than 0.5% of Americans listed Ebola as the most urgent issue, as the threat of the virus has subsided in both the U.S. and West Africa. Similar short-lived spikes in the responses to this question have occurred regarding other recent health threats, including the H1N1/swine flu outbreak in 2009 and anthrax and bioterrorism attacks in 2001.

Mentions of the cost of healthcare jumped to 30% in 1992, possibly in response to Bill Clinton's making healthcare cost a major campaign issue; however, AIDS was the most-cited health problem that year, with 41% naming it. Mentions of cost and access increased again at the start of the new millennium, underscoring the degree to which Americans have become as concerned or more concerned with healthcare basics than specific diseases in recent years. From 2007 until 2013, Americans were more likely to name access than cost, but since 2013, cost has surpassed access as the most frequently cited urgent health problem.

The Cost of and Access to Healthcare: 1987-2015

What would you say is the most urgent health problem facing this country at the present time? [OPEN-ENDED]

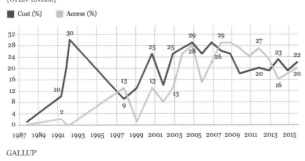

GALLUP'

Gallup has found no significant changes in mentions of cost and access since the Affordable Care Act was passed in 2010. While far fewer Americans lack insurance today than in 2013, one in five Americans still name access to healthcare or cost as the most urgent health problem.

Obesity, Cancer Most Frequently Named Diseases

Americans are more likely to name obesity or cancer as the most urgent problem facing the U.S. than other illnesses and diseases, including the flu, AIDS and heart disease. While mentions of cancer were near 20% in the early 2000s, they have dropped since then and have remained at 15% or less over the last decade.

Mentions of obesity increased from 1% in 1999 to as high as 16% in 2012. They dropped slightly last year, perhaps because Americans were more concerned with Ebola, but have increased again slightly in 2015, to 15%. Gallup and Healthways found that the obesity rate among U.S. adults reached 27.7% in 2014, the highest rate in seven years of tracking it.

Mentions of Obesity and Cancer as the Most Urgent U.S. Health Problem Since 1999

Open-ended

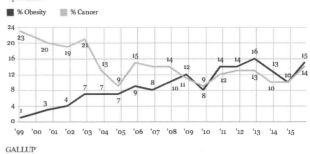

GALLUP'

Bottom Line

Americans continue to be most likely to name healthcare access or cost as the most urgent health issues facing the U.S., surpassing physical health ailments. In the 1980s and 1990s, AIDS was the dominant issue, and cancer ranked no lower than second from 1999 to 2002.

The Obama administration has made a major effort to address healthcare cost and access by passing the Affordable Care Act. Since its major provisions went into effect, there has been a drop in the percentage of Americans who lack health insurance. But the law probably did not affect the healthcare situation for the large majority of Americans, most of whom get health insurance through an employer or Medicare. The percentages mentioning both cost and access are down from the later years of George W. Bush's administration, even though they remain the top overall issues.

Survey Methods

Results for this Gallup poll are based on telephone interviews conducted Nov. 4–8, 2015, with a random sample of 1,021 adults, aged 18 and older, living in all 50 U.S. states and the District of Columbia. For results based on the total sample of national adults, the margin of sampling error is ±4 percentage points at the 95% confidence level. All reported margins of sampling error include computed design effects for weighting.

DESPITE HAVING HEART ATTACK, MANY SMOKE, ARE OBESE

by Alyssa Davis

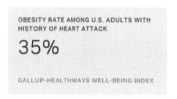

OBESITY RATE AMONG U.S. ADULTS WITH HISTORY OF HEART ATTACK

35%

GALLUP-HEALTHWAYS WELL-BEING INDEX

Story Highlights

- *Those who have had a heart attack less likely to exercise than those who haven't*
- *Those who have survived a heart attack more likely to experience stress*
- *Eating habits similar among those who have and haven't had a heart attack*

WASHINGTON, D.C.—Americans who have had a heart attack may not be making the necessary lifestyle changes to reduce their risk of having another one. Those who have had a heart attack are significantly more likely than those who never have had a heart attack to smoke, be obese and experience stress. And those who have survived a heart attack are much less likely to exercise regularly.

Health Habits of U.S. Adults, by Heart Attack Status

History of heart attack is based on answering "yes" to the following question: "Have you ever been told by a physician or nurse that you have had a heart attack?" Results are shown after controlling for age, race, ethnicity, income, education, region, marital status and children in household.

	History of heart attack	No history of heart attack	Difference
	%	%	(pct. pts.)
Smoke	22	17	+5
Are obese	35	27	+8
Experienced stress "yesterday"	52	41	+11
Exercise 30+ minutes, 3+ days per week	46	52	-6

Gallup-Healthways Well-Being Index
January 2014-June 2015

GALLUP

Medical research shows that patients who have had a heart attack are at higher risk for having another one. While individuals cannot change some risk factors for having a heart attack—increasing age, being male, hereditary factors and having a family history of heart disease—they can make lifestyle changes that may reduce their risk for, or even reverse, cardiac disease. These changes include eating a heart-healthy diet; engaging in regular, moderate physical activity; quitting smoking; maintaining a healthy weight; and minimizing stress.

These findings, collected as part of the Gallup-Healthways Well-Being Index from January 2014 through June 2015, do not follow the same people over time and cannot speak to whether those who have had a heart attack are practicing healthier behaviors than they were before they had a heart attack. It is possible that, as a group, those who have had a heart attack at some point in their lifetime have healthier habits now than they did before they had a heart attack. But these findings do show that, overall, Americans who have survived a heart attack are still less likely to practice key healthy behaviors than those who have not had a heart attack.

Even after controlling for key demographic differences between those who have had a heart attack and those who haven't—such as age, race or ethnicity, gender and income—these differences hold.

Self-Reported Eating Habits Similar for Both Groups

While those who have had a heart attack fall short on a number of important healthy behaviors, their self-reported eating habits are similar to those of Americans who have not had a heart attack. Both groups are about as likely to say they practiced healthy eating all day "yesterday" and to say they eat the recommended number of servings of fruits and vegetables each week.

Eating Habits of U.S. Adults, by Heart Attack Status

History of heart attack is based on answering "yes" to the following question: "Have you ever been told by a physician or nurse that you have had a heart attack?" Results are shown after controlling for age, race, ethnicity, income, education, region, marital status and children in household.

	History of heart attack	No history of heart attack	Difference
	%	%	(pct. pts.)
Ate healthy all day "yesterday"	61	63	-2
Eat 5+ servings of fruits, vegetables 4+ days a week	59	57	+2

Gallup-Healthways Well-Being Index
January 2014-June 2015

GALLUP

Still, about two in five people who have had a heart attack say they did not practice healthy eating the day before being interviewed and that they do not consume the recommended amount of fruits and vegetables.

On a positive note, nine in 10 people who have had a heart attack say they have a personal doctor, higher than the 83% found among those who have not had a heart attack. This is an encouraging sign that those who have had a heart attack may have a physician regularly monitoring their cardiac health and helping them manage their risk for another heart attack.

Implications

The percentage of U.S. adults who report having had a heart attack has declined over the seven years Gallup and Healthways have measured it, from 4.5% in 2008 to 3.9% in 2014. While the overall drop in this figure is positive news, many people who have had a heart attack may not be making the lifestyle changes that could prevent or reverse cardiac disease, given their higher smoking and obesity rates, higher stress levels and poorer exercise habits compared with those who have never had a heart attack. Not making these lifestyle changes could lead to higher healthcare costs and utilization, putting a financial strain on the economy, healthcare systems and families.

The percentage who report having had a heart attack varies widely by state—from a low of 2.4% in Utah to a high of 7.7% in West Virginia. Hospitals, employers and insurance companies, especially those in states with high percentages of residents who report that they have had a heart attack, can provide heart attack survivors and those at risk with the ongoing education, resources and support they need to help them make positive changes. And given that nine in 10 Americans who have experienced a heart attack report having a personal doctor, physicians are uniquely positioned to reinforce the lifestyle changes patients should make to prevent another heart attack.

"Heart disease is preventable and usually even reversible for most people by making comprehensive lifestyle changes—eat well, stress less, move more, love more," said Dr. Dean Ornish, president of the Preventive Medicine Research Institute. "A new paradigm of healthcare—lifestyle medicine—empowers people to address and transform these underlying causes of heart disease."

Family and friends also can play an important role in encouraging those who have had a heart attack to improve their health habits. Previous Gallup and Healthways research shows that having a heart attack doubles the odds of being diagnosed with depression. People who have had a heart attack often need social support to manage the numerous lifestyle changes they need to make and to cope with the depression and stress that can accompany such a major health event.

Ultimately, though, it is up to those who have had a heart attack to commit to lifestyle changes that could prevent further heart disease—not just immediately after a heart attack, but for the rest of their lives.

Survey Methods

Results are based on telephone interviews conducted Jan. 2, 2014–June 30, 2015, as part of the Gallup-Healthways Well-Being Index survey, with a random sample of 265,369 adults, aged 18 and older, living in all 50 U.S. states and the District of Columbia. For results based on the total sample of national adults, the margin of sampling error is ±0.24 percentage points at the 95% confidence level. For results based on the total sample of people who have had a heart attack, the margin of sampling error is ±1.08 percentage points at the 95% confidence level. All reported margins of sampling error include computed design effects for weighting.

November 19, 2015
AMERICANS' OWN HEALTHCARE RATINGS LITTLE CHANGED SINCE ACA

by Frank Newport

Story Highlights

- *Americans' views of cost and quality of their healthcare little changed*
- *Ratings are positive for majority of Americans*
- *Overall, little apparent impact of ACA on these attitudes*

PRINCETON, N.J.—Americans' overall satisfaction with the total cost they pay for their healthcare has been generally stable over the past 14 years. The 57% who now say they are satisfied is close to the 58% average across the 15 times Gallup has asked the question since 2001. In November 2001, satisfaction hit a high of 64%, partly reflecting the rally effect after 9/11. The low point was 54% in 2006.

Americans cite cost as the most urgent health problem facing the U.S. today. One might expect that their satisfaction with healthcare costs would drop after the Affordable Care Act (ACA) brought more previously uninsured people into the system and made changes to coverage. However, satisfaction with healthcare costs has remained

relatively stable. The current 57% who are satisfied is lower than the 62% measured in November 2009—the year before the ACA was signed into law.

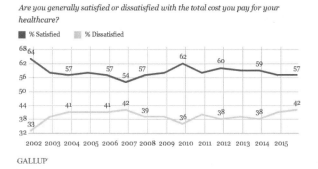

Are you generally satisfied or dissatisfied with the total cost you pay for your healthcare?

GALLUP

These data are from Gallup's annual Health and Healthcare survey conducted Nov. 4–8. Subsequent stories will look at trends in Americans' views of the U.S. healthcare system more broadly and attitudes about the appropriate government role in the nation's healthcare system.

Not surprisingly, Americans who get their insurance through a government program such as Medicare or Medicaid are more satisfied with the cost of their insurance than are those who have private insurance. Previous Gallup research has shown that those with government plans are also more likely than those with private plans to be satisfied with the way the healthcare system is working in general.

Americans' Satisfaction With Their Cost of Healthcare, by Type of Insurance
Are you generally satisfied or dissatisfied with the total cost you pay for your healthcare?

	% Satisfied
National adults	57
Medicare/Medicaid/Government	66
Private insurance	53

GALLUP

The percentage of Americans who have health insurance has increased by more than five percentage points in the past several years, likely as a result of the ACA, but there has been no positive uptick in Americans' ratings of their healthcare coverage. About two-thirds of Americans rate their coverage as excellent or good, and relatively few—10% in the latest survey—rate it as poor. One slight change is a drop from 30% in 2013 to 25% this year in the percentage of Americans who rate their coverage as excellent, and a simultaneous five-point increase to 22% in those who rate it as "only fair."

There is little difference in these healthcare coverage ratings among those with government and private insurance.

Americans have become somewhat less likely to rate the quality of healthcare they receive as excellent and more likely to rate it as good compared with two years ago. Excellent ratings dropped from 39% to 31%, while good ratings are up five points to 45%. The gap between good and excellent ratings has returned to where it was between 2001 and 2008, which represents a shift from the more evenly matched good and excellent ratings observed over the past five years. Despite this shift, the percentage in the combined excellent/good group is down only three points. Smaller percentages rate their healthcare quality as only fair or poor, broadly similar to previous years.

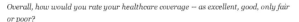

Overall, how would you rate your healthcare coverage -- as excellent, good, only fair or poor?

■ % Excellent ■ % Good ▨ % Only fair ▨ % Poor

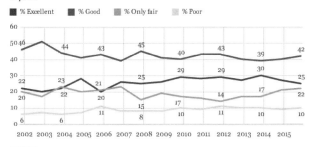

GALLUP

Overall, how would you rate the quality of healthcare you receive -- as excellent, good, only fair or poor?

■ % Excellent ■ % Good ▨ % Only fair ▨ % Poor

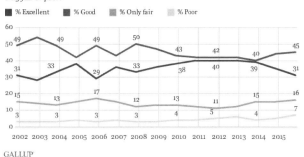

GALLUP

Bottom Line

The ACA was passed into law in March 2010, and many of its provisions have taken effect in the years since. These include the requirement that individuals must have health insurance or pay a fine, and the rollout of the state and federal exchanges from which Americans can purchase their insurance. Other provisions have mandated that all healthcare policies include certain types of coverage, that coverage cannot be denied because of pre-existing conditions and that young Americans are allowed to be covered under their parents' policies until age 26.

While the individual mandate portion of the ACA has clearly had an impact on lowering the percentage of Americans who are uninsured, Americans' attitudes about their healthcare coverage, its cost and the quality of healthcare they receive have changed little since the law went into effect. Much of this could reflect the reality that the ACA was not intended to change healthcare for the majority of Americans who already had healthcare coverage. But if the legislation did improve the situation for smaller percentages of the public who didn't previously have coverage or who had inadequate policies, it's not evident in these data.

From an overall perspective, the results show that more than two-thirds of Americans continue to rate their healthcare coverage and the quality of their healthcare as excellent or good. These are positive results, although their interpretation in the end depends on expectations. Some might argue that positive ratings should optimally reach closer to 100%, although Americans' health and economic situations are so different, and the healthcare system is so complex, that substantially increasing positive ratings may be a goal that is difficult to achieve.

Fewer than six in 10 Americans are satisfied with the cost of their healthcare, a category that subsumes coverage costs per se,

as well as deductibles and co-pays. This level of satisfaction has remained fairly constant over the past 14 years, suggesting that it is a needle that is hard to move, short of an even more radical restructuring of the overall system than has occurred with the ACA.

Survey Methods

Results for this Gallup poll are based on telephone interviews conducted Nov. 4–8, 2015, with a random sample of 1,021 adults, aged 18 and older, living in all 50 U.S. states and the District of Columbia. For results based on the total sample of national adults, the margin of sampling error is ±4 percentage points at the 95% confidence level. All reported margins of sampling error include computed design effects for weighting.

November 20, 2015
RATINGS OF U.S. HEALTHCARE QUALITY NO BETTER AFTER ACA

by Rebecca Riffkin

Story Highlights

- *53% of Americans rate healthcare quality in U.S. positively*
- *One in three rate U.S. healthcare coverage positively*
- *Fewer than one in four satisfied with cost of healthcare*

WASHINGTON, D.C.—Fifty-three percent of Americans rate the quality of healthcare in the U.S. as "excellent" or "good." This is similar to what Gallup has found since 2013, but is down from the more positive ratings of 2008 to 2012.

Americans' Ratings of Healthcare Quality in U.S. Level Since 2013
Overall, how would you rate the quality of healthcare in this country?

■ % Excellent/Good

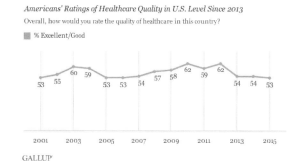

GALLUP

From 2005 to 2007, a slim majority of Americans rated the quality of healthcare in the U.S. as excellent or good. But this percentage increased slightly in 2008 after President Barack Obama was elected, reaching a high of 62% in November 2010 and again in 2012 just after he was elected to his second term. Those higher ratings could reflect optimism about Obama's promises to reform healthcare and the passage of the Affordable Care Act (ACA). However, since November 2013, shortly after the ACA insurance exchanges first opened, no more than 54% of Americans have rated the quality of healthcare in the U.S. as excellent or good.

Americans rate U.S. healthcare *coverage* far less positively than they do healthcare *quality*. The percentage of Americans rating U.S. healthcare coverage as excellent or good increased from 26% in 2008 to 38% in 2009. Since then, the percentage who view healthcare coverage in the U.S. positively has varied slightly from year to year, but remains higher than before Obama took office.

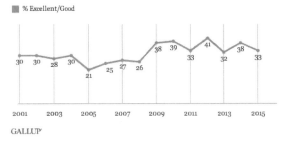

EXCELLENT/GOOD RATINGS OF ASPECTS OF U.S. HEALTHCARE

COVERAGE 33%   QUALITY 53%

GALLUP POLL, NOV. 4-8

Ratings of Healthcare Coverage in U.S. Generally Stable Since 2009
Overall, how would you rate healthcare coverage in this country?

■ % Excellent/Good

30 30 28 30 21 25 27 26 38 39 33 41 32 38 33

2001 2003 2005 2007 2009 2011 2013 2015

GALLUP

Fewer Than One in Four Satisfied With U.S. Healthcare Costs

Americans' satisfaction with the total cost of healthcare in the U.S. remains low, with 21% saying they are satisfied. Twenty-eight percent were satisfied in 2001, but satisfaction fell after that, rising again only in 2009, to 26%. This increase too may reflect optimism about the possibilities of Obama's healthcare reform. However, satisfaction has since slipped.

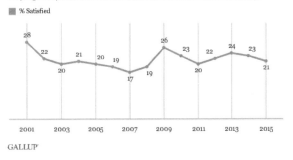

Fewer Than One In Four Satisfied With the Cost of Healthcare in the U.S.
Are you generally satisfied or dissatisfied with the total cost of healthcare in this country?

■ % Satisfied

28 22 20 21 20 19 17 19 26 23 22 20 24 23 21

2001 2003 2005 2007 2009 2011 2013 2015

GALLUP

Bottom Line

Although Americans were more positive about the cost, quality and coverage of U.S. healthcare in the early years of the Obama's first term, that optimism has faded to some degree. Americans' ratings of healthcare coverage are not high, but remain higher than they were in George W. Bush's second term. This may have something to do with the ACA, especially as the U.S. uninsured percentage has dropped since the ACA exchanges opened. The ACA may not have had such obviously positive effects on cost and quality, which Americans generally regard as no better than before Obama took office.

At the same time, Americans continue to rate their personal healthcare positively overall, although again without much improvement since the recent healthcare reform took effect. Americans are more negative about the healthcare system in the U.S. in general as opposed to their own healthcare. A similar phenomenon is found when Americans rate personal or local conditions compared with national conditions in areas such as education, government and crime.

Survey Methods

Results for this Gallup poll are based on telephone interviews conducted Nov. 4–8, 2015, with a random sample of 1,021 adults, aged 18 and older, living in all 50 U.S. states and the District of Columbia. For results based on the total sample of national adults, the margin of sampling error is ±4 percentage points at the 95% confidence level. All reported margins of sampling error include computed design effects for weighting.

November 23, 2015
IN U.S., 51% SAY GOVERNMENT SHOULD ENSURE HEALTHCARE COVERAGE

by Justin McCarthy

Story Highlights

- *First time a majority has held this view since 2008*
- *Most still prefer private insurance system to government-run system*

WASHINGTON, D.C.—U.S. adults are slightly more likely to say it is the responsibility of the federal government to ensure all Americans have health insurance coverage (51%) than to say it is not the government's responsibility (47%). The percentage who believe the government has that obligation is up six percentage points from 2014. This year marks the first time since 2008 that a majority of Americans say the government is responsible for making sure all citizens have health insurance.

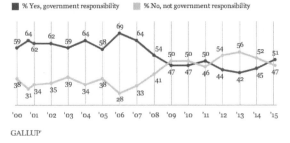

Views on the Role of Government to Ensure Americans Have Health Insurance
Do you think it is the responsibility of the federal government to make sure all Americans have healthcare coverage, or is that not the responsibility of the federal government?

■ % Yes, government responsibility   ■ % No, not government responsibility

59 64 62 59 64 58 69 64 54 50 50 50 54 56 52 51
62 38 31 34 35 39 34 38 28 33 41 47 47 46 44 42 45 47

'00 '01 '02 '03 '04 '05 '06 '07 '08 '09 '10 '11 '12 '13 '14 '15

GALLUP

From 2000 to 2008, between 54% and 69% of Americans said ensuring healthcare coverage for all citizens was the responsibility of the federal government. But the issue grew more divisive in 2009, as President Barack Obama worked to enact the Affordable Care Act, which Congress passed in 2010. Between 2009 and 2011, Americans were split nearly evenly on the matter. Then from 2012 to 2014, public opinion shifted, with slight majorities saying healthcare coverage was *not* the government's responsibility.

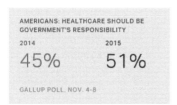

AMERICANS: HEALTHCARE SHOULD BE
GOVERNMENT'S RESPONSIBILITY

2014   2015

45%   51%

GALLUP POLL, NOV. 4–8

The latest poll was conducted Nov. 4–8 as part of Gallup's annual Health and Healthcare survey.

The percentage who feel the government should have this responsibility has increased across most key demographic groups since 2014, including lower-income Americans (+13 points), 50- to 64-year-olds (+12 points), Democrats and independents who lean Democratic (+9 points) and whites (+8 points). Across three of the country's four regions, this view has increased by seven points or more; the South is the only region where there has been no such change.

Americans who approve of the Affordable Care Act are more than three times as likely as those who disapprove of the law to say healthcare coverage should be the government's responsibility, 80% versus 26%, respectively.

Views on the Role of Government to Ensure Americans Have Health Insurance, Among Demographic Groups

Do you think it is the responsibility of the federal government to make sure all Americans have healthcare coverage, or is that not the responsibility of the federal government?

% Yes, government responsibility

	2014	2015	Change
	%	%	(pct. pts.)
National adults	45	51	+6
Whites	36	44	+8
Nonwhites	66	65	-1
18 to 29	61	68	+7
30 to 49	47	50	+3
50 to 64	36	48	+12
65+	38	38	0
Republicans/Leaners	24	22	-2
Democrats/Leaners	70	79	+9
Approve of Affordable Care Act	79	80	+1
Disapprove of Affordable Care Act	22	26	+4
East	50	60	+10
Midwest	42	51	+9
South	44	45	+1
West	44	51	+7
Household income $75,000+	39	45	+6
Household income $30,000 to $74,999	45	50	+5
Household income less than $30,000	51	64	+13

Nov. 4-8, 2015

GALLUP

Less than half of whites, Americans aged 50 and older, Republicans and independents who lean Republican, Southerners and higher-income Americans say healthcare coverage is the federal government's responsibility.

Americans Still Favor Private Insurance System

Although U.S. adults lean toward the view that the government should ensure all Americans have healthcare coverage, they do not endorse a government-run system, which exists in most other Western nations. When given a choice, 55% say they prefer a system mostly based on private insurance, as the U.S. has now, while 41% would prefer a government-run system. The percentage favoring a private system is down from 61% last year.

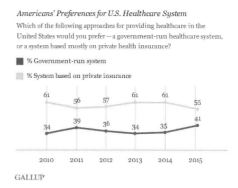

Americans' Preferences for U.S. Healthcare System

Which of the following approaches for providing healthcare in the United States would you prefer -- a government-run healthcare system, or a system based mostly on private health insurance?

■ % Government-run system
▒ % System based on private insurance

GALLUP

Despite receiving Medicare, which is mostly paid for by the government, senior citizens are the least likely to favor a government-run system (31%). The only age group in which a majority favor a government-run healthcare system are those younger than 30 (53%). Support for a government-run system drops with each subsequent age group.

Americans' Preferences for U.S. Healthcare System, Among Age Groups

Which of the following approaches for providing healthcare in the United States would you prefer -- a government-run healthcare system, or a system based mostly on private health insurance?

	Government-run system	System based on private insurance
	%	%
18 to 29	53	45
30 to 49	41	56
50 to 64	38	58
65+	31	63

Nov. 4-8, 2015

GALLUP

Bottom Line

Though Americans' views on the government's role in healthcare coverage have fluctuated in recent years, they remain just as contentious now as they were prior to the passage of the Affordable Care Act.

The latest result is the most favorable toward the view that the government should be responsible for healthcare coverage since the government took arguably the most significant step in that direction through passing the healthcare law. Still, Americans remain divided on the matter, and continue to favor a system based mostly on private health insurance to a totally government-run system.

Americans' views on the government's responsibility for ensuring healthcare coverage have changed during the Obama administration, with Americans less in favor of the government having that role than before. These data are important to monitor as Obama leaves office, especially because the fate of the healthcare law may depend on the outcome of the 2016 presidential election. Its existence is all but assured if a Democrat wins, but is far less certain if a Republican is elected.

Survey Methods

Results for this Gallup poll are based on telephone interviews conducted Nov. 4–8, 2015, on the Gallup U.S. Daily survey, with a random sample of 1,021 adults, aged 18 and older, living in all 50 U.S. states and the District of Columbia. For results based on the total sample of national adults, the margin of sampling error is ±4 percentage points at the 95% confidence level. All reported margins of sampling error include computed design effects for weighting.

November 23, 2015
AMERICANS AGAIN OPPOSED TO TAKING IN REFUGEES

by Jeffrey M. Jones

Story Highlights

- *60% oppose accepting Syrian refugees; 37% in favor*
- *Historically, Americans have rarely favored accepting refugees*
- *Eight in 10 Republicans oppose taking in Syrian refugees*

PRINCETON, N.J.—Americans, by 60% to 37%, oppose plans for the U.S. to take in at least 10,000 Syrian refugees who are trying to escape the civil war in their country. This is in keeping with Americans' historical tendency to oppose taking in large numbers of refugees, something that has been evident in similar situations as far back as the 1930s.

Support for the United States' Taking in Refugees, Gallup Polls

Date	Refugees' home country (details of situation)	% Favor/ Approve/ Support	% Oppose/ Disapprove/ Do not support
2015	Syria (at least 10,000)	37	60
1999	Kosovo (several hundred)	66	30
1979	Vietnam (Indochinese or "boat people")	32	57
1958	Hungary (160,000)	33	55
1947	Europe (10,000)	24	57
1946	Europe (including Jews -- President Truman asking Congress to allow more)	16	72
1939	Germany (children)	26	67
	AVERAGE	33	57

GALLUP

Last week, the House of Representatives passed a bill to tighten the federal government's screening requirements on refugees from Syria. This action came after many governors said their states would refuse to take these refugees. Many in favor of halting the refugee program cite increased concerns about terrorism in the wake of the terrorist attacks in Paris earlier this month.

MAJORITY IN U.S. DISAPPROVE OF PLAN
TO TAKE IN SYRIAN REFUGEES

APPROVE

DISAPPROVE

37%

60%

GALLUP POLL, NOV. 20-21

Despite the specific concerns about possible terrorism associated with accepting Syrian refugees, Americans' opposition to the current plan is in line with public opinion on refugee situations in the past. Across seven different refugee situations since 1939 for which Gallup has a basic support or opposition measure, the average level of public support has been 33% and the average level of opposition has been 57%.

Of these seven situations, the only one a majority of Americans supported involved Kosovo refugees in 1999. However, support may have been higher because the question mentioned that only several hundred refugees were being accepted, and the question was asked after the government had already taken that action.

Americans are a bit more positive when asked if the Syrian refugees would be welcomed if they came to their community—49% say they would be welcomed and 46% say they would not be. However, that is a slightly more negative assessment than Gallup found in a 1979 poll asking about Southeast Asian refugees, also known as the "boat people." At that time, 57% of Americans said those refugees would be welcomed in their community and 30% said they would not be.

In 1979 as well as now, many more said refugees would be welcomed in their community than were in favor of having them enter the U.S. This could indicate that Americans are expressing positive sentiments about their local community as much as support for the policy on taking in refugees when asked whether refugees would be welcomed.

Republicans Least Supportive of Taking In Syrian Refugees

Politics are a major influence on Americans' views about Syrian refugees. The majority of Democrats, 57%, approve of the plan for the U.S. to take the refugees, but a far larger majority of Republicans, 84%, disapprove. Independents' views are similar to the national average. These partisan differences are similar to what occurred in the House vote on the Syrian refugee bill, with nearly all Republicans voting in favor of the measure to tighten requirements for those refugees to gain entry to the U.S., and most Democrats voting against it.

Opinions on Syrian Refugees Coming to U.S., by Political Party

	Democrats %	Independents %	Republicans %
Plan to take in at least 10,000 Syrian refugees			
Approve	57	37	15
Disapprove	40	58	84
Syrian refugees would be welcomed in your community			
Yes, welcomed	60	49	38
No, not welcomed	34	46	56

Nov. 20-21, 2015

GALLUP

Roughly six in 10 Democrats approve of the plan and say Syrian refugees would be welcomed in their local community. Republicans and, to a lesser degree, independents are more inclined to believe Syrian refugees would be welcomed than to approve of letting them into the U.S. in the first place. Notably, though, a majority of Republicans still say the refugees would not be welcomed where they live.

Implications

Last week's House bill passed with enough votes to override an expected veto from President Barack Obama. However, as of now it is not clear whether the Senate will take up the measure, let alone pass it.

If the president does move forward on his plans to take in at least 10,000 Syrian refugees, he would be doing so without the American public's support. However, that would hardly be unprecedented, as Americans historically have not been supportive of plans to bring refugees to the U.S., and presidents have sometimes acted to take in refugees despite public opposition.

Why Americans have historically not been supportive of accepting refugees is unclear. To some degree it could be related to their more general views on having large numbers of new people enter the country, whether that be immigrants coming to the U.S. by choice or refugees coming to escape a troubled situation in their home country.

Americans have consistently said that immigration to the United States is a good thing. However, in the past 50 years Gallup has never found more than about a quarter of Americans calling for an increase in immigration levels; typically they have favored keeping the levels where they are, but at times a majority has called for a decrease.

Survey Methods

Results for this Gallup poll are based on telephone interviews conducted Nov. 20–21, 2015, on the Gallup U.S. Daily survey, with a random sample of 1,013 adults, aged 18 and older, living in all 50 U.S. states and the District of Columbia. For results based on the total sample of national adults, the margin of sampling error is ±4 percentage points at the 95% confidence level. All reported margins of sampling error include computed design effects for weighting.

November 24, 2015
AMERICANS EVENLY SPLIT ON SENDING TROOPS TO FIGHT ISLAMIC STATE

by Lydia Saad

Story Highlights

* *As many in U.S. favor sending ground troops as are opposed*
* *Prior to now, a majority of Americans opposed sending ground troops*
* *Support is up among Republicans and independents, not Democrats*

PRINCETON, N.J.—Since the Islamic State terrorist attacks in Paris and Beirut, Americans' reaction to sending U.S. ground troops to assist groups fighting Islamic militants has shifted from majority opposition to an even divide. Forty-seven percent of Americans now favor committing U.S. ground troops to Iraq and Syria for this purpose, while 46% are opposed. In early November, opponents surpassed supporters by 10 percentage points.

The latest survey was conducted a little over a week after the Islamic State group killed nearly 200 civilians in attacks in Paris and Beirut, and following reports that Islamic militants were responsible for bombing a Russian passenger jet over Egypt on Oct. 31, killing all 224 on board. In response to these acts of terrorism, Russia and

France have intensified their airstrikes against Islamic State targets in Syria, and French President Francois Hollande is attempting to assemble a global coalition to defeat the militant group.

Americans' Support for Sending Ground Troops to Iraq and Syria
Would you favor or oppose the United States sending ground troops to Iraq and Syria in order to assist groups in those countries that are fighting the Islamic militants?

	% Favor	% Oppose	% No opinion
Nov 22-23, 2015	47	46	7
Nov 4-8, 2015	43	53	4
Sept 20-21, 2014 ^	40	54	6

^ Asked on Gallup Daily tracking after question about approval of military action U.S. was taking against Islamic militants in Iraq and Syria

GALLUP

Domestically, President Barack Obama recently announced that while the U.S. fight against the Islamic State group will intensify, his position against committing U.S. ground troops hasn't changed. At the same time, several Republican presidential candidates, including Jeb Bush and Donald Trump, have advocated for significant troop deployment.

AMERICANS WHO FAVOR SENDING GROUND TROOPS TO IRAQ/SYRIA

NOV. 4-8   NOV. 22-23

43%   47%

GALLUP DAILY TRACKING

In line with these divergent positions, Republicans' support for committing U.S. troops has increased by close to 10 percentage points since early November, to 65%—while Democrats' support is unchanged at 37%. Independents' support is up slightly to 44%.

Americans' View of Sending U.S. Ground Troops to Iraq and Syria, by Party ID
% Favor

	Nov 4-8, 2015	Nov 22-23, 2015	Change
	%	%	(pct. pts.)
Republicans	56	65	+9
Independents	39	44	+5
Democrats	37	37	0

GALLUP

Even as Americans opposed sending U.S. ground troops to fight the Islamic State group in Iraq and Syria in 2014, Gallup polling from a year ago showed 60% broadly in favor of U.S. "military action" against the group. That figure was slightly higher than the percentage supporting U.S. military action against Libya in 2011, but below percentages supporting U.S. military action in Iraq in 2003 and in Afghanistan in 2001.

Bottom Line

Although a majority of Americans have opposed sending ground troops to fight Islamic militants for the past year, as many are now in favor as are opposed, largely driven by an increase in support among Republicans. This follows several violent attacks that, experts say, mean the Islamic State group is no longer just a regional threat in the Middle East. While the United States' recent experience in Afghanistan and Iraq may be causing many to recoil from another U.S. military venture in the Middle East, that could change if future attacks hit closer to home.

Survey Methods

Results for this Gallup poll are based on telephone interviews conducted Nov. 22–23, 2015, on the Gallup U.S. Daily survey, with a random sample of 1,017 adults, aged 18 and older, living in all 50 U.S. states and the District of Columbia. For results based on the total sample of national adults, the margin of sampling error is ±4 percentage points at the 95% confidence level. All reported margins of sampling error include computed design effects for weighting.

November 27, 2015

FEWER AMERICANS SAY THEY WANT TO LOSE WEIGHT

by Justin McCarthy

Story Highlights

- *Forty-one percent would like to stay at current weight*
- *Fewer than one in four "seriously trying" to drop pounds*
- *Americans twice as likely to want to lose weight as to be seriously trying*

WASHINGTON, D.C.—As Americans enjoy Thanksgiving leftovers this year, about half (49%) say they would like to lose weight. This is down from readings near 60% from 2001 to 2008.

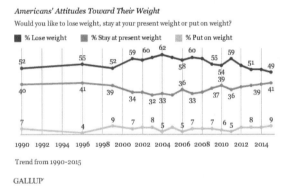

Americans' Attitudes Toward Their Weight

Would you like to lose weight, stay at your present weight or put on weight?

The latest update of Gallup's annual Health and Healthcare poll, conducted Nov. 4–8, finds that for the first time in at least 25 years, less than half of Americans want to lose weight. Gallup polls from the 1950s found that only about a third of Americans wanted to lose weight.

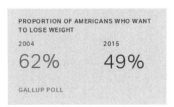

Along with the decrease in the percentage of Americans wanting to lose weight in recent years, there has been an accompanying increase in the proportion who say they would like to stay at their present weight—currently 41%. About one in 10 adults (9%) say they would like to *put on* weight.

As part of the Gallup-Healthways Well-Being Index, Gallup calculates Americans' body mass index (BMI) scores based on respondents' self-reported height and weight. The obesity rate ticked up to 27.7% in 2014, the highest rate recorded since Gallup and Healthways began tracking it in 2008. Still, Americans' desire to lose weight has not increased.

In addition to being less likely to say they *want* to lose weight in recent years, fewer Americans say they are making a concerted effort to do this. Less than a quarter of adults (24%) report they are "seriously trying to lose weight." This is the lowest reading since 2002, though it is similar to the 25% to 30% of adults who said they were "seriously" trying from 2003 through 2014.

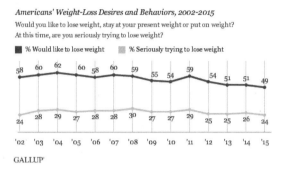

Americans' Weight-Loss Desires and Behaviors, 2002-2015

Would you like to lose weight, stay at your present weight or put on weight? At this time, are you seriously trying to lose weight?

Americans Have Become Less Likely to Say They Are Overweight Since 1990

When asked to describe their weight, 37% say they are "very" or "somewhat overweight." This has generally declined since 1990, when about half of adults (48%) said they were overweight. Meanwhile, 5% say they are "very" or "somewhat underweight."

Americans, however, are most likely to describe their weight as "about right" (56%)—consistent with readings since 2009. From 1990 to 2008, this figure was in a lower range, from 46% to 54%.

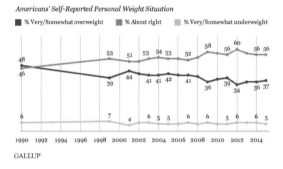

Americans' Self-Reported Personal Weight Situation

The overwhelming majority of those who say they are overweight also report wanting to lose weight. Over the past decade, between 90% and 96% of those who describe themselves as overweight have said they wanted to drop some pounds. This suggests that the decline in the percentage of Americans wanting to lose weight is more attributable to fewer people saying they are overweight than to overweight people being less likely to say they want to lose weight.

Bottom Line

Obesity in the United States has become a greater concern in the medical community and in society at large. In recent years, Gallup and Healthways have documented a slight but notable increase in the percentage of Americans who can be classified as obese, based on BMI calculations that use self-reports of height and weight. And obesity has ranked near the top of the list when Americans are asked to name the most urgent health problem facing the U.S.

Even so, the percentage of Americans who want to lose weight has dipped below the 50% mark for the first time in at least two decades, and a solid majority continue to say their weight is "about right." It is unclear whether those self-assessments are based on Americans' success in losing weight, or on a change in their thinking about what constitutes a healthy weight. Americans who are slightly above a normal weight, by BMI standards, may think of themselves as being "about right" and not urgently needing to lose weight.

Survey Methods

Results for this Gallup poll are based on telephone interviews conducted Nov. 4–8, 2015, with a random sample of 1,021 adults, aged 18 and older, living in all 50 U.S. states and the District of Columbia. For results based on the total sample of national adults, the margin of sampling error is ±4 percentage points at the 95% confidence level. All reported margins of sampling error include computed design effects for weighting.

November 30, 2015
COST STILL DELAYS HEALTHCARE FOR ABOUT ONE IN THREE IN U.S.

by Andrew Dugan

Story Highlights

- *31% have delayed medical care because of cost, unchanged from 2014*
- *Figure has not fallen since ACA reforms*
- *Americans more likely to put off care for serious condition*

WASHINGTON, D.C.—Slightly fewer than one in three Americans (31%) say that they or a family member have put off any sort of medical treatment in the past year because of the cost. This is essentially unchanged from the 33% who said this in 2014, and the figure has remained steady for the past decade. The majority of Americans (68%) say they did not have to put off care because of the cost.

These results come from Gallup's annual Health and Healthcare poll, conducted Nov. 4–8. In recent years, Americans have consistently cited healthcare cost as one of the top two "most urgent health problems" facing the U.S., and fewer than one in four Americans are satisfied with the cost of healthcare nationally. Since 2001, at least 19% of Americans—and much closer to a third beginning in 2006—have found the cost of some healthcare services so prohibitive that they or a family member has had to postpone a medical procedure.

The 2010 Affordable Care Act had the twin objectives of expanding health insurance to cover the uninsured and making healthcare more affordable. The Gallup-Healthways Well-Being Index has found that the uninsured rate has fallen considerably since the law was passed. In the third quarter of 2015, the rate stood at 11.6%, compared with 16.4% in early 2010.

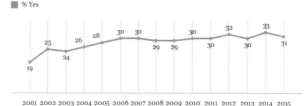

Percentage of Americans Putting Off Medical Treatment Because of Cost

Within the last 12 months, have you or a member of your family put off any sort of medical treatment because of the cost you would have to pay?

■ % Yes

GALLUP

Given these goals and the apparent success of the law in accomplishing the former, it would seem logical for fewer national adults to report that they or a family member has delayed medical treatment simply because of cost. But this has not happened; instead, the percentage has held statistically constant since the law was passed in 2010.

PERCENTAGE IN U.S. WHO HAVE PUT OFF MEDICAL CARE BECAUSE OF COST

31%

GALLUP POLL, NOV. 4–8

While the uninsured rate has declined, a little over one in 10 still are without health insurance. Not surprisingly, this group is especially sensitive to healthcare costs, with 53% of those interviewed in 2014 or 2015—i.e., the post-mandate period—saying they have had to forgo medical care. This rate is comparable to figures from aggregated samples in 2012–2013 and 2010–2011, when the number of uninsured adults was much greater. This suggests that those who remain uninsured over the last two years are not systematically different in this regard than in the past, despite their dwindling numbers.

Putting Off Medical Treatment Because of Cost Among U.S. Adults Without Insurance

Within the last 12 months, have you or a member of your family put off any sort of medical treatment because of the cost you would have to pay?

	2010-2011	2012-2013	2014-2015
	%	%	%
Yes	53	57	53
No	47	43	45

Aggregated Gallup data

GALLUP

Americans Still More Likely to Put Off Care for Serious Conditions

As has been the case nearly every year that Gallup has asked this question, Americans who put off treatment are more likely to say they did this for a serious condition (19%) than a nonserious one (12%). Nationally, the share of adults saying they were delaying treatment for a serious condition has climbed since this question was first asked in 2001, reaching a record 22% last year before edging down to 19% this year. Conversely, the percentage of U.S. adults putting off treatment for a nonserious condition has remained relatively stable.

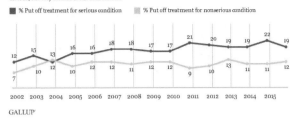

Putting Off Treatment for a Serious vs. Nonserious Condition in U.S.

When you put off this medical treatment, was it for a condition or illness that was -- very serious, somewhat serious, not very serious or not at all serious?

■ % Put off treatment for serious condition   ▨ % Put off treatment for nonserious condition

GALLUP

Bottom Line

A major aim of the ACA is to make healthcare affordable for all Americans, by requiring individuals to have health insurance and barring insurance companies from denying coverage to those with pre-existing conditions. The law has other provisions that are designed to limit the cost of healthcare services, but despite all these measures, a consistent third of the country say that in the past year, they or their family has had to delay medical treatment. The ACA has achieved objectives considered important by the policymakers who crafted the law—most notably, ensuring that a greater a number of Americans have medical insurance—but on this cost-related metric, its influence has not been felt.

Survey Methods

Results for this Gallup poll are based on telephone interviews conducted Nov. 4–8, 2015, with a random sample of 1,021 adults, aged 18 and older, living in all 50 U.S. states and the District of Columbia. For results based on the total sample of national adults, the margin of sampling error is ±4 percentage points at the 95% confidence level. All reported margins of sampling error include computed design effects for weighting.

December 01, 2015
GOP HAS MADE GAINS IN PARTY PREFERENCE SINCE THE SUMMER

by Jeffrey M. Jones

Story Highlights

- *Party preferences closely split—43% Democratic and 41% Republican*
- *Democrats had seven-point advantage in April*
- *Preferences reached parity in August*

PRINCETON, N.J.—Americans' party preferences are closely divided, with 43% identifying as Democrats or leaning Democratic and 41% identifying as Republicans or leaning Republican. The parties have been essentially tied since August, representing a shift from months prior when Democrats had the party affiliation advantage.

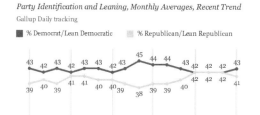

Party Identification and Leaning, Monthly Averages, Recent Trend
Gallup Daily tracking

■ % Democrat/Lean Democratic ▪ % Republican/Lean Republican

GALLUP

The results are based on Gallup Daily tracking interviews with approximately 15,000 Americans each month. Gallup asks Americans to say whether they identify politically as a Republican, an independent or a Democrat. More say they are independents (38%) than say they are either Democrats (30%) or Republicans (27%). All independents are then asked if they lean more toward the Republican or Democratic Party. Party "leaners" overwhelmingly vote for their preferred party, so the combined measure of party identifiers plus leaners gives a better sense of the relative strength of each party, especially because most election contests come down to a choice of a Republican or a Democratic candidate.

Democrats began the year with a slight edge in party affiliation, 43% to 40%. That gap expanded in April, to seven points (45% to 38%), when many of the presidential candidates announced their intentions to run. At that time, Hillary Clinton, the presumed Democratic front-runner, was easily the most popular candidate from either party in the field.

The Democratic advantage in party affiliation began to shrink in late spring, as Clinton became increasingly entangled in a scandal over her use of a private server to send and receive classified emails when she was secretary of state. The controversy took a toll on her image—by July, more Americans said they had an unfavorable than favorable opinion of Clinton.

While Clinton's image was suffering, the Republican field received increased media attention. Businessman Donald Trump, in particular, attracted media coverage for a succession of brash remarks and controversial policy statements, particularly on immigration.

The Republican Party's first presidential candidate debate, held in early August, earned record television ratings for a presidential primary debate. By the end of the month, an equal percentage of Americans identified and leaned Republican as identified or leaned Democratic. Since August, the Republican Party has held four presidential candidate debates, compared with two for the Democrats, keeping the GOP in the spotlight.

AMERICANS IDENTIFYING AS OR LEANING REPUBLICAN

APRIL   NOVEMBER
38%   41%

GALLUP DAILY TRACKING, 2015

Party preferences had been tied at 42% from August through October—the high for Republicans and leaners in Gallup's seven-year party identification trend. Democrats have regained a slight edge in November, 43% to 41%.

Implications

With just one month remaining until the start of the next presidential election year, the two parties are highly competitive in terms of the percentage of Americans aligned with each.

While some observers may have predicted that the controversial statements and positions of leading GOP candidates such as Trump and Ben Carson could hurt the party's image, these results show that on the contrary, the Republican Party's standing relative to the Democratic Party has improved since the spring.

Given usual Republican advantages in election turnout, having party preferences closely divided among national adults would be a sign of a potentially strong Republican year. But as the 2015 trend shows, party preferences can shift over the course of a year, and one party can gain, or lose, an advantage fairly quickly.

Survey Methods

Results for this Gallup poll are based on telephone interviews conducted Nov. 1–30, 2015, on the Gallup U.S. Daily survey, with a random sample of 14,212 adults, aged 18 and older, living in all 50 U.S. states and the District of Columbia. For results based on the total sample of national adults, the margin of sampling error is ±1 percentage point at the 95% confidence level. All reported margins of sampling error include computed design effects for weighting.

December 03, 2015
U.S. GALLUP GOOD JOBS RATE 44.9% IN NOVEMBER

by Ben Ryan

Story Highlights

- *Nov. 2015 Gallup Good Jobs almost full point higher year on year*
- *Unemployment lowest Gallup has measured in any November*
- *More part-time workers wanting full-time jobs*

WASHINGTON, D.C.—The Gallup Good Jobs (GGJ) rate in the U.S. was 44.9% in November. This is down slightly from the rate measured during the past three months (45.3%), but still the highest Gallup has measured for any November since tracking began in 2010.

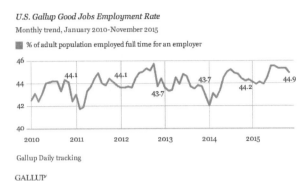

U.S. Gallup Good Jobs Employment Rate

Monthly trend, January 2010-November 2015

■ % of adult population employed full time for an employer

Gallup Daily tracking

GALLUP

The GGJ metric—previously labeled "Payroll to Population" or "P2P"—tracks the percentage of the U.S. adult population, aged 18 and older, who work for an employer for at least 30 hours per week. Gallup does not count adults who are self-employed, work fewer than 30 hours per week, are unemployed or are out of the workforce as payroll-employed in the GGJ metric.

The latest results are based on Gallup Daily tracking interviews with 28,373 Americans, conducted Nov. 1–30 by landline telephone and cellphone. GGJ is not seasonally adjusted.

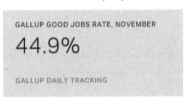

GALLUP GOOD JOBS RATE, NOVEMBER

44.9%

GALLUP DAILY TRACKING

Workforce Participation at 67.5% in November

The percentage of U.S. adults participating in the workforce in November was 67.5%. This is down only slightly from the rate in October (67.7%) and is tied with September.

Gallup's workforce participation measure averaged 67.7% between January 2010 and June 2013, but since then has averaged about one percentage point lower, at 66.8%. Higher participation rates in the past several months, however, may signal returning strength in the labor market. Gallup defines workforce participation as the percentage of adults, aged 18 and older, who are working or who are not working but are actively looking for work and are available for employment.

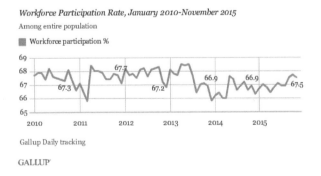

Workforce Participation Rate, January 2010-November 2015

Among entire population

■ Workforce participation %

Gallup Daily tracking

GALLUP

Unemployment at 5.7%

Gallup's unadjusted U.S. unemployment rate was 5.7% in November, statistically even with October's 5.6% and the lowest in any November since Gallup began tracking the measure in January 2010. Gallup's U.S. unemployment rate represents the percentage of adults in the workforce who did not have any paid work in the past seven days, either for an employer or themselves, and who were actively looking for and available to work.

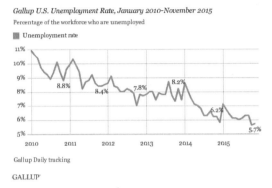

Gallup U.S. Unemployment Rate, January 2010-November 2015

Percentage of the workforce who are unemployed

■ Unemployment rate

Gallup Daily tracking

GALLUP

Unlike Gallup's GGJ rate, which is a percentage of the total population, the unemployment rates that Gallup and the U.S. Bureau of Labor Statistics (BLS) report are percentages of the labor force. While both Gallup and BLS data are based on surveys with large sample sizes, the two have important methodological differences—outlined at the end of this article. Additionally, the most discussed unemployment rate released by the BLS each month is seasonally adjusted, while Gallup reports unadjusted numbers. Although Gallup's unemployment numbers strongly correlate with BLS rates, the BLS and Gallup estimates of unemployment do not always track precisely on a monthly basis.

Underemployment Rises to 14.6%

Gallup's measure of *underemployment* in November was 14.6%, up 0.8 points from October. However, this rate is still lower than in any November since Gallup began tracking it daily in 2010. Gallup's U.S. underemployment rate combines the percentage of adults in the workforce who are unemployed (5.7%) with those who are working part time but desire full-time work (8.9%).

While unemployment was almost unchanged in November, the rate of "involuntary" part-time work rose by 0.7 points. This rate has risen more than a full point since September, when it was the lowest Gallup had measured since tracking began in January 2010 (7.8%). Involuntary part-time employment has been relatively constant over the past six years, never registering more than 10.1% but only once falling below 8.0%.

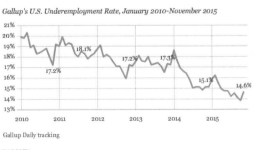

Gallup's U.S. Underemployment Rate, January 2010-November 2015

Gallup Daily tracking

GALLUP

Bottom Line

Gallup's November labor market indicators were slightly less rosy than those in October, but still show positive movement year on year. The nominal rates for full-time employment for an employer and workforce participation were both down from October, and unemployment and underemployment were both up. However, compared with November 2014, GGJ and workforce participation were up and unemployment was down. The apparent weakening in Gallup's nominal labor market figures over the past month is primarily a seasonal effect as the calendar year draws to a close.

Survey Methods

Results for this Gallup poll are based on telephone interviews conducted Nov. 1–30, 2015, on the Gallup U.S. Daily survey, with a random sample of 28,373 adults, aged 18 and older, living in all 50 U.S. states and the District of Columbia. For results based on the total sample of national adults, the margin of sampling error is ±1 percentage point at the 95% confidence level. All reported margins of sampling error include computed design effects for weighting.

December 03, 2015

U.S. CONSUMER SPENDING STRONG DURING THANKSGIVING WEEK

by Lydia Saad

Story Highlights

- *Consumers' reported daily spending averaged $112 over Black Friday weekend*
- *That is similar to same period in 2012 and 2013, but up from prior years*
- *Biggest spending occurred on Black Friday*

PRINCETON, N.J.—U.S. consumers' self-reported daily spending jumped from an average $90 in the first three weeks of November to $112 over the four-day retail spending bonanza following Thanksgiving that starts on Black Friday and ends on Cyber Monday. This level of holiday weekend spending is similar to what Gallup has found each of the past three years, while it is significantly higher than the spending averages found during the more economically depressed period from 2009 to 2011.

Americans' Pre- and Post-Thanksgiving Daily Spending Estimates
Based on averages of daily estimate of amount spent "yesterday"

	November Pre-Thanksgiving	Black Friday-Cyber Monday	Change
2015	$90	$112	$22
2014	$93	$115	$22
2013	$89	$108	$19
2012	$69	$102	$33
2011	$69	$95	$26
2010	$63	$93	$30
2009	$64	$89	$25
2008	$94	$121	$27

GALLUP

The jump in spending during the four days after Thanksgiving has not been quite as sizable in the past three years as it was from 2009 through 2012, but that could simply be because overall consumer spending was more depressed in those earlier years. It could also be a reflection of holiday sales ramping up earlier in recent years, thus inflating the pre-Thanksgiving figures.

Additionally, a day-by-day review shows that consumers reported spending an average of $147 on Black Friday but then dipped to $99 on Saturday, $99 on Sunday and $102 on Cyber Monday. Thus, it appears Black Friday remains the primary shopping event of this time period.

Gallup's spending measure asks consumers to estimate how much they spent on retail goods or services "yesterday," either in person or online, not counting home or vehicle purchases. The figures for the Black Friday weekend are based on consumers' reports from Saturday through Tuesday about their previous day's spending.

Spending Can Vary in December

Americans' self-reported spending figures always increase over the Black Friday weekend, making it one of the highest spending periods of the year, and this year's estimate is a robust one. However, the true strength of the holiday retail season will be indicated by the extent to which weekly spending estimates remain at or near this level throughout December.

Americans averaged $101 in daily spending during the last full week of November, based on interviewing from Monday, Nov. 23, through Sunday, Nov. 29. This is the figure that spending in upcoming weeks should be compared with in order to assess the retail climate.

December spending remained fairly strong in 2008 and 2014 and, to a lesser extent, in 2013. It actually rose substantially in 2012—but that could have been an artifact of the early timing of Thanksgiving and Black Friday that year, altering consumers' spending patterns.

Americans' Daily Spending Estimates -- Weekly Averages Over Holiday Period
Based on averages of daily estimate of amount spent "yesterday"

	November week 4	December week 1	December week 2	December week 3	December week 4
2015	$101				
2014	$110	$98	$104	$101	$97
2013	$100	$103	$82	$106	$91
2012	$67	$90	$75	$104	$63
2011	$83	$70	$78	$78	$83
2010	$79	$66	$66	$77	$85
2009	$69	$75	$73	$74	$70
2008	$92	$95	$94	$93	$68

GALLUP

Notably, despite being a fairly solid number relative to recent daily spending reports, the $101 daily average spending for the last week of November this year is not consistent with Americans' highly robust estimate of the total amount they will spend on gifts this season. Whether that's because they have scaled back their plans or because they still have much shopping to do is not clear, but will become evident in the coming weeks.

Bottom Line

The holiday retail season appears to be off to a promising start, with Americans' self-reports of daily spending over the Black Friday period averaging $112. This is not quite the level of spending that would have been predicted based on Americans' wide-eyed November holiday spending forecast, but it does set retailers up for solid sales, should spending hold near this level in December.

Survey Methods

Results for consumer spending in the last week of November are based on telephone interviews conducted Nov. 23–29, 2015, on the Gallup U.S. Daily survey, with a random sample of 3,045 adults, aged 18 and older, living in all 50 U.S. states and the District of Columbia. For results based on the total sample of national adults, the margin of sampling error for the spending mean is ± $10.

All reported margins of sampling error include computed design effects for weighting.

December 04, 2015
MORE AMERICANS SAY HEALTH PREMIUMS WENT UP OVER PAST YEAR

by Justin McCarthy

Story Highlights

- *36% who pay premiums say costs went up "a lot"—a new high*
- *Fewer insured Americans say employers pay full cost*

WASHINGTON, D.C.—Nearly three in four American adults (74%) who pay all or some of their health insurance premiums say the amount they pay has gone up over the past year. This percentage is up marginally from the 67% who last year said their costs increased, but it is generally in line with what Gallup has found in yearly updates since 2003.

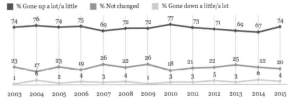

Self-Reports of Cost Changes Among Adults Who Pay All or Some of Their Health Premiums
Over the past year, has the amount YOU paid for your family's health insurance -- [ROTATED: gone up a lot, gone up a little, not changed, gone down a little (or) gone down a lot]?

Asked of those who say they pay all or part of their health premiums

GALLUP

These latest data, from Gallup's annual Health and Healthcare poll, come as many insurers have raised premiums—as well as deductibles, co-pays and coinsurance—for plans under the Affordable Care Act (ACA). Meanwhile, growth in national spending on healthcare has accelerated, increasing 5.3% in 2014, according to a report from the Centers for Medicare and Medicaid Services. According to the American Academy of Actuaries, premium costs, in general, will increase for the next several years because of various market factors, and Americans should plan for such increases.

Yearly increases have been the norm, but Americans are feeling them more sharply than usual. Since 2003, the large majority of adults who pay all or some of their premiums have consistently

reported that their costs have gone up. However, until now, many more said the costs went up "a little" than "a lot." In the latest poll, the two figures are nearly tied, with 38% saying costs went up a little and 36% saying a lot. The shift comes from an eight-percentage-point increase this year in those saying their costs rose a lot, bringing it to the highest Gallup has measured since first asking the question in 2003.

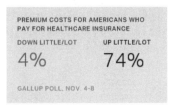

PREMIUM COSTS FOR AMERICANS WHO PAY FOR HEALTHCARE INSURANCE

DOWN LITTLE/LOT   UP LITTLE/LOT
4%   74%

GALLUP POLL, NOV. 4-8

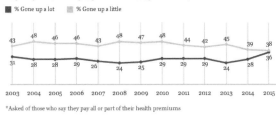

Self-Reports of Cost Changes Among Adults Who Pay All or Some of Their Health Premiums
Over the past year, has the amount YOU paid for your family's health insurance -- [ROTATED: gone up a lot, gone up a little, not changed, gone down a little (or) gone down a lot]?

■ % Gone up a lot   ☐ % Gone up a little

Asked of those who say they pay all or part of their health premiums

GALLUP

Insured Adults Have Taken on More of the Premium Costs Since 2001

Americans with healthcare insurance are also seeing less support from employers in paying premiums. More than a quarter of insured adults (28%) say they pay the full amount of their premiums, on the high of the trend dating back to 2001. Meanwhile, 10% say an employer pays all of the cost of their premiums, which is down by more than half from the high of 24% in 2001, but fairly consistent with recent figures.

Burden of Premium Costs of Americans' Health Insurance
Who pays the cost of premiums on your health insurance? Do you or someone in your household pay the total cost, does an employer pay the total cost or is the cost shared between the employer and you or someone in your household?

■ % Self/ household pays all   ☐ % Employer pays all   ☐ % Costs are shared

Asked of those who say they have private health insurance

GALLUP

That leaves the majority of insured Americans sharing the costs of their insurance with an employer. But the current figure of 58% is on the low end of the trend since 2001. Much of that decline occurred in the past two years since implementing the ACA.

Bottom Line

Though Americans are still more likely to be satisfied than dissatisfied with their personal healthcare costs, the latest poll indicates they are more likely to be grappling with higher premium costs than in previous years.

Healthcare costs remain a top issue for Americans and one that about a third say led them to put off medical treatment for themselves or a relative. While they have become more amenable to the concept of the government being responsible for providing healthcare, Americans remain overall disapproving of the Affordable Care Act.

What Americans pay for their healthcare premiums has not noticeably improved since the ACA's implementation, and experts have stressed that a rise in premiums will continue for several years. Meanwhile, the White House contends that recent premium increases would have been larger if not for the ACA.

Survey Methods

Results for this Gallup poll are based on telephone interviews conducted Nov. 4–8, 2015, on the Gallup U.S. Daily survey, with a random sample of, aged 18 and older, living in all 50 U.S. states and the District of Columbia. For results based on the total sample of 518 adults with private health insurance, the margin of sampling error is ±5 percentage points at the 95% confidence level. For results based on the total sample of 457 adults who pay all or part of their health premiums, the margin of sampling error is ±6 percentage points at the 95% confidence level. All reported margins of sampling error include computed design effects for weighting.

December 04, 2015
CLINTON'S DEMOCRATIC IMAGE ADVANTAGE OVER SANDERS EXPANDS

by Frank Newport

Story Highlights

- *Clinton has a 21-percentage-point net favorable advantage over Sanders*
- *Both men and women now see Clinton more positively than Sanders*
- *Sanders has better image among those 18–29 than does Clinton*

PRINCETON, N.J.—Hillary Clinton's net favorable rating among Democrats and Democratic-leaning independents in November averaged 21 percentage points higher than Sanders's, up from a 13-point advantage in September and early October.

Images of Hillary Clinton and Bernie Sanders, Among Democrats/Leaners

	Favorable	Unfavorable	Familiarity	Net favorable
	%	%	%	(pct. pts.)
HILLARY CLINTON				
Nov 1-30, 2015	76	18	94	+58
Sep 12-Oct 10, 2015	73	22	95	+51
BERNIE SANDERS				
Nov 1-30, 2015	51	14	65	+37
Sep 12-Oct 10, 2015	49	11	60	+38

Gallup Daily tracking

GALLUP

Both candidates have seen a slight uptick in their favorable ratings among all Democrats since Gallup's last update, which was based on data collected Sept. 12–Oct. 10, just before the first Democratic debate on Oct. 13. But while Clinton's unfavorable percentage has edged downward, Sanders's has increased slightly. The result? The gap between Clinton's and Sanders's net favorable ratings has expanded.

Sanders has gained five points in familiarity; even so, only two-thirds of Democrats know enough about the Vermont senator to have an opinion of him, compared with Clinton's nearly universal familiarity.

Clinton Gains Among Men, But Still Lags Among 18- to 29-Year-Olds

Clinton has a significant image advantage among men and women, as well as those 30 and older. But young Democrats still constitute a problem spot for Clinton, whose image among 18- to 29-year-olds is significantly less positive than Sanders's.

Clinton's net favorable image among Democratic men has undergone a significant change, going from a net favorable rating of +43 to +54. Sanders's image among men dropped from +44 to +39 over the same period, with the net result that Clinton has moved from a -1 net favorable deficit versus Sanders among men to a +15 advantage in the latest update.

Clinton has not seen this type of gain among 18- to 29-year-old Democrats, however. Her +39 rating among this group in November is up only four points from late September and early October. Meanwhile, Sanders's net favorable rating among young Democrats increased by seven points. That leaves Clinton with an 11-point deficit vis-à-vis Sanders among those 18–29, three points larger than the previous reading.

Clinton has extended her already large image advantage among all three groups aged 30 and older, and has a particularly strong positive image among Democrats 50 and older.

Net Favorable Ratings of Clinton and Sanders, Among Democrats/Leaners by Demographic Group

	Sep 12-Oct 10, 2015 (pct. pts.)	Nov 1-30, 2015 (pct. pts.)	Change
HILLARY CLINTON			
All Democrats	51	58	+7
Men	43	54	+11
Women	57	61	+4
18 to 29	35	39	+4
30 to 49	56	62	+6
50 to 64	59	64	+5
65+	56	66	+10
BERNIE SANDERS			
All Democrats	38	37	-1
Men	44	39	-5
Women	34	35	+1
18 to 29	43	50	+7
30 to 49	41	39	-2
50 to 64	34	28	-6
65+	34	31	-3

Gallup Daily tracking

GALLUP

Bottom Line

Clinton is both well known and well liked among Democrats nationally, and her image improved in November compared with a month earlier. The image of Sanders, her principal opponent, was stagnant over the same period. His favorable rating is now 25 points lower than Clinton's, while his unfavorable percentage is roughly the same. Sanders is hindered in that a third of Democrats do not know enough about him to have an opinion, compared with only 6% of Democrats who don't have an opinion of Clinton.

Sanders is 74, six years older than Clinton. But likely at least in part because of his more liberal views, he retains a pocket of strength with 18- to 29-year-old Democrats, among whom he continues to enjoy an image that is more favorable than hers. Sanders was viewed as favorably among men as was Clinton a few months ago, but Clinton is now better liked among both gender groups.

The next Democratic debate is Saturday, Dec. 19, and it is possible that the images of both of these candidates among Democrats could change as a result. At this point in the campaign, however, Clinton continues to have the clear image advantage.

Survey Methods

Results for this Gallup poll are based on telephone interviews conducted Nov. 1–30, 2015, on the Gallup U.S. Daily survey, with a random sample of 1,628 U.S. adults identifying as Democrats or independents who lean Democratic, aged 18 and older, living in all 50 U.S. states and the District of Columbia who rated Hillary Clinton, and 1,592 who rated Bernie Sanders. For results based on these samples, the margin of sampling error is ±4 percentage points at the 95% confidence level.

December 07, 2015
HALF OF OVERWEIGHT IN U.S. NOT SERIOUSLY TRYING TO LOSE WEIGHT

by Jim Norman

Story Highlights

- *31% think their weight is 20+ pounds more than it should be*
- *Only about half of these are seriously trying to lose weight*
- *Chances of being overweight affected by age, gender, income*

WASHINGTON, D.C.—More than three in 10 American adults (31%) say they weigh at least 20 pounds more than their "ideal" weight, and almost all of these (90%) want to do something about it. But less than half (48%) say they are "seriously trying to lose weight."

Overweight Americans: Know It, Do Not Like It, but ...

How Americans who are over their ideal weight feel about their weight, what to do about it

	1 to 19 pounds overweight	20 or more pounds overweight
Percentage who consider themselves overweight	27%	85%
"Would like to lose weight"	58%	90%
"Seriously trying to lose weight"	24%	48%

Health and Healthcare survey
Nov. 4-8, 2015

GALLUP'

In its annual Health and Healthcare survey, Gallup asks Americans to report their weight, and later, to say what their ideal weight should be. In 2015, the average weight for U.S. adults was 176 pounds, including an average 196 pounds for men and 155 pounds for women. The reported ideal weight is 161 pounds for national adults—183 pounds for men and 139 pounds for women. Americans weigh an average of 15 pounds more than their perceived ideal weight.

For the group reporting their weight as 20 pounds or more above their ideal, the average self-reported actual weight was 213 pounds, including an average 237 for men and 193 for women.

These results generally echo findings from four previous Health and Healthcare surveys conducted from 2011 to 2014. Combining the results from the last five surveys allows a more in-depth look at how Americans view their actual weight compared with how much they think they should weigh:

- About half of Americans (48%) estimate they are within 10 pounds of what they consider their ideal weight—18% are at their ideal weight, 23% are no more than 10 pounds over it and 8% are no more than 10 pounds under it.
- Among those under the age of 30, 14% estimate that they weigh at least 10 pounds *less* than what they should. That drops to 5% for those in their 30s, and less than 4% for those in their 40s and above.

Chances of Being Overweight Affected by Age, Gender, Income

Gallup's last five annual Health and Healthcare polls (2011–2015) show that age, income, gender and education all are significant factors in whether someone exceeds his or her preferred weight by at least 20 pounds.

Percentage of Americans 20 or More Pounds Over Their Ideal Weight, by Subgroup

	20 or more pounds overweight
All	32%
Men	29%
Women	35%
Less than $30,000 annual income	37%
$30,000 to $74,999 annual income	33%
$75,000+ annual income	28%
No college	34%
Some college	33%
College degree only	29%
Postgraduate work	25%
18 to 29	21%
30 to 39	35%
40 to 49	34%
50 to 59	38%
60 to 69	40%
70+	27%

Averages from five Health and Healthcare surveys, 2011-2015

GALLUP'

In addition to the basic subgroup findings, the larger data set allows for a look at some smaller subgroups. Among the findings:

- Women of all ages are more likely than men to estimate they are at least 20 pounds overweight. The differences are most pronounced for those in their 20s and 50s.
- Unmarried men (25%) are less likely than married men (32%) to say they are at least 20 pounds overweight, while there is

basically no difference between unmarried women (36%) and married women (35%).

- Those without insurance, those with private insurance and those with Medicaid or Medicare are all about as likely to be 20 pounds or more overweight.

Bottom Line

Questions about how close people are to their ideal weight are dependent on the individual's idea of what that weight should be. Even with that in mind, the evidence from five years of Gallup polls clearly shows that a large percentage of Americans see themselves as overweight. It is possible or likely that people may be somewhat less than accurate in disclosing their weight in a telephone interview; even so, a substantial 31% of Americans say they are 20 pounds heavier than their self-defined ideal weight. Further, though most of those who are overweight realize they are, the far lower percentage who are doing something about it is not increasing over time.

Methodology

Results for this Gallup poll are based on telephone interviews conducted in 2011, 2012, 2013, 2014, and most recently, Nov. 4–8, 2015. The aggregated sample for the five polls contains 4,915 adults, aged 18 and older, living in all 50 U.S. states and the District of Columbia. For results based on the total sample of national adults, the margin of sampling error is ±3 percentage points at the 95% confidence level.

December 09, 2015
U.S. SMALL-BUSINESS OWNERS' OPTIMISM AGAIN EDGES DOWNWARD

by Coleen McMurray and Frank Newport

Story Highlights

- *Wells Fargo/Gallup Small Business Index is down to 54*
- *The index peaked at 71 in the first quarter of 2015*
- *Small-business owners are relatively positive about hiring*

PRINCETON, N.J.—U.S. small-business owners continue to be less optimistic about their financial situations in the fourth quarter than they were at the beginning of 2015. The Wells Fargo/Gallup Small Business Index declined modestly but steadily in the second and third quarters of this year, after its significant rise in the first quarter.

In the quarterly small-business survey conducted Nov. 9–13, the overall index score, which measures small-business owners' optimism, dipped to 54, continuing a downward trend from 59 in the third quarter, 64 in the second quarter and 71 in the first quarter of this year. The last time the index declined for at least three consecutive periods was from Quarter 3, 2007, through Quarter 1, 2009. The index has lost the ground it gained late last year and early this year, but remains higher than the 49 recorded in the third quarter of 2014, before the most recent spike in small-business optimism.

The index consists of two parts—evaluations of present business conditions and expectations about the future. Both components have been declining in roughly parallel tracks this year, suggesting that the dip in small-business optimism is more of a general pattern than one that reflects disproportionate concern about the present or the future.

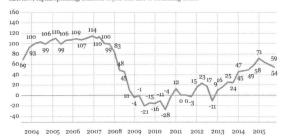

Wells Fargo/Gallup Small Business Index

The Small Business Index consists of owners' ratings of their business' current situation and their expectations for the next 12 months, measured in terms of their overall financial situation, revenue, cash flow, capital spending, number of jobs and ease of obtaining credit.

Index conducted since August 2003 and quarterly from December 2003-November 2015

GALLUP

Wells Fargo/Gallup Small Business Index

■ % Present situation   ▨ % Future expectations

GALLUP

The continuing drop in the index reflects the following:

- Expectations that company revenue will increase are the lowest since Quarter 4, 2013. Currently, 47% of small-business owners report that they expect their revenue to increase, compared with 51% in the third quarter. Optimism about revenue growth has not been this low since 44% anticipated increases two years ago.
- Owners' expectations for their businesses' financial situations in the next 12 months dropped modestly. Currently, 70% of small-business owners expect their financial situation in a year to be very or somewhat good, compared with 74% in the prior two quarters. While not a significant change, the small decrease contributes to the overall pattern of decline.
- Positive reports of revenue have changed little. In the third quarter and now, 39% of small-business owners reported that their company's revenues increased over the past 12 months, down significantly from 49% in January, although down only modestly from 42% in the second quarter.

Hiring Expectations Tick Up

Even as the overall index has declined, the 26% of owners who say the number of jobs at their company will be increasing over the next 12 months is actually higher now than it was in the robust first quarter of this year, and is tied for the highest since 2007.

Small-business owners typically are more likely to report they will add jobs than subtract them. Even during the recession and recent periods of high unemployment, owners were still about as likely to say they believed they would increase their staff as to say they would decrease it. But the gap between expectations of increasing and decreasing staff is now one of the largest seen since before the recession. As is usually the case, the vast majority of owners, roughly two-thirds, expect the number of workers at their company to stay the same.

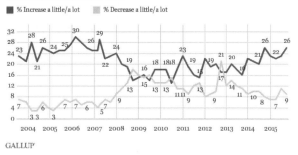

Expectations for Overall Number of Jobs in Your Company, Next 12 Months
Wells Fargo/Gallup Small Business Index

The survey also asks owners if they have hired or fired workers over the past 12 months, and 17% report that they have hired over the past year, while 14% say they have let workers go, leaving the significant majority who say they have not changed the size of their workforces.

Bottom Line

Small-business owners' optimism about business and financial conditions has continued its modest path of erosion in the fourth quarter of 2015, although the Wells Fargo/Gallup Small Business Index remains high relative to its low levels from 2008 through late last year. Despite this downtick, owners are as positive about adding new jobs over the next 12 months as they have been in eight years.

Survey Methods

Results are based on telephone interviews with 606 U.S. small-business owners in all 50 states, conducted Nov. 9–13, 2015. The margin of sampling error is ±4 percentage points at the 95% confidence level.

December 09, 2015
AFTER TERROR ATTACKS, U.S. SATISFACTION FALLS TO 13-MONTH LOW

by Rebecca Riffkin

Story Highlights

- *Satisfaction drops seven percentage points from last month*
- *Fewest Americans satisfied since November 2014*
- *Democrats had largest drop in satisfaction, 15 points*

WASHINGTON, D.C.—After the recent terrorist attack in San Bernardino, California, Americans' satisfaction with the way things are going in the U.S. dropped seven percentage points to 20%. This is the lowest level of satisfaction recorded since November 2014, but still above the all-time low of 7% in October 2008.

The San Bernardino attack, which occurred just before this Dec. 2–6 survey, almost certainly accounts for some of the downturn in satisfaction. In the attack, 14 victims died and many were

wounded, and it was considered so significant that President Barack Obama addressed the incident and its aftermath in a rare prime-time speech on Sunday night.

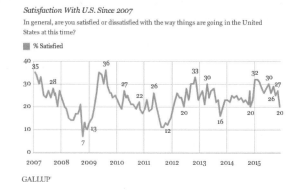

Satisfaction With U.S. Since 2007
In general, are you satisfied or dissatisfied with the way things are going in the United States at this time?

A seven-point month-to-month drop in satisfaction is rare but not unprecedented. Satisfaction dropped seven points in 2013 during the October partial government shutdown. It plummeted 12 points in the fall of 2008 as the economy crumbled, falling to the all-time low of 7% in mid-October of that year.

The recent high point in satisfaction is 32% in January and February of this year, the highest since the end of 2012. Satisfaction levels have been lower for the rest of this year. But despite month-to-month fluctuations, at least 25% of Americans have been satisfied each month until the December reading.

AMERICANS SATISFIED WITH THE WAY THINGS ARE GOING IN U.S.	
NOVEMBER	DECEMBER
27%	20%
GALLUP POLL	

Democrats' Satisfaction Declines Most

Satisfaction has dropped among all major demographic groups since early November, but not equally. Among Republicans, consistently the group least likely to be satisfied, satisfaction dropped four points, similar to independents' five-point decline. Satisfaction among Democrats dropped by a much larger 15 points. Democrats' November satisfaction was among the highest for any group, and thus it had more room to fall.

Satisfaction With the U.S. by Demographic Group
In general, are you satisfied or dissatisfied with the way things are going in the United States at this time?

	November 2015	December 2015	Difference
	% Satisfied	% Satisfied	Pct. pts.
Men	27	25	-2
Women	27	15	-12
18 to 34	30	19	-11
35 to 54	28	24	-4
55+	25	16	-9
Republicans	13	9	-4
Independents	26	21	-5
Democrats	42	27	-15
Whites	21	15	-6
Nonwhites	41	30	-11

GALLUP

Satisfaction among women and younger Americans dropped by double digits from November to December, leaving a significant gender gap on this measure, with men significantly more likely than women to be satisfied. White Americans remain less likely to be satisfied than nonwhite Americans, probably because whites are more likely to be Republicans.

Bottom Line

While the San Bernardino mass shooting was likely the primary factor in the drop in Americans' satisfaction with the way things are going in the U.S., it was not the only troubling news that could have driven the decline. Paris was hit by a terrorist attack on Nov. 13 that killed more than 120 people and prompted calls for a tougher U.S. strategy against the Islamic State group. In the U.S., a shooting at a Planned Parenthood clinic on Nov. 27 resulted in the deaths of three people. And a video of a white Chicago police officer killing a black teenager, who appeared to be walking away from him, was made public in late November. Meanwhile, in Baltimore, the trial began for one of the officers accused of being responsible for the death of Freddie Gray earlier this year.

But not all the news was negative. The government last Friday released a strong jobs report for November, prompting many to predict that the Federal Reserve will raise interest rates next week. If the stock market and economy appear to be improving in December, satisfaction could go up again.

Still, the major issue of the moment is terrorism. Americans' satisfaction with the way things are going in the country will most likely continue to reflect their perceptions of the way the terrorism situation is being handled, as long as the perceived threat remains high.

Survey Methods

Results for this Gallup poll are based on telephone interviews conducted Dec. 2–6, 2015, with a random sample of 824 adults, aged 18 and older, living in all 50 U.S. states and the District of Columbia. For results based on the total sample of national adults, the margin of sampling error is ±4 percentage points at the 95% confidence level. All reported margins of sampling error include computed design effects for weighting.

December 10, 2015
IN U.S., YOUNG ADULTS' CIGARETTE USE IS DOWN SHARPLY

by Nader Nekvasil and Diana Liu

Story Highlights

- *Young adults now no more likely to smoke than those aged 30 to 64*
- *Young adults' use of smokeless tobacco, pipes and cigars above average*
- *Young adults most likely to use three or more forms of tobacco*

WASHINGTON, D.C.—The smoking rate for 18- to 29-year-olds in the U.S. has dropped 12 percentage points to 22% over the past decade, more than twice the drop seen for any other age group. In the early 2000s, young adults were significantly more likely to smoke than their older counterparts. But now smoking rates are similar among young adults and those aged 30 to 49 and 50 to 64.

Percentage of U.S. Adults Who Smoke Cigarettes, by Age Group
Have you, yourself, ever smoked cigarettes in the past week? (% Yes)

	2001-2005	2006-2010	2011-2015	Change over past decade
	%	%	%	(pct. pts.)
18 to 29	34	28	22	-12
30 to 49	28	25	23	-5
50 to 64	24	22	21	-3
65+	11	11	11	0
National average	25	22	20	-5

Results shown are from Gallup's annual Consumption Habits poll, conducted each July.

GALLUP

Seniors remain much less likely to smoke than younger adults, and their smoking rates have not budged over the past decade.

These findings, collected as part of Gallup's annual Consumption Habits poll each July, align with those found in a recent Centers for Disease Control and Prevention study, which found that cigarette smoking has dropped most sharply among 18- to 24-year-olds.

At first glance, this dramatic drop in cigarette smoking among young adults appears to be encouraging news. It could mean that antismoking efforts are effective at preventing young adults from lighting up and possibly developing a lifelong addiction.

But new data from the Gallup-Healthways Well-Being Index, collected Jan. 2–Oct. 18, 2015, suggest that this decline might also be related to young adults switching to non-cigarette tobacco alternatives. Young adults' use of three other types of tobacco—cigars, pipes and smokeless tobacco—is well above the averages for all other age groups.

The use of non-cigarette forms of tobacco shows a consistent pattern by age, with young adults being the most likely of all age groups to use smokeless tobacco, to smoke pipes and to smoke cigars. The percentage who use any of those forms of tobacco is lower among each succeeding age group.

Method of Tobacco Use Among U.S. Adults, by Age Group
Do you use any of the following tobacco products: cigarettes, cigars, pipes, smokeless/chew/snuff?

	18 to 29	30 to 49	50 to 64	65+	National average
	%	%	%	%	%
Cigarettes	18.4	19.6	18.6	9.3	17.0
Cigars	4.1	2.4	1.7	0.9	2.3
Pipe tobacco	1.6	0.7	0.5	0.4	0.8
Smokeless tobacco	5.4	4.3	2.8	1.7	3.6

Jan. 2-Oct. 18, 2015
Gallup-Healthways Well-Being Index

GALLUP

Since 2014, Gallup and Healthways have asked tobacco consumers to specify which forms of the product they use: cigarettes, cigars, pipe tobacco, smokeless tobacco, chew or snuff. Given the limited trend, Gallup and Healthways cannot determine whether young adults' use of non-cigarette tobacco alternatives has increased over time. But the data do show that young adults are more likely than those in all other age groups to use all types of non-cigarette alternatives.

Smokeless tobacco is the most common alternative to cigarettes among all age groups and is used by 5.4% of young adults, almost two points above the national average.

Cigar smoking is the next most popular tobacco form, used by 4.1% of young adults, versus 2.3% of Americans overall. Additionally, although relatively few people in any age group smoke pipes, the 1.6% found among young adults is twice the national average. It is possible that those interviewed may have considered water pipes, also known as hookahs, in their responses for "pipes." According to the CDC, between 2011 and 2014, high school students' use of hookahs showed a statistically significant increase, while their current use of more traditional products such as cigarettes and cigars decreased, resulting in no change in overall tobacco use.

An American Cancer Society report found that while cigars have previously been associated with older adults, most new cigar users are in fact young adults. Additionally, the CDC found that the greater appeal of cigar smoking among 18- to 29-year-olds may be attributed to the use of flavoring in many brands, and the fact that some cigars are less costly than cigarettes because state and local governments tax them differently. Furthermore, the popularity of specialty cigar shops may encourage social smoking and a connoisseur culture that is especially appealing to young adults.

Young Americans More Likely to Use Multiple Forms of Tobacco

Gallup combined the responses to the four tobacco items to see how many Americans are using multiple forms of tobacco. Overall, 20.4% of Americans use two or more forms, while 2.5% use three or more.

Multiple Methods of Tobacco Use Among U.S. Adults, by Age Group
Percentage of U.S. adults who use multiple methods of tobacco

	18 to 29	30 to 49	50 to 64	65+	National average
	%	%	%	%	%
Two or more methods	23.0	23.5	21.6	11.5	20.4
Three or more methods	4.9	2.8	1.7	0.6	2.5

Jan. 2-Oct. 18, 2015
Gallup-Healthways Well-Being Index

GALLUP'

Twenty-three percent of 18- to 29-year-olds report using at least two forms of tobacco, similar to the use of multiple forms reported by middle-aged adults and about double the percentage reported by seniors. Far fewer young adults, 4.9%, use three or more types of tobacco, but this is significantly greater than any of the older age groups and nearly double the national average.

Bottom Line

Experimentation among young adults may be one possible explanation for their higher rate of non-cigarette tobacco use and their use of three or more forms of tobacco. According to a 2014 focus group study published in an Oxford University journal that studied the increase of e-cigarette use, the top reasons for young adults to experiment with tobacco alternatives are curiosity, appealing flavors and peer influences. Government regulations and increased taxation on cigarettes also may be leading young adults to embrace alternative methods of tobacco consumption.

Another possibility is that public smoking bans unwittingly may be contributing to the increased use of alternative tobacco products. In its most recent report on smokeless tobacco, the American Cancer Society attributes the increased use of alternative tobacco products among young adults to state and local smoking bans. The report states that tobacco companies are specifically marketing smokeless tobacco as an alternative to public tobacco consumption in places where smoking is not allowed. According to the report, smoking bans could be contributing to the "dual use" of tobacco among young adults.

With social stigma and government regulations on cigarette use continuing to increase, and a tendency for the young to experiment being an established characteristic of their age group, young adults have begun to seek alternatives to cigarettes. While previous Gallup research has shown that a majority of Americans—young adults included—are receptive to measures limiting cigarette smoking in public, the gradual decline in cigarette use may simply be the corollary of the rising use of smokeless tobacco and other alternative methods of tobacco consumption.

Gallup and Healthways will continue to monitor changes in tobacco consumption by subgroup and will report on e-cigarette use in the months ahead.

Survey Methods

Results for the cigarette-smoking trend are based on telephone interviews aggregated from Gallup polls conducted each July from 2011 through 2015, with a total random sample of 5,987 adults, aged 18 and older, living in all 50 U.S. states and the District of Columbia. For results based on the total sample of national adults, the margin of sampling error is ±1 percentage point at the 95% confidence level.

For results based on the sample of 792 18- to 29-year-olds, the margin of sampling error is ±4 percentage points at the 95% confidence level.

For results based on the sample of 1,448 30- to 49-year-olds, the margin of sampling error is ±3 percentage points at the 95% confidence level.

For results based on the sample of 1,829 50- to 64-year-olds, the margin of sampling error is ±3 percentage points at the 95% confidence level.

For results based on the sample of 1,918 adults aged 65 and older, the margin of sampling error is ±3 percentage points at the 95% confidence level.

Results for non-cigarette tobacco alternatives are based on telephone interviews conducted Jan. 2–Oct. 18, 2015, as part of the Gallup-Healthways Well-Being Index survey, with a random sample of 142,890 adults, aged 18 and older, living in all 50 U.S. states and the District of Columbia. For results based on the total sample of national adults, the margin of sampling error is ±0.32 percentage points at the 95% confidence level. All reported margins of sampling error include computed design effects for weighting.

For results based on 18- to 29-year-olds, Gallup surveyed 18,464 adults at a ±0.81 margin of sampling error at the 95% confidence level.

For results based on 30- to 49-year-olds, Gallup surveyed 33,566 adults at a ±0.61 margin of sampling error at the 95% confidence level.

For results based on 50- to 64-year-olds, Gallup surveyed 41,202 adults at a ±0.58 margin of sampling error at the 95% confidence level.

For results based on adults aged 65 and older, Gallup surveyed 47,267 adults at a ±0.55 margin of sampling error at the 95% confidence level.

December 10, 2015
DONALD TRUMP WELL-KNOWN,
BUT NOT WELL-LIKED

by Andrew Dugan

Story Highlights

- *Trump's net favorable stands at -27, well below others*
- *Ben Carson has seen largest gain in overall public familiarity*
- *Chris Christie's image improves modestly*

WASHINGTON, D.C.—The 2016 presidential candidates who are the most familiar to U.S. adults—Donald Trump, Hillary Clinton and Jeb Bush—also rank among the least-liked, in terms of their unfavorable rating exceeding their favorable rating. Trump vies with Clinton as the race's best-known candidate, but he is by far the least liked of the field, with 59% viewing him unfavorably and 32% favorably, yielding a net favorable score of -27.

Familiarity and Favorable Ratings of 2016 Presidential Candidates, Based on National Adults
Ranked by % familiar

	% Familiar (have an opinion)	% With favorable opinion	% With unfavorable opinion	Net favorable (pct. pts.)
Hillary Clinton	94	45	49	-4
Donald Trump	91	32	59	-27
Jeb Bush	78	32	46	-14
Chris Christie	69	32	37	-5
Ben Carson	66	36	30	6
Bernie Sanders	66	34	32	2
Marco Rubio	61	33	28	5
Ted Cruz	61	29	32	-3
Mike Huckabee	60	30	30	0
Carly Fiorina	49	26	23	3
John Kasich	43	21	22	-1

Nov. 23-Dec. 7, 2015

GALLUP

These ratings are based on Gallup's latest two-week rolling average, from Nov. 23–Dec. 7, 2015, largely before Trump made controversial remarks about Muslims entering the U.S. on Monday.

Bush rounds out the three most well-recognized presidential candidates, with 78% of Americans having an opinion of him. Like Trump, Bush's image is deeply underwater, as his unfavorable rating exceeds his favorable rating by 14 percentage points. By comparison, Clinton's image problem is more subdued, with a net favorable of -4. But her net-negative favorable score represents a significant slide from her score of +11 in March, when she was not only the best-known but also the best-liked candidate.

When Gallup first began tracking candidate images on July 8, several candidates were already known by a solid majority of Americans. In addition to Clinton, Trump and Bush, more than half of Americans were familiar with Chris Christie, Mike Huckabee and Ted Cruz. A little over half of Americans (52%) knew Marco Rubio. But several candidates were known only to a minority of Americans, including Ben Carson, Bernie Sanders, Carly Fiorina and John Kasich.

But over the past several months—particularly after four Republican presidential debates and two Democratic debates—Americans' familiarity with many candidates has grown considerably. Carson has seen the largest gain in the percentage of Americans able to rate him, from 36% in the initial reading to 66% today. That 30-percentage-point gain compares with a 22-point increase for Sanders. Fiorina has registered a 19-point gain, while Kasich and

Rubio have seen more modest gains over the campaign, at 14 points and 9 points, respectively.

Familiarity of 2016 Presidential Candidates, Based on National Adults
Selected two-week rolling averages
% Familiar, with an opinion

	Jul 8-21, 2015 %	Nov 23-Dec 7, 2015 %	Change (pct. pts.)
Ben Carson	36	66	30
Bernie Sanders	44	66	22
Carly Fiorina	30	49	19
John Kasich	29	43	14
Marco Rubio	52	61	9
Hillary Clinton	89	94	5
Jeb Bush	73	78	5
Chris Christie	65	69	4
Ted Cruz	58	61	3
Donald Trump	88	91	3
Mike Huckabee	59	60	1

GALLUP

Despite their gains in familiarity, Fiorina (49%) and Kasich (43%) are known to less than half of the population—the only two candidates Gallup tracks to not meet that threshold.

Christie Has Largest Gain in Popularity

The candidates' net favorable scores, a key gauge of popularity, have not moved as dramatically as their familiarity scores. Compared with when Gallup began tracking these measures in early July, Christie's negative net favorable score has improved by a modest four points to reach -5, the biggest gain of any candidate from either party. Meanwhile, Bush's net favorable score has fallen 11 points, the most of any candidate, from -3 in July to -14 today, giving him the second-worst score of any candidate—behind Trump.

Other candidates—namely Clinton, Fiorina, Rubio and Carson—experienced significant improvements in their net favorable score at points over the summer and fall, but have since fallen back to where they stood in July. Only four candidates have a net favorable score in positive territory—Carson, Rubio, Fiorina and Sanders.

Favorability of 2016 Presidential Candidates, Based on National Adults
Selected two-week rolling averages
"Net favorable" (pct. pts.)
Ranked by change

	Jul 8-21, 2015 (pct. pts.)	Nov 23-Dec 7, 2015 (pct. pts.)	Change (pct. pts.)
Chris Christie	-9	-5	4
Ted Cruz	-4	-3	1
Mike Huckabee	-1	0	1
Hillary Clinton	-3	-4	-1
Carly Fiorina	4	3	-1
Marco Rubio	6	5	-1
Bernie Sanders	4	2	-2
Donald Trump	-24	-27	-3
John Kasich	3	-1	-4
Ben Carson	12	6	-6
Jeb Bush	-3	-14	-11

GALLUP

Bottom Line

Several GOP candidates, as well as Democratic contender Bernie Sanders, have become more familiar to Americans over the past five months. But no candidate has significantly bolstered his or her image.

On the Republican side, Carson, Rubio and Fiorina can at least boast of slightly positive net favorable scores, but this relative popularity must be considered along with their lower name recognition. Cruz and Christie, meanwhile, have slightly negative favorability scores. Trump and Bush, who began the campaign as well-known figures, have not seemed to benefit from their familiarity. Bush has seen his popularity deteriorate since July, while Trump, despite his ability to dominate media coverage, has seen no improvement in his public image, which was already in poor shape in July.

On the Democratic side, Sanders enjoys slightly better bragging rights over his rival Clinton on national favorability, but again his lower name recognition raises the question of whether he can maintain his modest likability if he were to become better known. Clinton, on the other hand, saw her popularity tumble as she re-entered the public arena earlier this year, after enjoying a period of widespread public acclaim during her stint as secretary of state and in the year after her tenure as chief diplomat. But, more recently, even as she has faced high levels of scrutiny for email practices when she was in the president's Cabinet and congressional inquiries into her response to the Benghazi attacks in 2012, Clinton's favorable ratings have remained mostly steady, if slightly negative.

This presidential cycle is replete with well-known candidates, but none are extremely well liked by the public. There are some candidates who enjoy modest levels of popularity among U.S. adults, but they also tend to be the lesser-known candidates.

Survey Methods

Results for this Gallup poll are based on telephone interviews conducted Nov. 23–Dec. 7, 2015, on the Gallup U.S. Daily survey, with a random sample of 6,603 adults, aged 18 and older, living in all 50 U.S. states and the District of Columbia. Each candidate was rated by a random subset of respondents during this period with sample sizes for each candidate ranging approximately from 1,800 to 1,950 respondents. For results based on the total sample of national adults rating each candidate, the margin of sampling error is ±2 percentage points at the 95% confidence level. All reported margins of sampling error include computed design effects for weighting.

December 11, 2015
TRUST IN GOVERNMENT TO PROTECT AGAINST TERRORISM AT NEW LOW

by Justin McCarthy

Story Highlights

- *Fifty-five percent confident in U.S. government protection*
- *About half of Americans say they worry about becoming a victim*
- *Two in three say terrorist acts in U.S. likely in coming weeks*

WASHINGTON, D.C.—In the week after the deadly shootings in San Bernardino, California, Americans' confidence in the federal government's ability to protect citizens from acts of terrorism has dropped to a new low of 55%.

Confidence in the U.S. government to protect citizens from terrorism is down 12 percentage points since June, and is now 33 points lower than the 88% who said they had a "great deal" or "fair amount" of confidence shortly after 9/11.

These data, collected Dec. 8–9, come just days after the San Bernardino shootings and as more details emerge about the shooters' identities and alleged connections to radical Islamic ideology.

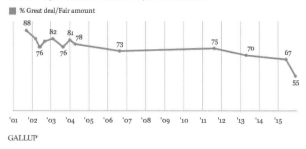

Confidence in U.S. Government to Protect Citizens From Terrorism

How much confidence do you have in the U.S. government to protect its citizens from future acts of terrorism -- a great deal, a fair amount, not very much or none at all?

The new low continues the gradual erosion in confidence over the past 14 years. But the peculiarities of the latest shootings may particularly affect Americans' views of what their government can do to prevent such events, because one of the shooters was a U.S.-born Muslim, while the other was a woman and a mother—a statistical anomaly among terrorists' profiles. Most prior perpetrators of terrorist attacks in the U.S. were young males.

Despite the sharp drop in confidence in the government to protect citizens from terrorism, Americans are no more likely to worry that they or their family members will be terrorism victims than they were six months ago. About half (51%) say they are "very" or "somewhat" worried that they or a relative will be a victim, similar to the 49% in June.

The current percentage who are worried that they will be affected by terrorism is higher than all but a few figures from Gallup's trend—and all of those came right after the 9/11 attacks, when between 51% and 59% said they worried for themselves and their family members. Although the latest figure is not significantly different from the 49% measured earlier this year, that figure in turn was higher than had been seen in recent years, most likely reflecting Americans' increasing concern about the rise of the Islamic State.

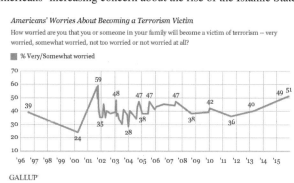

Americans' Worries About Becoming a Terrorism Victim

How worried are you that you or someone in your family will become a victim of terrorism -- very worried, somewhat worried, not too worried or not worried at all?

Two in Three Say Terrorist Acts in U.S. Likely in Coming Weeks

The percentage of Americans who believe it is "very" or "somewhat likely" that acts of terrorism will take place in the U.S. in the next several weeks (67%) has increased sharply, by 22 points, since June. The current figure is the highest on this measure since early 2003, just after the U.S.-led invasion of Iraq began. The dramatic increase may reflect both the San Bernardino shootings and the attacks in Paris last month.

The peak for this measure was shortly after the 9/11 attacks, when 85% of Americans felt another terrorist attack was imminent. Since then, expectations for such attacks have reached the current level only at the start of the Iraq War in March 2003 and after the U.S. killed Osama bin Laden in May 2011.

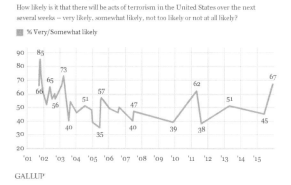

Perceived Likelihood of Acts of Terrorism Occurring in Next Few Weeks
How likely is it that there will be acts of terrorism in the United States over the next several weeks -- very likely, somewhat likely, not too likely or not at all likely?

▨ % Very/Somewhat likely

GALLUP

Bottom Line

Americans' heightened sense of the possibility of future terrorist attacks and their weakened trust in the government's ability to combat terrorism may have, in part, prompted President Barack Obama's Oval Office address this week, when he spoke about the threat of terrorism and his administration's work against it. Still, several Republican presidential candidates have criticized the president's response to the attacks and the administration's handling of the threat of terrorism in general.

Americans' confidence in the government and in institutions in general has floundered in recent years. But their lower confidence in the government's ability to keep them safe may not be as much a blaming of government ineptitude as it is a better understanding of the challenging nature of the threats now hiding within the U.S.

Americans' views of the likelihood of terrorist attacks have previously shot up after an attack, only to settle back down again. One key to understanding the public's views on this issue at this point will be monitoring whether that same pattern recurs, or whether this time the fear of a new attack stays high for an extended period of time.

Survey Methods

Results for this Gallup poll are based on telephone interviews conducted Dec. 8–9, 2015, on the Gallup U.S. Daily survey, with a random sample of 1,013 adults, aged 18 and older, living in all 50 U.S. states and the District of Columbia. For results based on the total sample of national adults, the margin of sampling error is ±4 percentage points at the 95% confidence level. All reported margins of sampling error include computed design effects for weighting.

December 14, 2015
FINANCIAL WELL-BEING AND SOCIAL RELATIONSHIPS CLOSELY LINKED

by Jade Wood and Rebecca Riffkin

Story Highlights

• *Strong social relationships and high financial well-being linked*
• *Link holds across income levels*

WASHINGTON, D.C.—Americans' financial well-being is closely linked to their perceptions of their social relationships. Almost nine in 10 Americans who are thriving in their financial well-being agree that their relationship with their spouse, partner or closest friend is stronger than ever. But this drops to six in 10 among those who are suffering in financial well-being.

Americans' Assessment of Closest Relationship,
by Financial Well-Being Status
On a five-point scale, where 5 means strongly agree and 1 means strongly disagree, please rate your level of agreement: Your relationship with your spouse, partner or closest friend is stronger than ever. Figures shown are the percentage who rate 4 or 5.

	% Agree relationship with spouse, partner or closest friend is stronger than ever
Thriving in financial well-being	87
Struggling in financial well-being	77
Suffering in financial well-being	61

Jan. 1, 2014-June 30, 2015
Gallup-Healthways Well-Being Index

GALLUP

Financial well-being is one of the five interrelated elements of well-being in the Gallup-Healthways Well-Being Index, along with purpose, social, community and physical well-being. Gallup and Healthways classify respondents as thriving, struggling or suffering in each well-being element:

• Thriving: Well-being that is strong and consistent in a particular element
• Struggling: Well-being that is moderate or inconsistent in a particular element
• Suffering: Well-being that is low and inconsistent in a particular element

To assess financial well-being, Gallup and Healthways ask U.S. adults about their ability to afford food and healthcare, whether they have enough money to do everything they want to do, whether they worried about money in the past week and their perceptions of their standard of living compared with those they spend time with. Importantly, thriving in financial well-being does not mean having a high income, but instead consistently managing one's finances to reduce stress and increase financial security. Nationally, 41% of Americans were thriving in financial well-being in the first half of 2015, up slightly from 39% in 2014.

The link between financial well-being and social relationships holds across income levels. In other words, Americans' perceptions of their social relationships improve as their financial well-being improves, regardless of their income level. Upper-income and lower-income Americans are both more likely to report their relationship is stronger than ever if they are thriving in financial well-being than if they are suffering.

Bottom Line

The interplay between financial well-being, income and strength of relationships is multidirectional and complex. One's sense of financial well-being and the experiences which accompany it— stress level, effort to acquire necessities, sense of security and stability—interact with interpersonal relationships and how people relate to others in their lives.

Relationship Between Financial Well-Being and Social Relationships, by Income

On a five-point scale, where 5 means strongly agree and 1 means strongly disagree, please rate your level of agreement: Your relationship with your spouse, partner or closest friend is stronger than ever. Figures shown are the percentage who rate 4 or 5.

	Annual income under $36,000	Annual income $36,000-$89,999	Annual income $90,000 or more
	% Agree relationship is stronger than ever	% Agree relationship is stronger than ever	% Agree relationship is stronger than ever
Thriving in financial well-being	83	87	89
Struggling in financial well-being	72	79	79
Suffering in financial well-being	57	66	63

Jan. 1, 2014-June 30, 2015
Gallup-Healthways Well-Being Index

GALLUP'

The strength of the direction of this relationship is unclear, however. One possibility is that financial well-being influences social relationships. For instance, financial stress overall can negatively affect interactions with family and friends. But strong financial well-being may strengthen relationships, as not worrying about money removes a significant potential source of conflict.

Another possibility is that social relationships influence financial well-being. For example, a divorce or separation can cause financial difficulties. But strong relationships may ease the psychological burden of coping with financial stress, such as having friends who are willing to offer support.

"We find that one of the first signs of positive behavior change in our financial well-being programs is discernible improvement in people's immediate relationships surrounding money, especially the relationship with their spouse," says Brian Hamilton, Vice President of Financial Wellness, Ramsey Solutions. "We get feedback every day from couples whose marriages were saved by getting on the same page with their money."

The relationship Americans have with their finances and the management of their money has a significant effect on their personal relationships—for high-income and low-income alike. Financial well-being is more than income alone. Americans with high incomes who do not successfully manage their money and who do not live within their means could have low financial well-being—and those with moderate or low incomes who manage their money well and live within their means could have high financial well-being.

Overall, these results distinctly illustrate that financial well-being and strong relationships are linked, regardless of income.

Survey Methods

Results are based on telephone interviews conducted Jan. 1, 2014–June 30, 2015, as part of the Gallup-Healthways Well-Being Index survey, with a random sample of 97,851 adults, aged 18 and older, living in all 50 U.S. states and the District of Columbia. For results based on the total sample of national adults, the margin of sampling error is ±0.3 percentage points at the 95% confidence level. All reported margins of sampling error include computed design effects for weighting.

December 14, 2015
AMERICANS NAME TERRORISM AS NO. 1 U.S. PROBLEM

by Rebecca Riffkin

Story Highlights

- *16% name terrorism as the most important U.S. problem*
- *Republicans more likely than Democrats to name terrorism*
- *Mentions of the economy as top problem are lowest since 2007*

WASHINGTON, D.C.—After the deadly terrorist attacks in Paris and San Bernardino, California, Americans are now more likely to name terrorism as the top issue facing the U.S. than to name any other issue—including those that have typically topped the list recently, such as the economy and the government. About one in six Americans, 16%, now identify terrorism as the most important U.S. problem, up from just 3% in early November.

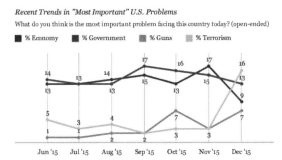

Recent Trends in "Most Important" U.S. Problems
What do you think is the most important problem facing this country today? (open-ended)

■ % Economy   ■ % Government   ■ % Guns   ■ % Terrorism

Shown are problems listed by at least 7% of Americans in December 2015

GALLUP'

This is the highest percentage of Americans to mention terrorism in a decade, although it is still lower than the 46% measured after 9/11. Before 2001, terrorism barely registered as the most important problem facing the country.

After 9/11, terrorism faded as the top problem, although mentions have spiked after major terrorist incidents. In 2004, mentions rose as high as 19% after the Madrid train bombings, and then jumped again to 17% in 2005 after the London train and bus bombings. Since 2007, less than 10% of Americans—sometimes less than 1%—have mentioned terrorism in Gallup's monthly updates, although mentions did spike again to 8% in early 2010 after the failed "underwear bombing."

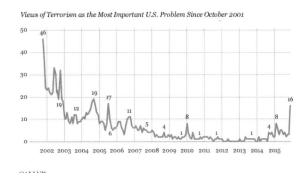

Views of Terrorism as the Most Important U.S. Problem Since October 2001

GALLUP

In January 2015, mentions of terrorism as the most important U.S. problem increased to 8% a few weeks after the *Charlie Hebdo* attacks in Paris. However, they soon fell and remained between 6% and 2% until December. The most recent polling was conducted Dec. 2–6, just after the San Bernardino attacks, and a few weeks after the Paris attacks that killed at least 130 people and are considered the worst terrorist attack in Europe in 11 years.

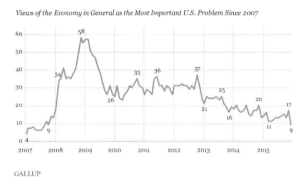

MENTIONS OF TERRORISM AS MOST
IMPORTANT PROBLEM IN U.S.

NOVEMBER 2015   DECEMBER 2015

3%   16%

GALLUP POLL, DEC. 2-6

Republicans are more likely than Democrats to say terrorism is the most important problem facing the U.S. And there has been a much greater rise in Republican concern about terrorism over the last month than among members of other party groups. Currently, 24% of Republicans name terrorism as the most important problem, compared with 9% of Democrats and 15% of independents. In November, 4% of Republicans, 3% of Democrats and 2% of independents named terrorism as the top problem.

Mentions of the Economy as Most Important Problem Are Lowest Since 2007

In December, 9% of Americans listed the economy in general terms as the most important problem, the lowest percentage to mention the issue since the end of 2007, before the depths of the recession took hold. Mentions of the economy increased sharply in 2008 and 2009, reaching an all-time high of 58% at the end of 2008. While mentions of the economy have dropped since then, it has remained one of the most frequently named issues.

Views of the Economy in General as the Most Important U.S. Problem Since 2007

GALLUP

In December, 21% of Americans mentioned *some aspect of the economy* as the most important problem, the lowest such percentage since mid-2007 and down significantly from 39% in November. This significant drop in December does not suggest a dramatic shift in the way Americans are viewing the economy, but instead indicates that terrorism concerns have, at least temporarily, occupied more space in Americans' minds when they are asked to name the top problem facing the U.S.

Mentions of Guns Also Increased in December

In December, 7% of Americans named guns or gun control as the most important U.S. problem. This is up from 3% in November, but the same as the October percentage. Before 2013, guns were rarely mentioned as the most important problem. But at the beginning of 2013, after the Sandy Hook Elementary shootings, mentions

increased to 6%, though they ultimately fell once again. The issue has generally been overshadowed by problems such as the economy and the government, which historically far more Americans have named than guns.

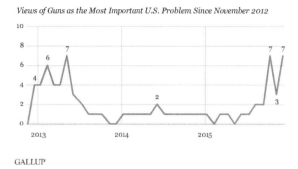

Views of Guns as the Most Important U.S. Problem Since November 2012

GALLUP

Bottom Line

The terrorist attacks in San Bernardino and Paris have altered how Americans view the problems facing the U.S. Satisfaction with the way things are going in the U.S. dropped significantly to a 13-month low in December, and Americans' trust in the government to protect them from terrorism is the lowest Gallup has measured. The data reviewed here show that terrorism has now become the single most frequently mentioned issue when Americans are asked to name the most important problem.

In the past, mentions of terrorism as the most important U.S. problem have quickly fallen after a major incident. But two major attacks in short succession, at a time when concern about terrorism was already elevated given the threat of the Islamic State, have Americans on edge. President Barack Obama himself made a rare Oval Office address shortly after the San Bernardino attacks, to discuss terrorism and how he hopes to combat it. Whether terrorism remains atop the list of Americans' concerns or recedes in the coming months likely will depend on the government's response to the terror threat as well as the occurrence, or the lack, of major attacks in the U.S. or elsewhere.

Survey Methods

Results for this Gallup poll are based on telephone interviews conducted Dec. 2–6, 2015, with a random sample of 824 adults, aged 18 and older, living in all 50 U.S. states and the District of Columbia. For results based on the total sample of national adults, the margin of sampling error is ±4 percentage points at the 95% confidence level. All reported margins of sampling error include computed design effects for weighting.

December 15, 2015
ANTI-TERROR: VISA CONTROL, AIRSTRIKES SEEN AS MOST EFFECTIVE

by Frank Newport

Story Highlights

- *Visa overhaul, military options seen as most effective in fighting terrorism*

- *Americans also see banning gun sales to those on no-fly list as effective*
- *Preventing Muslims from entering U.S. seen as least effective of any on list*

PRINCETON, N.J.—When asked about 11 ways to combat terrorism, Americans are most likely to say overhauling the nation's visa waiver program and intensifying airstrikes against the Islamic State, or ISIS, are effective measures. Establishing a religious test to ban Muslims from entering the U.S. ranks last.

Effectiveness of Actions to Combat Terrorism

How effective do you think each of the following will be in the U.S. campaign against terrorism -- very effective, somewhat effective, not too effective or not at all effective?

	% Very effective/ Somewhat effective
Increase U.S. airstrikes against the Islamic State or ISIS to take out their leaders, heavy weapons and infrastructure	79
Overhaul the federal visa waiver program to provide tighter screening for people who come to the U.S. temporarily for travel or business	79
Ban gun sales to people on the federal no-fly watch list	71
Send more U.S. special operations forces to fight the Islamic State or ISIS	70
Send large numbers of U.S. ground troops to Syria and Iraq to fight the Islamic State or ISIS	59
Intensify diplomatic efforts to pursue ceasefires and a political resolution to the Syrian war	56
Provide more U.S. training and equipment to Iraqi and Syrian forces fighting the Islamic State or ISIS	55
Pass new laws making it harder to buy assault weapons	55
A new law that would prevent any Muslim from entering the U.S.	38
Require Muslims, including those who are U.S. citizens, to carry a special ID	32
A new law that would impose a religious test for entering the U.S., banning those who identify their religion as Muslim	28

Dec. 11-12, 2015

GALLUP

Gallup tested Americans' views of the effectiveness of several current or proposed anti-terrorism measures Dec. 11–12, about 10 days after the Dec. 2 mass shooting in San Bernardino, California, that left 14 dead in what was apparently an attack inspired by Islamic extremism. Since the shooting, Gallup research has shown a sharp increase in the percentage of Americans naming terrorism as the nation's most important problem, as well as an increase in the percentage of Americans who believe it is likely that further acts of terrorism will occur in the coming weeks. At the same time, Gallup has seen a sharp decrease in Americans' confidence in the U.S. government to protect its citizens from such attacks.

Aware of this increased public concern, President Barack Obama addressed the nation on Dec. 6, outlining a number of steps to combat terrorism that are either already underway or that he wants enacted. Meanwhile, a day after Obama's speech, presidential candidate Donald Trump championed one of the policies that Obama had rejected in his speech—instituting a religious test to bar Muslims from entering the U.S.

This latest study updated a question format Gallup had originally used in a Sept. 21–22 survey conducted immediately after the 9/11 terrorist attacks. The list included a series of 11 actions the U.S. could take to combat terrorism, most of which Obama mentioned in his Dec. 6 speech in one way or another. Complete results appear at the end of this article.

Here are four key conclusions from the results:

1. **Military options are high on the list. Within that sphere, Americans see the use of airstrikes and special operations forces as more effective than the introduction of ground forces or doing more to arm rebel forces.**

The study includes four proposals related to the use of military action against the Islamic State. More than half of Americans see all as potentially effective. Intensified use of airstrikes is clearly perceived to be the most effective of the four measured, followed in order of perceived effectiveness by sending more U.S. special operations forces to fight the Islamic State, sending large numbers of U.S. ground troops to fight Islamic State militants, and providing more training and equipment to Iraqi and Syrian forces fighting the Islamic State.

2. **While many Americans see the effort to tighten up the visa waiver program as potentially effective in fighting terrorism, the concepts of targeting Muslims by preventing them from entering the U.S. or forcing them to carry a special ID are much less likely to be perceived as effective.**

Americans view Trump's proposal to ban Muslims from entering the U.S. as the least effective of any of the proposals tested.

The survey includes two different wordings of this idea. One wording references a new law that would "prevent any Muslim from entering the U.S." while the second references a new law that would "impose a religious test for entering the U.S., banning those who identify their religion as Muslim." This second wording approximates how Obama described—and objected to—the proposal in his speech, and just 28% of Americans believe it would be effective in preventing terrorism. The "religious test" wording scores 10 percentage points lower than the "prevent" wording. Both, as noted, are at the bottom of the list.

The question on the effectiveness of requiring Muslims to carry a special ID stems from a proposal Gallup asked about in a different context just after 9/11. This idea—along with the two wordings of the proposal to ban Muslims from entering the U.S.—appears at the bottom of the effectiveness list.

Overall, the two ideas related to profiling Muslims—either by preventing them from entering the U.S. or forcing them to carry an ID—are the only proposals tested whose perceived effectiveness is below 50%.

3. **Americans view the idea of preventing individuals on the no-fly list from buying guns as more effective than attempting to limit the sale of assault weapons.**

Two gun-control proposals are included on the list. Banning gun sales to individuals on the federal no-fly list is among the four most effective proposals tested, with a 71% effectiveness rating. Americans perceive new laws making it harder to buy assault weapons as less effective, at 55%.

4. **Democrats see gun control as most effective, while Republicans see visa overhaul and military operations as most effective.**

There are differences in the ways in which Republicans and Democrats rate the effectiveness of the proposals. The top four most effective proposals according to Republicans and Republican-leaning independents include reforming the visa waiver program and three military options—increased airstrikes, more special operations forces and introducing U.S. ground troops to fight Islamic State militants. For Democrats and Democratic leaners, the two most effective proposals relate to gun control—barring those on the no-fly list from buying guns, and limiting the sale of assault weapons—followed by airstrikes and reforming the visa waiver program.

The biggest distinction across party lines comes in views of banning assault weapons, with 78% of Democrats viewing it as effective, compared with 31% of Republicans. There is also a 26-point difference between Republicans and Democrats in the perceived effectiveness of preventing Muslims from entering the U.S., with Republicans more likely to see it as effective. Still, this proposal ranks fairly low on Republicans' list.

Bottom Line

American government leaders have no shortage of possible options to use in the battle against acts of terrorism in the U.S., and presidential candidates running for office themselves have no shortage of ideas about what they would do if elected. As far as the American public is concerned, a number of different options would be at least somewhat effective in combatting terrorism—including, in particular, tightening up the nation's visa waiver program, intensifying airstrikes against the Islamic State, banning individuals on the government's no-fly list from being able to buy guns, and sending more special operations forces to fight Islamic militants.

Notably, less than half of Americans think proposals to profile Muslims, either by preventing them from entering the country or by requiring them to carry special identification, would be effective.

Effectiveness of Actions to Combat Terrorism

How effective do you think each of the following will be in the U.S. campaign against terrorism -- very effective, somewhat effective, not too effective or not at all effective?

	% Very effective	% Somewhat effective	% Not too effective	% Not at all effective
Overhaul the federal visa waiver program to provide tighter screening for people who come to the U.S. temporarily for travel or business	46	33	11	9
Increase U.S. airstrikes against the Islamic State or ISIS to take out their leaders, heavy weapons and infrastructure	44	35	11	7
Ban gun sales to people on the federal no-fly watch list	42	29	9	16
Send more U.S. special operations forces to fight the Islamic State or ISIS	38	32	14	14
Pass new laws making it harder to buy assault weapons	34	21	14	30
Send large numbers of U.S. ground troops to Syria and Iraq to fight the Islamic State or ISIS	26	33	22	17
Intensify diplomatic efforts to pursue ceasefires and a political resolution to the Syrian war	25	32	20	19
A new law that would prevent any Muslim from entering the U.S.	22	16	18	42
Provide more U.S. training and equipment to Iraqi and Syrian forces fighting the Islamic State or ISIS	18	37	23	18
Require Muslims, including those who are U.S. citizens, to carry a special ID	16	16	20	46
A new law that would impose a religious test for entering the U.S., banning those who identify their religion as Muslim	15	14	16	52

Dec. 11-12, 2015

GALLUP'

Survey Methods

Results for this Gallup poll are based on telephone interviews conducted Dec. 11–12, 2015, on the Gallup U.S. Daily survey, with a random sample of 1,016 adults, aged 18 and older, living in all 50 U.S. states and the District of Columbia. Each item was asked of approximately half the sample, with item selection determined at random. For results based on the national adult sample rating each item, the margin of sampling error is ±5 percentage points at the 95% confidence level. All reported margins of sampling error include computed design effects for weighting.

Each sample of national adults includes a minimum quota of 60% cellphone respondents and 40% landline respondents, with additional minimum quotas by time zone within region. Landline and cellular telephone numbers are selected using random-digit-dial methods.

December 16, 2015

MARKET VOLATILITY A GROWING CONCERN FOR U.S. INVESTORS

by Jim Norman

Story Highlights

- *62% of U.S. investors are concerned by stock market volatility*
- *In February, 53% of investors were concerned*
- *Little change in confidence, optimism about stock market*

WASHINGTON, D.C.—More than six in 10 U.S. investors (62%) now say they are concerned about the stock market's volatility, according to a new Wells Fargo/Gallup Investor and Retirement Optimism Index survey. In February, before the huge stock market fluctuations in late summer and fall, a bare majority of 53% expressed concern.

Market Volatility Sparks Concerns

How concerned are you about the recent volatility in the stock market?

	Jan 30-Feb 9, 2015	Oct 30-Nov 8, 2015
Very concerned	14%	18%
Somewhat concerned	39%	44%
Not too concerned	33%	28%
Not at all concerned	13%	10%

Wells Fargo/Gallup Investor and Retirement Optimism Index surveys

GALLUP'

Eighteen percent of U.S. investors now say they are "very" concerned about market volatility, up slightly from 14% in February; another 44% are "somewhat concerned," an increase from 39%. At the same time, the rising concern has not adversely affected investors' long-term confidence in stocks as a place to save and invest for retirement—43% now say they have "a great deal" or "quite a lot" of confidence, compared with 40% in February.

Two other key measures of investors' views also changed little:

- Forty-four percent of investors in February said they were optimistic about the stock market's performance "over the next 12 months"; 45% are optimistic now.

- Looking at the larger picture of all financial markets, including stocks, 58% of investors said in February that "now is a good time to invest"; 54% feel that way now.

While overall views about whether it is a good time to invest in financial markets did not change significantly, investors who are very concerned about the market's recent ups and downs are much more likely to think it is a bad time to invest in financial markets (75%) than those who are somewhat concerned (39%) or are not too or not at all concerned (31%).

Investors' Outlook Tied to Level of Concern
Investor optimism about financial markets tied to level of comfort with market's fluctuations

	Very concerned about volatility	Somewhat concerned about volatility	Not too/Not at all concerned about volatility
Good or bad time to invest in financial markets?			
Good time	23%	57%	66%
Bad time	75%	39%	31%

Wells Fargo/Gallup Investor and Retirement Optimism Index survey, Oct. 30–Nov. 8, 2015

GALLUP

The most recent findings are from the fourth quarter Wells Fargo/Gallup Investor and Retirement Optimism survey of U.S. investors conducted Oct. 30–Nov. 8. For this survey, investors are defined as U.S. adults who have at least $10,000 invested in stocks, bonds or mutual funds, either in an investment account or a retirement fund—a definition that approximately 40% of U.S. adults fit.

Investors Brace for More Market Volatility at Start of New Year

Nearly three in four (74%) investors expect the market to be "somewhat" (58%) or "highly" (16%) volatile at the start of 2016. Americans with more than $100,000 invested are more likely to predict volatility (79%) than are those with smaller investments (68%).

Those expecting volatility at the start of 2016 are more likely to say they will buy stocks in hopes of taking advantage of low prices (30%) than to say they will sell stocks to protect from further losses (15%).

That would fit the pattern among stock owners in August, when the most extreme recent market fluctuations occurred. In that month, the Dow Jones Industrial Average plummeted more than 1,100 points—the Dow's biggest percentage drop in more than five years. One in four stock owners (25%) in the most recent poll say they reacted to the August volatility by buying stocks, almost twice as many as say they sold off stocks (14%).

In addition to buying or selling stocks as a response to the August fluctuations, half of stock owners say they reviewed their portfolio online, half say they paid closer attention to the market than usual and a third consulted with a financial adviser. Investors who consulted a financial adviser during that time were more likely to sell and to buy than those who didn't seek advice.

Investors Who Sought Financial Advice in August Market Dive Were More Active
During the period of market volatility in late August, which, if any, of the following did you do?

	Paid closer attention to the market	Sold some stocks	Bought some stocks
Investors who consulted with a financial adviser	57%	23%	40%
Investors who did not consult with a financial adviser	46%	10%	18%

Wells Fargo/Gallup Investor and Retirement Optimism Index survey, Oct. 30–Nov. 8, 2015

GALLUP

Bottom Line

As investors look back at the recent huge swings in the stock market and forward to the rise in interest rates the Federal Open Market Committee approved on Wednesday, it's not surprising that their concerns about stock market volatility have risen. However, those concerns do not appear to have had a major effect on long-term confidence in stocks as a good investment, nor have they made investors more eager to sell than to buy stocks.

Survey Methods

Results for the Wells Fargo/Gallup Investor and Retirement Optimism Index survey are based on questions asked Oct. 30–Nov. 8, 2015, on the Gallup Daily tracking survey, of a random sample of 1,018 U.S. adults having investable assets of $10,000 or more.

For results based on the total sample of investors, the margin of sampling error is ±4 percentage points at the 95% confidence level. All reported margins of sampling error include computed design effects for weighting.

December 16, 2015
AMERICANS MORE WORRIED ABOUT TERRORISM THAN MASS SHOOTINGS

by Art Swift

Story Highlights

- *47% say they are worried about being a victim of terrorism*
- *38% say they are worried about being a victim of a mass shooting*
- *Republicans more worried than Democrats about mass shootings, terrorism*

WASHINGTON, D.C.—More Americans are "very" or "somewhat" worried that they or a family member will become a victim of an Islamic State–inspired terrorist attack (47%) than they are about becoming a victim of a mass shooting (38%). But a majority of Americans say they are not worried about either potential event.

Worries About Being a Victim of a Mass Shooting or Terrorism in the U.S.
How worried are you that you or someone in your family will become a victim of a mass shooting -- very worried, somewhat worried, not too worried, or not worried at all?

How worried are you that you or someone in your family will become a victim of an act of mass terrorism planned by or inspired by the Islamic State or ISIS -- very worried, somewhat worried, not too worried, or not worried at all?

	% Very worried	% Somewhat worried	% Not too worried	% Not worried at all
Mass shooting	11	27	35	27
Terrorism, planned or inspired by the Islamic State	17	30	27	26

Dec. 11-12, 2015
NOTE: Each question asked of a half sample

GALLUP

These results, from a Gallup poll conducted Dec. 11–12, are similar to those from another Gallup trend, which makes no mention of ISIS, and shows 51% currently saying they worry about being a victim of terrorism.

Americans may perceive that there have been an increasing number of "mass shootings" in the U.S. in recent years. This subject is under debate because there is not a commonly accepted definition for mass shootings. Shootingtracker.com defines mass shootings as "an event or related series of events where four or more people are shot, likely without a cooling-off period." At the other end of the spectrum, *Mother Jones* defines a mass shooting as "a single incident in a public place, excluding gang activity, armed robbery or domestic violence, in which four or more people are killed." Based on shootingtracker.com's definition, there were 353 mass shootings from Jan. 1 through Dec. 5 of this year. But based on *Mother Jones'* definition, there were four. Other definitions place the number somewhere in the middle on that spectrum.

AMERICANS VERY/SOMEWHAT WORRIED
ABOUT BECOMING A VICTIM OF ...

A MASS SHOOTING   TERRORISM

38%   47%

GALLUP POLL, DEC. 11-12

There have been far fewer terrorist attacks in the United States, as opposed to more general mass shootings, but this month the issue gained prominence with the terrorist action in San Bernardino, California. Police say a husband and wife were "radicalized" by the Islamic State and carried out an attack at the Inland Regional Center, where 14 people were killed and 21 injured in shootings and an attempted bombing. This attack followed a coordinated Islamic State attack on multiple locations in Paris in November. Both of these events are examples of terrorist attacks that could be considered "mass shootings" by certain definitions of the term.

Republicans More Worried Than Democrats About Terrorism and Mass Shootings

Looking at political party identification, 64% of Republicans and Republican-leaning independents say they are "very" or "somewhat" worried about themselves or a family member being a victim of a terrorist attack by the Islamic State, while 35% of Democrats and Democratic-leaning independents say the same.

Republicans are also more worried than Democrats about a mass shooting, 46% versus 32%, respectively. But a slim majority of Republicans and a commanding majority of Democrats say they are "not too" worried or "not at all" worried about such an event.

Worries About ISIS-Inspired Terrorism and Mass Shootings
By political party

	% Very worried	% Somewhat worried	% Not too worried	% Not worried at all
ISIS-INSPIRED TERRORISM				
Democrats/Leaners	11	24	35	28
Republicans/Leaners	23	41	19	18
MASS SHOOTINGS				
Democrats/Leaners	11	21	39	29
Republicans/Leaners	13	33	32	23

Dec. 11-12, 2015

GALLUP

Bottom Line

While mass shootings seem to be a common aspect of American life nowadays, and terrorist attacks are relatively rare, more Americans say they are worried about being victimized by the latter than the former. This may be because the definition of a mass shooting is a subject of debate, or because memories of catastrophic attacks, such as 9/11, on American soil still loom large in the public consciousness.

American leaders have offered solutions to these problems, ranging from curbing sales of certain weapons and expanded background checks to reduce mass shootings, to increased U.S. military bombings overseas and greater intelligence gathering in the U.S. to combat the Islamic State. Gallup has asked Americans about a wide variety of actions to fight terrorism, from increasing airstrikes against ISIS and overhauling the federal visa waiver program, to requiring Muslims to carry a special ID and even banning those who identify as Muslim from entering the country. While Americans say the last two options are not effective in fighting ISIS, it is clear that during this political season, elected officials and politicians will be searching to assuage the fears of an uneasy electorate about the terrorism threat.

Survey Methods

Results for this Gallup poll are based on telephone interviews conducted Dec. 11–12, 2015, on the Gallup U.S. Daily survey, with a random sample of 1,016 adults, aged 18 and older, living in all 50 U.S. states and the District of Columbia. Both items were asked of a randomly selected half sample of respondents. The margin of sampling error is ±5 percentage points at the 95% confidence level. All reported margins of sampling error include computed design effects for weighting.

December 17, 2015
U.S. QUALITY JOB OUTLOOK IN 2015 BEST SINCE 2007

by Rebecca Riffkin

Story Highlights

- *Average of 42% in 2015 said good time to find a quality job*
- *First time the annual average over 40% since before the recession*
- *All key subgroups improved views of the job market in 2015*

WASHINGTON, D.C.—In 2015, an average of 42% of Americans said it was a good time to find a quality job. This is the most positive assessment of the job market since 2007, and up substantially from averages near 10% from 2009 through 2011.

Gallup began asking this question in August 2001 and has asked it monthly since October 2001. The annual average saying it is a good time to find a quality job has been higher than 40% only three times, in 2006, 2007 and now in 2015. Optimism about quality job prospects dropped dramatically between 2007 and 2008 and bottomed out at an average of 10% in 2009. Each year since then, job market assessments have improved at least slightly. The largest increase was evident this past year, during which unemployment levels have been the lowest the government has measured since 2007.

On a monthly level, the percentage of Americans who said it was a good time to find a quality job reached as high as 45% in January and September 2015, slightly below the all-time high of 48% in January 2007. In the latest monthly measurement from Dec. 2–6, 44% of Americans say it is a good time to find a quality job.

Percentage in U.S. Saying Now Is a Good Time to Find a Quality Job, Yearly Averages
Thinking about the job situation in America today, would you say that it is now a good time or a bad time to find a quality job?

■ % Good time

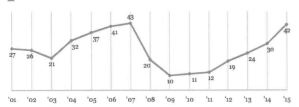

'01 '02 '03 '04 '05 '06 '07 '08 '09 '10 '11 '12 '13 '14 '15

2001 was only August-December, all other years have data for all 12 months

GALLUP

Perceived Job Prospects Better in 2015 Than in 2014 for All Key Subgroups

Among all major subgroups, the percentage saying it is a good time to find a quality job was higher in 2015 than it was in 2014, with nearly every group showing a double-digit increase.

One's political affiliation greatly influences assessments of the job market, as a majority of Democrats (53%) say now is a good time to find a quality job, compared with 32% of Republicans and 40% of independents. Democrats have also shown a larger increase in "good time" ratings since last year than Republicans and independents.

Percentage of Americans Saying Now Is a Good Time to Find a Quality Job, Annual Averages by Subgroup
Thinking about the job situation in America today, would you say that it is now a good time or a bad time to find a quality job?

	% Good time in 2014	% Good time in 2015
Men	32	45
Women	27	39
18-29	38	52
30-49	33	46
50-64	25	37
65+	22	32
White	25	38
Black	40	52
Hispanic	40	51
College graduate	32	47
Not a college graduate	29	40
Less than $30,000	28	37
$30,000-$74,999	29	42
$75,000-$99,999	30	44
$100,000-$249,999	34	48
$250,000 or more	40	54
Republican	24	32
Independent	27	40
Democrat	38	53
Working	33	48
Not working	26	35

GALLUP

Blacks and Hispanics are more likely to say it is a good time to find a quality job than whites. And younger Americans are more likely to be optimistic than older Americans. However, party identification could be influencing these differences, as younger Americans and nonwhites are more likely to be Democrats. Higher-income Americans, those with a college degree, men and working Americans remain most likely to say it is a good time to find a quality job. Perceptions of the job market improved across the board, rather than among only a few groups.

Bottom Line

The increase in the percentage of Americans who say it is a good time to find a quality job aligns with improvements in other Gallup economic measures. The Gallup Good Jobs rate has been slightly higher most months in 2015 than in comparable months in the past few years. Moreover, Gallup's Job Creation Index has been steady at a record high for most of 2015. Additional Gallup measures show that other aspects of the economy may still be fragile, however. Average consumer spending remains higher than Gallup found in 2009 through 2012 but has yet to cross the $100 threshold last reached in 2008. Americans' perceptions of the economy generally are down significantly from where they were at the end of last year and the beginning of this year. While the job market in the U.S. looks far better than it did in the aftermath of the Great Recession, not all economic measures have recovered to prerecession levels.

Survey Methods

Results for this Gallup poll are based on telephone interviews conducted in 2015 with a random sample of 12,137 adults, aged 18 and older, living in all 50 U.S. states and the District of Columbia. For results based on the total sample of national adults, the margin of sampling error is ±1 percentage point at the 95% confidence level. All reported margins of sampling error include computed design effects for weighting.

December 17, 2015
CONGRESSIONAL JOB APPROVAL AVERAGES MEAGER 16% IN 2015

by Jeffrey M. Jones

Story Highlights

- *2015 average two points above all-time low from 2013*
- *Sixth consecutive year approval averages below 20%*
- *Republicans' approval of Congress no higher than Democrats' approval*

PRINCETON, N.J.—Americans' approval of Congress averaged 16% in 2015, just slightly better than the 14% average recorded in 2013, the lowest in Gallup's four-decade trend. This marks the sixth consecutive year, and the seventh in the last eight years, in which fewer than 20% of Americans approved of Congress.

Gallup's yearly congressional job approval averages reflect ratings measured every month since 2001 and periodic ratings from 1974 through 2000.

In Gallup's most recent measurement, from a Dec. 2–6 poll, 13% of Americans approve of the job Congress is doing.

Congress historically has not had high approval ratings, with the average across all measurements since 1974 at just 32%. Congress's average job approval rating has exceeded 50% just twice since 1974, in 2001 and 2002 following the rally in support for government leaders after the Sept. 11 terrorist attacks.

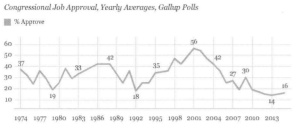

Congressional Job Approval, Yearly Averages, Gallup Polls

% Approve

Note: Gallup did not ask about congressional job approval in 1984 and 1985.

GALLUP

There have been other times, like now, when Congress's approval rating has averaged below 20%, including in 1979 and 1992 during recessionary economic times. But unlike the current era, those prior sub-20% readings did not persist.

The more negative evaluations of Congress in recent years partly reflect the economic struggles the nation has faced during that time. But even as Americans' confidence in the economy has improved since the 2007–2009 recession, their ratings of Congress have stayed low.

Americans' largely negative reviews of Congress, thus, are driven by more than just the health of the economy. The public appears to be frustrated with the federal government's seeming inability to address the problems facing the country, with attempts to address issues such as immigration or the economy ending in a partisan stalemate. In recent years, when Gallup has asked Americans to name the most important problem facing the country, dissatisfaction with the government has consistently ranked among the top issues. In 2015, it received more mentions, on average, than any other issue, edging out the economy.

Republicans Not Celebrating GOP Control of Congress

Americans who identify politically as Republican were slightly more approving of Congress earlier in the year, as their party enjoyed majority control of both houses of Congress for the first time since 2007.

But that greater power did not lead to passing Republican-favored legislation. Republicans may be blaming their leaders for this, as both Senate Majority Leader Mitch McConnell and former Speaker of the House John Boehner had higher unfavorable than favorable ratings from their own party's supporters, something highly unusual in ratings of any political figure.

Republicans' frustration is evident in that they have been at least somewhat less likely than Democrats to approve of the job Congress is doing each month since June.

The net result of these party trends is that average approval ratings of Congress this past year were equally poor among the major party groups—17% of Democrats, 15% of independents and 15% of Republicans.

The lack of a party difference in ratings of Congress is inconsistent with the historical norm when one party has had control of both the House and Senate. Gallup data going back to 1993 typically show the majority party's supporters give Congress much higher ratings than supporters of the minority party. This lack of strong support from either party is contributing to the lower overall approval rating.

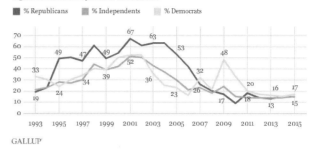

Congressional Job Approval, Yearly Averages by Party Since 1993, Gallup Polls

Figures shown are for Republicans and Democrats

■ % Republicans   ■ % Independents   ░ % Democrats

GALLUP

Since 1993, one party has had control of both houses of Congress in 17 of 23 years. The exceptions were 2001–2002, when Vermont Sen. Jim Jeffords defected from the GOP and aligned with the Democrats to give them the operating majority in the Senate, and from 2011 to 2014, when Republicans had a majority in the House and Democrats a majority in the Senate.

Prior to this year, in the four periods when one party had majority control of both houses of Congress, the Republican-Democratic gap in ratings of Congress has ranged from a low of 10 percentage points in 1993–1994 to 30 points from 2003 to 2006. The average party gap in those four periods is 18 points.

Differences in Congress Approval Ratings by Party, During Periods of One-Party Control of Congress

Years	Majority party	Average % approval, Republicans	Average % approval, Democrats	Republican-Democratic gap (pct. pts.)
1993-1994	Democratic	21	32	-10
1995-2000	Republican	52	36	16
2003-2006	Republican	55	25	30
2007-2010	Democratic	18	33	-15
2015	Republican	15	17	-2

GALLUP

Implications

Americans' views of Congress in 2015 were little changed despite their slightly more positive economic outlook and the change in party control of the Senate. For a brief period early in the year, the GOP's control of both houses helped Republicans be more positive about Congress. But that did not last, and by year's end, Republicans were less positive about Congress than were Democrats, despite the GOP's hold on the institution.

In the past, partisans may have been happy just to have their party in control of Congress, but now it appears Republicans take little solace in their party's majority status if it does not produce results in the form of passing legislation they favor. Republicans' poor ratings of Congress are a major reason for the institution's lower overall approval rating.

Former Speaker Boehner was the target of much of the party's frustration, leading to his resignation this fall. Now new Speaker of the House Paul Ryan will attempt to move the GOP agenda forward. Unlike Boehner and Senate Majority Leader McConnell, Republicans view Ryan positively overall. How long that positive view will last remains to be seen, especially considering that the Republicans' chances for seeing their favored legislation become law remain very slim as long as a Democratic president is in office.

Survey Methods

Results for this Gallup poll are based on telephone interviews conducted in 2015 with a random sample of 12,137 adults, aged 18 and older, living in all 50 U.S. states and the District of Columbia. For results based on the total sample of national adults, the margin of sampling error is ±1 percentage point at the 95% confidence level. All reported margins of sampling error include computed design effects for weighting.

December 18, 2015
ENGAGED EMPLOYEES LESS LIKELY TO HAVE HEALTH PROBLEMS

by Jim Harter and Amy Adkins

Story Highlights

- *Actively disengaged employees report more unhealthy days*
- *Engagement may be as important as age for health*
- *Active disengagement negatively affects productivity*

WASHINGTON, D.C.—U.S. employees who are actively disengaged at work are more likely than their engaged peers to say they experience health issues ranging from physical pain to depression.

Employee Engagement and Health
% Yes

	Actively disengaged	Engaged
	%	%
Experienced physical pain yesterday	23	14
Experienced stress yesterday	56	32
Diagnosed with high blood pressure	19	15
Diagnosed with high cholesterol	15	11
Diagnosed with depression	16	9
Obese (based on reported height/weight)	28	24

Controlling for age, gender, marital status, education, income, race and work category
Gallup-Healthways Well-Being Index

GALLUP

Actively disengaged employees also report more "unhealthy" days, or days in which health issues limited their activity. On a monthly basis, actively disengaged employees have 2.17 unhealthy days, compared with 1.25 unhealthy days for engaged employees.

U.S. EMPLOYEES' NUMBER OF UNHEALTHY DAYS PER MONTH

ENGAGED
1.25

ACTIVELY DISENGAGED
2.17

GALLUP-HEALTHWAYS WELL-BEING INDEX

Gallup categorizes workers' engagement based on their ratings of key workplace elements that predict important organizational performance outcomes. Engaged employees are involved in, enthusiastic about and committed to their work. Actively disengaged employees are not just unhappy at work; they are busy acting out their unhappiness. Every day, these workers undermine what their engaged coworkers accomplish. Gallup's extensive research shows that employee engagement strongly connects to business outcomes essential to an organization's financial success, such as productivity, profitability and customer engagement.

These findings, collected as part of the Gallup Employee Engagement tracking series and Gallup-Healthways Well-Being Index from January 2014 through September 2015, are statistically controlled for other demographic differences, including respondents' age. These results do not necessarily indicate that engagement *causes* better health, but they do show that there is a strong relationship between levels of engagement at work and health.

Health Is as Much About Engagement as It Is About Age

Young workers who are actively disengaged report more unhealthy days than older but engaged employees do. On average, actively disengaged employees aged 20 to 29 have 1.82 unhealthy days per month. This number is higher than it is for engaged employees in all older age groups. For example, engaged employees aged 40 to 49 experience 1.28 unhealthy days per month, and engaged employees aged 50 to 59 experience 1.57 unhealthy days.

Number of Unhealthy Days per Month, by Age and Engagement Level

	Actively disengaged	Engaged
Under 20	1.37	0.84
20 to 29	1.82	0.92
30 to 39	2.11	1.20
40 to 49	2.37	1.28
50 to 59	2.53	1.57
60 to 69	2.31	1.56
70 to 79	2.27	1.80

Controlling for gender, marital status, education, income, race and work category
Gallup-Healthways Well-Being Index

GALLUP

Gallup has found similar relationships between work engagement by age and other health issues, including physical pain and stress. While just 16% of engaged employees aged 50 to 59 say they experienced physical pain "yesterday," 23% of actively disengaged employees aged 30 to 39 say the same. And 33% of engaged employees aged 40 to 49 say they experienced stress yesterday, compared with 63% of actively disengaged employees aged 20 to 29.

Active Disengagement Costs Organizations

As actively disengaged employees experience more unhealthy days than their peers, they end up costing their companies more in lost productivity. A Gallup analysis finds that an engaged worker aged 40 to 49 costs his or her employer $127.76 per month in lost productivity due to unhealthy days, while an actively disengaged worker in the same age range costs $236.20—an 85% increase.

Cost of Lost Productivity, by Age and Engagement Level
Monthly cost per employee due to unhealthy days

	Actively disengaged	Engaged
Under 20	$136.83	$83.25
20 to 29	$181.35	$91.48
30 to 39	$209.77	$119.73
40 to 49	$236.20	$127.76
50 to 59	$252.02	$156.16
60 to 69	$230.49	$155.87
70 to 79	$226.47	$179.04

Controlling for gender, marital status, education, income, race and work category
Gallup-Healthways Well-Being Index

GALLUP

Bottom Line

Many factors can influence the health of employees, and in some cases, workers with pre-existing health issues may be more likely to miss work and be less engaged. A lack of engagement is not always responsible for a decline in physical or mental health; it is possible that poor health precedes poor engagement.

The data in the current study do not determine the direction of causation. But a previous Gallup study shows that workplace engagement does affect employees' physiological state to some degree. Researchers examined the daily mood and cortisol (stress hormone) levels of engaged and actively disengaged employees and discovered that engaged employees experience more moments of happiness and interest, and fewer moments of stress and sadness, during the course of their workday.

The researchers found higher levels of morning cortisol for less engaged employees on workdays, with no difference on weekends. These findings suggest that an individual's work situation affects his or her mood, which then connects to physiological stress.

While the data from the present study are cross-sectional and not longitudinal, research that has looked at the relationship between workplace engagement and health issues over time has found substantial connections between employee perceptions of the work environment and various health problems such as coronary heart disease, inflammation and depression.

As organizations continue to seek ways to reduce healthcare costs, they often turn to wellness programs or incentives to help employees better manage health issues. But they should not discount the role of employee engagement in creating a healthier workforce. Gallup research shows that engaged employees are more likely than actively disengaged employees to participate in wellness programs offered by their organizations. Engagement is a catalyst for higher well-being—it helps put employees in a mindset that encourages them to make healthy decisions.

To achieve the greatest amount of change, leaders should look for ways to integrate purpose, social, financial, community and physical well-being principles through company-sponsored benefits and manager education programs. High engagement and high well-being have an "additive effect," and when employees achieve both, their organizations benefit immensely. These employees miss fewer days due to illness, are less likely to leave their companies and are more likely to say they are adaptable to change and are performing at an "excellent" level.

Survey Methods

Results are based on telephone interviews conducted January 2014–September 2015 on the Gallup Employee Engagement tracking survey and the Gallup-Healthways Well-Being Index survey, with a random sample of 140,579 U.S. adults employed full or part time for an employer, aged 18 and older, living in all 50 U.S. states and the District of Columbia.

For results based on the total sample of employed adults, the margin of sampling error is ±1 percentage point at the 95% confidence level. All reported margins of sampling error include computed design effects for weighting.

December 21, 2015
AMERICANS' FAITH IN HONESTY, ETHICS OF POLICE REBOUNDS

by Lydia Saad

Story Highlights

- *Majority again rate police highly on honesty, ethical standards*
- *Figure had fallen to 48% in 2014, after plunge among nonwhites*
- *Nurses retain top spot as the most highly rated profession*

PRINCETON, N.J.—After dipping to 48% in 2014 amid a national firestorm over police treatment of young black men, the rating Americans give the honesty and ethical standards of police has rebounded to 56%. This is more consistent with the 54% to 58% ratings Gallup found between 2010 and 2013.

Americans' Ratings of Honesty and Ethics of Police -- 1977-2015

Please tell me how you would rate the honesty and ethical standards of people in these different fields -- very high, high, average, low or very low? Police officers

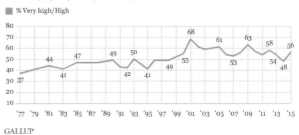

GALLUP

Four in 10 nonwhites now rate the ethical standards of police as very high or high—a sharp increase from the 23% who held this view in 2014. A steep drop in nonwhites' ratings of the police in 2014 was the sole cause of the profession's overall ratings dip last year. While nonwhites' attitudes have not rebounded to their pre-2014 levels, the slight increase in whites' positive views of the police this year, from 59% to 64%, coupled with the rise in nonwhites' ratings, pushes the overall percentage back to the "normal" range seen in recent years.

Honesty/Ethics Ratings of Police Officers, by Race

Percentage rating the honesty and ethical standards of police officers "very high" or "high"

GALLUP

This year's results are based on a Dec. 2–6 poll in which Gallup asked Americans to rate the honesty and ethics of the police and workers in 20 other professions.

Nurses Still No. 1, Congress Among the Lowest

Nurses have topped Gallup's Honesty and Ethics ranking every year but one since they were added to the list in 1999. The exception is 2001, when firefighters were included on the list on a one-time basis, shortly after the Sept. 11 terrorist attacks. (Firefighters earned a record-high 90% honesty and ethics rating in that survey.)

With an 85% honesty and ethics rating—tying their high point—nurses have no serious competition atop the Gallup ranking this year. Pharmacists and medical doctors constitute the next tier, with about two-thirds of Americans viewing each highly, followed by high school teachers at 60% and police officers at 56%.

Less than half of Americans consider clergy (45%), funeral directors (44%) or accountants (39%) to be highly ethical. Still, Americans are much more likely to view these professions positively than negatively.

Journalists, bankers and building contractors have closely split images, while lawyers, real estate agents, labor union leaders, business executives, stockbrokers, advertising practitioners and car salespeople all have low "high/very high" ratings and are more likely to be viewed negatively than positively. Still, at least four in 10 Americans consider the honesty and ethics of these professions to be "average," rather than low. On the other hand, there is little good news in the numbers for members of Congress, telemarketers and lobbyists. Solid majorities of Americans consider the honesty and ethics of these professions to be low or very low, while fewer than one in 10 believe they have high ethics.

Gallup's 2015 Honesty and Ethics of Professions Ratings

Please tell me how you would rate the honesty and ethical standards of people in these different fields -- very high, high, average, low or very low?

Sorted by very high/high

	Very high/ High	Average	Low/ Very low
	%	%	%
Nurses	85	13	1
Pharmacists	68	27	5
Medical doctors	67	27	5
High school teachers	60	29	9
Police officers	56	29	14
Clergy	45	39	11
Funeral directors	44	41	9
Accountants	39	51	7
Journalists	27	42	30
Bankers	25	49	24
Building contractors	25	55	17
Lawyers	21	44	34
Real estate agents	20	53	25
Labor union leaders	18	41	36
Business executives	17	47	32
Stockbrokers	13	42	39
Advertising practitioners	10	46	39
Car salespeople	8	41	49
Members of Congress	8	27	64
Telemarketers	8	34	56
Lobbyists	7	27	60

Dec. 2-6, 2015

GALLUP

It is noteworthy that the clergy continue to earn their lowest ratings since Gallup first asked this question in 1977. Since 2013, less than half of Americans have believed clergy have very high or high honesty and ethical standards, with the 45% measured this year being the lowest yet.

Americans' Ratings of Honesty and Ethics of Clergy -- 1977-2015

Please tell me how you would rate the honesty and ethical standards of people in these different fields -- very high, high, average, low or very low? Clergy

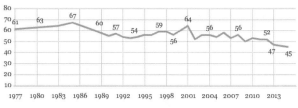

GALLUP

Bottom Line

The overall image of the police is largely restored to what it was before incidents in Ferguson and elsewhere in 2014 spawned the Black Lives Matter movement against police behavior. However, it is a tenuous recovery as the police's rating among nonwhites is still not fully repaired. That could partly reflect additional controversies over police behavior that have erupted in 2015, including the death of Freddie Gray—a young black man who died while in police custody in Baltimore. As long as events like these continue to make news or spread through social media, the police's image may continue to suffer among minorities, even if the profession's overall image remains high because of whites' positive views.

Meanwhile, the clergy's image continues to sag. Even the popularity of Pope Francis has yet to undo the damage that declining religiosity and numerous church and televangelist scandals over the years have seemingly done.

Members of Congress, lobbyists and telemarketers have shown no improvement at the bottom of the list, while nurses, pharmacists, medical doctors and high school teachers remain untarnished at the top.

Survey Methods

Results for this Gallup poll are based on telephone interviews conducted Dec. 2–6, 2015, with a random sample of 824 adults, aged 18 and older, living in all 50 U.S. states and the District of Columbia. For results based on the total sample of national adults, the margin of sampling error is ±4 percentage points at the 95% confidence level. All reported margins of sampling error include computed design effects for weighting.

December 22, 2015
BIG GOVERNMENT STILL NAMED AS BIGGEST THREAT TO U.S.

by Rebecca Riffkin

Story Highlights

- *More name big government as threat than big business, big labor*
- *Percentage naming government as threat down from record high in 2013*

- *Republicans still more likely than Democrats to say government is threat*

WASHINGTON, D.C.—When asked to choose among big government, big labor and big business, Americans overwhelmingly name big government as the biggest threat to the country in the future. The 69% choosing big government is down slightly from a high of 72% in 2013, the last time Gallup asked the question, but is still one of the highest percentages choosing big government in Gallup's 50-year trend.

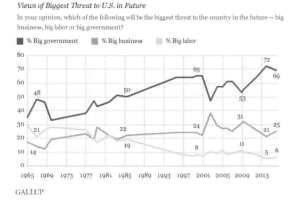

Views of Biggest Threat to U.S. in Future

In your opinion, which of the following will be the biggest threat to the country in the future -- big business, big labor or big government?

■ % Big government   ■ % Big business   ■ % Big labor

GALLUP

While Americans have always seen big government as a bigger threat than big business or big labor, the percentage naming it was significantly lower prior to 1990, when a much larger segment of Americans saw big labor as the greatest threat. By 2000, the percentage naming big government rose to 65%, as mentions of big labor fell into the single digits. A brief uptick in concerns about big business in 2002, probably prompted by several high-profile business scandals such as Enron, offset some concerns about big government. More recently, concerns about business and labor have drifted down while concerns about big government have climbed back up to nearly 70%.

The large increase in the percentage naming big government as the biggest threat in 2013 may have resulted from the rollout of the Affordable Care Act and Edward Snowden's revelations about government monitoring of communications.

Republicans Remain Most Likely to Say Government Poses the Biggest Threat

Almost nine in 10 Republicans, 88%, say big government is the biggest threat to the future of the country, far exceeding the 67% of independents and 53% of Democrats who say the same. Since 1985, Republicans have been more likely than Democrats and independents to name big government as the biggest threat. One notable exception occurred in 2005, when mentions of big government were tied across the three groups. This may have been due to U.S. involvement in a prolonged war in Iraq, as well as the Bush administration's struggle to respond adequately to Hurricane Katrina.

While a majority of Democrats say that big government poses the biggest threat, many more Democrats (41%) than independents (25%) or Republicans (7%) say big business is the biggest threat.

Bottom Line

While down slightly from 2013, 69% of Americans say big government is the biggest threat to the country in the future. This comes at a time when Americans name the government as one of the three most important problems facing the country and when 75% of Americans perceive widespread corruption in the government.

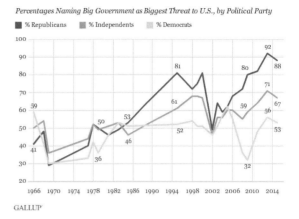

Percentages Naming Big Government as Biggest Threat to U.S., by Political Party

■ % Republicans   ■ % Independents   ■ % Democrats

GALLUP

Further, only 8% of Americans in June said they have "a great deal" or "quite a lot" of confidence in Congress, far below the 24% who said they have that much confidence in organized labor and 21% in big business. But slightly more Americans said they have confidence in the presidency and the Supreme Court than said they have confidence in organized labor or big business.

Half of Americans say the federal government poses an immediate threat to rights and freedoms, and Congress' job approval continues to languish—perhaps explaining why so many see big government as the biggest threat to the country.

Survey Methods

Results for this Gallup poll are based on telephone interviews conducted Dec. 2–6, 2015, on the Gallup U.S. Daily survey, with a random sample of 824 adults, aged 18 and older, living in all 50 U.S. states and the District of Columbia. For results based on the total sample of national adults, the margin of sampling error is ±4 percentage points at the 95% confidence level. All reported margins of sampling error include computed design effects for weighting.

December 23, 2015

U.S. FLIERS' SATISFACTION WITH TICKET PRICES NOSEDIVES

by Andrew Dugan

Story Highlights

- *Percentage of fliers satisfied with ticket prices fell 14 pts. since 2007*
- *81% of fliers satisfied with airlines' on-time performance*
- *55% of adults say they did not fly last year, up from 48% in 2012*

WASHINGTON, D.C.—U.S. adults who have flown in the past year remain at least as satisfied as they were in 2007 with many aspects of airline travel—except with what they pay to fly. While a slim majority (51%) still say they are satisfied with the price they pay for tickets, this satisfaction is down 14 percentage points from 2007, despite only modest increases in the average domestic airfare over that time.

How Adults Who Have Flown in the Past Year Rate Different Aspects of the Flying Experience

Now thinking about some specific aspects of flying today, please say whether you are generally satisfied or dissatisfied with each one. How about -- [RANDOM ORDER]?
% saying "satisfied"
Ranked by 2015 totals

	2007	2015	Change
The courtesy of the check-in and gate agents	88	95	+7
The courtesy of the flight attendants	92	94	+2
The process of buying a ticket	N/A	90	--
The airlines' on-time performance	69	81	+12
The schedules, including the options for getting where you want to go	79	80	+1
The speed and reliability of luggage systems at airports	75	78	+3
The procedures for going through security checkpoints	69	73	+4
The airlines' efforts to deal with problems of flight delays/cancellations	56	62	+6
The price you pay for tickets	65	51	-14
The comfort of the seats on the airplanes	47	45	-2

Dec. 2-6, 2015

GALLUP

These findings come from a Dec. 2–6 Gallup poll of 405 adults who have flown on an airplane in the past year. These results do not speak to customers' perceptions of any one airline company in particular, but instead offer general views on the various components of the flying experience.

The flying public remains least satisfied with the comfort of the seats on the airplanes (45%), the only aspect of the experience for which satisfaction drops to less than a majority. Analyses of decades of data for the major airline carriers seem to support the notion that over time, airline seats have gotten smaller and are stacked more closely together.

Overall, however, Americans who flew in the past year give high marks to nearly all aspects of the flying experience. Fliers continue to be most pleased with the courtesy of the staff on the ground and in the air—95% say they are generally satisfied with the courtesy of the check-in and gate agents, while 94% are happy with the courtesy of the flight attendants.

Ninety percent of airline travelers are satisfied with the ticket-buying process, which the industry has revolutionized in recent years. Travelers can now buy tickets in a multitude of ways from the airline or choose from a proliferation of travel websites that promise to help users find the cheapest ticket available to get to their destination. Interestingly though, even as these online sites are responsible for a larger percentage of overall bookings, travelers are less, not more, satisfied with ticket prices.

Of all aspects of the flying experience, satisfaction with airlines' on-time performance saw the largest improvement, climbing 12 points since 2007 to 81%. Department of Transportation data on flight delays of any type provide one explanation—flight delays have generally been on the decline and, in particular, the monthly on-time arrival rate for October 2015 was near a 20-year high.

Fliers are largely satisfied with most other aspects of air travel, including the air schedules (80%), the speed and reliability of luggage systems (78%) and the procedures for getting through checkpoints (73%). A comparatively smaller majority were satisfied with how airlines handle flight delays or cancellations (62%).

Majority of Americans Did Not Fly Last Year

Fifty-five percent of Americans say they did not take any trips on a commercial airliner in the past 12 months, a seven-point increase from 2007. However, this figure is still broadly in line with estimates

from previous Gallup surveys extending back to 2000. This increase comes amid falling gas prices, which are at their lowest levels since 2009. While a declining fuel price should theoretically make air travel and driving more affordable, it has minimally affected the cost of airplane tickets. At the same time, 57% of U.S. households say lower pump prices have made a notable difference in their finances.

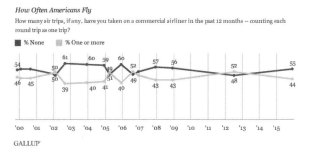

How Often Americans Fly

How many air trips, if any, have you taken on a commercial airliner in the past 12 months -- counting each round trip as one trip?

GALLUP

Forty-four percent of U.S. adults flew last year, which is comparable with rates measured in late 2007 and 2008. But those who are flying are doing more of it; the average number of flights adults took over the past year is 4.6, up from 4.2 in 2012 and the highest figure since December 2006.

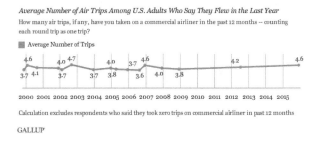

Average Number of Air Trips Among U.S. Adults Who Say They Flew in the Last Year

How many air trips, if any, have you taken on a commercial airliner in the past 12 months -- counting each round trip as one trip?

Calculation excludes respondents who said they took zero trips on commercial airliner in past 12 months

GALLUP

Bottom Line

From delays to long security lines to cramped seating arrangements, air travel fills many Americans with anxiety and dread. But air travelers are generally satisfied with most aspects of the experience, particularly with the courtesy of the airline personnel. While flight delays are never a welcome development for any traveler, more fliers are satisfied with airlines' on-time performance than have been in the past.

The comfort of airline seating remains the least satisfying part of air travelers' journeys, and fliers' satisfaction with ticket prices is falling. These findings contrast with the relative positivity with which passengers view other aspects of air travel.

Fliers' satisfaction with specific aspects of the flying experience is significantly different from how engaged fliers might be as customers of the airlines. Gallup research has shown that customer engagement is the most important factor in predicting brand loyalty and return purchases, and that engagement can vary substantially across airline brands.

Survey Methods

Results for this Gallup poll are based on telephone interviews conducted Dec. 2–6, 2015, with a random sample of 824 adults, aged 18 and older, living in all 50 U.S. states and the District of Columbia. For results based on the total sample of national adults, the margin of sampling error is ±4 percentage points at the 95% confidence level. For results based on the total sample of 405 adults who have flown on a plane in the past year, the margin of sampling error is ±6 percentage points at the 95% confidence level. All reported margins of sampling error include computed design effects for weighting.

December 24, 2015
PERCENTAGE OF CHRISTIANS IN U.S. DRIFTING DOWN, BUT STILL HIGH

by Frank Newport

Story Highlights

- *75% of Americans identify with a Christian religion*
- *Christian identification is down from 80% in 2008*
- *5% of Americans identify with a non-Christian religion, little changed*

PRINCETON, N.J.—On the eve of Christmas 2015, a review of over 174,000 interviews conducted in 2015 shows that three-quarters of American adults identify with a Christian religion, little changed from 2014, but down from 80% eight years ago. About 5% of Americans identify with a non-Christian religion, while 20% have no formal religious identification, which is up five percentage points since 2008.

Religious Identification in the U.S., 2008-2015

	Christian religion	Non-Christian religion	None
	%	%	%
2008	80.1	5.3	14.6
2009	80.0	4.8	15.3
2010	79.1	4.4	16.4
2011	77.9	4.7	17.5
2012	77.3	4.9	17.8
2013	76.8	5.3	17.8
2014	75.7	5.2	19.0
2015*	75.2	5.1	19.6

*Through Dec. 20, 2015
Gallup Daily tracking

GALLUP

These results are based on interviews conducted each year since 2008 as part of Gallup Daily tracking. The general trends in the data over this eight-year period are clear: As the percentage of Americans identifying with a Christian religion has decreased, the percentage with no formal religious identification has increased. The small percentage of Americans who identify with a non-Christian religion has been essentially constant over this time period.

PERCENTAGE OF AMERICANS WHO
IDENTIFY AS CHRISTIAN

75%

GALLUP DAILY TRACKING

The downtick in the percentage of the U.S. population identifying as Christian over the past eight years is a continuation of a trend that has been evident for decades. In Gallup surveys in the 1950s, over 90% of the adult population identified as Christian, with only a small percentage claiming no religious identification at all or identifying with a non-Christian religion.

Despite these changes, America remains a predominantly Christian nation, and with 94% of those who identify with a religion saying they are Christian.

The broad Christian category includes Catholics, Protestants, Mormons and non-denominational Christians. In 2015, 24% of Americans identify as Catholic, 50% as Protestant or as members of another non-Catholic Christian religion, and 2% as Mormon.

Christian Percentage Is Lowest Among Young Americans

The percentage of Christians is highest among older Americans and decreases with each progressively younger age group. This trend reflects the high number of "nones"—those without a formal religious identity—in the younger generations, as well as a higher proportion of non-Christians among them.

Religious Identification in the U.S. by Age, 2015

	Christian	Non-Christian	None
	%	%	%
18-24	62	7	31
25-29	62	7	32
30-34	67	7	26
35-39	71	6	23
40-44	74	6	21
45-49	79	5	16
50-54	81	4	15
55-59	81	4	15
60-64	82	4	14
65-69	83	4	13
70-74	85	4	11
75-79	88	3	9
80-84	89	4	8
85-89	88	4	8
90+	86	4	10

Gallup tracking through Dec. 20, 2015

GALLUP

One key to the future of Christian representation in the U.S. population will be shifts in the religious identification of today's youngest cohorts. Traditionally, Americans have become more likely to identify with a religion as they age through their 30s and 40s and get married and have children. If this pattern does not occur in the same way it has in the past, the percentage of Christians nationwide will likely continue to shrink.

Bottom Line

America remains a predominantly Christian nation, with three-quarters of all adults identifying with a Christian faith, and with over 90% Christian representation among those who say they are a member of any kind of religion. A major religious trend in the U.S., however, has been the increasing number of Americans who say they do not have a formal religious identification. This expansion has been accompanied by the shrinkage in the number of people who identify as Christian. More than 95% of Americans identified as Christian in the 1950s, and 80% did so as recently as eight years ago. While the 5% of the population who identify with a non-Christian faith is higher than it was decades ago, it has not shown significant change over the past eight years.

Survey Methods

Results for this Gallup poll are based on telephone interviews conducted from 2008 to 2015 on the Gallup U.S. Daily survey, with random samples of adults, aged 18 and older, living in all 50 U.S. states and the District of Columbia. The sample sizes of those interviewed were over 350,000 for the years 2008 through 2012, and over 170,000 for the years 2013 through 2015. The 2015 sample consists of interviews conducted through Dec. 20, 2015. For results based on the total sample of national adults for each year, the margin of sampling error is ±1 percentage point at the 95% confidence level. All reported margins of sampling error include computed design effects for weighting.

December 28, 2015
THE 2015 YEAR IN REVIEW AT GALLUP.COM

by Art Swift

Story Highlights

- *Gallup presents the most noteworthy stories of 2015*
- *The 2016 presidential campaign dominates headlines*
- *Corruption, LGBT community, Pope Francis top of mind for Americans*

WASHINGTON, D.C.—In its efforts to deliver analytics and advice to help leaders solve their most pressing problems, Gallup asks the world what it is thinking on the topics that matter and shares those results on Gallup.com. There was no shortage of important topics in 2015, which proved to be an intriguing, complex and turbulent year: A politically independent Vermont senator surged in the Democratic presidential race, same-sex marriage became law in all 50 states, and Russia's leadership received the lowest approval ratings worldwide for the eighth consecutive year.

The following are among the top stories on Gallup.com for 2015:

The Big Lie: 5.6% Unemployment—Amid talk of "falling unemployment" in the U.S. fueled by an "economic recovery," Gallup Chairman and CEO Jim Clifton explored what the government's unemployment figure really means and how inaccurate it is in modern-day America.

Sanders Surges, Clinton Sags in U.S. Favorability—Campaigns for the 2016 presidential election were in full swing in 2015. Some observers coined this past summer the "Summer of Sanders" as favorable ratings doubled for the Democratic socialist from Vermont. Hillary Clinton, who enjoyed high favorability as secretary of state, saw her image tilt negative, her worst rating since December 2007.

75% in U.S. See Widespread Government Corruption—Three in four Americans in 2014 perceived corruption as widespread in the U.S. government, up from roughly two in three Americans in 2007 and 2009. The trend has been largely stable since 2010, but the percentage of U.S. adults who see corruption as pervasive has not dropped below majority levels in the past decade.

Americans Greatly Overestimate Percent Gay, Lesbian in U.S.—Same-sex marriage became legal across the U.S. in June. One month earlier, Gallup found that the U.S. public estimated 23% of Americans are gay or lesbian. In reality, the percentage is about 4%. The higher estimate may be attributable to increased media portrayals of gay characters in movies and on television, along with the high-profile legal battle over gay marriage.

In U.S., 58% Back Legal Marijuana Use—Americans are still very much in favor of legalizing marijuana, as Gallup found continued majority support for such a measure in 2015. Millennials and Generation Xers primarily fueled this support, but many baby boomers also said they favor legalizing marijuana.

Americans Name Government as No. 1 U.S. Problem—Gallup asks Americans each month to name the most important problem facing the U.S. In March, 18% identified "government" as the nation's top problem, with the economy and unemployment trailing behind. Later in the year, after terrorist attacks in Paris and San Bernardino, California, terrorism topped the list.

Russia Receives Lowest Approval in World; U.S. Highest—Russia's leadership received the lowest approval ratings worldwide for the eighth consecutive year in 2014. Countries affiliated with the West, particularly NATO countries, soured on Russia dramatically. At the same time, Russians and people in many of its former republics all felt much more negatively about the leadership of the U.S., the EU and Germany. However, U.S. leadership garnered the highest approval ratings worldwide, slightly outpacing Germany.

In U.S., Socialist Presidential Candidates Least Appealing—Considering a list of various groups, from Catholics to Mormons and gays to Muslims, Americans said in June that a socialist presidential candidate was the least appealing. Forty-seven percent said they would support a socialist for president; all other groups received theoretical majority support.

In U.S., Support for Tea Party Drops to New Low—Support for the Tea Party movement appeared to drop in October, with only 17% of Americans considering themselves Tea Party supporters. A record 54% said they neither support nor oppose the movement. While the Tea Party's influence may have faded in 2015, this article detailed reasons why this political group may bounce back in the presidential election year.

Pope Francis's Favorable Rating Drops in U.S.—In advance of his first trip to the U.S., Pope Francis experienced a dip in popularity from the last time Gallup asked Americans about the pontiff in 2014. This drop occurred among both liberals and conservatives, and Catholics and Protestants. On average, Americans still rated Francis more favorably than his predecessor, Pope Benedict XVI.

Employees Want a Lot More From Their Managers—In April, Gallup reported that one in two U.S. adults have left their job to get away from their manager—and improve their life overall—at some point during their career.

Obsolete Annual Reviews: Gallup's Advice—As the year began winding down, and year-end reviews were in season, Gallup found that many large organizations have experienced the dysfunction of once-a-year performance conversations—and they're ditching the practice.

December 28, 2015

CLINTON MOST ADMIRED WOMAN FOR RECORD 20TH TIME

by Jeffrey M. Jones

PRINCETON, N.J.—Americans again name Hillary Clinton and President Barack Obama the woman and man living anywhere in the world they admire most. Both win by wide margins over the next-closest finishers, Malala Yousafzai for women and Pope Francis and Donald Trump for men.

Most Admired Woman and Man, 2015

What [woman/man] that you have heard or read about, living today in any part of the world, do you admire most? And who is your second choice?

	% Mentioning
MOST ADMIRED WOMAN	
Hillary Clinton	13
Malala Yousafzai	5
Oprah Winfrey	4
Michelle Obama	4
Carly Fiorina	2
Queen Elizabeth II	2
Angela Merkel	2
Elizabeth Warren	1
Aung San Suu Kyi	1
Condoleezza Rice	1
Sarah Palin	1
Ellen DeGeneres	1
MOST ADMIRED MAN	
Barack Obama	17
Pope Francis	5
Donald Trump	5
Bernie Sanders	3
Bill Gates	2
Ben Carson	1
The Dalai Lama	1
George W. Bush	1
Bill Clinton	1
Rev. Billy Graham	1

Dec. 2-6

Note: Combined first and second mentions. Top 10 finishers shown based on total mentions. Rice, Palin and DeGeneres tied for 10th place.

GALLUP

Although Clinton and Obama each led this year's poll by significant margins, the percentage mentioning each as most admired is slightly lower than the percentages they have received in the past. Across the eight times Obama has been most admired man, an average 23% of Americans have named him, while in the 20 times Clinton has been most admired woman, an average 16% have named her.

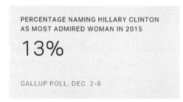

PERCENTAGE NAMING HILLARY CLINTON AS MOST ADMIRED WOMAN IN 2015

13%

GALLUP POLL, DEC. 2-6

The top 10 list for men includes three presidents (Obama, George W. Bush and Bill Clinton), three current presidential candidates (Trump, Vermont Sen. Bernie Sanders and Dr. Ben Carson), and three religious and spiritual leaders (Pope Francis, the Dalai Lama and the Rev. Billy Graham). The only top 10 male finisher who doesn't fall into one of those categories is Microsoft founder and philanthropist Bill Gates.

Trump's surprisingly strong and often controversial presidential campaign has made him a prominent news figure this year and, thus, top-of-mind for many Americans. This helps explain his strong showing when Gallup asks Americans, in an open-ended fashion, to name the man they admire most. The successful businessman has finished in the top 10 four other times, including from 1988 through 1990 and in 2011.

The 10 most admired women are an eclectic mix of political figures (Clinton, fellow 2016 presidential candidate Carly Fiorina, Massachusetts Sen. Elizabeth Warren, German Chancellor Angela Merkel, former Secretary of State Condoleezza Rice and former Alaska Gov. Sarah Palin), human rights leaders (Yousafzai of Pakistan and Aung San Suu Kyi of Myanmar), and television personalities (Oprah Winfrey and Ellen DeGeneres). Queen Elizabeth of England and Michelle Obama, who hold largely ceremonial positions in the government, also finished among the leading women.

Clinton Named Most Admired More Than Any Other Woman or Man

Clinton has been the most admired woman each of the last 14 years, and 20 times overall, occupying the top spot far longer than any other woman or man in Gallup's history of asking the most admired question. Since 1993, the year she was first named most admired woman, Clinton has stayed in the news as first lady, U.S. senator, secretary of state and a two-time presidential candidate.

Former first lady Eleanor Roosevelt was named most admired woman 13 times during her lifetime, putting her second to Clinton in terms of first-place finishes. Dwight Eisenhower has 12 No. 1 finishes, the most for any man. Obama, the most admired man each of the last eight years, is now tied with Bill Clinton and Ronald Reagan for top overall finishes among men.

Most Times Named Most Admired Woman, 1948-2015

	Number of times
Hillary Clinton	20
Eleanor Roosevelt	13
Margaret Thatcher	6
Jacqueline Kennedy	5
Mother Teresa	4
Golda Meir	3

GALLUP

Most Times Named Most Admired Man, 1946-2015

	Number of times
Dwight Eisenhower	12
Barack Obama	8
Bill Clinton	8
Ronald Reagan	8
George W. Bush	7
George H.W. Bush	4
Richard Nixon	4
Lyndon Johnson	4

GALLUP

Americans usually name the sitting U.S. president as the most admired man. The only men to win the distinction at least four times were all presidents. The tendency to name the sitting president as most admired man has acted as a cap on the number of total times a man can win the honor at eight, or the number of years elected presidents can serve.

So far, Eisenhower is the only man to win more than eight times. In addition to the eight years he served as president from 1953 to 1961, the World War II hero was also named most admired the year he was first elected president (1952), and three other years when the incumbent president was generally unpopular (1950, 1967 and 1968).

Obama can join Eisenhower as winning most admired more than eight times if he stays relatively popular during his final year in office, having also won in 2008, the year he was elected, when incumbent President George W. Bush was unpopular.

Graham, Queen Elizabeth Extend Records for Top 10 Finishes

While Hillary Clinton has the most appearances at No. 1 by a wide margin, her total of 24 top 10 placements is well behind the leaders in that category—Graham with 59 and Queen Elizabeth with 47.

Most Top 10 Finishes, Most Admired Woman, 1948-2015

	Number of times
Queen Elizabeth II	47
Margaret Thatcher	34
Jacqueline Kennedy	28
Oprah Winfrey	28
Hillary Clinton	24
Mamie Eisenhower	21
Barbara Bush	20
Margaret Chase Smith	20
Nancy Reagan	19
Mother Teresa	18
Clare Boothe Luce	18

GALLUP

Most Top 10 Finishes, Most Admired Man, 1948-2015

	Number of times
Billy Graham	59
Ronald Reagan	31
Jimmy Carter	28
Pope John Paul II	27
Bill Clinton	24
Dwight Eisenhower	21
Richard Nixon	21
George H.W. Bush	20
Harry Truman	20
Nelson Mandela	20
Edward Kennedy	18

GALLUP

Graham has been among the top 10 most admired men every year since 1955 except for 1962, in addition to 1976 when Gallup did not ask the question. Despite that impressive record, he has never placed first, but ranked second from 1969 through 1974 and again in 1997 and 1999. Graham is now 97 and generally out of the public eye, but still this year made the cutoff for the top 10.

Queen Elizabeth, now 89, placed in the top 10 in 1948, the first year Gallup asked Americans to name the most admired woman. Unlike Graham, she has not maintained a spot in the top 10 each year, but she has still amassed 47 such appearances in the last 67 years. She, like Graham, has never won the top overall honor, placing second in 1952, 1957, 1958 and 1962.

After Graham and Queen Elizabeth, Winfrey and Jimmy Carter are the living people with the next highest number of top 10 appearances, at 28. Winfrey also never has been named the most admired woman, but she has been second or third every year since 1997. Carter was most admired man in 1977, 1978 and 1979. He last finished in the top 10 in 2013.

Implications

Hillary Clinton has set many historical standards in Gallup's most admired woman and man polling. She has been named most admired woman 14 consecutive years and 20 times overall, both records. She ranks among the leaders in top 10 finishes but still trails a few women who rose to prominence at a young age, lived a long life, or both, including Queen Elizabeth, Margaret Thatcher, Jacqueline Kennedy and Winfrey.

Clinton is the front-runner for the 2016 Democratic presidential nomination. Given the prominence of presidents and ex-presidents in the most admired lists, if Clinton succeeds in her presidential bid, she would certainly continue to add to her long list of records in Gallup's most-admired polling. This would include joining Eisenhower as the only two people who have ever been named most admired man or woman before being elected president.

Survey Methods

Results for this Gallup poll are based on telephone interviews conducted Dec. 2–6, 2015, with a random sample of 824 adults, aged 18 and older, living in all 50 U.S. states and the District of Columbia.

For results based on the total sample of national adults, the margin of sampling error is ±4 percentage points at the 95% confidence level. All reported margins of sampling error include computed design effects for weighting.

December 29, 2015
GALLUP'S TOP 10 WELL-BEING DISCOVERIES OF 2015

by Alyssa Davis

Story Highlights

- *The U.S. uninsured rate continues to fall*
- *The obesity rate inches up again*
- *Young black males suffer a well-being deficit*

WASHINGTON, D.C.—Gallup published nearly 60 articles in 2015 about Americans' health and well-being. Through its year-round daily surveys, the Gallup-Healthways Well-Being Index provides the most up-to-date data and insights available on Americans' purpose, social, financial, community and physical well-being. The following list includes Gallup editors' picks for the top 10 most important findings from 2015.

- The uninsured rate among U.S. adults continues to fall. Gallup and Healthways have the most up-to-date data available on the U.S. uninsured rate. In the third quarter, 11.6% of U.S. adults were without health insurance, down significantly from 13.4% in the same quarter a year ago and 18.0% two years ago, just before the Affordable Care Act took effect. The uninsured rate continues to drop in 2015 in most states.
- Actively disengaged employees are more likely to have health issues. Disengaged workers are more likely than their engaged peers to report experiencing physical pain, high blood pressure and depression. They also report having more days per month when health issues limited their activities: 2.17 unhealthy days for actively disengaged employees versus 1.25 for engaged employees. Gallup found that an actively disengaged worker aged 40 to 49 costs his or her employer 85% more in lost productivity because of unhealthy days than an engaged employee in the same age range.
- Nearly two in 10 Americans say they take drugs to relax almost every day. West Virginians are most likely to report using drugs or medications (including prescription drugs) that alter their mood or help them relax. Southern states make up six of the top 10 highest drug use states. Those who use drugs that affect their mood almost every day have lower well-being than those who don't.
- Young adults' cigarette use declined significantly over the past decade. The smoking rate for 18- to 29-year-olds, which used to be the highest among all age groups, is now equal to that of their older counterparts. But this steep decline from 34% from 2001 to 2005 to 22% from 2011 to 2015 may be linked to young adults taking up other forms of tobacco use, such as cigars, pipes and smokeless tobacco.
- Heart attack survivors may not be making necessary lifestyle changes. Those who have had a heart attack are significantly

more likely to smoke, to be obese and to experience stress than those who have never had a heart attack. And those who have survived a heart attack are much less likely to exercise regularly.

- Young black males in the U.S. suffer a well-being deficit. Young black males as a group have higher unemployment, lower graduation rates, less access to healthcare and higher incarceration rates than other groups in the U.S. And in 2014, the deaths of several young black men during incidents with police became headline news. Gallup and Healthways found that on average, black men aged 18 to 34 have lower well-being than white, Asian and Hispanic men in the same age range. Young black males also have more negative outlooks on their lives than do young males who aren't black.

- The U.S. obesity rate continues to inch up. The obesity rate among U.S. adults in 2014 hit 27.7%, up more than two percentage points from 2008 and the highest rate recorded in seven years of tracking. More Americans who were previously overweight moved into the obese category. Americans aged 65 and older have experienced the sharpest rise in obesity since 2008.

- Getting more sleep is associated with higher well-being. Getting more hours of sleep is linked to having higher overall well-being, with the relationship peaking at eight hours and leveling off thereafter. Those who usually sleep seven hours per night have a 4.8-point advantage in their Well-Being Index score over those who typically sleep for six hours. But more than four in 10 adults report getting less than seven hours of sleep per night.

- Well-being and employee engagement have additive benefits. Employees who are engaged at work *and* have *high* well-being consistently outperform their peers who are engaged but have *low* well-being across a variety of business and health outcomes.

- Heart attacks and depression are closely linked. Americans who have had a heart attack are twice as likely as those who have not to say they are currently being treated for.

December 31, 2015
AMERICANS' PERCEIVED TIME CRUNCH NO WORSE THAN IN PAST

by Frank Newport

Story Highlights

- *48% of Americans today say they don't have enough time*
- *This is about average on this measure since 2001*
- *Working Americans, those with children least likely to have enough time*

PRINCETON, N.J.—Despite the fast-paced, multitasking, constantly-in-touch life many Americans live today, the 48% who say they do not have enough time to do what they want to do is not much different from the 47% average over the past 14 years. Further, the percentage is slightly lower than it was in the 1990s.

This latest update is based on Gallup's Dec. 2–6 Lifestyle poll, which can be compared to the eight times Gallup previously asked this question each December between 2001 and 2008. During that period, the average percentage saying they did not have enough time

was 47%, essentially the same as in 2015. Since 2001, the highest "not enough time" percentage is 49%, and the lowest is 41%.

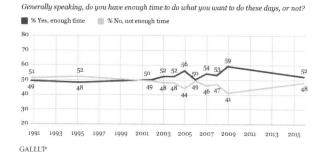

When Gallup asked the question in September 1990 and in March 1995, slightly more than half of Americans said they did not have enough time.

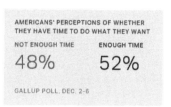

Workers, Those With Children and Younger Women Most Time-Pressured

About six in 10 working Americans (61%) say they do not have enough time to do what they want, compared with 32% of those who are not working. Having young children also appears to be an important factor in Americans' perceptions of time pressure. Sixty-one percent of those with children younger than 18 say they do not have enough time, while 42% of those without young children report the same.

Generally speaking, do you have enough time to do what you want to do these days, or not?

	Yes, enough time	No, not enough time
	%	%
TOTAL	52	48
GENDER		
Male	56	44
Female	49	51
AGE		
18-29	46	54
30-49	45	55
50-64	46	54
65+	78	21
GENDER AND AGE		
Male 18-49	52	48
Male 50+	61	39
Female 18-49	39	61
Female 50+	59	40
CHILDREN YOUNGER THAN 18		
Yes	39	61
No	58	42
EMPLOYMENT		
Working	39	61
Not working	68	32

Dec. 2-6, 2015

GALLUP'

Women's role in caring for children could factor into the wide gender disparity in time pressure among younger Americans. Sixty-one percent of women younger than age 50 report not having enough time, compared with 48% of younger men who say the same. There is almost no gender difference in perceived time pressure between men and women aged 50 and older.

A low 21% of those aged 65 and older say they do not have enough time to do what they want, reflecting the fact that having young children and working are widely associated with younger Americans. There is little difference in not having enough time among those younger than age 65.

Bottom Line

A recent *Economist* article posits that "time poverty" may be as much a result of perception as the reality of not having enough time. Gallup data, however, do not support the hypothesis that Americans' perceived time pressure has been increasing—at least not based on the trends over the past 25 years. The percentage of Americans who say they do not have enough time has stayed basically the same since 2001 and is slightly lower now than two measures recorded in the 1990s.

This finding fits with other data showing that Americans actually have more leisure time today than they did in the past, based on their spending fewer hours working and in normal household activities. There are big differences in time use across segments of the population, however, supporting Gallup's findings that certain categories of Americans—those who are working or responsible for young children in particular—perceive themselves as much more time-pressured than others.

Finally, because there are no comparable data showing how Americans in past generations would have responded to this question, there is no precise way of knowing whether the nearly half of Americans who today say they don't have enough time is higher or lower than at previous points in America's almost 240-year history.

Survey Methods

Results for this Gallup poll are based on telephone interviews conducted Dec. 2–6, 2015, with a random sample of 824 adults, aged 18 and older, living in all 50 U.S. states and the District of Columbia. For results based on the total sample of national adults, the margin of sampling error is ±4 percentage points at the 95% confidence level. All reported margins of sampling error include computed design effects for weighting.

Index

image of, 319–20
sales personnel in, honesty and ethical standards of, 468

baby boomers
    customer service and, 424
    ideology and, 37–38
    percentage in workplace, 34–36
    trust businesses to keep personal information private and, 178
    workplace engagement and, 36
banker(s), honesty and ethical standards of, 468
banks and banking
    confidence in, 217–18
        ideology and, 238
        trends in, 228–29
    customer service and, 423, 424
    image of, 319–20
        trends in, 324–25
bars, racial discrimination and, 285
beer, 273
Benedict XVI, favorability ratings, 266, 386
Benghazi incident, Clinton, Hillary, and, 181
Bernanke, Ben, confidence in, 157
beverages
    coffee, daily consumption, 278–79
    soda drinking habits, 286–87
    See also alcohol/alcoholic beverages
Biden, Joe
    favorability ratings, 94, 98, 111, 112, 121, 300, 379–80
    opinion of, 300
    would like to see run in 2016, 300
big business
    confidence in, 217–18, 245
        ideology and, 238
    as economic negative, 232
    as threat, 469
bill paying, worry about, 149
bipartisanship, support for, 30
Black Friday, 447
blacks
    affirmative action and, 323
    Affordable Care Act and, 135
    candidate matchups and, 415, 417–18
    Catholic, 353
    civil rights laws and, 295
    civil rights progress and, 294–95
    Clinton, Hillary, and, 295–96, 379
    college costs and, 144
    confidence in police and, 226
    death penalty and, 382
    Democratic Party and, 405–6
    exercise and, 278
    good/bad time to find a quality job, 464
    government and, 374
    haves and have-nots and, 313
    healthcare and, 285
    immigrant path to citizenship and, 302
    immigration and, 299, 333
    obesity and, 33
    police and, 285, 290–91
    race as most important issue and, 214
    race relations and, 292

Republican candidates and, 296
Sanders, Bernie, and, 379
satisfaction with quality of life and, 285–86
satisfaction with way blacks are treated, 287
single/never married and, 210
struggle to afford food and, 208
treatment of
    perceptions of, 285
    satisfaction with, 287–88
Trump, Donald, and, 296
unemployment and, 7, 154–55
uninsured and, 3, 139, 250, 373
well-being and, 20–21, 96–97, 405–6
would support for president, 227, 228
    religion and, 231
BMI (body mass index), 32–33
    See also obesity
Boehner, John, favorability ratings, 91–92, 301–2, 383, 404, 433
bonds, as best long-term investment, 155–56
Bradley, Bill, 121
Bryant, John Hope, 97
budget deficit, federal, as most important issue, 1, 65, 259, 308, 345, 425
    race and, 214
building contractors, honesty and ethical standards of, 468
Bush, Barbara, admiration of, 474
Bush, George H. W.
    admiration of, 473, 474
    approval ratings, 49
Bush, George W., 80
    admiration of, 473
    approval ratings, 17, 26, 48–49, 150, 265, 396
    can manage government effectively, 147
    confidence in presidency and, 219
    energy and, 108–9
    environment and, 108–9
Bush, Jeb
    blacks and, 296
    familiarity with, 102–3, 271, 316
    favorability and familiarity ratings, 131–33, 289–90, 332, 455
    favorability ratings, 94, 102–3, 111, 112, 271, 281, 315–16, 331–32, 403, 414, 415
    gender gap and, 309
business and industry
    customer service and, 423–24
    emissions standards for, support for, 30
    executives
        depression and, 142
        honesty and ethical standards of, 468
    owners, depression and, 142
    regulation of, 347–48
    trust to keep personal information secure, age and, 177–78

cable television, spending on, 190–91
California
    drug use in, 125
    economic confidence in, 52
    ideology in, 49
    Obama, Barack, and, 44–45
    obesity in, 194
    older adults' well-being in, 256

party identification in, 46
teacher engagement in, 18
unemployment in, 57
uninsured in, 73, 297
Canada, opinion of, 99
cancer, as most urgent health problem, 434
capital punishment. *See* death penalty
Carson, Ben
    admiration of, 473
    blacks and, 296
    favorability and familiarity ratings, 94, 102–3, 111, 112, 271, 289–90, 315–16, 331–32, 402–3, 414–15, 455
    gender gap and, 309
    government and, 375
    Hispanics and, 318
    LGBT individuals and, 188
Carter, Jimmy, 231
    admiration of, 474
    approval ratings, 49
Catholics
    Biden, Joe, and, 380
    confidence in religion and, 222
    demographics of, 352–53
    Francis I and, 266, 385–86
    identification with, 352
    marijuana use and, 268
    nontraditional presidential candidates and, 230–31
    party identification of, 353
    population of, 352
    would support for president, 227, 228
        religion and, 231
Chafee, Lincoln
    blacks and, 296
    favorability and familiarity ratings, 270, 317
    Hispanics and, 318, 319
    ideology and, 223
children
    extramarital, as morally acceptable, 196
        gender and, 224–25
        trends in, 199–200
    girls can learn computer science, 430–32
    school safety and, 320–21
        worry about, 407
    work/stay home preference and, 371–72
China
    economic power of, as threat, 58
        trends in, 78–79
    favorability ratings, 79
    as greatest enemy of U.S., 61, 72, 79
    opinion of, 99
    Trump, Donald, and, 258
Christians/Christianity, identification with, 471–72
Christie, Chris
    blacks and, 296
    favorability and familiarity ratings, 94, 102–3, 111, 112, 272, 289–90, 315–16, 331–32, 403, 414, 415, 455
    gender gap and, 309
    Hispanics and, 318
Christmas
    mood and, 13

spending on, 429–30
    forecast versus actual, 430
    trends in, 391
Christopher, Warren, favorability ratings, 307
church/church attendance
    alcohol and, 272
    Catholics and, 352–53
    confidence in, 217–18, 222
        ideology and, 238–39
    Jews and Obama and, 138
    marijuana use and, 268
    satisfaction with religious influence and, 55
    states and, 62–63
circuses, animal treatment and, 185
civil liberties, anti-terrorism and, 212–13
civil rights
    laws on, need for, 295
    progress of, 294–95
clergy, honesty and ethical standards of, 468
clerical workers
    depression and, 142
    workplace engagement and, 36
climate change
    Obama, Barack, and, 304
    weather and, 93, 116–17
    worry about, 104, 117, 118
        trends in, 116
    See also global warming
Clinton, Bill
    admiration of, 473, 474
    approval ratings, 17, 26, 48–49, 150, 265, 396
    can manage government effectively, 147
    confidence in presidency and, 219
    favorability ratings, 181
Clinton, Hillary Rodham
    admiration of, 473, 474
    Benghazi incident and, 181
    blacks and, 295–96
    candidate matchups, 258
    debates and, 417–18
    demographics of, 270
    economy and, 182, 183
    email issues, 181, 341–43
    favorability and familiarity ratings, 93–95, 97–99, 111–12, 181–82, 269–70, 317, 378–79, 414, 415, 449–50, 455
    foreign affairs and, 182–83
    government and, 182, 183
    healthcare and, 182, 183
    Hispanics and, 318, 319
    ideology and, 223
    immigration and, 182, 183
    income inequality and, 182, 183
    race relations and, 182, 183
    as secretary of state
        favorability ratings, 307
        opinion of, 183
    social class and, 161
    strengths of, 182–83
    terrorism and, 182, 183
    trends in, 121–22

cloning, as morally acceptable, 196
   age and, 203
clothing, stores, customer service and, 423, 424
coffee, daily consumption, 278–79
cohabitation, LGBT individuals and, 158, 413
college
   availability of, 144
   community, quality of, 229–30
   costs, 144–45
      as most important financial problem, 27
      worry about, 148
   diversity and, 401–2
   four-year, quality of, 229–30
   historically black colleges, well-being and, 400
   online, quality of, 229–30
   public
      diversity and, 401–2
      military service members and, 419
   veterans and, 419–20
   as worth cost, 360–61
   See also education
Colorado
   church attendance in, 62
   drug use in, 125
   economic confidence in, 52
   obesity in, 194
   Payroll to Population rate and, 57
   unemployment in, 57
   uninsured in, 73
   well-being in, 66
communication, smartphone versus computer and, 246
community
   feel safe in
      metro areas and, 166–67
      unemployment and, 154
      well-being and, 167
   pride in
      metro areas and, 178–80
      unemployment and, 154
   recognition for giving back to, metro areas and, 178–79
community well-being
   historically black colleges and, 400
   housing is ideal and, 233
   metro areas and, 130–31
   obesity and, 195
   states and, 66
   unemployment and, 154
computer industry, image of, 319–20
   trends in, 322
computers
   girls' confidence with, 430–32
   use of, 245–46
Confederate flag, 247–48
   display in South, 247
Congress
   approval ratings, 12, 59–61, 180, 354–55, 421–22, 464–65
      trends in, 12, 59–60, 180, 301, 421, 465
   confidence in, 217–19
      ideology and, 238
   corruption and, 359–60

knowledge of
   approval and, 355
   party ratings and, 369
members of
   honesty and ethical standards of, 467–68
   own
      image of, 359–60
      opinion of, 359–60
   as most important issue, 1, 259, 308
   as out of touch, 359–60
   special interests and, 359–60
   See also Democrats in Congress; Republicans in Congress
Connecticut
   actively disengaged employees in, 105
   church attendance in, 62
   ideology in, 49
   job creation in, 53–54
   Obama, Barack, and, 44
   obesity in, 194
   older adults' well-being in, 255
   party identification in, 46
   unemployment in, 57
   uninsured in, 73
conservatives
   Biden, Joe, and, 380
   candidate matchups and, 134, 270, 417–18
   Clinton, Hillary, and, 98, 379
   Confederate flag and, 248
   confidence in institutions and, 238–39
   confidence in police and, 226
   crime perceptions and, 394
   economic, 193–94
   Francis I and, 266, 385–86
   generational groups and, 37–38
   global warming and, 151–52
   government and, 374
   gun control and, 387
   identification with, 8–9
      trends in, 9
   ISIS and, 423
   LGBT in population and, 192
   NRA and, 395
   Palestinian state and, 74
   party identification of, 9
   Republican Party and, 205–6
   Sanders, Bernie, and, 379
   social, 193–94
      extramarital births and, 200
      morality and, 204–5
   states and, 49–50
   Supreme Court and, 346–47
   Tea Party and, 398
   terrorism versus civil liberties and, 213
   wealth distribution and, 171
   wealth redistribution and, 172
construction workers
   depression and, 142
   workplace engagement and, 36
consumers, spending and, 190–91, 409, 447
   needs versus wants, 190–91

trends in, 409
convenience stores, customer service and, 423, 424
corporations
    greed of, as economic negative, 232
    influence of, satisfaction with, 24
    tax system, perceptions of, 144
corruption
    Congress and, 359–60
    as most important issue, 308
cost of living, as most important financial problem, 27
courts, as most important issue, 259, 425
    See also judicial system
credit cards
    investors and, 344
    small businesses and, 293–94
    theft
        reported incidents, 396–97
        worry about, 397, 406–7
    worry about, 149
crime
    feel safe in community, unemployment and, 154
    feel safe walking alone at night, 399
    local, perceptions of, 399
    as most important issue, 1, 259
        race and, 214
    perceptions of, 393–94, 399
        feel safe walking alone at night and, 421
        versus reality, 393
    satisfaction with, 24
    seriousness of, 394
    victimization rates, 410–11
        demographics of, 416
        perceptions of, 393–94
        trends in, 410
    worry about, 104, 406–7
criminal justice system
    confidence in, 217, 218
        ideology and, 238
    reform, support for, 30–31
    satisfaction with, 173
Cruz, Ted
    Affordable Care Act and, 135
    blacks and, 296
    favorability and familiarity ratings, 94, 102–3, 111, 112, 133,
        271, 289–90, 315–16, 331–32, 403, 414, 415, 455
    gender gap and, 309
    Hispanics and, 318
Cuba
    diplomatic relations with, 67–68
    opinion of, 99, 100
        trends in, 67
    trade embargo with, lifting, support for, 30, 68
    travel to, 68
Cuomo, Andrew, 114
customer service, business and industry and, 423–24

Dalai Lama, admiration of, 473
death penalty
    fairness of imposition, 382
    frequency of imposition, 382–83

as morally acceptable, 196, 206–7
    trends in, 206
support for, 382–83
    trends in, 382
debt, investors and, 343–44
defense
    satisfaction with, 173
    spending on, 69–70
        trends in, 70
DeGeneres, Ellen, admiration of, 473
Delaware
    actively disengaged employees in, 105
    ideology in, 50
    job creation in, 53–54
    Obama, Barack, and, 44
    older adults' well-being in, 255
    party identification in, 46
Democratic Party
    abortion and, 51
        trends in, 201
    affirmative action and, 323
    Affordable Care Act and, 253
    Afghanistan and, 216–17
    animal rights and, 185
    banks and, 325
    better job of handling most important issue, 345, 351
    Biden, Joe, and, 380
    blacks and, 405–6
    Boehner, John, and, 301–2, 383
    business regulation and, 347–48
    candidate characteristics and, 227
    candidate issue positions and, 425
    candidate matchups and, 270, 415, 417–18
    candidates
        blacks and, 295–96
        favorability and familiarity ratings, 97–99, 111–12, 121–22,
            317, 455
        Hispanics and, 318, 319
        would like to see run, 300
    Catholics and, 353
    class identification and, 161
    Clinton, Bill, and, 181
    Clinton, Hillary, and, 98, 111, 181, 183, 342, 449–50
    concealed weapons and, 389
    Confederate flag and, 247–48
    confidence in banks and, 229
    confidence in police and, 226
    Congress and, 60, 180, 422, 465
    crime perceptions and, 394
    death penalty and, 207
    debates and, 417–18
    defense spending and, 70
    doctor-assisted suicide and, 197
    drugs and traffic safety and, 242
    economy and, 351
    energy and, 122
    environment and, 115–16, 118, 136–37
    favorability ratings, 100–101, 264
        trends in, 101
    federal government and, 354

financial situation and, 22
foreign trade and, 90
fracking and, 114
gay marriage and, 261
    trends in, 186–87
global warming and, 119–20, 151–52
good/bad time to find a quality job, 11, 263, 464
government and, 349–50, 363–64, 374
government responsibility to ensure healthcare coverage, 439
government role and, 370
gun control and, 387–88
identification with, 4–5, 244, 445
    states and, 45–47
    trends in, 5, 244
ideology and, 9, 223
    economic, 194
    social, 193
image of, 351
immigrant path to citizenship and, 302–3
immigration and, 38, 333
Internet industry and, 322
Iran and, 304
Iran nuclear weapons and, 80
Iraq War and, 216–17
ISIS and, 423, 441
Israel and, 71
Jews and, 2–3
judicial branch and, 346–47
Kennedy, Anthony, and, 261–63
Kerry, John, and, 307
labor and, 310
LGBT acceptance and, 31–32
LGBT as nature/nurture, trends in, 188
LGBT in population and, 192
LGBT morality and, 189
marijuana use and, 267–68
mass shootings and, 463
McConnell, Mitch, and, 301–2
media and, 362
most important issue and, 308
Netanyahu, Benjamin, and, 91
Obama, Barack, and, 64, 109, 190, 304, 428–29
one-party control and, 377
opinion of, 352
Palestinian state and, 74
personal financial situation and, 145–46
pharmaceutical industry and, 340
Planned Parenthood and, 381
poverty and, 174
proud to be American, 243
refugees and, 440
Republican Party and, 101, 352
Republicans in Congress and, 17, 157, 369
Roberts, John, and, 261–63
Sanders, Bernie, and, 449
satisfaction of, 19–20
satisfaction with equality and mobility and, 40
satisfaction with government and, 176
satisfaction with security and, 23
satisfaction with U.S. and, 19–20, 452

satisfaction with way blacks are treated, 288
Scalia, Antonin, and, 261–63
single/never married and, 210
Supreme Court and, 259–60, 368
tax cuts and, 28
taxes and, 28
terrorism and, 351
terrorism approaches and, 460–61
terrorism versus civil liberties and, 213
third party and, 358–59
threats to country and, 469
Trump, Donald, and, 257–58
U.S. as economic leader and, 84
United Nations and, 78
values and, 363
voting issues and, 184
wealth distribution and, 171
wealth redistribution and, 172
well-being and, 405–6
Democrats in Congress
    approval ratings, 368–69
    confidence in, 156, 157
depression
    heart attack and, 14–15
    history of, professionals and, 142
    professionals and, 141–42
diabetes, as most urgent health problem, 434
discrimination
    blacks and, 285
    Hispanics and, immigrant status and, 314–15
    perceptions of, trends in, 288
dishonesty, as most important issue, 259
District of Columbia
    actively disengaged employees in, 105
    economic confidence in, 52
diversity, college experience and, 401–2
divorce, as morally acceptable, 196
    gender and, 224–25
doctor(s)
    depression and, 142
    honesty and ethical standards of, 468
doctor-assisted suicide
    as morally acceptable, 196
        trends in, 198
    support for
        terminology and, 197
        trends in, 197–98
domestic issues, government and, confidence in, 353–54
drivers and driving, alcohol and drugs and, 242–43, 251–52
drugs
    driving and, 242–43, 251–52
    as most urgent health problem, 434
    See also marijuana
drug use
    states and, 125
    well-being and, 125
    worry about, 104

Ebola virus
    mood and, 14

as most urgent health problem, 434
economic conditions
    Clinton, Hillary, and, 182, 183
    confidence in, 12–13, 219, 409–10
        community groups and, 356–58
        gas prices and, 219–20
        metro areas and, 107–8
        states and, 52–53
        trends in, 13, 220, 410
    Democratic Party and, 351
    Gallup Good Jobs rate, 445–47
    government and, satisfaction with, 173
        trends in, 175–76
    as haves and have-nots, 312–14
        view society as, 313
    ideology and, 193–94
    as most important financial problem, 27
    as most important issue, 1, 65, 95–96, 259, 308, 344, 425, 458
        race and, 214
        trends in, 1, 459
    negative aspects of, 232
    Obama, Barack, and, 63, 304, 428–29
    outlook for, 410
    Payroll to Population rate, 6–7
        trends in, 6
    positive aspects of, 231
    Republican Party and, 351
    satisfaction with, 23–25
    Trump, Donald, and, 257–58
    as voting issue, 183–84
    worry about, 104
education
    Affordable Care Act and, 253
    alcohol and, 272–74, 276
    Biden, Joe, and, 380
    class identification and, 161
    Clinton, Hillary, and, 111, 379
    college education, worth of, 360–61
    college types, quality of, 230
    concealed weapons and, 389
    Confederate flag and, 248
    confidence in police and, 226
    federal worker financial well-being and, 86
    financial situation and, 22
    global warming and, 119–20
    gluten-free foods and, 269
    good/bad time to find a quality job, 464
    government and, satisfaction with, 173
    haves and have-nots and, 313
    image of, 319–20
    Internet industry and, 322
    Jewish party identification and, 2
    Jews and Obama and, 138
    LGBT in population and, 192
    lifelong learning and, 276
    marijuana use and, 268
    as most important issue, 1, 65, 259, 308, 345, 425
        race and, 214
    Obama, Barack, and, 304
    Palestinian state and, 74

Republican Party and, 101
    retirement expectations and, 165
    Sanders, Bernie, and, 379
    satisfaction with, 24
    single/never married and, 210
    smartphone checking frequency and, 249
    telecommuting and, 311
    terrorism versus civil liberties and, 213
    vaccines and autism and, 89
    weight and, 450
    worried about being laid off, 153
    as worth cost, 360–61
Edwards, John, 98–99
    favorability ratings, 121
Egypt, opinion of, 99, 100
Eisenhower, Dwight D.
    admiration of, 473–74
    approval ratings, 26, 48–49, 150, 265, 396
Eisenhower, Mamie, admiration of, 474
election of 2016
    candidate matchups, 98–99, 102–3, 111–12, 121–22, 131–33, 269–70, 280–81, 315–17, 331–32, 414–15, 417–18, 455
    immigration and, 333–34
    issues in, 183–84
electric and gas utilities, image of, 319–20
electronics, spending on, 190–91
Elizabeth II, queen of Great Britain, admiration of, 473, 474
email
    Clinton, Hillary, and, 181, 341–43
    smartphones and, 246
emotional health, daily mood, 13–14
employer-based health insurance, 4
employment
    actively disengaged employees, 36–37
        health and, 466–67
        metro areas and, 336
        states and, 105
        teachers and, 10, 43–44
            states and, 18–19
        trends in, 90
    baby boomers and, 34–36
    discrimination and, race and, 285
    engaged employees, 36–37
        health and, 466–67
        managers and, 126–27
        teachers and, 10, 43–44
            states and, 18–19
        trends in, 90
    Gallup Good Jobs rate, 445–47
    government and, satisfaction with, 173
        trends in, 175–76
    part-time
        baby boomers and, 35
        unwilling, 426
            financial well-being and, 425–27
    Payroll to Population rate
        metro areas and, 112–14
        states and, 57–58
    productivity losses

job creation and, 241, 371, 412

labor and, 310

obesity and, 33

proud to be American, 243

single/never married and, 210

well-being and, 21

winter temperature and, 93

Georgia

church attendance in, 62

teacher engagement in, 18

workplace engagement in, 105

Germany

opinion of, 99

refugees from, support for, 440

GI Bill, college experience and, 419–20

Gilmore, Jim

favorability and familiarity ratings, 315–16, 331–32

Hispanics and, 318

Gingrich, Newt, favorability ratings, 433

global warming

causes of

education and political affiliation and, 119–20

party and ideology and, 152

seriousness of

education and, 120

timeframe of, 116

education and, 120

party and ideology and, 151–52

trends in, 117

worry about, 116, 117, 118

education and, 120

See also climate change

gold, as best long-term investment, 155–56

Gore, Al, 121

government

business regulation and, 347–48

Clinton, Hillary, and, 182, 183

dissatisfaction with, as most important issue, 65, 95–96, 259, 308, 344, 425, 458

race and, 214

environment and, 136–37

healthcare and, 172–73

health insurance and, 438–40

jobs with, hiring/letting go, 371, 412

as most important issue, 1

as most urgent health problem, 434

Obama, Barack, and, 170

one-party control of, 376–78

congressional approval ratings and, 465

poverty and, satisfaction with, trends in, 173–74

power of, 374–75

satisfaction with, 24

trends in, 374

worry about, 104

president and, approval ratings and, 146–47

role of, 363–64

political affiliation and, 370

satisfaction with, trends in, 25

size of

satisfaction with, 24

worry about, 104

surveillance programs, satisfaction with, 24

terrorism and, 211–12, 456–57

civil liberties and, 212–13

trends in, 211

as threat, 349–50, 468–69

trends in, 469

trust in, issues and, 456–57

values and, 363

as voting issue, 184

Graham, Billy, admiration of, 473, 474

Graham, Lindsey

blacks and, 296

favorability and familiarity ratings, 272, 281, 289–90, 315–16, 331–32

gender gap and, 309

Hispanics and, 318

Great Britain, opinion of, 99

Greenspan, Alan, confidence in, 157

groceries

industry, image of, 319–20

spending on, 375–76

stores, customer service and, 423, 424

Guantanamo Bay prison, closure of, support for, 30

gun(s)

concealed carry, 389–90

mass shootings, worry about, 462–63

as most important issue, 425, 458

trends in, 459

ownership of, 388

concealed carry and, 389

feel safe walking alone at night, 420

gun control as voting issue and, 387

NRA and, 395

policy on, satisfaction with, trends in, 25

as voting issue, 386–87

gun control

background checks, 389–90

ban on purchase by no-fly list, effectiveness against terrorism, 460–61

handgun ban, 388

laws should be more/less strict, 388

as most important issue, 425

as voting issue, 386–87

happiness, 14

Hastert, Dennis, favorability ratings, 433

hate crimes, worry about, 407

Hawaii

church attendance in, 62

drug use in, 125

economic confidence in, 52

ideology in, 49

Obama, Barack, and, 44

obesity in, 194

party identification in, 46

well-being in, 66

healthcare

access to

as most urgent health problem, 433–34

Kasich, John
　　blacks and, 296
　　favorability and familiarity ratings, 272, 289–90, 315–16,
　　　　331–32, 403, 414, 415, 455
　　gender gap and, 309
　　Hispanics and, 318
Kelly, Megyn, 309
Kennedy, Anthony, favorability ratings, 261–63
Kennedy, Edward, admiration of, 474
Kennedy, Jacqueline, admiration of, 473, 474
Kennedy, John F., 231
　　approval ratings, 49
Kentucky
　　actively disengaged employees in, 105
　　church attendance in, 62
　　drug use in, 125
　　economic confidence in, 52
　　job creation in, 53–54
　　Obama, Barack, and, 44–45
　　obesity in, 194
　　Payroll to Population rate and, 57
　　uninsured in, 73, 297
　　well-being in, 66
Kerry, John, 100, 303
　　favorability ratings, 306–7
Keystone XL pipeline, 136
Kosovo, refugees from, support for, 440

labor (organized; unions)
　　as biggest threat, 469
　　confidence in, 217, 218
　　　ideology and, 238, 239
　　government and, satisfaction with, 173
　　　trends in, 175–76
　　health insurance coverage, 4, 139, 251, 373
　　　satisfaction with, 417
　　job satisfaction and, 338–39
　　leaders of, honesty and ethical standards of, 468
　　members, 311
　　Obama, Barack, and, 329
　　power of, 310
　　　outlook for, 310
　　support for, 29, 310
lakes, pollution of, worry about, 117, 118
Latinos/as. See Hispanics
law enforcement. See police
laws, as most important issue, 259, 425
lawyer(s)
　　honesty and ethical standards of, 468
　　image of, 319–20
leadership
　　as most important issue, 308
　　Obama, Barack, and, 170
legislative branch, trust in, 346
LGBT individuals and issues
　　acceptance of, satisfaction with, 24
　　　trends in, 25, 31–32
　　cohabitation versus marriage, 158, 413
　　metro areas and, 109–11
　　as morally acceptable, 188–89, 196
　　　gender and, 224

trends in, 189
　　nature/nurture, 188
　　in population, estimates of, 191–92
　　would support for president, 227, 228
　　　religion and, 230
　　See also gay marriage
liberals
　　Biden, Joe, and, 380
　　candidate matchups and, 270, 417–18
　　Clinton, Hillary, and, 98, 379
　　Confederate flag and, 248
　　confidence in institutions and, 238–39
　　confidence in police and, 226
　　crime perceptions and, 394
　　Democratic Party and, 223
　　economic, 193–94
　　　Democratic Party and, 223
　　Francis I and, 266, 385–86
　　generational groups and, 37–38
　　global warming and, 151–52
　　government and, 374
　　gun control and, 387
　　identification with, 8–9
　　　trends in, 9
　　ISIS and, 423
　　LGBT in population and, 192
　　morality and, 196
　　NRA and, 395
　　Palestinian state and, 74
　　party identification of, 9
　　Republican Party and, 205–6
　　Sanders, Bernie, and, 379
　　social, 193–94
　　　Democratic Party and, 223
　　　extramarital births and, 199–200
　　　morality and, 204–5
　　Supreme Court and, 346–47
　　Tea Party and, 398
　　terrorism versus civil liberties and, 213
　　wealth distribution and, 171
　　wealth redistribution and, 172
Life Evaluation Index, 20–21
liquor, 273
lobbyists, honesty and ethical standards of, 468
Louisiana
　　church attendance in, 62
　　drug use in, 125
　　economic confidence in, 52
　　ideology in, 49
　　obesity in, 194
　　workplace engagement in, 105
Luce, Clare Boothe, admiration of, 474
Lynch, Loretta, 180

mail
　　look forward to checking, 127–28
　　satisfaction with delivery, 173
　　types of, reactions to, 127–28
Maine
　　church attendance in, 62
　　job creation in, 53–54

older adults' well-being in, 256
  unemployment in, 57
managers
  depression and, 141–42
  high talent, 126–27
  workplace engagement and, 36, 126–27
Mandela, Nelson, admiration of, 474
manufacturing workers
  depression and, 142
  workplace engagement and, 36
marijuana
  driving and, 242–43, 251–52
  ever tried, 267–68
    trends in, 267
  legalization of, 391–92
    driving and, 242–43, 251–52
    trends in, 391
  use of, 251, 267
marital status
  Clinton, Hillary, and, 111
  financial worry and, 148, 149
  LGBT individuals and, 157–58, 412–14
  single, demographics of, 210
  struggle to afford food and, 208
  trends in, 210–11
marriage
  extramarital affairs, as morally acceptable, 196
    age and, 203
    gender and, 224
  polygamy, as morally acceptable, 196
  trends in, 210–11
  See also divorce; gay marriage
Maryland
  drug use in, 125
  economic confidence in, 52
  ideology in, 49
  Obama, Barack, and, 44
  party identification in, 45–46
  Payroll to Population rate and, 57
  uninsured in, 73
Massachusetts
  church attendance in, 62
  economic confidence in, 52
  ideology in, 49–50
  Obama, Barack, and, 44
  obesity in, 194
  party identification in, 45–46
  teacher engagement in, 18
McCain, John, 133, 280
McCarthy, Gina, 136
McCarthy, Jenny, 89
McConnell, Mitch, favorability ratings, 301–2, 404–5
media
  trust in, 362–63
    trends in, 362
  women and computer science in, 431
Medicaid, 4, 139, 251, 373
  Affordable Care Act and, 428
  expansion, states and, 73, 297
  satisfaction with, 417
  satisfaction with healthcare costs and, 436

medical system
  confidence in, 217, 218
    ideology and, 238
  finding cures for diseases, as most important issue, 434
Medicare, 4, 139, 251, 373
  Affordable Care Act and, 428
  satisfaction with, 24, 417
    trends in, 25
  satisfaction with healthcare costs and, 436
Meir, Golda, admiration of, 473
Memorial Day, mood and, 13
men
  admiration of, 473–74
  affirmative action and, 323
  Affordable Care Act and, 253
  alcohol and, 272–73, 276
  animal rights and, 185
  baby boomers in workforce and, 35
  best long-term investment and, 156
  Biden, Joe, and, 380
  candidate matchups and, 270, 309
  Clinton, Bill, and, 181
  Clinton, Hillary, and, 111–12, 181, 379, 449
  coffee and, 278
  concealed weapons and, 389
  confidence in police and, 226
  confidence in retirement savings and, 129
  crime perceptions and, 394
  divorce as morally acceptable, 225
  exercise and, 278
  extramarital affairs as morally acceptable, 224
  extramarital children as morally acceptable, 225
  fat or salt avoidance and, 274
  financial situation and, 22
  financial worry and, 149
  gluten-free foods and, 269
  good/bad time to find a quality job, 11, 263–64, 464
  Internet industry and, 322
  Jewish party identification and, 2
  Jews and Obama and, 138
  job satisfaction and, 330–31
  labor and, 310
  LGBT in population and, 192
  marijuana use and, 267–68
  morality and, 224–25
  obesity and, 33
  Palestinian state and, 74
  Planned Parenthood and, 381
  pornography as morally acceptable, 224
  Republican Party and, 101
  Sanders, Bernie, and, 379, 449
  satisfaction with U.S. and, 452
  school safety and, 321
  single/never married and, 210
  smartphone bond and, 254, 255
  smartphone checking frequency and, 249
  smoking bans and, 280
  sports fans and, 221
  struggle to afford food and, 208
  terrorism versus civil liberties and, 213
  time pressures and, 475

unemployment and, 154–55
vaccines and autism and, 89
weight and, 450
well-being and, 21, 96–97
work/stay home preference and, 372
worried about being laid off, 153
mental health
as most urgent health problem, 434
professionals and depression, 141–42
Merkel, Angela, admiration of, 473
metro areas
community pride in, 178–80
concealed weapons and, 389
confidence in police and, 226
crime perceptions and, 394
crime victimization and, 416
economic confidence and, 107–8, 356–58
feel safe in community and, 166–67
feel safe walking alone at night, 420
ideal housing and, 232–34
job creation in, 106–7
LGBT population and, 109–11
marijuana use and traffic safety and, 252
obesity in, 198–99
Payroll to Population rate and, 112–14
well-being in, 130–31
workplace engagement and, 335–36
Mexico
opinion of, 99
Trump, Donald, and, 257–58
Michigan
actively disengaged employees in, 105
job creation in, 53–54
older adults' well-being in, 255
teacher engagement in, 18
well-being in, 66
Middle East
as greatest enemy of U.S., 61, 72
sympathies in, 71
Palestinian state and, 74
as threat, 58
military
college experience and, 419–20
confidence in, 217, 218
ideology and, 238
effectiveness against terrorism, 460–61
health insurance coverage, 4, 139, 251, 373
satisfaction with, 417
satisfaction with healthcare costs and, 436
as No. 1 power, 68–69
importance of, 69
satisfaction with, 24, 173
strength of, 70
millennials
customer service and, 424
ideology and, 37–38
trust businesses to keep personal information private and, 177–78
workplace engagement and, 36–37
miners
depression and, 142

workplace engagement and, 36
minimum wage, raising, support for, 29
Minnesota
economic confidence in, 52
obesity in, 194
Payroll to Population rate and, 57
Mississippi
Catholics and, 353
church attendance in, 62
drug use in, 125
economic confidence in, 52
ideology in, 49
job creation in, 53–54
obesity in, 194
Payroll to Population rate and, 57
uninsured in, 297
well-being in, 66
workplace engagement in, 105
Missouri
actively disengaged employees in, 105
drug use in, 125
economic confidence in, 52
Obama, Barack, and, 45
obesity in, 194
well-being in, 66
moderates
Biden, Joe, and, 380
candidate matchups and, 270, 417–18
Clinton, Hillary, and, 98, 379
Confederate flag and, 248
confidence in institutions and, 238–39
confidence in police and, 226
crime perceptions and, 394
economic, 193–94
Francis I and, 266, 385–86
generational groups and, 37–38
global warming and, 151–52
government and, 374
gun control and, 387
identification with, 8–9
trends in, 9
ISIS and, 423
LGBT in population and, 192
NRA and, 395
Palestinian state and, 74
party identification of, 9
Republican Party and, 205–6
Sanders, Bernie, and, 379
social, 193–94
extramarital births and, 200
morality and, 204–5
states and, 49–50
Supreme Court and, 346–47
Tea Party and, 398
terrorism versus civil liberties and, 213
wealth distribution and, 171
wealth redistribution and, 172
Modi, Narendra, 100
money
lack of
as most important financial problem, 27

marijuana use and, 267–68
Palestinian state and, 74
police and, 467
satisfaction with U.S. and, 452
school safety and, 321
terrorism versus civil liberties and, 213
North Carolina
church attendance in, 62
teacher engagement in, 18
unemployment in, 57
North Dakota
actively disengaged employees in, 105
drug use in, 125
economic confidence in, 52
ideology in, 50
job creation in, 53–54
Obama, Barack, and, 44
party identification in, 46
Payroll to Population rate and, 57
unemployment in, 57
uninsured in, 297
North Korea
favorability ratings, trends in, 72
as greatest enemy of U.S., 61, 72
opinion of, 99
as threat, 58, 72
nuclear weapons, Iran and, 80
nurses
depression and, 142
honesty and ethical standards of, 467–68

Obama, Barack
admiration of, 473–74
Afghanistan and, 216
approval ratings, 34, 189, 264–65, 395–96
    economy and, 428–29
    healthcare and, 428–29
    issues and, 63–64, 303–4
    partisan gap in, 48–49
    seventh year, 17
    states and, 44–45
    trends in, 26
    twenty-fifth quarter, 150–51
    union members and, 329
    yearly averages, 25–26
can manage government effectively, 146–47, 170
climate change and, 304
confidence in
    economy and, 156–57
    seventh year, 218–19
economy and, 63, 304, 428–29
    confidence in, 156–57
education and, 304
energy and, 108–9
environment and, 108–9, 136, 152
favorability ratings, 91–92, 189–90
    trends in, 64
foreign affairs and, 63, 304
global respect for, 76–77
has clear plan for solving country's problems, 170
healthcare and, 428–29

honesty and, 170
immigration and, 304
influence of, 16–17
Iran and, 303–4
ISIS and, 441
Jews and, 137–38
leadership and, 170
race relations and, 304
religion and, 62–63
State of the Union address, support for proposals, 29–31
Syria and, 440–41
terrorism and, 304
Trump, Donald, and, 256–57, 258
understands problems Americans face in daily lives, 170
unions and, 329
Obama, Michelle, admiration of, 473
Obamacare. *See* Affordable Care Act
obesity
heart attack and, 435
as most urgent health problem, 434
states and, 194–95
trends in, 32–33
well-being and, 33, 195
office workers
depression and, 142
workplace engagement and, 36
Ohio
actively disengaged employees in, 105
teacher engagement in, 18
well-being in, 66
oil industry, image of, 319–20
trends in, 319
Oklahoma
church attendance in, 62
economic confidence in, 52
ideology in, 49
job creation in, 53–54
Obama, Barack, and, 44
obesity in, 194
older adults' well-being in, 256
workplace engagement in, 105
O'Malley, Martin, 121
blacks and, 296
favorability and familiarity ratings, 270, 317
Hispanics and, 318, 319
ideology and, 223
opportunities, satisfaction with, 24, 39–41
trends in, 25, 40
Oregon
church attendance in, 62
drug use in, 125
ideology in, 49
job creation in, 53–54
older adults' well-being in, 255
Payroll to Population rate and, 57
uninsured in, 73, 297
Ornish, Dean, 436

Pakistan
as greatest enemy of U.S., 61, 72
opinion of, 99

Palestinian Authority
  opinion of, 71, 99
  sympathy with, 71
Palestinian state, support for, 74–75
  trends in, 74
Palin, Sarah, admiration of, 473
parents
  financial worry and, college costs and, 148
  time pressures and, 475
  vaccines and autism and, 89
  worry and, school safety and, 320–21
partisan gap
  global warming and, 151–52
  Supreme Court and, 260
party identification, 4–5, 244, 445
  Catholics and, 353
  Jews and, 2–3
  Obama, Barack, and, 64
  states and, 45–47
  trends in, 5, 244
Pataki, George
  blacks and, 296
  favorability and familiarity ratings, 271–72, 289–90, 315–16,
      331–32
  gender gap and, 309
  Hispanics and, 318
patriotism, proud to be American, 243
Paul, Rand
  blacks and, 296
  favorability and familiarity ratings, 94, 102–3, 111, 112,
      133–34, 271, 289–90, 315–16, 331–32
  gender gap and, 309
  Hispanics and, 318
Payroll to Population rate, 6–7
  metro areas and, 112–14
  states and, 57–58
  trends in, 6
  See also Gallup Good Jobs rate
Pelosi, Nancy, favorability ratings, 433
Pennsylvania
  actively disengaged employees in, 105
  older adults' well-being in, 255
  teacher engagement in, 18
Perry, Rick
  blacks and, 296
  favorability and familiarity ratings, 94, 102–3, 111, 112, 271,
      281, 289–90, 315–16, 331–32
  gender gap and, 309
  Hispanics and, 318
pharmaceutical industry, image of, 319–20
  trends in, 339–40
pharmacists
  customer service and, 423, 424
  honesty and ethical standards of, 468
physical well-being
  historically black colleges and, 400
  housing is ideal and, 233
  metro areas and, 130–31
  states and, 66
Planned Parenthood, opinion of, 380–81
plant species, extinction of, worry about, 117, 118

police
  blacks' perceptions of, 285, 290–91
  confidence in, 217, 218
    ideology and, 238–39
    trends in, 225–26
  Hispanics' perceptions of, 314–15
  honesty and ethical standards of, 467
  presence in community, preferred level of, 291
political affiliation
  abortion and, 51
    trends in, 201
  affirmative action and, 323
  Affordable Care Act and, 253
  Afghanistan and, 216–17
  animal rights and, 185
  banks and, 325
  Biden, Joe, and, 380
  Boehner, John, and, 301–2, 383
  business regulation and, 347–48
  candidate characteristics and, 227
  candidate issue positions and, 424–25
  class identification and, 161
  Clinton, Bill, and, 181
  Clinton, Hillary, and, 111, 181, 183
  concealed weapons and, 389
  Confederate flag and, 247–48
  confidence in banks and, 229
  confidence in police and, 226
  Congress and, 60, 180, 421–22, 465
  crime perceptions and, 394
  death penalty and, 207
  defense spending and, 70
  Democrats in Congress and, 369
  doctor-assisted suicide and, 197
  drugs and traffic safety and, 242
  economic confidence and, 357
  energy and, 122
  environment and, 115–16, 118, 136–37
  federal government and, 354
  financial situation and, 22
  foreign trade and, 90
  fracking and, 114
  gay marriage and, 261
    trends in, 186–87
  global warming and, 119–20, 151–52
  good/bad time to find a quality job, 11, 263, 464
  government and, 349–50, 363–64, 374
  government responsibility to ensure healthcare coverage, 439
  government role and, 370
  gun control and, 387–88
  ideology and, 223
    economic, 194
    social, 193
  immigrant path to citizenship and, 302–3
  immigration and, 38, 333
  Internet industry and, 322
  Iran and, 304
  Iran nuclear weapons and, 80
  Iraq War and, 216–17
  ISIS and, 423, 441
  Israel and, 71

Putin, Vladimir, 100

quality of life, satisfaction with, 24
    race and, 285–86
Quayle, Dan, 199

race
    affirmative action programs for, 323–24
    Affordable Care Act and, 135, 253
    alcohol and health and, 276
    Biden, Joe, and, 380
    candidate matchups and, 417–18
    civil rights laws and, 295
    civil rights progress and, 294–95
    Clinton, Bill, and, 181
    Clinton, Hillary, and, 111, 181, 379
    coffee and, 278
    college costs and, 144
    Confederate flag and, 248
    confidence in police and, 226
    death penalty and, 382
    exercise and, 278
    fat or salt avoidance and, 274
    financial situation and, 22
    financial worry and, 148, 149
    gluten-free foods and, 269
    good/bad time to find a quality job, 11, 263, 464
    government and, 374
    government responsibility to ensure healthcare coverage, 439
    haves and have-nots and, 313
    immigrant path to citizenship and, 302
    immigration and, 299, 333
    marijuana use and, 267–68
    obesity and, 33
    Palestinian state and, 74
    police and, 285, 290–91, 467
    Sanders, Bernie, and, 379
    satisfaction with U.S. and, 452
    school safety and, 321
    single/never married and, 210
    struggle to afford food and, 208
    terrorism versus civil liberties and, 213
    unemployment and, 7, 154–55
    uninsured and, 3, 139, 250, 373
    well-being and, 20–21, 96–97
race relations, 291–92
    Clinton, Hillary, and, 182, 183
    discrimination venues, 285
    as most important issue, 259, 308, 345, 425
        race and, 214
    Obama, Barack, and, 304
    optimism on, 292
    satisfaction with, 23–25, 287–88
        trends in, 25
    as voting issue, 184
    worry about, 103–4
racism, as most important issue, 1, 258–59, 308, 345, 425
    trends in, 259
radio industry, image of, 319–20

rain forests, loss of, worry about, 117, 118
Reagan, Ronald
    admiration of, 473, 474
    approval ratings, 26, 48–49, 150, 265, 396
real estate
    agents, honesty and ethical standards of, 468
    as best long-term investment, 155–56
    image of, 319–20
    now is a good/bad time to buy, 158–59
        trends in, 159
    prices will increase/decrease, 159
refugees, support for, 440–41
religion
    Biden, Joe, and, 380
    confidence in, 217–18, 222
        ideology and, 238–39
    identification with, 471–72
    influence of, satisfaction with, 24, 55
    marijuana use and, 268
    as most important issue, 259
    nontraditional presidential candidates and, 230–31
    satisfaction with, 55–56
        trends in, 55
rent, as retirement income, 163
repair personnel
    depression and, 142
    workplace engagement and, 36
Republican Party
    abortion and, 51
        trends in, 201
    affirmative action and, 323
    Affordable Care Act and, 253
    Afghanistan and, 216–17
    animal rights and, 185
    banks and, 325
    better job of handling most important issue, 345, 351
    Biden, Joe, and, 380
    Boehner, John, and, 301–2, 383
    business regulation and, 347–48
    candidate characteristics and, 227
    candidate issue positions and, 424–25
    candidate matchups and, 415
    candidates
        blacks and, 296
        favorability and familiarity ratings, 102–3, 131–33, 270–72, 280–81, 289–90, 315–17, 331–32, 402–3, 414–15, 455
        gender gap and, 309
        government and, 375
        Hispanics and, 318–19
    Catholics and, 353
    class identification and, 161
    Clinton, Bill, and, 181
    Clinton, Hillary, and, 111, 181, 183
    concealed weapons and, 389
    Confederate flag and, 247–48
    confidence in banks and, 229
    confidence in police and, 226
    Congress and, 60, 180, 421–22, 465

optimism and, 235
savings
    expectations of, 162–66
    investor confidence and, 128–29
    as most important financial problem, 27
    spending on, 190–91
    worry about, 149
See also Social Security
Rhode Island
Catholics and, 353
drug use in, 125
ideology in, 50
job creation in, 53–54
Obama, Barack, and, 44
party identification in, 46
unemployment in, 57
uninsured in, 297
Rice, Condoleezza
admiration of, 473
favorability ratings, 307
rivers, pollution of, worry about, 117, 118
Roberts, John, favorability ratings, 261–63
Romney, Mitt, management experience of, 147
Roosevelt, Eleanor, admiration of, 473
Roosevelt, Franklin, Social Security and, 305
Rouhani, Hassan, 80–81
royalties, as retirement income, 163
Rubio, Marco
blacks and, 296
favorability and familiarity ratings, 94, 102–3, 111, 112, 131–33, 271, 289–90, 315–16, 331–32, 403, 414, 415, 455
gender gap and, 309
government and, 375
Hispanics and, 318
LGBT individuals and, 188
rural areas
concealed weapons and, 389
confidence in police and, 226
crime perceptions and, 394
crime victimization and, 416
economic confidence and, 356–58
feel safe walking alone at night, 420
Russia
conflict with Ukraine, as threat, 58–59
as greatest enemy of U.S., 61, 72
    trends in, 61–62
military power of, as threat, 58, 61
opinion of, 59, 99, 100
    trends in, 61, 100
Trump, Donald, and, 258
Ryan, Paul, 404, 422
favorability ratings, 432–33

sale pricing, 367
sales personnel
depression and, 142
workplace engagement and, 36
salt, consumption of, 274

same-sex marriage. *See* gay marriage
San Bernardino, CA, attack, 452–53
Sanders, Bernie
admiration of, 473
blacks and, 296
favorability and familiarity ratings, 94, 98, 111, 112, 269–70, 317, 378–79, 414, 415, 449, 455
    debates and, 418
    demographics of, 270
Hispanics and, 318, 319
ideology and, 223
Santorum, Rick
blacks and, 296
favorability and familiarity ratings, 94, 102–3, 111, 112, 272, 289–90, 315–16, 331–32
gender gap and, 309
Hispanics and, 318
satellite television, spending on, 190–91
satisfaction, 19–20, 23–25
with abortion policies, 51–52
    trends in, 51
with economic conditions, 23–25
with global position of U.S., 76
with government work in healthcare, 172–73
with health insurance coverage, by type, 417
with immigration, 38–39
    trends in, 39
with jobs, 325–26
    gender and, 330–31
    government workers and, 334–35
    union members and, 338–39
with opportunities, 39–41
with quality of life, race and, 285–86
with race relations, 23–25, 287–88
with religion, 55–56
    trends in, 55
with security, 22–23
with standard of living, 8
with taxes, 27–28
    trends in, 28
with U.S., 19–20, 96, 307–8, 452–53
    trends in, 308
Saudi Arabia
as greatest enemy of U.S., 61, 72
opinion of, 99
savings
as best long-term investment, 155–56
gas prices and, 215
lack of, as most important financial problem, 27
retirement
    expectations of, 162–66
    investor confidence and, 128–29
    as most important financial problem, 27
    spending on, 190–91
    worry about, 149
Scalia, Antonin, favorability ratings, 261–63
school(s)
confidence in, ideology and, 238
safety at, worry about, 320–21, 407

uninsured and, 3, 139, 250, 373
well-being and, 21, 405–6
Williams, Brian, 362
wine, 273
Winfrey, Oprah, admiration of, 473, 474
winter weather, 92–93
climate change and, 93, 116–17
Wisconsin
economic confidence in, 52
job creation in, 53–54
unemployment in, 57
women
admiration of, 473–74
affirmative action and, 323
Affordable Care Act and, 253
alcohol and, 272–73, 276
animal rights and, 185
baby boomers in workforce and, 35
best long-term investment and, 156
Biden, Joe, and, 380
candidate matchups and, 270, 309
Clinton, Bill, and, 181
Clinton, Hillary, and, 111–12, 181, 379, 449
coffee and, 278
concealed weapons and, 389
confidence in police and, 226
confidence in retirement savings and, 129
crime perceptions and, 394
divorce as morally acceptable, 225
exercise and, 278
extramarital affairs as morally acceptable, 224
extramarital children as morally acceptable, 225
fat or salt avoidance and, 274
feel safe walking alone at night, 420–21
financial situation and, 22
financial worry and, 149
gluten-free foods and, 269
good/bad time to find a quality job, 11, 263–64, 464
Internet industry and, 322
Jewish party identification and, 2
Jews and Obama and, 138
job satisfaction and, 330–31
labor and, 310
LGBT in population and, 192
marijuana use and, 267–68
morality and, 224–25
obesity and, 33
Palestinian state and, 74
Planned Parenthood and, 381
pornography as morally acceptable, 224
Republican Party and, 101
Sanders, Bernie, and, 379, 449

satisfaction with U.S. and, 452
school safety and, 321
single/never married and, 210
smartphone bond and, 254, 255
smartphone checking frequency and, 249
smoking bans and, 280
sports fans and, 221
struggle to afford food and, 208
terrorism versus civil liberties and, 213
time pressures and, 475
Trump, Donald, and, 309
vaccines and autism and, 89
weight and, 450
well-being and, 21
work/stay home preference and, 371–72
trends in, 372
worried about being laid off, 153
would support for president, 227, 228
religion and, 231
work environment
assault worries in, 407
boss, satisfaction with, 325
physical safety of, satisfaction with, 325
union members and, 338
workforce participation rate, 446
workplace engagement, 36–37
college and, 402
diversity and, 402
health problems and, 466–67
metro areas and, 335–36
states and, 104–6
teachers and, 10, 43–44
states and, 18–19
trends in, 90–91, 384–85
worry, 103–4
crimes and, 406–7
Wyoming
actively disengaged employees in, 105
drug use in, 125
economic confidence in, 52
ideology in, 50
Obama, Barack, and, 44
older adults' well-being in, 256
party identification in, 45–46
Payroll to Population rate and, 57
unemployment in, 57
well-being in, 66

Yellen, Janet, confidence in, 156, 157
Yousafzai, Malala, admiration of, 473

zoos, animal treatment and, 185